# CLARK'S
# KENTUCKY
# ALMANAC

## AND BOOK OF FACTS

## Second Edition

*A comprehensive publication with contemporary and historical information, infused with many photos, facts, and archival treasures that make up the rich and exciting history of Kentucky*

The **Clark** Group

CLARK'S
# KENTUCKY ALMANAC
### AND BOOK OF FACTS
## Second Edition

ISBN 1-883589-77-0 (softcover)
ISBN 1-883589-78-9 (casebound)

Published and distributed by The Clark Group
Printed in the United States of America

To order online, log on to www.kyalmanac.com
To order by telephone, call 1-800-944-3995

| | |
|---|---|
| Florence Huffman | Editor-in-Chief |
| Robert G. Clark | Publisher |
| Sam Stephens | Marketing & Public Relations |
| Jennifer Kash | Production Manager |
| Sid Webb | Photo Editor |
| Scott Risner | Graphic Design Consultant |
| Kelly Elliott | Graphic Design & Production |
| John A. McGill | Sports Editor |
| Tom Wallace | Associate Sports Editor |
| Carla Bryan | Associate Production Manager |
| Robert Seelbach | Associate Production Manager |
| Mark Reinhardt | Associate Editor |
| Beth Beasley | Associate Editor |
| Barbara Mabry | Associate Editor |

# Table of Contents

# *Flight 5191*

## A Dedication

*The tragedy of Comair Flight 5191 in the early morning hours on Sunday, Aug. 27, 2006 will live forever in the hearts and minds of the victims' families and friends. As so many have thought, if only we could turn back time and undo this terrible event, we would do it gladly. The hand of time will eventually begin to lessen the deep pain of the tragedy but will never heal the heartbreak of the loss on that fateful morning in Lexington.*

*We dedicate this Second Edition of Clark's Kentucky Almanac as a lasting memorial of those forty-nine individuals who perished, with the hope that in some small way the grief of losing family members and loved ones will forever be shared by many and will help to provide strength and courage for families and friends to carry on.*

*The Clark Group, Lexington, Kentucky*

# Acknowledgements

## *Contributing Writers*

**Jeffrey Abbott**, President, Louisville Stoneware
**Kandie Adkinson**, Secretary of State's Office
**David Adkisson**, President & CEO, Kentucky
Chamber of Commerce
**Todd Allen**, President, Bed & Breakfast Association
of Kentucky
**James G. Amato**, Director, Lexington Sister Cities
Commission
**Bill Ambrose**, Historian
**Karen Angelucci**, Gardener & Author
**Bob Arnold**, Executive Director, Kentucky
Association of Counties (KACO)
**Bob Babbage**, President, Babbage CoFounder
**Dr. Yvonne Honeycutt Baldwin**, Professor of
History, Dept. of Geography, Government, and
History (Chair), Morehead State University
**James R. Bean, M.D.**
**Dr. Royal Berglee**, Associate Professor of
Geography, Dept. of Geography, Government,
and History, Morehead State University
**Laura Biagi**, Writer
**Steven Block**, Louisvillian, Arts Supporter
**Robert Boles**, Writer & Producer
**Dr. Zachary J. Bortolot**, Assistant Professor of
Geography, Dept. of Geography, Government,
and History, Morehead State University
**Ed Bowen**, President, Grayson-Jockey Club
Research Foundation, Inc
**Bill Bright**, Curator, Kentucky Military History
Museum
**Bill Bryant**, News Editor, WKYT-TV, Channel 27
**Ron Bryant**, Historian
**Kim Bunnell**, Circuit Judge, Fayette Circuit Court
**Anne Butler,PhD.**, Kentucky State University
**Jim Carroll**, Kentucky Dept. of Parks
**Lindy Casebier**, Executive Director, Kentucky Office
for Arts & Cultural Humanities
**Bill Caylor**, President, Kentucky Coal Association
**Jerry Cecil**, Kentucky's Civilian Aide to the
Secretary of the U.S. Army
**Billy C. Clark**, Appalachian Author & Educator
**Robert G. Clark**, Publisher
**Thomas D. Clark** (1903-2005), Kentucky Historian
Laureate
**Martha Layne Collins**, Executive Director,
Kentucky World Trade Center
**Glen Conner**, Professor, Western Kentucky
University, State Climatologist Emeritus
**Bill Cooke**, Museum Director, International
Museum of the Horse
**Dr. Gary Cordner**, Dean (Ret.), College of Justice &
Safety
**Al Cross**, Political Writer, Director, Institute for
Rural Journalism & Community Issues
**Stephanie Darst**, Kentucky State Fair
**David & Lalie Dick**, Authors & Publishers, Plum Lick
Publishing Inc.
**Michelle Edwards**, Marion County Tourism
Commission
**Kadie Engstrom**, Education Coordinator, The Belle
of Louisville
**Lt. Mike Fields**, Dept. for Fish & Wildlife Resources
**Dr. Stuart Foster**, Professor, Western Kentucky

University, and Kentucky State Climatologist
**Virginia "Ginni" Fox**, Education Advocate &
Consultant
**Gatewood Galbraith**, Attorney & Historian
**Jon Gassett**, Commissioner, Dept. for Fish &
Wildlife Resources
**Jerry Gibson**, Historian, Journalist
**Dr. James M. Gifford**, CEO & Senior Editor, Jesse
Stuart Foundation
**Joanne Glasser**, President, Eastern Kentucky
University
**Jerrell Goodpaster**, Writer & Hiking Authority
**Tolley Graves**, Executive Director, American
Saddlebred Museum
**Trey Grayson**, Secretary of State of Kentucky
**William Crawford Green**, Professor of Government,
Dept. of Geography, Government, and History,
Morehead State University
**Col. Claude E. Hammond**, Astronomical
Consultant
**Tom Hicks**, Marketing Administrator, AAA,
Louisville
**Janet Steele Holloway**, Executive Director, Women
Leading Kentucky
**Gary Huddleston**, Communications Director,
Kentucky Farm Bureau
**Charlie Hughes**, Poet, Wind Publications
**Lynda Jeffries**, CEO, International Book Project
**Loyal Jones**, Author, Director (Ret.), Appalachian
Center at Berea College
**Dr. Steve Jones**, Professor, Murray State University
**Chris Kellogg**, Strategic Communications
Resources
**Jack Kelly**, CEO, World Games 2010 Foundation
**Nancy Jo Kemper**, Kentucky Council of Churches
**Dr. Thomas J. Kiffmeyer**, Associate Professor of
History, Dept. of Geography, Government, and
History, Morehead State University
**Dr. James Klotter**, Professor of History, Georgetown
College, and Kentucky State Historian
**Margaret A. Lane**, Author & Consultant
**Ed Lawrence**, Kentucky Arts Council
**Robert Lawson**, Executive Director, Kentucky
Music Hall of Fame
**John Lina**, Honorary Consul of France (Louisville)
**Sylvia Lovely**, Executive Director, Kentucky League
of Cities
**Barbara Mabry**, Poet
**Benita McCoy Lyons**, Owner, It's The Real McCoy, Inc.
**Dr. Pearse Lyons**, President, Alltech
**Mark Maloney**, Sports Writer
**Tom Martin**, Editor in Chief, Business Lexington
**William E. Matthews**, Historian & Co-Owner, Back
Home in Kentucky
**Dr. Michael B. McCall**, President, Kentucky
Community & Technical College System
**John A. McGill**, Writer
**Dr. Christine E. McMichael**, Assistant Professor of
Geography, Dept. of Geography, Government,
and History, Morehead State University
**Keven McQueen**, Author, Professor of English,
Eastern Kentucky University

**Andrew C. Meko**, President & CEO, Kentucky Association of Manufacturers

**Dr. Lynwood Montell**, Author & Professor, Western Kentucky University

**Nick Nicholson**, President & CEO, Keeneland

**Dr. Gary O'Dell**, Assistant Professor of Geography, Dept. of Geography, Government, and History, Morehead State University

**Chester Powell**, Poet

**Kerry Prather**, Biologist, Kentucky Dept. of Fish & Wildlife Resources

**O. Leonard Press**, founder of Kentucky Educational Television

**James Ramsey, PhD.**, President, University of Louisville

**Diana Ratliff**, Shaker Village of Pleasant Hill

**Joe Reagan**, President & CEO, Greater Louisville Inc.

**Billy Reed**, Sportswriter, Editor

**Mark Reinhardt**, Writer

**BG (Ret.) James E. Shane, Jr.**, Executive Director, Kentucky Commission on Military Affairs

**Patsy Sims**, Author

**Herb Sparrow**, Executive Director, The Group Travel Leader Inc.

**Thomas E. Stephens**, Kentucky Historical Society

**Bob Stewart**, former Commissioner, Kentucky Dept. of Travel

**Maj. Gen. Donald C. Storm**, Adjutant General of Kentucky

**Marvin E. Strong, Jr.**, Secretary, Economic Development Cabinet

**Charles Thompson**, Kentucky Humanities Council

**Lisa Thompson**, Dept. for Libraries & Archives

**Dr. Lee Todd**, President, University of Kentucky

**John Trowbridge**, Military Historian

**Bernie Vonderheide**, President, Kentuckians for Nursing Home Reform

**Tom Wallace**, Author & Writer

**Sue Weant**, Executive Director, Partners for Family Farms

**Paul Wesslund**, Kentucky Living Magazine

**Clarence R. Wyatt**, Pottinger Associate Professor of History, Centre College

# Special Thanks

2010 Alltech FEI World Equestrian Games, Scott Lowery
Alltech, Billy Frey
Mat Arnold, Supporter
Back Home In Kentucky Magazine Inc., Jerlene Rose, Editor & William E. Matthews
Wanda Bertram, Editor
Kimberly N. Bunnell, Supporter
Dan & Lesa Clark, Supporters
Lisa Clark, Editor & Supporter
Ameila Clark, Supporter
Clark Planning Services, Kathy Heltman
Robert Coomer, Photographer
Danville-Boyle County Convention & Visitors Bureau, Carolyn Crabtree
Darklight Imagery, Chris Anderson
Gateway Press
W. James Host, Supporter
Jesse Stuart Foundation
Kaiser Family Foundation
Kentucky Archaeological Survey
Kentucky Association of Counties, Cathy Jones
Kentucky Association of Manufacturers, Marty Kish & Sharon Fincel
Kentucky Book Fair, Connie Crowe
Kentucky Chamber of Commerce, Jim Ford, Seth Flynn & Sara Vaught
Kentucky College & University Sports Information Directors
Kentucky Commerce Cabinet, George Ward, Secretary; Creative Services, Jon Vaden & Brian Moore
Kentucky Commission on Military Affairs, Stacey Games
Kentucky Department of Fish & Wildlife Resources, Tim Slone, Dave Baker & Norm Minch
Kentucky Department of Libraries & Archives
Kentucky Department of Military Affairs, Jason LeMay & Gina Vaile
Kentucky Department of Tourism, Randy Fiveash, Commissioner; Kathy Yount, Marge Bateman
Kentucky Film Commission, Dian Knight
Kentucky Economic Development Cabinet, René True
Kentucky Education Cabinet, Tim Thornberry

Kentucky Geological Survey, William M. Andrews, James C. Currens, Cortland F. Eble & Brandon Nuttall
Kentucky Heritage Council, Diane Comer
Kentucky High School Athletic Association, Phyllis Sallee
Kentucky Historical Society, Kent Whitworth & Charlene Smith
Kentucky Horse Park, John Nicholson
Kentucky Humanities Council
Kentucky Living Magazine
Kentucky Museum of Art & Craft
Kentucky State University, Betsy Morelock
Kentucky Tourism Council, Marcheta Sparrow
Kentucky Virtual Library
Kentucky Women's State Golf Association
Kentucky World Trade Center, Ying Juan Rogers & Ben Golden
Lexington Herald-Leader, Mary Epple & Norma White
Lexington Sister Cities Commission, Kay Sargent
Ric McGee, Author & Editor
Morehead State University Folk Art Center
Murray State University, Kevin Britton
Northern Kentucky University Native American Studies, Dr. Ken Tankersley
Jim Ogle, Gray Television, Topeka, Kansas
Owensboro-Daviess County Tourist Commission, David Edds
Random House Publishing Group, Jennifer Jones
Bob & Mary Seelbach, Supporters
Patty Strange, Editor
TOUR Southern and Eastern Kentucky, Vicki Kidd & Karen Back
United States Equestrian Federation, Jeannie Putney
University of Kentucky, Jay Blanton & Whitney Hale
University Press of Kentucky
Univerity of Louisville, John Drees & John Chamberlin
Ursuline Sisters of Mount Saint Joseph, Sister Ruth Gehres
Tom Wallace, Editor
Esther Webb, Editor & Supporter
WaxWorks/VideoWorks, Clayton Nichols
Wind Publications, Charlie Hughes

*A very special thanks to our sponsors and advertisers!* (See page 749)

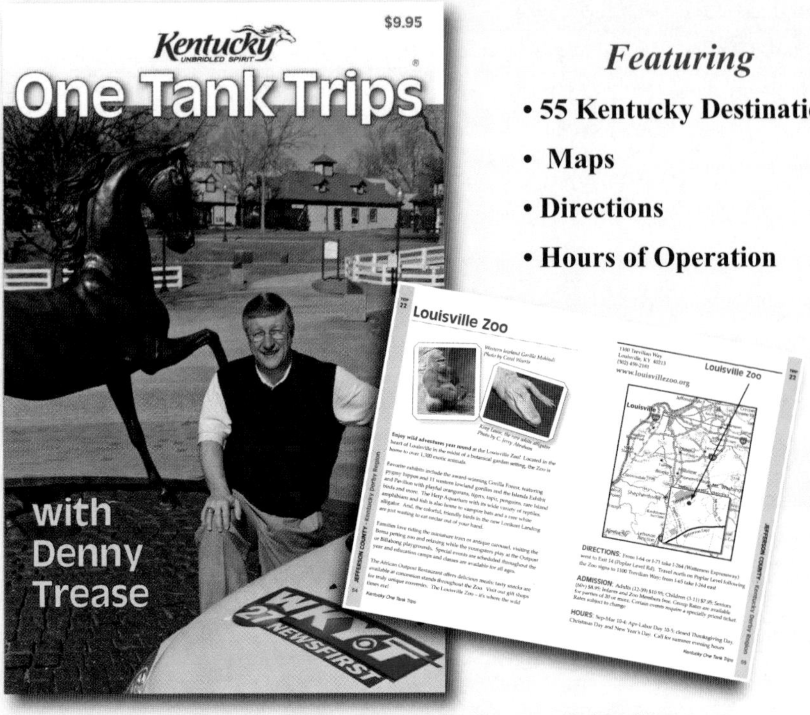

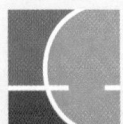

After 20 years, Toyota Motor Manufacturing, Kentucky has helped boost the local economy throughout the Commonwealth with a current investment, to date, of...

# $5,400,000,000

TOYOTA georgetown

TOYOTA MOTOR MANUFACTURING, KENTUCKY, INC.
www.toyotageorgetown.com

TOYOTA
MOTOR MANUFACTURING
20 Years
forever forward
Kentucky

# .completely about Kentucky

Seeking an elusive piece of information about Kentucky? Visit *kybiz.com* – your web portal to Kentucky.

*kybiz.com* is designed to help visitors link with data-rich web sites providing valuable and up-to-date information about Kentucky.

Plus, at *kybiz.com* you'll find exclusive, searchable archives and the current issue of *The Lane Report*, Kentucky's business news source for 20 years.

Managed by

www.kybiz.com

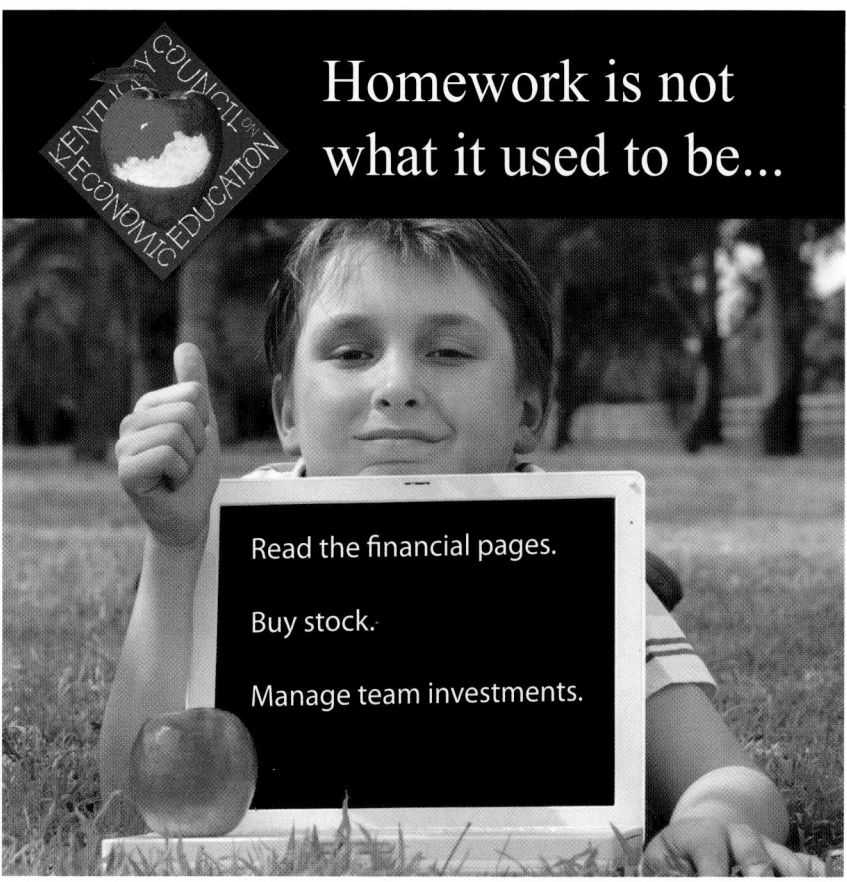

# Homework is not what it used to be...

Read the financial pages.

Buy stock.

Manage team investments.

## An investment education for a lifetime.

The Kentucky Council on Economic Education (KCEE) champions the teaching and learning of economics and personal finance.

KCEE serves all Kentucky schools providing student programming, teacher training and classroom resources.

Support Economic Education and KCEE with an individual or corporate contribution. For information call 1-800-436-3266.

*The Take Stock in Kentucky program is sponsored by Hilliard Lyons.*

**Kentucky Council on Economic Education**
**www.econ.org**

together

we

**Grow** • Every day is a new opportunity to give your best performance. At Ashland, our vision is to enable growth and add value to all we touch. Our people and products are hard at work improving processes, solving problems, and helping customers and communities worldwide to grow and succeed.

ASHLAND®

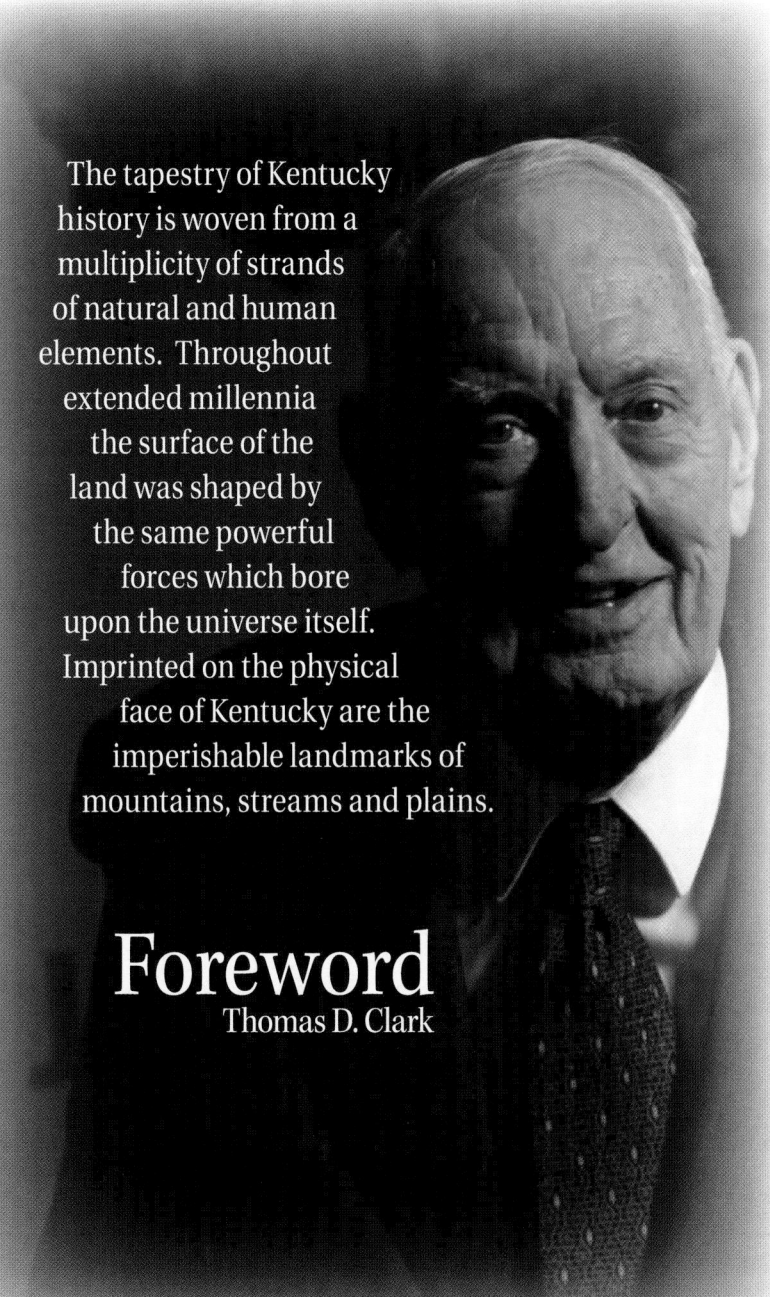

The tapestry of Kentucky
history is woven from a
multiplicity of strands
of natural and human
elements. Throughout
extended millennia
the surface of the
land was shaped by
the same powerful
forces which bore
upon the universe itself.
Imprinted on the physical
face of Kentucky are the
imperishable landmarks of
mountains, streams and plains.

# Foreword
Thomas D. Clark

Lying beneath the surface has rested a rich resource of minerals. It may be true that archeologists, anthropologists, and historians have only a general idea of earliest human occupation of the land. There remains positive evidence of the existence of a primitive stone age human presence, documented by a generous littering of stone artifacts, cliff hieroglyphics, and soot stains of cliff dwellers.

All across primeval Kentucky there spewed up through fissures in the earth chemicals, which created salt licks and salt-ladened streams. Throughout untold ages herbivorous

Explorer Dr. Thomas Walker built the first cabin in Kentucky. Replica on original site near Barbourville.
Source: Sid Webb

animals gathered at the licks and tramped trails across the land in doing so. The licks and connecting trails in the future played active roles in the settlement of Kentucky, and even in the opening of many of its arterial highways.

By gradual processes of population and economic expansion, and international rivalry, an Anglo-American civilization spread westward. Kentucky was the first state to be hacked out of the vast American frontier. Because of this fact the act of pioneering in the virginal backwoods became precedental in the future spread of American civilization. This fact was reflected in folkways, economies, politics, and international rivalries.

A basic theme in the history of Kentucky pioneering was, and remains, land. With the lingering direct ties of colonial Virginia and with the Atlantic Ocean, plus a modest population, there was little if any adventuring into the back country. A slight breakthrough came in 1671 when colonial Governor William Berkeley made Abraham Wood responsible for exploring areas to the west. General Wood's mission was to determine whether or not a stream beyond the Allegheny Ridge flowed into a great south sea. Wood's men discovered instead the New River and its fall line. This stream became a landmark in future explorations.

General Wood's exploration could hardly be called a major geographical breakthrough. The "dark" western littoral remained undisturbed until 1716 when Governor Alexander Spotswood, stimulated somewhat by Indian legend, led a party of gentlemen trail riders up to a peak ride in the Blue Ridge Mountains to look into the Shenandoah Valley and speculate on whether or not the river they saw flowed into a northern lake. They drank toasts to all members of the royal family and went home to be knighted into the Order of the Golden Horseshoe.

Gradually during the mid-decades of the eighteenth century the western country came into focus. Many of its rich natural resources were highly visible, and so were the potential profits to be garnered from the trade in Indian goods. It is significant in the opening of Kentucky history that two speculative land and Indian trade companies became active. First, the Loyal Land Company of Virginia sought to establish an imperial-sized claim to western lands. In 1750 that company employed Dr. Thomas Walker, a surveyor (among his other areas of interest), to lead an exploratory party to the southwest and the great webwork of Tennessee River streams. This mounted party traveled down the Buffalo-Indian path, and water courses to stand on April 13, 1750 in the saddle of the gap across the rock spine of the front face of the Appalachian Highlands. The Walker party, however, failed to penetrate the western country deep enough to reach the rich cane lands of the inner bluegrass. They departed the western country up the streams and mountain coves by way of Pound Gap and the great valley to Charlottesville. Dr. Walker's most important contributions to Kentucky history were making a written record of the existence of the great passways through the mountains into the land on the waters of the Ohio and Mississippi river systems, the naming of the gap, the mountain range, and the first river system he visited for the "Bloody" hero of Culloden, the Duke of Cumberland. The final entry in his journal tabulated the number of bears, deer, elk, and turkeys the party slaughtered.

A more aggressive band of speculators were those Virginians and Englishmen who formed the Ohio Company of Virginia. The list of names of members of this company was virtually synonymous with the leadership of colonial Virginia, containing such names as George and Lawrence Washington, Thomas Nelson, John Taylor, Thomas Cresap, Thomas Lee, and others. Their interest in the west was the Indian trade, land, and French and Indian activities. The company employed Christopher Gist, an experienced surveyor, to visit the western river valley in 1750 to discover and describe possible land sites for the establishment of settlements, to observe Indian activities, and to travel down the Ohio River to its fall line. Like Thomas Walker, Christopher Gist kept a rather full journal of his travels. There was one exception, Gist made numerous magnetic compass readings along the way. For twenty-nine days Christopher Gist wandered through the northern and upper rim of pres-

ent Kentucky. He went up the central branch of the Kentucky River and left the region by way of Pound Gap, never having seen much of the bluegrass area.

With the visitation of the two-company land explorers and the rising tempo of the com-

**Christopher Gist exploring wilderness**
*Source: The Picture Collection of the
New York Public Library*

mercial trading with the western tribes, there came a host of other viewers. In this manner the Kentucky frontier gradually came into focus. After the late fall of 1775, cabins and crude frontier fortresses came into view. As settlements advanced so did the administrative responsibilities of the commonwealth of Virginia. Its General Assembly took the first political step into the region by the creation of Kentucky County late in December 1776. This was the first time the name Kentucky was officially applied to the region.

At this juncture in Kentucky history, it must be emphasized that land, with its high magnetic attraction, became a central matter of attention. It may well be argued that no other element in Kentucky's history has continuously and consistently evoked such a volume of documentation, stirred so much human anxiety and anger, or provoked such a body of litigation and court decisions. From the moment the first wandering land claimant hacked evidence of his claim on a white oak tree, the ill-managed distribution of land warrants or "patents" has meant confusion. Unhappily, Kentucky fell heir to the ancient mode of land marking known as "metes and bounds." It would be folly to call metes and bounds a survey system of precision.

Neither the crown government nor colonial Virginia ordained an orderly plan for land management and disposal. This failure became visible at the end of the French and Indian War as documented in King George's Proclamation of 1763. King George's proclamation shifted the burden of paying French and Indian war veterans from the exchequer to newly acquired western lands.

Following settlement in 1775, that part of the west in the Ohio Valley became heavily involved in British activities in the American Revolution. The isolated Kentucky settlements were exposed to British-Indian raids and attacks, such as those which occurred against Ruddell's Station and Martin's Station on the Stoner Fork of the Licking River. Internally Boonesboro, Harrod's Town, and Bryan's Station barely escaped destructive assaults. The major phase of Kentucky in the American Revolution was the campaign that George Rogers Clark and his thin line of militiamen conducted against the western British-Indian posts of Kaskaskia, Cahokia, and Vincennes, and Clark's subsequent drive against the Shawnee-Wyandott villages north of the Ohio. The stunning attack against Kentucky, however, was the woeful defeat of the frontier militia in the

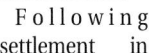
TAKING FIRST VIEW OF "THE BEAUTIFUL LEVEL OF KENTUCKY"

**Daniel Boone mural at the Capitol**
*Source: Ky. Dept. for Libraries & Archives*

**George Rogers Clark**
*Source: Kentucky Historical Society*

Battle of Blue Licks, August 19, 1782. Ironically, this battle occurred almost a year after Lord Cornwallis surrendered British forces at Yorktown.

No precise date can be stated as to that period when the raw pioneering process ended, and Kentuckians became involved in attending to the affairs of a rapidly expanding population. By the same token, it is doubtful that a full list of frontiersmen and women can be identified as bona fide pioneers in the heroic sense–the most readily sustainable fact that the exploration and settling of the virgin Kentucky frontier was not a single individual achievement.

Because of an historical-literary bit of luck, the name of Daniel Boone became almost synonymous with that of the American westward movement. Without any intent to denigrate that reputation of the old woodsman, faithfulness to the documentary record shows that Kentucky produced a host of pioneers of significant importance. There were Benjamin Logan, James Harrod, Simon Kenton, George Rogers Clark, Michael Bedinger, Isaac Shelby, and a host of others. There were the long-wandering hunter-Indian traders who became sources of first-hand information about the land and environment. Much less noted, but of monumental importance on the Kentucky frontier, were the land speculators who exercised a major influence in the settlement of Kentucky. There are few facts, if any, more fully documented than the omnivorous greed in the claiming of Kentucky lands.

In a much broader historical sense, land has been one of the major economic, political, and social elements in the commonwealth. It has filled that psychological and spiritual niche in the human psyche called "space." Following the opening decades of the nineteenth century, Kentuckians came to place great emphasis on the provincial as giving one an in-born sense of special heritage and belonging.

By 1790, Kentucky farmers and merchant traders had developed a rich commerce in tobacco, hemp, cured meats, lard, whiskey, corn, and small grains. Flatboats were drifted out of creeks and rivers into the main Ohio-Mississippi rivers flatboat trade. The name "Mill Road" was early attached to roads leading to creekbed sites of grain mills. By 1811, and almost miraculously, most of the prime, good land in central Kentucky had been claimed, the forest cleared away, and cultivated fields and grassy meadows were yielding rich harvests of field crops and herds and droves of livestock.

Equally important was the early development of driving herds of cattle, sheep, and horses over land by way of Cumberland Ford and the Atlantic coastal market. Literally thousands of hogs were driven that way. This rising commerce in agricultural products and the use of the western rivers as outlet channels involved the western Virginia counties in deep concern about the Spanish control of the Lower Mississippi, an issue which was to have a bear-

**Gov. Isaac Shelby**
*Source: Ky. Historical Society*

**First Constitution of Kentucky**
*Source: Ky. Dept. for Libraries & Archives*

ing on the formation of the Commonwealth of Kentucky.

Between 1775 and 1810, there was a phenomenal increase in the tide of emigration westward. At the same time, there was a growing dissatisfaction with Virginia's administration of its western counties. Involved in this condition was protection against Indian raids, remoteness from the capital in Richmond, and the expense of transporting court cases to the state capital for adjudication. The most immediate problem in 1784 was protecting the Kentucky settlements against Indian raids. This was the principle subject discussed in the first regional assembly in Danville in 1784. A second meeting (convention) was convened in 1785 in which the suggestion of separation from Virginia and creating an independent state was discussed. Involved in this proposition was a series of issues: the format of self government, sentimentalities regarding the Virginia attachment, the protection of the entangled mass of original land titles, the protection of an established court system, and the great and vexing problem of Spanish control of the lower central river system. Debaters, in convention and through the columns of the newly established *Kentucke Gazette*, discussed all these issues in extensor.

After all the debating in the ten conventions, the first Kentucky Constitution was written in a remarkably short period of time–less than a month. George Nicholas has been called "The Father of the Constitution," and the document reflects rather faithfully the second constitution of Pennsylvania and the one of Virginia. President George Washington temporarily approved the admission to the union of the new commonwealth. The date, June 1, was an arbitrary one. Officially Congress did not approve the admission until its fall session.

The operational government of Kentucky was formed in Lexington on June 4, 1792. Isaac Shelby had been chosen governor. On June 7, following the inaugural ceremony, the General Assembly held its first meeting. In Shelby's first message he admonished legislators to establish a judicial system and, "By your humanity as well as your duty will induce you to pass laws to compel the proper treatment of slaves, agreeable to the direction of the Constitution." The governor then asked that a revenue system be instituted, and that a permanent seat of government be located at an early date.

Location of the permanent seat of the Kentucky government was a complicated issue caused by sectionalism north and south of the Kentucky River, and competition among various towns and strategic sites. A committee of twenty-one names was selected, and militia officers struck off names until a group of only five was left. During the remainder of 1792 this committee met and considered various sites and finally settled on the Kentucky River village of Frankfort. This place was chosen for several reasons: it was near the center of the population, it was on a navigable stream, there was

some political finagling, and some citizens, including General James Wilkinson, made generous contributions of land and building materials for the construction of a state house. There was not unanimous approval of Frankfort as the capital. Between 1793 and 1904 there were recurring efforts to move the capital to Louisville.

Columns of the *Kentucke Gazette* down to 1794 contained notations of Indian raids in the state. In some instances land surveyors reported that they were hesitant about going into the woods because of these threats. Anthony Wayne's major drive against the northern lake tribes ended in the battle of Fallen Timbers and the subsequent Treaty of Greenville.

A more significant matter, however, was the activities of the British and Indians in the Lake Erie rim, incidents of violation of the freedom of the seas, and a possible threat against the vital port of New Orleans. All these issues were of major public concern. It was as an advocate of embargo of British importations of British goods, and the potential threat on the Great Lakes frontier that Henry Clay attracted national attention as a "Warhawk."

Kentucky became involved in the War of 1812 on both the lakes and gulf fronts. Isaac Shelby in 1812, and in his second term as governor, received permission from the Kentucky General Assembly to leave the state and command the state's militia forces on the Great Lakes front. Overwhelming success in the Battle of the Thames was a veritable "hero maker,"

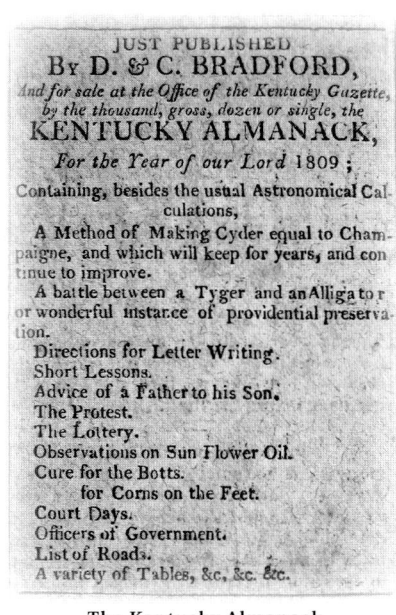

**The Kentucky Almanack
Advertisement published in the
Kentucky Gazette, January 10, 1809**
*Source: Photo from Lexington
Public Library Collection*

as was the Battle of New Orleans. Being a veteran of either of these battlefronts was a carte blanche assurance of political success.

The War of 1812 and its aftermath had tremendous influence in almost every area of life, none more so than being victimized by the great financial panic of 1819, and its lingering problems. This was an era in Kentucky history when the entire economic and political structures were thrown into chaos, wounds were inflicted upon the body politic, ones which required years to heal.

**Flatboat**
*Source: Ky. Historical Society*

In 1792, Kentucky had approximately 90,000 inhabitants and by 1820 this number had expanded impressively to 220,000 individuals. By the latter date, Kentucky, like Virginia, had become a mother state feeding population into the new developing states, west and south. The white population steadily comprised approximately three-fourths of the numbers, and black slaves approximately a quarter of the total population. The history of slavery in Kentucky was, from the beginning, as indicated in Governor Shelby's address to the first General Assembly, a complex human and economic issue. By 1820, slave labor had ceased to be of major importance when weighed against the expansion of the cotton and sugar growing activities of the gulf coastal South. Stamped indelibly in the annals of Kentucky is the stain of the interstate slave trade, a practice fully documented in the contemporary press, in pamphlets, travel accounts, and anti-slavery literature, plus modern studies of the subject. Three contemporary publications merit consideration: Harriett Beecher Stowe's, Uncle Tom's Cabin; Cassius M. Clay's newspaper, The True American; and Stephen Foster's, My Old Kentucky Home, Good Night, originally entitled, Poor Uncle Tom, Goodnight. By 1850, it was reasonably clear that slavery was perhaps a vanishing institution. Kentucky, however, had long been a focal center of critical viewing of the institution, and, subsequently, of the Underground Railway activities. The long stretch of the Ohio River became a line of passage into the land of freedom. Finally, slaves were freed with the ratification of the Thirteenth Amendment of the federal Constitution.

**First Lady Suzan Shelby**
*Source: Ky. Historical Society*

As indicated, the lands in central Kentucky and along the central Tennessee border were highly productive of vital field crops and livestock. Since 1778 the trade, downriver and overland, of these products was profitable. Historically this trade had evolved through the flatboat, steamboat, and opening railway era.

Transported as dead weight, freight was hempen goods, tobacco, small grains, cured meats, and whiskey. A precious material in the interstate trade was salt, refined from numerous licks and sites. This trade was a major factor in the rise of Louisville as a market center, and in tying many Kentucky commercial interests to the Lower South.

During the decades of 1810-1840, Kentucky farmers shaped the image of Kentucky as a prime livestock producing area. The explorers, Thomas Walker and Christopher Gist, penetrated the western wilderness on horseback. So did Daniel Boone and John Findley. The horse, draft and sporting, became a fact in Kentucky history from the beginning. Native cattle were driven west from Virginia, but at an early date improved breeds of English stock were imported to graze in blue grass pastures. This was true of hogs, sheep, and later, mules. Central counties, such as Bourbon, Clark,

View of Cumberland Gap from
Kingdom Come State Park
Source: Southern & Eastern Kentucky Tourism
Development Association

Woodford, Franklin and Fayette, became nationally famous as agriculture, livestock, and sporting horse breeding centers.

In the same degree, Kentucky in the first half of the nineteenth century and in its human ranks, produced an impressive body of political, scientific, and business leaders. No doubt but that the confusion which arose over land issues was influential in the development of a distinguished western country bar. The names of lawyers such as George Nicholas, Humphrey Marshall, John Breckinridge, Caleb Wallace, Henry Clay, John J. Crittenden, and a host of others enjoyed national status. In the field of science were Dr. Ephraim McDowell, Dr. Samuel Brown, Dr. Benjamin Dudley, John J. Audubon, the eccentric Constantine Rafinesque, Robert Peter, and Daniel Drake. The Kentucky governors, 1792 to 1865, comprised an interesting collection of personalities. Most of them were appreciable landholders, lawyers, men with military experience, and some with only limited formal educational backgrounds. Members of the General Assembly, all male, ranged from individuals with reasonably good native qualifications to none at all. All of these facts had a distinct bearing on the course of Kentucky's history.

Just as individuals left their imprints on the first half of the nineteenth century, so did many internal changes – the geographical and geological physical nature of the surface of the state. These features effected the social, economic, cultural, and political actions of the population. In no area was this more distinctly revealed than in the breaking of the natural barriers, and the lacing of the state with a webwork of roads. These ranged from the opening of the road to Cumberland Gap, the road from Maysville south by way of Paris, Lexington, Harrodsburg south to Nashville, Tennessee, and the ancient Midland Trail from Ashland to the Falls of the Ohio. Many of the internal roads followed animal and Indian trails, but by no means all of them. County court order books are filled with the matter of appointing committees to locate the rights of way of roads, their openings, and maintenance. In the steeper mountainous areas many roads were along streambeds.

It may be said that the opening of the modern age of transportation history in Kentucky occurred in 1811 when Nicholas Roosevelt piloted the little sternwheeler New Orleans into Louisville. In time, sternwheel boats plied many of the major Kentucky streams. As a matter of fact, Kentucky administrative and legislative officials became blinded to the dawning of the railway age. In 1831, the Lexington and Ohio Railway Company was chartered to build a line from Lexington to some point below Louisville on the Ohio. It was not until March 1850 that Kentucky really entered the interstate railway age when the Louisville and Nashville Railway was planned to connect the two cities. Four major issues confronted Kentuckians in the decade 1840 to 1850, issues which had lingered since the creation of the state. They were the devisement and support, both financially and academically, of a school program. Slavery, as Governor Shelby indicated in his message to the first Kentucky General Assembly, was a matter of public concern and responsibility. Then there was the highly tangible matter of sharp sectional divisions of an irregular, geographically-shaped, landed commonwealth. Throughout three quarters of a century, the people and officials sought answers to these problems, none of which demanded more imagination and public attention than establishing schools without first creating a basis of fiscal support. From the very opening of the western lands to settlement, there was a realization that some degree of learning was mandatory for success. Timidly, the Virginia General Assembly in May 1781 appropriated three tracts of escheated lands (lands owned by British subjects at the time of the Revolution). There were eighteen thousand acres in the three tracts "donated from this of a public school or seminary of learning." In the body of the act appeared the eloquent dedication of funds from the sale of the lands, "Might some day be a valuable fund for the education of youth, and it being the interest of this commonwealth always to promote and encourage every design which

**Henry Clay**
*Source: Library of Congress*

may tend to the improvement of the mind and the diffusion of useful knowledge, even among the most remote citizens, whose situation a barbarous neighborhood and a savage intercourse might otherwise render unfriendly to science." This was the first, and somewhat snobbish, tribute to a need for education even on the wild Kentucky frontier. No mention was made in either of the first two Kentucky Constitutions of education. In December 1794, in its second meeting, the Kentucky General Assembly chartered the Kentucky Academy in connection with the state's land grant law, which appropriated to each new county 6,000 acres of unclaimed public lands. This was a noble gesture, which fell far short of achieving its purpose.

Repeatedly up to 1849 citizens and legislators undertook to organize a public school system, and find a painless way to support it. Educational needs were extensively discussed in the constitutional convention of 1849 with no clear academic mandate being written into the new document, this despite all the previous attempts to effect real advancement. It might be a futile endeavor to try and determine which decade in Kentucky's history might be considered a seminal one. Certainly the one 1850-1860 would have to be given serious attention. Statistically this was an age of coming into political and social maturity. Measured objectively and statistically it was not only one of prosperity, but one of rich promise. The land had become highly productive, livestock breeding and production had reached a zenith, and, under the new constitution the

**Battle of Richmond Re-enactment**
*Photo: Sid Webb*

financial future of the state appeared brighter. The half century mark (1850) revealed how far Kentucky had advanced in many governmental areas since 1792. The population of 980,405 souls indicated a distinctive increase, despite the fact the opening and operation of the Erie Canal had directed much of the western population flow around Kentucky. Much of Kentucky in 1850 was still a virgin frontier, and basically unproductive of either revenue income or a stable domestic economy. The impact of this condition was to be reflected many times over in sharp regional and cultural differentiations.

It may be true that one of the tragic moments in Kentucky history was centered in the disruptive national issues which threatened the existence of the union of states in the latter half of the 1850s decade. This was reflected in the efforts of the state's leaders such as Henry Clay, John Jordan Crittenden, George D. Prentice, Robert Jefferson Breckinridge and others to find compromises and assurances of national unity. In 1860 Kentucky found itself in a key strategic position geographically, politically, economically, and emotionally. Kentucky

had almost everything to lose in the divisive political debates in the issues pertaining to slavery, and in the internal unity of its people and sections. In this connection, the question of whether Kentucky in 1860 was southern or northern has little pertinence. It was, as it had been formed, a border state caught in a binding political and economic triangle. It occupied a strategic geographical position which was vital to both North and South. It had vital agricultural productive capacity plus a generous blessing of natural resources such as salt, coal, timber, and iron ore. Too, it was tied to both sections by highway, railway, and river connections. In the convulsive moment of secession of the southern states in 1861, Kentucky's leadership was divided over the issue of secession. A strong core of leadership led by such persons as George D. Prentice, Albert Gallatin Hodges, John Jordan Crittenden, and Robert J. Breckinridge temporarily managed to keep Kentucky neutral. Internally, Governor Beriah Magoffin and a substantial body of Kentuckians were pro southern. Kentucky's position of neutrality was quickly violated by both southern and northern forces. Kentucky never seceded. The history of Kentucky's involvement in the Civil War has evoked the production of a modest library of biographies, histories of battles, essays, maps, and edited diaries. There were at lest three strategic battles, and numerous skirmishes, fought in the state. In the full measure of the fundamental meanings of the Civil War in Kentucky is to be reckoned in the sectional and partisan divisions among the people, the disruption of the state's economy, internal strife caused, first, by runaway guerilla activities, disruption of what might have been educational progress, and in the rise of a stifling partisanship in state politics to say nothing of the abuses of constitutional rights of citizens by high-handed military actions.

The post-Civil War period, down to the opening of the twentieth century, was in many respects one of reconstruction. It was an era of recovering markets for Kentucky agriculture, timber, and mineral resources, of expanding an internal system of railroads, of renewing the crusade for expanding the public school system, and of dealing with crime and civil upheavals. One of the most important events in this era was voter approval of the calling of a fourth constitutional convention to revise many of the restrictive elements in the third constitution, to bring Kentucky's government into alignment with the fundamental changes wrought in the nation by adoption of the 13th, 14th, and 15th amendments to the United States Constitution. The four volumes containing the proceedings of the convention mirror the times and issues confronting Kentucky at the close of the nineteenth century. For more than a century the fourth Kentucky Constitution has been a subject of public debate, court decisions, and campaigns to redraft it. The document has been amended numerous times, with the complete rewriting of the judicial article making substantial changes in this division of Kentucky constitutional history.

**Tobacco Field**
*Photo: Sid Webb*

During the decade, 1890-1900, there were sharp political divisions over monetary-agrarian-bipartisan matters. Within the Democratic Party there was division over all of the above issues plus the emerging dominance of a strong factional conflict between Senator William Goebel of northern Kentucky and the more conservative pro-Confederate-southern faction in state political control. In 1895 William O. Bradley was elected as Kentucky's first Republican governor. There was that dark political moment in the Democratic Convention in the famous Louisville Music Hall when William Goebel was nominated the party's candidate for the governorship. The Republicans nominated their attorney general, William S. Taylor, as their gubernatorial candidate. The gubernatorial election of 1899 was one of the most hotly contested in Kentucky's gubernatorial history. The popular vote seemed to favor Taylor, the Republican, but the vote was challenged by the Democrats on several grounds. While that debate occurred, Goebel was shot. He died four days later. The assassination of the Democratic candidate for governor, William Goebel, divided the people into angry partisan groups, and, along with the recurring mountain blood feuds, gave the state an image of runaway savagery. The victorious Republican governor-elect William S. Taylor, was unseated after a long, bitter court fight. The young bachelor Democrat lieutenant governor was elevated to the office. In all the bitterness and court trials, three Republicans were tried, and two went to prison. All were later paroled. This crime colored political affairs and Kentucky's image for at least three decades. Beyond this, no one can say beyond all evidentiary support who fired the rifle shot which did so much public damage.

The commonwealth was caught up in a second threat of anarchy. There occurred in the dark-fired tobacco-growing region of the state guerilla warfare, known as the Black Patch War, between the farmers and the tobacco corporate managers over marketing practices and ruinously low prices. It took more than a decade to quell this disturbance.

In the same interval of time there occurred

a vigorous campaign to improve the status of education. Teachers colleges were chartered to prepare more effective teachers. At the same time a quasi-public-private campaign was conducted to supplement public efforts. This was to be a major concern throughout the century.

Later, a group of principals who represented school districts which had received less support than was guaranteed them under the "Equal Opportunity Clause" of the 1890 constitution filed a lawsuit. The Franklin County Circuit Court and the Supreme Court declared the operation of the school system unconstitutional. The Kentucky General Assembly in 1990 enacted the massive House Bill 940. This act outlined the general purpose and a new direction of education in the future. To an encouraging extent the omnibus legislation placed the management of educational management beyond local and state partisan political controls. Fundamentally the Kentucky Education Reform Act (KERA), measured by many criteria, is the most far-reaching piece of social and cultural legislation ever enacted by the Kentucky General Assembly. The test of this lies in the impressive gains Kentucky has made against its traditional bottom rail educational rating, and in several of the national comparative scales.

In no era did Kentucky make more historical and economic changes in the 20th century than in the area of farming and in the agrarian folkways of rural life. Tobacco, burley and dark leaf, prevailed during the century as Kentucky's leading staple cash crop. The growing and marketing of the leaf underwent at least three crisis stages, and, after, periods of readjustment. Advancements were made in combating plant diseases and parasitic infestations. Tobacco growing and sales reflected the impact of two world wars. But other factors soon affected the fortunes of towns, banks, service enterprises, and even the romantic glow of the crop and its sales. The closing quarter of the twentieth century saw a sharp change in the tobacco industry, a change wrought by revelations that smoking was injurious to personal health. At the close of the century a major question was the survival of tobacco production, and the search for a new staple crop. Generally the major farming activities were shifted to the lands of central and western Kentucky. Farms were mechanized, and plant

**Governor Martha Layne Collins welcomes Toyota executives to Georgetown for the Ground breaking ceremony on May 5, 1986**
*Source: Toyota Motor Manufacturing Kentucky*

breeders introduced more productive varieties of grains, soy beans, and hay crops.

A major change in the last half of the twentieth century was the disappearance of the family farm. By mid-twentieth century corporate farms began to appear in Kentucky, producing chickens and hogs. There were even modest adventures in the production of shrimp and catfish. Certainly the state held on to a respectable ranking in the field of livestock production, and to the breeding, sales, and racing of the major breeds of sporting horses. A mid-twentieth century Kentucky underwent far-reaching changes in the fields of civil and human rights.

Historically the state in the 1870s granted full voting privileges to its African American population, but it failed to extend full educational advantages. In 1949 the indefensible Day Law, effective in 1904, was challenged by the NAACP in the lawsuit *Lyman Johnson v. University of Kentucky*. Johnson, a Jefferson County school teacher, won the case permitting him to take graduate courses in the university. The big change, however, came after the United States Supreme Court rendered its decision in 1954 in *Brown v. Board of Education,* which removed racial barriers in the nation's public schools. There were some aftermath disturbances in Clay, Sturgis, and Louisville. In 1966 Governor Edward T. Breathitt Jr. signed the Kentucky Civil Rights Act into law.

In the industrial areas the mining of coal in both the western and eastern fields was colored by periods of genuine prosperity, and at others, by a sagging national and world economy. The eastern coal field especially, was fraught with labor unrest and, on occasion, by violence. The physical mining procedures underwent phenomenal changes by the introduction of machines, which caused marked displacement of human miners. A major change in mining procedures was reflected in the introduction of strip mining procedures, which wrought fundamental changes in the topography of lands in both the eastern and western fields, provoking a fierce reaction from hoards of environmentalists. Documenting the changes are the abandoned coal mining villages, the shrunken ranks of miners, the negation of the "broad-form deed," and the mode of transporting coal.

No change in the 20th century reached so deep into human lives as the introduction of electric energy, private and public. The passage by the United States Congress in 1933 of the Tennessee Valley Authority (TVA) was to have a marked impact on Kentucky, even though it offered service to only a limited part of the state. The rural electrification laws and the favorable court decisions in the 1940s that allowed the organization of the Rural Electrification Administration (REA) districts, the building of a network of power lines across the state, and the availability of electricity to every rural home was a revolutionary advance in the Kentucky way of life.

The Federal Aid Highway Act of 1956 in many respects realigned highway development in Kentucky. Slicing across two sections of the state are the arterial limited interstate roads I-75 and I-65, plus links of I-24 and I-

Children and Adults take a tour and learn about coal mining
*Source: Southern & Eastern Kentucky Tourism Development Association*

71. The Kentucky Highway Authority used the Kentucky bonding power to construct a series of toll roads to be liquidated by use collections. Construction of the Western Kentucky, the Mountain and the Bluegrass parkways, plus the eastern Daniel Boone Parkway, made substantial progress in penetrating Kentucky's historical isolated regions, and proved to be a more tightly lacing together of all parts of the state.

The persuasion of Governor Martha Layne Collins that the Japanese Toyota Automobile manufacturer locate a plant in Georgetown, plus the Ford Motor Company operation in Louisville, and the General Motors plant in Bowling Green moved Kentucky deeper into the modern industrial world. Not only were main manufacturing plants located in state, but also there was the major develop-

**Late Ky. Poet Laureate
Joy Bale Boone**
*Source: Lexington Herald-Leader*

**Dr. James Klotter, State
Historian of Kentucky**
*Source: Lexington Herald-Leader*

**Ky. novelist Robert Penn
Warren**
*Source: Lexington Herald-Leader*

**Ky. novelist, Barbara
Kingsolver**
*Source: Lexington Herald-Leader*

**Late Ky. writer, James Still**
*Source: Lexington Herald-Leader*

ment of satellite supply industries, which were located in various places about the state.

Just as Kentucky underwent changes in its agrarian way of life, in its breaking of isolative physical barriers, and in considerable transitions from a basically rural-agrarian state to an urban service-industrial one, it underwent impressive advances in the areas of the human services and humanities. It would be challenging to fully appraise the advances made in the area of basic medical care. The establishment of a medical school and hospital in the University of Kentucky, and the advancements made in the University of Louisville medical school have been reflected in the advancement of human welfare, and possibly in an expansion of the life span of the populace.

Kentuckians made important advances during the twentieth century in the areas of the liberal arts. During the century an older order of authors passed on and a younger and more expansive one took over. This was the era which produced such significant renascent figures as Elizabeth Madox Roberts, Robert Penn Warren, Elizabeth Chevalier, A.B. Guthrie, Harriette Arnow, Jesse Stuart, James Still, Wendell Berry, Bobbie Ann Mason, and Janice Holt Giles as creative writers. There came on the scene a host of historians and non-fiction writers including John F. Day, William H. Townsend, J. Winston Coleman, Jr., Lowell Harrison, David Dick, Harry

Caudill, William Ellis, Charles Roland, Edward (Mack) Coffman, Tracy Campbell, and a host of others.

The creation of the University Press of Kentucky opened a progressive challenge for the publication of regional books. In the last half of the century library expansion and availability in Kentucky went from a limited number of inadequately stocked public libraries, horseback book conveyers, and bookmobiles, to the establishment of local and county libraries. In Frankfort, the severely limited state library system was revitalized. In the closing two centuries the annual Book Fair in Frankfort has increased many-fold the sale and distribution of books.

Kentucky, following the Great Depression, experienced a renaissance of the fine arts in the fields of music, graphics, and sculpture. The state claimed a central role in country music in all its forms in the performing arts in places like Louisville, Owensboro, Bowling Green, Lexington, and Danville.

No aspect of Kentucky history and human dedication has been more consistent than the absorbing interest in politics. This interest has not been solely based in the fundamentals of theoretical functioning democratic principles so much as in the great stone yard of rigid partisanism. John Adair, governor of Kentucky (1820-1824) could march onto the Kentucky political scene in 2005 and not feel completely out of place. He was an active party to partisan bickering, and in almost two centuries few, if any, revisionary changes have occurred.

In spite of all the deterrent features in the history of Kentucky politics, Kentucky produced a remarkable number of individuals in the twentieth century who rendered major service to the state and nation. During the century a coterie of governors created appreciable images of statesmanship in such areas of governmental reform, civil rights, economic development, education, and interstate relations. Each governor has to be evaluated within the context of his times and the leadership he supplied, not in a popularity poll. At the local levels of government there were officials who

**Governor John Adair**
*Source: Ky. Historical Society*

achieved reforms in both organization and projection reforms. Nationally Kentuckians became members of the Supreme Court, of diplomatic services, and as leaders in both houses of Congress. There were state legislators who on many occasions exhibited genuine statesmanship.

**Governor
Simon Bolivar Buckner**
*Source: Ky. Historical Society*

On the flip side of Kentucky's political history has been the ever-lurking virus of partisanism. Kentucky opened the twentieth century deadlocked in a vicious spasm of partisan hatred, which resulted in an image-destroying act of violence. Almost by rote it has opened the twenty-first century a victim of the same witless virus.

Once more, possibly no historian or political analyst could even in the most general terms, state fully the positives and negatives of Kentucky's history. It is safe, however, to assume the costs of failure to take full advantage of

centuries Kentuckians created a vigorous, often colorful mosaic of history. They made a veritable kaleidoscopic response to place, and social and environmental influences. They established government entities at all levels, nurtured institutions, tolerated defiances of law, made enormous patriotic responses to state and nation in moments of crises, and glorified the past, without fully developing a knowledge of local and state history.

Eighteenth-century citizens brought cultural baggage in their move west and a deep-seated love of politics – politics, which bor-

**Tunnel at Cumberland Gap**
*Source: Lexington Herald-Leader*

opportunities along the way have been considerable when translated in human terms. The wanton waste of opportunity to advance the welfare of human institutions caused by fruitless partisan bickering and neglect has been unconsciously great at times. It is an irony of Kentucky history that in a state that reveres the name of Henry Clay, the word "compromise" long ago became archaic.

We might stand on the mountain pinnacle towering over Cumberland Gap with the scales of history in hand and ask the question, "How well have Kentuckians fared in their virgin western Eden?" The answer would surely have to be stated in parts. Over two and a half

dered on being an all-season pastime. The quests have remained a Kentucky constant. Governors Simon Bolivar Buckner and William O. Bradley might well sit at a table on which rests a bottle of bourbon whiskey and conclude Kentucky politics and Kentucky politicians have changed little since they lived in the Governor's Mansion over a century ago.

Collectively Kentucky has undergone deep fundamental changes which may be best symbolized by the construction of a single generation house, in a new suburban rural community, alongside a decaying tobacco barn, all of this giving a fresh connotation to Stephen Collins Foster's deep spiritual lament.

# *State Song*

"My Old Kentucky Home" was written and set to music by Stephen Collins Foster in 1850 and published in 1853 by Firth, Pound, and Company of New York. Designated Kentucky's state song by an act of the Kentucky legislature in 1928, the original lyrics were changed in 1986 by a bill sponsored by Rep. Carl Hines (Democrat-Louisville), the only black member of the House, explaining the words were offensive. Stephen Foster, a professional songwriter of unparalleled skill and technique, wrote hundreds of songs. "Beautiful Dreamer," written in 1862 and published after his death in 1864, remains an all-time favorite. Stephen Foster was born in Lawrenceville, PA on July 4th, 1826 and died on January 13, 1864.

## CONTEMPORARY LYRICS (1986)

The sun shines bright on my old Kentucky home
'Tis summer, the people are gay
The corn top's ripe and the meadow's in bloom
While the birds make music all the day
The young folks roll on the little cabin floor
All merry, all happy and bright
By'n by hard times come a-knocking at the door
Then my old Kentucky home, good night.

*Weep no more my lady,*
*oh weep no more today.*
*We will sing one song for the old Kentucky home,*
*for the old Kentucky home far away.*

They hunt no more for the 'possum and the coon,
On meadow, the hill and the shore,
They sing no more by the glimmer of the moon,
On the bench by that old cabin door.
The day goes by like a shadow o'er the heart,
With sorrow where all was delight.
The time has come when the people have to part,
Then my old Kentucky home, good night.
The head must bow and the back will have to bend
Wherever the poor folks may go
A few more days and the trouble will end,
In the field where sugar-canes may grow.
A few more days till we totter on the road,
Then my old Kentucky home, good night.

**Statue of composer Stephen Collins Foster at My Old Kentucky Home State Park**
*Photo: Sid Webb*

*Source: www.lrc.ky.gov/kidspages/kentucky.htm*

# We're proud of what we put into the environment. And even prouder of what we don't.

To us, conservation is about energy. Energy saved by insulating homes through Project Warm. Energy dedicated to replenishing natural resources through Reforest the Bluegrass. And energy provided to our customers using one of the world's cleanest generating stations. Because when it comes to the environment, you have to give more than you take.

**Customers First. Energy that lasts.**

# State Profile

**Nickname:** *The Bluegrass State*
**Population - 2000 Census:** *4,041,769;* **2005 Est.:** *4,163,360;* **2030 Projection:** *4,554,998*
**Race: White - 3,640,889 (90.1%); Black/African American - 295,994 (7.3%); Hispanic - 59,939 (1.5%)**
**Civilian veterans - 380,618 (12.6% of Kentuckians over 18 years)**
**High School Graduates - 74.1%; Bachelor's Degree or Higher - 17.1%**
**Median Household Income: $33,672**
**Geographic Size**: *40,395 square miles*

**US Census metropolitan areas are within or extend into Kentucky:**
*Bowling Green; Cincinnati-Middletown (KY-OH-IN), including part of northern Kentucky; Clarksville (TN)-Hopkinsville; Elizabethtown; Evansville (IN)-Henderson; Huntington (WV)-Ashland; Lexington-Fayette; Louisville; and Owensboro.*
Source: http://www.uky.edu/KentuckyAtlas/kentucky.html

| Industry | Number | Percent |
|---|---|---|
| Agriculture, forestry, fishing & hunting & mining | 59,729 | 3.3 |
| Construction | 129,618 | 7.2 |
| Manufacturing | 315,774 | 17.6 |
| Wholesale Trade | 60,854 | 3.4 |
| Retail Trade | 217,164 | 12.1 |
| Transportation & warehousing & utilities | 108,783 | 6 |
| Information | 39,303 | 2.2 |
| Finance, insurance & real estate | 97,350 | 5.4 |
| Professional, scientific, management | 111,878 | 6.2 |
| Educational, health & social services | 365,605 | 20.3 |
| Arts, entertainment, recreation, accommodation  & food service | 129,973 | 7.2 |
| Other Services (except public administration) | 85,150 | 4.7 |
| Public administration | 77,128 | 4.3 |

*Source: http://ksdc.louisville.edu*

| Kentucky Gross State Product (GSP), by Component: 1995, 2000, and 2001 GSP: Current Dollars (In Millions of Dollars) | | | |
|---|---|---|---|
| Industry | 1995 | 2000 | 2001 |
| Total Gross State Product | 91,472 | 117,233 | 120,266 |
| Private industries | 78,522 | 101,566 | 103,632 |
| Agriculture, forestry, & fishing | 1,874 | 2,681 | 2,498 |
| Mining | 2,426 | 1,986 | 2,235 |
| Construction | 3,588 | 5,500 | 5,635 |
| Manufacturing | 25,848 | 30,891 | 30,297 |
| Transportation & public utilities | 7,574 | 9,433 | 9,905 |
| Wholesale trade | 5,332 | 7,502 | 7,461 |
| Retail trade | 8,300 | 10,947 | 11,369 |
| Finance, insurance, & real estate | 9,979 | 13,731 | 14,152 |
| Services | 13.599 | 18,895 | 20,081 |
| Government | 12,950 | 15,667 | 16,633 |

*Source: U.S. Census*

**Sharing in Kentucky's heritage.**

Kentucky Power has been a part of Kentucky's history for 85 years. Serving 175,000 customers in 20 eastern counties, we are a part of the rich heritage that makes the region special. And we plan to be here well into the future. By investing millions of dollars in environmental improvements at our power plant, and millions more in our energy delivery system, we are investing in Kentucky, its people and a bright future. When it comes to serving the Commonwealth, *Kentucky Power is there, always working for you.*

**AEP**

**KENTUCKY POWER®**

*A unit of American Electric Power*

*www.KentuckyPower.com*

# State Flag & Symbols

**Capital:** *Frankfort*
**State Seal,** *adopted 1792*
**State Motto:** *"United We Stand, Divided We Fall," adopted 1942*
**Official Latin Motto:** *"Deo gratiam habeamus" ("Let us be grateful to God"), adopted 2002*
**State Flag,** *adopted 1918*
**State Bird:** *Cardinal (Cardinalis cardinalis), adopted 1926*
**State Fossil:** *Brachiopod, adopted 1986*
**State Butterfly:** *Viceroy Butterfly (Limenitis archippus), adopted 1990*
**State Wild Animal Game Species:** *Gray Squirrel (Sciurus carolinensis), adopted 1968*
**State Horse:** *Thoroughbred (Equus caballus), adopted 1996*
**State Fish:** *Kentucky Spotted Bass, adopted 1956*
**State Fruit:** *Blackberry (Rubus allegheniensis), adopted 2004*
**State Flower:** *Goldenrod (Soldiago gigantea), adopted 1926*
**State Rock:** *Kentucky Agate, adopted 2000*
**State Gemstone:** *Freshwater Pearl, adopted 1986*
**State Soil:** *Crider Soil Series, adopted 1990*
**State Mineral:** *Coal, adopted 1998*
**State Tree:** *Tulip Poplar (Lirodendroan tulipifera), adopted 1994*
**State Musical Instrument:** *Appalachian Dulcimer, adopted 2001*
**State Song:** *"My Old Kentucky Home" - modern version, adopted 1986/1988*
**State Bluegrass Song:** *"Blue Moon of Kentucky," adopted 1988*

*Source: Kentucky Department for Libraries and Archives*

*Photos: Betty Hall & Sid Webb*

# The Home Builders Association of Kentucky – Celebrating 50 years of housing Kentucky

## Building or remodeling a home is one of the major investments you will make in your lifetime

The Home Builders Association of Kentucky sponsors a statewide Registered Builder and Remodelor Program, and, its members must adhere to strict guidelines in an effort to protect the consumer.

When choosing a Registered Builder or Remodelor you can be assured that you will receive a written contract, and a warranty covering structural items for at least one year.

Registered Builders and Remodelors carry all of the proper insurance and attend continuing education classes each year to keep up with latest industry trends and codes.

**When thinking of building or remodeling contact the local Home Builders Association in your area and ask for a list of Registered Builders or Remodelors.**

Find out more about housing in Kentucky by calling
**1-800-489-4225**
or visit our website at
**www.hbak.com**

# Top News Stories of 2005-2006

Bill Bryant

*2005-2006 in Kentucky included triumphs, tragedies and new challenges for the Bluegrass State as well as continuing political drama.*

**Tragedy came to Kentucky in different ways.** On August 27, 2006, Comair Flight 5191 crashed at Blue Grass Airport in Lexington, killing all but one of the 49 people onboard. The lone survivor was the plane's first officer; two other crewmembers including the pilot died. As the investigation got underway, it was immediately clear that the commuter jet, bound for Atlanta, had taken off on the wrong runway. Commercial pilots are supposed to use the airport's 7,000-foot runway. But in the predawn darkness, Flight 5191 roared down Runway 26, a much shorter general aviation runway. Unable to get airborne for more than a brief time from the 3,500-foot runway, the plane ran through a fence, clipped some trees and crashed, killing most people onboard instantly. The airplane—fuselage and cockpit separated from the tail of the plane—burned. At last report, the copilot is expected to recover, although he continues in serious condition. Questions have been raised regarding the air traffic control tower, which had only one of the two required air traffic controllers on duty that morning.

**The state's mining industry also had a tough year.** In the worst Kentucky coal mine disaster since 1989, five miners were killed in an explosion in Harlan County at the Kentucky Darby mine in May. Reports from the investigation indicated a methane gas leak into the section of the mine where the miners were working. The methane gas was somehow ignited, leading to the blast. Again, questions were raised whether standard procedures were followed.

**Blue Grass Airport director Michael Gobb wiped away tears after visiting a memorial to honor those who died in the Comair Flight 5191.**
*Photo: David Stephenson, Lexington Herald-Leader*

# WE GREW UP IN KENTUCKY.

## SO WE'RE GLAD TO HELP TELL ITS STORY.

Founded in Northern Kentucky, Tier 1 Performance Solutions is proud to have played a role in the creation of the 2006 Kentucky Almanac. We're experts when it comes to the organization and delivery of information—whether you need to train your sales force, spread corporate strategy throughout your organization, or catalogue over a century's worth of state history into a single volume.

Our combination of consulting, customizable software, and development services helps you translate your vision into the knowledge and information your people need to perform.

Tier 1 Performance: we turn your vision into results.

**Learning Solutions**
· E-Learning
· Classroom Training
· Instructional Design

**Change Management**
· Communications
· Train the Trainer
· Program Management

**Knowledge Management**
· Document Management
· Content Management
· Intranets and Portals

**Solution Accelerators**
· Learning Management Systems
· Content Management Systems
· Document Management Systems

PERFORMANCE SOLUTIONS

**www.tier1performance.com**

6 E 5th St | Covington, KY 41011
859.663.2114

In order to lessen the likelihood of an explosion from methane gas, which is prevalent in mines, miners are to barricade themselves in the section where they work. Evidence suggested the miners had not barricaded themselves in their work area.

**Kentucky continued to fight some apparently self-inflicted health struggles.** The Centers for Disease Control and Prevention said the commonwealth was first in the nation in the rate of cancer deaths, which appears to confirm the link between tobacco and cancer since Kentucky also leads the U.S. in numbers of adult smokers. State officials blamed smoking, poor diets and lack of awareness of available screenings and resources for that figure.

Addressing the harmful health effects of second-hand smoke, nearly a dozen cities have followed Lexington and Louisville's lead in enacting local indoor smoking bans, although debates were often contentious. Lexington led the way in 2003 when the Lexington Fayette Urban County Council passed an ordinance banning all smoking in most public buildings—restaurant and bar owners were most concerned about decline in revenues. One of the most restrictive smoking bans in Kentucky was passed by Henderson. Ashland passed a comparable ban, and Frankfort, the state's capital, prohibits smoking in public buildings. The Kentucky legislature also increased Kentucky's cigarette tax from 3 cents a pack to 30 cents in an effort to reduce smoking. Kentucky had the lowest cigarette tax in the nation: a smoker could save as much as 30 cents by purchasing a pack in Kentucky. As the top of the leading causes of death in the commonwealth, which is preventable, tobacco use takes the lives of nearly 8,000 Kentuckians annually. The health care cost is staggering at $1.4

A "Smoke-Free" ordinance sticker on the front window on a slow night at Buster's on Main St. in Lexington on June 17, 2004.
*Source: Lexington Herald-Leader*

billion per year.

**Gov. Ernie Fletcher, the first Republican to hold the office since 1971, had a difficult year in 2005-2006.** He was indicted by a Franklin County grand jury in May 2006 on misdemeanor charges—accused of rewarding jobs to political supporters that were specifically protected by the state merit system. The scandal involved a number of his closest appointees, for whom he issued pardons, leading to heated debates in the Franklin Circuit Courthouse between lawyers from the Attorney General's Office and Fletcher defense attorneys. Fletcher's approval ratings within the state dropped as he appeared headed for a public trial. Democratic Attorney General Greg Stumbo also came under attack by some who questioned his motives for the tough investigation into the Fletcher administration. This allegation was fueled in part when Stumbo declined to remove himself as a potential challenger to Fletcher for the governor's office.

After months of wrangling, the governor's attorneys and prosecutors came to an agreement that dropped the criminal charges. Under the agreed order, Fletcher

**People smoking at the bar at Trumps Sports Bar and Grill, 286 Southland Dr. in Lexington, KY, Thursday, July 1, 2004. People are still smoking at the establishment, where ash trays are still available, despite Lexington's smoking ban.**
*Photo: Charles Bertram, Lexington Herald-leader*

# Receive a Kentucky Almanac with a subscription to the Lexington Herald-Leader!

Subscribe to the Herald-Leader and get the Kentucky Almanac–2nd Edition or give a gift subscription and get the Kentucky Almanac. Whatever you decide, keep the Almanac. If you have a copy, give it as a gift to relatives, friends or business associates!

## For fast service, call now at 1-800-224-0518!

■ ■ ■ ■ ■ ■ ■ ■ ■ ■ ■ ■ ■ ■ ■ ■ ■ ■ ■ ■ ■ ■ ■ ■ ■

Or complete, clip and return this form with your payment information to:

Lexington Herald-Leader, Circulation - R. White
100 Midland Avenue • Lexington, KY   40508-1999

☐ **Daily paid subscription**
(All 7 days, Monday-Sunday)
Save $11.85! • Daily & Sunday $48
*($16/month for 3-months w/Kentucky Almanac)*
SD7PKY07*

☐ **Weekend paid subscription**
(4 days, Friday-Monday)
Regular rate • Weekend $36
*($12/month for 3-months w/Kentucky Almanac)*
SD4PKY07*

☐ **Please charge my:**
○ debit card or ○ credit card: ○ VISA   ○ MASTER CARD   ○ DISCOVER ○ AMEX

__ __ __ __ / __ __ __ __ / __ __ __ __ / __ __ __ __   Expires: __ __ __ __ / __ __ __ __

☐ **Please see attached check payment**

NAME _____

ADDRESS _____

CITY _____ STATE _____ ZIP _____

EMAIL _____ PHONE _____
*(required for verification)*

SIGNATURE _____ DATE _____

This offer is valid only for subscribers who have not been an active subscriber in the last 31 days. KY Almanac–2nd Edition is only eligible for paid subscriptions at the time service is started. Available while supplies last. Offer expires March 31, 2007.

*After three months, regular rate of $19.95 for daily service applies. Weekend rate is already the regular rate of $12. Or, continue to save with EZpay by calling 1-800-224-0518.

060713-002-KB

acknowledged "mistakes" by his administration but insisted the actions were unintentional. The governor also acknowledges that the attorney general's investigation was proper, although he never conceded any criminal conduct on his part. Gov. Fletcher continues his bid for re-election to the governor's office.

Gov. Fletcher faced serious, life-threatening health problems throughout February and March, 2006. Hospitalized for gallstones, he experienced complications from gallbladder surgery. Gov. Fletcher was readmitted on March 9th, 2006 for what his doctors called a "life-threatening blood-clot." The condition was extremely serious—to the extent that Gov. Fletcher transferred power to Lt. Governor Steve Pence before undergoing a procedure to dissolve the clot.

**Natural disasters took a decisive toll on Kentucky.** A November 2005 tornado touched down in Henderson County, which led to 25 deaths in the area that includes Evansville, Ind. There was significant damage to Ellis Park race track in Henderson County—the tornado, with peak winds of 200 mph, was the deadliest U.S. tornado in the 2005 tornado season. In September of 2006, heavy rains and flash flooding hit Central Kentucky hard. Two young women were killed as they were swept into floodwaters before the eyes of law enforcement officers while walking near the campus of the University of Kentucky in downtown Lexington. The total number of fatalities was eight, most from motor vehicles being swept away from rushing powerful floodwaters on roadways.

**Even some bright spots for the Commonwealth were tempered:** the famed Kentucky Derby proved eventful in May with a decisive win by "Barbaro," a heavy favorite in the Preakness Stakes that looked promising for a "Triple Crown." But, before a shocked crowd of 100,000 fans, Barbaro broke down at the start of the Preakness shattering his right hind leg at the ankle. His racing career was finished but veterinarians have struggled to save his life from complications from the injuries. As this almanac goes to print, Barbaro continues to improve.

**The horse industry brought Kentucky into the world spotlight when it was announced that the 2010 World Equestrian Games will be held at the Kentucky Horse Park.** This is the first time in the

**Help was on the way shortly after Barbaro broke down during the early stages of the Preakness Stakes at Pimlico Race Course in Baltimore, Md., on May 20, 2006.**
*Source: Lexington Herald-Leader*

# Lexington born and read.

At Smiley Pete Publishing, we bring you the latest information from the vibrant local communities where we live and work and from the people who make things happen.

history of the games that the event will take place outside Europe. And, paraequestrian events for athletes with disabilities will be included in the FEI Games™. Then, Alltech, a worldwide leader in the field of animal nutrition and based in Nicholasville, announced its $10 million donation to 2010 Alltech FEI Games™. The Games could bring 500,000 visitors to the state and have a $100 million economic impact. If these projections materialize, the FEI Games™ will take precedent as the largest sporting event to be held in the commonwealth.

**Kentuckians continued to serve and in some cases die in Operation Enduring Freedom (Afghanistan) and Operation Iraqi Freedom.** Kentucky soldiers were deployed to Iraq, Afghanistan and other locations in America's increasingly controversial global war on terrorism.

Gov. Ernie Fletcher spoke to the 483 soldiers of the Kentucky National Guard 1st Battalion, 149th Infantry Division that were dispatched to Iraq, at a farewell ceremony at Knox Central High School in Barbourville, Kentucky on June 29, 2006. The soldiers, from all over Eastern Kentucky, is the largest call up from Kentucky for the Iraq War. Kentucky National Guard troops were also sent to the U.S.-Mexican border to help deal with a flood of illegal immigration, another issue that sparked national and local debates.

**Kentucky's economy seemed to be defying some national downsizing.** While Ford Motor Company of Louisville announced major layoffs and plant closings around the country, it opted to keep the Louisville operations intact, at least for now. And, Louisville-based UPS announced in May 2006 that it will nearly double its capacity in Louisville, a move that is expected to bring 5,000 new jobs to the region. The UPS WorldPort expansion will result in a $1 billion investment at the facility and expand the existing shipping facility by more than 1 million square feet and increase all aspects of the capacity for volume shipping. UPS is

Governor Ernie Fletcher, First Lady Glenna Fletcher, David O'Connor - Olympic gold medalist and President of the United States Equestrian Federation and Jim Host, chairman of the World Games 2010 Foundation, Inc. celebrate World Equestrian Games announcement.
Source: Kentucky Commerce Cabinet

Kentucky's number one employer.

**Kentuckians showed their generous and giving spirit by helping the victims of Hurricane Katrina.** Hurricane Katrina was the costliest and one of the deadliest hurricanes in U.S. history. The sixth-strongest Atlantic hurricane ever recorded and the third-strongest landfalling U.S. hurricane ever recorded, Katrina hit in late August 2005 and devastated the north-central Gulf Coast region. The catastrophic effects on the city of

Sgt. Travis Thompson, Somerset, with his daughter Hanna Thompson who holds a yellow ribbon prior to ceremony for 483 soldiers of the Kentucky National Guard 1st Battalion, 149th Infantry Division who are being dispatched to Iraq.
Photo: Frank Anderson,
Lexington Herald-Leader

# ALL OVER THE BLUEGRASS
# WE SPEAK ONLY ONE LANGUAGE

## *exposure*

AS THE LEADER IN TOURISM MARKETING WE OFFER A
PASSPORT TO READERS THROUGHOUT THE BLUEGRASS

## 859-543-1014

TRAVELHOST OF THE BLUEGRASS

New Orleans led Kentucky National Guard troops, law enforcement officers from the Ky. Dept. of Fish and Wildlife Resources, and other emergency responders to the area. But Kentuckians were also busy at home, collecting money and necessities to send to victims. Many volunteers went to the hurricane-ravaged area to help residents rebuild and thousands of displaced victims came to Kentucky seeking refuge from the disaster.

**Kentuckians also kept a close eye on the U.S. Supreme Court's rulings regarding the public display of the Ten Commandments.** The court issued split decisions in a number of cases before it that left questions about whether or not it is legal to post the documents in government buildings. The Supreme Court's ruling in two Kentucky cases were clear—the posting of framed copies on the walls of two rural Kentucky courthouses is prohibited, while a 6-foot-tall granite monument on the grounds of the Texas Capitol in Austin was approved. The Supreme Court ruled that the Texas monument was a less blatantly religious statement, which had a secular, historical and educational meaning as part of a group of similar markers on the state grounds. These court decisions were the first Ten Commandments rulings from the nation's highest court in 25 years. Supreme Court Justice Stephen G. Breyer cast the decisive vote, expressing his view that the "basic purposes" of the First Amendment prohibits the creation of a state religion.

**Kentucky voters finished the year by choosing from among the most candidates ever running for public office.** Decisions were made about mayors, judges and other local officeholders as well as the state legislature and representation in Congress. Meanwhile the state awaits the 2007 statewide elections that will include the always colorful race for governor.

**Law enforcement officers with the Kentucky Department of Fish and Wildlife rescued a Louisiana resident in their boat in New Orleans, LA, Monday, September 5, 2005.**
**L-Captain Frank Floyd and R- Homer Pigman (cq)**
*Source: Charles Bertram, Lexington Herald-Leader*

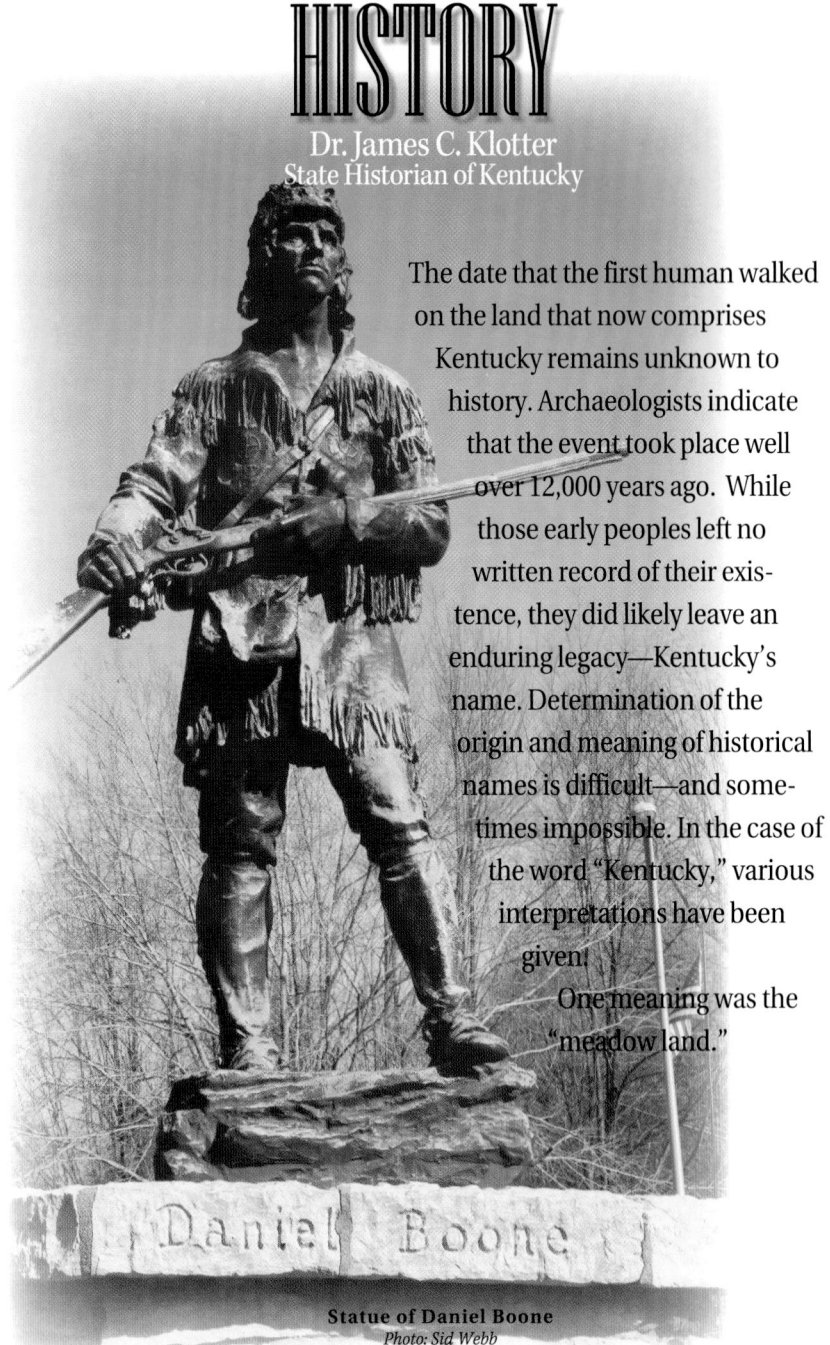

# HISTORY

Dr. James C. Klotter
State Historian of Kentucky

The date that the first human walked on the land that now comprises Kentucky remains unknown to history. Archaeologists indicate that the event took place well over 12,000 years ago. While those early peoples left no written record of their existence, they did likely leave an enduring legacy—Kentucky's name. Determination of the origin and meaning of historical names is difficult—and sometimes impossible. In the case of the word "Kentucky," various interpretations have been given.

One meaning was the "meadow land."

**Statue of Daniel Boone**
*Photo: Sid Webb*

To early Indians who lived in the area, Kentucky furnished abundant game, fertile land and pleasant climate. Many tribal nations had long made this land their old Kentucky home. Yet by the time the first European explorers visited the region, this place of first contact between cultures became a place of death for Native-Americans, as deadly microbes killed thousands. Disease swept over the land, tribal boundaries changed, and other factors intruded to mean that this land, once filled with Native-American homes, now had few permanent Indian settlements by the 1760s. Several tribes still regarded the region as their hunting ground, however.

**Constitution Square, Danville**
*Photo: Sid Webb*

As the two cultures met in this middle ground of Kentucky, another of its names grew up: "Dark and Bloody Ground." In the 1750s and the 1760s, land-hungry explorers, such as Christopher Gist and Dr. Thomas Walker, and then Long Hunters, among them Daniel Boone, James Harrod and Simon Kenton, first brought to the East stories of the richness of this seemingly unclaimed land beyond the mountains. A young man who would soon conquer the Northwest Territory, George Rogers Clark, proclaimed "a richer and more beautiful country than this I believe has never been seen in America." Attracted by the promise of what has been called the "Kentucky myth of plenty," eager settlers, imbued with "Kentucky Fever," flocked to the area just as the Revolutionary War broke out. Settlements erected at Harrodsburg in 1774 and Boonesborough and Stanford in 1775 met resistance. Indians fought this intrusion into their happy hunting ground. Bloodshed resulted and filled the first decade of settlement with death and sorrow. Native-Americans, and European settlers and their African-American slaves, all mourned their losses.

Peace finally did come to Kentucky and another meaning of its name reflected its promise to newcomers. It was "the land of tomorrow." Men and women who had been simply protecting and constructing wilderness homes now turned to building a state. By 1790, these Kentucky counties of Virginia had 73,000 people (16 percent of them slaves) and sought separation from the Mother State. After flirting briefly with independence, Kentucky, in 1792, finally joined the union as the fifteenth state—and first one west of the mountains. Revolutionary war hero Isaac Shelby became its first governor. He would later serve a second term and lead Kentucky forces in battle in the so-called Second American Revolution, the War of 1812.

In the period from 1800 to 1860, Kentucky was one of the most important states in the young republic. In 1840, its population ranked sixth in the nation. A diversified agricultural base gave Kentucky a sound economic foundation: it stood first in hemp production (then used in rope and bagging) and wheat; second in tobacco, corn, hogs and mules; third in flax; and fourth in rye. Its political leadership also gave the state much influence in national circles: John Breckinridge served as the first federal cabinet-level member from west of the Alleghenies; Richard M.

**Abe Lincoln**
*Photo: Sid Webb*

Johnson and John Cabell Breckinridge functioned as vice presidents (Breckinridge the youngest ever); President Zachary Taylor, although not a Kentuckian by birth, lived in the state many years (and is buried here); and, of course, the "Great Pacificator," three-time presidential candidate Henry Clay, gained fame for his compromises designed to avert conflict. The state's cultural advancement gave Lexington its title as "the Athens of the West," while Louisville's booming river and business trade made

**Battle of Perryville reenactment**
*Source: Tour Southern & Eastern Kentucky*

it one of the largest cities in the South and West. Overall, Kentucky had a reputation as a forward-looking commonwealth, a place for the ambitious and the eager.

Yet, lurking below the surface of prosperity lay elements that would disrupt the state and nation. For this commonwealth that was the first in the nation to allow people to vote without owning property did not give equal rights to many of those who lived in its borders. Slavery had existed in Kentucky since the earliest settlers came from Virginia, and by 1830 almost one-fourth of the population lived in bondage. The commonwealth had the third highest number of slaveholders among the slave states. Most held only a few slaves—the state ranked third lowest in the average number of slaves. But the voices of those denied human rights, the cries from the slave auction block, the search for freedom by bondsmen such as Henry Bibb and Josiah Henson, showed that the existence of even one person in slavery could "cause the very heart to sicken." If Kentucky had survived earlier crises with the Indians, the British, and political factions, it

now had to face the questions of slavery or emancipation, secession or nationalism. Its greatest crisis was yet to come.

The cost of deciding those momentous questions was great. With ties to both North and South, Kentucky knew that war would tear the state apart. Divided sentiment meant divided families fighting each other. Household after household saw one son ride north, another south. For the commonwealth, the conflict became truly "the Brothers' War." As many as 100,000 Kentucky soldiers (23,000 of them African-American) fought for the Union, which the state supported in 1861; perhaps another 40,000 went to the Confederate cause. Of all those men, 30,000 never returned from the battlefield.

Two natives of the state symbolized all the wartime divisions, for both Presidents Abraham Lincoln and Jefferson Davis were born in the commonwealth, less than eight months and eighty miles apart. Both sought to win their home state for their cause. At first the state declared itself neutral, and the land saw three separate entities—the United States, the Confederate States, and Kentucky. But such a stance could not continue, and Kentucky finally abandoned neutrality and remained in the Union. However, disgruntled southern sympathizers formed a rump government, with its capital at Bowling Green. The state soon became a star in both flags. Fighting first broke out in Kentucky in the winter of 1861-1862. Confederate losses ended their control, and the bloody Battle of Perryville in late 1862 marked the Confederacy's high-water mark in Kentucky. After that conflict, the Confederate army made no serious threats to retake Kentucky, and so the excesses that often accompany military rule fell chiefly on the Union side. In addition, Confederates who did enter the state (chiefly the raiders of Gen. John Hunt Morgan) presented a dashing, heroic front to most of the populace. Though only partly correct, such an image contrasted with that of Federal leaders who had to deal with the daily problems that Morgan never faced. Thus the southern cavalier image grew more attractive.

Union policies regarding slavery compounded northern problems. While Lincoln's Emancipation Proclamation did not directly affect Kentucky, ostensibly a loyal state, news of that declaration created resentment among state leaders. Even devoted unionists questioned and criticized the administration's policies, particularly after Kentucky slaves began enlisting in the army in return for their freedom.

The commonwealth slowly turned anti-administration and even pro-southern in sympathy. Soon after the end of hostilities in 1865, a newspaper remarked that Kentucky had waited until after the war to secede. And so it seemed, for the vanquished in war soon became the victors in postwar politics. Since Kentucky did not undergo Reconstruction, ex-Confederates quickly gained power, and for the next three decades dominated Democratic party councils, until Republicans registered their first gubernatorial triumph in 1895. (From then until the 1930s the two parties contested on a reasonably equal basis for major offices, but the effects of the Great Depression and the actions of the New Deal would again make the state solidly Democratic until the later decades of the 20th Century, when a realignment of voting patterns began to emerge.)

That same period saw marked changes in the Kentucky character. Despite many problems, the state continued its cultural advances. Kentucky novelists such as James Lane Allen and John Fox Jr. "The Little Shepherd of Kingdom Come", and then later, Elizabeth Madox Roberts, Harriette Arnow, Jesse Stuart and Robert Penn Warren (winner of three Pulitzer Prizes and the nation's first poet laureate) gave the state a firm foundation in regional literature. Newspapermen such as Henry Watterson, the colorful editor of the Louisville *Courier-Journal*, left their imprint on the nation. To a lesser extent, artists—including the nationally known Frank Duveneck and the regionalist Paul Sawyier—and a wide range of those who produced folk art, offered citizens of the commonwealth attractive alternatives.

Reenactment of Lewis & Clark exploration docked at Louisville
*Source: Sid Webb*

Yet during the same period, the effects of the war, depression and general stagnation stripped some of the veneer of antebellum prosperity from the land. The postwar introduction of the new burley tobacco increasingly oriented the agrarian economy to one crop and subjected it to its vagaries of price. Despite Louisville's presence as a supplier of the South, the state did not keep pace with the rapid industrial advancement and urbanization of America. (Not until 1970 would Kentucky have more urban dwellers than rural—a half century after the United States made that transformation.) On top of all this, violence erupted in the form of a dozen or more so-called feuds, giving the state an image it found hard to overcome. The assassination of a governor in 1900, violent farm protests in the Black Patch War, plus later coal-oriented conflicts added to the stereotype. Ironically, Kentucky now ranks very low in those statistics regarding violent crime.

Labor union conflicts, failures of leadership, more than a decade of Prohibition, the Great Depression, and then World War II, all added to the problems that Kentuckians faced. State citizens in search of work migrated to northern cities, the Appalachian area continued poor as the coal industry remained depressed, and the state's financial poverty made educational support difficult.

Slowly some change again came to the Bluegrass State. Improved transportation and additional industry

**Portal 31 Mine in Harlan County**
*Source: Tour Southern & Eastern Kentucky*

beginning in the 1950s gradually started to reverse population losses. A parks system attracted tourism while bettering recreational facilities for Kentuckians. Coal gained an increasingly important share in the national energy program and prices spiraled upward in the 1970s. The state slowly and basically changed from an agricultural base to an industrial one—by the 21st Century it ranked third among the states in the production of motor vehicles, for example.

Regarding civil rights, Kentucky had adopted a policy of segregation following the Civil War, though it never disenfranchised its black voters, as did the deeper South. The first Afri-

can-American legislator, Charles Anderson Jr., took office in the 1930s. Following the 1954 U.S. Supreme Court decision outlawing public school segregation, the state's mostly peaceful integration made it, for a time, a symbol of success and model for the South in the ensuing struggle for equal rights. But later riots in the state soon showed that much of that change was more symbolic than real. Still, Kentucky's passage of the first state Civil Rights Act and the first Fair Housing Act in the South showed that it remained a place of paradox.

Through it all, Kentuckians continued to enjoy the world around them. Hunting and fishing, always popular pastimes, competed with other sports for attention. Indicative of what one writer has called the state's ability to reconcile "red-eye, racing, and religion," the people increasingly supported the breeding and racing of thoroughbreds. Beginning as a small affair in 1875, the Kentucky Derby grew in popularity as the years passed. Newer sports made their appearance and one, basketball, made particularly rapid strides. The state's nationally known teams both divided and bound citizens together.

At times seemingly a part of Kentuckians' recreation, politics continued to attract attention, and the state produced respected and influential statesman. Folksy, personable Alben Barkley ("the Veep") served as senate majority leader under Franklin D. Roosevelt and vice president under Harry Truman, while Fred Vinson represented the state as Chief Justice of the U.S. Supreme Court. Also on the national scene, men such as Earle Clements, John Sherman Cooper, Wendell Ford and Mitch McConnell took leadership positions

**Henry Clay**
*Source: Library of Congress*

and left their imprint on national affairs.

On the state homefront, Kentucky had earlier taken a leadership role in the struggle for women's rights, through the efforts of Laura Clay, Madeline McDowell Breckinridge, and others. Once women gained the right to vote in 1920, political involvement followed. Kentucky had one of the first eight women to serve in Congress—Katherine Langley—and one of the first half-dozen women governors in America—Martha Layne Collins.

With party struggles, political scandals and lively election contests continuing to the present, Kentucky politics indicates that the conclusion of Judge James Mulligan's famous poem still reflects reality:

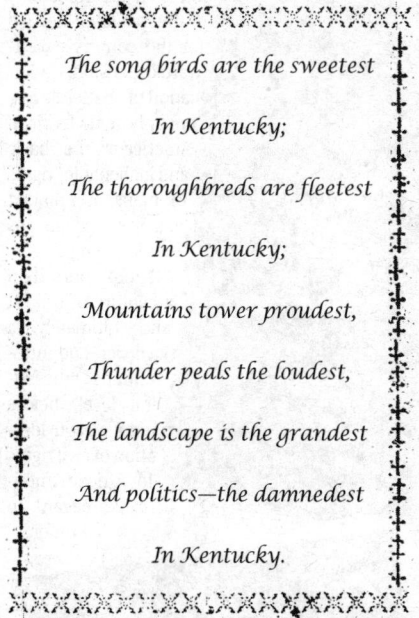

*The song birds are the sweetest*

*In Kentucky;*

*The thoroughbreds are fleetest*

*In Kentucky;*

*Mountains tower proudest,*

*Thunder peals the loudest,*

*The landscape is the grandest*

*And politics—the damnedest*

*In Kentucky.*

And so, in the first decade of the 21st Century, the commonwealth continues to reflect its past, as it looks to the future. It stands exactly in the middle of the states in population, and its 4,041,769 residents (in 2000) rank high in the nation in the percentage of native-born people who still live in the state of their birth. The traditional commonwealth remains a place still tied to the ideals of the family farm, small town life, and a sense of place, but another side of Kentucky reflects all the elements of modern America. This land of contrast still searches to see what it needs to do to achieve its dream to be "the land of tomorrow."

## "Well, I never!"

Two natives of the state symbolized all the wartime divisions, for both Presidents Abraham Lincoln and Jefferson Davis were born in the commonwealth, less than eight months and eighty miles apart. Both sought to win their home state for their cause. At first the state declared itself neutral, and the land saw three separate entities—the United States, the Confederate States, and Kentucky. But such a stance could not continue, and Kentucky finally abandoned neutrality and remained in the Union. However, disgruntled southern sympathizers formed a rump government, with its capital at Bowling Green. The state soon became a star in both flags. Fighting first broke out in Kentucky in the winter of 1861-1862. Confederate losses ended their control, and the bloody Battle of Perryville in late 1862 marked the Confederacy's high-water mark in Kentucky.

# HISTORY

## *Civil Rights*

Anne S. Butler, Ph.D.

When the newly formed Commonwealth of Kentucky chartered its first Constitution in 1792, it incorporated Article IX, a provision that sanctioned slavery under the rule of law.

Article IX "obliged the owners of slaves to treat them with humanity, to provide for their necessary clothing and provision, and to abstain from all injuries to them extending to life or limb." Another provision enabled the legislature to "pass laws to permit the owners of slaves to emancipate them." Although many citizens opposed the adoption of slave codes for the new state, their political strength was insufficient to stop the migration of slavery into the Commonwealth. Despite the continuing efforts of anti-slavery forces, a second Constitution was adopted in 1799 codifying the practice of slavery and thereby insuring its continuation.

Source: Kentucky State University

It was the retention of slavery through the end of the Civil War that set the stage for prolonged efforts by African-Americans, both free and enslaved, to secure basic civil liberties. Adoption of slave codes in the Constitutions of 1792, 1799, and 1850, signaled a three-fold aim among most lawmakers and the proslavery factions they represented. The inherent aims of the framers of the constitution were: to protect and promote the interests of slaveholders throughout the southern colonies; to recognize and support the importance of slavery for commercial interests in the northeast; and to ensure availability of the free labor needed for the country's westward expansion. Codification of chattel slavery not only denied African Americans the basic and inalienable "rights of man," it branded enslaved people as inferior beings.

It took more than a century of protest and ultimately a civil war, and interventions at the federal level, before serious consideration of civil rights for African Americans began to unfold

Martin Luther King with Gov. Ned Breathitt
Source: Kentucky Department of Libraries & Archives

within the Commonwealth. Among the enslaved population, however, neither the rule of law nor their status as "chattel property" was strong enough to extinguish the visions and hopes they held for liberty. Thus began individual and collective actions to acquire full access to the democratic ideals and practices governing a civil society. These efforts reached a high-water mark during the Civil War when 24,703 enslaved men in Kentucky joined the war effort both to preserve the union and secure freedom for themselves and their families. This number represented the third largest contingency of African American men in the nation that joined the war effort.

A series of promising steps following the Civil War gave the appearance that both the Nation and the Commonwealth were ready to bestow civil rights to all citizens. Chief among these steps was the abolishment of slavery, in December 1865, through federal ratification of the Thirteenth Amendment. Subsequently, passage of the federal Civil Rights Act of 1866, and adoption of the Fourteenth and Fifteenth Amendments to the United States Constitution, bestowing citizenship to former slaves and voting rights for men, provided small, but significant victories. African Americans would realize, however, that the same proverbial winds bringing positive and progressive changes are often buttressed by winds of resistance.

**Whitney Young, Jr.**
*Source: Kentucky Dept. of Libraries & Archives*

Disparate treatment in public modes of transportation provided a venue for a civil rights protest in Louisville in 1870. While African American women were allowed seats on the inside of street cars, their male companions were not allowed to sit with them. Instead, the men were required to stand on platforms outside the box cars. Filing a suit against this disparate treatment in federal court resulted in a victory for Horace Pierce, Robert and Samuel Clark, each a respected business owner residing in the city. The legal actions of these men resulted in elimination of the offensive practice among all local carriers.

Passage of the federal Civil Rights Act of 1875, also initially provided the appearance of access to a wider spectrum of public accommodations, including the "full enjoyment of the accommodations, advantages, facilities and privileges of inns, public conveyances on land or water, theaters and other places of public amusement." Almost as soon as the Act was published, the response to the bill in Kentucky was negative. One columnist writing for the March 7, 1875, issue of the *Lexington Weekly Press* commented that "The Negro is now endowed with all the political privileges, *miscalled rights*, which it is possible for him or any other man to possess in this country." The columnist made clear his disdain for such legislation and that of many of his readers.

Numerous strategies were designed to stifle or block African American access to the public accommodation measures contained in the 1875 Act. One of the most overt forms of opposition was the passage of a bill in the General Assembly, during its 1891 session, requiring separate coaches for African American and white passengers using interstate railroad transportation. A "separate, but equal" policy widely employed in other southern states would gain a foothold in Kentucky slowing progress in transportation, housing and employment, as well as in educational arenas.

In response to this proposed legislation mandating separate rail cars, a statewide committee was formed to fight against passage of such an unfair bill. Known as the Anti-Separate Coach Movement, the committee was unsuccessful in persuading the General Assembly that such legislation was both retrogressive and in violation of the federal Civil Rights Act. When the case was heard in the U.S. District Court, a ruling was issued on June 4, 1894, declaring the actions of the General Assembly unconstitutional. Ten years later, the "separate but equal" strategy was again imposed by the General Assembly. Passage of its infamous "Day Law," in 1904, ended nearly 40 years of integrated education at Berea College. It was not until almost 50 years later that the "separate but equal" clause was ruled unconstitutional.

Once physical enslavement ended in the Nineteenth Century, the persistence of prejudice and racial discrimination remained a formidable foe throughout most of the first-half of the twentieth century. On March 4, 1964, civil rights activists in Kentucky staged a protest march on the State Capital with renewed demands for open accommodations. They were joined by Dr. Martin Luther King, Jr., Jackie Robinson and other civil rights leaders with state, regional and national profiles.    After much ideological struggle, the Kentucky General Assembly, under the leadership of Governor Ned Breathitt, passed the Civil Rights Act of 1966. This Act was hailed as "the strongest and most comprehensive civil rights bill passed by a southern state."

The civil rights being sought by African Americans were intrinsically rights of access to opportunities that held promise of increasing the quality of their lives.  These, at a basic level, included: the right to equal educational opportunities and access to public accommodations, the right to vote and participate in governance, the right to purchase land and homes free of segregated restrictions, and the right to testify in courts and to serve as jurors, as well as the right to fair competition in the marketplace. Throughout much of the last part of the twentieth century, African Americans were joined in their quest for civil rights by many other groups who experienced similar inequities.

## A KENTUCKY CIVIL RIGHTS TIMELINE

**1792** - Kentucky admitted to union; first state constitution establishes legality of slavery.

**1794** - Kentucky statute gives free or freed Negroes legal equality to whites.

**1798-1799** - Law concerning "Slaves, Free Negroes, Mulattos, and Indians" and second Kentucky Constitution change status of free people of color by placing limitations on their rights, including voting and self-defense.

**1855** - Berea College founded by abolitionist Rev. John G. Fee to provide interracial education.

**1859** - Fee is forced to close the school and leave Kentucky following John Brown's raid on Harper's Ferry, Va.

**1863** - President Abraham Lincoln issues the Emancipation Proclamation, but his native state of Kentucky is unaffected because the proclamation frees slaves only in those states that have seceded from the Union.

**1864** - Camp Nelson, S. of Nicholasville, becomes the most important Union recruiting station and training camp for African Americans.

**1865** - Slavery ends nationwide, including in Kentucky, after the critical number of states ratify the 13th Amendment to the U.S. Constitution. The first great African-American migration begins.

**1866** - Berea College is reestablished by Fee and others, including African Americans from the Camp Nelson refugee camp.

**1870** - Members of Quinn Chapel A.M.E. Church in Louisville organize Kentucky's first known protest of racial discrimination, challenging segregation on local streetcars. This action and other early black protests would spark other actions demanding the rights to testify in court against whites, to serve on juries, and to vote.

**1896** - In *Plessy v. Ferguson*, U.S. Supreme Court rules that "separate but equal" treatment for blacks and whites under the law is constitutional.

**1904** - The Day Law takes effect, segregating both public and private schools across Kentucky.

**1908** - U.S. Supreme Court upholds Kentucky's Day Law. Justice John Marshall Harlan again dissents, protesting that the ruling puts racial prejudice ahead of civil liberties.

**1914** - The NAACP opens a branch in Louisville to protest lynching and mob violence against blacks and to fight a new housing ordinance reinforcing racial segregation.

**1917** - U.S. Supreme Court declares the 1914 Louisville residential segregation ordinance unconstitutional in *Buchanan v. Warley*.

**1935** - Charles W. Anderson is the first African American elected to the Kentucky House of Representatives since Reconstruction.

**1941** - Louisville sit-in protests segregated library.

**1945** - Baseball Commissioner A.B. "Happy" Chandler allows the Dodgers to sign Jackie Robinson as the first African American to play in the modern major leagues. Chandler agrees.

**1948** - Lyman T. Johnson files suit against the University of Kentucky for admission.

**1949** - UK admits the first black students to its graduate and professional schools.

**1950** - The Day Law is amended to allow individual colleges to decide whether to admit African Americans if no comparable course is taught at Kentucky State College.

**1954** - U.S. Supreme Court, in *Brown v. Board of Education of Topeka*, abolishes segregated public schools.

**1955** - Remaining state colleges opened to all applicants.

**1957** - Kentucky High School Athletics Association allows accredited African-American high schools to become members and to participate in state tournaments.

**1959** - NAACP Youth Council pickets Louisville's Brown Theater when its management refuses to admit African Americans to see *Porgy and Bess.*

**1960** - African Americans in Louisville organize a voter registration campaign to replace city officials, capped by a rally where Dr. Martin Luther King Jr. of the Southern Christian Leadership Conference speaks to thousands.

Young people in Louisville form a chapter of the Congress on Racial Equality and begin demonstrations at downtown businesses.

General Assembly establishes Kentucky Commission on Human Rights and prohibits discrimination in state employment.

**1961** - Kentuckian Whitney Young Jr. becomes executive director of the National Urban League.

**1963** - Gov. Bert Combs issues a Governor's Code of Fair Practice against segregation in state government and state contracts.

**1964** - U.S. Congress passes federal Civil Rights Act. Lack of support in the Kentucky legislature for a strong public accommodations bill leads to a mass march on Frankfort.

**1965** - At a major conference on civil rights in Louisville, Gov. Edward Breathitt pledges support for a strong civil rights bill addressing employment as well as public accommodations.

**1966** - General Assembly passes the Kentucky Civil Rights Act, and King calls it "the strongest and most comprehensive civil rights bill passed by a Southern state."

**1967** - Mae Street Kidd of Louisville is elected to the Kentucky House of Representatives.

Open housing ordinances are passed in Covington and Kenton County, and the Fayette County Fiscal Court bans discrimination in housing in Lexington and the county. One of the first acts of Louisville's new Board of Aldermen is to pass a strong ordinance against housing discrimination, replacing the weaker, voluntary one.

**1968** - Georgia Powers of Louisville is elected to the Kentucky Senate. The General Assembly adds housing discrimination to the enforcement section of the state Civil Rights Act. A protest against police mistreatment in Louisville turns violent, and a week of disturbances ends in the arrests of six African Americans—dubbed the "Black Six"—on charges that they conspired to blow up Ohio River oil refineries. After more than two years of demonstrations and court hearings, all charges against the six would be dismissed.

**1969** - The Kentucky Commission on Human Rights opens centers in Louisville and Lexington to help African Americans moving into new neighborhoods. A group of black students, inspired by the Black Power movement, takes over a building at the University of Louisville to force changes on campus.

**1970** - The Jefferson County Fiscal Court extends enforcement of Louisville's local housing law to the county.

**1975** - Cross-district busing to equalize the racial makeup of Louisville's public schools sparks sometimes violent reactions, which eventually subside after two years.

**1976** - Correcting a historical oversight, the General Assembly, after a campaign led by Kidd, ratifies the 13th, 14th, and 15th Amendments to the U.S. Constitution—more than 100 years after they became law.

**1996** - The state constitution is amended to remove provisions for a poll tax and segregated schools.

*Source: Kentucky Educational Television (KET)*

*Whitney M. Young, Jr.* (1921-1971), educator and civil rights leader, lived in a simple two-story wooden house on the campus of the Old Lincoln Institute near Simpsonville (a National Historic Landmark) until he was 15. He spent most of his career working to end employment discrimination in the South and turning the National Urban League from a relatively passive civil rights organization into one that aggressively fought for justice. In 1968, President Johnson honored Young with the highest civilian award. — **MEDAL OF FREEDOM**—

# HISTORY

# *The Struggle for Racial Equality*

### William Crawford Green

Three constitutional moments in the struggle for racial equality have been defined by Kentuckians: Abraham Lincoln, John Marshall Harlan and Frederick M. Vinson. Their contributions are rooted in the Declaration of Independence which announced the "self-evident" truth "that all men are created equal." Prior to the Civil War, Thomas Jefferson's revolutionary principle was limited to white men by the authors of the Constitution and by the Supreme Court's decision in *Dred Scott v. Sanford* (1857), which held that African Americans were property, not persons.

In the midst of the Civil War, Abraham Lincoln used the Declaration of Independence to remake the meaning of the Constitution. According to Garry Wills, "the very heart of his Gettysburg Address is a nation conceived in liberty by its dedication to the Declaration's critical proposition of

The Constitution was formally corrected in 1868 by the Fourteenth Amendment which provides that no state shall deny "any person the equal protection of the laws." In *Plessy v. Ferguson* (1896), the Supreme Court rejected the spirit of Lincoln's Declaration and decided that the Fourteenth Amendment permitted state governments to provide separate public facilities for whites and African Americans as long as those facilities were physically equal.

In his *Plessy* dissent, Justice John Marshall Harlan (from Danville) argued that the separate but equal doctrine violated the Declaration's conception of human equality to which he gave explicit constitutional meaning when he declared: "Our Constitution is color-blind " And by this declaration, he meant "all citizens are equal before the law." Harlan was also the lone dissenter in *Berea College v.*

**Jefferson Davis, President of the Confederate States**
*Source: Kentucky Department of Tourism*

**United States President Abraham Lincoln**
*Source: Kentucky Historical Society*

human equality." In Lincoln at Gettysburg, Wills argues: "Lincoln not only put the Declaration in a new light as a matter of founding law, but also put its central proposition, equality, in a newly favored position as a principle of the Constitution. When he spoke about government 'of the people, by the people, and for the people,' he was saying that America is a people addressing its great assignment as that was accepted in the Declaration." As a consequence, "the Declaration means what Lincoln told us it means, as a way of correcting the Constitution."

*Kentucky* (1908) when the Supreme Court went even further and upheld the Day Law which prohibited the private college from educating white and African-American students together.

When Justice Harlan died three years later, Frederick M. Vinson (from Louisa) had just graduated from Centre College. While he served in Congress and then in the Franklin D. Roosevelt administration, the regime of racial segregation began to slowly erode. After Vinson became chief justice in 1946, the Supreme Court took decisive action against racial discrimination. In education, housing, criminal justice, transportation, voting rights, and labor relations, its decisions began to redefine the constitutional meaning of equality.

In *Sweatt v. Painter* (1950), Vinson's unanimous opinion held that racially separate public law schools violated the Fourteenth Amendment, because he had used intangible criteria to define equal protection; they were "those qualities which are incapable of objective measurement including reputation of the faculty, experience of the alumni, standing in the community, traditions, and prestige." Vinson's new definition of equal protection meant that the Court would no longer decide whether racially separate public schools were physically equal, but would condemn them because of their intangible differences. As a result, his view of equality quietly consigned Plessy's doctrine of separate but equal to the constitutional trash can, affirmed Harlan's dissents, and permitted us, as a people, to rededicate ourselves to the "great task" which Lincoln told us we had accepted in the Declaration.

When the Supreme Court issued its unanimous 1954 decision in *Brown v. Board of Education* declaring unconstitutional racially separate public elementary and secondary schools, Chief Justice Earl Warren's opinion rejected any reliance on a comparison of physical factors in determining whether the schools were equal. Instead, he used the intangible criteria in Vinson's *Sweatt* opinion to hold that racially separate schools denied African-American children equality of educational opportunity, because they "generate a feeling of inferiority which affects the motivation of a child to learn." Then Warren boldly drove Vinson's definition of intangible equality to its logical conclusion: "Separate educational facilities are inherently unequal."

With this stoke of judicial creativity, Chief Justice Warren's *Brown* opinion, firmly rooted in the contributions of three Kentuckians, initiated a constitutional revolution in civil rights which has come to address government discrimination based on race, gender, age, illegitimacy, sexual preference, and mental retardation.

*William Crawford Green is Professor of Government at Morehead State University. His research and publications address state and federal constitutional law and public policy issues.*

**Chief Justice Earl Warren**
*Source: Kansas Bar Association*

## Equal Protection under the Law

In 1954, the U.S. Supreme Court issued a ruling that changed the law, and the lives of every American. The court ruled that racially separate schools denied African-American children equality of educational opportunity, because they "generate a feeling of inferiority which affects the motivation of a child to learn." Chief Justice Earl Warren boldly drove Vinson's definition of intangible equality to its logical conclusion: "Separate educational facilities are inherently unequal."

**Chief Justice Fred Vinson**
*Source: U.S. Supreme Court*

## HISTORY

# *Thomas D. Clark Center for Kentucky History*   Thomas E. Stephens

The Kentucky Historical Society was founded on April 22, 1836, by 16 "patriotically inclined Kentucky gentlemen," who met in the secretary of state's office at the state capitol (now Old State Capitol) in Frankfort.

Their efforts were in response to a pioneer era letter concerning Daniel Boone that was published two years earlier in the Frankfort Commonwealth. The new society resolved "to collect and preserve authentic information and facts connected with the early history of the State."

KHS was incorporated in Louisville on Feb. 16, 1838. After 11 years in the state's largest city, the society languished, and its sizable collection was incorporated into one of many efforts to establish what would become the Louisville Free Public Library.

The Kentucky Historical Society remained dormant for more than a quarter century until a group of history enthusiasts met to reorganize it on Oct. 31, 1878, in the Capital Hotel in Frankfort. The group obtained a new state charter from the legislature—"secured and held sacred"—that made the society custodian of the state's historical treasures. Two rooms "over the Auditor's Office, in the third story" of the present Old State Capitol Annex were reserved for the society's use.

After another lapse, the Kentucky Historical Society was revived under its state charter in 1896 by Mrs. Jennie Chinn Morton of Frankfort. Working with Gov. J.C.W. Beckham, Mrs. Morton won public printing status for a history journal, the Register of Kentucky State Historical Society, which began publication in January 1903. In his dual role as the state's chief magistrate and KHS president, Gov.

**Grand opening of the Kentucky History Center in April 1999**
*Source: Gene Burch*

Beckham secured, on March 16, 1906, an annual $5,000 state appropriation by the legislature. The act also mandated the publishing of the Register and officially established that Kentucky's governors would serve as the society's presidents ex-officio.

Gov. Augustus E. Willson granted the society four rooms in the newly completed state capitol in 1909, where the collection could grow. The society built on the state's collection of battle flags and portraits of "Governors, statesmen, and other famous men and women of Kentucky." One particular effort was the commissioning of gubernatorial portraits that would later become the KHS Hall of Governors. By this time, KHS had begun to be recognized by state government as the custodian of Kentucky's treasures, received the collection of paintings from the then-abandoned Old State Capitol and began collecting military equipment. KHS also published its first book in 1910, "Kentucky: Mother of Governors," by John Wilson Townsend.

Mrs. Morton died suddenly on Jan. 9, 1920, and Mrs. Jouett Taylor Cannon was elected secretary-treasurer. She led the society for the next 26 years. One of Cannon's first acts was to move the KHS headquarters. At the behest of Gov. Edwin P. Morrow and Lt. Gov. S. Thruston Ballard, the state sinking fund commissioners had the Old State Capitol repaired and renovated. The building, constructed in 1828-30, would become the society's most enduring symbol and provide space for all of its functions for the next five decades

By 1943, the society's library boasted more than

14,000 books and pamphlets, and the museum contained more than 2,600 items, including the portrait and battle flag collections, sculpture and numerous relics and other items of interest. One important addition during this period was the acquisition of the silver service used on the retired battleship U.S.S. Kentucky, which was arranged by Lt. Gov. Thruston Ballard. Ballard also drummed up support for the society and personally helped rescue precious old state records for the use of genealogists.

In August 1948 the society founded the Kentucky Historical Markers Committee, which in conjunction with the state highway department, began to place markers at significant sites throughout the state. A new state charter that altered the society's functions and titles was enacted in 1960.

The meteoric rise in family history brought the addition of a genealogical quarterly, Kentucky Ancestors, which debuted in July 1965 with Mrs. Anne Walker Fitzgerald as editor. Kentucky Ancestors incorporated genealogical features formerly in the Register and added others over the years.

KHS expanded into the Old State Capitol Annex—ironically its headquarters in the 1880s—in 1974, and the old capitol entered the first phase of its conversion to a museum. The Kentucky Military History Museum also opened in 1974, in the Old State Arsenal.

By 1987, however, the society had been adding to its collections and responsibilities for 13 years in the same space and was almost literally bursting at the seams. It was estimated that more than 90 percent of the museum's collection was in storage, unable to be adequately conserved or displayed. Under the leadership of Director James C. Klotter, KHS secured state funding for a new home, the Kentucky History Center.

Through the assistance of Gov. Brereton Jones, the general Assembly in 1992 approved construction of a Kentucky History Center. The project would eventually grow to $29 million, including $7 million in additional funds raised though the Kentucky Historical Society Foundation Inc. for the permanent exhibit, special equipment and furnishings, technology and landscaping.

KHS also enjoyed a groundswell of public support, in addition to corporate contributions. To celebrate its 10th anniversary in Kentucky, Toyota Manufacturing, USA of Georgetown and Toyota Motor Co. of Japan, donated $1 million to the project.

Opening on April 10, 1999, the history center is a 167,000-square-foot state-of-the-art museum and research library and provides office space and other facilities on a 3.7-acre block shared by the Old Governor's Mansion. It was named The Thomas D. Clark Center for Kentucky History on July 9, 2005, during festivities honoring the life of Thomas D. Clark (1903-2005), the state's former historian laureate.

Located at 100 West Broadway, the History Center is the focal point of the society's campus, which offers numerous learning opportunities to students, historians, genealogists and anyone else interested in Kentucky's past. Programs and activities include the Kentucky Junior Historical Society, the Kentucky Folklife Festival, a museum theatre program and Elderhostels for seniors and also weekend and summertime programs for children. The campus extends northwest to the Old State Capitol and southeast to the Old State Arsenal on Main Street, home to the Kentucky Military History Museum.

The History Center museum's $2.8 million permanent exhibit, A Kentucky Journey, employs a remarkable blend of more than 3,000 historic artifacts, sights and sounds to bring the state's glorious past to present generations. This chronological walk through time boasts life-size environments, state-of-the art technology and 14 interactive displays. Another area, Pure Kentucky, highlights the lives and contributions of famous Kentuckians.

More than 30,000 genealogists and other patrons use the society's research library each year. The facility is an important resource that maximizes both access to and security of the more than 90,000 volumes, microfilm and files in the collection. Tables are equipped for laptop computer use. Internet workstations allow for access to the KHS catalog, commercial databases and the Online Public Access Catalog.

For more information, visit history.ky.gov. Online visitors can search the library's more than 80,000 published works, browse the manuscript and photographic collections or order genealogical research through the museum shop.

**Renamed the Thomas D. Clark Center for Kentucky History in 2006**
*Source: Kentucky Historical Society*

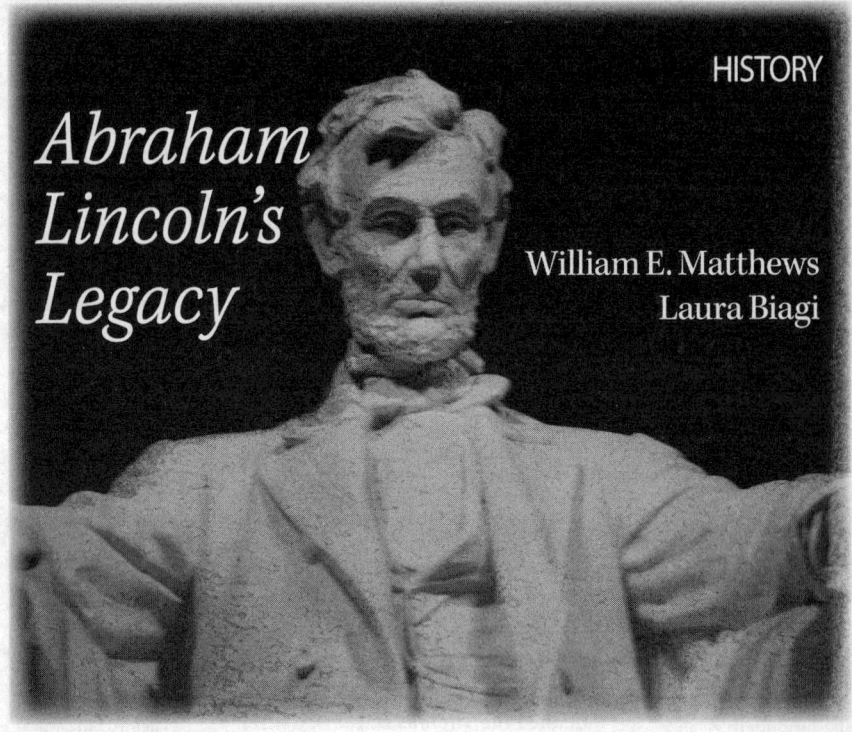

# Abraham Lincoln's Legacy

HISTORY

William E. Matthews
Laura Biagi

In the face of civil war, Abraham Lincoln resolved to preserve his country with fierce determination and a fearless spirit. His efforts and convictions to preserve the Union have since made him one of America's greatest leaders and a lasting legacy throughout the United States.

Though his life in Kentucky amounted to merely his first eight years, Abraham Lincoln felt the mark of his native origins throughout his entire life. His humble "backcountry" years in Kentucky formed the values and experiences that would later shape his life and his legacy.

Abraham Lincoln was born on February 12, 1809, a few miles south of Hodgenville in what is now Larue County. His parents, Thomas Lincoln and Nancy Hanks, had moved to the 348-acre Sinking Spring Farm on Nolin Creek the previous year with their daughter Sarah. Lincoln's parents were well-respected. Thomas Lincoln, a skilled carpenter, had built the one-room log cabin in which Lincoln was born. The values of Lincoln's parents, as well as those promulgated by the anti-slavery church they attended, may have influenced Lincoln's own aversion to slavery.

When Lincoln was two, trouble with a prior land claim forced the family to move to nearby Knob Creek, where they leased 30 acres. The lives of Lincoln and his family were very difficult. Though Lincoln only briefly attended school in Kentucky, he learned to read, write, and perform basic arithmetic at a young age.

Four years later another land claim challenged the Lincoln homestead. In 1816 they moved to Indiana when Lincoln was eight years old. After 14 years on the Indiana frontier, the Lincolns moved again, arriving in Illinois when Lincoln was 21.

Lincoln's education derived largely from his own efforts. After briefly serving in the Black Hawk War, he entered politics in the Illinois legislature. During this time, he taught himself law and soon became a well-respected attorney.

In 1842 Lincoln married fellow Kentuckian Mary Todd. They had four boys, only one of whom survived to adulthood. Soon after their marriage, Lincoln was elected to the U.S. House of Representatives as a member of the Whig party.

After a political hiatus, Lincoln returned to politics in 1858 when he ran for U.S. senator against

Stephen A. Douglas. In the now-famous Lincoln-Douglas debates, Lincoln challenged Douglas to a series of disputes that focused on the morality of slavery. Although Lincoln lost the senate election, his debating skills won him national fame. As a result, Lincoln acquired the nomination for president from the newly-formed, antislavery Republican Party in 1860.

During the Democrats' own convention to elect a presidential nominee, they split into Northern and Southern factions. Thanks largely to this political split, Lincoln received the majority of votes and on March 4, 1861, he was sworn in as the 16th president of the United States.

In the weeks that preceded the election, the South had warned it would not tolerate Lincoln as president. Although Lincoln did not advocate the abolition of slavery in already-formed states, the South felt threatened by his presidency. South Carolina was the first state to secede from the Union in December 1860. Mississippi, Florida, Georgia, Louisiana, Alabama, and Texas followed shortly thereafter. Together, these states formed a new nation called the Confederate States of America. Kentuckian Jefferson Davis was inaugurated president of this new union in February 1861, one month after his resignation from the U.S. Senate.

**Ford Theater, Washington, D.C.**
*Photo: Sid Webb*

In his first inaugural address, Lincoln expressed his determination to keep the Union intact, as well as his conviction that the Southern states had acted unconstitutionally. "You can have no conflict without being yourselves the aggressors," he declared. "You have no oath registered in Heaven to destroy the government, while I shall have the most solemn one to 'preserve, protect and defend' it."

When Confederate troops in South Carolina fired on Fort Sumter in April 1861, the Civil War began. Lincoln subsequently asked Union state governors to contribute 75,000 troops to "preserve the Union." Virginia, Tennessee, North Carolina, and Arkansas did not approve of the invasion of these troops into their borders to attack their fellow Southern states. Consequently, they joined the Confederacy soon after Lincoln's measures went into effect. Border states Kentucky, Maryland, Delaware, and Missouri stayed in the Union.

Kentucky's loyalty was very important to Lincoln. "I hope to have God on my side, but I must have Kentucky," he supposedly remarked. At first Lincoln's home state declared itself neutral, but eventually Kentucky sided with the Union.

In the face of war, Lincoln used his presidential powers more strongly than any other president before him. Without Congress' approval, he declared a blockade, increased funds for weapons, and suspended the writ of habeas corpus, which protected those who might be imprisoned unlawfully. During the war, he placed 18,000 presumed Confederate sympathizers in jail without trial.

His strategy focused upon establishing a quick, aggressive war while maintaining Washington D.C.'s safety. Lincoln appointed several generals-in-chief throughout the war. In 1864 he finally selected Ulysses S. Grant.

Perhaps Lincoln's most remembered actions during the war were his speeches, delivered to rally support in the North. Lincoln's dedication address at Gettysburg, Pa. on November 19, 1863, captivated the crowd and has since become one of the most famous speeches throughout history.

On January 1, 1863, Lincoln issued the Emancipation Proclamation, which freed all slaves in the Confederate states. The act served as an economic ploy to weaken the South at its agricultural base and as moral propaganda for northern abolitionists. Those Union states that still held slaves, however, including Kentucky, Maryland, Delaware, and Missouri, were allowed to keep them.

Lincoln presided over other important acts in addition to wartime measures like the Emancipation Proclamation. His Homestead Act of 1862 allowed for the purchase of millions of acres in the West at very low cost. The Morrill Land-Grant Colleges Act of 1862 provided for the erection of an agricultural university in each state (in Kentucky, there are two such universities—Kentucky State University and University of Kentucky). Lincoln instigated the first income tax in 1862. The building of the first transcontinental railroad was supported in the Pacific Railway Acts of 1862 and 1864. Finally, the National Banking Acts of 1863, 1864 and 1865 formed a system of national banks.

Lincoln's reelection to a second term of office appeared secure in 1864. The Union had been victorious in the battles of Gettysburg, Vicksburg and Chattanooga the previous year, and when Lincoln appointed Grant as general-in-chief in March, many believed the war would soon be over. That spring, however, battles developed into stalemates with heavy losses, and Lincoln's reelection became less favorable.

Just in time, the successful siege of Atlanta by Union Maj. Gen. William Tecumseh Sherman propelled Lincoln back into popularity. Lincoln was reelected with an astounding 212 of 233 electoral votes. In a moving second inaugural address, he declared his hopes for peace and a speedy end to the war.

During the last stretch of war, however, Union forces grew more and more aggressive. Grant led sieges against Petersburg and Richmond, while Sherman marched through Georgia. Finally, on April 9, 1865, Confederate Gen. Robert E. Lee surrendered to Grant at the Appomattox Court House, Virginia. Lee's surrender signaled the war's end.

Lincoln's goal was to make peace with the South generously. In a speech soon after Lee's surrender, Lincoln urged the crowd to "join in doing the acts necessary to restoring the proper practical relations between these [Southern] states and the Union." Lincoln's plans, however, would not be fulfilled by him.

On April 14, 1865, Lincoln and his wife attended a play at the Ford's Theatre in Washington D.C. John Wilkes Booth, a Confederate sympathizer, snuck into their balcony and shot Lincoln from behind while he was distracted. Lincoln was carried to a home across the street where his doctor attended him. He died nine hours later. Booth escaped, he was caught, shot and killed after an extensive manhunt.

The memory of Abraham Lincoln, Kentucky native and extraordinary president, continues. As president, he faced one of the most difficult and momentous phases of our nation's history. His strength, perseverance and beliefs established a standard for American freedom and equality, and fashioned the enduring nation that stands committed to its values today. Lincoln's spirit lives on in the heart of the America he created, and in the hearts of his fellow Kentuckians.

# The Gettysburg Address

Abraham Lincoln
**Gettysburg, Pennsylvania**
November 19, 1863

*"Four score and seven years ago our fathers brought forth on this continent, a new nation, conceived in Liberty, and dedicated to the proposition that all men are created equal.*

*Now we are engaged in a great civil war, testing whether that nation, or any nation so conceived and so dedicated, can long endure. We are met on a great battle-field of that war. We have come to dedicate a portion of that field, as a final resting place for those who here gave their lives that that nation might live. It is altogether fitting and proper that we should do this.*

*But, in a larger sense, we can not dedicate—we can not consecrate—we can not hallow—this ground. The brave men, living and dead, who struggled here, have consecrated it, far above our poor power to add or detract. The world will little note, nor long remember what we say here, but it can never forget what they did here. It is for us the living, rather, to be dedicated here to the unfinished work which they who fought here have thus far so nobly advanced. It is rather for us to be here dedicated to the great task remaining before us—that from these honored dead we take increased devotion to that cause for which they gave the last full measure of devotion—that we here highly resolve that these dead shall not have died in vain—that this nation, under God, shall have a new birth of freedom—and that government of the people, by the people, for the people, shall not perish from the earth."*

## HISTORY

# Dearly Beloved – The Vows of a Lincoln Legacy

Robert G. Clark

On a perfect mild summer day this past June (2006) more than 1,000 Kentuckians celebrated the 200th anniversary of the marriage of Thomas Lincoln and Nancy Hanks, parents of Abraham Lincoln, our 16th president. This celebration marked the first Kentucky event in a three-year celebration of the Abraham Lincoln Bicentennial, scheduled to officially start in February 2008. The exchange of vows was held at Lincoln Homestead State Park near Springfield.

The story, presented as an outdoor play, featured Abraham Lincoln recalling his past in a conversation with his son. Produced by the Kentucky Historical Society Museum Theater, the performance was titled "Dearly Beloved: The Vows of a Lincoln Legacy." The play told the story of the simple union between two people whose son would become one of the world's great leaders.

The performance began with U.S. Presidential candidate Abraham Lincoln (played by H. Kevin Lanham) sitting at a table responding to letters he received inquiring about his past and his roots. The wedding day of Thomas Lincoln and Nancy Hanks was one highlight of the performance. Lincoln's parents had a profound influence on his life; Lincoln said that everything he was or ever would be he credited to his mother, Nancy.

**200th Anniversary reenactment of the Thomas Lincoln and Nancy Hanks wedding**
*Photo: Bobby Clark*

As Lincoln campaigned for president from his home in Springfield, Ill., his political opponents tried to discredit him by proving he was illegitimate. Lincoln was asked repeatedly to write a biography addressing questions about his past. Lincoln and his supporters searched tirelessly to prove that his parents were married, but they were looking in the wrong place—within a few years after Lincoln's tragic death, the proof was found in Springfield, Ky. Afterwards, there was no shortage of testimonies about the Lincoln-Hanks marriage. These statements, in the form of affidavits, provided the historical basis for the production of the play.

"Dearly Beloved" was an inspiring tale of a man, a woman and their son who would change the world. The play was written and directed by Greg Hardison.

*Abraham Lincoln Bicentennial*

The official public Lincoln Bicentennial Commemoration launches February 2008 and closes February 2010, with the climax of the commemoration taking place on February 12, 2009, the 200th anniversary of Lincoln's birth. Across Kentucky and the country, communities, organizations and individuals have already begun to plan parades, museum exhibitions, performances, art installations and much more. Check on www.lincolnbicentennial.gov/planning/ for updates.

HISTORY

# *Women in Kentucky History*

Janet Steele Holloway

Women have asserted their influence in business, education, the arts and public service throughout the commonwealth since the 1700s, and contemporary women are making lasting contributions today. We name but a few here, and send our thanks to the many women throughout Kentucky for their work and contributions to family, community, commonwealth and nation.

**Dr. Lilialyce Akers** has been a major catalyst for change, encouraging the passage of the Kentucky Equal Rights Amendment and marching in D.C. to support the national ERA. She attended the UN's Earth Summit in Rio de Janeiro and was later named Program Chair for the national conference on sustainable development. Akers is a representative to the UN Commission on Women; her work on the BPW Foundation has provided mature women with scholarships to improve their education and advance their careers. **Nelda Barton-Collings,** a leading business woman in eastern Kentucky, owns banks, newspapers, nursing homes, a pharmacy and is widely recognized for her contributions to Kentucky and the nation. As the Republican National Committee Woman from Kentucky for 28 years, and the first female chair of the Kentucky Chamber of Commerce, Barton-Collings is still breaking down barriers for other women.

**Martha Layne Collins** became the only female governor in Kentucky history in 1983. Born in Bagdad, Ky., she started out as a schoolteacher, became clerk of the Supreme Court and later, lieutenant governor. In 1984 she served as chairperson of the Democratic National Convention. Her emphasis on education and economic development brought about major changes in the commonwealth, laying the foundation for educational reform and bringing Toyota Motor Manufacturing to Kentucky. Ten years after coming to Kentucky, Toyota chose the Commonwealth as the home of its North American headquarters. Collins continues her commitment to education and economic development through her positions as Executive Scholar in Residence at Georgetown College and Director of the Kentucky World Trade Center.

**Governor Martha Layne Collins congratulates Toyota Motor Manufacturing Kentucky on 20 years of service Kentucky**
*Source: Toyota Motor Manufacturing Kentucky*

**Mary Lucille Caudill Little (1909-2002)** made arts and education more available to Kentuckians through her more than $21 million in contributions to these fields. She founded the Lexington Children's Theatre and Studio Players, the Bluegrass Girl Scout Council, the Lexington Symphony and Lexington Philharmonic, Central Kentucky Youth Orchestra, the Living Arts and Science Center, and more. She gave millions to enrich the fine arts collections at the University of Kentucky and Transylvania University.

**Katherine Graham Peden (1926-2006)** had a string of firsts in her legacy: the first woman appointed as commissioner of commerce in Kentucky; the first Kentucky woman nominated as a U.S. Senate candidate; an appointment by President Kennedy to serve on the first President's Commission on the Status of Women. She served as the national president of Business and Professional Women's Clubs and was active for decades in economic growth issues at the national and state level.

**Georgia Powers** became the first African-American and the first woman to be elected to the Kentucky Senate in 1967. As senator, she chaired two legislative committees (Health and Welfare and Labor and Industry) where she pushed for legislation on public accommodations, open housing, and other issues of concern to people of color, women, children, and the poor. She fought for the Equal Rights Amendment resolution, the Displaced Homemaker's Law, and a law to increase the minimum wage in Kentucky. Powers was also the first black woman to serve on the Jefferson County Democratic Executive Committee.

**Former state senator Georgia Powers**
*Source: Kentucky Department for Libraries & Archives*

*Jane Stephenson* began the New Opportunity School for Women in Berea for financially distressed, out-of-work Appalachian women with little work experience or traditional job skills. The program she initiated and ran for a decade creates a setting where women can develop new skills and the confidence to build a better life. Graduates have gone on to pursue higher education and positions in public service. Stephenson is the author of "Courageous Paths: Stories of Nine Appalachian Women."

**Anne Lewis, Mimi Pickering, Elizabeth Barret,** and **Justine Richardson** are four of Appalshop's most prolific filmmakers. Though Lewis and Pickering are not Kentucky natives, these women have done much to promote Eastern Kentucky history and culture through their films. Anne Lewis' 1989 film "On Our Own Land" received the Alfred I. DuPont/Columbia University Award for Independent Broadcast Journalism. Lewis' other film credits include "To Save the Land and People" (1999), "His Eye is on the Sparrow" (1999), "Evelyn Williams" (1995), "Justice in the Coalfields" (1995), "Fast Food Women" and more. Pickering, a recipient of a Guggenheim Fellowship, has films that include "Chemical Valley" (1991), "Dreadful Memories: The Life of Sarah Ogan Gunning" (1988), and "Buffalo Creek Revisited" (1984). Richardson grew up in Whitesburg and her first Appalshop film, "Girls' Hoops" (1998), documented the history of girls' high school basketball in Kentucky. Barret, a native of Hazard, received a Rockefeller Foundation film/video/multimedia fellowship in 1998. Her films include "Stranger With A Camera" (2000), "Long Journey Home" (1987), "Coalmining Women" (1982) and more.

**Mary Lucille Caudill Little made contributions of more than $21 million to arts and education organizations**
*Source: Lexington Herald-Leader*

# HISTORY
# *Lewis & Clark*

When Thomas Jefferson dreamed of sending an exploring party into the American West, he asked George Rogers Clark, the hero of the Revolution in the West. Twenty years later, in March 1801 Thomas Jefferson became the third president. That same month, a young army officer named Meriwether Lewis became Jefferson's private secretary. Lewis and William Clark—the youngest brother of Gen. George Rogers Clark—actually did what the future president proposed to George Rogers Clark.

In 1783, Kentucky was the Western frontier of the nation. It was the "First West"—the first land to be settled beyond the Appalachian Mountains. Kentucky became the first western state and a major supplier of settlers and goods for lands that would become future states to the north, south and west.

It was an area of intrigue by foreign powers—the 1780s and 1790s witnessed attempts by the Spanish to influence Kentucky politics. French agents sought to enlist Kentuckians against the Spanish in Louisiana. And across the Ohio River, although the American Revolution had ended, the British encouraged hostility of American Indians for their continuing war with Kentuckians.

Then, an account of a Scotsman's journey across Canada prompted Jefferson to activate his plan of sending an exploring party up the Missouri. In early 1803 Congress approved $2,500 for what was called a commercial and scientific undertaking. Jefferson dispatched Lewis to lead the expedition;

and Lewis appointed William Clark the co-leader. He and Lewis met at Louisville to prepare for the journey.

Nine young men from Kentucky were key figures in the expedition: William Bratton, private, served as a blacksmith and hunter; John Colter, private, served the expedition as a hunter; Joseph and Reubin Fields, privates, both of whom were born in Virginia; Charles Floyd, sergeant, was the only man to die during the expedition; George Gibson, private, served as a marksman, hunter, and fiddle player; Nathaniel Pryor, sergeant, was born in Virginia in 1772; George Shannon, private, served as a hunter; John Shields, private, served as gunsmith, carpenter and hunter; and York, the black slave who was William Clark's companion since childhood, was the first African American to cross the continent from coast to coast.

Upon their return four years later, Lewis and Clark were treated as heroes. Lewis and Clark put names to the land, and people were lured to those places. As historian Bernard DeVoto put it, "theirs was the first report on the West, on the United States over the hill and beyond the sunset. ...It satisfied desire, and it created desire: the desire of a westering nation."

*Summary of "Kentucky and the Lewis & Clark Expedition," reprinted with permission by Back Home in Kentucky, Inc., "Lewis & Clark Bicentennial Edition."*

**Reenactment of Lewis & Clark Discovery exploration docked at Louisville**
*Photo: Sid Webb*

# HISTORY
# *Cassius Marcellus Clay*

### Dr. Gary O'Dell

The annals of Kentucky's history are full of colorful characters whose exploits often seem the stuff of legend, but the reality of Cassius Marcellus Clay, a cousin of Henry Clay, transcends folklore. He was egotistic, opinionated, and hot-tempered. With a reputation for blind courage and violence, he was an abrasive, combative and often dangerous man. Yet Clay also possessed the exquisite manners of a Southern gentleman. He was one of those rare men in the South before the Civil War—a member of the landed gentry who rejected his slave-holding heritage to advocate elimination of slavery. Toward this goal he dedicated his talents as an orator, political propagandist and strategist, and sought political power to bring his vision to reality. His rewards were few,

**Cassius Clay**
*Source: Lithograph, c April 1846
Engraved by Hoffy from a
daguerreotype by Plumbo*

for in the process, he made many enemies and was denied significant offices and appointments. In the end, when his mission had been accomplished and slavery abolished, he spent the remainder of his life without a guiding purpose, honored by his countrymen but becoming more and more eccentric.

Clay was born in Madison County on October 19, 1810, on the family's 2,000-acre estate, known as White Hall, which he inherited in 1828. As a young man, he attended several schools in Kentucky. Clay enrolled in Yale University in 1831, and set on a course that changed his life. While at Yale, he attended several anti-slavery lectures, but what most impressed him about the North was its industry and prosperity. Clay returned

Cassius Marcellus Clay inherited the estate, known as White Hall, in 1828
*Source: Kentucky Historical Society*

to Kentucky infected with a desire to bring about an end to slavery on economic grounds—he advocated economic diversity and industrialization, convinced that a system based on slave labor and an agrarian economy was retarding progress. Clay favored gradual emancipation and compensation to slave owners. Not until the eve of the Civil War did he change his opinion, when he came to believe that force was the only solution.

Clay married Mary Jane Warfield in 1833 and was elected as state representative from Madison County in 1835 and again in 1837. Soon after, he moved his family to Lexington in order to run for the more influential seat from Fayette County. Denouncing the slave system, he ran on a platform supporting free labor and industrialization—using statistics to show that free states were more prosperous than slave

**Cassius M. Clay**
*Source: Engraving From Allen Thorndike Rice, Reminisces of Abraham Lincoln*

in 1844, and in 1845 established an anti-slavery newspaper, the True American, in Lexington. Anticipating violence, he fortified the building with sheet iron and set up two cannons facing the door. His opponents waited until Clay fell ill, when a "Committee of Sixty" descended upon his office, dismantled the press and shipped it to Cincinnati. Because of the hostility he provoked, Clay took to arming himself heavily whenever he left home, usually carrying a brace of pistols and his trademark Bowie knife. Over the years leading up to the war, he was involved in numerous altercations, ranging from formal duels to bloody brawls.

Clay had come to the attention of Abraham Lincoln, but never realized his dream of becoming Lincoln's running mate. After Lincoln's election, Clay expected to be rewarded with a cabinet post. Pres. Lincoln, however, considered Cassius to be too radical, and instead shipped him off as ambassador to Russia (1861-1862 and 1863-1869). Clay's mission to Russia was successful; he socialized easily with the nobility, and was able to win political support for the Union.

Returning to the U.S., Clay remained sporadically active in politics, but with the abolition of slavery accomplished he no longer had a firm direction. He retired to White Hall in 1875, divorced his wife of almost 50 years in 1878, and ended all political participation by 1884. He became increasingly paranoid and reclusive, turning his home into a virtual fortress, ignoring or abusing visitors, or, on occasion, shooting at them. In 1894, at the age of 84, Clay scandalized his neighbors when he married a 15 year-old orphan. She only remained a few months, however, and in 1898 he divorced her for separation.

In the summer of 1903, Clay fell ill. One day in July, annoyed by a large fly buzzing around his sickroom, he ordered a servant to bring his rifle. Cassius propped himself up in bed, took aim, and eliminated the fly with a single shot. A few days later, on July 22, the man known as the "Lion of White Hall" was no more.

**Building on N. Mill Street, east side, where Cassius Clay ran his anti-slavery paper "The True American," Lexington**
*Source: Kentucky Virtual Library*

states. He narrowly won the election, but alienated the entire planter class by his anti-slavery views.

This victory gave Clay the last elected office he would ever hold. He remained active as political gadfly and campaigned for organization of an Emancipation Party. Clay freed his own slaves

# Military History

Bill Bright

The Kentucky Military History Museum is housed in the Old State Arsenal in Frankfort, a fitting site for this collection of military memorabilia including uniforms, weapons, flags and personal items once belonging to members of the state's armed forces.

The building itself is rich in history. It sits high above the Kentucky River, overlooking the capital's downtown area, its fortress-like architecture belying its designated use as an arsenal. It was the third arsenal that the state had, the first having been outgrown and the second having been destroyed by fire in 1836. By 1850 Kentucky's legislature deemed it necessary to have an arsenal once again, so $8,000 was appropriated in order to have

one built.

The architect for the new arsenal was Frankfort resident Nathanial C. Cook, who had designed several other public buildings in Kentucky including courthouses and churches. His design for the arsenal depicted a striking two-story, red brick building resembling a crenellated castle in the popular Gothic Revival style. Although severely damaged by fire in 1934, the building that we see today is much how Cook designed it to look from the outside.

Upon completion of construction the building became the primary depot for some 12,000 weapons. These weapons would be used to equip Kentucky's troops as well as the local citizenry.

**Kentucky Military History Museum**
*Source: Gene Burch*

The arsenal also served as a cartridge factory during the Civil War. Indeed, Union troops from Kentucky, Indiana, Ohio and Michigan were all supplied with ammunition made by the ladies of Frankfort. During the 1862 capture of Frankfort by Confederate forces, the cartridge factory ceased operation. However, recent research has proven that after Confederate forces left Frankfort in 1862, the cartridge factory resumed operations and continued to provide ammunition until the end of the war.

Only once in its history did the State Arsenal actually come under fire. That was in 1864 when the Confederates once again tried to capture the capital. Gunners on the arsenal lawn exchanged shots with Confederate cavalrymen on the opposite bank of the Kentucky River, but the attack failed.

After the Civil War the arsenal resumed its function as munitions storehouse, supplying troops of the Kentucky State Guard in several riots, the Spanish-American War, the Mexican Border Campaign and World War I. In 1934 a fire of indeterminate origin gutted the interior of the building and destroyed its contents. The exterior brick walls remained serviceable, and a new interior was constructed.

By the early 1970s the Department of Military Affairs had built a new complex called Boone Center, rendering the State Arsenal redundant. Meanwhile, the Kentucky Historical Society's restoration of the Old State Capitol had displaced the extensive collection of weapons and other military relics once housed there. So, in 1973, officials of both agencies decided to place this collection in the State Arsenal, thus creating the Kentucky Military History Museum.

The museum, jointly operated by the Kentucky Department of Military Affairs and the Kentucky Historical Society, chronicles more than two centuries of military service from the frontier era of the Kentucky Militia through to the present day. Displays include an impressive collection of firearms, edged weapons, artillery, uniforms, flags, photographs, personal items, and other equipment that illustrate the Commonwealth's martial heritage, plus exhibits of the cartridge factory, Kentucky inventors and Medal of Honor recipients.

## A time to mourn...

### AS OF SEPT. 15, 2006,
### 44 KENTUCKIANS HAVE BEEN KILLED IN IRAQ SINCE 2003.

| | | |
|---|---|---|
| Michael D. Acklin II | Santiago M. Halsel | James E. Powell |
| William A. Allers III | James William Harlan | Tatjana Reed |
| Jason E. Ames | Michael Ray Hayes | George S. Rentschler |
| Jason Lee Bishop | Christopher T. Heflin | Scott C. Rose |
| Gary B. Coleman | Robert L. Henderson II | Robert J. Settle |
| Chase Johnson Comley | James T. Hoffman | James A. Sherrill |
| Lance S. Cornett | Jonathan A. Hughes | Jusine D. Sims |
| Clinton W. Cubert | Charles Jason Jones | Joseph M. Tackett |
| Matthew L. Deckard | Sean M. Langley | Joshua K. Titcomb |
| Robert V. Derenda | Clarence D. McSwain | Eric L. Toth |
| Nicholas J. Dieruf | Scott A. Messer | Christopher T. Warndorf |
| Stephen P. Downing | Ryan J. Montgomery | Jeffery L. Wiener |
| Robert W. Ehney | Deshon E. Otey | Ronnie D. Williams |
| James W. Gardner | Christopher W. Phelps | David Neil Wimberg |
| Jeffrey C. Graham | Darrin K. Potter | |

# Kentucky in the War of 1812

William E. Matthews

Kentucky had been a state for only 20 years when the U. S. Congress declared war against Britain in June 1812. Anti-British feelings had been slowly mounting for several years over disputes about U.S. neutrality during the wars between Britain and France and its allies starting back in 1793.

During this period U.S. ships were frequently boarded, their crews impressed, and their cargoes confiscated. Particularly galling to Americans was British insistence on the right to seize British-born citizens aboard U.S. ships.

With Kentuckians already peeved by what was perceived as congressional indifference to blatant British interference with American shipping, their mood for war was heightened by the Nov. 11, 1811, battle at Tippecanoe between Indian followers of Tecumseh and a military detachment under Indiana Territorial Governor William Henry Harrison.

The Congressional Declaration of War in 1812 spurred Kentuckians into action and during the course of the two and a half-year war the Commonwealth provided more than 25,000 regulars, militia and volunteers to the American cause. Almost 20 percent of those who fought the British in the War of 1812 were Kentuckians.

Unlike other states whose troops were mostly used to garrison installations and guard borders, most Kentuckians actually got into combat. Consequently, casualties were high.

Kentuckians entered the fray full of optimism which was tempered substantially when Detroit was surrendered to the British in August 1812.

In January 1813, 1,300 Kentuckians under the command of Gen. James Winchester attacked the British-guarded town of Frenchtown on the River Raisin. About 1,000 Kentuckians took over the small settlement. On Jan. 22 the British counterattacked and over 500 Kentuckians were captured, more than 100 killed, and many others wounded or missing. Later, Indians massacred as many as 65 badly-wounded Kentuckians left at Frenchtown when the British withdrew.

Defeat at the River Raisin dampened Kentuck-

ians' ardor for war and when Gov. Isaac Shelby asked for 3,000 men to help Harrison, only a few responded.

But the Americans, led by Kentucky Sen. Richard M. Johnson's cavalry regiment, Shelby's 3,500 volunteers and about 120 regulars, won a convincing victory at the Battle of the Thames, routing 3,000 Indians and capturing most of the British regulars. Tecumseh himself was slain during the battle.

The deadliest battle of the war, on Jan. 8, 1815, at New Orleans was, ironically, fought after the warring parties had signed the Treaty of Ghent 15 days before, on Dec. 24, 1815. Kentuckians who fought at the Battle of New Orleans had been placed at the very center of the British attack, and inflicted heavy casualties on the attackers.

After the war, Kentuckians could take pride in helping rid the British from the upper northwest and of being an integral part of the defense of New Orleans.

Among the Kentuckians who distinguished themselves during the War of 1812 were:

**John E. King**, a general who led the only brigade in the 5th Regiment under the command of William Rennick; **James M. Meade**, who was killed at the Battle of the River Raisin. **John Montgomery Edmonson**, who formed a company of volunteer riflemen and joined Lt. Col. John Allen's 1st Rifle Regiment of the Kentucky militia; **John Simpson**, who served under Col. John Allen in the 1st Rifle Regiment; **Nathaniel Gray Smith Hart**, captain of the Lexington (Ky.) Light Infantry, organized a company of about 100 men to fight the British; **Paschal Hickman**, a lieutenant in the Kentucky Militia, was among 65 soldiers massacred by Indians following the British-Indian victory at Frenchtown; and **William Russell**, who was a member of the Virginia legislature that passed the act separating Kentucky from the Commonwealth of Virginia, distinguished himself in the War of 1812.

*Sources: The Kentucky Encyclopedia, The New History of Shelby County, The Louisville Encyclopedia*

# Kentucky in the Civil War

## William E. Matthews

Native son Abraham Lincoln is reported to have said that he "hoped to have God on his side, but I must have Kentucky."

Historian James M. McPherson wrote that the War divided Kentucky "more tragically than any other state; for Kentuckians it was truly a war between and among brothers."

McPherson concludes that it is scarcely an exaggeration to say that the Confederacy would have won the war if it could have gained Kentucky, and, conversely, that the Union's success in retaining Kentucky as a base for invasions of the Confederate heartland gave Mr. Lincoln the state he had to "have," and preserved the United States of America.

In the election of 1860, two of the four candidates were Kentuckians. John C. Breckinridge, Lexington native and former vice president, ran on the Southern Democrat ticket. He was opposed by Republican nominee Abraham Lincoln, an attorney born near Hodgenville. When the ballots were cast, most Kentuckians voted for Tennessean John Bell, whose platform was based on the preservation of the Union. Lincoln received a total of 1,364 votes in Kentucky. Of these only five came from Fayette County, the home of his in-laws.

As Southern states began leaving the Union toward the end of 1860, Kentucky faced turmoil. Democratic Gov. Beriah Magoffin believed in the legality of slavery and secession. Like most Kentucky Democrats, Magoffin thought that Southern rights had been violated.

**Military map of Frankfort, Ky.**
*Source: Library of Congress*

Following the fall of Fort Sumter, in April, 1861, President Lincoln asked for 75,000 troops to crush the rebellion. Gov. Magoffin replied defiantly, "Kentucky will furnish no troops for the wicked purpose of subduing her sister Southern States." Magoffin turned down a similar request from Confederate President Jefferson Davis, also a native Kentuckian. Many, if not most, Kentuckians longed for Kentucky to stay neutral.

On May 16, 1861, the Kentucky House of Representatives declared that Kentucky should remain neutral, and though the governor and senate approved this policy, hopes of mediation were dashed by the state elections of Aug. 5, 1861, when Southerners boycotted the election, enabling Unionist candidates to score a sweeping victory.

The first blood to be shed in Kentucky came at Barbourville on Sept. 19, 1861, when troops under the command of Gen. Felix K. Zollicoffer defeated a small Union detachment. Zollicoffer reported that 18 Federalists had been killed while he lost only two men. Local historians, however, document the loss of only one soldier on each side.

The Battle of Barbourville is one of 11 major battles fought in Kentucky, according to the National Park Service. While there were innumerable other skirmishes, such as the one at Sacramento, where Nathan Bedford Forrest first found fame, and Tebbs Bend where John Hunt Morgan's men were repulsed, the Park

**Gen. Garfield at the Battle of Pound Gap**
*Source: Back Home in Kentucky Magazine*

Service has designated only the following as "major" battles: Barbourville, Camp Wildcat Mountain, Ivy Mountain, Paducah, Cynthiana, Munfordville, Rowletts Station, Columbus-Belmont, Middle Creek, Richmond and Perryville.

The confrontation at Perryville on Oct. 8-9, 1862, represented the largest concentration of forces on both sides in Kentucky. The Confederates won a tactical victory, but strategically they were overwhelmed. Their invasion of Kentucky was ended, and the hopes of a Confederate Kentucky were lost forever.

Thinking that Kentucky would be a fertile recruiting ground, the Confederates brought 20,000 rifles into the state, but only about 2,500 Kentuckians signed on. One Southerner complained that Kentuckians were "too well off to fight." The war ended on April 9, 1865, with Robert E. Lee's surrender at Appomattox to Ulysses S. Grant.

The cost to the nation, and especially to Kentucky, was enormous. While precise figures will never be established, more than 100,000 Kentuckians answered Mr. Lincoln's call, while somewhere between 25,000 and 35,000 responded to Jefferson Davis' call. Of these more than 100,000 troops, nearly 30,000 died. It is believed that about 10,000 died in battle; the rest fell victim to disease, accidents and exposure.

It has been said that Kentucky seceded from the Union after the Civil War. Kentucky and Delaware voted against ratification of the 13th amendment, which abolished slavery. But when the amendment was eventually ratified, slavery finally came to a legal end in the two recalcitrant states.

Stuart Sanders, until recently the Director of Interpretation for the Perryville Battlefield Association, writes, "Kentucky's opinion of the Federal government became increasingly antagonistic. Although the Southern Democrats were defeated in the election of 1860, by 1867 the population had become fiercely Democratic. The 14th Amendment, which protected the civil rights of freemen, and the 15th amendment, which gave the vote to African Americans, was met with hostility. Anger spread into the polls. Many Kentuckians who had served the Confederacy were elected to the state legislature and the U. S. Congress. Simon Bolivar Buckner, a general in the Southern army, was elected governor in 1887."

The Union also had its heroes. Ulysses S. Grant and James A. Garfield, who first found fame at Paducah and Middle Creek respectively, were elected president of the United States.

In Volume III of Kentucky's Civil War 1861-1865, published by Back Home In Kentucky, Civil War researcher Lisa Matthews writes: "It is indisputable that Kentucky played an important, if not integral role in the War. Of the Border States, Kentucky was the most significant because of its river systems and railroads.

"It can also be argued that residents of border states suffered more acutely as brother faced off against brother, neighbor against neighbor. Social events were cancelled, business relationships foundered, and churches split along battle lines

"THE SECESSION WOLF" offering to lead Kentucky, "Or any other State," out of the Union. "That's what's the matter."

Published by Jos. Gates, Cincinnati.

**"The Secession Wolf" political cartoon**
*Source: Library of Congress*

that remained entrenched long after the war was over.

"These divisions within families, communities, and regions demonstrate how individual loyalties were tested far beyond traditional bounds."

One Confederate soldier summed up the experience in three mere words when he wrote, after his experience at the Battle of Perryville, "Oh, wretched war!"

## HISTORY
# *Kentuckians in Action*

### Maj. Gen. Donald C. Storm

**KENTUCKY NATIONAL GUARD
IN TIMES OF WAR AND PEACE**

The Kentucky National Guard is a military institution whose existence antedates the United States itself. Although the name "National Guard" was not applied to a state militia until 1824, the fundamental concept of a state or local military organization has existed since 1636, when the Colony of Massachusetts formed a regiment of "trained bands."

Kentucky National Guard, which is made up of elements of Army and Air Guard units, is one component of the U.S. Army, which consists of the Active Army, Army National Guard, and the Army Reserves. The National Guard is composed of civilian citizen-soldiers who serve their country, state and communities, on a part-time basis. The

For Federal missions the President of the United States serves as their Commander-in-Chief.

Throughout her history, Kentuckians have cherished the tradition of rendering military duty with zeal—Kentucky's history teems with incidents of self-sacrifice unsurpassed in daring and achievement. Kentuckians have answered the call to arms

(Top) The St. Matthews Armory, Part Headquarters Co., First Regiment. Kentucky's National Guard furnished the Army with many trained men in World Wars I and II.
(Left) The 138th Field Artillery Regiment training at Ft. Knox with the French 75 MM Gun, prior to their overseas deployment for the First World War (WWI)
*Source: Kentucky National Guard*

National Guard has a unique dual mission that consists of both federal and state roles. For state missions, the Governor, through the State Adjutant General, commands National Guard forces. The Governor can call the National Guard into action during local or statewide emergencies, such as storms, fires, earthquakes or civil disturbances.

in all wars and conflicts of our country. The Kentucky National Guard has the distinction of being one of the oldest military forces in the U.S. Its history dates back to 1775, when Kentucky was known as Fincastle County, a part of western Virginia. The first "organized" militia company west of the Allegheny Mountains was established in Fayette

County and called the "Lexington Light Infantry." They were organized prior to Kentucky statehood and were the honor guard for Isaac Shelby when he came into Lexington for his first inauguration, in 1792. The primary mission of these early militiamen was to serve as a self-protective association against the frequent hostile attacks of American Indians and foreign forces when Kentucky was the western frontier.

Records of the U.S. War Department document Kentucky's participation. For example, in World War One a

plies to the Gulf Coast in response to Hurricanes Katrina and Rita. Currently Kentucky Guard personnel are securing our nation's southwestern

**Sgt. First Class Gerald Smith (left) and Staff Sgt. Troy Holley (right) held Old Glory at the Kentucky National Guard Air Base in Louisville. Members of the 2123rd Transportation Company, Kentucky Army National Guard returned from Iraq**
*Photo: David Perry, Lexington Herald-Leader*

**Friends and relatives waved to a formation of UH-60 Blackhawk helicopters as they carried soldiers mobilized for the Iraq War**
*Photo: David Perry, Lexington Herald-Leader*

total of 84,172 persons from Kentucky served in the U.S. Army. This total included 80,009 enlisted men, 3,747 commissioned officers, 241 nurses, 153 army field clerks, and 22 U.S. Marine Cadets. A breakdown of these figures show that there were 12,759 men in the regular Army, 7,518 National Guardsmen, 2,526 in the Reserve Corps, 2,734 volunteers, and 58,635 drafted men. Seven Kentuckians were Army major generals, nine were brigadier generals, and 23 were colonels.

Today, Kentucky National Guard is comprised of over 7,000 soldiers and airmen in the Army and Air National Guard. Since September 11, 2001, the Kentucky National Guard has deployed over 8,000 soldiers and airmen in support of the Global War on Terrorism. Both Army and Air Guard units have deployed to Afghanistan and Iraq in support of the Global War on Terrorism; and upon their return to the U.S., flew rescue personnel and critical sup-

border with their involvement in Operation Jump Start. While conducting these missions the Kentucky National Guard was still continuing its state mission here in the Commonwealth.

Kentucky guardsmen have served in humanitarian missions in far-off places such as Bosnia and Guatemala; assisted Kentuckians in recovery from massive flooding along the Ohio River; provided water purification in western Kentucky; health care assistance in eastern Kentucky; and shelter from snowstorms at its armories.

Kentucky National Guard eased the struggles of the birth of our country and Commonwealth—from growing pains of westward expansion, world turmoil, civil strife, and domestic emergencies, and now the Global War on Terrorism. The skill and proficiency with which the Kentucky Guard has served our nation and state further demonstrates the fact that it is, and will continue to be, a necessary and indispensable organization for the continued existence of the Commonwealth of Kentucky.

*Maj. Gen. Donald C. Storm is Kentucky's Adjutant General.*

# Kentuckians in Wars & Conflicts

| WAR OR CONFLICT | IN ACTION | CASUALTIES |
|---|---|---|
| American Revolution | ** | ** |
| War of 1812 | 24,000 | 1,200 |
| Texas Independence | 600* | 75* |
| Mexican War | 4,694 | 612 |
| Civil War | | |
| Union | 115,760 | 12,774 |
| Confederate | 35,000-38,000*** | 10,4000*** |
| Spanish-American War | 6,065 | 89 |
| Mexican Punitive Expedition | 2,394 | 1 |
| WWI | 95,575 | 2,418 |
| WWII | 306,362 | 7,932 |
| Korean Conflict | 88,273 | 1,025 |
| Vietnam Conflict | 125,000 | 1,066 |
| Persian Gulf War | 1,321**** | 6 |

* = Figures are estimates, no other data available
** = No Figures For Kentuckians in the American Revolution because Kentucky was a part of Virginia; (recall, Kentucky became a state in 1792).
*** = Figures are estimates, there are no authoritative figures for Confederate forces.
**** = Kentucky National Guard only, the deaths are from all branches of service.

### KENTUCKY NATIONAL GUARD MOBILIZATIONS AND DEPLOYMENTS SINCE 9/11

(As of 10/3/06)

| | OPERATION NOBLE EAGLE | OPERATION ENDURING FREEDOM | OPERATION IRAQI FREEDOM |
|---|---|---|---|
| ARMY | 1,266 | 977 | 4,731 |
| AIR | 0 | 572 | 1,038 |
| TOTAL | 1,266 | 1,549 | 5,769 |

## 8,584 Mobilizations since 9/11

Note: these figures include multiple deployments. Two individuals from the air guard have been deployed nine times. Air Guard deployments typically are shorter in duration, from one to six months whereas Army deployments are typically one-year deployments.

Source: Kentucky Department of Military Affairs, Kentucky Military Records and Research Branch

# Civil War Battleground Sites
*William E. Matthews*

## 1861
\*Sept. 19  Battle of Barbourville
*(Barbourville)*
\*Oct. 21   Battle of Wildcat Mountain
*(near London)*
Oct. 23    Battle of Saratoga Springs
*(near Eddyville)*
\*Nov. 8    Battle of Ivy Mountain
*(near Prestonsburg)*
\*Dec. 17   Battle of Rowlett's Station
*(near Munfordville)*
Dec. 27    Battle of Sacramento
*(Sacramento)*

## 1862
\*Jan. 10   Battle of Middle Creek
*(near Prestonsburg)*
\*Jan. 19   Battle of Mill Springs
*(Nancy)*
\*July 17 – First Battle of Cynthiana
*(Cynthiana)*
Aug. 17 – Battle of London
*(London)*
\*Aug. 29-30 – Battle of Richmond
*(Richmond)*
\*Sept. 14-17 – Battle of Munfordville
*(Munfordville)*
Sept. 19 – Battle of Panther Creek
*(near Owensboro)*
Sept. 21 – Battle of Woodsonville
*(near Munfordville)*
Sept. 27 – Battle of Augusta *(Augusta)*
\*Oct. 8 – Battle of Perryville *(Perryville)*

Dec. 23-Jan. 2 – John Hunt Morgan's
   Christmas Raid into Kentucky
Dec. 30 – Battle of New Haven

## 1863
Mar. 22 – Battle of Mt. Sterling
Mar. 30 – Battle of Dutton's Hill *(near
Somerset)*
July 2-26 – John Hunt Morgan's Raid
   through Kentucky, into Indiana, Ohio
July 4 – Battle of Tebb's Bend *(near
Campbellsville)*
July 4 – Battle of Lebanon *(Lebanon)*
July 30 – Battle of Irvine

## 1864
\*Mar. 25 – Battle of Paducah
May 30 – John Hunt Morgan begins last
   raid into Kentucky
June 11-12 –Second Battle of Cynthiana

Nov. 8 – Kentucky joins New Jersey and
   Delaware as the only states to cast
   electoral votes for Democratic candidate
   George B. McClellan. Abraham Lincoln is
   re-elected in a landslide.

## 1865
April 9 – Gen. Robert E. Lee surrenders at
   Appomattox Courthouse in Virginia.
* *Designated "major" Civil War sites by the
National Park Service*

Oct. 7 – At 7 P.M., Gen. Buell sends special written orders to Gen. Thomas, in part as follows: 'The 3d corps, Gilbert's, is within 3 ½ miles of Perryville, the calvary being nearer, perhaps 2 ½ miles.  From all the information received to-day it is thought the enemy will resist our advances in to Perryville.  They are said to have a strong force in and around the place.  We expect to attack and carry the place to-morrow.  March at 3 o'clock precisely, to-morrow morning, without fail; and if possible get all the canteens filled, and have the men cautioned to use water in the most sparing manner.  Every officer must caution his men on this point. ...
*(From Collins' Historical Sketches, Vol. II, Page 113.)*

# Congressional Medal of Honor

*John Trowbridge*

The Congressional Medal of Honor, our country's highest award for military valor, is given only to those who have acted with supreme courage and total disregard for their own safety in the face of the most hazardous conditions.

The Medal is an award that only a comparative handful of men in the world are entitled to wear. It is bestowed by act of Congress and reflects our nation's gratitude to those who, in moments of uncommon risk, offered everything they had in its defense, including life itself.

The Medal is but a humble token, a gesture of recognition for sacrifices that cannot be repaid in worldly goods. Of the men and women of all branches of our armed forces who have been awarded the Congressional Medal of Honor for 'conspicuous gallantry' while defending our nation, many did not live to have the honor bestowed on them personally. These recipients died in the actions for which they were cited.

To them, 'above and beyond the call of duty,' were not mere words but self-sacrifice in the face of almost certain death. Their reward was the knowledge that they were acting in the tradition of the highest ideals of the military and the United States.

Those who live to wear the medal do so proudly and yet with the spirit of humility befitting true heroes. They share the highest glory of which it is a symbol, yet hold it in solemn trust for comrades less fortunate.

Whether they lived or died, our nation is richer for their actions.

*Information gathered from numerous sources including, Center of Military History, The Congressional Medal of Honor Society, and The Congressional Record.*

# Kentucky Congressional Medal of Honor Recipients

*(Recipients were in the Army unless indicated)*

### Civil War 1861-1865
Captain William P. Black; Private John C. Callahan; Sergeant John S. Darrough; Private John Davis; Drummer William H. Horsfall; Private Aaron Hudson; Private Henry B. Mattingly; Sergeant Francis M. McMillen; Navy Landsman Daniel Noble; Private Oliver P. Rood; Sergeant Andrew J. Smith; Private William Steinmetz; Doctor Mary E. Walker; Major John F. Weston; Colonel James A. Williamson

### Indian Campaigns 1870-1891
Second Lieutenant Thomas Cruse; First Sergeant William L. Day; Corporal John J. Givens; Private William M. Harris; Captain John B. Kerr; Private Franklin M. McDonald; Private George D. Scott; Sergeant Thomas Shaw; Private Thomas W. Stivers; Private Thomas Sullivan; Saddler Otto E. Voit; Sergeant Brent Woods

### Actions in Peacetime 1871-1910
Navy Seaman Edward W. Boers; Navy Watertender Edward A. Clary; Navy Quarter Gunner George Holt

### Wars of American Expansion 1897-1902
Colonel J. Franklin Bell; First Lieutenant Benjamin F. Hardaway; Private James J. Nash

### World War I 1917-1919
Sergeant Willie Sandlin

### World War II 1941-1945
Marine Corps Corporal Richard E. Bush; Technical Sergeant Morris E. Crain; Marine Corps Private First Class Leonard F. Mason; Marine Corps Reserve Private First Class Wesley Phelps; Private Wilburn K. Ross; Marine Corps Private First Class Luther Skaggs Jr.; Staff Sergeant Junior J. Spurrier; Sergeant John C. Squires

### Korean War 1950-1953
Marine Corps Captain William E. Barber; Marine Corps Private First Class William B. Baugh; Corporal John W. Collier; First Lieutenant Carl H. Dodd; Second Lieutenant Darwin K. Kyle; Private First Class David M. Smith; Private First Class Ernest E. West

### Vietnam War 1961-1975
Sergeant Charles C. Fleek; Staff Sergeant Don Jenkins; Private First Class Billy L. Lauffer; Sergeant First Class Gary L. Littrell; Second Lieutenant John J. McGinty III; Private First Class David P. Nash; Marine Corps Lance Corporal Joe C. Paul

*Source: http://www.medalofhonor.com/ KentuckyRecipients.htm; Photo Source: U.S. Army.*

## HISTORY

# Jack Jouett, The Other Ride

## Donald Norman Moran

Every school child in America knows the famous poem from the pen of Henry Wadsworth Longfellow, "Listen, My children, and you shall hear - of the midnight ride of Paul Revere... ." But, what of the "other" ride? Long neglected by history, it undoubtedly had a greater impact on the outcome of the American Revolution then did Paul Revere's ride. The following is a brief story of one of the most daring rides in American history.

Capt. Jack Jouett, of the Virginia Militia, looked the part of a hero—he stood 6-ft. 4-in. tall, weighed 220 pounds and was described as "handsome." It was said of him that he "evidenced muscular developement and not adiposity." Capt. Jouett was stationed in the Charlottesville area. Late on the evening of June 3rd of 1781, Captain Jouett was asleep on the lawn in front of the "Cuckoo Tavern." He was awakened by the sound of horsemen; sitting up, he observed a large unit of the dreaded "White Coats," British Dragoons under the command of Col. Banastre Tarleton's. Tarleton himself, a British Calvary officer known to be quite ruthless in fighting the American patriots, was leading the cavalry column.

Jouett quickly realized the objective of the British force: the Virginia General Assembly was in session at Charlottesville, some 40 miles away—Gov. Thomas Jefferson, Patrick Henry, and many other notorious Patriot 'rebels' were there. The Patriots were virtually helpless, as most of Virginia's fighting men were with Gen. George Washington; the local militia was ill-equipped and too few to stop Tarleton. The enormity of the situation sat squarely on Capt. Jouett's shoulders; he alone had to save the General Assembly. It was utterly impossible—a 40-mile horseback ride in the middle of the night over rough terrain. Col. Tarleton certainly had advance scouts on the road to Charlottesville, hence that route was denied to Jouett. He chose the tangled Virginia backwoods.

A speedy horse, a strong will, and the aid of a full moon gave Capt. Jouett some advantage. At the light of dawn he arrived at Jefferson's home, Monticello, where he awoke Gov.

**Jack Jouett house, Versailles**
*Photos: Sid Webb*

Jefferson and the Virginia legislators who were staying at Monticello. Then, the captain turned and galloped to Charlottesville to spread the alarm. The assemblymen at Charlottesville scattered, but only after voting to reconvene.

In 1782 Jouett migrated to Harrodsburg, Ky. He married and had a family (including son Matthew Jouett, a famous painter). Jouett became involved in gaining statehood for what is now Kentucky, and later imported fine horses and cattle from England. Capt. Jouett died in 1822 at the home of his daughter in Bath County, Ky.

*Reprinted with permission from "The Valley Compatriot," Feb 1984. Donald Norman Moran, Ed.*

# HISTORICAL SOCIETIES & MUSEUMS

| COUNTY | HISTORICAL SOCIETY/MUSEUM | CONTACT | ADDRESS | CITY | ZIP | PHONE |
|---|---|---|---|---|---|---|
| Adair | Adair County Historical Society/ Adair Public Library | Lila Ford, President | PO Box 613, 307 Greensburg St | Columbia | 42728 | (270) 384-2472 |
| Allen | Allen County Historical Society | Rosemary Harper, President | 301 N 4th St | Scottsville | 42164 | (270) 237-3026 |
| Anderson | Anderson County Historical Society | | PO Box 212 | Lawrenceburg | 40342 | (502) 839-1815 |
| Ballard | Ballard-Carlisle County Historical Society | Kathleen Rolland, Director | PO Box 279 | Wickliffe | 42087 | (270) 335-3323 |
| Ballard | Barlow House Museum | | 509 Broadway, Hwy 60 | Barlow | 42024 | (270) 334-3010 |
| Ballard | Wickliffe Mounds | | 94 Green St. Hwy 60 | Wickliffe | 42087 | (270) 335-3681 |
| Barren | Bell's Tavern Historical Park | | Old W Dixie Hwy | Park City | 42160 | (270) 749-5695 |
| Barren | S Central KY Historical & Genealogical Society | | PO Box 157 | Glasgow | 42142 | (270) 651-9114 |
| Barren | South Central Kentucky Cultural Center | | 200 W Water St | Glasgow | 42141 | (270) 651-9792 |
| Barren | South Central KY Historical Society | | PO Box 157 | Glasgow | 42142 | |
| Bell | American Association-Middlesboro Museum | | Visitor's Center | Middlesboro | 40965 | |
| Bell | Bell County Historical Society | Jerry Browning, President | PO Box 1344 | Middlesboro | 40965 | (606) 242-0005 |
| Bell | The Coal House Museum | | 106 N 20th St | Middlesboro | 40965 | (606) 248-1075 |
| Bell | The Lost Squadron Museum | | 1420 Dorchester Ave | Middlesboro | 40965 | (606) 248-1149 |
| Boone | Big Bone Lick State Park Museum | | 3380 Beaver Rd | Union | 41091 | (859) 384-3522 |
| Boone | Boone County Historical Society | Don Clare, Curator | 8100 Ewing St | Florence | 41042 | |
| Boone | Rabbit Hash Historical Society and Museum | | 11646 Lower River Rd | Union | 41091 | (859) 586-6431 |
| Bourbon | Hopewell Museum | Betsy Kephart, Director | 800 Pleasant St | Paris | 40361 | (859) 987-7274 |
| Boyd | Eastern KY Genealogical Society | Mark Meinhart | Box 1544 | Ashland | 41105 | |
| Boyd | Highlands Museum and Discovery Center | Nancy Smith, Director | 1620 Winchester Ave | Ashland | 41101 | (606) 329-8888 |
| Boyle | Danville/Boyle County Historical Society | | Constitution Square | Danville | 40422 | |
| Boyle | McDowell House Museum and Apothecary Shop | | 125 S Second St | Danville | 40472 | (859) 236-2804 |
| Bracken | Bracken County Historical Society | George Cummins, President | PO Box 307 | Brooksville | 41004 | (606) 735-3337 |
| Breathitt | Breathitt County Historical & Genealogy Society | Nancy E. Herald, President | 1024 College Ave | Jackson | 41339 | (606) 666-7722 |
| Breckinridge | Breckinridge County Historical Society | David W. Hayes, President | PO Box 498 | Hardinsburg | 40143 | (270) 756-2867 |
| Breckinridge | Breckinridge County Historical Society Museum | | Main St | Hardinsburg | 40143 | (270) 756-2347 |
| Breckinridge | Hartman Cooperage Museum, Jim Beam Distillery | | 149 Happy Hollow Rd | Clermont | 40110 | (502) 543-9877 |
| Bullitt | Bullitt County Genealogical Society | Barbara Bosley, President | PO Box 950 | Shepherdsville | 40165 | (502) 957-3332 |
| Bullitt | Bullitt County History Museum | David Strange, Director | 300 S Buckman PO Box 206 | Shepherdsville | 40165 | (502) 921-0161 |
| Bullitt | Mt. Washington Historical Society Museum | | 434 Riverview Dr | Mt. Washington | 40047 | (502) 538-7660 |
| Butler | Butler County Hist. and Gen.Society | June | PO Box 435 | Morgantown | 42261 | (270) 526-5971 |
| Butler | Green River Museum | Ardell Jarratt, Director | 108 N Church St | Woodbury | 42288 | |
| Caldwell | Adsmore Museum | Gale Cherry, President | 304 N Jefferson | Princeton | 42445 | (270) 365-3114 |
| Caldwell | Caldwell County Historical Society | | 206 Jefferson St | Princeton | 42445 | (270) 365-0582 |
| Caldwell | Caldwell County Railroad Historical Museum | | 116 Edwards St | Princeton | 42445 | (270) 762-4771 |
| Calloway | Wrather West Kentucky Museum | Kate Reeves, Manager | 100 Wrather Museum Murray State University | Murray | 42071 | |
| Campbell | Campbell County Historical and Genealogical Society | Kenneth A. Reis, President | 19 E Main St | Alexandria | 41001 | (859) 635-6407 |
| Campbell | Newport Aquarium WAVE Foundation | Doug Allender, Director | 1 Aquarium Way | Newport | 41071 | (859) 491-3467 |
| Campbell | NKU Museum of Anthropology | | 221 Landrum Acad. Center | Highland Heights | 41076 | |
| Carroll | Butler-Turpin Historic Home | | 1068 Hwy 227 | Carrollton | 41008 | (502) 732-4384 |
| Carroll | Port William Historic Home | | 714 Highland Ave | Carrollton | 41008 | |
| Carter | Carter County Historical and Genealogical Society | Janet Bentley, President | PO Box 1128 | Grayson | 41143 | |
| Casey | Bicentennial Heritage of Casey County | Gladys C. Thomas, President | 147 Wolford Street | Liberty | 42539 | (606) 787-6194 |
| Christian | Christian County Historical Society | Charles R. Jackson, President | 1110 Bethel St | Hopkinsville | 42240 | |
| Christian | Don F. Pratt Memorial Museum | | Building 5702 Tennessee Ave | Ft. Campbell | 42223 | (270) 798-4986 |
| Christian | Pennyroyal Area Museum | Donna Stone, Executive Director | 217 E 9th St PO Box 1093 | Hopkinsville | 42241 | (270) 887-4270 |
| Clark | Bluegrass Heritage Museum | Jim Pitts | 217 S Main St | Winchester | 40391 | (859) 745-1358 |

# HISTORICAL SOCIETIES & MUSEUMS

| COUNTY | HISTORICAL SOCIETY/MUSEUM | CONTACT | ADDRESS | CITY | ZIP | PHONE |
|---|---|---|---|---|---|---|
| Clark | Clark County Historical Society | | 122 Belmont | Winchester | 40391 | (859) 744-6616 |
| Clark | Holly Rood Clark Mansion | | 122 Belmont | Winchester | 40391 | (859) 744-6616 |
| Clay | Clay County Genealogy and Historical Society | | PO Box 394 | Manchester | 40962 | (606) 598-5507 |
| Clinton | Clinton County Historical Society | | Rt 4 Box 638 | Albany | 42602 | (606) 387-5519 |
| Crittenden | Ben Clements Mineral Museum | Bill Frazier, Chairman of the Board | 205 N Walker St | Marion | 42064 | (270) 965-4263 |
| Crittenden | Bobby Wheeler Museum, Crittenden County Historical Society | | W Carlisle St | Marion | 42064 | (270) 965-9657 |
| Crittenden | Crittenden County Historical Society | Myrle Dunning, Director/Treasurer | PO Box 25 | Marion | 42064 | (270) 965-4666 |
| Daviess | Daviess County Historical Society | Sheila E. Heflin, Director | PO Box 80 | Livermore | 42301 | (502) 684-0211 |
| Daviess | International Bluegrass Music Museum | Gabrielle Gray, Executive Director | 207 E Second St | Owensboro | 42303 | (270) 926-7891 |
| Daviess | Owensboro Area Museum of Science and History | Jeffery Jones, Executive Director | 122 E Second St | Owensboro | 42303 | (270) 687-2732 |
| Edmonson | Edmonson County Historical Society | | 8621 Brownsville Rd | Brownsville | 42210 | (502) 597-3140 |
| Elliott | Cultural Heritage Center | Laurell Gorge, Director | Old 7 and 32 PO Box 653 | Sandy Hook | 41171 | (606) 738-5543 |
| Estill | Estill County Historical & Genealogy Society | Diane Rogers, President | PO Box 221 | Irvine | 40472 | (859) 723-3806 |
| Fayette | American Saddlebred Museum | Tolley Graves, President | 4083 Iron Works Pike | Lexington | 40511 | (859) 259-2746 |
| Fayette | Ashland, The Henry Clay Estate | | 120 Sycamore Rd | Lexington | 40502 | (859) 266-8581 |
| Fayette | Aviation Museum of Kentucky | Alice McCormick, Operations Manger | PO Box 4118 4316 Hanger Dr Bldg 13 | Lexington | 40544 | (859) 231-1219 |
| Fayette | Explorium | Sara Holcomb, Director | 440 W Short St | Lexington | 40507 | (859) 258-3253 |
| Fayette | Fayette County Genealogical Society | Debbie Steuert, Director | 800 Apache Trl | Lexington | 40503 | (859) 224-9406 |
| Fayette | Headley-Whitney Museum | | 4435 Old Frankfort Pk | Lexington | 40510 | (859) 255-6653 |
| Fayette | Hunt Morgan House | | 201 N Mill St | Lexington | 40507 | (859) 233-3290 |
| Fayette | International Museum of the Horse | Bill Cook | 4089 Iron Works Pike | Lexington | 40511 | (859) 233-4303 |
| Fayette | Kentucky Hemp Museum | | PO Box 8551 | Lexington | 40533 | (606) 873-8957 |
| Fayette | Kentucky Horse Park | | 4089 Iron Works Pike | Lexington | 40511 | (800) 678-8813 |
| Fayette | Lexington History Museum Inc | Ed Houlihan, Director | PO Box 116  215 W Main St | Lexington | 40507 | (859) 254-0530 |
| Fayette | Mary Todd Lincoln House | | 578 W Main St | Lexington | 40507 | (859) 233-9999 |
| Fayette | UK Basketball Museum | Van Florence, Executive Director | PO Box 89 | Lexington | 40588 | (859) 225-5670 |
| Fayette | University of Kentucky Art Museum | Kathy Walsh-Piper, Director | 116 Singletary Center Rose and Euclid Aves | Lexington | 40506 | (859) 257-5716 |
| Fayette | William S Webb Museum of Anthropology | George Crothers, Director | 1020A Export St | Lexington | 40506 | (859) 257-8208 |
| Fleming | Fleming County Historical Society | Brenda Plummer, Director | 290 W Water St | Flemingsburg | 41041 | |
| Fleming | Fleming County Museum Society | | PO Box 24 | Flemingsburg | 41041 | |
| Floyd | Floyd County Historical and Genealogical Society | Bertha Daniels, Director | PO Box 982 | Auxier | 41653 | |
| Floyd | Samuel May House | | 1001 Wilkinson Blvd | Prestonsburg | 41653 | (606) 886-3863 |
| Franklin | Buffalo Trace Distillery Museum | Chris McCrory, Director | 103 Jackson Hall, KSU | Frankfort | 40601 | (502) 223-7641 |
| Franklin | Center of Excellence for the Study of Ky. African Americans | Dr. Anne Butler | | Frankfort | 40601 | (502) 597-6315 |
| Franklin | Kentucky Historical Society | Kent Whitworth, Executive Director | 100 W Broadway | Frankfort | 40601 | (502) 564-1792 |
| Franklin | Kentucky Military History Museum | Bill Bright, Curator | 120 E Main St | Frankfort | 40601 | (502) 564-3265 |
| Fulton | Fulton County Historical Society | Margaret Adams, President | PO Box 1031 | Fulton | 42041 | (270) 838-6961 |
| Fulton | Warren Thomas Black History Museum | | 603 Moulton St | Hickman | 42050 | (270) 236-2535 |
| Gallatin | Gallatin County Historical Society | | PO Box 165 | Warsaw | 41095 | |
| Gallatin | Peak-Corkran House | Jaqueline Mylor, President | PO Box 1241 | Warsaw | 41095 | (859) 567-6941 |
| Garrard | Garrard County Historical Society | | 208 Danville St | Lancaster | 40444 | |
| Grant | Grant County Historical Society | Ruby Miller, Director | PO Box 33 | Mason | 41054 | (859) 824-7181 |
| Graves | Graves County Historical Society | | Rt 1 Box 171 | Cunningham | 42035 | |
| Graves | Western Kentucky Museum | | Old Ice House, 120 N 8th St | Mayfield | 42066 | (270) 247-6971 |
| Grayson | Grayson County Historical Society | | PO Box 84 | Leitchfield | 42755 | (270) 230-8989 |
| Grayson | Jack Thomas House, Grayson County Historical Society | | 122 E Main St | Leitchfield | 42755 | (270) 230-8989 |
| Green | Green County Historical Society | | PO Box 276 | Greensburg | 42743 | |

## HISTORICAL SOCIETIES & MUSEUMS

| COUNTY | HISTORICAL SOCIETY/MUSEUM | CONTACT | ADDRESS | CITY | ZIP | PHONE |
|---|---|---|---|---|---|---|
| Greenup | McConnell House | | 1023 Riverside Dr | Wurtland | 41144 | (606) 833-9098 |
| Hancock | Hancock County Agricultural Museum at Lewisport | L R Waltman | Lewisport City Hall | Lewisport | 42351 | |
| Hancock | Hancock County Historical Society | | PO Box 667 | Hawesville | 42348 | (270) 927-8095 |
| Hancock | Hancock County Museum Inc. | | PO Box 605 110 River St | Hawesville | 42348 | (270) 927-8672 |
| Harden | Ft Duffield Park Civil War Site | | US 31W at Salt River Dr | West Point | 40177 | (502) 922-4574 |
| Hardin | Children's Museum of E town | Angela Wilcox, Director | 447 King's Way | Elizabethtown | 42701 | (270) 360-9696 |
| Hardin | Hardin County Historical Society | | 209 W Dixie Ave | Elizabethtown | 42701 | (270) 737-4126 |
| Hardin | Patton Museum of Cavalry and Armor | | Off US Hwy 31 W | Ft Knox | 40121 | (502) 943-8977 |
| Hardin | Schmidt Museum of Coca-Cola Memorabilia | Roy Minagawa, Director | 109 Buffalo Creek Dr | Elizabethtown | 42701 | (270) 234-1100 |
| Hardin | Swopes Cars of Yesteryear Museum | | 1100 N Dixie Ave | Elizabethtown | 42701 | (270) 765-2181 |
| Harlan | Harlan County Genealogical Society | | PO Box 1498 | Harlan | 40831 | |
| Harlan | Kentucky Coal Mining Museum | Bobbie Gothard, Curator | PO Box A 231 Main St | Benham | 40807 | (606) 848-1530 |
| Harrison | Cynthiana-Harrison County Museum | Martha S Barnes, President | PO Box 411 112 S Walnut St | Cynthiana | 41031 | (859) 234-7179 |
| Harrison | Harrison County Historical Society | Phillip Naff | 1490 Annerman Pk | Cynthiana | 41031 | (859) 234-5835 |
| Hart | American Cave Museum and Hidden River Cave | | 119 E Main St | Horse Cave | 42749 | (270) 786-1466 |
| Hart | Battle for the Bridge Civil War Site | | 940 S Dixie Hwy | Munfordville | 42765 | (270) 524-0101 |
| Hart | Hart County Historical Society | | PO Box 606 | Munfordville | 42765 | (270) 524-0101 |
| Henderson | Henderson County Historical and Genealogical Society | Netta Mullin, Director | PO Box 303 | Henderson | 42420 | |
| Henry | Henry County Historical Society | Shirely Sills, Director | PO Box 570 | New Castle | 40050 | |
| Hickman | Hickman County Historical Society | | RR 1 Box 70 | Clinton | 42031 | |
| Hickman | Hickman County Museum | | 221 E Clay St | Clinton | 42031 | (270) 653-6948 |
| Hopkins | Historical Society of Hopkins County | | 107 S Union St | Madisonville | 42431 | |
| Jackson | Jackson County Historical Society | Ken Williams, Director | 299 Hooten Rd | McKee | 40447 | (606) 287-7672 |
| Jefferson | Callahan Museum, American Printing House for the Blind | | 1839 Frankfort Ave | Louisville | 40206 | (800) 223-1839 |
| Jefferson | Cathedral Heritage Foundation | | 429 W Muhammad Ali Blvd | Louisville | 40202 | (502) 558-5336 |
| Jefferson | Col. Harland Sanders Museum | | 1441 Gardiner Ln | Louisville | 40213 | (502) 874-8353 |
| Jefferson | Filson Historical Society | | 1310 S Third St | Louisville | 40208 | (502) 635-5083 |
| Jefferson | Frazier Historical Arms Museum | B J Davis, Manager of Education | 829 W Main St | Louisville | 40202 | (502) 412-2220 |
| Jefferson | Historic Middletown Museum | | 726 Waterford Rd | Louisville | 40207 | (502) 254-4303 |
| Jefferson | Jeffersontown Historical Museum | | 10635 Watterson Trail | Jeffersontown | 40299 | (502) 261-8290 |
| Jefferson | Kentucky Derby Museum | Sherry Srose, COO | 704 Central Ave Churchill Downs | Louisville | 40208 | (502) 637-1111 |
| Jefferson | Little Loomhouse, Lou Tate Foundation | | 328 Kenwood Hill Rd | Louisville | 40214 | (502) 367-4792 |
| Jefferson | Louisville Science Center | Scott Alvey, Asst Dir | 727 W Main St | Louisville | 40202 | (502) 561-6100 |
| Jefferson | Louisville Slugger Museum | Bill Williams | 800 W Main St | Louisville | 40202 | (877) 775-8443 |
| Jefferson | Muhammad Ali Center | Michael Fox, President/CEO | 144 N Sixth St | Louisville | 40202 | (502) 584-9254 |
| Jefferson | Portland Museum | Nathalie Andrews, Executive Director | 2308 Portland Ave | Louisville | 40212 | (502) 776-7678 |
| Jefferson | SW Jefferson County Historical Society | | 13700 Sandray Blvd | Louisville | 40201 | |
| Jefferson | Thomas Edison House | | 729-31 E Washington St | Louisville | 40202 | (502) 585-5247 |
| Jefferson | Whitehall Historic House, Historic Homes Foundation | | 3110 Lexington Rd | Louisville | 40206 | (502) 897-2944 |
| Jessamine | Camp Nelson Heritage Park | | Ky Hwy 3026/US Hwy 27 | Nicholasville | 40356 | (859) 881-9126 |
| Jessamine | Jessamine County Historical Society | George Dean, Director | 504 W Maple St | Nicholasville | 40356 | (859) 885-4871 |
| Johnson | Johnson County Historical Society | | 444 Main St | Paintsville | 41240 | |
| Johnson | Kentucky Highway 23 Country Music Museum | | US Hwy 23 | Paintsville | 41502 | (800) 542-5790 |
| Johnson | Mountain Homeplace | | Paintsville Lake Park | Staffordsville | 41256 | (606) 297-1850 |
| Johnsons | Coal Miner's Museum, Van Lear Historical Society | | 78 Miller's Creek Rd | Van Lear | 41265 | (606) 789-8540 |
| Kenton | Behringer Crawford Museum | Laurie Risch, Executive Director | PO Box 67 1600 Montague St | Covington | 41011 | (859) 491-4003 |
| Kenton | Erlanger Historical Society | | 3313 Crescent Ave | Erlanger | 41018 | (859) 727-2630 |

Clark's Kentucky Almanac Second Edition

## HISTORICAL SOCIETIES & MUSEUMS

| COUNTY | HISTORICAL SOCIETY/MUSEUM | CONTACT | ADDRESS | CITY | ZIP | PHONE |
|---|---|---|---|---|---|---|
| Kenton | Kenton County Historical Society | John Boh, Secretary | 507 Russell Street | Covington | 41011 | (859) 341-2802 |
| Kenton | Oldenburg Brewery Archives & Museum | | I-75 & Buttermilk Pk | Ft. Mitchell | 41011 | (859) 341-0461 |
| Kenton | Vent Haven Museum | | 33 W Maple St | Ft. Mitchell | 41011 | (859) 341-0461 |
| Kenton | Vent Haven Museum | Lisa Sweasy, Curator | 33 W Maple St | Ft. Mitchell | 41011 | (859) 341-0461 |
| Knott | Knott County Historical and Genealogical Society | David Smith, Director | PO Box 1023 | Hindman | 41822 | (606) 785-5751 |
| Knox | Knox County Historical Society | | 601 N. Main St. | Barbourville | 40906 | |
| Knox | Knox Historical Museum | | PO Box 1446 196 Daniel Boone Dr | Barbourville | 40906 | (606) 546-4300 |
| Larue | Larue County Historical Society | | PO Box 361 | Hodgenville | 42748 | |
| Larue | The Lincoln Museum | | 66 Lincoln Sq | Hodgenville | 42748 | (270) 358-3163 |
| Laurel | Col. Sanders Café Museum | | 688 US 25W & 25E | Corbin | 40701 | (606) 528-2163 |
| Laurel | Laurel County Historical Society | | PO Box 816 | London | 40743 | |
| Laurel | Mountain Life Museum, Levi Jackson State Park | William Meaders, Director | 998 Levi Jackson Mill Rd | London | 40744 | (606) 878-8000 |
| Lee | Lee County Historical Society | | PO Box V | Beattyville | 41311 | |
| Leslie | Leslie County Historical Society | John Wilson | PO Box 9 | Hyden | 40840 | (859) 374-7828 |
| Letcher | C.B Caudill Store/History Center | Gaynell Begley, Proprietor | 7822 Hwy 7S | Whitesburg | 41858 | (606) 633-3281 |
| Letcher | Letcher County Historical & Genealogical Society | | PO Box 312 | Whitesburg | 41858 | |
| Letcher | Zegeer Coal-Railroad Museum | | PO Box 4 | Jenkins | 41537 | (606) 832-4676 |
| Lewis | Lewis County Historical Society | | PO Box 212 | Vanceburg | 41179 | |
| Lincoln | Vanceburg Depot Museum | | 615 2nd St | Vanceburg | 41179 | (606) 796-3044 |
| Lincoln | L & N Depot Museum | Luzia Foster, President | 1866 Depot St | Stanford | 40484 | (859) 365-0207 |
| Lincoln | Lincoln County Historical Society | Joyce Woodyard, President | PO Box 570 | Stanford | 40484 | (606) 365-2536 |
| Livingston | Livingston County Historical Society | | PO Box 96 | Smithland | 42081 | (270) 928-4656 |
| Livingston | Livingston County Welcome Center and Museum | | 117 State St | Smithland | 42081 | (270) 928-4656 |
| Livingston | Morris Toy Museum | | 1007 1st St | Smithland | 42081 | (270) 988-3591 |
| Logan | Auburn Museum | Eloise Haddon, President | 433 W Main St | Auburn | 42206 | (270) 542-4677 |
| Logan | Historic Russellville Visitors' Center-Bibb House Museum and 1817 Saddle Factory Museum | | 280 E Fourth St | Russellville | 42276 | (270) 726-4181 |
| Logan | Historic Russllville | Judy Lyne, President | PO Box 853 | Russellville | 42276 | (270) 726-2206 |
| Logan | Shaker Museum at South Union | Tommy Hines, Director | PO Box 177 | Auburn | 42206 | (270) 542-4167 |
| Logan | Shaker Museum at South Union | | 850 Shaker Museum Rd | South Union | 42283 | (270) 542-4167 |
| Lyon | Lyon County Historical Society | | PO Box 894 | Eddyville | 42038 | |
| Madison | Berea College Mus. App.Center | Mary Katherine Edwards, Director | CPO 2196 | Berea | 40404 | (859) 985-3373 |
| Madison | Ft Boonesborough State Park/Kentucky River Museum | Chris Miller, College Curator | 4375 Boonesboro Rd | Richmond | 40475 | (859) 527-3131 |
| Madison | Irvinton House Museum | | 345 Lancaster Ave | Richmond | 40475 | (859) 626-1422 |
| Madison | Madison County Historical Society | Charles Hay, Director | PO Box 5066 | Richmond | 40476 | |
| Madison | White Hall State Historic Site | | 500 White Hall Shrine Rd | Richmond | 40475 | (859) 626-9178 |
| Magoffin | Magoffin County Historical Society | | Box 222 | Salyersville | 41465 | (606) 349-1607 |
| Marion | Loretto Archives Heritage Room | | 515 Nerinx Rd | Loretto | 40037 | (270) 865-5811 |
| Marion | Maker's Mark Distillery and Museum | Mary Perry, Director | 3350 Burks Springs Rd | Loretto | 40037 | (270) 865-2099 |
| Marion | Marion County Historical Society | | 201 E Main St | Lebanon | 40033 | (270) 692-4698 |
| Marshall | Marshall County Historical Genealogical Society | Michael Ragsdale | PO Box 373 | Benton | 42025 | (502) 527-4749 |
| Martin | Martin County Historical Society | Evelynn Cassady, President | PO Box 501 | Inez | 41224 | |
| Mason | Harriet Beecher Stowe Slavery to Freedom Museum | Marsha H Jones, Secretary | 2124 Old Main St | Washington | 41056 | (606) 759-7411 |
| Mason | Mason County Historical Society | | c/o Mason County Museum 215 Sutton | Maysville | 41056 | (606) 564-5865 |
| Mason | Musem County Museum | Sue Ellen Grannis, Curator | 215 Sutton St | Maysville | 41056 | (606) 564-5865 |
| Mason | Old Washington | | 2215 Old Main St | Washington | 41096 | (606) 759-7411 |
| McCracken | Alben Barkley Museum | Martha Beck | 533 Madison St | Paducah | 42001 | (270) 534-8264 |

## HISTORICAL SOCIETIES & MUSEUMS

| COUNTY | HISTORICAL SOCIETY/MUSEUM | CONTACT | ADDRESS | CITY | ZIP | PHONE |
|---|---|---|---|---|---|---|
| McCracken | Market House Museum | | PO Box 12 121 Market St Sq | Paducah | 42001 | (270) 443-7759 |
| McCracken | McCracken County Geneological and Historical Society | | 4640 Buckner Ln | Paducah | 42001 | |
| McCracken | Metropolitan Hotel Museum | Sharon Poat, Treasurer | 446 Kinkead St | Paducah | 42003 | (270) 443-9229 |
| McCracken | Museum of the American Quilters Society | | 215 Jefferson St | Paducah | 42001 | (270) 442-8856 |
| McCracken | Paducah Railroad Museum | | 3rd and Washington St | Paducah | 42001 | (270) 442-4032 |
| McCracken | River Heritage Museum | Julie Harris, Director | 117 S Water St | Paducah | 42001 | (270) 575-9958 |
| McCracken | The Tilghman Heritage Foundation | | 631 Kentucky Ave | Paducah | 42003 | (270) 575-1870 |
| McCreary | Blue Heron Mining Community | | Hwy 742 | Stearns | 42005 | (606) 376-3787 |
| McCreary | McCreary County Historical and Genealogical Society | | PO Box 400 | Whitley City | 42653 | |
| McCreary | Stearns Museum | | PO Box 452 | Stearns | 42647 | (606) 376-5730 |
| McLean | Forrest's Orphans Museum | Fred Wilhite | PO Box 10 | Calhoun | 42327 | (270) 785-4594 |
| McLean | McLean County Historical & Genealogy Muesum | | 540 Main St Box 34 | Calhoun | 42327 | (270) 273-9760 |
| Menifee | Menifee County Roots | | PO Box 114 | Frenchburg | 40322 | (606) 768-3323 |
| Mercer | Harrodsburg Histoical Society | | PO Box 316 | Harrodsburg | 40330 | (606) 734-5985 |
| Metcalfe | Metcalfe County Historical Society | Kay Harbison, President | Box 910 | Edmonton | 42129 | |
| Monroe | Old Mulkey Meeting House State Historic Site | | 1819 Old Mulkey Rd | Tompkinsville | 42167 | (270) 487-8481 |
| Montgomery | Montgomery County Historical Society | Ray F Shear, President | 607 Elmwood Dr | Mt. Sterling | 40353 | (859) 498-0119 |
| Morgan | Memory Hill Foundation | | 89 Memory Hill Ln | West Liberty | 41472 | (606) 743-3330 |
| Morgan | Morgan County Historical Society | Laberta Potter, President | PO Box 900 Rt 1 | West Liberty | 41472 | |
| Morgan | Morgan County History Museum | | Morgan St | West Liberty | 41472 | (606) 743-2588 |
| Muhlenberg | Duncan Cultural Center | | 122 S Cherry St | Greenville | 42345 | (270) 338-2605 |
| Muhlenberg | Every Brothers Monument | | 203 N 2nd St | Central City | 42330 | (270) 754-9603 |
| Muhlenberg | Muhlenberg County Genealogy & Local History Annex | Barry Edwards, Manager | PO Box 758 | Greenville | 42345 | (270) 338-5388 |
| Nelson | Bardstown Civil War Museum | Joe Masterson, Director | 310 E Broadway | Bardstown | 40004 | (502) 349-0291 |
| Nelson | Bardstown Historical Museum | Mary Ellyn Hamilton, Curator | 114 N 5th St Spalding Hall | Bardstown | 40004 | (502) 348-2999 |
| Nelson | Doll Museum | | | Bardstown | 40004 | |
| Nelson | Heaven Hill Distillery Museum | Lynn Grant, Director | 1311 Gilkey Run Rd | Bardstown | 40004 | (502) 337-1000 |
| Nelson | Kentucky Railway Museum | Greg Matthews, Executive Director | PO Box 240 | New Haven | 40051 | (502) 549-5470 |
| Nelson | Nelson County Genealogical Roundtable | | PO Box 409 | Bardstown | 40004 | (502) 348-5652 |
| Nelson | Oscar Getz Museum | Mary Ellyn Hamilton, Curator | 114 N 5th St | Bardstown | 40004 | (502) 348-2999 |
| Nicholas | Nicholas County Historical Society | Joan Conley, President | PO Box 222 101 Market St | Carlisle | 40311 | (606) 289-9135 |
| Ohio | Bill Monroe Homeplace | Campbell "Doc" Mercer | PO Box 429 6210 HWY 62 | Rosine | 42320 | (270) 274-9181 |
| Ohio | Fordsville Historical Society Museum | | Old Train Depot, 32 Ridge Rd | Fordsville | 42343 | (270) 298-7452 |
| Ohio | Ohio County Historical Society | JT Boling, Director | Box 44 | Hartford | 42347 | (270) 298-3444 |
| Ohio | Ohio County Historical Society Museum | | 415 Mulberry St | Hartford | 42347 | (270) 298-3177 |
| Oldham | Oldham County Historical Society | Nancy Theiss, Director | 106 N. Second St. | LaGrange | 40031 | (502) 222-0826 |
| Owen | Owen County Historical Society | Katie Gibson, President | PO Box 84 | Owenton | 40359 | |
| Owen | Owen County Historical Society, J.C. Harsough Museum | | 206 Main St | Owenton | 40359 | (502) 484-2321 |
| Pendleton | Pendleton County Historical Society | | PO Box 130 | Falmouth | 41040 | |
| Perry | Bobby Davis Museum and Park | Martha Quigley, Director | 234 Walnut St | Hazard | 41701 | (606) 439-4325 |
| Perry | Perry County Historical Society | | 148 Chester St | Hazard | 41701 | |
| Pike | Big Sandy Heritage Center | Everett Johnson, Director | PO Box 1041 773 Hambley Blvd | Pikeville | 41501 | (606) 218-6050 |
| Pike | Elkhorn City Railroad Museum | | 100 Pine St | Elkhorn City | 41522 | (606) 754-8300 |
| Pike | Pike County Historical/Genealogical Society | | PO Box36 | Somerset | 42502 | |
| Powell | Red River Historical Society | Larry Meadows | 220 Powell Road | Clay City | 40312 | |
| Pulaski | Mill Springs Battlefield National Historic Landmark | | PO Box 814 | Somerset | 42502 | (606) 679-1859 |
| Pulaski | Pulaski County Historical Society | | PO Box 36 | Somerset | 42501 | (606) 679-8401 |

# HISTORY

## HISTORICAL SOCIETIES & MUSEUMS

| COUNTY | HISTORICAL SOCIETY/MUSEUM | CONTACT | ADDRESS | CITY | ZIP | PHONE |
|---|---|---|---|---|---|---|
| Robertson | Robertson County Historical Society | William Wheaton, Past President | PO Box 282 | Mt. Olivet | 41064 | (606) 256-9814 |
| Rockcastle | Bittersweet Cabins Museum | Carol Bryant, Director | Hwy 25 | Renfro Valley | 40473 | (859) 433-3208 |
| Rockcastle | Brush Arbor Appalachian Pioneer Log Village | Jerry Hayes | PO Box 57 | Renfro Valley | 40473 | (606) 256-1000 |
| Rockcastle | Kentucky Music Hall of Fame | | 2590 Richmond Rd | Renfro Valley | 40473 | |
| Rockcastle | Rockcastle County Historical Society | | PO Box 930 | Mt. Vernon | 40456 | |
| Rowan | Rowan County Historical Society | Gary Lewis, V.P. | 236 Allen Ave PO Box 60 | Morehead | 40351 | |
| Russell | Russell County Historical Society | Mary Donna Foley, Director | PO Box 544 | Jamestown | 42629 | |
| Scott | Georgetown & Scott County Museum | John Toncray, Director | 229 E Main St | Georgetown | 40324 | (502) 863-6201 |
| Scott | Scott County Historical Society | Ann Bevins, Director | 119 N Hamilton St PO Box 1064 | Georgetown | 40324 | |
| Shelby | Shelby County Historical Society | Bill Matthews, Director | 104 Bradford Ln PO Box 444 | Shelbyville | 40066 | |
| Simpson | African American Heritage Center | | 500 Jefferson St. | Franklin | 42134 | (270) 586-0099 |
| Simpson | Octagon Hall Museum and Archives | | 6040 Bowling Green Rd | Franklin | 42134 | (270) 586-9343 |
| Simpson | Simpson County Archives and Museum | | 206 N College St | Franklin | 42134 | (270) 586-4228 |
| Simpson | Simpson County Archives/Historical Society | | 206 N College St | Franklin | 42134 | (270) 586-4228 |
| Spencer | Spencer County Historical and Genealogical Society | | PO Box 266 | Taylorsville | 40071 | (502) 477-2980 |
| Taylor | Atkinson-Griffith House | | Green River Lake | Campbellsville | 42178 | (270) 465-4463 |
| Taylor | Hiestand House Museum Inc | Betty Gorin, Board Member | 112 Kensington Way PO Box 4021 | Campbellsville | 42718 | (270) 465-3786 |
| Taylor | Taylor County Historical Society Inc | | PO Box 14 | Campbellsville | 42718 | |
| Todd | Todd County Library | | 302 E Main St | Elkton | 42220 | (270) 265-9071 |
| Trigg | Homeplace 1850 | | Visitors Center, Land Between the Lakes | Golden Pond | 42211 | (270) 924-2233 |
| Trigg | Trigg County Historical Society | | PO Box 1008 | Cadiz | 42211 | (270) 522-6988 |
| Trimble | Preston Plantation | | 341 Watson Landing Rd & Venard Rd | Milton | 40045 | (502) 268-5858 |
| Trimble | Trimble County Historical Society | | PO Box 128 | Smithfield | 42544 | |
| Union | Camp Breckinridge Museum | Vicki Ricketts, Director | 1116 N Village Sq | Morganfield | 42437 | (270) 389-1082 |
| Union | Union County Historical Society | | 130 E Geiger | Morganfield | 42437 | (270) 389-1901 |
| Warren | Barren River Imaginative Museum of Science | Charles Phillips, Director | 1229 Center St | Bowling Green | 42101 | (270) 843-9779 |
| Warren | National Corvette Museum | Wendell Strode, Executive Director | 350 Corvette Drive | Bowling Green | 42101 | (270) 781-7973 |
| Warren | The Kentucky Museum | Timothy Mullin, Director | 1 Big Red Way, Western Kentucky University | Bowling Green | 42101 | (270) 745-2592 |
| Wayne | Wayne County Historical and Genealogical Society | Phillip Catron, Chairman | PO Box 320 | Monticello | 42633 | |
| Webster | Providence Museum and Learning Center | | 500 S Broadway | Providence | 42450 | |
| Webster | Webster County Historical and Genealogical Society | Lowell Childress, President | 1005 W Main St | Providence | 42450 | (270) 667-5022 |
| Whitley | Corbin Genealogical Society | Joyce Culver, Director | 99 Boone Ave PO Box 353 | Corbin | 40701 | |
| Whitley | Cumberland Falls State Res Park Blair Museum. | Bret Smitty, Director | 7351 Hwy 90 | Corbin | 40701 | (606) 528-4121 |
| Whitley | Cumberland Inn Museum | David Maggard, General Manager | 649 S 10th St | Williamsburg | 40769 | (800) 315-0286 |
| Wolfe | Wolfe County Historical Museum | | Main St | Campton | 41301 | (606) 668-3113 |
| Woodford | Bluegrass Railway Museum | Winfrey Adkins, President | PO Box 27 175 Beasley Dr | Versailles | 40383 | (859) 873-2476 |
| Woodford | Jouett House, Woodford County Heritage Commission | | Craig's Creek Rd | Versailles | 40383 | (859) 873-7902 |
| Woodford | Midway Museum | David Hume, President | PO Box 4592 | Midway | 40347 | (859) 846-4214 |
| Woodford | Woodford County Historical Society | Danna Estridge, Curator | 121 Rose Hill | Versailles | 40383 | (859) 873-3623 |
| Woodford | Woodford Reserve's Labrot and Graham Distillery | | 7855 McCracken Pk | Versailles | 40383 | (859) 879-1812 |

*Source: Kentucky Historical Society and Family Guide to Kentucky Museums and*

*Historic Sites - 2004, published by Back Home in Kentucky Magazine.*

# History & Tax Lists – Buried Treasure

Kandie Adkinson

Buried in microfilm cabinets in Kentucky's research libraries are dusty rolls of microfilm simply labeled "Tax Lists." Arranged by county in chronological order, tax lists are a veritable hidden treasure for researchers studying Kentucky's history, culture and land title. As census information is collected decennially (every 10 years), data derived from the annual collection of taxes provides a better insight into the household of the taxpayer and his acquisition of property, both real and personal. Free males 21 years of age or older were enumerated (and named) on tax lists if they own one horse. Women were included on tax lists if they were the head-of-the-household. Free Blacks were named on tax lists decades before the Civil War. The number of town lots, wheeled carriages, jewelry, tavern licenses and billiard tables—yes, billiard tables were taxed or the owner faced severe penalties—provide insight into Kentucky's developing society. The number of livestock, the value of hemp and other agricultural products provide insight into Kentucky's agrarian society. (It is interesting to note that tax collectors were local residents; would taxpayers withhold taxable items to avoid taxation or would they be more likely to report everything so they could be considered "the richest person in the county?") In later years, the numbers of school age children reported on tax lists are invaluable for researchers tracing the development of Kentucky's educational system.

This article provides excerpts from selected Kentucky Tax Laws regarding the collection of state taxes—the same type of state taxes, aka "permanent revenue," that Kentuckians pay today. These abstracts do not pertain to city, county or federal taxes. Tax records do not cease to exist after 1840; research libraries have tax list microfilm through the early 1890's for many Kentucky counties.

### Excerpts From Early Kentucky Legislation Regarding The Tax Process

1792 (June 26) – Shortly after attaining state-hood, the Kentucky General Assembly passed legislation (effective July 1, 1792) establishing "Permanent Revenue." Tax rates were set for land ("whether the land be claimed by patent or by entry only"), slaves, horses and mules, covering horses, cattle, coaches and carriages, billiard tables, and retail stores. Commissioners were appointed to make a "true & perfect account of all persons & of every species of property belonging to or in his possession or care, within that district." Under this Act, the number of commissioners within a county was determined by the legislature; the county court then assigned each commissioner a certain district to canvass. Commissioners were paid six shillings a day; they were exempt from militia service. The commissioners were required to make four alphabetical lists reciting tax information that had been collected; columns identifying the number of all free males above the age of 21 (within the household) and those subject to county levies were to be added. The lists were distributed by the last day of October (annually) as follows: (1) Commissioner's file; (2) County clerk for laying the county levy & fixing the poor rates; (3) High Sheriff for tax collection; and (4) State Auditor for use in tax litigation involving the county sheriff.

1793 (Dec. 21) – The Kentucky General Assembly passed legislation allowing taxpayers to report land they owned in other counties to the tax commissioner for their resident county and district. Out-of-state landowners could list their holdings with any tax commissioner within Kentucky. Taxpayers were to list the acreage and county for each tract they owned. Additionally, the legislature divided the lands into three classes by "quality," i.e. first, second and third-rate. First-rate land was taxed at three shillings, second-rate land was taxed at one shilling and six pence, and third-rate land at nine pence per 100 acres. "And the rich lands in Fayette County shall be considered as the standard of first-rate land."

*Source: Littell's Statute Law of Kentucky.*

# HISTORY
# *Historical Markers*

The Kentucky Historical Highway Marker Program, administered by the Kentucky Historical Society in cooperation with the Kentucky Transportation Cabinet, commemorates historic sites, events and personalities throughout the Commonwealth. Through the program, the wealth of history which is Kentucky's past is made accessible to the public as they travel along the state's roadways – in excerpts which stimulate an interest in the history of local communities. The plaques are on-the-spot history lessons that add drama and interest to the countryside for native Kentuckians as well as tourists. The goal of the Kentucky Historical Highway Marker Program is to connect events and personalities with their place, to bring the past to life and to increase the awareness of what we owe to those who came before us. The subjects of the more than 1,750 markers in Kentucky are varied. There are markers that tell of a duel of honor, a seven-year-old boy who served as a drummer in the Revolutionary War and the 1937 Ohio River flood. Others highlight "moonlight" schools that were established to combat illiteracy, an Indian academy and the first state-supported school for the hearing impaired in the US. Consider these examples:

## Campbellsville College
Marker Number: 1924
Location: Entrance to campus,
200 W. College St., Campbellsville
Description: Founded as Russell Creek Academy by Russell Creek Assoc. of Baptists in 1906. C.R. Hoskins sold ten-acre site for $1,000. On founding committee were J.L. Atkinson, J.R. Davis, George Durrett, James Garnett, Jr., S.E. Kerr, W.R. Lyon, B.W. Penick, Alexander Shively, W.T. Underwood, and H.C. Wood. Presented by Campbellsville College.

## John Bradford
Marker Number: 1864
Location: 1916 Iron Works Pike, Lexington
Description: Built on this property Flemish bond brick home, "Fairfield," ca. 1785-1800. Earlier a surveyor, Bradford became publisher and editor of Kentucky Gazette, state's first newspaper, printed Aug. 11, 1787. Active in public life, he served as

**Historical Marker for John Bradford**
**Kentucky's first printer**
*Photo: Sam Stephens*

trustee of city and Transylvania Univ., in Ky. legislature, and as Fayette Co. sheriff. His early Ky. "Notes" are a valued source on era.

## Hazen A. Dean (1899-1984)
(Marker Number: 1747)
County: Daviess
Location: Owensboro, at Settle Memorial Methodist Church
Description: First Kentuckian to receive "70 Continuous Years of Service Award" from Boy Scouts of America, 1983. Scoutmaster for over 50 years; with Owensboro's oldest troop, 24, from 1949 till death. Among many honors, he received Scoutmaster's Key and Silver Beaver awards. Recognized for having 86 Eagle Scouts, most in nation; received Lt. Governor's Outstanding Kentuckian Award, 1982.

# HISTORY

# *Milestones & Timeline*

Dr. James Klotter

**Pre-1750**

10000 B.C. or before – First people come to what is now Kentucky

1000-1750 – Late Prehistoric Period, with small villages, trade networks, and developed religions

Late 1600s-1750s – Sporadic contact between Native peoples and European explorers brings disease that kills thousands of Indians

**1750-1800**

1750 – Thomas Walker and Christopher Gist make separate trips to explore Kentucky

1755 – Mary Ingles taken to Kentucky as captive, probably first English woman in area

1767 – Daniel Boone's first trip to Kentucky

1774 – James Harrod's first attempt at settlement; abandoned later

1775 – Fort Harrod established as first permanent English settlement

1775 – Daniel Boone blazes Wilderness Road

1776 – Kentucky County established as part of Virginia

1778-79 – George Rogers Clark's N.W. Campaign

1780 – Present-day Transylvania University is chartered

1780 – Kentucky County is divided into three counties – Fayette, Jefferson, and Lincoln

1782 – Battle of Blue Licks marks last major conflict between settlers and Native Americans within Kentucky

1784 – John Filson's *Discovery, Settlement, and Present State of Kentucke* appears

1787 – *Kentucke Gazette*, first newspaper, is published

1792 – Kentucky becomes 15th state, with Isaac Shelby as first governor

1798-99 – Kentucky Resolutions passed, support theory of nullification

1799 – Kentucky's second constitution adopted

**1800-1850**

1800 – Kentucky population is 220,955

1801 – Great Revival changes face of religion

1807 – Thomas Todd of Kentucky is first from the state to be named to U.S. Supreme Court

1807-19 – John James Audubon lives in Kentucky

1808 – Jefferson Davis is born in Kentucky

1808 – Bardstown becomes center of first Catholic diocese west of the mountains

1809 – Dr. Ephraim McDowell performs first ovariotomy operation in world

1809 – Abraham Lincoln born in Kentucky

1811 – New Madrid Earthquake hits West Kentucky

1812-14 – War of 1812

1818 – Jackson Purchase added

1819 – Centre College chartered

1820 – Death of Daniel Boone

1823 – Kentucky School for the Deaf established, first such state-supported school in the U.S.

1824 – Henry Clay runs for president, but loses

1825 – Choctaw Academy for Native Americans revived in Scott County, closes in 1842

1829 – Georgetown College chartered, fifth Baptist college in U.S.

1832 – Henry Clay is defeated for presidency by Andrew Jackson

1836 – Death of Simon Kenton

1836 – Richard M. Johnson of Kentucky is elected vice president of the U.S.

1838 – Kentucky establishes a public school system

1838 – "Trail of Tears," Indian removal west

1842 – Kentucky School for the Blind set up; sixth one in U.S.

1844 – Henry Clay runs for president a third time and loses to James K. Polk

1846-48 – Mexican War

1848 – Zachary Taylor is elected president

**1850-1900**

1850 – Kentucky population is 982,405, ranking it eighth among the states

1850 – Zachary Taylor dies, is buried in Louisville

1850 – Kentucky's third constitution adopted

1852 – "Uncle Tom's Cabin" appears, is set in Ky.

1852 – Death of Henry Clay

1853 – "My Old Kentucky Home" is published; becomes state song in 1928

1855 – "Bloody Monday" election-day riots in Louisville kill some 20 people, mostly immigrants

1856 – John C. Breckinridge elected vice president

1860 – John C. Breckinridge runs for president, but loses to Abraham Lincoln

1861 – Kentucky declares itself neutral at start of Civil War, then, in Sept., officially remains in the union. Supporters of the Confederacy set up a separate government

1862 – Major battles at Mill Springs, Richmond, and Perryville

1865 – Civil War ends; 13th Amendment to the U.S. Constitution officially frees Kentucky slaves

1865 – Current-day University of Kentucky established

1868 – Louisville *Courier-Journal* formed; under editor Henry Watterson it becomes nationally known, continues status under Binghams

1875 – First Kentucky Derby

1870s-1903 – Numerous feuds take place across eastern Kentucky

1887 – Kentucky State University opens

1888 – State Treasurer "Honest Dick" Tate disappears with state funds

1888 – Kentucky Equal Rights Association formed, first in South

1891 – Kentucky's fourth and present constitution adopted

1898 – Spanish-American War

**1900-1950**

1900 – Assassination of William Goebel in disputed election. Named governor after he was shot.

1900 – Kentucky population is 2,147,174

1903 – Of 10 books on best seller list, five are written by Kentuckians

1904 – Day Law segregates Berea College, last integrated college in the South

1905-1909 – "Black Patch War" in tobacco fields

1906 – Eastern Kentucky University and Western Kentucky University formed

1911 – Death of Justice John Marshall Harlan

1911 – First "Moonlight School" opened by Cora Wilson Stewart, to help adult illiterates

1912 – Kentucky's last county, McCreary, formed

1917-18 – U.S. involvement in World War I

1918 – Fort Knox established

1918-19 – Great influenza epidemic kills thousands

1920 – Kentucky women get the right to vote

1922 – First woman, Mary Flanery, serves in legislature

1922 – WHAS, state's first radio station, on air

1922 – Morehead State University and Murray State University created

1923 – Last member of Shaker religion in Kentucky dies

1924 – Ashland Oil formed

1925 – Frontier Nursing Service established

1927 – Katherine Langley elected as first woman from Kentucky to serve in Congress

1929 – Great Depression begins

1930s – Labor conflicts in coal fields give "Bloody Harlan" its name

1933 – Thomas Hunt Morgan wins Nobel Prize.

1937 – Great Ohio River flood

1937 – Alben Barkley selected as Majority Leader of U.S. Senate

1941 – Mammoth Cave becomes national park

1941 – Thomas Merton, Kentucky's most famous religious writer, enters Gethsemani monastery

1941-45 – U.S. involvement in World War II

1945-51 – Happy Chandler serves as baseball commissioner

1946 – Fred Vinson of Kentucky named Chief Justice of the U.S.

1948 – University of Kentucky wins the first national basketball championship for the state

1948 – Alben Barkley elected U.S. vice president

1948 – 1st television station in state, WAVE, starts

**1950-2006**

1950 – Kentucky population is 2,944,806

1950-53 – Korean War

1954 – U.S. Supreme Court declares racial segregation illegal

1955 – Amendment to Kentucky constitution gives 18 year-olds the right to vote

1960 – Sales tax goes into effect

1960s – "War on Poverty"

1961-75 – Vietnam War

1961 – Whitney Young Jr. named head of National Urban League

1964 – Martin Luther King Jr. leads march on Frankfort in support of civil rights

1966 – Kentucky passes Civil Rights Act, first in the South

1968 – Northern Kentucky University formed

1970 – Census shows that the state is more urban than rural for the first time

1975 – Passage of a state amendment that revises the state judicial system

1977 – Beverly Hills nightclub fire in Southgate, 165 perished

1980 – Opening of Corvette plant in Bowling Green

1980 – Death of Colonel Harland Sanders

1983 – Martha Layne Collins elected as first woman governor

1987 – Opening of Toyota plant near Georgetown

1989 – Kentucky reestablishes lottery

1989 – Death of Kentucky writer and U.S. Poet Laureate Robert Penn Warren

1990 – Kentucky Education Reform Act (KERA) passed

2000 – Kentucky population is 4,041,769

2001 – Worst terrorist attacks in U.S. history, nearly 3,000 killed when four hijacked jets slammed into the twin towers of New York's World Trade Center, the Pentagon and a field in Pennsylvania

2002 – Death of Triple Crown winner Seattle Slew, one of the most successful stallions in history

2003 – U.S. invasion of Iraq; Ernie Fletcher elected governor, 1st Republican governor in 32 years

2006 – Comair Flight 5191 crash in Lexington, 49 of 50 on board perished

# INDIGENOUS PEOPLES OF KENTUCKY

The Proto-Historic period in Kentucky is the time following the arrival of the first Europeans to America and before the arrival of the first settlers. During this period, native inhabitants of Kentucky did not have much direct contact with Europeans, but they were greatly affected by the dislocation of other American Indian groups caused by the intrusion of the English, French, and Spanish explorers. Measles, smallpox, and other diseases had the most devastating effect on the lives of the American Indians. Estimates place the mortality rate of some American Indian groups as high as 75 percent as a result of European diseases. By the time the first settlers moved to Kentucky following the Revolutionary War, much of the land was used as a hunting ground by the Shawnee, Cherokee, and other tribal groups. Soon, settlers pushed these remaining tribes from their lands.

But, Native American Indians called Kentucky home for more than 12,000 years. To date more than 22,000 Native American archaeological sites have been documented—these sites range from small seasonal camps to burial mounds, from rock art to large villages that were occupied by hundreds of people. When Kentucky was declared the 15th state on June 1, 1792, more than 20 Indigenous Nations held legal claims to the land, including the Cherokee, Chickasaw, Chippewa, Delaware, and numerous other tribes.

More information visit www.heritage.ky.gov/kas.htm. The KAS is a joint program of the Kentucky Heritage Council and the University of Kentucky Department of Anthropology.

Sources: "Archaeology at Mammoth Cave," by Guy Prentice, National Park Service archeologist , www.mammoth.cave.national-park.com/info.htm, and Kenneth Barnett Tankersley, Ph.D., Anthropology and Native American Studies Program, Northern Kentucky University.

# State Government & Politics

## CONSTITUTIONAL OFFICERS

The **Governor** serves as the chief administrator of the state and, in addition to other powers and duties, acts as Commander-in-Chief of state military forces, appoints executive officers and members of boards and commissions, and has the power to grant pardons and commutations. As chief administrator of Kentucky, the Governor ensures that state government provides needed services to the citizens of the Commonwealth at minimum cost to the taxpayers. Some of the agencies attached to the Governor's office include: **Military Affairs Commission, Office of the State Budget Director; Department of Veterans' Affairs; Commission on Human Rights; Governor's Office for Local Development; Department of Military Affairs; Homeland Security** and **Commission on Women**.

**Ernie Fletcher
Governor**

The **Lieutenant Governor** is a constitutional officer elected jointly with the Governor. The Lieutenant Governor is to assume the duties and responsibilities of the Office of the Governor should the Governor be impeached or removed from Office, die, fail to qualify, resign, or be unable to discharge the duties of that office. Additional duties of the Lieutenant Governor include serv-

**Steve Pence
Lt. Governor**

ing on various boards and commissions.

The **Secretary of State** is the constitutional officer entrusted with filing, maintaining, and preserving the important documents and records of the Commonwealth. The Secretary also keeps the Seal of the Commonwealth and affixes it to all communications and commissions issued in the name of the state. The State Board of Elections administers the election laws of the state and supervises the registration and purgation of voters. The role of the Kentucky Registry of Election Finance is to assure the integrity of the Commonwealth's electoral process. The office is responsible for the registration and incorporation of businesses, both domestic and foreign, profit and non-profit, including the administration of documents of merger, dissolution, and name changes.

**Trey Grayson
Secretary of State**

The **Attorney General,** serves as the Commonwealth's constitutional chief law enforcement office who performs a range of legal, investigative, and administrative duties. The Office has five major programmatic areas: **Criminal Services, Advocacy Services, Civil Services,** the **Uninsured Employers Fund,** and the **Prosecutor's Advisory Council Services, which manages** the state's Unified Prosecutorial System.

**Greg Stumbo
Attorney General**

**Jonathan Miller**
**State Treasurer**

The **State Treasurer** manages the Treasury Department, which is the central administrative agency responsible for the receipt and custody of all revenues collected by state government and for writing all checks and disbursing state funds. The Disbursements and Accounting division receives all funds of the Commonwealth including fees, grants, taxes, federal funds, fees from officials in counties over 75,000 in population, and fees from various boards and commissions. The Abandoned Property program receives unclaimed property reports from holders and potential holders of unclaimed property, collects unclaimed property, and pursues the location.

**Crit Luallen**
**State Auditor**

The **Auditor of Public Accounts** is the constitutional officer responsible for auditing all state agencies and county governments. The Auditor must examine the management and control of all institutions and public works in which the state has financial interest or legal power. The Auditor must examine the management and control of all institutions and public works in which the state has financial interest or legal power. The Auditor's Office is responsible for assisting state and local officials in establishing and maintaining proper accounting records, internal controls, and administrative controls over public funds.

**Richie Farmer**
**Agriculture**

The **Department of Agriculture** is headed by the **Commissioner of Agriculture**, an elected Constitutional Officer. The Department includes the **Office for Consumer and Environmental Protection, Office of State Veterinarian** and **Office for Agricultural Marketing and Product Promotion**. The Department develops and manages programs that promote Kentucky-produced agricultural products, conducts research and development of new and expanded outlets for Kentucky's agricultural products, agricultural education, agritourism development, farm safety and farmland preservation.

The **Commerce Cabinet's** mission is to capitalize on the natural assets of the Commonwealth and draw from resources in business development, tourism, outdoor attractions, arts, and cultural heritage. Some of the cabinet's agencies are the **Departments of Tourism, Parks, and Fish and Wildlife Resources, State Fair Board, Kentucky Horse Park**, **Arts Council, Artisan Center at Berea, Heritage Council, Center for the Arts, Humanities Council, Historical Society, Craft Marketing Program, Energy Policy, Sports Authority,** and **Arts & Cultural Humanities**.

**George Ward**
**Commerce**

The **Cabinet for Economic Development** is governed by the Kentucky Economic Development Partnership. The Partnership's strategic plan states that its mission is to "create more and higher quality opportunities for all Kentuckians by building an expanding sustainable economy." Cabinet includes the **Department for Commercialization and Innovation, Department for Existing Business Development, Department for New Business Development, Department**

**Gene Strong**
**Economic Development**

of Regional Development, Department of Financial Incentives, Commission on Small Business Advocacy and Bluegrass State Skills Corporation.

The Cabinet's goal is to reduce unemployment and increase per capita income; create an infrastructure necessary to support knowledge-based and technology-driven firms; recruiting businesses to locate new facilities in Kentucky and create a globally-competitive business environment in Kentucky.

The **Education Cabinet** was created by combining departments and offices from the former Education, Arts and Humanities Cabinet and the former Workforce Development Cabinet. The cabinet includes: **Kentucky Authority for Educational Television (KET); Environmental Education Council; Departments for Education, Libraries and Archives, Vocational Rehabilitation, and Employment Services; Teachers' Retirement System; Education Professional Standards Board; Career and Office of Technical Education and Council on Postsecondary Education (CPE).**

Laura Owens
Education

CPE serves as the representative agency in matters of postsecondary education and in this role brings a statewide perspective to postsecondary education issues and planning. The council has the responsibility both for guiding the system and serving as an advocate for postsecondary education as a part of the total education enterprise. The agency is also responsible for Adult Education.

In 1990 the General Assembly reconstituted the **Kentucky Department of Education (KDE)** and required the implementation of the Kentucky Education Reform Act. The KDE is headed by a Commissioner of Education appointed by the Kentucky Board of Education. The Kentucky Supreme Court's 1989 mandate to equalize funding for public school pupils regardless of economic circumstances or place of birth, created a new mechanism for distributing state support to local school districts. The Support Education Excellence in Kentucky (SEEK) program replaced the Minimum Foundation and Power Equalization programs.

The **Environmental and Public Protection Cabinet** is charged with the protection and preservation of land, air and water resources, supervision and regulation of industries providing services to the citizens of the Commonwealth and the administration of rules concerning employer-employee relationships. The Cabinet includes **Petroleum Storage Tank Environmental Assurance Fund; Department for**

Teresa Hill
Environmental &
Public Protection

**Environmental Protection; Department for Natural Resources; Office of Mine Safety and Licensing; Environmental Quality Commission; Kentucky Nature Preserves Commission; Board of Claims; Crime Victims' Compensation Board; Offices of Alcoholic Beverage Control (ABC), Financial Institutions, Insurance, Housing, Buildings & Construction, Charitable Gaming, Worker's Claims, Kentucky Horse Racing Authority; Public Service Commission; Board of Tax Appeals; Boxing & Wrestling Authority; Department of Labor; and Mine Safety Review Commission.**

The **Finance and Administration Cabinet** is responsible for managing the financial resources of the Commonwealth and providing central administrative services to agencies of state and local government. The Cabinet's duties

John Farris
Finance
& Administration

include construction of state facilities, property management, tax administration and collection, management of the Commonwealth's information technology systems, expenditure control, and state purchasing. The Cabinet includes: **Department of Revenue; Kentucky**

Teachers' Retirement System Board of Trustees; Offices of Equal Employment Opportunity & Contract Compliance, Controller, Financial Management and Material and Procurement Services; Department for Facilities and Support Services; and Commonwealth Office of Technology.

**Mark Birdwhistell
Families & Children**

The **Health and Family Services Cabinet** is the primary state agency responsible for leadership in protecting and promoting the health and well being of all Kentuckians through the delivery of quality health and human services. The Cabinet includes: **Departments for Medicaid Services, Mental Health/ Mental Retardation** Services, Public Health, Disability Determination Services and Community Based Services; Commission for Children with Special Health Care Needs and Office of Certificate of Need.

The **Justice and Public Safety Cabinet**. The Cabinet is responsible for the overall administration of the cabinet, provision of legal services,

**Norman Arflak
Justice & Public
Safety**

development of legislation, regulation, policy, and coordination of activities within and among the Cabinet departments and agencies. The Cabinet has seven departments: **Justice Administration, State Police, Juvenile Justice, Criminal Justice Training, Corrections, Department of Public Advocacy,** and **Vehicle Enforcement**. The **Kentucky State Police** is the statewide law enforcement agency of the Commonwealth. State Troopers are assigned to 16 regional posts across the State. The State Police is responsible for the enforcement of criminal and traffic laws, along with white-collar crime, organized crime, electronic crime, racketeering, and drug-related crime. The State Police also provide protection

for the Governor, Lieutenant Governor, their families, and property.

The **Personnel Cabinet** is responsible for recruiting, counseling, testing, and certifying persons for employment with the Commonwealth; maintaining the classification and compensation system; auditing and certifying state payrolls; preparing and maintaining the official personnel and payroll records; and coordinating and implementing employee performance evaluation systems.

**Brian Crall
Personnel**

It is comprised of five appropriation units: **General Operations, Public Employees Deferred Compensation Authority**, the **Workers' Compensation Benefits and Reserve, Government Training**, the **State Salary and Compensation Fund**, and the **State Group Health Insurance Fund**. The cabinet has an Office of Government Training.

**The Transportation Cabinet** is responsible for maintaining and improving transportation services in the Commonwealth. All modes of transportation are addressed by the cabinet, including air transportation, railroads, waterways, public transit, and highways. The Cabinet receives funding from the State Road Fund, proceeds from bonds issued by the Kentucky Turnpike Authority, and federal aid apportionments for highways.

**Bill Nighbert
Transportation**

The departments include **Administrative Services, Aviation, Vehicle Regulation, Intergovernmental Programs**, and **Highways**.

*Note: The agency listing for each cabinet is not a comprehensive list of governmental units.*

*Source: 2006-2008 Budget of the Commonwealth, www.osbd.ky.gov.*

## STATE GOVERNMENT & POLITICS
# *Governors & Their Terms*

### Governor Isaac Shelby
Term: 1792-1796
Party: Jeffersonian Republican
Resident KY County: Lincoln
Election Returns: N/A
Born: 12/11/1750 - Died: 7/18/1826
Occupations: Farmer, Surveyor, Soldier

### Governor James Garrard
Term: 1796-1804
Party: Jeffersonian Republican
Resident KY County: Bourbon
Election Returns:
James Garrard - 8,390 (39.4%);
Christopher Greenup - 6,745 (31.7%); Benjamin
Logan - 3,995 (18.8%); Thomas Todd - 2,166
(10.2%)
Born: 1/14/1749 - Died: 1/19/1822
Occupations: Farmer, Miller, Whiskey Maker,
Solider, Baptist Minister

### Governor Christopher Greenup
Term: 1804-1808
Party: Jeffersonian Republican
Resident KY County: Mercer/
Fayette
Election Returns:
Christopher Greenup (Unopposed) 25,917
Born:1750 - Died: 4/17/1818
Occupations: Surveyor, Lawyer, Land Speculator

### Governor Charles Scott
Term: 1808-1812
Party: Jeffersonian Republican
Resident KY County: Woodford
Election Returns:
Charles Scott - 22,050 (61.3%); John
Allen - 8,430 (23.4%); Green Clay - 5,516 (15.3%)
Born: 4/1739 - Died: 10/22/1813
Occupations: Farmer, Miller, Soldier

### Governor Isaac Shelby
Term: 1812-1816
Party: Jeffersonian Republican
Resident KY County: Lincoln
Election Returns:
Isaac Shelby - 30,362 70.9%;
Gabriel Slaughter - 12,464 29.1%
Born: 12/11/1750 - Died: 7/18/1826
Occupations: Farmer, Surveyor, Soldier

### Governor George Madison
Term: 1816
Party: Jeffersonian Republican
Resident KY County: Franklin
Election Returns: George Madison
(Unopposed)
Born: 6/1763 - Died: 10/14/1816
Occupations: Soldier, Public Servant

### Governor Gabriel Slaughter
Term: 1816-1820
Party: Democratic Republican
Resident KY County: Mercer
Election Returns: Succeeded Gov.
George Madison, who died while
holding office (1816)
Born: 12/12/1767 - Died: 9/19/1830
Occupations: Farmer, Soldier

### Governor John Adair
Term: 1820-1824
Party: Democratic Republican
Resident KY County: Mercer
Election Returns:
John Adair - 20,493 (32.8%;)
William Logan - 19,947 (32.0%;)
Joseph Desha - 12,419 (19.9%); Anthony Butler
- 9,567 (15.3%)
Born: 1/9/1757 - Died: 5/19/1840
Occupations: Farmer, Soldier

### Governor Joseph Desha
Term: 1824-1828
Party: Jeffersonian Republican
Resident KY County: Mason
Election Returns:
Joseph Desha - 38,463 (59.5%);
Christopher Tompkins 22,300 (34.5%); William
Russell 3,899 (6.0%)
Born: 12/9/1768 - Died: 10/12/1842
Occupations: Farmer, Soldier

### Governor Thomas Metcalfe
Term: 1828-1832
Party: National Republican (Whig)
Resident KY County: Nicholas
Election Returns:
Thomas Metcalfe - 38,940 (50.5%);
William T. Barry 38,231 (49.5%)
Born: 3/10/1780 - Died: 8/18/1855
Occupation: Stonemason

### Governor John Breathitt
Term: 1832-1834
Party: Jacksonian Democrat
Resident KY County: Logan
Election Returns:
John Breathitt - 40,780 (50.9%);
Richard Buckner 39,269 (49.1%)
Born: 9/9/1786 - Died: 2/21/1834
Occupations: Surveyor, Lawyer

### Governor James Turner Morehead
Term: 1834-1836
Party: Whig
Resident KY County: Warren
Election Returns: Succeeded Gov.
John Breathitt, who died while holding office
(1834)
Born: 5/24/1797 - Died: 12/28/1854
Occupation: Lawyer

### Governor James Clark
Term: 1836-1839
Party: Whig
Resident KY County: Clark
Election Returns:
James Clark - 38,591 (55.8%)
Matthew Flournoy - 30,576 (44.2%)
Born: 1/16/1779 - Died: 8/27/1839
Occupations: Lawyer, Judge

### Governor Charles Anderson Wickliffe
Term: 1839-1840
Party: Whig
Resident KY County: Nelson
Election Returns: Succeeded Gov.
James Clark, who died while holding office (1839)
Born: 6/8/1788 - Died: 10/31/1869
Occupations: Soldier, Lawyer

### Governor Robert P. Letcher
Term: 1840-1844
Party: Whig
Resident KY County: Garrard
Election Returns:
Robert P. Letcher - 54,892 (58.4%);
Richard French - 39,160 (41.6%)
Born: 2/10/1788 - Died: 1/24/1864
Occupation: Lawyer

### Governor William Owsley
Term: 1844-1848
Party: Whig
Resident KY County: Lincoln
Election Returns:
William Owsley - 59,792 (52.1%);
William O. Butler - 55,089 (48.0%)
Born: 3/24/1782 - Died: 12/9/1862
Occupations: Teacher, Deputy Surveyor, Deputy
Sheriff, Lawyer, Judge

### Governor John J. Crittenden
Term: 1848-1850
Party: Whig
Resident KY County: Logan
Election Returns:
John J. Crittenden - 64,982 (53.4%);
Lazarus Powell 56.675 (46.6%)
Born: 9/10/1786 - Died: 7/26/1863
Occupation: Lawyer

### Governor John L. Helm
Term: 1850-1851
Party: Whig
Resident KY County: Hardin
Election Returns: Succeeded Gov.
John J. Crittenden, who resigned
(1850)
Born: 7/4/1802 - Died: 9/8/1867
Occupation: Lawyer

### Governor Lazarus Powell
Term: 1851-1855
Party: Democrat
Resident KY County: Henderson
Election Returns:
Lazarus Powell - 54.821 (48.8%);
Archibald Dixon 54,023 (48.1%)
Born: 10/6/1812 - Died: 7/3/1867
Occupation: Lawyer

### Governor Charles Slaughter Morehead
Term: 1855-1859
Party: American ("Know-Nothing")
Resident KY County: Franklin
Election Returns:
Charles Morehead 69,8- 70 (51.6%); Beverley Clark 65,570 (48.4%)
Born: 7/7/1802 - Died: 12/21/1868
Occupation: Lawyer

### Governor Beriah Magoffin
Term: 1859-1862
Party: Democrat
Resident KY County: Mercer
Election Returns:
Beriah Magoffin - 76,631 (53.2%);
Joshua Bell - 67,504 (46.8%)
Born: 4/18/1815 - Died: 2/28/1885
Occupation: Lawyer

### Governor James F. Robinson
Term: 1862-1863
Party: Democrat
Resident KY County: Scott
Election Returns: Succeeded Gov. Beriah Magoffin, who resigned (1862)
Born: 10/4/1800 - Died: 10/31/1882
Occupations: Farmer, Lawyer

### Governor Thomas E. Bramlette
Term: 1863-1867
Party: Democrat
Resident KY County: Jefferson
Election Returns:
Thomas Bramlette - 68,422 (79.6%); Charles Wickliffe - 17,503 (20.4%)
Born: 1/3/1817 - Died: 1/12/1875
Occupations: Lawyer, Soldier, Judge

### Governor John L. Helm
Term: 1867
Party: Democrat
Resident KY County: Hardin
Election Returns:
John Helm - 90,216 (65.7%); Sidney Barnes - 33,939 (24.7%); William Kinkead - 13,167 (9.6%)
Born: 7/4/1802 - Died: 9/8/1867
Occupation: Lawyer

### Governor John W. Stevenson
Term: 1867-1871
Party: Democrat
Resident KY County: Kenton
Election Returns: Succeeded Gov. John Helm, who died while in office (1867)
Born: 5/4/1812 - Died: 8/10/1886
Occupation: Lawyer

### Governor Preston H. Leslie
Term: 1871-1875
Party: Democrat
Resident KY County: Barren
Election Returns:
Succeeded Gov. John Stevenson, who resigned (1871), then elected to office in 1871 election.
Preston Leslie - 126,455 (58.6%); John Harlan - 89,083 (41.4%)
Born: 3/8/1819 - Died: 2/7/1907
Occupations: Deputy Clerk, Farmer, Lawyer

### Governor James B. McCreary
Term: 1875-1879
Party: Democrat
Resident KY County: Madison
Election Returns:
James McCreary - 126,976 (58.3%); John Harlan - 90,795 (41.7%)
Born: 7/8/1838 - Died: 10/8/1918
Occupations: Soldier, Lawyer

### Governor Luke Blackburn
Term: 1879-1883
Party: Democrat
Resident KY County: Jefferson
Election Returns:
Luke Blackburn 125,399 (55.4%); Walter Evans 81,881 (36.2%); C.W. Cook 18,954 (8.4%)
Born: 7/16/1816 - Died: 9/14/1887
Occupation: Doctor

### Governor James Proctor Knott
Term: 1883-1887
Party: Democrat
Resident KY County: Marion
Election Returns:
James Knott 133,615 (60.0%); Thomas Morrow 89,181 (40.0%)
Born: 8/29/1830 - Died: 6/18/1911
Occupation: Lawyer

### Governor Simon Bolivar Buckner

Term: 1887-1891
Party: Democrat
Resident KY County: Hart
Election Returns:
Simon Buckner - 143,466 (50.7%); William Bradley - 126,754 (44.8%)
Born: 4/1/1823 - Died: 1/8/1914
Occupations: Soldier, Businessman, Newspaperman

### Governor John Young Brown

Term: 1891-1895
Party: Democrat
Resident KY County: Henderson
Election Returns:
John Young Brown - 144,168 (49.9%); Andrew Wood - 116,087 (40.1%); S.B. Erwin - 25,631 (8.9%)
Born: 6/28/1835 - Died: 1/11/1904
Occupation: Lawyer

### Governor William O. Bradley

Term: 1895-1899
Party: Republican
Resident KY County: Garrard
Election Returns:
William Bradley - 172,436 (48.3%); Parker Hardin - 163,524 (45.8%)
Born: 3/18/1847 - Died: 5/23/1914
Occupation: Lawyer

### Governor William S. Taylor

Term: 1899-1900
Party: Republican
Resident KY County: Butler
Election Returns:
William Taylor - 193,727 (48.1%); William Goebel - 191,331 (47.5%)
Born: 10/10/1853 - Died: 8/2/1928
Occupations: Teacher, County Clerk, Lawyer, Farmer

### Governor William Goebel

Term: 1900
Party: Democrat
Resident KY County: Kenton
Election Returns: Appointed by the General Assembly after Gov. William Taylor's election was declared unconstitutional
Born: 1/4/1856 - Died: 2/3/1900
Occupation: Lawyer
Note: Kentucky Governor assassinated while holding office

### Governor John Crepps Wickliffe (J.C.W.) Beckham

Term: 1900-1907
Party: Democrat
Resident KY County: Nelson
Election Returns: By special election, succeeded Gov. William Goebel, who was assasinated while holding office.
Special Election
John Beckham - 233,197 (49.9%); John Yerkes - 229,468 (49.1%)
1903 Regular Election
John Beckham - 229,014 (52.1%); M.B. Belknap - 202,862 (46.2%)
Born: 8/5/1869 - Died: 1/9/1940
Occupations: Principal of Public Schools, Lawyer

### Governor Augustus E. Willson

Term: 1907-1911
Party: Republican
Resident KY County: Jefferson
Election Returns:
Augustus Willson - 214,478 (51.2%); Hager - 196,428 (46.9%)
Born: 10/13/1846 - Died: 8/24/1931
Occupation: Lawyer

### Governor James B. McCreary

Term: 1911-1915
Party: Democrat
Resident KY County: Madison
Election Returns:
James McCreary - 226,549 (53.7%); E.C. Orear - 195,672 (46.3%)
Born: 7/8/1838 - Died: 10/8/1918
Occupations: Soldier, Lawyer

### Governor Augustus Owsley Stanley

Term: 1915-1919
Party: Democrat
Resident KY County: Henderson
Election Returns:
Augustus Stanley - 219,991 (49.1%); Edwin Morrow - 219,520 (49.0%)
Born: 5/21/1867 - Died: 8/12/1958
Occupations: Teacher, Lawyer

### Governor James Dixon Black

Term: 1919
Party: Democrat
Resident KY County: Knox
Election Returns: Succeeded Gov. Augustus Stanley, who resigned
Born: 9/24/1849 - Died: 8/5/1938
Occupations: Teacher, President of Union College, Lawyer

### Governor Edwin P. Morrow

Term: 1919-1923
Party: Republican
Resident KY County: Pulaski
Election Returns:
Edwin Morrow - 254,472 (53.8%);
James Black - 214,134 (45.3%)
Born: 11/28/1877 - Died: 6/15/1935
Occupation: Lawyer

### Governor William J. Fields

Term: 1923-1927
Party: Democrat
Resident KY County: Carter
Election Returns:
William Fields - 356,045 (53.3%);
Charles Dawson - 306,277 (45.8%)
Born: 12/29/1874 - Died: 10/21/1954
Occupations: Farmer, Businessman, Lawyer

### Governor Flem D. Sampson

Term: 1927-1931
Party: Republican
Resident KY County: Knox
Election Returns:
Flem Sampson - 399,698 (52.1%);
John Beckham - 367,698 (47.9%)
Born: 1/25/1875 - Died: 5/25/1967
Occupations: Bank President, Teacher, Judge,
Lawyer

### Governor Ruby Laffoon

Term: 1931-1935
Party: Democrat
Resident KY County: Hopkins
Election Returns:
Ruby Laffoon - 438,513 (54.3%);
William Harrison - 366,982 (45.4%)
Born: 1/15/1869 - Died: 3/1/1941
Occupation: Lawyer

### Governor A.B. ("Happy") Chandler

Term: 1935-1939
Party: Democrat
Resident KY County: Woodford
Election Returns:
A.B. Chandler - 556,262 (54.5%); King Swope
- 461,104 (45.1%)
Born: 7/14/1898 - Died: 6/15/1991
Occupations: Coach, Lawyer, Baseball
Commissioner

### Governor Keen Johnson

Term: 1939-1943
Party: Democrat
Resident KY County: Madison
Election Returns: Succeeded Gov.
A.B. Chandler, who resigned (1939)
1939 Election; Keen Johnson - 460,834 (56.5%);
King Swope - 354,704 (43.5%)
Born: 1/12/1896 - Died: 2/7/1970
Occupations: Soldier, Journalist, Businessman

### Governor Simeon S. Willis

Term: 1943-1947
Party: Republican
Resident KY County: Boyd
Election Returns:
Simeon Willis - 279.144 (50.5%); J.
Lyter Donaldson - 270,525 (48.9%)
Born: 12/1/1879 - Died: 4/2/1965
Occupations: Teacher, Lawyer, Judge

### Governor Earle C. Clements

Term: 1947-1950
Party: Democrat
Resident KY County: Union
Election Returns:
Earle Clements - 387,795 (57.2%);
Eldon Dummit - 287,756 (42.5%)
Born: 10/22/1896 - Died: 3/12/1985
Occupations: Coach, Teacher, Soldier, Deputy,
Sheriff, Public Servant

### Governor Lawrence W. Wetherby

Term: 1950-1955
Party: Democrat
Resident KY County: Jefferson
Election Returns: Succeeded Gov.
Earle Clements, who resigned (1950)
1951 Election; Lawrence Wetherby - 346,345
(54.6%); Eugene Stiler - 288,014 (45.4%)
Born: 1/2/1908 - Died: 3/27/1994
Occupations: Lawyer, Judge

### Governor A.B. ("Happy") Chandler

Term: 1955-1959
Party: Democrat
Resident KY County: Woodford
Election Returns:
A.B. Chandler - 451,647 (58.0%); Edwin Denney
- 322,671 (41.5%)
Born: 7/14/1898 - Died: 6/15/1991
Occupations: Coach, Lawyer, Baseball
Commissioner

### Governor Bert T. Combs
Term: 1959-1963
Party: Democrat
Resident KY County: Floyd
Election Returns:
Bert Combs - 516,549 (60.6%); John
M. Robsion - 336,456 (39.4%)
Born: 8/13/1911 - Died: 12/4/1991
Occupation: Lawyer

### Governor Edward ("Ned") Breathitt
Term: 1963-1967
Party: Democrat
Resident KY County: Christian
Election Returns: Edward Breathitt
- 449,551 (50.7%); Louie B. Nunn - 436,496 (49.3%)
Born: 11/26/1924 - Died: 10/14/03
Occupation: Lawyer

### Governor Louie B. Nunn
Term: 1967-1971
Party: Republican
Resident KY County: Barren
Election Returns:
Louie B. Nunn - 454,123 (51.2%);
Henry Ward - 425,674 (48.0%)
Born: 3/8/1924 - Died: 1/29/04
Occupations: Soldier, Lawyer

### Governor Wendell Ford
Term: 1971-1974
Party: Democrat
Resident KY County: Daviess
Election Returns:
Wendell Ford - 470,720 (50.6%);
Tom Emberton - 412,653 (44.3%); Born: 9/8/1924
Occupations: Soldier, Businessman

### Governor Julian Carroll
Term: 1974-1979
Party: Democrat
Resident KY County: McCracken
Election Returns: Succeeded Gov.
Wendell Ford, who resigned (1974)
1975 Election; Julian Carroll -
470,159 (62.8%); Robert Gable - 277,998 (37.2%)
Born: 4/16/1931
Occupation: Lawyer

### Governor John Y. Brown, Jr.
Term: 1979-1983
Party: Democrat
Resident KY County: Fayette
Election Returns:
John Y. Brown - 558,088 (59.4%);
Louie B. Nunn - 381,278 (40.6%)
Born: 12/28/1933; Occupation: Businessman

### Governor Martha Layne (Hall) Collins
Term: 1983-1987
Party: Democrat
Resident KY County: Woodford
Election Returns:
Martha Layne Collins - 561,674 (54.6%); Jim
Bunning - 454,650 (44.2%)
Born: 12/7/1936
Occupation: Teacher

### Governor Wallace Wilkinson
Term: 1987-1991
Party: Democrat
Resident KY County: Fayette
Election Returns:
Wallace Wilkinson - 504,367
(64.9%); John Harper - 273,035
(35.1%)
Born: 12/12/1941 - Died: 7/5/2002
Occupations: Farmer, Businessman

### Governor Brereton C. Jones
Term: 1991-1995
Party: Democrat
Resident KY County: Woodford
Election Returns:
Brereton Jones - 540,468 (64.7%);
Larry Hopkins - 294,452 (35.3%)
Born: 6/27/1939
Occupation: Businessman

### Governor Paul E. Patton
Term: 1995-2003
Party: Democrat
Resident KY County: Pike
Election Returns:
1995 Election; Paul Patton
- 500,787 (51.1%)Larry Forgy
- 479,227 (48.9%)
1999 Election; Paul Patton - 352,099 (60.6%);
Martin & Cornelius - 128,788 (22.2%); Galbraith &
Lyons - 88,930 (15.3%); Others 6,934 (1.2%)
Born: 5/26/1937
Occupations: Engineer, Businessman

### Governor Ernie Fletcher
Term: 2003-
Party: Republican
Resident KY County: Fayette
Election Returns:
Ernie Fletcher 593, 058; Ben
Chandler 484,804
Born: 11/12/1952
Occupations: U.S. Congressman, physician, CEO
Medical Foundation, pastor of a Baptist church
*Source: www.kdla.ky.gov & Kentucky Historical Society*

## STATE GOVERNMENT & POLITICS

# Assassination of Governor William Goebel

### William Crawford Green

On a cold January 30, 1900, a man stood at an open window in the Kentucky Secretary of State's office. As William Goebel walked by on his way to the State Capitol building next door, the man raised his rifle, shot, and mortally wounded Goebel. Why was William Goebel murdered and who was his assassin?

Goebel's assassination can be traced to the disputed election of 1899 which Goebel, the Democratic president pro-tempore of the State Senate and gubernatorial candidate, had initially lost to William Taylor, the Republican candidate. The election results were challenged, but on December 12, the State Board of Elections declared Taylor the winner and three days later he took the oath of office. The Democrats, a majority in the newly elected legislature, decided to contest the Board of Elections' decision by relying upon the Goebel Election Law which allowed the General Assembly to be the final judge of the elections for governor and lieutenant governor. The legislature met on January 2, 1900 and subsequently selected a committee which began to hear evidence on January 15 concerning fraudulent election results in Louisville and forty counties. While the committee met over the next two weeks, tensions increased in Frankfort, encouraged by Republican and Democratic partisans.

**Kentucky Governor William Goebel was the first and only governor assassinated while in office**
*Source: Kentucky Historical Society*

Goebel was shot before the legislative election committee had reached its decision, but that evening as he lay dying in the Capitol Hotel, the committee met and decided, on a partisan vote, to recommend that he be chosen governor and J.C.W. Beckman lieutenant governor. Aware that the General Assembly would endorse the committee's recommendation, Governor Taylor claimed that a state of insurrection existed, called out the militia, and adjourned the legislature. Democrats disputed the constitutionality of the governor's action and, denied access to the State Capitol, met in the Capitol Hotel, adopted the committee report, and declared Goebel governor. Shortly thereafter, Chief Justice James Hazelrigg swore in a dying Goebel who then issued a proclamation to remove the militia and reconvene the General Assembly.

Goebel's death, four days later on February 3, and the swearing in of J.C.W. Beckman as governor did not end the debate over who was legally governor. His death did, however, lead legislators from both parties to meet on February 6 and agree that Goebel had been legally elected and Beckham had legally succeeded him as governor. Governor Taylor would not sign the agreement, because he believed that he had been legally elected. Two weeks later, however, he agreed to allow the courts to decide the issue and so did Governor Beckham.

Louisville Circuit Judge Emmett Field upheld the legislature's decision. The Republicans appealed. On April 6, the Court of Appeals, then Kentucky's supreme court, upheld Judge Field's decision. Once again, the Republicans appealed. On May 21, 1900, the U.S. Supreme Court denied review, because the case did not involve a federal legal issue. On hearing the news, Governor Taylor, fearing arrest, fled to Indiana and despite efforts to extradite him, never returned to Kentucky. The struggle over political power had ended, but the inquiry into who had assassinated Goebel was just beginning.

The General Assembly appropriated $100,000 to investigate, indict, and prosecute cases which would be deeply influenced by partisan judges and juries. Twenty persons were accused, sixteen indicted, three of them were promised immunity and became prosecution witnesses. Of the remaining thirteen, five were tried, two of whom were acquitted and three convicted.

The Republican Secretary of State Caleb Powers, who was believed to have planned the assassination, was convicted in his 1900, 1901, 1903 trials, but his 1907 trial produced a deadlocked jury. All his appeals failed, but he was pardoned in 1909. James Howard, thought to be the assassin, was convicted in his 1900, 1902 and 1903 trials and sentenced to life imprisonment. After his appeals failed, he began serving a life sentence, but he was also pardoned in 1909. Henry Youtsey, suspected of being the intermediary between Powers and Howard, was tried in 1900, found guilty, and began serving his life sentence, but he was paroled in 1916 and pardoned in 1919.

Who assassinated the only governor in American history? It may have been a single assassin or there may have been a conspiracy involving Powers, Youtsey, and Howard, but because the testimony was too unreliable and the people involved in the trials too partisan, we will never know.

*Source: James C. Klotter, William Goebel: The Politics of Wrath, Lexington, KY: University Press of Kentucky, 1977. William Crawford Green is Professor of Government at Morehead State University. His research and publications address state and federal constitutional law and public policy issues.*

**As William Goebel walked by on his way to the State Capitol building next door, an unknown assailant shot and mortally wounded Goebel**
*Source: Kentucky Department of Tourism*

Trey Grayson, Secretary of State

## STATE GOVERNMENT & POLITICS
# *Historical Elections*

Kentucky's rich history reveals a tradition of strong political leaders, dominated by the governor's leading role. From the election of Isaac Shelby as the first governor of the Commonwealth, Kentucky governors have wielded clout and power.

In its early history, influential governors such as John Breathitt (1832) and James Clark (1836) mapped the state's political history by using their terms in office to set the stage for their party's eventual rise in power, such as Breathitt's Democratic Party—or for their party's domination, as was the case with Clark's Whig Party (the party of statesman Henry Clay). The strength of this early two-party system lasted at least until the late 1850s. Kentucky would not see evidence of a vigorous two-party political system until the election of William O. Bradley in 1894, as the first Republican governor. Such a dynamic two-party system would be absent for much of the 20th century.

As a border state in the Civil War, Kentucky's gubernatorial leadership became critical to its place in history. If Beriah Magoffin's (1859) influence were greater, he might have taken the state out of the Union. His resignation in 1862 due to disagreements with the legislature over Kentucky's role in the war assured the Commonwealth would stay in the Union. Just a few years later Thomas Bramlette (1863) would heal Kentucky's Civil War wounds

**Gov. A. B. "Happy" Chandler**
*Source: Happy Chandler Foundation*

**Gov. Louie B. Nunn**
*Source: Governor Louie B. Nunn Foundation*

**Gov. Martha Layne Collins**
*Source: Kentucky Dept. for Libraries & Archives*

by pardoning most ex-Confederate soldiers and restoring some civil rights to former slaves. He also worked to create the public university that would eventually become the University of Kentucky.

In 1883 perhaps one of the most influential and efficient administrations came into power through the leadership of J. Proctor Knott, who completely reformed Kentucky's antiquated tax code, thereby stabilizing its economy during a most difficult time.

While some elections helped to stabilize Kentucky, others sent it into disarray. In 1899 Republican William S. Taylor was elected governor only to have the election deemed unconstitutional by the Democratic legislature. The legislature, in turn, elected Democrat William Goebel (1899) as governor. Shortly thereafter Goebel became the only governor in American history to die in office as a result of an assassination. These events nearly brought Kentucky to its own Civil War.

In 1934 one of Kentucky's most popular governors, A.B. "Happy" Chandler (1935 and 1955), used his time as acting governor to call a special session of the General Assembly to change the gubernatorial election process. (At that time, when governors left the Commonwealth, the lieutenant governor assumed acting governor status.) The following year, Chandler used this change, the addition of a run-off election in the primary, to win the

Democratic nomination and eventually the governorship.

Later in the century the civil rights movement swept across the country, and two Kentucky governors, Bert T. Combs (1959) and Ned Breathitt (1963), took steps to push the state toward equality for all of its citizens. Combs established the state's first human rights commission and desegregated all public accommodations; his successor passed the equal employment opportunity bill, which further removed barriers against minorities.

The latter half of the 20th century saw a partial return to one-party rule, but elections such as Simeon Wills (1943), Louie Nunn (1967) and Ernie Fletcher (2003) indicated a growing competitive spirit among parties and their candidates. In 1984 a competitive two-party system was solidified through the election of Mitch McConnell to the U.S. Senate. This election served as a catalyst to the resurgence of the Republican Party in Kentucky. The increased competition from two parties, along with more affluent candidates, gave rise to the multimillion-dollar campaigns that first became evident in the election of John Y. Brown, Jr. (1979).

Some of Brown's successors set other records for the Commonwealth. In 1983 Martha Layne Collins became the first woman to be elected governor. In 1999 Paul Patton became the first governor to be elected to two consecutive terms since the 19th century.

Beyond the governor's race, however, there were a number of elections that made a significant impact on the Commonwealth. In 1896 Emma Guy Cromwell became the first woman elected to a statewide office as the state librarian. She later became the first woman in the country to be elected as a state secretary of state. In 1935 Charles W. Anderson was the first African American elected to the Kentucky House of Representatives since Reconstruction. Later he sponsored bills to fund out-of-state tuition for black students denied higher education in Kentucky. In 1967 Georgia Powers made history by becoming the first African American woman elected to the Kentucky Senate.

These leaders shared a vision of a brighter Kentucky and a commitment to public service. Through their civic engagement we reap great benefits. Today the challenge is to follow in their pioneering footsteps and sow the seeds for tomorrow's change. Each election reaffirms a commitment to democracy and to the unbridled spirit of those who paved the way.

**Governor Isaac Shelby**
*Source: Kentucky Historical Society*

**Governors Ned Breathitt, Bert Combs, Wendell Ford,
Lawrence Wetherby and Happy Chandler**
*Source: Happy Chandler Foundation*

## STATE GOVERNMENT & POLITICS

# *State Capitol*

### Chris Kellogg

Approaching her century mark, Kentucky's majestic state capitol sits on a bluff above the Kentucky River valley, its recently restored lantern and dome lighted at night, visible from points throughout Franklin County. Referred to as the New State Capitol, this is the fourth state house since Kentucky became a commonwealth in 1792. Construction began in 1904 and was completed in 1910 in time for the General Assembly to meet. The following June dedication ceremonies were held amid great pomp and circumstance on Capitol Avenue. The building opened to the public in 1909. It has been on the National Register of Historic Places since the early 1970s.

Irreplaceable by today's standards, the building was designed by the distinguished architect Frank Mills Andrews for a total cost of $1.8 million (by comparison the 1998-1999 restoration of the dome cost $2 million). Its beaux arts style includes elements of classical architecture and is a combination of

Photo: Sid Webb

Greek architecture with the highly ornate elegance of French styling. The first floor was largely used as public space where day-to-day business was conducted. The governor's office was on the second floor where the state reception room is located now.

Today there are more than 350 offices carved out of the three-story building and in the attic and basement, which were intended for storage. The first or executive floor includes the offices of the governor, lieutenant governor, secretary of state and the attorney general. The dome, which towers seven stories over the rotunda, is modeled after the one above Napoleon's tomb in Paris, France. A statue of Abraham Lincoln in the center of the rotunda stands above other famous Kentuckians: Henry Clay, Alben Barkley, Ephraim McDowell and Jefferson Davis. Elsewhere on the first floor are likenesses of Thelma Stovall, Happy Chandler and Colonel Sanders.

Massive marble stairways modeled after the Paris Grand Opera House lead to the second floor, or the judicial floor, where the Supreme Court, the state law library and the state reception room are located. The state reception room, restored in 1994, was designed in the Louis XIV period and includes a handwoven Austrian carpet designed for the room when the capitol was built. French-style furniture, elegant murals and intricate faux finishes adorn the room. Portraits of state Supreme Court justices line the grand halls, which afford expansive views of other areas of the building. The court chamber was the most expensive room when the capitol was constructed at a cost $25,000. It has solid Honduras mahogany paneling and an elegant coffered ceiling covered in "Old Dutch" metal leafing.

The Kentucky House of Representatives and Senate chambers are located on opposite ends of the third floor. Entrances are highlighted by decorative lunettes of frontier scenes with Daniel Boone painted in oil by T. Gilbert White. Both chambers continue the classical styles of the building and are furnished with mahogany desks and leather-upholstered chairs. Offices of the leadership are also here.

## STATE GOVERNMENT & POLITICS

# *Kentucky's Executive Mansions* Margaret A. Lane

Kentucky is unique among the 50 states in operating two executive residences, both listed on the National Register of Historic Sites, and both still in use today.

Kentucky's executive mansion story began in 1798, when the state's second governor, James Garrard, and his family reportedly paraded down Frankfort hill in a "coach and four horses" to take

For the next 40 years, after the 1914 construction of the new mansion, the old house survived three auctions and several fires; it housed renters and state offices, and then was abandoned until Gov. Simeon Willis, in 1946, ordered its preservation. Ten years later, Lt. Gov. Harry Waterfield became the first of 10 Kentucky lieutenant governors to occupy the mansion, and the old house once again

*Photo: Sid Webb*

residence in the newly built federal farmhouse at 410 High Street. Known in Frankfort as the old Governor's Mansion, the Government House, and in the early years the "Palace," the three-story brick residence, located within walking distance of the Old Capitol, served as the seat of government for more than 50 years, and provided a residence for 37 Kentucky governors from 1798 until 1914.

became a private and official residence, serving as a gathering place for social and political guests. During the past three years, the old house has once again undergone a major restoration, resulting in new mechanical systems, an updated kitchen, and exterior and interior interpretation reflecting the era of the early 1840s. Having celebrated its 200th birthday in 1998, the old mansion remains steadfastly anchored on High and Clinton Streets, and reportedly is the oldest official residence still in use in the U.S. today.

When James McCreary returned to the Kentucky governorship in 1911 for a second term, he soon realized that the old 1798 Governor's Mansion was not an appropriate domicile for Kentucky's chief

*Photo: Sid Webb*

executive. Its sagging windows stared upon the dreary scene of the penitentiary, the flour mill, and the ragged slopes of the palisades. Gov. McCreary, an admirer of all things French, led the Sinking Commission (state officials responsible for overseeing the fiscal affairs of the state) to engage E.A. and C. C. Weber's firm of Fort Thomas to plan a French-inspired governor's residence. Thus, on a knoll adjacent to Kentucky's grand new marble and stone state capitol rose a 25-room mansion of brick and limestone, inspired by Marie Antoinette's French villa.

On January 21, 1914, Gov. McCreary welcomed throngs of well-wishers and curiosity seekers to an open house to inaugurate the grand new "palace." Records reflect this notation: "…. the Sinking Fund Commission reported to the General Assembly that the new mansion had been erected and furnished at a cost of $94,902.40. The commission hoped the legislators would be pleased with the Mansion that has been erected, which will, for more than a hundred years, be the home of the various Governors of the State of Kentucky."

Thomas Clark wrote, in The People's House:

"The arrival before its portal every four years of a new governor and his or her spouse and children marked the opening of an era of some degree of change. There has come a veritable kaleidoscopic mixture of gubernatorial and family personalities. In many respects, the houses have sheltered a microcosm of Kentucky domestic life. Children have been born; governors and their wives have died. Relatives have come for extended visits; weddings have been celebrated; and, on occasion, young couples have moved in to live with their parents. There have been fires and other tragedies, and even moments of tension with neighbors. Depending upon the inclinations of governors and their wives, there have been teas, levees, dinners, receptions, and balls."

During his 1979-1983 term, Gov. John Y. Brown Jr. and first lady, former Miss America Phyllis George Brown, organized the Save the Mansion Commission to address major mechanical, electrical and decorative issues in the 65-year-old mansion. More than $3.5 million was expended to rewire, refinish, refurbish, and re-landscape, returning the house and grounds to a semblance of its original Beaux-Arts splendor.

Kentucky's current governor, Ernie Fletcher, and first lady Glenna Fletcher, have recognized the need for another renovation, as the 20-year-old mechanical systems, much used kitchen, and worn carpets require major attention. Building on the efforts of former first lady, Judi Patton, Mrs. Fletcher is raising private funds to support the effort.

Ever the socio-political center of Kentucky politics, the mansions are open to the public several days per week, and they have been admired by hundreds of thousands of visitors from all over the world.

## STATE GOVERNMENT
# *State Legislature*                    Bob Babbage

### OUR GENERAL ASSEMBLY—CONTINUED GROWTH TO SIGNIFICANCE

While expanding its presence in the political orbit, Kentucky's General Assembly is producing its share of stars.

Attention increasingly centers on Senate President David L. Williams (R-Burkesville) as well at the House speaker, Jody Richards (D-Bowling Green). Both labor to grow their respective majorities. Each figures into the list of possible challengers in the 2007 race for governor of Kentucky.

Speaker Richards narrowly lost the Democratic nomination in 2003. This was also the year that

Now with its highly visible personalities and varying priorities, the 100 representatives and 38 senators have become an invigorated locus of increasing power, the nexus of epic confrontations of will and direction.

Sequestered in a Free Conference Committee at the tail end of the 2006 session, the House and Senate finally agreed to a budget. The Assembly had failed to give Governor Paul Patton, a two-term Democrat, his last executive spending plan, raising unique questions about executive power to use unbudgeted revenue.

Likewise, Governor Ernie Fletcher, the first

**Senate President David Williams speaks to reporters during the 2006 Regular Session of the Kentucky General Assembly**
*Source: Legislative Research Commission*

**Speaker of the House Jody Richards speaks to reporters during the 2006 Regular Session of the Kentucky General Assembly**
*Source: Legislative Research Commission*

Rep. Greg Stumbo, the long-serving House majority leader, was elected Attorney General. Stumbo, too, figures into future political calculus.

Republican to hold the top seat in 32 years, could not get legislative approval for his first two-year budget in 2004.

How did the state's lawmakers move from a once compliant status to become an equal, at times dominating, branch of state government in this modern generation?

Just three decades ago in 1975 Governor Julian Carroll, now a state senator, rewarded legislative allies with chairmanships. This was the time-honored tradition.   Carroll

(left-right) Senators David E. Boswell, Jr., D-8; Jerry P. Rhoads, D-6; Daniel Mongiardo; and Julian M. Carroll, D-7 talk during a break.
Source: Legislative Research Commission

himself has been House speaker and presided over the Senate as lieutenant governor.

The Kenton Amendment to the antiquated state constitution, championed by the late House Speaker William G. Kenton in 1978, re-sequenced legislative races out from under the election of the governor.

When John Y. Brown, Jr. became chief executive in 1979, he had no interest in traditional legislative control, freeing the legislative bodies to select their own leaders.

Other reforms coincided. A subset of legislators, dubbed the Black Sheep Squadron, prodded lawmakers toward an active agenda. KET, the Kentucky educational television network, put the legislature on TV in summary broadcasts, now with live webcasts, broadening public awareness.

A massive overhaul of education, driven from a court decision, put House and Senate leaders front and center. The combined efforts of President Williams and Speaker Richards led to a major change when voters approved annual sessions of the legislature, starting in 2001, a question rejected by the electorate in three prior votes.

While these seminal advances in process have created a more visible, meaningful bully pulpit, the most dramatic seismic shift came in 1996 when a coalition of Senate Republicans joined disaffected

Democrats to take control of the state Senate. Republicans then won control of the upper chamber outright -- and kept it.

Uniquely, Kentucky maintains a non-partisan staff working on issues covering the entire range of public subjects. This differs, and is preferred, from Congress and some states, where committee staffs are divided and highly partisan, according to Bobby Sherman, who heads the Legislative Research Commission.

Kentucky is far out of balance with regard to women in the General Assembly when compared to other states with just 16 members. A dozen serve in the House, including nine Democrats, while of the five senators, four are Republicans.

As Senate president pro tem, Republican Katie Kratz Stine is the highest ranking female on the capitol's third floor. Democrat Ruth Ann Palumbo, elected in 1990, is the longest serving woman.

Minority Floor Leader Rep. Jeffrey Hoover, R-83 confers with Rep. Marie L. Rader, R-89
Source: Legislative Research Commission

African American members number only six with a single member in the Senate, Louisville Democrat Gerald Neal.

Numerous legislators are mentioned for consideration for statewide office at present, including David Boswell, Dr. Daniel Mongiardo, R.J. Palmer, Damon Thayer and Ed Worley – all from the Senate.

House members on candidate lists include Rocky Adkins, Bob Damron, Jeff Hoover, Lonnie Napier, Steve Nunn, Tommy Thompson, and Ken Upchurch.

Given the high profile of critical decisions in policy added to the fabric of politics, look for even greater prominence for leading legislators.

*Bob Babbage, Secretary of State 1992-96, heads Babbage Cofounder, a government relations firm.*

## KY SENATE

| SENATOR (Party-District) | ADDRESS1 | ADDRESS2 | CITY | ZIP | PHONE | CAPITOL PHONE | FAX | EMAIL |
|---|---|---|---|---|---|---|---|---|
| Walter Blevins Jr (D-27) | 777 Broadway | | West Liberty | 41472 | (606) 743-1212 | (502) 564-8100 | (606) 743-1214 | http://lrc.ky.gov/mailform/s027.htm |
| Charlie Borders (R-18) | | PO Box Q | Russell | 41169 | (606) 327-4507 | (502) 564-8100 | | http://lrc.ky.gov/mailform/s018.htm |
| David E Boswell Sr (D-8) | 5591 Panther Creek Dr | | Owensboro | 42301 | (270) 926-8000 | (502) 564-8100 | (270) 926-9047 | david.boswell@lrc.ky.gov |
| Tom Buford (R-22) | 105 Crosswoods Pl | | Nicholasville | 40356 | (859) 885-0606 | (502) 564-8100 | (502) 564-0456 | http://lrc.ky.gov/mailform/s022.htm |
| Julian M Carroll (D-7) | | PO Box 1491 | Frankfort | 40601 | (502) 223-3806 | (502) 564-8100 | (502) 227-4849 | julian.carroll@lrc.ky.gov |
| Perry B Clark (D-37) | 5716 New Cut Rd | | Louisville | 40214 | | (502) 564-8100 | | http://lrc.ky.gov/mailform/s037.htm |
| Julie Denton (R-36) | 1708 Golden Leaf Way | | Louisville | 40245 | | (502) 564-8100 | (502) 564-6543 | julie.denton@lrc.ky.gov |
| Carroll Gibson (R-5) | | PO Box 506 | Leitchfield | 42755 | (270) 230-5866 | (502) 564-8100 | | http://lrc.ky.gov/mailform/s032.htm |
| Brett Guthrie (R-32) | 1005 Wrenwood Dr | | Bowling Green | 42103 | (270) 781-0049 | (502) 564-8100 | | dhangel@bellsouth.net |
| Denise Harper Angel (D-35) | 2521 Ransdall Ave | | Louisville | 40204 | (502) 452-9130 | (502) 564-8100 | (502) 452-9130 | http://lrc.ky.gov/mailform/s026.htm |
| Ernie Harris (R-26) | | PO Box 1073 | Crestwood | 40014 | | (502) 564-8100 | | http://lrc.ky.gov/mailform/s021.htm |
| Tom Jensen (R-21) | 303 S Main St | | London | 40741 | | (502) 564-8100 | | |
| Ray S Jones II (D-31) | 324 W Main | PO Drawer 3850 | Pikeville | 41502 | (606) 432-5777 | (502) 564-8100 | (606) 432-5154 | http://lrc.ky.gov/mailform/s031.htm |
| Dan Kelly (R-14) | 3274 Gondola Dr | | Springfield | 40069 | (859) 336-7723 | (502) 564-2450 | | dan.kelly@lrc.ky.gov |
| Alice Forgy Kerr (R-12) | | | Lexington | 40513 | (859) 223-3274 | (502) 564-8100 | | alice.kerr@lrc.ky.gov |
| Robert J (Bob) Leeper (I-2) | 229 S Friendship Rd | | Paducah | 42003 | (270) 554-9637 | (502) 564-8100 | (270) 554-5337 | bob.leeper@lrc.ky.gov |
| Vernie D McGaha (R-15) | 4787 W Hwy 76 | | Russell Springs | 42642 | | (502) 564-8100 | | http://lrc.ky.gov/mailform/s015.htm |
| Daniel Mongiardo (D-30) | 200 Medical Ctr Dr Ste 2N | | Hazard | 41701 | (606) 439-4466 | (502) 564-8100 | (606) 439-1941 | daniel.mongiardo@lrc.ky.gov |
| Gerald A Neal (D-33) | One Riverfront Plz | 401 W Main St Ste 1807 | Louisville | 40202 | (502) 584-8500 | (502) 564-8100 | (502) 584-1119 | http://lrc.ky.gov/mailform/s033.htm |
| R J Palmer II (D-28) | 1391 McClure Rd | | Winchester | 40391 | (859) 745-7604 | (502) 564-8100 | (859) 737-2348 | rj.palmer@lrc.ky.gov |
| Joey Pendleton (D-3) | 905 Hurst Dr | | Hopkinsville | 42240 | (270) 885-1639 | (502) 564-2470 | (502) 564-5508 | joey.pendleton@lrc.ky.gov |
| Jerry P Rhoads (D-6) | 9 E Center St | | Madisonville | 42431 | (270) 825-1490 | (502) 564-8100 | (270) 821-8512 | jerry.rhoads@lrc.ky.gov |
| Dorsey Ridley (D-4) | 4030 Hidden Creek Dr | PO Box 2002 | Henderson | 42420 | (270) 869-8400 | (502) 564-8100 | | dorsey.ridley@lrc.ky.gov |
| Richard (Dick) Roeding (R-11) | 2534 Kearney Ct | | Lakeside Park | 41017 | | (502) 564-8100 | (859) 331-1238 | http://lrc.ky.gov/mailform/s011.htm |
| Richie Sanders Jr (R-9) | 901 Maple Leaf Dr | | Franklin | 42134 | | (502) 564-2450 | | richie.sanders@lrc.ky.gov |
| Ernesto Scorsone (D-13) | 511 W Short St | | Lexington | 40507 | (859) 254-5766 | (502) 564-8100 | (859) 255-5508 | ernesto.scorsone@lrc.ky.gov |
| Dan (Malano) Seum (R-38) | 1107 Holly Ave | | Fairdale | 40118 | | (502) 564-2450 | (502) 749-2859 | dan.seum@lrc.ky.gov |
| Tim Shaughnessy (D-19) | 250 E Liberty Ste 103 | | Louisville | 40202 | (502) 584-1920 | (502) 564-8100 | | tim.shaughnessy@lrc.ky.gov |
| Katie Kratz Stine (R-24) | 21 Fairway Dr | | Southgate | 41071 | | (502) 564-3120 | | http://lrc.ky.gov/mailform/s024.htm |
| Robert Stivers (R-25) | 207 Main St | | Manchester | 40962 | (606) 598-2322 | (502) 564-8100 | (606) 598-2357 | robert.stivers@lrc.ky.gov |
| Gary Tapp (R-20) | 2154 Buzzard Roost Rd | | Waddy | 40076 | | (502) 564-8100 | | gary.tapp@lrc.ky.gov |
| Damon Thayer (R-17) | 102 Grayson Way | | Georgetown | 40324 | (859) 621-6956 | (502) 564-8100 | (502) 554-5508 | damon.thayer@lrc.ky.gov |
| Elizabeth J Tori (R-10) | 2851 S Wilson Rd | | Radcliff | 40160 | (270) 351-1829 | (502) 564-2450 | (270) 351-1829 | elizabeth.tori@lrc.ky.gov |
| Johnny R Turner (D-29) | | PO Box 5 | Drift | 41619 | | (502) 564-6136 | | johnnyray.turner@lrc.ky.gov |
| John (Jack) Westwood (R-23) | 2072 Lakelyn Ct | | Crescent Springs | 41017 | (859) 344-6154 | (502) 564-8100 | (859) 344-1878 | jack.westwood@lrc.ky.gov |
| David L Williams (R-16) | | PO Box 666 | Burkesville | 42717 | (270) 864-5636 | (502) 564-3120 | | http://lrc.ky.gov/mailform/s016.htm |
| Kenneth W Winters (R-1) | 1500 Glendale Rd | | Murray | 42071 | (270) 759-5751 | (502) 564-8100 | (270) 759-5751 | johnnyray.turner@lrc.ky.gov |
| Ed Worley (D-34) | | PO Box 659 | Richmond | 40475 | (859) 623-6524 | (502) 564-2470 | (859) 623-6557 | http://lrc.ky.gov/mailform/s034.htm |

Source: The Kentucky Directory Gold Book 2006-2007

## KY HOUSE OF REPRESENTATIVES

| REPRESENTATIVE (Party-District) | ADDRESS1 | ADDRESS2 | CITY | ZIP | PHONE | CAPITOL PHONE | FAX | EMAIL |
|---|---|---|---|---|---|---|---|---|
| Royce W Adams (D-61) | 580 Bannister Rd | | Dry Ridge | 41035 | (859) 824-3387 | (502) 564-8100 | (859) 824-7589 | royce.adams@lrc.ky.gov |
| Rocky Adkins (D-99) | | PO Box 688 | Sandy Hook | 41171 | (606) 928-3433 | (502) 564-5565 | (606) 929-5913 | rocky.adkins@lrc.ky.gov |
| Adrian K Arnold (D-74) | 4600 Paris Pk | | Mt Sterling | 40353 | | (502) 564-8100 | | http://lrc.ky.gov/mailform/h074.htm |
| John A Arnold Jr (D-7) | 1301 N Lee St | PO Box 124 | Sturgis | 42459 | (270) 333-4641 | (502) 564-8100 | | john.arnold@lrc.ky.gov |
| Eddie Ballard (D-10) | | PO Box 1736 | Madisonville | 42431 | (270) 821-4767 | (502) 564-8100 | | eddie.ballard@lrc.ky.gov |
| Joe Barrows (D-56) | 152 Stout Ave | | Versailles | 40383 | | (502) 564-7756 | | http://lrc.ky.gov/mailform/h056.htm |
| Sheldon E Baugh (R-16) | 252 W Valley Dr | | Russellville | 42276 | (270) 726-7616 | (502) 564-8100 | (270) 726-7618 | sheldon.baugh@lrc.ky.gov |
| Carolyn Belcher (D-72) | 51 Blevins Valley Rd | | Owingsville | 40360 | (606) 674-2417 | (502) 564-8100 | | carolyn.belcher@lrc.ky.gov |
| Joe Bowen (R-13) | 2031 Fieldcrest Dr | | Owensboro | 42301 | (270) 683-0236 | (502) 564-8100 | (270) 685-0840 | joe.bowen@lrc.ky.gov |
| Kevin D Bratcher (R-29) | 10215 Landwood Dr | | Louisville | 40291 | | (502) 564-8100 | | kevin.bratcher@lrc.ky.gov |
| Scott W Brinkman (R-32) | 6001 Two Springs Ln | | Louisville | 40207 | (502) 560-4244 | (502) 564-8100 | (502) 627-8744 | http://lrc.ky.gov/mailform/h032.htm |
| James E Bruce (D-9) | 6750 Ft Campbell Blvd | | Hopkinsville | 42240 | | (502) 564-8100 | | http://lrc.ky.gov/mailform/h009.htm |
| Thomas J Burch (D-30) | 4012 Lambert Ave | | Louisville | 40218 | | (502) 564-8100 | | tom.burch@lrc.ky.gov |
| Denver Butler (D-38) | 6712 Morocco Dr | | Louisville | 40214 | | (502) 564-8100 | | repbutler@aol.com |
| Dwight D Butler (R-18) | | PO Box 9 | Harned | 40144 | (270) 756-5931 | (502) 564-8100 | | butlerdd@bbtel.com |
| James R Carr (R-8) | 205 Fairfoix Ave | | Hopkinsville | 42240 | | (502) 564-8100 | | james.carr@lrc.ky.gov |
| Michael E Cherry (D-4) | 803 S Jefferson St | | Princeton | 42445 | | (502) 564-8100 | (270) 365-7801 | mike.cherry@lrc.ky.gov |
| Larry Clark (D-46) | 5913 Whispering Hills Blvd | | Louisville | 40219 | | (502) 564-7520 | | larry.clark@lrc.ky.gov |
| Hubert Collins (D-97) | 72 Collins Dr | | Whitinsville | 41274 | (606) 297-3361 | (502) 564-8100 | (606) 297-3361 | http://lrc.ky.gov/mailform/h097.htm |
| James R Comer (R-53) | 407 4th St Blvd | | Tompkinsville | 42167 | | (502) 564-8100 | | jcomer@scrtc.com |
| Howard Cornett (R-94) | 20 El Paso Dr | | Whitesburg | 41858 | (606) 832-4827 | (502) 564-8100 | | http://lrc.ky.gov/mailform/h094.htm |
| Tim Couch (R-90) | | PO Box 710 | Hyden | 41749 | (859) 229-4219 | (502) 564-8100 | (606) 672-8998 | http://lrc.ky.gov/mailform/h090.htm |
| Jesse Crenshaw (D-77) | 121 Constitution | | Lexington | 40507 | (859) 259-1402 | (502) 564-8100 | (859) 259-1441 | http://lrc.ky.gov/mailform/h077.htm |
| Ronald E Crimm (R-33) | | PO Box 43244 | Louisville | 40253 | (502) 245-2218 | (502) 564-8100 | (502) 245-3811 | ron.crimm@lrc.ky.gov |
| Robert R Damron (D-39) | 231 Fairway W | | Nicholasville | 40356 | (859) 229-4219 | (502) 564-2217 | (502) 564-2222 | robert.damron@lrc.ky.gov |
| Jim DeCesare (R-21) | 136 Cedar Trail Ave | | Bowling Green | 42101 | (270) 792-5779 | (502) 564-8100 | | dj951@insightbb.com |
| Milward Dedman (R-55) | 300 S Chiles St | | Harrodsburg | 40330 | (859) 734-2880 | (502) 564-8100 | (859) 734-4946 | mdedman@bellsouth.net |
| Mitchel (Mike) Denham (D-70) | 306 Old Hill City Rd | | Maysville | 41056 | | (502) 564-8100 | | http://lrc.ky.gov/mailform/h070.htm |
| Bob M DeWeese (R-48) | 6206 Glen Hill Rd | | Louisville | 40222 | | (502) 564-4334 | | bob.deweese@lrc.ky.gov |
| Jon E Draud (R-63) | 3081 Lyndale Ct | | Edgewood | 41017 | (859) 572-5757 | (502) 564-8100 | (859) 341-3887 | jon.draud@lrc.ky.gov |
| Ted (Teddy) Edmonds (D-91) | 1257 Beattyville Rd | | Jackson | 41339 | | (502) 564-8100 | | http://lrc.ky.gov/mailform/h091.htm |
| C B Embry Jr (R-17) | | PO Box 1215 | Morgantown | 42261 | | (502) 564-8100 | | http://lrc.ky.gov/mailform/h017.htm |
| Bill Farmer (R-88) | 3361 Squire Oak Dr | | Lexington | 40515 | (859) 272-1425 | (502) 564-8100 | (859) 272-1579 | http://lrc.ky.gov/mailform_temp/farmer.htm |
| Joseph M Fischer (R-68) | 126 Dixie Pl | | Ft Thomas | 41075 | (513) 794-6442 | (502) 564-8100 | | joe.fischer@lrc.ky.gov |

# KY HOUSE OF REPRESENTATIVES

| REPRESENTATIVE (Party-District) | ADDRESS1 | ADDRESS2 | CITY | ZIP | PHONE | CAPITOL PHONE | FAX | EMAIL |
|---|---|---|---|---|---|---|---|---|
| David W Floyd (R-50) | 102 Maywood Ave | | Bardstown | 40004 | (502) 349-6214 | (502) 564-8100 | | david.floyd@lrc.ky.gov |
| Danny R Ford (R-80) | | PO Box 1245 | Mt Vernon | 40456 | (606) 679-2212 | (502) 564-8100 | | danny.ford@lrc.ky.gov |
| Jim Gooch Jr (D-12) | 714 N Broadway Ste B-2 | | Providence | 42450 | (270) 667-9900 | (502) 564-8100 | (270) 667-5111 | jim.gooch@lrc.ky.gov |
| Derrick W Graham (D-57) | Capitol Annex Rm 451B | | Frankfort | 40601 | (502) 875-8655 | (502) 564-8100 | (502) 564-6834 | http://lrc.ky.gov/mailform/h057.htm |
| J R Gray (D-6) | 3188 Mayfield Hwy | | Benton | 42025 | (270) 527-8376 | (502) 564-8100 | (502) 564-6543 | jr.gray@lrc.ky.gov |
| W Keith Hall (D-93) | 155 McCoy Caney Rd | | Phelps | 41553 | (606) 835-4666 | (502) 564-8100 | (606) 835-4999 | http://lrc.ky.gov/mailform/h093.htm |
| Mike Harmon (R-54) | | PO Box 458 | Junction City | 40440 | (859) 238-9717 | (502) 564-8100 | (781) 846-1098 | mikeharmon@yahoo.com |
| Mary C Harper (R-49) | 5550 N Preston | | Shepherdsville | 40165 | | (502) 564-8100 | | http://lrc.ky.gov/mailform/h049.htm |
| Melvin B Henley (R-5) | 1305 S 16th St | | Murray | 42071 | (270) 753-3855 | (502) 564-8100 | | henlem02@charter.net |
| Jimmy Higdon (R-24) | 507 W Main | | Lebanon | 40033 | (270) 692-3881 | (502) 564-8100 | (270) 692-1111 | jimmyhigdon@alltel.net |
| Charlie Hoffman (D-62) | 406 Bourbon St | | Georgetown | 40324 | (502) 863-4807 | (502) 564-8100 | | charlie.hoffman@lrc.ky.gov |
| Jeffrey Hoover (R-83) | | PO Box 985 | Jamestown | 42629 | (270) 343-5588 | (502) 564-5413 | (270) 343-5590 | jeff.hoover@lrc.ky.gov |
| Dennis Horlander (D-40) | 1806 Farnsley Rd Ste 6 | | Shively | 40216 | (502) 447-4715 | (502) 564-8100 | | horlander1@aol.com |
| Joni Jenkins (D-44) | 2010 O'Brien Ct | | Shively | 40216 | | (502) 564-8100 | | jonijenkins@aol.com |
| Dennis Keene (D-67) | 1040 Johns Hill Rd | | Wilder | 41076 | (859) 912-2096 | (502) 564-8100 | (859) 428-2658 | http://lrc.ky.gov/mailform__temp/h067.htm |
| Thomas Robert Kerr (R-64) | 5415 Old Taylor Mill Rd | | Taylor Mill | 41015 | (859) 431-2222 | (502) 564-8100 | | thomas.kerr@lrc.ky.gov |
| Stan Lee (R-45) | | PO Box 2090 | Lexington | 40588 | (859) 252-2202 | (502) 564-8100 | | stan.lee@lrc.ky.gov |
| Jimmie Lee (D-25) | 901 Dogwood Dr | | Elizabethtown | 42701 | (270) 765-6222 | (502) 564-8100 | (859) 259-2927 | jimmie.lee@lrc.ky.gov or jolu25@msn.com |
| Gross C Lindsay (D-11) | | PO Box 19 | Henderson | 42419 | (270) 827-9824 | (502) 564-8100 | | http://lrc.ky.gov/mailform/h011.htm |
| Gerry Lynn (R-27) | 46 Lakeshore Pkwy | | Brandenburg | 40108 | (270) 422-4343 | (502) 564-8100 | (270) 422-1622 | http://lrc.ky.gov/mailform__temp/h027.htm |
| Paul H Marcotte (R-60) | 10674 Palestine Dr | | Union | 41091 | | (502) 564-8100 | | http://lrc.ky.gov/mailform/h060.htm |
| Mary Lou Marzian (D-34) | 2007 Tyler Ln | | Louisville | 40205 | | (502) 564-8100 | | marylou.marzian@lrc.ky.gov |
| Thomas M McKee (D-78) | 1053 Cook Rd | | Cynthiana | 41031 | | (502) 564-8100 | (859) 234-3332 | tom.mckee@lrc.ky.gov |
| Charles (Chuck) Meade (D-95) | | PO Box 222 | Allen | 41601 | (606) 874-9100 | (502) 564-8100 | (606) 874-9102 | http://lrc.ky.gov/mailform/h095.htm |
| Reginald K Meeks (D-42) | | PO Box 757 | Louisville | 40201 | (502) 852-3042 | (502) 564-8100 | | srmeeks42@aol.com |
| Charles Miller (D-28) | 3608 Gateview Cir | | Louisville | 40272 | (502) 937-7788 | (502) 564-8100 | (502) 749-7815 | charles.miller@lrc.ky.gov |
| Harry Moberly Jr (D-81) | | PO Box 721 | Richmond | 40475 | (859) 622-1501 | (502) 564-8100 | | harry.moberly@lrc.ky.gov |
| Russ Mobley (R-51) | 900 Holly St | | Campbellsville | 42718 | | (502) 564-8100 | | russmobley@alltel.neet |
| Brad Montell (R-58) | 543 Main St | PO Box 1016 | Shelbyville | 40066 | (502) 633-7017 | (502) 564-8100 | | brad.montell@lrc.ky.gov |
| Lonnie Napier (R-36) | 302 Danville St | | Lancaster | 40444 | (859) 792-2535 | (502) 564-8100 | | lonnie.napier@lrc.ky.gov |
| Rick G Nelson (D-87) | Rt 3 Box 686 | | Middlesboro | 40965 | (606) 248-8828 | (502) 564-8100 | (606) 248-8828 | rick.nelson@lrc.ky.gov |
| Fred Nesler (D-2) | 400 St Rt 440 | | Mayfield | 42066 | | (502) 564-8100 | | fred.nesler@lrc.ky.gov |
| Stephen R Nunn (R-23) | 136 Fairway Pl | | Glasgow | 42141 | (270) 651-4865 | (502) 564-8100 | (270) 651-4751 | snnnstaterep@glasgow-ky.com |
| David Osborne (R-59) | | PO Box 8 | Prospect | 40059 | | (502) 564-8100 | (502) 564-6834 | david.osborne@lrc.ky.gov |

## KY HOUSE OF REPRESENTATIVES

| REPRESENTATIVE (Party-District) | ADDRESS1 | ADDRESS2 | CITY | ZIP | PHONE | CAPITOL PHONE | FAX | EMAIL |
|---|---|---|---|---|---|---|---|---|
| Darryl T Owens (D-43) | 1300 W Broadway | | Louisville | 40203 | (502) 584-6341 | (502) 564-8100 | (502) 584-6342 | owenscommish@aol.com |
| Ruth Ann Palumbo (D-76) | 10 Deepwood Dr | | Lexington | 40505 | | (502) 564-8100 | | ruthann.palumbo@lrc.ky.gov |
| Don Pasley (D-73) | 5805 Ecton Rd | | Winchester | 40391 | (859) 749-2976 | (502) 564-8100 | | http://lrc.ky.gov/mailform/h073.htm |
| Tanya Pullin (D-98) | 1026 Johnson Ln | | South Shore | 41175 | (606) 932-2505 | (502) 564-8100 | (502) 564-5640 | http://lrc.ky.gov/mailform/h098.htm |
| Marie L Rader (R-89) | | PO Box 323 | McKee | 40447 | (606) 287-3300 | (502) 564-8100 | (606) 287-3300 | marie.rader@lrc.ky.gov |
| Rick Rand (D-47) | | PO Box 273 | Bedford | 40006 | (502) 225-3286 | (502) 564-8100 | (502) 255-9911 | http://lrc.ky.gov/mailform/h047.htm |
| Frank Rasche (D-3) | 2929 Jefferson St | | Paducah | 42001 | (270) 443-6206 | (502) 564-8100 | (270) 442-6565 | http://lrc.ky.gov/mailform/h003.htm |
| Jon David Reinhardt (R-69) | 323 Poplar Thicket Rd | | Alexandria | 41001 | | (502) 564-8100 | | jondavid.reinhardt@lrc.ky.gov |
| Jody Richards (D-20) | 817 Culpeper St | | Bowling Green | 42103 | (270) 781-9946 | (502) 564-2363 | (270) 781-9963 | jody.richards@lrc.ky.gov |
| Steven Riggs (D-31) | 8108 Thornwood Rd | | Louisville | 40220 | | (502) 564-8100 | (502) 564-6543 | http://lrc.ky.gov/mailform/h031.htm |
| Tom Riner (D-41) | 1143 E Broadway | | Louisville | 40204 | | (502) 564-8100 | | tom.riner@lrc.ky.gov |
| Steven J Rudy (R-1) | 3430 Blueridge Dr | | W Paducah | 42086 | (270) 462-3156 | (502) 564-8100 | (270) 462-3158 | steven@rudysfarmcenter.com |
| Terry Shelton (R-19) | 7725 N Jackson Hwy | | Magnolia | 42757 | (270) 528-5654 | (502) 564-8100 | (270) 528-5654 | http://lrc.ky.gov/mailform_temp/h019.htm |
| Charles L Siler (R-82) | 3570 Tackett Creek Rd | | Williamsburg | 40769 | (606) 549-0900 | (502) 564-8100 | | charles.siler@lrc.ky.gov |
| Arnold Simpson (D-65) | 112 W 11th St | | Covington | 41011 | (859) 261-6577 | (502) 564-8100 | | arsimp@yahoo.com |
| Ancel Smith (D-92) | 1812 Wiley Fork Rd | | Leburn | 41831 | (606) 785-3844 | (502) 564-8100 | | http://lrc.ky.gov/mailform/h092.htm |
| Brandon Smith (R-84) | 350 Kentucky Blvd | | Hazard | 41701 | | (502) 564-8100 | (606) 436-2398 | http://lrc.ky.gov/mailform/h084.htm |
| John Will Stacy (D-71) | | PO Box 135 | West Liberty | 41472 | | (502) 564-8100 | (606) 743-1516 | |
| Kathy W Stein (D-75) | 183 N Upper St | | Lexington | 40507 | (859) 225-4269 | (502) 564-8100 | (859) 254-0491 | kathy.stein@lrc.ky.gov - |
| Jim Stewart (R-86) | 141 KY 223 | | Flat Lick | 40935 | | (502) 564-8100 | | jim.stewart@lrc.ky.gov |
| Tommy Thompson (D-14) | | PO Box 458 | Owensboro | 42302 | (270) 926-1740 | (502) 564-8100 | (270) 685-3242 | tommy.thompson@lrc.ky.gov |
| Tommy Turner (R-85) | 175 Clifty Grove Church Rd | | Somerset | 42501 | | (502) 564-8100 | | tommy.turner@lrc.ky.gov |
| Kenneth H Upchurch (R-52) | | PO Box 991 | Monticello | 42633 | (606) 340-8490 | (502) 564-4334 | | ken.upchurch@lrc.ky.gov |
| John Vincent (R-100) | | PO Box 2528 | Ashland | 41105 | (606) 329-8338 | (502) 564-8100 | (606) 325-8199 | john.vincent@lrc.ky.gov |
| Jim Wayne (D-35) | 1280 Royal Ave | | Louisville | 40204 | | (502) 564-8100 | | |
| John (Mike) Weaver (D-26) | 131 Mayer Ln | | Elizabethtown | 42701 | | (502) 564-8100 | | http://lrc.ky.gov/mailform/h026.htm |
| Robin L Webb (D-96) | 404 W Main St | | Grayson | 41143 | (606) 474-5380 | (502) 564-8100 | | robin.webb@lrc.ky.gov |
| Ron Weston (D-37) | 423 Chieftain Dr | | Fairdale | 40118 | | (502) 564-8100 | | ron.weston@lrc.ky.gov |
| Susan Westrom (D-79) | 220 N Homestead Ct | PO Box 22778 | Lexington | 40522 | (859) 266-7581 | (502) 564-8100 | | susan.westrom@lrc.ky.gov |
| Rob Wilkey (D-22) | | | Scottsville | 42164 | (800) 582-3454 | (502) 564-8100 | (270) 781-7192 | robwilkey@aol.com |
| Addia Kathryn Wuchner (R-66) | | PO Box 911 | Burlington | 41005 | (859) 525-6698 | (502) 564-8100 | (859) 525-6698 | addia.wuchner@lrc.ky.gov |
| Brent Yonts (D-15) | | PO Box 370 | Greenville | 42345 | (270) 338-0816 | (502) 564-8100 | (270) 338-1639 | brent.yonts@lrc.ky.gov |

*Source: The Kentucky Directory Gold Book 2006-2007*

## STATE GOVERNMENT & POLITICS

# *Judiciary*

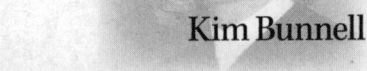

Kim Bunnell

Over the course of history, the judicial system of Kentucky, which is called the Court of Justice, has changed numerous times. Since 1976 there have been four separate levels of court in Kentucky—each having very defined responsibilities to hear certain types of cases. Trial courts are divided into Circuit Court, which has general jurisdiction, and District Court, which has limited jurisdiction. The appellate courts include the Supreme Court and the Court of Appeals.

Kentucky's four-tier court system was established by the passage of the Judicial Article to the Kentucky Constitution in 1975, which took effect July 15, 1976. The Judicial Article created the Court of Justice as an independent branch of government separate from the Executive and Legislative branches and from local county and city governments.

Kentucky's trial courts first hear the facts and issue judgments on those facts. Appeals courts may be asked to review the judgment of another court to see if a mistake was made. An appeals court generally cannot hear any new evidence or call witnesses, rather it must rule on what was presented to the trial court. Kentuckians have the right to one appeal per lawsuit. Beyond this one "matter of right" to appeal, a further appeal is discretionary and the appellate court may refuse to review the case.

The Supreme Court is the state court of last resort and the final interpreter of Kentucky law. Appeals involving the death penalty, life imprisonment or imprisonment for 20 years or more go directly from Circuit Court to the Supreme Court.

All other appeals must first be heard by the Court of Appeals, except those so exceptional that the Supreme Court will grant a request to bypass the Court of Appeals.

Circuit Court hears civil matters involving more than $4,000, criminal cases (capital offenses and felonies), dissolution of marriage, adoptions, termination of parental rights, land dispute title problems and contested probates of wills. Family Court 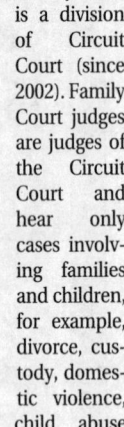 is a division of Circuit Court (since 2002). Family Court judges are judges of the Circuit Court and hear only cases involving families and children, for example, divorce, custody, domestic violence, child abuse and neglect cases.

District Court, often referred to as "the people's court," has limited jurisdiction—specifically, juvenile matters, city and county ordinances, guardianship, conservatorship, voluntary or involuntary commitment, misdemeanor and traffic offenses, probates of wills, felony preliminary hearings and civil cases involving $4,000 or less. Appeals from District Court decisions are made to the local Circuit Court.

*Kim Bunnell is a Circuit Judge in the Fifth Division of Fayette Circuit Court. Source: Kentucky Court of Justice, http://courts.ky.gov/courts/*

# *Kentucky Supreme Court*

Front row from left to right: William E McAnulty Jr, Joseph E Lambert (Chief Justice) and John D Minton Jr. Back row from left to right: Will T Scott, John C Roach, J William Graves and Donald C Wintersheimer.

**1st District**
**Justice John William (Bill) Graves**
Capitol Bldg Rm 216    222 Kentucky Ave
700 Capitol Ave          PO Box 993
Frankfort 40601          Paducah 42002
(502) 564-4163           (270) 575-7039
FAX (502) 564-2665

**2nd District**
**Justice John D Minton Jr**
Capitol Bldg Rm 223    Warren Co Justice Ctr
700 Capitol Ave          1001 Center St Rm 204
Frankfort 40601          Bowling Green 42101
(502) 564-4159           (270) 746-7867
FAX (502) 564-2665

**3rd District**
**Chief Justice Joseph E Lambert**
Capitol Bldg Rm 231    101 Rockcastle Judicial Ctr
700 Capitol Ave          PO Box 989
Frankfort 40601          Mt Vernon 40456
(502) 564-4162           (606) 256-9030
FAX (502) 564-1933

**4th District**
**Justice William E McAnulty Jr**
Capitol Bldg Rm 201    700 W Jefferson St
700 Capitol Ave          Ste 1000
Frankfort 40601          Louisville 40202
(502) 564-4157           (502) 595-3199
FAX (502) 564-2665

**5th District**
**Justice John C Roach**
Capitol Bldg Rm 245    155 E Main St Ste 200
700 Capitol Ave          Lexington 40507
Frankfort 40601          (859) 246-2220
(502) 564-6753
FAX (502) 564-2665

**6th District**
**Justice Donald C Wintersheimer**
Capitol Bldg Rm 239    PO Box 387
700 Capitol Ave          Covington 41012
Frankfort 40601          (859) 292-6300
(502) 564-4165
FAX (502) 564-2665

**7th District**
**Justice Will T Scott**
Capitol Bldg Rm 226    PO Box 1316
700 Capitol Ave          Pikeville 41502
Frankfort 40601          (606) 432-2030
(502) 564-4168
FAX (502) 564-2665

**Clerk of the Court**
**Susan Stokley Clary**
Capitol Bldg Rm 235
700 Capitol Ave
Frankfort 40601
(502) 564-5444
FAX (502) 564-2665
susanclary@kycourts.net

# Kentucky Court of Appeals

## 1st Appellate District

**Judge Rick A Johnson** — 1st Div
2380 St Rt 45 N
Mayfield 42066
(270) 247-1052

**Judge Donna L Dixon** — 2nd Div
US Bank Bldg Ste 406B
333 Broadway
Paducah 42001
(270)556-3465

## 2nd Appellate District

**Judge Jeff S Taylor** — 1st Div
Corporate Centre No A102
401 Frederica St
Owensboro 42303
(270) 687-7116

**Vacant** — 2nd Div

## 3rd Appellate District

**Vacant** — 1st Div

**Judge Michael L Henry** — 2nd Div
205 W Columbia St
Somerset 42501
(606) 677-4226

## 4th Appellate District

**Judge Thomas B Wine** — 1st Div
700 W Jefferson St Ste 1010
Louisville 40202
(502) 595-3430

**Judge Lisabeth Hughes Abramson** — 2nd Div
700 W Jefferson St Ste 1020
Louisville 40202
(502) 595-3440

## 5th Appellate District

**Judge Laurance B VanMeter** — 1st Div
1999 Richmond Rd Ste 5
Lexington 40502
(859) 246-2053

**Judge Glenn E Acree** — 2nd Div
Tate Bldg
125 Lisle Industrial Ave
Lexington 40511
(859) 246-2734

## 6th Appellate District

**Judge Daniel T Guidugli** — 1st Div
1 Moock Rd Ste 4
Newport 41071
(859) 291-9966

**Judge Wilfrid A Schroder** — 2nd Div
2734 Chancellor Dr Ste 109
Covington 41017
(859) 292-6574

## 7th Appellate District

**Chief Judge Sara W Combs** — 1st Div
323 E College Ave, PO Box 709
Stanton 40380
(606) 663-0651

**Judge David Barber** — 2nd Div
2980 KY Rt 321
Prestonsburg 41653
(606) 889-1710

## Clerk of the Court
**Hon Samuel Givens Jr**
60 Democrat Dr
Frankfort 40601
(502) 573-7920

## Did you Know?

The Kentucky Supreme Court is the court of last resort and the final interpreter of state law. It consists of seven justices that hear appeals of decisions from the lower courts and issue decisions or "opinions" on cases. The Court of Appeals is exactly what its title implies. Nearly all cases come to it on appeal from a lower court. If a case is tried in District or Circuit court, and the losing parties involved are not satisfied with the outcome, they may ask for a higher court to review the correctness of the trial court's decision.

*Source: Kentucky Court of Justice, www.kycourts.net*

# Circuit Judges

| COUNTY | CIRCUIT | DIVISION | TITLE | JUDGE | PHONE |
|---|---|---|---|---|---|
| Adair | 29th | 1st Div | Circuit Judge | James G Weddle | (606) 787-6991 |
| Allen | 49th | 1st Div | Circuit Judge | William R Harris | (270) 586-8058 |
| Anderson | 53rd | 1st Div | Circuit Judge | Charles R Hickman | (502) 647-5234 |
| Ballard | 1st | 1st Div | Circuit Judge | Vacant | (270) 335-5189 |
| Barren | 43rd | 1st Div | Circuit Judge | Phillip O Patton | (270) 651-2744 |
| Barren | 43rd | 2nd Div | Family Court Judge | Mitchell W Nance | (270) 651-9923 |
| Bath | 21st | 1st Div | Circuit Judge | William B Mains | (606) 784-5190 |
| Bath | 21st | 2nd Div | Circuit Judge | Beth Lewis Maze | (859) 498-0488 |
| Bell | 44th | 1st Div | Circuit Judge | James L Bowling Jr | (606) 337-5949 |
| Boone | 54th | 1st Div | Circuit Judge | Anthony N Frohlich | (859) 334-3270 |
| Boone | 54th-- | 2nd Div | Family Court Judge | Linda Rae Bramlage | (859) 334-3520 |
| Bourbon | 14th | 1st Div | Circuit Judge | Robert G Johnson | (502) 570-0947 |
| Bourbon | 14th | 2nd Div | Circuit Judge | Paul F Isaacs | (502) 863-4781 |
| Boyd | 32nd | 1st Div | Circuit Judge | Marc I Rosen | (606) 739-5844 |
| Boyd | 32nd | 2nd Div | Circuit Judge | C David Hagerman | (606) 739-6122 |
| Boyle | 50th | 1st Div | Circuit Judge | Darren W Peckler | (859) 239-7009 |
| Boyle | 50th | 2nd Div | Family Court Judge | Bruce Petrie | (859) 239-7090 |
| Bracken | 19th | 1st Div | Circuit Judge | John W McNeill | (606) 564-9736 |
| Breathitt | 39th | 1st Div | Circuit Judge | William Larry Miller | (606) 668-7590 |
| Breckinridge | 46th | 1st Div | Circuit Judge | Sam H Monarch | (270) 756-6278 |
| Breckinridge | 46th | 2nd Div | Circuit Judge | Robert A Miller | (270) 422-7800 |
| Bullitt | 55th | 1st Div | Circuit Judge | Thomas L Waller | (502) 543-4776 |
| Butler | 38th | 1st Div | Circuit Judge | Ronnie C Dortch | (270) 298-7250 |
| Caldwell | 56th | 1st Div | Circuit Judge | Bill Cunningham | (270) 388-5182 |
| Calloway | 42nd | 1st Div | Circuit Judge | Dennis R Foust | (270) 527-1480 |
| Campbell | 17th | 1st Div | Circuit Judge | Julie Reinhardt Ward | (859) 292-6301 |
| Campbell | 17th | 2nd Div | Circuit Judge | Fred A Stine V | (859) 292-6303 |
| Campbell | 17th | 3rd Div | Family Court Judge | Michael D Foellger | (859) 292-6717 |
| Carlisle | 1st | 1st Div | Circuit Judge | Vacant | (270) 335-5189 |
| Carroll | 15th | 1st Div | Circuit Judge | Stephen L Bates | (859) 824-7516 |
| Carter | 37th | 1st Div | Circuit Judge | Vacant | |
| Carter | 37th | 2nd Div | Family Court Judge | Kristi Hogg-Gossett | (606) 475-1801 |
| Casey | 29th | 1st Div | Circuit Judge | James G Weddle | (606) 787-6991 |
| Christian | 3rd | 1st Div | Circuit Judge | Edwin M White | (270) 889-6536 |
| Christian | 3rd | 2nd Div | Circuit Judge | John L Atkins | (270) 889-6537 |
| Christian | 3rd | 3rd Div | Family Court Judge | Judy A Hall | (270) 889-6038 |
| Clark | 25th | 1st Div | Circuit Judge | Julia H Adams | (859) 737-7263 |
| Clark | 25th | 2nd Div | Circuit Judge | William T Jennings | (859) 624-4750 |
| Clark | 25th | 3rd Div | Family Court Judge | Jean C Logue | (859) 625-0601 |
| Clark | 25th | 4th Div | Family Court Judge | Jeffrey M Walson | (859) 737-7491 |
| Clay | 41st | 1st Div | Circuit Judge | R Cletus Maricle | (606) 598-5251 |
| Clay | 41st | 2nd Div | Family Court Judge | Gene Clark | (606) 599-0948 |
| Clinton | 40th | 1st Div | Circuit Judge | Eddie C Lovelace | (606) 387-5986 |
| Crittenden | 5th | 1st Div | Circuit Judge | C René Williams | (270) 639-5506 |
| Crittenden | 5th | 2nd Div | Family Court Judge | William E Mitchell | (270) 639-5094 |
| Cumberland | 40th | 1st Div | Circuit Judge | Eddie C Lovelace | (606) 387-5986 |
| Daviess | 6th | 1st Div | Circuit Judge | Henry M Griffin III | (270) 687-7226 |
| Daviess | 6th | 2nd Div | Circuit Judge | Thomas O Castlen | (270) 687-7228 |
| Edmonson | 38th | 1st Div | Circuit Judge | Ronnie C Dortch | (270) 298-7250 |
| Elliott | 37th | 1st Div | Circuit Judge | Vacant | |
| Elliott | 37th | 2nd Div | Family Court Judge | Kristi Hogg-Gossett | (606) 475-1801 |
| Estill | 23rd | 1st Div | Circuit Judge | William W Trude Jr | (606) 723-3320 |
| Fayette | 22nd | 1st Div | Family Court Judge | Timothy N Philpot | (859) 246-2703 |
| Fayette | 22nd | 2nd Div | Circuit Judge | Gary D Payne | (859) 246-2214 |
| Fayette | 22nd | 3rd Div | Circuit Judge | James Ishmel Jr | (859) 246-2218 |
| Fayette | 22nd | 4th Div | Circuit Judge | Pamela R Goodwine | (859) 246-2216 |
| Fayette | 22nd | 5th Div | Circuit Judge | Mary C Noble | (859) 246-2212 |
| Fayette | 22nd | 6th Div | Family Court Judge | Jo Ann Wise | (859) 246-2786 |
| Fayette | 22nd | 7th Div | Circuit Judge | Sheila R Isaac | (859) 246-2531 |
| Fayette | 22nd | 8th Div | Circuit Judge | Thomas L Clark | (859) 246-2533 |
| Fayette | 22nd | 9th Div | Family Court Judge | Kimberly Nell Bunnell | (859) 246-2210 |
| Fleming | 19th | 1st Div | Circuit Judge | John W McNeil | (606) 564-9736 |
| Floyd | 31st | 1st Div | Circuit Judge | Danny P Caudill | (606) 889-1653 |
| Floyd | 31st | 2nd Div | Circuit Judge | John David Caudill | (606) 889-1900 |
| Floyd | 31st | 3rd Div | Family Court Judge | Julie M Paxton | (606) 889-1676 |
| Franklin | 48th | 1st Div | Circuit Judge | Samuel G McNamara | |
| Franklin | 48th | 2nd Div | Circuit Judge | Thomas Wingate | (502) 564-8382 |
| Franklin | 48th | 3rd Div | Family Court Judge | Orville Reed Rhorer | (502) 564-2278 |
| Fulton | 1st | 1st Div | Circuit Judge | Vacant | (270) 335-5189 |
| Gallatin | 54th | 1st Div | Circuit Judge | Anthony W Frohlich | (859) 334-3270 |
| Gallatin | 54th | 2nd Div | Family Court Judge | Linda Rae Bramlage | (859) 334-3520 |
| Garrard | 13th | 1st Div | Circuit Judge | Hunter Daugherty | (859) 885-6722 |
| Grant | 15th | 1st Div | Circuit Judge | Stephen L Bates | (859) 824-7516 |
| Graves | 52nd | 1st Div | Circuit Judge | Timorthy C Stark | (270) 247-8726 |
| Grayson | 46th | 1st Div | Circuit Judge | Sam H Monarch | (270) 756-6278 |
| Grayson | 46th | 2nd Div | Circuit Judge | Robert A Miller | (270) 422-7800 |
| Green | 11th | 1st Div | Circuit Judge | Douglhas M George | (606) 336-3903 |
| Greenup | 20th | 1st Div | Circuit Judge | Lewis Dunn Nicholls | (606) 473-7165 |

## CIRCUIT JUDGES, CONTINUED

| COUNTY | CIRCUIT | DIVISION | TITLE | JUDGE | PHONE |
|---|---|---|---|---|---|
| Hancock | 38th | 1st Div | Circuit Judge | Ronnie C Dortch | (270) 298-7250 |
| Hardin | 9th | 1st Div | Family Court Judge | Thomas Steven Bland | (270) 766-5003 |
| Hardin | 9th | 1st Div | Family Court Judge | Pamela Addington | (270) 766-5293 |
| Hardin | 9th | 2nd Div | Circuit Judge | Janet P Coleman | (270) 766-5039 |
| Hardin | 9th | 3rd Div | Circuit Judge | Kelly Mark Easton | (270) 766-5259 |
| Harlan | 26th | 1st Div | Circuit Judge | Ron (Ronnie) Johnson | (606) 573-3242 |
| Harrison | 18th | 1st Div | Circuit Judge | Robert W McGinnis | (859) 234-3431 |
| Harrison | 18th | 3rd Div | Family Court Judge | David E Melcher | (859) 234-0190 |
| Hart | 10th | 1st Div | Circuit Judge | Charles E Simms | (270) 348-7313 |
| Henderson | 51st | 1st Div | Circuit Judge | Stephen A Hayden | (270) 827-1295 |
| Henderson | 51st | 2nd Div | Family Court Judge | Sheila Nunley-Farris | (270) 869-0460 |
| Henry | 12th | 1st Div | Circuit Judge | Karen A Conrad | (502) 222-1692 |
| Henry | 12th | 2nd Div | Family Court Judge | Timothy Edward Feeley | (502) 222-2490 |
| Hickman | 1st | 1st Div | Circuit Judge | Vacant | (270) 335-5189 |
| Hopkins | 4th | 1st Div | Circuit Judge | Susan Wesley McClure | (270) 824-7422 |
| Jackson | 41st | 1st Div | Circuit Judge | R Cletus Maricle | (606) 598-5251 |
| Jackson | 41st | 2nd Div | Family Court Judge | Gene Clark | (606) 599-0948 |
| Jefferson | 30th | 10th Div | Circuit Judge | Kathleen V Montano | (502) 595-4327 |
| Jefferson | 30th | 10th Div | Family Court Judge | Paula Sherlock | (502) 595-4699 |
| Jefferson | 30th | 11th Div | Circuit Judge | Geoffrey P (Geoff) Morris | (502) 595-4400 |
| Jefferson | 30th | 12th Div | Circuit Judge | Kenneth Conliffe | (502) 595-3012 |
| Jefferson | 30th | 13th Div | Circuit Judge | Ann O'Malley Shake | (502) 595-3011 |
| Jefferson | 30th | 1st Div | Circuit Judge | Barry Willett | (502) 595-4054 |
| Jefferson | 30th | 1st Div | Family Court Judge | Joan L Byer | (502) 595-4656 |
| Jefferson | 30th | 2nd Div | Circuit Judge | James M Shake | (502) 595-4062 |
| Jefferson | 30th | 2nd Div | Family Court Judge | Hugh Smith Haynie Jr | (502) 595-4996 |
| Jefferson | 30th | 3rd Div | Circuit Judge | Lisabeth H Abramson | (502) 595-4919 |
| Jefferson | 30th | 3rd Div | Family Court Judge | Patricia FitzGerald Walker | (502) 595-4326 |
| Jefferson | 30th | 4th Div | Circuit Judge | Denise M Clayton | (502) 595-4604 |
| Jefferson | 30th | 4th Div | Family Court Judge | Dolly W Berry | (502) 595-4969 |
| Jefferson | 30th | 5th Div | Circuit Judge | Willaim D Kemper | |
| Jefferson | 30th | 5th Div | Family Court Judge | Eleanore M Garber | (502) 595-4988 |
| Jefferson | 30th | 6th Div | Circuit Judge | Martin F McDonald | (502) 595-4311 |
| Jefferson | 30th | 6th Div | Family Court Judge | Jerry B Bowles | (502) 595-4993 |
| Jefferson | 30th | 7th Div | Circuit Judge | Stephen K Mershon | (502) 595-4103 |
| Jefferson | 30th | 7th Div | Family Court Judge | Joseph W O'Reilly, Chief | (502) 595-4993 |
| Jefferson | 30th | 8th Div | Circuit Judge | Thomas B Wine | (502) 595-4294 |
| Jefferson | 30th | 8th Div | Family Court Judge | Kevin L Garvey | (502) 595-4043 |
| Jefferson | 30th | 9th Div | Circuit Judge | Judith McDonald-Burkman | (502) 595-4356 |
| Jefferson | 30th | 9th Div | Family Court Judge | Stephen M George | (502) 595-4998 |
| Jessamine | 13th | 1st Div | Circuit Judge | Hunter Daugherty | (859) 885-6722 |
| Johnson | 24th | 1st Div | Circuit Judge | Vacant | (606) 789-6861 |
| Johnson | 24th | 1st Div | Family Court Judge | John David Preston | (606) 788-7154 |
| Kenton | 16th | 1st Div | Circuit Judge | Steven R Jaeger | (859) 292-6538 |
| Kenton | 16th | 2nd Div | Circuit Judge | Vacant | (859) 292-6533 |
| Kenton | 16th | 3rd Div | Circuit Judge | Gregory M Bartlett | (859) 292-6530 |
| Kenton | 16th | 4th Div | Circuit Judge | Patricia M Summe | (859) 292-6531 |
| Knott | 36th | 1st Div | Circuit Judge | Kim Cornett Childers | (606) 785-3842 |
| Knott | 36th | 3rd Div | Family Court Judge | Julie M Paxton | (606) 889-1676 |
| Knox | 27th | 1st Div | Circuit Judge | Gregory A Lay | (606) 864-2850 |
| Knox | 27th | 2nd Div | Circuit Judge | Roderick Messer | (606) 878-8111 |
| Larue | 10th | 1st Div | Circuit Judge | Charles C Simms III | (502) 348-7313 |
| Laurel | 27th | 1st Div | Circuit Judge | Gregory A Lay | (606) 864-2850 |
| Laurel | 27th | 2nd Div | Circuit Judge | Roderick Messer | (606) 878-8111 |
| Lawrence | 24th | 1st Div | Family Court Judge | John David Preston | (606) 788-7154 |
| Lawrence | 24th | 2nd Div | Circuit Judge | Vacant | (606) 789-6861 |
| Lee | 23rd | 1st Div | Circuit Judge | William W Trude Jr | (606) 723-3320 |
| Leslie | 41st | 1st Div | Circuit Judge | R Cletus Maricle | (606) 598-5251 |
| Leslie | 41st | 2nd Div | Family Court Judge | Gene Clark | (606) 599-0948 |
| Letcher | 47th | 1st Div | Circuit Judge | Samuel T Wright III | (606) 633-2259 |
| Lewis | 20th | 1st Div | Circuit Judge | Lewis Dunn Nicholls | (606) 473-7165 |
| Lincoln | 28th | 1st Div | Circuit Judge | David A Tapp | (606) 677-4091 |
| Lincoln | 28th | 2nd Div | Circuit Judge | Jeffrey T Burdette | (606) 677-4098 |
| Lincoln | 28th | 3rd Div | Family Court Judge | Debra Hembree Lambert | (606) 677-4186 |
| Livingston | 56th | 1st Div | Circuit Judge | Bill Cunningham | (270) 388-5182 |
| Logan | 7th | 1st Div | Circuit Judge | Tyler Gill | (270) 726-2242 |
| Lyon | 56th | 1st Div | Circuit Judge | Bill Cunningham | (270) 388-5182 |
| Madison | 25th | 1st Div | Circuit Judge | Julia H Adams | (859) 737-7263 |
| Madison | 25th | 2nd Div | Circuit Judge | William T Jennings | (859) 624-4750 |
| Madison | 25th | 3rd Div | Family Court Judge | Jean C Logue | (859) 625-0601 |
| Madison | 25th | 4th Div | Family Court Judge | Jeffrey M Walson | (859) 737-7491 |
| Magoffin | 36th | 1st Div | Circuit Judge | Kim Cornett Childers | (606) 785-3842 |
| Magoffin | 36th | 3rd Div | Family Court Judge | Julie M Paxton | (606) 889-1676 |
| Marion | 11th | 1st Div | Circuit Judge | Douglas M George | (859) 336-3903 |
| Marshall | 42nd | 1st Div | Circuit Judge | Dennis R Foust | (270) 527-1480 |
| Martin | 24th | 1st Div | Family Court Judge | John David Preston | (606) 788-7154 |
| Martin | 24th | 2nd Div | Circuit Judge | Vacant | (606) 789-6861 |
| Mason | 19th | 1st Div | Circuit Judge | John W McNeil | (606) 564-9736 |

## CIRCUIT JUDGES, CONTINUED

| COUNTY | CIRCUIT | DIVISION | TITLE | JUDGE | PHONE |
|---|---|---|---|---|---|
| McCracken | 2nd | 1st Div | Circuit Judge | R Jeffrey Hines | (270) 575-7292 |
| McCracken | 2nd | 2nd Div | Circuit Judge | Craig Z Clymer | (270) 575-7400 |
| McCracken | 2nd | 3rd Div | Family Court Judge | Cynthia E Sanderson | (270) 575-7133 |
| McCreary | 34th | 1st Div | Circuit Judge | Jerry D Winchester | (606) 528-3013 |
| McCreary | 34th | 2nd Div | Circuit Judge | Paul E Braden | (606) 528-3013 |
| McLean | 45th | 1st Div | Circuit Judge | David H Jernigan | (270) 338-5930 |
| Meade | 46th | 1st Div | Circuit Judge | Sam H Monarch | (270) 756-6278 |
| Meade | 46th | 2nd Div | Circuit Judge | Robert A Miller | (270) 422-7800 |
| Menifee | 21st | 1st Div | Circuit Judge | William B Mains | (606) 784-5190 |
| Menifee | 21st | 2nd Div | Circuit Judge | Beth Lewis Maze | (859) 498-0488 |
| Mercer | 50th | 1st Div | Circuit Judge | Darren W Peckler | (859) 239-7009 |
| Mercer | 50th | 2nd Div | Family Court Judge | Bruce Petrie | (859) 239-7090 |
| Metcalfe | 43rd | 1st Div | Circuit Judge | Phillip R Patton | (270) 651-2744 |
| Metcalfe | 43rd | 2nd Div | Family Court Judge | Mitchell W Nance | (270) 651-9923 |
| Monroe | 40th | 1st Div | Circuit Judge | Eddie C Lovelace | (606) 387-5986 |
| Montgomery | 21st | 1st Div | Circuit Judge | William B Mains | (606) 784-5190 |
| Montgomery | 21st | 2nd Div | Circuit Judge | Beth Lewis Maze | (859) 498-0488 |
| Morgan | 37th | 1st Div | Circuit Judge | Vacant | |
| Morgan | 37th | 2nd Div | Family Court Judge | Kristi Hogg-Gossett | (606) 475-1801 |
| Muhlenberg | 45th | 1st Div | Circuit Judge | David H Jernigan | (270) 338-5930 |
| Nelson | 10th | 1st Div | Circuit Judge | Charles C Simms III | (502) 348-7313 |
| Nicholas | 18th | 1st Div | Circuit Judge | Robert W McGinnis | (859) 234-3431 |
| Nicholas | 18th | 3rd Div | Family Court Judge | David E Melcher | (859) 234-0190 |
| Ohio | 38th | 1st Div | Circuit Judge | Ronnie C Dortch | (270) 298-7250 |
| Oldham | 12th | 1st Div | Circuit Judge | Karen A Conrad | (502) 222-1692 |
| Oldham | 12th | 2nd Div | Family Court Judge | Timothy Edward Feeley | (502) 222-2490 |
| Owen | 15th | 1st Div | Circuit Judge | Stephen L Bates | (859) 824-7516 |
| Owsley | 23rd | 1st Div | Circuit Judge | William W Trude Jr | (606) 723-3320 |
| Pendleton | 18th | 1st Div | Circuit Judge | Robert W McGinnis | (859) 234-3431 |
| Pendleton | 18th | 3rd Div | Family Court Judge | David E Melcher | (859) 234-0190 |
| Perry | 33rd | 1st Div | Circuit Judge | William (Bill) Engle III | (606) 435-6004 |
| Pike | 35th | 1st Div | Circuit Judge | Eddy Coleman | (606) 433-7554 |
| Pike | 35th | 2nd Div | Circuit Judge | Steven D Combs | (606) 433-7551 |
| Pike | 35th | 3rd Div | Family Court Judge | Larry Thompson | (606) 433-7061 |
| Powell | 39th | 1st Div | Circuit Judge | William Larry Miller | (606) 668-7590 |
| Pulaski | 28th | 1st Div | Circuit Judge | David A Tapp | (606) 677-4091 |
| Pulaski | 28th | 2nd Div | Circuit Judge | Jeffrey T Burdette | (606) 677-4098 |
| Pulaski | 28th | 3rd Div | Family Court Judge | Debra Hembree Lambert | (606) 677-4186 |
| Robertson | 18th | 1st Div | Circuit Judge | Robert W McGinnis | (859) 234-3431 |
| Robertson | 18th | 3rd Div | Family Court Judge | David E Melcher | (859) 234-0190 |
| Rockcastle | 28th | 1st Div | Circuit Judge | David A Tapp | (606) 677-4091 |
| Rockcastle | 28th | 2nd Div | Circuit Judge | Jeffrey T Burdette | (606) 677-4098 |
| Rockcastle | 28th | 3rd Div | Family Court Judge | Debra Hembree Lambert | (606) 677-4186 |
| Rowan | 21st | 1st Div | Circuit Judge | William B Mains | (606) 784-5190 |
| Rowan | 21st | 2nd Div | Circuit Judge | Beth Lewis Maze | (859) 498-0488 |
| Russell | 57th | 1st Div | Circuit Judge | Vernon Miniard Jr | (270) 343-2131 |
| Scott | 14th | 1st Div | Circuit Judge | Robert G Johnson | (502) 570-0947 |
| Scott | 14th | 2nd Div | Circuit Judge | Paul F Isaacs | (502) 863-4781 |
| Shelby | 53rd | 1st Div | Circuit Judge | Charles R Hickman | (502) 647-5234 |
| Simpson | 49th | 1st Div | Circuit Judge | William R Harris | (270) 586-8058 |
| Spencer | 53rd | 1st Div | Circuit Judge | Charles R Hickman | (502) 647-5234 |
| Taylor | 11th | 1st Div | Circuit Judge | Douglas M George | (859) 336-3903 |
| Taylor | 11th | 2nd Div | Circuit Judge | Allen Ray Bertram | (270) 465-6603 |
| Todd | 7th | 1st Div | Circuit Judge | Tyler Gill | (270) 726-2242 |
| Trigg | 56th | 1st Div | Circuit Judge | Bill Cunningham | (270) 388-5182 |
| Trimble | 12th | 1st Div | Circuit Judge | Karen A Conrad | (502) 222-1692 |
| Trimble | 12th | 2nd Div | Family Court Judge | Timothy Edward Feeley | (502) 222-2490 |
| Union | 5th | 1st Div | Circuit Judge | C René Williams | (270) 639-5506 |
| Union | 5th | 2nd Div | Family Court Judge | William E Mitchell | (270) 639-5094 |
| Warren | 8th | 1st Div | Circuit Judge | Steve Alan Wilson | (270) 746-7412 |
| Warren | 8th | 2nd Div | Circuit Judge | John Grise | (270) 746-7408 |
| Warren | 8th | 2nd Div | Family Court Judge | Catherine Rice Holderfield | (270) 746-7190 |
| Warren | 8th | 3rd Div | Family Court Judge | Margaret R Huddleston | (270) 746-7144 |
| Washington | 11th | 1st Div | Circuit Judge | Douglas M George | (859) 336-3903 |
| Wayne | 57th | 1st Div | Circuit Judge | Vernon Miniard Jr | (270) 343-2131 |
| Webster | 5th | 1st Div | Circuit Judge | C René Williams | (270) 639-5506 |
| Webster | 5th | 2nd Div | Family Court Judge | William E Mitchell | (270) 639-5094 |
| Whitley | 34th | 1st Div | Circuit Judge | Jerry D Winchester | (606) 528-3013 |
| Whitley | 34th | 2nd Div | Circuit Judge | Paul E Braden | (606) 528-3013 |
| Wolfe | 39th | 1st Div | Circuit Judge | William Larry Miller | (606) 668-7590 |
| Woodford | 14th | 1st Div | Circuit Judge | Robert G Johnson | (502) 570-0947 |
| Woodford | 14th | 2nd Div | Circuit Judge | Paul F Isaacs | (502) 863-4781 |

*Source: Kentucky Directory Gold Book 2006-2007*

# District Judges

| COUNTY | DISTRICT | DIVISION | JUDGE | PHONE |
|--------|----------|----------|-------|-------|
| Adair | (29th) | 1st Div | Roger P Elliott | (606) 787-6761 |
| Allen | (49th) | 1st Div | Frank H Wakefield II | (270) 586-8717 |
| Anderson | (53rd) | 1st Div | Linda S Armstrong | (502) 633-4130 |
| Anderson | (53rd) | 2nd Div | Michael Harrod | (502) 633-6313 |
| Ballard | (59th) | 1st Div | Louis Keith Myers | (270) 335-5138 |
| Barren | (43rd) | 1st Div | Barlow Ropp | (270) 651-9839 |
| Bath | (21st) | 1st Div | William E (Bill) Lane | (859) 498-6622 |
| Bath | (21st) | 2nd Div | John R Cox | (606) 784-6888 |
| Bell | (44th) | 1st Div | Robert Vincent Costanzo | (606) 337-1149 |
| Boone | (54th) | 1st Div | Michael P Collins | (859) 334-2230 |
| Boone | (54th) | 2nd Div | Charles T Moore | (859) 334-2230 |
| Bourbon | (14th) | 1st Div | Mary Jane Wilhoit Phelps | (859) 879-9871 |
| Bourbon | (14th) | 2nd Div | Vanessa Dickson | (859) 987-5562 |
| Boyd | (32nd) | 1st Div | George W Davis III | (606) 739-5444 |
| Boyd | (32nd) | 2nd Div | Gerald Brock Reams Jr | (606) 739-5525 |
| Boyle | (50th) | 2nd Div | Jeff L Dotson | (859) 734-6343 |
| Bracken | (19th) | 1st Div | William (Todd) Walton | (606) 845-1037 |
| Breathitt | (39th) | 1st Div | Kenny Profitt | (606) 663-4123 |
| Breckinridge | (46th) | 1st Div | Tom Lively | (270) 259-6785 |
| Breckinridge | (46th) | 2nd Div | Shan Embry | (270) 259-5890 |
| Bullitt | (55th) | 1st Div | Rebecca S Ward | (502) 543-2243 |
| Bullitt | (55th) | 2nd Div | A Bailey Taylor | (502) 543-2243 |
| Butler | (38th) | 1st Div | Renona Carol Browning | (270) 298-3223 |
| Butler | (38th) | 2nd Div | John M McCarty | (270) 298-3223 |
| Caldwell | (56th) | 1st Div | James Rodman Redd III | (270) 365-6656 |
| Caldwell | (56th) | 2nd Div | Jill Clark | (270) 522-7979 |
| Calloway | (42nd) | 1st Div | Jeanne Carroll | (270) 753-0059 |
| Campbell | (17th) | 1st Div | Gregory T Popovich | (859) 292-6322 |
| Campbell | (17th) | 3rd Div | Karen A Thomas | (859) 292-6322 |
| Carlisle | (59th) | 1st Div | Louis K Myers | (270) 335-5138 |
| Carroll | (15th) | 1st Div | James L Purcell | (859) 824-0189 |
| Carroll | (15th) | 2nd Div | Thomas M Funk | (859) 824-0189 |
| Carter | (37th) | 1st Div | Kimberly I Gevedon | (606) 473-3866 |
| Casey | (29th) | 1st Div | Roger P Elliott | (606) 787-6761 |
| Christian | (3rd) | 1st Div | James G Adams Jr | (270) 889-6544 |
| Christian | (3rd) | 2nd Div | Arnold B Lynch | (270) 889-6544 |
| Clark | (25th) | 2nd Div | Brandy Oliver Brown | (859) 624-4719 |
| Clark | (25th) | 3rd Div | Bill Clouse | (859) 624-4719 |
| Clay | (41st) | 1st Div | Renee H Muncy | (606) 672-3350 |
| Clay | (41st) | 2nd Div | Oscar Gayle House | (606) 598-6170 |
| Clinton | (40th) | 1st Div | Robyn Edmond Williams | (270) 866-4500 |
| Clinton | (40th) | 2nd Div | James (Mike) Lawson | (606) 387-8682 |
| Crittenden | (5th) | 1st Div | Thomas E Simpson | (270) 389-0644 |
| Cumberland | (60th) | 2nd Div | Steve D Hurt | (270) 864-5600 |
| Daviess | (6th) | 1st Div | Lisa Jones | (270) 687-7216 |
| Daviess | (6th) | 2nd Div | David C Payne | (270) 687-7214 |
| Daviess | (6th) | 3rd Div | Joseph (Joe) Castlen III | (270) 687-7217 |
| Edmonson | (38th) | 1st Div | Ranona Carol Browning | (270) 298-3223 |
| Edmonson | (38th) | 2nd Div | John M McCarty | (270) 927-8800 |
| Elliott | (37th) | 1st Div | Kimberly I Gevedon | (606) 473-3866 |
| Estill | (23rd) | 1st Div | Ralph E McClanahan II | (606) 723-2000 |
| Fayette | (22nd) | 1st Div | Joseph Bouvier | (859) 246-2247 |
| Fayette | (22nd) | 2nd Div | Thomas Bruce Bell | (859) 246-2247 |
| Fayette | (22nd) | 3rd Div | Maria Ransdell | (859) 246-2247 |
| Fayette | (22nd) | 4th Div | David F Hayse | (859) 246-2247 |
| Fayette | (22nd) | 6th Div | Megan Lake Thornton | (859) 246-2247 |
| Fleming | (19th) | 1st Div | William (Todd) Walton | (606) 845-1037 |
| Floyd | (31st) | 1st Div | James R Allen | (606) 889-1816 |
| Floyd | (31st) | 2nd Div | Eric D Hall | (606) 889-1661 |
| Franklin | (48th) | 1st Div | Thomas D Wingate | (502) 564-7073 |
| Franklin | (48th) | 2nd Div | William (Guy) Hart Jr | (502) 564-7073 |
| Fulton | (1st) | 1st Div | Hunter B Whitesell II | (270) 236-2839 |
| Gallatin | (54th) | 1st Div | Michael Collins | (859) 334-2230 |
| Gallatin | (54th) | 2nd Div | Charles T Moore | (859) 334-2230 |
| Garrard | (13th) | 1st Div | Bill Oliver | (859) 885-5615 |
| Garrard | (13th) | 2nd Div | Janet Carroll Booth | (859) 885-5615 |
| Grant | (15th) | 1st Div | James L Purcell | (859) 824-0189 |
| Grant | (15th) | 2nd Div | Thomas M Funk | (859) 824-0189 |
| Graves | (52nd) | 1st Div | Deborah Hawkins Crooks | (270) 247-0580 |
| Grayson | (46th) | 1st Div | Tom Lively | (270) 259-6785 |
| Grayson | (46th) | 2nd Div | Shan Embry | (270) 259-5890 |
| Green | (11th) | 1st Div | James L Avritt Jr | (270) 699-9951 |
| Green | (11th) | 2nd Div | Connie Phillips | (270) 465-8424 |
| Greenup | (20th) | 1st Div | Robert B Conley | (606) 473-6339 |
| Hancock | (38th) | 1st Div | Renona C Browning | (270) 298-3223 |
| Hancock | (38th) | 2nd Div | John M McCarty | (270) 298-3223 |
| Hardin | (9th) | 1st Div | John David Simcoe | (270) 766-5004 |
| Hardin | (9th) | 2nd Div | Kimberly Winkenhofer Shumate | (270) 766-5005 |

## DISTRICT JUDGES, CONTINUED

| COUNTY | DISTRICT | DIVISION | JUDGE | PHONE |
|---|---|---|---|---|
| Harlan | (26th) | 1st Div | Phillip A Hamm | (606) 573-7209 |
| Harrison | (18th) | 2nd Div | William D Probus | (859) 234-1918 |
| Hart | (10th) | 1st Div | Clyde Derek Reed | (270) 358-9501 |
| Henderson | (51st) | 1st Div | Robert K Wiederstein | (270) 826-4755 |
| Henderson | (51st) | 2nd Div | Kenton J Watson | (270) 826-4755 |
| Henry | (12th) | 1st Div | Jerry D Crosby | (502) 222-7447 |
| Henry | (12th) | 2nd Div | Jerry D Crosby | (502) 222-7447 |
| Hickman | (1st) | 1st Div | Hunter B Whitesell II | (270) 236-2839 |
| Hopkins | (4th) | 1st Div | W Logan Calvert | (270) 824-7513 |
| Hopkins | (4th) | 2nd Div | Robert F Soder | (270) 824-7512 |
| Jackson | (41st) | 1st Div | Renee H Muncy | (606) 672-3350 |
| Jackson | (41st) | 2nd Div | Oscar Gayle House | (606) 598-6170 |
| Jefferson | (30th) | 10th Div | Sheila Anne Collins | (502) 595-4995 |
| Jefferson | (30th) | 11th Div | Matthew K Eckert | (502) 595-4992 |
| Jefferson | (30th) | 12th Div | Angela Bisig McCormick | (502) 595-3314 |
| Jefferson | (30th) | 13th Div | Joan (Toni) A Stringer | (502) 595-4960 |
| Jefferson | (30th) | 14th Div | Jacquelyn Eckertt | (502) 595-4983 |
| Jefferson | (30th) | 15th Div | Anne Haynie | (502) 595-4611 |
| Jefferson | (30th) | 16th Div | Audra J Eckerle | (502) 595-4990 |
| Jefferson | (30th) | 17th Div | Judith A Bartholomew | (502) 595-4162 |
| Jefferson | (30th) | 1st Div | Paula Fitzgerald | (502) 595-4994 |
| Jefferson | (30th) | 2nd Div | Kevin W Delahanty | (502) 595-4957 |
| Jefferson | (30th) | 3rd Div | Claude Prather | (502) 595-4610 |
| Jefferson | (30th) | 4th Div | Michele Stengel | (502) 595-4989 |
| Jefferson | (30th) | 5th Div | Donald E Armstrong Jr | (502) 595-4632 |
| Jefferson | (30th) | 6th Div | Sean R Delahanty | (502) 595-4991 |
| Jefferson | (30th) | 7th Div | William (Bill) Ryan | (502) 595-4997 |
| Jefferson | (30th) | 8th Div | Deborah Deweese | (502) 595-4696 |
| Jefferson | (30th) | 9th Div | Janice Martin | (502) 595-4999 |
| Jessamine | (13th) | 1st Div | Bill Oliver | (859) 885-5615 |
| Jessamine | (13th) | 2nd Div | Janet Carroll Booth | (859) 885-5615 |
| Johnson | (24th) | 1st Div | Susan M Johnson | (606) 297-9581 |
| Johnson | (24th) | 2nd Div | John Kevin Holbrook | (606) 297-9583 |
| Kenton | (16th) | 1st Div | Ann Ruttle | (859) 292-6576 |
| Kenton | (16th) | 2nd Div | Frank Trusty II | (859) 292-6561 |
| Kenton | (16th) | 3rd Div | Douglas J Grothaus | (859) 292-6576 |
| Kenton | (16th) | 4th Div | Martin J Sheehan | (859) 292-6561 |
| Knott | (36th) | 1st Div | Dennis B Prater | (606) 785-3078 |
| Knox | (27th) | 1st Div | John Knox Mills | (606) 864-7241 |
| Knox | (27th) | 2nd Div | Michael Caperton | (606) 864-7241 |
| Larue | (10th) | 1st Div | Clyde Derek Reed | (270) 358-9501 |
| Laurel | (27th) | 1st Div | John Knox Mills | (606) 864-7241 |
| Laurel | (27th) | 2nd Div | Michael Caperton | (606) 864-7241 |
| Lawrence | (24th) | 1st Div | Susan M Johnson | (606) 789-8636 |
| Lawrence | (24th) | 2nd Div | John Kevin Holbrook | (606) 789-8636 |
| Lee | (23rd) | 1st Div | Ralph E McClanahan II | (606) 723-2000 |
| Leslie | (41st) | 1st Div | Renee H Muncy | (606) 672-3350 |
| Leslie | (41st) | 2nd Div | Oscar Gayle House | (606) 598-6170 |
| Letcher | (47th) | 1st Div | James T (Jim) Wood Jr | (606) 633-4222 |
| Lewis | (20th) | 1st Div | Robert B Conley | (606) 473-6339 |
| Lincoln | (13th) | 1st Div | Bill Oliver | (859) 885-5615 |
| Lincoln | (13th) | 2nd Div | Janet Carroll Booth | (859) 885-5615 |
| Livingston | (56th) | 1st Div | James Rodman Redd III | (270) 365-6656 |
| Livingston | (56th) | 2nd Div | Jill Clark | (270) 522-7979 |
| Logan | (7th) | 1st Div | Sue Carol Browning | (270) 726-8080 |
| Lyon | (56th) | 1st Div | James Rodman Redd III | (270) 365-6656 |
| Lyon | (56th) | 2nd Div | Jill Clark | (270) 522-7979 |
| Madison | (25th) | 2nd Div | Brandy Oliver Brown | (859) 624-4719 |
| Madison | (25th) | 3rd Div | Bill Clouse | (859) 624-4719 |
| Magoffin | (36th) | 1st Div | Dennis B Prater | (606) 785-3078 |
| Marion | (11th) | 1st Div | James L Avritt Jr | (270) 699-9951 |
| Marion | (11th) | 2nd Div | Connie Phillips | (270) 465-8424 |
| Marshall | (58th) | 1st Div | Jack M Telle | (270) 527-3390 |
| Martin | (24th) | 1st Div | Susan M Johnson | (606) 789-8636 |
| Martin | (24th) | 2nd Div | John Kevin Holbrook | (606) 789-8636 |
| Mason | (19th) | 1st Div | William (Todd) Walton | (606) 845-1037 |
| McCracken | (2nd) | 1st Div | Donna L Dixon | (270) 575-7261 |
| McCracken | (2nd) | 2nd Div | Bard Kevin Brian | (270) 575-7261 |
| McCreary | (34th) | 1st Div | Cathy E Prewitt | (606) 528-4430 |
| McCreary | (34th) | 2nd Div | Daniel Ballou | (606) 549-5669 |
| McLean | (45th) | 1st Div | Brian W Wiggins | (270) 338-0995 |
| Meade | (46th) | 1st Div | Tom Lively | (270) 259-6785 |
| Meade | (46th) | 2nd Div | Shan Embry | (270) 259-5890 |
| Menifee | (21st) | 1st Div | William E (Bill) Lane | (859) 498-6622 |
| Menifee | (21st) | 2nd Div | John R Cox | (606) 784-6888 |
| Mercer | (50th) | 1st Div | Jeff L Dotson | (859) 734-6343 |
| Metcalfe | (43rd) | 1st Div | Barlow Ropp | (270) 651-9839 |
| Monroe | (60th) | 2nd Div | Steve D Hurt | (270) 864-5600 |

## DISTRICT JUDGES, CONTINUED

| COUNTY | DISTRICT | DIVISION | JUDGE | PHONE |
|---|---|---|---|---|
| Montgomery | (21st) | 1st Div | William E (Bill) Lane | (859) 498-6622 |
| Montgomery | (21st) | 2nd Div | John R Cox | (859) 784-6888 |
| Morgan | (37th) | 1st Div | Kimberly I Gevedon | (606) 473-3866 |
| Muhlenberg | (45th) | 1st Div | Brian W Wiggins | (270) 338-0995 |
| Nelson | (57th) | 1st Div | Robert W Heaton | (502) 348-2012 |
| Nicholas | (18th) | 2nd Div | William D Probus | (859) 234-1918 |
| Ohio | (38th) | 1st Div | Ranona Carol Browning | (270) 298-3223 |
| Ohio | (38th) | 2nd Div | John M McCarty | (270) 298-3223 |
| Oldham | (12th) | 1st Div | Diana Wheeler | (502) 222-7447 |
| Oldham | (12th) | 2nd Div | Jerry D Crosby | (502) 222-7447 |
| Owen | (15th) | 1st Div | James L Purcell | (859) 824-0189 |
| Owen | (15th) | 2nd Div | Thomas M Funk | (859) 824-0189 |
| Owsley | (23rd) | 1st Div | Ralph E McClanahan II | (606) 723-2000 |
| Pendleton | (18th) | 2nd Div | William D Probus | (859) 234-1918 |
| Perry | (33rd) | 1st Div | Leigh Anne Stephens | (606) 435-6007 |
| Pike | (35th) | 1st Div | Darrel Mullins | (606) 433-7562 |
| Pike | (35th) | 2nd Div | Kelsey E Friend | (606) 433-7561 |
| Powell | (39th) | 1st Div | Kenny Profitt | (606) 663-4123 |
| Pulaski | (28th) | 1st Div | Jeffery Scott Lawless | (606) 677-4112 |
| Pulaski | (28th) | 2nd Div | Kathryn G Wood | (606) 677-4112 |
| Robertson | (18th) | 2nd Div | William D Probus | (859) 234-1918 |
| Rockcastle | (28th) | 1st Div | Jeffery Scott Lawless | (606) 677-4112 |
| Rockcastle | (28th) | 2nd Div | Kathryn G Wood | (606) 677-4112 |
| Rowan | (21st) | 1st Div | William E (Bill) Lane | (859) 498-6622 |
| Rowan | (21st) | 2nd Div | John R Cox | (606) 784-6888 |
| Russell | (40th) | 1st Div | Robyn Edmond Williams | (270) 866-4500 |
| Russell | (40th) | 2nd Div | James (Mike) Lawson | (606) 387-8682 |
| Scott | (14th) | 1st Div | Mary Jane Wilhoit Phelps | (859) 879-9871 |
| Scott | (14th) | 2nd Div | Vanessa M Dickson | (859) 987-5562 |
| Shelby | (53rd) | 1st Div | Linda S Armstrong | (502) 633-4130 |
| Shelby | (53rd) | 2nd Div | Michael Harrod | (502) 633-0486 |
| Simpson | (49th) | 1st Div | Frank Wakefield | (270) 586-8717 |
| Spencer | (53rd) | 1st Div | Linda S Armstrong | (502) 633-4130 |
| Spencer | (53rd) | 2nd Div | Michael Harrod | (502) 633-0486 |
| Taylor | (11th) | 1st Div | James L Avritt Jr | (270) 699-9951 |
| Taylor | (11th) | 2nd Div | Connie Phillips | (270) 465-8424 |
| Todd | (7th) | 1st Div | Sue Carol Browning | (270) 726-8080 |
| Trigg | (56th) | 1st Div | James Rodman Redd III | (270) 365-6656 |
| Trigg | (56th) | 2nd Div | Jill Clark | (270) 522-7979 |
| Trimble | (12th) | 1st Div | Diana Wheeler | (502) 222-7447 |
| Trimble | (12th) | 2nd Div | Jerry D Crosby | (502) 222-7447 |
| Union | (5th) | 1st Div | Thomas E Simpson | (270) 389-0644 |
| Warren | (8th) | 1st Div | Catherine Rice Holderfield | (270) 746-7405 |
| Warren | (8th) | 2nd Div | Brent J Potter | (270) 746-7060 |
| Warren | (8th) | 3rd Div | Sam C Potter Jr | (270) 746-7028 |
| Washington | (11th) | 1st Div | James L Avritt Jr | (270) 699-9951 |
| Washington | (11th) | 2nd Div | Connie Phillips | (270) 465-8424 |
| Wayne | (40th) | 1st Div | Robyn Edmond Williams | (270) 866-4500 |
| Wayne | (40th) | 2nd Div | James (Mike) Lawson | (606) 387-8682 |
| Webster | (5th) | 1st Div | Thomas E Simpson | (270) 389-0644 |
| Whitley | (34th) | 1st Div | Cathy E Prewitt | (606) 528-4430 |
| Whitley | (34th) | 2nd Div | Daniel Ballou | (606) 549-5669 |
| Wolfe | (39th) | 1st Div | Kenny Profitt | (606) 663-4123 |
| Woodford | (14th) | 1st Div | Mary Jane Wilhoit Phelps | (859) 879-9871 |
| Woodford | (14th) | 2nd Div | Vanessa Dickson | (859) 987-5562 |

*Source: Kentucky Directory Gold Book 2006-2007*

## Well, What about that?

FAMILY COURT — Kentucky voters gave Family Court a resounding victory in November 2002 when the constitutional amendment passed in all 120 counties with more than 75 percent of the vote. Family Court judges handle all family law matters, like dissolution of marriage, child custody, support and visitation, paternity, adoption, domestic violence, dependency, neglect and abuse. ...

*Source: Kentucky Court of Justice, www.kycourts.net*

# State Government & Politics
## *Kentucky Politics*

Commentary by Al Cross

The moonlight falls the softest
in Kentucky;
The summer days come oftest
in Kentucky;
Friendship is the strongest,
Love's light glows the longest,
Yet wrong is always wrongest
in Kentucky.

. . . Orators are the grandest
in Kentucky.
Officials are the blandest
in Kentucky.
Boys are all the fliest.
Danger ever nighest,
Taxes are the highest
in Kentucky.

. . . Song birds are the sweetest
in Kentucky.
The thoroughbreds are fleetest
in Kentucky.
Mountains tower proudest,
Thunder peals the loudest,
The landscape is the grandest
And politics – the damndest,
in Kentucky.

*First, middle and last stanzas of*
*In Kentucky, 1902,*
*by James Henry Mulligan*

When Lexington's Judge Mulligan
wrote those words, Kentucky
politics certainly were the
damndest. Two years
before, Kentucky had
become the only state in
which a governor was the
victim of an assassin.
   It is still the only such
state and still often
seems to be struggling
to relieve itself of other
dubious distinctions.
   In 1902, Kentucky
still lacked the
"efficient" sys-
tem of public

**Statue of Gov. William Goebel, assassinated in 1900**
*Photo: Sid Webb*

education promised by the 1890 amendments to the state's constitution. Kentucky leaders couldn't figure out what to do with gambling, which was keeping its horse industry going as automobiles replaced equine transport. As a gambling ban was debated, so was Prohibition, which was to drive the state's other big "sin" industry underground a few years later.

Today, the constitution is much amended but still largely in effect, and it appears there is no longer momentum behind the 1990 education reforms that stemmed from the courts' interpretation of the efficiency clause. Some estimate gambling in adjoining states is draining a billion dollars a year from Kentucky, as political leaders dither about it. The "sin business" that kept rural Kentucky going for most of the 20th century, tobacco, is largely a spent force, with the end of federal quotas and price supports, and beyond cattle, we have seen little impact from the cigarette-firm money allocated to build a new farm economy.

Yet, if Kentucky's political system continues to fail its people, why? Perhaps because those in the system have become more concerned with staying in the system. Instead of the next election being about the sort of government we will have, our government is too often about what sort of election we will have.

**(left) Gov. Wendell H. Ford and (above) Gov. John Y. Brown**
Source: Kentucky Department of Tourism

Partisan competition and gridlock are ingrained in Kentucky. After the state elected its first Republican governor in 1895, the legislature deadlocked for 103 ballots and failed to elect a U.S. senator. But partisanship has become incessant in the modern era, in which legislators serve longer, party control of the General Assembly is divided, governors can succeed themselves, success comes most often to candidates well-funded by lobbying interests, and even legislative elections are big-money affairs driven by broadcast advertising.

Partisan competition took a back seat to competition between Democratic factions and gubernatorial campaigns in the 60 years from 1943 to 2003, when Kentucky elected only one Republican governor. That was Louie B. Nunn, who undercut his party and his own political career by pushing a 1968 sales-tax increase. The increase continued the progressive policies of Gov. Edward Breathitt (who had defeated him in 1963) and Gov. Bert Combs (who had succeeded former Gov. and Sen. Earle Clements as head of the progressive Democratic faction that opposed the faction headed by A.B. "Happy" Chandler, who was governor twice, U.S. senator and commissioner of baseball).

The bifactional system died with the 1979 primary. Millionaire John Y. Brown Jr. won it as an anti-politician with his new wife, former Miss America Phyllis George, defeating candidates from various elements of the party. Since then, Democratic primary candidates for governor have always had more than one opponent.

But while Democrats ruled Frankfort, Kentuckians voted Republican in 10 of the state's 14 elections for president and senator from 1952 to 1972. That reflected the essential conservatism of the state's voters, which Republicans capitalized upon after economic concerns were trumped by social issues – beginning with the 1973 U.S. Supreme Court decision legalizing abortion.

Kentucky is one of the most religious states – and Republicans gained further when national Democrats supported gay rights and a Democratic president and Democratic governor admitted infidelity in 1998 and 2002, respectively. Gun control was important, too, and was key in historically Democratic West Kentucky's election of its first Republican congressman, Ed Whitfield, in 1994. Republicans won on "God, gays and guns" and finally on tobacco, after Bill Clinton tried to regulate nicotine as a drug.

Clinton narrowly carried Kentucky twice, following a pattern that had begun in 1952, in which the state voted Republican for president unless a Southerner headed the Democratic ticket. That trend stopped cold in 2000, when Republican George W. Bush of Texas carried the state by 15 percentage points over Al Gore, who was nominally from Tennessee but to most Kentuckians seemed less like a neighbor than Clinton's vice president. The race in Kentucky would have been closer if Gore's campaign had not virtually abandoned the state.

In 2004, John Kerry lost the state by 20 points after making only minimal effort here, other than a successful fundraiser in Louisville (the only Kentucky place of any size he won).

## THE MCCONNELL ERA

The architect of Republican success in Kentucky was Mitch McConnell, who narrowly won re-election as Jefferson County judge-executive in 1981 but used smart strategy and Ronald Reagan's national success in 1984 to oust a Democratic U.S. senator.

After McConnell won re-election in 1990, he guided Republicans to victories in federal races, beginning with the 1994 special election of Ron Lewis in the 2nd Congressional District, the forerunner of that fall's national GOP landslide. In regular elections since 1996, Republicans have won five of the state's six House seats, and in 1998 GOP Rep. Jim Bunning won the Senate seat of retiring Democrat and former governor, Wendell Ford.

The night McConnell escaped defeat in 1981, Ford smelled trouble. He told pollster Harrison Hickman, "We'll rue the day we didn't beat this guy." Three years later, McConnell narrowly ousted Walter "Dee" Huddleston, who had managed Ford's 1971 campaign for governor and had defeated Nunn for the Senate in 1972.

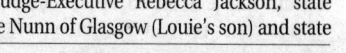

**Sen. Mitch McConnell and his wife, U.S. Secretary of Labor Elaine L. Chao**
*Source: U.S. Senator Mitch McConnell*

The hallmark of McConnell's campaign were ads in which bloodhounds searched for Huddleston, putting a humorous, memorable point on McConnell's argument that Huddleston had missed votes to make speeches. The ads were produced by Roger Ailes, who now runs Fox News. Their underlying argument, that Huddleston hadn't done much in the Senate, capitalized on the Democrat's relatively low profile and vote for the treaty that gave up the Panama Canal.

McConnell and Ford were opposites who never got along in their 14 years together in the Senate. Ford disliked McConnell's cold, technical and impersonal approach to politics, while the newcomer dismissed Ford as an old-fashioned hack who was never really happy in the Senate and longed to be governor again. In their final face-off, over competing tobacco bills in 1998, McConnell narrowly prevailed.

Ford was the whip, or assistant leader, of his party caucus in the Senate. McConnell now holds that post for the Republicans, and is in line to become Senate majority leader after the 2006 elections, when Bill Frist of Tennessee gives up the job and his Senate seat to run for president. McConnell would break Ford's 24-year record service by a Kentucky senator if he is re-elected in 2008.

## CURRENT STATE POLITICS

Even as Gov. Paul Patton was coasting to re-election in 1999 (the first governor in 200 years to serve two terms in succession, thanks to a 1992 constitutional amendment), his Democratic Party's control of Frankfort was broken when two state senators became Republicans. The GOP-controlled Senate, led by strong President David Williams of Burkesville, stymied Patton's agenda and killed a centerpiece Democratic program – public subsidies for gubernatorial slates that observed a campaign spending limit. McConnell, a leading national foe of such systems, had said it made a Republican victory in the 1999 race impossible, and openly told Republicans not to run.

Patton could not seek a third term in 2003, but hoped to oust Bunning in 2004. However, Patton's political career crashed when he first denied, and then tearfully admitted, infidelity with a political appointee whose nursing home later came under state investigation. Those were the underlying facts of the campaign theme of Republican Ernie Fletcher, who vowed to "clean up the mess in Frankfort."

Fletcher, a congressman from Lexington, ran with McConnell's encouragement and a McConnell running mate – top senatorial aide Hunter Bates, who pulled out after a judge ruled he had resided too much in Washington and not enough in Kentucky. Bates was replaced by U.S. Attorney Steve Pence, a McConnell appointee who won fame by prosecuting legislators and lobbyists in a big federal sting a decade earlier.

Fletcher won the primary over former Jefferson County Judge-Executive Rebecca Jackson, state Rep. Steve Nunn of Glasgow (Louie's son) and state

Sen. Virgil Moore of Leitchfield. He won a 10.1-percentage-point victory over Attorney General Ben Chandler of Versailles, Happy's grandson, who had been adverse to Patton but found that it was not a good time to be a Democrat.

Chandler had also been hurt by the final flurry in the Democratic primary. About three and a half days before the polls opened, record-spending multimillionaire Bruce Lunsford ceased his campaign and threw his support to state House Speaker Jody Richards of Bowling Green, creating an anti-Chandler wave that nearly propelled Richards to a huge upset. Chandler looked weak, and a post-election poll showed him trailing Fletcher. He never caught up.

In 2004, Chandler won a special election to fill Fletcher's congressional vacancy, defeating state Sen. Alice Forgy Kerr of Lexington.

**Gov. Ernie Fletcher**
*Source: Kentucky Commerce Cabinet, Creative Services*

## FACTS AND FIGURES, THE PAST AND THE FUTURE

Kentucky's Republican trend has been reflected not just in elections, but in voter-registration statistics and polls of party preference, which are better long-term measurements than individual elections.

In 1983, Kentucky had nearly five registered Democrats for every two Republicans. Today, that ratio of 2.5-to-1 has declined to less than 1.6-to-1. Polls that ask voters to which party they feel closer, regardless of registration, no longer show a clear Democratic advantage.

The trend is not just the result of social issues and McConnell strategy, but the gradual passing of voters who came of age and formed their political beliefs during the Democratic presidencies of Franklin Roosevelt in 1933-1945 and Harry Truman, who succeeded Roosevelt and was elected in his own right in 1948, with Sen. Alben Barkley of Kentucky as vice president. Roosevelt's legacies, which included the federal tobacco program, rural electrification, the Tennessee Valley Authority, Corps of Engineers lakes and Social Security, were strong in Kentucky.

The impacts of those legacies and the Roosevelt generation were last felt in a big way in 1995, when Patton narrowly defeated Larry Forgy. The difference was a larger-than-expected turnout, driven by a well-funded and smartly run Democratic Party campaign that operated outside the spending limit and federalized the election.

Democrats' turnout and broadcast messages focused on supposed Republican threats to Roosevelt-era programs and featured Kentucky versions of the "Dole-Gingrich" ads that Clinton used to great effect, beginning a few weeks earlier. Clinton and Patton had the same media consultant, the late Bob Squier. The message was so important to Patton that on a final-week swing through southern Kentucky, where Democrats could not afford to buy spots on Nashville television, he preceded his speeches by playing his party's commercials on a TV set sitting in the bed of a pickup truck.

Forgy blamed his loss on Democratic chicanery – later, Patton's campaign manager (who had become his chief of staff) and his labor liaison were indicted on charges of getting unions to pay the labor aide to run a parallel campaign aimed at union members. Courts upheld the indictment, despite arguments – including one from McConnell – that the 1992 campaign law violated First Amendment freedoms. But Patton, already mired in a sex scandal, pardoned his allies, ending the criminal case.

Fletcher was elected on Patton's scandal, and support from the rest of the state's congressional delegation. That unusual path to the governorship left him without a strong base. That showed in 2005, when Attorney General Greg Stumbo, a Democrat, investigated the administration's hiring practices and Fletcher plummeted in the polls. Nine Fletcher appointees were indicted on misdemeanor charges of politicizing career employment. He issued a pardon for anyone in the probe, except himself, but later fired some of the indicted aides. In 2006, he was indicted on three misdemeanor charges, and leading Republicans questioned his re-election prospects. But his stock in the GOP rose after Stumbo dropped the charges in return for Fletcher's statements that the evidence strongly indicated wrongdoing by the administration, that he accepted responsibility without acknowledging wrongdoing, and that the investigation was proper – contrary to his repeated charges it was political. The deal also helped Stumbo, who had said he wouldn't run against Fletcher as long as he was prosecuting him. Once again, Kentucky's politics were the damndest.

*Al Cross, veteran political writer, is the director of the Institute for Rural Journalism and Community Issues at the University of Kentucky.*

## STATE GOVERNMENT & POLITICS

# *Honorable Order of Kentucky Colonels*

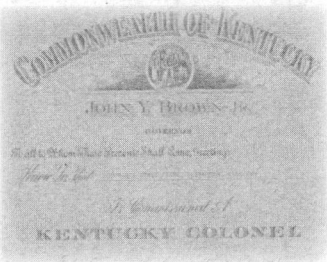

From the beginning, the Honorable Order of Kentucky Colonels has had the advancement of Kentucky and Kentuckians as its guiding principal. "The beginning" was late one Saturday afternoon in May of 1931 when a group of Colonels wishing to organize into a formal unit met with Governor Flem Sampson. The Governor directed the attendees to "formulate a society to more closely band together this group into a great non-political brotherhood for the advancement of Kentucky and Kentuckians." Today, nearly 75 years later, the Honorable Order continues to exemplify the ideals spelled out in that organizational meeting.

The title Kentucky Colonel has been around since 1813. The Kentucky Militia had just returned from a highly successful "War of 1812" campaign that resulted in control of the Northwest being returned to the U.S. When the militia disbanded, Governor Isaac Shelby commissioned Charles S.

**Kentucky Col. Ben Labree, curator of "My Old Kentucky Home" with Col. Thomas P. Henry, President of the American Automobile Association**
*Photo: Frank C. Dunn, Kentucky Virtual Library*

Todd, one of his officers in the campaign, as an AID-DE-CAMP with the rank and grade of Colonel.

Early Colonels served military roles. In the late1800s, the position took on a more ceremonial function. By the late 1800s, the title had become more of an honorary one. In the late 1920s, a group of Colonels talked about forming a "society," and Governor Flem Sampson gave his blessings several years later in 1931. Ruby Laffoon, who had an innate sense of public relations—and an affinity for Hollywood stars—became governor in 1932. Soon thereafter, Laffoon met with Colonel Anna Bell Ward

Olsen who owned movie theaters across Kentucky. A representative of theater owners nationwide, also a Kentucky Colonel, accompanied Colonel Olsen. Out of the meeting a "new" organization to be called the Honorable Order of Kentucky Colonels evolved. Laffoon appointed Colonel Olsen as Secretary and Keeper of the Great Seal.

Colonel Olson enthusiastically invited Colonels from around the world to become members of the Order. Social events coincided with the Kentucky Derby, and Governor Laffoon started appointing Colonels with the same zeal. Hollywood personalities such as Mae West, Clark Gable, Bing Crosby and Fred Astaire became Colonels and embraced the idea of the Honorable Order.

The Order would have a major impact on Kentucky when the disastrous Great Flood of 1937 struck. New York-based Colonels collected five dollars from each member; Colonel Fred Astaire held benefits to raise money for Kentucky. The charitable side of the Order grew rapidly, and Colonels continue to contribute to the goal of benefiting Kentucky and Kentuckians. Since 1951, as an IRS-recognized 501 (c) 3 charity, the Order has distributed over 5000 grants to charitable and educational agencies. For the last dozen years, the Order's Board of Trustees has distributed approximately 1.5 million dollars each year. Colonels living in every state in the nation as well as Colonels in nearly thirty-six nations abroad contribute money to the Order.

*Source: www.kycolonels.org*

**VOTER REGISTRATION - PARTY AFFILIATION - DATE: 8/15/06**

| COUNTY | NO. PRECINCTS | DEMOCRAT | REPUBLICAN | OTHER | MALE | FEMALE | TOTAL REGISTERED |
|---|---|---|---|---|---|---|---|
| ADAIR | 16 | 3,693 | 8,060 | 442 | 5,933 | 6,259 | 12,195 |
| ALLEN | 13 | 4,303 | 7,054 | 556 | 5,734 | 6,178 | 11,913 |
| ANDERSON | 14 | 9,706 | 4,112 | 576 | 6,889 | 7,505 | 14,394 |
| BALLARD | 13 | 5,027 | 757 | 154 | 2,861 | 3,077 | 5,938 |
| BARREN | 24 | 15,882 | 8,562 | 1,327 | 12,048 | 13,721 | 25,771 |
| BATH | 12 | 7,506 | 835 | 215 | 4,210 | 4,346 | 8,556 |
| BELL | 34 | 10,151 | 9,890 | 604 | 9,654 | 10,991 | 20,645 |
| BOONE | 58 | 25,300 | 35,729 | 7,981 | 32,841 | 36,167 | 69,010 |
| BOURBON | 18 | 9,340 | 2,772 | 626 | 5,985 | 6,753 | 12,738 |
| BOYD | 47 | 20,894 | 11,352 | 2,045 | 15,907 | 18,383 | 34,291 |
| BOYLE | 25 | 11,538 | 5,667 | 1,071 | 8,511 | 9,763 | 18,276 |
| BRACKEN | 8 | 4,761 | 986 | 189 | 2,922 | 3,014 | 5,936 |
| BREATHITT | 21 | 9,813 | 619 | 179 | 5,251 | 5,359 | 10,611 |
| BRECKINRIDGE | 15 | 7,220 | 5,747 | 651 | 6,711 | 6,904 | 13,618 |
| BULLITT | 44 | 26,536 | 15,831 | 3,426 | 22,129 | 23,661 | 45,793 |
| BUTLER | 12 | 1,706 | 6,752 | 201 | 4,175 | 4,484 | 8,659 |
| CALDWELL | 13 | 7,154 | 1,884 | 288 | 4,438 | 4,887 | 9,326 |
| CALLOWAY | 28 | 15,876 | 5,477 | 1,657 | 10,836 | 12,174 | 23,010 |
| CAMPBELL | 66 | 26,299 | 24,893 | 6,062 | 26,663 | 30,577 | 57,254 |
| CARLISLE | 7 | 3,345 | 478 | 74 | 1,868 | 2,029 | 3,897 |
| CARROLL | 11 | 5,933 | 778 | 260 | 3,353 | 3,618 | 6,971 |
| CARTER | 23 | 10,970 | 6,466 | 805 | 8,917 | 9,324 | 18,241 |
| CASEY | 15 | 1,999 | 8,458 | 231 | 5,213 | 5,475 | 10,688 |
| CHRISTIAN | 46 | 22,898 | 10,327 | 2,384 | 15,867 | 19,742 | 35,609 |
| CLARK | 25 | 15,291 | 6,674 | 1,199 | 10,951 | 12,213 | 23,164 |
| CLAY | 20 | 1,760 | 13,339 | 222 | 7,517 | 7,804 | 15,321 |
| CLINTON | 13 | 1,650 | 5,322 | 97 | 3,410 | 3,659 | 7,069 |
| CRITTENDEN | 12 | 3,246 | 2,671 | 283 | 2,972 | 3,228 | 6,200 |
| CUMBERLAND | 9 | 969 | 4,488 | 144 | 2,691 | 2,910 | 5,601 |
| DAVIESS | 85 | 39,358 | 18,233 | 3,749 | 28,521 | 32,819 | 61,340 |
| EDMONSON | 10 | 2,412 | 5,260 | 191 | 3,946 | 3,917 | 7,863 |
| ELLIOTT | 7 | 4,826 | 158 | 66 | 2,486 | 2,564 | 5,050 |
| ESTILL | 15 | 4,177 | 5,404 | 374 | 4,879 | 5,076 | 9,955 |
| FAYETTE | 250 | 87,270 | 61,501 | 15,964 | 75,829 | 88,906 | 164,735 |
| FLEMING | 18 | 6,975 | 2,433 | 294 | 4,743 | 4,959 | 9,702 |
| FLOYD | 42 | 27,636 | 2,678 | 505 | 15,091 | 15,727 | 30,819 |
| FRANKLIN | 44 | 24,303 | 5,632 | 1,460 | 14,233 | 17,116 | 31,395 |
| FULTON | 13 | 4,096 | 691 | 224 | 2,168 | 2,842 | 5,011 |
| GALLATIN | 8 | 3,819 | 1,241 | 248 | 2,616 | 2,692 | 5,308 |
| GARRARD | 13 | 3,980 | 6,296 | 570 | 5,272 | 5,574 | 10,846 |
| GRANT | 23 | 8,778 | 4,731 | 1,315 | 7,190 | 7,634 | 14,824 |
| GRAVES | 30 | 18,333 | 3,773 | 751 | 10,685 | 12,169 | 22,857 |

**VOTER REGISTRATION - PARTY AFFILIATION - DATE: 8/15/06**

| COUNTY | NO. PRECINCTS | DEMOCRAT | REPUBLICAN | OTHER | MALE | FEMALE | TOTAL REGISTERED |
|---|---|---|---|---|---|---|---|
| GRAYSON | 23 | 5,709 | 10,530 | 800 | 8,266 | 8,773 | 17,039 |
| GREEN | 10 | 3,178 | 4,864 | 192 | 4,017 | 4,217 | 8,234 |
| GREENUP | 32 | 16,140 | 8,117 | 1,361 | 12,308 | 13,300 | 25,618 |
| HANCOCK | 10 | 3,673 | 1,932 | 201 | 2,876 | 2,929 | 5,806 |
| HARDIN | 55 | 32,325 | 21,795 | 5,142 | 27,731 | 31,528 | 59,262 |
| HARLAN | 35 | 15,629 | 4,508 | 364 | 9,811 | 10,689 | 20,501 |
| HARRISON | 17 | 8,863 | 2,558 | 464 | 5,672 | 6,213 | 11,885 |
| HART | 19 | 8,341 | 3,467 | 364 | 5,873 | 6,299 | 12,172 |
| HENDERSON | 42 | 21,602 | 5,439 | 1,515 | 13,256 | 15,295 | 28,556 |
| HENRY | 20 | 7,275 | 2,537 | 472 | 4,945 | 5,339 | 10,284 |
| HICKMAN | 6 | 3,108 | 443 | 100 | 1,712 | 1,939 | 3,651 |
| HOPKINS | 40 | 22,132 | 6,875 | 1,264 | 14,042 | 16,228 | 30,271 |
| JACKSON | 14 | 1,083 | 8,062 | 206 | 4,609 | 4,742 | 9,351 |
| JEFFERSON | 516 | 266,528 | 153,151 | 42,148 | 208,802 | 253,024 | 461,827 |
| JESSAMINE | 35 | 14,728 | 11,942 | 2,041 | 13,559 | 15,151 | 28,711 |
| JOHNSON | 31 | 6,574 | 8,993 | 396 | 7,781 | 8,182 | 15,963 |
| KENTON | 108 | 43,798 | 43,816 | 12,458 | 46,995 | 53,075 | 100,072 |
| KNOTT | 30 | 11,301 | 422 | 150 | 5,820 | 6,052 | 11,873 |
| KNOX | 30 | 7,242 | 14,244 | 463 | 10,463 | 11,485 | 21,949 |
| LARUE | 12 | 6,566 | 2,620 | 392 | 4,635 | 4,943 | 9,578 |
| LAUREL | 45 | 8,892 | 28,296 | 1,269 | 18,532 | 19,924 | 38,457 |
| LAWRENCE | 18 | 6,093 | 4,312 | 427 | 5,300 | 5,530 | 10,832 |
| LEE | 10 | 2,039 | 3,113 | 93 | 2,579 | 2,666 | 5,245 |
| LESLIE | 17 | 924 | 8,216 | 169 | 4,604 | 4,705 | 9,309 |
| LETCHER | 32 | 12,612 | 3,378 | 247 | 7,873 | 8,364 | 16,237 |
| LEWIS | 14 | 2,191 | 7,104 | 271 | 4,761 | 4,802 | 9,566 |
| LINCOLN | 17 | 8,905 | 6,726 | 591 | 7,793 | 8,427 | 16,222 |
| LIVINGSTON | 10 | 5,736 | 1,077 | 212 | 3,455 | 3,570 | 7,025 |
| LOGAN | 20 | 11,894 | 3,443 | 852 | 7,523 | 8,666 | 16,189 |
| LYON | 6 | 4,661 | 944 | 189 | 2,858 | 2,936 | 5,794 |
| MCCRACKEN | 54 | 30,082 | 12,020 | 2,771 | 20,471 | 24,401 | 44,873 |
| MCCREARY | 18 | 3,006 | 7,616 | 428 | 5,390 | 5,660 | 11,050 |
| MCLEAN | 8 | 4,776 | 1,496 | 268 | 3,180 | 3,360 | 6,540 |
| MADISON | 56 | 25,795 | 17,524 | 3,746 | 22,089 | 24,973 | 47,065 |
| MAGOFFIN | 14 | 6,510 | 2,694 | 85 | 4,597 | 4,692 | 9,289 |
| MARION | 17 | 10,190 | 1,522 | 304 | 5,730 | 6,286 | 12,016 |
| MARSHALL | 25 | 16,503 | 4,774 | 754 | 10,626 | 11,405 | 22,031 |
| MARTIN | 14 | 2,259 | 6,633 | 146 | 4,474 | 4,563 | 9,038 |
| MASON | 20 | 7,753 | 2,965 | 694 | 5,324 | 6,086 | 11,412 |
| MEADE | 18 | 10,959 | 5,002 | 1,048 | 8,244 | 8,764 | 17,009 |
| MENIFEE | 6 | 4,089 | 681 | 182 | 2,493 | 2,459 | 4,952 |
| MERCER | 17 | 10,717 | 4,049 | 763 | 7,318 | 8,211 | 15,529 |

**VOTER REGISTRATION - PARTY AFFILIATION - DATE: 8/15/06**

| COUNTY | NO. PRECINCTS | DEMOCRAT | REPUBLICAN | OTHER | MALE | FEMALE | TOTAL REGISTERED |
|---|---|---|---|---|---|---|---|
| METCALFE | 12 | 4,018 | 2,890 | 293 | 3,507 | 3,684 | 7,201 |
| MONROE | 12 | 1,061 | 7,205 | 117 | 4,071 | 4,312 | 8,383 |
| MONTGOMERY | 17 | 12,664 | 3,559 | 561 | 8,007 | 8,777 | 16,784 |
| MORGAN | 12 | 8,219 | 647 | 78 | 4,402 | 4,542 | 8,944 |
| MUHLENBERG | 27 | 16,430 | 4,441 | 893 | 10,350 | 11,414 | 21,764 |
| NELSON | 27 | 17,875 | 6,797 | 2,294 | 12,826 | 14,140 | 26,966 |
| NICHOLAS | 5 | 4,593 | 586 | 153 | 2,588 | 2,743 | 5,332 |
| OHIO | 25 | 7,755 | 7,478 | 724 | 7,666 | 8,291 | 15,957 |
| OLDHAM | 34 | 14,053 | 19,211 | 3,549 | 17,820 | 18,991 | 36,813 |
| OWEN | 13 | 5,709 | 1,483 | 270 | 3,718 | 3,744 | 7,462 |
| OWSLEY | 8 | 745 | 2,655 | 39 | 1,709 | 1,729 | 3,439 |
| PENDLETON | 12 | 6,241 | 2,800 | 537 | 4,697 | 4,881 | 9,578 |
| PERRY | 37 | 16,078 | 4,034 | 359 | 9,984 | 10,485 | 20,471 |
| PIKE | 57 | 33,790 | 9,321 | 1,122 | 21,488 | 22,742 | 44,233 |
| POWELL | 11 | 7,012 | 1,965 | 307 | 4,534 | 4,750 | 9,284 |
| PULASKI | 58 | 10,917 | 27,949 | 2,198 | 19,667 | 21,393 | 41,064 |
| ROBERTSON | 5 | 1,437 | 208 | 33 | 840 | 838 | 1,678 |
| ROCKCASTLE | 14 | 2,073 | 8,715 | 389 | 5,478 | 5,699 | 11,177 |
| ROWAN | 18 | 9,022 | 3,243 | 709 | 6,194 | 6,780 | 12,974 |
| RUSSELL | 16 | 3,036 | 9,315 | 282 | 6,081 | 6,552 | 12,633 |
| SCOTT | 35 | 15,057 | 8,993 | 1,463 | 12,200 | 13,313 | 25,513 |
| SHELBY | 33 | 14,131 | 8,252 | 1,525 | 11,289 | 12,617 | 23,908 |
| SIMPSON | 13 | 7,728 | 2,447 | 805 | 5,112 | 5,867 | 10,980 |
| SPENCER | 11 | 6,186 | 3,577 | 544 | 5,112 | 5,195 | 10,307 |
| TAYLOR | 20 | 8,159 | 7,430 | 641 | 7,617 | 8,611 | 16,230 |
| TODD | 13 | 6,414 | 1,179 | 219 | 3,729 | 4,083 | 7,812 |
| TRIGG | 14 | 6,594 | 2,473 | 423 | 4,594 | 4,896 | 9,490 |
| TRIMBLE | 12 | 4,904 | 1,059 | 249 | 3,079 | 3,133 | 6,212 |
| UNION | 16 | 8,332 | 1,160 | 329 | 4,648 | 5,173 | 9,821 |
| WARREN | 63 | 32,947 | 20,209 | 4,008 | 26,645 | 30,515 | 57,164 |
| WASHINGTON | 14 | 5,435 | 2,180 | 225 | 3,750 | 4,089 | 7,840 |
| WAYNE | 19 | 5,169 | 8,109 | 389 | 6,673 | 6,994 | 13,667 |
| WEBSTER | 14 | 7,734 | 1,201 | 275 | 4,376 | 4,834 | 9,210 |
| WHITLEY | 36 | 6,280 | 18,099 | 958 | 12,289 | 13,046 | 25,337 |
| WOLFE | 8 | 4,906 | 441 | 97 | 2,688 | 2,756 | 5,444 |
| WOODFORD | 16 | 10,212 | 5,321 | 1,118 | 7,782 | 8,868 | 16,651 |
| STATE TOTALS | 3518 | 1,562,026 | 1,000,543 | 173,837 | 1,289,713 | 1,446,530 | 2,736,406 |

*Source: Secretary of State - http://elect.ky.gov/stats/regstat.htm*

## GENERAL FUND SUMMARY
## 2006-2008 EXECUTIVE BUDGET

| RESOURCES | Enacted FY 2007 | Enacted FY 2008 |
|---|---|---|
| Beginning Balance | 544,874,100 | 434,187,000 |
| Consensus Revenue Forecast | 8,341,200,000 | 8,675,700,000 |
| Tobacco Settlement- Phase 1 | 88,800,000 | 94,000,000 |
| Continuation of Revenue Measures | 7,600,000 | 7,900,000 |
| Other Resources | 44,142,500 | 87,652,400 |
| Small Business AMC Relief | (1,870,000) | (6,080,000) |
| Non-Participating Manufs. Assignment | 132,833,800 | 84,589,200 |
| Fund Transfers | 132,833,800 | 84,589,200 |
| **Total Resources** | **9,192,580,400** | **9,397,348,600** |
| **Continued Appropriations Reserve** | | |
| Budget Reserve Trust Fund | 119,015,100 | 151,815,100 |
| Tobacco Settlement-Phase 1 | 12,305,200 | 9,508,700 |
| Executive Branch | 7,288,300 | 3,167,600 |
| Legislative Branch | 6,828,400 | 5,299,600 |
| Judicial Branch | 6,411,600 | 4,351,600 |
| **Total Continued Appropriations Reserve** | **151,848,600** | **174,142,600** |
| **TOTAL RESOURCES** | **9,344,429,000** | **9,572,091,200** |
| | | |
| **APPROPRIATIONS** | | |
| **Executive Branch** | | |
| Regular Operating | 8,377,670,200 | 9,014,177,200 |
| Tobacco Settlement-Phase 1 | 88,800,000 | 94,000,000 |
| Special Bills (SB 82 in FY 2007 & 2008) | 400,000 | 400,000 |
| Other – Dedicated Revenues | 2,200,000 | 2,200,000 |
| Budgeted Lapse | (57,000,000) | (43,000,000) |
| Capital Projects | 22,145,800 | 11,103,000 |
| **Total Executive Branch** | **8,434,216,000** | **9,067,304,200** |
| **Judicial Branch** | **244,588,600** | **279,376,500** |
| **Legislative Branch** | **46,788,800** | **50,182,200** |
| **TOTAL APPROPRIATIONS** | **8,725,593,400** | **9,396,862,900** |
| | | |
| **BALANCE** | **618,835,600** | **175,228,300** |
| **Continued Appropriations Reserve** | | |
| Budget Reserve Trust Fund | 151,815,100 | 142,324,800 |
| Tobacco Settlement-Phase 1 | 12,305,200 | 9,508,700 |
| Executive Branch | 7,288,300 | 3,167,600 |
| Legislative Branch | 6,828,400 | 5,299,600 |
| Judicial Branch | 6,411,600 | 4,351,600 |
| **Total Continued Appropriations Reserve** | **184,648,600** | **164,652,300** |
| **ENDING BALANCE** | **434,187,000** | **10,576,000** |

## ROAD FUND SUMMARY
## 2006-2008 EXECUTIVE BUDGET

| | Enacted FY 2007 | Enacted FY 2008 |
|---|---|---|
| **RESOURCES** | | |
| Beginning Balance | 1,493,500 | |
| Consensus Revenue Forecast | 1,223,125,400 | 1,239,614,400 |
| Road Fund Revenue Initiative | 15,599,900 | 22,317,500 |
| **TOTAL RESOURCES** | **1,240,178,800** | **1,261,931,900** |
| | | |
| **APPROPRIATIONS** | | |
| **Transportation Cabinet** | | |
| Revenue Sharing | 214,886,100 | 244,276,700 |
| Aviation | 4,000,000 | 4,000,000 |
| Highways | 667,409,400 | 670,193,200 |
| Vehicle Regulation | 17,396,100 | 18,269,900 |
| Debt Service | 162,710,2000 | 181,143,200 |
| General Administration and Support | 69,217,100 | 70,072,400 |
| Capital Projects | 9,035,000 | 6,795,000 |
| **Subtotal** | **1,171,653,900** | **1,194,750,400** |
| Justice & Public Safety Cabinet | 63,974,900 | 63,881,500 |
| Finance and Administration Cabinet | 3,650,000 | 2,400,000 |
| Environmental Protection | 300,000 | 300,000 |
| Treasury | 250,000 | 250,000 |
| Homeland Security | 350,000 | 350,000 |
| **TOTAL APPROPRIATIONS** | **1,142,714,600** | **1,180,376,500** |
| | | |
| **ENDING BALANCE** | **0** | **0** |

*Source: Office of State Budget Director, http://www.osbd.ky.gov.*

## CAPITAL CONSTRUCTION SUMMARY
### 2006-2008 EXECUTIVE BUDGET

| | Enacted FY 2007 | Enacted FY 2008 | New Authorization |
|---|---|---|---|
| **SOURCE OF FUNDS** | | | |
| **Executive Branch** | | | |
| General Fund | 22,145,800 | 11,103,000 | 33,248,800 |
| Restricted Funds | 1,624,482,956 | 32,150,000 | 1,660,952,956 |
| Federal Funds | 179,399,084 | 22,190,000 | 201,589,084 |
| Bond Fund | 1,394,691,000 | | 1,394,691,000 |
| Road Fund | 10,285,000 | 6,795,000 | 17,080,000 |
| Agency Bond Fund | 267,537,000 | | 267,537,000 |
| Capital Construction Surplus | 4,107,000 | 1,045,000 | 5,152,000 |
| Investment Income | 10,900,000 | 10,810,000 | 21,710,000 |
| Other Funds | 249,138,000 | 17,868,000 | 267,006,000 |
| Emergency, Repair Maintenance & Replacement | 1,700,000 | | 1,700,000 |
| **TOTAL SOURCE OF FUNDS** | **3,764,385,840** | **101,961,000** | **3,870,666,840** |
| **EXPENDITURES BY CABINET** | | | |
| **Executive Branch** | | | |
| General Branch | 643,451,8000 | 34,304,000 | 677,755,800 |
| Commerce | 154,080,000 | 15,925,000 | 170,005,000 |
| Economic Development | 37,500,000 | | 37,500,000 |
| Department of Education | 73,075,000 | 675,000 | 73,750,000 |
| Education Cabinet | 18,092,000 | 400,000 | 18,492,000 |
| Environmental and Public Protection | 32,300,000 | 6,800,000 | 39,100,000 |
| Finance and Administration | 185,801,000 | 7,704,000 | 193,505,000 |
| Health and Family Services | 29,249,000 | 1,500,000 | 30,749,000 |
| Justice and Public Safety | 8,197,000 | 1,650,000 | 9,847,000 |
| Postsecondary Education | 2,572,965,040 | 26,208,000 | 2,603,493,040 |
| Transportation | 9,675,000 | 6,795,000 | 16,470,000 |
| **TOTAL EXPENDITURES** | **3,764,385,840** | **101,961,000** | **3,870,666,840** |

## TOBACCO SETTLEMENT-PHASE I SUMMARY
### 2006-2008 EXECUTIVE BUDGET

| | Enacted FY 2007 | Enacted FY 2008 |
|---|---|---|
| **Revenue** | **175,000** | **175,000** |
| | | |
| **Rural Development- (50%)** | | |
| Governor's Office of Agriculture Policy | 17,469,800 | 20,065,100 |
| Finance and Administrative Cabinet Debt Service | 17,842,700 | 17,847,400 |
| Environmental and Public Protection Cabinet | | |
| Natural Resources | 9,000,000 | 9,000,000 |
| **Subtotal** | **44,312,500** | **46,912,500** |
| | | |
| **Health Improvement- (25%)** | | |
| Office of Drug Control Policy (KY ASAP) | 1,816,800 | 1,923,400 |
| Health and Family Services | | |
| Public Health - Smoking Cessation | 2,215,600 | 2,345,600 |
| Council on Postsecondary Education | | |
| Lung Cancer Research Program/ Ovarian Cancer Screening | 4,431,200 | 4,691,200 |
| Environmental and Public Protection Cabinet | | |
| Insurance (Kentucky Access) | 13,692,700 | 14,496,000 |
| **Subtotal** | **22,156,300** | **23,456,200** |
| | | |
| **Early Childhood Development- (25%)** | | |
| Education | | |
| Early Childhood Development Services | 1,388,400 | 1,508,400 |
| Health and Family Services Cabinet | | |
| Community Based Services | 6,970,400 | 7,420,400 |
| Human Support Services | 100,000 | 100,000 |
| Public Health | 11,785,300 | 12,375,500 |
| Mental Health/Mental Retardation | 800,000 | 800,000 |
| Children with Special Health Care Needs | 312,100 | 352,000 |
| Postsecondary Education | | |
| Kentucky Higher Education Assistance Authority | 800,000 | 900,000 |
| **Subtotal** | **27,156,200** | **23,456,200** |
| | | |
| **TOTAL TOBACCO SETTLEMENT-PHASE 1** | **88,800,000** | **94,000,000** |

**KENTUCKY STATE GOVERNMENT EMPLOYMENT AND PAYROLL DATA: MARCH 2005**

| FUNCTION | FULL-TIME EMPLOYEES | FULL-TIME PAYROLL | PART-TIME EMPLOYEES | PART-TIME PAYROLL | PART-TIME HOURS | EQUIVALENT EMPLOYMENT | MARCH PAYROLL |
|---|---|---|---|---|---|---|---|
| Financial administration | 2,608 | 8,991,977 | 21 | 32,494 | 1,050 | 2,614 | 9,024,471 |
| Other government administration | 1,008 | 4,478,219 | 440 | 828,938 | 27,906 | 1,177 | 5,307,157 |
| Judicial and Legal | 4,377 | 14,444,175 | 826 | 1,464,740 | 103,170 | 4,998 | 15,908,915 |
| Police Protection - Officers | 996 | 3,380,460 | 0 | 0 | 0 | 996 | 3,380,460 |
| Police - Other | 1,321 | 4,660,779 | 0 | 0 | 0 | 1,321 | 4,660,779 |
| Correction | 3,855 | 9,724,224 | 154 | 83,760 | 2,008 | 3,867 | 9,807,984 |
| Highways | 5,046 | 15,375,845 | 56 | 108,938 | 4,776 | 5,074 | 15,484,783 |
| Public Welfare | 6,803 | 19,505,717 | 0 | 0 | 0 | 6,803 | 19,505,717 |
| Health | 2,157 | 7,126,594 | 84 | 89,563 | 5,525 | 2,189 | 7,216,157 |
| Hospitals | 5,497 | 16,868,725 | 368 | 1,243,917 | 61,404 | 5,848 | 18,112,642 |
| Social insurance administration | 1,054 | 3,214,484 | 1 | 2,774 | 80 | 1,054 | 3,217,258 |
| Parks and recreation | 1,437 | 3,171,606 | 142 | 123,270 | 16,682 | 1,537 | 3,294,876 |
| Natural resources | 3,365 | 10,534,300 | 969 | 1,115,429 | 94,424 | 3,913 | 11,649,729 |
| Higher Ed Instructional | 8,406 | 48,222,323 | 6,964 | 9,169,450 | 499,115 | 11,341 | 57,391,773 |
| Higher Ed - Other | 16,253 | 50,264,308 | 13,661 | 6,631,813 | 634,113 | 20,008 | 56,896,121 |
| Other education | 2,719 | 9,944,945 | 148 | 106,352 | 6,084 | 2,756 | 10,053,297 |
| All other and unallocable | 3,706 | 11,606,440 | 80 | 83,504 | 4,830 | 3,735 | 11,689,944 |
| Total | 70,608 | 241,515,121 | 23,914 | 21,086,942 | 1,461,167 | 79,231 | 262,602,063 |

**STATE GOVERNMENT EMPLOYMENT AND PAYROLL DATA: MARCH 2005 (US, Kentucky, and surrounding states)**

| STATE NAME | POPULATION | FULL-TIME EMPLOYEES | FULL-TIME PAYROLL | PART-TIME EMPLOYEES | PART-TIME PAYROLL | PART-TIME HOURS | EQUIVALENT EMPLOYMENT | MARCH PAYROLL |
|---|---|---|---|---|---|---|---|---|
| United States | 281,421,906 | 3,658,859 | 14,510,933,884 | 1,419,409 | 1,550,636,537 | 95,634,091 | 4,208,522 | 16,061,570,421 |
| Illinois | 12,419,293 | 111,422 | 475,142,271 | 47,976 | 44,741,225 | 3,571,380 | 132,934 | 519,883,496 |
| Indiana | 6,080,485 | 75,802 | 266,227,905 | 37,271 | 38,106,480 | 2,993,192 | 92,934 | 304,334,385 |
| Kentucky | 4,041,769 | 70,608 | 241,515,121 | 23,914 | 21,086,942 | 1,461,167 | 79,231 | 262,602,063 |
| Missouri | 5,595,211 | 81,512 | 251,614,610 | 26,864 | 21,458,676 | 1,808,338 | 91,801 | 273,100,286 |
| Ohio | 11,353,140 | 111,785 | 436,925,793 | 66,531 | 65,676,295 | 4,321,821 | 136,370 | 502,602,088 |
| Tennessee | 5,689,283 | 73,487 | 238,759,896 | 25,511 | 21,618,068 | 1,571,752 | 82,786 | 260,377,964 |
| Virginia | 7,078,515 | 102,148 | 376,734,153 | 47,518 | 47,635,211 | 3,062,804 | 119,548 | 424,369,364 |
| West Virginia | 1,808,344 | 34,934 | 106,449,253 | 9,395 | 7,500,346 | 463,042 | 37,710 | 113,999,599 |

Source: http://ftp2.census.gov/govs/apes/05stall.xls

# Historical Documents

# KENTUCKY GAZETTE

## Ron Bryant

On August 11, 1787, John Bradford (1749-1830) published the first issue of the *Kentucke Gazette*. As the first newspaper west of the Allegheny Mountains, the *Gazette* provided not only a source for news, but also a printing establishment for the western frontier. Although the paper did not report a great deal of local news, it did serve as a means to advertise local goods and services, and reprint articles of national and international importance.

The need for a printer on the Kentucky frontier became apparent during the second statehood convention in 1785. Delegates to the convention wanted a forum to publish their work and to help unify public opinion. A newspaper would serve their purpose to report to the citizens of Kentucky their efforts to achieve separation from Virginia and to form a new state.

Delegates to the statehood convention appointed a committee made up of John

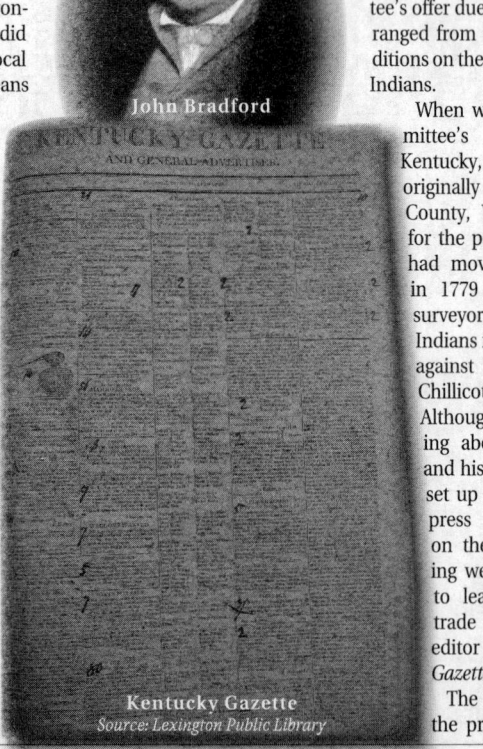

John Bradford

Kentucky Gazette
Source: Lexington Public Library

Coburn, Christopher Greenup and James Wilkinson to persuade a printer to come Kentucky. They endeavored to convince John Dunlap of Philadelphia and Miles Hunter of Richmond to settle on the frontier. Both refused the committee's offer due to concerns that ranged from unhealthful conditions on the frontier to fear of Indians.

When word of the committee's failure reached Kentucky, John Bradford, originally of Fauquier County, Virginia, applied for the position. Bradford had moved to Kentucky in 1779 and became a surveyor. He fought the Indians in the campaigns against the Shawnee at Chillicothe and Piqua. Although he knew nothing about printing, he and his brother Fielding set up the first printing press and newspaper on the frontier. Fielding went to Pittsburgh to learn the printing trade from John Scull, editor of the *Pittsburgh Gazette*.

The Bradford's had the printing press and

type brought from Philadelphia and down the Ohio River to Limestone (now Maysville). Packhorses then carried the printing materials over land to Lexington. With the assistance of Thomas Parvin, an immigrant schoolteacher who had some printing experience, Bradford published the first issue of the *Kentucke Gazette*. The first issue had an apology from Bradford regarding the delay in publication and one advertisement. These two contributions were the only local items in the paper.

Printing on an 18th century press was a laboriously slow process. The sheets of paper measured 8 by 10 inches and were inked with "dog skin" balls (animal skins). The press could only produce 50 to

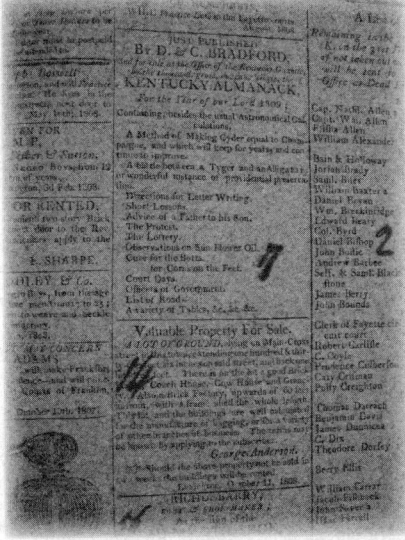

**Kentucky Gazette**
*Source: Lexington Library*

60 sheets per hour. The pages of the *Gazette* then had to be dried or else they would smear.

For the first few issues of his paper, Bradford dealt mostly with advertisements and copies of other news articles reporting on national affairs and international affairs. Scarcity of paper may have contributed to the lack of local news, or it may have been easier to reprint articles from other newspapers. The *Gazette* did publish letters from citizens on various issues of the day. It also published congressional debates and the proceedings of the Kentucky General Assembly. The *Gazette* print shop published numerous books, broadsides and pamphlets. One of Bradford's most enduring contributions to the printed word was a series of 66 articles on Kentucky history known as Bradford's

"Notes on Kentucky." Published between August 1825 and January 1829, these invaluable recollections of Kentucky's past are still used by historians and enjoyed by new generations of readers.

In the March 7, 1789, issue of the paper, Bradford changed the spelling on the masthead from *Kentucke* to *Kentucky Gazette*. As times became more settled, the *Gazette* began to publish more local news. From 1792 to 1798 (excepting 1796) Bradford served as public printer for the commonwealth. Until 1795 the *Gazette* was the only newspaper published within 500 miles of Lexington. The paper became a weekly, then a biweekly and at last a triweekly publication. It was originally delivered to subscribers by post rider and then by mail.

Bradford published more than just the *Gazette*. As public printer he printed state documents, including some of the first volumes of the *Acts of the Kentucky General Assembly*. In time he became an excellent printer and more of a journalist. In 1788 he began publication of the *Kentucky*

XXXXXXXXXXXXXXXXXXXX

The Kentucke Gazette published

letters from citizens on various issues

of the day as well as congressional

debates and proceedings of the

Kentucky General Assembly.

XXXXXXXXXXXXXXXXXXXX

*Almanac* (1788-1807). This annual publication contained information on the weather as well as astronomy and materials of general interest.

He remained the editor and owner of the *Gazette* until 1802, when he gave ownership of the paper to his son Daniel. In 1809 Daniel sold the paper to Thomas Smith, and in 1814 Smith sold the *Gazette* to Fielding Bradford Jr. In 1825 John Bradford again became editor of the *Gazette*, holding the position until 1827 when Albert G. Merriwether succeeded him.

The *Kentucky Gazette* continued publication from August 11, 1787, until December 29, 1848. No copy of the first issue of the paper has ever been found. The second issue of August 18, 1787, is known to be a near copy of the first edition. Another Lexington newspaper used the name from 1866 to 1910. In 1995, the *Kentucky Gazette* was revived and edited by Lowell Reese as a Frankfort-based political newspaper.

# HISTORICAL DOCUMENTS
# *Constitution of Kentucky*

## CONSTITUTION OF KENTUCKY

### PREAMBLE

We, the people of the Commonwealth of Kentucky, grateful to Almighty God for the civil, political and religious liberties we enjoy, and invoking the continuance of these blessings, do ordain and establish this Constitution.

### BILL OF RIGHTS

That the great and essential principles of liberty and free government may be recognized and established, we declare that:

Sec. 1. Rights of life, liberty, worship, pursuit of safety and happiness, free speech, acquiring and protecting property, peaceable assembly, redress of grievances, bearing arms. All men are, by nature, free and equal, and have certain inherent and inalienable rights, among which may be reckoned:

First: The right of enjoying and defending their lives and liberties.

Second: The right of worshipping Almighty God according to the dictates of their conscience.

Third: The right of seeking and pursuing their safety and happiness.

Fourth: The right of freely communicating their thoughts and opinions.

Fifth: The right of acquiring and protecting property.

Sixth: The right of assembling together in a peaceable manner for their common good, and of applying to those invested with power of government for redress of grievances or other proper purposes, by petition, address or remonstrance.

Seventh: The right to bear arms in defense of themselves and of the State, subject to the power of the General Assembly to enact laws to prevent persons from carrying concealed weapons.

Sec. 2. Absolute and arbitrary power denied. Absolute and arbitrary power over the lives, liberty and property of freemen exists nowhere in a republic, not even in the largest majority.

Sec. 3. Men are equal; no exclusive grant except for public services; property not to be exempted from taxation; grants revocable. All men, when they form a social compact, are equal; and no grant of exclusive, separate public emoluments or privileges shall be made to any man or set of men, except in consideration of public services; but no property shall be exempt from taxation except as provided in this Constitution, and every grant of a franchise, privilege or exemption, shall remain subject to revocation, alteration or amendment.

Sec. 4. Power inherent in the people; right to alter, reform or abolish government. All power is inherent in the people, and all free governments are founded on their authority and instituted for their peace, safety, happiness and the protection of property. For the advancement of these ends, they have at all times an inalienable and indefeasible right to alter, reform or abolish their government in such manner as they may deem proper.

Sec. 5. Right of religious freedom. No preference shall ever be given by law to any religious sect, society or denomination; nor to any particular creed, mode of worship or system of ecclesiastical polity; nor shall any person be compelled to attend any place of worship, to contribute to the erection or maintenance of any such place, or to the salary or support of any minister or religion; nor shall any man be compelled to send his child to any school to which he may be conscientiously opposed; and the civil rights, privileges or capacities of no person shall be taken away, or in any wise diminished or enlarged, on account of his belief or disbelief of any religious tenet, dogma or teaching. No human authority shall, in any case whatever, control or interfere with the rights of conscience.

Sec. 6. Elections to be free and equal. All elections shall be free and equal.

Sec. 7. Right of trial by jury. The ancient mode of trial by jury shall be held sacred, and the right thereof remain inviolate, subject to such modifications as may be authorized by this Constitution.

Sec. 8. Freedom of speech and of the press. Printing presses shall be free to every person who undertakes to examine the proceedings of the General Assembly or any branch of government, and no shall ever be made to restrain the right there of. Every person may freely and fully speak, write and print on any subject, being responsible for the abuse of that liberty.

Sec. 9. Truth may be given in evidence in prosecution for publishing matters proper for public information; jury to try law and facts in libel prosecutions. In prosecutions for the publication of papers investigating the official conduct of officers or men in public capacity, or where the matter published is proper for public information, the truth there of may be given in evidence; and in all indictments for libel the jury shall have the right to determine the law and the facts, under the direction of the court, as in other cases.

Sec. 10. Security from search and seizure; conditions of issuance of warrants. The people shall be secure in their persons, houses, papers and possessions, from unreasonable searches and seizure; and no warrant shall issue to search any place, or seize any person or thing, without describing them as nearly as may be, nor without probable cause supported by oath or affirmation.

Sec. 11. Rights of accused in criminal prosecution; change of venue. In all criminal prosecutions the accused has the right to be heard by himself and counsel; to demand the nature and cause of the accusation against him; to meet the witnesses face to face, and to have compulsory process for obtaining witnesses in his favor. He cannot be compelled to give evidence against himself, nor can he be deprived of his life, liberty or property, unless by the judgment of his peers or the law of the land; and in prosecutions by indictments or information, he shall have a speedy public trial by an impartial jury of the vicinage; but the General Assembly may provide by a general law for a change of venue in such prosecutions for both the defendant and the Commonwealth, the change to be made to the most convenient county in which a fair trial can be obtained.

Sec. 12. Indictable offense not to be prosecuted by information; exceptions. No person, for an indictable offense, shall be proceeded against criminally by information, except in cases arising in the land or naval forces, or in the militia, when in actual service, in time of war or public danger, or by leave of court for oppression or misdemeanor in office.

Sec. 13. Double jeopardy; property not to be taken for public use without just compensation. No person shall, for the same offense, be twice put in jeopardy of his life or limb, nor shall any man's property be taken or applied to public use without just compensation being previously made to him.

Sec. 14. Right of judicial remedy for injury; speedy trial. All courts shall be open, and every person for an injury done him in his lands, goods, person or reputation, shall have remedy by due course of law, and right and justice administered without sale, denial or delay.

Sec. 15.　Laws to be suspended only by General Assembly.　No power to suspend laws shall be exercised unless by the General Assembly or its authority.

Sec. 16.　Right to bail; habeas corpus.　All prisoners shall be bailable by sufficient securities, unless for capital offenses when the proof is evident or the presumption great: and the privilege of the writ of habeas corpus shall not be suspended unless when, in case of rebellion or invasion, the public safety may require it.

Sec. 17.　Excessive bail or fine, or cruel punishment, prohibited.　Excessive bail shall not be required, nor excessive fines imposed, nor cruel punishment inflicted.

Sec. 18.　Imprisonment for debt restricted.　The person of a debtor, where there is not strong presumption of fraud, shall not be continued in prison after delivering up his estate for the benefit of his creditors in such manner as shall be prescribed by law.

Sec. 19.　Ex post facto law or law impairing the obligation of contract forbidden.　No ex post facto law, nor any law impairing the obligation of contracts, shall be enacted.

Sec. 20.　Attainder, operation of restricted.　No person shall be attainted of treason or felony by the General Assembly, and no attainder shall work corruption of blood, nor, except during the life of the offender, forfeiture of estate to the Commonwealth.

Sec. 21.　Descent in case of suicide or casualty. The estate of such persons as shall destroy their own lives shall descend or vest as in cases of natural death; and if any person shall be killed by casualty, there shall be no forfeiture by reason thereof.

Sec. 22.　Standing armies restricted; military subordinate to civil; quartering soldiers restricted.　No standing army shall, in time of peace, be maintained without the consent of the General Assembly; and the military shall, in all cases and at all times, be in strict subordination to the civil power; nor shall any soldier, in time of peace, be quartered in any house without the consent of the owner, nor in time of war, except in a manner prescribed by law.

Sec. 23.　No office of nobility or hereditary distinction, or for longer than a term of years. The General Assembly shall not grant any title of nobility or hereditary distinction, nor create any office the appointment of which shall be for a longer time than a term of years.

Sec. 24.　Emigration to be free.　Emigration from the state shall not be prohibited.

Sec. 25.　Slavery and involuntary servitude forbidden.　Slavery and in-voluntary servitude in this State are forbidden, except as punishment for crime, whereof the party shall have been duly convicted.

Sec. 26.　General powers subordinate to Bill of Rights; laws contrary there to are void.　To guard against transgression of the high powers which we have delegated, We Declare that everything in this Bill of Rights is excepted out of the general powers of government, and shall forever remain inviolate; and all laws contrary thereto, or contrary to this Constitution, shall be void.

*For a complete copy of the Kentucky Constitution visit www.lrc.ky.gov/legresou/constitu/intro.htm*

## It's a Kentucky Thing!
## Sec. 4 of the Kentucky Bill of Rights.

"All power is inherent in the people, and all free governments are founded on their peace, safety, happiness and the protection of property."

# FEDERAL GOVERNMENT
## *National Spotlight Shines on Kentuckians in Congress*

### Bob Babbage

For Kentuckians in Congress 2007 is a year of almost unmatched importance.

Every second November dreams are made and dreams are dashed in a single evening between suppertime and just after dark as votes become apparent.

But the stars are aligned for top Kentuckians to be stars no matter what. Despite the relative size of Kentucky's delegation its members are set to move global issues and make Bluegrass history.

Mitch McConnell is so familiar among Kentuckians in politics that he is known by his first names – Whip, Senator or, simply Mitch. In conversations it's routinely asked, "Where is McConnell on this?" Clearly 2007 is the year for McConnell on the national stage. He moves to the head of the U.S. Senate Republicans adding "Leader" to his list of familiar monikers.

No Kentuckian has reached this status since the legendary Alben Barkley, who served as majority leader over a half century ago. The Paducah Democrat was also etched in American history as Truman's vice president.

Rising through the ranks through the position of whip, the assistant floor leader and head-counter,

Senator McConnell has become a fixture on Sunday news shows, a master of the Senate. McConnell receives wide credit as one of the nation's best prepared and hard-working lawmakers as confirmed in a 2006 survey of staff on the Hill. Moreover, observers say he uniquely gauges the will of his colleagues alongside the vectors of public sentiment to turn large ideas and legislation into law and policy.

Throughout 2006 four of Kentucky's six U.S. House members were mentioned as prospects for higher office just as U.S. Senator Bunning declared his interest in the 2010 race for a third term.

Rep. Ben Chandler (D-Lexington), who lost the 2003 race for governor to Ernie Fletcher, is a leading Democrat for the future. Ironically he holds the U.S. House seat that Fletcher held before winning the Governor's office in Frankfort. Chandler was formerly attorney general and state auditor for Kentucky. Chandler's standing in Washington opens a path to power within the time-honored committee system and seniority process.

"Chandler's Choice" – another run for governor or a prized assignment in Washington – has many waiting to see what's in store for 2007 as the Almanac goes to press.

Kentucky's prime example of rising to the upper echelon of influence is Congressman Harold Rogers (R-Somerset). Coming up through the Appropriations Committee over his 26 years of service, Rogers came to chair the transportation subcommittee, which directs nationwide spending on highways.

Of late Rogers has chaired homeland security spending at a critical time in the formation of national security policy and programs. The 13 subcommittee chairs are nicknamed "the college of cardinals" in Washington, a reference to the revered prelates of the Roman Catholic Church. Rogers, addressed as "Mr. Chairman" in national circles, is at the apex of congressional decision making, and could go higher.

**Gov Martha Layne Collins, Sen John Sherman Cooper and Sen Edward "Ted" Kennedy at the dedication of the John Sherman Cooper bust at the capital rotunda. Frankfort, Kentucky, October 12, 1987**
*Source: Kentucky Virtual Library*

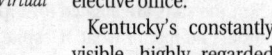

**Bust of John Sherman Cooper by John Tuska**
*Source: Kentucky Virtual Library*

Anne M. Northup and Edward Whitfield are often mentioned as tested, seasoned Republicans who could move up.

Whitfield (R-Hopkinsville) is in his sixth term. The 63 year-old lawyer is active on Energy and Commerce, a key committee, and made headlines in 2006 with House passage of an animal cruelty bill, addressing the slaughter of horses. Whitfield formed and led a large nationwide coalition.

Northup (R-Louisville) serves on Appropriations, now in her fifth term. She has been at the forefront of financial decisions impacting her region, especially the move for two new bridges across the Ohio River. Northup, a teacher by training, made a name for herself in the Kentucky legislature, before going to Washington from a highly competitive district.

Ron Lewis won a historic Kentucky special election, which opened a Kentucky political wave for Republicans. Lewis was a college professor, small business owner and most notably a minister before coming to Congress. His committee is Ways and Means.

Accumulating seniority has placed Lewis, Northup and Whitfield in upper circles.

Along the Ohio River from Covington to Ashland runs Kentucky's most fought-for congressional seat. As a Kentucky freshman Geoff Davis, a West Point graduate, served on Armed Services and Financial Services. Former Congressman Ken Lucas, who clashed with Davis in 2002 before leaving Congress in 2004, would gladly serve again in the seat, making the Davis-Lucas struggle a regular Kentucky political feud.

The chronological dean of the delegation at age 75 is Senator Jim Bunning. The famous major league pitcher of two no-hitters is no quitter, outlining his interest in re-election in 2010. The Hall of Fame member served in the halls of Frankfort, both the House and Senate, before going to the U.S. House. He is active on banking issues in the Senate, having also been an investment advisor in between baseball and elective office.

Kentucky's constantly visible, highly regarded delegation follows in a storied tradition, according to Ron Bryant, a gifted Kentucky historian in Frankfort.

Alongside Barkley in the last century came John Sherman Cooper (R-Somerset). He served in the U.S. Senate for partial terms, 1946-49 and 1952-55. During the period of 1956-73 Cooper as Senator was considered one of the most independent minds in Washington, working closely with both his own party and leading Democrats. President Johnson named him to the Warren Commission. He became a vocal critic of U. S. policies in Vietnam, clashing with Johnson. Cooper co-sponsored the formation of the Appalachian Regional Commission, a pillar in Johnson's Great Society domestic policy. Newsweek named him the Senate's most able Republican.

Senator Cooper died in 1991 and is buried in Arlington National Cemetery.

Henry Clay (1777-1852) served in the House, becoming Speaker, the Senate and as Secretary of State when the nation was deciding fundamental questions of human respect and federal unification. The "Great Compromiser" was known for the words "I'd rather be right than president." Three times Clay failed to win the top office in the land.

In addition to his preserved estate in Lexington one finds Clay's statue in the Jefferson County Courthouse rotunda, along with his famous U.S. Capitol portrait hanging in the Senate Majority Whip's office.

Breckinridge is a longstanding name in Kentucky political annals. John Breckinridge, a Virginian, became one of Kentucky's finest statesmen. His support of Thomas Jefferson may have been his contribution to the country. In 1798 he introduced the Kentucky

Resolutions, which, with the Virginia Resolutions, had been penned by Jefferson.

This laid the groundwork for the theory of nullification, and then the theory of secession.

William Cabell Preston Breckinridge (1837-1904) was a Democrat in the U.S. House, serving 10 years. He earned the term "silver tongued orator of the South." Breckinridge became the champion of the New South and an ardent advocate for free trade and individual rights. His formal career was ended by a personal scandal.

Like Breckinridge and Chandler, Brown is a name found in Kentucky public leadership. John Brown (1757-1837) was Virginia-born, not uncommon since the states were originally joined. He served

Top: Pres. Franklin Roosevelt, Gov. Lafoon, and V.P. Alben Barkley. Below: Senator Alben W. Barkley at the dedication of West Liberty High School, May 24, 1937
*Source: Kentucky Virtual Library*

as the Virginia representative from the Kentucky District in the Continental Congress of 1787-88, going then to serve in the U. S. House and Senate. Twice he was president pro tempore of the Senate. However, he was involved in the so-called Spanish Conspiracy and with the Aaron Burr Conspiracy, both of which damaged his political standing.

He built one of Frankfort's most distinctive structures, Liberty Hall.

Others from the Bluegrass impacted the leading questions of their day concerning nationhood. George Mortimer Bibb (1776-1859) backed President Andrew Jackson, but they fell out over the "Force Bill" which was used to intimidate South Carolina into submission after the state threatened to leave the Union over the establishment of a high tariff.

Senator John Jordan Crittenden (1786-1863) of Versailles authored the Crittenden Compromise and is remembered for working to keep the Union together. Later he was governor. Garrett Davis of Montgomery County (1801-1872) was a critic of secession and helped keep Kentucky in the Union.

Two Kentucky Senators also backed the union of the states. Humphrey Marshal (1760-1841) was an outspoken Federalist. John Rogers Underwood (1791-1876) was a staunch unionist and emancipationist.

Like their predecessors throughout history, those who serve Kentucky in Washington in this era face monumental issues, working from exceptional vantage points under the national spotlight.

Bob Babbage, Kentucky's Secretary of State, 1992-96, heads Babbage Cofounder, a government relations firm.

# Kentuckians in Congress

### SENATOR MITCH MCCONNELL (R)

In 2004 Senator Mitch McConnell was unanimously re-elected Majority Whip by his Republican colleagues. As Majority Whip, McConnell is the second ranking Republican in the US Senate. First elected to the Senate in 1984, McConnell was the only Republican challenger in the country to defeat a Democrat incumbent, and the first Republican to win a statewide race in Kentucky since 1968. McConnell's landslide victory in 2002 is also one for the record books — he won a fourth term with 65 percent of the vote, the largest margin of victory for a Republican in Kentucky history.

Born on February 20, 1942, and reared in south Louisville, McConnell graduated in 1964 with honors from the University of Louisville. A graduate from the University of Kentucky College of Law, he worked on Capitol Hill as an intern for Senator John Sherman Cooper; as chief legislative assistant to Senator Marlow Cook; and as deputy assistant attorney general under President Gerald R. Ford. Before being elected to the U.S. Senate, McConnell served as County Judge-Executive in Jefferson County from 1978 - 1985.

Senator McConnell is married to U.S. Secretary of Labor, Elaine Chao. He is the father of three daughters.

Mitch McConnell (R)
US Senator, Senate Majority Whip
361A Russell Senate Ofc Bldg
Washington DC 20510
(202) 224-2541
FAX (202) 224-2499
http://mcconnell.senate.gov/index.cfmc

### SENATOR JIM BUNNING (R)

Elected to serve a second term as U.S. Senator in 1984, Senator Jim Bunning was first elected to the U.S. Senate in 1998. He had won by a mere 6,766 votes. In 2004 he won by a margin almost 3 ½ times larger than his victory in 1998; he also won 73 of Kentucky's 120 counties and secured 873,507 votes — the most votes ever for a U.S. Senate candidate from Kentucky.

Reared in Northern Kentucky and a graduate of Xavier University, Bunning had a successful 17-year career as a Major League Baseball player. Pitching primarily for the Detroit Tigers and Philadelphia Phillies, Bunning's record won him a seat in the Baseball Hall of Fame in 1996. He was the second pitcher in history (Cy Young was the first) to record 1,000 strikeouts and 100 wins in both the American and National leagues. Retiring in 1971, Bunning was second on the all-time strikeout list—second only to Walter Johnson.

Bunning's political career began in 1977 when he served on the Fort Thomas City Council. In 1979, he was elected to the Kentucky State Senate and then, in 1986, Bunning was elected to the U.S. House of Representatives where he served for 12 years.

Bunning and his wife, Mary, have nine children and 35 grandchildren; they make their home in Southgate.

Jim Bunning (R)
US Senator
SH-316 Hart Senate Ofc Bldg
Washington DC 20510
(202) 224-4343
FAX (202) 228-1373
http://bunning.senate.gov/index.cfm

## REPRESENTATIVE ED WHITFIELD
## (R-FIRST DISTRICT)

First elected to Congress in 1984, Congressman Ed Whitfield is serving his sixth term as U.S. Representative for the 34 counties of Kentucky's First Congressional District.

A native of Hopkinsville, Whitfield earned a bachelor's degree and a law degree from the University of Kentucky. He served as a 1st Lieutenant in the 100th Division of the U.S. Army Reserves. A practicing attorney in Hopkinsville, Whitfield also operated an oil distributorship in the west Kentucky coalfields. He served in the Kentucky House of Representatives from 1974-75.

In 1979, he became counsel to the president of Seaboard System Railroad in Washington, D.C. Four years later, he was named vice president of State Relations for CSX Corp; and then vice president for Federal Railroad Affairs. Whitfield served as Legal Counsel to the Chairman of the Interstate Commerce Commission (ICC) from 1991 to 1993.

Married to the former Connie Harriman, Whitfield has a daughter, two grandchildren and a Scottish terrier.

Ed Whitfield (R)
US Representative - First District
301 Cannon House Ofc Bldg
Washington DC 20515
(202) 225-3115 • FAX (202) 225-3547
ed.whitfield@mail.house.gov
http://whitfield.house.gov/

## REPRESENTATIVE RON LEWIS
## (R-SECOND DISTRICT)

Ron Lewis has represented Kentucky's Second District since 1994. The Second District is home to Fort Knox, Mammoth Cave National Park, the birthplace of Abraham Lincoln, and over 50,000 people who depend on agriculture for a living.

The son of a tobacco farmer, Lewis was born Sept. 14, 1946, in Greenup County. He has a bachelor's degree in history and political science; and a master's degree in higher education. Lewis also attended the Southern Baptist Seminary prior to being ordained a minister.

Lewis married the former Kayi Gambill in 1966. They have two children, Ronald Brent and Allison Faye, and live in Cecilia.

Ron Lewis (R)
US Representative - Second District
2418 Rayburn House Ofc Bldg
Washington DC 20515
(202) 225-3501 • FAX (202) 226-2019
ron.lewis@mail.house.gov
http://www.house.gov/ronlewis/

## REPRESENTATIVE ANNE M. NORTHUP
## (R-THIRD DISTRICT)

Anne M. Northup was elected to represent the Third Congressional District of Kentucky in 1996. She returned to Congress in 1998, 2000, 2002, and 2004. Before her election to Congress, she represented the 32nd Legislative District in the Kentucky House of Representatives for nine years, where she served five consecutive terms from 1987-1996. Congresswoman Northup is a member of the Congressional Coalition on Adoption and traveled to China to work on eliminating growing bureaucratic obstacles that threatened to reduce the number of Chinese orphans available to American families for adoption.

Congresswoman Northup graduated from Saint Mary's College in 1970 with a bachelor of arts degree in economics and business. She has years of service on community boards, is a recipient of numerous civic awards and is an active community volunteer. She has been married to Woody Northup, a small business owner, for over 35 years, and together the Northups have six children.

Anne Northup (R)
US Representative -Third District
2459 Rayburn House Ofc Bldg
Washington DC 20515
(202) 225-5401 • FAX (202) 225-5776
rep.northup@mail.house.gov
http://northup.house.gov/index.asp

## REPRESENTATIVE GEOFF DAVIS
## (R-FOURTH DISTRICT)

Elected in 2004, Congressman Geoff Davis represents Kentucky's Fourth District, which is the northern part of the state bordering West Virginia, Ohio and Indiana.

Upon graduation from high school, Davis enlisted in the U.S. Army and received an appointment to the U.S. Military Academy at West Point. He served as a helicopter flight commander in the 82nd Airborne Division, and later ran U.S. Army Aviation Operations for Peace Enforcement between Israel and Egypt. Davis is a former Army Ranger and senior parachutist.

In 1992, Davis started a consulting firm specializing in lean manufacturing and high technology systems integration. He and his wife Pat live in Hebron with their six children.

Geoff Davis (R) - US Representative
Fourth District
1541 Longworth House Ofc Bldg
Washington DC 20515
(202) 225-3465 • FAX (202) 225-0003
http://geoffdavis.house.gov/

## REPRESENTATIVE HAROLD "HAL" ROGERS
## (R-FIFTH DISTRICT)

In his 25th year on Capitol Hill, Congressman Harold "Hal" Rogers was elected to Congress in 1980 and is currently serving his 13th term representing Kentucky's Fifth Congressional District. Rogers has a reputation as a skillful insider with significant influence over federal budget policy in a wide range of areas.

Rogers' congressional district consists of 29 counties in southern and eastern Kentucky. Born in rural Kentucky, Rogers earned his bachelor's and law degrees from the University of Kentucky. An attorney by profession, he stepped into the public arena during the 1960s by promoting industrial development in Somerset. In 1969, he was elected as Commonwealth Attorney for two Kentucky counties and served in that position for 11 years.

Rogers was married to Shirley McDowell Rogers for 37 years until her death in 1995. Together, they reared three children, Anthony, Allison and John. Rogers remarried Cynthia Doyle Rogers in 1999; they make their home in Somerset.

Harold Rogers (R)
US Representative - Fifth District
2406 Rayburn House Ofc Bldg
Washington DC 20515
(202) 225-4601 • (202) 225-0940
talk2hal@mail.house.gov
http://www.house.gov/rogers/

## REPRESENTATIVE BEN CHANDLER
## (D-SIXTH DISTRICT)

Ben Chandler was first elected in a special election in February 2004 to represent Kentucky's Sixth District in the U.S. House of Representatives. He won a full 2-year term in 2004 with 59 percent of the vote.

Before his election to Congress, Chandler served two terms as Kentucky's Attorney General. In 1995, he became the youngest Attorney General in the nation and was reelected in 1999 without opposition. He previously served a four-year term as Kentucky State Auditor.

Chandler graduated from the University of Kentucky with a bachelor's in history and holds a law degree from the University of Kentucky College of Law.

Born on September 12, 1959, Chandler lives in Woodford County with his wife Jennifer and their three children, Lucie, Albert IV and Branham.

Ben Chandler (D)
US Representative
Sixth District
1504 Longworth House Ofc Bldg
Washington DC 20515
(202) 225-4706 9 • FAX (202) 225-2122
http://chandler.house.gov/

FEDERAL COURTS

| COURT | JUDGES/OFFICERS | ADDRESS1 | ADDRESS2 | CITY | ST | ZIP | PHONE |
|---|---|---|---|---|---|---|---|
| Supreme Court of the US (The) | John G Roberts Jr, Chief Justice | US Supreme Court Bldg | 1 1st St NE | Washington | DC | 20543 | (202) 479-3211 |
| Supreme Court of the US (The) | Stephen G Breyer, Associate Justice | US Supreme Court Bldg | 1 1st St NE | Washington | DC | 20543 | (202) 479-3211 |
| Supreme Court of the US (The) | Ruth Bader Ginsburg, Associate Justice | US Supreme Court Bldg | 1 1st St NE | Washington | DC | 20543 | (202) 479-3211 |
| Supreme Court of the US (The) | Anthony M Kennedy, Associate Justice | US Supreme Court Bldg | 1 1st St NE | Washington | DC | 20543 | (202) 479-3211 |
| Supreme Court of the US (The) | Samuel Anthony Alito Jr, Associate Justice | US Supreme Court Bldg | 1 1st St NE | Washington | DC | 20543 | (202) 479-3211 |
| Supreme Court of the US (The) | Antonin Scalia, Associate Justice | US Supreme Court Bldg | 1 1st St NE | Washington | DC | 20543 | (202) 479-3211 |
| Supreme Court of the US (The) | David H Souter, Associate Justice | US Supreme Court Bldg | 1 1st St NE | Washington | DC | 20543 | (202) 479-3211 |
| Supreme Court of the US (The) | John Paul Stevens, Associate Justice | US Supreme Court Bldg | 1 1st St NE | Washington | DC | 20543 | (202) 479-3211 |
| Supreme Court of the US (The) | Clarence Thomas, Associate Justice | US Supreme Court Bldg | 1 1st St NE | Washington | DC | 20543 | (202) 479-3211 |
| Supreme Court of the US (The) | William K Suter, Clerk of the Court | US Supreme Court Bldg | 1 1st St NE | Washington | DC | 20543 | (202) 479-3211 |
| Supreme Court of the US (The) | Sally M Rider, Admin Assistant to the Chief Judge | US Supreme Court Bldg | 1 1st St NE | Washington | DC | 20543 | (202) 479-3211 |
| Supreme Court of the US (The) | Frank D Wagner, Reporter of Decisions | US Supreme Court Bldg | 1 1st St NE | Washington | DC | 20543 | (202) 479-3211 |
| Supreme Court of the US (The) | Judith A Gaskell, Librarian | US Supreme Court Bldg | 1 1st St NE | Washington | DC | 20543 | (202) 479-3211 |
| Supreme Court of the US (The) | Pamela Talkin, Marshal | US Supreme Court Bldg | 1 1st St NE | Washington | DC | 20543 | (202) 479-3211 |
| Supreme Court of the US (The) | Kathleen L Arberg, Public Information Officer | US Supreme Court Bldg | 1 1st St NE | Washington | DC | 20543 | (202) 479-3211 |
| US Court of Appeals, Sixth Circuit | Danny J Boggs, Chief Judge | 220 US Cthse | 601 W Broadway | Louisville | KY | 40202 | (502) 625-3900 |
| US Court of Appeals, Sixth Circuit | Ralph B Guy Jr, Senior Judge | 540 Potter Stewart US Cthse | 100 E 5th St | Cincinnati | OH | 45202 | (513) 564-7000 |
| US Court of Appeals, Sixth Circuit | Damon J Keith, Senior Judge | 540 Potter Stewart US Cthse | 100 E 5th St | Cincinnati | OH | 45202 | (513) 564-7000 |
| US Court of Appeals, Sixth Circuit | Cornelia G Kennedy, Senior Judge | 540 Potter Stewart US Cthse | 100 E 5th St | Cincinnati | OH | 45202 | (513) 564-7000 |
| US Court of Appeals, Sixth Circuit | Gilbert S Merritt, Senior Judge | 540 Potter Stewart US Cthse | 100 E 5th St | Cincinnati | OH | 45202 | (513) 564-7000 |
| US Court of Appeals, Sixth Circuit | David A Nelson, Senior Judge | 540 Potter Stewart US Cthse | 100 E 5th St | Cincinnati | OH | 45202 | (513) 564-7000 |
| US Court of Appeals, Sixth Circuit | Alan E Norris, Senior Judge | 540 Potter Stewart US Cthse | 100 E 5th St | Cincinnati | OH | 45202 | (513) 564-7000 |
| US Court of Appeals, Sixth Circuit | James L Ryan, Senior Judge | 540 Potter Stewart US Cthse | 100 E 5th St | Cincinnati | OH | 45202 | (513) 564-7000 |
| US Court of Appeals, Sixth Circuit | Eugene E Siler Jr, Senior Judge | 310 S Main St Ste 333 | | London | KY | 40741 | (606) 877-7930 |
| US Court of Appeals, Sixth Circuit | Richard F Suhrheinrich, Senior Judge | 540 Potter Stewart US Cthse | 100 E 5th St | Cincinnati | OH | 45202 | (513) 564-7000 |
| US Court of Appeals, Sixth Circuit | Deborah L Cook, Judge | 540 Potter Stewart US Cthse | 100 E 5th St | Cincinnati | OH | 45202 | (513) 564-7000 |
| US Court of Appeals, Sixth Circuit | Alice M Batchelder, Judge | 540 Potter Stewart US Cthse | 100 E 5th St | Cincinnati | OH | 45202 | (513) 564-7000 |
| US Court of Appeals, Sixth Circuit | Eric L Clay, Judge | 540 Potter Stewart US Cthse | 100 E 5th St | Cincinnati | OH | 45202 | (513) 564-7000 |
| US Court of Appeals, Sixth Circuit | R Guy Cole Jr, Judge | 540 Potter Stewart US Cthse | 100 E 5th St | Cincinnati | OH | 45202 | (513) 564-7000 |
| US Court of Appeals, Sixth Circuit | Martha Craig Daughtrey, Judge | 540 Potter Stewart US Cthse | 100 E 5th St | Cincinnati | OH | 45202 | (513) 564-7000 |
| US Court of Appeals, Sixth Circuit | Julia Smith Gibbons, Judge | 540 Potter Stewart US Cthse | 100 E 5th St | Cincinnati | OH | 45202 | (513) 564-7000 |
| US Court of Appeals, Sixth Circuit | Richard Allen Griffin, Judge | 540 Potter Stewart US Cthse | 100 E 5th St | Cincinnati | OH | 45202 | (513) 564-7000 |
| US Court of Appeals, Sixth Circuit | Ronald Lee Gilman, Judge | 540 Potter Stewart US Cthse | 100 E 5th St | Cincinnati | OH | 45202 | (513) 564-7000 |
| US Court of Appeals, Sixth Circuit | Boyce F Martin Jr, Judge | 209 US Cthse | 601 W Broadway | Louisville | KY | 40202 | (502) 625-3800 |
| US Court of Appeals, Sixth Circuit | David W McKeague, Judge | 540 Potter Stewart US Cthse | 100 E 5th St | Cincinnati | OH | 45202 | (513) 564-7000 |
| US Court of Appeals, Sixth Circuit | Karen Nelson Moore, Judge | 540 Potter Stewart US Cthse | 100 E 5th St | Cincinnati | OH | 45202 | (513) 564-7000 |
| US Court of Appeals, Sixth Circuit | John M Rogers, Judge | 540 Potter Stewart US Cthse | 100 E 5th St | Cincinnati | OH | 45202 | (513) 564-7000 |
| US Court of Appeals, Sixth Circuit | Jeffrey S Sutton, Judge | 540 Potter Stewart US Cthse | 100 E 5th St | Cincinnati | OH | 45202 | (513) 564-7000 |
| US Court of Appeals, Sixth Circuit | James Higgins, Circuit Executive | 503 Potter Stewart US Cthse | 100 E 5th St | Cincinnati | OH | 45202 | (513) 564-7200 |
| US Court of Appeals, Sixth Circuit | Leonard Green, Clerk US Court of Appeals | 540 Potter Stewart US Cthse | 100 E 5th St | Cincinnati | OH | 45202 | (513) 564-7000 |
| Administrative Offices of the US Courts | Leonidas Ralph Mecham, Director | Office of Public Affairs | | Washington | DC | 20544 | (202) 502-2600 |
| US Sentencing Commission | Judge Ricardo H Hinojosa, Chair | 1 Columbus Cir NE | | Washington | DC | 20002 | (202) 502-4500 |
| US District Court Clerk, Eastern District | Leslie G Whitmer, Clerk of the Court | 101 Barr St Rm 206 | PO Drawer 3074 | Lexington | KY | 40588 | (859) 233-2503 |
| US District Court Clerk, Eastern District | Mark Armstrong, Chief Deputy | 101 Barr St Rm 206 | PO Box 3074 | Lexington | KY | 40588 | (859) 233-2503 |
| US District Court Clerk, Eastern District | Christina Riley, Deputy in Charge | 336 Carl Perkins Federal Bldg | 1405 Greenup Ave | Ashland | KY | 41101 | (606) 329-8652 |
| US District Court Clerk, Eastern District | Lynn Battaglia, Deputy in Charge | 35 W 5th St | PO Box 1073 | Covington | KY | 41012 | (859) 392-7925 |
| US District Court Clerk, Eastern District | Shirley Middleton, Deputy in Charge | 313 John C Watts Federal Bldg | 330 W Broadway | Frankfort | KY | 40601 | (502) 223-5225 |
| US District Court Clerk, Eastern District | Shirley W Allen, Deputy in Charge | 310 S Main St | PO Box 5121 | London | KY | 40745 | (606) 877-7910 |
| US District Court Clerk, Eastern District | Malinda Bevins, Deputy in Charge | 110 Main St Ste 203 | | Pikeville | KY | 41501 | (606) 437-6160 |
| US District Court, Eastern District | Joseph M Hood, Chief Judge | 101 Barr St Ste 219 | PO Box 2227 | Lexington | KY | 40588 | (859) 233-2415 |

Clark's Kentucky Almanac Second Edition

## FEDERAL COURTS

| COURT | JUDGES/OFFICERS | ADDRESS1 | ADDRESS2 | CITY | ST | ZIP | PHONE |
|---|---|---|---|---|---|---|---|
| US District Court, Eastern District | William O Bertelsman, Senior Judge | 35 W 5th St Rm 505 | PO Box 1012 | Covington | KY | 41012 | (859) 392-7900 |
| US District Court, Eastern District | Karl S Forester, Senior Judge | 101 Barr St Ste 219 | PO Box 2165 | Lexington | KY | 40588 | (859) 233-2625 |
| US District Court, Eastern District | G Wix Unthank, Senior Judge | | PO Box 5112 | London | KY | 40741 | (606) 878-2731 |
| US District Court, Eastern District | Henry R Wilhoit Jr, Senior Judge | 320 Federal Bldg | 1405 Greenup Ave | Ashland | KY | 41101 | (606) 329-2592 |
| US District Court, Eastern District | David L Bunning, Judge | 35 W 5th St Rm 410 | PO Box 232 | Covington | KY | 41011 | (859) 392-7907 |
| US District Court, Eastern District | Karen K Caldwell, Judge | US District Cthse | 330 W Broadway Ste 354 | Frankfort | KY | 40601 | (502) 875-4777 |
| US District Court, Eastern District | Jennifer B Coffman, Judge | 101 Barr St Ste 136 | PO Box 2228 | Lexington | KY | 40588 | (859) 233-2453 |
| US District Court, Eastern District | Danny C Reeves, Judge | US District Cthse | 310 S Main St Ste 434 | London | KY | 40741 | (606) 877-7960 |
| US District Court, Eastern District | Gregory F Van Tatenhove, Judge | US District Cthse | 110 Main St Ste 210-H | Pikeville | KY | 40501 | (606) 437-7338 |
| US District Court, Eastern District | J B Johnson Jr, Magistrate Judge | US District Cthse | 310 S Main St | London | KY | 40741 | (606) 877-7940 |
| US District Court, Eastern District | Peggy E Patterson, Magistrate Judge | 210 Carl Perkins Federal Bldg | 1405 Greenup Ave | Ashland | KY | 41101 | (606) 329-2952 |
| US District Court, Eastern District | James B Todd, Magistrate Judge | 101 Barr St Ste 417 | PO Box 2058 | Lexington | KY | 40588 | (859) 233-2697 |
| US District Court, Eastern District | J Gregory Wehrman, Magistrate Judge | 35 W 5th St Ste 375 | PO Box 1299 | Covington | KY | 41012 | (859) 392-7909 |
| US Bankruptcy Court Clerk, Eastern District | Jerry D Truitt, Clerk of the Court | Community Trust Bank Bldg | 100 E Vine St Ste 200 | Lexington | KY | 40507 | (859) 233-2608 |
| US Bankruptcy Court, Eastern District | Joe Scott, Chief Judge | | PO Box 1111 | Lexington | KY | 40588 | (859) 233-2608 |
| US Bankruptcy Court, Eastern District | William S Howard, Judge | | PO Box 576 | Lexington | KY | 40588 | (859) 233-2465 |
| US Bankruptcy Court, Eastern District | Joe Lee, Judge | | PO Box 1111 | Lexington | KY | 40588 | (859) 233-2814 |
| US Probation Office, Eastern District | Rozel L Hollingsworth, Chief Probation Officer | 100 E Vine St Ste 600 | PO Box 1780 | Lexington | KY | 40588 | (859) 233-2646 |
| US District Court Clerk, Western District | Jeffery A Apperson, Clerk of Court | 601 W Broadway Rm 106 | | Louisville | KY | 40202 | (502) 625-3500 |
| US District Court Clerk, Western District | Vanessa Armstrong, Chief Deputy | 601 W Broadway Rm 106 | | Louisville | KY | 40202 | (502) 625-3528 |
| US District Court Clerk, Western District | Celia Furlong, Deputy in Charge/Case Administrator | 241 E Main St Ste 120 | | Bowling Green | KY | 42101 | (270) 393-2500 |
| US District Court Clerk, Western District | Patti May, Deputy in Charge | 126 Federal Bldg | 423 Frederica St | Owensboro | KY | 42301 | (270) 689-4400 |
| US District Court, Western District | Joan Moore, Deputy in Charge | 501 Broadway St Ste 127 | | Paducah | KY | 42001 | (270) 415-6400 |
| US District Court, Western District | John G Heyburn II, Chief Judge | Gene Snyder Cthse Rm 239 | 601 W Broadway | Louisville | KY | 40202 | (502) 625-3620 |
| US District Court, Western District | Edward H Johnstone, Senior Judge | Gene Snyder Cthse Rm 262 | 601 W Broadway | Louisville | KY | 40202 | (502) 625-3660 |
| US District Court, Western District | Judge Johnstone's Paducah Office | Federal Bldg Rm 217 | 501 Broadway St | Paducah | KY | 42001 | (270) 415-6450 |
| US District Court, Western District | Jennifer B Coffman, Judge | Gene Snyder Cthse Rm 252 | 601 W Broadway | Louisville | KY | 40202 | (502) 625-3680 |
| US District Court, Western District | Judge Coffman's Lexington Office | | PO Box 2228 | Lexington | KY | 40588 | (859) 233-2453 |
| US District Court, Western District | Joseph H McKinley Jr, Judge | 423 Frederica St Rm 206 | | Owensboro | KY | 42301 | (270) 689-4430 |
| US District Court, Western District | Judge McKinley's Bowling Green Office | 241 E Main St Rm 207 | | Bowling Green | KY | 42101 | (270) 393-2440 |
| US District Court, Western District | Thomas B Russell, Judge | Gene Snyder US Cthse Rm 202 | 601 W Broadway | Louisville | KY | 40202 | (502) 625-3640 |
| US District Court, Western District | Judge Russell's Bowling Green Office | 241 E Main St Rm 207 | | Bowling Green | KY | 42101 | (270) 393-2440 |
| US District Court, Western District | Judge Russell's Paducah Office | 501 Broadway St Rm 121 | | Paducah | KY | 42001 | (270) 415-6430 |
| US District Court, Western District | Charles R Simpson III, Judge | Gene Snyder US Cthse Rm 247 | 601 W Broadway | Louisville | KY | 40202 | (502) 625-3600 |
| US District Court, Western District | Dave Whalin, Magistrate Judge | US Cthse Rm 117 | | Louisville | KY | 40202 | (502) 625-3830 |
| US District Court, Western District | E Robert Goebel, Magistrate Judge | | | Owensboro | KY | 42301 | (270) 689-4450 |
| US District Court, Western District | Judge Goebel's Bowling Green Office | 241 E Main St Rm 207 | | Bowling Green | KY | 42101 | (270) 393-2440 |
| US District Court, Western District | W David King, Magistrate Judge | 501 Broadway St Rm 330 | | Paducah | KY | 42001 | (270) 415-6470 |
| US District Court, Western District | James D Moyer, Magistrate Judge | Gene Snyder Cthse Rm 208 | 601 W Broadway | Louisville | KY | 40202 | (502) 625-3930 |
| US Bankruptcy Court Clerk, Western District | Diane S Robl, Clerk of Court | 601 W Broadway Ste 450 | | Louisville | KY | 40202 | (502) 627-5700 |
| US Bankruptcy Court, Western District | Joan L Cooper, Chief Judge | 601 W Broadway | | Louisville | KY | 40202 | (502) 627-5525 |
| US Bankruptcy Court, Western District | Thomas H Fulton, Judge | 601 W Broadway | | Louisville | KY | 40202 | (502) 627-5550 |
| US Bankruptcy Court, Western District | David T Stosberg, Judge | 601 W Broadway | | Louisville | KY | 40202 | (502) 627-5575 |
| US Probation Office, Western District | Patrick Craig, Chief Probation Officer | 601 W Broadway Ste 400 | | Louisville | KY | 40202 | (502) 681-1000 |
| US Probation Office, Western District | Patrick Craig, Chief Probation Officer | 2530 Scottsville Rd Ste 22 | PO Box 51607 | Bowling Green | KY | 42101 | (270) 842-6109 |
| US Probation Office, Western District | Jeffery T Litchfield, Supervising Officer | 607 Hammond Plz | FtCampbell Blvd | Hopkinsville | KY | 42240 | (270) 885-4853 |
| US Probation Office, Western District | Jeffery T Litchfield, Supervising Officer | 309 Federal Bldg | 423 Frederica St | Owensboro | KY | 42301 | (270) 684-2351 |
| US Probation Office, Western District | Ronnie E Golden, Supervising Officer | 2625 Wayne Sullivan Dr | | Paducah | KY | 42003 | (270) 442-7824 |

*Source: The Kentucky Directory Gold Book 2006-2007*

# FEDERAL GOVERNMENT
# *Military Installations*

Jerry Cecil

Kentucky's role in national security is apparent in its two federal military installations, Fort Knox and Fort Campbell. However, long before these bases were established, Kentucky played a significant role and displayed an unflinching commitment to national defense. Early soldiers and frontiersmen such as Gen. George Rogers Clark and Daniel Boone defended against foreign designs to claim the territory west of the Appalachians. After the American Revolution, European nations threatened the Ohio River valley with attempts to reclaim territory. Kentuckians responded willingly and rallied behind Gen. Andrew Jackson in the War of 1812. Kentucky, technically neutral during the Civil War, was a key component to the strategies of both the Union and Confederacy; the state was at the forefront of providing supplies, troops and military posts to restore the Union. During WWII, Camp Zachary Taylor, near Louisville, served as a recruiting and training base including medical personnel for the famed Barro hospital unit.

Fort Knox covers 109,000 acres in Hardin, Meade, and Bullitt counties. In 1918 the first 40,000 acres for Camp Knox, named for Gen. Henry T. Knox, were purchased. The reservation was renamed Fort Knox in 1932. (Results of the 2005 BRAC decisions are covered elsewhere.) Units located on Fort Knox include active duty Army organizations, Army Reserve, National Guard and U.S. Marine Corps.

Fort Campbell opened in 1942 to provide training areas and housing for the Army during WW II. Fort Campbell was named after William B. Campbell, a Tennessee statesman and brigadier general of the U.S. Volunteers during the Civil War. Nearly two-thirds of the 105,000 acres of post are in Tennessee, but the post office is located in Kentucky, and identification lies with Kentucky.

The geographic and strategic national importance of Fort Knox and Fort Campbell continued to grow in the early 1960s as America entered the Vietnam War, and remains steady today especially in light of the threat of global terrorism.

Blue Grass Army Depot, situated on almost 14,000 acres near Richmond, was established to

**(Top) Fort Knox**
*Source: Kentucky Department for
Libraries & Archives*
**(left) M1-A1 Tank**
*Source: Kentucky Commission on
Military Affairs*

store and repair equipment after WW II. BGAD supplies ammunition and personal protection equipment; it is used for the storage of conventional explosive munitions as well as assembled chemical weapons (many scheduled for destruction in this decade). BGAD's companion depot, Lexington Army Depot, was closed in the 1980s.

Kentucky Army and Air National Guard maintain a network of military installations funded by state and federal funds. The Kentucky Reserves form an important pillar for national security. Each service – Army, Navy, Air Force, Marines, Coast Guard—maintains Reserve centers in Kentucky. The Coast Guard, part of the new Transportation Security Agency, performs missions on lakes and rivers, provides search and rescue, boat inspections, and interdictions of contraband.

*Jerry Cecil is Kentucky's Civilian Aide to the Secretary of the U.S. Army.*

# FEDERAL GOVERNMENT

# *Future Growth of Kentucky's Defense Industry* BG (Ret.) James E. Shane

## BASE REALIGNMENT AND CLOSURE (BRAC)

Historically, during the period of 1988–2005, the Base Realignment and Closure (BRAC) process was used as a restructuring and downsizing tool for the Department of the Defense (DoD). The purpose was to transform the military into meeting the challenges of the 21st century. During the decades of 1980 and 1990, Kentucky lost 13,000-plus jobs and declined $234 million dollars in payroll due to BRAC rounds and downsizing initiatives by DoD. In 1997 the Kentucky Commission on Military Affairs was established to reverse this negative trend impacting Kentucky's military. The recent 2005 round was signed by Pres. Bush as one of the most comprehensive BRAC recommendations in our country's history, which included 190 recommendations and 837-related closures and realignments.

The economic impact of BRAC 2005 on Kentucky has been universally positive along with other recent force structure decisions. These changes not only alter the forces assigned to Fort Knox, they will dramatically transform the personnel demographics by exchanging lower rank, transient student personnel for more senior, permanent military and civilian personnel. Fort Campbell will lose an Aviation Battalion, but gain a fourth Brigade Combat Team for the 101st Airborne Division (Air Assault). Fort Knox will undergo major transformation with the move of the Armor Center and School to Fort Benning, Georgia; establishment of the Army's Personnel Center of Excellence at Fort Knox—to include the re-stationing of the Army's Human Resources Command from Alexandria, Virginia—and other elements from St. Louis and Indianapolis; the move of the 84th Army Reserve Readiness Training Center from Fort McCoy, Wisconsin; activation of an Infantry Brigade Combat Team; a Deployable Command Post; 19th Engineer Battalion; and other smaller units from overseas

locations. Blue Grass Army Depot, in Richmond, will assume ammunition maintenance functions from the Red River Army Depot, Texas, and could experience significant increase in sensitive supply and maintenance functions from an approximate 33 percent increase in DoD special operations forces envisioned in the 2006 Quadrennial Defense Review.

## MORE ABOUT THE COMMISSION

The Kentucky Commission on Military Affairs is a separate administrative body of state government, which is attached to the office of the Governor. The Commission serves in an advisory capacity to the Governor, the Kentucky General Assembly and the Congressional Delegation. Its primary mission is to grow Kentucky's defense industry by protecting military installations and activities from the threat of downsizing—while sustaining and promoting military business opportunities, which enhance economic growth. And, the Commission assists small businesses that seek business opportunities with the defense industry. The Commonwealth has seen substantial growth in defense spending since the Commission's enactment in 1997. Today's military industry contributes over $5-plus billion dollars to Kentucky's economy. Its functions contribute to the overall economic strategy of the state.

Our world changed following the tragic attack on our country that occurred on 11 September 2001. The Global War on Terrorism has resulted in major changes designed to enhance our nation's security. The ongoing transformation of our military forces and the creation of the Department of Homeland Security are just two of the many initiatives resulting from the challenges of this ongoing conflict.

The Commission recognized that a strategic approach was necessary to guide our efforts to preserve and grow the federal military presence and the defense community in the Commonwealth. The Commission's Strategic Plan helped guide efforts that achieved overwhelmingly positive results from the BRAC 2005 process. As a result of this coordinated implementation effort, the Commonwealth of Kentucky will receive billions of dollars in economic growth and add thousands of new jobs.

Significant changes continue throughout federal government, and our challenge is to again adapt and respond to these changes. While today's environment is much different than the one that existed a few short years ago, it continues to provide both challenges and opportunities. Our response must be both aggressive and flexible, taking into account the needs of the nation and the Commonwealth of Kentucky.

To contact the Kentucky Commission on Military Affairs, please call (502) 564-0269 or visit http://kcma.ky.gov.

---

**BRAC KENTUCKY IMPACT**

- No Kentucky military installation closures
- Significant gains resulting from realignment:
  - 2 - Infantry Brigades (Ft Campbell & Ft Knox)
  - 7 - New Commands (Ft Knox)
  - 1 - Deployable Command Post (Ft Knox)
  - 32 - Detachments (Ft Knox)
  - 2 - New Armed Forces Reserve Centers

---

**BRAC ECONOMIC IMPACT**
(CURRENT ESTIMATES)

- 5,000 + military/civilian jobs
- $254 million annual salary increase
- $500 + million new military construction
- $250 million construction for Residential Community Initiative
- $15 - $20 million annual state tax revenue

---

## DOD PRIME CONTRACT AWARDS BY MAJOR PROCUREMENT PROGRAM($) , FY2005

| MAJOR PROCUREMENT PROGRAM (in thousands of dollars) | TOTAL DOLLARS | ARMY DOLLARS | NAVY DOLLARS | AIR FORCE DOLLARS | DLA DOLLARS * | CORP OF ENG $ * | ODA DOLLARS * |
|---|---|---|---|---|---|---|---|
| US TOTAL (in millions of dollars) | 236,985.8 | 70,048.1 | 62,774.7 | 51,670.8 | 23,112.5 | 4,384.4 | 24,995.3 |
| KENTUCKY TOTAL - All Programs | 4,299,757.0 | 750,307.9 | 221,126.2 | 110,673.7 | 441,517.2 | 120,521.8 | 2,655,610.2 |
| Aircraft Engines & Spares | 12,020.4 | 456.8 | 30.8 | 11,407.5 | 96.8 | 28.4 | 0.0 |
| Aircraft Frames & Spares | 80,691.1 | 11,646.7 | 14.2 | 36,430.9 | 1,312.3 | 328.1 | 30,958.8 |
| All other Supplies & Equip | 170,841.6 | 42,520.6 | 29,541.9 | 20,095.7 | 61,741.1 | 3,275.2 | 13,667.1 |
| Ammunition | 4,656.4 | 3,363.6 | 1,292.9 | 0.0 | 0.0 | 0.0 | 0.0 |
| Building Supplies | 79.0 | 56.6 | 15.1 | 0.0 | 0.0 | 7.3 | 0.0 |
| Combat Vehicles | 15,236.3 | 14,805.4 | 0.0 | 0.0 | 430.9 | 0.0 | 0.0 |
| Construction | 359,686.8 | 245,341.6 | 468.5 | 739.5 | 8,900.0 | 104,161.9 | 75.3 |
| Construction Equipment | 1,582.4 | 16.9 | 0.0 | 375.6 | 947.0 | 41.0 | 202.0 |
| Containers & Handling Equip | 11,631.6 | 10,896.4 | 735.2 | 0.0 | 0.0 | 0.0 | 0.0 |
| Electronics & Communications Equip | 25,566.5 | 6,388.8 | 4,265.1 | 12,229.8 | 2,400.8 | 38.6 | 243.6 |
| Materials Handling Equipment | 1,123.1 | 832.9 | 78.0 | 7.0 | 0.0 | 183.9 | 21.3 |
| Medical & Dental Supplies & Equip | 48,103.9 | 7,085.0 | 300.4 | 30.2 | 39,862.5 | 17.5 | 808.2 |
| Missile & Space Systems | 13,092.6 | 4,230.6 | 7,810.0 | 979.0 | 73.0 | 0.0 | 0.0 |
| Non-Combat Vehicles | 11,661.3 | 10,963.9 | 0.0 | 0.0 | 249.5 | 448.0 | 0.0 |
| Other Aircraft Equip | 24,380.5 | 193.5 | -10.9 | 23,469.4 | 637.2 | 0.3 | 91.0 |
| Other Fuels & Lubricants | 14,584.1 | 0.0 | 10.2 | 0.0 | 14,574.4 | -0.5 | 0.0 |
| Petroleum | 33,223.3 | 72.0 | 0.0 | 0.0 | 33,159.9 | -8.5 | 0.0 |
| Photographic Supplies & Equip | 21.5 | 13.3 | 0.0 | 4.2 | 0.0 | 4.1 | 0.0 |
| Production Equip | 1,196.1 | 173.8 | 0.0 | 0.0 | 1,022.3 | 0.0 | 0.0 |
| Services | 3,032,217.9 | 375,359.9 | 29,719.7 | 3,385.6 | 4,832.7 | 11,996.9 | 2,606,923.2 |
| Ships | 6,261.9 | 9.7 | 6,185.5 | 0.0 | 66.7 | 0.0 | 0.0 |
| Subsistence | 25,863.9 | 831.8 | 0.0 | 0.0 | 22,415.3 | 0.0 | 2,616.8 |
| Textiles, Clothing & Equipage | 264,658.9 | 14,162.9 | 279.2 | 1,508.7 | 248,705.3 | 0.0 | 2.8 |
| Transportation Equip | 98.0 | 98.0 | 0.0 | 0.0 | 0.0 | 0.0 | 0.0 |
| Weapons | 141,277.9 | 787.4 | 140,390.4 | 10.6 | 89.5 | 0.0 | 0.0 |

*Source:* http://siadapp.dior.whs.mil/procurement/historical_reports/geographic/P06-P09/FY2005/P06-P09-State-Maj-Procurement-2005.xls.

* DLA=Defense Logistics Agency; CORP OF ENG =Army Corps of Engineers; and ODA=Original Design Activity

# FEDERAL EXPENDITURES BY COUNTY, 2004

| COUNTY | RETIREMENT/ DISABILITY (INDIVIDUALS) | OTHER DIRECT PAYMENTS (INDIVIDUALS) | DIRECT PAYMENTS (NOT INDIVIDUALS) | GRANTS | PROCUREMENT CONTRACTS | SALARIES & WAGES | TOTAL DIRECT EXPENDITURES OR OBLIGATIONS | TOTAL EXPENDITURES (DEFENSE) | TOTAL EXPENDITURES (NON DEFENSE) | DIRECT LOANS | GUARANTEED/ INSURED LOANS | INSURANCE |
|---|---|---|---|---|---|---|---|---|---|---|---|---|
| Adair | 41,605,162 | 29,056,084 | 873,883 | 36,103,307 | 584,366 | 2,837,157 | 111,059,959 | 1,255,998 | 109,803,961 | 3,851,738 | 2,814,471 | 561,576 |
| Allen | 44,618,541 | 20,457,709 | 889,641 | 35,815,304 | 530,061 | 2,077,765 | 104,389,021 | 1,353,000 | 103,036,021 | 3,324,633 | 2,942,463 | 1,163,413 |
| Anderson | 42,499,770 | 13,427,013 | 165,321 | 23,449,992 | 561,693 | 2,635,114 | 82,738,903 | 2,527,536 | 80,211,367 | 1,884,850 | 18,079,126 | 4,761,135 |
| Ballard | 28,548,713 | 16,602,057 | 2,512,318 | 8,466,150 | 532,664 | 2,055,092 | 58,716,994 | 938,731 | 57,778,263 | 61,883 | 1,928,756 | 6,355,110 |
| Barren | 92,823,025 | 39,413,119 | 1,939,685 | 46,229,945 | 16,140,799 | 7,652,076 | 204,198,649 | 5,797,131 | 198,401,518 | 802,821 | 12,714,829 | 2,568,055 |
| Bath | 30,306,404 | 11,244,285 | 687,263 | 41,659,677 | 448,746 | 1,805,073 | 86,151,448 | 783,200 | 85,368,248 | 440,496 | 1,986,333 | 4,545,296 |
| Bell | 99,945,673 | 53,393,564 | 815,522 | 73,534,193 | -159,386,447 | 9,771,922 | 78,074,427 | 3,060,214 | 75,014,213 | 370,684 | 10,567,847 | 28,408,351 |
| Boone | 180,035,471 | 53,614,675 | 237,183 | 30,670,929 | 63,125,737 | 76,847,242 | 404,531,237 | 61,686,541 | 342,844,696 | 1,493,810 | 106,442,494 | 8,048,872 |
| Bourbon | 46,960,173 | 22,482,376 | 4,035,910 | 21,503,030 | 70,378,554 | 2,329,110 | 167,689,153 | 40,370,078 | 127,319,075 | 753,758 | 8,239,199 | 16,115,780 |
| Boyd | 175,788,258 | 86,705,253 | 803,157 | 69,265,129 | 16,385,002 | 34,103,316 | 383,050,115 | 11,912,667 | 371,137,448 | 420,005 | 9,791,897 | 24,661,455 |
| Boyle | 75,232,656 | 31,758,916 | 695,064 | 31,780,800 | 1,799,306 | 5,723,174 | 146,989,916 | 4,797,124 | 142,192,792 | 53,900 | 12,650,917 | 3,371,194 |
| Bracken | 21,362,074 | 10,396,508 | 376,737 | 11,342,038 | 397,546 | 1,849,073 | 45,523,976 | 661,000 | 44,862,976 | 559,830 | 2,038,530 | 10,292,371 |
| Breathitt | 48,413,801 | 23,237,721 | 443,859 | 57,481,938 | 396,608 | 4,036,891 | 134,010,818 | 1,207,000 | 132,803,818 | 710,201 | 242,852 | 6,443,800 |
| Breckinridge | 54,254,839 | 22,478,035 | 2,980,101 | 25,174,195 | 1,557,819 | 3,608,292 | 110,053,281 | 4,316,678 | 105,736,603 | 2,022,147 | 4,488,213 | 7,436,412 |
| Bullitt | 108,402,599 | 38,250,712 | 225,785 | 26,466,427 | 312,557,895 | 4,243,667 | 490,147,085 | 289,118,496 | 201,028,589 | 1,588,220 | 69,996,551 | 57,513,991 |
| Butler | 29,887,203 | 16,636,105 | 1,799,944 | 19,552,684 | 401,887 | 1,745,073 | 70,022,796 | 933,341 | 69,089,455 | 553,272 | 1,913,496 | 4,076,093 |
| Caldwell | 40,617,978 | 18,474,896 | 2,919,459 | 14,798,514 | 895,730 | 2,749,928 | 80,456,505 | 1,888,520 | 78,567,985 | 353,014 | 772,888 | 6,829,224 |
| Calloway | 87,005,361 | 49,657,296 | 3,864,556 | 26,786,351 | 2,708,575 | 5,684,567 | 175,706,706 | 5,866,678 | 169,840,028 | 501,755 | 6,499,463 | 18,569,596 |
| Campbell | 202,474,800 | 110,784,035 | 1,321,998 | 89,994,853 | 16,860,765 | 21,411,366 | 442,847,817 | 13,210,190 | 429,637,627 | 217,000 | 39,789,753 | 38,746,070 |
| Carlisle | 15,717,785 | 8,985,449 | 2,499,754 | 5,058,819 | 276,387 | 1,195,382 | 33,733,576 | 468,357 | 33,265,219 | 8,000 | 2,989,066 | 8,914,691 |
| Carroll | 24,382,813 | 12,532,248 | 575,579 | 16,605,006 | 3,410,617 | 2,663,073 | 60,169,536 | 4,657,078 | 55,512,458 | 1,879,233 | 3,368,979 | 7,327,030 |
| Carter | 74,838,315 | 35,073,691 | 389,095 | 51,995,153 | 17,019,545 | 5,336,002 | 184,651,801 | 19,271,907 | 165,379,894 | 2,732,031 | 15,450,091 | 17,486,085 |
| Casey | 37,341,298 | 18,567,256 | 577,135 | 29,550,815 | 507,740 | 1,870,419 | 88,414,663 | 1,131,000 | 87,283,663 | 662,804 | 1,247,146 | 3,046,206 |
| Christian | 151,889,721 | 66,107,239 | 10,747,911 | 72,289,257 | 363,961,048 | 1,083,219,194 | 1,748,204,984 | 1,441,425,688 | 306,779,296 | 1,142,184 | 31,569,393 | 75,401,266 |
| Clark | 91,931,603 | 30,904,729 | 996,931 | 55,670,293 | 3,018,724 | 7,805,166 | 190,327,446 | 5,550,703 | 184,776,743 | 1,769,663 | 12,416,905 | 15,674,712 |
| Clay | 65,977,857 | 32,286,120 | 248,196 | 78,021,756 | 35,051,329 | 19,409,620 | 230,994,878 | 33,409,921 | 197,584,957 | 1,710,996 | 844,952 | 5,430,128 |
| Clinton | 22,323,358 | 22,189,982 | 178,042 | 29,215,476 | 458,986 | 2,440,564 | 76,806,408 | 756,441 | 76,049,967 | 40,190,550 | 601,785 | 110,421 |
| Crittenden | 26,870,734 | 15,510,741 | 2,268,485 | 11,686,392 | 414,110 | 2,126,910 | 58,877,372 | 1,401,000 | 57,476,372 | 50,000 | 3,718,676 | 3,067,068 |
| Cumberland | 19,884,271 | 14,026,262 | 405,715 | 21,699,902 | 333,077 | 1,020,036 | 57,369,263 | 1,062,304 | 56,306,959 | 30,680 | 671,852 | |
| Daviess | 236,041,872 | 113,270,566 | 5,300,014 | 95,694,093 | 6,354,583 | 19,512,493 | 476,173,621 | 13,280,959 | 462,892,662 | 3,092,870 | 34,895,553 | 146,007,681 |
| Edmonson | 25,491,521 | 12,141,383 | 474,087 | 14,155,603 | 4,217,367 | 9,089,382 | 65,569,343 | 2,058,540 | 63,510,803 | 368,784 | 1,051,473 | 769,007 |
| Elliott | 13,586,579 | 6,041,757 | 171,696 | 13,784,283 | 134,115 | 512,691 | 34,231,121 | 127,000 | 34,104,121 | 80,260,121 | 74,000 | 769,849 |
| Estill | 48,472,122 | 26,163,315 | 425,603 | 29,783,649 | 736,446 | 2,684,564 | 108,265,699 | 2,366,332 | 105,899,367 | 578,305 | 1,503,516 | 1,625,292 |
| Fayette | 541,247,596 | 308,116,817 | 3,587,654 | 378,464,947 | 508,539,322 | 217,255,713 | 1,957,212,049 | 493,686,067 | 1,463,525,982 | 84,439,125 | 177,291,595 | 71,904,755 |
| Fleming | 36,328,049 | 14,893,400 | 1,870,912 | 36,749,929 | 717,908 | 2,799,947 | 93,360,145 | 775,024 | 92,585,121 | 562,024 | 18,224,263 | 4,717,726 |
| Floyd | 146,380,704 | 71,587,634 | 5,203,240 | 77,620,703 | 10,438,207 | 11,544,674 | 322,775,162 | 8,507,210 | 314,267,952 | 6,603,894 | 2,245,633 | 108,062,351 |
| Franklin | 229,783,177 | 67,383,020 | 13,202,943 | 1,017,845,362 | 5,012,597 | 32,593,250 | 1,365,820,349 | 41,351,462 | 1,324,468,887 | 21,008,748 | 23,782,150 | 58,979,864 |
| Fulton | 27,398,435 | 15,798,621 | 3,744,876 | 18,760,312 | 1,285,811 | 2,657,005 | 69,645,060 | 243,490 | 68,401,570 | 228,400 | 2,664,198 | 15,363,767 |
| Gallatin | 15,283,017 | 7,512,839 | 110,088 | 50,591,715 | 1,272,145 | 1,469,546 | 76,239,985 | 1,851,166 | 74,388,819 | 1,903,070 | 2,282,909 | 7,197,827 |
| Garrard | 38,008,844 | 13,591,323 | 412,955 | 14,566,118 | 480,368 | 1,880,255 | 68,939,863 | 1,404,000 | 67,535,863 | 333,045 | 8,111,430 | 3,209,987 |

# FEDERAL EXPENDITURES BY COUNTY, 2004

| COUNTY | RETIREMENT/ DISABILITY (INDIVIDUALS) | OTHER DIRECT PAYMENTS (INDIVIDUALS) | DIRECT PAYMENTS (NOT INDIVIDUALS) | GRANTS | PROCUREMENT CONTRACTS | SALARIES & WAGES | TOTAL DIRECT EXPENDITURES OR OBLIGATIONS | TOTAL EXPENDITURES (DEFENSE) | TOTAL EXPENDITURES (NON DEFENSE) | DIRECT LOANS | GUARANTEED/ INSURED LOANS | INSURANCE |
|---|---|---|---|---|---|---|---|---|---|---|---|---|
| Grant | 51,337,178 | 20,137,625 | 313,150 | 21,312,414 | 1,084,846 | 3,249,474 | 97,434,687 | 1,551,882 | 95,882,805 | 2,700,765 | 14,431,282 | 529,852 |
| Graves | 106,600,699 | 56,792,602 | 8,111,818 | 38,298,374 | 9,066,834 | 11,448,258 | 230,318,585 | 3,535,774 | 226,782,811 | 1,703,966 | 32,222,885 | 32,222,885 |
| Grayson | 68,821,944 | 32,438,665 | 1,868,834 | 45,424,797 | 1,030,695 | 4,762,511 | 154,347,446 | 4,312,053 | 150,035,393 | 955,068 | 3,467,141 | 2,590,822 |
| Green | 28,681,964 | 16,998,315 | 796,747 | 14,965,449 | 344,388 | 1,477,728 | 63,264,591 | 589,100 | 62,675,491 | 534,000 | 965,136 | 308,064 |
| Greenup | 120,333,094 | 49,451,348 | 687,623 | 33,215,923 | 4,303,926 | 3,905,991 | 211,897,905 | 6,509,055 | 205,388,850 | 503,594 | 7,356,922 | 34,795,813 |
| Hancock | 18,877,439 | 7,057,818 | 627,606 | 8,784,948 | 347,853 | 1,388,564 | 37,084,228 | 934,000 | 36,150,228 | 149,422 | 4,331,173 | 9,463,723 |
| Hardin | 350,847,838 | 77,673,251 | 2,447,414 | 57,380,730 | 5,881,025 | 485,222,854 | 979,453,112 | 558,729,516 | 420,723,596 | 4,453,188 | 89,085,659 | 32,003,799 |
| Harlan | 221,179,862 | 52,788,306 | 545,071 | 64,859,571 | 51,968,568 | 7,143,756 | 398,485,134 | 3,412,319 | 395,072,815 | 219,238 | 1,287,898 | 35,540,878 |
| Harrison | 45,988,359 | 17,785,157 | 758,715 | 22,846,830 | 1,027,402 | 4,379,438 | 92,785,901 | 3,248,044 | 89,537,857 | 2,247,630 | 7,555,927 | 15,457,930 |
| Hart | 39,884,690 | 20,382,885 | 882,626 | 28,225,483 | 546,626 | 2,182,601 | 92,104,911 | 1,339,000 | 90,765,911 | 288,567 | 3,140,700 | 2,054,762 |
| Henderson | 112,740,704 | 59,313,729 | 5,064,550 | 51,047,925 | 4,849,482 | 6,936,314 | 239,952,704 | 7,386,132 | 232,566,572 | 604,603 | 11,388,711 | 42,363,777 |
| Henry | 32,971,189 | 19,075,872 | 633,465 | 19,836,636 | 735,065 | 3,206,802 | 76,459,029 | 1,634,230 | 74,824,799 | 1,968,984 | 9,269,878 | 3,184,908 |
| Hickman | 11,263,905 | 7,780,592 | 3,714,694 | 6,369,975 | 273,351 | 1,106,873 | 30,509,390 | 304,564 | 30,204,826 | 131,200 | 1,905,405 | 15,144,034 |
| Hopkins | 141,606,498 | 57,587,736 | 4,015,659 | 48,520,962 | 89,659,996 | 10,602,459 | 351,993,310 | 5,751,872 | 346,241,438 | 790,722 | 8,391,076 | 11,870,528 |
| Jackson | 34,162,576 | 18,413,824 | 461,587 | 34,761,881 | 41,251,968 | 2,134,255 | 131,186,091 | 41,331,600 | 89,854,491 | 408,901 | 19,381,504 | 3,771,666 |
| Jefferson | 1,707,294,967 | 993,542,689 | 28,621,130 | 832,759,020 | 1,574,472,140 | 412,319,337 | 5,549,009,283 | 1,606,286,767 | 3,942,722,516 | 22,567,112 | 587,917,310 | 604,584,330 |
| Jessamine | 75,955,106 | 26,434,525 | 473,863 | 28,225,425 | 8,911,516 | 5,315,796 | 145,316,231 | 3,210,005 | 142,106,226 | 2,267,140 | 56,052,167 | 12,025,072 |
| Johnson | 72,886,368 | 35,313,307 | 971,662 | 53,596,581 | 2,334,664 | 3,418,672 | 168,521,254 | 2,763,088 | 165,758,166 | 3,295,831 | 10,264,564 | 40,064,721 |
| Kenton | 321,703,540 | 167,369,422 | 3,927,571 | 125,916,445 | 30,071,264 | 185,461,403 | 834,449,645 | 20,436,599 | 814,013,046 | 738,730 | 113,212,325 | 39,603,325 |
| Knott | 44,885,305 | 25,615,558 | 91,984 | 44,051,807 | 1,331,922 | 2,870,928 | 118,847,504 | 919,794 | 117,927,710 | 189,098 | 2,640,039 | 3,073,889 |
| Knox | 76,548,779 | 42,882,690 | 268,723 | 80,253,213 | 1,159,406 | 10,033,834 | 211,146,645 | 2,739,329 | 208,407,316 | 743,369 | 2,119,113 | 10,833,859 |
| Larue | 36,250,092 | 18,213,568 | 1,486,062 | 14,943,930 | 980,247 | 2,450,419 | 74,324,318 | 2,828,370 | 71,495,948 | 92,513 | 4,171,428 | 4,681,802 |
| Laurel | 125,829,445 | 48,792,709 | 505,660 | 65,072,948 | 7,140,578 | 19,620,708 | 266,962,048 | 6,349,657 | 260,612,391 | 9,039,684 | 11,328,783 | 680,923 |
| Lawrence | 42,853,977 | 21,447,437 | 312,893 | 31,555,245 | 586,443 | 2,317,255 | 99,073,250 | 1,309,612 | 97,763,638 | 546,675 | 654,931 | 5,256,149 |
| Lee | 23,534,841 | 12,809,953 | 150,198 | 20,126,150 | 398,743 | 1,241,055 | 58,260,940 | 500,000 | 57,760,940 | 388,716 | 58,400 | 3,982,099 |
| Leslie | 40,151,027 | 21,560,643 | 37,517 | 32,765,567 | 602,124 | 1,834,255 | 96,951,133 | 221,000 | 96,730,133 | 113,991 | 73,000 | 2,429,824 |
| Letcher | 84,704,812 | 41,280,403 | 207,302 | 51,742,901 | 1,363,344 | 4,737,329 | 184,036,091 | 932,300 | 183,103,791 | 116,932 | 448,023 | 4,517,500 |
| Lewis | 34,556,727 | 16,887,311 | 1,086,238 | 26,209,488 | 298,159 | 1,178,055 | 80,215,978 | 762,000 | 79,453,978 | 1,192,025 | 915,938 | 11,005,218 |
| Lincoln | 62,243,092 | 26,974,899 | 832,820 | 41,189,610 | 748,171 | 8,963,802 | 140,952,394 | 7,968,000 | 132,984,394 | 500,884 | 9,778,697 | 2,819,117 |
| Livingston | 30,841,507 | 15,607,015 | 2,281,132 | 9,412,079 | 33,638,032 | 4,351,765 | 96,131,530 | 20,437,971 | 75,693,559 | 146,050 | 1,487,657 | 3,818,106 |
| Logan | 66,954,826 | 39,255,398 | 6,480,979 | 36,670,772 | 889,428 | 3,488,147 | 153,739,550 | 2,944,325 | 150,795,225 | 3,035,515 | 21,397,963 | 32,049,107 |
| Lyon | 26,113,896 | 9,972,737 | 1,046,024 | 6,427,952 | 400,251 | 1,652,219 | 45,633,079 | 1,714,656 | 43,918,423 | 212,682 | 629,762 | 2,400,756 |
| McCracken | 188,200,079 | 96,015,078 | 5,450,175 | 70,919,546 | 978,145,418 | 52,557,321 | 1,391,287,617 | 11,875,491 | 1,379,412,126 | 1,088,956 | 21,919,542 | 23,291,020 |
| McCreary | 49,368,907 | 26,872,856 | 99,432 | 35,971,020 | 16,676,874 | 17,964,401 | 146,953,490 | 15,680,868 | 131,272,622 | 338,435 | 1,018,274 | 2,134 |
| McLean | 26,944,389 | 14,337,933 | 3,787,702 | 12,036,164 | 397,365 | 1,778,073 | 59,281,626 | 1,090,524 | 58,191,102 | 312,346 | 1,279,366 | 17,377,603 |
| Madison | 157,023,373 | 81,319,172 | 1,259,310 | 110,935,511 | 17,757,309 | 46,281,598 | 414,576,273 | 62,177,385 | 352,398,888 | 1,296,213 | 42,895,216 | 9,630,935 |
| Magoffin | 36,437,146 | 19,948,406 | 1,382,247 | 38,392,508 | 1,102,341 | 1,265,728 | 98,528,376 | 842,232 | 97,686,144 | 3,077,850 | 320,973 | 8,457,616 |
| Marion | 40,633,475 | 20,440,486 | 1,758,884 | 33,397,346 | 781,953 | 3,189,474 | 100,221,618 | 1,047,989 | 99,173,629 | 513,400 | 4,912,448 | 2,760,775 |
| Marshall | 99,669,650 | 40,480,626 | 2,827,982 | 18,891,037 | 2,596,272 | 5,056,857 | 169,522,424 | 4,195,828 | 165,326,596 | 401,110 | 6,652,981 | 8,224,340 |
| Martin | 50,211,503 | 16,368,684 | 1,200,360 | 35,999,695 | 2,965,943 | 18,978,382 | 125,724,567 | 1,063,198 | 124,661,369 | 7,100,535 | 10,355,458 | 28,488,510 |
| Mason | 40,242,217 | 21,933,653 | 1,351,649 | 25,096,616 | 645,141 | 3,891,947 | 93,161,223 | 1,811,578 | 91,349,645 | 439,180 | 6,757,755 | 6,110,978 |

## FEDERAL EXPENDITURES BY COUNTY, 2004

| COUNTY | RETIREMENT/ DISABILITY (INDIVIDUALS) | OTHER DIRECT PAYMENTS (INDIVIDUALS) | DIRECT PAYMENTS (NOT INDIVIDUALS) | GRANTS | PROCUREMENT CONTRACTS | SALARIES & WAGES | TOTAL DIRECT EXPENDITURES OR OBLIGATIONS | TOTAL EXPENDITURES (DEFENSE) | TOTAL EXPENDITURES (NON DEFENSE) | DIRECT LOANS | GUARANTEED/ INSURED LOANS | INSURANCE |
|---|---|---|---|---|---|---|---|---|---|---|---|---|
| Meade | 64,134,219 | 17,207,021 | 1,332,592 | 13,355,236 | 613,625 | 2,349,438 | 98,992,131 | 8,633,435 | 90,358,696 | 156,650 | 15,604,341 | 4,333,167 |
| Menifee | 18,026,305 | 7,078,158 | 100,485 | 10,913,103 | 3,621,756 | 16,004,691 | 55,744,498 | 15,934,843 | 39,809,655 | 772,738 | 1,033,951 | 447,045 |
| Mercer | 55,044,559 | 19,449,233 | 800,699 | 19,525,535 | 706,089 | 5,114,620 | 100,640,735 | 4,371,000 | 96,269,735 | 531,175 | 6,379,130 | 4,926,958 |
| Metcalfe | 24,638,807 | 12,859,707 | 541,592 | 17,824,368 | 518,055 | 1,756,583 | 58,139,112 | 743,816 | 57,395,296 | 163,679 | 839,831 | 699,479 |
| Monroe | 31,992,248 | 22,391,570 | 637,244 | 33,826,637 | 463,342 | 2,948,583 | 92,259,624 | 1,600,103 | 90,659,521 | 169,239 | 1,213,589 | 546,476 |
| Montgomery | 56,770,068 | 25,157,837 | 1,023,121 | 25,743,092 | 751,414 | 4,675,262 | 114,120,794 | 1,564,000 | 112,556,794 | 1,754,722 | 9,217,153 | 4,219,016 |
| Morgan | 32,355,201 | 15,865,968 | 205,140 | 31,075,374 | 591,084 | 1,868,746 | 81,961,513 | 299,088 | 81,662,425 | 1,386,402 | 2,605,071 | 4,232,837 |
| Muhlenberg | 98,289,496 | 44,699,117 | 2,103,828 | 29,452,458 | 86,645,759 | 44,563,876 | 305,754,534 | 8,630,082 | 297,124,452 | 570,821 | 4,568,535 | 4,967,807 |
| Nelson | 79,440,552 | 34,902,369 | 1,533,535 | 34,839,164 | 6,695,373 | 7,128,698 | 164,539,691 | 10,921,325 | 153,618,366 | 1,711,248 | 27,649,921 | 10,596,680 |
| Nicholas | 18,293,419 | 9,470,439 | 1,882,912 | 11,160,579 | 248,466 | 2,201,546 | 43,257,361 | 1,702,000 | 41,555,361 | 580,700 | 1,711,508 | 5,527,516 |
| Ohio | 63,135,786 | 29,389,763 | 2,481,660 | 21,915,344 | 1,239,094 | 5,267,021 | 123,428,668 | 1,889,743 | 121,538,925 | 751,957 | 3,948,263 | 7,389,539 |
| Oldham | 55,204,428 | 21,810,606 | 504,792 | 13,548,534 | 1,454,288 | 5,392,222 | 97,914,870 | 6,353,873 | 91,560,997 | 1,646,850 | 28,051,227 | 49,556,779 |
| Owen | 19,197,962 | 10,572,743 | 344,705 | 10,515,273 | 347,853 | 1,394,564 | 42,373,100 | 267,000 | 42,106,100 | 420,336 | 2,526,257 | 3,031,628 |
| Owsley | 17,521,574 | 10,507,432 | 78,944 | 20,805,665 | 231,902 | 879,709 | 50,025,226 | 273,000 | 49,752,226 | 440,331 | 77,103 | 888,647 |
| Pendleton | 29,217,931 | 13,867,974 | 272,262 | 10,666,810 | 909,558 | 1,688,746 | 56,623,281 | 826,883 | 55,796,398 | 433,256 | 4,674,727 | 30,115,346 |
| Perry | 104,458,398 | 46,579,457 | 415,778 | 70,463,622 | 10,746,553 | 9,689,487 | 242,353,295 | 2,688,233 | 239,665,062 | 684,801 | 1,124,046 | 32,538,176 |
| Pike | 242,350,093 | 96,559,283 | 580,710 | 156,203,418 | 6,257,268 | 17,880,914 | 519,831,686 | 3,242,434 | 516,589,252 | 522,310 | 6,171,370 | 148,827,837 |
| Powell | 29,499,998 | 9,900,871 | 586,968 | 19,567,144 | 486,067 | 2,083,401 | 62,124,449 | 683,000 | 61,441,449 | 949,969 | 1,336,196 | 5,868,036 |
| Pulaski | 186,078,469 | 61,262,335 | 1,380,320 | 131,005,743 | 3,785,449 | 12,301,068 | 395,813,384 | 9,178,237 | 386,635,147 | 1,490,561 | 14,508,267 | 4,615,785 |
| Robertson | 5,282,380 | 3,064,593 | 181,423 | 3,342,045 | 66,257 | 301,345 | 12,238,043 | 192,000 | 12,046,043 | 14,800 | 203,903 | 1,275,923 |
| Rockcastle | 39,528,418 | 19,399,185 | 258,871 | 33,727,345 | 871,175 | 1,872,419 | 95,657,413 | 1,178,701 | 94,478,712 | 220,840 | 1,578,759 | 1,612,377 |
| Rowan | 48,165,587 | 33,092,808 | 548,926 | 51,185,602 | 1,692,414 | 6,606,456 | 141,291,793 | 4,044,995 | 137,246,798 | 47,621,237 | 6,371,798 | 17,408,660 |
| Russell | 48,050,564 | 22,615,825 | 510,550 | 40,595,640 | 1,453,228 | 3,073,928 | 116,299,735 | 3,479,570 | 112,820,165 | 4,440,756 | 22,442,606 | 541,462 |
| Scott | 62,819,853 | 25,887,300 | 1,402,761 | 23,291,081 | 1,152,192 | 3,802,061 | 118,355,248 | 3,314,299 | 115,040,949 | 358,400 | 35,393,411 | 14,427,439 |
| Shelby | 62,954,486 | 24,919,582 | 1,423,879 | 34,142,567 | 1,062,505 | 5,748,790 | 130,251,809 | 3,436,510 | 126,815,299 | 1,134,550 | 30,040,069 | 7,587,740 |
| Simpson | 35,706,701 | 20,843,778 | 2,873,853 | 15,194,574 | 657,841 | 2,075,765 | 77,352,512 | 1,155,780 | 76,196,732 | 1,071,458 | 4,167,685 | 11,392,868 |
| Spencer | 23,661,589 | 8,536,648 | 405,044 | 6,787,182 | 544,047 | 1,839,583 | 41,774,093 | 1,335,808 | 40,438,285 | 616,238 | 11,374,989 | 3,459,734 |
| Taylor | 69,015,527 | 34,133,531 | 1,423,436 | 25,547,859 | 13,926,502 | 5,709,147 | 149,756,002 | 16,351,136 | 133,404,866 | 174,429 | 7,429,026 | 1,044,752 |
| Todd | 25,938,611 | 15,963,565 | 4,376,229 | 18,116,657 | 399,141 | 2,001,073 | 66,795,276 | 1,671,000 | 65,124,276 | 2,276,003 | 4,107,585 | 16,854,221 |
| Trigg | 46,472,322 | 17,119,613 | 2,213,247 | 12,994,942 | 2,810,815 | 5,507,746 | 87,118,685 | 4,859,414 | 82,259,271 | 1,641,060 | 5,278,810 | 8,289,062 |
| Trimble | 18,078,447 | 8,488,997 | 186,076 | 6,081,207 | 331,288 | 1,369,728 | 34,535,743 | 397,000 | 34,138,743 | 594,950 | 2,369,104 | 3,274,805 |
| Union | 39,949,198 | 20,230,846 | 6,246,330 | 15,535,257 | 220,759,686 | 2,979,947 | 305,701,264 | 1,351,960 | 304,349,304 | 3,324,505 | 2,751,333 | 12,716,258 |
| Warren | 203,069,070 | 113,613,070 | 4,535,289 | 97,116,561 | 13,338,618 | 29,163,235 | 460,835,843 | 18,190,179 | 442,645,664 |  | 85,458,378 | 20,283,914 |
| Washington | 26,426,854 | 14,200,142 | 975,761 | 26,699,992 | 430,675 | 2,256,746 | 70,990,170 | 663,000 | 70,327,170 | 1,172,750 | 2,968,481 | 3,844,734 |
| Wayne | 49,980,175 | 27,777,058 | 641,726 | 50,702,385 | 7,980,807 | 2,399,583 | 139,481,734 | 9,389,288 | 130,092,446 | 530,645 | 1,639,250 | 1,112,061 |
| Webster | 39,822,194 | 17,466,096 | 4,111,203 | 14,434,596 | 6,079,627 | 2,573,620 | 84,487,336 | 950,000 | 83,537,336 | 130,600 | 1,419,234 | 8,601,617 |
| Whitley | 147,065,028 | 67,473,215 | 671,118 | 71,930,127 | 26,229,328 | 8,602,848 | 321,971,664 | 26,788,237 | 295,183,427 | 898,869 | 4,530,359 | 9,725,893 |
| Wolfe | 22,450,669 | 9,528,310 | 72,564 | 25,248,748 | 480,368 | 1,889,255 | 59,669,914 | 253,000 | 59,416,914 | 292,728 | 636,262 | 361,151 |
| Woodford | 50,145,038 | 15,652,776 | 1,375,976 | 11,751,583 | 505,124 | 2,862,498 | 82,707,995 | 2,695,983 | 80,012,012 | 269,506 | 11,201,902 | 19,781,597 |

Source: http://harvester.census.gov/cffr/asp/Geography.asp

# FEDERAL GOVERNMENT OFFICES IN KENTUCKY

## EXECUTIVE AGENCIES

| DEPARTMENT | DIVISION | CITY | PHONE | FAX | WEB SITE |
|---|---|---|---|---|---|
| Agriculture, US Dept of, Farm Services Agency | FSA-KY State Office | Lexington | (859) 224-7601 | (859) 224-7691 | www.fs.fed.us/r8/boone |
| Agriculture, US Dept of, Forest Service | Daniel Boone National Forest | Winchester | (859) 745-3100 | (859) 737-3867 | www.fs.fed.us/r8/boone |
| Agriculture, US Dept of, Forest Service | Procurement Service | Winchester | (859) 745-3131 | (859) 745-4710 | |
| Agriculture, US Dept of, Forest Service | Cumberland Ranger District, Morehead Office | Morehead | (606) 784-6428 | (606) 784-6435 | |
| Agriculture, US Dept of, Forest Service | Cumberland Ranger District, Stanton Office | Stanton | (606) 663-2852 | (606) 663-9097 | |
| Agriculture, US Dept of, Forest Service | London Ranger District | London | (606) 864-4163 | (606) 878-0811 | |
| Agriculture, US Dept of, Forest Service | Redbird Ranger District | Big Creek | (606) 598-2192 | (606) 598-3648 | |
| Agriculture, US Dept of, Forest Service | Stearns Ranger District | Whitley City | (606) 376-5323 | (606) 376-3734 | |
| Agriculture, US Dept of, Forest Service | Frenchburg Job Corps Center | Frenchburg | (606) 768-2111 | (606) 768-3080 | |
| Agriculture, US Dept of, Forest Service | Pine Knot Job Corps Center | Pine Knot | (606) 354-2176 | (606) 354-2170 | |
| Agriculture, US Dept of, Natural Resources Conservation Service | NRCS-KY State Office | Lexington | (859) 224-7350 | (859) 224-7399 | www.ky.nrcs.usda.gov |
| Agriculture, US Dept of, Natural Resources Conservation Service | NRCS-Area 1 Office | Madisonville | (270) 825-2414 | (270) 825-2428 | |
| Agriculture, US Dept of, Natural Resources Conservation Service | NRCS-Area 2 Office | Frankfort | (502) 695-5203 | (502) 695-7996 | |
| Agriculture, US Dept of, Natural Resources Conservation Service | NRCS-Area 3 Office | Mt Sterling | (859) 498-8907 | (859) 497-9677 | |
| Agriculture, US Dept of, Research Education & Economics | Agriculture Research Service (Forage Animal Production Research) | Lexington | (859) 257-1647 | | |
| Agriculture, US Dept of, Research Education & Economics | Agricultural Statistics Service KY Field Office | Louisville | (800) 928-5277 | (502) 582-5114 | www.nass.usda.gov |
| Agriculture, US Dept of, Rural Development (RD) | RD-KY State Office | Lexington | (859) 224-7300 | (859) 224-7340 | www.rurdev.usda.gov/ky |
| Agriculture, US Dept of, Rural Development (RD) | RD-Area I | Princeton | (270) 365-6530 | (270) 365-7842 | www.rurdev.usda.gov/ky |
| Agriculture, US Dept of, Rural Development (RD) | RD-Area II | Columbia | (270) 384-6431 | (270) 384-6351 | www.rurdev.usda.gov/ky |
| Agriculture, US Dept of, Rural Development (RD) | RD-Area III | Shelbyville | (502) 633-3294 | (502) 633-0552 | www.rurdev.usda.gov/ky |
| Agriculture, US Dept of, Rural Development (RD) | RD-Area IV | Morehead | (606) 784-6447 | (606) 784-2076 | www.rurdev.usda.gov/ky |
| Agriculture, US Dept of, Rural Development (RD) | RD-Area V | London | (606) 864-2172 | (606) 878-7717 | www.rurdev.usda.gov/ky |
| Commerce, US Dept of | Economic Development Administration (EDA) | Lexington | (859) 224-7426 | (859) 224-7427 | www.doc.gov/eda/ |
| Commerce, US Dept of | International Trade Administration (ITA) | Louisville | (502) 582-5066 | (502) 582-6573 | www.ita.doc.gov |
| Defense, US Dept of, Dept of the Army | Army Corps of Engineers, US (USACE) | Louisville | (502) 315-6106 | (502) 315-6109 | www.usace.army.mil |
| Defense, US Dept of, Dept of the Army | Army Corps of Engineers, US (USACE) | Bee Spring | (270) 286-4511 | (270) 286-8615 | www.usace.army.mil |
| Defense, US Dept of, Dept of the Army | Army Corps of Engineers, US (USACE) | Calhoun | (270) 273-3152 | (270) 273-3107 | www.usace.army.mil |
| Defense, US Dept of, Dept of the Army | Army Corps of Engineers, US (USACE) | Grayson | (606) 474-5107 | (606) 474-2089 | www.usace.army.mil |
| Defense, US Dept of, Dept of the Army | Army Corps of Engineers, US (USACE) | Kuttawa | (270) 362-8159 | (270) 362-7403 | www.usace.army.mil |
| Defense, US Dept of, Dept of the Army | Army Corps of Engineers, US (USACE) | Morehead | (606) 784-9709 | (606) 784-2400 | www.usace.army.mil |
| Defense, US Dept of, Dept of the Army | Army Corps of Engineers, US (USACE) | Pineville | (606) 337-6162 | (606) 337-2646 | www.usace.army.mil |
| Defense, US Dept of, Dept of the Army | Army Corps of Engineers, US (USACE) | Van Lear | (606) 886-6709 | (606) 886-3483 | www.usace.army.mil |
| Defense, US Dept of, Dept of the Army | Army Corps of Engineers, District Contracting Division | Louisville | | | |
| Defense, US Dept of, Dept of the Army | Property & Fiscal Office for KY | Frankfort | (502) 607-7426 | (502) 607-1436 | |
| Defense, US Dept of (DOD), Dept of the Navy (USN) | Naval Surface Warfare Center, Port Hueneme Detachment | Louisville | (502) 364-5052 | (502) 364-5361 | |
| Health & Human Services, US Dept of (HHS) | Food & Drug Administration (FDA) | Louisville | (502) 425-0069 | (502) 425-0450 | www.fda.gov/ |
| Homeland Security, US Dept of | US Coast Guard Marine Safety Unit | Owensboro | (270) 442-1621 | (270) 442-1633 | www.uscg.mil |
| Homeland Security, US Dept of | US Coast Guard Marine Safety Unit | Paducah | (859) 223-2358 | (859) 223-1819 | www.uscg.mil |
| Homeland Security, US Dept of | US Secret Service | Lexington | (502) 582-5171 | (502) 582-6329 | www.secretservice.gov |
| Homeland Security, US Dept of | US Secret Service | Louisville | | | www.secretservice.gov |
| Homeland Security, US Dept of | US Customs & Border Protection (CBP) | Ft Mitchell | (859) 578-4600 | (859) 578-4606 | www.cbp.gov |

# FEDERAL GOVERNMENT OFFICES IN KENTUCKY

## EXECUTIVE AGENCIES

| DEPARTMENT | DIVISION | CITY | PHONE | FAX | WEB SITE |
|---|---|---|---|---|---|
| Homeland Security, US Dept of | US Customs & Border Protection (CBP) | Louisville | (502) 366-3398 | (502) 368-5319 | www.cbp.gov |
| Homeland Security, US Dept of | Immigration & Customs Enforcement | Louisville | (502) 582-6526 | (502) 582-6373 | www.dhs.gov |
| Housing & Urban Development, US Dept of (HUD) | KY State Office | Louisville | (502) 582-5251 | (502) 582-6074 | www.hud.gov |
| Housing & Urban Development, US Dept of (HUD) | KY Housing Corp | Frankfort | (502) 564-9946 | (502) 564-9964 | www.kyhousing.org |
| Housing & Urban Development, US Dept of (HUD) | KY Housing Corp | Frankfort | (800) 633-8896 | (502) 564-9964 | www.kyhousing.org |
| Housing & Urban Development, US Dept of (HUD) | KY Housing Corp | Louisville | (502) 585-5451 | | www.kyhousing.org |
| Housing & Urban Development, US Dept of (HUD) | KY Housing Corp | Frankfort | (502) 564-9946 | (502) 564-9964 | www.kyhousing.org |
| Interior, US Dept of (DOI) | Fish & Wildlife Service (FWS) | Benton | (270) 527-5770 | (270) 527-5330 | |
| Interior, US Dept of (DOI) | National Parks Service, Abraham Lincoln Brithplace | Hodgenville | (270) 358-3137 | (270) 358-3874 | www.nps.gov/maca/index.htm |
| Interior, US Dept of (DOI) | National Parks Service, Mammoth Cave | Mammoth Cave | (270) 758-2254 | (270) 758-2349 | www.nps.gov/maca/index.htm |
| Interior, US Dept of (DOI) | Surface Mining Reclamation, Office of | Lexington | (859) 260-8402 | (859) 260-8410 | |
| Interior, US Dept of (DOI) | Surface Mining Reclamation, Office of | Ashland | (606) 324-2828 | (606) 324-2846 | |
| Interior, US Dept of (DOI) | Surface Mining Reclamation, Office of | London | (606) 878-6440 | (606) 878-6049 | |
| Interior, US Dept of (DOI) | Surface Mining Reclamation, Office of | Madisonville | (270) 825-4500 | (270) 821-1232 | |
| Interior, US Dept of (DOI) | Surface Mining Reclamation, Office of | Pikeville | (606) 432-8145 | (606) 432-5041 | |
| Interior, US Dept of (DOI) | Geological Survey, Water Resources Division | Louisville | (502) 493-1900 | (502) 493-1909 | http://water.usgs.gov/ |
| Justice, US Dept of (DOJ) | US Attorney, Eastern District | Lexington | (859) 233-2661 | (859) 233-2666 | www.usdoj.gov/usao/offices |
| Justice, US Dept of (DOJ) | US Attorney, Western District | Louisville | (502) 582-5911 | (502) 582-5097 | |
| Justice, US Dept of (DOJ) | US Marshals Service, Eastern District | Lexington | (859) 233-2513 | (859) 233-2517 | |
| Justice, US Dept of (DOJ) | US Marshals Service, Eastern District | Ashland | (606) 329-2587 | (606) 329-2559 | |
| Justice, US Dept of (DOJ) | US Marshals Service, Eastern District | Covington | (859) 392-7918 | (859) 392-7924 | |
| Justice, US Dept of (DOJ) | US Marshals Service, Eastern District | Frankfort | (502) 223-5608 | (502) 223-2745 | |
| Justice, US Dept of (DOJ) | US Marshals Service, Eastern District | London | (606) 864-6993 | (606) 878-9310 | |
| Justice, US Dept of (DOJ) | US Marshals Service, Eastern District | Pikeville | (606) 437-6524 | (606) 432-8457 | |
| Justice, US Dept of (DOJ) | US Marshals Service, Western District | Louisville | (502) 588-8000 | (502) 588-8005 | |
| Justice, US Dept of (DOJ) | US Marshals Service, Western District | Bowling Green | (270) 901-2100 | (270) 901-2110 | |
| Justice, US Dept of (DOJ) | US Marshals Service, Western District | Ft Campbell | | | |
| Justice, US Dept of (DOJ) | US Marshals Service, Western District | Ft Knox | (502) 624-2086 | | |
| Justice, US Dept of (DOJ) | US Marshals Service, Western District | Owensboro | (270) 852-2640 | (270) 852-2650 | |
| Justice, US Dept of (DOJ) | US Marshals Service, Western District | Paducah | (270) 415-1700 | (270) 415-1710 | |
| Justice, US Dept of (DOJ) | Drug Enforcement Administration (DEA) | Lexington | (859) 233-2479 | (859) 233-2590 | www.dea.gov |
| Justice, US Dept of (DOJ) | Drug Enforcement Administration (DEA) | Louisville | (502) 582-5908 | (502) 582-5535 | www.dea.gov |
| Justice, US Dept of (DOJ) | FMC Lexington | Lexington | (859) 255-6812 | (859) 253-8821 | |
| Justice, US Dept of (DOJ) | FCI Ashland | Ashland | (606) 928-6414 | (606) 928-3635 | |
| Justice, US Dept of (DOJ) | FCI Manchester | Manchester | (606) 598-1900 | (606) 599-4115 | |
| Justice, US Dept of (DOJ) | USP Big Sandy | Inez | (606) 433-2400 | (606) 433-2577 | |
| Justice, US Dept of (DOJ) | USP McCreary | Pine Knot | (606) 354-7000 | (606) 354-7190 | |
| Justice, US Dept of (DOJ) | Federal Police Services | Louisville | (502) 582-5455 | (502) 569-3869 | |
| Justice, US Dept of (DOJ) | Alcohol Tobacco Firearms & Explosives, Bureau of (ATF) | Ashland | (606) 329-8092 | (606) 325-5251 | www.atf.gov |
| Justice, US Dept of (DOJ) | Alcohol Tobacco Firearms & Explosives, Bureau of (ATF) | Bowling Green | (270) 781-7090 | (270) 842-5941 | www.atf.gov |
| Justice, US Dept of (DOJ) | Alcohol Tobacco Firearms & Explosives, Bureau of (ATF) | Lexington | (859) 219-4508 | (859) 219-4516 | www.atf.gov |

# FEDERAL GOVERNMENT OFFICES IN KENTUCKY

## EXECUTIVE AGENCIES

| DEPARTMENT | DIVISION | CITY | PHONE | FAX | WEB SITE |
|---|---|---|---|---|---|
| Justice, US Dept of (DOJ) | Alcohol Tobacco Firearms & Explosives, Bureau of (ATF) | Lexington | (859) 219-4508 | (859) 219-4516 | www.atf.gov |
| Justice, US Dept of (DOJ) | Alcohol Tobacco Firearms & Explosives, Bureau of (ATF) | London | (606) 878-3011 | (606) 862-8296 | www.atf.gov |
| Justice, US Dept of (DOJ) | Alcohol Tobacco Firearms & Explosives, Bureau of (ATF) | Louisville | (502) 753-3450 | (502) 753-3451 | www.atf.gov |
| Justice, US Dept of (DOJ) | Alcohol Tobacco Firearms & Explosives, Bureau of (ATF) | Louisville | (502) 753-3500 | (502) 753-3501 | www.atf.gov |
| Justice, US Dept of (DOJ) | Alcohol Tobacco Firearms & Explosives, Bureau of (ATF) | Louisville | (502) 753-3550 | (502) 753-3551 | www.atf.gov |
| Justice, US Dept of (DOJ) | Federal Bureau of Investigation (FBI) | Ashland | (606) 329-8516 | (606) 324-7740 | www.fbi.gov |
| Justice, US Dept of (DOJ) | Federal Bureau of Investigation (FBI) | Bowling Green | (270) 781-4734 | (270) 842-9710 | www.fbi.gov |
| Justice, US Dept of (DOJ) | Federal Bureau of Investigation (FBI) | Ft Mitchell | (859) 341-3901 | (859) 426-3359 | www.fbi.gov |
| Justice, US Dept of (DOJ) | Federal Bureau of Investigation (FBI) | Elizabethtown | (270) 765-7213 | (270) 766-1408 | www.fbi.gov |
| Justice, US Dept of (DOJ) | Federal Bureau of Investigation (FBI) | Frankfort | (502) 223-3644 | (502) 223-1188 | www.fbi.gov |
| Justice, US Dept of (DOJ) | Federal Bureau of Investigation (FBI) | Hopkinsville | (270) 885-8272 | (270) 887-9772 | www.fbi.gov |
| Justice, US Dept of (DOJ) | Federal Bureau of Investigation (FBI) | Lexington | (859) 254-4038 | (859) 254-9652 | www.fbi.gov |
| Justice, US Dept of (DOJ) | Federal Bureau of Investigation (FBI) | London | (606) 878-8922 | (606) 862-2119 | www.fbi.gov |
| Justice, US Dept of (DOJ) | Federal Bureau of Investigation (FBI) | Louisville | (502) 583-3941 | (502) 569-3869 | www.fbi.gov |
| Justice, US Dept of (DOJ) | Federal Bureau of Investigation (FBI) | Owensboro | (270) 926-3441 | (270) 686-8290 | www.fbi.gov |
| Justice, US Dept of (DOJ) | Federal Bureau of Investigation (FBI) | Paducah | (270) 442-8050 | (270) 442-2962 | www.fbi.gov |
| Justice, US Dept of (DOJ) | Federal Bureau of Investigation (FBI) | Pikeville | (606) 432-1226 | (606) 432-1846 | www.fbi.gov |
| Labor, US Dept of (DOL) | Federal Contract Compliance Programs, Office of | Louisville | (502) 582-6275 | (502) 582-6182 | www.dol.gov/esa/ofccp_org.htm |
| Labor, US Dept of (DOL) | Coal Mine Workers Compensation, Black Lung | Pikeville | (800) 366-4599 | (606) 432-3574 | |
| Labor, US Dept of (DOL) | Coal Mine Workers, Division of | Mt Sterling | (800) 366-4628 | (859) 498-5787 | |
| Labor, US Dept of (DOL) | Wage & Hour Division | Louisville | (866) 487-9243 | | www.dol.gov/esa/whd |
| Labor, US Dept of (DOL) | Wage & Hour Division | Bowling Green | (270) 781-1245 | | www.dol.gov/esa/whd |
| Labor, US Dept of (DOL) | Wage & Hour Division | Ft Wright | | | www.dol.gov/esa/whd |
| Labor, US Dept of (DOL) | Wage & Hour Division | Lexington | (866) 487-9293 | | www.dol.gov/esa/whd |
| Labor, US Dept of (DOL) | Wage & Hour Division | Paducah | | | www.dol.gov/esa/whd |
| Labor, US Dept of (DOL) | Apprenticeship & Training, Bureau of | Louisville | (502) 582-5223 | (502) 625-7081 | |
| Labor, US Dept of (DOL) | MSHA (Coal)-Barbourville | Barbourville | (606) 546-5123 | (606) 546-6394 | |
| Labor, US Dept of (DOL) | MSHA (Coal)-Barbourville | Barbourville | (606) 546-5123 | (606) 546-6394 | |
| Labor, US Dept of (DOL) | MSHA (Coal)-Beaver Dam | Beaver Dam | (270) 274-9628 | (270) 274-9629 | |
| Labor, US Dept of (DOL) | MSHA (Coal)-Elkhorn City | Belcher | (606) 754-4187 | (606) 754-9491 | |
| Labor, US Dept of (DOL) | MSHA (Coal)-Harlan | Harlan | (606) 573-3400 | (606) 573-1774 | |
| Labor, US Dept of (DOL) | MSHA (Coal)-Hazard | Hazard | (606) 439-2396 | (606) 439-1851 | |
| Labor, US Dept of (DOL) | MSHA (Coal)-Hindman | Hindman | (606) 785-4191 | (606) 785-0997 | |
| Labor, US Dept of (DOL) | MSHA (Coal)-Madisonville | Madisonville | (270) 821-4180 | (270) 825-0949 | |
| Labor, US Dept of (DOL) | MSHA (Coal)-Madisonville | Madisonville | (270) 821-4180 | (270) 825-0949 | |
| Labor, US Dept of (DOL) | MSHA (Coal)-Martin | Martin | (606) 285-3281 | (606) 285-0255 | |
| Labor, US Dept of (DOL) | MSHA (Coal)-Morganfield | Morganfield | (270) 389-3134 | (270) 389-9814 | |
| Labor, US Dept of (DOL) | MSHA (Coal)-Phelps | Phelps | (606) 456-3438 | (606) 456-4167 | |
| Labor, US Dept of (DOL) | MSHA (Coal)-Pikeville | Pikeville | (606) 432-0944 | (606) 437-9988 | |
| Labor, US Dept of (DOL) | MSHA (Coal)-Whitesburg | Whitesburg | (606) 633-4882 | (606) 633-9277 | |
| Labor, US Dept of (DOL) | MSHA (Metal & Non-Metal) | Lexington | (859) 276-1384 | | |

# FEDERAL GOVERNMENT OFFICES IN KENTUCKY

## EXECUTIVE AGENCIES

| DEPARTMENT | DIVISION | CITY | PHONE | FAX | WEB SITE |
|---|---|---|---|---|---|
| Labor, US Dept of (DOL) | Occupational Safety & Health Administration (OSHA) | Frankfort | (502) 227-7024 | (502) 227-2348 | www.osha.gov |
| Labor, US Dept of (DOL) | Employee Benefits Security Administration | Ft Wright | (859) 578-4680 | (859) 578-4688 | www.dol.gov/ebsa |
| Labor, US Dept of (DOL) | Veterans Employment & Training Service (VETS) | Frankfort | (502) 564-7062 | (502) 564-1476 | www.dol.gov/vets/ |
| State, US Dept of | KY Consular Center | Williamsburg | (606) 526-7401 | (606) 526-7684 | www.state.gov |
| Transportation, US Dept of (DOT) | Federal Aviation Administration (FAA) | Lexington | (859) 233-2509 | (859) 233-2774 | www.faa.gov |
| Transportation, US Dept of (DOT) | Federal Aviation Administration (FAA) | Louisville | (502) 753-4200 | (502) 582-6735 | www.faa.gov |
| Transportation, US Dept of (DOT) | Federal Aviation Administration (FAA) | Owensboro | (502) 375-7360 | | www.faa.gov |
| Transportation, US Dept of (DOT) | Federal Aviation Administration (FAA) | Paducah | (270) 744-6622 | (270) 744-8044 | www.faa.gov |
| Transportation, US Dept of (DOT) | Federal Aviation Administration (FAA) Airport Traffic Control Tower | Louisville | (502) 753-3680 | (502) 753-3690 | |
| Transportation, US Dept of (DOT) | Federal Aviation Administration Sector Field (FAA) | Louisville | (502) 375-7360 | | |
| Transportation, US Dept of (DOT) | Federal Highway Administration (FHWA) | Frankfort | (502) 223-6720 | (502) 223-6735 | www.fhwa.dot.gov |
| Transportation, US Dept of (DOT) | Federal Railroad Administration (FRA) | Louisville | (502) 261-7198 | | www.fra.dot.gov |
| Treasury, US Dept of | Comptroller of the Currency | Louisville | (502) 429-3422 | (502) 429-0339 | www.occ.treas.gov/ |
| Treasury, US Dept of | Internal Revenue Service (IRS) | Covington | | (606) 292-5387 | www.irs.gov |
| Treasury, US Dept of | Treasury Inspector General for Tax Administration Office (TIGTA) | Louisville | (502) 582-5299 | (502) 625-7501 | |
| Treasury, US Dept of | Criminal Investigation Division | Louisville | (502) 572-2140 | (502) 572-2142 | |
| Treasury, US Dept of | Associate Area Council | Louisville | (502) 582-5471 | (502) 582-6579 | |
| Treasury, US Dept of | IRS Collection | Louisville | (502) 582-6700 | | |
| Treasury, US Dept of | IRS Appeals | Louisville | | | |
| Treasury, US Dept of | IRS Examination | Louisville | | (502) 582-5307 | |
| Treasury, US Dept of | IRS District Council | Louisville | | | |
| Treasury, US Dept of | Taxpayer Advocate Service | Louisville | (502) 582-6030 | (502) 582-6463 | |
| Veterans Affairs, US Dept of (VA) | Regional Office | Louisville | (800) 827-1000 | | |
| Veterans Affairs, US Dept of (VA) | Vet Center | Louisville | (502) 634-1916 | (502) 636-4002 | |
| Veterans Affairs, US Dept of (VA) | VA Medical Center | Lexington | (859) 233-4511 | | |
| Veterans Affairs, US Dept of (VA) | VA Medical Center | Louisville | (502) 287-4000 | (502) 287-6225 | |
| Veterans Affairs, US Dept of (VA) | VA Vet Center | Lexington | (859) 253-0717 | | |
| Veterans Affairs, US Dept of (VA) | VA Vet Center | Louisville | (502) 634-1916 | | |
| Veterans Affairs, US Dept of (VA) | VA Outpatient Clinic | Hanson | (270) 322-8019 | (270) 322-8957 | |
| Veterans Affairs, US Dept of (VA) | VA Community Based Outpatient Clinic | Bellevue | (859) 392-3840 | | |
| Veterans Affairs, US Dept of (VA) | VA Community Based Outpatient Clinic | Paducah | (270) 444-8465 | (270) 443-8198 | |

*Source: The Kentucky Directory Gold Book 2006-2007*

# FEDERAL GOVERNMENT OFFICES IN KENTUCKY

## INDEPENDENT AGENCIES

| DEPARTMENT | DIVISION | CITY | PHONE | FAX | WEB SITE |
|---|---|---|---|---|---|
| (None) | KY Representative to ARC | Frankfort | (502) 564-2611 | (502) 564-2517 | |
| Corp for National & Community Service (CNCS) | Learn & Serve, KY State Office | Louisville | (502) 582-6384 | (502) 582-6386 | www.learnandserve.org |
| Equal Employment Opportunity Commission (EEOC) | (None) | Louisville | (502) 582-6082 | (502) 582-5895 | www.eeoc.gov |
| General Services Administration (GSA) | GSA, SE Sunbelt Region | Bowling Green | (270) 782-6928 | | |
| General Services Administration (GSA) | Federal Protective Service Division, Physical Security & Law | Louisville | (502) 582-5455 | (502) 582-6868 | |
| General Services Administration (GSA) | KY Property Management Center | Louisville | (502) 582-6436 | (502) 582-6868 | |
| General Services Administration (GSA) | Public Buildings Service (PBS) | Louisville | (502) 582-6436 | (502) 582-6868 | |
| General Services Administration (GSA) | Public Buildings Service (PBS) | Owensboro | (270) 684-2939 | | |
| General Services Administration (GSA) | Public Buildings Service (PBS) | Paducah | | | |
| Occupational Safety & Health Review Commission (OSHRC) | (None) | Frankfort | (502) 573-6892 | (502) 573-4619 | www.oshrc.gov |
| Railroad Retirement Board (RRB) | District Office | Louisville | (502) 582-5208 | (502) 582-5518 | www.rrb.gov/default.asp |
| Small Business Administration (SBA) | KY District Office | Louisville | (502) 582-5971 | (502) 582-5009 | www.sba.gov/ky |
| Small Business Development Centers (SBDC) | KY Small Business Development Center | Ashland | (606) 329-8011 | (606) 324-4570 | www.ksbdc.org |
| Small Business Development Centers (SBDC) | KY Small Business Development Center | Bowling Green | (270) 745-1905 | (270) 745-1931 | www.ksbdc.org |
| Small Business Development Centers (SBDC) | KY Small Business Development Center | Somerset | (877) 358-7232 | (859) 622-1413 | www.ksbdc.org |
| Small Business Development Centers (SBDC) | KY Small Business Development Center | Elizabethtown | (270) 765-6737 | (270) 769-5095 | www.ksbdc.org |
| Small Business Development Centers (SBDC) | KY Small Business Development Center | Louisville | 888-475-SBDC | (502) 574-4771 | www.ksbdc.org |
| Small Business Development Centers (SBDC) | KY Small Business Development Center | Hopkinsville | (270) 886-8666 | (270) 881-9366 | www.ksbdc.org |
| Small Business Development Centers (SBDC) | KY Small Business Development Center | Lexington | (859) 257-7666 | (859) 257-1751 | www.ksbdc.org |
| Small Business Development Centers (SBDC) | KY Small Business Development Center | Morehead | (606) 783-2895 | (606) 783-5020 | www.ksbdc.org |
| Small Business Development Centers (SBDC) | KY Small Business Development Center | Highland Heights | (859) 442-4281 | (859) 442-4285 | www.ksbdc.org |
| Small Business Development Centers (SBDC) | KY Small Business Development Center | Owensboro | (270) 926-8085 | (270) 684-0714 | www.ksbdc.org |
| Small Business Development Centers (SBDC) | KY Small Business Development Center | Pikeville | (606) 432-5848 | (606) 432-8924 | www.ksbdc.org |
| Small Business Development Centers (SBDC) | KY Small Business Development Center | Paintsville | (606) 788-6007 | (606) 789-5623 | www.ksbdc.org |
| Small Business Development Centers (SBDC) | KY Small Business Development Center | Paducah | (270) 443-1746 | (270) 442-9152 | www.ksbdc.org |
| Small Business Development Centers (SBDC) | KY Small Business Development Center | Murray | (270) 809-2856 | (270) 881-9366 | www.ksbdc.org |
| Small Business Development Centers (SBDC) | KY Small Business Development Center | Middlesboro | (888) 225-7232 | (606) 242-4514 | www.ksbdc.org |
| Social Security Administration (SSA) | KY Offices | Frankfort | (800) 772-1213 | | www.socialsecurity.gov |
| Social Security Administration (SSA) | Hearings & Appeals, Office of | Paducah | (270) 443-0440 | (270) 441-7911 | |
| Social Security Administration (SSA) | Hearings & Appeals, Office of | Lexington | (859) 233-2653 | (859) 233-2402 | |
| Social Security Administration (SSA) | Hearings & Appeals, Office of | Louisville | (502) 582-6446 | (502) 582-6819 | |
| Social Security Administration (SSA) | Hearings & Appeals, Office of | Middlesboro | (606) 248-5320 | (606) 248-6866 | |
| Social Security Administration (SSA) | Inspector General, Office of | Frankfort | (502) 564-2888 | (502) 564-6546 | |
| Tennessee Valley Authority (TVA) | Shawnee Fossil Plant | West Paducah | | | |

*Source: The Kentucky Directory Gold Book 2006-2007*

# FEDERAL GOVERNMENT
# *National Cemeteries*

## THE NATIONAL CEMETERY SYSTEM

In the U.S., development of national cemeteries began as the Civil War was waged, which tried and tested the very existence of a young nation. During the early years of the war, the dead were buried in fields and churchyards, or close to the hospitals and camps where they died. The number of dead soon exceeded that of any previous conflict of the North American continent.

In 1862, Pres. Abraham Lincoln signed legislation authorizing the creation of national cemeteries, "...for the soldiers who shall die in the service of the country." These cemeteries were the beginning of what is now known as the National Cemetery System.

At the end of the Civil War, search and recovery teams visited hundreds of battlefields, churchyards and other locations where hasty combat interments had been made. More than a quarter of a million remains were disinterred. The reinterment process took five years to complete and by 1870, 73 national cemeteries were under the jurisdiction of the federal government.

Today there are a total of 130 national cemeteries — they stand as enduring testimonials to the appreciation of a grateful nation.

**Lexington National Cemetery**
*Photo: Sid Webb*

## KENTUCKY NATIONAL CEMETERIES

**Camp Nelson National Cemetery**
6980 Danville Rd
Nicholasville, KY 40356
Phone: (859) 885-5727
www.cem.va.gov/CEM/cems/nchp/campnelson.htm
No. of interments thru FY 2005: 12,034

**Cave Hill National Cemetery**
701 Baxter Ave
Louisville, KY 40204
Phone: (502) 893-3852
www.cem.va.gov/CEM/cems/nchp/cavehill.htm
No. of interments thru FY 2005: 5,967

**Danville National Cemetery**
277 North First St
Danville, KY 40442
(This cemetery is within Bellevue Cemetery)
Phone: (859) 885-5727
www.cem.va.gov/CEM/cems/nchp/danvilleky.htm
No. of interments thru FY 2004: 394

**Lebanon National Cemetery**
20 Highway 208
Lebanon, KY 40033
Phone: 859 885 5727, (270) 692-3390
www.cem.va.gov/CEM/cems/nchp/lebanon.htm
No. of interments thru FY 2005: 4,699

**Lexington National Cemetery**
833 West Main St
Lexington, KY 40508
(859) 885-5727
www.cem.va.gov/CEM/cems/nchp/lexington.htm
No. of interments thru FY 2005: 1,390

**Mill Springs National Cemetery**
9044 West Highway 80
Nancy, KY 42544
(859) 885-5727
www.cem.va.gov/CEM/cems/nchp/millsprings.htm
No. of interments thru FY 2005: 3,011

**Zachary Taylor National Cemetery**
4701 Brownsboro Rd
Louisville, KY 40207
Phone: (502) 893-3852
www.cem.va.gov/CEM/cems/nchp/zacharytaylor.htm
No. of interments thru FY 2004: 13,321

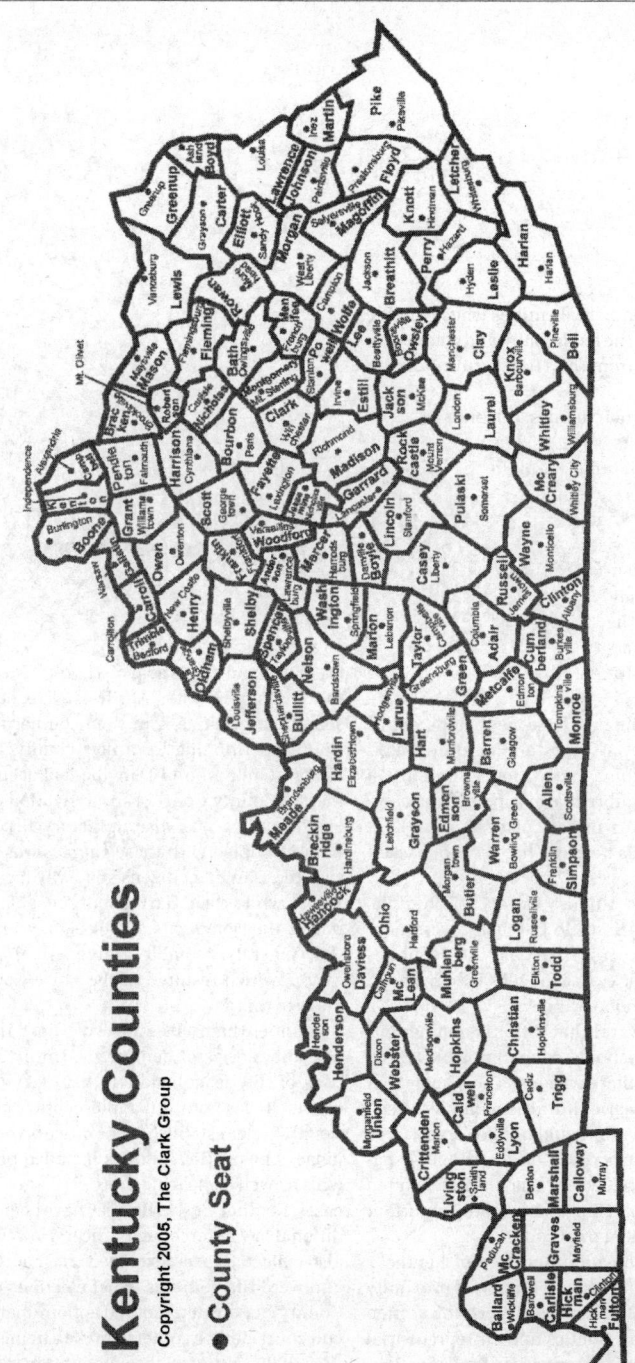

# Kentucky Counties

Copyright 2005, The Clark Group

● County Seat

Bob Arnold

# Counties of Kentucky

They are governmental entities whose history stretches back to the feudal shire and whose very name is derived from the 11th century Norman tongue.

In Kentucky, their names celebrate American patriots such as Washington, Marshall and Franklin. They commemorate our earliest pioneers, Kenton and Boone. Likewise, they recall the laurel bushes in our state's southeast and the jasmine flowers that bloom in the Bluegrass.

They are counties—those geographic units formed by surveyor's lines and nature's waterways. They are home to deep forests and urban skylines, thoroughbred farms and college campuses. They evoke a pride of place as old as Kentucky itself and as new as a high school basketball rivalry.

Once the westernmost county of Virginia, Kentucky itself is home to 120 such governmental units—a far cry from that handful of counties carved for Kentucky's scant 100,000 citizens in 1792, when statehood was new.

It was only natural that Virginia and her offshoot, Kentucky, should cling to this most English of governmental divisions. The climate that fostered an 18th agricultural economy lent itself as the proper governmental unit to serve a large area. Also, Kentucky was unlike the less spacious New England, where a harsh climate often necessitated that villages be more important units of government than counties.

But later, the creation and size of Kentucky counties were often a combination of proximity to the county seat and political mechanics, often based on partisan politics and entrepreneurial goals. An example is chronicled in Professor Rob-

ert M. Ireland's 1976 gem of a book, "The County in Kentucky History." Dr. Ireland recounts the 1834 saga of citizens in then-southern Mercer County petitioning for a new county. Citizens living in and around Danville had accused the Mercer County Court of "over taxation, fraudulent elections and discriminatory fiscal planning." Coupled with these charges was the fact that the Danville citizens generally favored the Whigs while their Harrodsburg neighbors supported the Democrats. It took eight years before the General Assembly granted final authorization, which resulted in the Boyle County we know to this day.

Counties themselves may have been the original laboratories of democracy. Until 1850, justices of the peace made up Kentucky's county courts. It was not until a mid-century constitutional change established the office of the county judge, whose official duties included probating wills as well as hearing petty civil and criminal cases. Kentucky's sheriffs may have been the traditional law enforcement officer. However, they also collected taxes, executed trial court orders, and were the counties' chief elections officers. County clerks often secured appointment as circuit court clerks in order to make a living wage.

By 1900 counties throughout America were

James Madison   George Washington

Abraham Lincoln   John Breathitt

the nation's character was changing and so were her counties.

A new century has ushered in new challenges to Kentucky's counties and their officials. The old charges to oversee county roads, operate jails, deliver emergency and disaster relief services, and maintain administrative support continue. All the while, new topics such as immigration, economic development, and cyber-crime confront our county leaders. The Kentucky county of the 21st century must respond to questions such as workforce training and technological infrastructure (while keeping an eye on expanding global markets) if it wishes to attract businesses that bring expanding employment and new tax revenues.

The history of each Kentucky county is a unique chapter in our commonwealth's story. As each chapter has its roots in the

experiencing change, Kentucky's with them. Nationally, fewer officials were appointed, more being selected through the ballot box. Increasing numbers of county officials were on salary, thus eliminating the dependence on the fee system for their incomes.

Counties evolved as the 20th century evolved, and the post-war era gave rise to the age of suburbia, interstate highways and automobile commuting. Counties implemented sweeping changes including professional accounting systems, as well as bidding and procurement systems. Likewise, civil service employment dethroned age-old political patronage. The post-war, suburb-dwelling, auto-commuting public flocked to unincorporated areas, yet they continued to expect the schools, parks, hospitals, fire and police protection, and garbage collection they had received as urbanites. Once again,

past, it has its theme clearly eyeing the future. As each county is unique, so too are its citizens. The pioneer paths of the 1780s have given way to the internet highway. The log cabin hearth has yielded to questions of energy efficiency. Frontier feuds have eclipsed into urban-rural strategic planning.

At the core of this evolution is the Kentucky county. Its elected leaders are our neighbors and its aspirations are our own. We each share in our county's achievements and we all shoulder our county's burdens. This Old World unit of government has evolved into a new millennium partner in progress that melds government with technology, leaders with their vision and is tied to the aspirations and quests of its citizens.

*Bob Arnold is Executive Director/CEO of the Kentucky Association of Counties.*

# Cities

Sylvia Lovely

"Thus ...
we will transmit this city
greater and more beautiful
than it was transmitted to us."

That excerpt from the ancient Athenian Oath of citizenship says it best. The heart and soul of citizenship and thus the highest order of human responsibility to one another is inexplicably bound to the idea of "city." In fact the Greek word civitas, meaning citizenship, is the word from which city is derived.

So what is this thing called city and why devote a chapter of this almanac to it? I dare say that when the first almanac was written in 1792, a chapter on cities probably didn't exist. The American republic was founded as a reaction against the overly rigid rules and laws of the British monarchy.

Those who relocated across the pond did so in an act of defiance against the tyranny of rules and regulations and in favor of wide-open spaces and small informal gatherings. As a result, city was not a favorable concept because it suggested rigid rules and government. People who had settled in Kentucky likewise had a strong independent nature and didn't take kindly to being governed from afar—part of the reason that its settlers struggled to separate themselves from being governed by Virginia and establish their own state.

And while the notion of America's indepen-

**Statue of York the black slave of the Lewis and Clark expedition, Louisville, Ky.**
*Photo: Sid Webb*

to the stunning inventions that have paralleled the evolution of civil society. Even in the heady frontier American West where individualism was prized, cowhands gathered to share tales of lonely nights and high noon adventure on the plains.

Here in Kentucky, from Paducah to Ashland, and from the more rural Williamsburg to the urban Covington, we identify with each of our 400-plus cities. The truth is that as people we are born alone but seek the remainder of our time on earth searching for warmth and comfort and a higher level of civilization—through togetherness.

In the past few decades, Kentucky has steadily transformed into a state that now has a larger urban than rural population. Consider these items:

· More than 80 percent of Kentucky jobs are inside city limits.
· U.S. Census-designated Metropolitan and Micropolitan counties are now home to more than two-thirds of the state's population.
· Metro Louisville and Lexington-Fayette County now account for nearly one-fourth of the people in Kentucky.
· Urbanized land makes up just a shade more than 3 percent of Kentucky, but almost 60 percent of the population lives there.

Happily, this growth need not threaten our rural heritage. Instead, it has the capacity to enhance both urban and rural areas. More and more, our cities are serving as regional centers for rural communities. Meanwhile, the drive to get broadband access to our most remote areas is yet another way that all of Kentucky's population can be in a position to benefit in an age in which access to the Internet is becoming more and more crucial to thrive.

Our cities also have the capacity to grow as economic engines that can raise the quality of life for all people in the Commonwealth.

Today, there are 18,000 cities and towns across the U.S., and they are at yet another crossroads. Just as is true for Kentucky, more people live in urban America than in the wide-open spaces. Our world has changed and so have cities and their role in our lives. America's heartland continues to empty out and the coasts fill up and become congested and compromised in the quality of life that they offer.

dent and adventurous spirit still thrives today, so do the organizing principles of city. Cities have survived, although that shouldn't surprise us.

Cities continue to evolve and have flourished throughout history for reasons that have never changed since the beginning of time. Cities began as gathering places for worshiping gods and revering the dead—where stability of place was a requirement. For the same reasons, they were where children were reared, crops were raised and cultural and religious symbols were erected.

The critical mass of workers could come together in cities to synergize their work, leading

Sprawl in the form of suburbs and "exurbs" that have extended outside the traditional boundaries of cities has led to increased discussion on the role of cities.

America in particular has an uneasy relationship with her cities. In a nation founded by rugged individualists, we have come together to form cities large and small, but that sense of individualism has historically given us a difficult time in fully embracing the idea of cities.

But in an era in which transition can come fast and frequently, there is a growing sense of the importance of cities.

**Downtown Lexington Fountain**
*Photo: Sid Webb*

The events of 9/11 along with the proliferation of information and televised images of unrest throughout the world have instilled an unprecedented fear of the loss of connection with one another. For that reason, our cities—where togetherness equates with civilized society—are threatened. But they are also the places where we can reinvigorate our sense of connection to each other and to values we hold dear.

Our work as citizens of the 21st century is cut out for us. Experts tell us that the paradox of the 21st "global" century will be that "local" is where we begin. We have become more and more aware of the fragility of our world and our own local places.

With deliberate intent, a base of knowledge, and newfound leadership, we can redefine city. It remains as it has been throughout history as the very heart, soul and repository of our collective spirit. But the notion of city must take into account the new forces—economic, social, and global—that the 21st century has generated.

In the year 2050, it is forecast that people will have gravitated to just eight "super cities" throughout the nation. Those super cities would know no boundaries—state or local. They must sort out the issues raised by the sheer numbers of people who gravitate to them, and manage the ills that come with fast and unplanned growth. And while Kentucky is not considered a site for one of those super cities, it is a place of unprecedented opportunity.

We have the opportunity to meet the yearning of people for city life that isn't based largely on unprecedented population growth, but is planned and promoted to meet the needs of people. It will involve connecting people with one another and the outside world, embracing what is new and different and building economic prosperity with the idea that people are the greatest natural resource in a world where they can live and work anywhere.

Wherever we choose to live, there remains in each of us a fundamental need to connect with others and have a place we can call home—a place of security and familiarity, a place where we believe

## Well, what about that ...

In the year 2050, it is forecast that people will have gravitated to just eight "super cities" throughout the nation. Those super cities would know no boundaries—state or local. They must sort out the issues raised by the sheer numbers of people who gravitate to them, and manage the ills that come with fast and unplanned growth. And while Kentucky is not considered a site for one of those super cities, it is a place of unprecedented opportunity.

we can make a difference as individuals and an even greater one as neighbors. In short, we need that sense of community that encourages citizenship and the sense of responsibility to each other that the Athenian Oath implies.

To effectively engage in making our communities better requires strong citizenship, and thus city comes back into the picture—not necessarily as a boundary-defined entity but as a concept and an ideal. That ideal is to strive to reach the highest achievements that benefit all.

We should engage ourselves locally, community by community, in a discussion of what is important in our lives and how best to enhance those aspects. In an age of high mobility when it is easier to leave one city or town for another, such community-building is not an easy task.

But it is possible. And it is necessary. If we don't take advantage of our ability to fashion a better community or city—and with it a better life—we run the risk of being left behind in a world that thrusts change upon us constantly.

Cities help anchor us, deal with change, and make our leaders more accountable. But only when we understand our shared reliance on cities, and each other, can we make government serve us better.

At their best, cities are a collection of neighborhoods and communities that are as much a manifestation of spirit and intent as they are actual places. We would do well to memorize the Athenian Oath and remember our ultimate responsibility: to leave our cities more beautiful and thriving for future generations.

*Sylvia Lovely is Executive Director of the Kentucky League of Cities and Executive Director & CEO of the NewCities Institute, www.klc.org.*

Mall, Newport, Ky.
Photo: Sid Webb

> Wherever we choose to live, there remains in each of us a fundamental need to connect with others and have a place we can call home—a place of security and familiarity, a place where we believe we can make a difference as individuals and an even greater one as neighbors. In short, we need that sense of community that encourages citizenship and the sense of responsibility to each other that the Athenian Oath implies.

# Adair County
# Columbia

Once a part of Green County, Adair County was formed in 1801. It is located in the Western Appalachian area, which contributes to its 407 square miles of rolling landscape. Adair County is watered by the 8,200-acre Green River Lake, as well as by Russell Creek. The 44th county of Kentucky, it was named in honor of the colorful Gen. John Adair, a South Carolinian who came to Kentucky and Ft. Harrod in 1786. During the War of 1812, he fought at the Battle of the Thames, and commanded the Kentucky rifle brigade at the Battle of New Orleans. Gen. Adair later went on to serve as Kentucky's eighth governor from 1820-1824. Adair County sits at an elevation of 738 feet above sea level.

The city of Columbia was chosen as the county seat on June 28, 1802. Rumor has it that the city was named for Christopher Columbus, but nobody knows for certain. Daniel Trabue was one of the earliest settlers to the area and one of the founders of Columbia. Trabue was a jack-of-all-trades—he served as sheriff, justice of peace, trustee, operator of a mill, inn and store, and was also a writer. Other early settlers included Col. James Knox, William Caldwell, William Montgomery and Col. William Casey (great-grand-

**Gen. John Adair**
*Source: KYVL Kentucky Virtual Library*

father of Mark Twain, who came to Adair County in 1789).

Confederate Gen. John Hunt Morgan was no stranger to Adair County. After his Christmas Raid of 1862-63, Morgan passed through Columbia on his way to Tennessee. And at Tebb's Bend, Morgan fought Union soldiers as he trekked north to Indiana and Ohio on July 4, 1863.

Adair County has had many notable residents: Thomas Bramlette was the governor of Kentucky from 1863-67; Col. Frank Wolford was the commander of the Union's 1st Kentucky Cavalry—that is, until he was dismissed for criticizing Pres. Lincoln; Jane Lampton Clemens was the mother of Samuel Clemens, Ed Diddle was a winning coach of the Western Kentucky University Hilltoppers; and Janice Holt Giles was the author of historical novels set in the Green River area about the American frontier.

Adair County is home to several historic landmarks including the John Field House (1812) where the parents of Mark Twain once lived (the front room was earlier used for the girls' portion of old Robertson Academy, Columbia's first school), the Benjamin Logan House, the Trabue-Russell House and the courthouse are also noteworthy.

# Allen County
# Scottsville

Allen County, the 57th county in order of formation, was carved out of Warren and Barren counties on Jan. 11, 1815. The land is rather hilly with timber in abundance. It is well-watered by the Barren River (once known as the Big Barren), which originates in Allen and Monroe counties. The elevation in the county ranges from 445 to 966 feet above sea level with a land area of 346.12 square miles.

The county received its name from Lt. Col. John Allen who died in the War of 1812. John Allen came to Kentucky with his father in 1779 when he was eight years old, settling near Danville. He commenced the study of law in 1791 in Virginia, returning to Kentucky to settle in Shelbyville and practice law. When war broke out in 1812, John Allen raised a regiment of riflemen; Lt. Col. Allen's regiment formed the left wing of the American force at the fatal battle of the river Raisin on Jan. 22, 1813. He was one of nine officers at that battle for whom Kentucky counties were named.

Scottsville, the county seat of Allen County, began as a stop on the stage route south of Louisville. The site was selected for its location near a spring, called the Public Spring, which was situated on the old Cumberland Settlement Trace from Nashville to Glasgow. Scottsville was named in honor of Gov. Charles Scott, an aide to Gen. George Washington, and the fourth governor of Kentucky.

Exploration of the county occurred before 1770. The Barren River area attracted fur-hunters and explorers. Stories of success in the fur trade and the bountiful land of Kentucky spurred settlement. Daniel Boone was in the area and carved his initials on a tree with the date 1777. There was early development of oil wells, limestone quarrying and clay mining, cotton was once grown in abundance.

**Public Spring, Scottsville**
*Source: Allen County Historical Society*

Scottsville and Allen County saw considerable action by both sides in the Civil War. On Dec. 8, 1863, Confederate forces of 200 under Col. John M. Hughs attacked Scottsville, and secured a quantity of stores, saddles, bridles, and a 500-stand of small arms. Twelve days earlier the force had attacked Monticello, seeking supplies; they captured (then paroled) a garrison of 153 men.

Allen County has 50 miles of shoreline along the Barren River Lake. The lake, a 10,000-acre reservoir, was built by the U.S. Corp of Engineers for flood control. It is surrounded by rolling hills and a 2,000-acre hardwood forest.

Allen County is the birthplace of the first woman elected to a political office in Kentucky, Emma Guy Cromwell, who served as secretary of state (1926-1927). Allen County is also the home of the Dollar General Company, which started in 1939. J.L. Turner and his son Cal Turner formed J.L. Turner & Son, wholesalers of basic dry goods.

# Anderson County
# Lawrenceburg

Anderson County, 82nd in order of county formation, was formed in 1827 out of parts of Franklin, Mercer and Washington counties. It is bounded on the east by the Kentucky River and is well-watered by the Salt River and its tributaries. Elevation ranges from 469 to 940 feet above sea level with a land area of 202.67 square miles. The McAfee brothers, James McCoun, Jr., and Samuel Adams were the first white men to explore this land, in 1773. The area was settled in the late 1770s and early 1780s by many of the early settlers from Ft. Harrod, who traveled north to claim land.

Anderson County was named in honor of Richard Clough Anderson, born in 1788 in Louisville (in the then district of Kentucky). He was the nephew of the celebrated Gen. George Rogers Clark. A learned man, he served in the state legislature and in the U.S. Congress; Anderson was appointed by Pres. Monroe as the first minister plenipotentiary to the Republic of Columbia.

Lawrenceburg, the county seat of Anderson county, was established in 1820 and named after Capt. James Lawrence, U.S. Navy Capt. Lawrence's last words on board the *Chesapeake* were, "Don't give up the ship." The post office opened in 1817 as Lawrenceburgh, and was renamed Lawrenceburg in 1827.

On October 8, 1862, during the Civil War, while the brutal Battle of Perryville was being fought to the south in Boyle County, Confederates skirmished with a rear-guard Union force under the command of Gen. J. W. Sill near Lawrenceburg. The following day, battle-weary Confederates under command of Maj. Gen. Edmund Kirby-Smith camped near the Mercer County line before withdrawing from Kentucky. Various skirmishes in the county were fought between partisan guerrillas and local Union Home Guard units.

Anna Mac Clarke (1919-44), a 1937 graduate of Lawrenceburg's Colored High School, enlisted in the U.S. Army and later became the only African American in the 15th Officer Training Class at Ft. Des Moines, Iowa. In 1943, she was first black WAAC assigned to duty with an all-white company as the platoon commander.

Anderson County is home to Four Roses Bourbon Distillery and Wild Turkey Bourbon Distillery, two of only eight working bourbon distilleries in Kentucky. In the late 1870s there were 13 distilleries in the county. Anderson County is home to the largest acreage of winery in the commonwealth – Lover's Leap Vineyard and Winery.

**Anderson County Courthouse**
*Photo: Sid Webb*

# Ballard County
## Wickliffe

Established in 1842, Ballard County was 93rd in the order of county formation. Ballard County, carved out of McCracken and Hickman Counties, contains 251.16 square miles. It is situated across from Cairo, Ill. and bounded on the north by the Ohio River and on the west by the Mississippi River. The county was named in honor of Capt. Bland Ballard who came to Ky. from Virginia in 1779 when he was 18 years old. A soldier in many campaigns, he devoted his life to protecting the frontier. Capt. Ballard served as a scout for Gen. George Rogers Clark and fought in the battles of Fallen Timbers (1793), Tippecanoe (1811), and River Raisin (1813). He served in the Ky. Legislature for five terms.

Wickliffe is the county seat of Ballard County. Blandville was originally established as the county seat in 1842, and continued as such for 40 years until 1882, when the courthouse burned. Wickliffe then became the county seat.

The Wickliffe Mounds, an archaeological site of a prehistoric village of the Mississippian Mound Builders, is a major attraction. The antique village was a complex settlement with a central plaza and permanent houses. The site is located on a bluff overlooking the Mississippi River and was occupied from about 1100 to 1350 A.D. It is now a state historic site.

Other attractions include the Ballard and Boatwright Wildlife Management Areas located in the Mississippi River floodplain along the Ohio River. The combined acreage is over 16,000 acres, which includes Swan Lake, the state's largest natural lake. Both areas contain bottomland hardwoods, interspersed with numerous oxbow lakes, tupelo and cypress tree swamps, and agricultural fields. The Barlow House Museum, a classic 11-room Queen Anne house, was built by the son of Thomas Jefferson Barlow, one of the first families to settle in the "wilderness" territory of Ballard County. Ft. Jefferson was built in 1780 by Gen. George Rogers Clark as part of an impressive plan of settlement, conceived by Gov. Patrick Henry of Virginia and later pursued by and named for Gov. Thomas Jefferson. The fort was to protect U.S. claims to its western border and serve as a key trading post. It was abandoned in 1781 after an attack by the Chickasaw, angered over settlement of the land without their consent. It was resettled after the Jackson Purchase was acquired. Ft. Jefferson was also one of the first Kentucky positions occupied by Union troops.

**Swan Pond**
*Source: Kentucky Virtual Library*

# Barren County
# Glasgow

Barren County was formed in 1799 from parts of Green and Warren counties. The county takes its name from what is generally termed the barrens or prairies, which abound in the region. According to Collins' Historical Sketches, "The county embraces almost every description of soil and surface." The sub-soil is a clay, founded on limestone, with a fair

Wigwam Village
Source: John Perkins

Spring on Gorin's land, sufficient to water the town. Many early settlers came from Virginia—soldiers and officers of the Revolutionary War who had been granted land "south of the Green River" in payment for their services.

When the War of 1812 raged, Barren County provided many soldiers; and those same Revolutionary War soldiers volunteered yet again. During the Civil War, Barren County was the site of the Civil War's first Kentucky federal death, on Oct. 10, 1861. A Union company slipped through a graveyard at night to arrest a local Southern sympathizer. Ten poorly equipped recruits from the Confederate camp had been sent to guard him; they were attacked, but defeated the Union enemy. Later, two of Kentucky raids by Confederate Gen. John Hunt Morgan's cavalry routed through Glasgow (July 10 and December 25, 1862).

number of mineral springs. The elevation in the county ranges from 465 to 1,068 feet above sea level with a land area of 490.97 square miles. Henry Skaggs and two companions trapping beaver in the winter of 1770-71 were probably the first white men in the area. Named Long Hunters due to the long period away from their homes in the East, they came through Cumberland Gap in 1769.

Glasgow, the seat of Barren County, was founded in 1799 with the county. It was named for the city in Scotland. John Gorin, a Revolutionary War soldier, donated 150 acres of land in July of 1799 for the purpose of establishing the town as the county seat. The town site was chosen because of the Big

The county has been home to many distinguished individuals including: two governors, Gov. Preston Leslie (1819-1907) and Gov. Louie B. Nunn (1924-2004); Luska Twyman(1913-1988), the first African American elected to a full term as mayor of a Ky. city (Glasgow, from 1968-1985); Billy Vaughn (1919-1991), the popular musician; Four-Star Gen. Robert Dougherty, Commanding General of the Strategic Air Command; Arthur Crock (1886-1974), called the dean of Washington newsmen; Diane Sawyer of ABC; and Johnny Depp, movie star, have Barren County ties.

# Bath County
# Owingsville

Bath County was formed from Montgomery County in 1811. It lies on the Licking River and presents a diversified surface—hilly, undulating and level. Rich and fertile soil lies on a base of limestone, with iron and coal in the south and east of the county; forests and rolling farmland edge into the foothills of the Appalachian Mountains. The county was named for its many mineral (often sulphur) springs.

As with much of Kentucky, the county's rich history precedes that first recorded by hunters, surveyors and scouts like Daniel Boone, who is said to have rescued his daughter and two of her friends from the Indians near the Bath County community of Wyoming. Before modern Indian tribes appeared, Mound Builders left evidence of their time here in the form of famous mounds, and the remains of an ancient fort, much of which has been destroyed by time and cultivation.

At one time, two iron furnaces (including the Bourbon Iron Works, the first iron blast furnace in Ky., 1791) and one forge in the county manufactured about 2,000 tons of iron per year. The Olympian Springs Hotel, a resort and spa originally known as Mud Lick, dated back to the late 1700s. Kentucky's first stage coach line, in 1803, ran from Lexington to Olympian Springs. The resort closed in the early part of the 20th century.

These ventures made the area a center for commerce and hospitality that drew such notables as Henry Clay and purportedly, King Louis Phillippe of France. Owingsville, the county seat, was named for Col. Thomas D. Owings, who fought in the Revolutionary War, and was an associate owner in the Bourbon Iron Works, 1795-1822. Iron Works Pike, Owingsville to Lexington, was built to haul iron from this area to the Bluegrass, there being no nearby river route.

The county has been home to many notable people including Revolutionary War hero Capt. John "Jack" Jouette, who is buried in Owingsville. Jouette, a true Revolutionary War hero, rode 40 miles overnight

**The Owings House**
**Built between 1811 and 1814**
**by Iron Master Thomas Deye Owings**
*Source: Carol Rison*

to warn Pres. Thomas Jefferson, Patrick Henry and other legislators of the British approach, June 3, 1781; Confederate Gen. John Bell Hood; two governors Alvin Hawkins of Tennessee, and Claude Matthews of Indiana; writers William Lightfoot Visscher and Col. John A. Joyce; soldier/diplomat Major Gen. Henry Tureman Allen; Joe Creason, noted Kentucky journalist; and artist Joel T. Hart.

# Bell County
## Pineville

Bell County, the 112th in order of formation, was organized in May, 1867. It was formed from parts of Harlan and Knox counties, and a portion of Whitley County in 1870-1871. It is a very mountainous and rugged terrain with streams cutting through deep valleys, dominated by two mountain ridges, Pine and Cumberland mountains. The elevation in the county ranges from 975 to 3,500 feet above sea level with a land area of 360.77 square miles. Bell County is strategically located where

**P-38 Lost Squadron Museum in Middlesboro**
*Source: Southern and Eastern Kentucky Tourism Development Association*

Kentucky meets Tennessee and Virginia at the famed Cumberland Gap.

Bell County (originally Josh Bell County) was named in honor of Joshua F. Bell (1811-70), a Kentucky politician and great-grandson of Dr. Thomas Walker, known as the first white man to have led an exploration into interior Kentucky. An historical marker designates the ford where, on April 17, 1750, Dr. Walker and a party of Virginians first viewed the river he named for the Duke of Cumberland. Known as the "Narrows," this area became a significant gateway for travelers on the Wilderness Road. Kentucky's

late Historian Laureate, Thomas Clark, maintained that Bell County contained the third most important geological feature in American history (he ranked the passageway formed by the Cumberland Gap behind Plymouth Rock and Boston Harbor in significance).

Pineville, the seat of Bell county, is situated on the bank of the Cumberland River where it cuts through Pine Mountain. It was settled in 1781 as Cumberland Ford.

Bell County contains another unique geological feature: the impact crater of a huge meteorite in which the town of Middlesboro is built entirely within its 10.9 square-mile crater. It is the only city within the northern hemisphere to have been built within a meteorite crater.

During the Civil War, the Gap was continuously occupied by one side or the other, changing hands four times; the area suffered the deprivations caused by foraging armies. However, no large battles were fought within the county.

In the late 1880s there was a huge developmental boom fueled by foreign investment and the recognition of the wealth of untapped mineral and forest resources in the county. A British land company bought 90,000 acres in and around Bell County. Railroads raced to connect the county with the outside world. Investors plowed millions into a planned city, which they called Middlesborough after the British steel center by that name. Multiple industries announced plans for factories and from 1889, the city boomed. Then several factors, topped off by the Panic of 1893, caused a "bust." In the years that followed, the county gradually rebounded, primarily by exploiting its vast coal resources.

# Boone County
# Burlington

Boone County was established out of Campbell County on December 13, 1798. Named in honor of Col. Daniel Boone, the distinguished pioneer, it became the 30th of Kentucky's 120 counties. Situated in a bend of the Ohio River, the county is generally hilly, with a considerable quantity of level land. The elevation in the county ranges from 455 to 964 feet above sea level with a land area of 246.26 square miles.

Burlington, the county seat of Boone County, was founded in 1799 as Craigs Camp, named for one of the owners of the land. The name was changed to Wilmington in 1800 and finally to Burlington, probably in 1816. (Burlington is no longer incorporated.) Florence, the largest city in the county, was settled as a fur-trading post and was alternatively named Pole-Cat, Crossroads, and Maddentown. It was renamed Connersville for Jacob Conner in 1828 and finally incorporated as Florence (for Conner's wife) in 1830. In stagecoach days it was a popular stop for travelers, being 10 miles out of Covington on the long journey to Lexington.

All along the 39 mile Ohio River shoreline there is archaeological evidence of prehistoric native culture. It was a logical and practical choice to settle here: the Ohio River provided water; there was lush vegetation, mineral springs and salt licks, game and transportation. Later, the French claimed this part of the Ohio Valley; meanwhile, the English colonies were beginning to look westward over the Appalachians for new rich lands to settle. The struggle for land now involved three separate nations – the French, the English and the Native Americans—they all claimed the same real estate. This led to the French and Indian War (1754-1763), resulting in the surrender to England of all claims by France to the Ohio River Valley.

Big Bone Lick, known as the "Graveyard of the Mastadons," is located in a valley that contains about 100 acres. Big Bone was a salt lick where many prehistoric animals (like the mastodon, mammoth and arctic elephant) sank into mud there and their bones were pre-

Inside the Cincinnati/Northern Kentucky
International Airport
*Source: Jake Mecklenborg*

served for over thousands of years. Notable Americans such as Thomas Jefferson and Benjamin Franklin personally examined the fossils, many of which are on display today at Big Bone Lick State Park Museum.

Boone County was the northern-most county in a border state with close proximity to Cincinnati. Its citizens favored slavery in a slave-holding state, while the state officially remained neutral during the Civil War. Boone County proudly claimed military leaders and enlistees in each army. There were minor skirmishes in the county, one in Florence and one at Snow's Pond in Walton; however, there was considerable guerilla activity and unrest with the underground railway and the escape provided to runaway slaves.

# Bourbon County
# Paris

Bourbon County was the fifth county created from Fayette County in 1786, six years before statehood. One of the original nine counties shaped while Kentucky was still a part of Virginia, it was named for the royal French family who aided the American colonies in the War of Independence. The elevation in the county ranges from 715 to 1,050 feet above sea level with a land area of 291.43 square miles.

Paris, the county seat of Bourbon County, is situated on the important turnpike road that led early travelers from Maysville to Lexington. The town was established by the Virginia legislature in 1789 under the name of Hopewell. It was also called Bourbonton, after the county in which it lies, but received its present name from the city of Paris in France, to express the good feelings that existed toward the French nation for the assistance during the revolution.

Confederate Gen. John Hunt Morgan's cavalry came to Paris on July 18, 1862, after its Cynthiana victory. A citizens' group held out for days but finally surrendered. Warned of a Union force nearby, the Confederate forces escaped pursuit and returned to Tenn. Paris was occupied in Sept. 1862, during the Confederate threat north.

Paris was home to Hon. Garrett Davis (1801-1872), lawyer, state legislator and congressman, who played a leading role in preventing the 1861 secession of Kentucky; Garrett Morgan (1877-1963), who invented the tri-color traffic signal and a gas mask worn in rescue work; Mae Street Kidd (1904-99), born in Millersburg, served as a representative in the Ky. state legislature from 1968-85; and William H. McGuffey (1800-1873), famous for his eclectic series of children's readers.

Bourbon County is known for fine-looking historical buildings including the courthouse, modeled after the U.S. Capitol. Maj. Joseph Duncan built Duncan Tavern, a three-story tavern, in 1788. He hosted many famous Kentuckians there. The John Fox, Jr. Library is also located in this building. It was named in honor of the famous author who wrote "The Little Shepherd of Kingdom Come," which was among the first books published in the U.S. to sell 1,000,000 copies.

**Bourbon County Courthouse**
*Photo: Sid Webb*

Hopewell Museum, a Beaux Arts building built in 1909 as the U.S. Post Office, is now a history and art museum. The last military school still in operation in Kentucky—the Millersburg Military Academy—has been in continuous operation since 1893. Claiborne Farm was the birthplace, home and final resting place of Secretariat (the Triple Crown winner was the only Kentucky Derby winner to finish in less than two minutes).

# Boyd County
# Catlettsburg

Boyd County, formed in 1860, was the 107th county established in Kentucky. It was named in honor of Linn Boyd, former U.S. Congressman. Boyd was elected as the state's lt. governor; however, he died shortly after winning office. The county is bounded on the east by the Big Sandy River and on the north by the Ohio River. The elevation ranges from 515 to 1,140 feet above sea level and has a land area of 160.17 square miles.

The county seat is at Catlettsburg and was incorporated in 1858. It is located at the confluence of the Ohio and Big Sandy rivers. It was named for Alexander and Horatio Catlett, early settlers of the area who arrived about 1798. The southern part of the city was once known as Hampton City, a separate town from Catlettsburg. Another major city in the area is Ashland, which was first known as Poage Settlement. It was settled by the Poage family of Virginia. They had received a land grant from Gen. James Wilkinson, who served as senior officer of the U.S. Army (1796-1798). They also founded the first church in the area, Bethesda, which was Presbyterian. The Poage family built the Clinton Iron Furnace in 1832.

During the Civil War, a Union post was located in Catlettsburg. Its purpose was to protect the Ohio River traffic—this post became a supply base as well as a communication center for Union forces serving in the Big Sandy area. Troops under Col. James A. Garfield drove Confederate forces from the area with a victory at Middle Creek in the winter of 1861-62. Col. Garfield went on to become the 20th president of the U.S. In 1864, the area was once again cleared of Confederate troops by Kentucky Union forces under the leadership of Col. George W. Gallup.

In 1921 Mary Elliott Flanery became the first woman elected to the Kentucky legislature. She was elected to the House of Representatives out of Boyd County. She was concerned with woman suffrage, marriage and divorce laws and education reform. A bronze marker was placed in the house chamber at her seat, number 40, upon her death in 1933.

Boyd County is known for its industries and iron furnaces. In 1854, the Kentucky Iron, Coal and Manufacturing Co. was formed in response to the increase of industrialists in the area. Many immigrants flocked to the area with hopes of employment at the furnaces. These furnaces include the Amanda Furnace, Ashland Furnace, Buena Vista Furnace, Clinton Furnace, Norton Furnace, Oakland Furnace, Princess Furnace, and Sandy Furnace.

**Paramount Theater, Ashland**
*Source: Kentucky Department of Tourism*

# Boyle County
# Danville

Boyle County, the 94th county in order of formation, was established in 1842. It was, however, one of the earliest counties to be colonized when James Harrod built a cabin in present-day Danville in 1774. Located in the center of Kentucky, Boyle County presents well-watered, rolling bluegrass pastureland. The elevation ranges from 740 to 1,364 feet above sea level and the area is 181.90 square miles. The county was named for Judge John Boyle. He served as judge on the Kentucky Court of Appeals and as judge of the U.S. District Court for Kentucky.

Danville, the seat of justice, was formed by Walker Daniel in 1783. The first post office in Kentucky opened in Danville in 1792. Constitution Square on Danville's Main Street is a state shrine, with reproductions of the first post office west of the Alleghenies, courthouse, jail and meeting hall. On this site, beginning in 1784, ten conventions were held over the following eight years in an effort to gain separation from Virginia and establish statehood. The Kentucky Constitution was written here and on June 1, 1792, Kentucky was admitted to the Union.

**McDowell House**
*Source: Danville-Boyle County Convention & Visitors Bureau*

Another well-known town is Perryville, which was incorporated on January 17, 1817. It was named for Commodore Oliver Hazard Perry who was victorious at the Battle of Lake Erie in 1813. On October 8, 1862, the Battle of Perryville took place, one of the fiercest and bloodiest battles of the Civil War. Under the command of Gen. Braxton Bragg, 16,000 Confederates fought 22,000 Federals under Gen. Don Carlos Buell. Bragg withdrew, knowing his troops faced superior forces. More than 7,600 men were wounded or killed, earning it the title "Gettsyburg of the West."

**Perryville horse silhouette**
*Source: Clay Jackson*

Many homes, schools and churches were used as hospitals and morgues, including the Boyle County Courthouse. After this battle, Confederate forces never returned to Kentucky in extreme force. Today, the battlefield is the Perryville Battlefield Historic Site.

One of the most notable surgeons hails from Boyle County. Dr. Ephraim McDowell performed the first ovariotomy abdominal operation on Jane Todd Crawford in his house on Christmas Day, 1809. Riding 60 miles on horseback, Crawford came from Green County to have a 22-pound tumor removed without the aid of anesthetic. McDowell's home and adjoining apothecary shop are both open to the public.

Lottie Moon was also from Boyle County. Moon was a dynamic Southern Baptist missionary who spent nearly 40 years in China teaching and ministering. She taught at the Caldwell Female Institute, which later became a part of Centre College. Centre College, established in 1819, has had many distinguished alumni and claims victory over Harvard in football in the early 1920s.

# Bracken County
## Brooksville

Bracken County was the 23rd county formed in Kentucky and was organized in 1796. The Ohio River bounds it on the north. The land is high and generally hilly. The elevation ranges from 455 to 980 feet above sea level and the land area is 203.22 square miles. It was named after William and Matthew Bracken, early explorers and hunters.

The county seat is Brooksville, which was originally known as Woodward's Cross Roads in the late 1700s. The seat was moved from Augusta in 1839 and renamed Brooksville. It was named for David Brooks, the legislature who introduced the bill for the seat change.

During the Civil War, 6,000 Union troops held the district but moved out in Sept. 1862 leaving a handful of Home Guards to defend the area. Confederate Gen. Basil W. Duke, along with 350 Morgan Raiders, attacked Augusta on September 27. It is said that bloody fighting raged in the streets. Many buildings were burned before Gen. Duke withdrew with heavy losses. The Confederate troops were forced to return to Falmouth and abandon their intended raid into Ohio.

A bitter Civil War duel was fought here, one of the last in Kentucky. It was fought under the "code duello" and took place on May 8, 1862 between William T. Casto and Col. Leonidas Metcalfe of Nicholas County. Casto, a lawyer, was a former Maysville mayor and Metcalfe commanded a Kentucky regiment. Casto, an ardent Secessionist who sent the challenge, was fatally wounded while Metcalfe was not hit.

German immigrants brought grape cultivation and wine production to the area. Bracken County was the leading wine-producing county in the U.S. during the 1870s. They furnished over 30,000 gallons annually, which was half the entire national production. Disastrous winters and blight brought setbacks and the wine industry faded.

Augusta, an important river port and location of Augusta College, is said to have been built over the early Native American burial ground.

Source: SouthEast Telephone

Augusta College was founded in 1822 and was known as the first established Methodist college in the world.

Several notable people were from Bracken County including John Gregg Fee, a leader in the anti-slavery movement and founder of Berea College. He advocated low-cost education for "all persons of good moral character," regardless of their race. Dr. Joshua Taylor Bradford, a world famous surgeon, was born and made his home in Bracken County. Arnold Gragston helped many slaves escape captivity. An African American himself, he rowed slaves from Dover (Mason County) across the Ohio River during the night.

# Breathitt County
# Jackson

Breathitt County was the 89th county formed in Kentucky and was created on April 1, 1839, out of territory taken from Clay, Perry and Estill. It was named for Gov. John Breathitt, who died in office at the age of 47. The county is located on the headwaters of the Kentucky River at the foothills of the Appalachian Mountains. Much of the land is in commercial forests, with scenic mountains and valleys. The soil is based on red clay and abounds in coal and iron ore. The elevation ranges from 650 to 1,600 feet above sea level and the land area is 494 square miles.

Source: SouthEast Telephone

The county seat is Jackson, which near the center of the county on the North Fork of the Kentucky River. It was founded in 1839 with the county and was called Breathitt Town. In 1845, it was renamed in honor of Pres. Andrew Jackson, the seventh president of the U.S., who had passed away that year.

Civil War violence divided Breathitt County, which was equally divided between the Unionists and Confederates. Long running feuds and political disagreements were reignited by shootings, thefts and other actions during the war. The county garnered national attention from a series of bloody post-Civil War feuds. These feuds were the Little-Strong feuds, Hargis-Marcum-Cockrell feud, as well as many others. These feuds led to the county being widely known as "Bloody Breathitt."

The Lexington and Eastern railroads entered the county on July 15, 1891. Jackson was the southern terminus. Breathitt County grew as business continued to prosper. This prosperity brought many people to Jackson. The population in Breathitt boomed. Timber tracts brought speculation and investment from lumbermen. Until 1925 the largest sawmill in the world operated at Quicksand under the brand Mowbray and Robinson Company. Owner E.O. Robinson (of Ft. Thomas) later donated 15,000 acres of property at Quicksand to the University of Kentucky as the Robinson Agricultural Experiment Substation and Robinson Forest.

During World War I, Breathitt County earned national prominence. It was the only county in Kentucky to fill its quota of service men by volunteers. Not a single man had to be drafted from Breathitt County. Breathitt County is the only county in the U.S. to hold this record. An historical marker in the courthouse lawn notes, "Kentuckians ranked among the highest in the nation in physical fitness."

Lee's Junior College, now associated with the community and technical college system, was established in 1884 as Jackson Academy.

# Breckinridge County
## Hardinsburg

Breckinridge County was established on December 9, 1799 and was the 39th county in order of formation. It was named in honor of John Breckinridge, an attorney and statesman. He served as state attorney-general and state representative before becoming a U.S. senator. Mr. Breckinridge was U.S. attorney-general in the administration of Pres. Thomas Jefferson in 1805. The elevation ranges from 383 to 920 feet above sea level. With a land area of 572.41 square miles, Breckinridge County is the sixth largest of Kentucky's 120 counties.

The county seat is at Hardinsburg. It was named after Capt. William "Big Bill" Hardin. It was incorporated in 1800. Another major town in the area is Cloverport. A health resort, known as Tar Springs, flourished in the 1840s. A 100-foot cliff existed here from which tar bubbled, while 11 springs of mineral waters flowed from its base. Each spring had a different type of mineral water. These springs were used by Native Americans. Wiley B. Rutledge, who was a Justice of the U.S. Supreme Court, was born at the Tar Springs resort in 1894.

When Abraham Lincoln was just seven years old, his family sought and found help in this county. In the fall of 1816 they crossed the Ohio River on a log raft ferry near Cloverport on the way to Indiana. Stopping near the city limits of Hardinsburg, Lincoln's family rested in a cabin for about three weeks. Neighbors were generous and provided the family with food.

In 1851 coal oil was first produced in Breckinridge County. A plant was built in 1857 and was reputed to be the first of its kind in the world. The mine was known for its extensive veins of cannel coal. Cannel coal is a type of coal containing a large amount of hydrogen. When ignited, it burns easily with a bright light

**Aerial photo of Hardinsburg**
*Source: David Hayes*

and leaves little ash.

The mine was owned by the English; it is believed that King Edward VII, the Prince of Wales, was an investor. Coal was transported to England via New Orleans for the manufacture of gas. However, due to a disastrous fire, the discovery of petroleum, and the Civil War, the mine operation came to an end.

During the Civil War, 22 Kentucky courthouses were burned. The courthouse at Hardinsburg was not spared. On December 28, 1864, guerrillas set fire to the courthouse at Hardinsburg. Luckily, citizens saved the building and the court records. Confederate forces arrived, but allowed the public to keep arms for their defense.

# Bullitt County
# Shepherdsville

Bullitt County was formed in 1797, and named in honor of Kentucky's first lieutenant governor, Alexander Scott Bullitt (1800-1804). Bullitt County was created from Jefferson and Nelson counties. Its western boundary extends to near the mouth of Salt River, and is watered by that stream and its tributaries. The Rolling Fork of Salt River washes its southwest border. The county is fertile and the surface is rolling with variegated and beautiful scenery. The elevation in the county ranges from 385 to 998 feet above sea level in a land area of 299.08 square miles.

Explorers entered this area early—due to natural roads created by the herds of buffalo, deer and elk that migrated here for the "salt licks." Salt and wild game in search of it were critical to the survival of settlers and Native Americans—these places were often the sites of battles between them. Frontiersmen Daniel and Squire Boone were among many who forged thick-forested hills following herds to the salt licks.

Bullitt's Lick, named for Capt. Thomas Bullitt was the site of the first commercial industry in Kentucky—salt production. It served all Kentucky, Illinois and Tennessee territories, shipping salt on flatboats down the Salt, Ohio, and Mississippi rivers on to New Orleans. Shepherdsville was incorporated in 1793 by Adam Shepherd on the Salt River near the licks. The Shepherdsville post office opened in 1806. Old Stone Bank, built in 1830, is believed to be the first bank west of the Alleghenies.

Iron production was another pioneer industry in Bullitt County. During the first half of the 19th century, 30-foot tall stone furnaces, heated by huge quantities of wood and charcoal, smelted iron out of the native rock ore 24 hours a day. Significant remains of two of these old iron furnaces still exist.

In September 1861 Union Gen. William Tecumseh Sherman and 4,000 men headquartered at the railroad to secure Muldraugh Hill from Confederate soldiers bound for Louisville.

Near the end of the 18th Century, the Beam family discovered the smoothness in the limestone water in the Clermont area and began making Jim Beam Bourbon. Today after more than 200 years of continuous operations, Jim Beam produces among the finest bourbons in the world. From 1826 to 1870 Paroquet Springs was one of the most noted health and pleasure resorts in the South. People came from far distances to partake of its rich mineral waters and to luxuriate in the superior accommodations of the day.

James T. Morehead, governor from 1823-1836, was born near Shepherdsville in 1797. In 1929 a successful businessman and visionary formed the Bernheim Foundation and purchased over 14,000 acres of land. Bernheim Arboretum and Research Forest is internationally recognized for its work with native-habitat rehabilitation. Alma Lesch (1917-1999), a native of Bullitt County, was an internationally known fiber artist.

**Bullitt County Courthouse**
*Source: Bullitt County History Museum*

# Butler County
# Morgantown

Butler County was formed on January 18, 1810 from portions of Logan and Ohio Counties. It was named in memory of Gen. Richard Butler. The county was the 53rd county in order of formation and contains 444 square miles of land. The elevation in the county ranges from 385 to 810 feet above sea level. The county seat is Morgantown.

Gen. Richard Butler was born in 1743 in Ireland and came to America in 1760. He served as an officer during the Revolutionary War. He was killed on St. Clair's expedition against American Indians into Ohio country in 1791.

Descriptions from early settlers described "a wild, untouched virgin forest with a cover of numerous species of trees, many being 100 feet high and five and six feet in diameter." Game was abundant—but no resource was more dominant than the Green River, which runs through Butler County. It proved to be a major factor in the growth of the county.

Morgantown, the county seat of Butler County, is west of the Green River. On June 11, 1810 a body of 11 justices of the peace, duly commissioned by Gov. Charles Scott, met to select officers for the newly formed county.

Butler County was home to William S. Taylor (1853-1928). A Republican, Taylor was declared winner over Sen. William Goebel and inaugurated as governor on Dec. 12, 1899. When Democrats contested the election, controversy and extreme bitterness led to Sen. Goebel's being shot on Jan. 30, 1900. For some 160 days Taylor served as governor, two-thirds of that time unofficially. Goebel succumbed to his wounds, and when courts decided against him, Taylor left the state for Indianapolis.

In 1833 Kentucky inaugurated a navigation system for the Green and Barren rivers. This system was completed in 1842, and in the following 20-year period, Butler County's population doubled.

After this period of growth, the Civil War began and slowed development. Butler County witnessed minor incidents during the war including a skirmish at Big Hill, near Morgantown on October 29, 1861. Another skirmish took place the following day at Woodbury where Confederate soldiers had established camp. A

**Butler County Courthouse**
*Source: Ky. Dept. of Libraries & Archives*

Civil War Monument was dedicated in May 1907; this monument lists Butler Countians who fought on both sides and is believed to be one of only two existing memorials that honors both Confederate and Union soldiers.

Adm. Claude C. Bloch, a native of Butler County, attended public schools and Ogden College in Bowling Green; he graduated from Annapolis in 1899. The career of this naval officer spanned the Spanish-American War and World Wars I and II. He served as Commander in Chief, U.S. Fleet, 1938-40.

During the annual Green River Catfish Festival, numerous tagged catfish are released into the river. Anglers from far and wide attempt to snag one of these tagged catfish for cash prizes, the top prize being $50,000.

# Caldwell County
# Princeton

Formed in 1809, Caldwell County was the 51st county established in Kentucky. Located on the Cumberland and Tennessee rivers, the elevation ranges from 339 to 767 feet above sea level with a land area of 346.98 square miles. Also nearby are Kentucky Lake, Lake Barkley and the Land

**Caldwell County courthouse under construction**
*Source: Kentucky Department of Libraries & Archives*

Between the Lakes National Recreation Area.

Caldwell County was named in honor of Gen. John Caldwell. He moved from Virginia to Kentucky in 1781. Gen. Caldwell rose from the rank of common soldier to major general in the Kentucky militia. Gen. Caldwell was elected lieutenant governor in September 1804. He died soon there after in November 1804.

Incorporated in 1817, Princeton is the county seat of Caldwell County. It is near a springs at the head of Eddy Creek. The town was originally called Eddy Grove, but was renamed Princetown in 1817 for Capt. William Prince, a Revolutionary War veteran who settled in the area around 1797. The name was later shortened to Princeton. Prince made his 200-acre land claim in 1798 and built Shandy Hall, a two-story frame home on a

bluff above Big Spring, a stream of underground water that emerges from a limestone bluff. The original county seat was Eddyville (now the seat of Lyon County).

As in much of the wilderness in Kentucky, the first paths blazed through this western county were "traces," or notches axed into trees to mark routes. The traces often followed trails worn down by buffalo, and later traveled by Native Americans and settlers. Three such traces, the Saline, Eddy (Palmyra-Princeton Trail), and Varmint traces, converged at Big Spring. In 1838 the Cherokee Indians camped near the "Varmintrace" Road on their 1200-mile "Trail of Tears." The forced trek, which began in the Great Smoky Mountains, led westward to Indian Territory. Princeton has two sites on the trail: Big Springs Park and the Champion-Shepherdson House.

During the Civil War Confederate irregular troops operated in Caldwell County. These Partisan Rangers, led by Brig. Gen. Adam R. Johnson, fought skirmishes and disrupted Union communications and supply lines. Most Caldwell County Confederates enlisted in Gen. Adam Johnson's Partisan Rangers. In August 1864, Gen. Johnson attacked a Union regiment at Grubb's Crossroad (about 6 miles from Princeton), and was permanently blinded. In December 1864 Confederate Gen. Hylan B. Lyon invaded western Kentucky with 800 men. His mission was to enforce the Confederate draft law and divert U.S. Army forces from Nashville. Over a period of 23 days, Gen. Lyon burned seven courthouses used by Union forces. Union troops fled Princeton as Gen. Lyon marched from Eddyville. The courthouse in Princeton was burned on December 15, but the court records were saved.

# Calloway County
# Murray

Calloway County was formed in 1823, and is situated immediately below and on the waters of the Tennessee River. The surface of more than half the county is level bottomland. Calloway County was the base of land-office operations forming the Jackson Purchase in 1818—now being Kentucky's eight and Tennessee's 20 westernmost counties. The elevation in the county ranges from 359 to 640 feet above sea level with a land area of 386.25 square miles.

Calloway County is named after Col. Richard Callaway, a noted lawgiver and defender of the frontier. Col. Calloway came to Kentucky with Daniel Boone in 1776. One of the founders of Boonesborough, it is said he instilled confidence in success among other settlers. In one year, 1777, he was appointed a colonel of the Ky. Militia and elected as a representative of Ky. County in the General Assembly of Virginia. He was killed at Boonesborough in 1780.

Murray, the seat of justice of Calloway County, was settled before 1825 and was known variously as Williston, Pooltown, and Pleasant Hill before being incorporated as Murray in 1844. Murray was named in the memory of John L. Murray. It replaced Wadesboro as the county seat in 1843. A land rush around Wadesboro followed the 1818 purchase of 8,500 square miles of territory bordered by three great rivers, (the Tennessee, Ohio and Mississippi) that we know as the Jackson Purchase. Negotiations were led by Generals Andrew Jackson and Issac Shelby

**Pogue Library**
*Source: Murray Tourism Commission*

(later to become Kentucky's first governor). They paid the Chickasaws $300,000 for their tribal real estate, then a wilderness, and these lands went to settlers by grant and purchase.

Ft. Heiman was one of three forts built to exert control over the Cumberland and Tennessee rivers, which had a significant impact on the Civil War. Located in extreme southwest Calloway County, Ft. Heiman was seized by Confederate Gen. Forrest in the fall of 1864. Using field cannon his cavalrymen sank two Union river transports, captured another plus a gunboat, and commandeered them. In this strange encounter between Confederate Calvary and the Union Navy, Forrest's gunners were repeating a trick they learned three years earlier when they engaged the big Federal gunboat Conestoga in a 7-hour ship-to-shore battle, at Canton in Trigg County. The gunboat retreated down river.

Calloway County is home to Murray State University, Kentucky Lake and the birthplace of radio (based upon pioneer experiments by Nathan Bowman Stubblefield [born in 1860]). Stubblefield successfully demonstrated wireless voice transmission as early as 1892. His early patents were granted that year; however, other patents took precedence and the honor of inventing radio went to others.

# Campbell County
# Alexandria &
# Newport

In 1794 Campbell County became the 19th county of Kentucky. It was carved from Scott, Harrison and Mason counties; later Boone, Kenton, parts of Pendleton and Bracken counties were carved from Campbell County. The county received its name in honor of Col. John Campbell, a native of Ireland who came to Kentucky at an early period. Col. Campbell, a Revolutionary War officer, received a grant of 4,000 acres of land from Virginia. The county lies on the Ohio River, immediately above the Licking River. The face of the county is diversified— level river bottomlands, rich and productive, while the uplands are hilly. Elevation ranges from 455 to 920 feet above sea level with a land area of 151.55 square miles. The county seats are Alexandria and Newport.

Newport was established as the county seat in 1796. Newport, is located near the confluence of the Ohio and Licking rivers. The town was founded in 1792 and named for Capt. Christopher Newport, who sailed the first English ship to Jamestown in 1607. Briefly, Wilmington (now in Kenton County) was the county seat. In 1840 when Kenton County was stricken off from Campbell, Alexandria was chosen as a central location for Campbell's courthouse, becoming the second seat of justice in the county.

In the 1850s an abolitionist, William Shreve Bailey, published the only antislavery newspaper in a slave state in the decade. Published in Newport, the last title for this paper was "The Free South." The press was attacked by mobs in 1851 and again in 1859, following Brown's raid on Harper's Ferry, Va.

When the Civil War began in 1861, Union enlistments totaled 800 for the Union to 200 for the Confederacy. No significant fighting occurred in Campbell County; however, a string of forts was constructed across the area to defend the urban region of Northern Kentucky and greater Cincinnati. In Campbell County a fort was built on John's Hill to prevent invaders coming north on the Licking River.

**Newport Aquarium**
*Photo: Sid Webb*

America's prohibition experiment in the 1920s gave birth to the growth of syndicate crime in the nation. Covington and Newport were significant national centers of such organized activity, which lasted for several decades.

Brig. Gen. John T. Thompson, inventor of the Thompson submachine gun, was born in Newport in 1860. A West Point graduate of 1882, he was an advocate of automatic weapons and improved many small arms. Gen. Thompson died in 1940, lamenting the notoriety of the Tommygun as a gangster weapon. William H. Horsfall (1847-1922) was one of the youngest Kentuckians to receive the Congressional Medal of Honor for service during the Civil War. Horsfall, born in Newport, was a drummer in Company G, First Ky. Infantry (USA).

# Carlisle County
## Bardwell

Carlisle County is located on the Mississippi River on the far western end of Kentucky and was originally part of Hickman County, which was formed in 1821. Established in 1886, Carlisle County was 119th in the order of county formation.

Carlisle, an attorney who practiced law in Covington and served as a legislator and lt. governor from 1871-1875. A member of the U.S. Congress, he served as Speaker of the House (1883-1889). Later he was a member of the U.S. Senate and served as the U.S. Secretary of Treasury under Pres. Grover Cleveland (1893-1897).

Bardwell, incorporated in 1879, is the county seat of Carlisle County. A courthouse in the Victorian style was erected. It survived until 1980 when it was consumed by fire. In 1982, a modern brick courthouse was completed in its place.

**Early broom factory**
Source: Ky. Dept. of Libraries & Archives

Carlisle County, along with Marshall, Calloway, McCracken, Graves, Hickman, Fulton and Ballard Counties, is part of the area known as the Jackson Purchase, which was added to the state in 1818 after the negotiations and treaty with the Chickasaw Indians. The county has a land area of 192.49 square miles and an elevation that ranges between 283 and 550 feet above sea level. While Carlisle County is mostly flat, there are a number of fresh water sources in the many creeks and streams that drain into the Mississippi River. Carlisle County is situated near the New Madrid Fault area and has often suffered the repercussions of earthquake activity.

The county was named in honor of John Griffin

Bardwell is a fifth class city with an approximate population of 795.

This far western land and its strategic location on the Mississippi River played an important role in the Civil War. In January 1862 Brig. Gen. Ulysses S. Grant sent 5,000 U.S. Army troops from Cairo, Ill. as a demonstration force against Columbus (in current day Hickman County and now the Columbus-Belmont State Park). Columbus was a heavily fortified Confederate stronghold on the Mississippi River. Combined forces led by Brig. Gen. J. S. McClernand marched from Ft. Jefferson at Wickliffe through the area to Milburn and back to Cairo, acquainting the U.S. Army with the area and inspiring confidence among many loyal Federal citizens.

# Carroll County
## Carrollton

In 1838 the 87th county of Kentucky was formed and named Carroll County. The Ohio River bounds Carroll County on the north at the mouth of the Kentucky River. The river bottom is fairly rolling and the land is hilly. With a land area of 130 square miles, the elevation of the county ranges from 420 to 940 feet above sea level.

Carroll County was formed out of Gallatin County. The town of Port William was established in 1794 as the county seat for

*Source: John Perkins*

says he, 'that there may be no mistake about that, I will save them the trouble of hanging two of us,' and instantly affixed his residence to his name, and by which he was ever afterwards known as 'Charles Carroll of Carrollton.'"

Carroll County's present courthouse was built in 1884. A brass plaque was placed on an interior wall marking the high water mark of the famous 1937 flood. The Coast Guard floated their boats through the hall until the water levels got too high for them to get their boats through the doors.

Point Park is located at the summit of the Ohio and Kentucky Rivers. In October 1754, James McBride came down the Ohio in a canoe and landed at the mouth of the Kentucky River. The great woodsman Simon Kenton camped at the point of these two rivers in 1771. In May of 1774 James Harrod and his companions made camp at this spot.

General Butler State Resort Park is located in Carrollton—the beautiful 791 acres surrounds a 30-acre lake and is the home of the Butler-Turpin State Historic House (c.1859). Col. Percival Butler was Kentucky's first adjutant general during Gov. Isaac Shelby's first term in office. He served until 1817, his office being in his Carrollton home. Butler also served under Maj. Gen. Samuel Hopkins during the War of 1812.

Gallatin. When Carroll County was formed, Port William became the county seat, but was renamed Carrollton. Both county and city were named in honor of Charles Carroll. Carroll was the only Catholic signer of the Declaration of Independence. This anecdote was told of Carroll in Collin's Historical Sketches: "Immediately after he placed his name to the Declaration of Independence, one of his friends jocularly remarked that if the British got hold of him, they would not know whether it were he or the Charles Carroll of Massachusetts, who had signed the declaration; consequently, they would be at a loss which to hang as the rebel. 'In order,'

Another historic home is the Masterson House. It was built by Richard and Sarah Masterson in the fall of 1790, and was the first two-story brick house to be built between Louisville and Cincinnati. Some speculate that it is the oldest two-story brick house still standing on the Ohio River between Pittsburgh and Cairo, Ill.

# Carter County
# Grayson

Carter County was created in 1838, bcoming the 88th county formed in Kentucky. It is located in northeastern Kentucky with a land area of 397 square miles and an elevation ranging from 542 to 1,300 feet above sea level. The area is well-watered by the Little Sandy River, the Little Fork of Little Sandy and Tygart creek. The county was named for Col. William Grayson Carter, a state senator from 1834-1838. Carter County was noted in its early years for five iron furnaces and its clay products industry that developed in the late 1800s.

Grayson is the county seat and is located on the Little Sandy River. Salt makers settled Grayson in the early 19th century. Originally known as Crossroads, it was renamed Grayson in 1838 upon becoming the seat of Carter County. Grayson was named in honor of the family of Col. William Grayson, the owner of a considerable amount of land in the area. A post office under the name Little Sandy Salt Works was opened in 1811, but was renamed Little Sandy in 1821, and finally relocated and renamed Grayson in 1840.

During the Civil War, Union forces under Gen. George W. Morgan, with 8,000 men, camped in Carter County in September 1862 on their retreat from Cumberland Gap. The Confederate Morgan's Raiders, knocking trees down across roads to block food and supplies, harassed the Union troops. However, reinforcements failed to reach the Confederates and they were forced to leave on October 1, 1862. They rejoined the main Confederate troops in Lexington. The Union troops traveled 200 miles to Greenup in just 16 days.

Pioneers drew salt from wells along the Little

Carter County native Tom T. Hall
Source: Eddie Pennington

Sandy River and the industry continued through 1850. Five stone furnaces were built in the east end of the county and used charcoal to make iron: Pactolus, Mount Savage, Star, Boon, and Iron Hills or Charlotte Furnace. The last one to close was Mount Savage in 1882.

In 1883 tobacco became a valuable crop. Entrepreneur William Malone lured several experienced growers from the Owen-Grant county area to relocate in Carter County. Between 1890 and 1925, tobacco warehousing and processing took place.

Many caves can be found beneath the forested hills in Carter County. Carter Caves was a major source of saltpeter during the War of 1812. Maintained as Carter Caves State Resort Park, nature has hidden more than 20 twisting caverns including Cascade Cave, where a 30-foot underground waterfall may be seen. Another cave that can be found is the Bat cave. Its name was derived in part to the innumerable swarms of bats that resided there.

## Bat Cave uncovered!

**The largest of a group of caves in Carter County got its name from the innumerous swarms of bats that live within. Perhaps Batman should look into finding a new secret hiding place.**

# Casey County
## Liberty

Casey County, the 46th county of Kentucky, was formed in 1807. The land varies between broad valleys with flat-topped ridges to dissected uplands. The main sources of water come from the Green River and the Rolling Fork of the Salt River. The elevation of the county ranges from 710 to 1,789 feet above sea level and the land area is 445.61 square miles. Casey County was named in honor of Col. William Casey of the Revolutionary War. Like many other Revolutionary War veterans, Casey received a land grant as payment for his military service. Casey is also known as the great-grandfather of Samuel L. Clemens (Mark Twain). Casey also helped frame the second Kentucky Constitution as a member of the state convention in Danville.

Mennonites in Casey County
Source: Tour Southern & Eastern Kentucky

Liberty, the county seat, is located near the center of the county. It was established in 1806 and its name was chosen out of patriotic sentiment. It became the county seat two years later. The Liberty Post Office opened in 1814. The present courthouse is not the original, in fact, it is the third one to be built. It was completed in 1889. In 1939, a "Doughboy" statue was dedicated there to commemorate the deaths of 32 Casey County natives during World War I.

Around 1781 the family of Capt. Abraham Lincoln (grandfather of Pres. Abraham Lincoln) settled in the area. The Lincolns lived on 800 acres of land on the Green River for two and a half years. Capt. Lincoln's heir, Mordecai Lincoln, sold the land to Christopher Riffe in 1803 for 400 pounds sterling. Riffe accompanied Col. William Casey to Kentucky in 1784. He was the first state representative to hail from Casey County and served seven terms. Landowner Enoch Burdett accumulated 13,000 acres of timberland. Upon his death in 1875, his assets were sold to Eugene Zimmerman, a Cincinnati businessman. Zimmerman built a wooden train track from Kings Mountain to Staffordsville and developed the Cincinnati & Green River Railway Co. in 1884.

Civil War skirmishes never reached Casey County, but the county still played an important role. Casey County is credited for having produced one-third of the 1st Kentucky Cavalry, which was recruited by Col. Frank Wolford and Col. Silas Adams. The cavalry was active in many battles including the Battles of Lebanon, Mill Springs, and the infamous Battle of Perryville.

Casey County is known as "The Gate Capitol of the World" due to the fact that farm gate production is one of the county's main businesses.

# Christian County
# Hopkinsville

Christian County was formed in 1797 and was the 21st county in order of formation in Kentucky. It is the second largest and one of the wealthiest counties in the state. The land area is 721.32 square miles and the elevation ranges from 390 to 966 feet above sea level. Tennessee forms the southern boundary. The county was named in memory of Col. William Christian, a native of Virginia, pioneer, politician and a colonel in the Revolutionary War. In 1785 Christian moved his family to Jefferson County, where his war land grants totaled 9,000 acres. He was killed in 1786 while defending the frontier.

Hopkinsville is the county seat and was founded about 1796. It was first known as Christian Court House and Elizabeth, but was changed to Hopkinsville in 1804 in honor of Gen. Samuel Hopkins.

On December 12, 1864, during the Civil War, Confederate Gen. Hylan B. Lyon burned the county courthouse. All county records were saved. Confederate Gen. Nathan Bedford Forrest joined Gen. Charles Clark here with six cavalry companies. Forrest was stationed in Hopkinsville, where he made his home with his wife and daughter.

During the Lewis and Clark Expedition, Clark and his family made a stop at Allsbury's Tavern in Hopkinsville. The infamous Trail of Tears passes through the county, Hopkinsville being a major camp stop. While taking this brutal forced journey from their homes in the Great Smoky Mountains to western Indian Territory (now Oklahoma), many Cherokees became ill and died. Included in the deaths were chiefs Fly Smith and Whitepath. Their graves are marked on the bank of the Little River.

Confederate Pres. Jefferson Davis was born at Fairview (in present-day Todd County). A 351-foot monument was erected in his honor on the Christian-Todd County line. Vice Pres. Adlai Ewing Stevenson was born in Christian County. Stevenson served under Pres. Cleveland in 1892 and was Bryan's running mate in 1900. Stevenson was one of four Kentuckians who were vice presidents, along with Richard M. Johnson, John C. Breckinridge and Alben W. Barkley. Besides New York, Kentucky has been home to more vice presidents than any other state.

The Pennyrile Forest State Resort Park is made up of 862 acres, which includes a 55-acre lake. Also at home in Christian County is Fort Campbell and the 101st Airborne Division, just 15 miles south of Hopkinsville. The Don F. Pratt Museum is on the base and exhibits the history of the "Screaming Eagles." The Fort Campbell Memorial Park is dedicated to soldiers of the 1985 Gander, Newfoundland tragedy. The focal point is a sculpture of a member of the Multi-National Peacekeeping Force in the Sinai Desert.

**Jefferson Davis Monument**
*Source: Kentucky Virtual Library*

# Clark County
## *Winchester*

Clark County was established in 1793 and became the 14th county formed in Kentucky. It was named for Gen. George Rogers Clark who came from Virginia to the Kentucky territory in 1775. Clark commanded an expedition into Illinois territory to capture several British forts, holding the northwest for future U.S. settlement. The Red, Kentucky and Licking rivers flow through Clark County. It is bounded on the south by the Kentucky and Red rivers, on the west by Boone's Creek, and on the east by Lulbegrud Creek. The west end of the county is the genuine Bluegrass Region, and is exceedingly fertile. Clark County has a land area of 254.31 square miles and an elevation ranging from 549 to 1,120 feet above sea level.

The county seat is Winchester, which was founded in 1792 with the new county. It was built on 66 acres of land that was donated by John Baker, a frontiersman who owned 319 acres of land in the area. It was named for Baker's former home in Winchester, Virginia. Other towns considered for the county seat were Strode's Station and Hood's Station. Winchester won by one vote. The Winchester post office was opened in 1803.

During the Civil War, Confederate Gen. John H. Morgan

and his raiders destroyed arms in Winchester on July 19, 1862. Morgan and his men had done much damage to surrounding towns. In 1864 after two battles in Mt. Sterling, they passed through Winchester on their way to Cynthiana where they were finally defeated.

The "Indian Old Fields" were ancient corn fields discovered when the county was first settled, about 12 miles east of present-day Winchester. American Indians had cultivated these fields many years before European explorers ventured into Kentucky. Known as Eskippakithiki and often referred to as "Kentake," this area was a meeting place for traders and American Indian hunters. It was the last of the Shawnee Indian towns.

Gov. James Clark made his home in Clark County. He was governor of Kentucky from 1836 to 1839. Clark was also a member of Congress and a judge on the Court of Appeals. When Clark was a circuit judge, he rendered his famous decision that the relief laws were unconstitutional. This move led to his arraignment and impeachment before the legislature.

Daniel and Squire Boone, Alexander Neeley and John Stuart are responsible for naming the Lulbegrud Creek. These pioneers named it after "Lorbrulgrud" in Gulliver's Travels—the first known book brought to Kentucky. Eventually, the name was shortened to Lulbegrud.

*Photo: Sid Webb*

# Clay County
# Manchester

Clay County, established in 1806, was the 47th county formed in Kentucky. It lies on the south fork of the Kentucky River, and its tributaries spread through the county. The county's land area equals 471 square miles with an elevation ranging from 690 to 2,235 feet above sea level. Red Bird Fork was named for a legendary Cherokee Indian who, along with another Native American called Jack, was friendly with early settlers and permitted them to hunt in the area. Allegedly, Red Bird and Jack were killed in a battle protecting their furs and their bodies thrown into the river.

Clay County was named in honor of Gen. Green Clay (1757-1826). Green Clay came from Virginia to Kentucky in 1777. His education was exceedingly limited but he later entered the office of James Thompson, a commissioned surveyor, where he more thoroughly studied the principles and acquired the art of surveying. While the vast wilderness lands of Kentucky were being appropriated, it was the custom of the warrant holders to give one half to the individual who would survey the quantity called for by the warrant. Thus, Clay acquired large quantities of land. From 1793 to 1808 he served in the Kentucky House, Senate, and the Kentucky Constitutional Convention. In May 1813 Gen. Clay, along with 3,000 Kentuckians, held back British and Indians at Ft. Meigs during the last war between Great Britain and the U.S.

Manchester, the county seat, was established along Goose Creek in 1807 as Greenville, also named for Gen. Green Clay. It was renamed Manchester later that year since there was already a Greenville, Ky. Manchester was named for the great manufac-

turing town in England.

During the Civil War, sympathy for the Union and Confederate causes divided the county and control shifted between the two loyalties. Gen. George W. Morgan's Union forces oc-

*Source: Tour Southern & Eastern Kentucky*

cupied Cumberland Gap (June 18 to Sept. 17, 1862). Cut off from supplies and surrounded, Morgan withdrew with an estimated 8,000 men. The force camped in Clay County to perfect the organization for their retreat to the Ohio River. Within the next 30 days, Union forces moved into the county. Five hundred men worked 36 hours to destroy all county salt works, mainly owned by Unionists but used by Confederates too. Citizens loyal to the federal government were allowed to remove salt for their own needs on taking oath none of it would be used to benefit the Confederacy. The promise of compensation for the destroyed salt works failed in 1873 when Pres. Ulysses S. Grant vetoed a bill for compensation. Only four salt production sites survived the war. At one time, salt was the leading article of export and there were over 15 furnaces in the county. The last of the salt works finally closed in 1908.

# Clinton County
## Albany

Clinton County was established in 1835 out of Cumberland and Wayne counties. The 85th county in order of formation, it lies south of the Cumberland River and borders the Tennessee state line. It has a generally hilly landscape, an elevation ranging from 530 to 1,780 feet above sea level and a land area of 197.46 square miles. Poplar Mountain holds the highest elevation at 1,700 feet.

DeWitt Clinton (1769-1828), whose name this county bears, was a native of New York, and one of the most distinguished men in the U.S. In 1797, Clinton was elected a member of the New York Legislature; in 1801, he received the appointment of U.S. senator. He was mayor of New York until 1815. He served as governor of New York in 1817 and again in 1824. He died suddenly in February 1828, while sitting in his library, before completing his second term of office.

Albany, the county seat, was established in 1837. The name may be from the city in New York (the original county seat was at Paoli, two miles south). The community of Seventy-Six Falls was named for the height of the falls, at that time 76 feet—now 38 feet because of backwater of the Cumberland Lake. Like many courthouses at the time, the courthouse at Albany and all court records were destroyed by fire during the Civil War. Guerrillas were responsible for the burning of this courthouse.

Oil was discovered in Clinton County in 1819 by Adam Beaty while he was drilling for salt water on the Little South Fork of the Cumberland River. The Lether Hay No. 1 well on Ill Will Creek was a gusher at 1,055 feet, with flames shooting 300 feet into the sky on September 10, 1945.

There are some notable people from Clinton County including Kentucky Gov. Thomas E. Bramlette, who was born near Albany in 1817. Bramlette raised and commanded the 3rd Kentucky Infantry. He resigned his commission in 1862 and was appointed by Pres. Lincoln as U.S. district attorney. He was elected governor in 1863 and served until 1867.

Clinton County is also the birth site of Gov. Pres-ton H. Leslie. He was admitted to the Kentucky Bar in 1840 and served as a member of the Ky. House of Representatives and as a state senator for Kentucky. Leslie was chosen Speaker of the House in 1869 and succeeded Gov. Stevenson (Feb. 1871). He was elected governor of Kentucky in 1871. Leslie County was named for him.

Clinton County is home to Dale Hollow Lake State Resort Park; Dale Hollow Lake and its 28,000-acre reservoir sit amid unspoiled wilderness. Lake Cumberland, one of the largest, man-made lakes in the nation, also lies in the county. It was formed in the 1940s by damming a large section of the Cumberland River.

**76 Falls**
*Source: Tour Southern & Eastern Kentucky*

# Crittenden County
# Marion

On the 26th day of January in 1842, the legislature set apart a portion of Livingston County as Crittenden County. The new county, the 91st to be formed in Kentucky, was named in honor of John Jordan Crittenden (1787-1863), then governor and one of Kentucky's great statesmen. The county covers a land area of 362 square miles; the elevation ranges from 310 to 842 feet above sea level. The northwestern boundary is formed by the Ohio River.

John J. Crittenden served as chairman of the Democratic National Conventions that nominated Woodrow Wilson for president, 1912 and 1916. He served as attorney general under three presidents, in the U.S. Senate five times, and was noted for the Crittenden Compromise in 1860, a futile effort to avert civil war and preserve the Union.

Marion, the county seat of Crittenden County, was named in honor of Gen. Francis Marion, a Revolutionary war hero known as the "Swamp Fox."

The old Saline Trace, used by American Indians in pursuit of buffalo, deer and elk, cut through the northwestern section of Crittenden County—the large game animals crossed the Ohio River at this site enroute to the salt licks of Illinois. The trail continued on to the site of Weston on the Ohio River. Weston, or West-town as the early name implies, was an important river port for western Kentucky pioneers before the Jackson Purchase opened in the 1820s. Flynn's Ferry began operating at the Ohio crossing of the trail in 1803, making it an important route of migration and commerce.

The intersection of the two main roads of that day, Weston to Princeton and Caseyville to Marion, was vital to the free movement of troops during the Civil War; it was hotly contested by Confederate raiding parties and Union occupation forces until war's end. Guerrillas burned the courthouse at Marion in January 1865. The building was a total loss; although the walls stood, all county records were lost.

Crittenden County was once one of the nation's largest producers of fluorspar, used in making steel, aluminum, porcelain, optical lenses and glass products. The county has other mineral resources including coal, rock asphalt, zinc and oil. Crittenden Furnace was one of the county's pro-

**Gov. John C. Crittenden**
*Source: Library of Congress*

ductive ironworks. Built in 1847, it was the last of several ironworks operated by the Cobb and Lyon families, who came to the area about 1800 when Andrew Jackson told them of iron ore deposits in the county.

Crittenden County was home to two U.S. Senators, Ollie James (1871-1918, Democrat) and Wm. Jordan Deboe (1849-1927, first Kentucky Republican senator). Marion's two U.S. senators lived one block east at College and Depot Streets. Both were prominent political leaders of their day.

# Cumberland County
## *Burkesville*

In 1798 Cumberland County was the 32nd county formed in Kentucky. It was named for the Cumberland River, which flows through the entire county. Nearby Dale Hollow Lake is a source of

**Dale Hollow Lake**
*Source: Tour Southern & Eastern Kentucky*

water in the county. The Iroquois Indians deeded the land for Cumberland County to settlers in 1768. It borders the Tennessee state line and has a land area of 305.82 square miles.

Incorporated in 1810, Burkesville, the county seat, was named in honor of one of the original proprietors, Samuel Burks. Situated on the north bank of the Cumberland River, it was established in 1798 and was known as Cumberland Crossing and Burkesville.

The Old American Oil Well was situated three miles north of Burkesville. It was discovered in 1829 or 1830 by men boring for salt water. After boring through 175 feet of solid rock, they struck a vein of oil, which spouted up 55 feet above the surface. For several days, the stream threw oil out and was running into the Cumberland River, covering the surface of the water for miles. Proving the theory to be true, it was ignited and a spectacular "river of fire" erupted with flames literally covering the surface for miles. Flames reached the tops of the tallest trees along the riverbanks. Oil bottled from this well was widely sold for medicinal use in the U.S. and Europe under the trade name "American Oil." It is believed to have been the first oil well in America.

During the Civil War, citizens of Cumberland County primarily supported the Union cause. In the presidential election of 1860, Abraham Lincoln received seven votes, with 67 percent of the voters casting their ballots in favor of the Constitutional Union Party. When the Civil War began in 1861, many Cumberland County citizens joined the 5th Kentucky Cavalry under the command of Burkesville resident Col. David Haggard.

Several noteworthy people are from Cumberland County. Brig. Gen. John Edwards King (1757-1828) made his home two miles north of Burkesville. He had obtained a Revolutionary War land grant for his military service. Thomas Lincoln, father of Abraham Lincoln, made a claim for land in Cumberland County in May 1801. He was appointed county constable in 1802 and 1804.

Joel Cheek, the founder of Maxwell House Coffee Company, was born in Burkesville in 1852. At the age of 21, his father gave him a silver dollar, which he called a "freedom dollar" as a symbol of the boy's freedom to venture forth on his own. Stanley Pac, former Chairman and CEO of the General Dynamics Corporation, was born in Burkesville. He was a graduate of the U.S. Military Academy with a distinguished record. Pac made his number one priority at General Dynamics the establishment and enforcement of unquestionable standards of ethics.

# Daviess County
## Owensboro

Daviess County was erected in 1815 out of part of Ohio County and was the 58th to be formed in Kentucky. The Ohio River forms its northern border and the Green River its western. The soil is particularly adapted to tobacco and is well watered by the rivers. The elevation ranges between 347 and 680 feet above sea level and the area is 462.39 square miles. The county was named in honor of Col. Joseph Hamilton Daveiss, although due to an error by the enrolling clerk, the name is spelled differently. Daveiss was a distinguished attorney and soldier and is best known as the U.S. district attorney who prosecuted the treason case against Aaron Burr.

The county seat, Owensboro, was named in memory of Col. Abraham Owen. Owen was a member of Kentucky's constitutional convention. Owensboro was incorporated on Feb. 3, 1817 and is situated on the bank of the Ohio River. Originally spelled Owensborough, in 1893 it was shortened to Owensboro.

Due to the county's reliance on slave labor, most residents were in support of the Confederacy during the Civil War. Only seven residents voted in favor of Abraham Lincoln during the Presidential election. Only one formal battle took place in Daviess County, which was at Panther Creek. Like most courthouses at the time, the Daviess County Courthouse was destroyed by arson. During World War I, about 1,747 of the 80,000 enlisted men from Kentucky were from Daviess County. Seventy-one were killed in action while seventy-six others were wounded.

There are some interesting things to see in Daviess County. One is where Uncle Tom lived and is the site of the Riley family homeplace. They were

the owners of Josiah Henson, who was an overseer of Amos Riley's farms. He is one of the characters on which Harriet Beecher Stowe based her 1852 novel, Uncle Tom's Cabin. When Henson learned that his owner was planning on sell-

Cooking team preparing mutton International Bar-B-Q Festival, Owensboro
*Source: Kentucky Department of Tourism*

ing him, he escaped to Canada and lived there for the rest of his life.

Another historic interest is a giant sassafras tree. It is located on Frederica Street and was first mentioned for its size in 1883. It is believed to be 250-300 years old, measures over 100 feet tall, and has a circumference of 16 feet. It is registered with the American Forestry Association as the largest tree in the U.S., and could possibly be the largest in the world of its kind.

Owensboro is known as a festival city—it has over 20 annual community celebrations. They have barbecue, bluegrass, fine arts, fine dining and much more. Self-proclaimed to be the Bar-B-Q Capital of the World, Daviess County's claim to fame is barbecued mutton, with more being consumed per person here than any other place in the world.

# Edmonson County
## Brownsville

In 1825 Edmonson County was formed as the 79th county in Kentucky. The land is generally undulating, and in some

Green River ferry
Source: Kentucky Department of Tourism

places quite hilly. There are several sulphur springs in the county and a seemingly inexhaustible supply of coal. The county has a land area of 302.62 square miles; the elevation in the county ranges from 412 to 900 feet above sea level. The Green and Nolin rivers flow through the county. The Green River was dammed in 1963, creating the 5,800-acre Nolin Lake in the northeastern part of the county.

The county was named for Capt. John Edmonson (1764-1813), a native of Washington County, Virginia. He settled in Fayette County in 1790, raised a company of volunteer riflemen, and joined Col. John Allen's regiment in 1812. He was killed in the disastrous battle of the River Raisin on Jan. 22, 1813. Capt. Edmonson was one of nine leaders

killed during the War of 1812 for whom Kentucky counties were named.

Brownsville, the county seat, was established in 1828 and named in honor of Gen. Jacob Brown, Commanding General of the U.S. Army (1815-1821). Gen. Brown defended the New York state frontier against the British in the War of 1812.

Although the Green River region and Edmonson County are largely rural in nature, this county was a major producer of iron ore beginning in the 1790s. Generally, Kentucky ranked third in production of iron ore in the 1830s and 11th in 1965. The Nolin Furnace, also called the Baker Furnace after its ironmaster, John H. Baker, was built in 1848. The top of the stone stack, about 40 feet high originally, is still visible when water in the Nolin Reservoir is low. Using steam power and charcoal fuel, it produced pig iron, kettles, andirons and other articles from local ore. The last blast was in 1850. The charcoal-furnace era ended in the 1880s with the depletion of ore and timber and the beginning use of modern methods.

Edmonson County lies in the heart of Kentucky's cave land region. Ninety percent of Mammoth Cave National Park, acclaimed as the longest cave system in the world, lies within its boundary.

Floyd Collins, a local man, was the first person to explore Sand Cave. On Jan. 30, 1925, he was trapped by a fallen rock in a narrow passage of the cave, just 150 feet from the entrance. Rescuers were able to reach him with food and heat for a short time; however, shifting of the earth closed the passage and cut off aid. Engineers sank a 55-foot shaft but were not able to reach his lifeless body until February 16.

# Elliott County
## Sandy Hook

Elliott County was the 114th county to be established in Kentucky in 1869. Located in the northeastern part of the state, it is surrounded by heavily forested hills and the waters of the Big Sandy, Little Sandy and Licking rivers. The land area is 233.96 square miles and the elevation ranges from 645 to 1,340 feet above sea level. Elliott County was named in honor of Judge John M. Elliott, a native of Scott County, Virginia. He practiced law at Prestonsburg. He served in the Kentucky Legislature, was a representative in the U.S. Congress from 1853-1859 and again from 1861-1863. On Nov. 6, 1861, Elliott was indicted for treason along with 31 other people. According to Collins' Historical Sketches, in December 1861 he was expelled from the Kentucky Legislature for being "directly or indirectly connected with, and giving aid and comfort to, the Confederate army, repudiating and acting against the government of the United States and the Commonwealth of Kentucky." Elliott was a Confederate sympathizer and served as a member of the Regular Congress of the Confederate States until the downfall of the Confederacy. Once the Civil War had ended, he served as a circuit judge and was also on the Kentucky Court of Appeals. In 1879 a disappointed litigant in a land case decided by the court assassinated Elliott.

The county seat of Elliott County is Sandy Hook, it was established in the early 19th century. It was named for its location on the bend in the Little Sandy River. It became the county seat after the formation of Elliott County in 1869. In 1872, the name was changed to Martinsburg to honor John P. Martin. However, another community was already using that name, so it was changed back to Sandy Hook. The area was known to hunters and explorers around Revolutionary War times but settlement wasn't made until the great timber harvesting days of the 1820s.

During the Civil War, no major battles were fought in Elliott County. However, both the Confederate and Union forces raided and recruited in the area. Just south of Sandy Hook, seven unknown soldiers are buried. They were casualties of Confederate attacks on Union troops withdrawing from Cumberland Gap in September 1862.

Over time, Laurel Creek has carved its way through the sandstone and formed the Laurel Gorge. It is a major part of the Little Sandy Watershed and feeds Grayson Lake. In forming Laurel Gorge, it has also formed cliffs as high as 300 feet. A variety of rare species exists and steps towards a preservation project are underway.

It is surrounded by high hills on three sides, the waters from which shed outwardly into Big Sandy and Licking rivers, but inwardly to Little Sandy River, forming along its tributaries a succession of moderately rich and very pretty valleys...

# Estill County
# Irvine

Estill County, established in 1808, was the 50th county formed in Kentucky. It is situated on both sides of the Kentucky River and is generally broken and mountainous. Several types of trees grow in abundance including oak, walnut, cherry, hickory, poplar, cedar and pine. The elevation ranges from 566 to 1,511 feet

**Fitchburg Furnace on Ky. 975**
*Source: Lexington Herald-Leader*

above sea level with
an area of 253.93 square miles. The county was named in honor of Capt. James Estill. Estill was a soldier and frontiersman. On March 22, 1782, he fought one of the bloodiest battles against natives, known as Estill's Defeat, in what is now Montgomery County. Along with seven of his 25 pioneers, he was killed in violent combat with a band of marauding Wyandots.

The county seat is Irvine and is located along the northern bank of the Kentucky River. It was established in 1812 and named in memory of Col. William Irvine, and possibly his older brother too, Capt. Christopher Irvine. The Irvine brothers came to Madison County (from which Estill County was carved) in 1778 or 1779. They built Irvine's Sta-

tion near where the city of Richmond now stands. Like many others for whom Kentucky counties are named, William Irvine served as the clerk of county and circuit courts in the Virginia Legislature and the Kentucky constitutional conventions.

A native trading post and camping ground called "Ah-wah-nee" was located in Estill County. Shawnees hunted here and also attained their supply of lead in this area. Daniel Boone, Squire Boone and Joseph Proctor were the first pioneers to use this camp in 1769.

The Battle of Irvine was the only Civil War battle fought in this area. Confederate Col. John S. Scott and his troops arrived here on July 30, 1863. They originally planned to capture the 14th Kentucky Cavalry; however, they only held Irvine for a few hours. Union Col. W.P. Sanders and his force pursued Scott and captured some of his rear guards. Col. Scott's troops crossed the river, but fought with Col. Sanders' men from the other side. Scott eventually departed.

The Daniel Boone National Forest is in the midst of the scenic beauty of Estill County. It has many streams, natural arches and steep forest ridges. According to legend, Daniel Boone first looked at the Bluegrass while at Station Camp.

Like many other Kentucky counties, iron furnaces are found here. Built in 1869, Fitchburg Furnace is commonly known as Red River Furnace and is one of the largest of its kind in the world. It is operated by the U.S. Park Service and is still in great condition. It is 60-feet high and the base measures 40 feet by 80 feet. Over 1,000 men worked there when it was in operation.

# Fayette County
## Lexington

Fayette County was formed in 1780 by the state of Virginia, and is one of the three original counties that at one time comprised the whole of Kentucky. It received its name as a testimonial of gratitude to Gen. Gilbert Morier de La Fayette, France's largest supporter of the American Revolution in 1780. The surface of this county is gently undulating, and the soil is probably as rich and productive as any upon which the sun ever shone. The elevation in the county ranges from 549 to 1,070 feet above sea level in a land area of 284.52 square miles.

Lexington, the seat of justice in Fayette county, is one of Kentucky's two first-class cities. It was founded in the year 1776, and named for the Battle of Lexington, Mass. (the opening battle of the Revolutionary War). Explorers camped at McConnell Springs near the Town Branch of South Elkhorn Creek, west of what is now downtown Lexington. Permanent settlers began arriving in 1779 and the town was officially established by the Virginia Assembly in 1782. For several years Lexington served as the seat of government of the state. The Lexington post office opened in 1794.

In 1780 Transylvania Seminary, the first literary institution of the west, was established by the legislature of Virginia. Transylvania University was established by the Kentucky Legislature in 1798, by the amalgamation of Transylvania Seminary and Kentucky Academy.

Lexington is the home of many "firsts" west of the Allegheny Mountains. With the exception of the Pittsburgh Gazette, the Kentucky Gazette was the oldest newspaper west of the mountains. It was published in Lexington in 1787 by brothers John and Fielding Bradford. The following year, Bradford printed the first Kentucky Almanac.

In 1812 Henry Clay, beloved statesman known as "The Great Compromiser," built Ashland, a 400-acre estate in what is now the heart of Lexington. Lexington opened its first city school in 1834. When the 1890s rolled around, tobacco replaced hemp as the major cash crop. By the early 1900s, Lexington became the world's largest burley tobacco market.

In 1924 William Monroe Wright, founder of Calumet Baking Powder, joined with a number of farms to form Calumet Farm, home of eight Kentucky Derby champion Thoroughbreds. Legendary Keeneland Race Course opened to huge crowds in 1936, while planes began taking off from nearby Blue Grass Airport in 1942.

The governments of the city of Lexington and Fayette County merged in 1974, creating Kentucky's only urban county government until recently, when Louisville merged its city and county governments. The merger formed the Lexington-Fayette Urban County Government. An Urban Services Area boundary separates the urban center of the county from the surrounding rural area.

Lexington is well-known as the "Horse Capital of the World." It has the honor of hosting the World Equestrian Games, hosted by Alltech, in 2010.

**Calumet horse farm**
*Photo: Sid Webb*

# Fleming County
## Flemingsburg

Fleming County, the 26th county formed in Kentucky, was created in 1798. Fleming was the first of 13 counties established in 1798. It is located on the Licking River and the face of the county

**Ringo Mills covered bridge**
*Source:: Fleming County Historical Society*

is variegated and the soil as diversified as any in Kentucky. The western portion of the land is rolling, abounding in limestone and very productive soil; other portions are generally mountainous, interspersed with large creeks and fertile bottoms. Fleming County was later divided into Floyd and Rowan counties. The elevation ranges from 590 to 1,420 feet above sea level and the area is 350.84 square miles.

The county seat is Flemingsburg. It was founded and named by Maj. George Stockton, in honor of his half-brother Col. John Fleming (the county was also named in his honor). Fleming and Stockton came to the area in 1776 to mark and improve the land. They followed the buffalo trails from northeastern Kentucky to Blue Licks. Fleming was an officer in the Revolutionary War and built one of the first settlements, Fleming's Station, in 1790. Stockton also built a settlement in 1787

and called it Stockton Station.

The Civil War did not avoid Fleming County. Gen. John Hunt Morgan's Raiders retreated via Fleming County from their last raid on central Kentucky towns in 1862. A civilian contraband merchant and trader between the lines, James J. Andrews led a group of Union soldiers into Georgia and captured a confederate steam locomotive called the "General." However, the mission failed, the men were captured and Andrews hanged in Atlanta, Ga.

A Fleming County native, Franklin R. Sousley, was one of the heroes memorialized in Joe Rosenthal's flag-raising picture at Iwo Jima during World War II. Sousley helped raise the flag on Mt. Suribachi, but was later killed in battle. He is buried at Elizaville.

There were numerous covered bridges built in Fleming County. They were first built in the 1790s but did not become popular until after 1814. Originally designed to protect the bridge from weather, there were more than 400 covered bridges in Kentucky at one time. Many were destroyed during the Civil War. Three such covered bridges are the Goddard "White" Bridge, which has a 63-foot span; the Hillsboro Covered Bridge, with an 86-foot span; and the Ringo's Mills Bridge. Goddard Bridge is Kentucky's only surviving example of a Town lattice truss bridge, inspired by Connecticut engineer and architect Ithiel Town, who patented the design in 1820. A signature of the Town design, the bridge trusses are connected by wooden pegs, or treenails. Goddard is also one of only two covered bridges that remains open to traffic in the commonwealth and has been restored. It was placed on the National Register of Historic Places in 1975.

# Floyd County
# Prestonsburg

On Dec. 13, 1799 the General Assembly enacted a bill creating Floyd County from Fleming, Montgomery and Mason counties. On June 1, 1800, Floyd County became the 40th county in order of formation and was named for John Floyd, a pioneer explorer. The elevation in the county ranges from 580 to 2,320 feet above sea level with a land area of 394.29 square miles.

Col. John Floyd was born in Amherst County, Va., in 1750. In 1773 or 1774 he came to Kentucky on a surveying excursion, as a deputy of Col Wm. Preston, principal surveyor of Fincastle County, Va. Col. Floyd was alternatively a surveyor, a legislator and a soldier. Col. Floyd was killed in 1783.

Prestonsburg, the seat of justice, is located on the Levisa Fork of the Big Sandy River. It was founded in 1797 and was originally known as Preston's Station, for John Preston. It was renamed Prestonsburg in 1799 when it was made the seat of the newly formed Floyd county.

Archaeological evidence shows that the Big Sandy Valley was originally occupied by the Adena tribe, popularly known as Mound Builders (so named for their practice of creating earthen burial mounds and other earthworks). Salt springs were discovered by Daniel Boone and his companions while exploring Eastern Kentucky in the winter of 1767-68. Later called Young's Salt Works, these springs provided salt for pioneers in the valley and for troops on both sides during the Civil War.

The Civil War divided Floyd County. Prestonsburg was a Confederate stronghold, but Union victory was claimed in two Floyd County battles.

The Battle of Ivy Mountain, site of the first important Civil War engagement in the Big Sandy Valley, occurred on November 8, 1861, when Confederate forces led by Capt. Andrew Jackson May were defeated by Federal troops. The Battle of Middle Creek took place on January 10, 1862, and involved Union Col. James A. Garfield (who would become the 20th U.S. president in 1881). The battle began around noon, with Union troops fighting their way up the ridges and Confederate soldiers counterattacking down them. The turning point came

**Mountain Arts Center, Kentucky Opry Christmas**
*Source: Tour Southern & Eastern Kentucky*

at 4:00 p.m., when Garfield's reserves arrived from Paintsville. Faced with fresh Union troops and advancing shadows, Marshall withdrew his troops from the ridge and retreated.

Floyd County is the home of Jenny Wiley State Resort Park, the Mountain Arts Center (a state of the art performance theater and is home to the Kentucky Opry) and StoneCrest Golf Course, Kentucky's highest public championship golf course and built on a reclaimed strip mine. The Samuel May House in Prestonsburg, built in 1817, is the oldest brick house in the Big Sandy Valley.

# Franklin County
# Frankfort

Franklin County, the 18th county to be formed, was created on December 7, 1794. It was first established as a county by the Virginia Legislature in 1786; the first survey of 600 acres was made by Robert M'Afee in July 1773. The county was named for Benjamin Franklin, early American patriot, inventor and signer of the Declaration of Independence. Land was taken from Shelby, Mercer and Woodford counties to form Franklin County.

Franklin County lies on both sides of the Kentucky River. The face of the county is diversified, with some tall cliffs along the meandering course of the river. Archaeological excavations reveal proof of Indian villages in the county. The Alanant-O-Wamiowee trail crossed the Kentucky River near Leestown, the county's first settlement established by Hancock Lee in 1775, on a site about a mile from modern-day Frankfort.

Frankfort is the seat of justice for Franklin County, and the capital of the state of Kentucky. It was originally known as Frank's Ford and named in memory of Stephen Frank, an early pioneer. It is the final resting place of Daniel and Rebecca Boone—at its 1844-45 session, the Kentucky Legislature adopted measures to have the mortal remains of Boone and his wife removed from their place of burial in Missouri, for the purpose of public interment in the public cemetery overlooking the city. A procession, extending more than a mile in length, accompanied the coffins to the grave.

**Rotunda in the
new Capitol building**
*Source: Kentucky Historical Society*

One of the most beautiful capitols in the country, the Capitol was completed in 1910; its Beaux Arts design features 70 iconic columns, decorative murals and sculptures of Kentucky. A floral clock planted with thousands of colorful flowering plants is located on the lawn of the Capitol grounds; the face of this clock is 34 feet in diameter.

Both armies operated in Franklin County during the Civil War. Between Sept. 3 and Oct. 7, 1862, Confederate forces occupied Frankfort—the only pro-Union state capital captured by Confederate forces during the war. On June 10-11, 1864, a detachment of Gen. John Hunt Morgan's cavalrymen attacked Frankfort. The Peaks Mill militia company and other local soldiers successfully defended the town.

Distilling, a leading industry, was effectively shut down by prohibition in 1919. After the repeal of prohibition in 1935, five distilleries prospered in Franklin County. Today, Buffalo Trace Distillery is located on an ancient buffalo crossing that became a pathway for westward movement and is the oldest distilling site in the U.S. Kentucky history, 509 Shelby Street. Frank Lloyd Wright, recognized as the greatest American architect, designed his only house built in Kentucky, on Shelby Street, for Rev. Jesse R. Zeigler in 1910.

# Fulton County
# Hickman

In 1845 Fulton County was formed, thus becoming the 99th county of Kentucky. It was named for Robert Fulton. Fulton is best known for the "Clermont," one of the first steamboats, which went up the Hudson River in 1807. Fulton County is bounded to the west and north by the Mississippi River and to the south by the Tennessee state line. It is the most western county in Kentucky and is literally split in two by the Mississippi River. Madrid Bend, in the far western part of the county, is separated from the rest of the county by the bend in the Mississippi River. Fulton County, with a land area of 208.95 square miles, has the lowest elevation in the state, which ranges from 260 to 500 feet above sea level. It is a part of the Jackson Purchase, purchased by treaty from the Chickasaw Indians in 1818.

The county seat is Hickman, which was established by the Kentucky Legislature in 1834. It was originally known as Mills' Point in honor of James Mills, an early settler. The name was changed to Hickman in 1837. It was the maiden name of G.W.L. Marr's wife. Marr once owned the entire town and several thousand acres around it. Hickman is located 45 miles below the mouth of the Ohio River and on the bluffs above the Mississippi River. It is below the mouth of Bayou du Chien.

**Reelfoot Lake was created by the earthquake of 1811**

*Photo: Sid Webb*

Fulton County saw considerable action during the Civil War. In the winter of 1861-62 Lt. Col. T.H. Logwood commanded the Sixth Battalion of the Tennessee Cavalry—this force constructed and occupied a camp of wooden huts in the area. They spent the winter scouting and patrolling. A surprise attack by a Federal force in March 1862 was repulsed after a forceful skirmish. Forces under Gen. Nathan B. Forrest captured the Federal garrison at Union City on March 24, 1864. Forrest's cavalry then crossed the state line and a band of approximately 1,200 men traveled to Hickman. Here they raided the town, taking large quantities of supplies.

The legendary railroad engineer, John Luther "Casey" Jones, is perhaps one of the most famous residents of the county. Jones lived near Hickman as a youth and when he was 16 years old, lived beside the tracks of the Mobile & Ohio Railroad. Now abandoned, it is located in the central part of Fulton County in the town of Cayce.

In December 1811, an earthquake occurred that was the most alarming and extensive east of the Rocky Mountains. Its greatest force was spent in Fulton County. The 25,000-acre Reelfoot Lake was formed when several streams changed their courses.

# Gallatin County
# Warsaw

Gallatin, the 33rd county established, was formed in 1798 from parts of Franklin and Shelby counties. At that time Gallatin was a large county with its county seat at Port William (now Carrollton). Later, parts of Gallatin were pared off to create three additional counties: Owen in 1819, Trimble in 1836, and Carroll in 1838. Today Gallatin County is the smallest county in Kentucky with just under 100 square miles of land area—an

trading center and was referred to as the Great Landing. In 1814 Col. Johnson and Henry Yates purchased 200 acres to establish a river town to be named Fredericksburg, after Johnson's hometown in Virginia. By 1815 the town plat was completed. In 1831 the town was renamed Warsaw (there was already a Fredericksburg in Kentucky). In 1837 the Gallatin County seat moved from Port William to Warsaw.

A great river tragedy occurred in Gallatin County on Dec. 4, 1869, when two large passenger steamboats collided two miles above Warsaw. Barrels of kerosene carried on deck of one of the steamers ignited,

Albert Gallatin, pictured on $500 dollar bill, 1863
*Source: Darrell Maines*

elongated slice of territory in the beautiful and fertile Ohio River valley. It lies on the Ohio River with a generally hilly but well-timbered surface.

The county was named for Albert Gallatin, who was born in Geneva, Switzerland in 1761. An orphan, he graduated from the University of Geneva in 1779; at age 19 he and a young comrade left home to seek glory and fortune in America. He became a financier, prominent American statesman, and served as Secretary of the Treasury to President Thomas Jefferson.

Warsaw, the county seat, began as a landing on the Ohio River in 1798. In 1805 founder Col. Robert Johnson surveyed and built a road from this landing to his former home in Scott County. This Ohio River landing soon became a busy steamboat-

enveloping both boats in flames that spread across the river. A loss of 162 lives resulted from the terrible holocaust.

The Markland Dam, three and one-half miles from Warsaw, creates additional miles of shoreline; Craig's Creek Lake is the largest lake with a 1,000-acre reservoir. Two landmark buildings are located on High Street in Warsaw: Adams House—built in the mid-1800s—was the home of Lucy Dupuy Montz, the first woman licensed to practice dentistry in Kentucky; and a block away is the birthplace of Gov. Richard Yates. He served in the Illinois Legislature for three terms and in the U.S. Congress from 1851-55. As governor of Illinois (1861-65), he vigorously supported Abe Lincoln and his state exceeded the call for volunteers in the War Between the States.

# *Garrard County*
# *Lancaster*

Garrard County, the 25th in order of formation, was formed in 1796. The county was named in honor of the then governor of the state, James Garrard. Garrard County's 231 square miles of land consists of gently rolling to hilly terrain and is bounded by the Dix River, the Kentucky River, and 3,600-acre Herrington Lake. The elevation in the county ranges from 514 to 1,400 feet above sea level.

Lancaster, the county seat, is situated two and one-half miles from Dix River at the head of Sugar Creek, a branch of the Kentucky River. It was founded in 1797 and named for Lancaster, Pennsylvania.

Garrard County is home to three of Kentucky's governors: Gov. Robert Letcher, Gov. William Owsley and Gov. William O. Bradley (first Republican governor).

Carrie Nation was born in this county in 1846. Driven by bitterness from her first marriage to an alcoholic and with hatchet in hand, this famous Kentuckian harassed saloon owners across the nation. She began her militant crusade in Kansas in 1899, smashing furniture, mirrors and bottles. Carry Nation gave direction to the anti-liquor movement, which led to Prohibition (1920-33). Her methods landed her in jail 30 times. She died in 1911 and the words, "She hath done what she could," are engraved on her monument.

Harriet Beecher Stowe, author of "Uncle Tom's Cabin," visited the home of Gen. Thomas Kennedy while gathering material for her book. A statesman and politician, Gen. Kennedy owned a plantation of 7,000 acres and 200 slaves at the time of his death in 1836. The legendary cabin of Uncle Tom was behind the mansion. Stowe's book inflamed anti-slavery sentiment throughout the North and deep resentment in the South, with its publication in 1851.

In August of 1861,

Public meeting in Lancaster in the 1st Southern National Bank meeting room on the town square
*Source: John Perkins*

Camp Dick Robinson was established seven miles north of Lancaster as the first Union enlistment station south of the Ohio River. Many Union troops from central and eastern Kentucky entered Federal service here. During the war, enlistments from Garrard County ran approximately three to one in favor of the Union. Camp Dick Robinson was later relocated to Jessamine County for better protection against invading Confederate troops and renamed Camp Nelson after its founder. After the war, the completion of the Stanford-Richmond line of the Louisville & Nashville Railroad (now CSX Transportation) in 1868 through Lancaster spawned growth in the city. The railroad helped Lancaster grow into a prosperous market town, but by the 1930s the line suffered from truck and auto competition, which caused the Richmond-Lancaster and the Stanford-Lancaster branches to be abandoned.

# Grant County
## Williamstown

Grant County, the 67th county established in Kentucky, was created in 1820 from the western part of Pendleton County, called the "Dry Ridge." The dry ridge, which runs through the county, is a rib of the great Cumberland Mountain, and divides the Licking and Kentucky rivers. Covering an area of 259 square miles, Grant County forms a parallelogram, 22 by 22 and one-half miles. It has an average elevation of 1,000 feet above sea level. The land is

Rustic Mullins log cabin
Photo: Sid Webb

mostly rolling plains, with a few hilly areas. The eastern part of the county is watered and drained by tributaries of the Licking River; the western portion, by tributaries of the Kentucky River.

Mr. John M'Gill, publisher of a small gazetteer of Kentucky in 1832, stated that this county was named for Col. John Grant, who came from North Carolina in 1779 to settle Grant's Station. However, others have asserted the county was named in honor of Col. Grant's brother, Samuel Grant. Yet another source argues that one legislator brought up the issue of a new county so often, and repeatedly asked the legislature to "grant" him a hearing, that the county was named Grant.

Williamstown was established in 1820 as the county seat of the newly formed Grant county and named for William Arnold, a captain in the Revolutionary War, who donated land for the town. (The name Philadelphia was considered but rejected.) The site had been the location of the pioneer Littell's Station. The Williamstown Court House post office opened in 1822. Crittenden is an early town dating from stagecoach days along Lexington-Cincinnati Pike.

Philanthropist and professor Curtis C. Lloyd established Lloyd Reservation here in a 300-acre woodland. He was buried on the reservation where years earlier he had erected his tombstone with this inscription: "Born in 1859. Died 60 or more years later. The exact number of days, months and years he lived nobody knows and nobody cares. Monument erected by himself, for himself, during his own life, to gratify his own vanity. What fools these mortals be."

The county was the source of some military action during the Civil War. A small Confederate force raided Williamstown in 1864, hoping to seize reported large sums of Federal money said to be have been cashed in banks there. Finding the money removed, the Confederates seized a Union firearms store. Later, south of Williamstown, three Confederates were brought from Lexington and executed in reprisal for guerrilla slayings of two Union sympathizers.

# Graves County
# Mayfield

Forming a perfect rectangle in the center of the Jackson Purchase, Graves County was formed in 1824, and named in memory of Maj. Benjamin Franklin Graves. It is the largest of eight counties taken out of the original Purchase area of Hickman County. Containing a land area of 555.59 square miles, Graves County is the eighth largest county in the state and the only county framed by four straight lines. The elevation in the county ranges from 321 to 580 feet above sea level.

Maj. Graves came to Fayette County in 1791 from Virginia at age 20. A farmer, he was elected to the Ky. General Assembly in 1801 and 1804. In 1812 when war was declared against Great Britain, he was among the first to volunteer his services. He received the appointment of major, and proved himself an active, vigilant and gallant officer. He was killed during the battle of River Raisin, Mich., on Jan. 22, 1813.

Mayfield is the seat of Graves County and was settled about 1819. The town was named for Mayfield Creek, which was possibly named for George Mayfield, a settler who was killed there. The post office opened in 1823.

Graves County hosted Camp Beauregard—a training base for Confederate troops from six states between 1861-1862. Severe epidemics caused a heavy mortality rate. Fancy Farm Picnic, held at St. Jerome's Church, is a premier political event. This annual event began in 1834 as a family picnic under the limbs of the "Lying Oak." Suspended during the Civil War, the event resumed in 1880 as a prime chance for politicians to stump before Election Day.

In May 1861, delegates of seven Kentucky and 20 of Tennessee's westernmost counties met in Mayfield, voted to secede from the Union and form a Confederate state. With Tennessee's vote to secede from the Union on June 8, 1861, the proposal was abandoned.

Confederate Gen. Nathan B. Forrest with a main body of cavalry passed through Mayfield to, and from, a destructive raid on Paducah in March 1864. Confederate Gen. Abraham Buford's division camped here and Kentucky regiments were given leave to visit their homes to enlist recruits.

**Edana Locus House**
*Source: Mayfield Tourism Commission*

Alben Barkley (1877-1956), was born in Graves County on November 24, 1877. A life-long leader in the Democratic Party, Barkley was elected prosecuting attorney for McCracken Co. in 1905, county judge in 1909, U.S. congressman in 1912, and U.S. senator in 1926. He was the majority leader of the U.S. senate longer than any other man. He was vice president under Harry Truman.

Mayfield is famous for the Wooldridge monuments, a rare statuary designed by Col. Henry Wooldridge. Wooldridge devoted 16 statutes to the memory of his family and his life. The collection includes his mother, brother, two girlfriends of his youth, his favorite dogs, a deer, a fox and Wooldridge himself, sitting astride his favorite horse, Fop.

# Grayson County
## Leitchfield

Grayson County was formed in 1810, thus becoming the 54th county formed in Kentucky. It was named for Col. William Grayson who served as an aide to Gen. George Washington during the Revolutionary War.

**Grayson County Courthouse**
*Source: Kentucky Virtual Library*

numerous principal sources of water Big Clifty, Little Clifty, Short, Bear, Canoloway and Caney creeks. The Rough and Nolin rivers form the northern and southeastern borders.

The county seat is at Leitchfield and was established in 1810. The widow of Maj. David Leitch donated the land for Leitchfield. In 1813 the post office opened as Litchfield (of which the pronunciation is reflected) or Grayson Court House. The spelling of the town was changed to Leitchfield in 1877. It is said that there is not another town in the entire world with exactly this same name.

Adjacent to Leitchfield was a 5,000-acre tract of land purchased by George Washington as an investment in November 1798. It was noted on Filson's 1784 map of Kentucke that there was an "abundance of iron ore" here. Gen. A. Spotswood visited the area and reported back to Washington, who died in 1799 before being able to visit and develop the land.

During the Civil War, along with many other courthouses, the courthouse at Leitchfield was burned by Confederate troops under command of Gen. Nathaniel Lyon. The burning was executed in order to harass and delay Federal troops in their pursuit. The courthouse at Leitchfield was destroyed twice more due to arson by 1936.

Grayson Spring was once a celebrated watering place and summer resort. It was located five miles from Leitchfield. This resort flourished for over 100 years and thrived on the mineral springs that were first discovered in 1800.

The Jack Thomas House was built in 1810 by Jack Thomas, the first county official and county/circuit court clerk. Thomas served from the time of the founding of Grayson County until 1851. His house is known as the earliest brick residence built in Grayson County. Thomas was born in a house built by Thomas Lincoln, Pres. Lincoln's father.

Grayson was also a member of the Virginia Assembly, the Continental Congress, and the first U.S. Senate. Grayson County has an elevation ranging from 395 to 963 feet above sea level and a land area of 503.68 square miles. Situated in the western middle section of the state, there are

# Green County
# Greensburg

Formed from parts of Lincoln and Nelson Counties in 1792, Green County was the 16th county created in the state of Kentucky. It was named in honor of Gen. Nathaniel Greene, of Revolutionary War fame. Since its creation the following counties have been taken entirely from Green County: Cumberland in 1798, Adair in 1801, and Taylor in 1848. The following counties were taken in part from Green County: Pulaski and Barren in 1796, Hart in 1819 and Metcalfe in 1860. Green River flows through the center of this county with its gently rolling land and valleys with many streams. The elevation in the county ranges from 490 to 1,045 feet above sea level. The land area is 288.66 square miles.

**L&N Depot at Greensburg**
*Source: Tour Southern & Eastern Kentucky*

Gen. Greene, in memory of whom this county was named, helped plan the defense of New York; he fought at Trenton, Brandywine and Monmouth; sent south by Gen. George Washington, Gen. Greene's Carolina campaign forced the British to leave Charleston in 1782.

Long Hunters explored the Green County area in 1770. Greensburg, the county seat, was established by John Glover in 1780. It began as Glover's Station and was renamed Greensburg in 1794 with the formation of the new county. The second Green County Courthouse, built in 1802 and in use until 1931, is the oldest public building still standing in Kentucky.

Green County was the scene of military activity during the Civil War. As the war progressed, guerrilla raids became frequent. In October 1863 a Confederate guerrilla force occupied Greensburg and terrorized its residents. On November 19, 1864, six Confederates were executed in the western part of the county in retaliation for the murder of two Union men. Camp Ward, a Union recruitment station, was established in Greensburg by Gen. William T. Ward, a resident.

In 1958 Green County experienced an extensive oil boom; in 1959 there were over 700 oil wells in the county. By 1969 over 20 million barrels of oil had been produced in the county, but after that year production declined sharply.

Green County has been home to many famous people, among them Union generals E. H. Hobson and William T Ward; the Rev. David Rice, pioneer Presbyterian minister; Mentor Graham, Abraham Lincoln's teacher in Ill.; Mary Owens, Lincoln's sweetheart; William H Herndon, anti-slavery advocate and Lincoln's law partner in Ill.; Rueben Creel, U.S. Consul to Mexico; and Jane Todd Crawford who agreed to unheard-of operation by surgeon Dr. Ephraim McDowell of Danville, without anesthesia on Christmas Day 1809.

# Greenup County
# Greenup

Greenup County was formed in 1804 and was the 45th county in order of formation. It is located on the mouth of the Little Sandy River and is bounded on the north by the Ohio River. It has a land area of 346.11 square miles and an elevation ranging from 485 to 1,200 feet above sea level. It was named for Christopher Greenup, a Kentucky governor, lawyer and an officer in the Revolutionary War. He was one of the first two members of the U.S. Congress from Kentucky.

The county seat is Greenup, which was established in 1803 along with the county. It was originally named Greenupsburg, but was shortened to Greenup in 1872 to prevent further inconvenience from confusing it in the U.S. mail with Greensburg in Green County. The Greenup Court House post office opened in 1811 and renamed Greenup in 1872.

Bennett's Mill Bridge is one of Kentucky's longest wooden covered bridges. It is a one-span bridge measuring 195 feet long. It was built by B.F. Bennett and his brother Pramley in 1855-56 to aide customers en route to their mill. It has never been painted and original footings and frame are still intact.

Raceland was a race track known as the "Million Dollar Oval." In 1924 a record crowd of 27,000 people filled the grandstand for the inaugural Raceland Derby. Kentucky Derby winner "Black Gold" and four other Kentucky Derby entrants were featured in the race. The 350-acre complex was built by J.O. Keene, who later built Lexington's Keeneland. The last season of racing at Raceland was in 1928. In 1937 the track was sold and torn down.

The grave of Lucy Virgin Downs rests in Greenup County. Downs was the first white child born to American parents west of the Alleghenies. She was born in 1767 and could remember George Washington visiting her father when he was surveying the land.

Jesse Stuart, the well-known teacher, author and poet laureate of Kentucky, was born in Greenup County. He lived most of his life in W-Hollow. Many of his short stories, books and poems were set in his home county. He received the Guggenheim fellowship and was nominated for a Pulitzer Prize in Poetry. He was honored with a marble shaft in the courthouse yard.

Country music singer and television actor Billy Ray Cyrus hails from Flatwoods in Greenup County. He does charitable work through the Billy Ray Cyrus Foundation.

Greenbo Lake State Resort Park, the Jesse Stuart Nature Preserve and several iron furnaces are found in Greenup County.

**Bennets Mill Bridge**
*Source: Greenup County Tourism Commission*

# Hancock County
# Hawesville

The 83rd county formed in Kentucky was Hancock County in 1829. It has a land area of 188.80 square miles and an elevation ranging from 358 to 840 feet above sea level. It is bounded on the north by the Ohio River. The county was named for John Hancock, patriot, statesman, soldier, and president of the Continental Congress. Hancock is best known as the first signer of the Declaration of Independence.

Hancock County was once considered the Sorghum Capital of the World, packaging and shipping over half a million gallons of sorghum syrup per year. But through the years, due to the crop's labor-intensive nature and decreasing market demands, production tapered down. Beginning in 2001 the county seat of Hawesville began hosting a sorghum festival.

Hawesville is located on the Ohio River. It was established along with the county and post office in 1829; it was incorporated in 1836. It was named for Richard Hawes, who provided the land for the town. Hawes' son, Richard, Jr., became the Confederate governor of Kentucky in 1862. The courthouse in Hawesville is the second oldest courthouse in Kentucky. Construction on it started in 1865 and was completed in 1867. However, the exterior has been restored as it was initially designed during the Civil War. Throughout the Civil War, Hawesville was a stronghold for Confederates and a refuge for guerrillas. By 1864 guerrillas had blocked entrances of several coal mines that were supplying Union steamboats. Capt. Edmond Morgan finally took action against the guerrillas by positioning his iron-plated steamer, Springfield, to open fire on Hawesville. To avoid shells, residents took cover in the stone-walled Catholic Church and inside the coal mines. Hawesville withstood much fire from other boats on the Ohio River as well.

Confederate guerrilla Capt. William Davison was born in Hawesville. His band of marauders terrorized residents along the Ohio River in western Kentucky. He died in 1865 and was finally laid to rest in the Hawesville Cemetery after the war.

Capt. John W. Cannon was also born in Hancock County. Cannon was a riverboat pilot and steamboat entrepreneur. He is best known for the Robert E. Lee, his steamboat that won over the Natchez in the steamboat race from New Orleans to St. Louis in 1870.

Abraham Lincoln won his first law case in Hawesville in 1827. Lincoln himself had been charged with operating a ferry without a license. He defended his own case in trial and won. Presiding Justice of the Peace Samuel Pate encouraged Lincoln to study law and even loaned him books.

**John Hancock**
*Source: Library of Congress*

# Hardin County
# Elizabethtown

Hardin County was created in November 1792 and was the 15th county formed in Kentucky. The county's early boundaries were the Rolling Fork on the east, the Green River on the west and south, and the Ohio River on the north. Since that early date 13 other Kentucky counties have been formed from the original land area. Today it has a land area of 627.98 square miles and an elevation ranging from 383 to 1,017 feet above sea level. It was named for Col. John Hardin, a defender of pioneer Kentucky from Nelson County.

The county seat is at Elizabethtown and was founded in 1795. The land was given by Col. Andrew Hynes and was named in honor of his wife, Elizabeth. The first post office was opened there in 1804 and may have been known as Hardin Court House. The first permanent settlements in Hardin County were established when Col. Andrew Hynes, Capt. Thomas Helm and Samuel Haycraft, each built a fort in 1780. The forts were a mile apart from each other. The settlement came to be known as Severns Valley, and when the Severns Valley Baptist Church was organized at least 17 families were living in the area.

During the Civil War Gen. John Hunt Morgan and his Morgan's Raiders caused much damage in Elizabethtown. On their second raid into Kentucky their goal was to destroy the L&N Railroad, the main channel for southbound Union troops. On December 28, 1862, they were successful in destroying two of the most important trestles, rendering the line impassable for two months. In just 11 days they destroyed $2,000,000 of U.S. property and wrecked an L&N line from Munfordville to Shepherdsville. The Elizabethtown stronghold was shattered and Federals were forced to surrender.

Two U.S. presidents hail from Hardin County. Abraham Lincoln was born in what was then Hardin County in 1809 and James Buchanan was a practicing lawyer at the Hardin County Bar in 1813. However, both had left Kentucky by 1816.

Camp Knox was established in 1918 as an artillery range on 21,722 acres acquired from Hardin County. It was named for Maj. Gen. Henry Knox. Knox organized artillery during the Revolutionary War. Mechanized cavalry training began in 1931 and in January 1932,

**The Hardin County History Museum is located in the former Elizabethtown Post Office built in 1931**
*Source: Kenny Tabb*

the name was changed to Fort Knox. Armored Force was created in 1940 and in 1941-42, 39,017 acres were added to the base. It is home to the U.S. Bullion Depository, also known as the "Gold Vault," and the Patton Museum of Armor and Cavalry. Millions of soldiers have trained here in cavalry and armor and have served in WW II, the Cold War, Korea, Vietnam and now Iraq.

Cavalry and infantry battalions were assigned to Elizabethtown under Gen. George Custer to suppress Ku Klux Klan activity and were successful. In 1873 Custer was ordered to Dakota, where the infamous "Custer's Last Stand" took place in June 1876.

# Harlan County
## Harlan

In 1819 Harlan County became the 60th county formed in Kentucky. It was the most southeastern county in the state for 48 years until Bell County was formed in 1867. It is bounded on the east and south by the Virginia state line. It has a land area of 467.20 square miles and an elevation ranging from 1,070 to 4,145 feet above sea level. The highest point in the state is found on Big Black Mountain, which runs along the Kentucky-Virginia border. Another popular mountain in the area is Stone Mountain, surmounted by a stupendous rock one mile long and 600 feet high on the northern border of Pine Mountain.

The county seat is at Harlan, located on the forks of the Cumberland River. It was originally known as Mount Pleasant, for a local Indian mound, and became the seat of the county in 1819. In 1828 the post office opened as Harlan Court House and was known as Spurlock by the postmaster. Mount Pleasant was renamed Harlan in 1865. Both the county and the seat were named for Maj. Silas Harlan. Harlan was born in Berkley County, Virginia and came to Kentucky in 1774. He commanded a company of spies under Gen. George Rogers Clark. Clark said of him: "He was one of bravest soldiers that ever fought by my side." Harlan built a stockade fort on the Salt River seven miles above Harrodsburg and called it Harlan's Station. Harlan died leading his troops at the battle of the Blue Licks.

During the Civil War Harlan County was an important passageway for Union and Confederate forces. Each force moved along routes that reflected the local sentiment—Union troops along the Poor Fork and Confederate troops along Clover Fork. Harlan County suffered great losses at the time. The courthouse at Harlan was burned along with many important papers and documents in the clerks' offices, the jail and many other houses were destroyed. Both soldiers and guerrillas committed the arson.

Harlan County is well known for its production of coal. After the Louisville & Nashville Railroad forged through the area, new

**Portal 31 Mine**
Source: Tour Southern & Eastern Kentucky

seams of coal were discovered. Many landowners became rich overnight. Coal towns filled the area and the population boomed. The crucial need for steel during World War I led to the founding of Lynch, built by the U.S. Steel Corp. in 1917. Lynch had the first fully electrified coal mine in the U.S. The location was chosen for the millions of tons of high-quality coal. However, due to innovations in mining, mechanized mining mergers and the reduction of operations, the population in Harlan County has deteriorated tremendously.

# Harrison County
# Cynthiana

On December 23, 1793 Harrison County became the 17th county formed in Kentucky. It lies on both sides of the South Licking River while the Main Licking River runs through a small portion of the northeastern part of the county. It has an elevation ranging from 540 to 1,060 feet above sea level and a land area of 309.68 square miles. The county was named in honor of Col. Benjamin Harrison who was a soldier in the Revolution and a representative from Bourbon County in the Kentucky legislature. Harrison was also present at the three conventions that produced Kentucky's first constitution. Many early inhabitants were Revolutionary War veterans who had received land grants as payment for their military service.

The county seat is at Cynthiana. Robert Harrison donated the land for the establishment of Cynthiana in 1793, and the town was named for his daughters, Cynthia and Anna. The Cynthiana post office opened in 1801 under the name Cinthiana, but the spelling was later changed. Cynthiana was originally settled as Hinkston's Station, but was later abandoned due to the frequent Indian raids—most of which were ignited by the British. It was then occupied by Issac Ruddell and his family, and renamed Ruddell's Station. Ruddle moved his family to the abandoned fort in order to better protect them against the Indians—the fortified fort became one of the largest and strongest in Kentucky.

Several battles were fought in Harrison County during the Civil War. The Battle of Cynthiana took place on July 18, 1862. It was then that Col. John Hunt Morgan defeated Federal forces here and captured the town. On June 1, 1864, Gen. Morgan and his raiders entered Kentucky on their last raid. They took Mt. Sterling on June 8 and lost it on June 9. Morgan's troops then captured Lexington on June 10 and finally Cynthiana on June 11. On June 12, 1864, Union troops under Gen. Stephen. G. Burbridge defeated Morgan and his Confederate troops. Morgan retreated to Virginia on June 20.

Two historic sites in Harrison County are the Old Log Court House and Stony Castle. Built in 1790 the Old Log Court House is the oldest house in Cynthiana. Henry Clay once practiced law here and Adam Keenan published the first city newspaper here in 1817. Stony Castle was the first post office between Lexington and Covington. Postmaster John Smith built it in 1807 on land granted to him by Patrick Henry. It survived the Civil War and was requisitioned by Gen. Morgan for his wounded troops.

**Flour mill near Cynthiana**
*Source: Kentucky Virtual Library*

# Hart County
## Munfordville

In 1819 Hart County became the 61st county formed in Kentucky. It is bounded on the west by the Nolin River and Lake and the Green River winds from east to west through the center. It has a land area of 415.93 square miles and an elevation ranging from 421 to 1,156 feet above sea level. It was named for Capt. Nathaniel G. T. Hart, a lawyer and business man who raised and commanded the Lexington Light Infantry in 1812. He was severely wounded at the Battle of Raisin and was taken prisoner by the British. Promised a safe trip home, Hart was betrayed by a British officer he had once befriended and died during an Indian escort home.

The county seat is at Munfordville. Established in 1816, the land for the town was given by Richard Jones Munford, for whom the town was named. It was once known as Big Buffalo Crossing but is now often called Munfordsville, even though the "s" is no longer in the official name. In 1820 the Munfordville Court House post office opened.

From 1857-59 the iron L&N Railroad bridge was constructed by engineer Albert Fink over the Green River. It was hailed as an engineering marvel; measuring 1,800-feet long it was the largest iron bridge in the U.S. at the time. Bacon Creek Bridge was also nearby and two Civil War battles were fought for control of these supply links between Louisville and Bowling Green. Confederate Gen. Simon B. Buckner ordered two spans of the L&N bridge to be destroyed to prevent Union use. The Battle of

Munfordville took place on September 14, 1862 and ended with Union troops under Col. Wilder surrendering to Gen. Bragg's Mississippi regiments. During the siege the Munfordville Presbyterian Church served as a hospital for wounded Union troops with the nurses' quarters next door. It was in Munfordville on October 27, 1861 that Gen. John Hunt Morgan and 84 of his soldiers were formally sworn

**Rolling field in Hart County**
*Source: John Perkins*

in as the Second Cavalry Regiment, Kentucky Volunteers, Confederate States of America. Originally part of the Lexington Rifles, they united with Confederates at the Green River. Their daring exploits branded them as "Morgan's Raiders."

One interesting site is the Old Munford Inn. It was built in 1810 on a pioneer trail by Thomas Munford, brother of Richard Jones Munford for whom the town is named. Many noteworthy guests have stayed here, one being Pres. Andrew Jackson enroute to his inauguration in 1829.

# Henderson County
## Henderson

Henderson County was formed in 1799 and was the 38th county formed in Kentucky. It is bounded on the north by the Ohio River and is also watered by the Green River. It has a land area of 440.12 square miles and an elevation ranging from 331 to 588 feet above sea level. It was named in honor of its founder Richard Henderson of North Carolina.

Henderson, along with Nathaniel Hart, James Luttrell and Daniel Boone, met with the entire tribe of Cherokee Indians and negotiated a land treaty. In it, all land between the Cumberland, Ohio and Kentucky rivers was transferred to Henderson's Transylvania Company for a generous sum. The Virginia legislature later cancelled this treaty and the area was renamed Kentucky County, Virginia. Henderson was compensated for his work with 200,000 acres of land on the Ohio River at the mouth of the Green River.

The county seat is at Henderson and was originally settled as Red Banks in the late 18th century. The town of Henderson was laid out for the Transylvania Company in 1797. It overlooks the Ohio River. In 1801 the Henderson post office opened.

During the Civil War, Brig. Gen. A. R. Johnson and 30 Confederate raiders seized Henderson on July 17, 1862. They captured guns, hospital supplies and several businesses before raiding Newburg, Ind. Because of a threat by Morgan's Raiders, Union headquarters in Louisville were unable to send reinforcements. Support finally arrived from Evansville on July 22 but Confederate troops had already abandoned the area.

Many notable people are from Henderson County. One is Albert B. "Happy" Chandler, a two-term governor of Kentucky who was elected baseball's second commissioner on April 24, 1945 by a unanimous vote of club owners. His six-year tenure encompassed some of the most significant developments in the game's history. In 1947 Chandler approved a contract to make Jackie Robinson the first African American player in the major league. In 1982 Chandler was elected into the Baseball Hall of Fame. Chandler played a major role as governor in the establishment of the University of Kentucky Medical Center, which was later renamed in his memory.

One of America's most famous ornithologists was John James Audubon, who lived in Henderson County. From 1810 to 1819 Audubon roamed the woods of Henderson County painting birds in their natural habitat. The Audubon State Park was named in his honor.

Mother's Day was first observed in Henderson County. Mary Towles Sasseen Wilson started the tradition with her school children in 1887 and it eventually obtained national observance. She was recognized by the Kentucky Legislature as the "originator of the idea." In 1914 Congress adopted the second Sunday of May as Mother's Day and deemed it a national holiday.

# Henry County
# New Castle

Henry County, the 31st county in order of formation, was established in 1799. It was taken entirely from Shelby County and its northern border is about 10 or 12 miles south of the Ohio River. It is bounded on the east by the Kentucky River. It has a land area of 289.32 square miles and an elevation ranging from 425 to 950 feet above sea level. It was named in honor of Patrick Henry, a patriot and orator whose most famous words were "Give me liberty or give me death." Henry was a member of the Continental Congress and opposed ratification of the U.S. Constitution without the Bill of Rights, which was later added.

The county seat is at New Castle, established in 1798. The origin of the name is unknown. In 1805 the New Castle post office was opened, perhaps under the name Henry Court House.

During the Civil War, cavalrymen under Henry County native Maj. George M. Jessee attacked provost marshal Robert Morris' home guard on September 21, 1862. The home guards surrendered several men, horses and arms. However, it was here on December 13, 1864 that Maj. Jessee and his Confederate forces were defeated after a skirmish with state troops led by Capt. J. H. Bridgewater. Gen. John Hunt Morgan and his raiders found shelter in the Old Pollard Inn on December 1, 1863 after escaping from an Ohio prison.

At one time Drennon Springs was one of the most popular watering places in Kentucky. American Indians discovered and used the springs for their medicinal properties. On July 26, 1773 Jacob Drennon and Matthew Bracken laid claim to the area. As governor of Virginia, Patrick Henry issued a patent to Gen. George Rogers Clark for 400 acres of land that included the springs on April 1, 1785. The Western Military Academy was located here in 1851.

Eminence College was originally chartered as a high school in 1856 and was given its name in 1861. It was one of Kentucky's first coeducational boarding schools. It had a commercial department and was a normal school for training teachers. The president of the college was Rev. W. S. Giltner, who also preached at the Eminence Christian Church. The college closed in 1895.

One of the most famous places in Henry County is Bethlehem. Here, thousands of Christmas cards are stamped with a scene of the wise men following the star. Church members use live animals as they present a living nativity scene of the first Christmas every year.

**Patrick Henry**

# Hickman County
# Clinton

Hickman County was formed in 1822 and was the 71st county formed in Kentucky. It is bounded on the west by the Mississippi River and was formed out of Chickasaw Territory. It has a land area of 244.44 square miles and an eleva-

Anchor and chain at Columbus, Belmont Park
Source: Kentucky Department of Libraries & Archives

tion ranging from 276 to 510 feet above sea level. Because the Mississippi River changed its course in the mid-1800s, the community of Wolf Island is now connected to Missouri. Hickman County is named for Capt. Paschal Hickman, who died in the War of 1812 following the Battle of the River Raisin in January 1813. Hickman was one of nine Kentucky officers who were killed in that war for whom Kentucky counties are named.

The seat of justice is at Clinton. The town was established in 1828 and replaced Columbus as the county seat in 1829. Clinton was incorporated in 1831—it is possible that it was named

for a Capt. Clinton but that fact is not known for certain. During the Civil War, Federal forces in the area were often harassed by enemy guerrillas who first raided Clinton on March 10, 1864. They took supplies and horses purchased for the Union troops.

It has been said that after the War of 1812 Columbus was considered for the site of the U.S. capital; however, there have been no records found to confirm this. Columbus is also known for being the first entire town in Kentucky to be relocated. In 1927 due to severe Mississippi River floods, Columbus was moved from the riverbanks to a bluff 200 feet above. The move was aided by the American Red Cross under the supervision of Marion Rust. While exploring the area for a new site, Rust found the remains of Confederate garrisons. He dreamed of having a Civil War memorial park and today that park is known as the Columbus-Belmont Battlefield State Park. The park is located on the Mississippi River and was the site of many battles fought during the Civil War.

Union and Confederate troops fought for control of the Mississippi River, leading to the Battle of Belmont on November 7, 1861. Another infamous event of the Civil War is known as the Gibraltar of the West. Under command of Gen. Leonidas Polk, Confederate troops fortified Iron Banks, a line of bluffs named by early French explorers. To block Union gunboats from moving southward, a huge chain was stretched across the Mississippi River and 140 cannons were set up along the riverbank. Union forces under Gen. Ulysses S. Grant overwhelmed Confederate troops at Belmont.

# Hopkins County
## Madisonville

In 1807 Hopkins county was established as the 49th county formed in Kentucky. It was named for Gen. Samuel Hopkins. Hopkins served with Gen. George Washington during the Revolutionary War; he came to Kentucky as a member of the Transylvania Company in 1797. He organized and was appointed to the first court in the original Henderson County. Hopkins County has a land area of 550.56 square feet and an elevation ranging from 345 to 729 feet above sea level.

land were given for the site by Daniel McGary and Solomon Silkwood, and named in honor and memory of Pres. James Madison. In 1809 the first post office was opened as Hopkins Court House.

During the Civil War, loyalty in Hopkins County was divided. The first shots of the war were fired at Burnt Mill Church in Webster County, which was originally part of Hopkins County. Like most other courthouses in Kentucky, Gen. Hyland B. Lyon burned the courthouse at Madisonville on December 17, 1864. Capt. L. D. Hockersmith, a member of Gen. John Hunt Morgan's cavalry, made his home in Hopkins County. He was captured and imprisoned at the Ohio State Prison by Federal troops during their raids through Ohio; however, he and five other officers escaped with Morgan through a tunnel they had shoveled. Confederate Gen. Nathan B. Forrest passed through Hopkins County with his cavalry on his way to Caseyville. On this foraging mission toward the Ohio River, Forrest and his troops found a large supply of hogs and took a few for themselves.

**Tobacco leaf**
*Photo: Sid Webb*

Coal mining is an important industry in the area. In 1869 the St. Bernard Coal Company opened the No. 11 Mine and by 1899 Hopkins County was producing over 1 million tons of coal per year, the first in Kentucky to do so.

The county seat is at Madisonville. It was founded in 1807 and incorporated in 1810. Forty acres of

World War II hero Navy Cmdr. D. W. "Mush" Morton grew up in Hopkins County. Morton was the commanding officer aboard the submarine Wahoo. This crew sank 31,890 tons of Japanese shipping in the Pacific. After leaving Pearl Harbor on September 9, 1943 Wahoo was lost through enemy action en route to the Sea of Japan. Morton was awarded four Navy Crosses and the Army Distinguished Service Cross.

Former Gov. Ruby Laffoon is also from Hopkins County. He was born in Madisonville on January 15, 1869 and was governor of Kentucky from 1931-1935. While in office he reorganized charitable and penal boards and recoded public education laws. Laffoon is credited for building more highways and bridges in Kentucky than in the previous 15 years.

# Jackson County
# McKee

The 105th county formed in Kentucky was Jackson County on April 25, 1858. It is situated on the headwaters of the Kentucky River and the Cumberland River. Most of the early settlers to the area were from the Carolinas and Virginias. The land is hilly and rolling and there are many small lime-

*Source: SouthEast Telephone*

stone caves in the northern part of the county. The early settlers used these caves to store food and other perishables. The settlers were also known for piping water from the limestone springs to their homes. Jackson County has a land area of 346.33 square miles and an elevation ranging from 650 to 1,633 feet above sea level. It was named in honor of Andrew Jackson, the seventh U.S. president. Jackson was the first president to be elected from west of the Appalachian Mountains.

The town of McKee is the county seat of Jackson County. It was founded in 1858 with the county. It was most likely named for Judge George R. McKee.

The McKee post office was also opened in 1858.

Past to present, Jackson County has traditionally been an agrarian community. The first settlers were hardy, resourceful people who did the best with available resources. They worked hard and cherished life through their faith and strength. The spirit of the early pioneers—their traditions and culture—still live in the hearts of present-day citizens. Many Jackson County residents are farmers, quilters, artists, doll makers, weavers, basket makers and potters.

The Daniel Boone National Forest covers over 56,000 acres of Jackson County and showcases much of the natural beauty of the area. Across the southwestern edge of the county is the Old Boone Trail, known by most Jackson County natives as the "Old State Road." It was the main county road from Big Hill to Maulden and was cut by oxen. It was often used to transport goods from Richmond and Lexington.

The Sheltowee Trace runs the entire length of the Jackson County along War Fork Creek. It was forged between the Shawnees of Ohio and the Cherokees of eastern Tennessee. The American Indians referred to it as Athiamiowee, which means "Path of the Armed Ones." Some of the first pioneers to travel this trail were Gabriel Arthur, Dr. Thomas Walker, Christopher Gist, Daniel Boone, and John Finley.

# Jefferson County
## Louisville

Jefferson—one of the original counties in the Kentucky territory of Virginia—is the most populous and most densely populated county in the state. The Virginia General Assembly formed Jefferson County out of Kentucky County, Virginia in 1780. The original 7,800 acres were bounded on the north by the Ohio River, east by the Kentucky River, and south and west by the Green River. Numerous Kentucky counties were formed from it and today Jefferson County has a land area of 385.09 square miles, and an elevation ranging from 383 to 902 feet above sea level. It was named for Thomas Jefferson, governor of Virginia and future president of the United States.

Louisville, founded by George Rogers Clark in 1778, was designated as the county seat in 1780. It is located at the Falls of the Ohio on the Ohio River. In 1779 the city was named in honor of King Louis XVI of France, who aided colonists during the Revolutionary War.

The 1,000-mile long and mile-wide Ohio River was considered impassable at only one point: the Falls of the Ohio at Louisville. The Falls of the Ohio was first officially recorded by a Colonial Government exploration in 1766, although it was known to American Indians and documented by French explorers. The opening of the Portland Canal made passage possible. The Lewis and Clark Expedition began at the Falls of the Ohio and moved westward.

During the Civil War, several skirmishes occurred in Jefferson County. Two in particular took place on September 27 and 30, 1862: Confederate forces had control of the state capitol and were threatening Louisville. Union forces drove Confederate troops back to Floyds Fork after the first clash. Three days later, Confederate troops were once again halted at the Union line. Both of these skirmishes were leading up to the infamous Battle of Perryville.

The Ohio River flood in January 1937 devastated Jefferson County. It covered three-fourths of Louisville and forced over 230,000 residents to evacuate. Ninety people died due to the record 57.15-feet Ohio River floodwaters.

**Watertower**
*Source: SouthEast Telephone*

Louisville is home to Churchill Downs where the Kentucky Derby is held—it is the most famous Thoroughbred horse race in the world. Also in Louisville is the Belle of Louisville, the oldest Mississippi-style sternwheel steamboat in America and still in operation today; the Louisville Slugger Museum & Factory, producer of baseball bats since the 1880s; Old Louisville, an elegant neighborhood lined with hundreds of Queen Anne, Colonial and Gothic Revival mansions; Actors Theatre; and the Muhammad Ali Center, a museum and monument to a Louisville favorite son.

In 2000 voters approved a merged city-county government to be known as Louisville/Jefferson County Metro Government, (Louisville Metro for short), effective in 2003.

# Jessamine County
# Nicholasville

Jessamine, the only one of the Kentucky's 120 counties with a feminine name, is located near the center of the state. This county was named by state legislator Col. John Price for the jessamine (jasmine) flower, grown widely in the area along the region's spring-fed creek that flows into the Kentucky River. Popular legend that the county was named for the daughter of a Scottish surveyor, Jessamine Douglas, is without foundation.

Jessamine County was formed from a part of Fayette County in 1798—a banner year for the creation of counties—becoming the 36th county in the state. It has a land area of 173.13 square miles and is one of the smallest in Kentucky having only 110,080 acres. The

**Bridge on Glass Mill Rd.**
*Source: Sid Webb*

elevation ranges from 497 to 1,072 feet above sea level. It is bounded on the east, south, and southwest by the Kentucky River. Although it became a county in 1798 it had no post office until 1806 and no railroad until 1857.

Nicholasville is the county seat of Jessamine County and was named for George Nicholas. Nicholas was one of the authors of Kentucky's first constitution and the first attorney general in Kentucky.

Levi Todd established the first and only fort in Jessamine County near Keene in 1779, one year before Lexington was built. At this time hostile American Indians, provided arms by the English, terrified settlers around this part of the state. It was for the personal safety of those at the fort that Todd felt compelled to abandon

the fort and seek protection from other forts around the Lexington area.

The first pioneer to enter the region was John Finley, a woodsman and hunter from North Carolina. Other hunters, with land grants issued by the British king for service in the French and Indian War, soon followed. On Finley's second trip, Daniel Boone accompanied him.

During the Civil War, Maj. Gen. William Nelson established the first Union recruiting center south of the Ohio River. It was originally located in Garrard County and called Camp Dick Robinson in honor of Capt. Dick Robinson, an uncompromising Union supporter. The camp was moved to the Jessamine side of the Kentucky River for better protection against invading Confederate troops. It was renamed Camp Nelson in honor of its creator. Nelson was killed in a dispute with fellow Union officer Jefferson Columbus Davis at the Galt House in Louisville on September 29, 1862. Camp Nelson was occupied until the end of the war and is now a U.S. military cemetery.

# Johnson County
# Paintsville

Johnson County was formed from parts of Lawrence, Floyd and Morgan counties in 1842 and named in honor of Col. Richard M. Johnson. The county is situated on the waters of the Sandy River. The surface is hilly, interspersed with fertile valleys with soil based upon sandstone. Elevation in the county ranges from 550 to 1,508 feet above sea level with a land area of 261.54 square miles.

Col. Richard M. Johnson, for whom the county was named, was a native of Kentucky. Johnson became a nationwide hero in 1813 because of the certainty that he personally killed the Indian Chief Tecumseh at the Battle of the Thames. Johnson was elected to the U.S. senate in 1819 and was vice president under Van Buren in 1837.

Dr. Thomas Walker camped at present site of Paintsville in 1750 on his expedition into the Kentucky wilderness. He discovered French cabins at the mouth of Paint Creek and named the river Louisa, honoring the daughter of King George II and sister of Duke of Cumberland. Over time, the name Louisa evolved to Levisa. The settlement, first known as Paint Lick Station, is the second oldest settlement in eastern Kentucky.

The abduction and captivity of young pioneer, Jenny Wiley, is now re-enacted at the outdoor amphitheater at Jenny Wiley State Resort Park. Young Jenny escaped after a year in captivity and followed a "dream" to safety here.

The Big Sandy River opened to steamboat traffic in 1837 beginning an era of economic, social and cultural contact with the rest of the nation. Manufactured goods could be delivered while fur hides and timber were sent downriver. Not even the arrival of the railroad a half-century later had as much impact on Johnson County as did the steamboats.

During the Civil War the fiscal court officially took a neutral stand. Neutrality, however, did not keep war from the county. The major skirmish took place between Col. James A. Garfield and Confederate Gen. Humphrey Marshall on Hager Hill. On a mission to dislodge Confederate forces from the area, Col. Garfield's troops reached Paintsville on Jan. 6, 1862. Gen. Marshall abandoned Hager Hill, and moving to Middle Creek he was overtaken on Jan. 10 by a large Union force, and retreated to Virginia.

The vision of John C. C. Mayo and the coal industry altered John-

**Stafford House Country Cottage**
*Source: Tour Southern & Eastern Kentucky*

son County's isolation—by 1880 Johnson County still had no paved roads, no banks, no railroad, no telephones, and no electricity. Between 1890 and 1910 Mayo's activity in buying, leasing and selling coal ushered in an era of economic progress.

Carl D. Perkins Rehabilitation Center provides comprehensive vocational rehabilitation services that enable Kentuckians with disabilities to achieve suitable employment and independence. In 1980, the U.S. Army Corps of Engineers dammed the juncture of Little Paint Creek and Open Fork creating Paintsville Lake, which covers more than 11,000 acres.

# Kenton County
## Covington &
## Independence

Kenton County, the 19th county in the order of formation, was formed in 1840 by a division of Campbell County. It was named in honor of the celebrated pioneer of the west, Gen. Simon Kenton. The Ohio River, Licking River and Dry Creek establish natural borders for the county's western edge. The elevation in the county ranges from 455 to 960 feet above sea level with a land area of 161.97 square miles.

Kenton County has two county seats, Covington and Independence, with courthouse centers in both cities. Most county business transpires at Covington.

The city of Covington, the largest city in Northern Kentucky, is situated on the Ohio River, across the river from Cincinnati, Ohio. It is immediately below the mouth of the Licking River. The city stands on historic ground known to French explorers 100 years before Christopher Gist decided to tie up his canoe at the confluence of the Ohio and Licking rivers in 1751. Many noted pioneers followed Gist, and finally the first permanent settlement was made in 1793. Covington was formed in 1815 and named for Gen. Leonard Wales Covington, a celebrated officer of the War of 1812.

Independence was formed in 1840 when Kenton County was established. It is widely believed it was so named to celebrate independence from Campbell County.

Ft. Mitchell, built in 1861, provided a major anchor in a line of seven forts defending Cincinnati from Confederate attack—at that time Cincinnati was the sixth largest city in the nation. These forts ran along hills around Covington, a radius of about 10 miles. The Confederate threat never materialized although Confederates reached the outskirts of Covington in 1862, only to be forced back by Union forces.

Half-a-dozen bridges now span the river, but the most notable is the Roebling bridge. The first bridge to span the Ohio River between Covington and Cincinnati, it was designed by John Roebling and opened in 1867. A prototype of Brooklyn Bridge, it was the longest suspension bridge in the world at the time.

Latonia Race Track (1883-1939) was known as one of world's foremost race tracks. After amassing substantial debts in the 1930s, Latonia Race Track closed after its last race on July 29, 1939. St. Mary's Catholic Cathedral on Madison Ave. was partly patterned after the Cathedral of Notre Dame; it opened in 1900. Devou Park covers 550 acres overlooking Covington, the river and the Cincinnati skyline. It contains a Civil War earthworks and the Behringer-Crawford Museum. The boyhood home of Dan Carter Beard, founder of the boy scouts of America, is on East Third in Covington. As a boy he drew inspiration from legends of Kentucky pioneers. Robert L. Surtees (1906-1985) made his home in Covington. Among his film credits are "Ben-Hur," "Oklahoma," "Doctor Dolittle," "The Graduate," and "The Sting."

**Main Strasse Village
in Covington**

*Source: SouthEast Telephone*

# Knott County
# Hindman

Knott County, created in 1884, was the 118th county in order of formation. It was formed from parts of Perry, Letcher, Floyd and Breathitt counties. The elevation in the county ranges from 675 to 2,360 feet above sea level with a land area of 352.19 square miles. Knott is the only Kentucky county that does not have a river within its boundaries or bordering it.

The county was named for J. Proctor Knott, Kentucky's governor at that time. Gov. Knott, famous as a humorous and satirical orator, served in the U.S. Congress for six terms. He served as the first law dean at Centre College (1891-1901).

Hindman, the county seat, was named for Lt. Gov. James Hindman. It is over 1,000 feet above sea level, but lies in a narrow valley at the forks of Troublesome Creek. A post office opened on the site in 1874 as McPherson.

The dramatic story of mountain schools is repeated in history of three such schools in Knott County, dedicated to the education of mountain children. Hindman Settlement School was founded in 1902 as the first rural social settlement school in Kentucky. The school played a vital role in preserving and promoting the literary and cultural heritage of southeastern Kentucky and Central Appalachia.

Pippa Passes is located in the eastern section of the county—its name reflected the literary tastes of its founder, a Boston teacher and her New England friends. Alice Lloyd founded her school as Caney Creek Community Center in 1917. It became Caney Junior College, and after Lloyd's death in 1962, the school was renamed Alice Lloyd College, honoring the founder who dedicated her life to the education of mountain youth.

Carr Creek Center, nine miles south of Hindman, was organized in 1920 by two other northerners, Olive V. Marsh and Ruth E. Watson, from Mass. Aided by the Daughters of the American Revolution, they carved this center of learning out of a wooded hillside overlooking rustic Carr Creek.

Knott County is the home of folk music scholar, Dr. Josiah H. Combs (1886-1960). He distinguished himself as an educator and collector of American folk music. Dr. Combs began his study of folklore at Hindman Settlement School and was one of two students in the first graduating class (1904). Dr. Combs received a Ph.D. degree from the Sorbonne in Paris in 1925. Hindman was the birthplace of Carl D. Perkins, Kentucky's beloved congressman from 1949 to 1984

**Kentucky Appalachian Artisan Center**
*Source: Tour Southern & Eastern Kentucky*

# Knox County
# Barbourville

Knox County was formed in 1800 and was the 41st county formed in Kentucky. It lies on both sides of the Cumberland River and has generally hilly and mountainous land. It has an elevation ranging from 890 to 2,322 feet above sea level and a land area of 387.66 square miles. Knox County was named in honor of Maj. Gen. Henry Knox, U.S. Secretary of War from 1785-1796. Knox joined the Continental Army in 1775 and was in command of artillery. He fought in several battles during the Revolutionary War including the Battles of Bunker Hill, Brandywine, and York-

Dr. Thomas Walker cabin
near Barbourville
Photo: Sid Webb

town. Fort Knox in Hardin County, home of the U.S. Army Armor Center and the Army Recruiting Command, is named in his honor.

The county seat is at Barbourville and was also established in 1800. James Barbour donated the land for the town. The Barbourville post office opened in 1804. Barbourville is located on the banks of the Cumberland River and is bordered by Richland Creek. Early travelers referred to it as "the town on the big bend of the Cumberland River." A floodwall was built after many years of disastrous floods to protect the town; the surrounding hills provide shelter from most severe storms. The nickname "Home of Governors" was given to Barbourville for the many people hailing from Knox County who have served as commanders in chief for Kentucky and several other states. James D. Black and Flem D. Sampson served as Kentucky governors.

Kentucky's first armed skirmish of the Civil War was fought in Barbourville on September 19, 1861. Both the Confederate and the Union troops suffered losses. Both forces occupied Barbourville at different points in the war. It was a temporary headquarters for Confederate Gen. Kirby Smith in 1862. Union Gen. U. S. Grant used the town when he was scouting the Wilderness Road for use as an invasion route in 1864.

In 1750 Dr. Thomas Walker built the first cabin in the Kentucky area, about six miles southeast of present-day Barbourville. Walker built this house as a requirement by the state of Virginia for staking claim to the territory. Walker wrote a description of the state in his journal and it is argued that this first documentation of Kentucky was in Knox County.

Knox County is home to Union College, which was incorporated in October 1879. The first degrees earned here were on June 9, 1893.

# LaRue County
## Hodgenville

Established on March 1, 1843, LaRue County was the 98th county established in order of formation. LaRue County was likely named in honor of John LaRue, who came to Kentucky in 1784 from the Shenandoah Valley of Virginia and settled in present day LaRue County. John's wife, Mary LaRue, was a mid-wife. She assisted Nancy Hanks Lincoln at the birth of her son, Abraham.

LaRue County is bounded to the north by the Rolling Fork of the Salt River and to the northwest by Middle Creek. Nolin River, its north and south forks and Otter Creek, provide additional water resources to the county. It has an elevation ranging from 421 to 1,080 feet above sea level and a land area of 263.20 square miles.

The county seat is at Hodgenville and is located on the site of Robert Hodgen's gristmill on the Nolin River. Hodgen's mill was built in 1789 near Phillips Fort, which was built in 1781 in what as then Hardin County. In 1818 Hodgenville was established and became the county seat in 1843 when LaRue County was established. The first post office opened in 1826 as Hodgensville but was renamed Hodgenville in 1904.

Confederate troops under command of Gen. Braxton Bragg swept through the area in September 1862 with a plan to capture Gen. Joseph Wheeler's Union forces. Hodgenville is the site of Camp Wickliffe (named in honor of Gov. Charles A. Wickliffe), chosen by Gen. William Nelson for its proximity to the supply depot at New Haven. On February 21, 1865 guerrillas burned the courthouse at Hodgenville; fortunately, all county records were saved. The courthouse had been used as barracks for Union soldiers.

The first settlement in LaRue County was Phillips Fort. Located on the North Fork of the Nolin River, the fortification was built in 1780 by Philip Phillips,

a surveyor from Pennsylvania. Phillips Fort was a place of refuge from hostile American Indians, but it was abandoned around 1786 when settlers felt safe to branch out to build homes.

**Pres. Abraham Lincoln & Son**
*Source: May 6, 1865 Edition of Harper's Weekly*

Pres. Abraham Lincoln was born on Feb. 12, 1809 near Hodgenville and began his formal education in a log cabin near Knob Creek. Lincoln and his sister Sarah attended ABC schools together and were taught by Zachariah Riney and Caleb Hazel. The Lincoln family lived on the old Cumberland Road; they left Kentucky for Indiana in 1816. The birthplace of Abraham Lincoln is a National Historic Site—a 15-member commission has been appointed to commemorate the 200th birthday of Abraham Lincoln in 2009, in order to emphasize the contribution of his thoughts and ideals to America and the world.

# Laurel County
# London

Laurel County, the 80th county formed in Kentucky, was established on December 1, 1825 with its first government taking office early in 1826. It was named for the abundant and beautiful growth of laurel bushes along its creeks and rivers. While exploring for the Loyal Land Company of England, Dr. Thomas Walker named the streams after different members of his party in 1750. Laurel County has a land area of 435.67 square miles and an elevation ranging from 723 to 1,760 feet above sea level.

The county seat is at London, which began as a settlement on the Wilderness Road north of Cumberland Gap. It was formed in 1826 and named for the great city of London, England. In 1831 the first post office was opened. John Jackson and his son Jarvis donated 25 acres of land for the settlement and were both active in the local government.

Thousands from all over Kentucky enjoy the Chicken Festival
*Source: Kentucky Department of Tourism*

They helped set up the government and build the courthouse and jail. When it came time to name the town the Pitman family, of Scottish decent, proposed Edinburgh while the Freeman family, of Irish decent, suggested Dublin. The Jacksons, who were of English decent, won the debate with the name London.

The Civil War Battle of London took place on August 17, 1862. Led by Col. J. S. Scott 500 Confederate cavalry attacked 200 Union troops under command of Col. L. C. Houk. The Union lost 13 men, 17 were wounded and 111 were captured. The Confederacy lost two men and four were wounded. Col. Houk was forced back to Gen. George W. Morgan's main Union force at the

Cumberland Gap. Being cut off from supplies, Morgan's forces retreated to Ohio 30 days later. Laurel County was also the location of Camp Wildcat, a crucial fortified position for each army. The Union forces wanted to prevent Confederate attack in Kentucky and the Confederate forces wanted to prevent Union advance into Tennes-

see. On October 21, 1861 Gen.Felix K. Zollicoffer led 7,500 Confederates in an attack on the camp of 5,000 of Gen. Albin Schoepf's Union soldiers. The Union advantage in the Rockcastle Hills stopped Confederate troops and forced them to retreat back to Tennessee.

In 1775 the Boone Trace was a well-known packhorse trail blazed by Daniel Boone and his company while en route to Boonesborough from Cumberland Gap. It was a single path road for horses and was the sole transportation route from the south for 20 years. It was used until 1796 when the Wilderness Road was built. A principle highway for 80 years, the Wilderness Road was maintained as a turnpike "toll road."

# Lawrence County
# Louisa

Lawrence County was formed in 1821, and named in honor of Capt. James Lawrence who was mortally wounded in a battle between the Chesapeake and the Shannon on June 1, 1813, off the coast of Boston. His famous last words aboard the Chesapeake were, "Don't give up the ship." Lawrence County is situated on the waters of the Big Sandy River and is abundant with coal and iron ore. The surface is hilly and broken but with fertile soil, particularly along the whole valley of the Big Sandy. Lawrence County has a land area of 418.78 square miles and an elevation ranging from 515 to 1,320 feet above sea level.

The county seat is at Louisa, which is located at the convergence of the Tug and Levisa forks of the Big Sandy River. In 1789 a settlement at The Point was attempted. West of The Point a settlement called Balclutha existed for a short while. The settlement that eventually became Louisa began about 1815. Louisa was named for the Levisa Fork of the Big Sandy River—so named by Dr. Thomas Walker in honor of the wife of the Duke of Cumberland, Louisa.

During the Civil War, in December 1861, Louisa was occupied due to river traffic by Union forces under Gen. James A. Garfield, who later became the 20th U.S. president. Confederate forces made several attempts to capture the city on March 12 and 25-26, 1863. Southern partisans raided the area on November 5, 1864. Many stores were looted; two steamers and several houses were burned. Nearby Fort Bishop was built during the Civil War by Union forces to protect against Confederate raids. It was named for Capt. William Bishop of the 100th Ohio Infantry who was killed in action in May of 1864.

The first giant cooling tower in the Western Hemisphere was completed in 1962 in Lawrence County. When it was built it had the largest capacity of any single tower in the world with the ability to cool 120,000 gallons of water per minute for steam condensing.

**Lawrence County Courthouse, 1942**
*Photo: George Goodman, Kentucky Virtual Library*

Lawrence County is one of seven counties featured on the Country Music Highway—created to honor the extraordinary number of musicians who were born along a seven-county stretch in scenic Eastern Kentucky. Lawrence County native Ricky Skaggs, and his band, Kentucky Thunder, are seven-time International Bluegrass Music Association award winners. Lawrence County is also home of singer and songwriter, Larry Cordle. Most widely known as a writer, Larry Cordle has had songs recorded by Ricky Skaggs, Garth Brooks, Alison Krauss, Alan Jackson, George Strait, and many others.

# Lee County
## Beattyville

Lee County was formed in 1870 and was Kentucky's 115th county in order of formation. Lee County was named for the infamous Gen. Robert E. Lee. A graduate of West Point, Lee declined command in the Union army and resigned his commission in 1861. Later that year he was named military

**Gen. Robert E. Lee**

adviser to Confederate Pres. Jefferson Davis. Lee was the highest-ranking officer in the Confederacy and it is said, "...he was fearless among men. As a soldier, he had no superior and few equal." Lee went on to become the president of Washington College, which is known today as Washington and Lee University.

Lee County has an elevation ranging from 610 to 1,367 feet above sea level and a land area of 209.86 square miles. The face of the county is generally hilly and mountainous.

The county seat is at Beattyville—it is located on the forks of the Kentucky River. It was originally known as Taylors Landing but was renamed Beatty in honor of Samuel Beatty, an early settler and landowner, in 1850. It was incorporated as Beattyville in 1872.

The original county seat was at Proctor, across the river from Beattyville. It was named in honor of the Rev. Joseph Proctor and was the county seat from the time of its formation in 1870 until 1872 when it was moved to Beattyville.

Lee County is located on both sides of the Kentucky River, which forms there. It is also watered by the North, South and Middle forks of the Kentucky—the three unite to form the Kentucky River, which flows 255 miles to the Ohio River. The Kentucky River was an important element in commerce for Lee County steamboats. River traffic increased as locks and dams were built. Coal and timber were key exports.

During the Civil War from June 18 to September 17, 1862, about 9,000 of Gen. George W. Morgan's Union troops occupied the Cumberland Gap. They were completely cut off from supplies and were forced to begin a 200-mile retreat. They passed through Lee County in search of supplies. Unfortunately for the Union troops, Confederate forces had burned the flour mill the night before. However, the long trek from the Cumberland Gap to Greenup on the Ohio River was made in only 16 days, despite much harassment from Confederate Gen. John H. Morgan's Raiders.

# Leslie County
## Hyden

Leslie County was created in 1878 and was the 117th county formed in Kentucky. The surface of the county is rather rugged and mountainous. Located in the largest coal producing area in Kentucky, coal is an abundant resource. Elk were restored to Eastern Kentucky in 1998 and have since flourished in the environment—becoming the largest herd east of the Mississippi River. With a land area of 404.03 square miles it is watered by the Middle Fork of the Kentucky River and has an elevation ranging from 757 to 2,600 feet above sea level.

Leslie County was named in honor of Gov. Preston H. Leslie. Leslie was governor of Kentucky from 1871 until 1875. Ten years later Leslie became the governor of Montana Territory, and was appointed him U.S. District Attorney by Pres. Cleveland. Leslie died in 1907 and is buried in Montana.

The county seat is at Hyden, which was founded in 1878. It was named for state Sen. John Hyden. Hyden is located on the Middle Fork of the Kentucky River at the mouth of Rockhouse Creek. In 1879 the Hyden post office was opened.

Wendover is located about two miles south of Hyden in the central part of Leslie County. Mary Breckinridge founded the town in 1925 as her home and the headquarters for the Frontier Nursing Service. Midwives from England were sent to help bring medical service to the "remote hollows and hills of Clay, Leslie, and Perry counties." This service helped save the lives of hundreds of mothers and children. A 28-bed hospital was opened in Hyden in 1928. In 1939 the Frontier Graduate School of Midwifery was founded and is only one of three such schools in the U.S. This is the oldest and largest of the three schools. Nurse-midwives at the schools nurse the sick, attend births and teach the importance of sanitation, health and hygiene. Their techniques have been taught in South America, the Middle East and Southeast Asia.

The only Kentuckian to receive the Congressional Medal of Honor in World War I was Sgt. Willie Sandlin of Leslie County. Sandlin enlisted in the military in 1917 and served as a sergeant in the 132nd Infantry, 33rd Division. Sandlin was awarded the medal for his extraordinary bravery and his responsibility in putting three machine gun nests out of action at Bois de Forges, France, on September 27, 1918. After the war Sandlin returned to Leslie County, where he resided until his death on May 29, 1949.

**Fall day on Coon Creek**
*Source: SouthEast Telephone*
*Rick Pennington*

# Letcher County
## Whitesburg

Letcher County was created in 1842 and was the 95th county formed in Kentucky. It is located in the far southeastern portion of Kentucky on the Virginia border. The surface is rather rugged and mountainous and only Harlan County has a higher elevation. The elevation in Letcher County ranges from 940 to 3,720 feet above sea level and the land area is 339.04 square miles. The well-known Pine Mountain runs along the county line. Settlement in the area began around 1795. Also located in Letcher County is The Lilley Cornett Woods, one of the largest tracts of protected old-growth forest in Kentucky. The county was named for Gov. Robert P. Letcher, who served Kentucky from 1840 until 1844. Letcher was an officer in the War of 1812 and a presidential elector in 1836. He proclaimed the first Thanksgiving during his term as governor.

The county seat is at Whitesburg and it was named for Daugherty White, a legislator from Clay County. Stephen Hiram Hogg donated the land for the site. Whitesburg is located on the North Fork of the Kentucky River. It was founded with the county in 1842. The post office was opened as Whitesburgh Court House in 1843.

Many of the early settlers were deeply religious. After beholding the beauty and fertility of a Letcher County valley they decided to name the area Kingdom Come, words from "The Lord's Prayer." This was the setting for the novels written by John Fox, Jr. in the early 20th century, "The Little Shepherd of Kingdom Come" and "The Trail of the Lone-some Pine." Fox was born in December 1862 to a prominent family in Bourbon County. Kingdom Come State Park is found on the southwest border with Harlan County.

**Lilley Cornett Woods**
*Source: Tour Southern & Eastern Kentucky*

Two noted war heroes hail from Letcher County. Lt. Darwin K. Kyle of the U.S. Army was awarded a Congressional Medal of Honor for his service in the Korean War. Amid intensive fighting, Kyle rallied his men to renew attacks on the enemy. He died in the war on February 16, 1951. Francis Gary Powers was a part of the "U-2 Incident." Directed by the CIA, Powers and others flew U-2s over Russia and photographed missile, industrial, and nuclear test sites. His plane was disabled 1,300 miles over Russian on May 1, 1960. Powers parachuted to safety but was taken prisoner. He responded that his compass had malfunctioned; however, film was found among the plane wreckage. The Russians tried him for espionage and sentenced him to ten years imprisonment. In 1962 he was released in exchange for a Soviet spy. Powers was highly decorated by the CIA before dying in a civilian helicopter accident.

# Lewis County
# Vanceburg

Lewis County was organized on April 27, 1807 and was the 48th county formed in Kentucky. It is bounded to the north by the Ohio River and the surface of the county is generally hilly. Lewis County has a land area of 484.49 square miles and an elevation ranging from 485 to 1,400 feet above sea level. Lewis County was named in honor of Meriwether Lewis of the Lewis and Clark expedition. Lewis and William Clark began their exploration voyage to the Rocky Mountains in 1803 from Louisville. After the three-year journey Lewis returned and was appointed governor of the territory of Louisiana in 1806. Lewis died in 1809 at the age of 36; a great deal of uncertainty surrounded his death with questions of foul play or suicide.

The county seat is at Vanceburg, which is located on the banks of the Ohio River. Unlike many seats of justice, Vanceburg has not always held the position. Poplar Flat was the first county seat, followed by Clarksburg in 1809, and finally Vanceburg in 1864. Founded in 1797 Vanceburg was named for one of the original founders, Joseph Vance. The rush of settlers to the area led the small town to become an incorporated city. The Vanceburg post office was opened in 1815. Vanceburg was an important port and was less susceptible to floods due to it high location above the river.

**Meriwether Lewis**

The town is occasionally referred to as Alum City because of the nearby deposits of alum.

Cabin Creek was an early point of entry into Kentucky for explorers and pioneers. American Indians forded across the Ohio River and war roads led from its mouth to the Upper Blue Licks. They were marked with drawings of animals and the sun and moon. A 114-foot covered bridge spans across Cabin Creek.

From 1845 to 1860 one of the most popular health resorts along the Ohio River was at Esculapia Springs. The resort was easily accessible by boat and many out-of-state guests frequented the area. The mineral water from the spring was used for medicinal purposes. The resort was destroyed by fire in 1860 and business declined thereafter.

John Vance, Moses Baird and John Heath dug the first salt wells in 1794 in Salt Lick Creek. They were about 300-feet deep and supplied the surrounding regions with salt. For a time the salt licks were the most celebrated objects in the county.

The only Union memorial south of the Mason-Dixon line was erected by public subscription in Lewis County. The memorial was dedicated in 1884 to the county's 107 Union soldiers who lost their lives during the Civil War.

# Lincoln County
# Stanford

Lincoln County was established in 1780 and was one of the three original counties formed from Kentucky County, Virginia. It was named in honor of Gen. Benjamin Lincoln, a Revolutionary War officer and leader of the forces at Shays' Rebellion. Lincoln County played a key role in the naming of Kentucky's statehood. All constitutional conventions were held in Danville in then-Lincoln County, which is also where the Constitution of Kentucky was framed. Lincoln County has an elevation ranging from 760 to 1,440 feet above sea level and a land area of 336.26 square miles.

Lincoln County Courthouse
Photo: Sid Webb

The county seat is at Stanford, which was settled in 1775 by Benjamin Logan. It was originally known as Logan's Fort or St. Asaph (a name Logan gave). It is the second oldest permanent settlement with courthouse records dating back to 1781, the oldest records in the state. It is possible that the name Stanford was derived from Standing Fort, a name that may have been used for the station. It could also have been named for Stamford, England. The county seat was moved from Fort Harrod (now Harrodsburg) to Stanford in 1787 and the Stanford post office was opened in 1798.

During the Civil War Confederate Gen. J. H. Morgan's Raiders made their camp in Lincoln County after burning the Dix River Bridge near here on their return from Cynthiana. They also burned 120 Union wagons in the area and at Somerset. After the Battle of Perryville on October 8, 1862 Morgan's Raiders retreated to Tennessee through Lincoln County.

In 1827 the Crab Orchard Springs was a fashionable, renowned spa. Between 400-500 guests would visit the spa during the tourist season. This popular watering place was famed for its excellent mineral springs that were used for medical remedies, which were produced by evaporation of salts. Lack of patrons forced the resort to close in 1930.

Two notable military heroes hail from Lincoln County. Navy Lt. Caswell Saufley's flights were the first official U.S. demonstrations using airplanes for scouting purposes. Saufley Field near Pensacola, Fl. is named for him and for his innovations in aviation. PFC William B. Baugh of the U.S. Marine Corps was a member of an Anti-Tank Assault Squad when a hostile grenade landed in his truck on November 29, 1950. After shouting a warning to the soldiers in the truck, he put himself in harm's way to protect others from injury or death and suffered mortal injuries. Baugh was posthumously awarded the Congressional Medal of Honor for his service and bravery.

# Livingston County
## Smithland

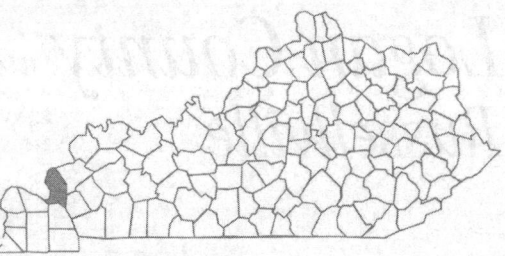

Livingston County was created in 1799 and was the 29th county formed in Kentucky. It was named for Robert R. Livingston, a distinguished statesman and a member of the committee to draft the Declaration of Independence. Livingston administered Pres. George Washington his oath into office as president of the new nation and was a partner in conducting the treaty for the cession of Louisiana to the U.S. Livingston County remains well watered by several rivers—it is bounded to the north by the Ohio River, to the south by the Tennessee River, and partially to the east by the Cumberland River. The elevation in the county ranges from 302 to 754 feet above sea level and the land area is 316.08 square miles.

The first county seat was at Eddyville, followed by Centerville and then Salem in 1809. It remained in Salem until 1842 when it was moved to its final place in Smithland. Smithland is located on the Ohio River at the mouth of the Cumberland River. It was incorporated in 1805 and the Smithland post office was opened in 1802. It was named to honor James Smith, an early explorer to the area.

Livingston County had an active role in the Civil War. In September 1861 Union forces occupied Smithland, a strategic town. The land at the confluence of the Ohio and Cumberland Rivers was a rendezvous point for troops in support of Gen. Grant's campaign against Fort Donelson. Two forts were built on the hills south of there and were used to command the two rivers. Throughout the war, Smithland was continuously used as a Union supply base. In Salem, Union troops under Capt. Hugh M. Hiett drove off a force of 300 Confederate soldiers under Maj. John T. Chenoweth. The skirmish took place on August 8, 1864 and lasted six hours.

The younger sister of Pres. Thomas Jefferson

**Kentucky Lake dam**
*Source: U.S. Army Corps of Engineers*

lies at rest in Livingston County. Lucy Jefferson Lewis was the wife of Dr. Charles L. Lewis, brother to explorer Meriwether Lewis. Dr. and Mrs. Lewis moved from Virginia to Kentucky in 1808 with their six children.

The tragic "Trail of Tears" journey in which the Cherokee Indians were forced to leave their homes in the Smoky Mountains and relocate to Oklahoma territory took place during the winter of 1838-1839. Mantle Rock in Livingston County was used as a shelter from the weather since there was no ferry traffic on the icy Ohio River. Many died under the 40-foot sandstone arch and were left behind while the others continued on the long enforced trek across the land.

# Logan County
## Russellville

Logan County was created in 1792 and was the 13th county formed in Kentucky. It was named in honor of Gen. Benjamin Logan, a pioneer who called the Danville Assembly in 1784, which ultimately led to Kentucky's independence from Virginia. Logan County was organized immediately after Kentucky's admission to the Union. It is bounded to the south by the Tennessee border and is watered by the Red, Cumberland, Muddy and Green rivers. It has a land area of 555.68 square miles and an elevation ranging from 395 to 868 feet above sea level.

**Centre family dwelling, Shaker Village and Museum at South Union**
*Source: Kentucky Department of Tourism*

The county seat is at Russellville and was possibly established in 1790 by William Cook. It was originally known as Cook's Station and Logan Court House. In 1798 it was renamed Russellville for Gen. William Russell, a prominent landowner. The Russellville post office was opened for use in 1801.

During the Civil War Confederate delegates from 64 counties in Kentucky met in Russellville for a Confederate State Convention. The result was their succession from the Union on November 20, 1861. On December 10, 1861 Kentucky was the 13th state admitted to the Confederate States of America.

Four of Kentucky's governors hail from Logan County. John Breathitt (1832-34), James T. Morehead (1834-36), John J. Crittenden (1848-50) and Charles S. Morehead (1855-59) all went on to lead as governors of Kentucky. Three other natives were governors in other states: Richard Call in Florida, Ninian Edwards in Illinois and Fletcher Stockdale in Texas.

Many other notable people claimed Logan County as their home. The first American to raise the flag on foreign soil was Lt. Presley N. O'Bannon of the U.S. Marine Corps. On April 17, 1805, O'Bannon led an attack on Barbary Coast pirates who were holding 180 American seamen for ransom. After resigning from the Marine Corps, O'Bannon moved to Logan County in 1807; he served in the Kentucky state legislature and state senate. Three Navy ships have been named USS O'Bannon in his honor.

Logan County native Col. James Bowie was a Texas Ranger and co-commander at the Alamo. Along with 187 other soldiers he chose to give his life rather than surrender. Three other Logan County natives were by his side: P. J. Bailey, D. W. Cloud and W. Fountleroy. The infamous battle cry, "Remember the Alamo" was a sign of Texas victory and freedom from Mexico in 1836. Bowie designed the Bowie Knife, a preferred weapon in frontier days. The notorious Jesse James gang made an appearance in Logan County on March 20, 1868, when the gang staged a holdup at the Southern Bank of Kentucky. Bank president N. Long was shot and wounded during the robbery. James and his gang escaped with over $9,000.

# Lyon County
## Eddyville

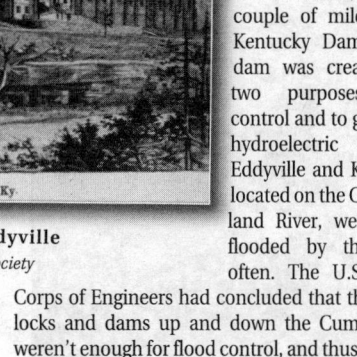

Lyon County was the 102nd county in order of formation in Kentucky, and was formed from the southwestern half of Caldwell County in 1854. The county was named in honor of Chittenden Lyon, who came to the area with his father Matthew Lyon in 1801. As a leader in Thomas Jefferson's Republican Party, Matthew Lyon was jailed and fined under the infamous Sedition Law for his criticism

**Branch Penitentiary, Eddyville**
*Source: Kentucky Historical Society*

of Pres. John Adams. When the election of 1800 was sent to the U.S. House of Representatives, Lyon cast the deciding vote for Jefferson from his jail cell.

Eddyville is the county seat of Lyon County. Matthew Lyon chose the site for his home, Eddyville, after visiting with his friend, Andrew Jackson, who recommended the area. In the spring of 1801 he sailed down the Ohio River and up the Cumberland to Caldwell County and founded Eddyville. First settled around 1798 and named for the eddies in the nearby Cumberland River, it first became the seat of justice of Livingston county in 1799, then the county seat of Caldwell county in 1809, and finally the seat of Lyon county when it was formed in 1854.

In 1811-12 Matthew Lyon built the hulls of several war vessels for the U.S. Government, which helped to build the iron and ship building industries in Eddyville. The goods could be floated down the Cumberland from Eddyville and eventually to the ocean.

Kentucky Dam was constructed on the Tennessee River by the Tennessee Valley Authority during the early 1940s. The resulting Kentucky Lake and later, Lake Barkley, has had a tremendous effect on development in Lyon County.

Barkley Dam was created on the Cumberland River, only a couple of miles from Kentucky Dam. The dam was created for two purposes—flood control and to generate hydroelectric power. Eddyville and Kuttawa, located on the Cumberland River, were both flooded by the river often. The U.S. Army Corps of Engineers had concluded that the small locks and dams up and down the Cumberland weren't enough for flood control, and thus, started buying property below the 378-foot sea level for the building of Barkley Dam and to create Lake Barkley. The decision would require the relocation of approximately 3,500 people and the towns of Eddyville and Kuttawa. Eddyville was moved 5-1/2 miles from its original site and Kuttawa was moved approximately one mile. Construction of Barkley Dam began in 1959. At 134 miles long with 1,004 miles of shoreline, Lake Barkley was fully impounded in 1966. Old foundations, sidewalks and streets of old Eddyville can be seen during Barkley's winter pool (when the lake is five feet lower).

# Madison County
# Richmond

Formed in 1785, Madison County was just the seventh in order of formation, and was originally a county of Virginia. It is situated in the eastern middle portion of the state, on the waters of the Kentucky River. It is the largest of the Bluegrass counties with 446 square miles, containing both geographical and cultural contrasts. At one side it touches the

**Madison County Courthouse**
*Photo: Sid Webb*

rolling Appalachian mountains, and on the other the lush Bluegrass.

Richmond, the seat of Madison County, was settled in 1785. The town was established in 1795 as the new county seat, replacing Milford. It was named for the town of the same name in Virginia.

Named after Pres. James Madison, the pages of Madison County's history are filled with colorful personalities and events. The old frontier Wilder-

ness Trail, on which legendary Daniel Boone and other pioneers traveled to establish Fort Boonesborough in 1775, goes through the county. Perhaps no other leader dominated the country's early history more than Gen. Green Clay, a classic example of a self-made entrepreneur who served as a model for aspiring farmers and businessmen. As a member of the county court

**Cassius Clay**
*Source: The New York Public Library, Astor, Lenox and Tilden Foundations*

for nearly 40 years, Clay used his political power to develop a vast economic empire, which included large estates, ferries, taverns and toll roads.

The Valley View Ferry is the oldest continuous business of record in Kentucky. On land acquired by John Craig in 1780 through a military warrant, the Virginia Assembly granted a perpetual and irrevocable franchise to establish a ferry in 1785. It is presently named for its location in the picturesque Valley View community.

During the antebellum period the region was primarily proslavery in its sentiment; however, it saw the establishment of an antislavery colony at Berea in the violent and turbulent 1850s by the abolitionist missionary John G. Gee and emancipationist Cassius M. Clay. The county also witnessed major battles during both the American Revolution and the Civil War, including the Battle of Richmond in 1862.

Madison County was the birthplace of Cassius M. Clay, Kit Carson, African American man-of-letters Henry Allen Laine, associate justice of the U.S. Supreme Court Samuel Freeman Miller, women's rights leaders Laura Clay and Belle H. Bennett, and five governors. In the 21st century, Madison County continues to be known for its institutions of higher education, Berea College and Eastern Kentucky University.

# Magoffin County
## Salyersville

Magoffin County was established in 1860, out of parts of Morgan, Johnson, and Floyd counties, and named in honor of Beriah Magoffin, then governor of Kentucky. It was the 108th county in order of formation. It is situated on the head waters of Licking River, and extends over, onto the waters of the Big Sandy. The Licking River runs for 60 miles, dividing the county nearly centrally from southeast to northwest. The land is marked by valleys and bottomlands among hilly terrain.

Magoffin County was first settled about 1800 by emigrants originally from South Carolina—John Williams, Archibald Prather, Clayton Cook, Ebenezer Hanna, and a few others. Some of them had previously attempted a settlement in 1794, but were driven back by natives. The settlers built their cabins and a fort about one mile below present-day Salyersville.

Salyersville, the seat of Magoffin county, is located on the Licking River. The original settlement was known as Prather's Fort, for one of the settlers. It was later renamed Adamsville for William Adams, a prominent local citizen, and renamed again as Salyersville, for Judge Samuel Salyers, after the formation of Magoffin county. The post office opened as Burning Spring in 1829, was moved and renamed Licking Station in 1839, moved and renamed Adamsville in 1849, and was finally renamed Salyersville in 1861.

During the Civil War the Union Army's 14th Kentucky Infantry operated in this area to scout and protect eastern Kentucky. Near Ivyton in 1863 Reuben Patrick, a detachment leader with the 14th, boldly detached a Confederate gun from its carriage and hid it in the woods while the posted Confederate guard slept. The Confederate force moved on and left the carriage.

In 1912 the Big Sandy and Kentucky River Railroad began operation, lessening the isolation of the area. As a result millions of board feet of lumber have been shipped to market from Magoffin County. The first oil well was completed on Sept. 4, 1919, bringing oil men and scouts to the county.

Each year in Salyersville, a founder's day celebration is sponsored by the Magoffin County Historical Society. The festival offers young people opportunities to enter contests and win prize money for excelling in academic subjects such as math, spelling, essay writing, and art. Also as part of the Founder's Day festivities, a family surname is selected each year and that family is honored for their contributions to the development of the county. A book of genealogy is prepared and the family surname is engraved on a marker in the Community Center lawn.

The Pioneer Village Cabin Complex near Salyersville attracts many visitors each year. The complex consists of 15 original log cabins that have been restored and preserved through the efforts of the Magoffin County Historical Society. These donated cabins are all original, and many date back to the early 1800s.

Beriah Magoffin, after whom this county was named, was born in Harrodsburg, Mercer co., Ky., April 18, 1815, and is therefore (1873) 58 years old. He still lives on the farm inherited from his father, of the same name, who was from County Down, Ireland.

# Marion County
# Lebanon

Marion County, created in 1834 from the southern part of Washington County, is in the geographical center of Kentucky. It contains approximately 343 square miles. Marion was the 84th county in the state and was named for General Francis Marion of Revolutionary fame.

The county seat of Lebanon was established in 1814 and named for the biblical Lebanon because of the abundant cedar trees surrounding it. Early settlers came largely from Virginia and Maryland. In 1776, James Sandusky built a station on Pleasant Run six miles north east of Lebanon. In 1778, Samuel Cartwright erected one 3 ½ miles north of Lebanon on the creek that bears his name. Peter Bradford settled what is now Bradfordsville.

**Marion County Courthouse**
*Source: SouthEast Telephone*

In 1785 "a league of 60 Catholic families was formed in Maryland, mostly residents of St. Mary's County, each pledged to emigrate to Kentucky within a specified time." About 25 families, led by Basil Hayden, settled on Pottinger's Creek in what is now Holy Cross in 1785. He donated land on which the first Catholic Church west of the Allegheny Mountains was built in 1792.

Farming was for nearly 200 years the main occupation. After clearing the land and building a cabin, most settlers planted an orchard and sugar crop for family use. They raised corn and tobacco for trade. Mills were soon found on various streams.

Blacksmith shops and distilleries sprung up all over the county. Grain, liquor and other products were floated down the Rolling Fork to Salt River and on to New Orleans. Hunting, trapping and fishing not only provided food but fur for trading. Raising horses and mules was a profitable business before, during and after the Civil War.

Records show that there are now about 1,500 farms in Marion County averaging 140 acres. Marion County has only in the past 30 years become a thriving industrialized county. An industrial foundation was formed in 1972 and an industrial park opened in 1973.

Maker's Mark Distillery is the oldest continuously operated distillery in America operating at its original site near Loretto. It is a National Historic Landmark and the county's greatest tourist attraction.

Marion County is also the home of The Loretto Sisters, a religious order, that was founded by Father Charles Nerinckx in 1812, near St. Charles Church in St. Mary. In 1824, they moved to their present Motherhouse near Loretto. The Loretto Sisters operated a boarding school for girls in Loretto and an academy at Calvary from 1816-1900.

Other famous Marion County residents include: J. Proctor Knott, Governor of Kentucky 1883-1887; Martin John Spalding, Bishop of Louisville (1848), Archbishop of Baltimore (1864); Edwin Carlile Litsey, poet laureate of Kentucky (1954); and Wallace Kelly, author.

# Marshall County
# Benton

Marshall County was formed in 1842 in the Jackson Purchase region and was the 92nd county formed in Kentucky. It is bounded on the north by the Tennessee River and on the east by the Kentucky Lake. It has a land area of 304.89 square miles and an elevation ranging from 302 to 550 feet above sea level. It was named in honor of John Marshall, Chief Justice of the U.S. Supreme Court. Marshall is known as the "principal founder of judicial review and of American system of constitutional law." He also served as a lieutenant in the Revolutionary War. George Washington once solicited Marshall to accept an appointment as his successor, but he respectfully declined.

The county seat is at Benton, which lies on the East Fork of Clark River. Benton was established in 1842 and was named for Senator Thomas Hart Benton. In June 1842 nine justices met at James Clark's home to organize the first Marshall County Court. Details of the meeting were destroyed by fire at the county clerk's office. The Benton post office was opened in 1842 and the town was incorporated in 1845.

During the Civil War two impromtu skirmishes took place in Marshall County. Two days before the Battle of Paducah on March 25, 1864 forces under Confederate Gen. Nathan B. Forrest were headed north from Mississippi when they happened upon Union troops, both forces in search of horses. A total of five men were killed in the skirmishes and were buried in the old Gilbert cemetery.

Some people of interest from Marshall County are: Arthur H. Davis was one of the earliest landowners in the Jackson Purchase area. Davis was a representative for Calloway County, now Marshall County, in the state legislature, as well as a justice of the peace and a sheriff. Davis was a general in the Kentucky militia.

James R. Lemon was the owner and editor of the Benton Tribune and Mayfield Messenger and authored a history of Marshall County. Lemon is

**John Marshall, Chief Justice of the United States (1801)**

responsible for founding Big Singing Day, which evolved from Southern Harmony, a popular hymn singing custom in the 1800s and still popular today. Music reading is simplified by using only four "shaped notes" and there is no accompaniment.

Joe Creason was born in Benton in 1918. He is known for often speaking of his birthplace as "the only town in Kentucky where I was born." This astounding journalist wrote dotingly of Kentucky in his column, "Joe Creason's Kentucky," in the Louisville Courier-Journal. This daily column won him widespread recognition and acclaim. Creason died in 1974 and is buried in Bethel, Kentucky.

# Martin County
# Inez

Martin County was founded on September 1, 1870, becoming the 116th county in order of formation. It lies at the foot of the Appalachian Mountains and consists of 231 miles of rugged mountain terrain that elevates to 1,606 feet above sea level. The Tug River flows down the eastern part and separates the county from West Virginia.

**Warfield Railroad Bridge**
Source: *Tour Southern & Eastern Kentucky*

Martin County was named for Col. John P. Martin who came to Kentucky in 1828 from his native Virginia. Col. Martin later served in the Ky. House of Representatives, U.S. Congress and finally as a state senator. Col. Martin was also a delegate to the unsuccessful Kentucky Peace Convention in September 1861.

Pioneers were drawn to the area by the virgin wilderness and its resources in the late 1700s and early 1800s. Pioneer James Ward, who fought against American Indians for the frontier lands with Thomas Walker and Daniel Boone, returned to the county around 1810 bringing his family to the area of what is now Inez.

Inez, now the county seat, is located at the forks of Rockcastle Creek. The town was built on a cornfield owned by Ward's daughter-in-law, Arminta Ward. The site has been known as Arminta Ward's Bottom and Eden (for its natural beauty). In 1873 the county seat was moved from Warfield to Eden. The Inez post office opened in 1874 and may have been named for the daughter of the first postmaster. The town eventually became known by the same name.

Martin County's primary resources are minerals, timber and coal. Mining continues to be a predominant industry in Martin County, with several large employers in the area. In recent years, the land once mined for coal has been reclaimed for other uses, including the Big Sandy Airport and Big Sandy Penitentiary.

A distinguished native of Martin County, Henry L. Clay, D.D. (1875-1964), was a teacher and later became ordained into the Methodist ministry. He was on the committee that formed the Methodist Church in 1939—uniting the Northern, Southern and Protestant Methodists.

Moses Stepp is an interesting character in Martin County's colorful history. As legend has it, the frontiersman fought American Indians and Tories in the western Carolinas and east Tennessee. Stepp was captured by the Cherokees and tortured (his ears were nailed to a tree), but he escaped. He then came to Martin County where he lived out the remaining years of his life. An ancient headstone at his gravesite shows he was born in 1735 and died in 1855.

# Mason County
# Maysville

Mason county was formed in 1789 as the 8th county in Kentucky—it was created out of Bourbon County. The county was named for George Mason, a distinguished Virginian who authored the Virginia Declaration of Rights in 1776, the foundation for the U.S. Bill of Rights. The county is bounded on the north by the Ohio River, and presents a bold range of hills, frequently uneven in a varied and beautiful landscape. The elevation in the county ranges from 485 to 1,000 feet above sea level with a total land area of 241 square miles.

Mason County was the northern counterpart of the Cumberland Gap as a point of entry into Kentucky and the west. Limestone Creek provided an excellent landing place for settlers' flatboats; the North Fork of the Licking River and its tributaries provided water for farming. The buffalo trace used by animals and American Indians to make their way to Blue Licks for salt provided access to interior Kentucky. The rich cane land drew settlers from Pennsylvania, Virginia, New Jersey, and Maryland.

Maysville, the seat of Mason county, is at the junction of Limestone Creek and the Ohio River. The site was first settled in the 1780s and was known as Limestone. The town was formed in 1787 and named Maysville for John May, a surveyor, clerk, and land owner in the area. The post office opened in 1794 as Limestone and was renamed Maysville about 1799.

Washington, four miles to the south, was established in 1786 and is said to be the first town named for George Washington, who appointed its first postmaster. This first post office west of the Alleghenies became the distributing point for mail for five states. Washington served as the seat of county government until 1848 when it was moved to Maysville.

Simon Kenton raised the first corn crop in 1775. Hemp became a major crop in the 19th century followed by tobacco in the 20th. Maysville was the second largest burley market in the world. Today, agricultural diversification is being expanded with tobacco diminishing as a

**Mason County Courthouse**
*Source: SouthEast Telephone*

cash crop.

The Theatrical Society performed at the courthouse in Washington in October of 1797. It continues today with The Maysville Players—established in 1962—and the oldest group of its kind in the state. The Washington Opera House is being restored—built in 1884 it featured such notable acts as Buffalo Bill Cody's Wild West Show.

Supreme Court Justice Stanley F. Reed, singer Rosemary Clooney, and Miss America 2000, Heather French Henry, are notable Kentuckians who have called Mason County home.

# McCracken County
## Paducah

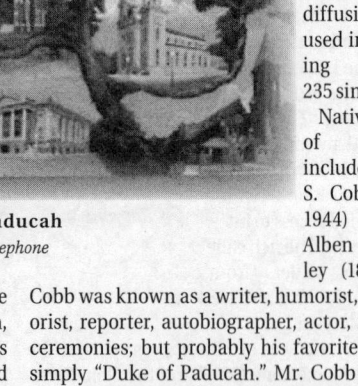

Located in the western part of Kentucky at the confluence of the Ohio and Tennessee rivers, McCracken County was destined to be in a crucial location during the Civil War. Comprised of 251.02 square miles in the 1818 Jackson Purchase, it is generally flat, with river-bottom soil. Although Wilmington was the first county seat when the county was formed in 1825, Paducah was made county seat in 1832.

Confederate Gen. Nathan B. Forrest attacked the fort on March 25, 1864; the Confederate forces were repulsed but burned riverfront warehouses and homes in range of the fort. Confederate Col. Albert P Thompson, of Paducah, was killed.

The Ohio River Flood of 1937 was the greatest natural disaster in the history of the U.S. and drove over one million people from their homes; over 90 percent of Paducah was inundated. Today the $8 million floodwall, built by the Army Corps of Engineers, protects the city, which has been the site of a $785 million gaseous diffusion plant used in producing Uranium 235 since 1954.

Native sons of reknown include Irvin S. Cobb (1876-1944) and Alben W. Barkley (1877-1956).

**Postcard from Paducah**
*Source: SouthEast Telephone*

The site for Paducah was chosen by Gen. George Rogers Clark during the American Revolution, with the first settlers arriving around 1821. Clark's brother, William, laid out the town in 1827 and selected the name Paducah in honor of the legendary Chickasaw leader, Paduke, who lived and hunted in the area.

Paducah was taken by Gen. Ulysses S. Grant in 1861; he built Fort Anderson, which he used as his base to take Fort Henry and Fort Donelson on the Tennessee and Cumberland rivers in Tennessee. This was the beginning of Gen. Grant's famous Mississippi Valley campaign, which split the Confederacy and led to its defeat.

Cobb was known as a writer, humorist, local colorist, reporter, autobiographer, actor, master of ceremonies; but probably his favorite title was simply "Duke of Paducah." Mr. Cobb said, "I'd rather be born in Paducah than be natural twins in any other city in the world." Alben W. Barkley was possibly Kentucky's most influential citizen in national politics in the 20th century. He was the 35th vice president under Pres. Harry Truman. While speaking in Lexington, Va., he suffered a massive heart attack and died. His last words were, "I would rather be a servant in the house of the Lord than sit in the seats of the mighty."

# McCreary County
## Whitley City

The last county formed in Kentucky was McCreary County in 1912 due to the inaccessibility of the industrial activity by the county seats. McCreary County is located between the Big South Fork and the main body of the Cumberland River. It is bounded on the south by the Tennessee state line. It has a land area of 427.70 square miles and an elevation ranging from 723 to 2,165 feet above sea level. McCreary County is located entirely within the Daniel Boone National Forest and includes the Big South Fork National River and Recreation Area.

Although the county was strongly in support of the Union during the Civil War, the county was named for Confederate army veteran James B. McCreary. McCreary was also a two-time Democratic governor of Kentucky. The county seat is at Whitley City and was chosen after two bitter elections between the northern and southern parts of the newly created McCreary County.

The first oil well in Kentucky was discovered in the McCreary County area in 1818. Marcus Huling and Andrew Zimmerman were drilling salt wells along the South Fork of the Cumberland River when they struck oil on land that was leased from Martin Beaty. Attempts were made to market the oil

**Heritage Days**
*Source: Tour Southern & Eastern Kentucky*

down river but were unsuccessful; so, the oil was barreled and hauled to Nashville for sale, primarily for medicinal use. Production reached 100 barrels daily.

In 1902 a group of entrepreneurs led by Justus S. Stearns arrived in the area and built a new town within 13 months of their arrival. The town was named Stearns. The people were well educated and financed. The town had an electrical generating plant and America's first all-electric saw mill.

Mining and lumber industries made the county prosperous until after World War II, when the federal government purchased over 70 percent of the land of McCreary County to form the Daniel Boone National Forest and the Big South Fork National River and Recreation Area. The lumber production slowed in McCreary County where the state's largest lumberyard was once located.

The Sandhill 4-H Conservation Camp is located in the Daniel Boone National Forest in McCreary County. It was established in 1959 and was the first of its kind in Kentucky. Here, youth are taught the importance of appreciating and caring for natural resources.

# McLean County
# Calhoun

McLean County was formed on January 28, 1854 and became the 103rd county of Kentucky. It is bisected by the Green River, which makes 70 percent of the county a flood plain. Agriculture has been an abundant source of income for many years. McLean County has a land area of 254.30 square feet and an elevation ranging from 345 to 660 feet above sea level.

The county was named in honor of Judge Alney McLean. McLean was born in Burke County, N.C. on June 10, 1779—he had several careers in his lifetime: surveyor, lawyer, politician, state representative and circuit judge. A captain in the War of 1812, McLean was elected in 1815 as a Republican to the Fourteenth Congress, elected to the Sixteenth Congress in March 1819 and finished his illustrious career as judge of the 14th district of Kentucky from 1821 until his death. Judge McLean was a presidential elector on the Clay ticket in 1824 and on the ticket of Clay and Sergeant in 1832.

The county seat is at Calhoun. It was originally established in 1785 as Rhoadsville by Soloman Rhoads. Rhoads built a fort here and the town was later known as Fort Vienna. It was named Calhoun in 1849 for Judge John Calhoun and five years later became the county seat.

McLean County was a place of excitement during the Civil War. On December 18, 1861 Confederate forces under Col. Nathan B. Forrest executed a surprise attack on Union forces under the command of Maj. Eli H. Murray. Dismounted men were ordered to attack both Union flanks while Forrest and the remaining mounted men drove straight to the center of the Union troops. Union troops were broken and many fled the area. After pursuing the scattering troops for four miles, Forrest returned to Hopkinsville. McLean County was also a Union campsite in

**McLean County Courthouse**
*Photo: Sid Webb*

July 1864, established to guard the critical area between the Cumberland and Green rivers.

The 1,350-foot Livermore Bridge is said to be the only river bridge in the world that begins and ends in the same county (McLean), spans two rivers (Green and Rough rivers), and crosses another county (Ohio). Another bridge of note is the Corp. James Bethel Gresham Memorial Bridge. It was named in honor of the first American killed in action during World War I. Gresham was born in McLean County in 1893 but moved to Indiana in 1901—where he enlisted in 1914. Pfc. Gresham was killed at the Battle of Sommerviller, Lorraine, on November 3, 1917.

# Meade County
## Brandenburg

Formed in 1823, the 76th county of Kentucky, Meade County was named after Capt. James Meade of Woodford County. A veteran of French and American Indian skirmishes and the Battle of Tippecanoe, Capt. Meade was killed in the War of 1812. Situated in the northwest middle part of the state, Meade is bounded in part by a great bend of the Ohio River. Two-thirds of the land—some 308.51 square miles—is "barrens," with much of the rest good river-bottoms. The elevation in the county ranges from 383 to 1,000 feet above sea level.

Brandenburg, the county seat, was named after Solomon Brandenburg, the owner of a large tract of land purchased in 1804. He built the Old Walnut Log Tavern, a double log house which served as courthouse, hotel, schoolhouse and home. Among the earliest steamboats built were three at his landing and ferry. A leading promoter, he helped the town become a major river port. Brandenburg developed on the banks of the Ohio around Brandenburg's tavern and ferry in the early 1800s. Many of the historic buildings in Brandenburg, a number of them antebellum, were destroyed in tornadoes that rampaged through Kentucky on April 3, 1974.

The first corn-grinding mill was built by Jonathan Essery, just below the mouth of Blue Spring Branch of Doe Run Creek. When it was enlarged in 1821, Abraham Lincoln's father, Thomas Lincoln, was said to have worked there as a carpenter or mason. It later was expanded into Doe Run Inn, a popular retreat today and part of the Doe Run Creek Historic District.

John James Audubon, artist, naturalist and ornithologist, spent a great deal of time sketching in 1820 in Meade County and its neighboring territory. His excursions led him to combine a love of art and science to produce his now-famous prints. Many sketches from this area were printed in "Birds of America," to which he owes his fame.

Gen. John Hunt Morgan's Raiders came through Meade County in 1863, crossing the river into Indiana at Brandenburg on captured steamers. Meade County was where the notorious guerilla Jerome Clarke, called Sue Mundy, was captured in 1865 by Union soldiers and put to death three days later in Louisville.

> **Captain Meade, when quite a youth, volunteered his services under the lamented Colonel Joseph H. Daveiss, in the Wabash expedition, and fought side by side with that gallant officer in the battle of Tippecanoe.**

Harold "Pee Wee" Reese (1918-1999) was born in Meade County. His major league debut was in 1940; Reese spent 16 years with the Dodgers in Brooklyn and L.A. (1940-58). His baseball career was interrupted by WWII service in the U.S. Navy. Credited with aiding Jackie Robinson's integration into major league baseball, Reese was elected to the Baseball Hall of Fame in 1984.

# Menifee County
# Frenchburg

Menifee County, 113th in order of formation, was formed from parts of Bath, Montgomery, Morgan, Powell and Wolfe counties in 1869. Named for Congressman Richard Hickman Menefee, a well-regarded statesman and successful lawyer, the misspelling of the county name occurred in the legislature when the county was chartered. Menifee County is heavily forested—its rugged terrain located in the Daniel Boone National Forest. Streams, cliffs, overlooks and natural stone arches typify the area. Grant's Arch, one such sandstone formation, stands 15-feet high and 51-feet long. Environments range from high cliffs to wetlands. The elevation in the county ranges from 670 to 1,428 feet above sea level with a land area of 203.90 square miles.

Evidence of early occupation by Native Americans is indicated. A large natural rock house (100-feet deep and 350-feet long) at the head of Sargent's branch was a one-time shelter. Indian Stairway is a set of footholds carved into the sloping cliff.

Richard H. Menefee, one of Kentucky's great orators who died at age 32, was the youngest person to have a county named for him in Kentucky. He was regarded as one of Kentucky's great orators. Born in Owingsville (1808), he was elected commonwealth attorney of 11th Judicial district, 1831; state representative, 1836-37; and

U.S. Representative, 1837-39. He died at age of 32; at his death, it was said that Kentucky lost "one of her proudest and fondest hopes."

Frenchburg, the seat of justice of Menifee county, is located near the center of the county. The city was named in honor of Judge Richard French, who was defeated by Menefee in a race for U.S. Congress in 1837. Frenchburg was founded in 1869; the Frenchburg post office opened in 1871.

Menifee has deposits of oil and coal, and was the site of pioneer iron furnaces in the early 1800s. Beaver Dam Furnace was erected in 1819 by J. T. Mason. It began operations under Robert Crockett, ironmaster. The furnace was a big truncated pyramid of sandstone blocks, 35 feet high with a 28-foot square base. It was water-powered. Some products were nails, "plough plates," kettles, skillets and flat irons. The goods were flatboated down river to the southern markets. The furnace went out of business, 1870-73.

Cave Run Lake was impounded in 1974 with 8,270 surface acres. The lake is known for producing trophy-size musky. Red River Gorge Geological Area is a 25,500-acre natural scenic wonder of sandstone cliffs, rock formations and magnificent wilderness. Sheltowee Trace National Recreational Trail lies within the county.

**Cabin near Gladie**
*Source: SouthEast Telephone*

# Mercer County
# Harrodsburg

Mercer is one of the nine counties established by Virginia in 1786. It was formed from 250.92 square miles of Lincoln County. Mercer County was named after Gen. Hugh Mercer, a Scotsman who was killed in the American Revolution. It is located near the geographic center of the state, on the waters of the Kentucky and Salt rivers. The surface is undulating, and the land generally of good quality—some portions very rich and the whole finely watered. The elevation in the county ranges from 483 to 1,000 feet above sea level.

Settlement of the area was begun in June of 1774 by a Pennsylvanian, James Harrod, and a company of 31 adventurers. They built five or six cabins near a boiling spring and called it Harrods Town (Harrodstown). American Indians— alarmed by the encroachment of settlers and surveyors—became hostile, so work had to be suspended. Harrods Town was the seat of Kentucky county, Virginia when it was formed in 1776, then the seat of Lincoln county, which was formed in 1780. It remained the county seat when Mercer county was formed in 1785. The Harrodsburgh post office, probably the second in Kentucky, opened in 1794 and its spelling was changed to Harrodsburg in 1894.

More than two hundred years later, Harrodsburg has the honor of being known as the oldest permanent settlement in Kentucky and the first English settlement west of the Alleghenies. The first corn raised in Kentucky was in 1775, by John Harman, in a field at the east end of Harrodsburg. Col. Daniel Boone, of the Kentucky militia, found the settlers on his way to the Falls of Ohio, being sent out by Gov. Dunmore to warn the surveyors in that region that the northern American Indians had become hostile.

When the whole state was known as

**Pleasant Hill, Shaker Community**
*Photo: Sid Webb*

Kentucky county, the first court ever held was convened in Harrodsburg on September 2, 1777. "Collin's Historical Sketches" records the population was 198 at the time: 85 men, 24 women, 12 children over ten years, 58 children under ten years, 12 slaves above ten years and 7 under ten years.

Pleasant Hill was a small village of rare beauty and neatness, situated on a commanding eminence about one mile from the Kentucky River. It belonged to an orderly and industrious religious society called Shakers, who thrived in Mercer County. Shaker Village of Pleasant Hill is fully restored to the order and beauty created by the Shakers.

# Metcalfe County
# Edmonton

Metcalfe, the 106th county established in Kentucky, was named in honor of Kentucky's 10th governor, Thomas Metcalfe. Metcalfe County was formed in 1860, primarily from Barren County, with smaller parts carved out of Hart, Green, Adair, Cumberland and Monroe counties. The elevation in the county ranges from 560 to 1,120 feet above sea level with a land area of 291 square miles.

Gov. Thomas Metcalfe (1780-1855) was born in Virginia, and served as a captain in the Ky. Volunteer forces during the War of 1812. He was elected to the U.S. Congress (1819-28) and served as governor from 1828-32.

The town of Edmonton was laid out in 1800 and named as the county seat after Edmund Rogers, who owned the land. He served in the Virginia campaign of the Revolutionary War; an early surveyor, he joined Gen. George Rogers Clark, his cousin, in 1783. A year later, he came south of Green River where he made earliest surveys on the Barren River and settled there.

**Construction of a building to house the gymnasium and auditorium of Edmonton High and Graded School, Edmonton, April 7, 1936**
*Source: Kentucky Virtual Library*

Shortly after Metcalfe County was established, the county courthouse was built. On March 15, 1865, a band of guerrillas looted the town and burned the courthouse. After rebuilding the courthouse, it was again burned on July 26, 1868. The present courthouse was begun on September 19, 1868 and was completed in October 1869.

John Filson located Big Blue Spring on his 1784 map of Kentucky as being between the Little and Big Barren Rivers in northwestern Metcalfe County. Two Indian trails crossed at Big Blue Spring. The "Great Warrior's Trail" extended from Cherokee settlements near Chattanooga to the Falls of the Ohio River.

An artesian well was discovered in 1845 by Ezekiel Neal while drilling for salt water. The water contained salt, sulphur, magnesium and iron; it was used by many for its medicinal value. It became the site of Beulah Villa Hotel, built in 1903 across from the sulphur well. The hotel was noted for spacious, wide verandas; a swinging bridge was erected from the main veranda to the well. The popular hotel closed in 1968.

Metcalfe County is the birthplace of Eugene W. Newman (1845-1923). His pen name, Savoyard, was given to the community formerly known as Chicken Bristle. Savoyard, a noted Washington columnist, authored sketches about the Pennyrile of Kentucky. Known as a great political writer, he won praise from his contemporaries for his understanding of people and his versatility.

Ed Porter Thompson was born in Metcalfe County in 1834. Elected Kentucky superintendent of public instruction, 1891 to 1895, Thompson was a noted educator, mathematician, author and linguist. His "History of the Orphan Brigade" is a most complete and valuable Civil War record. He died in 1903.

# Monroe County
## Tompkinsville

Monroe County was carved out of Barren and Cumberland counties in 1820 and named for just-elected Pres. James Monroe (of Monroe Doctrine fame). Monroe County is situated on the southern border with Tennessee, on the headwaters of Barren River. The land is quite diverse—hilly, undulating, level—and comprised of 330.81 square miles. Over the years it has been extensively logged. Zinc ore was found in 1856, and today there are oil and gas wells to enrich the county. Elevation in the county ranges from 495 to 1,141 feet above sea level.

Tompkinsville, the seat of Monroe County, is located near the center of the county at the intersection of three state highways. It was settled around the beginning of the 19th century and was originally known as Watsons Store, for the store opened by J.C. Watson in 1809. The town was renamed Tompkinsville to honor Daniel D. Tompkins, sitting U.S. vice president at the time. It was made the seat of the Monroe county soon after it was formed in 1819. The Tompkinsville post office opened in 1819.

Tompkinsville was laid out and situated on Mill Creek, nine miles from the Cumberland River, which runs through the county's southeast cor-

**Old Mulkey Meetinghouse**
*Photo: Sid Webb*

ner. Tompkinsville's courthouse was one of 22 Kentucky courthouses to be burned during the Civil War.

Indeed, Monroe County suffered severely during the War Between the States, more so than its neighboring counties. It was an almost constant battlefield for opposing forces—even after the war, guerrillas continued to raid and burn, especially in and around Tompkinsville. Late in the autumn of 1861 Gen. S.S. Stanton of Tennessee led Confederate troops into Monroe County to burn Camp Anderson; General Bragg's entire army came through in 1862; and, later the same year, it was ravaged by Col. John Hunt Morgan's Raiders, who encountered a Major Jordan of the Union Army and was forced to retreat.

Monroe County is notable because it is the only one of 2,957 counties in the entire United States in which the county is named for the president and the county seat for the vice president. Trees in the abundant forests of the county, also record the early visitors—one of the most interesting is D. Bone 1777. Other trees bear the same date but no names. Monroe County proved to be a thoroughfare for early settlers as well as soldiers in the Civil War.

# Montgomery County
# Mt. Sterling

Montgomery County, the 22nd county in order of formation, was formed in 1796. The county was named in memory of Gen. Richard Montgomery. Montgomery County lies on the waters of the Hinkston

**Montgomery County Courthouse**
*Source: SouthEast Telephone*

and Red rivers; it once stretched to the Virginia border. The county assumed its present size in 1869 with the formation of Floyd, Bath, Powell and Menifee counties from its land area. The southeastern half of the county is mountainous; most of the residue of the county is rich, limestone land, more broken and hilly but comprised of rich, productive soil. The elevation in the county ranges from 707 to 1,447 feet above sea level in a land area of 198.59 square miles.

Gen. Montgomery was a major general in the American Revolutionary army, and a native of Ireland. An advocate of colonial freedom, he commanded continental forces in the north, capturing first British colors in the war at Ft. St. Johns in 1775. Gen. Montgomery was killed at the Revolutionary

War battle of Quebec (1775) at the age of 38.

Mt. Sterling, the county seat, was founded on Hinkston Creek in 1792 on 640 acres of land. The town originally was called "Little Mountain" for a large mound located where Queen and Locust streets intersect. The mound was attributed to the Adena people, who inhabited the Ohio Valley around 800 B.C. to A.D. 700. Rituals involving cremation and mound building were central to Adena life. When the mound was excavated in 1845 and 1846, many curious things were found interspersed with human bones—among them were engraved stone tablets, copper breastplates, and a great number of large beads, some copper and others of ivory.

Mt. Sterling was renamed in 1792 for Stirling, Scotland, the home of one of the town founders. Mt. Sterling was the western terminus of the Mount Sterling-Pound Gap road, the longest pre-Civil War state road. It became the major overland route to Virginia and the east. Present-day US 460 follows the approximate route of the original road.

Mt. Sterling has a rich civil war history. Primarily a Union garrison town, it fell several times to Confederate forces commanded by Col. John Hunt Morgan. On March 22, 1863, about 300 Confederate cavalrymen captured the city, taking 438 prisoners, 222 wagon loads of military stores, 500 mules, and 1,000 stand of arms. A year later, on June 8, 1864, Confederate forces under Gen. John H. Morgan (on his last raid) attacked the Union camp here. Confederates took 380 prisoners and material; $59,000 taken from Farmers' Bank.

The home of Gen. John Bell Hood is located four miles west of Mt. Sterling. From here Hood (1831-1879) went to West Point; he resigned his commission in 1861 to join the Confederate Army.

# Morgan County
## West Liberty

Morgan County was formed in 1822, and named for Gen. Daniel Morgan, a distinguished officer of the Revolutionary War. It was created from parts of Floyd and Bath counties. Licking River flows through

that was to be called Liberty.

Morgan County differed from other coal counties in the eastern coalfields because of its rich veins of cannel coal — originally "candle" coal, so called

**Wrigley Arch**
*Source: Tour Southern & Eastern Kentucky*

because it burned easily, has a silky luster, and emits a bright flame like a candle. In the early 1900s cannel coal was favored for use in parlor grates when company came. Cannel City became a booming center with a landmark hotel, Hotel Delancey, dating to 1900. It served as the headquarters for the coal, timber and railroad industrialists, salesmen and showmen when the region was flourishing.

The first important Civil War engagement in eastern Kentucky occurred here in October 1861 when Union Brig. Gen. Wm. Nelson sur-

the center of the county in a northwestern direction. The headwaters of Little Sandy and Red rivers have their rise here. Morgan County lies on the face of the western slope of the Appalachian plateau, in the foothills of the Cumberland Mountain range. The face of the country is hilly, interspersed with fertile valleys. The soil is based on free stone, with red clay foundation. Iron ore, coal, alum and copperas and mineral and oil springs, abound in the county. The elevation ranges from 690 to 1,400 feet above sea level in a land area of 381.26 square miles.

In 1823 the county seat of West Liberty was established; it is located on the Licking River. It was settled in 1804 and became known as Wells Mill, for the mill of Edmund Wells. The town was renamed West Liberty when it became the seat of the new county. The name is thought to have been chosen because the town was west of the site of a proposed town

prised Confederate forces under Capt. Andrew May. Civilian secessionists were captured and jailed. In 1862 and 1864 the county saw skirmishes between Union and Confederate forces. Gen. George Morgan's Union forces came through the county from Cumberland Gap enroute to Greenup; they camped near West Liberty for two days in September 1872. After their last raid into Kentucky, Gen. John Hunt Morgan's calvarymen moved through West Liberty on their retreat to Virginia. The court house was destroyed by fire during the Civil War. The current courthouse was modeled after the colonial capital at Williamsburg, Va.

Cave Run Lake, an impoundment on the Licking River with an 8,270-acre reservoir, extends into Morgan County. The rugged areas of northern Morgan County are within the Daniel Boone National Forest and offer scenic cliffs, rock arches and waterfalls.

# Muhlenberg County
## Greenville

Kentucky's 34th county, Muhlenberg, was established in 1798 out of sections of Christian and Logan counties. It claims three river borders: the Breen, Pond and Mud rivers. Located in Kentucky's Western Coal Field, Muhlenberg's coal production and land reclamation operations are world-renowned. With an area of 482 square miles (about half farmland) the county's wealth comes from coal, gas, oil, limestone, and the quarrying of sand and gravel. The elevation above sea level ranges from 355 to 760 feet. Muhlenberg County encompasses 474.7 square miles.

Named in honor of Revolutionary War Gen. John Peter Gabriel Muhlenberg, the county was never visited by its namesake, but given its moniker by soldiers who fought with Muhlenberg at Monmouth, Germantown, Brandywine, Stony Point and Yorktown. A Lutheran minister, Gen. Muhlenberg's quote, "A time to preach and a time to fight," marks the end of his religious work and the beginning of his service in the Revolutionary War. After serving with honor, he later returned to Pennsylvania where he was elected to the U.S. Congress and became Collector of Customs in Philadelphia. His tombstone reads, "He was Brave in the Field, Faithful in the Cabinet, Honorable in all his transactions, a Sincere Friend and an Honest Man."

Greenville, the county seat, was founded in 1799 on land donated by William Campbell. It was named for Nathaniel Greene, an officer in the Revolutionary War who served with George Washington. Lake Malone State Park, with 374 acres and an 826-acre lake, is located 18 miles south of Greenville.

In keeping with its coal producing status, Muhlenberg County is home to one of the world's largest coal shovels. The Peabody Coal Company stripping shovel, located at the Sinclair Mine, took 11 months to build. It is 200-feet tall, with the capacity to remove 100,000 cubic yards of rock each day. The operator of this behemoth sits five stories above the ground in an air-conditioned cabin, which is reached via an elevator located in the center of the machine. Requiring the power of a 15,000-person city, the machine is wider than an eight-lane highway. The dipper alone is larger than a two-car garage.

Another point of interest in Muhlenberg County is Indian Knoll, located east of Greenville on the Green River across from the Paradise Steam Plant. An American Indian refuse receptacle from 3000-2000 B.C., thousands of American Indian relics have been discovered there.

**Old Courthouse, 1942**
*Source: Kentucky Virtual Library*

# Nelson County
# Bardstown

Formed by the Virginia Assembly in 1874 out of Jefferson County, Nelson County was the fourth county in order of formation. It was named after Thomas Nelson, who signed the Declaration of Independence and served as governor of Virginia in 1781, succeeding Thomas Jefferson. Marked by a diverse topography, Nelson County has an elevation of 390 to 1,090 feet above sea level and a land area of 422.63 square miles.

Bardstown, the county seat, was originally called

**John Fitch, first inventor of steamboats**

Salem, and is known as the second oldest town in Kentucky. It was situated on a 1,000 acre Revolutionary War tract granted to David Baird of Pennsylvania, who never visited his namesake—he sent his brother William to survey the land and lay out a town. In time the name changed to Bairdtown, and later Bardstown when incorporated by an act of the Virginia Assembly in 1788.

During the Civil War Bardstown was home to Bragg's confederate army of 28,000 who lived for weeks there before continuing on to Perryville.

Nancy Johnson was a member of the committee to select flag of the Confederacy; the one chosen was unfurled here in 1861 before some 5,000 people. The Lexington Rifles, under John Hunt Morgan, camped in Nelson County in Sept. 1861 and received the hospitality of local people. With additional recruits, horses and supplies they joined Confederates at Green River on September 30. The Rifles were mustered in as Second Cavalry Regiment, Ky. Volunteers, CSA; their division became renowned as "Morgan's Raiders."

Old Talbott Tavern, oldest hotel west of the Allegheny Mountains, is still in operation in Bardstown. St. Thomas Farm is claimed as the "cradle of the Catholic Church" in the west; here in 1811 Bishop B. J. Flaget and Benedict Father David pioneered St. Joseph's Cathedral, St. Joseph's College and Nazareth Academy. Gethsemani Abbey of the Order of Trappist Monks, noted for prayer, labor and silence, is located in New Haven.

Bardstown is home to Federal Hill, site of My Old Kentucky Home State Park and the "Stephen Foster Story," an outdoor musical drama. Foster's cousin, Judge John Rowan, lived at Federal Hill, and after a visit there, Foster is believed to have been inspired to write "My Old Kentucky Home," Kentucky's state song.

Heaven Hill Distillery, America's largest independent, family-owned producer and marketer of distilled spirits, is located in Bardstown. Founded at the end of Prohibition, it is now the seventh largest supplier of spirits in the U.S. Nelson County also holds claim to the Bernheim Arboretum and Research Forest, established in 1929 by Isaac W. Bernheim. Bernheim, a German immigrant, became a successful distiller and showed his gratitude to Kentucky by gifting its residents with the forest.

# Nicholas County
# Carlisle

Initially formed from sections of Mason and Bourbon counties, Nicholas County was the 42nd county named in 1799. Rich in limestone, the land is diverse with rich, productive soil. The Licking River forms part of the northeast boundary and runs through the county; Hinkson Creek borders Nicholas County on the south. The elevation ranges from 565 to 1,060 feet above sea level. The land area is 196 square miles.

Although still part of Virginia in 1789, the county was the site of one of the original 13 district courts located in Kentucky. Col. George Nicholas was appointed the first U.S. attorney in Kentucky by George Washington and gave Nicholas County its name in 1799. During the Revolutionary War Col. Nicholas was a Captain in Virginia. He was an admired member of the Virginia convention and helped ratify the federal Constitution. He has been called "Father of the Kentucky Constitution," and ultimately served as a professor of law at Transylvania College in Lexington.

Carlisle is the seat of justice. Originally located at Blue Licks and then Ellsville, the county seat finally settled in Carlisle in 1816. The original courthouse was built in 1800; the current courthouse dates from 1893.

Other interesting attractions in or near Carlisle include the Tollgate House, at the Bourbon County line, one of the last tollgates used in Kentucky. Daniel Boone's cabin, the last in which he and his wife Rebecca lived before moving to the Louisiana Territory (now Missouri) in 1799, was moved from Hinkston Creek and is now located northwest of Carlisle. The last battle of the Revolutionary War was fought at Blue Licks Battlefield, now a state park. Kentuckians battled British soldiers and American Indians in 1782 near the Blue Lick River, and fallen soldiers are commemorated with a monument at the park. One of those killed was Daniel Boone's son, whose father's words are immortalized on the monument: "Enough of honour cannot be paid."

Abundant salt springs at the Blue Licks Battlefield State Resort Park not only attracted Daniel Boone with its therapeutic waters, but years earlier drew prehistoric animals. Lower Blue Licks, a famous salt lick near Carlisle, was the site of Daniel Boone's capture by American Indians with 30 companions in 1778. In 1789 Lower Blue Licks was the only station on the old Smith Wagon Road between Limestone (now Maysville) and Lexington—a small fort was built there for protection by a settler named Lyons.

Forrest Retreat is the home of Gov. Thomas Metcalfe, a stonemason nicknamed "Old Stone Hammer." In 1797 Metcalfe laid the foundation of Kentucky first governor's mansion, later used by lieutenant governors.

If he [Col. George Nicholas] was not a transcendent orator according to the Demosthenian process of resolving eloquence into action alone, his powers of argumentation were of the highest order, and his knowledge of the laws and institutions of his country placed him in the first rank of the distinguished men by whose wisdom and patriotism they were established.

*Governor Morehead - 1792*

# Ohio County
# Hartford

Ohio County, the 35th county in order of formation, was established from part of Hardin County on December 17, 1798. The county was named for the Ohio River, which at one time formed its northern boundary. Several counties were carved out its original land area including Daviess County in 1815, parts of Butler and Grayson counties in 1820, Hancock County in 1829, and McLean County in 1854. The elevation in the county ranges from 365 to 800 feet above sea level and it has a land area of 594 square miles. The topography of Ohio County is undulating and well-suited for agriculture. It contains the sixth largest land area in Kentucky.

The county seat is at Hartford. It was established as a fort in 1782 on a bluff overlooking the Rough River. Gabriel Madison, who claimed a 4,000-acre Virginia land grant, donated a four-acre area for the town. Deer, also called harts, often crossed the river below the bluff and the settlement became known as the "hart's ford." The name Hartford derived from this description. It is considered the first fortified settlement in the lower Green River Valley, followed by Barnett's Station and Calhoun, in what is now McLean County. Daniel Boone and Joseph Barnett were among the first surveyors in the region.

During the Civil War, Ohio County was the scene of intense guerrilla activity. On July 21, 1864, a partisan force commanded by Capt. Dick Yates ambushed a detachment of Daviess County Home Guards at Rough River Creek. On February 20, 1865, a group of Grayson County Home Guards attacked an encampment of guerrillas near Hartford. On December 20, 1864, Confederate Gen. Hylan B. Lyon's troops captured the county seat of Hartford and burned the courthouse.

River traffic down the Green and Rough rivers promoted the county's growth. Hartford became a river port and mill town on the Rough River. The river traffic was disrupted during the Civil War and the advent of railroads dealt a serious blow to the county in the 1870s.

Large burial mounds found along the

Artist's rendering of "new" courthouse
Source: Kentucky Virtual Library

Green River in the southern part of the county indicate that the area was extensively occupied by prehistoric people. Excavations there in the late 1930s uncovered more than 1,200 skeletons at Indian Knoll.

Bill Monroe was born on Sept. 13, 1911, in Rosine. He is credited as "the Father of Bluegrass." He won the first Grammy award ever given for Bluegrass music in 1989, earned the Grammy's Lifetime Achievement award (1993) and was awarded a National Medal of Honor by Pres. Clinton (1995). Bill Monroe died on Sept. 9, 1996. The Rock and Roll Hall of Fame inducted him as an early influence of rock 'n' roll.

# Oldham County
## LaGrange

Oldham County was formed in 1824, the 74th in order of formation. Oldham County is located along and to the southeast of the Ohio River. The county was created from sections of Henry, Jefferson and Shelby counties. The western portion of the county is gently undulating, while the eastern section is broken and hilly. The elevation ranges from 420 to 920 feet above sea level and it has a land area of 190 square miles. The principal waterways in addition to the Ohio River are Harrod's Creek, Eighteen Mile Creek, Curry's Fork and Floyd's Fork.

The county was named for Col. William Oldham of Jefferson County, a Revolutionary War officer and a native of Virginia. Oldham was killed in 1794 while leading a regiment of Kentucky militia in the bloody and ill-fated St. Clair Indian Campaign on the Wabash River, Col. Oldham was one of over 800 killed in that battle.

Early settlers founded a trading center named Westport, located in a beautiful valley near the Ohio. It served as the county seat several times until it was relocated once and for all to LaGrange.

LaGrange, the county seat, was founded in 1827

**Film producer, D.W. Griffith**
*Source: Kentucky Virtual Library*

and named for the home of Gen. Marquis de Lafayette in honor of his services to America in the revolution. Pewee Valley (named for a small Pewee bird) was first established as Smith's Station in honor of Thomas Smith, president of Kentucky's first railroad. Pewee Valley was the setting of the famous "The Little Colonel" books and other fictional portrayals of life in Pewee Valley by Annie Fellows Johnston. Shirley Temple starred in The Little Colonel film in 1934. It is the site of the only state-owned cemetery for Confederate veterans of the Civil War who died while residents of the Kentucky Confederate Veterans Home.

The county is home to the Kentucky State Reformatory, Luther Luckett Correctional Complex, and the Roederer Farm Center, all near LaGrange; and the Kentucky Correctional Institute for Women and the Lonnie Watson Center, both near Pewee Valley.

D. W. Griffith (1875-1948) was a native of Oldham County and is buried here. He is renowned as a pioneer in the motion picture industry, creating dramatic and photographic effects with lighting and camera techniques. Griffith produced "Birth of a Nation," a controversial film drama of Civil War and the postbellum era. LaGrange is also the resting place of Rob Morris, founder of the Order of the Eastern Star.

# Owen County
# Owenton

In 1819 Owen County became the 63rd county formed in the state. Owen County was formed from parts of Franklin, Gallatin and Scott counties and was named, as was the county seat of Owenton, in honor of Col. Abraham Owen. The topography is rolling to hilly, with deep productive soil. Deciduous forests are extensive. The county is watered by Big Eagle Creek with numerous smaller streams. At one time many valuable mineral springs were found in the county. The county contains 354 square miles and ranges in elevation from 425 to 1,000 feet above sea level.

Col. Owen was born in Virginia in 1769; he immigrated to Shelby County in 1785. He was elected to the Kentucky legislature and attended the state constitutional conventions at Danville. Col. Owen was the first Kentuckian to join the command of Gen. Wm. Henry Harrison in the Indian campaign of upper Wabash Valley. Col. Owen fell at the side of Gen. Harrison at the battle of Tippecanoe in 1811.

Owen County became the home of Henry Sparks, a Revolutionary War soldier who served as Gen. George Washington's guard. He was discharged at Valley Forge in 1778 and came to Kentucky in 1795, settling in present-day Owen County in 1800.

When Owen County was organized, Heslerville, now Hesler, was chosen as its county seat. In 1822 the county seat was moved to a new location, where Owenton was established in 1828.

From the summer of 1862 to March 1865, the county was subjected to skirmishes and guerrilla warfare during the Civil War. Many residents were strongly sympathetic to the Confederate cause. During the course of the war, Federal troops had to fend off frequent attacks from Confederate forces at Lusby's Mill and Vanlandingham's farm, two very active recruiting camps. In 1864 a portion of New Liberty was destroyed by fire at an estimated loss of $120,000. Confederate Col. George M. Jessee gained control of most of the county by September 1864. Confederate Gen. John Hunt Morgan stopped at the home of a friend in Owen County on Nov. 30, 1863—after his escape from a Union prison in Ohio. Morgan made his way to Tenn., where he organized and led yet another raid into Kentucky in 1864.

After the war, the Democratic Party maintained control of the county for many years. "Sweet Owen" was the nickname given to the county in the early 1850s by Owen County native, John C. Breckinridge, U.S. congressman, senator, and vice-president of the U.S. in 1856 with James Buchanan as president.

## I didn't know that...

"The people of Owen county were almost unanimous in favor of the South; and Confederate soldiers were nearly always in the county, for concealment, for recruiting purposes, or for a dash upon their enemies. Many persecuted Southern Sympathisers and Southern soldiers escaping from northern prisons or cut off from their commands, found a temporary hiding-place in the thick undergrowth in several portions of the county. Mose Webster's most daring operations were, some of them, planned and carried out from or in Owen county. Few, if any, counties in the state furnished so many soldiers to the Confederate army, in proportion to population."

*From Collins' Historical Sketches, Vol. II, page 671.*

# Owsley County
## Booneville

Owsley County was formed in 1843 as the 96th county in order of formation of Kentucky counties. The South Fork of the Kentucky River roughly

**Faith Hill Community Center**
*Source: Tour Southern & Eastern Kentucky*

Judge William Owsley was born in Virginia in 1782; his parents moved to Lincoln County the next year. He studied law with Judge John Boyle and served in various judicial and legislative positions, as secretary of state from 1834-36.

Booneville, the county seat of Owsley County, is located on the South Fork of the Kentucky River. The site was once known as Boones Station—for Daniel Boone—and Moores Station, for a family of late 18th century settlers. Daniel Boone explored the area between 1769-71, returning in 1784 to survey about 50,000 acres. Elias Moore donated land for a seat of justice for the new county in 1843 and the town was incorporated as Booneville in 1846, in honor of Daniel Boone. John Renty Baker and John Abner were among the first settlers in Owsley County. The Bakers were involved in one of the longest and bloodiest family feuds in U.S. history. The feud lasted for 59 years and took over 100 lives before it ended.

During the Civil War, Owsley County led all Kentucky counties in the percentage of voters who enrolled in the Union army: slightly over 13 percent. Several times during the war, Union and Confederate forces passed through the county, among them the Union command of Gen. George W. Morgan as the force retreated from the Cumberland Gap to Greenup in 1862. Bands of lawless men rode into the county; in reprisal Owsley County men led similar raids into Wolfe and Breathitt counties.

Pebworth in Owsley County is the birthplace of Earle B. Combs, centerfielder for the New York Yankees from 1924-35, and coach between 1936-43. Combs helped the New York win 11 pennants and nine World Series. Combs (1899-1976) was elected to the Ky. Athletic Hall of Fame in 1963 and to the Baseball Hall of Fame in 1970.

bisects the county, flowing south to north. Despite the rugged terrain, much of the county is farmland. The county was named for Judge William Owsley, governor of Kentucky from 1844 to 1848. The elevation ranges from 650 to 1,720 feet above sea level and the county has an area of 198 square miles.

# Pendleton County
# Falmouth

Pendleton County was named after Edmund Pendleton (1721-1803), a member of the 125th Continental Congress. Nearly square in shape, it was created from portions of Campbell and Bracken counties in 1799, the 28th county in order of formation. The elevation in the county ranges from 455 to 960 feet above sea level and it has a land area of 281 square miles. The Ohio River borders Pendleton County for five miles along its northeastern border, and the South Fork and the main stream of the Licking River join at Falmouth and flow northward out of the county. The terrain consists of fertile river valleys surrounded by undulating hills.

It is thought that the first settlement in the county was at the fork of the Licking River around 1780. The settlement, which may have been known as Forks of Licking, became Falmouth, the county seat. Falmouth is located near the center of the county where the South Fork of the Licking River joins the main stem. It was chartered in 1793 and named for Falmouth, Virginia.

Licking River served as an important route for early exploration and settlement of Kentucky. In June 1780, acting under orders from British command at Detroit, Col. Henry Bird was sent to attack the frontier forts of Kentucky. His force included 300 British and Canadian rangers and between 600-1,000 American Indians including Shawnees, Ottawas, Hurons, Chippewas, Delawares, Mingoes and 'Taways. Col. Bird traveled into Pendleton County and up the Licking River. Word arrived that Gen. George Rogers Clark was

approaching, causing Bird's hasty retreat, but not before blasting the settlers' forts and stations, looting and killing hundreds. Over 400 captives were taken from Kentucky forts.

Source: John Perkins

During the Civil War two Confederate recruiters were captured and executed in the Peach Grove area of northern Pendleton County. In July 1862 a number of county citizens were arrested by Union forces during a crackdown against suspected Confederate sympathizers. In June 1863 a number of women were arrested at Demossville because they were believed to be potential spies who were "dangerous to the federal government." Falmouth was the site of a small skirmish on September 18, 1862, between 28 Confederates and 11 Home Guardsmen. Falmouth has been devastated by flooding at times throughout its history; major flooding of the Licking River in 1937, 1948, and 1964 and 1997 made flood control a major issue. Kincaid Lake State Park is an 850-acre park on Kincaid Lake, a 183-acre impoundment northeast of Falmouth.

# Perry County
# Hazard

Perry County, the 68th county in order of formation, was formed in 1821. The land surface is hilly and mountainous— elevation in the county ranges from 700 to 2,520 feet. The land abounds in timber, coal and natural gas. Perry County is drained by the north and middle forks of the Kentucky River and their tributaries.

The county and the county seat of Hazard were both named for naval hero Commodore Oliver Hazard Perry (1785-1819). Perry, the commander and hero in the battle of Lake Erie in 1813, reported the famous message: "We have met the enemy and they are ours." Victory gave the U.S. control of the lake and advanced its claims to the great Northwest. The defeat of the British on the lake was the first time in history that England had been forced to give up a naval squadron by surrender. Oliver Hazard Perry at that time was 28 years old.

The City of Hazard was founded in 1884 on land deeded to the town trustees by Elijah Combs and his wife, Sarah. Hazard has been subjected to severe flooding throughout its history. The 1957 flood was particularly disastrous.

The Civil War brought to the region an era of suffering and misery that lasted over a generation. Because the area was not of significant strategic value to either side, bands of bushwhackers roamed freely. Many of the guerillas were locals and their actions spread seeds of hatred that later led to vicious mountain feuds. A Confederate veteran, quoted in a county history, recalled the condition of Hazard when he returned from war: "the neglected farms, the roads and paths overgrown with weeds, and almost no business of any kind being carried on."

During the late 18th and early 19th century there had been some coal mining and tim-

**Buckhorn Log Cathedral**
*Source: Tour Southern & Eastern Kentucky*

bering in the mountains, but for the most part the inhabitants had mined only enough coal to heat their homes and had used logs for building houses and making tools. Any coal or timber for sale had to be floated down the Kentucky River on flatboats.

It was the railroad that opened Perry County to development. In 1911 at a time when the population of Hazard had increased to 500, the Louisville & Nashville Railroad (now CSX Transportation) extended its tracks into Perry County. By 1912 the railroad was completed and coal was being hauled out in trainloads of about 30 cars.

# Pike County
# Pikeville

Pike County, formed in 1821, was the 70th county established in order of formation. It is the easternmost county and the largest with a land area of 787.69 square miles. Elevation in the county ranges from 610 to 3,149 feet above sea level. The county is separated from West Virginia by the Tug Fork of the Big Sandy River, while the Levisa Fork of the Big Sandy bisects the county. Pine Mountain forms the border with Virginia. Pike County is part of the Central Appalachian Highlands, a well-dissected plateau with alternating steep, narrow ridges and narrow stream-made valleys extending in all directions.

The county was named for Gen. Zebulon M. Pike, the U.S. Army officer and explorer who discovered Pike's Peak. In 1805 the military commandant of the Territory of Louisiana ordered Lt. Pike on an exploring trip up the Mississippi from St Louis. Lt. Pike returned on the 30th of April, 1806 and accounts of his expeditions were published in 1810. They were of great interest to Americans, particularly to settlers west of the Mississippi.

Members of Maj. Andrew Lewis' ill-fated Big Sandy expedition of 1756 are believed to be the first recorded explorers of the area. Daniel Boone and a companion may have descended Shelby Creek in their 1767 search for the Bluegrass Region. The first known permanent settlement in Pike County was made in 1790 at the mouth of Sycamore Creek, on lower Johns Creek. By 1800 other settlements were being made on the Levisa in the vicinity of present-day Pikeville, the county seat.

Pikeville was founded in 1823 on the Levisa Fork of the Big Sandy River and was named, like the county, for Gen. Zebulon Pike. The town was always known as Pikeville, although the official name of the town and post office were Pike and Piketon at various times.

The infamous Hatfield-McCoy feud took place in Pike County and neighboring West Virginia.

**Pikeville College**
*Source: Tour Southern & Eastern Kentucky*

The feud resulted, in part, from Civil War conflicts, romantic entanglements, family-oriented discord, property and election disputes, mixed with mountain pride.

The Levisa Fork of the Big Sandy River historically encircled Pikeville, frequently flooding the city. The Pikeville Cut-through, completed in 1987, relocated the river eliminating flooding and creating additional room for development. It is one of the largest land removal projects of its time ever completed in the western hemisphere, moving a total of 12 million cubic yards of rock and dirt.

# Powell County
# Stanton

Powell County's 180.14-square-mile boundary, established in 1852 from Clark, Estill and Montgomery counties, was named for Kentucky Gov. Lazarus Powell, 1851-1855. It is located in the eastern Knobs region, between the rolling fertile Bluegrass and the hillier Cumberland Plateau with its vast stands of hardwoods (elevation 580-1,440 feet above sea level). Southeastern Powell County lies within the Daniel Boone National Forest and the Red River Gorge Geological Area. Red River meanders through the county, briefly forming the Powell-Estill County boundary before emptying into the Kentucky River between Clark and Estill counties.

The county seat is Stanton, originally called Beaver Pond. In 1852 the town and post office were renamed Stanton to honor State Representative Richard M. Stanton of Maysville. Civil War guerrillas burned the courthouse in 1863.

Iron ore was discovered in the area in the mid-1700s and one of the earliest iron forges, Red River Iron Works, was in Clay City. By 1805 it was producing quality products such as pots and nails, and cannonballs for the War of 1812. Virgin forests drew loggers to this land in the 1800s. Kentucky Union Railroad laid track in 1886 to export timber. Dana Lumber Company built a railroad tunnel in the Red River Gorge for transporting logs to a sawmill at Nada.

**Lakeside Trail**
*Source: Tour Southern & Eastern Kentucky*

Logs were floated down Red River to mills in Clay City. By 1889 Clay City had one of the largest timber processing plants in the country. It was destroyed by fire in 1906.

Powell County has no minable coal, but is a source of limestone mining and clay brick manufacturing, which are still in operation. The Clay City National Bank, built in 1889 from local brick, now houses the Red River Historical Society Museum.

The Louisville & Nashville Railroad Company offered passenger-train excursions to see the natural wonders of the area. With the decline of the lumber industry the rail lines were abandoned. Land (1,900 acres) for the Natural Bridge State Resort Park was donated to the state in 1926; it was the second park added to the state park system. All rail lines in the county were removed in 1942 to help the war effort.

The four lane Bert T. Combs Mountain Parkway opened to traffic in 1963. Two first ladies have visited here: Eleanor Roosevelt (1937) and Lady Bird Johnson (1967). Harriette Simpson Arnow, author of "The Dollmaker," attended Stanton Academy, a United Presbyterian Church school operated from 1908-1931. Sara Walter Combs, chief judge of the Kentucky Court of Appeals, resides here, as did her late husband, Gov. Bert Combs. Internationally known horse trainer Woody Stephens was born in Powell County.

# Pulaski County
## Somerset

Pulaski County, the 27th in order of formation, was formed in 1799 from portions of Green and Lincoln counties. It was named for Casimir Pulaski, a Polish patriot and soldier of liberty. He came to the U.S. when he learned of the colonies' fight for freedom—Gen. Pulaski was killed in action in 1779. The county is drained by the Cumberland and Rockcastle Rivers, and by South Fork, White Oak, Buck, Pitman, and Fishing Creeks. The elevation in the county ranges from 723 to 1,680 feet above sea level; it has a land area of 662 square miles, making it the third largest county in the state.

Somerset was established as the county seat in 1801. This site was picked because of the nearby Old Town Spring; the path to it became the town's most traveled street in order to drink from the spring. Thus a saying became popular, "Whoever drinks from the Old Town Spring will have wisdom and will always return to Somerset." Somerset was first named Point Isabel. It was settled 1800 by pioneers from the Carolinas and Virginia in 1800 (or thereabouts).

During the Civil War the Union Army set up a troop rendezvous and supply base here as a prelude to the East Tennessee campaign of Gen. Ambrose E. Burnside. The area became known as Camp Burnside in official dispatches and the name Burnside was retained after war. The Battle of Mill Springs was fought in Pulaski County. In the first hour, Gen. Zollicoffer was killed, which threw his Confederate regiments into confusion. Rallied by Gen. Crittenden, the battle continued for three hours. After Union reinforcements arrived, the Confederate forces retreated, fighting all day to reach the river. They evacuated camp during the night and withdrew into Tennessee.

A portion of Lake Cumberland lies within Pulaski County. It is one of the ten largest man-made lakes in the country. The lake covers over 63,000 acres with more than 1,200 miles of shoreline.

John Sherman Cooper (1901-1991)—lawyer, Army officer, diplomat, ambassador, consummate

**Clock on Somerset Town Square**
*Photo: Sid Webb*

statesman, and senator from Kentucky—was born in Somerset on August 23, 1901. He attended public schools at Somerset, Centre College, Yale College and Harvard Law School. Sen. Cooper was admitted to the bar in 1928 and commenced practice in his hometown. He was known as a liberal republican; his years of service in the senate were: 1946-1949; 1952-1955; 1956-1973.

Author Harriet Simpson Arnow and Edith Pearl Fitzgerald, a Broadway screenwriter and actress, are among the well-known people that have lived in Pulaski County.

# Robertson County
## Mount Olivet

Robertson County was formed in 1867, the 111th county created in the state. Elevation in the county ranges from 550 to 1,009 feet above sea level and it contains 100 square miles of mostly rolling hills. It is the least populous and second smallest county in the state. It was named for George Robertson (1790-1874), who served Kentucky and the U.S. with an illustrious career of public service; an attorney, he represented Kentucky

Robertson County Courthouse is listed on the National Register of Historic Places and is one of the few original courthouses in the state still in use
Source: Robertson County web site

**Simon Kenton**
Source: Kentucky Historical Society

times. The Indians called him "the man whose gun is never empty," because he was so adept at reloading his flintlock on the run. Long before Kenton and Boone came to the region, it was crossed by the old "Buffalo Trail," a well-worn trail used by American Indians from the north on their hunting forays into Kentucky.

MountOlivet, thecountyseat, was founded about 1820 and its name is of biblical origin. It is popularly thought that the original name was although this has not been documented. On Aug. 19, 1782, the bloody Battle of Blue Licks was fought by Kentucky pioneers against a superior force of American Indians and British-Canadians. It was the last major battle of the Revolutionary War. The battle occurred almost 10 months after the surrender of British Commander Cornwallis. The battle was a decisive victory for a force of 1,000 British regulars and Indians over 180 Kentucky militiamen.

in the U.S. Congress from 1817-21. Robertson County was formed from parts of Bracken, Harrison, Mason, Nicholas and Fleming counties.

The primary explorer and early protector of this region was Simon Kenton. Kenton, a contemporary of Daniel Boone, was captured by Shawnee Indians in 1778. They roped him, hands tied, to a galloping horse. He was also forced to run the "gauntlet" nine

On his last Kentucky raid, Confederate Gen. John Hunt Morgan and his Raiders entered the state on June 1, 1864, took Mt. Sterling on June 8, lost it on the 9th, and took Lexington on the l0th and Cynthiana on the 11th. Union forces, under Gen. S. G. Burbridge defeated the Raiders the next day. Morgan retreated through Robertson County, reaching Virginia on June 20.

# Rockcastle County
# Mount Vernon

Rockcastle County is often referred to as part of the foothills of the Appalachians. Created in 1810, Rockcastle County became the 52nd county in the state. One of only two counties not named after a person, it was named for the 75-mile long river that forms its southeastern boundary. The Rockcastle River was in turn named after a towering cliff called Castle Rock in 1767 by Isaac Lindsey, a hunter from South Carolina.

Dr. Thomas Walker passed through Rockcastle in 1750 on his foray to locate land for the Loyal Land Company of Virginia. Daniel Boone crossed here on his way to establish Fort Boonesboro in 1774. The game trail followed by Boone, known as the Wilderness Road, and another trail, the Madison branch, were improved to accommodate the large influx of settlers that would help lead Kentucky to statehood in 1792.

One of the earliest industries in the county was the manufacturing of saltpeter, a key ingredient in gunpowder. Today the remnants of this industry can be viewed at Great Saltpetre Cave. The manufacture of gunpowder played an important role in the War of 1812.

The Civil War divided Rockcastle households as it did much of the country. Because of the topography many landowners did not have large farms and slavery was on a much smaller scale than in the south. It is because of these two facts that most of the sons of Rockcastle fought for the Union. The first Civil War skirmish in Kentucky took place across the Rockcastle River at Wildcat Mountain on October 21, 1861. This section of modern Laurel County was originally part of Rockcastle County.

Rockcastle's share of prosperity came with the extension of railroad lines through the county after the Civil War. The natural resources of the county were virtually untouched until the railroad allowed timber, coal, limestone and agricultural products to be economically shipped out of the region.

**Quilters' Haven at Mount Vernon**
*Source: Tour Southern & Eastern Kentucky*

After the railroads, highways were built. In 1918 the Boone Way Association established a road that connected Mount Vernon, Livingston and Brodhead. This road followed roughly the path of the old Wilderness Trail; later this road would become US Highway 25. In the 1970s Interstate 75 was completed through the county, which revolutionized travel through the region and made it possible for Rockcastle residents to find work outside of the county and yet maintain their lifestyle and farms.

Mount Vernon, the county seat, was originally named White Rock; the name was changed to Mount Vernon to honor the residence of George Washington. The post office here was established in 1811 and the town was incorporated in 1818.

Daniel Boone National Forest, the only national forest completely within the boundary of Kentucky, was established in 1937—over 16,000 acres in Rockcastle County (non-contiguous) are set aside for recreation and conservation.

# Rowan County
# Morehead

Rowan County was formed in 1856 as the 104th county in Kentucky, from portions of Morgan and Fleming counties. The county was named in honor of Judge John Rowan (1773-1843), a distinguished attorney and judge who was a member of the U.S. House of Representatives and Senate. Judge Rowan served as the first president of the Ky. Historical Society, 1838-1843. He was buried

*Source: SouthEast Telephone*

at his home, Federal Hill in Bardstown, where it is believed his nephew Stephen Foster was inspired to write "My Old Kentucky Home." The county ranges in elevation from 625 to 1,435 feet above sea level in a land area of 281 square miles.

The county seat of Morehead was first known as Triplett. It was renamed for Charles Morehead, Kentucky governor from 1855-1859. Although the area was settled beginning in the early part of the 19th century, the city was not founded until 1856, when the county was formed.

During the Civil War, Gen. John Hunt Morgan and his Raiders camped here on their disastrous last raid into Kentucky. The Raiders took Mt. Sterling, Lexington and Cynthiana, but on June 12,

1864 Gen. S. G. Burbridge dispersed the Raiders. They never recovered from this defeat. As in many Kentucky counties, it was brother against brother and neighbor against neighbor. The courthouse was burned in 1864.

Bitterness and violence in Rowan County continued after the war—erupting again in 1884 in a conflict named the Tolliver-Marin Feud or Rowan County War, which continued until 1887. Deep-rooted political tensions over a circuit judge's race eventually resulted in a three-year period of violence, resulting in over 20 deaths and one faction seizing virtual control of the county. The state militia was sent in three times to restore order, and a state report suggested that Rowan County be abolished.

Moonlight Schools originated in Rowan County in 1911, the creation of by Mrs. Cora W. Stewart, "to emancipate from illiteracy those enslaved in its bondage." Volunteer rural teachers opened several of the schools throughout the county. The schools were open on evenings after day's work was done, but only on moonlit nights to facilitate travel to and from the schools in the dark. Teachers were hoping for 150 students, but 1,200 attended the first night.

On July 4, 1939, a tremendous flash flood struck Morehead. Twenty-five people drowned with property damage estimated at $5 million. A floodwall was built in order to prevent a repeat of the disastrous flooding. In 1973 the Army Corp of Engineers completed the Cave Run dam—the resulting Cave Run Lake, on the western edge of Rowan County, is over 8,000 acres in size and has been called the "Muskie Capital of the South."

# Russell County
# Jamestown

Formed in 1826 Russell County was the 81st county created in Kentucky. It is located on both sides of the Cumberland River, with a surface that is generally hilly and broken. The level bottom lands on the Cumberland are very fertile. It has an elevation ranging from 530 to 1,140 feet above sea level and a land area of 253.53 square miles. Russell County was named in honor of Col. William Russell. Russell fought in the Revolutionary War and participated in the American Indian campaigns of 1791 and 1794. Russell, a native of Virginia, moved to Kentucky after the war of Independence; he represented Kentucky in the legislature for 13 sessions (1792-1823).

Jamestown, the county seat of Russell County, was established in 1826. The land was donated by James Woodridge and was originally named Jacksonville in honor of Andrew Jackson. However, the name was changed to Jamestown in honor of James Woodridge. The Jamestown post office was opened in 1826.

Russell County saw action during the Civil War. In December 1861 Union Col. Frank Wolford and troops guarded forage collected and stored by Lieut. Silas Adams. On July 4, 1862 Col. Wolford and troops marched to Lebanon after staying in Russell County.

**County Courthouse at Jamestown, 1942**
*Photo: George Goodman, Kentucky Virtual Library*

On April 19, 1863, U.S. Lt. Col. William Riley ordered to Creelsboro to scout enemy strength. He surprised Confederate troops, taking 12 prisoners. On December 31, 1863, Union troops under Lt. Col. A. J. Cropsey arrived at Creelsboro with two gunboats and 40 sharpshooters. On November 22, 1861, Confederate Gen. Felix Zollicoffer reached Jamestown, anxious to secure a strong defensive position on Cumberland River to protect approaches to southeastern Ky. His plan to seize nine ferryboats along the river was defeated.

The county was the site of early industry along Greasy Creek. In addition to a paper mill, there were the Alex Dick and Geo. Lewis meat house, 1785; a grist mill, 1799; an iron furnace and forge, 1824; the Wooldridge's Roller Mill; a cotton and two woolen mills. The Farmers Woolen Mill, owned and operated by Esco Reese, was in operation until late 1940.

In the summer of 1888 a brilliant stone was found on the farm of Henry Burris. It was appraised as a gem-quality diamond, octahedral in form and 0.776 carat in weight. G. A. Schultz, the Louisville jeweler who appraised it, bought the stone for $20. The diamond is now on display in the Smithsonian Institution. No other diamonds have been found in area, although many have searched.

# Scott County
# Georgetown

Scott County, the 11th county formed in Kentucky and the 2nd after Kentucky achieved statehood, was created in 1792 out of a portion of Woodford County. It was named for Gen. Charles Scott, 1739-1813, an officer in the Revolutionary War and the fourth governor of Kentucky. The county has a land area of 285 square miles and ranges in elevation from 690 to 1,060 feet above sea level.

The county seat of Georgetown, originally George Town, was named after George Washington. It became a settlement in 1782 under the name of Lebanon, Virginia, and was renamed in 1790. Elijah Craig, a businessman and Baptist minister founded the town—building a sawmill, a gristmill and a fabric mill. He is considered the originator of Kentucky bourbon.

Early natives lived in Scott County as long as 10,000 years ago, hunting and fishing along the banks of Elkhorn Creek. There are a number of mounds from the Adena culture, who lived in the area from about 800 B.C. to 800 A.D. The first known exploration by non-natives was John Floyd's survey expedition from Virginia in 1774.

The Scott County town of Stamping Ground was named for the vast buffalo herds that had stamped down the ground around the spring. William McConnell and Charles Lecompte explored the area in April 1775.

The first Confederate governor of Kentucky,

George W. Johnson, was born in 1811 in Scott Co. An aide to Gen. John C. Breckinridge, Johnson fought and was killed as a private in the Battle of Shiloh, while still governor. Gen. John Hunt Morgan and his Raiders camped in Scott County during their July 1862 raid, destroying bridges, Union supplies and routing Home Guards.

Scott County is home to Toyota Motor Manufacturing Kentucky, which opened in 1986. It is the largest manufacturing facility of Toyota Motor Corp. In September 2006, TMMK reached a milestone when the five-millionth Camry rolled off the assembly line. The Camry has been the number one selling sedan in America in eight of the last nine years. The 2007 Camry hybrid, the first Toyota hybrid vehicle to be produced in North America, is under production.

Horses and tobacco have historically been important in the county. Scott County farms have been home to three Kentucky Derby winners: Kingman, Venetian Way and Winning Colors. The county is also known for producing the finest American Saddlebred horses. Scott county farms were among the first in the state to practice crop diversification, changing from tobacco to beef cattle and vegetables.

**Scott County Courthouse in Georgetown**
*Photo: Sid Webb*

# Shelby County
## Shelbyville

Formed from a part of Jefferson County, Shelby County was the third county established after Kentucky became a state in 1792. The county was named in honor of Isaac Shelby (1750-1826), Kentucky's first governor. Shelby served in the Revolutionary War, the American Indian campaigns and the War of 1812. He came to Kentucky in 1783 and was a member of the Danville constitutional conventions of 1784-92. Shelby County has a land area of 384.19 square miles and an elevation ranging from 550 to 1,188 feet above sea level.

Shelbyville, the county seat, was founded in 1792 and was also named for Gov. Isaac Shelby. The Shelbyville post office was opened in 1801. Shelbyville made the national press when Gen. Marquis de Lafayette and his entourage visited, dined and danced here in 1825. It was a return to the young republic for the noted Frenchman, a sentimental return to the country that he had fought for and helped create 50 years previously. Lafayette's visit occurred on May 13, 1825, during a trip to Frankfort and Lexington. Henry Clay and Judge John Rowan were in the party. An honorary guard of cavalry accompanied the procession out of Louisville and east on the old road through Middletown to Shelbyville. Adverse weather or difficult roads probably caused the overnight stop in Shelbyville.

In late October 1809 William Clark, his wife Julia, and their infant son, Meriwether Lewis Clark, were traveling through Shelbyville on their way home in Virginia. While eating lunch, Clark read in a Frankfort newspaper, The Argus of Western America, that expedition partner Meriwether Lewis had apparently killed himself 17 days earlier near Nash-

ville, Tennessee. Clark then wrote a heartfelt letter that night to his brother, Jonathan Clark, in Louisville about the newspaper article. Clark penned the letter to his brother at Shannon's Tavern in the

**Shelby County Courthouse**
*Source: SouthEast Telephone*

tiny community of Graefenburg in eastern Shelby County.

Former Gov. Martha Layne Collins, in her foreword to The New History of Shelby County wrote, "Shelby County is a special place. From the days when Indians roamed the forests, savannas, and waterways of what is now Kentucky to the present day, Shelby County has grown, developed and changed. Throughout these many years, history has been made which has created the character of this place, influencing its landscape, its people, its economy, its education, and the quality of life. Several years ago, the Shelby County Chamber of Commerce adopted a slogan, 'Good People, Good Land, Good Living.' The history of Shelby County is woven tightly into all three of these components."

# Simpson County
## Franklin

Simpson County was formed in 1819 out of portions of Logan, Warren and Allen counties, the 63rd county formed in Kentucky. The county contains 236 square miles of predominately rolling farm land. It ranges in elevation from

**Mule Days**
*Source: Simpson County archive file*

490 to 928 feet above sea level, and is drained by the Red and Big Barren rivers. The namesake of the county was Capt. John Simpson, one of Kentucky's officers in the War of 1812. He was one of nine officers killed at Battle of River Raisin in January 1813, for each of whom a Kentucky county was named. Captain Simpson also fought under "Mad Anthony" Wayne in the 1794 Battle of Fallen Timbers.

The southern border of Kentucky (except in the western portion of the state) is generally a straight east-west line. In Simpson County the border takes an almost triangular jag south—the origination of the jag is unknown, but there are several rumored explanations. One of the stories concerns Sanford Duncan, who lived near the border. Not wanting his

land divided by a state border, he plied the surveyors with food and drink. His hospitality worked: his land remained intact, all in Kentucky.

The county seat of Franklin was established in 1819 and named in honor of Benjamin Franklin. Three sites were considered, with an adequate water source a primary consideration. The owner of one site, William Hudspeth, dug a well on his land but it was dry. He secretly hauled water to fill the well and his site was chosen. Remarkably, the water primed the well and it served for many years.

During the Civil War, Confederate Gen. N. B. Forrest's cavalry camped on the farm of Stephen T. Barnes, a Union sympathizer, for three days in September 1862. Barnes claimed, the famished cavalrymen "ate him out of house and home." Forrest's cavalry was part of Gen. Braxton Bragg's invasion.

Confederate soldier Marcellus Jerome Clarke, later known as guerrilla "Sue Mundy" is buried in Simpson County. He enlisted in the Confederate Army in 1861 at age 17 and became part of Morgan's Cavalry in 1863. In 1865 he was captured, taken to Louisville and hanged, court-martialed as a guerrilla. His last words were "I believe in and die for the Confederate cause."

The best-known native of the county may be Col. Jim Bowie, who died in 1836 at the Alamo in Texas. Famous for his "Bowie Knife," he was born in Logan County in a part that is now Simpson County. Television and film actress Annie Potts is also a Simpson County native.

# Spencer County
## Taylorsville

Spencer county was formed in 1824 as the 77th county in the state. It was formed from portions of Bullitt, Nelson and Shelby counties. The county contains 186 square miles and ranges in elevation from 420 to 880 feet above sea level. The topography is rolling to hilly, with valleys as much as 250 feet deep cut by the Salt River. The county was named after Capt. Spear Spencer, who was born in Pennsylvania and moved to Kentucky in 1792, after Kentucky became a state. Capt. Spencer was a member of the "Cornstalk Militia," which, due to a shortage of rifles, drilled using corn stalks. Leading a unit known as Spencer's "Yellow Jackets," he joined Gen. William Henry Harrison's command in the Tippecanoe campaign, where he was killed in battle in November 1811.

Taylorsville is the county seat of Spencer County. It was founded in the late 1700s at the fork of the Salt River and Brashears Creek, and incorporated in 1829. The town was founded by and named for Richard Taylor, a miller, who owned and donated the tract of land on which the town was established. The first non-native settlers in the area of present-day Taylorsville arrived by boat up the Salt River.

There were no major battles in Spencer County during the Civil War, but considerable guerilla activity did occur. William Quantrill, sometimes under the alias Capt. Clarke, was the most notorious. He led several dozen men into Kentucky in January 1865. They raided a number of towns such as Danville, Hartford and Hustonsville over a four-month period. Federal troops were unable to apprehend Quantrill, so Union guerilla Edwin Terrill was hired for the job. Terrill and his men surrounded Quantrill's group in a barn in May 1865. Quantrill attempted to escape but he was severely wounded and captured. Although sentenced to hang, he died of his wounds at Louisville Military Prison Hospital.

Taylorsville Lake, impounded in 1982,

**Taylorsville Park**
*Source: Kentucky Department of Tourism*

was constructed on the Salt River by the Army Corps of Engineers to prevent the periodic flooding of Taylorsville. In addition to its flood-control value, the 3,050-acre lake provides excellent fishing and boating opportunities.

Spencer County was an agricultural county from the days of the first settlers. Primary crops in early times included corn, wheat, barley, livestock and hay. Later, tobacco became the major cash crop.

Spencer County, due in part to its proximity to Louisville, is the fastest growing county in Kentucky.

# Taylor County
# Campbellsville

Taylor County, the 100th county in order of formation, was named for Mexican War hero Gen. Zachary Taylor, who later became the 12th U.S. president. Taylor County was formed by the Kentucky legislature from Green County on March 1, 1848. The topography of Taylor County is gently undulating, in some places broken and hilly. The county is well timbered, and well watered by Pitman and Robinson creeks, and on the south by Green River. Elevation in the county ranges from 570 to 1,200 feet above sea level. The county has a land area of 269.83 square miles.

Campbellsville, the county seat, is situated just north of Green River Lake State Park. It was settled beginning around 1808 and established in 1817. The name is from brothers Adam and Andrew Campbell, who owned the site. The Campbellsville post office opened in 1817.

**Zachary Taylor**

Two early pioneers, Thomas Denton and William Stewart, built cabins on Sinking Creek, now called Pitman Creek, in 1780. Cumberland Trace was used by American Indians, hunters, and settlers alike. Years later, the Lexington and Nashville Road replaced the Cumberland Trace—and became the main route for stagecoaches delivering U.S. mail. According to Collins' Historical Sketches, the first settlers were almost entirely from Virginia and North Carolina; and about 150 families of "thrifty Pennsylvania farmers" settled in the county in 1869-1770.

Sanders Tavern, located about six miles east of Campbellsville, was owned and operated by Henry Sanders, Jr., as early as 1814. The 30-room inn was a famous stop for the six-horse stage coaches traveling the old Lexington and Nashville Road. Many notable persons were guests at the tavern, the most prominent of whom was Pres. Andrew Jackson on his way to Washington, September 27, 1832.

During the Civil War, Camps Hobson and Andy Johnson were both established in Taylor County. In December 1864, guerillas attacked Federal soldiers stationed at Campbellsville; and at another time made a charge on the town killing two Federal soldiers before resistance was effectual. On July 4, 1863, near Green River bridge on the Lebanon and Columbia turnpike, in the south corner of Taylor County, occurred one of the bravest assaults but bloodiest repulses of the war—the Confederate forces being driven off, with terrible slaughter, in only half an hour. The courthouse at Campbellsville was burned December 25, 1864 by Confederate forces.

The Army Corps of Engineers impounded the Green River in 1969 to control flooding in the basins of the Green and the Ohio rivers. Green River Lake State Park is considered a recreational paradise with its 8,200-acre lake.

# Todd County
# Elkton

When settlers in Logan and Christian counties asked the Kentucky Legislature to create a new county, the General Assembly formed Todd County on December 30, 1819. For years these settlers had found it almost impossible to reach the county seats of justice, so they were pleased. Todd County, the 64th county of Kentucky, was named in honor of Col. John Todd, a famous frontiersman who was instrumental in the creation of the new county.

Records show that early settlers arrived in the southern part of the county, west of what is now Guthrie, and built a fort similar to those in central Kentucky. Today, there is no trace of this fort. Elkton, the seat of Todd county, was settled early in the 19th century and named for the Elk Fork of Red River. The original town on Elk Fork was established about 1817 but was moved about one-half mile west in 1820 after the formation of the county.

Several localities were considered in deciding upon a county seat—Old Elkton, established in 1818 on Fork Creek and in a central location; Newburg, with a hotel and a site between Hopkinsville and Russellville; and New Elkton. After a bitter battle—almost a duel—Elkton was designated as county seat in May of 1820.

Todd is bounded on the south by the Tennessee line and is roughly oblong—about 30-miles long and 12-miles wide. Comprising 376.35 square miles, with land varying from 405 to 966 feet above sea level, the county is well-watered by Elk, West and East forks of Pond River, Whippoorwill, and Big, Little, and West Clifty creeks. The south and a portion of the north part of the county are level or gently rolling—the soil is based upon limestone and very productive, while the remainder is rolling and hilly, the soil of inferior quality but producing fine grass.

Robert Penn Warren—the first official poet laureate of the U.S.—was born in Guthrie on April 24, 1905. In 2005 our nation celebrated the 100th anniversary of Warren's birth. A Literary Arts series stamp was issued to recognize the achievements of Warren, a three-time recipient of the Pulitzer Prize, and the only writer to win the prize in poetry as well as fiction, "All the King's Men" in 1947. "All the King's Men" was adapted for film in 1949, and became an award-winning movie starring Broderick Crawford. The movie was remade in 2006 and featured leading stars Sean Penn, Jude Law, Anthony Hopkins and Kate Winslet.

## Well, I never...

Col. Todd's widow told this story after his death: "That, during the winter succeeding their marriage [in 1780], the provisions of the fort at Lexington became exhausted to such an extent, that, on her husband's return home with George [his aid] one night, almost famished with hunger, she had been able to save for him a small piece of bread, about two inches square, and about a gill of milk, which she presented to him; on which he asked, if there was nothing for George? She answered, 'not a mouthful.' He called George, and handed him the bread and the milk, without taking any of it for himself."

*Collins' Historical Sketches of Kentucky, Vol. II, page 730.*

# Trigg County
## Cadiz

Trigg County was established in 1820, the 66th county formed in the state. Trigg County, carved out of parts of Christian and Caldwell counties. It was named in honor of Col. Stephen Trigg, a native of Virginia who came to Kentucky in the fall of 1779, as a member of the court of land commissioners. In the spring of 1780 he returned to make a home. Col Trigg settled a station at the mouth of Dick's River; he died two years later at the battle of Blue Licks on Aug. 19, 1782.

The first census of 1820 listed Trigg County's population at 3,874 inhabitants. The first government was organized on May 15, 1820.

Trigg County is bordered on the south by the state of Tennessee. Nearly triangular in shape, it has about 443 square miles. The Cumberland River flows through the southwester part of the county, about eight and one-half miles from the Tennessee River. The surface is varied, from generally broken, but not mountainous, with rich and productive river and creek bottoms, and in parts hilly and undulating with a portion called barrens, which is highly cultivated. The soil is based on limestone, with red clay foundation. Elevation in the county ranges from 359 to 813 feet above sea level.

Nathan Futrell, reputed to be the youngest drummer boy in War of the American Revolution, came to Kentucky in 1799 and settled on Ford's Creek in 1820 where he farmed, set out the first apple orchard, built one of area's first grist mills, and was an official surveyor.

Cadiz, the seat of Trigg county, is located on the Little River. The area was settled late in the 18th century and Cadiz was established in 1820 to provide the county seat, although it was not immediately accepted as such. Unfortunately, the origin of the name is obscure.

During the Civil War, a man by the name of Jack Hinson swore revenge against the Union Army when two sons were executed as bushwhackers in 1862. From ambush he shot men in blue uniforms on gunboats and on land. Soon, there was a price on his head, but Hinson continued his vendetta until the close of the war. He guided Confederate Gen. Nathan Bedford Forrest of Tennessee in his last campaign in the area in the fall of 1864.

Trigg County lies within the Land Between the Lakes, a designated national recreation area under the management of the USDA Forest Service. When the Cumberland and Tennessee rivers were impounded to create Kentucky Lake and Lake Barkley, an inland peninsula was formed. In 1963, Pres. John F. Kennedy designated the peninsula Land Between The Lakes National Recreation Area to demonstrate how an area with limited timber, agricultural and industrial resources could be converted into a recreation asset that would stimulate economic growth in the region.

# Trimble County
# Bedford

Trimble County lies along the south bank of the Ohio River, and opposite Madison, Indiana. The Kentucky General Assembly established Trimble County in 1836, taking lands from Henry, Oldham, and Gallatin Counties; it was the 86th in order of formation. The new county lay on the banks of the Ohio River in the midst of rolling hills and almost midway between Louisville and Cincinnati. It was named for the Kentucky lawyer and U.S. Supreme Court Justice, Robert Trimble, who was appointed to the Supreme Court by Pres. John Quincy Adams in 1826. The formal government of Trimble County was first organized on March 27, 1837.

Two incorporated towns of Trimble County are quite historic. The river town of Milton, one of the oldest towns in Kentucky, was established by the Virginia Legislature in 1789, three years before Kentucky became a state. Milton was briefly the county seat, but yielded in 1837 to Bedford, first settled in 1805 by Richard Ball and chartered by Kentucky in 1816. Bedford was named in honor of Bedford, Virginia.

Trimble County was the scene of two of the most dramatic events in the history of early Kentucky: the flow of immigrants into Kentucky on flatboats to settle along the Ohio River and the flight of slaves through the "underground railroad" to freedom in the territory of the North. Abolitionist Delia Webster ran one such underground railroad station, on land bought with funds provided by Northern abolitionists in 1854. Slaveholders filed charges against her—Webster refused to leave Kentucky and was imprisoned. Following her release she was indicted again but escaped into Indiana.

Trimble County is now bordered on the southwest by Oldham County, the southeast by Henry, on the east by Carroll, and the west and north by the Ohio River—a felicitous location in the Outer Bluegrass. Containing only 148.85 square miles, it is therefore one of the smallest. Ranging from 420 to 970 feet above sea level, the land is hilly and

fertile, and the major crops have been tobacco, blackberries, corn, wheat, oats, hogs, and cattle. Tobacco production, as might be expected, is dwindling.

Mineral springs were discovered around 1840

...but the stormy life of a politician not being congenial to his disposition or taste, he (Judge Robert Trimble) ever afterwards refused to be a candidate for political office...

by Mr. and Mrs. Noah Parker, who found the water unusual in taste and of medicinal value. The Parkers soon erected the Bedford Springs and Hotel. The Parkers owned and managed the noted antebellum health resort, which fostered Bedford's growth. After the 1851 cholera epidemic, the resort declined. The former hotel burned in 1967.

# *Union County*
# *Morganfield*

Union county, the 55th formed in the state, was taken entirely from the western part of Henderson County, in 1811. Elevation in the county ranges from 320 to 673 feet above sea level, 637 in a land area of 345.10 square miles. It is bordered by the Ohio and Tradewater rivers, and Crittenden, Henderson, and Webster counties. The origin of the name is in doubt; but the general opinion is that it was so named because of the hearty unanimity with which the people assented to the proposed division of the old county. The

**Camp Breckinridge Museum & Arts Center**
*Source: Kentucky Department of Tourism*

face of the country is level, undulating, and in some parts hilly. The soil is good.

Morganfield, the seat of Union County, is located near the center of the county at the intersection of US 60 and KY 56. It was established in 1812 with the new county and named Morgan's Field for General Daniel Morgan. The Morganfield Court House post office opened in 1813. Abraham Lincoln's only political speech in his native state was delivered in Union County in 1840, at age 31. An elector from Illinois, he campaigned for Whig presidential candidate William Henry Harrison. From Shawneetown, across river, Lincoln led the parade. Young ladies

rode on floats drawn by white horses; a cannon discharged for a salute burst upon firing. Its breech is at the Kentucky Historical Society.

Many Native American burial and ceremonial mounds have been found in Union County. Relic collectors raided the graves, with more than 1,000 of the graves desecrated in 1987—the Kentucky legislature designated such activity a felony in 1988. A reburial ceremony for recovered remains was held in 1988 by an estimated 200 Native American Indians.

Union County was settled during the westward migration following the Revolutionary War. Numerous towns were incorporated along the Ohio River including the towns of Sturgis, Morgantown (the county seat), and Waverly.

Union countians were predominantly sympathetic to the Confederate cause—the slave population is estimated at over 2,000 in 1860. In July 1862 Union troops from a Federal gunboat on the Ohio River arrived in Caseyville and imprisoned all the residents, charging them with treason. Confederate Col. Nathan Bedford Forrest and his command entered the county in late 1861. On September 1, 1862, a Union detachment was defeated in a skirmish at Morganfield.

Nearby coal fields in Sturgis supplied fuel to power the steamboat Robert E. Lee in a race against the Natchez in 1870. Hailed as the greatest race in river history, the competition began in New Orleans and ended at St. Louis. Robert E. Lee won the championship of Mississippi River by six hours and 15 minutes. Both steamboat captains were natives of Kentucky.

Samuel Casey (1788-1859), a resident of Caseyville, served as the treasurer of U.S. from 1853-59, under Presidents Pierce and Buchanan.

# Warren County
# Bowling Green

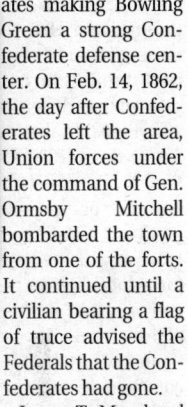

Warren County, the 24th formed in the state, was established in 1796 and named in honor of Gen. Joseph Warren, the hero of Bunker Hill. Big Barren River, which heads near the Cumberland River, runs through this county. The face of the country is gently undulating; the soil is fertile and productive, based mostly on red clay and limestone foundation. Warren County embraces about 545 square miles and elevation in the county ranges from 395 to 955 feet above sea level.

Maj. Gen. Joseph Warren, M.D., in honor of whom this county was named, was a distinguished patriot of the American Revolutionary war. He was born at Roxbury, near Bos-

**Kentucky Library & Museum (left) operates the 1815 Log House (above) located next door**
*Source: Kentucky Library & Museum*

because of its location on the Barren River and that river's link to the Mississippi River and the markets downriver in New Orleans.

Bowling Green was named the state capital of the Confederate State of Kentucky at the convention in Russellville on Nov. 20, 1861. Nine hills were fortified by the Confederates making Bowling Green a strong Confederate defense center. On Feb. 14, 1862, the day after Confederates left the area, Union forces under the command of Gen. Ormsby Mitchell bombarded the town from one of the forts. It continued until a civilian bearing a flag of truce advised the Federals that the Confederates had gone.

James T. Morehead (1797-1854), an attorney in Bowling Green, was Kentucky's first native son to become governor. He was born in Bullitt County, reared in Logan County, and read law under John J. Crittenden. Morehead served in the Ky. House of Representatives and was elected lieutenant governor. At Gov. John Breathitt's death, Morehead became chief executive, 1834-1836.

ton, in 1741—the son of a farmer, he entered Harvard University at age 14. Maj. Warren was killed by a random shot at the battle of Bunker Hill, in Boston, on June 17,1775.

Bowling Green, the seat of Warren County, is located on the Barren River. Bowling Green was founded in 1796 by Robert Moore who built a cabin at the Big Spring located there. This spring was the nucleus around which the town grew. Moore, his brother, George, and James Stewart posted a bond of 1,000 English pounds to establish the town in 1797. The town was originally named "Bolin Green," traditionally because of bowling grounds located on the site (or the name may be from Bowling Green, Virginia). In 1802 the post office opened as Bowling Green. Bowling Green first flourished

The first railroad in Kentucky ran from Bowling Green to the Double Springs on Green River. Reports indicate it was over a mile long, and was built about 1832 by James R. Skiles and Jacob Vanmeter.

The National Corvette Museum in Bowling Green features more than 50 Corvettes set in their own era. The Kentucky Museum and Library, located on the campus of Western Kentucky University, houses a rich collection of educational exhibits about Kentucky's history and heritage.

# Washington County Springfield

Washington County was formed in 1792, the first Kentucky county formed after Kentucky became a state, and the 10th overall. It was named for George Washington, who was then president of the United States. It has a land area of 301 square miles and an elevation ranging from 475 to 1,020 feet above sea level. The Salt River flows through and along the northern and northwestern border. Beech Fork also runs through the county and was important to early settlers.

Springfield, the county seat, was founded in 1793 by Matthew Walton, a legislator and Revolutionary War veteran. It was named for a local spring and is one of the oldest towns in Kentucky. The courthouse was built in 1816 and is the oldest in the state still in use. Among the records stored there is the marriage certificate of Pres. Abraham Lincoln's parents,

Source: SouthEast Telephone

Thomas and Nancy Hanks Lincoln. Thomas Lincoln's father, Abraham, Sr., and his family settled in the Beech Fork area of Washington County in 1782. Lincoln Homestead State Park, seven miles north, now marks the site of the log house where Reverend Jesse Head performed the marriage on June 12, 1806.

Settlers from Fort Harrod arrived in the area in 1775 in search of abundant game and salt. Sandusky's Station and Cartwright's Station were the earliest settlements. Subsequent settlers followed the Wilderness Trace, which stretched from the Cumberland Gap to Bardstown.

During the Civil War, Confederate Gen. John H. Morgan's cavalry moved through Springfield on raids in July and December 1862, and in July 1863. After the third raid Morgan's forces brought back Union prisoners from Ohio. The prisoners were released here so the Confederate troops could move faster. Both Confederate and Union forces moved through Springfield prior to the October 1862 Battle of Perryville—the Confederate force of 16,000 just passed through, but Union Gen. Buell made his headquarters there.

Saint Catharine College, founded in 1931, is a small liberal arts college. It is an independent, co-educational college founded in the traditions of the Catholic Church and the history and ministries of the Dominican orders. The Kentucky Sisters of Saint Dominic established the first school in a converted still house in 1823. In 1839 the Sisters applied for and obtained a charter to grant educational degrees. In 1904 a disastrous fire razed the Academy's building. A decision was made to immediately rebuild on a site adjacent to Bardstown Road. A statue marks the spot of the original building. The Academy grew into a Normal School and became the immediate forerunner of today's Saint Catharine College.

# Wayne County
# Monticello

Wayne County, the 43rd county in order of formation, was created in 1800. The South Fork of the Cumberland River bisects the county and a portion of Lake Cumberland provides hundreds of miles of shoreline in Wayne County. The county was named in honor of Revolutionary War officer "Mad Anthony" Wayne. Wayne's forces captured Stony Point, New Jersey in 1779, earning him a gold medal from Congress. He also negotiated the Treaty of Greenville in 1795, which ended the American Indian wars in the Old Northwest, Kentucky and Pennsylvania. The elevation in the county ranges from 723 to 1,788 feet above sea level in a land area of 459 square miles.

Monticello was established as the county seat when Wayne County was established. It was named for the home of Thomas Jefferson, who became President of the United States the year the county was formed. Surveyor and Revolutionary War veteran Joshua Jones laid out the town on land owned by William Beard.

Cherokee Chief Chuqualatague (Doublehead), the last chieftain in this area, lived along the Cumberland River. His descendants remain in the area. Pioneer Long Hunters camped in 1770 near what became Mill Springs, as did Daniel Boone in 1774. Mill Springs later became the home to the largest over-shot water wheel in the world, which is still in operation. In 1775 Benjamin Price established Price's Station, one of the earliest permanent settlements in the state. It was also one of the few in Kentucky to withstand American Indian attacks.

The largest Civil War battle in Wayne County occurred on January 19, 1862. Some 12,000 Union troops met and defeated 4,000 Confederate troops. Confederate Gen. Felix Zollicoffer was killed in the battle. The rout was so complete that Confederate Gen. Crittenden wrote: "From Mill Springs and on the first steps of my march officers and men, frightened by false rumors of the move-

ment of the enemy, shamefully deserted, and, stealing horses and mules to ride, fled to Knoxville, Nashville, and other places in Tennessee."

In July 1862 Confederate Gen. John H. Morgan and 900 cavalrymen raided 17 towns, including

**Mill Springs Mill**
*Source: Tour Southern & Eastern Kentucky*

Cynthiana, Paris, Winchester, Richmond and Somerset on his first foray into Kentucky. They passed through Wayne County on July 22 on their way back to Tennessee. This raid, which was approximately 1,000 miles in length, lasted 24 days and resulted in the destruction of Union arms and supplies.

# Webster County
# Dixon

Webster County, the 100th in order of formation, was created in 1860 out of parts of Henderson, Hopkins and Union counties. It was named for the famous orator, statesman and lawyer, Noah Webster. The county is bordered in part by two rivers: Tradewater River in the south and Green River in the north. Although both rivers are navigable, Green River is larger and much more useful for commercial shipping. The terrain in Webster County is mostly flat-lying, but is somewhat broken in the central portion. Soil is rich and productive in the county, which contains 335 square miles and ranges in elevation from 325 feet to 640 feet above sea level.

The county seat of Dixon was named for Archibald Dixon. Dixon was lieutenant governor of Kentucky (1844-1848) and a member of the U.S. Senate (1852-1855). Providence, however, is the largest community in Webster County.

The first settler in Webster County is thought to have been William Jenkins. A Virginian who obtained a land warrant for his Revolutionary War services. Although he was captured by American Indians, legend has it they came to like him so much they carefully plucked his hair so that he would not be scalped by warriors from other tribes. Webster Coun-

ty's most infamous residents were the Harp Brothers. These notorious outlaws committed murders, robberies and other crimes throughout Webster County over a 30-year period in the late 1700s and early 1800s. Micajah "Big" Harp was finally killed in July 1806 by a man whose wife and children had been slain by the Harps. He cut off Big Harp's head and as a warning to other outlaws, placed it on a pike next to the road.

There were no major Civil War battles in Webster County, but in September 1861 there was a skirmish between Union soldiers under Col. James F. Buckner and Confederate forces under Capt. Al Fowler. The rebel forces captured 25 soldiers. Later that year Confederate Gen. Nathan Bedford Forrest passed through Webster County with 300 cavalry on a reconnaissance and foraging mission, and helped themselves to a large number of hogs. There was also some activity by Johnson's Partisan Rangers, a cavalry unit formed in Western Kentucky that served under Confederate Gen. John H. Morgan.

Early in the county's history, before the roads were paved, each man was asked to spend a specified number of days each year working on the roads. Subsequently, a poll tax of $1.50 per adult man was enacted to maintain the roads.

**Daniel Webster**

# Whitley County
# Williamsburg

Whitley County was formed in 1818 from a section of Knox County. It was named in honor of an early pioneer and frontiersman, Col. William Whitley. Situated along the Tennessee state line, Whitley is drained by the Cumberland River and its tributaries; Laurel River forms part of the county's boundary line. The face of the county, excepting the river valleys, is hilly and broken. Elevation in the county ranges from 723 to 2,220 feet above sea level; the land area is 440.15 square miles.

Williamsburg, the county seat, is situated on the Cumberland River. The town of Whitley Court House was formed with the county and named, like the county, for William Whitley. The name of the town and post office were changed to Williamsburgh in 1882 and the spelling was changed to Williamsburg in 1890.

Dr. Thomas Walker, employed by Loyal Land Co., in 1750 led five Virginians through Cumberland Gap. The party built a cabin at the present-day site of Barbourville. Walker and two others went on to the Rockcastle River into Whitley County, and camped on April 25.

Corbin, the largest town in Whitley County, is on Lynn Camp Creek on the northeastern edge of the county, extending into Knox County. It began as Lynn Camp, named for William Lynn, around 1800; it was also known as Lynn Camp Station. The first post office at the site opened in 1883 as Cummins, in honor of Nelson Cummins, a town founder. It was renamed Corbin for Rev. James Corbin Floyd, in 1885. Corbin is the birthplace of the original Colonel Sanders Cafe and Museum.

Cumberland Falls is a wall of water 125-feet wide, falling 60 feet into a boulder-strewn gorge—known as the "Niagara of the South." The mist of the falls creates the only moonbow in the Western Hemisphere. It may be observed under a full moon and a clear sky. Generations of people have visited here to see this natural phenomenon.

Kentuckians in the Civilian Conservation Corps, included in Pres. Roosevelt's New Deal, helped develop Cumberland Falls State Park, blazing foot trails and erecting cabins. They also built DuPont Lodge, which was given to the state in 1934. Several years earlier the members of the Corbin Kiwanis Club built the Corbin-Cumberland Falls Road into Cumberland Falls.

Immediately behind the falling sheet of water, there is a cave in the surface of the rock; and a person can go almost across the river by this passage—through an arch formed on one side by the rock, and on the other by the flashing waters.

The Daniel Boone National Forest, originally named the Cumberland National Forest, was established in the 1930s with about 700,000 acres of land. This land is generally rugged and characterized by steep forested ridges, narrow valleys, and over thousands of miles of cliffline. Managed by the U.S. Dept. of Agriculture, Forest Service, the Daniel Boone National Forest is one of the most heavily used forests in the South, with over 5 million visitors annually.

# Wolfe County
# Campton

Wolfe County, located in eastern Kentucky, is the 110th county, encompassing about 223 square miles of hilly terrain. Hazel Green, a settlement dating from about 1800, was the first incorporated city (1856); but the more centrally located Campton was designated county seat when the Wolfe County was established in 1860 from Breathitt, Owsley and Powell counties. The county was named for Kentucky Sen. Nathaniel Wolfe, a highly regarded lawyer and advocate for neutrality in the Civil War.

About 14,317 acres of northwestern Wolfe County lie within the boundaries of Daniel Boone National Forest, known for its natural sandstone arches and precipitous cliffs. Natural resources include timber, oil, and some coal. Red River runs east-west through the county, and the North Fork of the Kentucky River forms its southern boundary. These waterways and several streams enrich the level land along the river and creek bottoms for the county's agricultural base.

**Wolfe County Courthouse, 1942**
*Source: Kentucky Virtual Library*

Early settlers came from mostly Virginia. The legendary Jonathan Swift and his "lost silver mine" in the 1760s gave the name to Swift Camp Creek. The county's first documented water mill was in operation in 1810 near Hazel Green.

During the Civil War, there was an unsuccessful attempt to change the county's name to honor the late Confederate Gen. Felix Kirk Zollicoffer who died in battle at Mill Springs on Jan. 19, 1862. The retreating army of Union Gen. George Morgan camped in Hazel Green on Sept. 23, 1862, on June 7, 1864, Gen. John Hunt Morgan's Cavalry passed near the area.

Pine Ridge (est. 1856) became a lodging center in 1889 after the Swan-Day Lumber Company acquired land forested with vast stands of hardwood timber in Wolfe and Powell counties. Swan-Day built the Mountain Central in 1907, a narrow-gauge railroad that ran from the L&E (Lexington and Eastern) in Powell County eastward along Pine Ridge to Campton. Wolfe County became known for its resort hotels in the late 19th and early 20th centuries, due to the logging industry and mineral springs that dotted the area. El Park Hotel (circa. 1890) at Torrent, flourished until the Great Depression and was destroyed by fire in 1935. At Swango Springs near Hazel Green, three hotels and several boarding houses were in operation by 1895. The largest was destroyed by fire in 1910 but mineral water was bottled and shipped from there until 1943. Communities that grew up around the logging industry became ghost towns when timber was depleted in the 1920s. The railroad ceased operation in 1928.

Christian mission societies established schools in Wolfe County to address the isolation and apparent poverty of the area, including Hazel Green Academy (1880), a branch campus of Kentucky Wesleyan Academy (1896-1912); and Alvan Drew School (1913-1947).

# Woodford County
## Versailles

Woodford County was formed in 1788, the 9th and last county created while what would become Kentucky was still part of Virginia. The county government was formed in 1789, which is the date most often used as the county's date of birth. Woodford County was named for Revolutionary War Gen. William Woodford, an officer in the Continental Army, who died while a British prisoner of war. Formed from a portion of Fayette County, Woodford has a land area of 191 square miles and is bordered on the east by the Kentucky River. The land is fertile and gently rolling; elevation ranges from 469 to 1,000 feet above sea level.

Versailles, the county seat, was originally called "Falling Spring" for the large stream that spewed from a grand cavern. It was renamed in 1792 after the city of Versailles, France by town founder Gen. Marquis Calmes, to commemorate French assistance in the Revolutionary War.

Jerome Clarke, called Sue Mundy, one of Morgan's Raiders, formed his own guerrilla band on Morgan's death in Sept. 1864. Clarke and band raided the county on November 1, 1864, killing Adam Harper. Four Confederate prisoners were executed in reprisal by Union forces. In 1865 Clarke returned with William Quantrill, another guerrilla leader, burned the depot here and stole 15 horses.

Woodford County Courthouse
Photo: Sid Webb

The Jack Jouett House, located off of McCowan's Ferry, was built by Jouett, a Revolutionary War hero who is known as the "Paul Revere of the South." Pisgah Presbyterian Church was organized in 1784, the first Presbyterian Church west of the Allegheny Mountains. James Parrish and Dr. Lewis Pendleton founded an orphan's school for girls in Midway that would become Midway College, the only women's college in Kentucky.

One of Kentucky's oldest distilleries is Labrot & Graham—renamed The Woodford Reserve Distillery in 2003. The distillery, completely restored by Brown-Forman Corporation, was built by Elijah Pepper around 1812. Woodford Reserve premium bourbon whiskey is the "official bourbon" of the Kentucky Derby and Breeder's Cup.

Woodford County was home to A. B. "Happy" Chandler, a colorful politician who served two terms as governor, with a U.S. senate term and a stint as U.S. baseball commissioner between them. As commissioner, he approved Jackie Robinson as the first black player in major league baseball. Chandler was elected to the National Baseball Hall of Fame in 1982.

Woodford County is also home to numerous, and famous, Thoroughbred horse farms such as Ashford Stud, Gainsborough Farm, Hurstland Farm, Stonewall Farm, Pin Oak Stud, Three Chimneys—forces in the Thoroughbred industry.

# County Essay Sources

Behind each county lies centuries of traditions, dedicated "pride of place," regional cultures, governmental units, and loyalties—the very essence of what holds these geographic units we call counties together. The essays presented here—with limitations imposed by space—are mere glimpses into the great stories behind the counties, county seats, and towns in Kentucky. May the words presented here kindle the drive to learn more.

"Collins' Historical Sketches of Kentucky, History of Kentucky" ( Vol. I and II), Lewis Collins and Richard H. Collins (Covington, Collins & Co., 1882); "Guide To Kentucky Bicentennial '74-'76," **William E. Matthews**, Pres., Landmark Community Newspapers, Inc. (Shelbyville: 1974); Kentucky Atlas & Gazetteer; "The Kentucky Encyclopedia"; **John E. Kleber**, Ed., The University Press of Kentucky (Lexington: 1992); Kentucky Historical Society; Historical Marker Database; Kentucky Secretary of State; Kentucky Dept. of Library and Archives; SouthEast Telephone; Kentucky Educational Television; US Army Corps of Engineers; Adair Co., **Lila Ford**; Allen Co., **H.D. Overholt**; Scottsville/Allen Co. Chamber of Commerce; Anderson Co., **Ann McBrayer Garrison**; Ballard Co., Ballard Co. Chamber of Commerce; Barren Co., South Central Kentucky Historical and Genealogical Society, Glasgow; Bath Co., **Linda Denton**; Bell Co., **Ann Matheny**, Bell Co. Historical Society; Boone Co., **Don Clare**; Bourbon Co., **Kellie West**; Boyd Co., **Ernest M. Tucker**; Boyle Co., **Carolyn Crabtree**; Bracken Co., **John Parker**, Bracken Co. Historical Society; Breathitt Co., **Stephen D. Bowling**, Breathitt Co. Library and Heritage Center; Breckinridge Co., **David Hayes**; Bullitt Co., **David Strange**, Bullitt Co. History Museum; Butler Co., N**ancy Cardwell**; Caldwell Co., City of Princeton; Calloway Co., Murray Tourism Commission, Murray-Calloway Co. Chamber of Commerce; Campbell Co., **W. Frank Steely**; Carroll Co., Carrollton-Carroll Co. Tourism Commission; Carter Co., **George Wolfford**; Casey Co., **Jan Banks**; Christian Co., Hopkinsville-Christian Co. Convention and Visitor's Bureau, Hopkinsville; Clark Co., City of Winchester, Ky.; Clinton Co., Albany-Clinton Co. Chamber of Commerce; Crittenden Co., **Brenda Underdown**; Cumberland Co., Burkesville-Cumberland Co. Chamber of Commerce; Edmonson Co., Edmonson Co. Chamber of Commerce; Estill Co., Estill.Net; Fayette Co., Commerce Lexington Inc.; Fleming Co., **Brenda Plummer**, **Mary Jane Scaggs**; Floyd Co., Floyd Co. Chamber of Commerce; Franklin Co., Capital City Museum; Gallatin Co., **David Hull**; Graves Co., **Wendy Hunter**; Green Co., **Ray Perkins**; **Carolyn Scott**, Green Co. Historical Society; Greenup Co., **Kelly Nelson**; Hancock Co., **Patsy R. Young**, Hancock Chamber of Commerce, Hancock Co.; Hardin Co., **Mary Josephine Jones**; Harrison Co., Historical Society of Harrison Co.; Hart Co., **Virginia Davis**; Henderson Co., **Netta Mullin**, Henderson Co. Historical & Genealogical Society, Inc.; Henry Co., **Pat Wallace**; Hickman Co., **Wanda Moon**; Hopkins Co., **J. Harold Utley**; Jackson Co., Jackson Co. Public Library; Jefferson Co., **Todd Hollenback**; Jessamine Co., **Howard C. Teater**, Jessamine Co. Genealogical & Historical Society; Johnson Co., Johnson Co. Public Library; Kenton Co., **John H. Boh**; Knott Co., **David R. Smith**; Knox Co., **Charles Reed Mitchell**; Laurel Co., **Jan Sparkman**; Lawrence Co., **Ruby Arrington**; Leslie Co., **Mary Ethel Wooton**; Letcher Co., **Merlene Davis Day**; Lewis Co., **Joan Godfrey**; Lincoln Co., Lincoln Co. Historical Society; Livingston Co., **Mary Lou Smith**; Logan Co., Logan Co. Chamber of Commerce; Lyon Co., Lyon Co. Chamber of Commerce, Lyon Co. Joint Tourism Commission; Madison Co., **Charles Hays**, Madison Co. Historical Society; Marion Co., **Veronica Hill**; Marshall Co., www.MarshallCounty.net; Martin Co., **Evelynn Cassady**, Martin Co. Historical Society; Mason Co., **Sue Ellen Grannis**; McLean Co., **Helen Anderson**; Menifee Co., **Lola Thomas**; Metcalfe Co., **Jerry Sampson**; Montgomery Co., **George Stone**; Morgan Co., **Linda Bradley**; Pendleton Co., **Mildred Belew**; Perry Co., **Martha Quigley**, Bobby Davis Museum & Park; Powell Co., **David Eugene Rule**; Pulaski Co., **Louann Hardy**; Rockcastle Co., **Duane D. Allen**, Rockcastle Co. Historical Society; Rowan Co., **Jack D. Ellis**; Scott Co., Georgetown-Scott Co. Chamber of Commerce Magazine & Lanham Media Service; Shelby Co., **William E. Matthews**; Simpson Co., **Dr. James Henry Snider**, **Nancy Thomas**, **Sara Jo Cardwell**, Simpson Co. Historical Society, Inc.; Spencer Co., **Hilda Snider**; Trigg Co., Cadiz-Trigg Co. Chamber of Commerce; Washington Co., Springfield-Washington Co. Chamber of Commerce; Wayne Co., **Harlan Ogle**, William Crenshaw Kennedy, Jr. Memorial Museum; Webster Co., **Lowell Childress**; Woodford Co., **Danna Estridge**, Woodford Co. Historical Society and Woodford Chamber of Commerce.

# COUNTIES AND JUDGE EXECUTIVES

| COUNTY | JUDGE/EXECUTIVE | ADDRESS1 | ADDRESS2 | CITY | ZIP | PHONE | FAX |
|---|---|---|---|---|---|---|---|
| Adair | Jerry Vaughan | Adair Co Cthse Annex | 424 Public Sq Ste 1 | Columbia | 42728 | (270) 384-4703 | (270) 384-9754 |
| Allen | Johnny Hobdy | City-Co Bldg | PO Box 115 | Scottsville | 42164 | (270) 237-3631 | (270) 237-9155 |
| Anderson | Anthony D Stratton | 137 S Main St | | Lawrenceburg | 40342 | (502) 839-3471 | (502) 839-8151 |
| Ballard | Bob Buchanan | 437 Ohio St | PO Box 276 | Wickliffe | 42087 | (270) 335-5176 | (270) 335-3010 |
| Barren | Davie Greer | 117 N Public Sq Ste 3A | | Glasgow | 42141 | (270) 651-3338 | (270) 651-2344 |
| Bath | Walter Shrout | Cthse Annex | PO Box 39 | Owingsville | 40360 | (606) 674-6346 | (606) 674-6658 |
| Bell | William (Bill) Kelley | Cthse Sq | PO Box 339 | Pineville | 40977 | (606) 337-3076 | (606) 337-9807 |
| Boone | Gary W Moore | 2950 Burlington Pk | PO Box 900 | Burlington | 41005 | (859) 334-2242 | (859) 334-3105 |
| Bourbon | Donnie R Foley | Bourbon Co Cthse | 301 Main St Rm 203 | Paris | 40361 | (859) 987-2135 | (859) 987-2316 |
| Boyd | Bill F Scott | Boyd Co Cthse | PO Box 423 | Catlettsburg | 41129 | (606) 739-4134 | (606) 739-5446 |
| Boyle | Tony Wilder | Boyle Co Cthse | 321 W Main St Ste 111 | Danville | 40422 | (859) 238-1100 | (859) 238-1108 |
| Bracken | Leslie Newman | Bracken Co Cthse | PO Box 264 | Brooksville | 41004 | (606) 735-2300 | (606) 735-2615 |
| Breathitt | Lewis H Warrix | Breathitt Co Cthse | 1137 Main St | Jackson | 41339 | (606) 666-3800 | (606) 666-3813 |
| Breckinridge | George Monarch | Co Cthse Annex | PO Box 227 | Hardinsburg | 40143 | (270) 756-2269 | (270) 756-2364 |
| Bullitt | Kenneth J Rigdon | Bullitt Co Cthse 1st Fl 300 S Buckman St | PO Box 768 | Shepherdsville | 40165 | (800) 672-5058 | (502) 543-1577 |
| Butler | Hugh C Evans | Butler Co Cthse | PO Box 626 | Morgantown | 42261 | (270) 526-3433 | (270) 526-2658 |
| Caldwell | Van Knight | 100 E Market St Rm 27 | | Princeton | 42445 | (270) 365-6660 | (270) 365-6637 |
| Calloway | Larry Elkins | Calloway Co Cthse | 101 S 5th St | Murray | 42071 | (270) 753-2920 | (270) 753-2911 |
| Campbell | Steven Pendery | Campbell Co Fiscal Court | 24 W 4th St | Newport | 41071 | (859) 292-3822 | (859) 292-3888 |
| Carlisle | John G Roberts III | 77 E Court St | PO Box 279 | Bardwell | 42023 | (270) 628-5451 | (270) 628-0190 |
| Carroll | Harold (Shorty) Tomlinson | Carroll Co Cthse 2nd Fl | 440 Main St | Carrollton | 41008 | (502) 732-7000 | (502) 732-7023 |
| Carter | Charles Wallace | Carter Co Cthse Rm 227 | 300 W Main St | Grayson | 41143 | (606) 474-5366 | (606) 474-6991 |
| Casey | Ronald D Wright | 625 Campbellsville St | PO Box 306 | Liberty | 42539 | (606) 787-6154 | (606) 787-6154 |
| Christian | Steve Tribble | 515 Weber St | | Hopkinsville | 42240 | (270) 887-4100 | (270) 885-7501 |
| Clark | John Myers | Clark Co Cthse Rm 103 3rd Fl | 34 S Main St | Winchester | 40391 | (859) 745-0200 | (859) 737-5678 |
| Clay | James G Garrison | 102 Richmond Rd Ste 201 | | Manchester | 40962 | (606) 598-2071 | (606) 598-7849 |
| Clinton | Donnie McWhorter | 100 S Cross St | | Albany | 42602 | (606) 387-5234 | (606) 387-7651 |
| Crittenden | Fred Brown | Crittenden Co Cthse | 107 S Main St | Marion | 42064 | (270) 965-5251 | (270) 965-5252 |
| Cumberland | Tim Hicks | Cumberland Co Cthse | PO Box 826 | Burkesville | 42717 | (270) 864-3444 | (270) 864-1757 |
| Daviess | Louis Reid Haire | Daviess Co Cthse | 212 St Ann St | Owensboro | 42303 | (270) 685-8424 | (270) 685-8469 |
| Edmonson | N E Reed | Edmonson Co Cthse | PO Box 353 | Brownsville | 42210 | (270) 597-2819 | (270) 597-2494 |
| Elliott | Charles R Pennington | Elliott Co Cthse Main St | PO Box 710 | Sandy Hook | 41171 | (606) 738-5821 | (606) 738-4509 |
| Estill | Wallace Taylor | Estill Co Cthse Rm 101 | | Irvine | 40336 | (606) 723-7524 | (606) 723-5471 |
| Fayette | Sandra Varellas | 167 W Main St Ste 1310 | | Lexington | 40507 | (859) 255-1790 | (859) 252-4476 |
| Fleming | Larry Foxworthy | Fleming Co Cthse | | Flemingsburg | 41041 | (606) 845-8801 | (606) 845-1312 |
| Floyd | Paul H Thompson | Floyd Co Cthse | | Prestonsburg | 41653 | (606) 886-9193 | (606) 886-1083 |
| Franklin | Robert Roach | 315 W Main St Ste 302 | | Frankfort | 40601 | (502) 875-8751 | (502) 875-8755 |
| Fulton | Harold M Garrison | 2004 S 7th St | | Hickman | 42050 | (270) 236-2594 | (270) 236-7904 |
| Gallatin | George W Zubaty | Gallatin Co Cthse Annex II | 149 S Central Ave | Warsaw | 41095 | (859) 567-5691 | (859) 567-4764 |
| Garrard | E J Hasty | Garrard Co Cthse | PO Box 144 | Lancaster | 40444 | (859) 792-3531 | (859) 792-2010 |
| Grant | Darrell L Link | Grant Co Cthse | 15 Public Sq Ste 3 | Williamstown | 41097 | (859) 823-7561 | (859) 428-4567 |
| Graves | Anthony Doyle (Tony) Smith | Graves Co Cthse | 101 N Main St | Mayfield | 42066 | (270) 247-3626 | (270) 247-1274 |
| Grayson | Gary L Logsdon | 10 Public Sq | 101 E South St Ste 1 | Leitchfield | 42754 | (270) 259-3159 | (270) 259-0512 |
| Green | Mary Ann Blaydes Baron | Green Co Cthse | 203 W Court St | Greensburg | 42743 | (270) 932-4024 | (270) 932-3635 |
| Greenup | Robert W Carpenter | Greenup Co Cthse Rm 102 | | Greenup | 41144 | (606) 473-6440 | (606) 473-9878 |
| Hancock | Jack B McCaslin | Hancock Co Admin Bldg | PO Box 580 | Hawesville | 42348 | (270) 927-8137 | (270) 927-8138 |
| Hardin | Harry Berry | Hardin County Cthse 3rd Fl | PO Box 568 | Elizabethtown | 42702 | (270) 765-2350 | (270) 737-5590 |
| Harlan | Joseph A Grieshop | 210 E Central St Ste 111 | | Harlan | 40831 | (606) 573-2600 | (606) 573-3522 |
| Harrison | Dean Peak | Harrison Co Cthse | PO Box 956 | Cynthiana | 41031 | (859) 234-7136 | (859) 234-6647 |
| Hart | Terry L Martin | Hart Co Cthse | 111 S Main St | Munfordville | 42765 | (270) 524-5219 | (270) 524-4647 |
| Henderson | Sandy Lee Watkins | Henderson Co Cthse | PO Box 490 | Henderson | 42420 | (270) 826-3971 | (270) 827-6002 |
| Henry | John Brent | Henry Co Cthse Annex | PO Box 202 | New Castle | 40050 | (502) 845-5707 | (502) 845-4916 |
| Hickman | Gregory D Pruitt | Hickman Co Cthse | 110 E Clay St Ste E | Clinton | 42031 | (270) 653-4369 | (270) 653-4360 |
| Hopkins | Patricia Hawkins | Hopkins Co Govt Bldg | PO Box 523 | Madisonville | 42431 | (270) 821-8294 | (270) 821-8295 |

## COUNTIES AND JUDGE EXECUTIVES

| COUNTY | JUDGE/EXECUTIVE | ADDRESS1 | ADDRESS2 | CITY | ZIP | PHONE | FAX |
|---|---|---|---|---|---|---|---|
| Jackson | Tommy Slone | | PO Box 339 | McKee | 40447 | (606) 287-8562 | (606) 287-7190 |
| Jefferson | Vacant | | | | | | |
| Jessamine | William Neal Cassity | Jessamine Co Cthse | 101 N Main St | Nicholasville | 40356 | (859) 885-4500 | (859) 885-2545 |
| Johnson | Roger T Daniel | 338 2nd St | PO Box 868 | Paintsville | 41240 | (606) 789-2550 | (606) 789-2555 |
| Kenton | Ralph Drees | Kenton Co Bldg | PO Box 792 | Covington | 41012 | (859) 392-1400 | (859) 392-1412 |
| Knott | Randy C Thompson | Knott Co Cthse | PO Box 505 | Hindman | 41822 | (606) 785-5592 | (606) 785-0966 |
| Knox | Raymond Smith | Knox Co Cthse | PO Box 173 | Barbourville | 40906 | (606) 546-6192 | (606) 546-6196 |
| LaRue | Tommy Turner | LaRue Co Cthse Ste 4 | 209 W High St | Hodgenville | 42748 | (270) 358-4400 | (270) 358-4528 |
| Laurel | Lawrence Kuhl | Laurel Co Cthse Rm 301 | 101 S Main St | London | 40741 | (606) 864-4640 | (606) 864-3867 |
| Lawrence | Phillip Carter | Lawrence Co Cthse | 122 S Main Cross St | Louisa | 41230 | (606) 638-4102 | (606) 638-0618 |
| Lee | L C (Bub) Reese | Lee Co Cthse | PO Box G | Beattyville | 41311 | (606) 464-4100 | (606) 464-4107 |
| Leslie | Kenneth Witt | Leslie Co Cthse | PO Box 619 | Hyden | 41749 | (606) 672-3200 | (606) 672-7373 |
| Letcher | Carroll A Smith | Letcher Co Cthse | 156 Main St Ste 107 | Whitesburg | 41858 | (606) 633-2129 | (606) 633-7105 |
| Lewis | Steven Applegate | Lewis Co Cthse | 514 2nd St | Vanceburg | 41179 | (606) 796-2722 | (606) 796-0822 |
| Lincoln | R W (Buckwheat) Gilbert | Lincoln Co Cthse | 102 E Main St | Stanford | 40484 | (606) 365-2534 | (606) 365-4514 |
| Livingston | Christopher Lasher | Livingston Co Cthse | PO Box 70 | Smithland | 42081 | (270) 928-2106 | (270) 928-3262 |
| Logan | John H Guion III | Logan Co Cthse | PO Box 365 | Russellville | 42276 | (270) 726-3116 | (270) 726-3117 |
| Lyon | Sara Jean Boyd | Lyon Co Cthse | PO Box 598 | Eddyville | 42038 | (270) 388-7311 | (270) 388-0715 |
| Madison | Kent Clark | Madison Co Cthse | 101 W Main St | Richmond | 40475 | (859) 624-4700 | (859) 624-9140 |
| Magoffin | Bill May | Magoffin Co Cthse | PO Box 430 | Salyersville | 41465 | (606) 349-2313 | (606) 349-2109 |
| Marion | David R Hourigan | 102 W Main St | | Lebanon | 40033 | (270) 692-3451 | (270) 692-9487 |
| Marshall | Mike Miller | Marshall Co Cthse | 1101 Main St | Benton | 42025 | (270) 527-4750 | (270) 527-4795 |
| Martin | Kelly E Callaham | | PO Box 309 | Inez | 41224 | (606) 298-2800 | (606) 298-4404 |
| Mason | James L (Buddy) Gallenstein | 221 Court St | | Maysville | 41056 | (606) 564-6706 | (606) 564-7315 |
| McCracken | Danny Orazine | McCracken Co Cthse | 300 S 7th St | Paducah | 42003 | (270) 444-4707 | (270) 444-4731 |
| McCreary | Blaine Phillips | McCreary Co Cthse | PO Box 579 | Whitley City | 42653 | (606) 376-2413 | (606) 376-9499 |
| McLean | Larry B Whitaker | McLean Co Cthse | PO Box 127 | Calhoun | 42327 | (270) 273-3213 | (270) 273-9985 |
| Meade | William Haynes | Meade Co Cthse | 516 Fairway Dr | Brandenburg | 40108 | (270) 422-3967 | (270) 422-3262 |
| Menifee | James Trimble | | PO Box 105 | Frenchburg | 40322 | (606) 768-3482 | (606) 768-2144 |
| Mercer | John D Trisler | Fiscal Court Bldg | 134 S Main St | Harrodsburg | 40330 | (859) 734-6300 | (859) 734-6345 |
| Metcalfe | Donald M Butler II | Metcalfe Co Cthse | PO Box 149 | Edmonton | 42129 | (270) 432-3181 | (270) 432-3726 |
| Monroe | Wilbur Graves | Monroe Co Cthse | 200 N Main St Ste C | Tompkinsville | 42167 | (270) 487-5505 | (270) 487-0591 |
| Montgomery | B D Wilson Jr | 44 W Main St | | Mt Sterling | 40353 | (859) 498-8707 | (859) 498-1040 |
| Morgan | Timothy Conley | Morgan Co Ofc Bldg | 450 Prestonsburg St | West Liberty | 41472 | (606) 743-3898 | (606) 743-3895 |
| Muhlenberg | Rodney Keith Kirtley | Muhlenberg Co Cthse | PO Box 137 | Greenville | 42345 | (270) 338-2520 | (270) 338-6116 |
| Nelson | Dean Watts | Old Cthse | PO Box 578 | Bardstown | 40004 | (502) 348-1801 | (502) 348-1873 |
| Nicholas | Larry D Tincher | Nicholas Co Cthse | PO Box 167 | Carlisle | 40311 | (859) 289-3725 | (859) 289-3705 |
| Ohio | Wayne Hunsaker | Ohio Co Cthse | PO Box 146 | Hartford | 42347 | (270) 298-4400 | (270) 298-4408 |
| Oldham | Mary Ellen Kinser | Oldham Co Fiscal Court Bldg | 100 W Jefferson St | LaGrange | 40031 | (502) 222-9357 | (502) 222-3210 |
| Owen | William P O'Banion | Owen Co Cthse | 100 N Thomas | Owenton | 40359 | (502) 484-3405 | (502) 464-1004 |
| Owsley | Cale Turner | Owsley Co Cthse | PO Box 749 | Booneville | 41314 | (606) 593-6202 | (606) 593-6381 |
| Pendleton | Henry W Bertram | 233 Main St Rm 4 | | Falmouth | 41040 | (859) 654-4321 | (859) 654-5047 |
| Perry | Denny Ray Noble | Perry Co Cthse | PO Box 210 | Hazard | 41702 | (606) 439-1816 | (606) 439-1686 |
| Pike | William M Deskins | Pike Co Cthse | 146 Main St | Pikeville | 41501 | (606) 432-6247 | (606) 432-6242 |
| Powell | Robert Ray (Bobby) Drake | Powell Co Cthse | PO Box 506 | Stanton | 40380 | (606) 663-2834 | (606) 663-2905 |
| Pulaski | Darrell Beshears | Pulaski Co Cthse | PO Box 712 | Somerset | 42502 | (606) 678-4853 | (606) 679-8642 |
| Robertson | Bradley Gifford | Court St | PO Box 76 | Mt Olivet | 41064 | (606) 724-5615 | (606) 724-5022 |
| Rockcastle | Buzz Carloftis | Rockcastle Co Cthse | PO Box 755 | Mt Vernon | 40456 | (606) 256-2856 | (606) 256-8104 |
| Rowan | Clyde Thomas | Rowan Co Cthse | 627 E Main St | Morehead | 40351 | (606) 784-5151 | (606) 784-3535 |
| Russell | Ronnie McFall | Russell Co Cthse | PO Box 397 | Jamestown | 42629 | (270) 343-2112 | (270) 343-2134 |
| Scott | George H Lusby | 101 E Main St | PO Box 973 | Georgetown | 40324 | (502) 863-7850 | (502) 863-7852 |
| Shelby | Rob Rothenburger | 419 Washington St | | Shelbyville | 40065 | (502) 633-1220 | (502) 633-7623 |
| Simpson | Jim Henderson | Main St | PO Box 242 | Franklin | 42135 | (270) 586-7184 | (270) 586-9505 |
| Spencer | David Jenkins | 12 W Main St | PO Box 397 | Taylorsville | 40071 | (502) 477-3205 | (502) 477-3206 |

## COUNTIES AND JUDGE EXECUTIVES

| COUNTY | JUDGE/EXECUTIVE | ADDRESS1 | ADDRESS2 | CITY | ZIP | PHONE | FAX |
|---|---|---|---|---|---|---|---|
| Taylor | Paul Patton | Taylor Co Cthse | 203 N Court St Ste 4 | Campbellsville | 42718 | (270) 465-7729 | (270) 789-3675 |
| Todd | Carl Knight | Todd Co Cthse | PO Box 355 | Elkton | 42220 | (270) 265-2451 | (270) 265-3277 |
| Trigg | Berlin S Moore Jr | 38 Main St | PO Box 672 | Cadiz | 42211 | (270) 522-8459 | (270) 522-7786 |
| Trimble | Randy Stevens | 123 Church St | PO Box 251 | Bedford | 40006 | (502) 255-7196 | (502) 255-4618 |
| Union | Frank J Etter | Union Co Cthse | PO Box 60 | Morganfield | 42437 | (270) 389-1081 | (270) 389-0406 |
| Warren | Michael O Buchanon | Warren Co Cthse | 429 E 10th St | Bowling Green | 42101 | (270) 843-4146 | (270) 781-2777 |
| Washington | John A Settles | Washington Co Cthse | PO Box 126 | Springfield | 40069 | (859) 336-5410 | (859) 336-5407 |
| Wayne | Bruce Ramsey | Wayne Co Cthse | PO Box 439 | Monticello | 42633 | (606) 348-4241 | (606) 348-6647 |
| Webster | James R (Jim) Townsend | Webster Co Cthse | PO Box 155 | Dixon | 42409 | (270) 639-5042 | (270) 639-7009 |
| Whitley | Burley J Foley | Whitley Co Cthse | PO Box 237 | Williamsburg | 40769 | (606) 549-6000 | (606) 549-6095 |
| Wolfe | Raymond Hurst | Wolfe Co Cthse | PO Box 429 | Campton | 41301 | (606) 668-3040 | (606) 668-3367 |
| Woodford | Joe D Gormley | Woodford Co Cthse Rm 200 | 103 S Main St | Versailles | 40383 | (859) 873-4139 | (859) 873-0196 |

*Source: The Kentucky Directory Gold Book 2006-2007*

**Autumn in Kentucky**
*Source: Kentucky Department of Tourism*

## Autumn Comes to Kentucky
*Charlie Hughes*

Drawn to nakedness and held
in the bare arms of ash and locust,
I am most alive in summer's death, awakened
each autumn by the chainsaw's scream, blood
stirred by great vees of geese.
I become as sharp and crisp as the taste
of woodsmoke on October's cool, clear wind.
I begin to speak in metaphor,
have the midnight eloquence
of the condemned
awaiting the morning's hangman.

A strange paradox, to be so alive, while
all around me life ending.

...

Tonight the sky will once again rise
in the east with wonder not seen in summer.
The trees will reach toward the heavens
where stars burn holes in the darkness.
Barns will cast dark shapes in the fescue
and the tin of their roofs will mirror
the brilliant moon, and I, in amazement,
will walk in this light and shadow
one last time before the snow.

*Reprinted with permission of Wind Publications, Autumn Comes to Kentucky from "Shifting for Myself," Charlie Hughes, Wind Publications, pages 74-75 (Nicholasville: 2002).*

## CITIES AND MAYORS — 1ST - 6TH CLASS CITIES

| CITY | CLASS | POP | COUNTY | MAYOR | ADDRESS | CITY | ZIP | PHONE | FAX |
|---|---|---|---|---|---|---|---|---|---|
| Adairville | 4 | 927 | Logan | James Wilkerson | PO Box 185 | Adairville | 42202 | (270) 539-6731 | (270) 539-5503 |
| Albany | 4 | 3053 | Clinton | John N (Nicky) Smith | 204 Cross St | Albany | 42602 | (606) 387-6011 | (606) 387-6105 |
| Alexandria | 4 | 8016 | Campbell | Daniel M McGinley | 8236 W Main St | Alexandria | 41001 | (859) 635-4125 | (859) 635-4127 |
| Allen | 6 | 350 | Floyd | Sharon S Woods | PO Box 510 | Allen | 41601 | (606) 874-2953 | |
| Anchorage | 4 | 2500 | Jefferson | W Thomas Hewitt | 1306 Evergreen Rd | Anchorage | 40223 | (502) 245-4654 | (502) 245-5651 |
| Arlington | 6 | 390 | Carlisle | Charles Burton | PO Box 399 | Arlington | 42021 | (270) 655-6811 | (270) 655-2261 |
| Ashland | 2 | 21586 | Boyd | Stephen Gilmore | 1700 Greenup Ave | Ashland | 41105 | (606) 327-2001 | (606) 327-2055 |
| Auburn | 5 | 1483 | Logan | Dewey Roche | 103 E Main | Auburn | 42206 | (270) 542-4149 | (270) 542-4143 |
| Audubon Park | 5 | 1543 | Jefferson | Michael Scalise | 3340 Robin Rd | Louisville | 40213 | (502) 637-5066 | (502) 637-1574 |
| Augusta | 4 | 1259 | Bracken | John Laycock | 219 Main St | Augusta | 41002 | (606) 756-2183 | (606) 756-2185 |
| Bancroft | 5 | 543 | Jefferson | Kimberly Reinhardt | 7608 Wesleyan Pl | Louisville | 40242 | (502) 425-8369 | |
| Barbourmeade | 5 | 1274 | Jefferson | Albert A Tomassetti | 3516 Breeland Ave | Louisville | 40241 | (502) 429-6141 | (502) 429-6141 |
| Barbourville | 4 | 3515 | Knox | W Patrick Hauser | 196 Daniel Boone Dr | Barbourville | 40906 | (606) 546-3914 | (606) 546-4543 |
| Bardstown | 4 | 10897 | Nelson | Dixie Hibbs | 220 N 5th St | Bardstown | 40004 | (877) 348-5947 | (502) 348-2433 |
| Bardwell | 5 | 790 | Carlisle | Joe C Ross | 265 Front St | Bardwell | 42023 | (270) 628-5415 | (270) 628-3246 |
| Barlow | 6 | 715 | Ballard | Ruth Negley | PO Box 309 | Barlow | 42024 | (270) 334-3500 | (270) 334-3564 |
| Beattyville | 6 | 1164 | Lee | Charles Beach III | PO Box 127 | Beattyville | 41311 | (606) 464-3631 | (606) 464-2123 |
| Beaver Dam | 4 | 3100 | Ohio | Mary Pate | 309 W 2nd | Beaver Dam | 42320 | (270) 274-7106 | (270) 274-5640 |
| Bedford | 6 | 743 | Trimble | Russell Dale Clifton | 147 Victory Ave | Bedford | 40006 | (502) 255-3684 | (502) 255-3222 |
| Beechwood Village | 5 | 1175 | Jefferson | Joyce Louden | 220 Sage Rd | Louisville | 40207 | (502) 893-5087 | |
| Bellefonte | 6 | 846 | Greenup | Thomas R (Tom) Bradley | 422 Bellefonte Princess Rd | Ashland | 41101 | (304) 529-5375 | |
| Bellemeade | 6 | 876 | Jefferson | Arthur (Wes) Amos | 108 Tristan Rd | Louisville | 40222 | (502) 425-0485 | |
| Bellevue | 4 | 6091 | Campbell | John Jack Meyer | 616 Poplar St | Bellevue | 41073 | (859) 431-8866 | (855) 261-8387 |
| Bellewood | 6 | 305 | Jefferson | Bruce Gale | 3907 Brookfield Ave | Louisville | 40207 | (502) 893-0237 | |
| Benham | 5 | 565 | Harlan | Betty Joy Howard | 463 Cumberland Ave | Benham | 40807 | (606) 848-5506 | (606) 848-5506 |
| Benton | 4 | 4189 | Marshall | Larry Spears | 1009 Main St | Benton | 42025 | (270) 527-8677 | (270) 527-2251 |
| Berea | 4 | 12738 | Madison | Steven Connelly | 212 Chestnut St | Berea | 40403 | (859) 986-8528 | (859) 986-7657 |
| Berry | 6 | 306 | Harrison | Vacant | PO Box 96 | Berry | 41003 | (859) 234-1268 | (859) 234-3185 |
| Blackey | 6 | 145 | Letcher | Don Adams | 265 Main St Loop | Blackey | 41804 | (606) 633-4111 | (606) 632-9808 |
| Blaine | 6 | 252 | Lawrence | Ella V Seals | PO Box 66 | Blaine | 41124 | (606) 652-9175 | |
| Bloomfield | 5 | 868 | Nelson | Ronnie Bobblett | 141 Depot St | Bloomfield | 40008 | (502) 252-8222 | (502) 252-9013 |
| Blue Ridge Manor | 6 | 628 | Jefferson | Albert M Hardesty | 120 Blue Ridge Rd | Louisville | 40223 | (502) 245-5139 | (502) 245-5106 |
| Bonnieville | 6 | 364 | Hart | Rose Bostic | 347 Campground Rd | Bonnieville | 42713 | (502) 531-5693 | |
| Booneville | 5 | 108 | Owsley | Charles Long | 1 Mulberry St | Booneville | 43314 | (606) 593-6800 | (775) 414-9363 |
| Bowling Green | 2 | 51294 | Warren | Elaine Walker | PO Box 430 | Bowling Green | 42102 | (270) 793-9055 | (270) 393-3698 |
| Bradfordsville | 6 | 316 | Marion | David Edelen | Main St | Bradfordsville | 40009 | (270) 337-3796 | (270) 337-2085 |
| Brandenburg | 5 | 2193 | Meade | Ronnie C Joyner | 737 High St | Brandenburg | 40108 | (270) 422-4981 | (270) 422-4983 |
| Bremen | 6 | 365 | Muhlenberg | Roy A Shaver | PO Box 334 | Bremen | 42325 | (270) 525-3493 | |
| Briarwood | 6 | 556 | Jefferson | William H Vaughan | 2006 Japonica Way | Louisville | 40242 | (502) 425-2515 | |
| Brodhead | 5 | 1199 | Rockcastle | Walter Lee Cash | 7 W Main St | Brodhead | 40409 | (606) 758-8635 | (606) 758-8635 |
| Broeck Pointe | 6 | 297 | Jefferson | Leonard P Wiseman | PO Box 22205 | Louisville | 40222 | (502) 426-4471 | (502) 426-4471 |
| Bromley | 5 | 923 | Kenton | James G Miller | 211 Rohman Ave | Bromley | 41016 | (859) 261-2498 | (859) 261-6791 |
| Brooksville | 6 | 615 | Bracken | John H Corlis | 320 Frankfort St | Brooksville | 41004 | (606) 735-2501 | (606) 635-2619 |
| Brownsboro Farm | 6 | 682 | Jefferson | Eric Cerro | 8455 Brownsboro Rd | Louisville | 40241 | (502) 426-1113 | |
| Brownsboro Village | 6 | 318 | Jefferson | Mark Joyce | PO Box 6635 | Louisville | 40206 | (502) 893-0344 | (502) 893-3757 |
| Brownsville | 5 | 1300 | Edmonson | Timothy M Houchin | PO Box 238 | Brownsville | 42210 | (270) 597-3814 | (270) 597-3274 |
| Buckhorn | 6 | 144 | Perry | Veda Wooton | 191 Buckhorn Ln | Buckhorn | 41721 | (606) 398-7381 | (606) 398-7912 |
| Burgin | 5 | 874 | Mercer | John D Brown | 117 Maple St | Burgin | 40310 | (859) 748-5220 | (859) 748-9900 |
| Burkesville | 5 | 1767 | Cumberland | Mike Irby | 214 Upper River St | Burkesville | 42717 | (270) 864-5391 | (270) 864-1795 |
| Burnside | 5 | 670 | Pulaski | Dean Lovins | PO Box 8 | Burnside | 42519 | (606) 561-4113 | (606) 561-6604 |
| Butler | 5 | 638 | Pendleton | Delbert Reid | 102 Front St | Butler | 41006 | (859) 472-5015 | (859) 472-5173 |
| Cadiz | 4 | 2516 | Trigg | Lyn Bailey | 63 Main St | Cadiz | 42211 | (270) 522-8244 | (270) 522-0025 |
| Calhoun | 5 | 819 | McLean | Thomas Fulkerson | 325 W 2nd St | Calhoun | 42327 | (270) 273-3092 | (270) 273-9717 |
| California | 6 | 82 | Campbell | Franklin D Smith | PO Box 25 | California | 41007 | (859) 635-7716 | |

# CITIES AND MAYORS — 1ST - 6TH CLASS CITIES

| CITY | CLASS | POP | COUNTY | MAYOR | ADDRESS | CITY | ZIP | PHONE | FAX |
|---|---|---|---|---|---|---|---|---|---|
| Calvert City | 4 | 2737 | Marshall | Lynn B Jones | PO Box 36 | Calvert City | 42029 | (270) 395-7138 | (270) 395-5554 |
| Camargo | 5 | 947 | Montgomery | Greg Beam | 4406B Camargo Rd | Mt Sterling | 40353 | (859) 498-9075 | |
| Cambridge | 6 | 193 | Jefferson | Camille Mills | 2907 Cambridge Rd | Louisville | 40220 | (502) 473-8043 | (502) 584-3091 |
| Campbellsburg | 6 | 712 | Henry | Carl Rucker | 8142 Main St | Campbellsburg | 40011 | (502) 532-6050 | (502) 532-0039 |
| Campbellsville | 3 | 10752 | Taylor | Brenda Allen | 100 Terri St | Campbellsville | 42718 | (270) 465-7011 | (270) 789-0251 |
| Campton | 6 | 424 | Wolfe | Gay Campbell | Main St | Campton | 41301 | (606) 668-3574 | (606) 668-7426 |
| Caneyville | 6 | 649 | Grayson | James P Embry | PO Box 222 | Caneyville | 42721 | (270) 879-8711 | (270) 879-3333 |
| Carlisle | 4 | 2045 | Nicholas | Eugene Kelley | 107 E Chestnut St | Carlisle | 40311 | (859) 289-3700 | (859) 289-7704 |
| Carrollton | 4 | 3830 | Carroll | Ann C Deatherage | 750 Clay St | Carrollton | 41008 | (502) 732-7051 | (502) 732-6738 |
| Carrsville | 6 | 63 | Livingston | Deana Jo Gerding | 1810 Fleet St | Carrsville | 42081 | (270) 988-3632 | |
| Catlettsburg | 4 | 1933 | Boyd | Donald Wellman | PO Box 533 | Catlettsburg | 41129 | (606) 739-0104 | (606) 739-5754 |
| Cave City | 4 | 1923 | Barren | Bob Y Hunt | 103 Duke St | Cave City | 42127 | (270) 773-2188 | (270) 773-4522 |
| Centertown | 6 | 325 | Ohio | Jeanene Reeneer | 816 Main St | Centertown | 42328 | (270) 232-5067 | (270) 232-5969 |
| Central City | 4 | 5823 | Muhlenberg | Hugh W Sweatt Jr | 214 N 1st St | Central City | 42330 | (270) 754-5097 | (270) 754-5745 |
| Clarkson | 6 | 820 | Grayson | Bonnie Henderson | 510 Millerstown St | Clarkson | 42726 | (270) 242-6997 | (270) 242-2841 |
| Clay | 5 | 1176 | Webster | Rick Householder | 9100 St Rt 132 W | Clay | 42404 | (270) 664-2444 | (270) 664-9185 |
| Clay City | 5 | 1337 | Powell | Jimmy Caudill | 4651 Main St | Clay City | 40312 | (606) 663-2224 | (606) 663-0672 |
| Clinton | 5 | 1389 | Hickman | Tommy Kimbro | City Hall | Clinton | 42031 | (270) 653-6419 | (270) 653-6422 |
| Cloverport | 5 | 1262 | Breckinridge | Tom Wheatley | 212 W Main St | Cloverport | 40111 | (270) 788-6632 | (270) 788-3751 |
| Coal Run Village | 5 | 556 | Pike | Phyllis S Muncy | 3515 N Mayo Trl | Pikeville | 41501 | (606) 437-6032 | (606) 437-6032 |
| Cold Spring | 4 | 4992 | Campbell | Mark Stoeber | 5694 E Alexandria Pk | Cold Spring | 41076 | (859) 441-9604 | (859) 441-4640 |
| Coldstream | 6 | 967 | Jefferson | Winfred McBroom | 9462 Brownsboro Rd No 140 | Louisville | 40241 | (502) 243-7002 | |
| Columbia | 4 | 4176 | Adair | Pat Bell | 116 Campbellsville St | Columbia | 42728 | (270) 384-6183 | (270) 384-3799 |
| Columbus | 5 | 235 | Hickman | Lynn Bencini | PO Box 121 | Columbus | 42032 | (270) 677-2701 | |
| Concord | 6 | 27 | Lewis | Lovell Polley | Rt 2 Box 510 | Vanceburg | 41179 | (606) 798-6921 | |
| Corbin | 3 | 8111 | Whitley/Knox | Eddie Amos Miller | PO Drawer 1343 | Corbin | 40702 | (606) 523-6520 | (606) 523-6500 |
| Corinth | 6 | 188 | Grant | William H Hill | 215 Thomas Ln | Corinth | 41010 | (859) 824-5922 | (859) 824-5922 |
| Corydon | 5 | 765 | Henderson | Larry Thurby | 5317 Rt 1 | Corydon | 42406 | (270) 533-6676 | (270) 533-6721 |
| Covington | 2 | 43010 | Kenton | Irvin T Callery | City Bldg | Covington | 41011 | (859) 292-2127 | (859) 292-2137 |
| Crab Orchard | 6 | 863 | Lincoln | Michael Ramey | 723 Meadowlark Dr | Crab Orchard | 40419 | (606) 355-2394 | |
| Creekside | 6 | 340 | Jefferson | Michael Cottman | 9903 Four Seasons Ln | Louisville | 40241 | (502) 412-1494 | |
| Crescent Springs | 4 | 3963 | Kenton | Claire F Moriconi | 739 Buttermilk Pk | Crescent Springs | 41017 | (859) 341-3017 | (859) 341-3518 |
| Crestview | 6 | 459 | Campbell | Janet Krebs | 14 Circle Dr | Crestview | 41076 | (859) 441-5898 | (859) 441-5898 |
| Crestview Hills | 5 | 3286 | Kenton | Paul W Meier | 50 Crestview Hills Mall Rd | Crestview Hills | 41017 | (859) 341-7373 | (859) 341-6993 |
| Crestwood | 5 | 2750 | Oldham | Dennis L Deibel | PO Box 186 | Crestwood | 40014 | (502) 241-7088 | (502) 241-3159 |
| Crittenden | 5 | 2554 | Grant | James Livingood | 104 N Main St | Crittenden | 41030 | (859) 428-2597 | (859) 428-2419 |
| Crofton | 5 | 834 | Christian | Michael Croft | PO Box 42 | Crofton | 42217 | (270) 424-5111 | (270) 424-9332 |
| Crossgate | 5 | 253 | Jefferson | Peggy W Swain | 1804 Crossgate Ln | Louisville | 40206 | (502) 426-3086 | (502) 426-3086 |
| Cumberland | 4 | 2355 | Harlan | Carl Hatfield | 402 W Main St | Cumberland | 40823 | (606) 589-2107 | (606) 589-2107 |
| Cynthiana | 4 | 6243 | Harrison | Virgie Florence Wells | PO Box 67 | Cynthiana | 41031 | (859) 234-7153 | (859) 234-0035 |
| Danville | 3 | 15428 | Boyle | John W D Bowling | 445 W Main St | Danville | 40423 | (859) 238-1200 | (859) 238-1236 |
| Dawson Springs | 4 | 2972 | Hopkins | Stacia Peyton | 200 W Arcadia Ave | Dawson Springs | 42408 | (270) 797-2781 | (270) 797-2221 |
| Dayton | 4 | 5619 | Campbell | Kenneth Rankle | 1203 Dayton Ave | Dayton | 41074 | (859) 491-1600 | (859) 491-3538 |
| Dixon | 6 | 609 | Webster | Colin E Todd | 10 N Main St | Dixon | 42409 | (270) 639-5088 | (270) 639-5864 |
| Douglass Hills | 4 | 5624 | Jefferson | Sheri Fetter | 11013 Finchley Rd | Louisville | 40243 | (502) 245-3600 | (502) 245-3648 |
| Dover | 6 | 322 | Mason | Ed Sidell | PO Box 161 | Dover | 41034 | (606) 882-2306 | |
| Drakesboro | 6 | 629 | Muhlenberg | Jesse Gibson | Main St | Drakesboro | 42337 | (270) 476-8986 | (270) 476-7714 |
| Druid Hills | 6 | 318 | Jefferson | Ben Franklin | 4006 Druid Hills Rd | Louisville | 40207 | (502) 637-0631 | (502) 637-0148 |
| Dry Ridge | 4 | 2163 | Grant | William W Cull | PO Box 145 | Dry Ridge | 41035 | (859) 824-3335 | (859) 824-3598 |
| Earlington | 4 | 1612 | Hopkins | Steve Everly | 305 E Clark St | Earlington | 42410 | (270) 821-4897 | (270) 383-2041 |
| Eddyville | 5 | 2378 | Lyon | Judith Stone | PO Box 744 | Eddyville | 42038 | (270) 388-2017 | (270) 388-5683 |
| Edgewood | 4 | 9400 | Kenton | John D Link | 385 Dudley Rd | Edgewood | 41017 | (859) 331-5910 | (859) 331-5912 |
| Edmonton | 5 | 1586 | Metcalfe | Howard D Garrett | 207 East St | Edmonton | 42129 | (270) 432-2811 | (270) 432-3949 |
| Ekron | 6 | 179 | Meade | Gwynne Ison | 307 4th St | Ekron | 40117 | (270) 828-3801 | |

## CITIES AND MAYORS—1ST - 6TH CLASS CITIES

| CITY | CLASS | POP | COUNTY | MAYOR | ADDRESS | CITY | ZIP | PHONE | FAX |
|------|-------|-----|--------|-------|---------|------|-----|-------|-----|
| Elizabethtown | 4 | 23109 | Hardin | David Willmoth Jr | 200 W Dixie Ave | Elizabethtown | 42702 | (270) 765-6121 | (270) 737-5362 |
| Elkhorn City | 4 | 1033 | Pike | Richard Vaughn Salyer | 395 Patty Loveless Dr | Elkhorn City | 41522 | (606) 754-5080 | (606) 754-8588 |
| Elkton | 4 | 1933 | Todd | John E Walton | 71 Public Sq | Elkton | 42220 | (270) 265-9877 | (270) 265-5816 |
| Elsmere | 4 | 8054 | Kenton | Billy Bradford | 910 Garvey Ave | Elsmere | 41018 | (859) 342-7911 | (859) 342-7910 |
| Eminence | 4 | 2252 | Henry | Douglas Bates | PO Box 163 | Eminence | 40019 | (502) 845-4159 | (502) 845-8066 |
| Erlanger | 3 | 16746 | Kenton | Marc T Otto Sr | 505 Commonwealth Ave | Erlanger | 41018 | (859) 727-2525 | (859) 727-7944 |
| Eubank | 6 | 371 | Pulaski | Frey Todd | 10 Depot St | Eubank | 42567 | (606) 379-2703 | (606) 379-2023 |
| Evarts | 5 | 1063 | Harlan | Burl Fee | 101 Harlan St | Evarts | 40828 | (606) 837-2477 | (606) 837-2093 |
| Ewing | 6 | 290 | Fleming | Vacant | PO Box 63 | Ewing | 41039 | (606) 267-4010 | (606) 564-2257 |
| Fairfield | 6 | 133 | Nelson | Mary Ellen Marquess | PO Box 42 | Fairfield | 40020 | (502) 348-3475 | (502) 348-3475 |
| Fairview | 4 | 147 | Kenton | Harold Parks | 8394 Decoursey Pk | Fairview | 41015 | (859) 291-7885 | (859) 291-4697 |
| Falmouth | 4 | 2098 | Pendleton | Gena Flaugher | 230 Main St | Falmouth | 41040 | (859) 654-4730 | (859) 654-3603 |
| Ferguson | 5 | 906 | Pulaski | James Muse | 414 Murphy Ave | Ferguson | 42533 | (606) 679-6800 | (606) 678-9638 |
| Fincastle | 6 | 910 | Jefferson | Raymond H Elms | 4411 Amelia Ct | Louisville | 40241 | (502) 429-6629 | (502) 429-6629 |
| Flatwoods | 5 | 7659 | Greenup | Bobby F Crager | 2513 Reed St | Flatwoods | 41139 | (606) 836-9661 | (606) 836-4222 |
| Fleming-Neon | 5 | 816 | Letcher | Susan Polis | Main St | Fleming-Neon | 41840 | (606) 855-7900 | (606) 855-7995 |
| Flemingsburg | 3 | 3087 | Fleming | Louie Flanery | PO Box 406 | Flemingsburg | 41041 | (859) 371-5491 | |
| Florence | 4 | 25449 | Boone | Diane Ewing Whalen | 8100 Ewing Blvd | Florence | 41042 | (270) 276-5268 | (859) 647-5411 |
| Fordsville | 6 | 544 | Ohio | Wilda G Hardesty | 66 Ratliff St | Fordsville | 42343 | (502) 261-0348 | (270) 276-5268 |
| Forest Hills | 6 | 507 | Jefferson | Kenneth W Griffin | 2401 Merriwood Dr | Louisville | 40269 | (859) 331-1212 | (502) 491-5567 |
| Fort Mitchell | 4 | 8162 | Kenton | Thomas E Holocher | PO Box 17157 | Ft Mitchell | 41017 | (859) 441-2964 | (859) 331-6102 |
| Fort Thomas | 4 | 15733 | Campbell | Mary H Brown | 140 Highland Ave | Ft Thomas | 41075 | (859) 331-1700 | (859) 441-3519 |
| Fort Wright | 4 | 5493 | Kenton | Gene Weaver | 409 Kyles Ln | Ft Wright | 41011 | (270) 434-3544 | (859) 331-0454 |
| Fountain Run | 6 | 233 | Monroe | Eldon Veach | 202 Main St | Fountain Run | 42133 | (502) 957-3359 | (270) 434-2211 |
| Fox Chase | 6 | 490 | Bullitt | Joe Laswell | 4814 Fox Chase Dr | Shepherdsville | 40165 | (502) 875-8500 | |
| Frankfort | 2 | 27281 | Franklin | William I May Jr | 315 W 2nd St | Frankfort | 40602 | (502) 586-4497 | (502) 875-8502 |
| Franklin | 4 | 8071 | Simpson | Jim Brown | PO Box 2805 | Franklin | 42135 | (270) 545-3925 | (270) 586-9419 |
| Fredonia | 5 | 414 | Caldwell | Mike Board | PO Box 58 | Fredonia | 42411 | (606) 768-3457 | (270) 545-3925 |
| Frenchburg | 6 | 565 | Menifee | Dwain E Benson | Rt 36 | Frenchburg | 40322 | (270) 472-1320 | (606) 768-6277 |
| Fulton | 4 | 2617 | Fulton | Edward Crittendon | PO Box 1350 | Fulton | 42041 | (270) 457-4561 | (270) 472-6526 |
| Gamaliel | 6 | 432 | Monroe | Roger Geralds | 298 Lil Taylor Rd | Gamaliel | 42140 | (502) 863-9800 | (270) 457-2901 |
| Georgetown | 6 | 19732 | Scott | Everette L Varney | 100 Court St | Georgetown | 40324 | (606) 728-2312 | (502) 863-9810 |
| Germantown | 6 | 151 | Bracken | Maude B Teegarden | 41077 Salem Rd | Germantown | 41044 | (502) 347-0161 | |
| Ghent | 3 | 386 | Carroll | William Mumphrey | 501 Main St | Ghent | 41045 | (270) 651-1777 | |
| Glasgow | 3 | 13829 | Barren | Darrell Pickett | 126 E Public Sq Ste 200 | Glasgow | 42141 | (859) 643-2211 | (270) 659-2114 |
| Glencoe | 6 | 249 | Gallatin | Michael Murphy | 112 N Main St | Glencoe | 41046 | (502) 893-3333 | (859) 643-2211 |
| Glenview | 6 | 625 | Jefferson | Gar Davis | 2211 Brownsboro Rd | Louisville | 40206 | (502) 426-9863 | (502) 897-6093 |
| Glenview Hills | 6 | 341 | Jefferson | Fred R Simon | 2908 Lightheart St | Louisville | 40222 | (502) 429-6988 | |
| Glenview Manor | 6 | 194 | Jefferson | Michael Patterson | 6 Glenwood Rd | Louisville | 40222 | (502) 426-2480 | |
| Goose Creek | 6 | 274 | Jefferson | Don Zitnik | 8709 Banbridge Rd | Louisville | 40242 | (502) 228-2377 | |
| Goshen | 5 | 945 | Oldham | Todd D Hall | 1111 Crestview | Goshen | 40026 | (502) 362-8272 | (502) 228-4277 |
| Grand Rivers | 5 | 339 | Livingston | Max Webb | 122 W Cumberland Ave | Grand Rivers | 42045 | (502) 484-2053 | (270) 362-2572 |
| Gratz | 4 | 94 | Owen | Charles Redmon | 583 Crittenden St | Gratz | 40359 | (502) 426-9561 | |
| Graymoor-Devondale | 4 | 2945 | Jefferson | John Vaughan | 1508 Valley Brook Rd | Louisville | 40222 | (606) 474-6651 | (502) 425-5721 |
| Grayson | 6 | 4017 | Carter | Leda Dean | 302 E Main St | Grayson | 41143 | (502) 228-3651 | (606) 474-6653 |
| Green Spring | 6 | 773 | Jefferson | William M Huff | 7103 Green Spring Dr | Louisville | 40241 | (270) 932-4298 | |
| Greensburg | 5 | 2413 | Green | George Cheatham | 105 W Hodgenville Ave | Greensburg | 42743 | (606) 473-7331 | (270) 932-7778 |
| Greenup | 5 | 1190 | Greenup | Charles Veach | 1005 Walnut St | Greenup | 41144 | (270) 338-3966 | (606) 473-7831 |
| Greenville | 4 | 4314 | Muhlenberg | Billie Ruth Lewis | PO Box 289 | Greenville | 42345 | (270) 483-2511 | (270) 338-3007 |
| Guthrie | 5 | 1424 | Todd | Albert Scott Marshall | 110 Kendall St | Guthrie | 42234 | (270) 322-8760 | (270) 483-9062 |
| Hanson | 6 | 625 | Hopkins | Charles Young | 7580 Hanson Rd | Hanson | 42413 | (270) 437-4910 | (270) 322-8575 |
| Hardin | 6 | 568 | Marshall | Randal Scott | PO Box 377 | Hardin | 42048 | (270) 756-2213 | (270) 437-4934 |
| Hardinsburg | 5 | 2429 | Breckinridge | Wayne Macy | 220 S Main St | Hardinsburg | 40143 | (606) 573-2912 | (270) 756-2029 |
| Harlan | 4 | 2018 | Harlan | Daniel E Howard | PO Box 783 | Harlan | 40831 | | (606) 573-9947 |

## CITIES AND MAYORS — 1ST - 6TH CLASS CITIES

| CITY | CLASS | POP | COUNTY | MAYOR | ADDRESS | CITY | ZIP | PHONE | FAX |
|---|---|---|---|---|---|---|---|---|---|
| Harrodsburg | 4 | 8041 | Mercer | Lonnie Campbell | 208 S Main St | Harrodsburg | 40330 | (859) 734-7705 | (859) 734-6231 |
| Hartford | 5 | 2640 | Ohio | Earl Russell | 116 E Washington St | Hartford | 42347 | (270) 298-3612 | (270) 298-3220 |
| Hawesville | 5 | 964 | Hancock | Charles M King | 395 Main St | Hawesville | 42348 | (270) 927-8707 | (270) 927-8184 |
| Hazard | 3 | 4847 | Perry | William D Gorman | 700 Main St | Hazard | 41702 | (606) 436-3171 | (606) 436-3252 |
| Hazel | 6 | 444 | Calloway | Harold Pittman | PO Box 184 | Hazel | 42049 | (270) 492-6464 | (270) 492-8862 |
| Hebron Estates | 5 | 1132 | Bullitt | Jerry Clark | 3407 Burkland Blvd | Shepherdsville | 40165 | (270) 955-4973 | |
| Henderson | 2 | 27574 | Henderson | Henry G Lackey | PO Box 716 | Henderson | 42419 | (270) 831-1200 | (270) 831-1206 |
| Hickman | 4 | 2410 | Fulton | Richard H White | PO Box 199 | Hickman | 42050 | (270) 236-2535 | (270) 236-2537 |
| Hickory Hill | 6 | 130 | Jefferson | Patricia J Rayburn | 3001 Creekside Dr | Louisville | 40241 | (502) 423-9302 | |
| Highland Heights | 4 | 6326 | Campbell | Charles W Roettger | 175 Johns Hill Rd | Highland Heights | 41076 | (859) 441-8575 | (859) 441-8293 |
| Hills and Dales | 6 | 157 | Jefferson | Ralph Johanson | 3209 Mt Rainier Dr | Louisville | 42024 | (502) 426-7948 | |
| Hillview | 4 | 7253 | Bullitt | James Eadens | 298 Prairie Dr | Louisville | 40229 | (502) 957-5280 | (502) 955-5673 |
| Hindman | 5 | 773 | Knott | Janice Jarrell | Main St | Hindman | 41822 | (606) 785-5544 | (606) 785-0799 |
| Hiseville | 6 | 226 | Barren | Bill Phillips | PO Box 149 | Hiseville | 42152 | (270) 453-2605 | (270) 453-2941 |
| Hodgenville | 4 | 2779 | Larue | Roger Truitt | PO Box 189 | Hodgenville | 42748 | (270) 358-3832 | (270) 358-9757 |
| Hollow Creek | 5 | 823 | Jefferson | Robert A Wagner Jr | 6410 Watch Hill Rd | Louisville | 40228 | (502) 231-0858 | |
| Hollyvilla | 6 | 494 | Jefferson | Charles David Clemons Sr | 10721 Charlene Dr | Fairdale | 40118 | (502) 363-4939 | |
| Hopkinsville | 2 | 28953 | Christian | Richard G Liebe | 101 N Main St | Hopkinsville | 42240 | (270) 887-4000 | (270) 890-0202 |
| Horse Cave | 4 | 2311 | Hart | JoAnne Smith | PO Box 326 | Horse Cave | 42749 | (270) 786-2680 | (270) 786-2688 |
| Houston Acres | 6 | 493 | Jefferson | Charles G Bartman | 4302 Martha Ave | Louisville | 40220 | (502) 454-3355 | (502) 957-4205 |
| Hunters Hollow | 6 | 380 | Bullitt | Linda S Parker | 11300 Angelina Rd | Louisville | 40229 | (502) 957-4205 | (502) 428-4889 |
| Hurstbourne | 4 | 3951 | Jefferson | Robert English | 8315 Salford Way | Louisville | 40222 | (502) 426-3327 | |
| Hurstbourne Acres | 5 | 1510 | Jefferson | Sean P Fore | 1808 Addington Ave | Louisville | 40220 | (502) 491-5419 | |
| Hustonville | 6 | 313 | Lincoln | Larry Doss | PO Box 172 | Hustonville | 40437 | (606) 346-2501 | (606) 346-4312 |
| Hyden | 6 | 197 | Leslie | Eugene Stewart | 22035 Main St | Hyden | 41749 | (606) 672-2300 | (606) 672-5810 |
| Independence | 3 | 17940 | Kenton | Chris Moriconi | 5409 Madison Pk | Independence | 41051 | (859) 356-5302 | (859) 356-6843 |
| Indian Hills | 4 | 2971 | Jefferson | Thomas O Eifler | PO Box 6289 | Louisville | 40206 | (502) 895-0005 | (502) 893-0330 |
| Inez | 6 | 451 | Martin | Dick Young | 142 Broadway | Inez | 41224 | (606) 298-7051 | |
| Irvine | 4 | 2738 | Estill | W T (Tom) Williams | 806 Michelle Way | Irvine | 40336 | (606) 723-2554 | (606) 723-2558 |
| Irvington | 5 | 1302 | Breckinridge | Ricky Lucas | 145 N Washington | Irvington | 40146 | (270) 547-6623 | |
| Island | 6 | 438 | McLean | Charles R Strole | 333 Broadway St | Island | 42350 | (270) 486-3992 | (270) 486-9303 |
| Jackson | 4 | 2412 | Breathitt | Michael D Miller | 202 Monument Sq | Jackson | 41339 | (606) 666-7069 | (606) 666-7046 |
| Jamestown | 5 | 1695 | Russell | June McGaha | 10416 Watterson Trl | Jamestown | 42629 | (270) 343-4594 | (270) 343-4929 |
| Jeffersontown | 2 | 26232 | Jefferson | Clay S Foreman | PO Box 127 | Jeffersontown | 40299 | (502) 267-8333 | (502) 267-0547 |
| Jeffersonville | 6 | 1851 | Montgomery | Richard Henderson | 853 Lakeside Dr | Jeffersonville | 40337 | (859) 498-5808 | (859) 497-6267 |
| Jenkins | 4 | 2322 | Letcher | Robert Pud Shubert | 794 Shelby St | Jenkins | 41537 | (606) 832-2142 | (606) 832-2362 |
| Junction City | 5 | 2178 | Boyle | Glen Harmon | 464 Kuhrs Ln | Junction City | 40440 | (859) 854-3900 | (859) 854-3900 |
| Kentonvale | 6 | 147 | Kenton | Michael Pendery | PO Box 83 | Kentonvale | 41015 | | |
| Kevil | 6 | 574 | Ballard | Charles Burnley | PO Box 5515 | Kevil | 42053 | (270) 462-3151 | (270) 462-3104 |
| Kingsley | 6 | 427 | Jefferson | Phyllis A Breuer | 82 Cedar St | Louisville | 40205 | (502) 452-2515 | (502) 452-2515 |
| Kuttawa | 5 | 622 | Lyon | Lee McCollum | PO Box 420 | Kuttawa | 42055 | (270) 388-7151 | (270) 388-7695 |
| LaCenter | 5 | 1036 | Ballard | Lewis Hicks | PO Box 240 | LaCenter | 42056 | (270) 655-5162 | (270) 665-9113 |
| LaFayette | 6 | 187 | Christian | Nancy A Reece | 410 W Jefferson St | LaFayette | 42254 | (270) 271-2185 | (270) 271-2859 |
| LaGrange | 4 | 5767 | Oldham | Elsie Carter | 258 N Ashbrook Cir | LaGrange | 40031 | (502) 222-1433 | (502) 222-5875 |
| Lakeside Park | 5 | 2869 | Kenton | Karen Gamel | 385 Circle Dr | Lakeside Park | 41017 | (859) 331-8707 | (859) 331-8707 |
| Lakeview Heights | 6 | 242 | Rowan | David Bolt | 101 Stanford St | Morehead | 40351 | (606) 784-5271 | (606) 780-7613 |
| Lancaster | 5 | 4091 | Garrard | Billy Carter Moss | PO Box 22294 | Lancaster | 40444 | (859) 792-2241 | (859) 792-3341 |
| Langdon Place | 6 | 982 | Jefferson | Carolyn S Weitlauf | 6132 Clubhouse Dr | Louisville | 40252 | (502) 426-3701 | (502) 426-3701 |
| Latonia Lakes | 6 | 307 | Kenton | William Dorgan Jr | 100 E Main | Latonia Lakes | 41015 | (859) 356-0417 | (859) 356-9111 |
| Lawrenceburg | 4 | 9396 | Anderson | Bobby Sparrow | PO Box 840 | Lawrenceburg | 40342 | (502) 839-5372 | (502) 839-5106 |
| Lebanon | 4 | 5884 | Marion | Gary D Crenshaw | 271 Main St | Lebanon | 40033 | (270) 692-6272 | (270) 692-4638 |
| Lebanon Junction | 5 | 1897 | Bullitt | George Halk | 314 W White Oak St | Lebanon Junction | 40150 | (502) 833-4311 | (502) 833-4688 |
| Leitchfield | 4 | 6419 | Grayson | William H (Turkey) Thomason | 204 S Main St | Leitchfield | 42755 | (270) 259-4034 | (270) 259-5858 |
| Lewisburg | 5 | 903 | Logan | Kenneth Whitson | | Lewisburg | 42256 | (270) 755-2516 | (270) 755-4829 |

# CITIES AND MAYORS — 1ST - 6TH CLASS CITIES

| CITY | CLASS | POP | COUNTY | MAYOR | ADDRESS | CITY | ZIP | PHONE | FAX |
|---|---|---|---|---|---|---|---|---|---|
| Lewisport | 5 | 1627 | Hancock | Chad Gregory | 1010 Market St | Lewisport | 42351 | | |
| Lexington | 2 | 266358 | Fayette | Teresa Isaac | 200 E Main St | Lexington | 40507 | (859) 258-3100 | (859) 258-3194 |
| Liberty | 5 | 1872 | Casey | Steve Sweeney | PO Box 127 | Liberty | 42539 | (606) 787-9973 | (606) 787-7992 |
| Lincolnshire | 6 | 155 | Jefferson | Lewis Hudson | 109 W 3rd St | Louisville | 40220 | (502) 454-3857 | (502) 895-6552 |
| Livermore | 5 | 1482 | McLean | Eldon Eaton | PO Box 654 | Livermore | 42352 | (270) 278-2113 | (270) 278-9092 |
| Livingston | 6 | 228 | Rockcastle | Curl McHargue | | Livingston | 40445 | (606) 308-2175 | |
| London | 4 | 7767 | Laurel | Ken Smith | 501 S Main St | London | 40741 | (606) 864-6995 | (606) 864-5184 |
| Lone Oak | 6 | 443 | McCracken | Frank M Galliher | 254 S Friendship Rd | Paducah | 42003 | (270) 554-5929 | (270) 534-8477 |
| Loretto | 6 | 643 | Marion | Robert G Miles | 9215 Loretto Rd | Loretto | 40037 | (270) 865-4174 | (270) 865-4422 |
| Louisa | 5 | 2038 | Lawrence | Teddy Preston | 215 N Main Cross St | Louisa | 41230 | (606) 638-4038 | (606) 638-3414 |
| Louisville | 1 | 699017 | Jefferson | Jerry Abramson | Louisville Metro Hall | Louisville | 40202 | (502) 574-2003 | (502) 574-5354 |
| Loyall | 5 | 776 | Harlan | Charles Wattenberger | 306 Carter St | Loyall | 40854 | (606) 573-6396 | (606) 573-2283 |
| Ludlow | 4 | 4409 | Kenton | Ed F Schroeder | 306 Stokesay St | Ludlow | 41016 | (859) 291-1243 | (859) 491-2966 |
| Lynch | 5 | 854 | Harlan | Thomas E Vicini | 6 E Main St | Lynch | 40855 | (606) 848-2873 | (606) 848-2147 |
| Lyndon | 4 | 10270 | Jefferson | Susan M Barto | 515 Wood Rd | Lyndon | 40222 | (502) 423-0932 | (502) 339-9722 |
| Lynnview | 5 | 965 | Jefferson | Lawrence Shaughnessy | 1241 Gilmore Ln | Louisville | 40213 | (502) 966-4086 | (502) 966-5507 |
| Mackville | 6 | 212 | Washington | Carl Gabhart | 151 N Church St | Mackville | 40040 | (859) 262-5175 | |
| Madisonville | 4 | 19340 | Hopkins | Karen L Cunningham | 37 E Center St | Madisonville | 42431 | (270) 824-2100 | (270) 821-6161 |
| Manchester | 4 | 1967 | Clay | Daugh K White | 239 Memorial Dr | Manchester | 40962 | (606) 598-3456 | (606) 599-1763 |
| Manor Creek | 6 | 224 | Jefferson | Paul Veatch | PO Box 22133 | Louisville | 40252 | (502) 425-3000 | (502) 425-2007 |
| Marion | 4 | 3047 | Crittenden | Michael D Alexander | 217 S Main St | Marion | 42064 | (270) 965-2266 | (270) 965-5235 |
| Martin | 4 | 639 | Floyd | Thomasine Robinson | 11729 Main St | Martin | 41649 | (606) 285-9335 | (606) 285-3309 |
| Maryhill Estates | 4 | 177 | Jefferson | Linda Jedlicki | 4116 Ormond Rd | Louisville | 40207 | (502) 895-3158 | |
| Mayfield | 3 | 10252 | Graves | Arthur Byrn | 211 E Broadway | Mayfield | 42066 | (270) 247-1981 | (270) 247-2485 |
| Maysville | 3 | 9011 | Mason | David Cartmell | 216 Bridge St | Maysville | 41056 | (606) 564-9411 | (606) 564-9416 |
| McHenry | 6 | 434 | Ohio | Dennis Chinn | 59 Hillard Moseley Rd | McHenry | 42354 | (270) 274-4831 | |
| McKee | 5 | 856 | Jackson | Dwight K Bishop | US 421 Main St | McKee | 40447 | (606) 287-8305 | (606) 287-7179 |
| Meadow Vale | 5 | 772 | Jefferson | Roy Fey | 9818 Boxford Way | Louisville | 40242 | (502) 425-8329 | |
| Meadowbrook Farm | 6 | 147 | Jefferson | Timothy (Tim) Roe | 2114 Ternwood Ct | Louisville | 40223 | (502) 429-9356 | |
| Meadowview Estates | 6 | 423 | Jefferson | Henry Glass | 2912 Meadowview Cir | Louisville | 40250 | (502) 459-3579 | |
| Melbourne | 6 | 451 | Campbell | Helen P Lutz | 7 Raintree Dr | Melbourne | 41059 | (859) 781-6664 | (859) 781-9444 |
| Mentor | 6 | 200 | Campbell | David Gearding | PO Box 3 | Mentor | 41007 | (859) 635-9365 | |
| Middlesboro | 3 | 10192 | Bell | Ben Hickman | PO Box 756 | Middlesboro | 40965 | (606) 248-6670 | (606) 248-1202 |
| Middletown | 4 | 6040 | Jefferson | J Byron Chapman | PO Box 43048 | Middletown | 40253 | (502) 245-2762 | (502) 245-6047 |
| Midway | 5 | 1614 | Woodford | Becky Moore | 101 E Main St | Midway | 40347 | (859) 846-4237 | (859) 846-4411 |
| Millersburg | 6 | 832 | Bourbon | Samuel (Sam) Chanslor | 5th St | Millersburg | 40348 | (859) 484-3899 | (859) 484-3901 |
| Milton | 6 | 597 | Trimble | Donald Oakley | 206 Peck Pk | Milton | 40045 | (502) 268-5224 | (502) 268-0224 |
| Minor Lane Heights | 5 | 1516 | Jefferson | Fred D Williams Sr | 11642 Reality Trl | Louisville | 40229 | (502) 893-3767 | (502) 290-5423 |
| Mockingbird Valley | 6 | 198 | Jefferson | John Hanley | 606 Club Ln | Louisville | 40207 | (502) 484-0672 | |
| Monterey | 6 | 175 | Owen | Dennis Atha | 10335 Hwy 127S | Monterey | 40359 | | |
| Monticello | 4 | 6080 | Wayne | Thurston Frye | PO Box 550 | Monticello | 42633 | (606) 348-5719 | (606) 348-0267 |
| Moorland | 4 | 465 | Jefferson | Brian Kidd | | Moorland | 40223 | (502) 836-0797 | |
| Morehead | 4 | 7589 | Rowan | Bradley H Collins | 105 E Main St | Morehead | 40351 | (606) 784-8505 | (606) 784-2216 |
| Morganfield | 4 | 3461 | Union | Jerry R Freer | 130 E Main St | Morganfield | 42437 | (270) 389-2525 | (270) 389-2157 |
| Morgantown | 5 | 2553 | Butler | Charles T Black | 117 N Main St | Morgantown | 42261 | (270) 526-3557 | (270) 526-6295 |
| Mortons Gap | 5 | 962 | Hopkins | Frank D Stafford | 102 S Main St | Mortons Gap | 42440 | (270) 258-5362 | (270) 258-5006 |
| Mount Olivet | 5 | 291 | Robertson | Philip Insko | PO Box 166 | Mt Olivet | 41064 | (606) 724-5816 | (606) 724-5816 |
| Mount Sterling | 4 | 6122 | Montgomery | Gary Williamson | 33 N Maysville St | Mt Sterling | 40353 | (859) 498-8725 | (859) 498-8727 |
| Mount Vernon | 5 | 2610 | Rockcastle | Clarice R Kirby | 125 Richmond St | Mt Vernon | 40456 | (606) 256-3437 | (606) 256-3443 |
| Mount Washington | 4 | 8718 | Bullitt | Frank Sullivan | PO Box 285 | Mt Washington | 40047 | (502) 538-4216 | (502) 538-4064 |
| Muldraugh | 5 | 1358 | Meade | Danny J Tate | 120 S Main St | Muldraugh | 40155 | (502) 942-2824 | (502) 942-2892 |
| Munfordville | 5 | 1605 | Hart | John Johnson | PO Box 85 | Munfordville | 42765 | (270) 524-2635 | (270) 524-3021 |
| Murray | 3 | 15270 | Calloway | Tom Rushing | 104 N 5th St | Murray | 42071 | (270) 762-0350 | (270) 762-0306 |
| Murray Hill | 6 | 620 | Jefferson | Eric Higdon | Goose Creek Rd | Louisville | 40252 | (502) 454-3083 | |

# CITIES AND MAYORS — 1ST - 6TH CLASS CITIES

| CITY | CLASS | POP | COUNTY | MAYOR | ADDRESS | ZIP | PHONE | FAX |
|---|---|---|---|---|---|---|---|---|
| Nebo | 6 | 222 | Hopkins | Wayne Kelley | 8695 Nebo Rd | 42441 | (270) 249-3116 | (502) 845-5702 |
| New Castle | 5 | 927 | Henry | James Brammell | 37 E Cross Main St | 40050 | (502) 845-5750 | |
| New Haven | 6 | 849 | Nelson | Tessie R Cecil | 379 Center St | 40051 | (502) 549-3569 | |
| Newport | 2 | 16086 | Campbell | Thomas Guidugli | 998 Monmouth St | 41071 | (859) 292-3666 | (859) 292-3669 |
| Nicholasville | 3 | 28878 | Jessamine | John P Martin | 517 N Main St | 40356 | (859) 885-1121 | (859) 881-0750 |
| Northaune Estates | 6 | 460 | Jefferson | Timothy (Tim) Kraus | 4020 Norbourne Blvd | 40207 | (502) 895-7731 | |
| North Middletown | 5 | 600 | Bourbon | Buddy Mers | 213 Liberty St | 40357 | (859) 362-7776 | (859) 362-7052 |
| Northfield | 5 | 985 | Jefferson | Jack Kaiser | 6401 Lime Ridge Ct | 40222 | (502) 425-3997 | |
| Nortonville | 5 | 1260 | Hopkins | James L Noel | 199 S Main St | 42442 | (270) 676-3384 | (270) 676-7067 |
| Norwood | 6 | 398 | Jefferson | Kenneth Schueler | 405 Hidden Oak Way | 40252 | (502) 426-2818 | |
| Oak Grove | 4 | 7601 | Christian | Colleen Ochs | PO Box 250 | 42262 | (270) 439-6552 | (270) 439-1201 |
| Oakland | 6 | 256 | Warren | William P Mansfield Jr | 701 N Vine St Box 145 | 42159 | (270) 563-4033 | |
| Old Brownsboro Place | 6 | 389 | Jefferson | Maurice H (Mick) Wagner | 7247 Heatherly Sq | 40242 | (502) 426-8447 | (606) 286-8538 |
| Olive Hill | 4 | 1820 | Carter | Danny Sparks | 415 Oak St | 41164 | (606) 286-5220 | (502) 243-0028 |
| Orchard Grass Hills | 5 | 1375 | Oldham | Jim Burke | PO Box 25 | 40014 | (502) 241-7963 | |
| Owensboro | 2 | 54067 | Daviess | Tom Watson | PO Box 10003 | 42302 | (270) 687-8550 | (270) 687-8585 |
| Owenton | 5 | 1466 | Owen | David M Wotier | 220 S Main St | 40359 | (502) 484-2322 | (502) 484-5156 |
| Owingsville | 4 | 1543 | Bath | Don Kincaid | 19 Goodpaster Ave | 40360 | (606) 674-6361 | (606) 674-3068 |
| Paducah | 2 | 25545 | McCracken | William F Paxton | 300 S 5th St | 42002 | (270) 444-8503 | (270) 443-5058 |
| Paintsville | 4 | 4132 | Johnson | Douglas Pugh | 101 Euclid Ave | 41240 | (606) 789-2600 | (606) 789-2602 |
| Paris | 3 | 9284 | Bourbon | Donald Kiser | 525 High St | 40361 | (859) 987-2110 | (859) 987-4640 |
| Park City | 5 | 535 | Barren | David Lyons | 388 Riherd Estate Rd | 42160 | (270) 749-5700 | |
| Park Hills | 4 | 2844 | Kenton | Michael J Hellmann | 1106 Amsterdam Rd | 41011 | (859) 431-6252 | (859) 431-6410 |
| Park Lake | 6 | 560 | Oldham | James Kramer | PO Box 310 | 40014 | (502) 243-0467 | |
| Parkway Village | 5 | 710 | Jefferson | Betty Shelton | 850 Parkway Dr | 40217 | (502) 636-2726 | (270) 475-9766 |
| Pembroke | 6 | 786 | Christian | Freddy Shelton | PO Box 308 | 42266 | (270) 475-9171 | (859) 332-7682 |
| Perryville | 5 | 756 | Boyle | Bruce Richardson | 216 S Buell St | 40468 | (859) 332-8361 | (606) 437-5106 |
| Pewee Valley | 5 | 1522 | Oldham | Clayton Stoess | 109 LaGrange Rd | 40056 | (502) 241-1964 | (606) 437-5106 |
| Pikeville | 3 | 6304 | Pike | Frank Justice | 118 College St | 41501 | (606) 437-5108 | (606) 437-5106 |
| Pineville | 4 | 2015 | Bell | Bruce Hendrickson | PO Box 688 | 40977 | (606) 337-2207 | (606) 337-7111 |
| Pioneer Village | 4 | 2598 | Bullitt | Gary W Hatcher | 3300 Cardinal Dr | 40229 | (502) 957-3800 | (502) 975-4580 |
| Pippa Passes | 6 | 294 | Knott | Richard Kennedy | 100 Purpose Rd | 41844 | (606) 368-6082 | (606) 368-6217 |
| Plantation | 5 | 906 | Jefferson | Becky Peak | PO Box 22698 | 40252 | (502) 425-4449 | (502) 425-4747 |
| Pleasureville | 6 | 885 | Henry | William Rodney Young | 111 Roberts St | 40057 | (502) 878-4273 | (502) 878-9952 |
| Plum Springs | 6 | 453 | Warren | Thomas Clayton | 124 Owl Dr | 42101 | (270) 843-1593 | |
| Poplar Hills | 6 | 404 | Jefferson | W Grayson Flood Jr | 201 Huntington Park Dr | 40213 | (502) 966-8088 | (502) 966-8666 |
| Powderly | 5 | 848 | Muhlenberg | Donald C Hancock | PO Box 106 | 42367 | (270) 338-5123 | (270) 338-4990 |
| Prestonsburg | 4 | 3714 | Floyd | Jerry S Fannin | 200 N Lake Dr | 41653 | (606) 886-2335 | (606) 886-0563 |
| Prestonville | 6 | 171 | Carroll | Tommy Couch | PO Box 306 | 41008 | (502) 732-4576 | |
| Princeton | 4 | 6412 | Caldwell | Vickie Hughes | 206 E Market St | 42445 | (270) 365-9575 | (270) 365-4661 |
| Prospect | 3 | 4853 | Jefferson | Joseph Kehlbeck | PO Box 1 | 40059 | (502) 228-1121 | (502) 228-9542 |
| Providence | 4 | 3554 | Webster | Eddie Gooch | PO Box 128 | 42450 | (270) 667-5463 | (270) 667-5125 |
| Raceland | 5 | 2443 | Greenup | Bill C Selvage Sr | 50 Bellifonte Rd | 41169 | (606) 836-5151 | |
| Radcliff | 2 | 21617 | Hardin | Sheila C Enyart | 411 W Lincoln Trail Blvd | 40159 | (270) 351-4714 | (606) 351-7329 |
| Ravenna | 5 | 680 | Estill | Charles Crowe | 609 Elm St | 40472 | (606) 723-3332 | (606) 723-3332 |
| Raywick | 6 | 148 | Marion | Marilyn Mullins | 5720 Raywick Rd | 40060 | (270) 692-2216 | (270) 349-6872 |
| Richlawn | 6 | 454 | Jefferson | Sandra Banta | PO Box 7786 | 40257 | (502) 893-3609 | (502) 581-6365 |
| Richmond | 4 | 30008 | Madison | Connie Lawson | 239 W Main St | 40476 | (859) 623-1000 | (859) 623-7618 |
| River Bluff | 6 | 420 | Oldham | Bryan Dillon | PO Box 792 | 40059 | (502) 426-1542 | |
| Riverwood | 6 | 477 | Jefferson | John DeWeese | 2105 Round Ridge Rd | 40207 | (502) 895-6942 | |
| Robards | 6 | 569 | Henderson | Ron Iler | 8933 N Easy St Loop | 42452 | (270) 521-7621 | |
| Rochester | 6 | 190 | Butler | Horace B Hammers | PO Box 125 | 42273 | (270) 934-3851 | |
| Rockport | 6 | 343 | Ohio | Kermit Geary | PO Box 184 | 42369 | (270) 274-9783 | |
| Rolling Fields | 6 | 654 | Jefferson | Bill Conway | 425 Club Ln | 40207 | (502) 895-5004 | (502) 895-5661 |

# CITIES AND MAYORS — 1ST - 6TH CLASS CITIES

| CITY | CLASS | POP | COUNTY | MAYOR | ADDRESS | CITY | ZIP | PHONE | FAX |
|---|---|---|---|---|---|---|---|---|---|
| Rolling Hills | 5 | 910 | Jefferson | Leslie Faust | 9405 Aylesbury Dr | Louisville | 40242 | (502) 426-7895 | |
| Russell | 4 | 3615 | Greenup | Bill Hopkins | 410 Ferry St | Russell | 41169 | (606) 836-9666 | (606) 836-3795 |
| Russell Springs | 5 | 2497 | Russell | Eric Selby | 72 High St | Russell Springs | 42642 | (270) 866-3981 | (270) 866-3860 |
| Russellville | 4 | 7235 | Logan | Shirlee Yassney | 168 S Main St | Russellville | 42276 | (270) 726-5001 | (270) 726-5043 |
| Ryland Heights | 6 | 820 | Kenton | Bob Miller | 9985 Decoursey Pk | Ryland Heights | 41015 | (859) 356-5862 | |
| Sacramento | 6 | 519 | McLean | Pam Jennings | PO Box 245 | Sacramento | 42372 | (270) 736-5114 | (270) 736-5042 |
| Sadieville | 6 | 289 | Scott | Robbie Wagoner | PO Box 129 | Sadieville | 40370 | (270) 857-4576 | (502) 857-4555 |
| Saint Charles | 6 | 390 | Hopkins | Louise Foe | PO Box 164 | St Charles | 42453 | (270) 669-9432 | |
| Saint Matthews | 4 | 17374 | Jefferson | Arthur K Draut | 4306 Churchill Rd | St Matthews | 40207 | (502) 893-2751 | (502) 895-0510 |
| Saint Regis Park | 4 | 1530 | Jefferson | William Bohnert | 4607 Stormon Ct | St Regis Park | 40250 | (502) 451-3776 | |
| Salem | 6 | 760 | Livingston | Andrew Fox | 111 Court St | Salem | 42078 | (270) 988-2600 | (270) 988-4662 |
| Salt Lick | 6 | 353 | Bath | Brad Frizzel | 200 Caney Ave | Salt Lick | 40371 | (606) 683-5041 | (606) 278-6683 |
| Salyersville | 4 | 1603 | Magoffin | Stanley Howard | PO Box 954 | Salyersville | 41465 | (606) 349-7990 | (606) 349-2449 |
| Sanders | 6 | 252 | Carroll | Jackie Ogden | 14373 Hwy 36 E | Sanderson | 41083 | (502) 347-9809 | |
| Sandy Hook | 5 | 681 | Elliott | James (Robby) Adkins | PO Box 274 | Sandy Hook | 41171 | (606) 738-6489 | (606) 738-5192 |
| Sardis | 6 | 149 | Mason | Bonnie Tuel | PO Box 14 | Sardis | 41056 | (606) 763-6693 | (606) 763-6693 |
| Science Hill | 6 | 649 | Pulaski | MacDonald M Phelps | PO Box 14 | Science Hill | 42553 | (606) 423-4109 | (606) 423-2384 |
| Scottsville | 4 | 4327 | Allen | Rob Cline | City County Bldg | Scottsville | 42164 | (270) 237-3238 | (270) 237-4922 |
| Sebree | 5 | 1565 | Webster | Jerry L Hobgood | 36 S Spring St | Sebree | 42455 | (270) 835-7501 | (270) 835-9807 |
| Seneca Gardens | 6 | 698 | Jefferson | James F (Jim) MacDonald | 2501 Denham Rd | Seneca Gardens | 40205 | (502) 451-8221 | |
| Sharpsburg | 6 | 303 | Bath | Roberta Shrout | PO Box 176 | Sharpsburg | 40374 | (606) 247-2931 | |
| Shelbyville | 4 | 10622 | Shelby | Tom Hardesty | 315 Washington St | Shelbyville | 40066 | (502) 633-0011 | (502) 633-4292 |
| Shepherdsville | 4 | 8737 | Bullitt | Joseph G Sohm | 170 Frank E Simon Ave | Shepherdsville | 40165 | (502) 543-2923 | (502) 543-6201 |
| Shively | 4 | 15258 | Jefferson | Sherry Sinegra Conner | PO Box 16007 | Shively | 40216 | (502) 449-5000 | (502) 449-5004 |
| Silver Grove | 5 | 1400 | Campbell | Vacant | 308 Oak St | Silver Grove | 41085 | (859) 441-6390 | (859) 441-4363 |
| Simpsonville | 5 | 1600 | Shelby | Steve Eden | 503 Garden Ct | Simpsonville | 40067 | (502) 722-5711 | (502) 722-0060 |
| Slaughters | 6 | 239 | Webster | Donald W Winstead | 51 W 2nd St | Slaughters | 42456 | (270) 884-7000 | (270) 884-7009 |
| Smithfield | 6 | 103 | Henry | Les Bryant | PO Box 22 | Smithfield | 40068 | (270) 845-6300 | |
| Smithland | 6 | 395 | Livingston | Thomas N (Tom) Cothron | PO Box 262 | Smithland | 42081 | (270) 928-4287 | (270) 928-2446 |
| Smiths Grove | 5 | 762 | Warren | Larry Steve Watt | 146 S Main St | Smiths Grove | 42171 | (270) 563-4014 | (270) 563-9315 |
| Somerset | 3 | 11972 | Pulaski | J P Wiles | 400 E Mt Vernon St | Somerset | 42502 | (606) 679-6366 | (606) 679-2481 |
| Sonora | 6 | 340 | Hardin | Larry D Copelin | 330 E Western Ave | Sonora | 42776 | | |
| South Carrollton | 6 | 184 | Muhlenberg | Jerry Barbee | PO Box 121 | South Carrollton | 42374 | | |
| South Park View | 6 | 201 | Jefferson | Eddie Rasnake | 9010 Vondine Dr | Louisville | 40219 | (859) 969-2069 | |
| South Shore | 5 | 1244 | Greenup | Ronald (Ronnie) Stone | PO Box 89 | South Shore | 41175 | (606) 932-4604 | |
| Southgate | 4 | 3475 | Campbell | Charles (Chuck) Melville | 122 Electric Ave | Southgate | 41071 | (859) 441-0075 | (859) 441-0244 |
| Sparta | 6 | 211 | Owen/Gallatin | Brenda Henry | 104 Main St | Sparta | 41086 | (859) 643-4000 | (859) 643-3500 |
| Spring Mill | 6 | 382 | Jefferson | Robert Schmitt | 6902 Peppermill Ln | Louisville | 40228 | (502) 231-0040 | |
| Spring Valley | 6 | 678 | Jefferson | Patrick Long | 7400 Lanfair Dr | Louisville | 40241 | (502) 339-7237 | |
| Springfield | 4 | 2777 | Washington | Mike Haydon | 127 W Main St | Springfield | 40069 | (859) 336-5440 | (859) 336-5455 |
| Stamping Ground | 6 | 622 | Scott | Jared Hollon | 3206 Main St | Stamping Ground | 40379 | (502) 535-6114 | (502) 535-6523 |
| Stanford | 4 | 3443 | Lincoln | Eddie Carter | 305 E Main St | Stanford | 40484 | (606) 365-4509 | (606) 365-1023 |
| Stanton | 4 | 3094 | Powell | Virginia Wills | PO Box 370 | Stanton | 40380 | (606) 663-4459 | (606) 663-4433 |
| Strathmoor Manor | 6 | 331 | Jefferson | Dennis Boyd | 2018 Emerson Ave | Louisville | 40255 | (502) 452-9104 | |
| Strathmoor Village | 6 | 622 | Jefferson | Dewey Cornell Jr | 2303 Emerson Ave | Louisville | 40205 | (502) 456-1620 | |
| Sturgis | 4 | 2027 | Union | Mike Cowan | 23 N Main St | Sturgis | 42459 | (270) 333-2166 | (270) 333-2724 |
| Sycamore | 6 | 160 | Jefferson | Cleveland A Parkins | 123 Sycamore Dr | Anchorage | 40223 | (502) 245-3766 | |
| Taylor Mill | 4 | 6786 | Kenton | Mark Kreimborg | 5225 Taylor Mill Rd | Taylor Mill | 41015 | (859) 581-2324 | (859) 581-0015 |
| Taylorsville | 6 | 1125 | Spencer | Walter E Hahn Sr | 106 Maple St | Taylorsville | 40071 | (502) 477-3235 | (502) 477-1310 |
| Ten Broeck | 6 | 141 | Jefferson | Robert Roos | 3704 Ten Broeck Way | Louisville | 40241 | (502) 425-7687 | (502) 425-7687 |
| Thornhill | 6 | 176 | Jefferson | Patricia Lay | 2309 Thornhill Rd | Louisville | 40222 | (502) 429-8467 | |
| Tompkinsville | 5 | 2634 | Monroe | Windell Carter | 207 Carter St | Tompkinsville | 42167 | (270) 487-6862 | (270) 487-6940 |
| Trenton | 5 | 416 | Todd | Craig Hines | PO Box 72 | Trenton | 42286 | (270) 466-3332 | (270) 466-3332 |
| Union | 5 | 3251 | Boone | Don Kirby | 984 Lakepointe Ct | Union | 41091 | (859) 384-4467 | (859) 384-7760 |

## CITIES AND MAYORS — 1ST - 6TH CLASS CITIES

| CITY | CLASS | POP | COUNTY | MAYOR | ADDRESS | CITY | ZIP | PHONE | FAX |
|---|---|---|---|---|---|---|---|---|---|
| Uniontown | 5 | 1072 | Union | Kevin Ferguson | 3rd & Main Sts | Uniontown | 42461 | (270) 822-4277 | (270) 822-4773 |
| Upton | 6 | 633 | Hardin/Larue | Debra Riggs | 438 N Walnut St | Upton | 42784 |  |  |
| Vanceburg | 6 | 1689 | Lewis | William T Cooper | PO Box 336 | Vanceburg | 41179 | (606) 796-3044 | (606) 796-6096 |
| Versailles | 4 | 7498 | Woodford | Fred Siegelman | PO Box 625 | Versailles | 40383 | (859) 873-4581 | (859) 873-5969 |
| Vicco | 6 | 321 | Knott/Perry | Harry Ward | PO Box 153 | Vicco | 41773 | (606) 476-2418 | (606) 476-2676 |
| Villa Hills | 4 | 948 | Kenton | Michael Sadouskas | 719 Rogers Rd | Villa Hills | 41017 | (859) 341-1515 | (859) 341-0012 |
| Vine Grove | 4 | 4169 | Hardin | Gary Minter | 300 W Main St | Vine Grove | 40175 | (270) 877-2422 | (270) 877-2875 |
| Wallins Creek | 6 | 242 | Harlan | Freddy Burke | PO Box 483 | Wallins Creek | 40873 | (606) 664-3093 |  |
| Walton | 5 | 2750 | Boone/Kenton | Phillip W Trzop | 40 N Main St | Walton | 41094 | (859) 485-4383 | (859) 485-9710 |
| Warfield | 6 | 276 | Martin | John Hensley | PO Box 261 | Warfield | 41267 |  | (606) 395-6423 |
| Warsaw | 4 | 3011 | Gallatin | Travis Simpson | 101 W Market St | Warsaw | 41095 | (859) 567-5900 | (859) 567-5931 |
| Water Valley | 6 | 320 | Graves | Murrel Stephens | Box 63 | Water Valley | 42085 | (270) 355-2294 |  |
| Watterson Park | 5 | 1040 | Jefferson | Norman R Liebert | 4264 Regina Ln | Watterson Park | 40213 | (502) 432-2993 | (502) 458-7613 |
| Waverly | 6 | 294 | Union | David Wolfe | 100 S Maple St | Waverly | 42462 | (270) 389-4270 |  |
| Wayland | 6 | 294 | Floyd | Tom Murphy | PO Box 181 | Wayland | 41666 |  |  |
| Wellington | 6 | 559 | Jefferson | William Newell | 2402 Manchester Rd | Louisville | 40205 | (502) 452-2458 | (502) 456-0727 |
| West Buechel | 5 | 1324 | Jefferson | Richard Richards | 3713 Marvin Ave | Louisville | 40218 | (502) 456-2822 |  |
| West Liberty | 4 | 3354 | Morgan | Robert W Nickell | City Hall | West Liberty | 41472 | (606) 743-3330 | (606) 743-2202 |
| West Point | 5 | 1045 | Hardin | Eric Duvall | 1501 Elm St | West Point | 40177 | (502) 922-4775 | (502) 922-0126 |
| Westwood | 6 | 616 | Jefferson | Robert M Groemling | 9003 Trentham Ln | Louisville | 40242 |  | (502) 254-2948 |
| Wheatcroft | 6 | 174 | Webster | Patsy J Clark | PO Box 7 | Wheatcroft | 42463 | (270) 664-2802 |  |
| Wheelwright | 6 | 1042 | Floyd | David Marlee Sammons | Box 175 | Wheelwright | 41669 | (606) 452-4202 | (606) 452-4203 |
| White Plains | 5 | 812 | Hopkins | Ronald D (Ronnie) Lewis | 161 Greenville Rd | White Plains | 42464 | (270) 676-8164 | (270) 676-8622 |
| Whitesburg | 5 | 1526 | Letcher | Nathan Baker | 72 Bentley Ave | Whitesburg | 41858 | (606) 633-8827 | (606) 633-3712 |
| Whitesville | 6 | 630 | Daviess | John Boarman | 10184 Hwy 54 | Whitesville | 42378 | (270) 233-4103 |  |
| Wickliffe | 5 | 792 | Ballard | Sylvio L Mayolo | 321 Court St | Wickliffe | 42087 | (270) 335-3557 | (270) 335-3557 |
| Wilder | 6 | 2880 | Campbell | Stanley Turner | 520 Licking Pk | Wilder | 41071 | (859) 581-8884 | (859) 581-0823 |
| Wildwood | 6 | 249 | Jefferson | Dwight Riggle | PO Box 24036 | Louisville | 40224 | (502) 339-7348 |  |
| Williamsburg | 4 | 5107 | Whitley | Roger (Roddy) Harrison | 116 N 2nd St | Williamsburg | 40769 | (606) 549-6033 | (606) 549-6080 |
| Williamstown | 5 | 3396 | Grant | Glenn V Caldwell | 400 N Main St | Williamstown | 41097 | (859) 824-6351 | (859) 824-6320 |
| Willisburg | 6 | 313 | Washington | Bruce Welch | 2952 Lawrenceburg Rd | Willisburg | 40078 | (859) 375-9215 |  |
| Wilmore | 4 | 5845 | Jessamine | Harold L Rainwater | 335 E Main St | Wilmore | 40390 | (859) 858-4411 | (859) 858-3595 |
| Winchester | 3 | 16412 | Clark | Dodd D Dixon | PO Box 40 | Winchester | 40392 | (859) 744-9815 | (859) 744-8822 |
| Windy Hills | 5 | 2509 | Jefferson | Louis A Phillips | 5614 Coach Gate Wynde | Louisville | 40207 | (502) 899-9971 | (502) 899-7645 |
| Wingo | 6 | 900 | Graves | Charles W Shelby | 9606 St Rt 45 S | Wingo | 42088 | (270) 376-5580 | (270) 376-2286 |
| Woodburn | 6 | 333 | Warren | Chip Jenkins | 9555 Three Springs Rd | Bowling Green | 42104 | (270) 529-9119 | (270) 846-4663 |
| Woodbury | 6 | 88 | Butler | Leroy J Klaas Jr | PO Box 50 | Woodbury | 42288 | (615) 585-6241 | (270) 526-6955 |
| Woodland Hills | 6 | 663 | Jefferson | Robert Robinson | PO Box 43032 | Middletown | 40253 | (859) 245-8869 |  |
| Woodlawn | 6 | 254 | Campbell | Ronald (Ron) Barth | 14 W Crescent Ave | Woodlawn | 41071 | (859) 781-7146 |  |
| Woodlawn Park | 5 | 1038 | Jefferson | Tim Robertson | 4254 Westport Ter | Louisville | 40207 | (502) 896-6499 | (502) 895-6620 |
| Worthington | 5 | 1679 | Greenup | Jerry Epling | 512 Ferry St | Worthington | 41183 | (606) 836-6821 | (606) 833-2993 |
| Worthington Hills | 6 | 1607 | Jefferson | Beth Kreakie | PO Box 22586 | Louisville | 40252 | (502) 243-8415 | (502) 243-8416 |
| Worthville | 6 | 221 | Carroll | Melanie Stewart | PO Box 123 | Worthville | 41098 | (502) 732-5937 |  |
| Wurtland | 6 | 1047 | Greenup | Donna K Hayes | 500 Wurtland Ave | Wurtland | 41144 | (606) 836-9166 | (606) 836-5544 |

Source: *The Kentucky Directory Gold Book 2006-2007*

POPULATION, HOUSING UNITS, AREA, AND DENSITY FOR 1-4 CLASS CITIES

| CITY | CLASS | COUNTY | POPULATION | | POPULATION BY RACE | | | HOUSING UNITS | AREA IN SQ MILES | | | DENSITY PER SQ MILE | |
|---|---|---|---|---|---|---|---|---|---|---|---|---|---|
| | | | 2000 CENSUS | 2005 EST | WHITE | BLACK | OTHER | | TOTAL | WATER | LAND | POP | HOUSING UNITS |
| KENTUCKY | | | 4,041,769 | 4,173,405 | 3,640,889 | 295,994 | 236,522 | 1,750,927 | 40,409 | 681 | 39,728 | 102 | 44 |
| Albany | 4 | Clinton | 2,220 | 2,288 | 2,184 | 1 | 35 | 1,165 | 3.40 | 0.00 | 3.40 | 653 | 343 |
| Alexandria | 4 | Campbell | 8,286 | 7,996 | 8,188 | 2 | 96 | 2,989 | 5.40 | 0.05 | 5.38 | 1,539 | 555 |
| Anchorage | 4 | Jefferson | 2,264 | 2,529 | 2,199 | 19 | 46 | 750 | 3.05 | 0.01 | 3.04 | 744 | 247 |
| Ashland | 2 | Boyd | 21,981 | 21,510 | 21,066 | 505 | 410 | 10,763 | 12.20 | 1.12 | 11.08 | 1,984 | 972 |
| Augusta | 4 | Bracken | 1,204 | 1,257 | 1,174 | 15 | 15 | 605 | 1.65 | 0.44 | 1.22 | 991 | 498 |
| Barbourville | 4 | Knox | 3,589 | 3,520 | 3,388 | 116 | 85 | 1,646 | 3.49 | 0.00 | 3.49 | 1,027 | 471 |
| Bardstown | 4 | Nelson | 10,374 | 10,984 | 8,518 | 1,563 | 293 | 4,488 | 7.22 | 0.05 | 7.18 | 1,445 | 625 |
| Beaver Dam | 4 | Ohio | 3,033 | 3,113 | 2,824 | 104 | 105 | 1,411 | 2.53 | 0.00 | 2.53 | 1,201 | 559 |
| Bellevue | 4 | Campbell | 6,480 | 6,022 | 6,376 | 14 | 90 | 2,936 | 0.94 | 0.00 | 0.94 | 6,904 | 3,128 |
| Benton | 4 | Marshall | 4,197 | 4,335 | 4,112 | 26 | 59 | 1,922 | 3.94 | 0.00 | 3.94 | 1,065 | 488 |
| Berea | 4 | Madison | 9,851 | 13,230 | 9,106 | 424 | 321 | 4,115 | 9.36 | 0.03 | 9.33 | 1,055 | 441 |
| Bowling Green | 2 | Warren | 49,296 | 52,272 | 39,842 | 6,267 | 3,187 | 21,290 | 35.60 | 0.20 | 35.40 | 1,392 | 601 |
| Calvert City | 4 | Marshall | 2,701 | 2,749 | 2,674 | 0 | 27 | 1,203 | 13.93 | 0.05 | 13.88 | 195 | 87 |
| Campbellsville | 3 | Taylor | 10,498 | 10,906 | 9,355 | 918 | 225 | 4,876 | 6.06 | 0.10 | 5.96 | 1,761 | 818 |
| Carlisle | 4 | Nicholas | 1,917 | 2,030 | 1,869 | 42 | 6 | 982 | 1.28 | 0.00 | 1.28 | 1,500 | 768 |
| Carrollton | 4 | Carroll | 3,846 | 3,861 | 3,615 | 86 | 145 | 1,709 | 2.26 | 0.01 | 2.24 | 1,715 | 762 |
| Catlettsburg | 4 | Boyd | 1,960 | 1,927 | 1,924 | 22 | 14 | 959 | 1.65 | 0.37 | 1.28 | 1,529 | 748 |
| Cave City | 4 | Barren | 1,880 | 2,054 | 1,706 | 134 | 40 | 914 | 4.32 | 0.00 | 4.32 | 435 | 212 |
| Central City | 4 | Muhlenberg | 5,893 | 5,785 | 5,190 | 629 | 74 | 2,313 | 5.23 | 0.00 | 5.23 | 1,126 | 442 |
| Columbia | 4 | Adair | 4,014 | 4,174 | 3,628 | 296 | 90 | 1,789 | 3.44 | 0.00 | 3.44 | 1,168 | 521 |
| Corbin | 3 | Knox/Whitley | 7,742 | 8,230 | 7,614 | 6 | 122 | 3,704 | 7.40 | 0.00 | 7.40 | 1,046 | 500 |
| Corbin (part) | 3 | Knox | 1,865 | | | | | 907 | 2.33 | 0.00 | 2.33 | 800 | 389 |
| Corbin (part) | 3 | Whitley | 5,877 | | | | | 2,797 | 5.07 | 0.00 | 5.07 | 1,159 | 551 |
| Covington | 2 | Kenton | 43,370 | 42,811 | 37,752 | 4,397 | 1,221 | 20,448 | 13.67 | 0.53 | 13.14 | 3,301 | 1,557 |
| Crescent Springs | 4 | Kenton | 3,931 | 3,975 | 3,766 | 54 | 111 | 1,760 | 1.43 | 0.00 | 1.43 | 2,741 | 1,227 |
| Cumberland | 4 | Harlan | 2,611 | 2,330 | 2,444 | 133 | 34 | 1,288 | 4.59 | 0.01 | 4.58 | 571 | 281 |
| Cynthiana | 4 | Harrison | 6,258 | 6,311 | 5,784 | 331 | 143 | 2,909 | 3.34 | 0.00 | 3.34 | 1,874 | 871 |
| Danville | 2 | Boyle | 15,477 | 15,409 | 12,949 | 2,015 | 513 | 6,734 | 15.80 | 0.01 | 15.79 | 980 | 427 |
| Dawson Springs | 4 | Caldwell/Hopkins | 2,980 | 2,953 | 2,912 | 28 | 40 | 1,353 | 3.95 | 0.01 | 3.94 | 756 | 343 |
| Dawson Springs (part) | 4 | Caldwell | 0 | | | | | 0 | 0.02 | 0.00 | 0.02 | 0 | 0 |
| Dawson Springs (part) | 4 | Hopkins | 2,980 | | | | | 1,353 | 3.93 | 0.01 | 3.92 | 760 | 345 |
| Dayton | 4 | Campbell | 5,966 | 5,556 | 5,866 | 27 | 73 | 2,401 | 1.66 | 0.34 | 1.33 | 4,495 | 1,809 |
| Douglass Hills | 4 | Jefferson | 5,718 | 5,597 | 5,105 | 397 | 216 | 2,553 | 1.33 | 0.00 | 1.33 | 4,286 | 1,914 |
| Earlington | 4 | Hopkins | 1,649 | 1,601 | 1,250 | 384 | 15 | 798 | 3.57 | 0.22 | 3.34 | 493 | 239 |
| Edgewood | 4 | Kenton | 9,400 | 8,913 | 9,155 | 36 | 209 | 3,149 | 4.18 | 0.01 | 4.18 | 2,251 | 754 |
| Elizabethtown | 4 | Hardin | 22,542 | 23,450 | 19,395 | 2,186 | 961 | 10,043 | 24.38 | 0.31 | 24.07 | 937 | 417 |

# POPULATION, HOUSING UNITS, AREA, AND DENSITY FOR 1-4 CLASS CITIES

| CITY | CLASS | COUNTY | POPULATION | | POPULATION BY RACE | | | HOUSING UNITS | AREA IN SQ MILES | | | DENSITY PER SQ MILE | |
|---|---|---|---|---|---|---|---|---|---|---|---|---|---|
| | | | 2000 CENSUS | 2005 EST | WHITE | BLACK | OTHER | | TOTAL | WATER | LAND | POP | HOUSING UNITS |
| Elkhorn City | 4 | Pike | 1,060 | 1,030 | 1,053 | 1 | 6 | 506 | 32.02 | 0.00 | 2.02 | 526 | 251 |
| Elkton | 4 | Todd | 1,984 | 1,941 | 1,633 | 311 | 40 | 928 | 2.07 | 0.00 | 2.07 | 959 | 449 |
| Elsmere | 4 | Kenton | 8,139 | 7,948 | 7,497 | 445 | 197 | 3,126 | 2.50 | 0.00 | 2.50 | 3,256 | 1,251 |
| Eminence | 4 | Henry | 2,231 | 2,257 | 1,865 | 260 | 106 | 998 | 2.15 | 0.01 | 2.15 | 1,039 | 465 |
| Erlanger | 3 | Kenton | 16,676 | 16,852 | 16,023 | 302 | 351 | 6,865 | 8.42 | 0.10 | 8.33 | 2,002 | 824 |
| Falmouth | 4 | Pendleton | 2,058 | 2,096 | 1,980 | 39 | 39 | 988 | 1.29 | 0.00 | 1.29 | 1,599 | 768 |
| Flatwoods | 3 | Greenup | 7,605 | 7,621 | 7,467 | 29 | 108 | 3,338 | 4.49 | 0.00 | 4.49 | 1,692 | 743 |
| Flemingsburg | 4 | Fleming | 3,010 | 3,104 | 2,791 | 152 | 67 | 1,434 | 2.65 | 0.09 | 2.55 | 1,178 | 561 |
| Florence | 3 | Boone | 23,551 | 26,349 | 21,771 | 629 | 1,151 | 10,322 | 9.90 | 0.03 | 9.87 | 2,386 | 1,046 |
| Fort Mitchell | 4 | Kenton | 8,089 | 7,605 | 7,836 | 80 | 173 | 3,744 | 3.13 | 0.00 | 3.13 | 2,582 | 1,195 |
| Fort Thomas | 4 | Campbell | 16,495 | 15,592 | 16,100 | 120 | 275 | 7,028 | 6.43 | 0.76 | 5.67 | 2,910 | 1,240 |
| Fort Wright | 4 | Kenton | 5,681 | 5,438 | 5,529 | 56 | 96 | 2,573 | 3.46 | 0.01 | 3.46 | 1,642 | 744 |
| Frankfort | 2 | Franklin | 27,741 | 27,210 | 22,704 | 4,078 | 959 | 13,422 | 15.01 | 0.28 | 14.73 | 1,883 | 911 |
| Franklin | 4 | Simpson | 7,996 | 8,079 | 6,476 | 1,340 | 180 | 3,609 | 7.44 | 0.00 | 7.44 | 1,075 | 485 |
| Fulton | 4 | Fulton | 2,775 | 2,564 | 1,869 | 816 | 90 | 1,388 | 2.83 | 0.01 | 2.82 | 983 | 492 |
| Georgetown | 4 | Scott | 18,080 | 19,988 | 16,033 | 449 | 1,598 | 7,209 | 13.72 | 0.00 | 13.72 | 1,318 | 525 |
| Glasgow | 3 | Barren | 13,019 | 14,062 | 11,576 | 1,074 | 369 | 6,153 | 14.76 | 0.01 | 14.75 | 883 | 417 |
| Graymoor-Devondale | 4 | Jefferson | 2,925 | 2,937 | 2,644 | 152 | 1,129 | 1,157 | 0.73 | 0.00 | 0.73 | 4,003 | 1,583 |
| Grayson | 4 | Carter | 3,877 | 3,986 | 3,812 | 20 | 45 | 1,538 | 2.50 | 0.00 | 2.50 | 1,549 | 615 |
| Greenville | 4 | Muhlenberg | 4,398 | 4,273 | 3,953 | 385 | 60 | 2,047 | 4.78 | 0.00 | 4.77 | 922 | 429 |
| Harlan | 4 | Harlan | 2,081 | 1,912 | 1,894 | 146 | 41 | 1,060 | 1.75 | 0.00 | 1.75 | 1,187 | 605 |
| Harrodsburg | 4 | Mercer | 8,014 | 8,126 | 7,126 | 603 | 285 | 3,709 | 5.31 | 0.00 | 5.31 | 1,511 | 699 |
| Hazard | 4 | Perry | 4,806 | 4,819 | 4,338 | 316 | 152 | 2,291 | 7.02 | 0.00 | 7.02 | 685 | 326 |
| Henderson | 2 | Henderson | 27,373 | 27,666 | 23,885 | 2,883 | 605 | 12,652 | 17.07 | 2.11 | 14.97 | 1,829 | 845 |
| Hickman | 4 | Fulton | 2,560 | 2,371 | 1,640 | 895 | 25 | 1,177 | 3.57 | 0.01 | 3.56 | 718 | 330 |
| Highland Heights | 4 | Campbell | 6,554 | 5,791 | 6,261 | 139 | 154 | 2,787 | 2.27 | 0.00 | 2.27 | 2,882 | 1,226 |
| Hillview | 4 | Bullitt | 7,037 | 7,349 | 6,889 | 26 | 122 | 2,460 | 4.16 | 0.00 | 4.16 | 1,690 | 591 |
| Hodgenville | 4 | Larue | 2,874 | 2,788 | 2,490 | 324 | 60 | 1,349 | 1.72 | 0.00 | 1.72 | 1,668 | 783 |
| Hopkinsville | 2 | Christian | 30,089 | 28,821 | 19,875 | 9,302 | 912 | 13,260 | 24.04 | 0.01 | 24.03 | 1,252 | 552 |
| Horse Cave | 4 | Hart | 2,252 | 2,314 | 1,822 | 404 | 26 | 1,091 | 2.97 | 0.00 | 2.97 | 758 | 367 |
| Hurstbourne | 4 | Jefferson | 3,884 | 3,939 | 3,552 | 117 | 215 | 1,887 | 1.87 | 0.00 | 1.87 | 2,077 | 1,009 |
| Independence | 3 | Kenton | 14,982 | 19,065 | 14,563 | 144 | 275 | 5,391 | 16.78 | 0.01 | 16.77 | 893 | 321 |
| Indian Hills | 4 | Jefferson | 2,882 | 2,977 | 2,758 | 50 | 74 | 1,162 | 1.98 | 0.01 | 1.97 | 1,460 | 589 |
| Irvine | 4 | Estill | 2,843 | 2,714 | 2,822 | 1 | 20 | 1,409 | 1.55 | 0.04 | 1.52 | 1,872 | 928 |
| Jackson | 4 | Breathitt | 2,490 | 2,413 | 2,445 | 14 | 31 | 1,111 | 2.75 | 0.09 | 2.66 | 935 | 417 |
| Jeffersontown | 2 | Jefferson | 26,633 | 26,100 | 23,101 | 2,305 | 1,227 | 11,220 | 9.96 | 0.01 | 9.95 | 2,676 | 1,127 |

**POPULATION, HOUSING UNITS, AREA, AND DENSITY FOR 1-4 CLASS CITIES**

| CITY | CLASS | COUNTY | POPULATION | | POPULATION BY RACE | | | HOUSING UNITS | AREA IN SQ MILES | | | DENSITY PER SQ MILE | |
|---|---|---|---|---|---|---|---|---|---|---|---|---|---|
| | | | 2000 CENSUS | 2005 EST | WHITE | BLACK | OTHER | | TOTAL | WATER | LAND | POP | HOUSING UNITS |
| Jenkins | 4 | Letcher | 2,401 | 2,297 | 2,352 | 26 | 23 | 1,122 | 8.56 | 0.02 | 8.54 | 281 | 131 |
| La Grange | 4 | Oldham | 5,676 | 6,046 | 5,135 | 289 | 252 | 2,330 | 3.79 | 0.04 | 3.75 | 1,515 | 622 |
| Lawrenceburg | 4 | Anderson | 9,014 | 9,403 | 8,500 | 370 | 144 | 3,733 | 3.71 | 0.00 | 3.71 | 2,427 | 1,005 |
| Lebanon | 4 | Marion | 5,718 | 5,959 | 4,453 | 1,139 | 126 | 2,555 | 4.41 | 0.00 | 4.41 | 1,297 | 579 |
| Leitchfield | 4 | Grayson | 6,139 | 6,462 | 5,932 | 96 | 111 | 2,797 | 8.80 | 0.03 | 8.77 | 700 | 319 |
| Lexington-Fayette | 2 | Fayette | 260,512 | 268,080 | 211,120 | 35,116 | 14,276 | 116,167 | 5.50 | 1.00 | 4.52 | 916 | 408 |
| London | 4 | Laurel | 5,692 | 7,787 | 5,466 | 104 | 122 | 2,676 | 7.71 | 0.00 | 7.71 | 738 | 347 |
| Louisville-Jefferson | 1 | Jefferson | 256,231 | 699,827 | 161,261 | 84,586 | 10,384 | 121,275 | 66.65 | 4.53 | 62.12 | 4,125 | 1,952 |
| Ludlow | 4 | Kenton | 4,409 | 4,647 | 4,341 | 17 | 51 | 1,888 | 1.24 | 0.38 | 0.86 | 5,142 | 2,202 |
| Lyndon | 4 | Jefferson | 9,369 | 10,248 | 8,022 | 854 | 493 | 4,934 | 3.45 | 0.00 | 3.45 | 2,719 | 1,432 |
| Madisonville | 4 | Hopkins | 19,307 | 19,273 | 16,644 | 2,170 | 493 | 8,889 | 18.50 | 0.73 | 17.80 | 1,085 | 500 |
| Manchester | 4 | Clay | 1,738 | 1,968 | 1,604 | 109 | 25 | 844 | 1.51 | 0.00 | 1.51 | 1,148 | 558 |
| Marion | 4 | Crittenden | 3,196 | 3,033 | 3,089 | 56 | 51 | 1,595 | 3.30 | 0.01 | 3.29 | 972 | 485 |
| Martin | 4 | Floyd | 633 | 636 | 616 | 0 | 17 | 339 | 0.47 | 0.00 | 0.47 | 1,358 | 727 |
| Mayfield | 3 | Graves | 10,349 | 10,288 | 8,338 | 1,377 | 634 | 4,907 | 6.68 | 0.00 | 6.68 | 1,550 | 735 |
| Maysville | 3 | Mason | 8,993 | 9,136 | 7,734 | 1,038 | 221 | 4,416 | 22.25 | 2.34 | 19.91 | 452 | 222 |
| Middlesborough | 3 | Bell | 10,384 | 10,164 | 9,641 | 509 | 234 | 4,955 | 7.64 | 0.00 | 7.64 | 1,359 | 649 |
| Middletown | 4 | Jefferson | 5,744 | 6,072 | 5,192 | 318 | 234 | 2,543 | 4.89 | 0.03 | 4.86 | 1,181 | 523 |
| Monticello | 4 | Wayne | 5,981 | 6,062 | 5,660 | 145 | 176 | 2,730 | 6.08 | 0.00 | 6.08 | 984 | 449 |
| Morehead | 4 | Rowan | 5,914 | 7,592 | 5,574 | 152 | 188 | 2,347 | 9.26 | 0.04 | 9.23 | 641 | 254 |
| Morganfield | 4 | Union | 3,494 | 3,430 | 2,877 | 567 | 50 | 1,581 | 2.12 | 0.03 | 2.09 | 1,672 | 756 |
| Mount Sterling | 4 | Montgomery | 5,876 | 6,317 | 5,235 | 513 | 128 | 2,768 | 3.44 | 0.00 | 3.44 | 1,709 | 805 |
| Mount Washington | 4 | Bullitt | 8,485 | 8,624 | 8,337 | 27 | 121 | 3,294 | 5.34 | 0.00 | 5.34 | 1,589 | 617 |
| Murray | 3 | Calloway | 14,950 | 15,538 | 13,180 | 1,017 | 753 | 6,622 | 9.70 | 0.00 | 9.70 | 1,542 | 683 |
| Newport | 2 | Campbell | 17,048 | 15,911 | 15,628 | 937 | 483 | 7,828 | 2.97 | 0.25 | 2.81 | 6,268 | 2,72 |
| Nicholasville | 3 | Jessamine | 19,680 | 23,897 | 18,313 | 862 | 505 | 7,783 | 8.51 | 0.03 | 8.48 | 2,320 | 917 |
| Oak Grove | 4 | Christian | 7,064 | 7,570 | 4,360 | 1,823 | 881 | 2,912 | 10.31 | 0.00 | 10.31 | 685 | 283 |
| Olive Hill | 4 | Carter | 1,813 | 1,823 | 1,790 | 3 | 20 | 886 | 2.01 | 0.00 | 2.01 | 904 | 442 |
| Owensboro | 2 | Daviess | 54,067 | 55,459 | 48,999 | 3,728 | 1,340 | 24,302 | 18.66 | 1.23 | 17.42 | 3,103 | 1,395 |
| Owingsville | 4 | Bath | 1,488 | 1,564 | 1,417 | 59 | 12 | 720 | 2.18 | 0.00 | 2.18 | 684 | 331 |
| Paducah | 2 | McCracken | 26,307 | 25,575 | 19,145 | 6,353 | 809 | 13,221 | 19.51 | 0.02 | 19.48 | 1,350 | 679 |
| Paintsville | 4 | Johnson | 4,132 | 4,141 | 4,028 | 27 | 77 | 1,901 | 5.26 | 0.00 | 5.26 | 786 | 362 |
| Paris | 3 | Bourbon | 9,183 | 9,334 | 7,735 | 1,167 | 281 | 4,222 | 6.81 | 0.02 | 6.80 | 1,351 | 621 |
| Park Hills | 4 | Kenton | 2,977 | 2,803 | 2,877 | 49 | 51 | 1,523 | 0.78 | 0.00 | 0.78 | 3,840 | 1,965 |
| Pikeville | 3 | Pike | 6,295 | 6,312 | 5,954 | 166 | 175 | 2,981 | 15.43 | 0.00 | 15.43 | 408 | 193 |
| Pineville | 4 | Bell | 2,093 | 2,014 | 1,941 | 90 | 62 | 961 | 1.44 | 0.00 | 1.44 | 1,452 | 667 |

# COUNTIES & CITIES

## POPULATION, HOUSING UNITS, AREA, AND DENSITY FOR 1-4 CLASS CITIES

| CITY | CLASS | COUNTY | POPULATION | | POPULATION BY RACE | | | HOUSING UNITS | AREA IN SQ MILES | | | DENSITY PER SQ MILE | |
|---|---|---|---|---|---|---|---|---|---|---|---|---|---|
| | | | 2000 CENSUS | 2005 EST | WHITE | BLACK | OTHER | | TOTAL | WATER | LAND | POP | HOUSING UNITS |
| Pioneer Village | 4 | Bullitt | 2,555 | 2,631 | 2,506 | 7 | 42 | 900 | 1.17 | 0.00 | 1.17 | 2,187 | 770 |
| Prestonsburg | 4 | Floyd | 3,612 | 3,706 | 3,522 | 12 | 78 | 1,683 | 11.07 | 0.20 | 10.87 | 332 | 155 |
| Princeton | 4 | Caldwell | 6,536 | 6,447 | 5,830 | 589 | 117 | 3,150 | 9.13 | 0.00 | 9.13 | 716 | 345 |
| Prospect | 4 | Jefferson/Oldham | 4,657 | 4,877 | 4,327 | 158 | 172 | 1,847 | 4.02 | 0.00 | 4.02 | 1,158 | 459 |
| Prospect (part) | 4 | Jefferson | 4,564 | | | | | 1,819 | 3.86 | 0.00 | 3.86 | 1,183 | 472 |
| Prospect (part) | 4 | Oldham | 93 | | | | | 28 | 0.16 | 0.00 | 0.16 | 573 | 173 |
| Providence | 4 | Webster | 3,611 | 3,549 | 2,958 | 59 | 594 | 1,754 | 6.17 | 0.02 | 6.15 | 587 | 285 |
| Radcliff | 2 | Hardin | 21,961 | 21,471 | 13,782 | 5,632 | 2,547 | 9,487 | 11.48 | 0.01 | 11.47 | 1,914 | 827 |
| Richmond | 2 | Madison | 27,152 | 30,893 | 23,976 | 2,246 | 930 | 11,857 | 19.25 | 0.14 | 19.12 | 1,420 | 620 |
| Russell | 4 | Greenup | 3,645 | 3,597 | 3,517 | 26 | 102 | 1,584 | 4.01 | 0.00 | 4.00 | 911 | 396 |
| Russellville | 4 | Logan | 7,149 | 7,271 | 5,622 | 1,331 | 196 | 3,458 | 10.64 | 0.00 | 10.64 | 672 | 325 |
| St. Matthews | 4 | Jefferson | 15,852 | 17,309 | 14,317 | 785 | 750 | 8,537 | 4.03 | 0.00 | 4.03 | 3,938 | 2,121 |
| St. Regis Park | 4 | Jefferson | 1,520 | 1,526 | 1,471 | 27 | 22 | 595 | 0.36 | 0.00 | 0.36 | 4,252 | 1,664 |
| Salyersville | 4 | Magoffin | 1,604 | 1,604 | 1,599 | 1 | 4 | 710 | 2.12 | 0.00 | 2.12 | 758 | 336 |
| Scottsville | 4 | Allen | 4,327 | 4,525 | 4,132 | 142 | 53 | 2,059 | 5.77 | 0.00 | 5.77 | 750 | 357 |
| Shelbyville | 4 | Shelby | 10,085 | 10,730 | 7,561 | 1,649 | 875 | 4,117 | 7.64 | 0.07 | 7.56 | 1,334 | 544 |
| Shepherdsville | 4 | Bullitt | 8,334 | 8,874 | 8,104 | 77 | 153 | 3,402 | 10.78 | 0.25 | 10.53 | 791 | 323 |
| Shively | 3 | Jefferson | 15,157 | 15,212 | 10,195 | 4,595 | 367 | 6,929 | 4.63 | 0.00 | 4.63 | 3,271 | 1,495 |
| Somerset | 3 | Pulaski | 11,352 | 12,136 | 10,689 | 416 | 247 | 5,428 | 11.29 | 0.01 | 11.27 | 1,007 | 482 |
| Southgate | 4 | Campbell | 3,472 | 3,356 | 3,328 | 25 | 119 | 1,665 | 1.43 | 0.00 | 1.43 | 2,439 | 1,170 |
| Springfield | 4 | Washington | 2,634 | 2,806 | 1,967 | 590 | 77 | 1,239 | 2.54 | 0.03 | 2.51 | 1,049 | 493 |
| Stanford | 4 | Lincoln | 3,430 | 3,452 | 3,086 | 278 | 66 | 1,522 | 3.09 | 0.01 | 3.08 | 1,115 | 495 |
| Stanton | 4 | Powell | 3,029 | 3,109 | 2,999 | 13 | 17 | 1,340 | 1.97 | 0.00 | 1.97 | 1,538 | 680 |
| Sturgis | 4 | Union | 2,030 | 2,008 | 1,796 | 196 | 38 | 973 | 1.51 | 0.00 | 1.51 | 1,343 | 644 |
| Taylor Mill | 4 | Kenton | 6,913 | 6,733 | 6,771 | 29 | 113 | 2,604 | 6.37 | 0.11 | 6.26 | 1,105 | 416 |
| Vanceburg | 4 | Lewis | 1,731 | 1,698 | 1,703 | 11 | 17 | 752 | 1.15 | 0.00 | 1.15 | 1,502 | 653 |
| Versailles | 4 | Woodford | 7,511 | 7,728 | 6,623 | 651 | 237 | 3,330 | 2.81 | 0.00 | 2.81 | 2,669 | 1,183 |
| Villa Hills | 4 | Kenton | 7,948 | 7,749 | 7,751 | 36 | 161 | 2,855 | 4.45 | 0.75 | 3.71 | 2,144 | 770 |
| Vine Grove | 4 | Hardin | 4,169 | 3,983 | 3,473 | 443 | 253 | 1,779 | 5.90 | 0.01 | 5.89 | 708 | 302 |
| West Liberty | 4 | Morgan | 3,277 | 3,349 | 2,603 | 596 | 78 | 758 | 4.43 | 0.00 | 4.43 | 739 | 171 |
| Williamsburg | 4 | Whitley | 5,143 | 5,162 | 4,961 | 89 | 93 | 2,118 | 4.77 | 0.10 | 4.66 | 1,103 | 454 |
| Wilmore | 4 | Jessamine | 5,905 | 5,826 | 5,582 | 114 | 209 | 1,740 | 2.64 | 0.00 | 2.64 | 2,239 | 660 |
| Winchester | 3 | Clark | 16,724 | 16,494 | 14,875 | 1,477 | 372 | 7,400 | 7.68 | 0.04 | 7.64 | 2,188 | 968 |

Source: U.S. Census Bureau, Census 2000 Summary File 1, http://factfinder.census.gov, http://ksdc.louisville.edu/kpr/popest, and The Kentucky Directory Gold Book 2006-2007

PERSONAL INCOME, RACE, BIRTHS, DEATHS AND UNEMPLOYMENT FOR KENTUCKY COUNTIES

| AREA NAME | 2004 | | | | | 2003 | | 2006* | 2000 | | |
|---|---|---|---|---|---|---|---|---|---|---|---|
| | ESTIMATED POPULATION | WHITE | BLACK | HISPANIC | OTHER RACES** | BIRTHS | DEATHS | UN-EMPLOYMENT | PERSONAL INCOME ($000) | PER CAPITA PERSONAL INCOME ($) | POVERTY LEVEL |
| Kentucky | 4,222,977 | 3,746,921 | 310,996 | 77,055 | 88,005 | 55,147 | 40,143 | 6.0% | 104,263,983 | 25,494 | 12.7% |
| Adair | 17,704 | 16,846 | 515 | 129 | 214 | 201 | 183 | 4.8% | 333,517 | 19,192 | 18.2% |
| Allen | 18,694 | 18,125 | 254 | 153 | 162 | 265 | 228 | 5.4% | 389,357 | 21,498 | 13.2% |
| Anderson | 20,307 | 19,424 | 485 | 208 | 190 | 242 | 168 | 5.0% | 484,252 | 24,766 | 4.8% |
| Ballard | 8,359 | 7,893 | 277 | 64 | 125 | 90 | 100 | 5.2% | 214,923 | 26,426 | 10.7% |
| Barren | 39,878 | 37,397 | 1,586 | 405 | 490 | 518 | 432 | 5.0% | 871,810 | 22,491 | 11.8% |
| Bath | 11,643 | 11,244 | 198 | 105 | 96 | 153 | 145 | 6.4% | 217,978 | 19,131 | 16.4% |
| Bell | 29,912 | 28,544 | 730 | 240 | 398 | 403 | 394 | 7.9% | 525,478 | 17,521 | 26.7% |
| Boone | 103,815 | 96,078 | 2,346 | 2,461 | 2,930 | 1,561 | 560 | 4.5% | 2,780,666 | 29,703 | 4.4% |
| Bourbon | 20,280 | 18,001 | 1,346 | 657 | 276 | 239 | 213 | 4.7% | 547,079 | 28,045 | 0.1% |
| Boyd | 50,436 | 47,784 | 1,349 | 693 | 610 | 621 | 590 | 6.0% | 1,280,980 | 25,795 | 11.5% |
| Boyle | 28,694 | 25,009 | 2,619 | 453 | 613 | 310 | 295 | 6.5% | 701,445 | 25,327 | 9.1% |
| Bracken | 8,750 | 8,613 | 51 | 43 | 43 | 105 | 77 | 5.6% | 176,492 | 20,887 | 7.6% |
| Breathitt | 16,045 | 15,760 | 67 | 108 | 110 | 192 | 180 | 7.3% | 279,501 | 17,559 | 28.1% |
| Breckinridge | 19,321 | 18,409 | 545 | 153 | 214 | 234 | 204 | 5.8% | 384,342 | 20,317 | 11.8% |
| Bullitt | 67,235 | 65,295 | 439 | 590 | 911 | 832 | 396 | 5.5% | 1,524,370 | 23,927 | 6.2% |
| Butler | 13,583 | 13,175 | 71 | 219 | 118 | 175 | 122 | 8.1% | 246,472 | 18,737 | 13.1% |
| Caldwell | 12,955 | 12,170 | 611 | 76 | 98 | 149 | 166 | 4.9% | 289,184 | 22,578 | 12.2% |
| Calloway | 35,329 | 32,542 | 1,299 | 540 | 948 | 356 | 365 | 4.8% | 822,506 | 23,927 | 9.8% |
| Campbell | 88,129 | 84,050 | 1,783 | 873 | 1,423 | 1,145 | 856 | 5.3% | 2,479,433 | 28,049 | 7.3% |
| Carlisle | 5,375 | 5,198 | 64 | 65 | 48 | 68 | 72 | 5.3% | 116,600 | 21,733 | 15.0% |
| Carroll | 10,740 | 10,012 | 202 | 396 | 130 | 163 | 127 | 5.6% | 236,769 | 23,036 | 10.4% |
| Carter | 27,620 | 27,163 | 56 | 161 | 240 | 323 | 283 | 7.8% | 481,942 | 17,798 | 19.2% |
| Casey | 16,377 | 15,880 | 70 | 318 | 109 | 198 | 196 | 6.6% | 289,067 | 18,276 | 20.7% |
| Christian | 73,761 | 51,242 | 16,596 | 3,112 | 2,811 | 1,495 | 609 | 6.7% | 1,666,017 | 23,444 | 12.1% |
| Clark | 34,826 | 32,383 | 1,616 | 449 | 378 | 431 | 299 | 4.9% | 905,655 | 26,944 | 8.4% |
| Clay | 24,604 | 22,871 | 1,213 | 350 | 170 | 305 | 242 | 9.1% | 361,297 | 14,798 | 35.4% |
| Clinton | 9,760 | 9,458 | 14 | 202 | 86 | 126 | 127 | 5.3% | 183,305 | 19,031 | 20.2% |
| Crittenden | 9,050 | 8,869 | 62 | 51 | 68 | 93 | 124 | 5.5% | 183,711 | 20,040 | 14.7% |
| Cumberland | 7,216 | 6,853 | 251 | 48 | 64 | 88 | 90 | 6.0% | 130,773 | 18,328 | 0.2% |
| Daviess | 93,639 | 86,599 | 4,284 | 1,052 | 1,704 | 1,356 | 878 | 5.1% | 2,325,761 | 25,310 | 9.4% |
| Edmonson | 12,015 | 11,751 | 77 | 94 | 93 | 127 | 121 | 5.2% | 197,760 | 16,728 | 14.2% |
| Elliott | 6,874 | 6,788 | 2 | 39 | 45 | 90 | 68 | 8.2% | 99,111 | 14,601 | 20.8% |
| Estill | 15,283 | 15,015 | 26 | 119 | 123 | 184 | 163 | 6.1% | 272,148 | 17,747 | 22.5% |
| Fayette | 278,617 | 217,734 | 36,416 | 12,259 | 12,208 | 3,765 | 1,944 | 4.3% | 8,681,237 | 32,932 | 8.2% |
| Fleming | 14,589 | 14,127 | 219 | 109 | 134 | 186 | 159 | 4.7% | 263,310 | 18,606 | 14.8% |
| Floyd | 42,665 | 41,477 | 587 | 286 | 315 | 567 | 521 | 6.7% | 828,370 | 19,568 | 26.9% |
| Franklin | 49,037 | 42,388 | 4,625 | 895 | 1,129 | 624 | 500 | 4.5% | 1,370,821 | 28,481 | 6.9% |
| Fulton | 7,415 | 5,561 | 1,718 | 58 | 78 | 75 | 114 | 6.8% | 169,217 | 22,398 | 20.1% |
| Gallatin | 8,093 | 7,752 | 131 | 114 | 96 | 133 | 83 | 5.3% | 162,705 | 20,828 | 11.6% |
| Garrard | 16,440 | 15,559 | 516 | 277 | 88 | 199 | 145 | 5.3% | 320,535 | 20,513 | 11.6% |
| Grant | 24,591 | 23,954 | 79 | 274 | 284 | 382 | 183 | 5.3% | 498,350 | 21,195 | 9.0% |

PERSONAL INCOME, RACE, BIRTHS, DEATHS AND UNEMPLOYMENT FOR KENTUCKY COUNTIES

| AREA NAME | 2004 ESTIMATED POPULATION | WHITE | BLACK | HISPANIC | OTHER RACES** | 2003 BIRTHS | 2003 DEATHS | 2006* UN-EMPLOY-MENT | 2000 PERSONAL INCOME ($000) | 2000 PER CAPITA PERSONAL INCOME ($) | POVERTY LEVEL |
|---|---|---|---|---|---|---|---|---|---|---|---|
| Graves | 38,850 | 35,093 | 1,697 | 1,449 | 611 | 479 | 465 | 6.7% | 818,459 | 22,070 | 13.1% |
| Grayson | 25,250 | 24,624 | 142 | 246 | 238 | 320 | 270 | 8.0% | 462,078 | 19,038 | 13.9% |
| Green | 11,811 | 11,264 | 300 | 144 | 103 | 124 | 135 | 5.0% | 210,960 | 18,091 | 15.2% |
| Greenup | 37,499 | 36,543 | 256 | 225 | 475 | 408 | 393 | 6.3% | 839,441 | 22,795 | 11.6% |
| Hancock | 8,549 | 8,325 | 80 | 90 | 54 | 105 | 68 | 4.9% | 170,526 | 20,219 | 11.4% |
| Hardin | 99,179 | 79,858 | 11,341 | 3,113 | 4,867 | 1,430 | 659 | 5.3% | 2,439,028 | 25,468 | 8.2% |
| Harlan | 32,158 | 30,576 | 830 | 231 | 521 | 397 | 465 | 8.0% | 564,389 | 17,354 | 29.1% |
| Harrison | 18,497 | 17,619 | 454 | 241 | 183 | 245 | 169 | 5.4% | 405,268 | 22,423 | 9.4% |
| Hart | 18,419 | 17,035 | 1,009 | 182 | 193 | 220 | 170 | 5.8% | 302,339 | 17,110 | 18.6% |
| Henderson | 46,046 | 41,537 | 3,292 | 620 | 597 | 616 | 430 | 4.1% | 1,140,611 | 25,356 | 9.7% |
| Henry | 16,182 | 14,992 | 562 | 411 | 217 | 218 | 130 | 5.5% | 355,919 | 23,222 | 10.4% |
| Hickman | 5,226 | 4,606 | 504 | 54 | 62 | 53 | 73 | 6.3% | 169,337 | 32,359 | 14.2% |
| Hopkins | 47,370 | 43,113 | 2,925 | 552 | 780 | 559 | 588 | 5.9% | 1,070,212 | 23,039 | 13.6% |
| Jackson | 13,695 | 13,523 | 17 | 73 | 82 | 174 | 165 | 8.0% | 198,954 | 14,588 | 25.8% |
| Jefferson | 716,055 | 538,246 | 138,796 | 16,025 | 22,988 | 9,783 | 7,078 | 5.5% | 23,300,262 | 33,466 | 9.5% |
| Jessamine | 42,910 | 40,050 | 1,363 | 597 | 900 | 580 | 304 | 4.2% | 1,036,492 | 25,429 | 8.4% |
| Johnson | 24,030 | 23,547 | 71 | 174 | 238 | 304 | 275 | 6.3% | 473,002 | 20,159 | 21.7% |
| Kenton | 155,066 | 143,148 | 6,406 | 2,176 | 3,336 | 2,407 | 1,327 | 5.1% | 4,600,382 | 30,332 | 7.1% |
| Knott | 17,696 | 17,320 | 131 | 114 | 131 | 184 | 182 | 6.4% | 302,466 | 17,047 | 26.2% |
| Knox | 32,136 | 31,192 | 333 | 224 | 387 | 473 | 351 | 6.7% | 574,617 | 18,139 | 29.6% |
| Larue | 13,628 | 12,911 | 429 | 143 | 145 | 157 | 162 | 5.0% | 326,908 | 24,295 | 12.6% |
| Laurel | 56,377 | 54,597 | 428 | 384 | 968 | 751 | 501 | 5.4% | 1,114,855 | 20,468 | 17.8% |
| Lawrence | 16,114 | 15,893 | 35 | 66 | 120 | 172 | 169 | 8.6% | 267,742 | 16,853 | 25.3% |
| Lee | 7,818 | 7,414 | 305 | 32 | 67 | 91 | 102 | 7.3% | 129,870 | 16,433 | 25.2% |
| Leslie | 12,119 | 11,977 | 11 | 76 | 55 | 122 | 145 | 9.4% | 215,272 | 17,513 | 30.2% |
| Letcher | 24,786 | 24,381 | 141 | 109 | 155 | 288 | 299 | 7.5% | 481,485 | 19,337 | 23.7% |
| Lewis | 13,891 | 13,693 | 44 | 71 | 83 | 160 | 155 | 7.0% | 208,424 | 15,057 | 23.5% |
| Lincoln | 25,141 | 23,982 | 635 | 320 | 204 | 297 | 238 | 6.4% | 445,770 | 18,458 | 16.4% |
| Livingston | 9,843 | 9,656 | 22 | 81 | 84 | 96 | 123 | 5.3% | 222,318 | 22,623 | 7.6% |
| Logan | 27,452 | 24,671 | 2,001 | 404 | 376 | 329 | 285 | 5.4% | 574,143 | 21,476 | 10.8% |
| Lyon | 8,266 | 7,530 | 604 | 61 | 71 | 49 | 94 | 5.8% | 163,653 | 20,095 | 10.2% |
| McCracken | 65,509 | 56,372 | 6,972 | 809 | 1,356 | 759 | 746 | 5.2% | 1,898,114 | 29,313 | 11.4% |
| McCreary | 17,171 | 16,718 | 142 | 116 | 195 | 244 | 194 | 10.6% | 255,317 | 14,912 | 26.1% |
| McLean | 10,104 | 9,894 | 43 | 122 | 45 | 115 | 120 | 8.2% | 262,270 | 26,351 | 13.7% |
| Madison | 77,052 | 71,148 | 3,248 | 844 | 1,812 | 967 | 533 | 4.5% | 1,527,134 | 20,808 | 12.0% |
| Magoffin | 13,517 | 13,375 | 25 | 61 | 56 | 186 | 117 | 10.1% | 231,129 | 17,389 | 31.2% |
| Marion | 18,949 | 16,789 | 1,691 | 221 | 248 | 285 | 176 | 5.6% | 390,066 | 21,105 | 15.8% |
| Marshall | 31,073 | 30,397 | 63 | 260 | 353 | 276 | 345 | 5.4% | 749,109 | 24,792 | 6.6% |
| Martin | 12,411 | 12,239 | 14 | 83 | 75 | 166 | 113 | 7.4% | 215,133 | 17,152 | 33.3% |
| Mason | 17,108 | 15,521 | 1,179 | 171 | 237 | 186 | 196 | 4.9% | 390,234 | 23,126 | 12.9% |
| Meade | 29,002 | 26,344 | 1,158 | 702 | 798 | 314 | 154 | 5.4% | 594,657 | 21,687 | 9.3% |
| Menifee | 6,843 | 6,637 | 93 | 77 | 36 | 90 | 61 | 7.2% | 102,838 | 15,356 | 23.4% |

PERSONAL INCOME, RACE, BIRTHS, DEATHS AND UNEMPLOYMENT FOR KENTUCKY COUNTIES

| AREA NAME | 2004 | | | | | 2003 | | 2006* | PERSONAL INCOME ($000) | 2000 | |
|---|---|---|---|---|---|---|---|---|---|---|---|
| | ESTIMATED POPULATION | WHITE | BLACK | HISPANIC | OTHER RACES** | BIRTHS | DEATHS | UN-EMPLOY-MENT | | PER CAPITA PERSONAL INCOME ($) | POVERTY LEVEL |
| Mercer | 21,824 | 20,272 | 809 | 331 | 412 | 267 | 235 | 5.5% | 483,495 | 22,911 | 10.0% |
| Metcalfe | 10,222 | 9,914 | 186 | 57 | 65 | 112 | 123 | 5.1% | 177,505 | 17,761 | 18.8% |
| Monroe | 11,907 | 11,250 | 324 | 247 | 86 | 136 | 142 | 5.1% | 224,023 | 19,098 | 20.0% |
| Montgomery | 23,912 | 22,591 | 787 | 283 | 251 | 339 | 210 | 5.5% | 496,987 | 21,398 | 12.5% |
| Morgan | 14,450 | 13,620 | 642 | 90 | 98 | 147 | 111 | 8.0% | 215,797 | 15,153 | 23.5% |
| Muhlenberg | 32,034 | 30,023 | 1,483 | 282 | 246 | 340 | 403 | 9.6% | 654,185 | 20,632 | 15.5% |
| Nelson | 40,846 | 37,617 | 2,201 | 440 | 588 | 567 | 301 | 5.2% | 1,000,785 | 25,732 | 10.0% |
| Nicholas | 7,121 | 6,981 | 60 | 45 | 35 | 86 | 88 | 6.4% | 145,341 | 21,052 | 9.7% |
| Ohio | 23,862 | 23,143 | 212 | 297 | 210 | 294 | 284 | 6.0% | 450,354 | 19,435 | 13.9% |
| Oldham | 53,028 | 48,949 | 2,286 | 928 | 865 | 580 | 274 | 4.7% | 1,580,063 | 32,120 | 2.9% |
| Owen | 11,410 | 11,046 | 129 | 110 | 125 | 136 | 129 | 5.0% | 198,508 | 18,053 | 12.1% |
| Owsley | 4,784 | 4,727 | 6 | 35 | 16 | 59 | 60 | 7.9% | 83,966 | 17,644 | 41.7% |
| Pendleton | 15,252 | 14,966 | 83 | 118 | 85 | 150 | 111 | 5.0% | 303,138 | 20,445 | 9.8% |
| Perry | 29,979 | 28,958 | 514 | 217 | 290 | 403 | 370 | 6.8% | 615,460 | 20,926 | 26.1% |
| Pike | 67,552 | 66,040 | 359 | 472 | 681 | 772 | 789 | 6.1% | 1,435,298 | 21,172 | 20.6% |
| Powell | 13,702 | 13,455 | 93 | 87 | 67 | 181 | 126 | 6.9% | 243,793 | 18,341 | 18.9% |
| Pulaski | 59,413 | 57,222 | 714 | 686 | 791 | 720 | 662 | 6.2% | 1,259,175 | 21,986 | 14.8% |
| Robertson | 2,345 | 2,268 | 6 | 37 | 34 | 21 | 32 | 5.1% | 39,657 | 17,227 | 17.5% |
| Rockcastle | 16,881 | 16,616 | 32 | 99 | 134 | 196 | 179 | 5.4% | 277,128 | 16,615 | 19.1% |
| Rowan | 22,458 | 21,352 | 343 | 282 | 481 | 270 | 181 | 4.9% | 430,716 | 19,309 | 15.9% |
| Russell | 16,978 | 16,624 | 114 | 140 | 100 | 191 | 193 | 5.7% | 315,432 | 19,139 | 20.4% |
| Scott | 38,782 | 35,173 | 2,061 | 753 | 795 | 548 | 238 | 4.5% | 993,257 | 28,022 | 7.3% |
| Shelby | 40,038 | 33,173 | 3,120 | 2,819 | 926 | 503 | 289 | 4.7% | 982,079 | 28,034 | 6.5% |
| Simpson | 17,061 | 14,905 | 1,668 | 170 | 318 | 222 | 169 | 5.4% | 383,939 | 23,107 | 8.5% |
| Spencer | 14,980 | 14,381 | 242 | 158 | 199 | 169 | 99 | 5.4% | 287,405 | 21,150 | 7.7% |
| Taylor | 23,726 | 22,071 | 1,221 | 247 | 187 | 268 | 244 | 4.5% | 473,473 | 20,391 | 14.2% |
| Todd | 12,093 | 10,765 | 1,014 | 230 | 84 | 189 | 136 | 8.0% | 242,358 | 20,121 | 14.7% |
| Trigg | 13,412 | 11,839 | 1,226 | 163 | 184 | 145 | 145 | 4.7% | 324,402 | 25,449 | 8.8% |
| Trimble | 9,178 | 8,937 | 28 | 131 | 82 | 109 | 82 | 7.0% | 147,889 | 17,109 | 10.0% |
| Union | 15,955 | 13,383 | 2,121 | 247 | 204 | 187 | 187 | 5.4% | 359,036 | 22,994 | 9.3% |
| Warren | 100,329 | 85,386 | 8,523 | 3,161 | 3,259 | 1,303 | 810 | 4.3% | 2,376,512 | 25,183 | 10.8% |
| Washington | 11,472 | 10,305 | 829 | 206 | 132 | 159 | 110 | 5.7% | 231,200 | 20,732 | 10.3% |
| Wayne | 20,895 | 19,896 | 305 | 495 | 199 | 233 | 233 | 6.4% | 346,422 | 17,231 | 24.6% |
| Webster | 14,666 | 13,389 | 623 | 536 | 118 | 195 | 165 | 4.7% | 358,051 | 25,417 | 12.6% |
| Whitley | 37,864 | 36,960 | 149 | 298 | 457 | 560 | 491 | 5.5% | 713,644 | 19,388 | 21.6% |
| Wolfe | 7,093 | 7,005 | 18 | 48 | 22 | 114 | 102 | 9.1% | 114,326 | 16,407 | 29.9% |
| Woodford | 25,019 | 22,376 | 1,278 | 1,058 | 307 | 328 | 193 | 3.7% | 803,775 | 34,135 | 5.2% |

Source: Regional Economic Information System, U.S. Bureau of Economic Analysis. (CA05N) Personal Income & Per Capita Personal Income Data, 2000

Vital Statistics from: http://ksdc.louisville.edu/sdc/vitalstats/vs1960_2003.xls

http://www.workforcekentucky.ky.gov/cgi/dataanalysis/AreaSelection.asp?tableName=Labforce, Jan 2006 Data

* Totals as of January, 2006

**Includes Indian, Asian, and Other

## COUNTIES WITH YEAR FORMED, COUNTY SEAT, AREA, POPULATION, & DENSITY

| COUNTY | YEAR FORMED | COUNTY SEAT(S) | AREA | POPULATION | | DENSITY | NO OF HOUSEHOLDS | |
|---|---|---|---|---|---|---|---|---|
| | | | | 2000 CENSUS | 2005 ESTIMATE | | 2000 CENSUS | 2005 ESTIMATE |
| KENTUCKY | | | 39,728.1 | 4,041,769 | 4,173,405 | 101.7 | 1,590,647 | 1,865,516 |
| Adair | 1802 | Columbia | 406.8 | 17,244 | 17,573 | 42.3 | 6,747 | 7,869 |
| Allen | 1815 | Scottsville | 346.1 | 17,800 | 18,706 | 51.4 | 6,910 | 8,371 |
| Anderson | 1827 | Lawrenceburg | 202.6 | 19,111 | 20,394 | 94.2 | 7,320 | 8,653 |
| Ballard | 1842 | Wickliffe | 251.1 | 8,286 | 8,277 | 32.9 | 3,395 | 3,966 |
| Barren | 1799 | Glasgow | 490.9 | 38,033 | 40,073 | 77.4 | 15,346 | 17,510 |
| Bath | 1811 | Owingsville | 279.4 | 11,085 | 11,626 | 39.6 | 4,445 | 5,218 |
| Bell | 1867 | Pineville | 360.7 | 30,060 | 29,665 | 83.3 | 12,004 | 13,751 |
| Boone | 1799 | Burlington | 246.2 | 85,991 | 106,272 | 349.1 | 31,258 | 41,781 |
| Bourbon | 1786 | Paris | 291.4 | 19,360 | 19,833 | 66.4 | 7,681 | 8,809 |
| Boyd | 1860 | Catlettsburg | 160.1 | 49,752 | 49,594 | 310.6 | 20,010 | 22,301 |
| Boyle | 1842 | Danville | 181.9 | 27,697 | 28,363 | 152.2 | 10,574 | 12,133 |
| Bracken | 1797 | Brooksville | 203.2 | 8,279 | 8,670 | 40.7 | 3,228 | 3,844 |
| Breathitt | 1839 | Jackson | 495.1 | 16,100 | 15,957 | 32.5 | 6,170 | 7,090 |
| Breckinridge | 1800 | Hardinsburg | 572.4 | 18,648 | 19,293 | 32.5 | 7,324 | 10,273 |
| Bullitt | 1797 | Shepherdsville | 299 | 61,236 | 68,474 | 204.7 | 22,171 | 27,249 |
| Butler | 1810 | Morgantown | 428 | 13,010 | 13,414 | 30.3 | 5,059 | 6,008 |
| Caldwell | 1809 | Princeton | 346.9 | 13,060 | 12,973 | 37.6 | 5,431 | 6,288 |
| Calloway | 1823 | Murray | 386.2 | 34,177 | 35,122 | 88.4 | 13,862 | 16,825 |
| Campbell | 1795 | Alexandria, Newport | 151.5 | 88,616 | 87,251 | 584.7 | 34,742 | 38,393 |
| Carlisle | 1886 | Bardwell | 192.4 | 5,351 | 5,329 | 27.7 | 2,208 | 2,573 |
| Carroll | 1838 | Carrolton | 130 | 10,155 | 10,454 | 78 | 3,940 | 4,554 |
| Carter | 1838 | Grayson | 410.6 | 26,889 | 27,306 | 65.4 | 10,342 | 12,071 |
| Casey | 1807 | Liberty | 445.6 | 15,447 | 16,290 | 34.64 | 6,260 | 7,499 |
| Christian | 1797 | Hopkinsville | 721.3 | 72,265 | 70,145 | 100.1 | 24,857 | 28,554 |
| Clark | 1793 | Winchester | 254.3 | 33,144 | 34,887 | 130.3 | 13,015 | 15,384 |
| Clay | 1807 | Manchester | 471 | 24,556 | 24,146 | 52.1 | 8,556 | 9,807 |
| Clinton | 1836 | Albany | 197.4 | 9,634 | 9,559 | 48.7 | 4,086 | 5,024 |
| Crittenden | 1842 | Marion | 362.1 | 9,384 | 8,984 | 25.9 | 3,829 | 4,555 |
| Cumberland | 1799 | Burkesville | 305.8 | 7,147 | 7,147 | 23.3 | 2,976 | 3,603 |
| Daviess | 1815 | Owensboro | 462.3 | 91,545 | 93,060 | 197.9 | 36,033 | 42,070 |
| Edmonson | 1826 | Brownsville | 302.6 | 11,644 | 12,030 | 38.4 | 4,648 | 6,360 |
| Elliott | 1869 | Sandy Hook | 233.9 | 6,748 | 6,902 | 28.8 | 2,638 | 3,244 |
| Estill | 1808 | Irvine | 253.9 | 15,307 | 15,089 | 60.2 | 6,108 | 7,037 |
| Fayette | 1780 | Lexington | 284.5 | 260,512 | 268,080 | 915.6 | 108,288 | 127,634 |
| Fleming | 1798 | Flemingsburg | 350.8 | 13,792 | 14,610 | 39.3 | 5,367 | 6,310 |
| Floyd | 1800 | Prestonsburg | 394.2 | 42,441 | 42,218 | 107.6 | 16,881 | 19,304 |
| Franklin | 1795 | Frankfort | 210.4 | 47,687 | 48,207 | 226.5 | 19,907 | 22,595 |
| Fulton | 1845 | Hickman | 208.9 | 7,752 | 7,217 | 37 | 3,237 | 3,741 |
| Gallatin | 1799 | Warsaw | 98.8 | 7,870 | 8,134 | 79.6 | 2,902 | 3,539 |
| Garrard | 1797 | Lancaster | 231.2 | 14,792 | 16,579 | 63.9 | 5,741 | 6,648 |
| Grant | 1820 | Williamstown | 259.9 | 22,384 | 24,610 | 86.1 | 8,175 | 10,226 |
| Graves | 1824 | Mayfield | 555.5 | 37,028 | 37,625 | 66.6 | 14,841 | 16,756 |
| Grayson | 1810 | Leitchfield | 503.6 | 24,053 | 25,189 | 47.7 | 9,596 | 12,907 |
| Green | 1793 | Greensburg | 288.6 | 11,518 | 11,588 | 39.9 | 4,706 | 5,453 |
| Greenup | 1804 | Greenup | 346.1 | 36,891 | 37,184 | 106.5 | 14,536 | 16,284 |
| Hancock | 1829 | Hawesville | 188.8 | 8,392 | 8,613 | 44.4 | 3,215 | 3,669 |
| Hardin | 1793 | Elizabethtown | 627.9 | 94,174 | 96,947 | 149.9 | 34,497 | 41,555 |
| Harlan | 1819 | Harlan | 467.2 | 33,202 | 31,614 | 71 | 13,291 | 15,477 |
| Harrison | 1794 | Cynthiana | 309.6 | 17,983 | 18,527 | 58 | 7,012 | 8,006 |
| Hart | 1819 | Munfordville | 415.9 | 17,445 | 18,319 | 41.9 | 6,769 | 8,264 |
| Henderson | 1799 | Henderson | 440.1 | 44,829 | 45,573 | 101.8 | 18,095 | 20,326 |
| Henry | 1799 | New Castle | 289.3 | 15,060 | 15,903 | 52 | 5,844 | 6,863 |
| Hickman | 1822 | Clinton | 244.4 | 5,262 | 5,075 | 21.5 | 2,188 | 2,516 |
| Hopkins | 1807 | Madisonville | 550.5 | 46,519 | 46,705 | 84.4 | 18,820 | 21,364 |
| Jackson | 1858 | McKee | 346.3 | 13,495 | 13,618 | 38.9 | 5,307 | 6,291 |
| Jefferson | 1780 | Louisville | 385 | 693,604 | 699,827 | 1801.1 | 287,012 | 322,329 |
| Jessamine | 1799 | Nicholasville | 173.1 | 39,041 | 43,463 | 225.5 | 13,867 | 17,505 |
| Johnson | 1843 | Paintsville | 261.5 | 23,445 | 24,001 | 89.6 | 9,103 | 10,410 |
| Kenton | 1840 | Covington, Independence | 161.9 | 151,464 | 153,665 | 935.1 | 59,444 | 68,315 |

| COUNTY | YEAR FORMED | COUNTY SEAT(S) | AREA | POPULATION | | DENSITY | NO OF HOUSEHOLDS | |
|---|---|---|---|---|---|---|---|---|
| | | | | 2000 CENSUS | 2005 ESTIMATE | | 2000 CENSUS | 2005 ESTIMATE |
| Knott | 1884 | Hindman | 352.1 | 17,649 | 17,561 | 50.1 | 6,717 | 7,905 |
| Knox | 1800 | Barbourville | 387.6 | 31,795 | 32,069 | 82 | 12,416 | 14,541 |
| Larue | 1843 | Hodgenville | 263.2 | 13,373 | 13,699 | 50.8 | 5,275 | 6,356 |
| Laurel | 1826 | London | 435.6 | 52,715 | 56,338 | 120.9 | 20,353 | 23,229 |
| Lawrence | 1822 | Louisa | 418.7 | 15,569 | 16,166 | 37.1 | 5,954 | 7,326 |
| Lee | 1870 | Beattyville | 209.8 | 7,916 | 7,709 | 37.7 | 2,985 | 3,455 |
| Leslie | 1878 | Hyden | 404 | 12,401 | 11,994 | 30.6 | 4,885 | 5,744 |
| Letcher | 1842 | Whitesburg | 339 | 25,277 | 24,434 | 74.5 | 10,085 | 11,840 |
| Lewis | 1807 | Vanceburg | 484.4 | 14,092 | 13,872 | 29 | 5,422 | 6,417 |
| Lincoln | 1780 | Stanford | 336.2 | 23,361 | 25,122 | 69.4 | 9,206 | 11,181 |
| Livingston | 1799 | Smithland | 316 | 9,804 | 9,760 | 31 | 3,996 | 4,959 |
| Logan | 1792 | Russellville | 555.6 | 26,573 | 27,169 | 47.8 | 10,506 | 12,087 |
| Lyon | 1854 | Eddyville | 215.7 | 8,080 | 8,160 | 37.4 | 2,898 | 4,386 |
| McCracken | 1825 | Paducah | 251 | 65,514 | 64,698 | 260.9 | 27,736 | 32,059 |
| McCreary | 1912 | Whitley City | 427.7 | 17,080 | 17,233 | 39.9 | 6,520 | 5,712 |
| McLean | 1854 | Calhoun | 254.3 | 9,938 | 9,926 | 39 | 3,984 | 7,469 |
| Madison | 1786 | Richmond | 440.6 | 70,872 | 77,749 | 160.8 | 27,152 | 15,340 |
| Magoffin | 1860 | Salyersville | 309.4 | 13,332 | 13,472 | 43 | 5,024 | 5,810 |
| Marion | 1834 | Lebanon | 346.3 | 18,212 | 18,939 | 52.5 | 6,613 | 7,968 |
| Marshall | 1842 | Benton | 304.8 | 30,125 | 30,967 | 98.8 | 12,412 | 31,485 |
| Martin | 1870 | Inez | 230.7 | 12,578 | 12,215 | 54.5 | 4,776 | 7,513 |
| Mason | 1789 | Maysville | 241.1 | 16,800 | 17,140 | 69.6 | 6,847 | 4,548 |
| Meade | 1824 | Brandenburg | 308.5 | 26,349 | 28,447 | 85.4 | 9,470 | 10,892 |
| Menifee | 1869 | Frenchburg | 203.9 | 6,556 | 6,809 | 32.1 | 2,537 | 3,855 |
| Mercer | 1786 | Harrodsburg | 250.9 | 20,817 | 21,610 | 82.9 | 8,423 | 9,894 |
| Metcalfe | 1860 | Edmonton | 290.9 | 10,037 | 10,197 | 34.5 | 4,016 | 4,763 |
| Monroe | 1820 | Tompkinsville | 330.8 | 11,756 | 11,660 | 35.5 | 4,741 | 5,468 |
| Montgomery | 1797 | Mount Sterling | 198.5 | 22,554 | 24,256 | 113.5 | 8,902 | 10,629 |
| Morgan | 1823 | West Liberty | 381.2 | 13,948 | 14,334 | 36.5 | 4,752 | 5,739 |
| Muhlenberg | 1799 | Greenville | 474.7 | 31,839 | 31,548 | 67 | 12,357 | 14,106 |
| Nelson | 1785 | Bardstown | 422.6 | 37,477 | 41,088 | 88.6 | 13,953 | 17,308 |
| Nicholas | 1800 | Carlisle | 196.6 | 6,813 | 7,027 | 34.6 | 2,710 | 3,132 |
| Ohio | 1799 | Hartford | 593.7 | 22,916 | 23,676 | 38.5 | 8,899 | 10,292 |
| Oldham | 1824 | La Grange | 189.1 | 46,178 | 53,533 | 244 | 14,856 | 19,299 |
| Owen | 1819 | Owenton | 352.1 | 10,547 | 11,374 | 29.9 | 4,086 | 5,554 |
| Owsley | 1843 | Booneville | 198 | 4,858 | 4,746 | 24.5 | 1,894 | 2,335 |
| Pendleton | 1799 | Falmouth | 280.5 | 14,390 | 15,125 | 51.2 | 5,170 | 5,937 |
| Perry | 1821 | Hazard | 342.1 | 29,390 | 29,452 | 85.8 | 11,460 | 13,272 |
| Pike | 1822 | Pikeville | 787.6 | 68,736 | 66,922 | 87.2 | 27,612 | 32,393 |
| Powell | 1852 | Stanton | 180.1 | 13,237 | 13,687 | 73.4 | 5,044 | 5,758 |
| Pulaski | 1799 | Somerset | 661.6 | 56,217 | 59,200 | 84.9 | 22,719 | 27,676 |
| Robertson | 1867 | Mount Olivet | 100 | 2,266 | 2,279 | 22.6 | 866 | 1,069 |
| Rockcastle | 1810 | Mount Vernon | 317.5 | 16,582 | 16,712 | 52.2 | 6,544 | 7,649 |
| Rowan | 1856 | Morehead | 280.8 | 22,094 | 22,226 | 78.6 | 7,927 | 9,349 |
| Russell | 1826 | Jamestown | 253.5 | 16,315 | 17,020 | 64.3 | 6,941 | 9,222 |
| Scott | 1792 | Georgetown | 284.7 | 33,061 | 39,380 | 116.1 | 12,110 | 15,248 |
| Shelby | 1792 | Shelbyville | 384.1 | 33,337 | 38,205 | 86.7 | 12,104 | 15,154 |
| Simpson | 1819 | Franklin | 236.1 | 16,405 | 17,021 | 69.4 | 6,415 | 7,609 |
| Spencer | 1824 | Taylorsville | 185.9 | 11,766 | 15,651 | 63.2 | 4,251 | 5,844 |
| Taylor | 1848 | Campbellsville | 269.8 | 22,927 | 23,754 | 84.9 | 9,233 | 10,269 |
| Todd | 1820 | Elkton | 376.3 | 11,971 | 11,944 | 31.8 | 4,569 | 5,255 |
| Trigg | 1820 | Cadiz | 443.1 | 12,597 | 13,349 | 28.4 | 5,215 | 6,982 |
| Trimble | 1837 | Bedford | 148.8 | 8,125 | 9,023 | 54.5 | 3,137 | 3,573 |
| Union | 1811 | Morganfield | 345.1 | 15,637 | 15,592 | 45.3 | 5,710 | 6,337 |
| Warren | 1797 | Bowling Green | 545.2 | 92,522 | 98,960 | 169.6 | 35,365 | 42,940 |
| Washington | 1792 | Springfield | 300.5 | 10,916 | 11,399 | 36.3 | 4,121 | 4,660 |
| Wayne | 1800 | Monticello | 459.4 | 19,923 | 20,352 | 43.3 | 7,913 | 9,901 |
| Webster | 1860 | Dixon | 334.7 | 14,120 | 14,161 | 42.1 | 5,560 | 6,409 |
| Whitley | 1818 | Williamsburg | 440.1 | 35,865 | 38,029 | 81.4 | 13,780 | 15,884 |
| Wolfe | 1860 | Campton | 222.7 | 7,065 | 7,070 | 31.7 | 2,816 | 3,411 |
| Woodford | 1789 | Versailles | 190.6 | 23,208 | 24,246 | 121.7 | 8,893 | 10,165 |

*Sources: www.uky.edu/KentuckyAtlas/kentucky-counties.html, ksdc.louisville.edu, and www.census.gov*

# Wet-Dry Counties

## It's a Kentucky Thing

It isn't that easy knowing where one can legally purchase a bottle of bourbon or a mug of Kentucky Ale. Out of Kentucky's 120 counties, the Office of Alcoholic Beverage Control lists 54 counties as dry (absolutely no legal liquor sales); 30 "wet" counties; 16 "moist" (wet cities within a dry county); 19 cities or counties with "limited" alcohol sales (sales of alcohol by the drink only in restaurants with at least 100 seating and 70 percent food sales); 13 wet for alcohol by the "drink only" at golf courses; and 13 small and farm wineries in a dry territory.

| COUNTY | STATUS | COUNTY | STATUS |
|---|---|---|---|
| ADAIR | DRY | KNOX | LTD |
| ALLEN | DRY | LARUE | DRY |
| ANDERSON | WET | LAUREL | LTD |
| BALLARD | LTD | LAWRENCE | DRY |
| BARREN | DRY | LEE | DRY |
| BATH | DRY | LESLIE | DRY |
| BELL | LTD | LETCHER | WI |
| BOONE | WET | LEWIS | M |
| BOURBON | WET | LINCOLN | DRY |
| BOYD | M | LIVINGSTON | DRY |
| BOYLE | LTD & WI & G | LOGAN | M |
| BRACKEN | WET | LYON | LTD |
| BREATHITT | DRY | McCRACKEN | WET |
| BRECKINRIDGE | DRY | McCREARY | DRY |
| BULLITT | WET | McLEAN | DRY |
| BUTLER | DRY | MADISON | M & G & WI |
| CALDWELL | WI | MAGOFFIN | WET |
| CALLOWAY | LTD & G | MARION | WET |
| CAMPBELL | WET | MARSHALL | LTD |
| CARLISLE | DRY | MARTIN | DRY |
| CARROLL | WET | MASON | WET |
| CARTER | DRY | MEADE | WET |
| CASEY | DRY | MENIFEE | DRY |
| CHRISTIAN | WET | MERCER | LTD |
| CLARK | WET | METCALFE | DRY |
| CLAY | DRY | MONROE | DRY |
| CLINTON | DRY | MONTGOMERY | M |
| CRITTENDEN | DRY | MORGAN | DRY |
| CUMBERLAND | DRY | MUHLENBERG | M |
| DAVIESS | WET | NELSON | WET |
| EDMONSON | DRY | NICHOLAS | WET |
| ELLIOTT | DRY | OHIO | DRY |
| ESTILL | DRY | OLDHAM | LTD & G |
| FAYETTE | WET | OWEN | WI |
| FLEMING | DRY | OWSLEY | DRY |
| FLOYD | WET | PENDLETON | M & G |
| FRANKLIN | WET | PERRY | WET |
| FULTON | WET | PIKE | M |
| GALLATIN | WET | POWELL | DRY |
| GARRARD | DRY | PULASKI | WI & LTD |
| GRANT | LTD | ROBERTSON | DRY |
| GRAVES | LTD & G | ROCKCASTLE | DRY |
| GRAYSON | DRY | ROWAN | M & WI |
| GREEN | DRY | RUSSELL | DRY |
| GREENUP | DRY | SCOTT | LTD & WI & G |
| HANCOCK | DRY | SHELBY | M & LTD & G |
| HARDIN | LTD & G | SIMPSON | LTD |
| HARLAN | M | SPENCER | DRY |
| HARRISON | WET | TAYLOR | DRY |
| HART | DRY | TODD | LTD |
| HENDERSON | WET | TRIGG | DRY |
| HENRY | M & WI | TRIMBLE | DRY |
| HICKMAN | DRY | UNION | WET & G |
| HOPKINS | M | WARREN | M |
| JACKSON | DRY | WASHINGTON | M & WI |
| JEFFERSON | WET | WAYNE | DRY |
| JESSAMINE | M & G & WI | WEBSTER | DRY |
| JOHNSON | DRY | WHITLEY | LTD |
| KENTON | WET | WOLFE | WET |
| KNOTT | DRY | WOODFORD | WET |

LTD = Limited, M = Moist, G = Golf, WI = Winery
Source: Kentucky Alcoholic Beverage Control Board

## COUNTIES & CITIES

# *What is a Commonwealth?*

In 1785 district residents of Kentucky County, Virginia, began petitioning the Virginia legislature for statehood. They wished the county to be recognized as a "free and independent state, to be known by the name of the 'Commonwealth' of Kentucky." On June 4th, 1792, Kentucky County, Virginia became officially the "Commonwealth of Kentucky."

When Kentucky joined the Union, the terms "commonwealth" and "state" were recognized by the U.S. government as being synonymous. Four states in the U.S. are titled commonwealths: Kentucky, Virginia, Pennsylvania and Massachusetts. The designation is an elected title deemed by the states' legislatures. To be a commonwealth rather than a state grants no differences legally or economically.

"Commonweal" is derived from the Anglo-Saxon "wela," meaning "sound and prosperous state." The term commonwealth had greater political meaning back in the time of Oliver Cromwell, when the British Parliament declared that government by a king was "unnecessary, burdensome, and dangerous," and further declared that the British nation would from then on be a commonwealth, or free state. To be a commonwealth meant that all power was vested in and derived from a equally free and independent people rather than a hierarchical and/or feudal system under a king. The basis for a commonwealth's success required each citizen to be an active participant in government, practitioners of civic virtue and socially responsible. The government essentially was to serve the people, rather than having the people serve the government.

This idea was one of the forerunners of democracy. The citizens of Virginia were the first to bring the term into U.S. government when its constitution declared the state independent of England and designated itself a newly formed commonwealth in 1776. Massachusetts and Pennsylvania soon followed. When the U.S. was granted separation from Great Britain and its monarchy, the term commonwealth lost its meaning in a democratically governed nation. Thus, the idea to be a state or to be a commonwealth in the U.S. became identical.

> The basis for a commonwealth's success required each citizen to be an active participant in government, practitioners of civic virtue and socially responsible. The government essentially was to serve the people, rather than having the people serve the government.

*Source: Kentucky Dept. of Libraries & Archives, www.kdla.ky.gov/resources/kycommonwealth.htm*

# Geology

### Dr. Gary O'Dell

**K**entucky displays a wide variety of physical landscapes, from the scenic mountain vistas of eastern Kentucky, to the gently rolling pastures of the central Bluegrass, to the fertile Mississippi River floodplains of extreme western Kentucky. These landscapes are the result of tectonic, erosional and depositional processes that have taken place over a very long span of time, and which are still modifying the landscape today. Kentucky's terrain is still a work in progress. If the geological record tells us anything, it is that landscapes are not static and unchanging, but dynamic and subject to dramatic alterations from a variety of geologic processes.

The shaping of Kentucky's landscape is a story written in the rocks for those who can interpret the geological text. Each layer is a page in the ancient history of the land. The rocks of the surface speak of more recent events; beneath these are tales deeply buried in place and in time, miles beneath the surface and representing a span of years greater than

**Chimney Rock near Danville**
*Source: Kentucky Department of Libraries & Archives*

our comprehension. To understand the forces and processes that produced modern-day Kentucky we must peel away layers of time and bedrock to recreate landscapes of hundreds of millions of years ago, when the world was a very different place. Kentucky's geologic history is part of a grand-scale drama, a story of continents slowly colliding to form giant supercontinents—and of those same giant masses rupturing and splitting apart—even as great oceans were created and destroyed.

Centered around Hudson Bay in Canada is a region of ancient granitic, igneous rock, which is the nucleus or "craton" of the original continent of North America known as the Canadian Shield. Some of the rocks of the Shield have been dated to more than four billion years in age. The North American continent grew around the Canadian Shield by the gradual process of accretion, as other land masses were brought into contact with the core region by movement of crustal plates. Around the margin of the core area is the relatively stable region known as the platform, which, while submerged, accumulated massive sediment deposits eroded from the craton. Kentucky is positioned on the platform of the southeastern margin of the Canadian Shield.

From approximately 1.3 to 1.0 billion years ago, during Precambrian time, this core region was located along the equator and its eastern edge was in the process of colliding with a continental block. The collision, which took place over several hundred million years, led to the formation of a supercontinent called Rodinia (homeland) by geologists, and a massive mountain-building event known as the Grenville Orogeny. The western edge of the collision zone, the Grenville Front, traverses central Kentucky, but is now buried beneath thousands of feet of sedimentary rock.

Rodinia remained stable for a long time, and the Himalaya-scale mountain ranges generated during the orogeny were leveled by erosion near sea level. About 700 million years ago, Rodinia began to split ("rift") apart in the vicinity of the previous suture zone, and a new ocean, the Iapetus, separated the parts of the former supercontinent. At the beginning of the Paleozoic Era, more than a half billion years ago, the crustal plates containing the continents of North America, Europe, and Africa were again on a collision course. The Iapetus Ocean, predecessor of the modern Atlantic, was shrinking as the ocean floor plunged beneath the eastern coastal margin of North America in a process known as subduction. Along the subduction boundary, as the subducting plate melted and magma rose to the surface, lines of volcanic islands were produced. As the continental masses converged, these island arcs and wedges of crustal material were compressed between them in several major episodes of mountain-building.

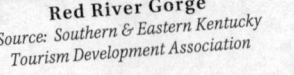

**Red River Gorge**
Source: Southern & Eastern Kentucky Tourism Development Association

During the later Paleozoic, beginning in the Pennsylvanian Period about 310 million years ago, a full contact collision began to occur that lasted for nearly 60 million years and created the supercontinent of Pangea. This supercontinent persisted for about 100 million years and then began to split apart during the Triassic Period of the Mesozoic Era. The rift that developed to separate the continents was the origin of the present-day Atlantic Ocean, which is still widening as the crustal plates move farther apart.

The major mountain-building episodes of the Paleozoic produced major deformations and disruptions of the crust. These earlier mountain ranges, uplifted by plate collisions—and ancestral to the modern Appalachian Mountains—no longer exist, having been leveled by erosion. The byproducts of their disintegration were deposited as sheets of sediment in adjacent oceans.

During the Paleozoic Era, which spanned nearly 300 million years, the region that is now Kentucky was covered by a shallow sea and only intermittently exposed. Much of the bedrock that is today at or near the land surface was deposited as sediments in this marine environment and was compressed and transformed to solid rock by the accumulating weight of overlying material. Because of their origin as marine deposits, the sedimentary bedrocks of Kentucky occur in layers that are more-or-less horizontal, except where they have been disturbed. Features associated with Precambrian tectonic events, such as the Grenville Front, lie buried beneath thousands of feet of sedimentary rocks. Reactivation of several of these lines of structural weakness in later eras resulted in fracturing of the sedimentary cover to produce fault zones, some of which are active today.

The type of sedimentary rock being deposited at any given time depended upon the nature of rock being eroded from adjacent highlands, prevailing environmental conditions and configuration of land and sea. Deposition of clastic sediments (sandstone, shale) dominated some eras and carbonates (limestone, dolomite) during others. This produced a stratigraphic sequence for Kentucky in which the lowermost Precambrian and early Paleozoic sedimentary rocks are of clastic origin, then a period of carbonate deposition—followed by more sandstones and shales— a thick sequence of carbonates in the middle to late Paleozoic, and, last, a layer of sandstones and other clastics. Embedded within the late Paleozoic rocks are seams of bituminous coal, derived from massive accumulations of organic matter in lowland swamps that represented the explosion of plant and animal life on land at this time.

The proto-Appalachian ranges that were uplifted by continental collisions during the Paleozoic were reduced to a flat, eroded plain in North America by the end of the Mesozoic. Regional uplift brought the Paleozoic marine sedimentary rocks of the interior to the surface, exposing them to weather and erosion. The uplift rejuvenated regional streams and rivers, which began to cut deeply into the plateau surface formed by sedimentary rock. Differential rates of weathering, according to the nature of the bedrock, developed a new mountainous topography influenced by ancient mountain roots, preserving the geologic structures of rocks folded and overthrust during previous orogenies—our present-day Appalachian Mountains. In eastern Kentucky, the Appalachian Mountains tend to be more erosional than tectonic in origin. Unlike the overthrust and folded mountains farther east, the Kentucky mountains are erosional remnants left by the carving of deep valleys into these horizontal rock strata rather than the product of an orogeny.

During the post-Grenville episodes of slow-motion tectonic violence, Kentucky's location on the cratonic platform was far enough to the west of the collision zone that the sedimentary rocks of the region were generally spared major distortions and faulting, except in the extreme southeast corner. Instead, the tectonic events that built mountains in the east produced a series of gradually diminishing waves in the bedrock of the continent westward away from the collision zone. In Kentucky, this flexing of the bedrock produced a slight structural upwarp, known as the Cincinnati Arch. The axis of the Arch runs diagonally through the state from Ohio through Tennessee, and is one of the defining features of Kentucky's overall geology.

The upward flex of the Arch is expressed more in the bedrock than in the topography. Millions of years of erosion—concurrent with and subsequent to the uplifts—have leveled the surface, cutting across rock layers and planing away the convexity. The structure of the Arch is revealed at the surface only by a very subtle upward bulge in the center as a consequence of exposed strata that have been more resistant to erosion than layers higher in the sequence. The Arch has two major domes: one centered nearly under Lexington called the Jessamine Dome, and another near Nashville. Because of the upward bulge of the rock structure and subsequent erosion, the oldest rocks in the state are exposed in the center of the Jessamine Dome (in the gorge of the Kentucky River) and become progressively younger as one travels outward in any direction.

The surface geology of Kentucky resembles a vast bull's eye target comprised of concentric rings of bedrock of similar age. Driving across Kentucky is like traveling through time, with tens of millions of years of bedrock time passing for every hour on the road. The oldest rocks at the center of the planed-down dome are limestones, formed in shallow tropical seas that dominated the region 500 million years ago during the Ordovician Period. Surrounding this center are younger rock belts of Silurian and Devonian age. During this geologic time period, less carbonate and a greater amount of silt and mud was deposited from eroding mountains to the east, so that shales and siltstones are dominant. Moving still further out from the central region, the traveler again enters a zone representing carbonate deposition; limestones deposited during the Mississippian Period, and, at last, Pennsylvanian sandstones with their seams of coal. The basins to either side of the Arch served as reservoirs for sediment accumulation, and the tremendous weight of these sediments augmented the tectonic downwarp to depress these areas still farther into the crust. The Ordovician strata exposed at the center of the Cincinnati Arch lie buried beneath more than 3,000 feet of sedimentary rock in the Appalachian Basin to the east and more than 4,000 feet of rock in the Illinois Basin to the west. Both sides of the Illinois Basin are present in Kentucky, so that the pattern of bedrock at the surface forms a series of roughly concentric circles similar to the pattern exhibited by the Jessamine Dome. On the Dome, however, rocks become older toward the center, whereas on the Basin the youngest rocks are toward the center. Only the western side of the Appalachian Basin is present in Kentucky, so that rock strata in the state continue dipping downward toward the east.

During the later Paleozoic Era, the eastern coastline of the Appalachian Basin was dominated by river deltas and wetlands, formed of river-borne sediments eroded from the ancestral Appalachians in the east. These were the coal swamps of the Pennsylvanian and Permian periods, in which organic matter accumulated and was eventually transformed to bituminous coal.

Pine Mountain Thrust Fault in the Pound Gap road cut near Jenkins, Letcher County
Source: Steve Greb, KY Geological Survey

Because of the Cenozoic uplift, the region was no longer underwater and accumulation of marine sediments ceased across most of the area that is now Kentucky. Deposition was replaced by erosion, and much of the uppermost Paleozoic bedrock was worn away to form the present day surface landscape. In far western Kentucky, however, beginning in the late Mesozoic, gradual subsidence along an ancient rift zone combined with higher sea levels than today allowed the ocean to invade the landmass along a broad corridor. Known as the Mississippi Embayment, this longitudinal dent in the southern margin of the continent stretches from Louisiana to Illinois. Since the Cretaceous Period, thousands of feet of marine sediments eroded from adjacent land areas accumulated in this depositional trough. As sea levels subsequently dropped and the ocean retreated from the embayment, particularly during the last 2 million years, the Mississippi River became established in this location.

Multiple episodes of recent Ice Age continental glaciation had other effects in Kentucky, although the landscape was directly impacted by ice sheets only in northern Kentucky. The direct effects of glaciation exist as a thin strip of till, outwash, and glacial lake deposits along the Ohio River from Kenton to Oldham counties. Glacial outwash deposits mixed with alluvium are found further westward along the river to the embayment area, which served as an outlet for an outpouring of meltwaters during periods of glacial retreat. Deposits of wind-blown silt and fine sand (loess) as much as 70-feet thick occur mixed with glacial deposits in some locations, and as a thin layer in much of western Kentucky. Massive ice sheets covering the lands bordering Kentucky to the north blocked existing rivers and caused a reorganization of regional drainage. The major rivers of Kentucky, including the Kentucky, Licking and Green, were forced to find shorter pathways to the sea. The reduction in the length of these rivers increased the gradient, or steepness of the flow path, so that the streams began downcutting their channels. Consequently, rivers in Kentucky were entrenched, and the residual alluvium of former flood plains exists in numerous locations as high-level terrace deposits above the present-day river courses.

In summary, during virtually the 300 million year span of the Paleozoic, the region that includes present-day Kentucky was under water—a depositional environment. Sediments eroded from land areas to the east, north, and west accumulated in this low area and were compacted and cemented to form thick layers of sedimentary rock. These initially flat-lying rock strata were disturbed by tectonic events to the east, producing an alternating series of upwarps and downwarps that are today visible in the rock structure. The region was uplifted during the Cenozoic and has remained dry land to the present day, so that no further accumulation of marine sediments occurred except in the area to the extreme west. As a result, Kentucky was transformed from a region of deposition to an erosional environment, and about 2,000 feet of accumulated sedimentary rock were subsequently worn away to produce the modern landscape.

# Fault Lines & Earthquakes
## Dr. Gary O'Dell

An earthquake is the result of a sudden movement along a geographic fault—stress builds along a fracture in the earth's crust until slippage occurs, releasing energy in the form of seismic waves. These waves radiate outward through the earth from the point of origin, or focus; the location on the surface directly above the focus is known as the epicenter. Generally, the longer movement along the fault is hindered, allowing stress to build, the greater will be the displacement along the fault and the associated severity of the quake. There are hundreds of earthquakes around the globe every day, most so slight that only sensitive instruments can detect the movement.

Most earthquakes take place near the boundaries of tectonic plates, but one in 10 is an intraplate quake, located far from an active plate margin. New Madrid Seismic Zone is one such region and is situated above a failed rift zone, which trends southwest to northeast from Arkansas, through southeast Missouri, western Tennessee, and western Kentucky to southern Illinois—but is deeply buried beneath Mississippi River alluvial deposits. About 750 million years ago, when the supercontinent Rodinia began to break apart, the rupture now occupied by the New Madrid zone ceased before a split took place. The rifting process produced a zone of weakness that persists today and is known as the Reelfoot Rift. Most of the fault systems in Kentucky appear to be related to failed rift zones associated with the breakup of the Rodinia supercontinent.

During the Mesozoic breakup of Pangaea, stretching of the earth's crust reactivated the long-dormant faults of the Reelfoot Rift, which were subsequently covered by many thousands of feet of sediments. Some geologists believe that recent episodes of continental glaciation—the Ice Ages—played a role in stimulating activity along the New Madrid Seismic Zone. The tremendous weight of ice sheets depressed the earth's crust during the last two million years. After the glaciers melted, the crust slowly rebounded upward toward its original position.

Several less active fault zones in Kentucky appear to be related to New Madrid fault zone. East of the Fluorspar District in western Kentucky is the Rough Creek Graben, which may be an extension of the Reelfoot Rift. The graben is a section of crust displaced downward between two east-west trending faults. Another inactive zone is the Lexington Fault System of central Kentucky, which traverses the Bluegrass from southwest to northeast. This system is related to the Paleozoic tectonic events that produced the Cincinnati Arch, and parallels the Arch along the eastern flank.

The most dramatic fault zone in Kentucky is the Pine Mountain Thrust Fault in southeastern Kentucky. Displacement along a thrust fault is primarily horizontal, rather than vertical. Thrust faults are the result of forces so extreme as to cause one section of the rock strata to be pushed up and over another. The Pine Mountain fault originated about 275 million years ago as one of a series of overlapping fault blocks generated by the collision of land masses that formed the Pangaea supercontinent. The horizontal displacement ranges from four to 11 miles, and created Pine Mountain (a ridge more than 100 miles long). Small earthquakes have occurred along this fault including a January 19, 1976 event that registered a magnitude of 4.0.

A previously unknown fault system was responsible for the strongest earthquake to originate within Kentucky during historic times. The 5.2 magnitude quake occurred on July 27, 1980—centered in Bath County, the quake was felt in 15 states and in Ontario, Canada. Property damage amounted to more than $3 million. Maysville, located on the Ohio River about 30 miles north of the epicenter, was most severely affected.

## STRONGEST EARTHQUAKES IN CONTINENTAL U.S. (Not Alaska)

| Location | Date | Time UTC | Magnitude |
|----------|------|----------|-----------|
| 1. New Madrid, MO | 1811 Dec 16 | 08:15 | 8.1 |
| 2. New Madrid, MO | 1812 Feb 07 | 09:45 | 8.0 |
| 3. Fort Tejon, CA | 1857 Jan 09 | 16:24 | 7.9 |
| 4. New Madrid, MO | 1812 Jan 23 | 15:00 | 7.8 |
| 5. Imperial Valley, CA | 1892 Feb 24 | 07:20 | 7.8 |
| 6. San Francisco, CA | 1906 Apr 18 | 13:12 | 7.8 |

Source: US Geological Survey

# ENVIRONMENT & NATURAL RESOURCES

# *Caves & Karst*

Dr. Gary O'Dell

In his 1784 book, "Discovery, Settlement and Present State of Kentucke," John Filson wrote: "Caves are found in this country amazingly large; in some of which you may travel several miles under a fine limestone rock, supported by curious arches and pillars: in most of them runs a stream of water." The size and splendor of Kentucky's caves are today still a source of amazement to visitors. Kentucky is home to Mammoth Cave, which, with more than 360 miles of mapped passageways, is the world's longest cave. Although Mammoth is certainly the most significant cave in the state, the geology of Kentucky has promoted the formation of many thousands of other caves contained within a distinctive landscape type known as "karst." Karst landscapes are characterized by subsurface drainage and landscape features such as sinkholes, sinking streams, caves and springs. In karst, the typical patterns of drainage by surface streams found elsewhere are absent or interrupted, since flow takes place underground through a network of conduits. This network develops as bedrock fractures are enlarged by the circulation of naturally acidic groundwater that slowly dissolves limestone, dolomite and other carbonate sedimentary rocks. Approximately half of Kentucky's land area displays such features and is considered karst terrain. Precipitation falling to the earth is naturally slightly acidic, the result of carbon dioxide and water vapor combining in the atmosphere to form carbonic acid. This acidity is increased as water filters through the soil and absorbs more carbon dioxide from organic matter. The relatively weak solution of carbonic acid in groundwater is capable of dissolving rocks such as limestone. Acidic water percolates downward through the soil cover and into the bedrock, following the network of joints and bedding planes. Vertical bedrock fractures, or joints, are largely the result of past tectonic stresses that have

Mammoth Cave
Source: Tour Southern & Eastern Kentucky

This "blue hole" or artesian spring in Allen County is one of the largest in Kentucky
Source: Gary O'Dell

cracked the rock layers, providing pathways for downward penetration of groundwater. Bedrock structure is thus an important control upon the conduit pathways that develops as acidic groundwater dissolves the rock. As vertical fractures just beneath the soil cover are enlarged by removal of the rock, eventually the soil slumps downward to form an enclosed depression known as a sinkhole. Water enters a karst conduit system through direct inlet points such as sinkholes and sinking streams, and by a more diffuse and widespread recharge that takes place beneath the soil. The enlargement of bedrock fractures creates an extensive plumbing system of tubes and conduits that carry groundwater to lower elevations, where it is discharged as springs. As the channel of a surface stream becomes wider and deeper downstream as tributaries join, the conduits in an underground system increase in diameter in a downstream direction.

There are four distinct cave regions in Kentucky: the Pine Mountain Karst Region, Inner Bluegrass Karst Region, Eastern Pennyroyal Karst Region and the Western Pennyroyal Karst Region. These four regions are differentiated primarily by the age of the carbonate rocks in which the cave and conduit systems are developed and by their geography.

The Pine Mountain Karst Region is a long narrow strip at the extreme southeastern corner of the state, representing a band of limestone of Mississippian age exposed at the northwestern edge of the Pine Mountain thrust fault.

The Inner Bluegrass Karst Region is very nearly centered on Lexington, a roughly circular area of limestones and dolomites of Ordovician age exposed by the weathering of the upward bulge of the Jessamine Dome. The rock strata are nearly horizontal, with a very slight dip away from the center in all directions except to the southeast where the Lexington

**"300 Springs" in Hart County**
*Source: Gary O'Dell*

Fault System comprises the boundary of the karst area. The rocks in the region tend to be rather thinly bedded, and often interbedded with shales, which tends to limit development of extensive cave networks. Although several hundred caves are known in the region, with few exceptions, most of these are short, low and wet.

The Eastern and Western Pennyroyal Karst Regions are both developed on carbonate sedimentary rocks of Mississippian age. These carbonate rocks are relatively pure, thickly bedded, and often of considerable vertical extent, allowing the development of multi-level cave systems and large passages. Carter Caves State Resort Park is located in the northern part of the Eastern Pennyroyal, and many large cave systems are found in the southeastern section. The most famous cave system in the world, Mammoth Cave, is found in the Western Pennyroyal Karst Region. The karst area stretches in an arc around the hilly, non-karst Western Coal Field region. The edge of the coalfield region is a dissected landscape of ridges and valleys in which cavernous limestones are capped by non-soluble sandstones and shales. The Mammoth Cave system is located in this area. The area around Mammoth Cave is probably the best-known and most intensively studied karst region in the world, and has been designated a World Heritage Region by the U.N. Educational, Scientific, and Cultural Organization.

The first explorers and settlers of Kentucky, as Filson noted, were greatly impressed by the many caves and abundant springs of clear water in this land. Spring water was then, as today, perceived as being the highest quality water supply, and the location of springs had a strong influence upon the early settlement pattern. As the land was surveyed, claimed and settled, first priority was given to tracts containing a significant spring. Individual settlements or stations were often situated in close proximity to a significant spring. In the Inner Bluegrass Karst Region, for example, communities originally sited to take advantage of a particular spring include Lancaster, Georgetown, Versailles, Paris and Lexington. Early deeds recorded in Kentucky courthouses exhibit a well-developed terminology describing karst features such as springs, "sinking springs," and "blue holes." Urban growth and land development upon a karst landscape also imposes certain problems not evident in other terrain types. Groundwater contamination by chemical pollutants and pathogenic organisms is a particular hazard. Karst aquifers exist at relatively shallow depths and are easily contaminated by a variety of causes, ranging from runoff of agricultural chemicals to leaking sewer lines. Since water flows swiftly through karst conduits and thus spends relatively little time underground there is only a slight reduction in potential pathogens, nor is there any filtration of the water flow as occurs in sand and gravel aquifers. Too often sinkholes are regarded by a property owner simply as a convenient place to dispose of trash or waste, unaware that what is dumped into a sinkhole today may show up in his neighbor's drinking water spring tomorrow.

# ENVIRONMENT & NATURAL RESOURCES
# *Physical Regions*                        Dr. Gary O'Dell

The present-day physical landscape of Kentucky, as we have seen, is a result of both ancient and recent geological processes. The accumulation of transported sediments during the Paleozoic, when this region was a shallow marine environment, produced a veneer of sedimentary strata thousands of feet in thickness over the much older basement rocks. Tectonic processes, involving the movement of crustal plates, fractured, warped and folded the rock layers to impose structural features within the bedrock mass. Because these structural features vary across the length and width of the Commonwealth, and because different types of sedimentary rocks vary in their resistance to weathering and erosion, there is a distinct pattern of variation of the surface landscape. Kentucky's 40,409 square miles of land and water can thus be divided into discrete physiographic regions according to characteristics of the topography. The five main physical regions of Kentucky, from east to west, are: the Eastern Kentucky Coal Field, the Bluegrass, the Mississippian Plateau, the Western Kentucky Coal Field, and the Mississippi Embayment. The physical regions of Kentucky are included within the larger geomorphic provinces of the United States. The Eastern Kentucky Coal Field is part of the Appalachian Plateaus that stretch from New York to Georgia; the Bluegrass, Mississippian Plateau and the Western Kentucky Coal Field are contained within the Interior Low Plateaus that include parts of southern Illinois, Indiana and Ohio; and the Mississippi Embayment is a section of the much larger Gulf Coastal Plain. Broadly speaking, the landscape of Kentucky consists of dissected highland plateaus, east and west, separated by escarpments from gently rolling plains in central and southern Kentucky. The plateau areas; the two coal field regions, are capped by sandstones and conglomerate rocks, which have eroded less rapidly than the limestones and shales of the Bluegrass and Mississippian plateau. The Eastern Kentucky Coal Field can

**Moonshiner's Arch in Menifee County**
*Source: Tour Southern & Eastern Kentucky*

be described as mountainous (part of the Appalachians), and the Western Kentucky Coal Field as hilly. The Bluegrass and the Mississippian Plateau are characterized by karst topography; a landscape of sinkholes, sinking streams, springs and caves resulting from the dissolution of carbonate bedrock by the percolation of acidic groundwater. The Mississippi Embayment is a low-lying dissected plain situated on thick deposits of Mesozoic and Cenezoic sand and gravel. Elevations range from more than 4,000 feet above sea level in the eastern mountains, between 800 to 1,000 feet in the Bluegrass, to less than 300 feet in the Embayment.

## EASTERN KENTUCKY COAL FIELD
### (Cumberland Plateau, Eastern Kentucky)

The Eastern Coal Field region, an area of about 10,500 square miles, is part of the Central Appalachian Mountains and has very mature and rugged terrain. The long-standing economic significance of numerous seams of bituminous coal is reflected in the name given to the region. The heavily forested topography consists of steep and narrow ridges separated by v-shaped valleys, with the mountain elevations increasing toward the southeast. Black Mountain in Harlan County is the highest point in the state, with an elevation of 4,145 feet. Cumberland Mountain, a narrow linear ridge, marks part of the southeastern boundary with Virginia, and is paralleled within Kentucky by the very similar Pine Mountain that continues the boundary with Virginia to the northeast. The steep northwestern face of Pine Mountain is the leading edge of an overthrust fault block shoved, in places, nearly a dozen miles past underlying strata during the Allegheny Orogeny in the late Paleozoic. These ridges, which were significant barriers to the pioneer settlement of the state, are cut by gaps in only a few locations, notably Cumberland Gap in the Cumberland Mountain and the Pineville Gap in Pine Mountain. The Pine Mountain ridge reaches a height of 3,200 feet in Letcher County. Northwest of Pine Mountain, the much larger area of mountainous terrain in Eastern Kentucky is of lesser height and is often referred to as the Cumberland Mountains (as distinct from the Cumberland Mountain of the Virginia border). These mountains are not of tectonic origin and are thus unlike the Pine and Cumberland ridges, and the folded and fault block mountains farther east. The mountains of the Eastern Coal Field, except in the southeast corner, are the result of a deep and intricate dissection by stream erosion of a plateau of relatively flat-lying sedimentary rocks. The western boundary of the Eastern Coal Field is defined by the Potts-

ville (Cumberland) Escarpment, which trends in a southwestern direction from Lewis County, on the Ohio River, toward the Tennessee border. The escarpment rises 200 to 300 feet from the adjacent terrain and is capped by sandstone and conglomerate rocks that are highly resistant to erosion. The edge of the escarpment is thoroughly dissected, and is bordered by conical hills known as "Knobs" that are erosional remnants left by the retreat of the escarpment. The escarpment area is very scenic, with many attractive stream-carved gorges, waterfalls, and natural arches produced by the narrowing of ridges. More than 450,000 acres of the Daniel Boone National Forest are located along the escarpment area, as are the Red River Gorge Geological Area and the nearby Natural Bridge State Park. The escarpment also contains numerous caves developed in limestone exposed by the erosion of the landscape. Most of the region is drained by four streams and their tributaries, all of which flow northward to the Ohio River: the Big Sandy River, which forms the boundary between Kentucky and West Virginia; the Licking River; the Cumberland River, which flows southward into Tennessee but returns to Kentucky in the western part of the state; and the Kentucky River, which is divided into three separate branches. Because of the very steep and rugged terrain, most communities in the region are located in floodplains. As a consequence, flooding is a serious hazard for these towns.

## BLUEGRASS

Adjacent to the Eastern Coal Field and sharing the Escarpment as a border is the Bluegrass region, which contains about 8,000 square miles and is subdivided into the Inner and Outer Bluegrass subregions. The fertile lands of the Bluegrass were the first to be settled by the pioneers, and in this region today resides most of the population of the state. Frankfort, the state capital, is located here, as are the two largest cities: Louisville and Lexington, and the metropolitan areas of Newport and Covington, across the Ohio River from Cincinnati. The region is named for a grass, *Poa pratensis*, that was introduced by the early settlers of the area, probably by accident. The Bluegrass is bordered to the north by the Ohio River and separated from the rest of the state by the Knobs, which extend completely around the region in a belt 10 to 15 miles wide from Lewis County in the east to Jefferson County in the west. The Knobs range from about 50 feet to nearly 1,000 feet in height, with the highest toward eastern Kentucky. The terrain is gently rolling, with a belt of low hills that separates the Inner from the Outer Bluegrass. The Bluegrass region is centered upon the Jessamine Dome, the highest point of the Cincinnati Arch, so that the older rocks in the middle are surrounded by irregular concentric bands of younger strata, wider to the north and west. The changing nature of the bedrock, nearly all of Ordovician age, accounts for the changing nature of the terrain. The Inner Bluegrass is a karst landscape of about 2,000 square miles situated upon limestone and characterized by numerous sinkholes and natural springs. Many sinkholes contain small ponds. Surrounding the Inner Bluegrass is the Eden Shale belt, sometimes called the Hills of the Bluegrass because the topography is more rugged and contains little level land. Because shale is the dominant bedrock, soils in this region are generally thin and infertile. The Outer Bluegrass encircles the region outside the shale belt, and, as a gently rolling karst plain, is very similar to that of the Inner Bluegrass. The Bluegrass region is drained by the Kentucky River and its tributaries, which, as they flow through the Bluegrass, are entrenched in sinuous meanders 200 to 300 feet below the adjacent uplands.

### MISSISSIPPIAN PLATEAU
### (Pennyroyal Plateau, Pennyrile Plateau)

The Mississippian Plateau, with 12,000 square miles, is the largest region of Kentucky and shares borders with all of the other regions. From the Pottsville Escarpment, which forms the eastern boundary, the region extends west to the Mississippi Embayment and northward to the Knobs of the Bluegrass and nearly encircles the Western Coal Field region. Except for the southern boundary with Tennessee, which is political, the geographic bounds of the region are derived from the underlying geologic structure. South and west from the Jessamine

Dome of the Cincinnati Arch is a broad belt of younger rock, of Mississippian age; this characteristic names the region. The Mississippian Plateau is separated from the Western Coal Field by an escarpment similar to the Pottsville Escarpment along the boundary with the Eastern Kentucky Coal Field, but of lesser relief. The topography of the region, and associated land use, is related to the surface bedrock. Where the bedrock is limestone, the terrain generally consists of gently rolling hills that are good farmland. Where resistant sandstone caprock still exists to protect the limestone from erosion, the terrain tends to be more rugged, cut up into steep hills and valleys. Since the rocks of the Missis-

**Kinlee Stables in Laurel County**
*Source: Tour Southern & Eastern Kentucky*

sippian Plateau are mainly limestones, a large proportion of the region is considered karst and contains many caves. Mammoth Cave is located in the Chester Upland that separates the Plateau from the Western Coal Field. The outer edge of the Chester Upland is the Dripping Springs Escarpment, which rises 150 to 300 feet above the surrounding landscape. Southeast from the escarpment is an area of complex sinkhole patterns known as the Sinkhole Plain, in which surface streams are almost entirely absent since the local drainage is underground. The early settlers referred to this area as the "Barrens," a term used for a grassland prairie. Northward from the Sinkhole Plain, the Mississippian Plateau is separated from the Bluegrass region by the Muldraugh's Hill limestone escarpment, at the base of which is the most extensive area of Knobs in the state. Much of the landscape of the eastern and central Mississippian Plateau is also karst. The eastern section of the Mississippian Plateau tends to have a more rugged topography, particularly near the border with the Eastern Coal Field and in the vicinity of the deeply entrenched Cumberland River, Lake Cumberland, and Dale Hollow Lake. North and west from the lakes, the terrain is more suitable for agriculture. Most of the Mississippian Plateau region is drained by the Green River and its tributaries, and to a lesser extent by the Cumberland River in the eastern and western parts of the region. The Mississippian Plateau topography extends southward into Middle Tennessee, where it is known as the Highland Rim.

## WESTERN KENTUCKY COAL FIELD

The 4,680 square-mile Western Kentucky Coal Field, like its eastern counterpart, owes its name to the long-standing economic significance of coal mining in the region. The Ohio River forms the northern border, and elsewhere the Coal Field is surrounded by the Mississippian Plateau region on all sides. The topography of the region is derived from the underlying structural downwarp feature, the Illinois Basin. The basin originated during the early Paleozoic, slowly subsiding as it accumulated a great thickness of marine sediments. Most of the 60,000 square-mile basin lies in Illinois and Indiana; only the southern tip extends into Kentucky. Since this is a basin, the oldest strata are on the perimeter, unlike the structure of the Jessamine Dome in the Bluegrass where the oldest rocks are in the center. The margin of the Western Coal Field is a narrow belt of rough, hilly land whose outer edge forms an escarpment, very similar to the Pottsville Escarpment bordering the Eastern Kentucky Coal Field but not as high. Within the rim of

hills is a lower interior of rolling hills. The region is drained by the Green, Tradewater and Ohio rivers. The Green and Tradewater rivers, and their tributaries, flow through wide valleys which contain an alluvial fill nearly 200 feet thick in places, deposited as floodplain and lake sediments during periods of glaciation when glacial outwash dammed the mouths of the rivers. Radical alterations of the topography have been made across broad areas by the surface mining of coal carried on extensively in the region.

## MISSISSIPPI EMBAYMENT
### (Jackson Purchase, Purchase)

The Embayment region is very unlike any other part of Kentucky in its geology and topography. The landscape is geologically the youngest and lowest terrain of the state, and, historically, the most recent territory incorporated into the Commonwealth. This region has traditionally been called The Jackson Purchase because it was acquired in 1818 from the Chickasaw Indians during the administration of Andrew Jackson. The 2,396 square-mile region is bounded by the Tennessee River and the impoundment of Kentucky Lake to the east, by the Ohio River to the north, and by the Mississippi River to the west. The Tennessee state line forms the southern boundary. There are some boundary anomalies along the Mississippi River border with Missouri. This boundary was originally established as a line down the center of the Mississippi river, but shifts over time in the course of the river have stranded small sections of Kentucky on what is now the opposite side of the river. An error in a 1780 survey created the Kentucky Bend enclave, a tract of about 5 square miles isolated within a hairpin bend of the Mississippi, completely separated from the rest of the state. The region is located at the head of the Mississippi Embayment, a depositional trough that formed during the late Mesozoic and accumulated thick deposits of marine sediments overlain by more recent deposits of alluvium and loess. Low hills and rolling plains of deeply weathered gravel in the eastern part slope gradually to low, flat plains of sand, gravel, silt and clay in the west. The landscape is poorly drained in the southern part, dissected by a network of low-gradient creeks and small rivers often bordered by wetland areas, but well-drained farmland is found to the north. In the west, the uplands end in a line of bluffs along the Mississippi River, 100 to180 feet high, overlooking the floodplain of the great river. The flows of the Ohio and Mississippi join just above Wickliffe in Ballard County, and the floodplains of these rivers exhibit many meander scars and oxbow lakes.

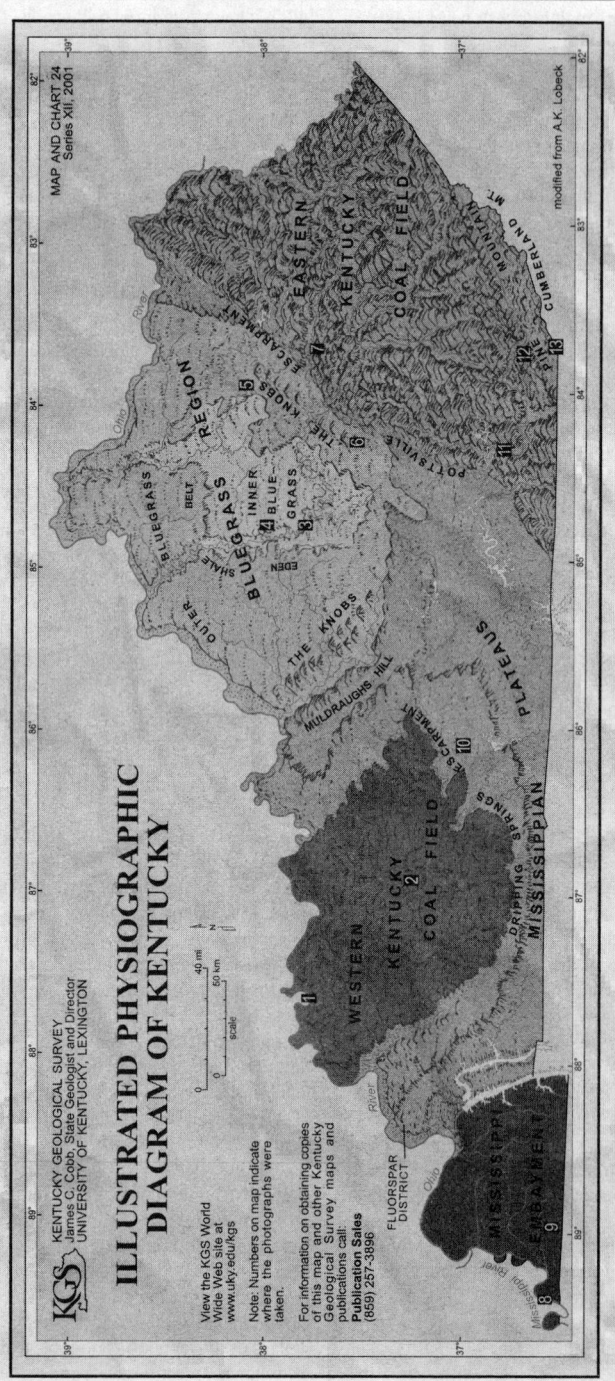

ILLUSTRATED PHYSIOGRAPHIC
DIAGRAM OF KENTUCKY

KENTUCKY GEOLOGICAL SURVEY
James C. Cobb, State Geologist and Director
UNIVERSITY OF KENTUCKY, LEXINGTON

View the KGS World
Wide Web site at
www.uky.edu/kgs

Note: Numbers on map indicate
where the photographs were
taken.

For information on obtaining copies
of this map and other Kentucky
Geological Survey maps and
publications call:
**Publication Sales**
(859) 257-3896

MAP AND CHART 24
Series XII, 2001

modified from A.K. Lobeck

## ENVIRONMENT & NATURAL RESOURCES

Dr. Gary O'Dell

# *Water Resources*

Kentucky is an exceptionally well-watered state. Nearly 90,000 miles of rivers and streams give the Commonwealth more flowing water than any other state except Alaska. Each year more than 100 million tons of commodities, mainly coal and grain, are shipped to and from Kentucky by way of more than 1,000 miles of navigable rivers. Seven hundred miles of streams in the state have been designated as "outstanding resource waters"

**Little Mud Lick Falls in Johnson County**
*Source: Tour Southern & Eastern Kentucky*

for their high water quality, and 114 miles in eight streams are protected as "wild rivers" under the provisions of the 1972 Kentucky Wild Rivers Act. The state contains more than 2,700 surface water impoundments, both natural and artificial, although nearly all of the larger lakes are of human construction. Approximately one-third of the impoundments are greater than 10 acres in size. As elsewhere in the nation, much of Kentucky's

wetland area has been reduced by development, from an estimated 1.5 million acres at the time of settlement to less than 640,000 acres today. Groundwater in bedrock and granular aquifers is an important water supply resource for communities and individual households.

## RIVERS

Nearly all streams within the state are contained within the Ohio River basin, which in turn is part of the Mississippi River system. Excepting only the headwaters of the Cumberland River, which initially flow southward to Tennessee, all of the major rivers in Kentucky flow to the north. The primary drainage basins in Kentucky are those of the Green River, Kentucky River, Cumberland River (upper and lower segments), Licking River, Salt River, Big and Little Sandy rivers, Tradewater River, Tennessee River and Tygarts Creek. In addition, substantial areas parallel to the courses of the Ohio and Mississippi drain directly to those rivers. The basins of the Kentucky, Licking, Salt, Tradewater, Little Sandy and Tygarts are entirely contained within the state, as is all but a fraction of the Green River drainage.

The Green River, the longest river in the state (370 miles), has the largest drainage area (9,430 square miles) and the greatest number of miles navigable to commercial shipping (108.5). Originating in Lincoln County at the eastern edge of the Mississipian Plateau, the river flows west, passing through Mammoth Cave National Park, and then turns northwest, flowing through the Western Coal Field to join the Ohio River across from Evansville. A series of locks and dams were built on the river, beginning in 1842, which once allowed river navigation as far as Bowling Green. The lowermost two locks and dams remain in service and facilitate a substantial amount of shipping, mainly coal and aluminum ore.

Although most of the Cumberland River flows through Tennessee, the beginning and end sections are located within the Commonwealth and are known as the Upper and Lower Cumberland River basins. The headwaters of the Cumberland River originate in the mountains of southeastern Kentucky. The Cumberland flows south and west for over 300 miles across the Eastern Coal Field region, crossing the Tennessee border in Monroe County, Kentucky, and returns to Kentucky in south-central Trigg County. The Upper Cumberland and its tributaries are exceptionally scenic: six of the state's eight wild rivers are found here, including 10.2 miles of the Big South Fork in Whitley County, one of the nation's finest stretches of whitewater. Cumberland Falls, sometimes called the "Niagara of the South," is located on the river at the border of McCreary and Whitley counties. The falls are 68 feet high and span about 125 feet.

The Licking River rises in southeastern Magoffin County in the Eastern Coal Field Region and follows a meandering course northwestward through the Bluegrass for 310 miles, joining the Ohio River in northern Kentucky opposite Cincinnati, where it separates the cities of Covington and Newport. The river was named for the many mineral springs near the river that attracted animals to salt licks. The river was an important transportation route for native Americans and during the settlement of Kentucky and a trade route during the 19th century.

The headwaters of the Kentucky River arise in the mountainous terrain of the Eastern Coal Field. The North Fork, Middle Fork and South Fork of the Kentucky flow northward from the vicinity of Pine Mountain, roughly parallel to each other, and join near Beattyville. From this confluence, the river flows northwestward for 255 miles through the Bluegrass Region to join the Ohio River at Carrollton in

northern Kentucky. The nearly 7,000-square-mile area of the Kentucky River basin is second largest in the state. Other major tributary streams include the Red River, Dix River, Elkhorn Creek and Eagle Creek. The Palisades, a 100-mile stretch of scenic limestone gorge, lies between Clays Ferry in Madison County and Frankfort. The river once provided access to the mineral and timber resources of the Coal Field, aided by a series of 14 locks and dams constructed on the river beginning in the early 19th century, but is today navigable only as far as Frankfort, a distance of 65 river miles from the mouth. The Kentucky is an important regional resource for 63 municipal water systems that withdraw from the river, supplying over 700,000 residents with water.

The Salt River rises in Boyle County, west of Danville, flows northward and then west to the Ohio River at West Point. The river was named for the saline licks and springs along the lower reaches of the stream. Early settlers established a salt works at Bullitt's Lick in 1779 and in several other locations.

The Big Sandy was named for the presence of many sand bars in the river channel. The main stem of the Big Sandy is a relatively short stretch of river, only 27 miles long, formed by the confluence of the Levisa Fork and Tug Fork at Louisa. The Big Sandy is navigable due to lock and dam construction, as are the lower parts of the Levisa and Tug Forks, and carries commercial shipping, primarily coal.

In northeastern Kentucky, Tygarts Creek and the Little Sandy River are the smallest of the Kentucky drainage systems of significance that flow to the Ohio River; both are less than 100 miles in length.

The Tennessee River is the largest tributary of the Ohio River, but only about 10 percent of its 620-mile length is within the Commonwealth, and most of that is impounded as Kentucky Lake.

The Tennessee flows into the Ohio River at Paducah. The Kentucky Dam is located about 22 miles from the river mouth, creating the largest impoundment in the eastern U.S., 184-mile-long Kentucky Lake. This lake is linked by a navigation canal to Lake Barkley, an almost equally large and parallel impoundment of the Cumberland River. The area is known as "Land Between the Lakes" National Recreation Area.

The Mississippi River forms a short section of Kentucky's far western boundary, flowing 49 miles from its confluence with the Ohio River at Wickliffe to the Tennessee state line. In addition, the Mississippi comprises another 15.5 miles of boundary for the Kentucky Bend enclave, a small area within a hairpin bend of the river not directly connected to another part of the state.

**Wolf Creek Dam
on the Cumberland River**
*Source: Sid Webb*

The Ohio River is one of the most important tributaries of the Mississippi, flowing 981 miles from the confluence of the Allegheny and Monongahela rivers in downtown Pittsburgh to join with the Mississippi near Wickliffe in far western Kentucky. The Ohio forms the boundary between West Virginia and Ohio and, for a distance of 665 miles, the northern boundary of Kentucky that separates it from Indiana and Illinois. Unlike most boundary rivers, the boundaries between states along the Ohio were established along the centerline of the river. This situation derives from the January 2, 1781, resolution of the General Assembly of Virginia that the Commonwealth of Virginia would cede to the U.S. all

those lands granted to it under the Virginia Charter "northwest of the river Ohio." This was interpreted to mean that Virginia owned the Ohio River to the far shore, a right of possession that was extended to Kentucky and West Virginia when those states were formed. In the years since the original boundary was established, many locks and dams have been built on the river to improve navigation.

During the settlement of Kentucky and the western territory, the Ohio River was a primary transportation route and remains today an important artery for commerce. The only significant navigation obstacle on the river is the Falls of the Ohio, a series of cascading rapids over limestone ledges that drops 26 feet in a 2-1/2 mile stretch of the river. The river barrier created a natural stopping point for travelers, and the city of Louisville was founded on the south side of the rapids. The first canal and locks around the Falls was completed in 1830 by a private stock company charted by the Commonwealth. In 1874 the canal and locks were appropriated by the U.S. government. The U.S. Army Corps of Engineers has widened and improved the original canal and locks and constructed an additional route to bypass the falls. About 20 barge tows pass through the canals and locks every day.

## LAKES

Since most of Kentucky lies south of the farthest glacial advance, there are few natural lakes of significant size within the state. Swan Lake in Ballard County is the largest natural lake wholly contained within Kentucky and is of about 300 acres extent. The lake is situated in the bottom land of the Ohio River, surrounded by cypress swamps and part of the 2,200 acre Swan Lake Wildlife Management Area. The far larger Reelfoot Lake, 15,500 acres at normal pool, is almost entirely within Tennessee, except for a tiny section that extends north into Fulton County, Kentucky. This is a very shallow lake, surrounded by cypress swamps and marshes and a habitat for bald eagles and is included within the Reelfoot National Wildlife Refuge.

Nearly all of Kentucky's larger lakes are artificial impoundments formed by the damming of a stream or river. With the exception of Kentucky Lake, managed by the Tennessee Valley Authority, these lakes are under the jurisdiction of the U.S. Army Corps of Engineers and the Kentucky Dept. of Fish and Wildlife

Resources. Most of these lakes were built during the 1960s and early 1970s for flood control, recreation and hydroelectric power generation. Lake Herrington, built in the 1920s, was the first major impoundment in the state and supplied hydroelectric power for many years. The most recent large impoundment was Cedar Creek Lake, a reservoir of 762 acres that finished filling in 2002. Kentucky Lake is one of the largest artificial lakes in the eastern U.S., although only a little more than a third of its 160,000 acres are contained within the Commonwealth. The largest lake entirely within Kentucky is Lake Cumberland in the southeastern section of the state, which contains over 50,000 acres at normal pool and more than 1,000 miles of shoreline. Five lakes in the state produce hydroelectric power – Kentucky, Cumberland, Barkley, Dale Hollow and Laurel lakes – with a total capacity of nearly 2.9 billion annual kilowatt-hours.

## WETLANDS

Kentucky's wetlands are an important natural resource that is often unappreciated by the general public. Wetlands are areas that may be flooded on a permanent, seasonal or occasional basis, or are saturated by groundwater seepage, and are characterized by specialized plants (hydrophytic) that are adapted to wet environments and soils (hydric) that are sufficiently wet during the growing season to develop anaerobic conditions in the upper part. Freshwater wetlands include marshes, swamps, bogs and fens. Wetlands were once perceived as undesirable wastelands, breeding grounds for mosquitoes and flies and sources of diseases and unpleasant odors. Because of this viewpoint, more than half of America's original wetlands have been destroyed, drained or filled for agriculture or development. More recently, we have come to understand that wetlands provide important benefits to people and the environment. Wetlands help to control water levels within watersheds, improve water quality, reduce flood damages, provide fish and wildlife habitats and support recreational activities.

About 2.5 percent of Kentucky is wetlands. At the time of settlement the state contained an estimated 1,566,000 acres of wetlands; today only about 637,000 acres remain – a 60 percent loss. Most of the wetland loss has occurred in the western part of the state as a result of conversion to cropland and pasture-land. The Kentucky Division of Water estimates that about 3,600 acres of existing wetland are lost annually, being drained or filled. Most of the wetlands of the state are privately owned. The 2005 General Assembly authorized the Environmental and Public Protection Cabinet to investigate the possibility of administrating the federal wetlands program at the state level, and the state has received a grant from the EPA to help fund development of a proposed program.

## GROUNDWATER

Nearly one-fifth of the earth's fresh water is contained underground, more than three times as much as can be found in all the rivers, streams and lakes combined. Groundwater is an important water-supply resource for the planet, and in Kentucky, more than 1.6 million citizens depend upon groundwater from wells and springs for drinking water and other household needs. Groundwater sources also supply commercial, agricultural and industrial uses in the state. The normal flow and dry-weather flow of Kentucky's rivers and streams is maintained by groundwater seepage. The use of groundwater in the state is increasing, although contamination from urban, industrial and agricultural sources poses an increasing threat to quality.

Just over half of Kentucky's public water supplies (226 of 435) depend upon groundwater sources, supplying a combined population of over 1.2 million persons. This represents about 30 percent of the total population. An estimated 400,000 persons are self-supplied, of which about 90 percent rely on groundwater from private wells and springs. Over 35,000 private water wells for domestic use have been drilled in Kentucky since 1985.

The Kentucky Division of Water has monitored groundwater quality across the state since 1995. Overall water quality is considered good, though impacts from human activity, primarily related to agriculture, occur in the karst regions where shallow conduit aquifers are particularly vulnerable to contamination. Pesticides are routinely detected in groundwater samples only in the karst regions. Local groundwater contamination from causes such as landfills, leaking underground storage tanks, Superfund and hazardous waste sites are of concern in Kentucky as elsewhere, but does not represent a widespread disruption of groundwater use.

## MAJOR RIVERS

| RIVER BASIN | TOTAL DRAINAGE AREA (mi) | DRAINAGE AREA IN KENTUCKY (sq. mi.) | TRIBUTARY STREAMS | LENGTH IN KENTUCKY (mi)* | DRAINAGE AREA IN KENTUCKY (sq. mi.) |
|---|---|---|---|---|---|
| Mississippi River | > 1.2 million | 40,424 total; 39,124 by Ohio River and tributaries; 1,300 by main stem and minor tributaries | Main stem and minor tributaries | 49 (main stem) | 329 |
| | | | Mayfield Creek | 63 | 436 |
| | | | Obion Creek | 60 | 320 |
| | | | Bayou du Chien | 33 | 215 |
| Ohio River | 204,000 | 39,124 | Major tributaries | see below | 34,974 |
| | | | Main stem and minor tributaries | 665 (main stem) | 4,150 |
| Green River | 9,233 | 8,810 | Main stem and minor tributaries | 366 (main stem) | 3,319 |
| | | | Barren River | 147 | 1,813 |
| | | | Pond River | 71 | 1,077 |
| | | | Nolin River | 92 | 798 |
| | | | Panther Creek | 31 | 726 |
| | | | Mud River | 50 | 375 |
| | | | Russell Creek | 66 | 373 |
| Kentucky River | 6,972 | 6,975 | Main stem and minor tributaries | 249 (main stem) | 2,330 |
| | | | North Fork | 134 | 1,750 |
| | | | South Fork | 78 | 560 |
| | | | Middle Fork | 95 | 519 |
| | | | Eagle Creek | 100 | 492 |
| | | | Elkhorn Creek | 18 | 487 |
| | | | Red River | 76 | 442 |
| | | | Dix River | 42 | 289 |
| Cumberland River | 17,913 | 5,180 Upper Cumberland | Main stem and minor tributaries | 238 (main stem) | 3,042 |
| | | | Rockcastle River | 50 | 764 |
| | | | Big South Fork | 63 | 405 |
| | | | Buck Creek | 41 | 294 |
| | | | Laurel River | 52 | 289 |
| | | | Poor Fork | 37 | 149 |
| | | | Martins Fork | 33 | 108 |
| | | | Clover Fork | 58 | 105 |
| | | 2,040 Lower Cumberland | Main stem and minor tributaries | 70 (main stem) | 1,439 |
| | | | Little River | 58 | 601 |
| Licking River | 3,712 | 3,710 | Main stem and minor tributaries | 267 (main stem) | 2,244 |
| | | | South Fork | 62 | 928 |
| | | | North Fork | 68 | 920 |
| | | | Slate Creek | | 308 |
| Salt River | 2,920 | 2,920 | Main stem and minor tributaries | 180 (main stem) | 1,450 |
| | | | Rolling Fork | 109 | 1,284 |
| | | | Floyds Fork | 62 | 262 |
| | | | Brashear Creek | 37 | |
| Big Sandy River | 4,288 | 2,290 | Main stem and minor tributaries | 26 (main stem) | 1,475 |
| | | | Levisa Fork | 127 | 448 |
| | | | Tug Fork | 94 | 264 |
| | | | Blaine Creek | 46 | |
| Tennessee River | 40,879 | 1,040 | Main stem and minor tributaries | 63 (main stem) | 362 |
| | | | Clarks River | 53 | 678 |
| Tradewater River | 943 | 943 | Main stem and minor tributaries | 67 (main stem) | 943 |
| Little Sandy River | 726 | 726 | Main stem and minor tributaries | 65 (main stem) | 572 |
| | | | East Fork | 36 | 154 |
| Tygarts Creek | 340 | 340 | Main stem and minor tributaries | 88 (main stem) | 340 |

* "Length" is length of stream section bearing that name. For example, the given length of Elkhorn Creek is for that section downstream from the junction of North Elkhorn Creek and South Elkhorn Creek, which merge to form Elkhorn Creek.

Primary sources: Carey, Daniel I. Catalog of hydrologic units in Kentucky. Kentucky Geological survey 2003. Online at http://kgsweb.uky.edu/download/rivers/CATHUCS.pdf;
U.S. Geological Survey, Hydrology of Kentucky. Online at http://kygeonet.ky.gov/kyhydro/viewer.htm;
U.S. Geological Survey, High Resolution National Hydrography Dataset (by Basin) Coverage Area: Kentucky. Online at: http://www.uky.edu/KGS/gis/kyhucepic.htm;
Dr. Steven Parkansky, Morehead State University; and
Erik Siegel, Kentucky Environmental Quality Commission

## MAJOR LAKES & DAMS

| LAKE | COUNTY LOCATION | STREAM IMPOUNDED | AREA (Acres)* | SHORELINE (Miles)* | DAM | DAM HEIGHT & WIDTH (Feet) | WHEN CONSTRUCTED | GENERATING CAP (kwh/year) |
|---|---|---|---|---|---|---|---|---|
| Kentucky Lake | Calloway, Lyon, Marshall, Trigg | Tennessee River | 160,300 total / 51,000 Kentucky | 2,064 total | Kentucky Dam | 206 by 8,422 | 1938 - 1944 | 1.3 billion |
| Lake Cumberland | Clinton, Laurel, Pulaski, Russell, Wayne | Cumberland River | 50,250 | 1,085 | Wolf Creek Dam | 258 by 5,736 | 1941 - 1943; 1946 - 1950 | 800 million |
| Lake Barkley | Caldwell, Livingston, Trigg | Cumberland River | 57,920 / 45,600 Kentucky | 1,004 total | Barkley Dam | 157 by 10,180 | 1959 - 1964 | 582 million |
| Barren River Lake | Allen, Barren, Monroe | Barren River | 10,000 | 300 | Barren River Lake Dam | 146 by 1,272 | 1961 - 1964 | |
| Cave Run Lake | Bath, Menifee, Morgan, Rowan | Licking River | 8,270 | 166 | Cave Run Lake Dam | 148 by 2,700 | 1969 - 1974 | |
| Green River Lake | Adair, Casey, Taylor | Green River | 8,210 | 250 | Green River Dam | 141 by 2,350 | 1964 - 1969 | |
| Nolin River Lake | Edmonson, Grayson, Hart | Nolin River | 5,795 | 172 | Nolin Dam | 166 by 980 | 1959 - 1963 | |
| Laurel Lake | Laurel, Whitley | Laurel River | 5,600 | 192 | Laurel Dam | 282 by 1,420 | 1964 - 1974 | 67 million |
| Rough River Lake | Breckinridge, Grayson, Hardin | Rough River | 5,100 | 220 | Rough River Dam | 132 by 1,590 | 1955 - 1958 | |
| Dale Hollow | Clinton, Cumberland | Obey River | 27,700 total / 4,933 Kentucky | 620 total / 112 Kentucky | Dale Hollow Dam | 200 by 1,717 | 1942 - 1943 | 127 million |
| Taylorsville Lake | Anderson, Nelson, Spencer | Salt River | 3,050 | 75 | Taylorsville Lake Dam | 163 by 1,280 | 1982 - 1983 | |
| Lake Herrington | Boyle, Mercer, Garrard | Dix River | 2,335 | 325 | Dix Dam | 287 by 1,080 | 1923 - 1925 | |
| Yatesville Lake | Lawrence | Blaine Creek | 2,242 | 93 | Yatesville Dam | 109 by 760 | 1984 - 1991 | |
| Grayson Lake | Carter, Eliot | Little Sandy River | 1,512 | 74 | Grayson Dam | 120 by 1,460 | 1965 - 1968 | |
| Buckhorn Lake | Leslie, Perry | Middle Fork, Kentucky River | 1,230 | 65 | Buckhorn Lake Dam | 162 by 1,020 | 1956 - 1961 | |
| Fishtrap Lake | Pike | Russell Fork | 1,131 | 43 | Fishtrap Lake Dam | 195 by 1,000 | 1962 - 1968 | |
| Dewey Lake | Floyd | John's Creek | 1,100 | 52 | Dewey Dam | 118 by 920 | 1946 - 1949 | |
| Paintsville Lake | Johnson, Morgan | Paint Creek | 1,139 | 57 | Paintsville Dam | 160 by 1,660 | 1976 - 1980 | |
| Lake Malone | Logan, Muhlenberg, Todd | Rocky Creek | 826 | 30 | Mud River MPS No. 51 | 56 by 610 | 1959 - 1961 | |
| Cedar Creek Lake | Lincoln | Cedar Creek | 762 | 23 | Cedar Creek Dam | 86 by 2,110 | 2000 - 2002 | |
| Lake Beshear | Caldwell, Christian | trib. Tradewater | 760 | 24 | Beshear Lake Dam | 38 by 550 | Completed 1962 | |
| Carr Creek Lake | Knott | Carr Creek | 710 | 24 | Carr Creek Dam | 130 by 720 | 1966 - 1976 | |
| Wood Creek Lake | Laurel | Wood Creek | 672 | 33.6 | Wood Crk Lake Dam | 163 by 800 | Completed 1968 | |
| Martin's Fork Lake | Harlan | Martins Fork | 340 | 10 | Martins Fork Dam | 97 by 504 | 1973 - 1978 | |
| Guist Creek Lake | Shelby | Guist Creek | 325 | 27 | Guist Crk Lake Dam | 60 by 1,010 | Completed 1961 | |
| Williamstown Lake | Grant | Grassy Creek | 300 | 13.5 | Williamstown Lake Dam | 55 by 680 | Completed 1956 | |
| Lake Linville | Rockcastle | Renfro Creek | 273 | 8.2 | Renfro Lake Dam | 72 by 1,100 | Completed 1978 | |
| Cannon Creek Lake | Bell | Cannon Creek | 243 | 7.7 | Cannon Crk Lake Dam | 125 by 900 | Completed 1972 | |
| Cranks Creek Lake (Herb Smith Lake) | Harlan | Cranks Creek | 219 | 9 | Cranks Crk Lake Dam | 120 by 635 | Completed 1963 | |
| Kincaid Lake | Pendleton | Kincaid Creek | 183 | 12.5 | Kincaid Lake Dam | 61 by 480 | Completed 1961 | |
| Greenbo Lake | Greenup | Claylick Creek | 181 | 7.6 | Greenbo Lake Dam | 70 by 570 | 1954 - 1955 | |

*Acreage and shoreline vary according to pool elevation of lakes. Figures represent summer pool.

Compiled by Dr. Gary A. O'Dell
Primary sources: U.S. Army Corps of Engineers, Kentucky Division of Water,
Kentucky Department of Fish and Wildlife Resources, Kentucky Department of Parks

This image shows the Teays River drainage that existed before the Ohio River.

Source: Emporia State University, Kansas, Earth Science Dept.

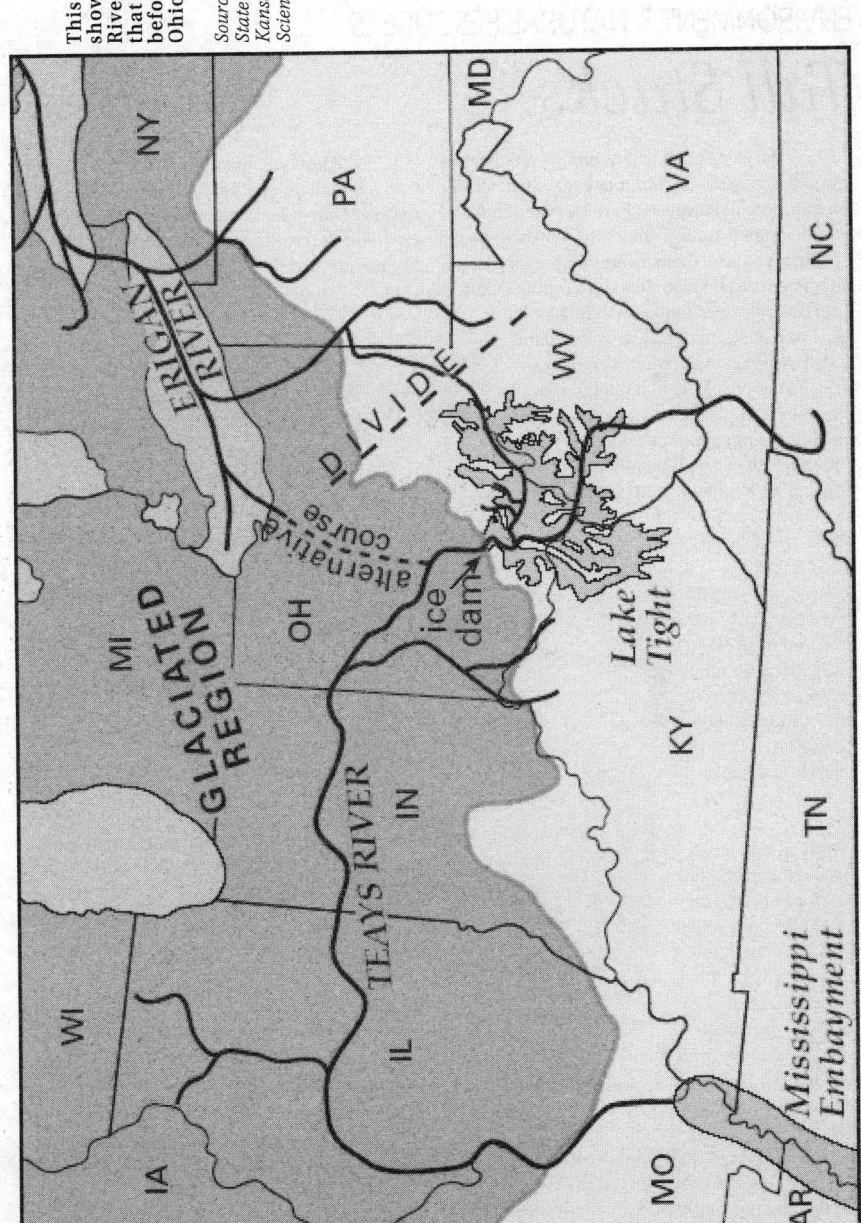

# ENVIRONMENT & NATURAL RESOURCES
# *Tall Stacks*

Kadie Engstrom

It was the same at all wharfs along every river of any size. One after another they came, steam whistles blaring, paddlewheels churning water, captains shouting orders to deck crews below. There might be as many as 50 of them in one day, bringing exotic things from distant places and loading merchandise of all kinds destined for ocean-side shipping ports and major markets. It was exciting and industrious, and it was how money was made, how people and products moved from place to place and how new settlements grew into important cities.

It was the heyday of steamboats and the building of Kentucky, and all the country. Waterways were the highways then, before reliable railroads and passable roads linked the U.S. Many of the commonwealth's largest cities today were major river ports in their beginnings – like Frankfort on the Kentucky River; Bowling Green on the Barren River; and Ashland, Covington, Louisville, Owensboro and Paducah on the Ohio River.

Most of the steamboats of the 1800s were built for work (and they were called all manner of things like packet boats or freight boats and towboats). Constructed primarily of wood, their stacks were tall so cinders from the fuel they burned flew up and away from their highly-flammable roofs and decks. They carried freight of all kinds – everything imaginable that was needed in a young supply-and-demand economy.

The steamboats of the 19th century are gone now, but they are not forgotten. Six steam-powered river vessels currently ply the inland waterways in the U.S. The oldest one, and the only one still operating that was built as a packet boat, is the Belle of Louisville at Louisville, Kentucky. She is the last of her kind, and she cruises today using boilers and steam engines just like she did when she was launched in 1914.

Only one type of event in the country today

**The 2003 Tall Stacks Celebration**
*Source: Belle of Louisville*

has recreated the steamboat era – "Tall Stacks," sponsored by Cincinnati, Ohio, and involving Newport and Covington. As many as 17 boats (that are steam-powered, were at one time steam-powered, or have never been steam-powered but were built to represent that era) gathered at Cincinnati in 1988, 1992, 1995, 1999, 2003 and 2006 to collectively give millions of people the opportunity to sense what it was like 150 years ago when steamboats ruled the rivers.

# ENVIRONMENT & NATURAL RESOURCES

## Dr. Royal Berglee

# *Minerals*

### Metallic, Non-metallic and Vein Minerals
### MINERAL MINING

Numerous metallic and non metallic mineral resources have been mined in Kentucky, including iron, titanium, phosphates, and vein minerals such as fluorite, barite, sphalerite, galena, gypsum and calcite. Vein mineral deposits occur in 20 counties in the central, western and southern Kentucky mineral districts. Iron ore has been used for steel products. Titanium is used as a high-strength alloy in aircraft and ship building. Phosphates are used as fertilizer. Vein minerals such as fluorite and barite are used in the steel and oil-field industries, respectively. Sphalerite and galena are metallic minerals used in automobiles, electronics and radiation protection. Gypsum has a very low thermal conductivity (hence its use in *drywall* as insulating filler).

Kentucky was a major center for mining iron, phosphates, barite and fluorite during the early 1900s. Occasionally, small operators still mine some of these mineral deposits, but currently no large commercial mines are operating in Kentucky. Principal mining companies have, however, conducted exploration activity. The geology of Kentucky is not favorable for the natural occurrence of large quantities of precious metals such as gold or silver, though they both have been found in the state. The same can be said for gemstones such as diamonds, which are not common in Kentucky's geological formations. A number of additional minerals can be found in the state but not in large enough quantities to be economically feasible to extract. For example, naturally occurring potassium nitrate (saltpeter) was once mined in various caves and similar locations in Kentucky to produce gunpowder.

### LIMESTONE AND DOLOSTONE

Limestone and dolostone, both carbonate rocks, can be found at the surface of 25 percent of Kentucky, mainly in the central and western regions. Kentucky has attained the

**Strip mine in western Kentucky**
*Photo: David Stephenson, Herald-Leader*

Kentucky Coal Mining Museum is located in a former coal mining camp in Benham, Harlan County
*Source: Kentucky Department of Tourism*

position of one of the nation's major producers of limestone. Since the year 2000, Kentucky has been rated as high as the fifth-largest stone producer in the United States. Kentucky produced 58.8 million short tons of limestone and dolostone in 1992, which had a value of $251.1 million, averaging $4.25 per ton. Stone is being produced at 72 open-pit quarries and 17 underground mines in 62 of the state's 120 counties. In recent years, the Reed Quarry in western Kentucky has been listed as the largest producer of crushed limestone in the U.S. The Reed Quarry has produced over 10 million short tons of crushed stone annually. Fine-grained dolomitic limestone of the Oregon Formation, which has been labeled Kentucky River marble, was once used as building stone for central Kentucky residences and commercial and public buildings.

Industrial and miscellaneous applications of limestone and dolostone include chemically pure

most region of the state. The largest market for sand, gravel and crushed stone produced in Kentucky is the construction industry, which includes aggregate for road construction and maintenance;

Source Ky Dept. of
Libraries & Archives,
WPA Collection

residential, commercial and government construction; riprap and jetty stone; and railroad ballast. Sand and gravel are obtained from the valley of the Ohio River from land-based pits in fluvioglacial and alluvial deposits and from the channels of the Ohio and Mississippi

**Coal miner**
Photo: Russell Lee — Source: Kentucky Virtual Library

Rivers by floating operations from bars, islands and other channel and bedload deposits in the streams themselves. Combined, these sources constitute more than three-fourths of the sand and gravel produced in Kentucky. Floating dredge operations provide the greatest amount. Sands and gravels are also found in numerous stream channels within the state.

stone for the manufacture of lime and cement, filter stone, sorbent stone for removing sulfur dioxide emissions from coal-burning plants, rock dust for explosion abatement in underground coal mines, and acid-water treatment. Agricultural uses include limestone applied to soils to adjust their pH, poultry grit, and mineral feed. The second and third largest lime plants in the U.S. are in Kentucky along the Ohio River in Mason and Pendleton counties.

### SAND AND GRAVEL

Sand and gravel deposits can mainly be found along the Ohio River Valley and in the western-

### CLAY

Current clay and shale supplies are being extracted primarily from deposits in the western coal fields and the Ohio River Valley. Of historical importance is the formerly large firebrick industry that developed around clay deposits found in the northeastern portion of the state; an example is the Olive Hill clay bed. Also, clay from the Irvine Formation (high-level fluvial deposits) in east-central Kentucky has been the source of raw material for a small but well-known pottery in Madison County for many years.

## SHALE

Commonly used locally for fill and for a base course for road construction, shales have also been used for the manufacture of face brick, drain tile and quarry or roofing tile. Shales on both the east and west sides of the Cincinnati arch are located near potential markets but appear to offer little possibility for structural clay products. Shales in northern Lewis County near the Ohio River appear to be relatively free of deleterious materials and offer potential for further exploitation. The carbon-rich Chattanooga-New Albany-Ohio shales constitute a present and potential energy resource. When oil shales are heated to 900 F, they can give off a gas similar to natural gas and a type of oil not much different from conventional crude oil.

## SANDSTONE

Often resistant to erosion, sandstone can be seen in places like rock outcroppings, ridges and cliff faces. Comprised of mineral grains and cemented together by silica, iron oxide or calcium carbonate, sandstone is porous and easily crushed into sand. Silica sands of high quality and purity are used in the glass industry for windows, light bulbs and containers. Glass sands have been extracted from deposits in Calloway County. Certain types of dense sandstone have been used for building stone throughout the state.

### Kentucky Coal Resources

Kentucky has two distinct coalfields: one in western Kentucky and one in eastern Kentucky. Each contains numerous deposits of bituminous coal of varied characteristics and mines of every type and size. Original resource estimates for western and eastern Kentucky were 41 and 64 billion tons respectively. The resources currently remaining after 200 years of mining are estimated to be 35.8 billion tons in western Kentucky and 52.3 billion tons in eastern Kentucky. Of Kentucky's 130.7 million tons of 2000 coal production, 80.2 million tons were produced by underground mining methods and 50.5 million tons were produced by surface mining methods.

*Electricity:* Average electricity costs in Kentucky were 4.1 cents per kilowatt-hour in 2001, the lowest in the U.S. Coal provides 51.8 percent of the electricity in the U.S. and 97 percent in Kentucky.

*Production:* Kentucky produced 131 million tons of coal in 2000, compared to the record production of 179 million tons set in 1990. Kentucky has been one of the top three coal producers in the U.S. for the last 50 years.

# Types of coal mining in Kentucky

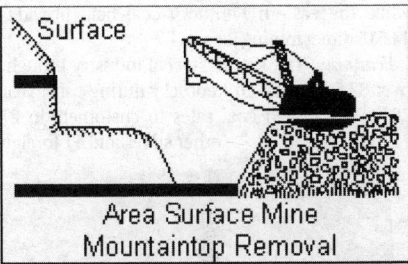

Area Surface Mine
Mountaintop Removal

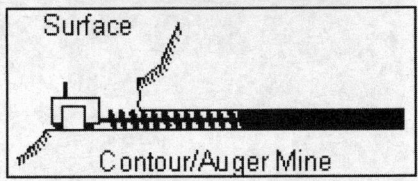

Contour/Auger Mine

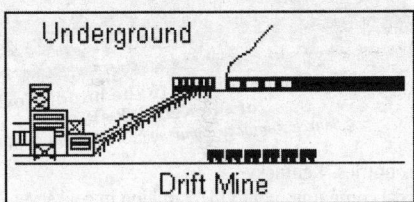

Drift Mine

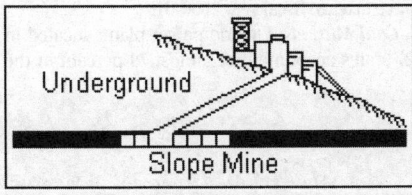

Slope Mine

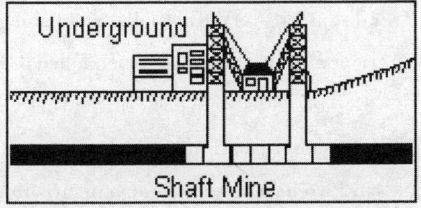

Shaft Mine

*Graphic Source: U.S. Department of Energy*

**Employment:** The Kentucky coal industry paid $678.4 million in direct wages in 2000, directly employing 14,812 persons and indirectly providing three additional jobs for every miner employed. The average weekly wage for coal miners in Kentucky was $880 during 2000. The Kentucky coal mining industry has a current work force of approximately 17,042 people directly employed in coal mining jobs. The western Kentucky coalfield directly employs approximately 2,524 persons, while the eastern Kentucky coal field provides 14,518 direct mining jobs.

**Economy:** The Kentucky coal industry brought over $2.5 billion into Kentucky during fiscal year 2000-01, through coal sales to customers in 27 other states and 11 foreign

**Coal haul sled in the middle fork of the Kentucky River**
*Source: Kentucky Department of Libraries & Archives*

countries. Kentucky coal companies paid $141.2 million in coal severance taxes in fiscal year 2000-01.

**Coal Markets:** Electric power plants located in 27 states accounted for almost 79 percent of the Kentucky coal sold during 2000. Approximately 80 percent of the coal produced in Kentucky is sold out-of-state each year.

**Coal Prices:** There are as many coal price averages as there are coal qualities.

Average Value of Kentucky Coal FOB Mine in 2002 was $27.77 dollars per ton.

**Eastern Coal Average = $29.04 per ton**
-- Underground = $29.77
-- Surface = $28.11

**Western Coal Average = $22.23 per ton**
-- Underground = $22.37
-- Surface = $21.81

**Kentucky Oil and Gas Production:** Oil production in Kentucky is most prominent in the western coalfield and south-central region. The eastern coalfield produces mostly natural gas. Kentucky has an estimated 18,000 producing oil wells and over 19,000 producing gas wells. The majority of those producing wells are in the "stripper" category, having daily production rates of 10 barrels of oil or 60,000 cubic feet of gas or less. Many wells are reported with initial daily production rates in excess of 100 barrels of oil or 580,000 cubic feet of gas. Daily production per well averages much lower, at around 0.5 barrels for oil and 19,000 cubic feet for gas. Since the year 2000, annual production has averaged 2.8 million barrels of oil and 85 billion cubic feet of natural gas with a total annual value of $457 million. On an annual basis, Kentucky only produces about 10 percent of the oil and natural gas consumed in the state.

## Well, what about that ...

Limestone covers 25 percent of Kentucky's land surface in central, south-central, and southwestern Kentucky. Sand and gravel occurs near the Ohio and Kentucky rivers and other major stream beds. Clays are found in the Jackson Purchase Region and also in eastern Kentucky near Rowan and Bell counties. Iron and phosphates occur in eastern and central Kentucky, titanium occurs in the Jackson Purchase Region, and vein minerals occur in central and western Kentucky.

*Source: Kentucky Geological Survey, www.uky.edu/KGS/coal/*

## EASTERN KENTUCKY COAL RESOURCES, 2004

| COUNTY | ORIGINAL | MINED | LOST | REMAINING |
|---|---|---|---|---|
| Bell | 3,194.70 | 302.69 | 302.69 | 2,589.32 |
| Boyd | 630.68 | 19.93 | 19.93 | 590.82 |
| Breathitt | 4,112.20 | 208.47 | 208.47 | 3,695.26 |
| Carter | 501.96 | 18.61 | 18.61 | 464.74 |
| Clay | 1,536.11 | 61.87 | 61.87 | 1,412.37 |
| Elliott | 316.32 | 9.87 | 9.87 | 296.58 |
| Floyd | 4,168.08 | 459.68 | 459.68 | 3,248.72 |
| Greenup | 204.87 | 10.42 | 10.42 | 184.03 |
| Harlan | 7,881.12 | 917.66 | 917.66 | 6,045.80 |
| Jackson | 375.87 | 11.31 | 11.31 | 353.25 |
| Johnson | 1,419.44 | 97.56 | 97.56 | 1,224.32 |
| Knott | 4,385.10 | 329.9 | 329.9 | 3,725.30 |
| Knox | 1,381.93 | 75.51 | 75.51 | 1,230.91 |
| Laurel | 408.04 | 35.95 | 35.95 | 336.14 |
| Lawrence | 2,024.68 | 26.81 | 26.81 | 1,971.06 |
| Lee | 363.98 | 8.49 | 8.49 | 347 |
| Leslie | 3,554.65 | 259.17 | 259.17 | 3,036.31 |
| Letcher | 3,692.80 | 558.17 | 558.17 | 2,576.46 |
| McCreary | 444.97 | 55.34 | 55.34 | 334.29 |
| Magoffin | 1,969.10 | 55.77 | 55.77 | 1,857.56 |
| Martin | 3,319.97 | 391.28 | 391.28 | 2,537.41 |
| Morgan | 849.4 | 15.22 | 15.22 | 818.96 |
| Owsley | 574.14 | 10.02 | 10.02 | 554.1 |
| Perry | 3,596.70 | 593.36 | 593.36 | 2,409.98 |
| Pike | 11,391.70 | 1,420.07 | 1,420.07 | 8,551.56 |
| Whitley | 987.44 | 91.4 | 91.4 | 804.64 |
| Wolfe | 443.92 | 7.16 | 7.16 | 429.6 |
| Other | 334.89 | 33.18 | 33.18 | 268.53 |
| Total | 64,064.76 | 6,084.87 | 6,084.87 | 51,895.02 |

## WESTERN KENTUCKY COAL RESOURCES, 2004

| COUNTY | ORIGINAL | MINED | LOST | REMAINING |
|---|---|---|---|---|
| Butler | 413.69 | 30.2 | 30.2 | 353.29 |
| Daviess | 1,330.32 | 62.33 | 62.33 | 1,205.66 |
| Henderson | 6,852.78 | 76.12 | 76.12 | 6,700.54 |
| Hopkins | 8,814.80 | 781.8 | 781.8 | 7,251.20 |
| McLean | 3,576.41 | 19.73 | 19.73 | 3,536.95 |
| Muhlenberg | 4,723.84 | 749.83 | 749.83 | 3,224.18 |
| Ohio | 1,824.55 | 266.72 | 266.72 | 1,291.11 |
| Union | 6,506.98 | 332.21 | 332.21 | 5,842.56 |
| Webster | 6,322.95 | 317.11 | 317.11 | 5,688.73 |
| Other | 623.08 | 25.44 | 25.44 | 572.2 |
| Total | 40,989.40 | 2,661.49 | 2,661.49 | 35,666.42 |

## KENTUCKY COAL PRODUCTION

| YEAR | UNDERGROUND | | SURFACE | | STATE TOTALS |
|---|---|---|---|---|---|
| | EASTERN KY | WESTERN KY | EASTERN KY | WESTERN KY | |
| 1960 | 32,041,487 | 12,851,108 | 4,622,417 | 18,552,641 | 67,067,653 |
| 1965 | 37,740,473 | 13,341,646 | 9,587,626 | 26,537,294 | 87,207,039 |
| 1970 | 44,068,538 | 19,430,489 | 28,527,422 | 33,281,946 | 125,308,395 |
| 1975 | 41,280,096 | 24,757,456 | 46,957,448 | 31,209,511 | 144,204,511 |
| 1980 | 59,603,430 | 19,558,157 | 49,582,095 | 21,400,291 | 150,143,973 |
| 1985 | 75,530,607 | 21,188,598 | 52,294,115 | 22,602,743 | 169,616,063 |
| 1990 | 81,577,417 | 27,375,465 | 49,393,390 | 21,026,997 | 179,373,269 |
| 1995 | 73,922,358 | 24,763,534 | 47,288,817 | 11,812,973 | 157,787,682 |
| 2000 | 59,956,626 | 21,543,143 | 44,335,363 | 6,010,856 | 131,845,988 |
| 2002 | 59,562,704 | 21,244,764 | 44,615,777 | 5,979,552 | 131,402,797 |
| 2003 | 52,952,957 | 19,055,260 | 40,751,963 | 4,360,719 | 117,120,899 |
| 2004 | 54,250,895 | 19,228,512 | 41,544,662 | 3,930,444 | 118,954,473 |

*Sources: www.coaleducation.org/Ky_Coal_Facts/coal_resources/ky_resources.htm; Kentucky Division of Mines and Minerals, Annual Reports, 1960-2002; Office of Mine Safety & Licensing, Annual Reports, 2003-2004.*

# ENVIRONMENT & NATURAL RESOURCES

# *Forests &*
# *Plant Life*

Dr. Zachary J. Bortolot

Forests are very important to Kentucky. Kentucky has 12.7 million acres of forested land, which covers 50 percent of the state's land area. Although 92 percent of the forested land is privately owned, there is also an extensive amount of publicly owned forest land, including 628,000 acres of National Forest land. In addition to the wildlife and recreational benefits of the forest, Kentucky's forest-related industries employ 30,000 Kentuckians and generate $2 billion of revenue each year.

*Source: Tour Southern & Eastern Kentucky*

## FOREST HISTORY

During the height of the last ice age 18,000 years ago, the forests of Kentucky were much different than they are now. In place of Kentucky's primarily broadleaf forests was a coniferous boreal forest similar to the forests found in northern Canada today. This forest was well adapted to the brutally cold climate that existed at that time. The boreal forest lasted until about 11,500 years ago, at which point the climate began to warm up and forests similar to Kentucky's modern forests began to appear. This transition was complete by about 10,000 years ago. Between 10,000 years ago and the arrival of large numbers of settlers of European descent, the region was occupied by several groups of Native Americans. The level of impact these groups had on Kentucky's forests varied quite a bit from one Native American group to another. Groups with a hunting and gathering-based culture had a minimal impact on the forests, whereas groups with extensive settlements

and agricultural production had much more of an impact. Examples of these impacts include a reduction in forest land as a result of harvesting for fuel and construction and agriculture-related burning.

Large numbers of settlers of European descent arrived in Kentucky about 200 years ago. With this new settlement came the widespread clearing of land for raising crops and livestock, building factories and mining. By 1900, the amount of forested land in Kentucky had been reduced from 23.1 million acres before settlement began to 10.0 million acres. Since 1900 there has been a slow increase in the amount of forested land, and currently there are 12.7 million acres of forest land. This increase is primarily due to the abandonment of poor quality farmland. Researchers predict that in the future, urban development will again reduce the amount of forested land in Kentucky. They predict that by 2020, 1.3 percent of the forested land will have been converted to other uses and by 2040, 3.4 percent will have been converted. Most of the forests found in Kentucky today are secondary growth forests of relatively recent origin.

Besides clearing the land, European settlers also changed the forests through the introduction of disease. One of the most important was the chestnut blight which affects the American chestnut tree. Prior to the introduction of the blight, American chestnut was one of the most common trees in Kentucky. The American chestnut tree was prized for its excellent timber and delicious nuts and was an important species for wildlife due to its reliable production of large quantities of food. The chestnut blight was accidentally brought to North America from Asia in 1904 by the Bronx Zoo in New York City. The disease spread to Kentucky in the 1930s and killed nearly all mature chestnut trees. Luckily other tree species have filled in the gaps left vacant by the disappearance of the American chestnut, but these trees are often not as valuable commercially or to wildlife.

# Blanton Forest State Nature Preserve

Blanton Forest, located on Pine Mountain in Harlan County, is the largest old-growth forest known in Kentucky. Trees that tower 100 feet above the forest floor are the same ones settlers saw as they came through the Cumberland Gap and moved westward into Kentucky in the 1700s. The forest is a union of past and present, one of the rare places where nature's scheme has gone unchallenged and unexploited.

Several distinct natural communities are found in Blanton Forest. The most diverse of these is the mixed mesophytic forest. This forest typically includes a variety of canopy trees such as sugar maple, beech, tulip poplar, basswood, hemlock, and several species of oaks and magnolias. It is found on moist, rich slopes and in some ravines. The larger ravines, or hollows, support a hemlock-dominated forest with a dense understory of rhododendrons. Drier sites on ridges support chestnut oak dominated forests as well as oak-pine forests. Small open seeps, often called bogs or mires, are filled with sphagnum moss, cinnamon ferns and wildflowers—located in the heads of some hollows on the south face of the mountain. Watts Creek, a stream within the preserve that supports a population of the federally threatened fish, Blackside dace, begins in one of these seeps.

Blanton Forest is named in honor of former owners, Grover and Oxie Blanton. The Blantons purchased the land in 1928 and passed it on to their daughters with the understanding that it would never be logged. The Blanton family's desire to protect the forest forever was fulfilled when the two parcels containing the old growth were acquired in 1995 and 2001 and dedicated as state nature preserves. The preserve is open to the public sunrise to sunset, all year.

At the present time the Blanton Forest Preserve design includes over 6,000 acres. A stewardship endowment has been established to generate the income needed to protect and preserve the forest for years to come. Visit the Kentucky Natural Lands Trust at www.knlt.org/ or www.naturepreserves.ky.gov to learn more about how to be a part of this great effort.

# Non-Forest Vegetation
*Dr. Christine E. McMichael*

## OVERVIEW

In addition to forests, which comprise the major vegetation community type in Kentucky, there are a number of other important plant communities that deserve mention – namely wetland and grass-dominated communities. Unfortunately, these communities occupy an ever-shrinking portion of Kentucky's landscape as our population grows and our urban areas continue to expand into natural areas.

## WETLAND COMMUNITIES
### Forested Wetlands

There are two major types of forested wetlands in Kentucky; swamp forests and floodplain forests. Swamp forests generally occupy areas that are either permanently or frequently covered with standing water; they are also associated with high water tables, sinkholes and depressions. These forested wetlands are found throughout Kentucky, but are most common in the western part of the state where bald cypress and water tupelo thrive in areas with deep standing water. Oak, sycamore, black gum and red maple species dominate swamp forests in central and eastern Kentucky where sinkholes provide suitable watery habitat. Localized depressions occurring within the eastern part of the state may contain swamp forest dominated by red maple, black gum, tulip tree and white oak. Floodplain forests are found along the banks of major waterways throughout the state, as well as in the adjacent floodplain areas, particularly in western and central Kentucky. Hardy trees such as black willow and sycamore are common canopy species in stream-bank communities, while a variety of vines and herbs thrive in the understory. Typically, there is a greater diversity of tree species associated with forested wetland communities in floodplain areas. In addition to containing species having statewide distributions such as American elm, red maple, black gum and green ash, floodplain forests also include species with more localized distributions – e.g., American beech in the Appalachians.

## NON FORESTED WETLANDS

Nonforested wetland communities can be found across the state, but are most common in central and western lowland areas that are fairly flat, generally (but not always) submerged in water and dominated by herbaceous and shrub vegetation. There are a number of nonforested wetland community types including those associated with standing water (ponds, lakes, reservoirs) or running water (streams and rivers), as well as those dominated by emergent vegetation (marshes and wet meadows) or shrubs. Some of the plants commonly found in standing water communities include the mosquito fern, bladderwort, water lily and alligator weed; rushes and sedges typify running water communities. Cattails, irises and cardinal-flowers may be found in emergent wetland communities, while buttonbush, pawpaw, willow, false indigo and highbush blueberry are common in shrub dominated wetlands.

Despite the range of important "services" they provide (e.g., flood control, water supply, fisheries and wildlife habitat), most wetland communities in Kentucky have been destroyed by, or are currently threatened by, ongoing human activities including agriculture and urban expansion.

## GRASS-DOMINATED COMMUNITIES

It is thought that prairie grasses began extending their range into Kentucky 4,000 years ago, but it is unclear whether their current distribution throughout the state is a relic of the last glacial retreat or a more recent result of the agricultural-related burning practices of Native American peoples. Today, grass-dominated communities are most common in the western and central areas of the state. The two major grassland regions in Kentucky include the Big Barrens in west central Kentucky and the hill prairies of central Kentucky. The Big Barrens region occupies flat to steep hilly terrain in the Shawnee Hills and is dominated by perennial grasses and herbs, with occasional shrubs and small trees. The rolling hill prairies of the Knobs and Bluegrass regions are thought to be remnants of tallgrass prairie communities. While little bluestem grass dominates these communities, other grasses are commonly found throughout these areas including big bluestem grass, gama grass and prairie cord grass. Flower-

ing plants found here include hairy sunflower, blazing stars, coneflowers and lobelia; common shrubs and small trees include red maple, sassafras, persimmon and mockernut hickory. Altogether, these grass-dominated communities cover a fairly small area within Kentucky, however they contain some of the state's rarest plants including Short's goldenrod, Eggert's sunflower, blue wild indigo, buffalo clover and Carolina larkspur.

### y'know what?

The U.S. Forest Service estimates that there are 6.7 billion trees in Kentucky. That's 1,700 trees for each person in Kentucky.

The most common tree in Kentucky is the red maple. There are 803 million of them.

Cumberland County has the most trees per person: 13,330. Fayette County has the fewest, "only" seven trees per person.

Kentucky's state tree is the yellow poplar, also known as the tulip poplar or tulip tree.

The largest tree in Kentucky is a 168-foot tall yellow poplar in McCreary County.

## KENTUCKY'S FEDERAL THREATENED & ENDANGERED SPECIES

| COMMON NAME | SCIENTIFIC NAME | FEDERAL STATUS |
|---|---|---|
| **Crustaceans** | | |
| Mammoth Cave Shrimp | Palaemonias ganteri | Endangered |
| **Mussels** | | |
| Catspaw | Epioblasma obliquata obliquata | Endangered |
| Clubshell | Pleurobema clava | Endangered |
| Cumberland Bean Mussel | Villosa trabalis | Endangered |
| Cumberland Elktoe * | Alasmidonta Atropurpurea | Endangered |
| Cumberlandian Combshell * | Epioblasma Brevidens | Endangered |
| Fanshell | Cyprogenia stegaria | Endangered |
| Fat Pocketbook | Potamilus capax | Endangered |
| Little-wing Pearlymussel | Pegias fabula | Endangered |
| Northern Riffleshell | Epioblasma tarulosa rangiana | Endangered |
| Orange-foot Pimpleback | Plethobasus cooperianus | Endangered |
| Oyster Mussel * | Epioblasma Capsaeformis | Endangered |
| Pink Mucket | Lampsilis abrupta | Endangered |
| Ring Pink | Obovaria retusa | Endangered |
| Rough Pigtoe | Pleurobema plenum | Endangered |
| **Fish** | | |
| Blackside Dace | Phoxinus cumberlandensis | Threatened |
| Duskytail Darter * | Etheostoma Percnurum | Endangered |
| Palezone Shiner | Notropis sp. | Endangered |
| Pallid Sturgeon | Scaphirhynchus albus | Endangered |
| Relict Darter * | Etheostoma Chienense | Endangered |
| **Birds** | | |
| Bald Eagle | Haliaeetus leucocephalus | Endangered |
| Interior Least Tern | Sterna antillarum athalassos | Endangered |
| Paregrine Falcon * | Falco Peregrinus | Endangered |
| Red-cockaded Woodpecker | Picoides borealis | Endangered |
| **Mammals** | | |
| Gray Myotis (bat) | Myotis grisescens | Endangered |
| Indiana Myotis (bat) | Myotis sodalis | Endangered |
| Virginia Big-eared Bat | Plecotus townsendii virginianus | Endangered |
| **Insects** | | |
| American Burying Beetle | Nicrophorus americanus | Endangered |
| **Plants** | | |
| Chaffseed | Schwalbea americana | Endangered |
| Cumberland Rosemary | Conradina verticillata | Threatened |
| Cumberland Sandwort | Minvartia cumberlandensis | Endangered |
| Price's Potato-bean | Apios priceana | Threatened |
| Running Buffalo Clover | Trifolium stoloniferum | Endangered |
| Short's Goldenrod | Solidago shortii | Endangered |
| Virginia Spiraea | Spiraea virginiana | Threatened |
| White-haired Goldenrod | Solidago albopilosa | Threatened |

*Included in some Federal listings*
*Source: Kentucky State Nature Preserves Commission*

# ENVIRONMENT & NATURAL RESOURCES
# *Wildlife Past & Present*

Dr. Gary O'Dell

## ICE AGE KENTUCKY

The period of earth history known as the Pleistocene—lasting from about 1.6 million to about 10,000 years before the present—was an age when great sheets of ice repeatedly spread across the upper part of the North American continent, alternately advancing and retreating. At the peak of the last glacial advance about 15,000

Mastodons at Big Bone Lick State Park (Replica)
*Source: KY Dept. of Parks*

years ago, the climate, vegetation, and animal life of the land known as Kentucky were quite different than today. A landscape altered by the cold, dry air flowing off the great ice massif, the glacier borderlands comprised open tundra grassland mixed with sparse boreal woodlands of stunted white spruce, aspen and birch.

Here, driven southward by the inexorable movement of the ice, roamed the Pleistocene megafauna. This was the era of giant mammals, far larger, and existing in greater variety than today.

During periods of glacial advance, the sea level was lowered by hundreds of feet, and a land bridge connected North America to Asia across the Bering Sea. The land bridge allowed an intermingling of species. From the Old World to the New came bison, mammoth, mastodon, musk-ox, and felines such as the American lion, jaguar, and saber-tooth cats. Species originating in North America spread to Asia included members of the deer family, horse, camel, and wolf.

Evidence of most megafauna species is found from fossils preserved in deposits in caves and sites such as the salt springs of Big Bone Lick and Blue Licks in northern Kentucky. The composition of biological communities during the Pleistocene varied with climatic shifts—during recessions of ice, the ecology included more species favoring a warmer climate.

In the near-Arctic landscape of Kentucky during the late Pleistocene, vast herds of foraging animals mingled peaceably. Bison, horse, and mammoth fed upon grasses, while caribou, stag-moose, musk-ox and mastodon browsed on tundra plants. The most common grazing species was the shaggy *Bison antiquus*, direct ancestor of the modern buffalo, but nearly a third larger. Today's magnificent thoroughbreds originated in North America more than 50 million years ago and were five-toed leaf browser about the size of a house cat—the horse gradually evolved to its larger modern form, with longer limbs and a single central toe on each foot. The horse became extinct at the end of the Pleistocene, but was reintroduced by the Spanish during the 16th century.

The wooly mammoth, *Mammuthus primigenius*, Columbia mammoth, *Mammuthus columbi*, and their cousin, the American mastodon, *Mammut americanum*, are mammals most symbolic of the Ice Age. The wooly mammoth was covered with a dense coat of hair, as much as 20-inches long, with a layer of fine dense wool beneath. A grown mammoth was comparable in size to the modern elephant, about six to eight tons in weight and 10- to 11-feet high at the shoulder.

Woodlands were occupied by pig-like peccaries, tapirs, and ground sloths. Certainly, one of the strangest prehistoric mammals was the ground-sloth, *Megalonyx jeffersonii*, which somewhat resembled an immense hamster larger than a grizzly bear.

Bison, commonly called Buffalo
Source: KY Dept. of Fish & Wildlife

Ice Age carnivores included giant short-faced bears, dire wolfs, American lions, jaguars, and the scimitar and saber-toothed cats. Bison, horses and mammoth provided the bulk of the diet for large predators—the giant short-faced bear was the largest and most powerful. This bear stood more than 11-feet tall when erect, and weighed about 1,500 pounds when heavy with autumn fat.

As the climate warmed and the ice sheet withdrew for the last time, a massive extinction took place from about 12,000 to 9,000 years before the present—nearly three-fourths of the large mammal genera in North America were eliminated. Vanished forever were the mammoth and mastodon, stag-moose, ground sloth, short-faced bears, dire wolves, American lion, scimitar and saber-toothed cats. Giant bison gradually evolved to the smaller modern bison. Jaguars, peccaries, and tapirs retreated southward. The woodland musk-ox was lost; horses and camels disappeared from the continent. In their absence, smaller mammals dominated North America: bison, elk, moose, pronghorn antelope, bighorn sheep, mountain goat, grizzly bear, and mountain lion. Bison became the largest land mammal of the continent.

Scientific explanations for the disappearance of the North American megafauna include epidemic diseases or overkill hunting by prehistoric humans. These circumstances did contribute to the decline, but the most likely cause seems to be the severe environmental disruption associated with the changing climate. As many herbivore species vanished, carnivores and scavengers dependent upon them likewise disappeared.

## PRE-SETTLEMENT WILDLIFE

Once the great North American ice sheet retreated, tundra and boreal forest migrated northward and gradually were reestablished across Canada. At the same time, warmer-climate hardwood forests returned from the southeastern coastal plains. By the time Europeans discovered North America, the ancient forests were domi-

Black bear enjoying the snow
Source: KY Dept. of Fish & Wildlife

nated by oak and chestnut—extending from southern New England along the Appalachians to the Mississippi valley.

West of the Appalachian mountains, the forest gave way to woodlands and savanna—a more open habitat maintained by grazing animals and by fires deliberately set by the paleo-Indian inhabitants to drive game and make land more productive. Early explorers found the savanna of central Kentucky a fertile place filled with grass and cane, dotted with clustered oak and ash, surrounded by rolling, wooded hills. To the west, the treeless prairie landscape was called the Big Barrens.

Early pioneers described vegetation and wildlife—but their main concern was upon game animals. Christopher Gist made one of the earliest records during 1750-1751 as he traveled down the Ohio River and through eastern Kentucky. He described the lands along the Ohio River bordering northeastern Kentucky as "rich fine and Level Land, well Timbered with large Walnut, Ash, Sugar Trees, Cherry Trees &c, it is well watered...and abounds with Turkeys Deer, and Elks and most sorts of Game particularly Buffaloes...."

Large mammals left an imprint upon the landscape, creating networks of well-trodden pathways as they moved from favored grazing lands to salt licks and watering places. The game trails were used by American Indians, by explorers and settlers.

Red Fox
Source: U.S. Fish and Wildlife Service

When Daniel Boone traveled from the Cumberland Gap to the Kentucky River, he and his party followed a bison path that became known as the Wilderness Road. The game trails often served as the foundations for wagon roads, railroad beds, and modern highways.

### KENTUCKY'S WILDLIFE TODAY

In the 15 years between the first Kentucky fortifications and the first U.S. Census in 1790, nearly 74,000 immigrants settled in the region; by 1820 more than half a million persons called Kentucky their home. The landscape at the time of settlement had been created through the interaction of climate, wildlife, and human agency; the ecology was altered to an even greater extent by the influx of population. Early inhabitants wielded axe and plow, transforming savanna woodlands into cropland and pasture. During the second half of the 19th century, the ancient forest of the Appalachian highlands was systematically stripped of its timber (nearly half was gone by 1900).

Unregulated hunting, habitat alterations, and competition from domestic livestock eliminated or greatly reduced populations of many of the most common large mammals. By 1800 woodland

bison and elk were rarely seen; by mid-century, mountain lions, black bear, red and gray wolves, bobcat, beaver, and wild turkey had nearly been exterminated.

Experimental projects have reintroduced certain species that were eliminated during the settlement period. In 1997 the Kentucky Dept. of Fish and Wildlife Resources began restoring elk to southeastern Kentucky—today we host the largest herd east of the Mississippi River. In the same year, the U.S. Geological Survey reintroduced black bears from the Great Smokey Mountain National Park into the Big South Fork area along the Kentucky-Tennessee border. Kentucky's wild turkey restoration project was so successful that it has been used as a national model. Bison, which once numbered less than 1,000 individuals, have

Bobcat (Felis Rufus), Salato
Source: KY Dept. of Fish & Wildlife

increased to an estimated 350,000 in North America today.

Smaller mammals commonly found in Kentucky include red and gray foxes, woodchuck, raccoon, mink, beaver, muskrat, opossum, spotted and striped skunk, eastern cottontail rabbit, gray squirrel, and eastern woodrat. Kentucky has many different species of bats, occupying diverse habitats from caves to barns. Among the most common bird species are the robin, cardinal, jay, wild turkey, ruffed grouse, barred owl, bobwhite, mourning dove, red-winged blackbird, eastern meadowlark, mockingbird, and summer tanager. Reptiles and amphibians include the red-spotted newt, dusky salamander, American toad, bullfrog, wood frog, box turtle, painted turtle, common snapping turtle, eastern garter snake, northern water snake, black rat snake, and copperhead. There are regional and habitat differences in the occurrence of these species, which are not distributed uniformly across the commonwealth.

## ENVIRONMENT & NATURAL RESOURCES
# *Wildlife Refuges*

### CLARKS RIVER NATIONAL WILDLIFE REFUGE

Clarks River National Wildlife Refuge is a beautiful bottomland hardwood forest lying along the East Fork of the Clarks River and is a seasonal home to over 250 different species of migratory birds. The refuge is located in the western Kentucky counties of Marshall, McCracken and Graves, between Paducah and Benton. The bottomlands are dominated with overcup oaks, bald cypress, and tupelo gum, and the slightly higher, better drained areas, are covered with willow oak, swamp chestnut oak, red oak, sweet gum, sycamore, ash and elm.

Clarks River National Wildlife Refuge is the only National Wildlife Refuge located solely within the State of Kentucky. It is located in close proximity to the National Recreational Area Land Between the Lakes and a number of state Wildlife Management Areas offering a multitude of outdoor activities.

The most significant resource values of this area are the wetland habitat complexes formed by the river, creeks, beaver ponds and natural ponding.

This natural wetland ecosystem is relatively intact and has high wildlife habitat values, particularly for migratory birds and other species representative of bottomland hardwood systems. The hardwood dominated forests are used as breeding, wintering and migration habitat by many species of neotropical migratory birds.

The refuge provides habitat for a natural diversity of wildlife associated with the Clarks River floodplain and includes: wintering habitat for migratory waterfowl, habitat for nongame migratory birds and opportunities for wildlife dependent recreation.

The refuge offers the public opportunities for hunting and fishing (special regulations do apply), wildlife observation and photography and hiking.

*For more information, call (270) 527-5770 or visit http://southeast.fws.gov/clarksriver.*

### THE CENTRAL KENTUCKY WILDLIFE REFUGE

The Central Kentucky Wildlife Refuge is a 500-acre preserve, located 13 miles from Danville in the Parksville (Boyle County) knob land and bordering a stretch of the beautiful North Rolling Fork. The refuge is open to all as a protected area for the enjoyment and study of nature in its many fascinating forms. It is set aside as a permanent sanctuary for plant and animal forms native to Central Kentucky to be enjoyed by future generations. The refuge depends upon donations and volunteer labor to operate; there is no paid staff.

The bird blind near the caretaker's home provides close-up views of feeding birds for study and photography. Birds include purple finches and house finches, evening grosbeaks, cardinals, towhees, Carolina chickadees, flickers and nuthatches, just to name a few.

*Source: Kentucky Department of Fish & Wildlife*

Hundreds of wildflowers grow and many animals such as deer, foxes, grey and fox squirrels, flying squirrels and more. The refuge has five main trails rated easy to strenuous.

*For information, call 800-755-0076.*

### WOLF RUN WILDLIFE REFUGE & EDUCATIONAL FACILITY

Wolf Run is a non-profit wildlife refuge in Central Kentucky. State and federally licensed, this refuge houses, heals and cares for abused, abandoned and injured wild and exotic animals. A 501(c)(3) non-profit organization, there is no paid staff and 100 percent of the profit is used in the care of the animals. The refuge houses everything from opossums to lions, and all in between. The refuge, located in Jessamine Co., is near Camp Nelson National Cemetery.

*For more information, call (859) 887-2256.*

ENVIRONMENT & NATURAL RESOURCES

# Wildlife Management Areas, Nature Preserves & Natural Areas

Most of the public wildlife areas listed in this guide are owned by various agencies of the state and federal government. Many areas were purchased with dollars from hunting and fishing license sales. Funding from the same sources pay for wildlife management programs on more than 70 percent of these areas. Kentucky's public-use lands total 1,602,978 acres, or 6.3 percent of the state.

Wildlife management practices on these areas provide food, cover and water for a wide variety of species. Since wild creatures are more active at dawn and dusk, these are the best times to watch wildlife. The widest variety of species can be seen during spring and fall migrations.

## PURCHASE REGION
**Reelfoot Lake National Wildlife Refuge** (2,500 acres): Fulton Co. (731) 538-2481
**Obion Creek WMA** (3,521 acres): Hickman, Fulton, Carlisle Cos. (270) 753-6913

**Meadwestvaco WMA** (3,600 acres): Hickman, Carlisle Cos. (270) 753-6913
**Winford WMA** (237 acres): Carlisle Co.
**Boatwright WMA** (6,975 acres): 9 units in Ballard, Carlisle Cos., Peal Unit (1,724 acres) (270) 224-2244
**Ballard Hunting Unit** (400 acres): Ballard Co., 4 mi. S. of Oscar off KY 1105 on Salle Crice Rd. Area is not part of Ballard WMA. No roads or trails within area. (270) 224-2244
**Ballard WMA** (8,473 acres): Ballard Co. (270) 224-2244
**West Kentucky WMA** (6,463 acres): McCracken Co. (270) 488-3233
**Ohio River Islands WMA** (1,375 acres): Livingston Co. (270) 753-6913
**Livingston County WMA**
**Kaler Bottoms WMA** (1,930 acres): Graves Co.
**Clarks River National Wildlife Refuge** (5,000 acres): Marshall Co. (270) 527-5770

**Golden Pond in the Land Between the Lakes**
*Photo: Charles Bertram, Lexington Herald-Leader*

Kentucky Lake WMA (3,500 acres): Calloway, Marshall, Lyon Cos.

Beechy Creek WMA (122 acres): Calloway Co.

Land Between the Lakes National Recreational Area (107,000 acres): Trigg, Lyon Cos., between Kentucky and Barkley lakes. (270) 924-2065

Lake Barkley WMA (5,429 acres): Trigg, Lyon, Livingston Cos.

Fort Campbell Military Reservation (85,000 acres): Christian, Trigg Cos. (270) 798-2175

Pennyrile State Forest (17,000 acres): Christian Co.

Tradewater WMA (724 acres): Hopkins-Christian County line, shares boundary with Pennyrile Forest

Jones-Keeney WMA (2,250 acres): Caldwell Co.

Clear Creek WMA

Wendell H. Ford RTC

## GREEN RIVER REGION

White City WMA (5,472 acres): Hopkins Co. (270) 273-3569 or 3568

Lee K. Nelson WMA (70 acres): Webster Co. Gift to Ky. Dept. Fish and Wildlife Resources from former wildlife biologist Lee K. Nelson

Higginson-Henry WMA (5,424 acres): Union Co. (270) 389-3580

Sloughs WMA (10,481 acres): 6 units in Henderson, Union Cos. (270) 827-2673

Green River State Forest

Daviess Demonstration Area (72 acres): Daviess Co., (270) 273-3569 or 3568

L. B. Davison WMA (150 acres): Ohio Co.

Peabody WMA (60,000 acres): Ohio, Muhlenberg Cos.

Yellowbank WMA (6,000 acres in 4 tracts): Breckinridge Co. (270) 547-6856

Rough River Lake WMA (3,425 land acres at summer pool): Portions of lake shoreline, Breckinridge, Grayson Cos. (270) 746-7130

Nolin River Lake WMA (5,210 land acres at summer pool): Portion of lake shoreline, Grayson, Edmonson, Hart Cos. (270) 746-7130

Barren River Lake WMA (10,100 land acres at summer pool): Barren, Allen Cos. (270) 646-5167

## BLUEGRASS REGION

Fort Knox Military Reservation (109,068 acres): Hardin, Bullitt, Meade Cos. (502) 624-2712

John C. Williams WMA (384 acres): Nelson Co. (502) 477-9024

Taylorsville Lake WMA (10,571 acres): Spencer, Anderson, Nelson Cos. (502) 477-9024

Central Kentucky WMA (1,847 acres): Madison Co. (859) 986-4130

Blue Grass Army Depot (14,596 acres): Madison Co.

(859) 625-6420

Dr. James C. Salato Wildlife Education Center (132 acres): Franklin Co. (800) 858-1549, M-F, 7:30 a.m.-5:30 p.m. Eastern Time

T. N. Sullivan WMA (155 acres): Franklin Co. (502) 535-6335

John A. Kleber WMA (2,605 acres): Owen, Franklin Cos. (502) 535-6335

**A Natural Arch**
*Source: Southern & Eastern Kentucky Tourism Development Association*

Dr. James R. Rich WMA (1,567 acres): Owen Co. (502) 535-6335

Kentucky River WMA (1,604 acres): Henry, Owen Cos., (502) 535-6335

Twin Eagle WMA (166 acres): Owen Co. (502) 535-6335

Curtis Gates Lloyd WMA (1,179 acres): Grant Co. (859) 428-2262

Mullins WMA (266 acres): Kenton Co. (859) 428-2262

Dr. Norman And Martha Adair WMA (631 acres): Boone Co. (859) 428-2262

## NORTHEAST REGION

Claude Cummins Property (100 acres): Mason Co. (606) 564-6706

Ohio River Islands National Wildlife Refuge (1,450 acres in 12 islands, 2 islands in Ky.) (304) 422-0752

Lewis County WMA (1,161 acres): Lewis Co. (606)

686-3312.

South Shore WMA

**Daniel Boone National Forest** (670,000 acres; 141,457 acres in the Northeast Region including Pioneer Weapons WMA).

**Fleming WMA** (2,070 acres): Fleming Co. (859) 289-2564.

**Clay WMA** (5,790 acres): Nicholas and Fleming Cos.

**Cumberland Gap, Bell Co.**
*Source: Southern & Eastern Kentucky Tourism Development Association*

(859) 289-2564

**Pioneer Weapons WMA** (7,610 acres): Bath, Menifee Cos. (606) 745-3100

**Tygarts State Forest** (800 acres): Carter Co.

**Grayson Lake WMA** (10,598 acres in land at summer pool): Carter, Elliott Cos. (606) 474-6856.

**Yatesville Lake WMA** (17,370 acres in land at summer pool): Lawrence Co. (606) 686-3312)

**Paintsville Lake WMA** (12,103 acres in land at summer pool): Johnson, Morgan Cos. (606) 297-6312

**Dewey Lake WMA** (9,870 acres in land at summer pool): Floyd Co. (606) 789-4521

**Fishtrap Lake WMA** (10,691 acres in lake at summer pool): Pike Co.

**George Washington-Jefferson National Forest** (961 acres; 116 acres are in Pike Co. The rest lies in the Southeast Region)

**SOUTHEAST REGION**

**George Washington-Jefferson National Forest** (961 acres): Pike Co. 845 acres and Letcher Co. 116 acres

**Hensley-Pine Mountain WMA** (6,000 acres): Letcher Co.

**Carr Creek Lake WMA** (2,849 acres): Knott Co. (606) 642-3308

**Addington Enterprises WMA** (16,000 acres): Breathitt, Knott, Perry Cos. (606) 378-3474

**Buckhorn Lake WMA** (3,480 acres): Lake shoreline in Perry Co. (606) 398-7154

**Redbird WMA** (25,529 acres): Leslie and Clay Cos.

**Beech Creek WMA** (1,260 acres): Clay Co.

Ataya Hardwoods WMA

**Kentenia State Forest** (3,624 acres): Harlan Co.

**Cranks Creek WMA** (2,167 acres): Harlan Co.

**Martins Fork Lake WMA** (1,394 acres): Harlan Co.

**Begley WMA** (20,000 acres): Bell, Harlan and Leslie Cos.

**Shillalah Creek WMA** (2,640 acres): Bell and Harlan Cos.

**Kentucky Ridge Forest WMA** (3,600 acres): Bell Co.

Ashland WMA

**Mill Creek WMA** (13,558 acres): Jackson Co.

**Daniel Boone National Forest** (670,000 acres): From Tenn. line in McCreary Co. N. to Fleming and Lewis Cos.

**Cane Creek WMA** (6,672 acres): Laurel Co.

Paul Van Booven WMA

Robinson Forest

**Beaver Creek WMA** (17, 347 acres): McCreary and Pulaski Cos.

**Big South Fork National River and Recreation Area** (55,000 acres): McCreary Co. Visitor Center, (606) 376-5073

**Lake Cumberland WMA** (39,484 acres in land at summer pool): Lake shoreline in Pulaski, Russell, Wayne, Clinton Cos. (606) 376-8083

**Dale Hollow Lake WMA** (3,130 acres): Lake shoreline in Cumberland, Clinton Cos. and Dale Hollow State Resort Park

**Mud Camp Creek WMA** (600 acres): Cumberland Co.

**R. F. Tarter WMA** (1,300 acres): Adair, Russell Cos.

**Dennis-Gray WMA** (70 acres): Adair Co.

**Green River Lake WMA** (20,500 acres): Taylor, Adair Cos. (270) 465-5039

Cedar Creek Lake WMA

Dix River WMA

Source: Kentucky Department of Fish and Wildlife Resources, (800) 858-1549

## STATEWIDE PRESERVES & NATURAL AREAS

A State Nature Preserve (SNP) is a legally dedicated area that has been recognized for its natural significance and protected by law for scientific and educational purposes. Dedicated State Nature Preserves are established solely to protect and preserve rare species and the natural environment. Public visitation is encouraged but closely regulated to protect the natural integrity of the preserve so that it may be passed on unimpaired to future generations.

Axe Lake Swamp SNP
Bad Branch SNP
Bat Cave SNP
Beargrass Creek SNP
Bissell Bluff SNA
Blackacre SNP
Blanton Forest SNP
Blue Licks SPNP
Boone County Cliffs SNP
Bouteloua Barrens SNP

Brigadoon SNP
Cascade Caverns SNP
Chaney Lake SNP
Crooked Creek Barrens SNP
Cumberland Falls SPNP
Cypress Creek SNP
Dinsmore Woods SNP
Eastview Barrens SNP
Flat Rock Glade SNP
Floracliff SNP
Frances Johnson Palk SNP
Goodrum Cave SNP
Hi Lewis Pine Barrens SNP
James E. Bickford SNP
Jesse Stuart SNP
Jim Scudder SNP

John B. Stephenson Memorial Forest SNP
John James Audubon SPNP
Julian Savanna SNP
Kingdom Come SPNP
Logan County Glade SNP
Lower Howard's Creek Heritage Park and SNP
Martin's Fork SNA
Metropolis Lake SNP
Natural Bridge SPNP
Newman's Bluff SNA
Obion Creek SNP
Pilot Knob SNP
Pine Mountain SPNP
Quiet Trails SNP
Raymond Athey Barrens SNP
River Cliffs SNP
Short's Goldenrod SNP
Six Mile Island SNP
Springhouse Barrens SNP
Stone Mountain SNA
Terrapin Creek SNP
Thompson Creek Glades SNP
Three Ponds SNP
Tom Dorman SNP
Vernon-Douglas SNP
*Woodburn Glade SNP*
* SPNP indicates State Park Nature Preserve
* SNA indicates State Natural Area

**Kentucky State Nature Preserves Commission**
(502) 573-2886

(top) Hi Lewis State Nature Preserve is a pine barrens on the south face of Pine Mountain in Harlan County. (bottom) Axe Lake State Nature Preserve is a cypress/tupelo swamp in Ballard County.
Source: Kentucky State Nature Preserves Commission

# ENVIRONMENT & NATURAL RESOURCES

# *Fisheries Resources*      Kerry Prather

All stream watersheds in Kentucky eventually flow into the Ohio River with the exception of a few minor streams that drain into the Mississippi River. There are about 14,000 miles of streams in Kentucky. The Ohio River makes up the entire northern border for a stream length of 664 miles and encompasses 39,210 square miles. Major reservoirs (≥ 500 acres) total 209,788 surface acres. Fish have preferences for either flowing streams or standing water (ponds, lakes and reservoirs). The term "fishery resources" includes freshwater mussels, crayfishes and fishes that have natural heritage and economic value.

The freshwater mussel fauna of Kentucky is one of the most diverse in the U.S. The state has 103 recognized species: 12 species are presumed extinct, 22 species listed by the U.S. Fish and Wildlife Service as endangered with eight of these considered extirpated from the state. Ohio River tributaries support some of the last strongholds of rare and endangered mussels. Kentucky has identified 46 mussel species that are considered species of greatest conservation need. Of these there are 20 species listed as globally rare and 25 species as rare within Kentucky. Habitat loss and exotic species are among factors that have con-

**Kentucky Darter (*Etheostoma rafinesquei*)**
*Photo: Matthew R. Thomas*

**Bottlebrush Crayfish**
**(*Barbicambarus cornutus*)**
*Photo: Guenter A. Schuster*

tributed to the downward spiral of mussel populations. Some of the state's most diverse populations of mussels are found in the Green River and tributaries to the upper Cumberland River. Mussel shells from Kentucky Lake and the Tennessee River are highly prized for their use in the foreign cultured pearl industry.

Crayfishes represent another imperiled aquatic group and one of the most poorly known. Some crayfish species display surprisingly brilliant hues of blue, green, orange, red, and yellow, sometimes in dazzling combinations. Crayfish forage on living and dead plant and animal matter, and are themselves fed upon by a variety of predators. Crayfish are susceptible to habitat damage caused by impoundments, stream channelization, pollution, and sedimentation. Kentucky has 52 known species and 1 undescribed species of crayfish.

The Mammoth Cave region offers the largest area for cave species in Kentucky. They are very vulnerable to pollution, particularly inadequately treated sewage, pesticides, and sedimentation. A cave species with state and federal protection status is the Mammoth Cave Shrimp (Palaemonias ganteri).

Kentucky has a diverse fish fauna being exceeded

only by Tennessee and Alabama. The Cumberland River drainage (7,220 square miles) supports the most diverse and unusual fish fauna in Kentucky. A total of 158 species occur, or once occurred, in the Kentucky portion of this drainage. Second in fish diversity is the Green River drainage (9,230 sq. mi.) with 150 fish species. The Green River is the largest watershed contained within state borders. Though smaller in size and diversity, Terrapin Creek, Running Slough, and the oxbows of the Mississippi River in western Kentucky harbor seven species not present in the rest of the state. In total, 236 species are known to occur or have

systematic approach to trout management began in 1983 with an inventory and rating of existing and potential trout streams. Commercial anglers are licensed through the KDFWR to use specialized gear to harvest "rough" fish species for commercial sale.

**(Top) Teaching the joy and excitement of fishing at an early age**
*Source: Kentucky Dept. of Fish & Wildlife Resources*
**(Left) A Wavyrayed Lampmussel**
*Photo: Monte McGregor*

occurred in the state, of which 10 are presumed extinct or extirpated from the state.

Kentucky has diverse fishing resources, sought by all types of anglers. Fishing is open all year long. Kentucky is on the southern home range of some typically northern species (Muskellunge, Smallmouth Bass, Walleye and Yellow Perch), and on the northern fringe of what are considered southern species (Spotted Bass, Redear Sunfish, and Blue Catfish).

**Jamie Sutherland catches a large mouth bass on private property in Scott County**
*Source: Robo Sutherland*

The temperate location allows for seasonal changes without prolonged ice cover on the state's waters during winter. The number of fish stocked in Kentucky waters in 2005 by KDFWR totaled 11,434,501.

Spotted (Kentucky) Bass (Micropterus punctulatus)—are generally distributed and common throughout the state. First described and named by Rafinesque in 1819 from the Ohio River, in Kentucky. The official "state fish" of Kentucky, Spotted Bass are found primarily in flowing streams and larger lakes. Rainbow trout have been utilized since 1952. The U.S. Fish and Wildlife Service established Brook trout in two streams from stockings in 1968. Brown trout were first stocked by the KDFWR in 1981. A

Commercial anglers reported harvesting 2,633,738 lbs. of fish and 17,014 lbs. of eggs in 2004.

Aquaculture is the culture of fishery resources, whether domestic or foreign, in controlled areas for food and profit by the private sector. The Kentucky Aquaculture Association (www.kaatoday.org) and the Kentucky Aquaculture Taskforce report that this is the fastest growing sector of agriculture worldwide and is a means to increase farm profits and expand farm enterprises.

For more information, visit Kentucky Department of Fish & Wildlife Resources (fw.ky.gov) and the Kentucky State Nature Preserves Commission, (www.naturepreserves.ky.gov).

# Cora Wilson Stewart

## Dr. Yvonne Honeycutt Baldwin

On a moonlit night in September of 1911, the superintendent of Rowan County schools, along with volunteer teachers, opened the district's 50 schools to adult pupils. Expecting three or four students per school, the teachers were overwhelmed by 1,152 pupils, all hoping to learn to read, write, and "cipher." From this experiment, Cora Wilson Stewart—first female superintendent of her county's schools and first female president of the Kentucky Education Association—created Moonlight Schools to educate rural adults. Unlike urban Americans and immigrants who had access to night schools, the rural population had little opportunity to make up schooling missed in their youth. The idea caught on quickly and Moonlight Schools were established in most school districts in Kentucky. The legislature created the Kentucky Illiteracy Commission in 1914. The first agency of its kind in the nation, the KIC, headed by Cora Wilson Stewart, undertook a campaign to eliminate illiteracy in the state by 1920.

Unwilling to use materials designed for children, Stewart created a three-volume series of primers for adults called "The Country Life Readers," and developed a grooved writing pad to teach proper penmanship. Responding to draft statistics and data showing that 25 percent of the nation's draft age men were functionally illiterate, she urged the nation to educate its young men before sending them to fight in a war they could not understand or support as long as they remained illiterate. She wrote the "Soldier's First Book" and urged families to develop literacy skills as well, so they could communicate with their soldier serving "over there." For illiterate women, she wrote "Mother's First Book," a parenting and homemaking how-to that taught reading while providing information about health, nutrition, and child care.

Using Kentucky as a model and draft statistics to illustrate the need for action, Stewart traveled the country urging clubwomen, church and civic organizations, and professional education associations at state and national levels to undertake the task of educating the nation's illiterates. Their motto became "each one teach one." Stewart organized and headed the National Illiteracy Crusade and was appointed chairman of the National Illiteracy Commission by Pres. Herbert Hoover.

After nearly 30 years crusading against illiteracy, assisted by some of the nation's best-known political and educational leaders, Stewart retired to Pine Bluff, Arkansas, and Tryon, North Carolina, where she died in 1958.

**68 pupils enrolled in a "moonlight school"**
*Source: Cora Wilson Stewart Photographic Collection, PA58M25, Special Collections and Digital Programs, University of Kentucky.*

*See Yvonne Honeycutt Baldwin, "Cora Wilson Stewart and the Moonlight Schools: Fighting for Literacy in America" (University Press of Kentucky, Lexington, 2006).*

Education

Virginia Fox

Students L-R Michael Sidney, Darion Waite, Micah Tatum, observing and measuring how long it takes for various pieces of butter to melt in a beaker
*Photo: Charles Bertram, Herald-Leader*

**K**entucky is the 2006 winner of the Frank Newman Award for State Innovation given by the Education Commission of the States in recognition of excellence in state education policy and policy-making. This award recognized Kentucky's depth, breadth and sustained focus of its education reform and improvement efforts over the past 15 years. Those efforts include K-12 reform, Higher Education Reform, teacher quality, P-16 efforts, online learning, technology planning and deployment.

Almost daily, the State Department of Education, Council on Post-secondary Education and Education Cabinet are contacted by other states to obtain information on how Kentucky has moved in such a short time from the bottom of the pack to the national average. While we have understandable pride in this accomplishment, Kentucky's goals are far more ambitious. We know that the competition is not just in surrounding states, or even the U.S.—we are preparing students to compete in the global economy.

Key educational investments approved by the 2006 General Assembly included more than $250 million in teacher pay, $47 million for pre-school, nearly $100 million for operating costs and new computer technology hardware, two additional instructional days to the school calendar, ACT testing for all high school juniors, and increased reading instruction for struggling readers through the Read To Achieve program.

Kentucky has world-class learning standards—and we have high accountability for our schools. Early in 2007 Kentucky will have the most sophisticated student tracking system in the country. Kentucky will also lead the nation with a high-speed electronic system that connects all K-12, postsecondary and workforce sites with voice, video and data.

The first public school system was set up in the state in 1838. Most Kentucky children could not attend classes regularly because of various factors: they were poor, were needed at home to help their families on the farm, lived in remote rural areas that did not have a school or teacher, or they were not allowed to attend because of their color. Then, as now, we struggled with financing education, hiring and retaining qualified teachers, compensating teachers, providing adequate instructional materials and textbooks.

But, the biggest drawback was indifference—and even opposition—to public education. Many Kentuckians simply did not see a need for education when they earned a living doing physical labor, and children were more valuable to their families working on the land. Most people did not want to pay taxes to support schools, or have attendance mandated.

Schools for women were fairly common in early Kentucky, however for the upper class. And, there were occasional schools for blacks, not many but a few. For a time, Kentucky black children were allowed to read and write—after 1850 Kentucky became more restrictive, much more like the Deep South where such education was forbidden.

When talk turns to sweeping education changes, most people think of the Kentucky Education Reform Act of 1990. Actually, when talk turns to education reform nationally, most education experts think of KERA. But before KERA, there was ground breaking legislation and attempts to move the state forward. Every generation has had education prophets literally crying in the Kentucky wilderness for accessible public education for all Kentuckians.

As early as 1821 there was movement toward establishing government funding of public education by way of a literary fund through a state bank called the Bank of Kentucky. Unfortunately, that venture failed. In 1837 the Kentucky legislature debated using surplus federal money from the sale of public lands to fund common schools, but that became embroiled in political bickering. The money that was designated for education was diverted for internal improvement, when transportation issues became a priority of the legislature.

In 1838 the state's first superintendent, Joseph J.

Bullock, was appointed and began gathering data on illiteracy in Kentucky. Even though he showed the profound need for basic education, Supt. Bullock did not receive the support necessary to develop a statewide system.

Even in 1845 when the legislature created a permanent office of superintendent of public education, a state board of education, and encouraged the creation of common schools in every county, there was no enforcement power to make these changes happen. However, this was a turning point—it was the first time legislators adopted an education provision in the Kentucky Constitution.

**Freedom School**
*Photo: Sid Webb*

Kentuckians approved the first state property tax for public education in 1848. The tax was 2 cents per $100 of taxable property. These and other revolutionary initiatives were lead by strong-willed Supt. Robert J. Breckinridge, who organized The Friends of Public Education. They met in 1851 to make recommendations on curriculum, length of school (which was only three months a year at that time) and standard textbooks, among other important issues.

Supt. Breckinridge felt the winds of change as the whole state moved to organize a complete general education system. Breckinridge wrote, "Many tens of thousands of the sons and daughters of the state have received the first elements of education—great multitudes of whom, but for these schools, would never have received any education at all. And perhaps more than all, a public sentiment, and what is better and deeper, a public principle, fixed, general, and earnest has been begotten in the mind and settled in the heart of our people, that the work is a good work, that it can be done, and shall be done." Finally, Breckinridge could see and feel that Kentuckians were starting to support schools financially, and truly to value education.

Unfortunately, the Civil War destroyed much of the progress that Breckinridge and The Friends of Public Education made during those years.

It wasn't until 1908 that Kentucky made school attendance mandatory in every county and required counties to organize high schools. At this point, there were less than 50 high schools with fewer than 5,000 students enrolled in the state. Two years earlier, the general assembly established two normal schools, Eastern and Western, to train teachers—creating a systematic approach to preparing classroom teachers.

Equal funding of schools was not mandatory until a 1949 amendment addressed the inadequate

**Technology is important in today's classrooms**
*Source: Kentucky Department of Education*

funding of schools in poor counties, and even then equal funding did not materialize. It was another 40 years before 66 school districts, seven boards of trustees and 22 public school students sued the state, demanding equal support of education for all students. The case, Rose v. Council for Better Education, went all the way to the Kentucky Supreme Court—and concluded in the 1989 ruling that the entire system of elementary and secondary public schools was unconstitutional because the Kentucky General Assembly was not providing an adequate and efficient system of public schools.

The resulting study by the legislature and dramatic statutory reforms in 1990 created the most sweeping educational reform act in the history of the U.S. The legislature totally revamped Kentucky's education system in the areas of finance, governance, and curriculum in an attempt to provide equal educational opportunities for all of Kentucky's children regardless of the property wealth of the district in which they lived.

As of the 2004-2005 school year, Kentucky had 176 school districts with 1,241 schools and more than 40,800 teachers instructing more than 656,000 students. In the school years around 1950, there were actually more school districts, with 237, and more schools, with 5,424 across the state and about 20,000 teachers. About 60 percent of those schools only had one teacher. The average teacher salary was $2,350 compared to $42,032 in 2004-2005. The state education budget in 1950 was $49 million compared to $3.092 billion in 2005.

Since 1990 Kentucky has been the focus of the education establishment. We have hosted visitors from throughout the country and the world—all wanting to see what we're doing and how it's working. Kentucky's education history is both rich and complex—understanding our past offers useful insights on our promising educational future.

Virginia "Ginni" Fox retired as Secretary of the Education Cabinet on Sept.1, 2006. Secy. Fox had previously retired from Kentucky Educational Television (KET) as executive director and CEO in Dec. 2002. Under Fox's leadership, KET became the first state network in the country to move from analog to digital broadcasting, initiated multiple channels, data casting and laid the foundation for a myriad of new digital services. As Secretary, Fox spearheaded the establishment of the Kentucky Education Network (KENS) a high speed telecommunications network that will provide two way voice, video and data to all K-12, postsecondary and workforce training sites in Kentucky.

**Virginia Fox**
*Source: Kentucky Department of Education*

# EDUCATION
# *KET*

O. Leonard Press

The decade of the 1950s was a period of educational ferment. There was growing acknowledgment of the woeful inequities and inadequacies in American education. State and federal governments undertook major corrective actions. In Kentucky, the Minimum Foundation Program, an attempt to equalize school funding, was passed in 1954. The same year, the U.S. Supreme Court declared the doctrine of "separate but equal" unconstitutional. Two years later, Kentucky's Day Law, compelling segregation in higher education, was declared unconstitutional by Kentucky's highest court.

Around the country, especially in the South where educational deficiencies were greatest and, consequently, the pressure for out-of-the box progress most pressing, the new technology of television was tried and proved promising.

It was against this backdrop that the plan for a statewide Kentucky educational television network, first drafted at the University of Kentucky's Radio-TV Department in 1958, took shape.

The Kentucky Educational Television Network (KET) grew out of the zeal of thousands of co-founders, citizens at all levels of influence from the schoolhouse to the state house, who promoted the idea with their legislators, with teachers and school administrators, and with a succession of governors. Finally, on September 23, 1968, ten years after conception, a string of TV transmitters from Murray to Ashland went on the air as the largest state educational TV network in the nation.

From the beginning, KET's primary mission was to provide educational enhancement for every child and every adult in the Commonwealth, no matter

**Gov. Bert Combs signs bill authorizing Kentucky Educational Television.**

Kentucky Governor Bert T. Combs at desk, Len Press at far right, (L to R) Bill Small, WHAS News Director; Ron Stewart, WBKY Chief Engineer; Harry King Lowman, Speaker of the House; Townes Ray, Majority Leader of the House; Wendell Butler, Superintendent of Public Instruction.
*Source: UK Radio Photographic Collection*

how rural or remote their schools and homes.

Early on, KET gained national recognition for outstanding production. Its GED series "GED ON TV" has enrolled more than 1.25 million adults throughout the nation since it was released in 1974. More than 120,000 Kentucky adults have so far registered in KET's college courses broadcast in partnership with Kentucky's colleges and universities.

To encourage a more informed citizenry, KET offers every home a front-row seat in the chambers of state government. Further, it provides penetrating insight into current events through analyses, such as "Comment on Kentucky" with Al Smith and "Kentucky Tonight" with Bill Goodman.

A pioneer in the use of new age technology, KET created one of the first systems in the nation for interactive teaching by satellite and the only one that, at once, connected every school building in the state and all its universities and libraries. KET's multi-casting Star Channels serve curriculum needs for students in many other states as well as in Kentucky.

From its inception, KET has been institutionally mindful of a concern best expressed by Kentucky's late historian laureate, Dr. Thomas D. Clark. "It is highly frustrating," Dr. Clark said, "to see Kentuckians fail to live up to the potential of their land and place." With its world-class staff and its advanced technology, KET is an instrument of education and cultural enrichment designed to address that very concern, to help fulfill the historical promise of this, our "land and place."
*Contributed by O. Leonard Press, founder of KET.*

# EDUCATION
# *Governor's Scholars Program*

## Clarence R. Wyatt

Kentucky Governor's Scholars Program is a five-week summer residential program for outstanding Kentucky students between their junior and senior years in high school. The program was established in 1983 under the administration of Gov. John Y. Brown. Gov. Brown and Lillian Press, founding executive director of the program, created the program in order to slow and reverse a growing trend, in which many of Kentucky's talented young people were leaving the commonwealth to pursue educational and career opportunities. The mission of the program is to enhance Kentucky's next generation of civic and economic leaders.

The program began on the campus of Centre College with 230 students. The Kentucky Governor's Scholars Program is the largest continuing governor's school program in the U.S. Since 1983, nearly 18,000 students have participated in the program.

Selected through a rigorous application process, Governor's Scholars come from across the commonwealth and reflect the demographics of Kentucky's high school population. The program brings scholars together with outstanding faculty members, residential advisors, and administrative staff drawn from Kentucky colleges and high schools, throughout the U.S., and from overseas. Each summer the program seeks to create a community of scholars, in which all the participants—students, faculty, and staff—create and pursue opportunities for intellectual, social, and personal growth that

**Lillian Press,**
**Founding Executive Director**
*Photo: Doug Prather*

cannot be developed within the confines of the typical high school curriculum and schedule. While the subject areas represent a range of topics, each aspect of the program is based upon a fundamental belief that teaching and learning best take place when students share responsibility for the process—both through a hands-on, experiential approach—and in shaping the focus of the experience.

Creating this opportunity each summer for more than 1,100 students and over 150 faculty and staff on three campuses requires significant financial support. A permanent staff, including current executive director Dr. Aris Cedeno, works year-round with teachers and administrators, state government officials, host campuses, and private donors to sustain and strengthen the program. The Kentucky General Assembly allocated over $1.7 million to support the 2006 session, comprising some 80 percent of the program's cost. Gifts from private donors—individuals, foundations, and corporations—supported the remainder of the program's budget. Students participate in the program free of charge.

While Kentucky's long-running effort to improve its educational system sometimes meets with mixed results, the Governor's Scholars Program, now planning for its 25th year, is a national model of such programs, a fact in which all Kentuckians should take great pride.

*Clarence R. Wyatt is the Pottinger Associate Professor of History at Centre College, Danville.*

# Education by the numbers (Public Schools)

**Number of school districts:** .........................................176
(26 female superintendents; 150 male; 2 minority)

**Number of public schools:** ....................................1,241
(Does not include dependent districts Ft. Campbell and
Ft. Knox, alternative schools or the Kentucky School for
the Deaf and Kentucky School for the Blind)

**Number of public schools by grade level:**

> **Elementary** - 751
> **Middle** - 228
> **High** - 230
> **Preschool** - 27
> **9th Grade** - 1

**Number of public school teachers**

(full-time equivalent).................................40,833.44 [2003-04]

**Number of public school students**
(actual headcount of enrolled
students on the last day of
the school year) ............................................................656,503

**Ethnicity of public school students**
> **White** - 85.3%
> **African American** - 10.5%
> **Hispanic** - 1.8%
> **Asian** - less than 1%
> **Native American** - less than 1%
> **Other** - 1.3%

**Number of employed certified staff,
minus teachers** (full-time equivalent) [2003-04] ............7,712.25

**Average teacher salary** [2003-04].................................$40,849

**Number of classified staff** (actual head count) [2003-04]..............49,249

**Average per-pupil current expense spending**
(excludes debt service, facilities and fund transfers)
.................................................................................$7,513

**Total SEEK budget**
.....................................................................$2.051 billion

**Total state education budget**
[FY 2005] ......................................................$3.092 billion

**Total federal education revenue**
...........................................................................$647 million

**Total local education revenue**
...........................................................................$1.620 billion

**Length of school year** .............................................. 185 days
(includes 4 days of professional development;
4 holidays; 2 planning days)

**Number of districts with alternative calendars** ...................................32
(Individual schools in Fayette and Jefferson Counties and
Ashland Independent also have alternative calendars.)

**Number of local school board seats** .............................. 882
(5 for each district; Jefferson County has 7 because of its size)

**Gender breakdown of local school board members:**

> **Male** - 554 (63%)
> **Female** - 305 (35%)
> **Not Reported** - 23 (2%)

**Racial breakdown of local school board members:**

> **White** - 804 (91%)
> **Non-White** - 36 (4%)
> **Not reported** - 42 (5%)

**State dropout rate**
[2003-04]......................................................................3.35%

**State retention rate**
[2003-04] .....................................................................3.27%

**State attendance rate** ...............................................94.26%
[2003-04]

**State graduation rate**................................................81.29%
[2003-04]

**Percentage of high school graduates
attending college, vocational/technical
schools, entering the military, employed
or a combination of the above**
[2003-04]..........................................................................96%

**Number of exceptional children ages 3-5** ....................................... 20,777
[as of December 2003]

**Number of exceptional children ages 6-21**
[as of December 2004].................................................83,564

**Percentage of networked schools with Internet access** ................ 100%

**Percentage of schools using e-mail** .............................100%

**Number of family resource/youth services centers** ........................... 782
(399 family resource; 233 youth services; 150 combined)

**Number of students served in extended
school services programs**.........................................187,049

**ESS grant monies provided to school districts**
[FY 2005].....................................................................$32 million

**Number of homeschools** ............................................9,534

**Number of homeschooled students** .............................. 12,170

*All numbers are for the 2004-05 school year un-
less otherwise noted.*
*Source: Kentucky Department of Education,
http://www.education.ky.gov/; for national
statistics, visit the National Center for Education
Statistics, http://nces.ed.gov/.*

## SCHOOL BOARDS

| COUNTY | DISTRICT | SUPERINTENDENT | ADDRESS1 | ADDRESS2 | CITY | ZIP | PHONE | FAX |
|---|---|---|---|---|---|---|---|---|
| County | District | Superintendent | Add1 | Add2 | City | Zip | Phone | Fax |
| Adair | Adair County Schools | Darrell Treece | 1204 Greensburg St | | Columbia | 42728 | (270) 384-2476 | (270) 384-5841 |
| Allen | Allen County Schools | Larry Williams | 238 Bowling Green Rd | | Scottsville | 42164 | (270) 237-3181 | (270) 237-3898 |
| Anderson | Anderson County Schools | Kim Shaw | 103 N Main St | | Lawrenceburg | 40342 | (502) 839-3406 | (502) 839-2501 |
| Ballard | Ballard County Schools | Ed Adami | 3465 Paducah Rd | | Barlow | 42024 | (270) 665-8400 | (270) 665-9844 |
| Barren | Barren County Schools | Jerry Ralston | 202 W Washington St | | Glasgow | 42141 | (270) 651-3787 | (270) 651-8836 |
| Barren | Caverna Independent Schools | Sam Dick | 1108 Cleveland Ave | PO Box 240 | Horse Cave | 42749 | (270) 773-2530 | (270) 773-2524 |
| Barren | Glasgow Independent Schools | Fred Carter | 405 W Main St | PO Box 1239 | Glasgow | 42142 | (270) 651-6757 | (270) 651-9791 |
| Bath | Bath County Schools | Nancy Hutchinson | | | Owingsville | 40360 | (606) 674-6314 | (606) 674-2647 |
| Bell | Bell County Schools | George W Thompson | 211 Virginia Ave | PO Box 340 | Pineville | 40977 | (606) 337-7051 | (606) 337-1412 |
| Bell | Middlesboro Independent Schools | Darryl Wilder | 220 N 20th St | PO Box 959 | Middlesboro | 40965 | (606) 242-8800 | (606) 242-8805 |
| Bell | Pineville Independent Schools | Mike White | 401 Virginia Ave | | Pineville | 40977 | (606) 337-5829 | (606) 337-9983 |
| Boone | Boone County Schools | Bryan Blavatt | 8330 US Hwy 42 | | Florence | 41042 | (859) 283-1003 | (859) 282-2376 |
| Boone | Erlanger-Elsmere Ind. Schools | Lawrence Bowman | 947 Donaldson Rd | PO Box 18548 | Erlanger | 41018 | (859) 283-6230 | (859) 283-6237 |
| Boone | Walton-Verona Independent Schools | Bill Boyle | 16 School Rd | | Walton | 41094 | (859) 485-4181 | (859) 485-1810 |
| Bourbon | Bourbon County Schools | Lana Fryman | 3343 Lexington Rd | | Paris | 40361 | (859) 987-2180 | (859) 987-2182 |
| Bourbon | Paris Independent Schools | Janice Cox Blackburn | 310 W 7th St | | Paris | 40361 | (859) 987-2160 | (859) 987-6749 |
| Boyd | Ashland Independent Schools | Phil Eason | 1420 Central Ave | | Ashland | 41101 | (606) 327-2799 | (606) 327-2705 |
| Boyd | Boyd County Public Schools | Howard K Osborne | 1104 Bob McCullough Dr | | Ashland | 41102 | (606) 928-4141 | (606) 928-4771 |
| Boyd | Fairview Independent Schools | Bill Musick | 2127 Main St | | Ashland | 41102 | (606) 324-3877 | (606) 324-2288 |
| Boyle | Boyle County Schools | Steve Burkich | 352 N Danville Bypass | | Danville | 40422 | (859) 236-6634 | (859) 236-8624 |
| Boyle | Danville Independent Schools | Robert E (Bob) Rowland | 152 E Martin Luther King Blvd | | Danville | 40422 | (859) 238-1300 | (859) 238-1330 |
| Bracken | Augusta Independent Schools | John Cordle | 307 Bracken St | | Augusta | 41002 | (606) 756-2545 | (606) 756-2149 |
| Bracken | Bracken County Schools | Anthony Johnson | 348 W Miami St | | Brooksville | 41004 | (606) 735-2523 | (606) 735-3640 |
| Bracken | Covington Diocese* | Lawrence Bowman | 948 Donaldson Rd | PO Box 18549 | Erlanger | 41019 | (859) 283-6231 | (859) 283-6238 |
| Breathitt | Breathitt County Schools | Arch Turner | 420 Court St | PO Box 750 | Jackson | 41339 | (606) 666-2491 | (606) 666-2493 |
| Breathitt | Jackson Independent Schools | Timothy D Spencer | 940 Highland Ave | | Jackson | 41339 | (606) 666-4979 | (606) 666-4350 |
| Breckinridge | Breckinridge County Schools | Evelyn Neely | 86 Airport Rd | | Hardinsburg | 40143 | (270) 756-3000 | (270) 756-8888 |
| Breckinridge | Cloverport Independent Schools | Josh Powell | 214 W Main St | PO Box 37 | Cloverport | 40111 | (270) 788-3910 | (270) 788-6290 |
| Bullitt | Bullitt County Schools | Michael M Eberbaugh | 1040 Hwy 44 E | | Shepherdsville | 40165 | (502) 543-2271 | (502) 543-3608 |
| Butler | Butler County Schools | Larry Woods | 203 N Tyler St | PO Box 339 | Morgantown | 42261 | (270) 526-5624 | (270) 526-5625 |
| Caldwell | Caldwell County Schools | Carrell Boyd | 612 W Washington St | PO Box 229 | Princeton | 42445 | (270) 365-8000 | (270) 365-5742 |
| Calloway | Calloway County Schools | Steve Hoskins | 2110 College Farm Rd | PO Box 800 | Murray | 42071 | (270) 762-7300 | (270) 762-7310 |
| Calloway | Murray Independent Schools | Bob Rogers | 208 S 13th St | | Murray | 42071 | (270) 753-4363 | (270) 759-4906 |
| Campbell | Bellevue Independent Schools | Wayne Starnes | 219 Center St | | Bellevue | 41073 | (859) 261-2108 | (859) 261-1708 |
| Campbell | Campbell County Schools | Anthony Strong | 101 Orchard Ln | | Alexandria | 41001 | (859) 635-2173 | (859) 448-2439 |
| Campbell | Covington Diocese* | Lawrence Bowman | 949 Donaldson Rd | PO Box 18550 | Erlanger | 41020 | (859) 283-6232 | (859) 283-6239 |
| Campbell | Dayton Independent Schools | Gary Rye | 200 Clay St | | Dayton | 41074 | (859) 491-6565 | (859) 292-3995 |
| Campbell | Fort Thomas Independent Schools | Larry Stinson (resigning 2007) | 28 N Ft Thomas Ave | | Ft Thomas | 41075 | (859) 781-3333 | (859) 442-4016 |
| Campbell | Newport Independent Schools | Michael Brandt | 301 E 8th St | | Newport | 41071 | (859) 292-3004 | (859) 292-3073 |
| Campbell | Silver Grove Independent Schools | Danny Montgomery | 101 W 3rd St | | Silver Grove | 41085 | (859) 441-3894 | (859) 441-4299 |
| Campbell | Southgate Independent Schools | Vacant | Wm Blatt & Evergreen | | Southgate | 41071 | (859) 441-0743 | (859) 441-8735 |
| Carlisle | Carlisle County Schools | Danny Brown | Rt 1 Box 237 | | Bardwell | 42023 | (270) 628-5476 | (270) 628-5477 |
| Carroll | Carroll County Schools | Carroll Yager | 813 Hawkins St | | Carrollton | 41008 | (502) 732-7070 | (502) 732-7073 |
| Carter | Carter County Schools | Darlene Gee | 228 S Carol Malone Blvd | | Grayson | 41143 | (606) 474-6696 | (606) 474-6125 |
| Casey | Casey County Schools | Linda Hatter | 1922 N US 127 | | Liberty | 42539 | (606) 787-6941 | (606) 787-5231 |
| Christian | Christian County Schools | Robert (Bob) Lovingood | 200 Glass Ave | PO Box 609 | Hopkinsville | 42240 | (270) 887-9131 | (270) 887-1267 |
| Christian | Fort Campbell Dependent Schools | Martha H Brown | 77 Texas Ave | | Ft Campbell | 42223 | (270) 439-1927 | (270) 439-3179 |
| Clark | Clark County Schools | Kenneth Edward Musgrove | 1600 W Lexington Ave | | Winchester | 40391 | (859) 744-4545 | (859) 745-3935 |
| Clay | Clay County Schools | Douglas Adams | 128 Richmond Rd | | Manchester | 40962 | (606) 598-2168 | (606) 598-7829 |
| Clinton | Clinton County Schools | Mickey McFall | Rt 4 Box 100 Hwy 127 | | Albany | 42602 | (606) 387-6480 | (606) 387-5437 |

## SCHOOL BOARDS

| COUNTY | DISTRICT | SUPERINTENDENT | ADDRESS1 | ADDRESS2 | CITY | ZIP | PHONE | FAX |
|---|---|---|---|---|---|---|---|---|
| Crittenden | Crittenden County Schools | John W Belt | 601 W Elm St | PO Box 420 | Marion | 42064 | (270) 965-3525 | (270) 965-9064 |
| Cumberland | Cumberland County Schools | John Hurt | 810 N Main St | PO Box 21510 | Burkesville | 42717 | (270) 864-3377 | (270) 864-5803 |
| Daviess | Daviess County Schools | Tom Shelton | 1622 Southeastern Pkwy | | Owensboro | 42304 | (270) 852-7000 | (270) 852-7010 |
| Daviess | Owensboro Diocese | Jim Mattingly | 600 Locust St | | Owensboro | 42301 | (270) 683-1545 | (270) 683-6883 |
| Daviess | Owensboro Independent Schools | Larry Vick | 1335 W 11th St | PO Box 129 | Owensboro | 42302 | (270) 686-1000 | (270) 684-5756 |
| Edmonson | Edmonson County Schools | Patrick Waddell | 100 Wildcat Way | PO Box 767 | Brownsville | 42210 | (270) 597-2101 | (270) 597-2103 |
| Elliott | Elliott County Schools | John Williams | Main St Chse Sq | PO Box 930 | Sandy Hook | 41171 | (606) 738-8002 | (606) 738-8050 |
| Estill | Estill County Schools | Hilbert Hensley | 253 Main St | | Irvine | 40336 | (606) 723-2181 | (606) 723-6029 |
| Fayette | Fayette County Schools | Stu Silberman | 701 E Main St | | Lexington | 40502 | (859) 381-4104 | (859) 381-4303 |
| Fayette | Lexington Diocese | Bernadette McManigal | 1310 W Main St | | Lexington | 40508 | (859) 253-1993 | (859) 254-6284 |
| Fleming | Fleming County Schools | Kelley F Crain | 211 W Water St | | Flemingsburg | 41041 | (606) 845-5851 | (606) 849-3158 |
| Floyd | Floyd County Schools | Paul W Fanning | 106 N Front Ave | | Prestonsburg | 41653 | (606) 886-2354 | (606) 886-8862 |
| Franklin | Frankfort Independent Schools | Judith M Lucarelli | 309 Shelby St Ste 201 | | Frankfort | 40601 | (502) 875-8661 | (502) 875-8663 |
| Franklin | Franklin County Schools | Monte E Chance (resigning 06/07) | 916 E Main St | | Frankfort | 40601 | (502) 695-6700 | (502) 695-6708 |
| Fulton | Fulton County Schools | Charles Holliday | 2780 Moscow Ave | | Hickman | 42050 | (270) 236-3923 | (270) 236-2184 |
| Fulton | Fulton Independent Schools | Dianne Owen | 313 Main St | | Fulton | 42041 | (270) 472-1553 | (270) 472-6921 |
| Gallatin | Gallatin County Schools | Dorothy Perkins | 600 Main St | PO Box 147 | Warsaw | 41095 | (859) 567-2828 | (859) 567-4528 |
| Garrard | Garrard County Schools | Raymond Woosley | 322 W Maple Ave | | Lancaster | 40444 | (859) 792-3018 | (859) 792-4733 |
| Grant | Grant County Schools | Donald Martin | 820 Arnie Risen Blvd | | Williamstown | 41097 | (859) 824-3323 | (859) 824-3508 |
| Grant | Williamstown Independent Schools | Charles Ed Wilson | 300 Helton St | | Williamstown | 41097 | (859) 824-7144 | (859) 824-3237 |
| Graves | Graves County Schools | Brady M Link Jr | 2290 St Rt 121 N | | Mayfield | 42066 | (270) 328-2666 | (270) 328-1561 |
| Graves | Mayfield Independent Schools | Lonnie Burgett | 709 S 8th St | | Mayfield | 42066 | (270) 247-3968 | (270) 247-3854 |
| Grayson | Grayson County Schools | Barry Anderson | 909 Brandenburg Rd | PO Box 4009 | Leitchfield | 42754 | (270) 259-4011 | (270) 259-4756 |
| Green | Green County Schools | Marshall Lowe | 206 W Court St | PO Box 369 | Greensburg | 42743 | (270) 932-5231 | (270) 932-3624 |
| Greenup | Greenup County Schools | John F Younce | 45 Musketeer Dr | | Greenup | 41144 | (606) 473-9819 | (606) 473-5710 |
| Greenup | Raceland-Worthington Independent Schools | Frank Melvin | 600 Ram Blvd | | Raceland | 41169 | (606) 836-2144 | (606) 833-5807 |
| Greenup | Russell Independent Schools | Susan Compton | 409 Belfont St | | Russell | 41169 | (606) 836-9679 | (606) 836-2865 |
| Hancock | Hancock County Schools | Scott Lewis | 83 St Rt 271 N | | Hawesville | 42348 | (270) 927-6914 | (270) 927-6916 |
| Hardin | Elizabethtown Independent Schools | John Millay | 219 Helm St | | Elizabethtown | 42701 | (270) 765-6146 | (270) 765-2158 |
| Hardin | Fort Knox Community Schools | Todd Curkendall | Crittenberger Central Staff Ofc | 281 Fayette Ave | Ft Knox | 40121 | (502) 624-2345 | (502) 624-4256 |
| Hardin | Hardin County Schools | Nannette Stovall Johnston | 65 W A Jenkins Rd | | Elizabethtown | 42701 | (270) 769-8800 | (270) 769-8888 |
| Hardin | West Point Independent Schools | Pamela Stephens | 209 N 13th St | PO Box 367 | West Point | 40177 | (502) 922-4617 | (502) 922-9372 |
| Harlan | Harlan County Schools | Tim Saylor | 251 Ball Park Rd | | Harlan | 40831 | (606) 573-4330 | (606) 573-5767 |
| Harlan | Harlan Independent Schools | David R Johnson | 420 E Central St | | Harlan | 40831 | (606) 573-8700 | (606) 573-8711 |
| Harrison | Covington Diocese* | Lawrence Bowman | 950 Donaldson Rd | | Erlanger | 41021 | (859) 283-6233 | (859) 283-6240 |
| Harrison | Harrison County Schools | Roy Woodward | 324 Webster Ave | PO Box 18551 | Cynthiana | 41031 | (859) 234-7110 | (859) 234-8164 |
| Hart | Hart County Schools | Ricky Line | 511 W Union St | | Munfordville | 42765 | (270) 524-2631 | (270) 524-2634 |
| Henderson | Henderson County Schools | Thomas Richey | 1805 2nd St | | Henderson | 42420 | (270) 831-5000 | (270) 831-5009 |
| Henry | Eminence Independent Schools | Donald Aldridge | 291 W Broadway | | Eminence | 40019 | (502) 845-5427 | (502) 845-2339 |
| Henry | Henry County Schools | Tim Abrams | 326 S Main St | | New Castle | 40050 | (502) 845-8600 | (502) 845-8601 |
| Hickman | Hickman County Schools | Steve Bayko | 416 Waterfield Dr | | Clinton | 42031 | (270) 653-2341 | (270) 653-6007 |
| Hopkins | Dawson Springs Independent Schools | Alexis Seymore | 118 E Arcadia Ave | | Dawson Springs | 42408 | (270) 797-3811 | (270) 797-5201 |
| Hopkins | Hopkins County Schools | James L Stevens | 320 S Seminary St | | Madisonville | 42431 | (270) 825-6100 | (270) 825-6062 |
| Jackson | Jackson County Schools | Ralph Hoskins | | PO Box 217 | McKee | 40447 | (606) 287-7181 | (606) 287-8469 |
| Jefferson | Anchorage Independent Schools | Larry R Harrison | 11400 Ridge Rd | | Anchorage | 40223 | (502) 245-8927 | (502) 245-2124 |
| Jefferson | Jefferson County Schools | Stephen Daeschner | 3332 Newburg Rd | PO Box 34020 | Louisville | 40232 | (502) 485-3011 | (502) 485-3991 |
| Jefferson | Louisville Diocese | Leisa Speer | Flaget Ctr | 1935 Lewiston Dr | Louisville | 40216 | (502) 448-8581 | (502) 448-5518 |
| Jessamine | Jessamine County Schools | Lu S Young | 871 Wilmore Rd | | Nicholasville | 40356 | (859) 885-4179 | (859) 887-4811 |

# SCHOOL BOARDS

| COUNTY | DISTRICT | SUPERINTENDENT | ADDRESS1 | ADDRESS2 | CITY | ZIP | PHONE | FAX |
|---|---|---|---|---|---|---|---|---|
| Johnson | Johnson County Schools | Steve Trimble | 253 N Mayo Trl | | Paintsville | 41240 | (606) 789-2530 | (606) 789-2506 |
| Johnson | Paintsville Independent Schools | Coy D Samons | 305 2nd St | | Paintsville | 41240 | (606) 789-2654 | (606) 789-7412 |
| Kenton | Beechwood Independent Schools | Fred Bassett | 50 Beechwood Rd | | Ft Mitchell | 41017 | (859) 331-3250 | (859) 331-7528 |
| Kenton | Covington Diocese* | Lawrence Bowman | 951 Donaldson Rd | PO Box 18552 | Erlanger | 41022 | (859) 283-6234 | (859) 283-6241 |
| Kenton | Covington Independent Schools | Jack Moreland | 25 E 7th St | | Covington | 41011 | (859) 392-1000 | (859) 292-5916 |
| Kenton | Erlanger-Elsmere Independent Schools | Michael Sander | 500 Graves Ave | | Erlanger | 41018 | (859) 727-2009 | (859) 727-5653 |
| Kenton | Kenton County Schools | Thomas T Hanner | 1055 Eaton Dr | | Ft Wright | 41017 | (859) 344-8888 | (859) 344-1531 |
| Kenton | Ludlow Independent Schools | Curtis Hall | 525 Elm St | | Ludlow | 41016 | (859) 261-8210 | (859) 291-6811 |
| Knott | Knott County Schools | Harold Combs | Rt 160 | | Hindman | 41822 | (606) 785-3153 | (606) 785-0800 |
| Knox | Barbourville Independent Schools | Larry Warren | 200 Daniel Boone Dr | | Barbourville | 40906 | (606) 546-3120 | (606) 546-3452 |
| Knox | Knox County Schools | Walter "T" Hulett | 208 College St | | Barbourville | 40906 | (606) 546-3157 | (606) 546-2819 |
| Larue | Larue County Schools | Sam Sanders | 296 E Hwy 30 | | Hodgenville | 42748 | (270) 358-4111 | (270) 358-3053 |
| Laurel | East Bernstadt Independent Schools | Homer Radford Jr | 275 S Laurel Rd | PO Box 128 | East Bernstadt | 40729 | (606) 843-7373 | (606) 843-6249 |
| Laurel | Laurel County Schools | Vacant | 50 Bulldog Ln | | London | 40744 | (606) 862-4600 | (606) 862-4601 |
| Lawrence | Lawrence County Schools | Jeff May | 242 Lee Ave | PO Box 607 | Louisa | 41230 | (606) 638-9671 | (606) 638-0128 |
| Lee | Lee County Schools | Frank Kincaid | 108 Maple St | PO Box 668 | Beattyville | 41311 | (606) 464-5000 | (606) 464-5009 |
| Leslie | Leslie County Schools | Larry Sparks | 9409 Hwy 805 | PO Box 949 | Hyden | 41749 | (606) 672-2397 | (606) 672-4224 |
| Letcher | Jenkins Independent Schools | John Shook | 224 Park St | PO Box 74 | Jenkins | 41537 | (606) 832-2183 | (606) 832-2181 |
| Letcher | Letcher County Schools | Anna Craft | 520 Plomann Ln | PO Box 159 | Whitesburg | 41858 | (606) 633-4455 | (606) 633-4724 |
| Lewis | Lewis County Schools | Maurice Reeder Jr | 305 Danville Ave | PO Box 265 | Vanceburg | 41179 | (606) 796-2811 | (606) 796-3061 |
| Lincoln | Lincoln County Schools | Teresa T Wallace | 2222 Bowling Green Rd | PO Box 219 | Stanford | 40484 | (606) 365-2124 | (606) 365-1660 |
| Livingston | Livingston County Schools | Jack Monroe | 355 S Summer St | | Smithland | 42081 | (270) 928-2111 | (270) 928-2112 |
| Logan | Logan County Schools | Marshall Kemp | 217 Jenkins Rd | PO Box 417 | Russellville | 42276 | (270) 726-2436 | (270) 726-8892 |
| Logan | Russellville Independent Schools | Roger D Cook | 3 Pirate Pkwy | | Russellville | 42276 | (270) 726-8405 | (270) 726-4036 |
| Lyon | Lyon County Schools | Lee Gold | 550 S Keeneland Dr | | Eddyville | 42038 | (270) 388-9715 | (270) 388-4962 |
| Madison | Berea Independent Schools | Gary Conkin | 109 Gardner Trr | PO Box 768 | Berea | 40403 | (859) 986-8446 | (859) 986-1839 |
| Madison | Madison County Schools | Mike Caudill | 755 E Main St | PO Box 109 | Richmond | 40476 | (859) 624-4500 | (859) 624-4508 |
| Magoffin | Magoffin County Schools | Joe Hunley | 86 High School Rd | | Salyersville | 41465 | (606) 349-6117 | (606) 349-3417 |
| Marion | Marion County Schools | Roger L Marcum | Rt 40 | | Lebanon | 40033 | (270) 692-3721 | (270) 692-1899 |
| Marshall | Marshall County Schools | Stephen Knight | 952 Donaldson Rd | PO Box 366 | Benton | 42025 | (270) 527-8628 | (270) 527-0804 |
| Martin | Martin County Schools | Mark Blackburn | 2nd & Limestone St | PO Box 18553 | Inez | 41224 | (606) 298-3572 | (606) 298-4427 |
| Mason | Covington Diocese* | Lawrence Bowman | 435 Berger Rd | PO Box 130 | Erlanger | 41023 | (859) 283-6235 | (859) 283-6242 |
| Mason | Mason County Schools | Tim Moore | 800 Caldwell St | | Maysville | 41056 | (606) 564-5563 | (606) 564-5392 |
| McCracken | McCracken County Schools | Tim Heller | 120 Raider Way | PO Box 2550 | Paducah | 42003 | (270) 538-4000 | (270) 538-4001 |
| McCracken | Paducah Independent Schools | Randy Greene | 283 Main St | | Paducah | 42002 | (270) 444-5600 | (270) 444-5607 |
| McCreary | McCreary County Schools | Ray M Ball | 1155 Old Ekron Rd | PO Box 245 | Stearns | 42647 | (606) 376-2591 | (606) 376-5584 |
| McLean | McLean County Schools | William Earl Melloy | 202 Back St | PO Box 337 | Calhoun | 42327 | (270) 273-5257 | (270) 273-5259 |
| Meade | Meade County Schools | Mitchell Crump | 140 Burgin/Danville Rd | PO Box 110 | Brandenburg | 40108 | (270) 422-7500 | (270) 422-5494 |
| Menifee | Menifee County Schools | Charles Mitchell | 371 E Lexington St | PO Box B | Frenchburg | 40322 | (606) 768-8002 | (606) 768-8050 |
| Mercer | Burgin Independent Schools | Richard Webb | | | Burgin | 40310 | (859) 748-4000 | (859) 748-4010 |
| Mercer | Harrodsburg Independent Schools | H M Snodgrass (Retiring 6/30/06) | 961 Moberly Rd | | Harrodsburg | 40330 | (859) 734-4364 | (859) 734-8404 |
| Mercer | Mercer County Schools | Bruce Johnson | 1007 W Stockton St | | Harrodsburg | 40330 | (859) 734-4364 | (859) 734-4852 |
| Metcalfe | Metcalfe County Schools | Pat Hurt | 309 Emberton St | PO Box 10 | Edmonton | 42129 | (270) 432-3171 | (270) 432-3170 |
| Monroe | Monroe County Schools | George Wilson | 700 Woodford Dr | | Tompkinsville | 42167 | (270) 487-5456 | (270) 487-5571 |
| Montgomery | Montgomery County Schools | Daniel Freeman | 460 Prestonsburg St | | Mt Sterling | 40353 | (859) 497-8760 | (859) 497-8780 |
| Morgan | Morgan County Schools | Joe Dan Gold | 510 W Main St | PO Box 489 | West Liberty | 41472 | (606) 743-8002 | (606) 743-8050 |
| Muhlenberg | Muhlenberg County Schools | R Dale Todd | 308 N 5th St | | Powderly | 42367 | (270) 338-2871 | (270) 338-0529 |
| Nelson | Bardstown Independent Schools | Brent Holsclaw | 1200 Cardinal Dr | | Bardstown | 40004 | (502) 331-8800 | (502) 331-8830 |
| Nelson | Nelson County Schools | Janice Lantz | | PO Box 2277 | Bardstown | 40004 | (502) 349-7000 | (502) 349-7004 |

## SCHOOL BOARDS

| COUNTY | DISTRICT | SUPERINTENDENT | ADDRESS1 | ADDRESS2 | CITY | ZIP | PHONE | FAX |
|---|---|---|---|---|---|---|---|---|
| Nicholas | Nicholas County Schools | Gregory A Reid | 395 W Main St | | Carlisle | 40311 | (859) 289-3770 | (859) 289-3777 |
| Ohio | Ohio County Schools | Soretta Ralph | 315 E Union St | PO Box 70 | Hartford | 42347 | (270) 298-3249 | (270) 298-3886 |
| Oldham | Oldham County Schools | Paul S Upchurch | 1350 N Hwy 393 | PO Box 218 | Buckner | 40010 | (502) 222-8880 | (502) 222-8885 |
| Owen | Owen County Schools | Mark Cleveland | 1600 Hwy 22 E | | Owenton | 40359 | (502) 484-3934 | (502) 484-9095 |
| Owsley | Owsley County Schools | Stephen Jackson | Court & Main | | Booneville | 41314 | (606) 593-6363 | (606) 593-6368 |
| Pendleton | Pendleton County Schools | J Robert Yost | 2525 Hwy 27 N | | Falmouth | 41040 | (859) 654-6911 | (859) 654-6143 |
| Perry | Hazard Independent Schools | Sandra Johnson | 325 Broadway | | Hazard | 41701 | (606) 436-3911 | (606) 436-2742 |
| Perry | Perry County Schools | John Paul Amis | 315 Park Ave | | Hazard | 41701 | (606) 439-5813 | (606) 439-2512 |
| Pike | Pike County Schools | Thomas Roger Wagner | 314 S Mayo Tr | PO Box 3097 | Pikeville | 41502 | (606) 433-9200 | (606) 432-3321 |
| Pike | Pikeville Independent Schools | Jerry Green | 401 N Mayo Trl | | Pikeville | 41501 | (606) 432-8161 | (606) 432-2119 |
| Powell | Powell County Schools | Lonnie Morris | 691 Breckinridge St | | Stanton | 40380 | (606) 663-3300 | (606) 663-3303 |
| Pulaski | Pulaski County Schools | Tim Eaton | 501 University Dr | PO Box 430 | Somerset | 42502 | (606) 679-1123 | (606) 679-1438 |
| Pulaski | Science Hill Independent Schools | Rick Walker | 6007 N Hwy 27 | | Science Hill | 42553 | (606) 423-3341 | (606) 423-3313 |
| Pulaski | Somerset Independent Schools | Wilson Sears Jr. | 305 N College St | PO Box 1055 | Somerset | 42502 | (606) 679-4451 | (606) 678-0864 |
| Robertson | Robertson County Schools | Charles Brown | Main St | PO Box 108 | Mt Olivet | 41064 | (606) 724-5431 | (606) 724-5921 |
| Rockcastle | Rockcastle County Schools | Larry Hammond | 245 Richmond St | | Mt Vernon | 40456 | (606) 256-2125 | (606) 256-2126 |
| Rowan | Rowan County Schools | Marvin Moore | 121 E 2nd St | | Morehead | 40351 | (606) 784-8928 | (606) 783-1011 |
| Russell | Russell County Schools | Scott Pierce | 404 S Main St | PO Box 440 | Jamestown | 42629 | (270) 343-3191 | (270) 343-3072 |
| Scott | Scott County Schools | Dallas J Blankenship | 2168 Frankfort Pk | PO Box 578 | Georgetown | 40324 | (502) 863-3663 | (502) 863-5367 |
| Shelby | Shelby County Schools | Elaine Farris | 1155 W Main St | PO Box 159 | Shelbyville | 40066 | (502) 633-2375 | (502) 633-1988 |
| Simpson | Simpson County Schools | Jim Flynn | 430 S College St | PO Box 467 | Franklin | 42135 | (270) 586-8877 | (270) 586-2011 |
| Spencer | Spencer County Schools | R Larry Holt | 207 W Main St | | Taylorsville | 40071 | (502) 477-3250 | (502) 477-3259 |
| Taylor | Campbellsville Independent Schools | Diana W Woods | 136 S Columbia Ave | | Campbellsville | 42718 | (270) 465-4162 | (270) 465-3918 |
| Taylor | Taylor County Schools | Gary Seaborne | 1209 E Broadway | | Campbellsville | 42718 | (270) 465-5371 | (270) 789-3994 |
| Todd | Todd County Schools | David A Eakles (retiring 8/1/06) | 804 S Main St | | Elkton | 42220 | (270) 265-2436 | (270) 265-5414 |
| Trigg | Trigg County Schools | Tim McGinnis | 202 Main St | | Cadiz | 42211 | (270) 522-6075 | (270) 522-7782 |
| Trimble | Trimble County Schools | Marcia Haney-Dunaway | 68 Wentworth Ave | PO Box 275 | Bedford | 40006 | (502) 255-3201 | (502) 255-5105 |
| Union | Union County Schools | Gerald Novak | 510 S Mart St | | Morganfield | 42437 | (270) 389-1694 | (270) 389-9806 |
| Warren | Bowling Green Independent Schools | Joe Tinius | 1211 Center St | | Bowling Green | 42101 | (270) 746-2200 | (270) 746-2205 |
| Warren | Warren County Schools | Dale Brown | 303 Lover's Ln | PO Box 51810 | Bowling Green | 42102 | (270) 781-5150 | (270) 781-2392 |
| Washington | Washington County Schools | Larry Graves | 120 Mackville Hill Rd | | Springfield | 40069 | (859) 336-5470 | (859) 336-5480 |
| Wayne | Monticello Independent Schools | Donnie Robison | 132 College St | | Monticello | 42633 | (606) 348-5311 | (606) 348-3664 |
| Wayne | Wayne County Schools | John Dalton | 534 Albany Rd | | Monticello | 42633 | (606) 348-8484 | (606) 348-0734 |
| Webster | Providence Independent Schools | Edwina Slack | 302 W Main St | | Providence | 42450 | (270) 667-7007 | (270) 667-7606 |
| Webster | Webster County Schools | James Kemp | 28 St Rt 1340 | | Dixon | 42409 | (270) 639-5083 | (270) 639-0117 |
| Whitley | Corbin Independent Schools | Marion (Ed) McNeel | 108 Roy Kidd Ave | | Corbin | 40701 | (606) 528-1303 | (606) 523-1747 |
| Whitley | Whitley County Schools | Lonnie Anderson | 300 Main St | | Williamsburg | 40769 | (606) 549-7000 | (606) 549-7006 |
| Whitley | Williamsburg Independent Schools | Dennis Byrd | 1000 Main St | | Williamsburg | 40769 | (606) 549-6044 | (606) 549-6076 |
| Wolfe | Wolfe County Schools | Stephen Butcher | Main St | PO Box 160 | Campton | 41301 | (606) 668-8002 | (606) 668-8050 |
| Woodford | Woodford County Schools | Paul Stahler | 330 Pisgah Pk | | Versailles | 40383 | (859) 873-4701 | (859) 873-1614 |

*Source: The Kentucky Directory Gold Book 2006-2007*

\* *The Covington Dioceses serves Boone, Bracken, Campbell, Harrison, Kenton and Mason counties*

# County & Independent School Districts

*Independent districts indicated with italicized type*

**120 School Districts**
**56 Independent School Districts**

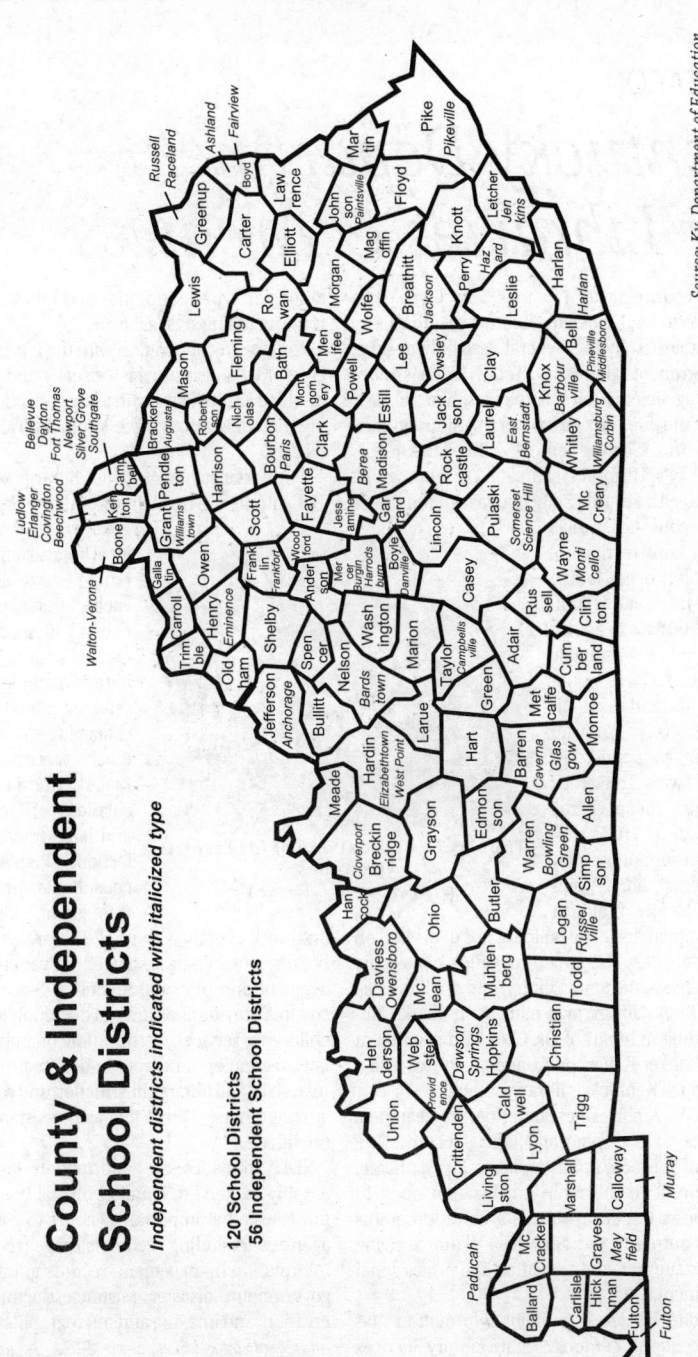

*Source: Ky. Department of Education*

## EDUCATION

# *Kentucky Department for Libraries & Archives*

The Department for Libraries & Archives dates its origins to 1825, when the Kentucky State Library was established by the General Assembly to serve the government in Frankfort. Today, KDLA is one of 10 state agencies in the U.S. that combines library, archival and public records programs, and is guided by the motto, "Serving Kentucky's Need to Know."

Kentucky's Historian Laureate Dr. Thomas D. Clark played a key role in the passage of the state's public records law in 1958 and in construction of KDLA. Clark began lobbying governors and legislators in the 1930s to appropriate funds for a suitable home for the state's public records and pled his case to every governor over a 40-year period. His tenacity was rewarded when Gov. Julian Carroll supported a $10.5 million appropriation for a combined library and archival facility of almost 140,000 square feet. The building was dedicated on October 8, 1982. The structure, which houses the State Archives, the State Library, and the Kentucky Talking Book Library, was named the Clark-Cooper building in honor of Dr. Clark and prominent Hazard banker C. Vernon Cooper, who was also a champion of Kentucky's library system.

**Thomas D. Clark at one of his favorite pastimes**
*Source: Jim Cummings, Pioneer Times*

At KDLA's Archives Research Room, researchers find access to local, state, and judicial records. The Friends of Kentucky Public Archives, Inc., a private, not-for-profit membership organization open to all, supports the department's archival programs through outreach and advocacy, planned giving and fiscal support, and education and professional development.

The State Library is a major information and referral center in Kentucky. State Library Services maintains information and resources sharing among all types of libraries and information centers – including state agencies.

Working in cooperation with the Library of Congress, KDLA also provides visually and physically disabled Kentuckians with a large selection of reading materials through the Kentucky Talking Book Library.

Kentuckians have public library services in 118 counties. The abilities of these libraries vary greatly; KDLA works with local library staffs and governing boards to enhance each public library's efforts. Resources available to Kentucky's public libraries include: reference services, interlibrary loan, cataloging assistance, quick access through KDLA's website, and circulation of multimedia and large print book collections. Regional library consultants are located throughout the state, and work directly with public librarians and their boards, providing assistance in a variety of management and planning functions. Statewide consultants provide assistance in bookmobile services, children's services, certification of public librarians, technology and automation, conservation of materials, and library construction and renovation, among others. Direct financial assistance is also provided.

KDLA provides the information government employees need to conduct official business and furnishes other important services to government agencies, including records storage, records and information management, records grants to local governments, disaster assistance, document preservation, and imaging and micrographics.

*Additional information about KDLA is available at http://www.kdla.ky.gov.*

# PUBLIC LIBRARIES

| LIBRARY | ADDRESS1 | ADDRESS2 | CITY, ZIP | PHONE | WEBSITE |
|---|---|---|---|---|---|
| Adair County Public Library | 307 Greensburg St | | Columbia, 42728 | 270-384-2472 | http://www.allencountylibrary.com/ |
| Allen County Public Library | 106 West Main St | | Scottsville, 42164 | 270-237-3861 | http://www.allencountylibrary.com/ |
| Anderson County Public Library | 114 North Main St | | Lawrenceburg, 40342 | 502-839-6420 | http://www.andersonpubliclibrary.org/ |
| Ballard/Carlisle/Livingston Public Library System | 24 West Main St | P.O. Box 428 | Bardwell, 42023 | 270-335-5059 | |
| Bath County Memorial Library | 8899 U.S. 42 | P.O. Box 380 | Owingsville, 40360 | 606-674-2531 | http://www.youseemore.com/bath/ |
| Boone County Public Library | | | Union, 41091 | 859-384-5550 | http://www.bcpl.org/ |
| Bowling Green Public Library | 1225 State St | | Bowling Green, 42101 | 270-781-4882 | http://www.bgpl.org/ |
| Boyd County Public Library | 1740 Central Ave | | Ashland, 41101 | 606-329-0090 | http://www.thebookplace.org/ |
| Bracken County Public Library | 310 West Miami St | | Brooksville, 41004 | 606-735-3620 | http://brackenlibrary.com |
| Breathitt County Public Library | 1024 College Ave | P.O. Box 305 | Jackson, 41339 | 606-666-5541 | http://www.breathittcountylibrary.com/ |
| Breckinridge County Public Library | 112 South Main St | P.O. Box 248 | Hardinsburg, 40143 | 270-756-2323 | |
| Butler County Public Library | 116 West Ohio St | P.O. Box 247 | Morgantown, 42261 | 270-526-4722 | |
| Calloway County Public Library | 710 Main St | | Murray, 42071 | 270-753-2288 | http://www.cc-pl.org/ |
| Campbell County Public Library | 3920 Alexandria Pike | | Cold Spring, 41076 | 859-781-6166 | http://www.carrollcolibrary.org |
| Carroll County Public Library | 136 Court St | | Carrollton, 41008 | 502-732-7020 | http://www.carrollcolibrary.org |
| Casey County Public Library | 238 Middleburg St | | Liberty, 42539 | 606-787-9381 | http://www.caseylibrary.org/ |
| Clark County Public Library | 370 South Burns Ave | | Winchester, 40391 | 859-744-5661 | http://www.clarkpublib.org |
| Clay County Public Library | 211 Bridge St | | Manchester, 40962 | 606-598-2617 | http://www.claycountypubliclibrary.org |
| Clinton County Public Library | 302 King Dr | | Albany, 42602 | 606-387-5989 | |
| Crittenden County Public Library | 204 West Carlisle St | | Marion, 42064 | 270-965-3354 | http://www.cumberlandlibrarylcd.com |
| Cumberland County Public Library | 114 Hill St | P.O. Box 440 | Burkesville, 42717 | 270-864-2207 | http://www.cumberlandlibrarylcd.com |
| Cynthiana-Harrison County Public Library | 104 North Main St | | Cynthiana, 41031 | 859-234-4881 | http://harrisonlibrary.org/ |
| Daviess County Public Library | 450 Griffith Ave | | Owensboro, 42301 | 270-684-0211 | http://www.dcpl.lib.ky.us/ |
| Duerson-Oldham Co. Public Library | 106 East Jefferson St | | LaGrange, 40031 | 502-222-1141 | http://www.oldhampl.org/ |
| Edmonson County Public Library | 503 Washington St | | Brownsville, 42210 | 270-597-2146 | |
| Estill County Public Library | 246 Main St | | Irvine, 40336 | 606-723-3030 | http://www.youseemore.com/estill/ |
| Fleming County Public Library | 303 South Main Cross | | Flemingsburg, 41041 | 606-845-7851 | http://www.youseemore.com/fleming |
| Floyd County Public Library | 161 North Arnold Ave | | Prestonsburg, 41653 | 606-886-2981 | http://www.fclib.org/ |
| Fulton County Public Library | 312 Main St | | Fulton, 42041 | 270-472-3439 | http://www.fultonlibrary.com |
| Gallatin County Public Library | 209 West Market St | P.O. Box 848 | Warsaw, 41095 | 859-567-2786 | http://www.gallatincountylibrary.org/ |
| Garrard County Public Library | 101 Lexington St | | Lancaster, 40444 | 859-792-3424 | http://garrardpublib.state.ky.us/ |
| George Coon Public Library | 114 South Harrison St | P.O. Box 230 | Princeton, 42445 | 270-365-2884 | |
| Goodnight Memorial Library | 203 South Main St | | Franklin, 42134 | 270-586-8397 | http://www.goodnightlibrary.org/ |
| Grant County Public Library | 201 Barnes Rd | | Williamstown, 41097 | 859-824-2080 | http://www.grantcountypubliclibrary.org |
| Graves County Public Library | 601 North 17th St | | Mayfield, 42066 | 270-247-2911 | http://www.gcpl.org |
| Grayson County Public Library | 130 East Market St | | Leitchfield, 42754 | 270-259-5455 | http://www.graysoncountylibrary.org |
| Green County Public Library | 116 South Main St | | Greensburg, 42743 | 270-932-7081 | http://www.gcpl.info |
| Greenup County Public Library | 614 Main St | | Greenup, 41144 | 606-473-6514 | http://greenuplib.state.ky.us/ |
| Hancock County Public Library | 240 Court Square | P.O. Box 249 | Hawesville, 42348 | 270-927-6760 | http://www.hancockcopubliclibrary.ky.gov |
| Hardin County Public Library | 100 Jim Owen Dr | | Elizabethtown, 42701 | 270-769-6337 | http://www.hcpl.info/ |
| Harlan County Public Library | 107 North Third St | | Harlan, 40831 | 606-573-5220 | http://www.harlancountylibraries.org/ |
| Harry M. Caudill Memorial Library | 220 East Main St | | Whitesburg, 41858 | 606-633-7547 | http://lcld.org |
| Hart County Public Library | 500 East Union St | P.O. Box 337 | Munfordville, 42765 | 270-524-1953 | http://www.hartcountypubliclibrary.org |
| Harvey Helm Memorial Library | 301 Third St | | Stanford, 40484 | 606-365-7513 | |
| Helen H. Rayburn Public Library | 422 Second St | | Vanceburg, 41179 | 606-796-2532 | |
| Henderson County Public Library | 101 South Main St | | Henderson, 42420 | 270-826-3712 | http://www.hcpl.org/ |

# PUBLIC LIBRARIES

| LIBRARY | ADDRESS1 | ADDRESS2 | CITY, ZIP | PHONE | WEBSITE |
|---|---|---|---|---|---|
| Henry County Public Library | 172 Eminence Terrace | | Eminence, 40019 | 502-845-5682 | http://www.youseemore.com/henry |
| Hickman County Memorial Library | 209 Mayfield Rd | | Clinton, 42031 | 270-653-2225 | |
| Hopkins County–Madisonville Public Library | 31 South Main St | | Madisonville, 42431 | 270-825-2680 | http://www.publiclibrary.org/ |
| Hopkinsville-Christian County Library | 1101 Bethel St | | Hopkinsville, 42240 | 270-887-4263 | http://hccpl.org |
| Jackson County Public Library | Second St | P.O. Box 160 | McKee, 40447 | 606-287-8113 | |
| Jessamine County Public Library | 600 South Main St | | Nicholasville, 40356 | 859-885-3523 | http://www.jesspublib.org/ |
| Johnson County Public Library | 444 Main St | | Paintsville, 41240 | 606-789-4355 | http://mywebpage.netscape.com/johnsoncolibrary/ |
| Kenton County Public Library System | 502 Scott Blvd | | Covington, 41011 | 859-962-4060 | http://www.kenton.lib.ky.us/ |
| Knott County Public Library | 238 Route 160 | P.O. Box 667 | Hindman, 41822 | 606-785-5412 | |
| Knox County Public Library | 206 Knox St | | Barbourville, 40906 | 606-546-5339 | |
| LaRue County Public Library | 201 South Lincoln Blvd | | Hodgenville, 42748 | 270-358-3851 | http://www.laruelibrary.org |
| Laurel County Public Library | 120 College Park Dr | | London, 40741 | 606-864-5759 | http://laurelcountypubliclibrary.org |
| Lawrence County Public Library | 102 West Main and Jefferson | P.O. Box 600 | Louisa, 41230 | 606-638-4497 | http://lawrencecountypubliclibrary.org |
| Lee County Public Library | 123 Center St | P.O. Box V | Beattyville, 41311 | 606-464-8014 | |
| Leslie County Public Library | 22065 Main St | P.O. Box 498 | Hyden, 41749 | 606-672-2460 | |
| Lexington Public Library | 140 East Main St | | Lexington, 40507 | 859-231-5504 | http://www.lexpublib.org/ |
| Lexington Public Library - Beaumont Branch | 3080 Fieldstone Way | | Lexington, 40513 | 859-231-5570 | http://www.lexpublib.org/ |
| Lexington Public Library - Eagle Creek Branch | 101 North Eagle Creek Dr | | Lexington, 40509 | 859-231-5560 | http://www.lexpublib.org/ |
| Lexington Public Library - Northside Branch | 1737 Russell Cave Rd | | Lexington, 40505 | 859-231-5590 | http://www.lexpublib.org/ |
| Lexington Public Library - Tates Creek Branch | 3628 Walden Dr | | Lexington, 40517 | 859-231-5580 | http://www.lexpublib.org/ |
| Lexington Public Library - Village Branch | 2185 Versailles Rd | | Lexington, 40504 | 859-231-5575 | http://www.lexpublib.org/ |
| Logan County Public Library | 201 West Sixth St | | Russellville, 42276 | 270-726-6129 | http://www.loganlibrary.org/ |
| Louisville Free Public Library | 301 York St | | Louisville, 40203 | 502-574-1600 | http://www.lfpl.org/ |
| Louisville Free Public Library - Bon Air Regional Branch | 2816 Del Rio Place | | Louisville, 40220 | 502-574-1795 | http://www.lfpl.org/ |
| Louisville Free Public Library - Crescent Hill Branch | 2762 Frankfort Ave | | Louisville, 40206 | 502-574-1793 | http://www.lfpl.org/ |
| Louisville Free Public Library - Fairdale Branch | 10616 West Manslick Rd | | Fairdale, 40118 | 502-375-2051 | http://www.lfpl.org/ |
| Louisville Free Public Library - Fern Creek Branch | 6768 Bardstown Rd | | Louisville, 40291 | 502-231-4605 | http://www.lfpl.org/ |
| Louisville Free Public Library - Highlands-Shelby Park Branch | 1250 Bardstown Rd | | Louisville, 40204 | 502-574-1672 | http://www.lfpl.org/ |
| Louisville Free Public Library - Iroquois Branch | 601 West Woodlawn Ave | | Louisville, 40215 | 502-574-1720 | http://www.lfpl.org/ |
| Louisville Free Public Library - Jeffersontown Branch | 10635 Watterson Trail | | Louisville, 40299 | 502-267-5713 | http://www.lfpl.org/ |
| Louisville Free Public Library - Middletown Branch | 200 North Juneau Dr | | Louisville, 40243 | 502-245-7332 | http://www.lfpl.org/ |
| Louisville Free Public Library - Okolona Branch | 7709 Preston Hwy | | Louisville, 40219 | 502-964-3515 | http://www.lfpl.org/ |
| Louisville Free Public Library - Portland Branch | 3305 Northwestern Pkwy | | Louisville, 40212 | 502-574-1744 | http://www.lfpl.org/ |
| Louisville Free Public Library - Saint Matthews/Eline Branch | 3940 Grandview Ave | | Louisville, 40207 | 502-574-1771 | http://www.lfpl.org/ |
| Louisville Free Public Library - Shawnee Branch | 3912 West Broadway | | Louisville, 40211 | 502-574-1722 | http://www.lfpl.org/ |
| Louisville Free Public Library - Shively/Newman Branch | 3920 Dixie Hwy | | Louisville, 40216 | 502-574-1730 | http://www.lfpl.org/ |
| Louisville Free Public Library - Southwest Regional Branch | 10375 Dixie Hwy | | Louisville, 40272 | 502-933-0029 | http://www.lfpl.org/ |
| Louisville Free Public Library - Western Branch | 604 South Tenth St | | Louisville, 40203 | 502-574-1779 | http://www.lfpl.org/ |
| Louisville Free Public Library - Westport Community Library | Westport Middle School | 8100 Westport | Louisville, 40222 | 502-394-0379 | http://www.lfpl.org/ |
| Lyon County Public Library | 261 Commerce St | P.O. Box 546 | Eddyville, 42038 | 270-388-7720 | |
| Madison County Public Library | 507 West Main St | | Richmond, 40475 | 859-623-6704 | http://www.madisonlibrary.org/ |
| Magoffin County Public Library | 141 Church St | P.O. Box 435 | Salyersville, 41465 | 606-349-2411 | |
| Marion County Public Library | 201 East Main St | | Lebanon, 40033 | 270-692-4698 | http://geocities.com/marioncountypubliclibrary/ |
| Marshall County Public Library | 1003 Poplar St | | Benton, 42025 | 270-527-9969 | http://www.marshallcolibrary.org |
| Martin County Public Library | Main St | P.O. Box 1318 | Inez, 41224 | 606-298-7766 | |
| Mary Wood Weldon Memorial Public Library | 107 West College St | | Glasgow, 42141 | 270-651-2824 | http://www.weldonpubliclibrary.org |

# PUBLIC LIBRARIES

| LIBRARY | ADDRESS1 | ADDRESS2 | CITY ZIP | PHONE | WEBSITE |
|---|---|---|---|---|---|
| Mason County Public Library | 218 East Third St | | Maysville, 41056 | 606-564-3286 | http://maysvillelibrary.com/ |
| McCracken County Public Library | 555 Washington St | | Paducah, 42003 | 270-442-2510 | http://www.mclib.net/ |
| McCreary County Public Library | 6 North Main St | P.O. Box 8 | Whitley City, 42653 | 606-376-8738 | http://www.mccrearylibrary.org/ |
| Meade County Public Library | 400 Library Place | | Brandenburg, 40108 | 270-422-2094 | http://www.meadereads.org/ |
| Menifee County Public Library | P.O. Box 49 | 1585 Main St | Frenchburg, 40322 | 606-768-2212 | |
| Mercer County Public Library | 109 West Lexington St | | Harrodsburg, 40330 | 859-734-3680 | http://www.mcplib.info/ |
| Metcalfe County Public Library | 200 South Main St | P.O. Box 626 | Edmonton, 42129 | 270-432-4981 | http://www.scrtc.com/~metcolib/ |
| Middlesborough–Bell Co. Public Library | 126 South 20th St | P.O. Box 1677 | Middlesborough, 40965 | 606-248-4812 | http://www.bellcountypubliclibraries.org |
| Morgan County Public Library | 151 University Ave | | West Liberty, 41472 | 606-743-4151 | http://www.youseemore.com/mcpl/ |
| Mount Sterling-Montgomery County Public Library | 241 West Locust St | | Mount Sterling, 40353 | 859-498-2404 | http://www.youseemore.com/mtsterling/ |
| Muhlenberg County - Central City Public Library | 108 East Broad St | | Central City, 42330 | 270-754-4630 | |
| Nelson County Public Library | 90 Court Square | | Bardstown, 40004 | 502-348-3714 | http://www.nelsoncopublib.org/ |
| Nicholas County Memorial Library | 223 North Broadway St | | Carlisle, 40311 | 859-289-5595 | http://www.nicholascountylibrary.com/ |
| Ohio County Public Library | 413 Main St | | Hartford, 42347 | 270-298-3790 | http://www.youseemore.com/Owen/ |
| Owen County Public Library | 118 North Main St | | Owenton, 40359 | 502-484-3450 | |
| Owsley County Public Library | #2 Action Place | P.O. Box 280 | Booneville, 41314 | 606-593-5700 | http://bourbonlibrary.org |
| Paris–Bourbon County Public Library | 701 High St | | Paris, 40361 | 859-987-4419 | http://www.pspl.org/ |
| Paul Sawyier Public Library | 305 Wapping St | | Frankfort, 40601 | 502-223-1658 | |
| Pendleton County Public Library | 228 Main St | P.O. Box 928 | Falmouth, 41040 | 859-654-8535 | http://perrycountylibrary.org |
| Perry County Public Library | 479 High St | P.O. Box 471 | Hazard, 41701 | 606-436-2475 | |
| Pikeville Public Library | 119 College St | | Pikeville, 41502 | 606-432-1285 | |
| Powell County Public Library | 725 Breckenridge St | | Stanton, 40380 | 606-663-4511 | http://www.geocities.com/powellcountylibrary |
| Pulaski County Public Library | 107 North Main St | P.O. Box 36 | Somerset, 42502 | 606-679-8401 | |
| Ridgway Memorial Library | 127 North Walnut St | P.O. Box 146 | Shepherdsville, 40165 | 502-543-7675 | http://www.bcplib.org |
| Robertson County Public Library | 148 North Main St | P.O. Box 282 | Mount Olivet, 41064 | 606-724-5746 | http://www.rcpl.state.ky.us/ |
| Rockcastle County Public Library | 60 Ford Dr | | Mount Vernon, 40456 | 606-256-2388 | http://www.rockcastlelibrary.com/ |
| Rocky J. Adkins Public Library | Main St | P.O. Box 750 | Sandy Hook, 41171 | 606-738-5796 | |
| Rowan County Public Library | 185 East First St | | Morehead, 40351 | 606-784-7137 | http://www.youseemore.com/rowan/ |
| Russell County Public Library | 94 North Main St | P.O. Box 970 | Jamestown, 42629 | 270-343-3545 | http://www.russellcountylibrary.com/ |
| Scott County Public Library | 104 South Bradford Lane | | Georgetown, 40324 | 502-863-3566 | http://www.scottpublib.org/ |
| Shelby County Public Library | 309 Eighth St | | Shelbyville, 40065 | 502-633-3803 | http://www.scplibrary.net |
| Spencer County Public Library | 168 Taylorsville Rd | | Taylorsville, 40071 | 502-477-8137 | http://members.iglou.com/scpl/ |
| Taylor County Public Library | 205 North Columbia Ave | | Campbellsville, 42718 | 270-465-2562 | http://www.taylorcountypubliclibrary.org/ |
| Todd County Public Library | 302 East Main St | | Elkton, 42220 | 270-265-9071 | http://www.angelfire.com/ky/toddcopl/ |
| Trigg County - John L. Street Library | 244 Main St | | Cadiz, 42211 | 270-522-6301 | http://www.tclibrary.org/ |
| Trimble County Public Library | 112 Hwy 42 East | P.O. Box 249 | Bedford, 40006 | 502-255-7362 | |
| Union County Public Library | 126 South Morgan St | | Morganfield, 42437 | 270-389-1696 | http://www.wcpl.ky.gov |
| Washington County Public Library | 210 East Main St | | Springfield, 40069 | 859-336-7655 | http://www.waynepubliclibrary.net |
| Wayne County Public Library | 159 South Main St | | Monticello, 42633 | 606-348-8565 | |
| Webster County Public Library | 101 State Route 132 East | P.O. Box 50 | Dixon, 42409 | 270-639-9171 | |
| Whitley County Public Library | 285 South Third St | | Williamsburg, 40769 | 606-549-0818 | http://www.whitleylibrary.org |
| William B. Harlan Memorial Library | 500 West Fourth St | | Tompkinsville, 42167 | 270-487-5301 | http://www.wbhmlibrary.org |
| Wolfe County Public Library | 176 Kentucky 15 North | P.O. Box 10 | Campton, 41301 | 606-668-6571 | http://www.wolfcountypubliclibrary.org |
| Woodford County - Logan Helm Woodford Co. Library | 115 North Main St | | Versailles, 40383 | 859-873-5191 | http://www.woodfordcountylibrary.org |

Source: http://www.kdla.ky.gov

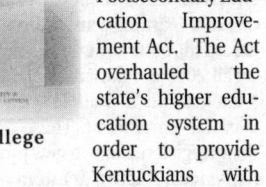

# Dr. Michael B. McCall

# EDUCATION
# *Colleges*
# *& Universities*

## THE TRANSFORMATION OF LEARNING AND WORK

Our economy is undergoing a profound transformation—one equivalent in scope and depth to the industrial revolution that occurred in the 19th century as our nation moved from an agrarian-based economy to a manufacturing economy. Technology is revolutionizing every aspect of our lives including...what we learn and how we learn it...where we work and how we work...and how we create wealth. Knowledge is at the core of this revolution and education is the key to success from both an organizational and individual perspective. In fact, schooling at all levels is fast becoming our nation's political and economic passion.

Technology has virtually erased all borders and created a worldwide marketplace where wealth is created by combining science and business to apply innovative ideas and technologies to services, products, and manufacturing processes. This New Economy has drastically changed the workplace by demanding that 21st century Americans work with their brains, not their hands. This demand is placing increasing pressure on American workers to get more education and embrace a philosophy of lifelong learning. Labor economist Tony Carnevale says, "We've moved from a system in which hard work and showing up for a job, the blue collar economy, was one way to make a living in America. Now the only way you can get ahead is by going to college some way or other and getting some form of postsecondary education or training."

Today's high school graduates face a very different workplace than the one their parents and grandparents faced several decades ago. Technology is changing the nature of work so rapidly that most Americans will hold an average of nine jobs between the ages of 18 and 34, and change their careers at least three times during their lifetime. In addition, this fast-changing economy is exposing vast numbers of workers to global labor competition. Because our economy is based increasingly on the handling of information, large amounts of work can be performed anywhere, and countries like China and India are turning out large numbers of well-educated young people fully qualified to work in an information-based economy.

Fortunately, Kentucky has been blessed with visionary leadership ever since Daniel Boone opened up the west to early pioneers in 1769 through the Cumberland Gap. In 1997 state leaders recognized that the only way Kentucky could succeed in the New Economy was to begin linking postsecondary education to economic development by opening up higher education paths to its citizens. The result of their vision was the 1997 Postsecondary Education Improvement Act. The Act overhauled the state's higher education system in order to provide Kentuckians with the knowledge and skills needed to succeed in an information-based economy. It essentially redefined the mission of Kentucky's public colleges and universities, giving each the flexibility to build on its strengths.

**Kentucky Community & Technical College System Office, Versailles**

For the University of Louisville and the University of Kentucky this meant committing their resources into research—developing knowledge that will open the door for new business and industries throughout the Commonwealth. The six regional universities were asked to focus their efforts on their unique educational expertise and concentrate on undergraduate, baccalaureate programs. However, the greatest change in the reform act was combining the state's community colleges and technical schools into one institution, creating the newest member of the state's postsecondary education family, the Kentucky Community and Technical College System (KCTCS). KCTCS, with its close community connections, has quickly become the largest provider of postsecondary education and workforce training in the state. Its 16 colleges and 65 campuses provide citizens with a quality and affordable education close to home and a seamless path from high school to postsecondary education and on into the workplace.

Kentucky's higher education reform efforts have changed the face of postsecondary education in the Commonwealth. What was once a narrow doorway for a privileged few is now an open gateway for every Kentuckian. We have moved from a K-12 system to a K-16 system. The future of not only our state but our nation depends on our citizens' ability to adapt to the constant, rapid changes in technology and the increased demands of a global economy.

The 1997 Postsecondary Education Improvement Act has given each of us with the educational tools for success. It is now in our hands to write a new future for our state, a future that links higher education to economic development and personal success.

*Dr. Michael B. McCall is President of the Kentucky Community and Technical College System.*

# Kentucky Community & Technical Colleges

The Postsecondary Education Improvement Act of 1997 created the Kentucky Community and Technical College System with a mission "to be the primary provider of two-year transfer and technical programs, workforce training for existing and new businesses and industries, and remedial and continuing education to improve the quality of life and employability of the citizens of the Commonwealth of Kentucky."

KCTCS comprises 16 colleges with over 65 campuses and other locations open or under construction. KCTCS colleges, branch campuses and distance learning centers are strategically located across the commonwealth.

Fall 2006 enrollment is estimated to be 87,286 students—an increase of 2.8 percent over the 2005 fall enrollment. These figures include students registered in two new programs: the **North American Racing Academy**—the first school for jockeys in the U.S. and the **Kentucky Coal Academy**—a mine training and safety program at four KCTCS campuses located in the coal fields.

The **NewCitizen Kentucky,** a collaboration between the NewCities Institute, Kentucky League of Cities and KCTCS is designed to lift the civic capacity of an entire state. New-Citizen Kentucky includes: A defined curriculum and interactive leadership experiences for KCTCS students; Programming and dialog opportunities for Kentucky's locally elected officials, specifically around issues such as regionalism and mutual cooperation; Research with Kentucky colleges and other entities on trends and issues that affect Kentuckians and communities; Curriculum development with universities; and Programs for citizens and the public.

Through KCTCS, Kentucky's two-year colleges work together to achieve academic excellence, economic growth and lifelong learning. As KCTCS carries out its mission, the focus is on changing lives—and Kentucky's future—for the better.

## KCTCS Colleges:

Ashland Community and Technical College—*Ashland*; Big Sandy Community and Technical College—*Paintsville, Pikeville, Prestonsburg*; Bluegrass Community and Technical College District—*Lawrenceburg, Lexington, Danville, Winchester*; Bowling Green Technical College—*Bowling Green, Glasgow*; Elizabethtown Community and Technical College—*Elizabethtown, Fort Knox*; Gateway Community and Technical College—*Covington, Edgewood, Highland Heights*; Hazard Community and Technical College—*Hazard, Jackson, Hindman*; Henderson Community College—*Henderson*; Hopkinsville Community College—*Hopkinsville, Fort Campbell*; Jefferson Community and Technical College—*Louisville, Shelbyville, Carrollton*; Madisonville Community College—*Madisonville, Central City*; Maysville Community and Technical College—*Maysville, Morehead, Cynthiana*; Owensboro Community and Technical College—*Owensboro*; Somerset Community College—*Somerset, London*; Southeast Kentucky Community and Technical College—*Cumberland, Middlesboro, Pineville, Whitesburg, Harlan*; West Kentucky Community and Technical College—*Paducah*.

# Colleges & Universities

## ALICE LLOYD COLLEGE

Alice Lloyd is a co-educational, private, four-year institution based on Christian principles and dedicated to leadership training. The college offers a tuition guarantee for qualified students from its 108-county central Appalachia service area. Valued at $6,360 per year and awarded for a total of 10 semesters, provided that reasonable progress is made toward the completion of a degree) this program is guaranteed to all students, regardless of income. Alice Lloyd College was founded by Alice Spencer Geddes Lloyd, who came to the mountains of Eastern Kentucky from her native Boston. She secured generous support of her friends on the east coast, voluntary teachers, and "faith as firm as a rock and aspirations as high as the mountains."

## ASBURY COLLEGE

Asbury College, founded in 1890, is a four-year, multi-denominational institution located 20 minutes in Wilmore. U.S. News & World Report ranked Asbury College among the top comprehensive colleges in the South for the last 13 years. Within the 17 academic departments, 49 majors are available, as well as several master's degrees in education, including alternative certification programs. With a commitment to academic excellence and spiritual vitality, Asbury College encourages 1,300 students to study, worship and serve together.

## BELLARMINE UNIVERSITY

Bellarmine University, nestled on 135 acres in Louisville's Highlands neighborhood, is ranked as one of the top universities in the South by U.S. News & World Report. Bellarmine, an independent Catholic liberal arts based university, offers undergraduate and graduate professional programs in business, education and health sciences. Also available are international programs and study abroad opportunities in 40 countries. Over 700 of 1,600 full-time undergraduates live on campus. In addition, there are 300 part-time undergraduate students and 600 graduate students.

## BEREA COLLEGE

Founded in 1855, Berea provides a high-quality liberal arts education within the context of a non-sectarian and inclusive Christian tradition. The college limits enrollment to 1,500, charges no tuition and takes 80 percent of its students from the Southern Appalachian area and Kentucky. Berea College seeks those who have high ability but limited financial resources. In addition to carrying a full academic load, students work 10-15 hours per week in a college job, which permits them to earn a portion of their educational expenses.

## BRESCIA UNIVERSITY

Brescia University, a liberal arts college located in Owensboro, offers 31 undergraduate degrees, nine pre-professional programs, a master's of science in management, and a master's of science in curriculum and instruction. Brescia is a NAIA school with 10 varsity sports competing in the Kentucky Intercollegiate Athletic Conference. Founded in 1950 by the Ursuline Sisters of Mount Saint Joseph, the university is committed to providing academic excellence and value-centered education in the Catholic tradition.

## CAMPBELLSVILLE UNIVERSITY

Founded in 1906 and affiliated with the Kentucky Baptist Convention, Campbellsville University is one of the fastest-growing Christian comprehensive universities in the South. The university has experienced an increase of 150 percent in student enrollment during the past decade. Much of this growth can be attributed to the expansion of academic and athletic programs as well as the addition of seven master's degree programs.

## CENTRE COLLEGE

Centre College is known for its outstanding liberal arts academic program and extraordinary career success of its graduates. Enrollment is around 1,100, and alumni span the range of occupations—from U.S. vice presidents, to Supreme Court justices (including a chief justice)—to the founder of the Hard Rock Café. The Centre record of accomplishment is based on rigorous academic standards and one-to-one teacher/student interaction. Centre College hosted the 2000 vice presidential debate, and the city of Danville was recently featured by Time magazine as one of the nation's outstanding small towns.

## GEORGETOWN COLLEGE

Chartered in 1829 and affiliated with the Kentucky Baptist Convention, Georgetown College is dedicated to teaching the liberal arts in a Christian environment; offering bachelor of science, arts and music education degrees, students can select a field of study from 37 majors and 28 minors. Georgetown also offers a graduate program in education. The college has forged a unique agreement with Oxford University in London, England, to allow its students, faculty and associates to participate in an academic partnership with Regent's Park, the Baptist college at Oxford.

## EASTERN KENTUCKY UNIVERSITY

For 100 years, Eastern Kentucky University has served as a beacon of hope for generations of students eager to better their lives, and for a region and commonwealth that have come to depend on it as an invaluable source of mind power and leadership. Founded in 1906 as a teachers' college, EKU has evolved into a leading comprehensive university with 168 academic degree programs, many nationally prominent. With an enrollment of approximately 16,000, and with more than 115,000 alumni, this university embraces a commitment to provide a high-quality education that is both affordable and accessible, and a learning environment where a caring faculty and staff put students and learning first.

## KENTUCKY CHRISTIAN UNIVERSITY

Founded in 1919, Kentucky Christian University's mission is to educate students for Christian leadership and service. The university, which is located in northeastern Kentucky, offers more than 20 baccalaureate majors and two master's degrees. KCU is recognized as one of the best comprehensive schools in the south by the U.S. News & World Report. KCU's students enjoy a high level of personal attention that is provided through the institution's low student-faculty ratio.

## KENTUCKY STATE UNIVERSITY

KSU's liberal arts programs draw upon the unique diversity of the institution and its African-American heritage. As an 1890 Land Grant institution, KSU is committed to providing quality research and other community outreach initiatives. The work of the Governmental Services Center meets the institution's statutory responsibility to serve public employees in the Commonwealth. With around 2,300 students, KSU provides students with a public liberal-arts stud-

ies vocation-oriented courses of instruction in such areas as business, computer sciences, medical technology, office administration, and nursing. Pre-professional programs in law, dentistry, medicine, veterinary medicine, optometry, allied health, and engineering are also offered.

## KENTUCKY WESLEYAN COLLEGE

High-quality teaching and a commitment to a career-oriented liberal arts education are hallmarks of Kentucky Wesleyan College. Established in 1858, the mission of the college, in partnership with the United Methodist Church, fosters a liberal arts education that nourishes, stimulates and prepares future leaders intellectually, spiritually, and physically to achieve success in life. Kentucky Wesleyan is home to nearly 700 students from 23 states and numerous foreign countries.

## LINDSEY WILSON COLLEGE

Founded in 1903 to train teachers for south central Kentucky, Lindsey Wilson College has evolved into a vibrant liberal arts college with 16 baccalaureate majors and a master's degree program. Lindsey Wilson is affiliated with the Kentucky Conference of the United Methodist Church. The campus is located on 45 partially wooded acres in Columbia, a small town about 20 miles from scenic Lake Cumberland.

## LOUISVILLE TECHNICAL INSTITUTE

Part of the Sullivan University System, Louisville Technical Institute offers students short-term career training in a number of hi-tech career fields. Students can pursue nine-month diplomas and certificates, or earn an associate degree in as little as 18 months. Students benefit from short career-oriented programs, small classes and hands-on training—while a four-day school week with day and evening classes provide convenient scheduling options for adult students. Programs include mechanical engineering, computer engineering technology and information system security.

## MIDWAY COLLEGE

Established in 1847, Midway College is Kentucky's only women's college. Midway offers baccalaureate degrees in 14 disciplines and associate degrees in four disciplines through the traditional day program. The college's School for Career Development meets the needs of working men and women by offering accelerated degree programs in the evening and at extension sites.

The college also offers online degree-completion programs through the new Midway Online College. Midway College's pillar degree programs are equine studies, business and organizational management, nursing, and teacher education.

## MID-CONTINENT UNIVERSITY

Mid-Continent is unique in study options: accelerated programs, double majored, dual enrollment for high school students, independent study, study abroad, and teacher certification. Also, extensive undergraduate evening and early morning classes. Remedial instruction and tutoring are available. Mid-Continent offers fields in liberal arts, accounting, business, counseling, criminal justice, e-business, education, finance, health care, information systems, management, marketing, MBA, nursing, technology, education.

## MOREHEAD STATE UNIVERSITY

Founded in 1887 as a church-sponsored school to train teachers, MSU is located in the Appalachian foothills. MSU offers 76 undergraduate degree programs and 12 pre-professional programs of study, as well as master's degrees. Art and music facilities provide cultural programs and activities for the campus and surrounding area. Morehead State has been recognized for the third consecutive year as one of the top public universities in the South in the 2007 edition of "America's Best Colleges" by U.S. News & World Report.

## MURRAY STATE UNIVERSITY

The 232-acre campus located in Murray is home to more than 9,920 students. With a full-time teaching faculty of 390, the university is a comprehensive institution comprised of five colleges and one school. Additionally, the university offers interactive television and web distance learning, extended campus, correspondence courses, and evening classes.

## NORTHERN KENTUCKY UNIVERSITY

NKU is located in Highland Heights, meeting the needs of the surrounding northern Kentucky region and providing associate, bachelor's, master's and pre-professional degree programs. Started in 1948 as an extension center of the University of Kentucky, and later part of the UK's Community College System, NKU became an autonomous senior institution in 1968. It now boasts 11,500 students and 1,200 faculty and staff.

## PIKEVILLE COLLEGE

Pikeville College is a private, four-year, liberal arts and sciences college in the heart of Appalachia. Founded in 1889 by Presbyterian ministers to provide educational opportunity to mountain youth, Pikeville College has played an integral role in the economic, academic, and social development of its area for more than a century. In addition to a range of undergraduate degrees, Pikeville also offers the Doctor of Osteopathic Medicine degree, through the Pikeville College School of Osteopathic Medicine.

## SAINT CATHARINE COLLEGE

St. Catharine College is an independent, co-educational college in the Dominican tradition. St. Catharine was formally founded in 1931, but dates its educational heritage to the formation of the Dominican sisters in 1822. The college offers certificate, associate and bachelor degrees in a variety of fields including humanities, social sciences, education, mathematics, natural sciences and business topics. Consistent with the Dominican tradition upon which it was founded, St. Catharine College fosters education grounded in the liberal arts values and is committed to the free pursuit of truth.

## SPALDING UNIVERSITY

Spalding University dates to 1814 when the Sisters of Charity of Nazareth established Nazareth Academy at Nazareth, near Bardstown, Kentucky. Spalding University is a Catholic, independent, coeducational, urban university located in downtown Louisville. Founded by the Sisters of Charity of Nazareth, it remains dedicated to value-oriented education and ethical principles. Spalding is now owned and operated by an independent board of trustees, broadly representative of the community that it serves.

## SPENCERIAN COLLEGE

Spencerian College, founded in 1892, is part of the Sullivan University System. It has a main campus in Louisville and branch campus in Lexington. Spencerian specializes in short-term career programs ranging leading to certificates, diplomas and associate degrees in allied health, business and technology. These career program offerings include radiology, nursing, cardiovascular, surgical and medical office technology, business office, accounting, electronic engineering technology, computer graphic design, architectural and mechanical computer-aided design.

## SULLIVAN UNIVERSITY

Sullivan University is a career college with campuses in Louisville, Lexington and Fort Knox—accredited to award associate, bachelor's, and master's degrees. With 6,000 students it is the largest, for-profit, private university in Kentucky. It is known for dispute-resolution and culinary arts programs. It offers an MBA and is preparing to offer a Doctor of Pharmacy degree. Its philosophy is to prepare quickly students by offering staircase programs: attain a career degree program in one year, an associate in another, and a bachelor's degree after two more.

## THOMAS MORE COLLEGE

Thomas More College, named for the English saint, scholar and statesman, is located on 60 acres in Crestview Hills. The suburban campus is eight miles south of Cincinnati, Ohio. Thomas More serves some 1,500 students. Although primarily from Greater Cincinnati and Northern Kentucky, students from some 12 states and six countries attend the college.

## TRANSYLVANIA UNIVERSITY

Chartered in 1780, Transylvania is the 16th oldest institution of higher learning in the U.S. and the first college west of the Allegheny Mountains. The private liberal-arts school, with an enrollment of 1,100 students, is consistently recognized by publications such as U.S. News & World Report, Peterson's Top Colleges for Science, and Barron's Best Buys in College Education. The student body consists of bright, highly motivated students who thrive partly with the low student/faculty ratio.

## UNION COLLEGE

Union College offers a liberal arts education to about 1,000 students. The college, affiliated with the United Methodist Church, was founded in 1879. Union's 100-acre campus is on the edge of the Appalachian Mountains. The famous Wilderness Road spans the east side of the campus and Cumberland Gap National Historic Park is nearby. It offers applied sciences, humanities, social sciences, natural sciences, as well as majors and areas of study in pre-professional, technical, and skills-oriented fields.

## UNIVERSITY OF KENTUCKY

UK is the principal research and graduate-degree granting institution in the commonwealth serving more than 30,000 students. It is a comprehensive land-grant institution located in Lexington. UK offers baccalaureate, professional, master's, specialist, doctoral, and post-doctoral programs and conducts joint doctoral programs in cooperation with other institutions. UK is ranked among the top 100 research universities in the nation. It also has medical, dental, nursing, and pharmacy schools, as well as allied health programs.

## UNIVERSITY OF LOUISVILLE

U of L is an urban, public, state-supported university that emphasizes undergraduate and graduate-level education, as well as research. With a student population of more than 22,000 undergraduates and graduates, the University of Louisville offers graduate, professional, baccalaureate, and associate degrees, as well as certificates, in more than 170 fields of study through 12 schools and colleges on three campuses: Belknap, Health Sciences, and Shelby. It also has a medical and a dental school. As the University of Louisville celebrated its bicentennial in 1998 it has become known especially for teaching, research, and service to its community and the advancement of educational opportunity for all citizens thereof. Its academic programs attract students from every state and from all over the world.

## UNIVERSITY OF THE CUMBERLANDS

University of the Cumberlands (formerly Cumberland College) is in its 117th year of operation. It offers undergraduate degrees in 38 major fields of study, 30 minors and nine pre-professional programs, as well as opportunities such as studying abroad. Cumberland, located in Williamsburg, is affiliated with the Kentucky Baptist Convention and has long been known for its outstanding academic programs and graduates who enter the work force well prepared for success and service.

## WESTERN KENTUCKY UNIVERSITY

WKU offers associate, baccalaureate, and masters degrees, and certificate programs. "The home of the Hilltoppers," Western's campus crowns a hill overlooking the city of Bowling Green and is proclaimed as one of the most beautiful in the nation. WKU offers liberal arts, engineering, business, education, health and human services, and nursing. Western has been an educational leader since its beginning. Its roots come from the Southern Normal School of Bowling Green, and Western has been broadening horizons throughout the region since its founding in 1906.

# Medical Schools

Kentucky has three medical schools: the University of Louisville School of Medicine, University of Kentucky College of Medicine, and the Pikeville College School of Osteopathic Medicine at Pikeville College.

The oldest medical school in Kentucky is the **University of Louisville School of Medicine**, which traces its beginnings to 1833 when the Louisville Common Council set up a committee to investigate establishing a medical college in the city. The Louisville Medical Institute began classes in temporary quarters in the fall of 1837. Nearly 16,000 medical students have earned the M.D. degree from the UofL School of Medicine. According to the National Institutes of Health ranking information for 2004, the UofL School of Medicine is now ranked 42nd among public schools for research funding received from NIH, Dept. of Neurology ranks 4th, the Dept. of Ophthalmology ranks 14th, and the Dept. of Anesthesiology ranks 20th. Anatomical Sciences and Pediatrics also are ranked in the top 30.

Recent milestones include:

· 1999 U of L surgeons perform the first human hand transplant in the U.S. at Jewish Hospital's Kleinert, Kutz Hand Care Center.

· 2001 U of L surgeons implant the first fully-implantable artificial heart at Jewish Hospital.

· 2005 U of L received approval for construction of a third biomedical research building, funded in part by a $39 million appropriation from the Kentucky Legislature and a $10.25 million federal earmark secured with the assistance of U.S. Senator Mitch McConnell.

The **University of Kentucky College of Medicine**, in Lexington, enrolled its first medical school class in 1960. Since then over 3,000 medical students have earned the M.D. degree from the UK College of Medicine. UK College of Medicine is ranked 31st among public schools for the research funding received from the National Institutes of Health (NIH), according to rankings for the 2004 fiscal year. In 2005, UK dedicated a $74.4 million Biomedical Biological Sciences Research Building.

Other NIH rankings based on 2004 fiscal year figures include:

· College of Medicine ranks 35th among public medical schools

· The Center on Aging ranks 3rd

· The Department of Physiology ranks 8th

· Molecular and Biomedical Pharmacology ranks 10th among public medical schools

· The Departments of Anatomy and Neurobiology;

· Microbiology, Immunology, and Molecular Genetics; Molecular and Cellular Biochemistry and Surgery also are ranked in the top 20.

**Pikeville College School of Osteopathic Medicine** is the 19th school of osteopathic medicine in the U.S. PCSOM is strongly supported by community leaders whose objective is to improve delivery of healthcare to underserved areas of Appalachia. The 1997 inaugural class of PCSOM—53 D.O.s—graduated in May 2001. D.O.s practice a "whole person" approach to health care; special attention is focused on the musculoskeletal system. Statistics indicate that while D.O.s make up only seven percent of the physicians in the U.S., they see about 18 percent of the patients. PCSOM is fully accredited by the American Osteopathic Association Bureau of Professional Education.

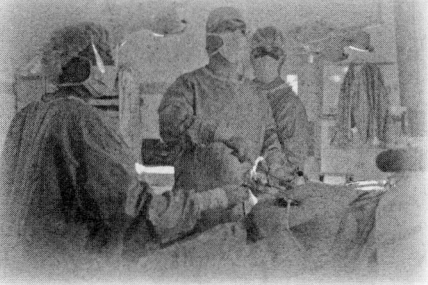

**Adrian Park, center, performs surgery at UK Hospital on 9/26/02 in Lexington. Assisting is Sharon Coles, surgical technician, left, and David Bullock, a 3rd year medical student.**
*Source: David Stephenson, Lexington Herald-Leader*

Sources: University of Louisville School of Medicine, www.louisville.edu/medschool/; University of Kentucky College of Medicine, www.mc.uky.edu/medicine/; and Pikeville College School of Osteopathic Medicine http://pcsom.pc.edu/ http://pcsom.pc.edu/.

# COLLEGES, UNIVERSITIES, COMMUNITY & TECHNICAL COLLEGES

| COLLEGE | PRESIDENT | ADDRESS | CITY | ZIP | PHONE | WEB PAGE |
|---|---|---|---|---|---|---|
| Alice Lloyd College | Joe Alan Stepp | 100 Purpose Rd | Pippa Passes | 41844 | (606) 368-2101 | www.alc.edu |
| Appalachian Graduate Consortium | John P Nelson | 147 Sycamore St | Pikeville | 41501 | | |
| Asbury College | William Crothers | 1 Macklem Dr | Wilmore | 40390 | (859) 858-3511 | www.asbury.edu |
| Asbury Theological Seminary | Jeff Greenway | 204 N Lexington Ave | Wilmore | 40390 | (800) 2-ASBURY | www.asburyseminary.edu |
| Ashland Community & Technical College, President's Office | Heather Shelton | 1400 College Dr | Ashland | 41101 | (800) 928-4256 | www.ashland.kctcs.edu |
| Bellarmine University | Joseph J McGowan | 2001 Newburg Rd | Louisville | 40205 | (800) 274-4723 | www.bellarmine.edu |
| Berea College | Larry D Shinn | CPO 2182 | Berea | 40404 | (859) 985-1000 | www.berea.edu |
| Big Sandy Community & Technical College, President's Office | George D Edwards | One Bert T Combs Dr | Prestonsburg | 41653 | (888) 641-4132 | www.bigsandy.kctcs.edu |
| Bluegrass Community & Technical College, President's Office | Jim Kerley | 209 Oswald Bldg, Cooper Dr | Lexington | 40506 | (866) 774-4872 | www.bluegrass.kctcs.edu |
| Bowling Green Technical College, President's Office | Lewis Burke Jr | 1845 Loop Ave | Bowling Green | 42101 | (800) 790-0990 | www.bowlinggreen.kctcs.edu |
| Brescia University | Vivian M Bowles | 717 Frederica St | Owensboro | 42301 | (270) 685-3131 | www.brescia.edu |
| Campbellsville University | Michael V Carter | 1 University Dr | Campbellsville | 42718 | (800) 264-6014 | www.campbellsville.edu |
| Centre College of Kentucky | John A Roush | 600 W Walnut St | Danville | 40422 | (859) 238-5200 | www.centre.edu |
| Clear Creek Baptist Bible College | Bill D Whittaker | 300 Clear Creek Rd | Pineville | 40977 | (866) 340-3196 | www.ccbbc.edu |
| Eastern Kentucky University | Joanne K Glasser | 521 Lancaster Ave | Richmond | 40475 | (800) 262-7493 | www.eku.edu |
| Elizabethtown Community & Technical College, President's Office | Thelma White | 600 College Street Rd | Elizabethtown | 42701 | (877) 246-2322 | www.elizabethtown.kctcs.edu |
| Gateway Community & Technical College, President's Office | G Edward Hughes | 300 Buttermilk Pk Ste 334 | Ft Mitchell | 41017 | (859) 441-4500 | www.gateway.kctcs.edu |
| Georgetown College | William H Crouch Jr | 400 E College St | Georgetown | 40324 | (502) 863-8000 | www.georgetowncollege.edu |
| Greater Cincinnati Consortium of Colleges & Universities | Janet S Piccirillo | 440 E McMillan St | Cincinnati | 45206 | | www.gcccu.org |
| Hazard Community & Technical College | Vicki Combs | One Community College Dr | Hazard | 41701 | (800) 246-7521 | www.hazcc.kctcs.edu |
| Henderson Community College, President's Office | Patrick R Lake | 2660 S Green St | Henderson | 42420 | (800) 696-9958 | www.henderson.kctcs.edu |
| Hopkinsville Community College, President's Office | James E Selbe | 720 North Dr | Hopkinsville | 42241 | (270) 707-3700 | www.hopkinsville.kctcs.edu |
| Jefferson Community & Technical College, President's Office | Anthony Newberry | 109 E Broadway | Louisville | 40202 | (502) 213-5333 | www.jefferson.kctcs.edu |
| Kentuckiana Metroversity | Jack Will | 200 W Broadway Ste 700 | Louisville | 40202 | | www.metroversity.org |
| Kentucky Christian College | Keith P Keeran | 100 Academic Pkwy | Grayson | 41143 | (606) 474-3000 | www.kcc.edu |
| Kentucky Community & Technical College System | Michael B McCall | 300 N Main St | Versailles | 40383 | (877) 528-2748 | www.kctcs.edu |
| Kentucky Mountain Bible College | Philip Speas | 855 KY Hwy 541 | Vancleve | 41385 | (800) 879-KMBC | www.kmbc.edu |
| Kentucky State University | Mary Evans Sias | 400 E Main St | Frankfort | 40601 | (502) 597-6000 | www.kysu.edu |
| Kentucky Wesleyan College | Anne C Federlein | 3000 Frederica St | Owensboro | 42302 | (270) 926-3111 | www.kwc.edu |
| Lexington Baptist College | David E Adams | 163 N Ashland Ave | Lexington | 40502 | (859) 252-1130 | |
| Lexington Theological Seminary | Robert Cueni | 631 S Limestone | Lexington | 40508 | (859) 252-0361 | www.lextheo.edu |
| Lindsey Wilson College | William T Luckey Jr | 210 Lindsey Wilson St | Columbia | 42728 | (800) 264-0138 | www.lindsey.edu |
| Louisville Bible College | Charles A McNeely | 8013 Damascus Rd | Louisville | 40291 | (502) 231-5221 | www.louisvillebiblecollege.org |

# COLLEGES, UNIVERSITIES, COMMUNITY & TECHNICAL COLLEGES

| COLLEGE | PRESIDENT | ADDRESS | CITY | ZIP | PHONE | WEB PAGE |
|---|---|---|---|---|---|---|
| Louisville Presbyterian Theological Seminary | Dean Thompson | 1044 Alta Vista Rd | Louisville | 40205 | (502) 895-3411 | www.lpts.edu |
| Louisville Technical Institute | David Keene | 3901 Atkinson Square Dr | Louisville | 40218 | (800) 844-6528 | www.louisvilletech.com |
| Madisonville Community College, President's Office | Judith L Rhoads | 2000 College Dr | Madisonville | 42431 | (270) 821-2250 | www.madisonville.kctcs.edu |
| Maysville Community & Technical College, President's Office | Augusta A Julian | 1755 US Hwy 68 | Maysville | 41056 | (606) 759-7141 | www.maycc.kctcs.edu |
| Metropolitan College | Dan Ash | 1000 Community College Dr | Louisville | 40272 | | |
| Mid Continent College | Robert Imhoff | 99 E Powell Rd | Mayfield | 42066 | (270) 247-8521 | www.midcontinent.edu |
| Midway College | William B Drake Jr | 512 E Stephens St | Midway | 40347 | (859) 846-4421 | www.midway.edu |
| Morehead State University | Wayne D Andrews | 150 University Boulevard | Morehead | 40351 | (606) 783-2221 | www.moreheadstate.edu |
| Murray State University | Kern Alexander | PO Box 9 | Murray | 42071 | (800) 272-4678 | www.murraystate.edu |
| Northern Kentucky University | James C Votruba | Nunn Dr | Highland Heights | 41099 | (859) 572-5100 | www.nku.edu |
| Owensboro Community & Technical College, President's Office | Jacqueline Addington | 4800 New Hartford Rd | Owensboro | 42303 | (866) 755-OCTC | www.octc.kctcs.edu |
| Pikeville College | Harold H Smith | 147 Sycamore St | Pikeville | 41501 | (606) 218-5250 | www.pc.edu |
| Portland Christian School of Bible Studies | J R Satterfield | 2500 Portland Ave | Louisville | 40212 | | |
| Saint Catharine College | William D Huston | 2735 Bardstown Rd | St Catharine | 40061 | (859) 336-5082 | www.sccky.edu |
| Simmons Bible College | Thomas H Peoples Jr | 1811 Dumesnil St | Louisville | 40210 | (502) 776-1443 | www.sbcollege.edu |
| Somerset Community College, President's Office | Jo Marshall | 808 Monticello St | Somerset | 42501 | (877) 629-9722 | www.somerset.kctcs.edu |
| Southeast Kentucky Community College, President's Office | W Bruce Ayers | 700 College Rd | Cumberland | 40823 | (888) 274-SECC | www.southeast.kctcs.edu |
| Southern Baptist Theological Seminary | R Albert Mohler Jr | 2825 Lexington Rd | Louisville | 40280 | (800) 626-5525 | www.sbts.edu |
| Spalding University | Jo Ann Rooney | 851 S 4th St | Louisville | 40203 | (502) 585-9911 | www.spalding.edu |
| Spencerian College, Lexington Campus | E G Clark | 1575 Winchester Rd | Lexington | 40505 | (859) 223-9608 | www.spencerian.edu/lexington |
| Spencerian College, Louisville Campus | Jan Gordon | 4627 Dixie Hwy | Louisville | 40256 | (502) 447-1000 | www.spencerian.edu |
| Sullivan University | A R Sullivan | 3101 Bardstown Rd | Louisville | 40205 | (502) 456-6504 | www.sullivan.edu |
| Sullivan University, Lexington Campus | David McGuire | 2355 Harrodsburg Rd | Lexington | 40504 | (800) 467-6281 | www.sullivan.edu |
| Sullivan University, Ft Knox Campus | Barbara Dean | 63 Quartermaster St | Ft Knox | 40121 | (270) 942-8500 | www.sullivan.edu |
| Thomas More College | Margaret Stallmeyer | 333 Thomas More Pkwy | Crestview Hills | 41017 | (800) 548-7044 | www.thomasmore.edu |
| Transylvania University | Charles L Shearer | 300 N Broadway | Lexington | 40508 | | www.transy.edu |
| Union College | Edward de Rosset | 310 College St | Barbourville | 40906 | (606) 546-4151 | www.unionky.edu |
| University of Kentucky | Lee T Todd Jr | 101 Gillis Bldg | Lexington | 40506 | (859) 257-9000 | www.uky.edu |
| University of Louisville | James R Ramsey | 102 Grawemeyer Hall | Louisville | 40292 | (800) 334-8635 | www.louisville.edu |
| University of the Cumberlands | James H Taylor | 6191 College Station Dr | Williamsburg | 40769 | (606) 549-2200 | www.ucumberlands.edu |
| West Kentucky Community & Technical College | Barbara Veazey | 4810 Alben Barkley Dr | Paducah | 42002 | (270) 554-9200 | www.westkentucky.kctcs.edu |
| Western Kentucky University | Gary A Ransdell | 1 Big Red Way St | Bowling Green | 42101 | (270) 745-0111 | www.wku.edu |

Source: *The Kentucky Directory Gold Book 2006*

EDUCATION

# *Higher Education is Key to Kentucky's Economic Future*

### James R. Ramsey, Ph.D.

Kentuckians celebrated in Spring 2006 when United Parcel Service announced a $1 billion expansion—and an additional 5,000 jobs—at its Louisville hub.

They cheered again when U.S. Secretary of Veterans Affairs R. James Nicholson announced that Louisville would be the site of a new $450 million VA hospital, one of only five new veterans hospitals in the nation.

Both announcements were significant for the health and economic welfare of the Louisville community.

And both occurred, in large part, because of the University of Louisville.

UPS cited Metropolitan College, the company's unique educational partnership with U of L, Jefferson Community and Technical College, and the university's Logistics and Distribution Institute as significant factors in its decision to expand in Louisville. Secretary Nicholson pointed to the university's medical research and its medical school's relationship to the current VA hospital as key to that agency's decision.

**Auguste Rodin's "The Thinker" on University of Louisville's campus**
*Source: University of Louisville*

These are just two examples of the role strong universities play in the economic development of their communities and their states.

U of L is not alone—Kentucky is blessed with a number of strong universities that have helped attract businesses to the commonwealth.

Universities boost economic development in other ways. They tend to be among the largest employers in their communities. They graduate talented students who go on to become entrepreneurs and government leaders. They attract millions of dollars in research funding. They produce products that can be commercialized. They spin off companies that bring jobs to communities.

And they do even more.

Not too long ago, Kentucky thrived as a manufacturing and agricultural state. While those industries are still important, they play a smaller role each year as the economy changes.

Noted author Richard Florida proposes that communities that wish to be successful in the future must develop a strong "creative class"—intelligent, well-educated people from many backgrounds who will spur economic development through new ideas and high-tech businesses. As Florida explains, cities with strong creative classes attract individuals who will be business, government and cultural leaders of the future. For Kentucky to thrive, it needs to develop the creative class.

The creative class is attracted to outstanding universities, particularly schools that have strong programs in a wide variety of areas, ranging from engineering, medicine and health fields to fine arts and music. Kentucky's universities offer the types of programs the creative class is seeking.

Attracting new businesses. Attracting outstanding people. All while offering today's students an outstanding education. This is a tall order, and it's one that the University of Louisville and all of Kentucky's institutions of higher education are taking seriously.

*Dr. James R. Ramsey is president of the University of Louisville.*

# GREAT·PARTNERS·IN·TIME

## EXPLORERS WITH HEART

### Lewis and Clark

In 1803 President Thomas Jefferson sent Meriwether Lewis and William Clark on a mission to

*Up the Jefferson,* courtesy of Mrs. John F. Clymer and the Clymer Museum.

find a waterway linking the Mississippi River and the Pacific Ocean. Their three-year odyssey into unknown territory not only marked the path for a new nation to expand westward, but charted America's future, too.

## U of L and the Kentucky Medical Community

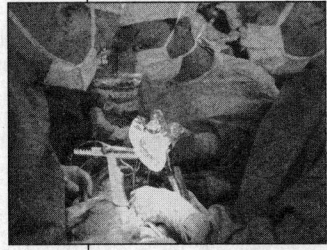

The University of Louisville and its medical partners across the state also are charting new territory. From the world's first self-contained artificial heart implant and better heart devices designed just for kids, to cancer vaccines and new insights into autism, U of L and the region's medical professionals are giving patients new hope for a normal life.

# EDUCATION

# *The Catalyst for a New Commonwealth*

Dr. Lee Todd

Policy makers who crafted the Commonwealth's revolutionary Postsecondary Education Improvement Act of 1997 (House Bill 1) understood the importance of higher education to Kentucky's future. They believed that states with Top 20 public research universities offered better opportunities for the citizens of those states.

In December 2005, the University of Kentucky released a Business Plan that makes clear the true benefits of building a Top 20 public research university right here in Kentucky.

The facts are clear: States with Top 20 universities are places where citizens are more educated, healthier, and more financially secure. Average household incomes are higher in states with Top 20 universities. The median income in these states is over $10,000 higher than we have in Kentucky. Fewer people live in poverty and fewer public dollars are spent on health care in these states. Seventeen percent of Kentuckians live in poverty–over one-third of them are children. In states with Top 20 universities, the rate is 12 percent.

Most important to Kentucky's long-term economic success is the fact that only 19 percent of our fellow Kentuckians have a bachelors degree or higher. The national average is 27 percent and it is 28 percent in states with Top 20 universities. Especially in a knowledge economy, a state that allows its workforce to lag behind in educational attainment is a state that willingly accepts economic failure.

Three-quarters of economic growth in the U.S. today is the result of technological advance and nearly all that advance is the result of university-based research. One just has to look at the nation's strong economic regions. States with thriving economies are built on intellectual property, on the education of their workforce, and their ability to retain the talented individuals in their communities.

If you examine what Boston's universities contributed to that region in the year 2000 alone, the results are staggering. Universities contributed $7.4 billion to the regional economy. It created a workforce of almost 50,000 university employees and 37,000 other workers, and a talent pool of more than 32,000 graduates. Innovative university research resulted in 264 patents, 280 commercial licenses, and numerous startup companies throughout the region.

Universities have a synergistic influence on an entire region, impacting much more than just the economy. As Richard Florida, Gary Gates, Brian Knudsen, and Kevin Stolarick point out in "The University and the Creative Economy," the university comprises a potential— and, in some places, actual— creative hub that sits at the center of regional development. It is a catalyst for stimulating the spillover of technology, talent, and tolerance into the community."

The desire to be the "creative hub" of Kentucky was at the heart of the Top 20 Business Plan. Over the next 14 years, the Business Plan calls on UK to increase its intellectual capital by adding 625 more faculty and 7,000 additional students. The plan also calls on UK to expand its research portfolio by $470 million by 2020, while increasing engagement in Kentucky's schools, farms, businesses, and communities.

That is what made the passage of House Bill 1 so important to the future of this state. The legislation is not only about building a strong and responsive postsecondary education system. It called on the University of Kentucky to provide better educational opportunities, develop better health care, diversify and strengthen Kentucky's communities, and create sustainable jobs that would be competitive in a global economy.

It called on the University of Kentucky to be the catalyst for a new Commonwealth.

*Dr. Lee Todd is President of the University of Kentucky.*

## EDUCATION

# *St. Catharine College*

If you haven't visited St. Catharine College lately then you really haven't seen St. Catharine. Major, exciting changes are underway at the picturesque campus in central Kentucky. Last December, seven students became the first to earn Bachelor's Degrees from Kentucky's Newest Four-Year College.

But the new Bachelor Degree programs in Business Management and Supervision and Health Sciences are not the only exciting changes underway at St. Catharine. St. Catharine started a Bachelor of Arts in Education and Bachelor of Science in Psychology in the fall of 2006. St. Catharine will also begin to offer more academic scholarships. Students with an ACT score of 21 or above and a GPA of 3.0 will automatically receive an academic scholarship, the amount to be determined by their score and GPA. Students with an ACT of 25 or above and a 3.0 GPA may apply for the Presidential Scholarship which is up to full tuition.

All the excitement at St. Catharine is not confined to the classroom, however, as the athletic programs are also expanding. In the fall of 2006, varsity volleyball and cheerleading began. These two new programs are in addition to the eight existing varsity sports that annually garner national attention.

Come join as at St. Catharine College – where the excitement continues.

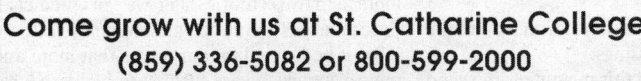

EDUCATION

# *The Good Life*

Joanne Glasser

Daniel Boone and his fellow explorers from the 18th century crossed through the Cumberland Gap in search of it.

They found it in the wide-open spaces, fertile soil and abundant wildlife of Kentucky.

It conjures different meanings today, but more

He could have been talking about higher education.

All across Kentucky, we see outstanding colleges and universities, and all the faculty, students and staff who grace their campuses, engaged in this exercise of vital powers along lines of excellence.

The goal of these learning communities? For each and every member, it's a life that affords them scope – a heightened awareness of the world around them, a renewed vision for a brighter tomorrow, and opportunities for service.

Just as Boone could never have envisioned

**President Glasser personally congratulates each graduate who attends Commencement**
*Source: Eastern Kentucky University*

than 200 years later, Kentuckians from our eastern mountains to our western flatlands are still seeking the elusive "good life."

For some, it means financial security.

For others, it means a summer weekend on a houseboat or a good book by a roaring winter fire.

For many of us, it just means having our family around to enjoy our blessings.

Aristotle once defined this pursuit of "the good life" as "the exercise of vital powers along lines of excellence, in a life affording them scope."

**Students at Eastern Kentucky University Fall 2005**
*Source: Eastern Kentucky University*

how important higher education would become more than two centuries later, we can't predict all the challenges that await our Commonwealth.

But it bodes well for our future that more and more Kentuckians are turning to higher education in their pursuit of "the good life."

*Joanne Glasser is President of Eastern Kentucky University.*

# Your Future Begins at EKU

If you have a passion for learning, Eastern Kentucky University has a place just for you.

Whether you're interested in arts and sciences, business and technology, education, health sciences, or justice and safety, choose from 168 degree programs and set yourself on a path to achieve your lifetime goals.

Are you ready for the challenge?

Where Students and Learning Come First

# EDUCATIONAL ATTAINMENT: YEARS OF SCHOOL COMPLETED, 1970-2000

| AREA | TOTAL PERSONS 25 YEARS AND OLDER | | | | 8 YEARS OF SCHOOL OR LESS | | | | HIGH SCHOOL | | | | 4 OR MORE YEARS OF COLLEGE | | | |
|---|---|---|---|---|---|---|---|---|---|---|---|---|---|---|---|---|
| | 1970 | 1980 | 1990 | 2000 | 1970 | 1980 | 1990 | 2000 | 1970 | 1980 | 1990 | 2000 | 1970 | 1980 | 1990 | 2000 |
| Kentucky | 1,713,298 | 2,086,692 | 2,333,833 | 2,646,397 | 44.8 | 31.3 | 19.0 | 11.7 | 38.5 | 53.1 | 64.6 | 74.1 | 7.2 | 11.1 | 13.6 | 17.1 |
| Adair | 7,629 | 9,291 | 9,885 | 11,270 | 69.4 | 52.2 | 36.6 | 23.6 | 21.6 | 34.6 | 46.3 | 60.1 | 3.4 | 5.3 | 7.4 | 10.9 |
| Allen | 7,749 | 8,779 | 9,463 | 11,643 | 66.7 | 48.7 | 32.2 | 18.9 | 23.8 | 38.5 | 51.1 | 64.5 | 2.6 | 5.0 | 4.6 | 9.1 |
| Anderson | 5,330 | 7,393 | 9,421 | 12,600 | 47.7 | 33.5 | 18.6 | 8.0 | 38.2 | 50.3 | 66.7 | 80.4 | 5.3 | 7.3 | 9.9 | 12.0 |
| Ballard | 5,186 | 5,521 | 5,328 | 5,766 | 41.7 | 29.6 | 16.8 | 9.9 | 39.3 | 53.4 | 64.2 | 76.3 | 2.7 | 7.7 | 8.7 | 10.6 |
| Barren | 16,676 | 20,864 | 22,627 | 25,751 | 58.7 | 43.0 | 28.8 | 16.3 | 29.6 | 44.0 | 54.5 | 69.5 | 4.9 | 8.0 | 8.3 | 11.1 |
| Bath | 5,183 | 5,908 | 6,341 | 7,451 | 65.1 | 49.6 | 36.1 | 22.8 | 21.6 | 35.6 | 46.3 | 59.0 | 3.3 | 6.4 | 6.2 | 10.1 |
| Bell | 16,696 | 19,319 | 19,644 | 20,042 | 61.9 | 49.7 | 33.5 | 25.0 | 25.2 | 36.2 | 46.7 | 56.6 | 5.5 | 6.5 | 9.3 | 9.0 |
| Boone | 16,536 | 25,095 | 35,347 | 54,166 | 32.5 | 17.9 | 9.3 | 4.8 | 47.0 | 65.3 | 76.4 | 85.1 | 6.7 | 11.8 | 15.3 | 22.8 |
| Bourbon | 10,481 | 11,628 | 12,332 | 13,015 | 40.7 | 31.1 | 16.4 | 9.3 | 41.8 | 53.6 | 64.0 | 75.4 | 6.6 | 9.2 | 11.8 | 13.5 |
| Boyd | 29,531 | 33,759 | 34,809 | 34,697 | 34.2 | 24.3 | 13.0 | 8.2 | 48.3 | 59.0 | 68.9 | 78.0 | 7.8 | 9.8 | 11.9 | 14.1 |
| Boyle | 11,967 | 14,648 | 16,693 | 18,491 | 37.9 | 28.6 | 16.2 | 9.5 | 44.3 | 55.6 | 65.4 | 76.6 | 9.8 | 12.6 | 14.4 | 19.3 |
| Bracken | 4,225 | 4,627 | 5,016 | 5,460 | 53.1 | 39.7 | 24.4 | 14.2 | 30.1 | 43.7 | 56.0 | 69.6 | 3.1 | 5.4 | 6.5 | 9.5 |
| Breathitt | 6,867 | 8,776 | 9,455 | 10,393 | 69.5 | 48.1 | 34.8 | 24.2 | 21.2 | 37.0 | 47.8 | 57.5 | 6.0 | 8.9 | 8.6 | 10.0 |
| Breckinridge | 8,254 | 9,892 | 10,615 | 12,501 | 60.2 | 44.1 | 28.1 | 15.9 | 26.4 | 42.1 | 56.7 | 68.9 | 2.0 | 5.7 | 6.3 | 7.4 |
| Bullitt | 12,335 | 22,177 | 28,596 | 39,307 | 44.7 | 26.8 | 15.0 | 7.8 | 34.9 | 53.0 | 64.7 | 76.0 | 3.1 | 5.8 | 6.3 | 9.2 |
| Butler | 5,584 | 6,504 | 7,252 | 8,488 | 68.6 | 52.6 | 34.9 | 20.3 | 20.3 | 34.6 | 46.6 | 60.7 | 3.1 | 3.1 | 5.1 | 6.4 |
| Caldwell | 8,022 | 8,625 | 8,928 | 9,265 | 45.4 | 34.7 | 19.0 | 11.3 | 37.2 | 49.5 | 61.9 | 73.1 | 4.4 | 7.6 | 8.2 | 10.0 |
| Calloway | 14,198 | 16,883 | 18,542 | 21,032 | 40.4 | 26.6 | 15.7 | 9.9 | 43.8 | 59.8 | 69.1 | 77.9 | 11.4 | 18.1 | 19.4 | 24.0 |
| Campbell | 47,257 | 47,773 | 52,731 | 57,184 | 39.7 | 26.3 | 12.7 | 7.1 | 40.1 | 55.6 | 71.0 | 80.8 | 5.7 | 9.8 | 14.9 | 20.5 |
| Carlisle | 3,399 | 3,457 | 3,508 | 3,690 | 47.6 | 32.1 | 19.2 | 11.9 | 34.3 | 52.5 | 62.3 | 73.4 | 2.1 | 4.6 | 6.6 | 10.6 |
| Carroll | 4,781 | 5,517 | 5,938 | 6,690 | 49.5 | 33.4 | 18.9 | 15.0 | 32.2 | 46.5 | 59.6 | 68.1 | 5.6 | 7.6 | 10.7 | 8.3 |
| Carter | 10,546 | 13,753 | 15,035 | 17,394 | 62.1 | 45.7 | 29.5 | 19.2 | 23.9 | 38.0 | 51.3 | 64.4 | 4.4 | 5.4 | 7.6 | 8.9 |
| Casey | 7,293 | 8,665 | 9,152 | 10,423 | 71.1 | 55.2 | 38.6 | 24.9 | 19.4 | 33.2 | 43.1 | 57.4 | 4.9 | 5.8 | 6.5 | 7.4 |
| Christian | 25,507 | 32,876 | 38,693 | 40,344 | 42.9 | 25.1 | 14.2 | 10.2 | 41.2 | 60.5 | 72.2 | 77.2 | 6.2 | 8.7 | 10.4 | 12.5 |
| Clark | 13,064 | 16,521 | 19,172 | 22,187 | 43.6 | 28.8 | 17.8 | 10.4 | 40.1 | 55.9 | 65.1 | 75.0 | 6.8 | 9.6 | 13.0 | 15.6 |
| Clay | 8,765 | 11,718 | 12,818 | 16,083 | 75.1 | 59.9 | 43.5 | 31.9 | 17.2 | 27.6 | 38.9 | 49.4 | 5.0 | 7.3 | 7.4 | 8.0 |
| Clinton | 4,738 | 5,588 | 5,987 | 6,594 | 74.4 | 55.3 | 34.1 | 29.3 | 17.5 | 30.5 | 44.4 | 53.5 | 3.1 | 4.7 | 6.6 | 8.0 |
| Crittenden | 5,264 | 5,776 | 6,102 | 6,460 | 53.6 | 40.0 | 24.4 | 17.6 | 33.5 | 45.4 | 59.6 | 67.0 | 3.6 | 5.9 | 5.1 | 7.3 |
| Cumberland | 4,106 | 4,551 | 4,583 | 4,972 | 73.1 | 61.3 | 43.6 | 28.2 | 18.4 | 29.0 | 39.5 | 56.0 | 4.3 | 6.7 | 6.1 | 7.1 |
| Daviess | 41,289 | 48,965 | 55,048 | 59,745 | 32.7 | 22.6 | 12.6 | 6.7 | 48.9 | 61.3 | 72.3 | 80.7 | 8.7 | 11.0 | 14.1 | 4.9 |
| Edmonson | 4,769 | 5,772 | 6,570 | 7,865 | 65.2 | 47.8 | 32.1 | 20.3 | 19.7 | 35.5 | 48.6 | 61.7 | 2.2 | 5.3 | 5.4 | 7.8 |
| Elliott | 3,095 | 3,742 | 3,912 | 4,422 | 74.5 | 55.0 | 37.0 | 27.1 | 18.8 | 31.3 | 44.0 | 52.6 | 3.4 | 7.1 | 5.6 | 7.1 |
| Estill | 6,964 | 8,301 | 9,170 | 10,189 | 65.5 | 50.5 | 35.5 | 25.1 | 23.1 | 38.4 | 46.5 | 58.5 | 2.9 | 6.5 | 5.4 | 6.9 |
| Fayette | 89,217 | 115,055 | 142,116 | 167,235 | 24.2 | 15.9 | 8.3 | 5.1 | 60.1 | 71.6 | 80.2 | 85.8 | 17.2 | 25.6 | 30.6 | 35.6 |
| Fleming | 6,583 | 7,326 | 7,946 | 9,154 | 60.2 | 48.3 | 31.1 | 20.5 | 27.9 | 40.2 | 53.8 | 66.5 | 3.3 | 6.3 | 8.7 | 8.8 |
| Floyd | 18,863 | 29,961 | 26,566 | 28,370 | 63.8 | 45.9 | 31.3 | 20.4 | 24.5 | 39.9 | 50.8 | 61.3 | 4.2 | 6.0 | 7.4 | 9.7 |
| Franklin | 19,347 | 25,064 | 28,819 | 32,388 | 35.1 | 22.7 | 12.0 | 8.7 | 51.0 | 64.0 | 76.0 | 78.8 | 11.9 | 18.0 | 21.3 | 23.8 |
| Fulton | 6,067 | 5,495 | 5,512 | 5,111 | 46.9 | 33.8 | 25.0 | 10.7 | 37.8 | 45.2 | 54.4 | 69.5 | 4.9 | 6.6 | 10.3 | 11.5 |
| Gallatin | 2,296 | 2,761 | 3,349 | 5,007 | 51.6 | 36.9 | 21.2 | 11.6 | 32.1 | 43.2 | 59.8 | 68.0 | 2.2 | 5.5 | 5.0 | 6.9 |
| Garrard | 5,592 | 6,741 | 7,776 | 9,951 | 51.3 | 36.8 | 26.0 | 13.3 | 31.9 | 44.5 | 54.3 | 69.4 | 4.7 | 7.2 | 6.3 | 10.5 |

## EDUCATIONAL ATTAINMENT: YEARS OF SCHOOL COMPLETED, 1970-2000

| AREA | TOTAL PERSONS 25 YEARS AND OLDER | | | | 8 YEARS OF SCHOOL OR LESS | | | | HIGH SCHOOL | | | | 4 OR MORE YEARS OF COLLEGE | | | |
|---|---|---|---|---|---|---|---|---|---|---|---|---|---|---|---|---|
| | 1970 | 1980 | 1990 | 2000 | 1970 | 1980 | 1990 | 2000 | 1970 | 1980 | 1990 | 2000 | 1970 | 1980 | 1990 | 2000 |
| Grant | 5,756 | 7,630 | 9,635 | 13,861 | 48.1 | 34.0 | 19.8 | 9.3 | 33.5 | 49.0 | 61.6 | 72.4 | 3.7 | 5.6 | 7.2 | 9.4 |
| Graves | 18,967 | 21,686 | 22,682 | 24,932 | 43.9 | 32.2 | 18.7 | 10.7 | 36.3 | 50.0 | 62.0 | 73.4 | 3.6 | 7.9 | 8.8 | 12.6 |
| Grayson | 9,200 | 12,203 | 13,615 | 15,940 | 66.4 | 49.1 | 32.0 | 20.3 | 21.7 | 37.2 | 48.3 | 62.8 | 4.0 | 5.6 | 6.1 | 7.7 |
| Green | 6,154 | 6,918 | 7,093 | 7,983 | 70.6 | 55.2 | 38.6 | 24.7 | 21.1 | 35.6 | 49.0 | 61.4 | 3.1 | 3.9 | 6.8 | 9.1 |
| Greenup | 17,403 | 22,402 | 24,051 | 25,323 | 43.4 | 27.1 | 18.6 | 10.5 | 38.9 | 57.1 | 64.7 | 75.1 | 4.3 | 9.1 | 11.1 | 11.5 |
| Hancock | 3,747 | 4,253 | 4,844 | 5,427 | 45.8 | 29.0 | 17.3 | 8.8 | 38.9 | 57.2 | 69.3 | 77.2 | 3.9 | 6.3 | 6.9 | 8.1 |
| Hardin | 28,263 | 39,986 | 49,643 | 58,358 | 32.7 | 20.9 | 12.1 | 6.7 | 51.7 | 66.5 | 75.3 | 82.3 | 7.5 | 10.9 | 12.9 | 15.4 |
| Harlan | 19,821 | 22,992 | 22,506 | 22,041 | 61.2 | 45.1 | 31.7 | 21.9 | 23.9 | 38.2 | 49.5 | 58.7 | 4.3 | 5.7 | 6.4 | 8.9 |
| Harrison | 8,408 | 9,271 | 10,490 | 12,000 | 46.1 | 34.8 | 19.5 | 10.7 | 37.2 | 46.9 | 62.4 | 74.2 | 6.2 | 7.3 | 8.6 | 10.6 |
| Hart | 8,005 | 9,123 | 9,659 | 11,474 | 63.6 | 47.8 | 34.6 | 21.0 | 23.0 | 37.2 | 45.3 | 58.2 | 3.2 | 6.4 | 5.2 | 7.0 |
| Henderson | 19,705 | 23,811 | 27,643 | 29,960 | 37.7 | 25.2 | 14.3 | 8.0 | 44.2 | 57.2 | 68.5 | 78.3 | 5.5 | 10.2 | 11.1 | 13.8 |
| Henry | 6,492 | 7,776 | 8,389 | 10,032 | 49.0 | 34.0 | 21.4 | 10.7 | 36.0 | 50.9 | 60.9 | 73.4 | 4.6 | 7.4 | 8.2 | 9.8 |
| Hickman | 3,741 | 3,830 | 3,852 | 3,734 | 45.1 | 30.3 | 23.0 | 15.0 | 34.6 | 53.2 | 56.8 | 64.4 | 2.6 | 7.5 | 7.6 | 8.8 |
| Hopkins | 22,200 | 27,410 | 29,896 | 31,464 | 47.1 | 34.3 | 20.9 | 12.8 | 35.5 | 49.7 | 62.5 | 71.3 | 5.0 | 7.5 | 9.6 | 10.6 |
| Jackson | 5,294 | 6,693 | 7,324 | 8,611 | 76.4 | 62.5 | 43.6 | 27.7 | 13.6 | 25.3 | 38.3 | 52.9 | 3.5 | 4.2 | 4.9 | 6.8 |
| Jefferson | 370,404 | 406,868 | 439,055 | 464,284 | 31.9 | 19.1 | 9.7 | 5.4 | 47.3 | 63.6 | 74.1 | 81.8 | 9.7 | 15.3 | 19.3 | 24.8 |
| Jessamine | 9,594 | 14,032 | 18,458 | 24,182 | 41.5 | 26.3 | 14.2 | 8.7 | 41.5 | 59.7 | 69.0 | 79.1 | 11.8 | 17.3 | 19.1 | 21.5 |
| Johnson | 9,923 | 13,944 | 14,571 | 15,735 | 62.8 | 44.7 | 28.1 | 18.0 | 25.2 | 42.8 | 54.7 | 63.8 | 4.5 | 7.4 | 9.3 | 9.3 |
| Kenton | 68,985 | 78,036 | 88,454 | 97,727 | 35.9 | 22.9 | 10.7 | 6.1 | 42.4 | 59.0 | 74.4 | 82.1 | 7.1 | 12.2 | 17.0 | 22.9 |
| Knott | 7,181 | 9,283 | 10,619 | 11,427 | 70.4 | 50.7 | 35.9 | 25.0 | 18.8 | 36.2 | 45.1 | 58.7 | 4.9 | 6.1 | 8.2 | 10.2 |
| Knox | 12,441 | 16,552 | 17,934 | 20,401 | 66.5 | 50.9 | 35.2 | 27.0 | 21.9 | 36.0 | 46.6 | 54.1 | 4.3 | 7.3 | 8.0 | 8.8 |
| Larue | 6,042 | 7,232 | 7,814 | 9,017 | 57.5 | 40.4 | 24.3 | 14.7 | 29.3 | 43.9 | 59.0 | 71.0 | 4.6 | 5.0 | 8.1 | 10.9 |
| Laurel | 14,566 | 21,732 | 27,037 | 34,431 | 61.4 | 43.5 | 27.6 | 18.1 | 26.8 | 42.5 | 52.7 | 63.9 | 5.3 | 6.7 | 8.2 | 10.6 |
| Lawrence | 6,080 | 7,982 | 8,677 | 10,256 | 64.2 | 48.9 | 36.0 | 23.7 | 23.2 | 36.0 | 46.4 | 58.2 | 3.8 | 5.5 | 6.2 | 6.6 |
| Lee | 3,562 | 4,544 | 4,654 | 5,381 | 70.3 | 49.8 | 37.7 | 25.6 | 16.6 | 34.6 | 43.4 | 50.9 | 2.8 | 5.7 | 5.8 | 6.3 |
| Leslie | 5,313 | 7,448 | 8,048 | 8,214 | 72.9 | 55.0 | 38.0 | 27.0 | 16.0 | 30.6 | 40.4 | 52.5 | 4.5 | 7.0 | 6.6 | 6.3 |
| Letcher | 12,154 | 16,618 | 16,645 | 16,930 | 66.5 | 46.5 | 33.6 | 22.7 | 19.3 | 37.9 | 45.6 | 58.5 | 3.1 | 6.7 | 6.7 | 7.7 |
| Lewis | 6,336 | 7,805 | 8,127 | 9,256 | 66.2 | 54.7 | 38.8 | 23.4 | 22.0 | 33.0 | 45.4 | 57.4 | 3.5 | 5.3 | 6.7 | 6.4 |
| Lincoln | 9,339 | 11,159 | 12,759 | 15,440 | 58.9 | 45.5 | 30.1 | 18.3 | 26.1 | 37.0 | 50.4 | 64.6 | 4.0 | 4.7 | 6.2 | 8.4 |
| Livingston | 4,565 | 5,723 | 6,200 | 6,851 | 56.3 | 33.0 | 21.2 | 10.2 | 29.8 | 50.9 | 63.1 | 74.3 | 3.0 | 5.4 | 5.4 | 8.4 |
| Logan | 12,653 | 14,495 | 15,856 | 17,471 | 52.3 | 38.9 | 24.9 | 15.4 | 31.7 | 45.1 | 57.7 | 68.5 | 4.7 | 6.6 | 8.1 | 9.6 |
| Lyon | 3,720 | 4,373 | 4,959 | 6,185 | 52.8 | 30.6 | 18.7 | 9.5 | 33.7 | 54.1 | 61.0 | 68.0 | 3.3 | 6.4 | 9.1 | 10.1 |
| McCracken | 34,129 | 38,193 | 42,531 | 45,038 | 32.7 | 22.1 | 11.7 | 7.4 | 47.8 | 62.9 | 73.1 | 80.3 | 7.4 | 11.5 | 14.3 | 18.1 |
| McCreary | 6,194 | 8,145 | 9,118 | 10,668 | 74.0 | 56.0 | 39.4 | 26.6 | 14.8 | 28.8 | 40.2 | 52.6 | 4.1 | 5.2 | 4.6 | 6.7 |
| McLean | 5,346 | 6,149 | 6,316 | 6,737 | 51.9 | 36.3 | 23.5 | 11.0 | 32.1 | 47.1 | 58.6 | 70.8 | 2.8 | 5.6 | 6.6 | 8.7 |
| Madison | 19,544 | 26,152 | 32,274 | 42,125 | 44.3 | 30.4 | 19.2 | 11.9 | 40.6 | 54.9 | 64.8 | 75.2 | 12.0 | 17.8 | 19.1 | 21.8 |
| Magoffin | 5,087 | 6,841 | 7,567 | 8,410 | 71.4 | 55.0 | 40.4 | 28.5 | 17.5 | 30.1 | 38.2 | 50.1 | 2.5 | 5.5 | 4.6 | 6.3 |
| Marion | 8,010 | 9,606 | 10,339 | 11,772 | 54.1 | 38.7 | 23.3 | 15.2 | 31.1 | 44.9 | 58.9 | 70.5 | 4.9 | 6.7 | 6.4 | 9.1 |
| Marshall | 12,120 | 16,184 | 18,824 | 21,278 | 42.9 | 28.5 | 16.2 | 8.4 | 39.5 | 56.4 | 67.6 | 76.9 | 4.1 | 8.4 | 9.6 | 13.7 |
| Martin | 4,389 | 6,874 | 7,208 | 7,835 | 75.5 | 50.4 | 35.3 | 25.0 | 13.9 | 34.5 | 44.4 | 54.0 | 3.8 | 5.9 | 6.0 | 9.0 |
| Mason | 9,947 | 10,708 | 10,895 | 11,372 | 35.2 | 33.8 | 19.0 | 10.1 | 37.4 | 49.2 | 60.7 | 73.3 | 4.8 | 9.7 | 10.2 | 14.4 |

## EDUCATIONAL ATTAINMENT: YEARS OF SCHOOL COMPLETED, 1970-2000

| AREA | TOTAL PERSONS 25 YEARS AND OLDER | | | | 8 YEARS OF SCHOOL OR LESS | | | | HIGH SCHOOL | | | | 4 OR MORE YEARS OF COLLEGE | | | |
|---|---|---|---|---|---|---|---|---|---|---|---|---|---|---|---|---|
| | 1970 | 1980 | 1990 | 2000 | 1970 | 1980 | 1990 | 2000 | 1970 | 1980 | 1990 | 2000 | 1970 | 1980 | 1990 | 2000 |
| Meade | 8,481 | 11,623 | 13,790 | 16,131 | 34.0 | 22.4 | 13.7 | 7.0 | 51.6 | 64.2 | 74.3 | 77.9 | 14.0 | 12.2 | 11.0 | 11.3 |
| Menifee | 2,075 | 2,761 | 3,122 | 4,213 | 73.6 | 54.8 | 34.8 | 23.2 | 15.8 | 31.8 | 46.0 | 57.6 | 2.9 | 4.2 | 4.9 | 8.4 |
| Mercer | 9,361 | 11,520 | 12,757 | 14,158 | 43.1 | 30.9 | 20.5 | 9.6 | 39.9 | 52.3 | 62.8 | 75.8 | 6.3 | 9.2 | 8.9 | 13.5 |
| Metcalfe | 2,075 | 5,370 | 5,873 | 6,729 | 72.8 | 55.5 | 39.8 | 24.7 | 17.3 | 33.1 | 45.2 | 58.0 | 3.3 | 5.2 | 5.0 | 6.6 |
| Monroe | 6,683 | 7,454 | 7,553 | 7,896 | 71.3 | 57.0 | 38.3 | 26.4 | 20.4 | 32.4 | 47.1 | 57.8 | 4.0 | 5.2 | 6.9 | 8.4 |
| Montgomery | 8,241 | 11,405 | 12,460 | 15,033 | 50.4 | 37.4 | 25.7 | 14.7 | 34.1 | 46.8 | 56.1 | 70.5 | 6.5 | 8.0 | 9.2 | 13.4 |
| Morgan | 5,454 | 6,680 | 7,325 | 9,321 | 70.4 | 55.5 | 39.1 | 24.5 | 20.5 | 30.5 | 44.1 | 56.4 | 4.8 | 6.3 | 6.7 | 7.7 |
| Muhlenberg | 16,062 | 18,947 | 20,133 | 21,676 | 51.9 | 37.1 | 24.9 | 15.5 | 30.8 | 44.8 | 54.9 | 65.8 | 3.2 | 6.5 | 6.2 | 8.1 |
| Nelson | 11,095 | 14,802 | 18,159 | 23,785 | 47.0 | 29.8 | 16.9 | 9.6 | 37.8 | 56.0 | 67.4 | 79.0 | 7.1 | 10.0 | 9.3 | 13.4 |
| Nicholas | 3,741 | 4,329 | 4,420 | 4,636 | 54.0 | 39.1 | 25.0 | 16.5 | 28.7 | 42.0 | 55.4 | 62.9 | 3.0 | 6.3 | 6.0 | 7.5 |
| Ohio | 10,930 | 12,863 | 13,562 | 15,237 | 55.9 | 38.3 | 25.5 | 15.9 | 28.3 | 44.1 | 53.1 | 67.0 | 3.5 | 5.1 | 6.2 | 7.4 |
| Oldham | 7,789 | 15,518 | 21,049 | 30,366 | 38.3 | 17.1 | 7.9 | 4.8 | 42.4 | 69.3 | 80.2 | 86.5 | 7.1 | 16.4 | 22.9 | 30.6 |
| Owen | 4,596 | 5,460 | 5,887 | 6,999 | 54.5 | 40.3 | 24.8 | 14.1 | 31.2 | 41.6 | 55.2 | 67.9 | 3.5 | 7.0 | 7.4 | 9.1 |
| Owsley | 2,680 | 3,237 | 3,187 | 3,242 | 76.8 | 59.5 | 49.1 | 33.8 | 12.6 | 29.3 | 35.5 | 49.2 | 4.4 | 6.9 | 9.8 | 7.7 |
| Pendleton | 5,523 | 6,238 | 7,336 | 9,081 | 49.5 | 36.1 | 20.1 | 10.8 | 34.1 | 47.5 | 60.1 | 72.8 | 3.1 | 6.0 | 6.8 | 9.7 |
| Perry | 12,941 | 17,943 | 18,362 | 19,596 | 62.9 | 47.9 | 32.5 | 21.5 | 24.2 | 37.3 | 47.6 | 58.3 | 5.1 | 6.0 | 6.7 | 8.9 |
| Pike | 31,121 | 43,648 | 44,941 | 46,153 | 64.0 | 45.3 | 31.5 | 21.3 | 23.4 | 38.3 | 50.2 | 61.8 | 4.1 | 6.2 | 7.7 | 9.9 |
| Powell | 3,896 | 5,973 | 7,012 | 8,485 | 66.8 | 50.8 | 33.8 | 23.9 | 21.9 | 34.0 | 50.1 | 56.1 | 3.4 | 5.5 | 5.3 | 6.5 |
| Pulaski | 20,038 | 27,175 | 32,512 | 38,430 | 59.3 | 43.1 | 28.5 | 18.1 | 28.8 | 44.5 | 56.2 | 65.6 | 5.2 | 7.1 | 9.2 | 10.5 |
| Robertson | 1,360 | 1,424 | 1,408 | 1,566 | 58.6 | 45.1 | 29.7 | 21.3 | 27.0 | 40.7 | 50.8 | 60.9 | 3.4 | 6.6 | 7.7 | 8.7 |
| Rockcastle | 6,490 | 8,008 | 9,249 | 11,109 | 69.9 | 53.1 | 37.9 | 24.4 | 19.7 | 34.4 | 44.9 | 57.7 | 3.6 | 6.2 | 5.9 | 8.3 |
| Rowan | 6,910 | 9,205 | 10,476 | 12,455 | 52.9 | 36.6 | 27.4 | 16.8 | 35.0 | 51.0 | 57.9 | 70.9 | 12.4 | 16.9 | 17.3 | 21.9 |
| Russell | 6,162 | 8,384 | 9,839 | 11,437 | 67.2 | 48.9 | 32.7 | 22.7 | 22.0 | 37.4 | 50.2 | 61.8 | 4.7 | 6.0 | 6.2 | 9.6 |
| Scott | 9,261 | 12,203 | 14,554 | 20,459 | 40.7 | 28.5 | 13.9 | 7.6 | 42.6 | 55.2 | 69.1 | 80.5 | 8.6 | 11.6 | 15.2 | 20.3 |
| Shelby | 10,882 | 13,909 | 16,318 | 22,096 | 42.7 | 28.3 | 14.8 | 8.0 | 40.1 | 55.1 | 69.9 | 79.1 | 6.1 | 11.3 | 12.9 | 18.7 |
| Simpson | 7,381 | 8,586 | 9,730 | 10,680 | 49.6 | 32.7 | 21.9 | 12.5 | 36.0 | 49.8 | 58.9 | 73.6 | 5.4 | 7.6 | 8.8 | 11.9 |
| Spencer | 2,923 | 3,455 | 4,343 | 7,672 | 62.2 | 43.9 | 25.9 | 12.1 | 25.1 | 39.7 | 57.5 | 75.4 | 3.9 | 5.4 | 9.9 | 11.1 |
| Taylor | 9,549 | 12,533 | 13,792 | 15,253 | 55.1 | 42.4 | 27.4 | 20.1 | 30.8 | 44.1 | 57.4 | 68.0 | 5.5 | 8.2 | 10.1 | 12.2 |
| Todd | 6,232 | 7,090 | 7,028 | 7,758 | 55.3 | 45.4 | 30.0 | 20.7 | 30.6 | 41.3 | 50.6 | 63.5 | 5.5 | 5.8 | 7.1 | 9.2 |
| Trigg | 4,984 | 5,956 | 7,223 | 8,897 | 56.0 | 36.9 | 22.4 | 10.6 | 28.6 | 49.0 | 58.9 | 72.1 | 3.8 | 9.4 | 11.4 | 12.0 |
| Trimble | 2,895 | 3,699 | 3,931 | 5,340 | 46.4 | 29.8 | 19.7 | 11.0 | 33.4 | 49.2 | 61.6 | 70.7 | 2.9 | 5.3 | 7.3 | 7.6 |
| Union | 7,682 | 8,864 | 9,408 | 9,524 | 36.9 | 24.1 | 12.5 | 8.1 | 43.4 | 56.4 | 68.1 | 76.9 | 5.7 | 6.7 | 8.9 | 10.9 |
| Warren | 28,146 | 38,216 | 46,161 | 56,069 | 40.5 | 25.4 | 15.0 | 7.8 | 45.6 | 63.1 | 70.9 | 80.3 | 10.6 | 16.6 | 19.2 | 24.7 |
| Washington | 5,725 | 6,135 | 6,669 | 7,144 | 52.3 | 38.9 | 26.2 | 17.1 | 34.2 | 45.9 | 57.8 | 68.8 | 5.0 | 8.6 | 7.5 | 13.3 |
| Wayne | 7,818 | 9,759 | 11,030 | 13,153 | 73.5 | 58.8 | 39.4 | 26.1 | 18.2 | 29.6 | 44.6 | 57.8 | 2.6 | 5.3 | 5.5 | 7.2 |
| Webster | 8,084 | 8,902 | 9,089 | 9,424 | 51.5 | 34.2 | 19.9 | 12.5 | 30.2 | 47.3 | 60.7 | 70.9 | 3.2 | 5.2 | 6.0 | 7.1 |
| Whitley | 13,472 | 18,554 | 20,195 | 22,708 | 58.7 | 44.0 | 28.8 | 19.0 | 26.9 | 40.5 | 53.0 | 61.3 | 5.5 | 8.7 | 11.3 | 13.4 |
| Wolfe | 2,994 | 3,688 | 4,052 | 4,571 | 75.4 | 57.9 | 38.8 | 25.9 | 16.6 | 26.8 | 42.8 | 53.6 | 3.3 | 6.7 | 7.7 | 10.6 |
| Woodford | 7,749 | 10,267 | 12,840 | 15,546 | 36.8 | 24.6 | 12.2 | 7.5 | 46.0 | 60.8 | 73.5 | 82.6 | 9.6 | 15.6 | 19.5 | 25.9 |

Produced by the Kentucky State Data Center
Sources: 1970, 1980, 1990, and 2000 Census of Population and Housing
http://ksdc.louisville.edu/sdc/census2000/educ 1970-200.xls

# EDUCATION
# *Adult Education and Literacy*

For all Kentuckians to prosper, every citizen must be prepared to function well in the workforce, the community and the home. Experts tell us that 80 percent of all jobs to be created over the next two decades will require some postsecondary education. Kentucky is far from ready for this new reality, with about 40 percent of working-age citizens functioning at the two lowest levels of literacy. According to 2004 census data, Kentucky ranks 44th in the nation in the percentage of adults with at least a high school education (81.8 percent).

Without a good education, Kentuckians can't compete for good jobs to make enough money to support their families and their children are less likely to succeed in school and beyond. This means the Commonwealth can't make a compelling case for companies opening or expanding their business in Kentucky.

Recognizing that an undereducated workforce is a hindrance on the state's economy, the 2000 General Assembly passed The Kentucky Adult Education Act. This legislation created a partnership between Kentucky Adult Education (KYAE) and the Council on Postsecondary Education, increased funding and set the stage for dramatic improvements in the educational status of adult Kentuckians who lacked a high school diploma, functioned at low levels of literacy or wanted to learn the English language.

In fiscal year 2004, 120,051 students enrolled in Kentucky Adult Education programs. This was more than double the number enrolled in 2000.

Kentucky Adult Education places a particular emphasis on family literacy because efforts to improve the educational attainment of children will fail without a strong outreach to their first teachers — their parents. Kentucky is one of only two states with family literacy programs in every county. KYAE partners with the Kentucky Institute for Family Literacy and the National Center for Family Literacy, which provides professional development and technical assistance to help improve Kentucky's family literacy program.

KYAE provides funds workforce education to meet the needs of business and industry. Many businesses are using KYAE's SkillMobiles — state-of-the-art mobile computer labs that feature online curriculum.

The first of its kind in the nation, the Kentucky Virtual Adult Education website (www.kyvae.org) allows adults to learn anywhere, anytime, at their convenience.

English-as-a-second language programs help adults become more fluent in English, pass U.S. citizenship tests, work on job-seeking skills and improve their ability to cope with society. With the help of Kentucky Department of Correction and federal funds, KYAE provides adult education in state prisons and local jails. In addition to adult basic education services, this program provides appropriate life skills courses.

KYAE has funded pilot programs designed to increase the number of GED graduates who move on to postsecondary education. The percentage of GED graduates who went on to college increased from 12 percent in 1998 to 19 percent in 2002. Kentucky's recent reforms have enhanced KYAE collaborations with other programs, agencies, educational systems and services.

*Source: Kentucky Adult Education.*

**A Moonlight school**
*Source: Kentucky Virtual Library*

## EDUCATION

# General Education Development (GED)

Sid Webb

The General Educational Development test was developed over 50 years ago to help returning veterans from WW II pick up their educations where they left off and enable them to continue on to college. A GED certificate is the equivalent of a high school diploma. Kentucky leads the nation in providing an alternative to high school dropouts who discover that good paying jobs are scarce for people who have not attained a high school education.

Nearly 35 years ago, KET, the public television network in Kentucky, developed a comprehensive television series to aid people in studying for the GED test. Since then, KET has remade the series twice, improving on it each time with feedback from both teachers and students.

Contrary to what many think, the GED is not an easy test. Its developers at the American Council on Education (ACE) see to that. Each time they remake the test and update it they ask high school seniors to take it. The pass/fail score for the test is set at a level that would have failed 25 percent of the high school seniors who took it.

While KET was making their first GED series a respected book company in New York formed a partnership with KET to publish and sell the GED videotapes and accompanying workbooks to other states. The partnership proved fruitful for KET. By the end of the decade adult education centers in every state in the union, including the U.S. military, were using the KET/GED series.

In the 70s, the use of videotapes was not common in homes. Videotape machines were bulky and expensive. By the early 80s, however, videotape machines had become small and affordable. More and more people had them in their homes. Now GED students who depended on TV for instruction could tape and replay at their convenience GED programs broadcast on KET and other stations. This widened the potential audience and changed the market dynamics.

KET had always partnered with the Kentucky Department of Education and schools in Kentucky, and during the 70s it had left the promotion and recruitment of GED students to the state department. KET felt it was reaching students in rural communities that were under-served by adult education programs; but when it took a hard look at what other states were accomplishing with its GED program, KET decided it time to take an active role in promoting the series in Kentucky.

About the same time, several things happened that gave new impetus to the GED series for KET. The network dropped its partnership with the book company and started publishing and distributing its own books. Secondly, ACE decided it was time to update and revise the GED test. Thirdly, there was a move on the national level to promote the KET/GED series as an important educational contribution that public television could do well.

KET decided to provide its new KET/GED series at no cost to other public TV stations across the nation to stir new life and enthusiasm into GED. KET also began actively enrolling, tracking and aiding GED-ON-TV students.

Today the KET/GED series is still going strong in Kentucky and attracting new students in the state and around the U.S. KET revised the GED series again in 2002 as part of the broader Workplace Literacy series. Each year about 1,000 people watch the series, take and pass the GED test in Kentucky.

In the past three decades KET estimates that as many as a million people in the nation may have gotten their GED certificates by using its series.

*Source: KET, The Kentucky Network*

Culture
& the Arts

*Lindy Casebier*

Rosemary Clooney

Jean Ritchie

KYA Artisan Center, Berea, KY

Loretta Lynn

David Wright - Windsor Chairmaker

The Judds

Louisville Ballet

Boots Randolph

John Lair

*Sources: Kentucky Artisan Center*
*Kentucky Music Hall of Fame*
*Kentucky Department of Tourism*

Kentucky is blessed with a rich artistic and cultural heritage. Through the years Kentuckians have led the way in sharing their extensive talents: Jesse Stuart, Robert Penn Warren, Wendell Berry, Joel Tanner Hart, Lionel Hampton, Rosemary Clooney, Bill Monroe, Loretta Lynn, the Everly Brothers, Ed Hamilton, Ricky Skaggs, John Michael Montgomery, Naomi, Wynonna & Ashley Judd, Diane Sawyer and Johnny Depp – to name a few. These Kentuckians have received national and international acclaim for their contributions. Every day many other talented Kentuckians make their artistic contribution to the commonwealth and the nation by sharing their gifts.

Kentucky's arts offerings are as diverse as our people, and can be found in every corner of the state. Bluegrass or blues, opera or opry, craft fairs or art museums—wherever your tastes may lead you, we've got it in the Bluegrass state.

In Kentucky, crafts are revered and the traditions live on in the pieces that grew out of necessity from early frontier days, like quilts and coverlets, baskets, furniture, pottery, brooms and dulcimers. That strong foundation in craft has also made way for contemporary expressions in sculpture, ceramics, jewelry, glass, metal and fiber arts. With the newly inaugurated Kentucky Artisan Center at Berea

**A display in the Kentucky Appalachian Artisan Center in Hindman**
*Source: Lexington Herald-Leader*

**A craftsman at work**
*Source: Tour Southern & Eastern Kentucky*

and the Berea College and the Kentucky Guild of Artist and Craftsmen's craft fairs, Berea earns its title as the Folk Arts and Crafts Capital of Kentucky. Centrally located in the state, this enclave of tradition is the gateway into a world of wonderful crafts that can be found from the hills and hollers of eastern Kentucky all the way west to the Mississippi River, including our urban centers.

When it comes to theatre and the performing arts, Kentucky has something for everyone including professional theatre, community theatre, summer stock, outdoor drama, touring companies and student productions.

The Music Theatre Louisville, performing at the Iroquois Amphitheater is a must see for family fun, along with The Jenny Wiley Theatre in Prestonsburg, the Ragged Edge Community Theatre in Harrodsburg, or the Walden Theatre with youth performers in Louisville. The Kentucky Repertory Theatre at Horse Cave is nationally acclaimed for artistic excellence. The Actors Guild of Lexington and Actors Theatre of Louisville produce high quality shows with some written by America's best playwrights.

Great theatre can also be found in Paducah, Bowling Green, Owensboro, Falmouth and in Elkhorn City.

The state strongly supports the performing arts, with the Kentucky Center (www.kentuckycenter.org) in Louisville as the cultural heart of the city, region, and state. It is a showcase for Kentucky performance and visual arts as well as for national and international performances in orchestra, theatre, dance, opera, jazz, and contemporary music.

The annual Great American Brass Band Festival in Danville
Source: Lexington Herald-Leader

Other venues include The Mountain Arts Center in Prestonsburg, which serves as home to the Kentucky Opry. The Paramount Arts Center in Ashland offers performances by artists from the Country Music Highway such as Ricky Skaggs, Loretta Lynn and Wynonna Judd, as does Renfro Valley Entertainment Center in Renfro Valley. Appalshop in Whitesburg offers an authentic view of Appalachian culture through performance, visual and media arts.

In Lexington, the University of Kentucky's Singletary Center for the Arts serves the greater Lexington community, and the Norton Center at Centre College's provides nationally acclaimed performances. Owensboro is home to the International Thumbpickers Hall of Fame, which honors a distinctive style of guitar playing that originated in the western coalfields.

With world-renowned works on display, the Speed Art Museum, in Louisville, is Kentucky's oldest and largest art museum with over 12,000 pieces in its permanent collection. Its collection spans 6,000 years, ranging from ancient Egyptian to contemporary art, and also includes a strong Kentucky collection of paintings, sculp-

ture and decorative arts.

The Owensboro Museum of Fine Art features a permanent collection of 19th-and 20th-century paintings and sculptures, decorative arts dating back as far as the 16th century, and the spectacular Stained Glass Gallery.

Visit the Museum of the American Quilters Society in Paducah, which houses the largest collection of art quilts in the world. Lexington's Headley-Whitney Museum tops the list for small treasures. Dedicated to the decorative arts, the museum's signature collection is comprised of intricately jeweled sculptures known as bibelots.

The Carnegie Center for Visual and Performing Arts in Covington has five art galleries showcasing local, regional and national artists. A wonderful blend of regional natural history, cultural history and art can be found at Covington's Behringer-Crawford Museum. In Paducah, the Yeiser Art Center's permanent collection of American, European, African and Asian art is highlighted each year by the prestigious "Fantastic Fibers" exhibition with a national call to fiber artists.

Lexington's oldest and largest visual arts organization, the Lexington Art League, offers regular exhibitions at the MetroLex Gallery of the National City Bank Building and their home base at the Loudon House.

Kentucky's cultural landscape is as varied as the high winding eastern mountain roads, the rolling hills of central Kentucky and the vast farms and lakes of the west. The Kentucky Arts Council can provide current contact information for any of the listed arts organizations or cultural attractions. Call 888-833-ARTS or kyarts@ky.gov.

**Inside the Kentucky Artisan Center**
Source: Kentucky Artisan Center

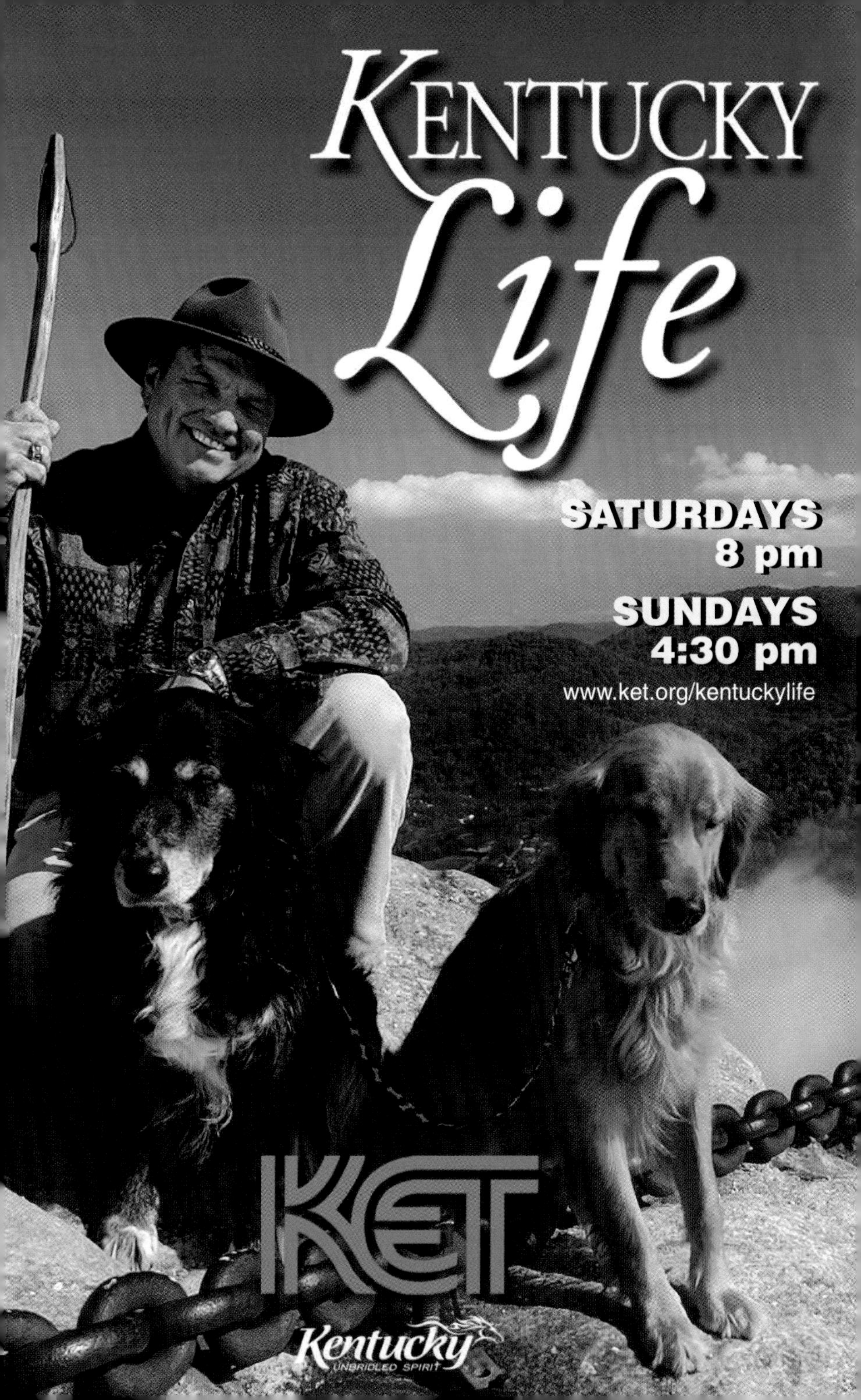

# KENTUCKY *Life*

**SATURDAYS**
8 pm

**SUNDAYS**
4:30 pm

www.ket.org/kentuckylife

KET

Kentucky
UNBRIDLED SPIRIT

# CULTURE & THE ARTS

# *Governor's Awards in the Arts*

Ed Lawrence

The Governor's Awards in the Arts are the commonwealth's most prestigious awards in the arts. Recipients are selected annually to honor individuals, organizations, businesses and government entities who have outstanding achievements in the arts or have made significant contributions to the arts in Kentucky, with the Milner Award being the highest honor.

The most recent recipient of the Milner Award, for outstanding individual commitment to the arts and their role in the economy, community and culture of Kentucky, was Glema Mahr of Madisonville. Mahr has been a devoted volunteer, and significant donor to the arts-programming endowment of the Madisonville Community College Glema Mahr Center for the Arts.

The National Award honored the Everly Brothers, from the Central City area, as Kentuckians who have achieved national acclaim for their artistic achievement. Don and Phil Everly have had such popular hits as "Wake Up Little Susie," "Bye Bye Love," and "All I Have to Do Is Dream."

The Artist Award honoring lifetime achievement in the arts went to Emmy Award winning musician, accompanist, arranger, composer and teacher Jay Flippin of Morehead.

Artique, with two galleries of fine contemporary craft in Lexington, received the Business Award for outstanding support of the arts.

The Baker Hunt Foundation, a non-profit arts school founded in 1922 to serve northern Kentucky area youth and adults, won the Community Arts Award, for its substantial impact on the community through the arts.

The Education Award honored Hazel Carver for her lifelong and significant contributions to the arts in education. She served for 35 years as band and choral director for Russellville High School, and is known as a legend in her own time in music education.

Marvin Finn, a living treasure of Louisville, received the Folk Heritage Award for his contributions to promoting and perpetuating Kentucky's unique artistic traditions. Folk artist Finn is best known for his colorful and imaginative hand-carved wood sculptures of animals, invoking associations with African Art.

The Government Award recipient is a flagship program for the commonwealth, the Governor's School for the Arts. Each summer this national model brings together 225 high school students and a community of arts professionals to participate in a rigorous, college–level training program in eight different arts disciplines. Kentucky Monthly, the magazine that celebrates the people, places and events of the state, received the Media Award for its notable commitment to bring the arts to the attention of the public.

The Kentucky Arts Council, a state agency in the Commerce Cabinet, administers the Governor's Awards in the Arts selection process. In partnership with the National Endowment for the Arts, the Arts Council invests in programs that develop vibrant communities, provide lifelong education in the arts and support arts participation.

*For more information about the Kentucky Arts Council; call 1-888-833-2787, e-mail kyarts@ky.gov or visit www.artscouncil.ky.gov.*

**Don and Phil Everly**
*Source: Kentucky Department for Tourism*

CULTURE & THE ARTS

# Poets, Writers, Novelists & Playwrights

## Kentucky's Poets Laureate

Bluegrass music, thoroughbred horses and bourbon may be among the first things to come to mind when people think of Kentucky. Poets laureate and distinguished writers. Kentucky is rich in accomplished writers, from Pulitzer-Prize winner (both poetry and prose) Robert Penn Warren to the flock of talented and acclaimed Kentucky writers publishing now—James Baker Hall, Wendell Berry, Bobbie Ann Mason,

**J. T. Cotton Noe**
*Source: Kentucky Virtual Library*

Kim Edwards—there seems to be unusually fecund soil for their growth and productivity. As 1999 Poet Laureate, Richard Taylor observes, "Kentucky is increasingly recognized as a state that has produced important national voices in fiction, drama, and poetry...a state that values its rich literary heritage."
Since 1926 Ken-

tucky has appointed 22 poets laureate, honoring these individuals and recognizing the art and importance of poetry. In 1986 Kentuckian Robert Penn Warren, one of America's most distinguished scholars and writers, was appointed U.S. Poet Laureate (he was the only three-time Pulitzer Prize winner). Kentucky's poets laureate have come from diverse backgrounds and occupations—farmers, lawyers, educators, homemakers, bankers, legislators, professors, and business people—all have made unique contributions to the illustrious literary tradition and heritage of Kentucky:

1926  J.T. Cotton Noe
1928  Edward G. Hill
1945  Louise Scott Phillips
1954  Edwin Carlisle Litsey
1954  Jesse Hilton Stuart
1956  Lowell Allen Williams
1974  Lillie D. Chaffin
1976  Tom Mobley
1978  Agnes O'Rear
1984  Clarence Clay
1984  Lee Pennington
1984  Paul Salyers
1986  Dale Faughn
1986  Jim Wayne Miller
1986  Henry E. Pilkenton
1990  James H. Patton
1995  James Still
1997  Joy Bale Boone
1999  Richard Taylor
2001  James Baker Hall
2003  Joe Survant
2005  Sena Jeter Naslund

**Richard Taylor**
*Source: KET The Kentucky Network*

*Reprinted with permission from Wind Publications, Poets Laureate of Kentucky, Betty J. Sparks (2004) and special thanks to the Kentucky Arts Council.*

# Notable Kentucky Authors

James Lane Allen
Joseph A Altsheler
Harriette Arnow
Prentice Baker
Donald Barickman
Garry Barker
Beverly Barlett
Wendell Berry
Emily Bingham
Sallie Bingham
Ed Bowen
Michelle Boisseau
Perry Bramlett
Cleanth Brooks
Devin Brown
Harry Brown
James Mason Brown
William Wells Brown
Patricia Parker Brunner
Warren Brunner
Charles Neville Buck
Roberta Bunnell
Ben Lucien Burman
Tracy Campbell
John Carloftis
Stephanie A Carpenter
Harry Caudill
Madison Cawein
Lillie Chaffin
Sherry Chandler
Billy C Clark

**Thomas D Clark**
Irvin S Cobb
Richard H Collins
Joe Coomer
Stephen Cope
Joseph S Cotter

Joseph Seamon Cotter Jr
Alfred Leland Crabb
Donna Valtri Crane
Joe Creason
Olive Tilford Dargan
Guy Davenport
Gwen Davenport

**David & Lalie Dick**
Linda Scott DeRosier
David Domine
Andy Doolen
Michael Dorris
Kathleen Driskell
Leon V Driskell
George Ecklund
Amy Edwards
Kim Edwards
Scott Elliott
Steve Flairty
Abraham Flexner
Charles Bracelon Flood
Leigh Anne Florence
John Fox Jr
Thomas Freese
Lucy Furman
Gatewood Galbraith
Jane Gentry
Janice Holt Giles
Joey Goebel
James B Goode
John Patrick Googan
Caroline Gordon
Sue Grafton
Jonathan Green
Jonathan Greene
Vivianne A Griffiths
AB Guthrie
James Baker Hall
Tom T Hall

Wade Hall
Elizabeth Hardwick
Anthony Harkins
Robert Hazel
Lynn Hightower
Harry L. Hinkle
Chris Holbrook
David Holland
Bruce Hopkins
Silas House
Charlie Hughes
Gwyn Hyman-Rubio
Fenton Johnson
Annie Fellows Johnston
Ann Jonas
Carridder Jones
Gayl Jones
Loyal Jones
Marcia Thornton Jones
Eleanor Mercein Kelly
Leatha Kendrick
Jack Kerley
David King

**Barbara Kingsolver**
John Kleber
Freda Klotter

**Jim Klotter**
Lisa Koger
Richard Krause
Laban Lacy

Margaret Lane

**Sylvia Lovely**
Loretta Lynn
George Ella Lyon

**Bobbie Ann Mason**
Jane Mayhall
Taylor McCafferty
Deborah Vansau McCauley

**Ed McClanahan**
Robert Emmett McDowell
John McGill
Jennie Taylor McHenry
Clark McMeekin
Keven McQueen
Teresa Medeiros
Thomas Merton
Jim Wayne Miller
Lynwood Montell
Rob Morris
James Hilary Mulligan
Beverly Graves Myers
Alana Nash
Sena Jeter Naslund

**John Jacob Niles**
Gurney Norman
Marsha Norman
Jayna & Kelli Oakley
Chris Offutt
Theodore O'Hara
Z Z Packer

**John Ed Pearce**
Lee Pennington
Yolanda Pierce
Joe A Porter
Eugenia Dunlap Potts
Betty Layman Receveur
Erik Reece
Billy Reed
Alice Hegan Rice
Cale Young Rice
Jean Ritchie
Karen Robards
Elizabeth Madox Roberts
Charles P Roland

**Gwyn Rubio**
Charles Semones
Anne Shelby
James Robert Sherburne
Bob Sloan

Effie Waller Smith
Frederick Smock
Mark Sohn
Jan Sparkman
Vince Staten
Tom Stephens
Albert Steward
Al Stewart
Albert Stewart
Martha Bennet Stiles
James Still
Louis Stout
Jesse Stuart
Lucinda Dixon Sullivan
Hollis Summers
Harold Tallant
Allen Tate
Walter Tevis
Samuel Thomas
Charles Thompson
Frank X Walker
Pamela Walker
Tom Wallace

**Robert Penn Warren**
Jan Watson

**Henry Watterson**
Amelia B Welby
Crystal Wilkinson
Shelia Williams
Geoge C Wolfe

*Source:s Eastern Kentucky University, Dept. of English, www.english.eku.edu/services/ kylit/default.htm; "Kentucky Encyclopedia," University Press of Kentucky 1992.*

David and Lalie Dick

## CULTURE & THE ARTS
# *Kentucky –*
# *A State of Mind*

One of the best things about living in Kentucky is the coming back after being gone for a while. When we turn in at the front gate, past the twin plum trees, through the row of blooming Bradford pears, toward the ancient water maples, we know in our bones, we've done the right thing.

We shouldn't be living anyplace else. This is where we belong—with the grassroots people.

This is homeland—a state of mind—which, or course, is possible in any land at any time. Yet, Kentucky is quietly out of the ordinary, providing a common ground encouraging human beings to reach within themselves and to be themselves in the way Kahlil Gibran described "beauty" in *The Prophet*:

*Beauty is eternity gazing at itself in a mirror.*
*But you are eternity and you are the mirror.*

Eternity in Kentucky is the movement of the Great Water Cycle. The mirror refracts in the cloud formations, the droplets coming to rest on blowing blades of bluegrass. Most Kentuckians live intimately in this eternity—clouds, sun, and the moisture.

There is no death.

Imagine, then, Kentucky—A State of Mind is an abiding closeness, an assembly of consciousness with nature and creatures of many kinds.

There's no mistaking home. The dogs come out to greet with licks and tail quivers. If they could talk they wouldn't say, "What did you bring us other than yourself?" If the walls of the mudroom could speak, they might say, "Come on in here, prop up your feet, and tell us a little, but not too much about the trip."

We call to mind the first sight of the mountains of Whitley County as we come up I-75 along Hell's Point Ridge past Jellico, then along Clear Fork of Cumberland River the haze beginning to take on an unmistakable Kentucky hue. Makes us want to roll the window down and breathe deeply!

There's much to do in our winter of content—appreciation of small treasures, the return to simple values, the building of a finer communication.

Let us live in Kentucky, a state of mind, in every season, through every storm, through every calm moment, sunrise to sunset.

When you're a Kentuckian a sustaining existence comes in the unfurling of the natural curl of life. It is well to remember, we do not live alone. Our companions are those who share our belief that we are united in trust and respect in and for the good life, the state of mind we call home.

## Quotes from David & Lalie Dick

"With Lalie, I found my "peace at the center" in the old house alongside Plum Lick Creek—we call it home sweet Kentucky—where there are no committees, consultants, or circular firing squads."
*Follow the Storm—A Long Way Home*
by David Dick

"Jesse was big, boisterous, and beset with a desire to write, no matter the consequences. He was as tough as a terrapin's shell—but underneath, he was tender and caring."
*Jesse Stuart—The Heritage*
by David Dick

"The miracle of Kentucky lies mainly in the loveliness of the seasonal movement. It is a treasure that is real."
*Home Sweet Kentucky*
by David and Lalie Dick

"He was a scroungy dog. His ribs showed. When he breathed, little puffs of dust rose up and settled back down on his crusted nose. He was a Camelot for fleas."
*The View from Plum Lick*
by David Dick

CULTURE & THE ARTS

# Kentucky Book Fair & Festival of Books

### Kentucky Book Fair in Frankfort Celebrates 25th Anniversary

The Kentucky Book Fair, founded in 1981, is one of Kentucky's premier literary events and one of the largest of its kind in the nation. Each year approximately 150 authors attend the Book Fair to autograph copies of their latest book. Between 4,000 and 5,000 patrons attend and gross sales annually top $120,000.

The Kentucky Book Fair provides an opportunity for the public to meet, talk with, and purchase personally autographed books from authors residing here in Kentucky and throughout

(Top) Tom Clark and Margaret Lane show off their new book — (left) Former First Lady Phyllis George and Connie Crowe at the Kentucky Book Fair
*Photo: Riggs Williams*

the country. This year marks the 25th anniversary of the fair, and it will continue a great tradition with a wonderful selection of authors as well as special symposiums and events for children.

The Book Fair is sponsored by The State Journal, Frankfort's daily newspaper, and co-sponsored by the Kentucky Department for Libraries and Archives and the University Press of Kentucky.

### Bluegrass Festival of Books

Joseph-Beth Group is one of the nation's strongest and most prosperous independent bookselling companies. Neil and Mary Beth Van Uum opened the first Joseph-Beth store in Lexington in November 1986. The original bookstore began with 37,000 titles in a 6,500-square-foot space. Twenty years later, an expanded and renovated Joseph-

Beth's is a 40,000-square-foot bookstore located in the heart of the Mall at Lexington Green provides customers with two stories of books and sidelines, expanded music and children's departments, and a full service restaurant overlooking the Lexington Green Lake. Joseph-Beth Booksellers has stores in Cincinnati and Cleveland, Ohio; Nashville, Memphis and Jackson Tenn.; Pittsburgh, Penn.; and the newest store opened in Charlotte, N.C. in April of 2005.

The Bluegrass Festival of Books, sponsored by Joseph-Beth Booksellers and the Lexington Herald-Leader, is held in late April at the Lexington Convention Center, in downtown Lexington. Book lovers can meet some of their favorite regional and national authors, attend special sessions, like "Small Space Gardening" with John Carloftis, participate in a writer's workshop, listen to authors' readings or musical, and there are childrens events too.

Other Kentucky communities host book fairs to celebrate books and encourage literacy including: Maysville Festival of Books, held annually in Dec. at the Maysville Community and Technical College in Maysville; Southern Kentucky Book Fest, held every April during National Library Week, at Sloan Convention Center in Bowling Green, and Western Kentucky Book Fair in October each year, in Sturgis.

All book fairs are free and open to the public; special events may require a fee and reservations.

*The 25th Anniversary poster was created and copyrighted by Bob Lanham, 2006.*

# CULTURE & THE ARTS

Robert S. Boles

# *Film & Television*

*"You've all been so nice and please tell everybody that I've enjoyed my stay here and appreciate the kindnesses of the Danville people."* - Elizabeth Taylor, Aug. 30, 1956, Kentucky Advocate.

Kentucky has a very rich heritage when it comes to the film industry. Successful films such as Raintree County, The Kentuckian, Seabiscuit, How the West was Won, Coal Miner's Daughter, Eight Men Out, and Stripes are but a few of the successful films that were filmed on location in the state.

Whether Hollywood filmmakers are looking for period towns, scenic outdoor areas or bluegrass horse farms, Kentucky has a wide variety of extraordinary locations to choose from. The choice was made early for two award-winning films in the late 1950s—April Love (1957) and Raintree County (1958). April Love, set in Central Kentucky, finds bad boy Pat Boone as a juvenile delinquent sent to his uncle's farm for rehabilitation. Along the way to recovery he meets Shirley Jones, and gets involved with drag-racers. The following year, Raintree County, written in the great tradition of civil war romance, was filmed in Danville. The dramatic plot was perfect for the stellar cast, which included Montgomery Clift, Elizabeth Taylor, Eva Marie Saint, Nigel Patrick, Lee Marvin, Rod Taylor and Agnes Moorehead. The world premiere of the film, directed by Edward Dmytryk, was held in October 1957 in Louisville. A two-week festival celebrating the 50th anniversary of the release of the MGM classic film Raintree County will be held July 24 -

**The "Welcome to Danville" parade for Elizabeth Taylor for the filming of Raintree County in 1956**
*Source: Guy Ingram, and the Raintree Festival Committee*

August 4, 2007 in Danville. See www.raintreecountyfestival.com for details.

Kentucky is known throughout the world for its thoroughbred industry, and that's especially true in Hollywood. Our horse farms, the 1,032-acre Kentucky Horse Park and our beautiful tracks, including Keeneland, Turfway Park and Churchill Downs, have been featured in a wide variety of commercials, television shows and feature films. Horse related feature films that were shot totally or partially in the commonwealth include Seabiscuit, The Thoroughbreds, Black Beauty, The Champions, Bluegrass, A Horse for Danny, Simpatico, Dreamer and many others.

Lexington, "The Horse Capital of the World," is located in the heart of central Kentucky and home to many world-famous farms. Lexington may be the town with the largest concentration of horse farms in the world, but the film industry learned long ago that Lexington has a lot more than just horses to offer. Scattered throughout the Lexington area are period neighborhoods, antebellum mansions, two universities and one of the largest basketball venues in the nation, Rupp Arena, and these are only a few of the city's assets that film makers have used over the years. In 1978 the feature film Steel was filmed on location at a downtown Lexington construction site. Other films that have been shot in central Kentucky include Seabiscuit and Dreamer.

Kentucky's largest river city is Louisville, home of the Kentucky Derby, the Belle of Louisville and

Tony-award winning Actors Theatre. Modern office towers contrast with historic neighborhoods, including blocks of Victorian homes such as Farmington, built in 1810 using a design by Thomas Jefferson. These venues have been used by film producers for decades. The recently released movie, Elizabethtown, was filmed in Oldham County and in Jefferson County.

Many of the communities in northern Kentucky reflect the ethnic backgrounds of Irish and German heritage. These period neighborhoods manifest the character and variety of an age not so long ago. These areas have also attracted Hollywood film companies. Films shot in this region include Little Man Tate, City of Hope and A Rage in Harlem to name a few. The blockbuster film, Rain Man, was also filmed at locations throughout northern Kentucky, and even required the closing of a nearby interstate for one scene.

Kentucky also has many small towns scattered throughout the state that evoke the charm of main street America. River towns along the Ohio River have welcomed Lost in Yonkers, a PBS American Playhouse version of Huckleberry Finn, and the television mini-series Centennial.

Many of Kentucky's small towns are well-preserved, intact period towns that frequently attract film producers. The Kentucky Main Street Program manages the revitalization of downtown areas statewide, providing towns with period appearances ranging from 1880-1920. Part of A League of Their Own was filmed in the Main Street community of Henderson, featuring the Soaper Hotel and a private home as a boarding house. Kentucky has many historic sites, including a wide variety of private homes and public buildings. The southern charm of Spindletop Hall welcomed the television mini-series Bluegrass. White Hall, a

Ken Curtis on location during the filming of "Black Beauty" released in 1977
Source: Kentucky Film Commission

Richard Chamberland in the mini-series "Centennial" shot on location at White Hall near Richmond
Source: Kentucky Film Commission

unique blend of Gothic, Georgian Revival and Italianate architectural styles, has been featured in the opening credits of the television series Sister Kate and in the mini-series Centennial.

Although Kentucky has more miles of navigable water than any other state except Alaska, Kentucky's waterlands aren't all rivers. In Western Kentucky, there are huge lakes that surround Land Between the Lakes National Recreation Area. Farther west, swamplands were featured in Norman Jewison's In Country as Vietnam.

Military bases have also been proven to be popular film locations through the years. Stripes was filmed at Fort Knox with the cooperation of the U.S. Army. The army base also worked with a major Hollywood studio to make the set realistic for the James Bond feature film Goldfinger.

## FILM STARS FROM KENTUCKY

**Ned Beatty** was born in Louisville and has appeared in over 100 films. His most recognized roles include Lex Luthor's henchman Otis in Superman, and as rape victim Bobby Trippe in Deliverance, his debut role. Beatty was nominated for an Academy Award for Best Supporting Actor in the movie Network.

**Rebecca Gayheart** was born in Hazard and is a coal miner's daughter. She left Kentucky at age 15 to start acting. Gayheart appeared in a series of commercials for Noxzema and then joined the cast of the soap opera Loving. Gayheart also had a role in the series Beverly Hills, 90210 and other TV shows. Gayheart has several film appearances.

**Grandpa Jones** was a banjo player and country and gospel music singer. Jones was born in Niagra and left Kentucky as a teenager and sang songs on the radio. His career led to Boston, MA where he met musician/songwriter Bradley Kincaid who gave him the nickname "Grandpa". He moved to Nashville, TN, and played the banjo and sang and joined the Grand Ole Opry. He was best known for his role on the popular TV show Hee Haw. Grandpa Jones was inducted into the Country Music Hall of Fame.

**Lily Tomlin** was born in Michigan but her mother moved them to Paducah during the Depression. She is an actress and comedian and became very well-known for her character on the TV show Laugh-In. Her most notable character was the wisecracking and snorting telephone operator Ernestine and her other famous character was a five-year-old brat Edith Ann, which she performed from an oversized rocking chair. Tomlin did stand-up comedy in nightclubs after college and had her first TV appearance on The Merv Griffin Show. She was a versatile actor and played the role of the secretary Violet Newstead in Nine to Five. More recently she has played a role on the popular TV series The West Wing. Recently, she was awarded the Mark Twain Prize for American Humor.

**Lee Majors** was born in Michigan and is an actor best known for playing the part of Steve Austin with bionic limbs in the television series The Six Million Dollar Man. Majors was adopted by his uncle and aunt after his mother was killed in an automobile accident. His new family moved to Middlesboro, where he graduated from Middlesboro High

Actress Sissy Spacek, country singer Loretta Lynn (front), Governor John Y. Brown, Jr. and First Lady Phyllis George Brown share a laugh at a news conference promoting the movie Coal Miner's Daughter
Source: Kentucky Film Commission

School and earned a degree from Eastern Kentucky University in Richmond. Majors had a role on the 1960s television show The Big Valley and years later starred in another popular series, The Fall Guy. Married several times his most famous marriage was to actress Farrah Fawcett.

**James Best** was born in Powderly and played the role of Sheriff Rosco P. Coltrane in the television series The Dukes of Hazzard.

**William Conrad** was born in Louisville and had a marvelous baritone voice. His large size, deep, resonant voice led to a number of noteworthy roles in radio drama, most prominently his originating the role of Marshal Matt Dillon on Gunsmoke.

**Foster Brooks** was born in Louisville. Brooks was an actor and comedian and was most famous for his ongoing portrayal of a drunken man in Las Vegas nightclub performances and television programs. He regularly appeared on The Dean Martin Show.

**George Timothy Clooney** is an actor born in Lexington and known for his former role in the long-running television drama ER. He started his acting career in a similarly named sitcom, E/R, and played a handyman on the series The Facts of Life. He had starring roles in Batman & Robin, The Perfect Storm, O Brother, Where Art Thou?, Ocean's Eleven and Ocean's Twelve.

**Nick Clooney** was born in Maysville and is a former television news anchorman and politician from the state of Kentucky. He is the brother of singer Rosemary Clooney and the father of noted actor George Clooney. He writes a column for The Cincinnati Post.

**Billy Ray Cyrus** was born in Flatwoods and is a country singer, best known for the hit single "Achy Breaky Heart". In 2001, Cyrus began playing the lead role on the PAX Network comedy-drama Doc. In 2004, Blender magazine selected Achy Breaky

Heart as the magazine's choice for second worst song ever.

**Ashley Judd** was born in California and is an actress. Her mother Naomi Judd and sister Wynonna Judd are country singers. She graduated with honors in 1990 from the University of Kentucky and is often seen at UK Basketball games. She earned early acclaim in Smoke and publicity in Heat. By the end of the 1990s, she managed to achieve significant fame and success as an actress in movies like Double Jeopardy and Someone Like You.

**Victor Mature** was a film actor born in Louisville and considered a handsome leading man. His best known role was Samson in Samson and Delilah. He played opposite stars like Betty Grable and Rita Hayworth. He served in World War II and played the role of Doc Holliday with Henry Fonda as Wyatt Earp.

**Annie Potts** was born in Nashville, TN, but grew up in Franklin and is a television and film actress. She is probably best known for her roles in the television sitcom Designing Women and in the movie Ghostbusters. She is currently a visiting professor of Drama at Stephens College in Missouri.

**Diane Sawyer** was born and raised in Glasgow and is a television journalist for ABC News and co-anchor of ABC's Good Morning America. She served as a reporter for WLKY-TV in Louisville, Kentucky. In 1970 she was hired by Ron Ziegler, White House press secretary for President Richard Nixon. In 1978, she became a political correspondent for CBS, becoming a co-anchor of the CBS Morning News in 1981. In 1984, she became a correspondent for 60 Minutes, where she stayed for five years. In 1989, she moved to ABC to co-anchor Primetime Live with Sam Donaldson.

**Rosemary Clooney** was a very popular singer and actress. She was born in Maysville. Rosemary's sister Betty and brother Nick (his son is George Clooney) all became entertainers. In

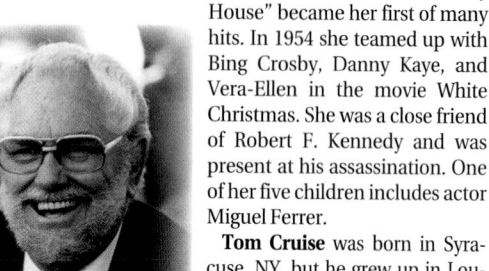

**Foster Brooks in December 1979**
*Photo: Frank Anderson, Lexington Herald-Leader*

**George Clooney in July 2002.**
*Photo: Frank Anderson, Lexington Herald-Leader*

1945, the Clooney sisters won a spot on Cincinnati's radio station WLW as singers. Rosemary's first recordings were in May of 1946 for Columbia Records. In 1951 her record of "Come On-a My House" became her first of many hits. In 1954 she teamed up with Bing Crosby, Danny Kaye, and Vera-Ellen in the movie White Christmas. She was a close friend of Robert F. Kennedy and was present at his assassination. One of her five children includes actor Miguel Ferrer.

**Tom Cruise** was born in Syracuse, NY, but he grew up in Louisville. He was known then as Tom Mapother. Cruise is an actor and producer who has starred in a number of top-grossing movies including his first leading role in a blockbuster movie Risky Business. He received Academy Award nominations for Born on the Fourth of July and Jerry Maguire, both as Best Actor; and for Magnolia, as Best Supporting Actor. In 1996, he became the first actor in history to star in five consecutive films that grossed $100 million in domestic release. The films were A Few Good Men, The Firm, Interview with the Vampire, Mission: Impossible, and Jerry Maguire.

**Kassie DePaiva** was born Katherine Virginia Wesley in Morganfield and is an actress on the soap opera One Life to Live. She started her soap opera career on Guiding Light. DePaiva is also a singer, and has released two albums: Naked and No Regrets.

**John Christopher Depp II** or Johnny Depp was born in Owensboro and is a well-known film actor. He dropped out of school to become a rock musician. Depp's film debut was in Wes Craven's A Nightmare on Elm Street as teenager Glen Lantz, who dies after being swallowed by a bed. In the late '80s, he starred in the TV police drama 21 Jump Street, and later he distinguished himself as an acclaimed lead actor in unique roles beginning with Edward Scissorhands in 1990. Other movies include The Curse of the Black Pearl, Donnie

Brasco and The Brave.

**Lynn Ryan** was born in Germany and is an actress known for playing the shapely Borg Seven of Nine on Star Trek: Voyager. Her father served in the military and raised the family on military bases all over the country until they finally settled in Paducah, when Ryan was 11. Early in her career she was on TV shows like Melrose Place and Matlock, and had a role in David E. Kelley's Boston Public. She gained national attention when details of her divorce proceedings with Jack Ryan, a candidate for the U.S. Senate, were unsealed by a California judge.

**Actor and comedian Jim Varney in February 1984**
*Photo: Frank Anderson, Lexington Herald-Leader*

**Roger Davis** is an actor who is best known for his role in the early 1970s television series, Alias Smith and Jones. Davis was born in Bowling Green, KY, and first appeared on television in 1959. He first gained attention playing multiple characters on the daytime gothic soap TV series Dark Shadows.

**Charles Napier** was born in Scottsville and is an actor usually known to play tough guys and military types. He made his film debut in Russ Meyer's Cherry, Harry & Raque.! Napier had roles in Silence of the Lambs, Rambo: First Blood Part II and in The Blues Brothers. Napier served in the military before becoming an actor.

**A.J. Bakunas** was a stunt man who died while filming the movie Steel. He was killed when his landing pad malfunctioned.

**David Llewelyn Wark (D.W.) Griffith** was born in Crestwood and became a famous film director and was best known for his film The Birth of a Nation. His father was a Confederate Army colonel and Civil War hero Jacob "Roaring Jake" Griffith. Griffith contributed or mastered techniques in the film industry. In addition, he worked on many of his best films with the legendary silent star Lillian Gish. The Birth of a Nation was very controversial and helped revive the Ku Klux Klan. Griffin founded United Artists along with Charlie Chaplin, Mary Pickford, and Douglas Fairbanks.

**Josh Hopkins** is an actor born in Lexington and is the son of former U.S. Congressman Larry Hopkins. His film and television credits include Ally McBeal, Cold Case and the movie The Perfect Storm.

**Irene Dunne** was born in Louisville and

**Actor Lee Majors of the "Six Million Dollar Man" TV show in September 1978 during the filming of the movie "Steel"**
*Photo: Ron Garrison, Lexington Herald-Leader*

**Actor Patricia Neal at the banquet room at the Continental Inn on October 9, 1978**
*Photo: Ron Garrison, Lexington Herald-Leader*

was a film actress and a major star through the 1930s. Later in her career she best known for her role in The Awful Truth and the original film of Anna and the King of Siam. In 1995, she was appointed one of five alternate U.S. delegates to the United Nations by President Dwight Eisenhower.

**Kelly Rutherford** starred on the TV series Melrose Place and was born in Elizabethtown. She became famous in Turkey for a role in the TV series Generations. She has had numerous TV roles and guest appearances

**Charles Albert Browning** with the nickname "Tod" was born in Louisville and attended Louisville Boys High School. He left home around 1900 to join a circus and became a clown and contortionist. He later became an actor for director D.W. Griffith. Browning played a crook in Griffith's movie Intolerance and served as an assistant director in the movie.

**James Albert Varney Jr.** was an actor born in Lexington and is best known for his character Ernest P. Worrell, which was used in numerous television commercials. His character became so popular that it became a TV series called Hey Vern, its

Ernest.

**Patricia Neal** was born in Packard, KY, and grew up in Tennessee. She appeared on Broadway and won a Tony Award for Voice of the Turtle and later appeared in her first film opposite Ronald Reagan in John Loves Mary. She had an affair with actor Gary Cooper that became public. Neal won the Academy Award for Best Actress for her role in the movie Hud. Neal did television work late in her career and appeared in a TV movie which became the pilot TV series The Waltons.

## FILMS SHOT IN KENTUCKY

- 1955 – The Kentuckian
- 1957 – April Love; Raintree County
- 1958 – Some Came Running
- 1962 – How the West Was Won
- 1964 – Goldfinger
- 1965 – The Great Race
- 1967 – The Film-Flam Man
- 1975 – Escape to Witch Mountain
- 1976 – The Treasure of Matecumbe; The Thoroughbreds; The Greatest
- 1977 – A Child of Glass; Black Beauty; Lawman Without a Gun
- 1978 – Centennial; Steel
- 1979 – Coal Miner's Daughter

**Actor Raymond Burr getting ready for a scene in the filming of the movie "Centennial" in 1978**
*Photo: Kentucky Film Commission*

- 1980 – Stripes
- 1981 – Rare Breed
- 1982 – The Act; And They're Off; Kentucky Woman
- 1983 – The Champions; The River Rat; Carnauba
- 1984 – Sylvester
- 1985 – Huckleberry Finn
- 1987 – Big Business; Bluegrass; Eight Men Out
- 1988 – Fresh Horses; Rain Man; In Country;

Next of Kin
- 1990 – A Rage in Harlem; Little Man Tate; City of Hope
- 1991 – The Pickle
- 1992 – Lost in Yonkers
- 1993 – Airborne
- 1995 – A Horse for Danny; Jimmy Crack Corn; Pharaoh's Army
- 1996 – Fire Down Below; Lawn Dogs
- 1997 – The Mighty; U S Marshals

**Workers from Keeneland install the gateway to the Paddock used in the movie "Seabiscuit," in a parking lot on East Main St. in Lexington, Friday, July 18, 2003**
*Photo: Charles Bertram, Lexington Herald-Leader*

- 1998 – The Insider; Nice Guys Sleep Alone; Simpatico
- 1999 – Madison
- 2000 – Traffic; Greatest Adventure of My Life
- 2002 – Zombie Planet; Paper Cut; Peoples; Fake ID; End of the Party; Finish Line; Coming Down the Mountain; Seabiscuit
- 2003 – Dance With a Vampire; Keep Your Distance; The Gray; Andy's Logic; Zombie Planet II; Breaking & Entering; Trade Paperback; Forever In Blackhills; Uncle Smiley's Comin' Home;
- 2004 – Stray; Sweet William; The Death Tunnel; Shadow's Light; Elizabethtown; Dreamer; Jimmy & Judy; A Second More; 12 Steps NOWHERE; The Perfect Stranger; The Deer Path
- 2005 – Saint Joseph College; The Humane Game; Wrong Number; Halloween; Life Without Harriett
- 2006 – Murderer (Short); Fair Trade (Short); Red Neck Fury; The Edison Death Machine; Blink; Voice (Short); Daniel Boone (Remake Segment); Into The Woods

*For more info, Kentucky Film Office, 800-345-5691*

## Robert Lawson

# *Music*

No one can question the fact that Kentucky is rich in music and musicians. From the early days of European settlers bringing their folk music traditions to the area as well as African American gospel and working songs, these are the building blocks of our rich musical heritage today.

The Kentucky Music Hall of Fame & Museum in Renfro Valley, honors the state's performers, songwriters, publishers, promoters, managers, broadcasters, comedians and other music professionals who have made significant contributions to the music industry in Kentucky and around the world.

**Sam Bush**
*Source: Kentucky Music Hall of Fame*

What follows is a list of artists, past and present, that have influenced and inspired our current musical environment.

**Akemon, David "Stringbean" (1915-1973)**
Place of Birth – Annville
Born into a musical family, young David was taught to play banjo by his father. His moniker "Stringbean" came from his tall and thin stature. In the 1940's Akemon became the banjo player with Bill Monroe using a two-finger style. In 1969 he became a founding member of the television show "Hee Haw."

**Baker, Kenny (b. 1926)**
Place of Birth: Jenkins
Kenny was born and grew up in the east Kentucky coal mining town of Jenkins. Both his father and grandfather were fiddlers. Baker made his recording debut with the Blue Grass Boys in 1957. Baker has made many solo recordings through the years and is considered one of the most influential fiddle players of modern times.

**Brown, Frank "Hylo" (1922 – 2003)**
Place of Birth: Johnson County
A Bluegrass and country singer, Frank Brown earned the nickname "Hylo" because of his considerable vocal range.

Brown joined Flatt and Scruggs becoming a featured vocalist. Due to their increasing popularity, Flatt and Scruggs formed a second group called the Timberliners with Brown as the frontman.

**Bush, Sam (b. 1952)**
Place of Birth: Bowling Green
Sam Bush expanded the known capabilities of the mandolin and the fiddle in a blend of bluegrass, soul, rock, jazz, and reggae. The founder, leader and member of the New Grass Revival and Strength in Numbers where he expanded the traditions even further. Bush was an integral member of Emmylou Harris' backup band the Nash Ramblers.

**Carlisle, Bill (1908 – 2003)**
Place of Birth: Wakefield
Bill Carlisle, in a duo with his brother Cliff, was a singer, comedian, guitarist, songwriter, and a showman. In the early 1920s he and his brother Cliff were performing in their family's band on WLAP in Lexington. While working in Knoxville he expanded his craft with his comic alter ego Hot Shot Elmer and had audiences laughing for years.

**Carson, Martha (b. 1921)**
Place of Birth: Neon
Born Irene Amburgey, "The First Lady of Gospel Music", Martha began as a guitar player with her sisters Jean and Berthey ("Mattie and Minnie") as "The Sunshine Sisters" in 1936. At the Renfro Valley Barn Dance, she and her sisters performed with Lily Mae Ledford in 1939 as the Coon Creek Girls (replacing some original members), and by themselves in 1940 as the Hoot Owl Holler Girls. Her single, "Satisfied," sold more than one-million copies. On the strength of "Satisfied," Martha was invited

to join the Grand Ole Opry in 1952.

Martha toured with Elvis Presley, Ferlin Huskey, Del Reeves, Little Jimmy Dickens, and Patsy Cline. Elvis also recorded "Satisfied" and borrowed Martha's dramatic set-ending stance of dropping to one knee and holding the mic stand at an angle. In 1996, a highway near Neon, Kentucky was named the "Martha Carson Highway" in her honor.

### Chapman, Steven Curtis (b. 1962)
Place of Birth: Paducah

Steven has been one of the biggest stars of contemporary Christian music since the late 1980s.

### Chesnut, Jerry (b. 1931)
Place of Birth: Harlan County

A guitarist and prolific song writer, Chesnut became a regular on Hee Haw in the 1970s. Some of his most famous songs are: "Another Place Another Time" written for Jerry Lee Lewis; "Good Year for the Roses" by George Jones; " The Wonders You Perform" by Tammy Wynette and "They Don't Make 'Em Like My Daddy Anymore" by Loretta Lynn. Elvis regarded Chesnut as his favorite songwriter recording 12 of his songs. Chestnut was a member of the 2006 induction class into the Kentucky Music Hall of Fame & Museum.

### Clooney, Rosemary (1928-2002)
Place of Birth: Maysville

Rosemary Clooney was a renowned pop, jazz, and blues singer on film and radio. She became a band vocalist and rose to instant fame with her recording of "Come-On-A-My-House." She starred in a number of films, most notably "White Christmas," co-starring with Bing Crosby. In the National Broadcaster's Hall of Fame, she won the "Pied Piper Award," describing her as "an American Musical Treasure." She was a member of the 2002 class inducted into the Kentucky Music Hall of Fame.

**Rosemary Clooney**
*Source: Kentucky Music Hall of Fame*

### Conlee, John B. (b. 1946)
Place of Birth: Versailles

John Conlee is one of the most respected vocalists to emerge during the urban cowboy era. Conlee was born on a tobacco farm in Versailles, and took up the guitar as a child, performing on local radio at age ten. Conlee's hits made the Top Ten 19 times through 1987.

### Coon Creek Girls
**Ledford, Lily May (1917 – 1985)**
Place of Birth: Pilot
**Ledford, Rosie (1923-1987)**
Place of Birth: Pilot

In 1917, Lily May Ledford (banjo) was born in the Red River Gorge area of Powell County, Kentucky. When the Renfro Valley Barn Dance was born, so was the world's first all girl string band, "The Coon Creek Girls" featuring Lily May Ledford, her sister Rosie, Esther Koehler, and Evelyn Lange. In 1939, they performed at the White House for President and First Lady, Franklin and Eleanor Roosevelt and King George IV and Queen Elizabeth of England. In 2002, they were inducted into the Kentucky Music Hall of Fame.

### Cousin Emmy (1903-1980)
Place of Birth: Lamb

Born Cynthia May Carver, Cousin Emmy became known as "the first hillbilly to own a Cadillac." She began recording for Decca in the late '40s, her album winding up a cherished item among folk music revivalists of the '60s. Showmanship was always a big deal with her, and she once played almost two dozen different instruments during her show.

### Crowe , J.D.  (b. 1936 )
Place of Birth: Lexington

One of bluegrass music's most talented and influential artist, James Dee Crowe, was born in Lexington in 1937. In the 1950s he played banjo with Jimmy Martin and Mac Wiseman. Jn the 1960s, he formed his own band, the Kentucky Mountain Boys. In 1971 he formed The New South and in 1975 released one of the most influential bluegrass records of all time. Crowe with The New South won a Grammy for their instrumental "Fireball" in 1983.

### Cyrus, Billy Ray (b. 1961)
Place of Birth: Flatwoods

Cyrus is a country singer, best known for the hit single "Achy Breaky Heart" in 1992, which helped renew the popularity of line dancing and made Cyrus a star. Cyrus continued to chalked up a string of top 40 singles, including "It Could Have Been Me" and "When I'm Gone."

**Davis, Skeeter (1931-2004)**
Place of Birth: Dry Ridge
Mary Frances Penick was born in a two-room cabin near Dry Ridge, KY, in 1931. Her grandfather, impressed by her energy, nicknamed her "Skeeter." Davis was a pioneering female vocalist in country music blazing the trail for female singers to follow. She and Betty Jack Davis began the Davis Sisters. Signed by RCA Victor they had their first hit with "I Forgot More Than You'll Ever Know."

**The Everly Brothers**
*Source: Kentucky Music Hall of Fame*

"Bye-Bye Love," reached number one on the country charts in less than a month and remained in the Top 10 for six months to become their first Gold record. "Bye-Bye Love" and "All I Have To Do Is Dream" are identified by the Rock and Roll Hall of Fame as two of "500 songs that shaped Rock and Roll." They were among the first inductees into the Rock and Roll Hall of Fame 1986, and in 2002, were inducted into the Kentucky Music Hall of Fame.

**DeShannon, Jackie (b. 1944)**
Place of Birth: Hazel
Jackie DeShannon (Sharon Myers) began singing country tunes at age six; by age 11, she hosted her own radio program. Considered the first female singer songwriter of the rock 'n' roll period, DeShannon wrote the soundtrack for Splendor in the Grass (1961); "Don't Doubt Yourself Babe" for The Byrds debut album; and in 1965, she recorded Bacharach and David's "What the World Needs Now Is Love." These hits were followed by "Put a Little Love in Your Heart" and "Bette Davis Eyes" (a worldwide Number 1 single for Kim Carnes in 1981 and a 1982 Grammy Award for Song of the Year for DeShannon).

**Duncan, Todd (1903-1998)**
Place of Birth: Danville
Duncan was the first Black vocalist to join the New York City Opera. Duncan, considered one of the groundbreaking figures in American art-song, sang the original Porgy in George Gershwin's Porgy and Bess. In 1934 Duncan started his opera career with a production of Mascagni's Cavalleria Rusticana with the Aeollian Opera, and sang with various black opera companies, when the opera stage was still segregated. Duncan was a 2006 inductee into the Kentucky Music Hall of Fame.

**Everly Brothers**
**Everly, Don (b. 1937)**
**Everly, Phil (b.1939)**
Place of Birth: Central City
The Everly Brothers hit the Top 10 singles chart 15 times and sold more than 35 million records in the first five years of their career. Their first hit

**Foley, Red (1910-1968)**
Place of Birth: Blue Lick
Clyde Julian, better known as "Red" Foley, was a native of Blue Lick, close to Berea. Foley was a country, gospel and pop artist. A member of the Grand Ole Opry (1946) & the Country Music Hall of Fame (1967), his song, "Peace in the Valley" was the first gospel record to sell a million copies. He was the first Kentuckian to be elected to the Country Music Hall of Fame (1967). He was a member of the 2002 induction class into the Kentucky Music Hall of Fame.

**Gayle, Crystal: (b. 1951)**
Place of Birth: Paintsville
One of the most popular and widely recognized female country singers of her era, Crystal Gayle, supported her trademark of nearly floor-length hair with a supple voice. Gayle was born Brenda Gail Webb in Paintsville, KY, in 1951. Her older sister was future superstar Loretta Lynn, Lynn's label, Decca, signed the young singer as soon as she was done with high school, but suggested a name change so as to avoid confusion with labelmate Brenda Lee. Lynn suggested the name Crystal, inspired by the Krystal hamburger chain, and Brenda adopted her middle name to come up with Crystal Gayle.

**Gillespie, Haven (1888 – 1975)**
Place of Birth: Covington
Haven Gillespie, one of the great Tin Pan Alley writers, is the composer and lyricist of the timeless classics "You Go To My Head," "Honey," "By the Sycamore Tree" and "Santa Claus is Coming to Town."

### Hall, Tom T. (b. 1936)

Place of Birth: Olive Hill

Tom T. Hall was a country and bluegrass singer, songwriter, storyteller and author. He began playing at age 10; his early musical work was on WMOR in Morehead. Hall's first two singles, "I Washed My Face in the Morning Dew" and "A Week in the County Jail" were Top 10 hits. His song, "Harper Valley P.T.A.," sung by Jeannie C. Riley went to number one on the U. S. Pop Charts. He was a member of the 2002 class inducted into the Kentucky Music Hall of Fame.

### Hampton, Lionel (1909 – 2002)

Place of Birth: Louisville

Hampton was the first jazz vibraphonist and was one of the jazz giants beginning in the mid-'30s. His big band in the early 1940s enjoyed hit records such as: "Sunny Side of the Street," "Central Avenue Breakdown," "Flying Home," and "Hamp's Boogie-Woogie."

### Hill, Mildred (1859-1916)
### Hill, Patty (1868-1946)

Place of Birth: Louisville

These sisters both taught nursery school or kindergarten. In 1893, Mildred wrote a melody, Patty added the lyrics and "Good Morning to All" was created. The original lyrics were Good morning to you, Good morning to you, Good morning, dear children, Good morning to all. The Hill sisters were granted the copyright to "Happy Birthday To You" in 1934.

### Jones, Grandpa (1913-1998)

Place of Birth: Niagra

Born Louis Marshall in Niagra, Grandpa Jones was given his "old" nickname at the age of 22, because he sounded like a "grumpy old man." A country music singer who excelled on his primary instrument, the banjo, he was equally known for his open comedy routines. He was one of the original cast members of the popular television show, "Hee Haw." Jones was elected to the Country Music Hall of Fame in 1978. He was a 2002 inductee into the Kentucky Music Hall of Fame.

### Judds, The
Judd, Naomi (b. 1946)
Place of Birth: Ashland
Judd, Wynonna (b. 1964)
Place of Birth: Ashland

Both Naomi Judd and her daughter, Wynonna, (born Christina Ciminella) are natives of Ashland. The mother and daughter duo were the most commercially successful duo in country music history, until the fame of Brooks & Dunn. Acclaimed as one of the most popular country music acts in the 1980s, the Judds sustained a run of 14 number-one singles from 1984 to 1989. Their debut single, "Had a Dream (For the Heart)," reached the country Top 20; the Judds' second single, "Mama He's Crazy," was a knockout hit that went all the way to number one and later won a Grammy for Best Country Vocal by a Duo or Group. The Judds were inducted into the Kentucky Music Hall of Fame in 2006.

**Lair, John (1894 – 1985)**

Place of Birth: Livingston

John Lair
Source: Kentucky Music Hall of Fame

Radio Pioneer, Folklorist, Writer, Entrepreneur and Founder Renfro Valley Barn Dance. Lair was instrumental in discovering and developing the talents of many country music performers such as Lulubelle, Karl & Harty, "Red" Foley, Doc Hopkins, Linda Parker, "Whitney" Ford, Lily Mae & the Coon Creek Girls, Merle Travis, Homer & Jethro, "Slim" Miller, and Old Joe Clark, among others.

On Nov. 4, 1939 John Lee Lair stepped to the microphone on the stage of the big barn and

**Grandpa Jones**
Source: Kentucky Music Hall of Fame

said: "This is the Renfro Valley Barn Dance, coming to you direct from a real barn in Renfro Valley, Kentucky--the first and only barn dance on the air presented by the actual residents of an actual community…"

## Loveless, Patty (b. 1957)
Place of Birth: Pikeville

One of the most popular female country singers of the 1990s, Patty Loveless rose to stardom thanks to her mix of honky tonk and emotive country ballads. She is a distant cousin of sisters Loretta Lynn and Crystal Gayle. Perhaps her crowning achievement was her album, "When Fallen Angels Fly." It won the Country Music Association's Album of the Year award and gave her four Top 10 singles.

## Lynn, Loretta (b. 1935)
Place of Birth: Butcher Hollow

Born in Butcher Hollow, Loretta Lynn is one of country music's most well-known personalities and performers. Her biography, "Coal Miner's Daughter," made her famous worldwide. In 1972, Lynn was the first woman to become the Country Music Association's Entertainer of the Year, and she shared the Vocal Duo of the Year award with Conway Twitty. Making the cover of Newsweek in 1973, Lynn was the first woman in country music to become a millionaire. She was inducted into the Kentucky Music Hall of Fame in 2002.

**Loretta Lynn**
*Source: Kentucky Music Hall of Fame*

## Montgomery Gentry
**Montgomery, Gerald Edward (Eddie) (b.1963)**
Place of Birth: Danville
**Gentry, Troy (b. 1967)**
Place of Birth: Lexington

Montgomery Gentry's first musical effort was in a band named Young Country. After several years with the band, Gentry left to try a solo career. In 1994, he was the opener for Patty Loveless, Tracy Byrd and John Michael Montgomery (Eddie's younger brother). He won the Jim Beam National Talent Contest. Later, Gentry forged a duo with Montgomery, building on their rowdy fan base in Kentucky clubs. They won the CMA vocal duo award in 2000.

## Montgomery, John Michael (b. 1965)
Place of Birth: Danville

John Michael Montgomery arrived on the country music scene in 1993 with a debut album, "Life's a Dance," that became the only million-seller on the country charts by a new artist that year. Its title was a No. 4 hit single and was followed by his first country chart-topper, "I Love the Way You Love Me." The follow-up album hit the top spot on both the country and adult contemporary charts and produced four more successful singles. At this point, Montgomery was one of the hottest artists in country music, appealing to lovers of both Garth Brooks and Lynyrd Skynyrd.

## Monroe, Bill (1911-1996)
Place of Birth: Rosine

Bill Monroe is rightly known as the "Father of Bluegrass." As a singer, songwriter and mandolin player, he is credited with developing and perfecting the Bluegrass music form and teaching it to many great artists. Monroe formed his first band, the Kentuckians, and then the Bluegrass Boys in the 40s. His song "Blue Moon of Kentucky" is an icon in the Bluegrass music world.

## Niles, John Jacob (1892-1980)
Place of Birth: Louisville

He began collecting folk songs at a young age and composed his first song by 1907. Although he specialized in folk music, he was trained at the Cincinnati Conservatory, sang with the Lyric Opera of Chicago, and studied in France. Among his better known folk compositions are "I Wonder As I Wander" and "Black is the Color of My True Love's Hair." He was inducted into the Kentucky Music Hall of Fame in 2006.

## Molly O'Day (1923 – 1987)
Place of Birth: Pike County

Born Lois LaVerne Williamson, Molly O'Day pioneered the position of solo female Country vocalist. She recorded 36 solo and duet numbers for Columbia (each considered a classic). O'Day started out in a string band playing guitar and singing, with her brothers "Skeets" on fiddle and "Duke" on banjo and later recorded songs by Alabama songwriter

Hank Williams for Columbia Records. Beginning in 1973, she and her husband had a daily Gospel record program at WMMN-FM Huntington.

## Osborne, The Brothers
## Osborne, Bobby (b. 1932)
## Osborne, Sonny (b. 1937)
Place of Birth: Hyden

The Osborne Brothers Invented the "High Lead Trio" style of Bluegrass music. In 1963, they joined the Grand Ole Opry and had several country chart successes including "Rocky Top," which has the distinction of being the state song in Tennessee. The first to play Bluegrass at the White House, they are the only band to win both the Country Music Association award and Bluegrass Vocal Group of the Year award in the same year. They were inducted into the Kentucky Music Hall of Fame in 2002.

## Osborne, Joan (b. 1963)
Place of Birth: Anchorage

Joan's early desire was filmmaking, which led her to New York City where she was a film student at New York University's prestigious film school. Faced with the daunting task of financing her own education, circumstances resulted in a lapse in enrollment. It was during this break that Joan found herself in a little blues bar singing Billie Holiday's "God Bless The Child" after a friend's late night dare. The realization of a great talent was, thus, born. What followed next was Joan's full blown induction into New York City's thriving blues and roots music scene. In 1992 she formed her own label, Womanly Hips, releasing the live-recorded Soul Show. Her album, "Relish," earned eight Grammy Award nominations, including one for Album of the Year.

## Price, Kenny (1931 – 1987)
Place of Birth: Florence

A man of many musical talents, singer and songwriter Kenny Price played drums, guitar, banjo, stand-up bass. Price learned to play on a Sears Roebuck catalog guitar at age five. Drafted into the Army in 1952, Price was stationed in Korea where he played with the USO Show. After his discharge from the Army, he attended the Cincinnati Conservatory of Music. His biggest hits were "Sea Of Heartbreak" (1972) and "Turn On Your Light" (1973). Price joined the cast of Hee Haw in 1973, singing in the Hee Haw Gospel Quartet with Roy Clark, Grandpa Jones and Buck Owens.

## Rambo, Dottie (b. 1934)
Place of Birth: Madisonville

Rambo is considered by many to be the queen of gospel music and a recording artist of international fame. Rambo started writing songs sitting on a creek bank near her Morganfield home when she was only eight years old. The Christian Country Music Association named Rambo Songwriter of The Century (1994), the CCMA presented her with the Living Legend award (2002). Rambo was a member of the 2006 class inducted into the Kentucky Music Hall of Fame.

**Osborne Brothers**
*Source: Kentucky Music Hall of Fame*

## Ritchie, Jean (b. 1922)
Place of Birth: Viper

Mountain Dulcimer Performer, Folk Singer, Songwriter. Jean Ritchie was the youngest of 14 children from a well-known family of traditional singers. Jean's father taught her to play the Mountain Dulcimer and she was first recorded in 1948. In 2002, she was inducted into the Kentucky Music Hall of Fame.

## Shultz, Arnold (1886-1931)
Place of Birth: Racine

Arnold Shultz was a blues guitarist and fiddler. He is credited as a major influence on white guitarists in western Kentucky and more noteably, on a young Bill Monroe. Shultz is buried in Morgantown Colored Cemetery.

## Skaggs, Ricky (b. 1954)
Place of Birth: Eastern Kentucky, reared in Cordell

An accomplished singer and mandolin player, Scaggs was a master by the age of 21. He began his professional career playing bluegrass in 1971, when he and friend, late country singer, Keith Whitley, were invited by Ralph Stanley to join his band. He performed with J.D. Rowe and the New South on their 1975 debut album, which has become one of the most influential bluegrass albums ever released.

As a member of Emmylou Harris' Hot Band in the late 70's, Ricky began exploring the country scene. He reached the top of the country charts in 1981 with the release of his own album, "Waitin' for the Sun to Shine," and in 1982 became the youngest member included in the Grand Ole Opry at that time. Ricky was awarded many honors throughout the 80's including the 1985 CMA entertainer of the year, four Grammy awards and dozens of other awards. At a time when the Nashville sound was becoming more and more popish, Ricky carried the torch for returning country to its traditional elements. He was a member of the 2006 class inducted into the Kentucky Music Hall of Fame.

**Sullivan, John Y. "Lonzo," (1919- 1967)**
**Sullivan, Rollin "Oscar" (b. 1917 )**
**Lonzo & Oscar**
Place of Birth: Edmonton
  Ranked as the Grand Ole Opry's premier musical comedy team for more than 25 years. There were really three "Lonzos," brother John being the first and most significant; then, Lloyd George (known as Ken Marvin) and was David Hooten. Lonzo & Oscar hit the Country singles chart with "I'm My Own Grandpa" in 1948.

**Travers , Mary (b. 1937)**
Place of Birth: Louisville
  Mary Travers was a major influence on the folk music scene during the 1960s and 1970s. Travers, a founding member of Peter, Paul And Mary, became one of the most commercially successful folk performers. She became an inspirational political spokesperson and performed at civil rights rallies with Dr. Martin Luther King and at numerous anti-Vietnam War demonstrations. She was a member of the 2006 class inducted into the Kentucky Music Hall of Fame.

**Mary Travers**
*Source: Kentucky Music Hall of Fame*

**Travis, Merle (1917-1983)**
Place of Birth:  Rosewood
  Travis was a guitar stylist, singer, and songwriter. The son of a tobacco farmer and coal miner, he and Grandpa Jones did many radio shows together and recorded as the Shepard Brothers. Travis's "Walkin' The Strings" is a highly regarded album of acoustic guitar solos. In 1948, he developed the solid-body guitar. He was elected to the Country Music Hall of Fame in 1977, and inducted into the Kentucky Music Hall of Fame in 2002.

**Merle Travis**
*Source: Kentucky Music Hall of Fame*

**Vaughn, Billy (1919-1991)**
Place of Birth: Glasgow
  Born Richard Smith Vaughn, Billy Vaughn is credited with being one of the top most popular orchestra leaders and pop music arrangers of the 1950s and early 60s. He began writing songs in his spare time as a barber, and later a factory worker in Glasgow. In 1952, he organized the musical group, "the Hilltoppers" with Jimmy Sacca, Don McGuire and Seymour Spiegelman. Their song, "Trying" became a hit record, and the group enjoyed almost a decade of success. Billy formed an orchestra in Gallatin, TN, and became Dot Records' top moneymaker with hits like "Melody of Love" and "Sail Along Silvery Moon," which sold over 3 million copies. Billy Vaughn became the first American artist to be awarded a gold record in Europe and the first musician to receive a platinum record for achieving sales well over 3 million. He was a member of the 2006 class inducted into the Kentucky Music Hall of Fame.

**Whitley, Keith (1955-1989)**
Place of Birth: Sandy Hook
  A talented new country singer and songwriter, Whitley was just beginning to emerge as a superstar at the time of his death in 1989. The first three singles from his hit album, "Don't Close Your Eyes" --"Don't Close Your Eyes," "When You Say Nothing At All," and "I'm No Stranger to the Rain" – all reached number one.

**Yoakam, Dwight (b. 1956)**
  Place of Birth: Pikeville; reared in Columbus, Ohio.
  When he began his career, Nashville was oriented towards pop UrbanCowboymusic,andYoakam's brand of Bakersfield honky tonk was not considered marketable. His debut LP was 1986's Guitars, Cadillacs, Etc., Etc. and it instantly launched his career. "Honky Tonk Man" and "Guitars, Cadillacs" were hit singles. Yoakam's song Readin', Writin', and Route 23 pays tribute to his childhood move from Kentucky, and is titled after a local expression describing the route that rural Kentuckians need to take to find a job.

## CULTURE & THE ARTS

# *Orchestras & Symphonies*

**Bowling Green Chamber Orchestra**
**(270) 846-2426**
　The Bowling Green Chamber Orchestra changes lives through music education and exciting concerts featuring a wide variety of music.

**Bowling Green Western Symphony Orchestra**
**(270) 745-7681**
　A cooperative venture between Western Kentucky University's Department of Music and the Bowling Green Western Symphony Orchestra Association, BGWSO is composed of Western students and faculty members as well as musicians from the surrounding region.

**Central Kentucky Youth Orchestra**
**(859) 254-0796**
　The Central Kentucky Youth Orchestras is one of the oldest, independently chartered, youth orchestras dating back to 1947.

**Centre College**
**(859) 238-5424**
　Centre's Music Program offers a wide variety of performance and academic opportunities. Any student may take private lessons, participate in ensembles, and take courses ranging from music theory and history to world music.

**Eastern Kentucky University**
**(859) 622-3266**
　The Eastern Kentucky University Symphony Orchestra is open to all string performers and to selected woodwind, brass and percussion performers by auditions.

**Lexington Philharmonic**
**(859) 233-4226; Toll Free: (888) 494-4226**
　LPO has a long and vibrant tradition that enhances thousands of lives each year through the beauty of timeless symphonic music.

**Louisville Orchestra**
**(502) 587-8681**
　Founded in 1937 by conductor Robert Whitney and Charles Farnsley, Mayor of Louisville, the Louisville Orchestra has been called the cornerstone of the Louisville arts scene.

**Louisville Youth Orchestra**
**(502) 896-1851**
　The Louisville Youth Orchestra (LYO), founded in 1958, provides an extraordinary musical experience for young people from grade school through age 21.

**Morehead State University**
**(606) 783-2473**
　The MSUO is composed of Morehead State University students and faculty members, as well as musicians from the surrounding region.

**Murray State University**
**(270) 762.6456**
　The Symphony Orchestra meets on Monday from 6:30 to 8:20, and on Thursday from 2:30 to 3:50 in the Fine Arts Building.

**Northern Kentucky Symphony Orchestra**
**(859) 431-6216**
　The Kentucky Symphony Orchestra offers the Northern Kentucky and Greater Cincinnati area unique, affordable symphonic experience in a relaxed setting.

**Owensboro Symphony**
**(270) 684-0661**
　The Owensboro Symphony Orchestra is a premier producer of live classical and pops music.

**Paducah Symphony Orchestra**
**(270) 444-0065**
　Founded in 1979, the Paducah Symphony Orchestra performs classical, pops and children's concerts featuring internationally recognized guest artists. A regional orchestra, it has played in Kentucky, southern Illinois, southwest Tennessee and southeast Missouri. The Orchestra also has a Children's Chorus and Symphony Chorus.

**University of Kentucky**
**(859) 257-4900**
　The school has achieved awards and national recognition for high-caliber education in opera, choral and instrumental music performance, as well as for music education, composition, theory and music history.

# SEPTEMBER'S SONG

*By Barbara Mabry*

The dark is flecked
with sound tonight,
confetti-bright and variegated.
The dark is crowded;
the hills press close,
the sky stretched taut
and random-pricked
where myriad stars shine through.
Cicadas orchestrate
        September's song,
and the wind laps
drying corn leaves
with a raspy tongue.
Autumn slips
        into Sourwood Hollow
on a moonless night
when the stars are bright
and the wind is restless
and the creek the tiniest
        thread of sound.
This night breathes
        a reverent requiem
        to summer.

CULTURE & THE ARTS

# Arts Impact on Louisville Growth

Steven Block

Charles P. Farnsley served as mayor of Louisville from 1948 to 1953 and is remembered as one of the most innovative mayors of his era. As mayor of Louisville, Farnsley pioneered the use of an occupational tax to fund local projects, and created the Louisville Fund (now the Louisville Fund for the Arts)—the oldest united arts fund in the country, which has raised over $130 million since its establishment in 1949.

More than one of Mayor Farnsley's innovative programs earned him a national reputation—but Farnsley understood earlier than most that "quality of life" issues were related in momentous ways to Louisville's economic growth. Mayor Farnsley recognized that "culture, industry, and retail business are woven together—that the progress of one affects the progress of the others." With this insight, he paved streets, built small parks, installed streetlights, and infused into Louisville a diverse array of artistic and cultural endeavors.

In late 1948, Charlie Farnsley was president of the Louisville Orchestra board. The orchestra, then slightly over a decade old, was still something of a new organization—particularly in its stature as a fledgling regional orchestra. Charlie Farnsley realized the need to raise enough funds not only to sustain the orchestra, but guarantee its growth too.

Charlie Farnsley, who would soon fill the unexpired term of Mayor Taylor, conceived a brilliant plan: the orchestra was reduced to 50 musicians and saved money by commissioning works of contemporary composers, cutting out the cost of guest soloists. Orchestra conductor, Robert Whitney, was behind the mayor, and the orchestra began commissioning works by contemporary American composers (mostly unknown to traditional orchestra patrons). And, it worked.

Mayor Farnsley, never one to think small, applied for—and got—an unheard of $500,000 grant from the Rockefeller Foundation in early 1953. The money was used to commission and record more new works, which were distributed on the orchestra's own First Edition label. This was the first time in America that an orchestra created its own record company.

Mayor Farnsley set much of this in motion, realizing that if we could focus on the "quality of life," Louisville could compete with larger cities like Indianapolis and Cincinnati. Mayor Farnsley's theme was revealed during an interview with this author when he served as the managing editor of the U of L student magazine. The resulting article was entitled, "Charles Farnsley—The Growth of Louisville," and opinions expressed by Mayor Farnsley over 50 years ago still resonate today.

The topic was the growth of industry and cultural interest in Louisville. Was there a direct relationship between the two or did they develop independently? Farnsley answered, "I think what it is, is a sudden upsurge of both. They have been developing right along. ... I definitely think they're an aid to one another right now and will continue to be. ...I think that in order to fulfill its role in modern life, the city must develop its raw materials in three areas—culture, industry and retail business." He continued, saying, "Culture and industry help one another.

**Speed Museum, Louisville**
*Source: Kentucky Department of Tourism*

Industry brings in more money and the money helps the cultural interests. One important thing that industry has brought about that helps the cultural interests immensely is the increase of income per capita. This amounts to putting more money in the hands of the individual to spend on cultural interests."

Although page limits are restricted, passing mention must be made about several cornerstones of Louisville's arts and cultural community. We start with the J.B. Speed Art Museum, which is Kentucky's oldest and largest art museum. The Speed was founded in 1925 by Mrs. James Breckinridge Speed as a memorial to her husband, a prominent Louisville businessman. It houses nearly 12,000 pieces in its permanent collection—all in a magnificent building.

The Kentucky Opera was created in 1952 and strongly supported by local patrons. It was led by Moritz von Bomhard and designated the State Opera of Kentucky in 1982. The Opera has moved over time, from the Columbia Auditorium to the Brown Theater, and now, all mainstage performances are held in Whitney Hall at the Kentucky Center for the Arts.

Louisville Ballet, the State Ballet of Kentucky, was founded in March 1952 as a civic ballet company. It was recently described by the Chicago Sun Times dance critic as one of the most exciting regional ballets in America. Louisville Ballet has 65 world premiere ballets to its credit, and a state-of-the-art facility for dance, drama and visual arts.

Actors Theatre of Louisville was founded by Richard Block in 1963 under the name Theatre Louisville. Designated in 1974 as the State Theatre of Kentucky, Actor's Theatre has been hailed as one of the finest resident professional theaters in the nation. And, over 40 years later, it is a big part of what is happening on restored 19th century Main Street.

A unique plan between Gov. John Y. Brown and the legislature led to a public/private partnership to build a performing acts center in Louisville. The Kentucky Center for the Arts opened in 1983. Nearly 20 years later, in 2000, the center has undergone a $4.5 million renovation.

**Actors Theater of Louisville**
*Source: Kentucky Department of Tourism*

For almost 70 years, UofL has encouraged the development of the visual arts in Louisville. The University's art department was founded in 1937, and it became the Allen R. Hite Art Institute in 1946, in gratitude for the bequest of Allen R. and Marcia S. Hite.

This is all the result of citizen participation in the arts, and in all cases, these efforts have had strong corporate support. We are fortunate to have corporations that never hesitate to get behind the arts. There's Humana Inc., which is one of the largest patrons of the arts in Louisville, including the Humana Festival of New American Plays. Brown-Forman Corporation stands behind the arts—the UofL art auction is a major event, which attracts artists from across the U.S., and gets bigger every year. Increasingly UPS, Philip Morris, and Brown Williamson (in the past) provided such support, not to mention the national corporations, General Electric and Ford.

We fast-forward over 50 years to the new 21C Museum Hotel—a museum hotel dedicated to collecting and showing 21st-century art. It demonstrates the continuing investment in the city's artistic and cultural attractions. Laura Lee Brown and her husband, Steve Wilson, are part of re-energizing Main Street because they share Mayor Farnsley's belief that art can create economic growth.

Louisville is experiencing a promising arts renaissance. Some might say that Louisville is taking on a new cultural identity—the new 21C Museum Hotel, UofL's Main Street Cressman Center, the New Center for Contemporary Art, the loft living rehabilitation of the Albert Kahn-designed Ford Factory. And, soon, the innovative Museum Plaza will offer Kentucky residents a distinctive new venue for arts, living, education and shopping.

And don't forget First Friday gallery hops on Market and Main streets attract as many as 7,000 people downtown, where renovation and new construction are flourishing.

Down Market Street, Bardstown Road, Frankfort Avenue—people "hop" on trolley cars to visit the galleries.

I bet Mayor Charlie Farnsley would really like it.

## CULTURE & THE ARTS
# *Craft & Folk Art*

Glass, steel, iron, fabric, fiber, clay, wood, sticks, beads, even coal…from time immemorial humans have found many ways to express their creativity, their dreams, their very souls. Out of the celebration of Kentucky's folklife naturally comes an interest in the crafts and folk art created by its people. We

Folk artist Minnie Adkins
at home, Isonsville
Photo: Sid Webb

Creations of folk artist Minnie Adkins
Photo: Sid Webb

humbly pay homage to all folk artists and whatever means they select to share their visions with us and thank them for their generosity in permitting a glimpse into their genius.

The Kentucky Artisan Center at Berea offers an outstanding opportunity to explore Kentucky artisan works and their stories — it offers Kentucky crafted items, recordings by Kentucky musicians, books by Kentucky authors, and specialty foods grown or produced in Kentucky. Berea is officially the "Crafts Capital" of Kentucky, recognition earned from a long-time tradition as a center of craftsmanship. At the heart of Berea and its crafts tradition is Berea College, where students do not pay tuition, but work ten to 15 hours per week in one of the college's industries. As part of the Berea College Crafts Program, students create fine furniture, woven items, ceramics, brooms and wrought iron pieces.

In 1980, former First Lady of Kentucky, Phyllis George, helped propel into the spotlight the amazing skills and talents of the state's artisans. The effort began when Kentucky crafts were featured in "Oh, Kentucky" shops at Bloomingdales department store in New York City. In 1981 the Kentucky Museum of Art and Craft, in Louisville, was organized as a non-profit organization to promote the rich art and craft heritage of Kentucky through three main areas of programming: exhibition, education, and support of artists through the retail Gallery Shop.

The Museum of Art and Craft has supported more than 400 artists and provided educational programs to more than 500,000 school children. The Museum is supported in part by the Fund for the Arts and Kentucky Arts Council, a state agency of the Commerce Cabinet. The Gallery Shop features the work of over 200 artists at any one time, offering work in all media from folk art to furniture.

In Morehead, the Kentucky Folk Art Center offers visitors one of the most unique and important cultural experiences to be found anywhere in Appalachia. From the fun and quirky to the fantastical, the folk art exhibited and conserved by the Folk Art Center is an engaging and vital piece of the region's history and contemporary culture.

With a growing permanent collection of nearly 1,000 works by regional folk artists, the Folk Art Center strives to preserve and promote a broader understanding of traditional and contemporary folk art through exhibitions that range in content from folk art works, such as textiles to contextually related subject matter, including photography and food traditions.

Events around the state celebrating the gifts from Kentucky hands include the biannual Arts and Crafts Fairs at the Folk Art Center, which creates a market for regional crafts people. "A Day in the Country" folk art show, formerly held on Minnie Adkin's farm in Elliott County, brings more than 50 folk artists to Morehead on the first Saturday of June each year. More than 100 artists and craft persons from Kentucky and surrounding states reveal their creations at each of the two annual Appalachian Arts and Crafts Fair on the first Saturday of December and the last Saturday of June in the Laughlin Health Building on the campus of Morehead State University, Morehead.

Another extremely popular event is Kentucky

**Loghouse Crafts**
*Source: Tour Southern & Eastern Kentucky*

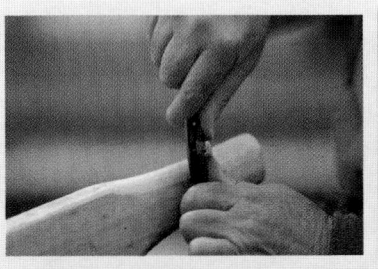

**Traditional Kentucky pattern on woven coverlet**
*Photo: Sid Webb*

Crafted: The Market, held annually at the Kentucky Fair and Exposition Center in Louisville. Now in its 24th year, the show is an extension of the Kentucky Craft Marketing Program (also established under George's leadership in 1981). The program's mission is, among other things, to develop the state's craft industry, support and empower Kentucky artisans and craftspeople, and create an economically viable environment for craft entrepreneurs.

Kentucky Crafted: The Market was selected as one of the Top 25 Art Fairs and Festivals in the country by "American Style Magazine," and, for the tenth time, the Southeast Tourism Society has named it one of the Top Twenty Events in the Southeast. More than 300 exhibitors participate offering fine traditional, folk and contemporary crafts, two-dimensional visual art, musical recordings, books and food products. The Market is a collaborative effort among several state agencies and cabinets, and generates $2-$3 million dollars in direct sales.

The craft industry in Kentucky contributes $252 million dollars to the state's economy and has an impact of additional $147 million dollars from out-of-state sales. Kentucky is recognized as a model for its craft programs and its role in the $14 billion national craft industry.

*Sources: The Kentucky Artisan Center, www.kentuckyartisancenter.ky.gov; The Kentucky Museum of Art and Craft, www.kentuckyarts.org/index.cfm; Kentucky Crafted: the Market, http://kycraft.ky.gov/; The Kentucky Folk Art Center at Morehead, www.morehead-st.edu/units/folkart.*

Sid Webb

originals and prints

Visit the online gallery
www.sidwebb.com
859-226-9943

# Preservation

Kentucky has a rich heritage expressed in its historic buildings, sites and cultural landscapes. Since 1966 the Kentucky Heritage Council / State Historic Preservation Office has been assisting individuals, communities and local governments with making historic preservation an important component of comprehensive community planning, and economic development. Making a concerted effort to preserve this heritage and the built environment is integral to building successful, thriving communities. At its heart, fostering a preservation ethic in Kentucky is essential to community revitalization and quality of life.

The Kentucky Heritage Council (KHC) is charged with identifying, preserving and protecting the historic resources of Kentucky, and seeking to build a greater awareness of Kentucky's past while ensuring it for the future. KHC has successfully encouraged the adaptive reuse of historic buildings in all contexts and advocated that historic preservation should be a key public policy initiative to encourage economic development, provide affordable housing, revitalize downtowns and neighborhoods, provide life-long learning opportunities and enhance Kentucky's quality of life.

KHC programs include surveying historic structures and archaeological sites, nominating properties to the National Register of Historic Places, rebuilding and revitalizing Kentucky Main Streets, and administering and overseeing federal rehabilitation tax incentives, Certified Local Governments, historic preservation grants, environmental review, archaeology programs, and public education and outreach.

KHC Executive Director David Morgan listens to First Lady Laura Bush at a Preserve America announcement
Source: Kentucky Heritage Council

Through the years, several special emphasis programs (including Civil War, Rural Preservation, Heritage Tourism, the African American Heritage Commission, the Native American Heritage Commission, Military Sites, Underground Railroad, and the Kentucky Archaeological Survey) have been developed and proven highly successful in reaching diverse audiences and expanding preservation efforts to encompass important new partners. These additional initiatives have made Kentucky a leader in the national historic preservation movement. For more information, see www.heritage.ky.gov.

The National Historic Preservation Act of 1966 authorized the National Park Service to create and maintain the National Register of Historic Places, the official federal listing of properties deemed to be of historic, cultural and architectural significance. Today among states, Kentucky has the fourth highest number of listings in the National Register with more than 3,100 districts, sites and structures totaling more than 41,000 historic features.

National Register listing can be applied to buildings, objects, structures, districts and archaeological resources. Properties proposed for listing must be significant in architecture, engineering, American history or culture, or possess a special role in the development of our country. Owners of National Register properties may qualify for federal or state tax credits for certified rehabilitation of these prop-

406	CULTURE & THE ARTS

erties or for making charitable contribution of preservation easements. For more information about the National Register in Kentucky, see www.heritage.ky.gov/national_register.htm

Introduced in 2003, Preserve America is a White House initiative that encourages and supports community efforts in historic preservation. Led by honorary chair First Lady Laura Bush, the program was developed in cooperation with the federal Advisory Council on Historic Preservation, the U.S. Department of the Interior, and the U.S. Department of Commerce to focus attention on President and Mrs. Bush's commitment to preserving our national heritage. Kentucky leads the nation with 67 designated communities and neighborhoods and one historic district. For more information about Preserve America, see www.preserveamerica.gov.

Created and administered by the Kentucky Heritage Council, the Kentucky Main Street Program is the oldest statewide downtown revitalization program in the nation, celebrating its 27th anniversary in 2006. Kentucky Main Street Program strategy is based on a four-point approach developed by the National Main Street Center of the National Trust for Historic Preservation, which emphasizes organization, promotion, design and economic restructuring within the context of historic preservation as principles for successful downtown revitalization.

Downtowns throughout Kentucky feature substantial historic resources embodied in their buildings and structures. Fortunately, the Kentucky Main Street Program's emphasis on historic preservation as a sound economic development strategy not only helps promote development along Main Street, but also creates a halo effect to encourage neighborhood investment and redevelopment. Fostering strong partnerships between the public and private sector to achieve downtown revitalization has been the key to this success.

Today more than 100 communities—a record number—participate in the Kentucky Main Street Program and reap the economic benefits of preserving the business core of their communities. For more information, see www.heritage.ky.gov/kyheritage_mainstreet.htm

National Historic Landmarks are nationally significant historic places designated by the Secretary of the Interior because they possess exceptional value or quality in illustrating or interpreting the heritage of the U.S. Today fewer than 2,500 historic places bear this national distinction. Working with citizens throughout the nation, the National Historic Landmarks Program draws upon the expertise of National Park Service staff, who nominate new landmarks and provide assistance to existing landmarks.

Ida Lee Willis was named the first Executive Director of the Kentucky Heritage Council / State Historic Preservation Office (formerly the Kentucky Heritage Commission) in 1966. Each year the Ida Lee Willis Memorial Foundation honors Mrs. Willis, widow of former Gov. Simeon Willis, by presenting awards in her name to individuals and organizations who have demonstrated an understanding of and an appreciation for the value of preserving and reusing Kentucky's historic and prehistoric resources. These awards include the Ida Lee Willis Memorial Award, given annually to the individual who has demonstrated outstanding dedication to the cause of historic preservation in the Commonwealth

The history of African American life in Kentucky is filled with a host of rich experiences. African American history in Kentucky has roots in the commonwealth's earliest history. The KHC and the Kentucky African American Heritage Commission are dedicated to preserving buildings and places important to the history of Kentucky African Americans. Kentucky offers an array of sites that tell the story of slavery, the Underground Railroad, Civil War, education (including an historically black college) and civil rights, as well as a variety of historically significant buildings and museums that promote local history. For more information, see www.kcaah.com.

Native Americans have called Kentucky home for more than 12,000 years. To date, more than 22,000 Native American archaeological sites have been documented in the state. These sites range from small seasonal camps to burial mounds, from rock art to large villages that were occupied by hundreds of people.

To learn more about the Native Americans who once called Kentucky home, visit exhibits on Kentucky prehistory at the Thomas C. Clark Center for History in Frankfort, the University of Kentucky William S. Webb Museum of Anthropology in Lexington or the Gladie Creek Cultural and Environmental Learning Center at the Daniel Boone National Forest. More information is also available from the Kentucky Archaeological Survey (KAS) web site, at www. heritage.ky.gov/kas.htm. The KAS is a joint program of the Kentucky Heritage Council and the University of Kentucky Department of Anthropology.

For more information on how you can help with the preservation and interpretation of historic places, contact the Kentucky Heritage Council / State Historic Preservation Office, 300 Washington Street, Frankfort, KY 40601, 502-564-7005 or see www.heritage.ky.gov.

# CULTURE & THE ARTS
# *Museums*
# *& Related Organizations*

## ART MUSEUMS

| MUSEUM | LOCATION | PHONE |
|---|---|---|
| Behringer-Crawford Museum | Covington | (859) 491-4003 |
| Bill Monroe Museum | Rosine | (270) 298-3551 |
| The Crane House | Louisville | (502) 635-2240 |
| Emma Reno Connor's Black History Gallery | Elizabethtown | (270) 769-5204 |
| Headley-Whitney Museum | Lexington | (859) 255-6653 |
| International Museum of the Horse | Kentucky Horse Park,Lexington | (859) 233-4303 |
| Janice Mason Art Museum | Cadiz | (270) 522-9056 |
| John James Audubon Museum & Nature Center | Henderson | (270) 826-2247 |
| Kentucky Derby Museum | Louisville | (502) 637-1111 |
| Kentucky Museum of Arts & Design | Louisville | (502) 589-0202 |
| Magoffin Co. Historical Society Pioneer Village | Salyersville | (606) 349-1607 |
| Mayfield/Graves County Art Guild | Mayfield | (270) 247-6971 |
| Museum of the American Quilter's Society | Paducah | (270) 442-8856 |
| Owensboro Museum of Fine Arts | Owensboro | (270) 685-3181 |
| Portland Museum | Louisville | (502) 776- 7678 |
| The Speed Art Museum | Louisville | (502) 634-2700 |

## UNIVERSITY ART MUSEUMS

| MUSEUM | LOCATION | PHONE |
|---|---|---|
| Berea College Museum | Berea | (859) 985-3373 |
| Clara M. Eagle Art Gallery | Murray State University, Murray | (270) 762-3052 |
| Fine Arts Center | Henderson Community College, Henderson | (270) 827-1867 |
| Godbey Appalchian Center | Southeast Community College | (606) 589-2145 |
| Kentucky Folk Art Center | Morehead State University, Morehead | (606) 783-2204 |
| The Kentucky Museum | Western Kentucky University, Bowling Green | (270) 745-2592 |
| Museum of Anthropology | Northern Kentucky University, Highland Heights | (859) 572-5259 |
| University of Kentucky Art Museum | University of Kentucky, Lexington | (859) 257-5716 |

## ART CENTERS

| ART CENTER | LOCATION | PHONE |
|---|---|---|
| Camp Breckinridge Museum and Arts Center | Moranfield | (270) 289-4420 |
| Dawson Springs Museum And Art Center | Dawson Springs | (270) 797-3503 |
| The Gateway Regional Center for the Arts | Mt. Sterling | (859) 498-6264 |
| Henderson Fine Arts Center | Henderson | (270) 831-9800 |
| Kentucky Artisan Center | Berea | (859) 985-5448 |
| Kentucky Center | Louisville | (859) 562-0100 |
| Kentucky Folk Art Center | Morehead | (606) 786-2204 |
| Living Arts and Sciences Center | Lexington | (859) 252-5222 |
| Minds Wide Open Art Center | Lexington | (859) 259-2637 |
| Richmond Area Arts Center | Richmond | (859) 624-4242 |
| Yeiser Art Center | Paducah | (270) 492-2453 |

## NON-PROFIT ORGANIZATIONS

| ORGANIZATION | LOCATION | PHONE |
|---|---|---|
| Arts Kentucky | Louisville | (502) 561-0701 |
| Kentucky Art & Craft Foundation | Louisville | (502) 589-0102 |
| Kentucky Arts Council | Frankfort | (502) 564-3757 |
| Kentucky Citizens for the Arts | Louisville | (502) 589-3116 |
| Kentucky Crafted | Frankfort | (502) 564-3757 |
| Lexington Art League | Lexington | (859) 254-7024 |
| Lexington Arts & Cultural Council | Lexington | (859) 225-2951 |
| Louisville Visual Art Association | Louisville | (502) 896-2146 |
| VSA Arts of Kentucky | Bowling Green | (270) 781-0872 |

## CULTURE & THE ARTS

# Kentucky Chautauqua

### Kentucky Humanities Council

**KENTUCKY CHAUTAUQUA —
BRINGING HISTORY TO LIFE**

"Kentucky Chautauqua," presented by the Kentucky Humanities Council, are historically accurate impersonations of 16 fascinating characters from Kentucky's past. Intended for audiences of 40 or more, Kentucky Chautauqua performances offer a unique combination of education and entertainment. KHC offers a limited number of reduced-cost ($125) Kentucky Chautauqua performances supported by the generosity of sponsors.

The characters are: Ruth Hanly Booe, Bourbon Ball Belle (1891-1973); George Rogers Clark, Revolutionary War Hero (1752-1818); Anna Mac Clarke, Military Pioneer (1919–1944); Catherine Conner, Political Powerhouse (1900-2002); Henry Clay, Kentucky's Great Statesman (1777–1852); Price Hollowell, Black Patch War Hero (1895–1975); Grandpa Jones, Country musician and Comic (1913–1998); Maxine Lacey, Toby Tent Show Actress (1916–1996); Lily May Ledford, Coon Creek Girl (1917–1985); Rose Will Monroe, Rosie the Riveter (1920–1997); Adolph Rupp, The Coach (1901–1977); Dinnie Thompson, No Ordinary Woman (1857–1939); Dr. Thomas Walker, Pioneer Physician (1715–1794); Simon Kenton, Frontiersman (1755–1836); John C. C. Mayo, Coal Baron (1864–1914); and Sallie Ward, Queen of Society (1827–1896).

Book Kentucky Chautauqua by calling (859) 257-5932 or by going to http://www.kyhumanities.org.

**Ruth Hanly Booe
(Kelly Brengelman)**
*Source: Kentucky
Humanities Council*

**Catherine Connor
(Suzi Schuhmann)**
*Source: Kentucky
Humanities Council*

Ruth Hanly Booe: Borbon Ball Belle (1891-1873): Ruth Booe, inventor of the world-famous bourbon ball, founded the Rebecca Ruth candy company of Frankfort. Her grandson now runs the business. Portrayed by Kelly Brengelman of Midway.

Catherine Conner: Political Powerhouse (1900-2002): Born on a farm in Bullitt County, Kentucky, Conner's political career carried her all the way to the inner councils of Franklin D. Roosevelt's White House. Portrayed by Suzi Schuhmann of Louisville.

Price Hollowell: Black Patch War Hero (1895-1975): Hollowell was just thirteen when the Night Riders attacked his family's farm in western Kentucky (Caldwell County). His testimony in court brought the villains to justice. Portrayed by Ethan Sullivan Smith of Cynthiana.

Rose Will Monroe: Rosie the Riveter (1920-1997): Monroe, a native of Pulaski County, Kentucky, was working in a bomber factory when she was picked to play World War II icon Rosie the Riveter in a film. Portrayed by Angela Bartley of Louisville.

Adolph Rupp: The Coach (1901-1977): The legendary coach's winning teams and genius for public relations made University of Kentucky basketball a statewide phenomenon. Portrayed by Edward B. Smith of Cynthiana.

Dr. Thomas Walker: Pioneer Physician (1715-1794): Walker, a politically well connected doctor and land speculator from Virginia, led the first English expedition into Kentucky in 1750. Portrayed by Danny W. Hinton of Livingston.

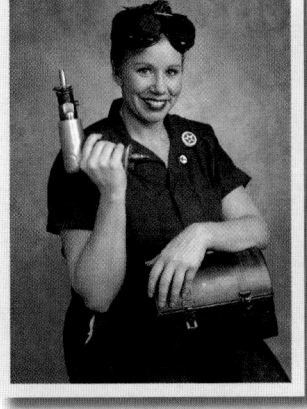

**Dr. Thomas Walker (Danny W. Hinton)**
*Source: Kentucky Humanities Council*

**Rose Will Monroe (Angela Bartley)**
*Source: Kentucky Humanities Council*

**Price Hollowell (Ethan Sullivan Smith)**
*Source: Kentucky Humanities Council*

**Adolph Rupp (Edward B. Smith)**
*Source: Kentucky Humanities Council*

## CULTURE & THE ARTS
# *Scratch Cooking*                    Benita McCoy Lyons

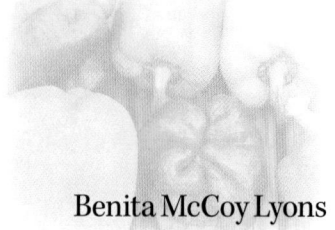

Scratch cooking is a hands-on approach to the way we prepare our daily meals using homemade foods with fresh ingredients that capture the original flavor of the recipe contents. In doing so, try avoiding pre-cooked or prepackaged products that may have unhealthy limits of additives and preservatives in them.

The definition of "scratch" cooking doesn't mean that every morsel has to be harvested from seed, and cooked all day. A watched pot never boils— I've been told. One theory is to evoke the beauty of the food. Find out what your favorite dishes are and learn every aspect and method of fixing that dish, and then add your own taste and style. Take a pinch of this or a dab of that. If you try to follow every recipe verbatim you will never have the feel of originality. Most good cooks make it easy by looking at cooking as a joy.

Cooking from scratch is a healthier way of eating and can incorporate the heritage of your ancestors into your lifestyle, making the beautiful and lost art of this method of cooking for friends and family a part of a well-balanced diet.

Benita is a descendant of the Hatfield-McCoy feud of American folklore, but she'd much rather feed a Hatfield than shoot one these days. Here are some good, old-fashioned recipes from her cookbooks. Take your time, and enjoy.

### FLORENE'S FRESH APPLE CAKE

**Batter**
1-1/4 c. cooking oil
3 c. flour
2 c. sugar
3 c. peeled and chopped apples
3 eggs
1 c. nuts, chopped, any variety
1 tsp. baking soda
2 tsp. vanilla
1 tsp. salt
Blend oil and sugar well, sift dry ingredients, and add to oil and sugar mixture. Beat eggs slightly and add to batter; add vanilla. Fold in apples and nuts. Grease and flour a tube or bundt pan. Bake at 250 degrees for 1-1/2 hours.

**Topping**
1 c. brown sugar
1/v c. evaporated milk
1 stick butter
1 tsp. vanilla
Cook ingredients to a full boil. Beat and cool. Spread on cake.

### RED TOMATO RELISH

12 ripe tomatoes, peeled and cored
6 large onions, chopped
6 green peppers, chopped
6 red peppers, chopped
3 banana peppers, chopped
2 c. sugar
3 c. apple cider vinegar
Stir all ingredients together and bring to a boil in a large cooker. Simmer for 45 minutes. Pour into clean dry jars, and cap with boiled lids. Seal
**Serve with soup beans or orange roughy fish. To serve over fish: pour salsa over fish and bake at 350 degrees for 35 minutes. You can add 1-2 cups chopped jalapeno peppers to make this salsa hot

### SALMON PATTIES

2 cans pink salmon, drained and de-boned.
1 egg
Salt and pepper to taste
1 c. crushed cracker crumbs
1 egg beaten
1 c. crushed cracker crumbs
Mix salmon, egg, salt and pepper, and cracker crumbs together. Roll in patties and dip into beaten egg and then into cracker crumbs. Fry in 1-inch oil on medium heat until well-browned.

## HOME-STYLE POTATO CHIPS

Wash and dry 6 medium potatoes; do not peel. Slice thin. Fry in a large skillet full of oil until crispy golden brown.

## COLE SLAW

1 head cabbage
1 small onion
1 carrot
1 green pepper
Grate all ingredients in a food processor.
In a small bowl mix together:
1 c. mayo, 3 tbsp. lemon juice,
1 tbsp. Mrs. Dash,
1 tbsp. sugar,
1 tbsp. salt, and salt and pepper to taste.
Stir together with cabbage mixture and chill before serving.

## AUNT JUANITA BLACKBURN'S MEXICAN CORNBREAD

1 c. yellow cornmeal (not self-rising)
½ c. Wesson oil
1 c. flour
1 c. chopped onion
¼ c. sugar
1 c. grated cheese
4 tsp. baking powder
1 chopped jalapeno pepper
½ tsp. salt
½ can cream style corn 2 eggs
¾ c. milk
Mix together as given above and turn into a greased skillet. Bake at 425 degrees for 20-30 minutes or until golden brown. Makes a big loaf.

In her cookbooks, "Scratch Cooking" and "Scratch Cooking 2," Benita McCoy Lyons shares her recipes, the recipes of family & friends, and the rich culinary traditions of her native Appalachia.

You may purchase her newest cookbook at www.kyalmanac.com or by calling 1-800-944-3995. To contact Benita go to www.kentuckyscratchcooking.com.

## CULTURE & THE ARTS

# *Food & Traditional Recipes*

### MINT JULEP

3 cups sugar
3 cups water
Sprigs of fresh mint
Crushed ice
Bourbon (not whisky)
Silver Julep Cups

Make a simple syrup by boiling sugar and water together for about five minutes. Cool and place in a covered container with eight - ten sprigs of fresh mint, and refrigerate overnight. Make one julep (only one) at a time by filling a julep cup with crushed ice, adding one tablespoon syrup and two ounces of Bourbon. Stir briskly with a spoon in order to frost the outside of the julep cup. Garnish with a sprig or two of fresh mint. Enjoy.

### SHAKER LEMON PIE

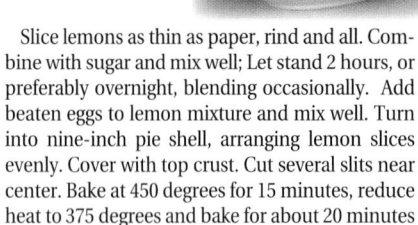

2 large lemons
4 eggs, well beaten
2 C sugar

Slice lemons as thin as paper, rind and all. Combine with sugar and mix well; Let stand 2 hours, or preferably overnight, blending occasionally. Add beaten eggs to lemon mixture and mix well. Turn into nine-inch pie shell, arranging lemon slices evenly. Cover with top crust. Cut several slits near center. Bake at 450 degrees for 15 minutes, reduce heat to 375 degrees and bake for about 20 minutes or until silver knife inserted near edge of pie comes out clean. Cool before service.

NOTE: In the 1800's lemons had a much thinner layer of rind than are found today. For this reason, look for a variety of lemons with a very thin rind.

*(From the Trustees House Daily Fare, Pleasant Hill, Kentucky. Compliments of Shaker Village at Pleasant Hill, http://www.shakervillageky.org)*

### SIMPLE SHAKER COOKIES

½ C butter
¾ C granulated sugar
1 egg
1 tsp vanilla
1-1/2 C flour
1 tsp baking powder
¼ tsp salt

Cream butter and sugar until well blended. Beat in egg and vanilla, mixing well. Sift dry ingredients together. Add to creamed mixture. Chill for at least two hours, then roll and cut on floured surface. (This dough can be rolled in a wax paper cylinder and sliced and baked after chilling. For cookie presses omit the chilling. Place on greased cookie sheet. Bake at 400 degrees until firm but not brown. This recipe has many uses. It's basic for fancy-shaped holiday cookies, plain icebox cookies or drop cookies.

*(Also from the Trustees House Daily Fare, Pleasant Hill, Kentucky.)*

**The Inn at
Shaker Village**
*Source: Shaker Village at
Pleasant Hill*

### WOODFORD PUDDING

1 C flour
½ C butter
1 tsp soda
1 tsp cinnamon
1 C sugar
1 C blackberry jam
½ C sour milk
3 eggs

Mix all together well. Bake in pudding dish at 375 degrees for 40 minutes or until lightly firm.

*(Also from the Trustees House Daily Fare, Pleasant Hill, Kentucky.)*

When issues that affect the future of agriculture come before Kentucky's governing bodies, who speaks up for farmers? Who promotes growth of agribusiness? Who defends the rural values and lifestyle that are so much the backbone of this great state? Since 1919, that has been a role played by Kentucky Farm Bureau. And it's no different today. With representatives and offices in all 120 counties, Kentucky Farm Bureau sees the big picture and understands the local issues. That's why people on the farm, in small towns, and even in major cities, benefit from the voice of Kentucky Farm Bureau.

## Yes, we
### represent
# special
## interests
## in Frankfort.
## Yours.

## BIG ON COMMITMENT.®

AGRICULTURE

Gary Huddleston

*Introduction*

Take everything you think you know about farming in Kentucky and re-examine it.

The state is dominated by small farms, you say? Consolidation and joint ventures have cut into that age-old maxim. Completely tobacco dependent? Less so all the time. Subsidies a big factor in most farmers' income, you've heard? With the tobacco program gone and livestock, by far our biggest income generator, a free-market enterprise, most producers nowadays get little or no government support.

Many of these questionable premises were dead-on truths not so long ago. But today's typical Kentucky farm, if that can even be defined considering the overall diversity of operations, is in a state of transition unlike any period in our history.

Every business seminar for the past decade has been headlined by a consultant who has preached the importance of managing change. That same exhortation is just as applicable to Kentucky agriculture, and the reasons are many. Tobacco's well-documented decline is a big one, considering the history of the crop in the state. Need for supplemental income for farmers is another, with many spouses working off the farm. And a drive toward diversification, fueled by a healthy share of Kentucky tobacco settlement dollars, is yet another.

What hasn't changed, however, is the devotion to agriculture by literally thousands of Kentucky families—a devotion that serves as an inseparable link to the soil despite the fickle nature of farmers' profit margins that makes every year's enterprise a gamble of the highest order. Those families may be growing cantaloupes instead of tobacco and keeping goats in the old hog barn, but they are just as committed to agriculture as were their forbears in generations past.

## HISTORY

Kentucky's farmers have throughout much of the state's history carried the economy of the commonwealth on their collective backs. But more often than not, slim monetary returns to individual families made for challenging financial times. Some of those fiscal difficulties tracked to obvious limiting factors—unpredictable weather, less than ideal terrain, and climate conditions that allowed crop-devouring pests to flourish. But at least one factor owed to the basic structure of Kentucky agriculture, the proliferation of small acreage farmsteads unsuited for anything more than a subsistence scale of income support.

Many small operations survived far longer than might have been predicted by the unique features of the federal tobacco program. Long considered the holy grail of Kentucky agriculture, the program limited production of both burley and dark tobaccos, and guaranteed a level of pricing that proved attractive for several decades, spreading tobacco dollars among thousands of Kentucky farmers and landowners. But even those generous provisions failed to keep pace with skyrocketing labor and input costs. Production limits became impediments to producers who wanted to expand. So by the onset of the millennium many growers were going to a place they had never gone before—asking that the program be terminated and that federal tobacco quotas and production histories be rewarded with a buyout to compensate program participants. That happened in 2004, the last crop grown under the program, and the torrent of resultant changes in the state's agriculture landscape is continuing to build steam.

But change is really nothing new to agriculture. Kentucky's earliest farms weren't profit centers, by any stretch of the imagination. They were designed to sustain the life of the farm family, providing virtually their entire food supply from salt-cured pork to fruits from the orchard, vegetables from the garden, and grain for both human and work animal consumption. Over the past half-century, that focus has been entirely transformed. Now the emphasis is more on cash than calories, with farmers concentrating on the financial return from crops and livestock. A century ago, Kentucky farm families got their meat from the smokehouse, dried fruits and vegetables from the cellar, and milk and eggs from their barn and chicken house. Now they go to the local grocery store for most of these staples, just like their urban counterparts. Marketing proceeds now go to the local bank, not the coffee can of yore.

Other changes affecting agriculture have been just as dramatic. Rural electrification and improvements in rural roads made huge improvements in farmers' lives. Mechanization took away some of the backbreaking work and allowed for greater yields. Crop protection chemicals boosted returns and further cut labor requirements. And farm organizations gave the agriculture sector a voice in public policy that until early in the 20th century was entirely lacking.

Perhaps the biggest change in agriculture, and to some the most unsettling, was the population shift from farms to cities that occurred between the early 1900s and the years following the end of World War II. Kentucky farm dwellers historically looked down on those who lived "in town," making clear their collective opinion that farm residents were a better, more upstanding group than their county seat kin. That notion was buttressed by the fact that from the founding days of the commonwealth, a large majority of citizens were farmers by trade. But by the late 1940s the younger generation of the day rejected that notion of agricultural permanence and departed the farms in surprising numbers, lured by the promise of higher wages and a more comfortable, less demanding lifestyle. Now, in Kentucky as elsewhere, the farm exodus has continued to the point that no more than 2 percent of citizens list farming as their occupation. This incredible demographic reversal is testament to the premise that, to many, the farming lifestyle looks better in the rearview mirror than it did in the precious present—especially on payday.

**Farmer's Market**
Source: Southern & Eastern Kentucky Tourism Development Association

**Blueberries**
Photo: Sid Webb

## TODAY'S FARMERS

Now that farmers are Kentucky's most prominent minority group, much has changed about how families earn a living on farms. But, those few who have survived in the honorable profession of food and fiber production say that they continue to be drawn to the fields by the same factors that were so alluring to their great-grandparents. The hearty lifestyle, independence that comes with self-employment, love of land and water, and the wholesomeness of the rural life experience—all these combine to hold today's farm families close to their agrarian roots. Yes, it's far different to follow a GPS tracking device when computing fertilizer application rates, or to operate a cab-enclosed combine through soybean fields than it was when mule power provided most of the push and pull through crop acreages. But it's the same thrill and sense of fulfillment when crops flourish and when bins fill at the end of the season. And it's every bit as satisfying when the son or daughter coming of age sits down with the parents and tells of their desire to continue into farming through yet another generation.

The current drive to diversify, or reinvent if you will, Kentucky's agriculture carries with it a sense of urgency. That urgency is born out of the intense desire by today's farming adults to ensure that future generations can choose a career in agriculture, with at least a reasonable chance of earning a "living wage." The investments being made in alternative enterprises by the state's Agriculture Development Fund are tailored to offer farmers, or future farmers, new ways to generate farm income. If beef calves are profitable, what about feeder steers or fed cattle? Corn and soybeans sell well as livestock feed ingredients, but the promise of higher demand from renewable fuel production is strong. Kentucky grapes, catfish, goats and prawns are finding their way into farm plans as supplemental income sources for enterprising producers. All these and many more new crops and products offer tantalizing potential for Kentucky's forward-thinking farm families.

For some rural entrepreneurs, it's not so much what they grow on their land, it's the prospect of merchandising the place itself. Rural bed-and-breakfasts are popping up as destinations for travelers in search of peaceful getaways. Sometimes the crops themselves can enhance a visitor's experience, such as a corn maze or a pick-your-own pumpkin patch. For others, a wagon ride through the property or even a pay lake for young fishermen may be the draw. Agritourism proponents have an enthusiasm about their subject matter

**Nancy Newsome, Princeton**
*Photo: Sid Webb*

that is contagious. Conferences promoting destination agriculture have become almost as common on extension service calendars as beef days or horticulture workshops.

## DEVELOPING ISSUES

Despite the budding optimism evident among agriculture's 21st century adherents, few doubt that the challenges of the future will be every bit as daunting as those in our state's farming past. Blending of suburban development and farming areas, where the so-called exurbs are pushing into active ag zones, is producing friction among these long-standing farming operations and their new neighbors. Political solutions to public policy problems as taxes and environmental restrictions are more challenging now that agriculture's voting strength has been diluted. And the global nature of some of the most serious threats to farmers, such as agriterrorism or animal disease outbreaks, place Kentucky's producers in a position of vulnerability not of their own making.

But farmers are adapting well to new realities, as they have throughout their history. They're taking a more activist stance in the political arena, working through Farm Bureau and other advocacy groups to hold public officials accountable for their decisions. Those same organizations are offering training to their agriculture members in activities as diverse as running for public office to serving as an agriculture spokesperson with news media or with urban groups. And farmers are embracing new technologies to help them become more efficient producers and marketers. In short, these agricultural innovators are making the necessary investments, both financial and intellectual, to compete successfully in their new environment. It's the natural response for a group who has led Kentucky through its first two centuries, and who plan to carve out an equivalent role for their beloved profession in the future. For most casual observers, farming is a cap-wearing, pickup-driving, mud-stomping lifestyle. To those who till and tend the crops and livestock, and have for generations, farming is life itself.

# Kentucky Farm Bureau – Established in November 1919

## AGRICULTURE

# *Gardening*

Karen Angelucci

### KENTUCKY WINTER GARDENING

Winter brings cold and snow—and our gratitude for warm homes and cozy fires. Now that the leaves have fallen and perennials are underground, it is time to evaluate the design of your landscape. Evergreens are scene savers thanks to their forever-green foliage. As long as the weather permits there will be chores outside. As you dream over plant catalogs, remember these secrets for winter gardening.

When night temperatures consistently stay below 50 degrees F., add 2 to 3 inches of mulch to gardens. Keep mulch away from trunks and stems to minimize damage from insects, animals and disease.

with woody and other perennial plants during dry spells, especially prior to a hard freeze. Order or plan to shop locally for seeds for the upcoming spring season. Make sure you buy seeds packed for the upcoming season.

Plan vegetable gardens and crop rotation for the upcoming season.

Repair garden tools, accessories, furniture, arbors, and trellises.

**(top) Cardinal in the winter**
*Photo: Betty Hall*
**(left) Lotus in a garden pond**
*Photo: Florence Huffman*

If the ground is not frozen, most deciduous trees and shrubs can be planted or transplanted.

If you trim foliage for your holiday decorations, be sure to prune properly so that the shrub will not be out of shape come spring.

Winter injury can be harsh on the landscape. Snow and ice, along with drying winds, can damage plants, as can road salt if you are an urban gardener. To avoid unwanted damage, choose plants for your landscape that are appropriate for your zone. Winter injury is more common in evergreen plants.

Harvest mistletoe to ensure lots of kisses during the holidays. To avoid damage, don't walk or drive on a frozen lawn.

Keep an eye on houseplants and remove any dead

Continue to clean herbaceous and perennial flowerbeds as needed.

Protect hardy Chrysanthemums with mulch or straw to aid in the over-wintering process. Do not cut dead foliage until spring.

Bulbs can be planted as long as the soil is not frozen.

Check garden for plants that have been lifted or heaved from the ground due to freezing and thawing. Reset the plant by pressing or tucking.

Leave snow on the garden as a protective blanket against icy winds.

Continue to water outdoor containers

or dying leaves. Also look for signs of insects—if you spot aphids, spray them with a solution of rubbing alcohol, a drop of dish soap and water. Due to the decrease in sunlight, routine fertilizing is not recommended until spring. Clean houseplants by sponging glossy-leafed plants and lightly brushing plants that have fuzzy or textured foliage with a soft brush.

Dream of spring. Don't forget to feed and supply water for our feathered friends who hang with us during the long cold months of winter.

## KENTUCKY SPRING GARDENING

Blue skies and warm air bring bursting buds, growing plants and flowers. Springtime arrives and warms our spirits—finally Kentucky is reborn. As Kentucky awakes from winter it brings with it a marvelous display of blooming flowers, trees and shrubs. Listed are a few secrets to springtime gardening in this great state.

Photos: Sid Webb

Prepare soil for planting by double digging or tilling the soil. Do not over-till and produce flour—this will decrease draining ability. Replenish gardens with organic matter and compost. If you have trouble with clay soil, amend it with sharp sand or granite meal, peat moss and topsoil.

Kentuckians are blessed with land laden with plenty of phosphorus and potassium, leaving nitrogen to be replenished. An all-purpose fertilizer such as 10-10-10 will meet most of soil needs. Kentucky's soil is rich in limestone and produces good plant growth. Grasses like timothy and alfalfa utilize the mineral elements and animals grazing on them enjoy the benefits, the primary one being strong bone development. Add 10-10-10 to garden beds and compost piles every 6 to 8 weeks throughout the growing season.

Deep watering to reach roots is more beneficial than just surface or foliage wetting. Water gardens early in the day to allow foliage to dry to decrease disease. Watering late in the day will increase disease due to excess moisture in the night. Minimize overhead watering to decrease spread of disease.

Hold off mulching until soil warms to 55 to 60 degrees F. Mulching now will only confuse plants. It will be better to mulch when soil temperature is warm.

**Sunflowers**
Source: Karen Angelucci

Don't be tempted to plant summer annuals until after Derby Day, the last frost date for most of Kentucky. Perennials can be divided now if the weather permits. The plants should be 2" to 4" tall before division.

Soak seeds in water overnight if they have a hard shell to speed germination. Marigold roots release a toxin that kills root nematodes. Knowing this, plant marigolds among vegetables to protect them.

Finish pruning chores on trees and shrubs. Prune spring-bloomers after bloom fades and before new growth.

Give established deciduous trees, broadleaf and needled evergreens a light application of fertilizer such as 10-10-10 now and again in the fall.

Young trees develop stronger trunks if not staked; let the tree sway with the wind.

Keep your eyes open for the Kentucky state butterfly, the viceroy, which overwinter around willow trees, even using the willow leaves as little blankets.

Since 1976 the Kentucky state tree has been the yellow poplar or tulip poplar (Liriodendron tulipifera). A member of the Magnolia family, its blooms are unique with yellow-green petals and an orange inner covering.

Harvest mint for a Kentucky Derby mint juleps.

## KENTUCKY SUMMER GARDENING

Kentucky summers bring bright sunshine and a kaleidoscope of color to the landscape. Roses reign with grace and charm, as hydrangeas continue to steal the show. Daylilies naturalize along road banks and the fields are full of chicory and Queen Ann's lace. The sun reddens as the sky grows hazy, and we frown on the sticky muggy days that lie before us. Here are a few secrets to summer gardening in Kentucky. Apply water to gardens if

Photos: Sid Webb

rainfall is inadequate. One inch of water is necessary every week—less frequent, deep watering will allow roots to grow deeper. Deep roots are more likely to survive drought than shallow roots. Remember, plants are 90 percent water.

Keep gardens weed-free—remove weeds before they bloom and set seed or they will multiple fast.

Use a scuffle hoe, stirrup hoe or your hands to remove weeds, roots and all. Weeding is easier if the soil is damp.

Fertilize gardens early in the summer with a light application of granular 10-10-10.

Completely remove cool-weather annuals such as pansies, and replace with warm-weather annuals such as Vinca or sage.

Pinch or cut leggy annuals to keep a more compact and healthy appearance. This stretches bloom time until September or October. Deadhead perennials to promote new blooms.

Collect and sprinkle seeds of hollyhocks, larkspur, Nigella, and foxgloves after the blooms fade and plant dies.

Surprisingly, many perennials and biennials benefit from having weak stems cut to the ground. Thinning allows for more air circulation and will reduce disease. Complete pinching fall-flowering perennials by mid-July to allow time to form flower buds prior to fall.

For optimum bloom size, replant and separate Irises every three years. The best time to replant is after the flowers fade through late summer. Divide spring-blooming perennials after blooms fade.

Herbs enhance the flavor of any dish. For the best flavor cut herbs after dew has dried on leaves in the morning. It's best to harvest herbs on a cool day before the plant blooms. After herbs bloom they lose the amount of oil that once concentrated in the leaves. Don't allow basil to form blooms—this decreases flavor in the leaves. Removing blooms encourages new growth. Harvest basil, mint, thyme, oregano, rosemary, lavender and sage for drying.

After spring harvest, cultivate the soil, sow seeds and set more transplants. Try successive planting of your favorite vegetables for a constant harvest until fall.

Harvest vegetables as they ripen. Harvest leafy vegetables, squash and cucumbers after the dew has dried, about mid-morning. Sugar content is highest in the afternoon in corn, peas and tomatoes, so they should be harvested then. Withhold water one week before harvesting cantaloupe, muskmelon and watermelons for sweeter fruit. Wait to transplant trees and shrubs this fall.

## KENTUCKY FALL GARDENING

When the Harvest Moon appears in our sky we realize that summer is drawing to an end. Cool winds of autumn blow in a stunning display of color and nature begins its resting period. The garden season wanes as cool weather approaches. Here are a few secrets to fall gardening in Kentucky.

Fall is a great time to create new and replenish established gardens. Roots grow best in the fall making this an important time to amend the soil, propagate and plant. A soil test can be done any time of year on flower and vegetable gardens as well as your lawn—but get test results before applying fertilizer or lime to your soil. Contact the county extension office—testing now will allow you to get results and amend soil before spring.

Tidy gardens by removing dead and diseased foliage. Removing debris is the best defense against next year's insects and disease. Add debris to compost pile; discard material with an insect or disease problem.

The more weeds you pull now—especially before seeds mature—the less you will have next spring.

Moisture is critical as plants prepare for dormancy. Keep newly planted plant material watered throughout dry periods.

Fall mulching isn't necessary. It is best to wait until ground temperatures become cold and stay cold to allow plants to prepare for winter before applying mulch.

Perennial planting, dividing and transplanting in early fall is ideal—wait until a cool, cloudy day or late in the day. Water plants well before digging and keep soil moist to aid root reestablishment after planting. Perennials need a few months of root growth before the ground freezes to survive the winter.

Plant perennials for fall color and interest, such as chrysanthemums, Japanese anemone, ornamental and native grasses, Russian sage, pansies and showy stonecrop.

Kentucky's state flower, the Goldenrod (Solidago) with its golden plumes can be seen this season. It was thought that masses of goldenrod in the field pointed the way to hidden treasure or maybe a water source. It was often planted near the front of the house to bring good luck.

Cut annuals to soil level when they die. Leave roots in the ground to add organic matter to nourish the soil. It's too late to prune trees and shrubs (it will trigger new growth that will be susceptible to winter kill). Transplant deciduous trees and shrubs when leaves start to change colors. Give established deciduous trees and shrubs a light application of 10-10-10 after leaves begin to fall. After the last rake of leaves mow the lawn at 2" to 2.5". The lower cut allows more energy to be directed toward root development.

*Karen Angelucci lives in Lexington with her family. She is the author of "Secrets of a Kentucky Gardener," Angelucci Garden Press, 2005. Her book is a practical, monthly journal providing easy-to-follow advice for Kentucky gardeners.*

2002 CENSUS OF AGRICULTURE UNITED STATES: Released June 3, 2004, by the National Agricultural Statistics Service (NASS), Agricultural Statistics Board, U.S. Department of Agriculture

## Table 1. Kentucky Summary Highlights: 2002

| | | |
|---|---|---|
| Farms | number | 86,541 |
| Land in farms | acres | 13,843,706 |
| Average size of farm | acres | 160 |
| Median size of farm | acres | 94 |
| **Estimated market value of land and buildings:** | | |
| Average per farm | | $294,056 |
| Average per acre | | $1,824 |
| **Estimated market value of all machinery and Equip.** | | |
| Average per farm | | $41,458 |
| **Farms by size:** | | |
| 1 to 9 acres | | 5,342 |
| 10 to 49 acres | | 24,758 |
| 50 to 179 acres | | 36,628 |
| 180 to 499 acres | | 14,950 |
| 500 to 999 acres | | 3,175 |
| 1,000 acres or more | | 1,688 |
| **Total cropland** | farms | 80,927 |
| | acres | 8,412,354 |
| **Harvested cropland** | farms | 65,815 |
| | acres | 4,978,994 |
| **Irrigated land** | farms | 3,606 |
| | acres | 36,751 |
| **Market value of agricultural products sold** | | $3,080,080,000 |
| Average per farm | | $35,591 |
| Crops | | $1,110,209,000 |
| Livestock, poultry, and their products | | $1,969,871,000 |
| **Farms by value of sales:** | | |
| Less than $2,500 | | 32,918 |
| $2,500 to $4,999 | | 11,778 |
| $5,000 to $9,999 | | 13,561 |
| $10,000 to $24,999 | | 13,154 |
| $25,000 to $49,999 | | 6,525 |
| $50,000 to $99,999 | | 3,486 |
| $100,000 or more | | 5,119 |
| **Government payments** | farms | 22,825 |
| | | $94,053,000 |
| **Total income from farm-related sources, gross before taxes and expenses** | farms | 33,083 |
| | | $210,952,000 |
| **Total farm production expenses** | | $2,604,069,000 |
| Average per farm | | $30,073 |
| **Net cash farm income of operation** | farms | 86,591 |
| | | $847,511,000 |
| Average per farm | | $9,788 |

## Table 1. Kentucky Summary Highlights: 2002 (cont'd)

| | | |
|---|---|---|
| **Principal operator by primary occupation:** | | |
| Farming | number | 46,939 |
| Other | number | 39,602 |
| **Principal operator by days worked off farm:** | | |
| Any | number | 49,176 |
| 200 days or more | number | 36,532 |
| **Livestock and poultry:** | | |
| Cattle and calves inventory | farms | 47,447 |
| | number | 2,395,476 |
| Beef cows | farms | 40,234 |
| | number | 1,125,183 |
| Milk cows | farms | 2,939 |
| | number | 120,748 |
| Cattle and calves sold | farms | 40,429 |
| | number | 1,291,026 |
| Hogs and pigs inventory | farms | 1,254 |
| | number | 385,811 |
| Hogs and pigs sold | farms | 1,220 |
| | number | 986,704 |
| Sheep and lambs inventory | farms | 1,230 |
| | number | 27,443 |
| Layers 20 weeks old and older inventory | farms | 2,197 |
| | number | 4,343,328 |
| Broilers and other meat-type chickens sold | farms | 669 |
| | number | 271,176,998 |
| **Selected crops harvested:** | | |
| Corn for grain | farms | 7,446 |
| | acres | 1,043,990 |
| | bushels | 108,721,040 |
| Corn for silage or greenchop | farms | 2,307 |
| | acres | 82,820 |
| | tons | 1,287,831 |
| Wheat for grain, All | farms | 2,145 |
| | acres | 318,856 |
| | bushels | 16,447,721 |
| Winter wheat for grain | farms | 2,145 |
| | acres | 318,856 |
| | bushels | 16,447,721 |
| Spring wheat for grain | farms | - |
| | acres | - |
| | bushels | - |

*Note: Some data based on survey samples.*
*Source: http://www.nass.usda.gov/census/census02*

# FARMER'S MARKETS

| COUNTY | MARKET | CONTACT | PHONE |
| --- | --- | --- | --- |
| Adair | Adair County Farmers Market | David Herbst | (270) 384-2317 |
| Allen | Allen County Farmers Market | Nina Jones | (270) 622-8029 |
| Anderson | Anderson County Farmers Market | Fred Chumbler | (502) 859-4845 |
| Barren | Cave City Farmers Market | Patricia Switzer | (800) 346-8908 |
| Bath | Bath County Farmers Market | Jimmie Thompson | (606) 683-2892 |
| Boone | Boone County Farmers Market | Don Talbert Jr | (859) 762-7736 |
| Bourbon | Paris-Bourbon County Farmers Market | Patricia Jones | (606) 987-6614 |
| Boyd | Boyd County Farmers Market | F. H. Bradley | (606) 324-4047 |
| Boyle | Boyle County Farmers Market | Treina Miller | (859) 236-2631 |
| Bracken | Bracken County Farmers Market | Alex Hyrcza | (606) 756-3971 |
| Breckinridge | Breckinridge County Farmer's Market | Carol M Hinton | (270) 756-2182 |
| Caldwell | Caldwell County Farmers Market | Ethelyne Fraley | (270) 388-9043 |
| Calloway | Murray Main Street Saturday Market | Deana Wright | (270) 759-9474 |
| Campbell | Campbell County Farmers Market | Don Sorrell | (859) 572-2600 |
| Carroll | Riverview Farmers Market | Jenny Urie | (502) 732-0472 |
| Carter | Carter County Farmers Market | Myron Evans | (606) 474-6686 |
| Christian | Bradford Square Farmers Market | Samantha Hancock | (270) 886-9777 |
| Clark | Winchester - Clark County Farmers Market | Shelia McCord | (859) 744-4360 |
| Crittenden | Marion Farmers Market | Rose Crider | (270) 704-0134 |
| Daviess | Owensboro Regional Farmers Market, Inc. | Earl & Peggy Castlen | (270) 264-1681 |
| Edmonson | Edmonson County Farmers Market | Whylie Willis | (270) 597-3133 |
| Elliott | Elliott County Farmers Market | Ben Meredith | (606) 738-6440 |
| Fayette | Lexington Farmers Market | Roland McIntosh | (859) 633-4059 |
| Franklin | Franklin County Farmers Market | Edie Greer | (502) 695-9035 |
| Garrard | Garrard County Farmers Market | Kathy Simpson | (859) 792-3828 |
| Grant | Dry Ridge Farmers Market | Jeff Nehring | (859) 824-0552 |
| Grant | Grant County Farmers Market | Rodney Stephenson | (859) 824-3355 |
| Hardin | Hardin County Farmers Market | Brenda Thomas | (270) 352-4829 |
| Harlan | Harlan County Farmers Market | Theresa Howard | (606) 573-4464 |
| Harrison | Harrison County Farmers Market | Alyson Arthur | (859) 234-3621 |
| Henderson | Green River Area Farmers Market | George Warren | (270) 826-9531 |
| Henry | Henry County Farmers Market | Mary Ellan Garrison | (502) 845-2811 |
| Hopkins | Dawson Spring Main Street Market | Emily Barbour | (270) 797-4248 |
| Hopkins | Pennyrile Area Farmers Market | Lisa Miller | (270) 821-3435 |
| Jackson | Jackson County Farmers Market | Juanitta Welborn | (606) 364-5482 |
| Jefferson | Bardstown Road Farmers Market | Ken Hubsch | (502) 647-1662 |
| Jefferson | Jeffersontown Farmers Market | Barbara Carby | (502) 267-1674 |
| Jefferson | Rowan Street Farmers Market | Holly Likes | (502) 829-5988 |
| Jefferson | Temple Farmers Market | Gerry Roncin | (502) 423-1818 |
| Jessamine | Jessamine County Farmers Market | Mary E. Stevens | (859) 887-2797 |
| Johnson | Johnson Co. Farmer's Market | Brian Jeffiers | (606) 789-8108 |
| Laurel | Laurel County Farmers Market | Glenn Williams | (606) 864-4167 |
| Lawrence | Lawrence County Farmers Market | John E. Sparks | (606) 638-9495 |
| Lee | Lee County Farmers Market | Neil Hoffman | (606) 593-6584 |
| Lewis | Lewis County Farmers Market | Dee Potter | (606) 757-2335 |
| Lincoln | Old Depot Farmers Market | Andrea Miller | (606) 365-4118 |
| Logan | Logan County Farmers Market | Marian Davis | (270) 726-6323 |
| Madison | Berea Farmers Market | Bill Best | (859) 986-3204 |
| Madison | Madison County Farmers Market | Myra E. Isbell | (859) 624-9573 |
| Marion | Marion County Farmers Market | Kathryn A. Alford | (859) 336-3711 |
| Martin | Martin County Farmers Market | Sue Sluss | (606) 298-7033 |
| Mason | Mason County Farmers Market | Bill Peterson | (606) 564-6808 |
| McCracken | Paducah Downtown Farmers Market | Rick Greenwell | |
| McLean | Calhoun Farmer's Market | Margaret Scott | (270) 273-3690 |
| Meade | Meade County Farmers Market | Jennifer Benham | (270) 422-4958 |
| Menifee | Menifee County Farmers Market | Marvinn Bolts | (606) 768-3866 |
| Mercer | Mercer County Farmers Market | Tony Shirley | (859) 734-4378 |
| Monroe | Monroe County Farmers Market | Kevin Lyons | (270) 487-5504 |
| Montgomery | Montgomery County Farmers Market | Gayle Arnold | (859) 498-1898 |
| Morgan | Morgan County Farmers Market | Karen Wright | (606) 743-7817 |
| Muhlenberg | Muhlenberg County Farmers Market | Darrell Simpson | (270) 338-3124 |
| Nelson | Bardstown Farmers Market | Carla Constant | (502) 348-5947 |
| Pendleton | Pendleton County Farmers Market | Dewey Peluso | (859) 472-5723 |
| Powell | Powell County Farmers Market | Mike Reed | (606) 663-6405 |
| Pulaski | Pulaski Growers Association | Twila VanHook | (606) 423-2939 |
| Rockcastle | Rockcastle Farmers Market | Noah C. Campbell | (606) 256-4040 |
| Rowan | Rowan County Farmers Market | Bob Marsh | (606) 784-5457 |
| Russell | Russell County Farmers Market | Dena Wright & Laura Miller | (270) 759-9474 |
| Scott | Scott County Farmers Market, Inc. | Mark Reese | (502) 863-0984 |
| Shelby | Shelby County Farmers Market | Doug & Holly Likes | (502) 829-5988 |
| Trigg | Cadiz/Trigg County Farmers Market | Carole Schafer | (270) 522-3269 |
| Warren | Bowling Green Farmers Market | Dorothy Richmond | (270) 782-8465 |
| Warren | Southern Kentucky Regional Farmers Market | Paul Wiediger | (270) 749-4600 |
| Wolfe | Wolfe County Farmers Market | Johnson & Kay Holbrook | (606) 668-3732 |
| Woodford | Woodford County Farmers Market | John Wilhoit | (859) 873-6861 |

Source: Kentucky Department of Agriculture, www.kyagr.com

# AGRICULTURE
# *Family Farms*

Sue Weant

The term "family farm" is not limited to simply one definition. But the concept of the family farm that is most precious to Kentucky is the "traditional" idea of farming—a relatively small farm owned and managed by one family and passed down from generation to generation to continue the rural livelihood that is so vital to us today. Your childhood memories of a family farm may stem from visiting your grandparent's farm and petting baby calves, cradling baby kittens, or gathering eggs as an angry hen clucked furiously nearby ...and there was the huge tobacco barn with its unique smell of curing tobacco. Remember? Oh, and don't forget Sunday dinner—when every fresh fruit and vegetable that could be beaten, or baked or scalloped was proudly served, along with fried chicken, roast beef or pork roast. Hard work was behind all of it.

The U.S. Department of Agriculture defines family farm as a farm with annual gross receipts of less than $250,000, and on which day-to-day labor and management is provided by the family who owns the land and farm assets. Family farms are the most basic, yet exceedingly important unit, of an agricultural economy. We are now living in a transitionary time involving family farms, as farmers who relied on tobacco as their cash crop are forced to diversify and find other ways to make their farms profitable.

According to Scott Smith, Dean of the College of Agriculture at the University of Kentucky, "It's almost as if we have two farming populations in this state: a small number of large globally competitive farms, and a large number of small family farms that usually involve off-farm employment and part-time work since their total sales often aren't enough to provide full support for a family."

The small farmer's troubles are catching the attention of consumers as many remember when nearby farms supplied their food needs without planting thousands of acres to make a living. Are those days gone? Are we are growing more dependent on foreign countries to supply our food, just as we are dependent for our oil supply. In Kentucky—one of five states where the majority of family farms are located—the struggle continues to keep farmland from being destroyed to make room for commercial construction as the latest generation of farmers steadily decreases.

The threat of losing our farms has precipitated the creation of non-profit organizations leading the charge to saving Kentucky's farms—Partners for Family Farms and Community Farm Alliance are at the forefront of this movement.

Welcome Hall Garden, Versailles
*Photo: Sid Webb*

# AGRICULTURE
# *Biotechnology*

## Dr. Pearse Lyons

Once considered the frontier and "wild west" when Daniel Boone and fellow pioneers crossed the Appalachian mountain range, Kentucky boasts a long and rich history. These days, the state is known as the Horse Capital of the World and plays host to "the greatest two minutes in sports," the annual Kentucky Derby on the first Saturday in May. From Churchill Downs and Keeneland to Colonel Sanders' secret recipe of 11 herbs and spices, Kentucky's brand resonates throughout the world. Generations of Kentuckians have raised tobacco, horses, cattle, and even corn for the production of the state's beloved bourbon. The one common denominator of these Kentucky traditions is agriculture.

As we move forward, we have the opportunity to embrace our state's past in order to build our future, using our strengths to move the commonwealth ahead in ways that were previously inconceivable. At Alltech, we see this opportunity in biotechnology. With the construction of the new Center for Animal Nutrigenomics and Applied Animal Nutrition, we are taking strides to make Kentucky the "Silicon Valley" of advanced agriculture. In the near future, it is likely that the food production industry will look to Kentucky to find the best ways to produce food—food that is safe for humans as well as the environment.

The possibilities are endless. By exploring and developing sciences like nutrigenomics – the study of how nutrition affects genes—we not only realize that everything we feed our animals affects their growth, but we also learn more about the world around us. With the global population rising at an unprecedented rate, the demand for food is increasing exponentially. We must become more efficient in all methods of food production in order to feed our people and also leave the world in good standing for future generations. That is but one role of biotechnology.

With a wealth of experience in producing bourbon, Kentucky will play an important role in the future of our country. A government mandate to produce 30 percent of transportation fuel from biofuels by 2030—thereby reducing our reliance on foreign oil—has provided Kentucky the opportunity to lead this charge. We cannot rely on corn-based ethanol to meet this mandate and also expect to grow enough grain or corn to provide for our animals.

**Alltech Headquarters, Nicholasville**
*Source: Alltech*

Research is currently underway to uncover ways of producing ethanol from cellulose, making it possible to turn any type of plant life into a source of energy.

The role of biotechnology is immense, and Kentucky is poised to reap the benefits. By embracing science and the potential for advanced agriculture, the state invites today's pioneer scientists to forge new, progressive trails. The lasting impact of biotechnology will to put Kentucky in the history books once again.

# AGRICULTURE
# *Hemp*

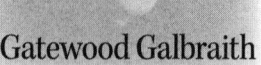

Gatewood Galbraith

Hemp is the name given to the Cannabis sativa plant when it is cultivated and used in its industrial and textile capacity. Hemp is as integral a part of Kentucky and its history as racehorses and bourbon. Hemp was Kentucky's first cash crop and was its largest cash crop for over 100 years (almost twice as long as tobacco held that distinction). Indeed, the Commonwealth was the world's largest hemp producer from 1810 until 1911.

The cannabis plant, also known as marijuana when cultivated for its medicinal and intoxicating properties, has been a valuable commodity to mankind for thousands of years. Civilizations

**Harvesting hemp**

have depended on hemp to create sails and rigging for ships and cloth for clothing. During the War of 1812, Napoleon's ill-fated invasion of Russia was prompted by his need to cut off shipments of hemp to England. Without hemp Great Britain's formidable navy would have been rendered useless within three months.

In addition to canvas, ropes, thread and linens, hemp can also be used to make fine paper with a useful life of centuries. Interestingly, the Vatican continues to print its most important documents on hemp paper.

When the colonists landed on the shores of North America, hemp was such an integral part of survival that a law was passed compelling citizens to grow hemp as a crop, and they could pay their taxes with it. The first pioneers passing into Kentucky through the Cumberland Gap brought hemp seeds for planting in order to furnish their day-to-day needs and to barter with.

Hemp cultivation is labor-intensive, and turning it into finished products became a major industry in Kentucky. The seeds were a valuable source of oil for paints, lubricants, inks and medicinal balms. The seedcake remaining after the oil was derived was a valuable food for humans and animals and today it is prized as birdseed.

Kentucky remained the world's largest producer of hemp until 1911, when it lost ground to cheaper imports and synthetic products such as nylon. After a long period of vilification of the cannabis plant, Congress outlawed growing cannabis in the 1937 Marijuana Tax Act. The hemp market was destroyed.

Hemp enjoyed a rebirth in 1941, and Kentucky farmers' income rose when its cultivation was encouraged to produce goods for the war effort including oil for motor lubrication of high altitude aircraft. Farmers in a seven-state area were required to view a 14-minute film produced by the U.S. military entitled "Hemp for Victory". Moreover, hemp farmers were exempt from the draft. However, as the Allies regained access to major oil supplies in 1944, the hemp program was discontinued, and marijuana was maligned again as criminal.

Nevertheless, cannabis is a very useful plant. Hemp can be converted to a biofuel called methanol, which may one day be a viable fuel source, and it is becoming more widely accepted as a medicine, with 11 states now allowing its use by prescription.

*Gatewood Galbraith is a Lexington Attorney and author.*

# Dr. Stuart Foster

# Climate & Seasons

Location plays a vital role in determining the distinct seasonal variations in Kentucky's climate. Its inland location on the North American continent contributes to seasonal swings in average temperature, while its position relative to the Gulf of Mexico contributes to ample precipitation that is well distributed throughout the year. Upper-level westerly winds, which steer storm systems across North America, also contribute to the variability of Kentucky's weather.

Average temperature has varied over the past century. While concerns about the quality of temperature observations over time raise questions about the assessment of temperature trends, nearly all of Kentucky's high temperature records were achieved in the early 1900s. The recent rise in average temperature since the late 1980s is more evident in the average winter temperatures than in the average summer temperatures, which remain unremarkable in comparison with historical observations. Currently, the mean annual temperature in Kentucky ranges from 53 F in the northeast to 59 F in the southwest.

Precipitation is generally abundant across Kentucky. Average annual precipitation increases from 42 inches in the north to 52 inches in the south. A strong precipitation gradient during the winter season is less evident over the summer months. After a relatively dry period through the mid-1900s, the average annual precipitation across Kentucky has increased by an average of nearly three inches over the past three decades.

## SPRING

Spring is an active weather season in Kentucky. While the warm, sunny days of spring are always welcome, springtime weather can be very changeable. Temperatures reaching above 80 F in early spring can be followed by temperatures dipping to near 20 F. The clash between cold, dry air masses from the north and warm, moist air masses from the south brings the risk of severe weather in the form of thunderstorms producing damaging winds, hail and tornadoes.

Average temperatures rise significantly throughout spring. Mid-spring daily high temperatures

**Snowy day on Main St., Lexington**
*Photo: Sid Webb*

average in the low to mid 70s across Kentucky with higher values to the south and west. In extreme cases, high temperatures above 90 F have been recorded as early as March, while subfreezing temperatures have been recorded up until the first of June. The average date of the last spring freeze ranges from early April in the southwest to early

May in the northeast.

While precipitation is distributed rather evenly throughout the year, Kentucky's wettest months on average occur during spring. May averaged more than 5 inches of rain across the state, with slightly higher amounts in the south and central portions of Kentucky. Though early spring snowstorms are not common, they can bring significant accumulations of heavy, wet snow.

## SUMMER

Summer days in Kentucky are typically quite warm. Weather prognosticators often bring out the three H's, forecasting "hazy, hot and humid, with the chance of an isolated, afternoon thunderstorm." As the upper-level winds weaken and migrate further north during the summer months, the passage of frontal systems becomes less frequent. Kentucky's summer weather is thus less changeable than during other seasons, and weather patterns often persist for several days or even weeks. When summertime frontal systems do move through Kentucky, cool and dry air from Canada brings pleasant conditions that may persist for a few days.

The average daily high temperature for July increases from about 86 F in the east to 90 F in the west. High temperatures exceed 90 F for an average of 20 days per year in the north and east and 40 or more days in the south and west. Temperatures occasionally exceed 100 F. Nighttime low temperatures average near 63 F in the east to 68 F in the west, but during a heat wave they may not dip below the 70s.

Summertime precipitation is produced largely from thunderstorms, though severe weather is less frequent than during spring. Moist, tropical air from the Gulf of Mexico helps to fuel thunderstorms and normally contributes sufficient rains to support crops and pastureland. Still, it is not uncommon for a location to go for a period of two weeks without measurable precipitation at some point during the summer.

## FALL

Fall, like spring, is a transitional season. Weather is influenced by a reduced flow of moist air from the south and by the more frequent passage of weak frontal systems bringing cool, dry air from the north. Together, these contribute to an increased frequency of warm, sunny days and cool, clear nights. While severe weather is possible during the fall, it is much less common than during spring. Instead, fair weather and colorful fall foliage make this a favorite time of year for many people.

Average temperatures decline steadily throughout fall. High temperatures drop from the mid to upper 70s in early fall to the mid to upper 40s by the time winter arrives. As during spring, weather patterns can be quite variable. Freezing temperatures have been recorded as early as September, while temperatures well into the 90s have been observed even in October. The average date of the first fall freeze ranges from early October in the northeast to late October in the southwest, resulting in an average growing season of 165 to 200 days.

Kentucky's driest season is fall. Thunderstorms are much less frequent than during summer, and the passage of frontal systems rarely brings heavy rain during early fall. October is normally the driest month of the year, averaging about 3.5 inches of rain in the west and less than 3 inches in the east. The remnants of occasional tropical storms add significantly to Kentucky's precipitation total during the fall. Average precipitation increases through November and into December, often providing relief from any dry spells that may have persisted through early fall.

## WINTER

Winters in Kentucky are typically mild. The polar jet stream is strong and plays a vital role in Kentucky's winter weather, bringing an increased frequency of cloudy days. When it moves north of Kentucky, the jet stream can bring spring-like temperatures in the midst of winter. When it dips to the south, it can usher in arctic air that sends the mercury plummeting. Further, it can steer storm systems bringing cold, steady rains or heavy snows across Kentucky.

The average daily high temperature for January ranges from 38 F in extreme northern Kentucky to 44 F along the Kentucky-Tennessee border. Daily low temperatures average near 20 F in the north and 25 F in the south and southwest. When polar air masses visit Kentucky, their stay is usually short. Subzero temperatures occur an average of five days in the north and only two days in the south. During many winters, temperatures never drop below zero.

Most winter precipitation is in the form of rain. Seasonal snowfall totals average from less than 10 inches in the south to more than 20 inches in the north. But totals can vary greatly from year to year. Some winters, particularly in the south, may pass without any significant accumulation. Meanwhile, seasonal accumulations of more than 2 or 3 feet occur periodically, typically reflecting a small number of heavy snow events. Snow seldom covers the ground for more than a week at a time in the south or more than two weeks in the north.

## CLIMATE & SEASONS
# *Weather Highlights*
## *2004-2006*

### Dr. Stuart Foster

**JAN 2004 33.2°F / 3.91 inches**

January temperatures and precipitation were near normal. Minor flooding and flash flooding occurred across central and eastern regions on the 2nd through the 4th, followed by minor river flooding in southwest through mid month. Heavy snow, with up to 7 inches in upland areas, occurred on the 9th in the east. Following an intrusion of arctic air, widespread freezing rain on the 25th caused power outages and traffic accidents. On the 26th, lightning strikes, including one at the Kentucky State Penitentiary at Eddyville, damaged buildings.

**FEB 2004 36.9°F / 2.82 inches**

February temperatures were near normal, and precipitation was slightly below normal. Thundersnow was reported on the 5th in the west, where 1 to 3 inches of wet snow fell. Flash flooding occurred in the east on the 5th and 6th. Minor flooding along rivers in the central and west was reported during mid month. Dry weather in the west during the final three weeks led to widespread grass and brush fires by month's end.

**MAR 2004 49.5°F / 4.28 inches**

March was warm with near normal precipitation. Flash flooding was widespread in the east from the 5th through the 7th, resulting in 2 deaths. A 6-inch snowfall was reported in Bell County on the 9th. Thunderstorm winds on the 20th caused damage at locations in the central and eastern regions. Dry, windy weather contributed to a wildfire in the Land-Between-the-Lakes area on the 28th.

**APR 2004 55.9°F / 4.69 inches**

April temperatures were near normal and precipitation was slightly above normal. A late sea-

Photo: Sid Webb

son snow on the 13th brought 2 to 4 inches over areas from the Mayfield to Hopkinsville and north to Owensboro, causing limited power outages and numerous traffic accidents that resulted in 4 fatalities. Minor flash flooding was reported in the east on the 13th and 14th. Severe thunderstorms on the 30th caused minor wind damage and flash flooding in the west.

**MAY 2004 69.2°F (6th warmest) / 8.31 inches (5th wettest)**

May was very warm and very wet. Severe weather at month's end caused widespread problems. Tornadoes in Fayette and Henry counties on the 27th caused considerable damage, while weaker tornadoes touched down in Henderson and Pulaski counties. Severe weather was also widespread on the 30th. Tornadoes were reported on the 29th and 30th in the west and on the 31st in the east. Overall damage was minor. Thunderstorms dumped heavy rain causing widespread flooding and flash flooding in the east, resulting in millions of dollars in damage.

**JUN 2004 72.3°F / 4.00 inches**

June temperatures and precipitation were near normal. Severe weather continued into the first days of the month. Minor flooding along the Ohio River continued from late May through the first third of June. On the 12th, thunderstorms contributed to flash flooding in the northern and eastern regions. Damage was greatest in Fleming and Letcher counties.

**JUL 2004 74.4°F / 5.67 inches**

July temperatures were below normal, while precipitation was above normal. The dominant weather for the month came in the form of severe thunderstorms. On the 5th and 6th, storms brought very strong winds, causing extensive power outages, fallen trees, and damage to structures. One week later on the 13th, another line of strong thunderstorms with damaging winds moved southeastward across the state. Damage and power outages were widespread over the central portion of the state.

## AUG 2004 71.2°F (6th coolest) / 4.10 inches

August was cool with near normal precipitation. Severe thunderstorms with damaging winds and hail were widespread on the 4th. Otherwise, there were no widespread outbreaks of severe weather.

## SEP 2004 68.8°F / 3.86 inches (1st wettest in east, 2nd driest in west)

September brought near normal temperatures, but it was a month of precipitation extremes. Many locations in central and western areas received barely a drop of rain the entire month. Meanwhile, the east was inundated by heavy rains brought by the remnants of Hurricane Frances, bringing 3 to 6 inches of rain on the 7th and 8th, and Hurricane Ivan, bringing similar totals on the 16th and 17th. These storms, during a normally dry time of year, caused minor flooding that was widespread in the eastern half of the State, and led to 1 death.

## OCT 2004 59.9°F / 4.83 inches (8th wettest)

October was warm and wet. A weak tornado was reported on the 15th in Caldwell County. Thunderstorms bringing strong winds and heavy rain moved through on the 18th causing minor damage.

## NOV 2004 50.4°F (9th warmest) / 5.83 inches

November was warm and wet. Still, there was very little active weather. Ashland reported some urban flooding at the result of heavy rains on the 4th.

## DEC 2004 36.4°F / 4.60 inches

December was near average in temperature and precipitation. However, it will be marked for the historic winter storm on the 22nd and 23rd. A combination of snow, sleet, and freezing rain moved northeastward across the western half of the state. Snow accumulated to record depths with 14 inches at Paducah to as much as 19 inches in Hancock County. Louisville received 9 inches, but Lexington received only a thin coating of ice. Farther south, ice and sleet accumulated more than 1 inch. Following the storm, low temperatures dropped below zero in many snow-covered areas.

## JAN 2005 39.1°F / 4.68 inches

January was warm with slightly above normal precipitation. The first part of the month was very warm, and some areas remained above freezing from December 29th through January 13th. Heavy rains in early January, combined with runoff from melting snow, caused flooding on the Ohio River and tributaries. Floodwaters were the highest since 1997, but damage was minor. A winter storm on the 20th dropped up to 5 inches of snow in northern Kentucky near the Ohio River. Another storm on the 22nd left 3-6 inches in the east.

## FEB 2005 40.6°F / 2.59 inches

February was warm with below normal precipitation. Two snowstorms in the east left significant accumulations. The first storm on the 10th left 6 inches on Black Mountain. The second storm on the 28th left 14 inches on Black Mountain.

## MAR 2005 42.9°F / 3.95 inches

March was cool with slightly below normal precipitation. A weak tornado touched down in Spencer County on the 19th. Severe weather on the 27th caused wind damage near Kentucky Lake, and hail accumulated to 4 inches depth in Calloway County. Minor flooding was reported in the western and central regions near the end of the month.

## Apr 2005 – 57.0 F / 5.27 inches

April was warmer and wetter than normal. Thunderstorms were widespread on the 22nd, with wind damage and some reports of minor hail damage. A weak tornado touched down briefly causing minor damage to businesses in Louisville. Heavy rains on the 30th caused flash flooding along streams in the east, with the greatest damage in Jackson.

## May 2005 – 61.5 F / 2.33 inches (9th driest)

May was cooler and very dry. A late season cold snap during the first days of May brought frost to low lying areas in the northwest. Thunderstorms producing high winds and hail did minor damage in the central and eastern areas on the 12th and 13th. More thunderstorms on the 19th resulted in damage from lightning, wind, hail, tornadoes, and flash flood. The most severe storms struck in the west, where tornadoes caused damage in Christian and Todd counties, and baseball size hail pelted Hopkins County. A weak tornado was also reported to the east in Wolfe County.

## Jun 2005 – 73.9 F / 2.74 inches

June was warmer and drier than normal. Thunderstorms with high winds developed over much of the state on the 14th, and a death was attributed to lightning in Pendleton County. On the 28th, a lightning strike caused a fire that burned a church to the ground in Harrison County.

**Jul 2005 – 77.3 F / 4.28 inches**

July was near average in both temperature and precipitation. Thunderstorms during the first week and again toward the end of the month caused only minor damage throughout the state.

**Aug 2005 – 78.3 F (8th warmest) / 6.07 inches (5th wettest)**

August was warm and wet, with much of the precipitation occurring near the end of the month. Storms produced heavy rains and flooding in western counties. Flash flooding in Madisonville and Princeton caused damage to houses and businesses on the 26th. A total of 8 to 11 inches of rain fell in the Hopkinsville over the 29th and 30th. A portion of this was due to the remnants of Hurricane Katrina. One fatality occurred in Hopkinsville, where well over 100 houses and businesses were damaged. Roads and schools were closed in Christian, Todd, and Trigg counties. Strong winds and heavy rain, attributed to Hurricane Katrina, resulting in downed trees and power lines in western counties. Earlier in the month, on the 7th, a fatality due to lightning was reported in Hancock County.

**Sep 2005 – 71.6 F / 1.29 inches**

September was warm and dry. It was a particularly quiet month weather-wise. The northeast showed signs of drought.

**Oct 2005 – 58.2 F / 0.97 inches (10th driest)**

October was warm, dry, and uneventful. No damage from severe or extreme weather was reported. Concerns about drought, particularly in the north and east, continued.

**Nov 2005 – 48.2 F / 3.28 inches**

November was warmer than normal with precipitation slightly below normal. Two tornadoes swept through western counties along the Ohio River on the 6th. One touched down in Henderson County before injuring eight people and causing extensive damage to a horse racing facility. Five people were injured by a second tornado that moved through Crittenden and Webster counties. A narrow band of thunderstorms along a stalled warm front on the 15th brought 5 to 10 inches of rain over a 24-hour period in Henderson and Union counties. Widespread flooding caused extensive damage to homes and businesses and closed schools. Strong winds in Fulton County and a weak tornado that moved through Graves and Calloway counties caused minor damage. Another tornado cut a path through Marshall and Lyon counties, killing one person and injuring 10 others. Significant damage was reported in the Kentucky Lake area. Another strong tornado injured 40 people and damaged or destroyed hundreds of houses in Hopkins County.

**Dec 2005 – 33.8 F / 2.36 inches**

December was colder and drier than normal. A winter storm moved across the Ohio River Valley on the 8th. Sleet and freezing rain followed by 1 to 3 inches of snow fell across northern Kentucky from west to east. Numerous accidents were reported, including one fatality in western Kentucky. Thunderstorms producing high winds and small hail caused minor damage in central and northeastern counties on the 28th.

**Jan 2006 – 43.0 F (4th warmest) / 5.72 inches**

January was much warmer than normal with above average precipitation. Thunderstorms were widespread on the 2nd. Tornadoes touched down in Adair, Hardin, Jefferson, Larue, and Lincoln counties. Two people were injured in Lincoln County. Up to four inches of snow fell across the southeast on the 14th. Heavy rain led to minor flooding and flash flooding on the 22nd and following days in areas throughout the state.

**Feb 2006 – 35.8 F / 2.22 inches**

February was cooler and dry. Heavy snow fell across the east on the 11th, with accumulations of 4 to 5 inches. Similar snowfall totals were recorded in some eastern counties on the 18th and 20th. Minor accumulations of snow developed over western counties on the 8th, 10th and 11th, and again on the 18th and 19th. Numerous accidents, but no injuries, were reported in conjunction with the wintry weather.

**Mar 2006 – 46.2 F / 3.53 inches**

March temperatures were near normal with below normal precipitation. Thunderstorms with high winds were widespread on the 9th. The storms were more severe in western counties, where minor flash flooding occurred and wind damage was more extensive. A rapid moving winter storm on the 21st brought in freezing rain that caused delays over portions of the north.

# WEATHER & CLIMATE

# *Temperature &*
# *Precipitation Records*   Dr. Stuart Foster

## KENTUCKY RECORD MAXIMUM DAILY TEMPERATURES

| TEMPERATURE | YEAR | MONTH | DAY | LOCATION |
|---|---|---|---|---|
| 83 F | 1907 | Jan | 20 | Loretto |
| 86 F | 1890 | Feb | 11 | Princeton |
| 94 F | 1929 | Mar | 24 | Hopkinsville |
| 98 F | 1925 | Apr | 24 | Farmers |
| 106 F | 1896 | May | 10 | Ashland |
| 110 F | 1936 | Jun | 29 | St. John's Academy |
| 114 F | 1930 | Jul | 28 | Greensburg |
| 113 F | 1930 | Aug | 5 | St. John's Academy |
| 110 F | 1925 | Sep | 6 | Beaver Dam |
| 98 F | 1953 | Oct | 1 | Frankfort & Hopkinsville |
| 90 F | 1902 | Nov | 14 | Pikeville |
| 87 F | 1982 | Dec | 3 | Pikeville |

## KENTUCKY RECORD MINIMUM DAILY TEMPERATURES

| TEMPERATURE | YEAR | MONTH | DAY | LOCATION |
|---|---|---|---|---|
| -37 F | 1994 | Jan | 19 | Shelbyville |
| -32 F | 1951 | Feb | 2 | Princeton |
| -14 F | 1960 | Mar | 6 | Bonnieville |
| 10 F | 1857 | Apr | 2 | Millersburg |
| 20 F | 1966 | May | 10 | Falmouth |
| 29 F | 1966 | Jun | 1 | Cumberland |
| 34 F | 1988 | Jul | 1 | Ashland |
| 36 F | 1946 | Aug | 31 | Clermont |
| 24 F | 1928 | Sep | 26 | Farmers |
| 10 F | 1962 | Oct | 27 | Dewey Dam |
| -9 F | 1929 | Nov | 30 | Shelbyville |
| -24 F | 1989 | Dec | 24 | Farmers |

## KENTUCKY RECORD GREATEST DAILY PRECIPITATION

| PRECIPITATION | YEAR | MONTH | DAY | LOCATION |
|---|---|---|---|---|
| 8.52" | 1966 | Jan | 2 | Mayfield |
| 6.20" | 1949 | Feb | 14 | Turkey Creek School |
| 10.25" | 1997 | Mar | 2 | Madisonville |
| 9.05" | 1911 | Apr | 30 | Edmonton |
| 6.00" | 1983 | May | 19 | Elkton |
| 10.40" | 1960 | Jun | 28 | Dunmor |
| 8.44" | 1965 | Jul | 24 | Middlesboro |
| 8.20" | 1982 | Aug | 31 | Gilbertsville Dam |
| 8.20" | 1982 | Sep | 2 | Jamestown |
| 5.60" | 1910 | Oct | 6 | Earlington |
| 6.66" | 1957 | Nov | 18 | Mammoth Cave |
| 6.16" | 1917 | Dec | 7 | Bowling Green |

## *"Well, what about that?"*

The word "plunge" is a descriptive word for occasions like those of 18 January 1996. In Bowling Green that day, a high temperature of 68 F was recorded. By the following day, the temperature had plunged 58 degrees to 10 F.

*Kentucky State Climatology Center, http://kyclim.wku.edu*

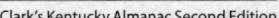

# WEATHER & CLIMATE
# Destructive Weather

Dr. Stuart Foster

## Floods

Kentucky, with nearly 90,000 miles of waterways ranging from small mountain streams to the broad Ohio and Mississippi rivers, is quite prone to flooding. A distinction can be drawn between river floods that inundate broad flood plains and flash floods that sweep through narrow stream valleys with little or no advance warning. River flooding results from an extended period of heavy precipitation over a large region and it is most common during the winter and early spring when weather systems become stalled or recurring storm systems move over Kentucky one after another. The best-known flood affecting Kentucky dates to January of 1937. Flash flooding can be highly localized and is particularly troublesome in upland watersheds in the Appalachians of eastern Kentucky. It is more likely to be associated with intense and sometimes persistent thunderstorms that bring copious amounts of rain in a short period of time.

The list below is not comprehensive, but it highlights some of the most destructive and deadly floods in Kentucky history.

**Accounts of Selected Kentucky Floods**

**1937** – January of 1937 brought hardship across Kentucky. Storm systems, one after another, trained along the nearly stationary boundary between air masses that stretched through the Ohio River Valley. More than 20 inches of rain fell

in areas of central Kentucky during the month, and totals of at least 15 inches were common throughout Kentucky and portions of neighboring states. The heaviest rains occurred from Jan. 17 to Jan. 23 and sent the Ohio River and its tributaries to levels that had never been seen. A final day of heavy rain on Jan. 24 sent floodwaters even higher. At the crest on Jan. 27, waters were 30 feet above flood stage in Louisville, and the river and its backwaters were as much as 20 to 25 miles wide. Towns all along the Ohio River were inundated. In Louisville alone, 175,000 people were evacuated to towns across Kentucky. Paducah was nearly deserted, as residents were forced to leave the city where floodwaters nearly 10 feet deep engulfed the downtown business district. Cities all along the Ohio River were left without drinking water, electricity and communication, and explosions started numerous fires. The flood exceeded previous devastating floods of 1883, 1884 and 1913, and no flood since has approached the magnitude of the 1937 event. Hundreds of people died in Kentucky as a result of the flood, and damage was estimated at $250 million.

**1939** – On the night of July 4th and early morning of July 5th, intense, localized thunderstorms dropped torrents of rain in the hills of Rowan and Breathitt counties. A storm lasting three hours

**Torrential Rain**
Photo: Charles Bertran, Lexington Herald-Leader

began at 9:30 p.m. in Rowan County and dumped anywhere from 4 to 10 inches of rain, according to unofficial gages. The storm left 25 people dead and destroyed 10,800 acres of crops, 5,000 chickens, 200 farm animals, 50 homes and 300 other farm buildings. Later that evening, a storm produced an even more deadly flash flood along Troublesome, Frozen, and Quicksand creeks in Breathitt County. The worst flooding was concentrated along Frozen Creek, where houses with unsuspecting families sleeping inside were swept into the floodwaters. Only the remnants of communities remained. A total of 51 people were found dead as the floodwaters receded.

**1957** – Late January of 1957 saw heavy rains spread across eastern Kentucky and parts of Tennessee, Virginia, and West Virginia causing widespread flooding. From 4.5 to 9 inches of rain fell on already saturated soils in the headwaters of the Big Sandy, Kentucky and Cumberland rivers. Rapidly rising floodwaters forced thousands to leave their homes without time to collect belongings. Hazard was one of 13 towns and many smaller communities to suffer heavy damage. Aid was rushed to the area as food and drinking water were in short supply, and electric power was out. Washed out roads and bridges forced supplies to be brought in by helicopter. Damage in the town of Pineville was limited by a floodwall. But in numerous other eastern Kentucky towns, homes were washed away and business districts were under water. The flood claimed five lives, left nearly 8,000 homeless and caused $50 million damage. The magnitude of the flood exceeded previous floods in 1927 and 1937, and it was compared to the flood of 1862.

**1977** – A storm system moving slowly northeastward brought 3 to 6 inches across southeastern Kentucky, with locally higher amounts reported up to 15 inches. Floodwaters swept through the Appalachian valleys from April 4 through April 7. Communities along the Upper Cumberland and Big Sandy rivers were hardest hit. The flood on the Upper Cumberland broke historical records. The floodwall and levee at Pineville was topped by floodwaters. Officials in Williamsburg, recognizing that their efforts would not save the town, moved documents from the courthouse as floodwaters threatened the building. Roads were blocked preventing people from trying to enter Harlan, Barbourville and Pineville. Communities along tributaries of the Big Sandy River, including Pikeville, Elkhorn City, Prestonsburg, South Williamson, Martin and Inez, also suffered extensive damage. In Pikeville, the hospital was surrounded by floodwaters, and patients had to be ferried by boat. Flooding was less extensive on the Kentucky and Licking rivers. Five deaths were reported, thousands were left homeless, and damage estimates reached as high as $175 million.

**1997** – March ushered in heavy rains across Kentucky. Upper level winds brought a steady flow of moisture-laden air into the Ohio River Valley. Rain that began falling on the last day of February intensified as March arrived, bringing more than 7 inches of rain to Louisville and over 5 inches to Lexington in one day. By March 3, rainfall totals had reached from 6 to 12 inches over much of central and northern Kentucky. The Licking River, a stream that normally runs 4 feet deep through the town of Falmouth, rose to 52 feet, some 24 feet above flood stage, nearly destroying the town, as residents fled in disbelief. The death toll in Kentucky reached 21, and damage was estimated as high as $500 million.

# Tornadoes

Severe thunderstorms producing dangerous lightning, damaging winds, large hail and tornadoes are most frequent during spring. These storms frequently form in warm, moist air in advance of an approaching cold front. They are more common in the afternoon and early evening hours but can occur at any time of day. The air-mass thunderstorms prevalent in midsummer are less likely to produce severe weather. But there are no certainties when it comes to severe weather. Thunderstorms producing hail and tornadoes have been reported in every month of the year in Kentucky, with an average of about 10 tornadoes per year.

Improved weather radar systems, better knowledge of the atmospheric conditions that lead to severe weather and the adoption of modern communication systems provide advance warning that helps to save lives. Many Kentuckians, however, will vividly recall the tornado outbreak of April 3, 1974, that brought devastation to communities scattered across the state with little or no warning of what was to come.

## SIGNIFICANT TORNADOES
### March 27, 1890

The myth that Louisville was protected from tornadoes was dispelled on the evening of March 27, 1890. Following a day when snow flurries swirled in the air, evening thunderstorms bore down on the city. Around 8 p.m., in the midst of vivid lightning display, a tornado touched down and ripped through residential and commercial districts before crossing the Ohio River into Indiana. The death toll in Louisville and environs reached 76, and 200 people were injured. Damage was estimated at more than $2 million, including tobacco warehouses, hotels and churches. On the same day, eight other tornadoes were also reported in western and southern Kentucky, killing another 44 people.

### May 27, 1917

An outbreak of tornadoes stretched from Alabama to Kentucky and westward into Arkansas. Heavy thunderstorms blew through western Kentucky in the late afternoon bringing destruction. A tornado crossed from Tennessee into Kentucky killing 68 people. The greatest loss of life was in Fulton County, where 42 people were killed, but Hickman, Carlisle and Graves counties also suffered losses from the storm.

### March 18, 1925

On the same day that the deadliest tornado in U.S. history cut a path through Missouri, Illinois and Indiana, four tornadoes struck Kentucky. The most deadly of these crossed from Tennessee into southeastern Allen County at about 5 p.m. and continued to move through Barren, Monroe and Metcalfe counties. Four deaths were reported near Scottsville in Allen County and six at Beaumont in Metcalfe County. Tornadoes in Jefferson and Oldham counties killed seven and injured 100. Near 6:30 p.m., another tornado passed through Marion, Washington, Mercer, Jessamine, Fayette and Bourbon counties, leaving two people dead and injuring 40.

### May 9, 1933

On an evening when severe thunderstorms brought damaging winds and hail across Kentucky, a midnight tornado left a path of destruction through Monroe, Adair, Cumberland and Russell counties in southern Kentucky. The tornado destroyed about 60 houses in Tompkinsville and left 17 people dead. Significant damage was also reported near Russell Springs, but most of the damage was in rural areas, where an estimated 100 barns were destroyed. A total of 36 deaths were reported in Kentucky, with additional fatalities in Tennessee.

### March 16, 1942

Tornadoes raked through the South and Midwest. In Kentucky, a tornado touched down in Muhlenberg County around 5:30 p.m. without warning, killing 11 people. The storm carved a path northeastward through Grayson, Hardin and Nelson counties, moving through Bardstown before dissipating. Fortunately, much of the path was through sparsely populated areas. A total of 24 deaths were reported, and 60 people were injured.

### April 3, 1974

Kentucky was one of 13 states in the South and Midwest that were hit by a massive outbreak of 148 tornadoes. At least 26 tornadoes struck Kentucky alone, killing 77 people and injuring another 1,377. Damage estimates exceeded $110 million. The most devastating tornado packed winds estimated at 260 miles per hour and tore a path 500 yards wide through the small town of Brandenburg in Meade County shortly after 4 p.m., leaving 31 people dead. Louisville was also hit, leaving a path of damage that included the Kentucky State Fair Grounds, Cherokee Park and suburban residential areas. Tornadoes, many with little or no advance warning, carved through southern and central Kentucky, leaving behind death and destruction in Boyle, Clinton, Franklin, Hardin, Madison, Nelson, Simpson and Warren counties. Pulaski County was hit by three tornadoes that evening before the storm system moved out of Kentucky.

# Droughts

Drought is commonly referred to as a "creeping" hazard. The onset of drought is difficult to identify, but when lawns have turned brown and crops withered in the field, the presence of a drought is easier recognized.

Definitions of drought abound. From a meteorological perspective, drought is defined as an extended period with deficit precipitation. Other definitions are based on observed impacts of drought. An agricultural drought reflects dry soil conditions that stunt the growth of crops and pasture. If the dry spell persists long enough, hydrological drought may become evident as water levels drop in reservoirs and streams and freshwater springs and groundwater wells cease to produce. In the case of severe droughts, water supplies of entire cities may be threatened.

Make no mistake: Drought is a recurrent feature of Kentucky's climate. Agricultural droughts can develop quickly during the spring and summer and can be localized in extent. Kentucky's most intense and widespread drought of record occurred through the summer of 1930. If drought is thought of in terms of its impacts on water availability, then one may conclude that Kentucky's growing population and growing demand for water make the state more vulnerable to drought than in the past.

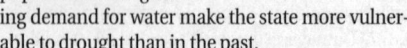
Photo: Sid Webb

about the change of temperature during the summer long, yet we have had nothing but suffocating hot and dry temperatures. Of course, if we got a tornado from the south and a blizzard from the north, all at the same time, the temperature might condescend to drop a few points, but at the present we will be skeptical about any chance until we really see it."

Precipitation remained below normal each month for the remainder of the year. The tobacco crop was worthless. Corn failed to pollinate, and cornstalks were cut for silage. Farmers, lacking feed and water, were forced to sell livestock for any price. Small streams were dry, and large ones had only pools of water in places. By winter, when water supplies are normally recharged, the shortage forced some municipalities to seek other sources of drinking water. Exceptionally dry weather through January left dirt roads dusty in some areas. It was not until late March that a return of more normal precipitation brought flow back to streams.

## SELECTED KENTUCKY DROUGHTS
### 1930

In contrast to many droughts whose beginnings can be traced to a dry spell that emerges through the late fall and winter months, the onset of the drought in 1930 was sudden and harsh. Dry weather in March of 1930 was followed by hot, dry weather in April. Temperatures reached above 90 F before midmonth, and the ground became too dry for farmers to work. Many areas received less than 1 inch of rain during the month. Drought quickly became evident in the north and lower Green River region. The shortage of stock water became severe in upland areas. Then came the worst. July and August brought record heat, including an all-time high of 114 F on the 28th of July at Greensburg. Meanwhile, Bowling Green experienced 22 days with temperatures over 100 F from early July through early August, as day after day passed without significant precipitation. A newspaper writer from the Russellville News-Democrat summarized the mood:

"Various reports are received, some predicting thundershowers for today, tomorrow, or the next day. However, there have been so many reports

### 1952-1954

The early 1950s was an extended period of generally dry weather. The onset of drought was evident in western Kentucky with each passing day of June 1952, which proved the warmest on record. The town of Hicksville in Graves County did not record a drop of precipitation the entire month. Hot, dry weather dominated the weather pattern. The temperature reached 110 F at both Murray and Princeton in July, and precipitation averaged half of the normal monthly total. Drought conditions spread into the central portion of Kentucky. Temperatures above 100 F became a frequent occurrence. Pasture and hay crops wilted in the hot, dry fields, and the fire danger was high. Farmers were forced to buy feed for their livestock, and many chose to reduce their herds. The dry weather continued through the fall and winter seasons with few exceptions and set the stage for persistent drought in 1953. Hot, dry weather returned in the summer of 1953, but farmers were more prepared for drought this time. Many had built silos and increased their allocation of pasture. But crops faired no better than the previous year. Temperatures that reached above 100 F in September remained in the 90s for several days in October. Louisville went 36 days in a row without rain beginning on Sept. 20. Water was increasingly in short supply, as below normal precipitation continued through December. A wet January helped to improve soil moisture into the spring of 1954, but a return of hot, dry weather by July quickly depleted the moisture available to crops and pasture. Drought was worse in the western areas. But the late summer and fall of 1954 brought a return to more normal precipitation, and heavy precipitation during January and February of 1955 marked the clear end to a prolonged drought.

**1999-2000**

Following a wet spring in 1998, a pattern of dry weather settled over Kentucky during the summer and fall of 1998. Though it received little attention, it helped set the stage for severe drought in the coming year. While January of 1999 brought above normal precipitation, the weather pattern again turned dry. By the end of June, a water shortage watch was issued for counties in the eastern and bluegrass regions, as drought moved westward into Kentucky. Precipitation during July averaged less than one-half of normal, while temperatures soared. Temperatures from the 90s to the 100s held over the second half of July. The maximum reading was 107 F at Rough River Lake. Conditions deteriorated rapidly, as the period of July through September was the driest on record statewide with an average of only 5.3 inches of rain. By the end of September, 96 of Kentucky's 120 counties had been placed under a water shortage warning, and the remaining counties were under a water shortage watch. Mandatory curtailments of water usage for some residential and commercial activities were implemented in some areas. The drought reduced crop yields, particularly for late season crops. Poor pasture and a shortage of water for livestock led many farmers to sell cattle and hogs. Precipitation returned to normal seasonal amounts throughout much of the state by the summer of 2000, but the dry pattern persisted in parts of southern and central Kentucky, and concerns about the availability of municipal water supplies continued in some areas through the end of the year.

## Ice & Snow

Kentucky normally enjoys mild winters but is vulnerable to a wide variety of hazardous winter weather, including snow, ice and arctic cold waves. Low-pressure systems that bring winter storms to Kentucky often track eastward across the southern United States before turning toward the northeast. Those that track along the western margin of the Appalachian Mountains are most likely to bring heavy precipitation. With cold air in place over Kentucky, the precipitation is often in the form of heavy snow, but it can also be freezing rain and sleet, resulting in destructive ice storms. Occasionally, a strong cold front will move into the region and send temperatures plunging below zero. Gusty winds often magnify the impact and create dangerous wind chills.

Many Kentuckians will recall the winter of 1977-1978, while a few still recall the winter of 1917-1918, as long cold winters willed plenty of snow. Those winters, along with a recollection of the

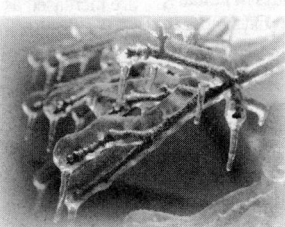

**Ice Storm**
*Source: Sid Webb*

winter storm of January 1994, are highlighted below.

**Winter of 1917-1918**

December ushered in a cold, snowy winter season. An early snowstorm on the 7th and 8th dumped a foot or more of snow across parts of Kentucky. The blizzard was followed by a period of extreme cold with temperatures dropping to near or below zero for several days. Farmers were snowbound and unable to bring poultry to market for the Christmas season. The average temperature of 26.5 F for December was some 11 F below normal. Snow returned before the end of the month, and December's totals ranged from 9 inches in southeastern Kentucky to 28 inches in the Louisville area, with an average of 17.3 inches across the state. Harsh winter conditions persisted through January. Temperatures as low as minus 20 F combined with winds of 30 miles per hour on Jan. 12 to produce the most severe weather conditions recalled since New Year's Day of 1864. Heavy snow returned.

Average snowfall across the state in January was 23.3 inches, while more than 30 inches fell in western and southern counties. The average temperature of 20.6 F for January was nearly 15 F below normal. Many stations reported temperatures of zero or below on 10 days during the month. The cold snap finally broke on Feb. 6, and snow that had covered the ground in some areas since early December began to melt.

## Winter of 1977-1978

A brief, early December cold snap brought light snow and subzero temperatures to parts of northern and central Kentucky on the 6th and 7th. But warm temperatures quickly returned as the mercury touched 60 F again before Christmas, and early January remained seasonably warm. The weather changed for the worse however, on January 16th and 17th, when a major winter storm dumped at least 10 inches of snow from western Kentucky through the north central portion of the state. Some of the heavier totals included 12 inches at Paducah, 16 inches at both Henderson and Louisville and 11 inches at Lexington and Covington. At La Grange in Oldham County, where 18 inches fell, accumulation from January storms reached a record depth of 31 inches on Jan. 20. Blizzard conditions returned on the 25th and 26th and roads were declared closed in all but the southeast counties. All told, snow fell somewhere in Kentucky on 19 days in January, 12 days in February, and even seven days more in March. With a heavy snow cover from mid-January and persistent snows in the following weeks, snow remained on the ground well into March at some northern locations. Owenton measured snow 15 inches deep on March 8, and La Grange still had 3 inches of snow cover as late as the 12th. Over the course of the winter, snowfall totals ranged from 31 inches at Scottsville, near the Kentucky-Tennessee border and 84 inches at La Grange. While there were no record-setting cold waves during the winter, the continued influx of polar air resulted in a long, cold winter. Cities ran short of road salt, and disruptions of river traffic due to icing at locations on the Ohio River delayed shipments. School children, particularly in rural areas, missed week upon week of classes. When spring finally arrived, it was a welcome sight indeed.

## January 1994

January of 1994 started out as a typical winter month in Kentucky. Light snow in the first week of the month was followed by warmer weather with temperatures reaching well into the 40s. The uneventful weather took a sudden and unexpected change beginning on the 16th. Heavy snow, accu-

mulating up to 3 inches per hour, blanketed the northern half of the state, covering Paducah with 15 inches, Louisville with 16 inches, Shelbyville with 19 inches, Lexington with 10 inches and Jackson with 15 inches. Unofficial totals in the northern counties reached 20 inches or more. To the south, accumulations of 4 to 8 inches fell on top of a thick coating of ice, as freezing rain and sleet preceded the snowfall. In Louisville, it was an all-time record snowfall.

Ice and snow was followed by frigid arctic air that rushed in over Kentucky. Temperatures plummeted, and Shelbyville broke the all-time record low temperature for Kentucky with a reading of minus 37 F on the morning of the 19th. Temperatures dropping to at least minus 30 F were also recorded at Cynthiana (minus 33 F), Falmouth (minus 30 F), Gray Hawk (minus 35 F), Manchester (minus 30 F), Somerset (minus 32 F) and West Liberty (minus 30 F).

The record-shattering burst of winter weather brought Kentucky to a near standstill. A state of emergency was declared. All interstate highways were ordered closed to all but emergency vehicles on the 17th, and they remained closed until the 20th. Emergency personnel struggled across the state to reach people in need. Schools and businesses were closed. Thousands were without power, many for several days. The danger of fire increased as people resorted to fireplaces and kerosene heaters to keep warm. Manufacturers depending upon just-in-time delivery of inventory were shut down, as the transportation industry struggled to deliver shipments.

Motorists are reminded never to drive through a water-covered roadway. It only takes a small amount of water over the driving surface to carry a vehicle off the roadway. Drivers should also use extreme caution when driving in and near flood prone areas. Be alert to rising water and water covering local roads.

Motorists are encouraged to call 511 or log on to www.511.ky.gov for the latest road conditions.

# Hurricanes Impact Kentucky's Climate In 2005

The summer of 2005 might have been remembered for a severe drought was it not for the remnants of two hurricanes, Dennis and Katrina, which brought heavy rains across large portions of Kentucky. May is normally the peak of the wet season in Kentucky. Based on climate normals, Kentucky averages 5.05 inches of precipitation in May. However, May of 2005 was unusually dry. With an average of 2.33 inches of rain statewide, it ranked as the 9th driest May on record dating to 1893. The month of June was almost as dry with a statewide average of 2.74 inches. Combined, the two-month average precipitation of 5.07 represented the 5th driest May and June combined.

Hurricane Dennis made landfall near the border between Alabama and Florida, moved into western Tennessee and Kentucky, and then meandered through the lower Ohio River Valley. The system produced soaking rains that persisted for several days. Some observing stations recorded precipitation for as many as 8 or 9 consecutive days beginning on July 11th, easily a record for that month. Total precipitation from Dennis ranged from 2 to 4 inches over the western half of Kentucky, while eastern areas generally received lighter amounts. Once the system moved out of the region, precipitation became scarce. The remainder of July and early August were hot and dry.

While Hurricane Katrina will long be remembered for the devastation that it brought to southern U.S. (especially the city of New Orleans)—it also left its mark on Kentucky. Katrina dumped copious rainfall over much of the western half of Kentucky. Outer bands from remnants of Katrina brought heavy rain over western Kentucky on August 29th, 2005. As much as eight inches fell in a narrow band across Christian and Todd counties. Slightly lower totals, ranging from 5 to 8 inches, were common throughout south central Kentucky. One fatality was reported in Hopkinsville, and local flooding produced extensive damage. The center of the low pressure passed over the lower Ohio River Valley on August 30th, with only minimum impact on the eastern portion of Kentucky. Katrina is considered the costliest and deadliest natural disaster in American history—an estimated 1,836 lives were lost in the hurricane and subsequent floods, with approximately $81.2 billion in damage.

Following Katrina, the weather pattern again turned warm and dry. Precipitation totals for the month of September averaged 1.29 inches, the 13th driest month on record. The statewide precipitation average for October was only 0.97 inches, making it the 10th driest October. Meanwhile, the two-month total of 2.26 inches ranked as the 5th driest.

If not for the remnants of Dennis and Katrina, the statewide precipitation total for May through October would likely have been the driest on record, breaking the record set in 1930 when Kentucky suffered through its most severe drought in recorded history.

*Sources: (1) National Weather Service Forecast Office, Paducah, Kentucky, "Katrina Produces Heavy Rainfall, Gusty Winds," http://www.crh.noaa.gov/pah/hydro/katrina.php and (2) NOAA, NCDC, Climatological Data, Kentucky, July 2005, Volume 100, Number 7, and (3) NOAA, NCDC, Climatological Data, Kentucky, August 2005, Volume 100, Number 8).*

**Railroad tracks run beside many of the areas that remain flooded in New Orleans, La. The RJ Corman Railroad Group performed much of the railroad repair caused by Hurricane Katrina**
*Photo: Charles Bertram, Lexington Herald-Leader*

## WEATHER & CLIMATE
# *Weather Records*
Dr. Stuart Foster

### 10 WARMEST YEARS

| Year | Avg Temp(°F) |
|------|--------------|
| 1921 | 59.2 |
| 1998 | 58.3 |
| 1931 | 57.9 |
| 1938 | 57.7 |
| 1922 | 57.7 |
| 1991 | 57.6 |
| 1933 | 57.5 |
| 1953 | 57.5 |
| 1990 | 57.5 |
| 1946 | 57.4 |

### 10 WARMEST SUMMERS**

| Year | Avg Temp(°F) |
|------|--------------|
| 1936 | 78.8 |
| 1952 | 77.9 |
| 1921 | 77.7 |
| 1934 | 77.5 |
| 1943 | 77.2 |
| 1914 | 77.1 |
| 1913 | 77.1 |
| 1901 | 77.0 |
| 2002 | 76.9 |
| 1900 | 76.9 |

### 10 WARMEST WINTERS*

| Year | Avg Temp(°F) |
|---------|--------------|
| 1931-32 | 44.7 |
| 1948-49 | 41.7 |
| 1949-50 | 41.5 |
| 1956-57 | 40.3 |
| 1951-52 | 40.2 |
| 1997-98 | 40.0 |
| 1952-53 | 40.0 |
| 1998-99 | 39.9 |
| 1936-37 | 39.8 |
| 2001-02 | 39.8 |

### 10 COLDEST YEARS

| Year | Avg Temp(°F) |
|------|--------------|
| 1917 | 52.6 |
| 1958 | 53.7 |
| 1976 | 53.8 |
| 1912 | 52.8 |
| 1978 | 53.9 |
| 1940 | 54.0 |
| 1963 | 54.0 |
| 1979 | 54.0 |
| 1966 | 54.2 |
| 1924 | 54.2 |

### 10 COLDEST SUMMERS**

| Year | Avg Temp(°F) |
|------|--------------|
| 1967 | 71.4 |
| 1992 | 71.8 |
| 1927 | 71.9 |
| 1976 | 72.1 |
| 1950 | 72.1 |
| 1915 | 72.3 |
| 1974 | 72.4 |
| 2004 | 72.6 |
| 1946 | 72.7 |
| 1961 | 72.7 |

### 10 COLDEST WINTERS*

| Year | Avg Temp(°F) |
|---------|--------------|
| 1977-78 | 27.1 |
| 1917-18 | 27.4 |
| 1976-77 | 28.2 |
| 1935-36 | 29.4 |
| 1962-63 | 29.4 |
| 1904-05 | 29.6 |
| 1901-02 | 30.3 |
| 1898-99 | 30.6 |
| 1939-40 | 30.8 |
| 1978-79 | 30.9 |

\* *(December, January, February)*
\*\* *(June, July, August)*
*Photo Source: Kentucky Historical Society*

Dr. Stuart Foster

# *Weather Records*

## *Hopkinsville sets record for wettest August*

Hopkinsville (Christian County) broke the record for greatest precipitation total for the month of August in Kentucky with 16.11 inches in 2005. The previous record was 15.50 inches at Alpha (Clinton County) in 1901.

County) recorded only 1.42 inches for the month.

Kentucky's climatic conditions also varied significantly during the month of August 2005. The first half of August was hot and dry, before much needed rains arrived in mid month. Precipitation

**Campbell County, Kentucky. Flood of 1937. Evacuating a family at Newport**
*Photo: George Goodman, Kentucky Virtual Library*

Much of Kentucky suffered from drought entering August. Precipitation across the state averaged only 1.72 inches in July that year, while temperatures averaged 4°F above normal, soaring as high as 112°F in Paducah on the 23rd.

The weather pattern changed in August, particularly over the southern half of the state. Precipitation totals exceeded 10 inches over much of southeastern Kentucky. It rained every day from August 10th through August 23rd at Alpha. Totals were much lower through the northern tier of counties along the Ohio River, where Owenton (Owen

from the remnants of Hurricane Katrina on the 29th and 30th brought heavy precipitation, with Hopkinsville reporting 6.47 inches for the 24 hours ending on the morning of the 30th and 10.19 inches total for the 29th through the 31st.

*Sources: (1) US Department of Agriculture, Climate and Crop Service, Weather Bureau, Kentucky Section, Report for August 1901, Volume 6, Number 8, and (2) U.S. Department of Commerce, National Oceanic and Atmospheric Administration, National Climatic Data Center, Climatological Data, Kentucky, August 2005, Volume 100, Number 8.*

## WEATHER & CLIMATE

# *Folklore Weather*

Glen Conner

Humans have long had a desire to foretell the weather based on what we can see and feel. There are many sayings about the weather that have been passed down through the generations. Some have a basis in fact but others don't: "If you wash your car, it is likely to rain." Such sayings are proof that faith in them persisted but not necessarily proof that they are true.

*Red skies at night, sailor's delight; red skies at dawning, sailor take warning.* The red clouds seen before sunset are reflecting the reds from sunlight. It must be clear to the west if the sunlight is making it through to them. Good weather must be coming because most weather systems move from the west.

Source: Sid Webb

*Count the fogs in August and that is the number of snows for the coming winter.* If that were true, then there could never be more than 31 snows in a winter. There is no predictive capability in this saying. However, the average number of fogs in August and the average number of days with an inch of snow or more on the ground are roughly similar. In weather, unlike mathematics, things equal to the same thing aren't necessarily equal to each other.

*Rainbow in the morning is the shepherd's warning.* A rainbow is only visible when the sun is behind you and the rain is in front of you. Because most rain events approach from the southwest, when you see a rainbow in the morning, it is from a rain shower that is approaching from the west.

Conversely, when you see a rainbow in the evening, it is from a rain shower that has passed and is going away from you.

*Damp salt is a sign of coming rain.* Salt does absorb moisture from the air and high humidity is a major ingredient in conditions that precede rain.

*When leaves show their undersides, be sure that rain betides.* The topsides of leaves are green but the undersides of leaves are a lighter color (poplar, sycamore, silver maple, etc.). An approaching thunderstorm is preceded by instability and rapidly changing wind direction, which can flip the leaves upside down.

*When the dew is on the grass, rain will not come to pass.* Dew forms during a cloudless night, which permits the Earth's surface to cool rapidly by radiation of heat, causing condensation to form on the grass. The presence of clear skies during the night is a good indicator of a rainless day to follow.

*Curls that kink are signs of rain.* Human hair is sensitive to changes in humidity. Rising relative humidity is associated with approaching rain events and people with curls may be the first to know.

*All signs fail in a drought.* This saying about sayings is true of most weather lore as well. Nevertheless, a remarkable number of them have some truth. Reduction of the activity of our enormously complicated weather patterns to a short saying seems unlikely. But, we love to try.

## WEATHER & CLIMATE
# *Climate Folklore*

### Glen Conner

Folklore has given us the names of hot spells and cool spells that are recurring periods of unseasonable weather. Some of those names are generally recognized across Kentucky. Recognition of their arrival is subjective rather than quantitative. People just know them when they see them!

***Indian Summer.*** The term Indian Summer may be the oldest of the climate lore seasons. The dictionary defines it as a period of warm temperature in early winter that is characterized by a cloudless sky that appears smoky or hazy. In Kentucky, a warm spell that follows some winter weather in November would be recognized as Indian Summer. The origin of the name is uncertain and debatable. One origin suggestion was that, in areas like Kentucky, Indian hunting parties were absent during winter but would return during the warm spell in November. Thus, the Indian Summer.

*Source: Sid Webb*

***January Thaw.*** A warm spell in late January that is sufficient in warmth and duration to thaw the ground after a period of it being frozen would be recognized as the January Thaw. In modern times, a warm spell in late January provides a welcomed temporary relief to winter. In earlier times, before paved roads, the January Thaw was not welcomed because the roads turned into mud and became impassable.

***Dogwood Winter.*** The dictionary defines Dogwood Winter as a brief spell of wintry weather in spring. In Kentucky, the climate lore refers to the very cold spell that comes while the dogwoods are in bloom. In the parts of Kentucky that do not have dogwoods, the same cold spell may be called Locust Winter because it occurs while the locust trees are in bloom.

***Blackberry Winter.*** When the prickly brambles of the Blackberry are in bloom, they are seen as large mounds of white blossoms. Once, those mounds of white were a common sight in the springtime countryside. The decline of home canning and the inclination toward mowed pastures have made blackberry patches a less common sight. Climate lore says that Blackberry Winter arrives while the blackberries are in bloom. They bloom sometime in early May after spring has fully arrived and cool periods have become more infrequent and shorter in duration. Kentuckians would see a cool spell during the blackberry bloom period as Blackberry Winter

***Dog Days.*** The name Dog Days comes from a Mediterranean reference to Sirius (the Dog Star) that rose and set with the sun for this period. The name and its summer period were adapted in climate lore to represent a long uninterrupted period of hot, sultry and muggy days in mid summer. Dog Days occur when the annual march of temperature reaches highest during the last two weeks of July. Rather than reaching a peak, it is more likely to plateau. Add an area of high pressure that remains over Kentucky for several consecutive days, builds up pollutants in its stable, stagnating air, and accumulates heat day after breezeless day. The result would be known as Dog Days.

*Contributed by: Glen Conner, Kentucky State Climatologist Emeritus*

# Astronomical Calendar 2007

Col. Claude E. Hammond

## The Kentucky Almanac Calendar for 2007

The third year after Bissextile or Leap Year
As of July 4th, 2007, the 231th of American Independence
The 218th of Federal Government
As of June 1, 2007, the 215th of this Commonwealth

### THE CALENDAR

A calendar is a system of organizing units of time for the purpose of reckoning time over extended periods. There are six principal calendars in current use. These are the Gregorian, Hebrew, Islamic, Indian, Chinese, and Julian Calendars. These calendars replicate astronomical cycles according to fixed rules.

The principal astronomical cycles are the day (based on the rotation of the Earth on its axis), the year (based on the revolution of the Earth around the Sun), and the month (based on the revolution of the Moon around the Earth). The complexity of calendars arises because the year does not comprise an integral number of days or an integral number of lunar months.

All times given are in Eastern Standard Time, so West Kentucky residents living in the Central Time Zone will need to subtract an hour when using information from Clark's Kentucky Almanac. Corrections are made in Almanac times for Daylight Savings Time, saving the reader additional calculating effort.

The times given are calculated, specifically for Frankfort, Kentucky's capital city.

### EXPLANATION OF CALENDAR PAGES

The first column shows the day of the Month (with Sunday in bold); the second Remarkable Days & Judgement of Weather, proverbs to live by and certain details of note; the second column shows the Moon's Phase & Astrological events; the third column shows the Moon's Place in the Zodiac; and the fourth through seventh columns indicate the Rising and Setting of the Sun and Moon.

### SIGNS OF THE ZODIAC

|  |  |  |
|---|---|---|
| ♋ | Cancer | The Crab |
| ♌ | Leo | The Lion |
| ♍ | Virgo | The Virgin |
| ♎ | Libra | The Balance |
| ♏ | Scorpio | The Scorpion |
| ♐ | Sagittarius | The Bowman |
| ♑ | Capricorn | The Goat |
| ♒ | Aquarius | The Waterman |
| ♓ | Pisces | The Fishes |
| ♈ | Aries | The Ram |
| ♉ | Taurus | The Bull |
| ♊ | Gemini | The Twins |

# JANUARY—hath 31 days.

| | REMARKABLE DAYS, JUDGEMENT OF WEATHER. | | | MOON PHASE LOCATION | ZODIAC SYMBOL | SUN RISE | SUN SET | MOON RISE | MOON SET |
|---|---|---|---|---|---|---|---|---|---|
| 1 | New Year's Day | | | | ♊ | 7:56am | 5:30pm | 3:28pm | 6:20am |
| 2 | Melting ice is bad for firewood and fast drivers. | | Mercury most distant from Earth | | ♋ | 7:56am | 5:31pm | 4:28pm | 7:25am |
| 3 | Earth closest to the Sun | | | Full Moon | ♋ | 7:56am | 5:32pm | 5:33pm | 8:20am |
| 4 | | | | | ♌ | 7:56am | 5:33pm | 6:41pm | 9:05am |
| 5 | | | | | ♌ | 7:56am | 5:33pm | 7:48pm | 9:41am |
| 6 | Old Christmas | | | | ♌ | 7:56am | 5:34pm | 8:52pm | 10:10am |
| 7 | Epiphany | | | | ♍ | 7:56am | 5:35pm | 9:53pm | 10:34am |
| 8 | Baptism | | | | ♍ | 7:56am | 5:36pm | 10:52pm | 10:56am |
| 9 | | | | | ♎ | 7:56am | 5:37pm | 11:50pm | 11:17am |
| 10 | | | | | ♎ | 7:56am | 5:38pm | - - - - - | 11:37am |
| 11 | | | | Last Quarter | ♎ | 7:56am | 5:39pm | 12:48am | 11:59am |
| 12 | | | | | ♏ | 7:56am | 5:40pm | 1:48am | 12:23pm |
| 13 | Gen. Humphrey Marshall, CSA, born in Frankfort, 1813. | | | | ♏ | 7:55am | 5:41pm | 2:49am | 12:51pm |
| **14** | | | | | ♐ | 7:55am | 5:42pm | 3:53am | 1:25pm |
| 15 | Martin Luther King Jr. Day | | | | ♐ | 7:55am | 5:43pm | 4:58am | 2:07pm |
| 16 | | | | | ♐ | 7:55am | 5:44pm | 6:01am | 3:00pm |
| 17 | Muhammed Ali born, Louisville, 1942 | | | | ♑ | 7:54am | 5:45pm | 7:00am | 4:02pm |
| 18 | | | | New Moon | ♑ | 7:54am | 5:46pm | 7:50am | 5:13pm |
| 19 | Robert E Lee Day | | | | ♒ | 7:53am | 5:47pm | 8:32am | 6:27pm |
| 20 | Alben Barkley becomes US Vice President, 1949. | | | | ♒ | 7:53am | 5:49pm | 9:08am | 7:42pm |
| **21** | Centre College founded, 1819. | | | | ♓ | 7:52am | 5:50pm | 9:38am | 8:56pm |
| 22 | Battle of the Raisin River, 1813. 400 Ky Soldiers perish. | | Moon closest to Earth this month | | ♓ | 7:52am | 5:51pm | 10:05am | 10:09pm |
| 23 | | | | | ♈ | 7:51am | 5:52pm | 10:30am | 11:20pm |
| 24 | Have your garden planned by today. | | | | ♈ | 7:51am | 5:53pm | 10:56am | - - - - - |
| 25 | Anti-Darwinism bill introduced in Ky Legislature, 1922. | | | | ♉ | 7:50am | 5:54pm | 11:24am | 12:32am |
| 26 | | | | | ♉ | 7:49am | 5:55pm | 11:57am | 1:45am |
| 27 | John James Audubon dies in New York (he should've stayed in Ky). | | | | ♊ | 7:49am | 5:56pm | 12:35pm | 2:59am |
| **28** | Judge Louis Brandeis, from Louisville, appointed to US Supreme Court, 1913. | | | | ♊ | 7:48am | 5:57pm | 1:22pm | 4:10am |
| 29 | | | | | ♋ | 7:47am | 5:59pm | 2:17pm | 5:16am |
| 30 | Franklin D. Roosevelt Day | | | | ♋ | 7:46am | 6:00pm | 3:19pm | 6:13am |
| 31 | Col. Jack Chinn, Mercer County's legendary horseman, dies. 1920. | | | | ♋ | 7:45am | 6:01pm | 4:26pm | 7:01am |

# FEBRUARY—hath 28 days.

| | REMARKABLE DAYS, JUDGEMENT OF WEATHER. | | | MOON PHASE LOCATION | ZODIAC SYMBOL | SUN RISE | SUN SET | MOON RISE | MOON SET |
|---|---|---|---|---|---|---|---|---|---|
| 1 | Donald Isaac Everly (of the Everly Bros) born in Brownie, Ky, 1937. | | | Full Moon | ♌ | 7:45am | 6:02pm | 5:33pm | 7:39am |
| 2 | Groundhog Day | | | Presentation | ♌ | 7:44am | 6:03pm | 6:38pm | 8:10am |
| 3 | Wm Lowther Jackson, CSA general and jurist, born in Louisville, 1825. | | | | ♍ | 7:43am | 6:04pm | 7:40pm | 8:36am |
| 4 | Abolitionist James Gillespie Birney born in Danville, 1792. | | | | ♍ | 7:42am | 6:05pm | 8:41pm | 8:59am |
| 5 | A spittoon is quaint only as long as it is clean. | | | | ♍ | 7:41am | 6:06pm | 9:39pm | 9:20am |
| 6 | February's wind cuts faster than a scared rabbit. | | | | ♎ | 7:40am | 6:08pm | 10:37pm | 9:40am |
| 7 | Lexington's John C Breckinridge made CSA Secretary of War, 1865. | | Moon furthest from Earth this month | | ♎ | 7:39am | 6:09pm | 11:36pm | 10:01am |
| 8 | Smith D Broadbent, West Ky's extrordi-nary agriculturist, born 1914. | | | | ♏ | 7:38am | 6:10pm | ----- | 10:24am |
| 9 | Beckham County formed from part of Carter County, 1904. Would be abolished in 80 days. | | Neptune & Earth farthest apart | | ♏ | 7:37am | 6:11pm | 12:36am | 10:50am |
| 10 | Saturn & Earth closest this year | | | Last Quarter | ♏ | 7:36am | 6:12pm | 1:38am | 11:20am |
| 11 | Have your garden soil tested. | | | | ♐ | 7:35am | 6:13pm | 2:42am | 11:58am |
| 12 | Lincoln's Birthday | | | | ♐ | 7:34am | 6:14pm | 3:45am | 12:45pm |
| 13 | George Rogers Clark died in Louisville, 1818. | | | | ♑ | 7:32am | 6:15pm | 4:45am | 1:42pm |
| 14 | Sts Cyril & Methodius | | Valentine's Day | | ♑ | 7:31am | 6:17pm | 5:38am | 2:48pm |
| 15 | Those flowers you got for Valentine's Day may fade, but true love will grow nonetheless. | | | | ♒ | 7:30am | 6:18pm | 6:24am | 4:01pm |
| 16 | Brooksville becomes seat of Bracken County, 1839. | | | | ♒ | 7:29am | 6:19pm | 7:03am | 5:17pm |
| 17 | | | | New Moon | ♓ | 7:28am | 6:20pm | 7:35am | 6:33pm |
| 18 | Chinese New Year (Gung Hay Fat Choy!) | | | | ♓ | 7:26am | 6:21pm | 8:04am | 7:49pm |
| 19 | President's Day | Washington's Birthday | Moon closest to Earth this mo., in conj. With Venus | | ♈ | 7:25am | 6:22pm | 8:31am | 9:03pm |
| 20 | Mardi Gras | | | | ♈ | 7:24am | 6:23pm | 8:58am | 10:18pm |
| 21 | Ash Wednesday | | | | ♉ | 7:23am | 6:24pm | 9:26am | 11:33pm |
| 22 | Agricultural & Mechanical College of Ky Founded, 1865. It would become the University of Kentucky. | | | | ♉ | 7:21am | 6:25pm | 9:58am | ------ |
| 23 | Calhoun, Ky, named for Judge John Calhoun, 1849. | | | | ♊ | 7:20am | 6:26pm | 10:35am | 12:48am |
| 24 | Mercury close to Earth | | | First Quarter | ♊ | 7:19am | 6:27pm | 11:19am | 2:02am |
| 25 | 1st Sunday of Lent | | | | ♊ | 7:17am | 6:28pm | 12:12pm | 3:10am |
| 26 | Talent's value is in its use. | | | | ♋ | 7:16am | 6:29pm | 1:12pm | 4:10am |
| 27 | Versailles founder, French nobleman the Marquis Calmes, dies, 1834. | | | | ♋ | 7:15am | 6:30pm | 2:16pm | 4:59am |
| 28 | I hope you're not Feb-u-weary! | | | | ♌ | 7:13am | 6:31pm | 3:23pm | 5:40am |

# MARCH—hath 31 days.

| | REMARKABLE DAYS, JUDGEMENT OF WEATHER. | | | MOON PHASE LOCATION | ZODIAC SYMBOL | SUN RISE | SUN SET | MOON RISE | MOON SET |
|---|---|---|---|---|---|---|---|---|---|
| 1 | Confederate Camp Bureaugard evacuated, Graves County, 1862. | | | | ♍ | 7:12am | 6:32pm | 4:28pm | 6:12am |
| 2 | Pea planting time! | | | | ♍ | 7:10am | 6:33pm | 5:30pm | 6:40am |
| 3 | | Total Lunar Eclipse (partially visible in Ky) | | Full Moon | ♍ | 7:09am | 6:35pm | 6:31pm | 7:03am |
| 4 | 2nd Sunday of Lent | | | | ♍ | 7:07am | 6:36pm | 7:30pm | 7:25am |
| 5 | Martin Luther King Jr led Ky's largest civil rights march to date, Frankfort, 1964. | | | | ♎ | 7:06am | 6:37pm | 8:28pm | 7:45am |
| 6 | Col James Bowie and 13 other Kentuckians die with 175 others defending the Alamo. | | | | ♎ | 7:05am | 6:38pm | 9:26pm | 8:06am |
| 7 | Wis Howard kills Bob Turner and the Howard-Turner feud begins, Harlan County, 1882. | | | | ♏ | 7:03am | 6:39pm | 10:26pm | 8:27am |
| 8 | Richard Callaway and Pemberton Rawlings killed by Indians, Callaway Creek, 1780. | | | | ♏ | 7:02am | 6:40pm | 11:27pm | 8:52am |
| 9 | Even the fastest horse can be slowed by a bad shoe. | | | | ♏ | 7:00am | 6:40pm | ---------- | 9:20am |
| 10 | Daniel Boone and others leave NC to colonize Boonesborough, 1775. | | | | ♐ | 6:59am | 6:41pm | 12:29am | 9:54am |
| 11 | 3rd Sunday of Lent | Daylight Savings Time begins | | Last Quarter | ♐ | 7:57am | 7:42pm | 2:32am | 11:36am |
| 12 | "Sue Mundy" (Marcellus Clarke) hanged for murder. Louisville, 1865. | | | | ♑ | 7:56am | 7:43pm | 3:32am | 12:27pm |
| 13 | To be hopeless is to be faithless | | | | ♑ | 7:54am | 7:44pm | 4:27am | 1:28pm |
| 14 | Casey Jones, engineer, born, Fulton County, 1864. | | | | ♑ | 7:53am | 7:45pm | 5:15am | 2:36pm |
| 15 | IDES | | | | ♒ | 7:51am | 7:46pm | 5:56am | 3:50pm |
| 16 | Dig and divide your mature rhubarb. | | | | ♒ | 7:50am | 7:47pm | 6:31am | 5:05pm |
| 17 | St Patrick's Day | | | | ♓ | 7:48am | 7:48pm | 7:01am | 6:20pm |
| 18 | 4th Sunday of Lent | Mercury nearest to Mars | | New Moon | ♓ | 7:47am | 7:49pm | 7:29am | 7:36pm |
| 19 | St Joseph | Moon nearest to Earth this mo. | | | ♈ | 7:45am | 7:50pm | 7:56am | 8:53pm |
| 20 | Ky Dept. of Agriculture founded, 1876. | | | | ♈ | 7:43am | 7:51pm | 8:24am | 10:10pm |
| 21 | First Day of Spring | | | Vernal Equinox | ♉ | 7:42am | 7:52pm | 8:55am | 11:29pm |
| 22 | The fool's pastime is sitting and wishing. | | | | ♉ | 7:40am | 7:53pm | 9:31am | -------- |
| 23 | Madison J Cawein, Louisville's great 19th Century poet, born 1865. | | | | ♊ | 7:39am | 7:54pm | 10:14am | 12:46am |
| 24 | Don't criticize what you can't improve. | | | | ♊ | 7:37am | 7:55pm | 11:05am | 1:59am |
| 25 | 5th Sunday of Lent | | | First Quarter | ♋ | 7:36am | 7:56pm | 12:04pm | 3:04am |
| 26 | Duncan Hines born, Bowling Green, 1880. | | | | ♋ | 7:34am | 7:57pm | 1:09pm | 3:57am |
| 27 | Annunciation | | | | ♌ | 7:33am | 7:58pm | 2:15pm | 4:41am |
| 28 | Beattyville incorporated, 1872. | | | | ♌ | 7:31am | 7:59pm | 3:20pm | 5:16am |
| 29 | Spring fever arrives! | | | | ♌ | 7:30am | 8:00pm | 4:23pm | 5:44am |
| 30 | Poison Ivy begins to grow: get out now and chop it with your hoe! | | | | ♍ | 7:28am | 8:00pm | 5:24pm | 6:08am |
| 31 | Tick Creek Massacre, 1788. | | | | ♍ | 7:27am | 8:01pm | 6:23pm | 6:30am |

## *APRIL—hath 30 days.*

| | REMARKABLE DAYS, JUDGEMENT OF WEATHER. | | | MOON PHASE LOCATION | ZODIAC SYMBOL | SUN RISE | SUN SET | MOON RISE | MOON SET |
|---|---|---|---|---|---|---|---|---|---|
| 1 | Palm Sunday | All Fools' | | | ♎ | 7:25am | 8:02pm | 7:21pm | 6:51am |
| 2 | Blues Great, Clifford Carlisle, dies in Lexington, 1983. | | | Full Moon | ♎ | 7:23am | 8:03pm | 8:19pm | 7:11am |
| 3 | Bees swarm when it's kind of warm. | Moon farthest from Earth this mo. | | | ♎ | 7:22am | 8:04pm | 9:18pm | 7:32am |
| 4 | Clean horseshoe pits for the season. | | | | ♏ | 7:20am | 8:05pm | 10:19pm | 7:56am |
| 5 | Folks cheer when spring weather is clear. | | | | ♏ | 7:19am | 8:06pm | 11:21pm | 8:23am |
| 6 | Good Friday | | | | ♐ | 7:17am | 8:07pm | --------- | 8:55am |
| 7 | Confederate Gov of Ky, George Johnson, killed at Shiloh, 1862. | | | | ♐ | 7:16am | 8:08pm | 12:23am | 9:34am |
| 8 | Easter Sunday | | | | ♐ | 7:14am | 8:09pm | 1:23am | 10:21am |
| 9 | Crappie start running. | | | | ♑ | 7:13am | 8:10pm | 2:19am | 11:17am |
| 10 | | | | Last Quarter | ♑ | 7:11am | 8:11pm | 3:08am | 12:21pm |
| 11 | The harder you work, the luckier you get. | | | | ♒ | 7:10am | 8:12pm | 3:51am | 1:30pm |
| 12 | Henry Clay born, 1777. | | | | ♒ | 7:09am | 8:13pm | 4:27am | 2:41pm |
| 13 | Alexander Bullitt, Ky Pioneer, dies at Oxmoor estate, near Louisville, 1816. | | | | ♓ | 7:07am | 8:14pm | 4:58am | 3:54pm |
| 14 | Three Forks Battalion of Ky Home Guards, 40 men, defeat guerrilla force of 75, Booneville, 1864. | | | | ♓ | 7:06am | 8:14pm | 5:26am | 5:08pm |
| 15 | 2nd Sunday of Easter | | | | ♈ | 7:04am | 8:15pm | 5:53am | 6:23pm |
| 16 | Julian Carroll born in McCracken County, 1931. | | | | ♈ | 7:03am | 8:16 p.m | 6:20am | 7:40pm |
| 17 | Moon closest to Earth this month | | | New Moon | ♉ | 7:01am | 8:17pm | 6:50am | 8:59pm |
| 18 | Too warm, then it'll storm. | | | | ♉ | 7:00am | 8:18pm | 7:24am | 10:19pm |
| 19 | A mind that refuses to think is like a biscuit refusing baking powder. | | | | ♊ | 6:59am | 8:19pm | 8:05am | 11:38pm |
| 20 | Augusta's Old Court Building burns, 1848. | | | | ♊ | 6:57am | 8:20pm | 8:54am | ------- |
| 21 | St Anselm | | | | ♋ | 6:56am | 8:21pm | 9:52am | 12:49am |
| 22 | 3rd Sunday of Easter | Boonesborough surveyed, 1775. | | | ♋ | 6:55am | 8:22pm | 10:57am | 1:49am |
| 23 | St George | Rosemary Clooney born in Maysville, 1928. | | | ♌ | 6:53am | 8:23pm | 12:04pm | 2:38am |
| 24 | | | | First Quarter | ♌ | 6:52am | 8:24pm | 1:11pm | 3:16am |
| 25 | St Mark | | | | ♌ | 6:51am | 8:25pm | 2:16pm | 3:47am |
| 26 | Carp and catfish spawn: Sharpen your gig! | | | | ♍ | 6:49am | 8:26pm | 3:17pm | 4:13am |
| 27 | April is a fine month, even if it rains, the ponies can still run. | | | | ♍ | 6:48am | 8:27pm | 4:17pm | 4:36am |
| 28 | Joseph Allen, hero of the War of 1812, dies in Hardinsburg, 1862. | | | | ♎ | 6:47am | 8:28pm | 5:15pm | 4:56am |
| 29 | 4th Sunday of Easter | Court of Appeals dissolves Beckham County, 1914. | | | ♎ | 6:46am | 8:29pm | 6:12pm | 5:17am |
| 30 | Alben Barkley dies after making speech at Washington & Lee University, 1956. | Moon farthest from Earth | | | ♎ | 6:45am | 8:29pm | 7:11pm | 5:38am |

## MAY—hath 31 days.

| | REMARKABLE DAYS, JUDGEMENT OF WEATHER. | | | MOON PHASE LOCATION | ZODIAC SYMBOL | SUN RISE | SUN SET | MOON RISE | MOON SET |
|---|---|---|---|---|---|---|---|---|---|
| 1 | | | | | ♏ | 6:43am | 8:30pm | 8:11pm | 6:01am |
| 2 | | | | Full Moon | ♏ | 6:42am | 8:31pm | 9:13pm | 6:26am |
| 3 | Harry Caudill, Appalachian author, born in Letcher County, 1922. | | | | ♐ | 6:41am | 8:32pm | 10:15pm | 6:57am |
| 4 | Historian J. Winston Coleman dies at his Lexington home, 1983. | | | | ♐ | 6:40am | 8:33pm | 11:17pm | 7:34am |
| 5 | Derby Day | | | | ♐ | 6:39am | 8:34pm | -------- | 8:19am |
| 6 | 5th Sunday of Easter | | | | ♑ | 6:38am | 8:35pm | 12:14am | 9:12am |
| 7 | If your horse didn't win, you'll say betting is a sin! | | | | ♑ | 6:37am | 8:36pm | 1:05am | 10:13am |
| 8 | Gradening in the Bluegrass begins in earnest. | | | | ♒ | 6:36am | 8:37pm | 1:49am | 11:19am |
| 9 | | | | Last Quarter | ♒ | 6:35am | 8:38pm | 2:26am | 12:28pm |
| 10 | Belle of Louisville begins renovations, 1962. | | | | ♓ | 6:34am | 8:39pm | 2:58am | 1:38pm |
| 11 | Comedian Foster Brooks born in Louisville, 1912. | | | | ♓ | 6:33am | 8:40pm | 3:26am | 2:49pm |
| 12 | Dogwoods start a show. | | | | ♓ | 6:32am | 8:41pm | 3:52am | 4:00pm |
| 13 | 6th Sunday of Easter | | | | ♈ | 6:31am | 8:41pm | 4:18am | 5:14pm |
| 14 | Mother's Day | | | | ♈ | 6:30am | 8:42pm | 4:46am | 6:30pm |
| 15 | You cannot bring back the past, but you can always help build the future. | Moon closest to Earth this mo. | | | ♉ | 6:29am | 8:43pm | 5:17am | 7:49pm |
| 16 | | | | New Moon | ♉ | 6:28am | 8:44pm | 5:54am | 9:09pm |
| 17 | Ascension | The Marquis de Lafayette visits Fayette County, which was named for him, 1825. | | | ♊ | 6:27am | 8:45pm | 6:39am | 10:25pm |
| 18 | May in Ky Is a tempestuous beauty. | | | | ♊ | 6:26am | 8:46pm | 7:35am | 11:33pm |
| 19 | James Dixon Black begins 7 month gubernatorial term, 1919. | | | | ♋ | 6:26am | 8:47pm | 8:38am | -------- |
| 20 | 7th Sunday of Easter | | | | ♋ | 6:25am | 8:48pm | 9:47am | 12:28am |
| 21 | Mountain business magnate Thomas Jefferson Asher born in Clay County, 1848. | | | | ♌ | 6:24am | 8:48pm | 10:57am | 1:12am |
| 22 | If you sing while you work, your soul benefits. | | | | ♌ | 6:23am | 8:49pm | 12:04pm | 1:47am |
| 23 | | | | First Quarter | ♍ | 6:23am | 8:50pm | 1:08pm | 2:15am |
| 24 | Jockey Don Brumfield born in Nicholasville, 1938. | | | | ♍ | 6:22am | 8:51pm | 2:09pm | 2:39am |
| 25 | St Bede | | | | ♍ | 6:22am | 8:52pm | 3:07pm | 3:01am |
| 26 | Lawyer Charles W Anderson Jr, first black Ky Colonel, born in Louisville, 1907. | | | | ♎ | 6:21am | 8:52pm | 4:05pm | 3:21am |
| 27 | 8th Sunday of Easter | Moon farthest from Earth this mo. | | | ♎ | 6:20am | 8:53pm | 5:03pm | 3:42am |
| 28 | Memorial Day | Beverly Hills Nightclub fire, near Newport, 1977. 165 perish. | | | ♏ | 6:20am | 8:54pm | 6:03pm | 4:04am |
| 29 | A good day to string up the hammock. | | | | ♏ | 6:19am | 8:55pm | 7:04pm | 4:29am |
| 30 | Actress Mary Anderson, from Louisville, dies in London, 1940. | | | | ♏ | 6:19am | 8:55pm | 8:07pm | 4:58am |
| 31 | Brides take cheer, grooms may fear, June is almost here. | | | | ♐ | 6:19am | 8:56pm | 9:09pm | 5:33am |

# JUNE—hath 30 days.

| | REMARKABLE DAYS, JUDGEMENT OF WEATHER. | | | MOON PHASE LOCATION | ZODIAC SYMBOL | SUN RISE | SUN SET | MOON RISE | MOON SET |
|---|---|---|---|---|---|---|---|---|---|
| 1 | | Kentucky Statehood Day (215 years!) | | Full Moon | ♐ | 6:18am | 8:57pm | 10:08pm | 6:16am |
| 2 | Strawberry picking time! | Mercury closest to Venus | | | ♑ | 6:18am | 8:57pm | 11:02pm | 7:07am |
| 3 | Trinity | Confederate Memorial Day and Jefferson Davis Day (Ky. Holidays) | | Mercury furthest east of Sun | ♑ | 6:17am | 8:58pm | 11:48pm | 8:06am |
| 4 | When June gets warm, it's true to form. | | | | ♒ | 6:17am | 8:59pm | --------- | 9:12am |
| 5 | St Boniface | John Allen commissioned Colonel of 1st Ky Rifles, 1812. | | | ♒ | 6:17am | 8:59pm | 12:27am | 10:20am |
| 6 | Fort Harrod established, 1774. | | | | ♒ | 6:17am | 9:00pm | 1:00am | 11:29am |
| 7 | Morning work prevents afternoon worries. | | Jupiter closest to Earth | | ♓ | 6:16am | 9:00pm | 1:29am | 12:39pm |
| 8 | | | | Last Quarter | ♓ | 6:16am | 9:01pm | 1:55am | 1:48pm |
| 9 | Rebecca Bryan born in Va, 1739. Later on, she'd marry Daniel Boone. | | | | ♈ | 6:16am | 9:02pm | 2:20am | 2:58pm |
| 10 | Body & Blood of Christ | Venus farthest east from Sun | | | ♈ | 6:16am | 9:02pm | 2:46am | 4:10pm |
| 11 | Second Battle of Cynthiana, 1864. | | | | ♉ | 6:16am | 9:03pm | 3:15am | 5:26pm |
| 12 | The promise of fast money is bait with a hook in it. | | Moon closest to Earth | | ♉ | 6:16am | 9:03pm | 3:48am | 6:43pm |
| 13 | Florence M Cantrill born, 1888: First woman in Ky Legislature. | | | | ♊ | 6:16am | 9:03pm | 4:28am | 8:00pm |
| 14 | Flag Day | Robert Anderson born, 1805 near Louisville. Defender of Fort Sumter in 1861. | | | ♊ | 6:16am | 9:04pm | 5:18am | 9:12pm |
| 15 | | | | New Moon | ♋ | 6:16am | 9:04pm | 6:18am | 10:14pm |
| 16 | Daniel Boone escapes the Shawnee, 1778. | | | | ♋ | 6:16am | 9:05pm | 7:26am | 11:03pm |
| 17 | Pete-Louis Rogers Browning born, 1861 -- the original "Louisville Slugger." | | Pluto closest to Earth | | ♌ | 6:16am | 9:05pm | 8:37am | 11:43pm |
| 18 | Gen. Simon Bolivar Buckner killed at Okinawa, 1945. | | | | ♌ | 6:16am | 9:05pm | 9:47am | --------- |
| 19 | Fish start to go to deeper water. | | | | ♌ | 6:16am | 9:05pm | 10:54am | 12:14am |
| 20 | Benjamin Helm Bristow born at Elkton, 1832. Later, he'd become US Solicitor General. | | | | ♍ | 6:16am | 9:06pm | 11:57am | 12:40am |
| 21 | Solstice | First Day of Summer | | | ♍ | 6:16am | 9:06pm | 12:57pm | 1:03am |
| 22 | | Thomas Barlow, inventor of the rifled cannon, Nicholas County native, died, 1865. | | First Quarter | ♎ | 6:17am | 9:06pm | 1:56pm | 1:25am |
| 23 | Irvin S Cobb born in Paducah, 1876. | | | | ♎ | 6:17am | 9:06pm | 2:54pm | 1:45am |
| 24 | Nativity of John the Baptist | Moon furthest from Earth | | | ♎ | 6:17am | 9:06pm | 3:53pm | 2:07am |
| 25 | He who works hardest in the sun rests best in the shade. | | | | ♏ | 6:17am | 9:07pm | 4:54pm | 2:31am |
| 26 | First known ad for bourbon whisky appears in the Paris Western Citizen, 1821. | | Mercury closest to Earth | | ♏ | 6:18am | 9:07pm | 5:56pm | 2:58am |
| 27 | There are many good speakers, but few good listeners. | | | | ♐ | 6:18am | 9:07pm | 6:58pm | 3:31am |
| 28 | St Irenaeus | A big dose of responsibility is good for the soul. | | | ♐ | 6:19am | 9:07pm | 7:59pm | 4:11am |
| 29 | Sts Peter & Paul | Breezy and sneezy. | | | ♑ | 6:19am | 9:07pm | 8:55pm | 5:00am |
| 30 | | Rare 'Blue Moon' this day | | Full Moon | ♑ | 6:19am | 9:07pm | 9:45pm | 5:57am |

## JULY—hath 31 days.

| | REMARKABLE DAYS, JUDGEMENT OF WEATHER. | | | MOON PHASE LOCATION | ZODIAC SYMBOL | SUN RISE | SUN SET | MOON RISE | MOON SET |
|---|---|---|---|---|---|---|---|---|---|
| 1 | Tis the month for fishin' and air conditionin'. | | | | ♑ | 6:20am | 9:07pm | 10:27pm | 7:02am |
| 2 | Wm Goodell Frost born, 1854. Became president of Berea College. | | | | ♒ | 6:20am | 9:06pm | 11:02pm | 8:11am |
| 3 | St Thomas | A watermelon iced down takes away the farmer's frown. | | | ♒ | 6:21am | 9:06pm | 11:32pm | 9:21am |
| 4 | Independence Day | | | | ♓ | 6:21am | 9:06pm | 11:59pm | 10:31am |
| 5 | "Uncle John" Shell, 134 years old, dies after being horse-kicked, Leslie County, 1922. | | | | ♓ | 6:22am | 9:06pm | ------ | 11:40am |
| 6 | Gen John Hunt Morgan's Confederates fight US troops all night: Bardstown, 1863. | | | | ♈ | 6:22am | 9:06pm | 12:24am | 12:50pm |
| 7 | Harriette Arnow, author, born in Wayne County, 1908. | Sun farthest from Earth for '07 | | Last Quarter | ♈ | 6:23am | 9:05pm | 12:49am | 2:00pm |
| 8 | The plastic surgeon, like Milton, seeks to find Paradise Lost. | | | | ♉ | 6:24am | 9:05pm | 1:16am | 3:12pm |
| 9 | James Campbell Cantrill, US & Ky Legislator, born in Georgetown, 1870. | Moon closest to Earth | | | ♉ | 6:24am | 9:05pm | 1:47am | 4:27pm |
| 10 | Too much sorrow is a waste. | | | | ♊ | 6:25am | 9:04pm | 2:23am | 5:43pm |
| 11 | Plan fall's cole crops. | | | | ♊ | 6:25am | 9:04pm | 3:08am | 6:55pm |
| 12 | Pioneer filmmaker Charles Browning born in Louisville, 1881: Inventor of the horror film. | | | | ♋ | 6:26am | 9:04pm | 4:03am | 8:00pm |
| 13 | Stable boys and lawyers sometimes have similar duties. | Moon & Mercury close | | | ♋ | 6:27am | 9:03pm | 5:06am | 8:54pm |
| 14 | AB "Happy" Chandler born, 1898. | Venus' brightest night in '07 | | New Moon | ♋ | 6:27am | 9:03pm | 6:16am | 9:37pm |
| 15 | Jackson connects to the Ky Union Rail Road, 1891. | | | | ♌ | 6:28am | 9:02pm | 7:27am | 10:12pm |
| 16 | Whether hot weather? | | | | ♌ | 6:29am | 9:02pm | 8:36am | 10:40pm |
| 17 | Chenoweth Massacre, Jefferson County, 1789. | | | | ♍ | 6:30am | 9:01pm | 9:41am | 11:05pm |
| 18 | WHAS, Ky's first radio station, goes on the air, Lousville, 1922. | | | | ♍ | 6:30am | 9:01pm | 10:44am | 11:27pm |
| 19 | At home, Louisville Grays beat Nashville: First pro baseball game west of the Alleghenies: 1865. | | | | ♎ | 6:31am | 9:00pm | 11:44pm | 11:48pm |
| 20 | Moon Day | Mercury farthest west from Sun | | | ♎ | 6:32am | 8:59pm | 12:43pm | ---- |
| 21 | Orlando Brown, Whig editor of 'The Frankfort Commonwealth,' died, 1867. | | | | ♏ | 6:33am | 8:59pm | 1:42pm | 12:09am |
| 22 | Great Catlettsburg Fire, 1878. | Moon farthest from Earth | | First Quarter | ♏ | 6:33am | 8:58pm | 2:42pm | 12:32am |
| 23 | Thomas Buford convicted of assassinating Judge Elliott, Owen County, 1879. | | | | ♏ | 6:34am | 8:57pm | 3:43pm | 12:58am |
| 24 | First livestock show in Ky, near Lexington, 1816. | | | | ♐ | 6:35am | 8:56pm | 4:45pm | 1:28am |
| 25 | St James | | | | ♐ | 6:36am | 8:56pm | 5:47pm | 2:05am |
| 26 | The two best occasions for Mint Juleps: At horse races and sunsets. | | | | ♐ | 6:37am | 8:55pm | 6:45pm | 2:50am |
| 27 | John Buford of Woodford County promoted to Brigadier General in US Army, 1862. | | | | ♑ | 6:38am | 8:54pm | 7:38pm | 3:44am |
| 28 | The fishin' hole has become the swimmin' hole by now. | | | | ♑ | 6:38am | 8:53pm | 8:23pm | 4:46am |
| 29 | Tis well into summer, thy neck is red, from bending over thy hoe and bowing thy head. | | | | ♒ | 6:39am | 8:52pm | 9:01pm | 5:55am |
| 30 | | | | Full Moon | ♒ | 6:40am | 8:51pm | 9:33pm | 7:06am |
| 31 | Whitney Young Jr born in Shelbyville, 1921. | | | | ♓ | 6:41am | 8:50pm | 10:02pm | 8:18am |

# AUGUST—hath 31 days.

| | REMARKABLE DAYS, JUDGEMENT OF WEATHER. | | MOON PHASE LOCATION | ZODIAC SYMBOL | SUN RISE | SUN SET | MOON RISE | MOON SET |
|---|---|---|---|---|---|---|---|---|
| 1 | Bell County established, 1867. | Mercury in Gemini | | ♓ | 6:42am | 8:49pm | 10:28pm | 9:29am |
| 2 | Clinton County Courthouse burns, 1980. | | | ♈ | 6:43am | 8:48pm | 10:53pm | 10:40am |
| 3 | Sophia Kindrick Alcorn born in Stanford, 1883: Pioneer educator of the blind and deaf. | | | ♈ | 6:43am | 8:47pm | 11:20pm | 11:51am |
| 4 | Desha Breckinridge born in Lexington, 1867: Great journalist and editor of 'The Lexington Herald.' | | Moon nearest Earth this mo. | ♉ | 6:44am | 8:46pm | 11:49pm | 1:04pm |
| 5 | Wendell Berry born in Henry County, 1934. | | | ♉ | 6:45am | 8:45pm | - - - - - | 2:18pm |
| 6 | Transfiguration | | Last Quarter | ♉ | 6:46am | 8:44pm | 12:23am | 3:32pm |
| 7 | First sermon in Louisville preached by Squire Boone, 1776. | | | ♊ | 6:47am | 8:43pm | 1:04am | 4:45pm |
| 8 | Jesse Stuart born in Greenup County, 1906. | Venus & Saturn close | | ♊ | 6:48am | 8:42pm | 1:55am | 5:51pm |
| 9 | Confederate guerillas capture Calhoun, 1862. | | | ♋ | 6:49am | 8:41pm | 2:54am | 6:47pm |
| 10 | Carl C Brenner, Ky's great landscape artist, born 1838. | | | ♋ | 6:50am | 8:39pm | 4:01am | 7:34pm |
| 11 | First issue of 'The Kentucke Gazette' appears, Lexington, 1787. | | | ♌ | 6:50am | 8:38pm | 5:10am | 8:11pm |
| 12 | | | New Moon | ♌ | 6:51am | 8:37pm | 6:20am | 8:41pm |
| 13 | Fogs in August born, send frosts upon November's morn. | | | ♍ | 6:52am | 8:36pm | 7:26am | 9:07pm |
| 14 | Last legal public hanging in the US Owensboro, 1936. | | | ♍ | 6:53am | 8:35pm | 8:30am | 9:30pm |
| 15 | Barry Bingham Sr died, 1988. | | | ♍ | 6:54am | 8:33pm | 9:31am | 9:51pm |
| 16 | Tories and Indians repelled at Bryan's Station, 1782. | | | ♎ | 6:55am | 8:32pm | 10:31am | 10:12pm |
| 17 | A wandering mind can sometimes get lost. | | | ♎ | 6:56am | 8:31pm | 11:30am | 10:34pm |
| 18 | James Graham Brown born, 1881; founder of the Brown Hotel. | | | ♏ | 6:57am | 8:29pm | 12:30pm | 10:59pm |
| 19 | Battle of Blue Licks, Robertson County, 1782. | | | ♏ | 6:58am | 8:28pm | 1:30pm | 11:27pm |
| 20 | Moon farthest from Earth this mo. | | First Quarter | ♏ | 6:58am | 8:27pm | 2:32pm | - - - - |
| 21 | Complaint and inaction are dreadful partners. | | | ♐ | 6:59am | 8:25pm | 3:33pm | 12:00am |
| 22 | Confidence is best when supported with hard work. | | | ♐ | 7:00am | 8:24pm | 4:33pm | 12:41am |
| 23 | John Shermon Cooper, legendary US Senator, born in Somerset, 1901. | | | ♑ | 7:01am | 8:23pm | 5:27pm | 1:30am |
| 24 | St Bartholomew | | | ♑ | 7:02am | 8:21pm | 6:15pm | 2:29am |
| 25 | Inability to handle money indicates other flaws. | | | ♒ | 7:03am | 8:20pm | 6:56pm | 3:34am |
| 26 | Unwilling to work, unhappy at life. | | | ♒ | 7:04am | 8:18pm | 7:31pm | 4:45am |
| 27 | Wm Campbell Breckinridge born, 1837: Editor, Col Of 9th Ky Cavalry (CSA) and later, civil rights advocate. | | | ♒ | 7:04am | 8:17pm | 8:02pm | 5:57am |
| 28 | | | Partial Lunar Eclipse   Full Moon | ♓ | 7:05am | 8:15pm | 8:29pm | 7:10am |
| 29 | Beheading of St John the Baptist | | | ♓ | 7:06am | 8:14pm | 8:55pm | 8:23am |
| 30 | Alexander Arthur, Middlesboro's founder, born 1846 in Glasgow, Scotland. | | | ♈ | 7:07am | 8:12pm | 9:22pm | 9:36am |
| 31 | School days are here: Parents cheer, kids shed a tear. | | Moon nears Earth | ♈ | 7:08am | 8:11pm | 9:51pm | 10:50am |

## SEPTEMBER—hath 30 days·

| | REMARKABLE DAYS, JUDGEMENT OF WEATHER. | | | MOON PHASE LOCATION | ZODIAC SYMBOL | SUN RISE | SUN SET | MOON RISE | MOON SET |
|---|---|---|---|---|---|---|---|---|---|
| 1 | Martin County formed, 1870. | | | | ♉ | 7:09am | 8:09pm | 10:24pm | 12:06pm |
| 2 | Adolph Rupp born, 1901. | | | | ♉ | 7:10am | 8:08pm | 11:03pm | 1:22pm |
| 3 | Labor Day | Long weekends are nice; Bring a cooler of ice. | | Moon in Pleiades | ♊ | 7:11am | 8:06pm | 11:51pm | 2:36pm |
| 4 | | | | Last Quarter | ♊ | 7:11am | 8:05pm | - - - - | 3:45pm |
| 5 | Blessed Mother Teresa | | | | ♋ | 7:12am | 8:03pm | 12:48am | 4:44pm |
| 6 | Summer's final weeks are to be savored. | | | | ♋ | 7:13am | 8:02pm | 1:52am | 5:32pm |
| 7 | The ninth month holds many surpises. | | | | ♌ | 7:14am | 8:00pm | 3:00am | 6:12pm |
| 8 | Dry weather and dry humor both have their proper place. | Moon & Venus close | | | ♌ | 7:15am | 7:59pm | 4:08am | 6:43pm |
| 9 | Col. Harland Sand-ers born, 1890. | | | | ♌ | 7:16am | 7:57pm | 5:15am | 7:10pm |
| 10 | John J Crittenden born, 1786, in Wood-ford County: Ky Gov, US Sen, Atty Gen. | | | | ♍ | 7:17am | 7:56pm | 6:19am | 7:34pm |
| 11 | | | | New Moon | ♍ | 7:17am | 7:54pm | 7:20am | 7:55pm |
| 12 | If the weather is mild the fish will go wild. | | | | ♎ | 7:18am | 7:53pm | 8:20am | 8:16pm |
| 13 | Rosh Hashana & Ramadan begin | | | | ♎ | 7:19am | 7:51pm | 9:19am | 8:38pm |
| 14 | Holy Cross | Kentucky History Day | | | ♏ | 7:20am | 7:49pm | 10:19am | 9:02pm |
| 15 | FCC grants license to WLAP radio station in Lexington, 1922. | Moon farthest from Earth this mo. | | | ♏ | 7:21am | 7:48pm | 11:19am | 9:28pm |
| 16 | John CC Mayo born, 1864: Developer of East Ky Coal fields. | | | | ♏ | 7:22am | 7:46pm | 12:20pm | 9:59pm |
| 17 | UK and NFL football great George Blanda born, 1927. | | | | ♐ | 7:23am | 7:45pm | 1:21pm | 10:36pm |
| 18 | Southern troops occupy Bowling Green, 1861. | | | | ♐ | 7:23am | 7:43pm | 2:21pm | 11:21pm |
| 19 | | | | First Quarter | ♑ | 7:24am | 7:42pm | 3:17pm | - - - |
| 20 | Lexington's Gen Benjamin Hardin Helm, CSA, killed at Chickamauga, 1863: Was Mary Todd Lincoln's half-brother., | | | | ♑ | 7:25am | 7:40pm | 4:06pm | 12:15am |
| 21 | St Matthew | | | | ♑ | 7:26am | 7:38pm | 4:50pm | 1:16am |
| 22 | UK founder John Bryan Bowman died, 1891. | | | | ♒ | 7:27am | 7:37pm | 5:27pm | 2:23am |
| 23 | First Day of Autumn | Venus very bright | | | ♒ | 7:28am | 7:35pm | 5:59pm | 3:33am |
| 24 | Black Patch War begins, Guthrie, 1904. | | | | ♓ | 7:29am | 7:34pm | 6:27pm | 4:45am |
| 25 | Best apples are now pickable. | | | | ♓ | 7:30am | 7:32pm | 6:54pm | 5:58am |
| 26 | | | | Full Moon | ♈ | 7:30am | 7:31pm | 7:21pm | 7:12am |
| 27 | Fishing by Autumn's first full moon usu-ally brings good luck. | | | | ♈ | 7:31am | 7:29pm | 7:50pm | 8:27am |
| 28 | St Wenceslas | Moon close to Earth | | | ♉ | 7:32am | 7:27pm | 8:22pm | 9:44am |
| 29 | US Gen Jeff Davis kills Gen Wm Nelson in dispute, Louisville, 1862. | Mercury farthest east from Sun. | | | ♉ | 7:33am | 7:26pm | 9:00pm | 11:03am |
| 30 | Thrilla in Manila' -- Ali defeats Frazier, 1975. | Moon very close to Pleiades | | | ♊ | 7:34am | 7:24pm | 9:46pm | 12:21pm |

# OCTOBER—hath 31 days.

| | REMARKABLE DAYS, JUDGEMENT OF WEATHER. | | MOON PHASE LOCATION | ZODIAC SYMBOL | SUN RISE | SUN SET | MOON RISE | MOON SET |
|---|---|---|---|---|---|---|---|---|
| 1 | Sen Joseph Blackburn born in Woodford County, 1838. | | | ♊ | 7:35am | 7:23pm | 10:41pm | 1:34pm |
| 2 | Rebecca Caudill, Harlan County author, died, 1985. | | | ♋ | 7:36am | 7:21pm | 11:44pm | 2:38pm |
| 3 | Bellarmine College (now University) opens in Louisville, 1950. | | Last Quarter | ♋ | 7:37am | 7:20pm | - - - - | 3:31pm |
| 4 | Pumpkins ripe, the weather chills, frost is showing on the hills. | | | ♌ | 7:38am | 7:18pm | 12:52am | 4:13pm |
| 5 | Battle of the Thames: Kentucky soldiers save the day: 1813. | | | ♌ | 7:39am | 7:17pm | 2:01am | 4:47pm |
| 6 | Louisville's Charles Browning, pioneer filmmaker, dies in California, 1962. | | | ♌ | 7:39am | 7:15pm | 3:07am | 5:15pm |
| 7 | Start drying gourds today. | | | ♍ | 7:40am | 7:14pm | 4:11am | 5:39pm |
| 8 | Columbus Day | Battle of Perryville, 1862. | | ♍ | 7:41am | 7:12pm | 5:13am | 6:01pm |
| 9 | Gen Edward Kirby-Smith, CSA, gets lost on way to relieve Bragg's forces at Perryville. | | | ♎ | 7:42am | 7:11pm | 6:12am | 6:22pm |
| 10 | Time to switch from mint juleps to hard cider. | | | ♎ | 7:43am | 7:09pm | 7:11am | 6:43pm |
| 11 | Oakland Race Course opens in Louisville, 1832. | | New Moon | ♎ | 7:44am | 7:08pm | 8:10am | 7:06pm |
| 12 | Lexington founder Robert Patterson leaves Fort Pitt for Kentucky, 1775. | | | ♏ | 7:45am | 7:06pm | 9:10am | 7:31pm |
| 13 | End of Ramadan | Levisa Fork River cut-through completed at Pikeville, 1987. | | ♏ | 7:46am | 7:05pm | 10:11am | 8:01pm |
| 14 | Holy Cross | Sow multiplier onions within the week. Moon farthest from Earth this mo. | | ♐ | 7:47am | 7:03pm | 11:12am | 8:36pm |
| 15 | John Bibb of Frankfort promoted to major after Battle of the Thames, 1813. | | | ♐ | 7:48am | 7:02pm | 12:12pm | 9:17pm |
| 16 | Cleanth Brooks, literary critic, born 1906, Murray. | | | ♐ | 7:49am | 7:01pm | 1:09pm | 10:07pm |
| 17 | St Ignatius | UK begins first university-owned radio station, 1940. | | ♑ | 7:50am | 6:59pm | 2:00pm | 11:04pm |
| 18 | Feel like fishing at the lake? First get finished with your rake. | | | ♑ | 7:51am | 6:58pm | 2:44pm | - - - - |
| 19 | Cassius Marcellus Clay born, 1810. | | First Quarter | ♒ | 7:52am | 6:56pm | 3:23pm | 12:07am |
| 20 | Gen John Hunt Morgan's men burn a Yankee wagon train at Cox's Creek, 1862. | | | ♒ | 7:53am | 6:55pm | 3:55pm | 1:14am |
| 21 | Jim Wayne Miller, Berea poet, born 1936. | | | ♓ | 7:54am | 6:54pm | 4:25pm | 2:23am |
| 22 | Gov Earl Clements born in Morganfield, 1896. | Mercury closest to Earth this mo. | | ♓ | 7:55am | 6:53pm | 4:52pm | 3:33am |
| 23 | Adlai Stevenson, U.S. Vice President, born in Christian County, 1835. | | | ♓ | 7:56am | 6:51pm | 5:18pm | 4:45am |
| 24 | Dann Byck, Louisville clothier, born 1899. | | | ♈ | 7:57am | 6:50pm | 5:46pm | 5:58am |
| 25 | When sunshine appears, it takes away the tears. | | | ♈ | 7:58am | 6:49pm | 6:16pm | 7:15am |
| 26 | Indian Corn should be picked by now. | | Full Moon | ♉ | 7:59am | 6:47pm | 6:52pm | 8:34am |
| 27 | Barbourville selected as seat of Knox County, 1800. | | | ♉ | 8:00am | 6:46pm | 7:36pm | 9:55am |
| 28 | St Simon & St Jude | Venus farthest W. of Sun | | ♊ | 8:01am | 6:45pm | 8:29pm | 11:14am |
| 29 | Centre 6, Harvard 0, 1921. | | | ♊ | 8:02am | 6:44pm | 9:31pm | 12:24pm |
| 30 | Mary Phelps Holley, early Lexington author & scholar, born 1784. | | | ♋ | 8:03am | 6:43pm | 10:40pm | 1:24pm |
| 31 | Halloween | Otis Singletary, former UK president, born, 1921. | | ♋ | 8:04am | 6:42pm | 11:51pm | 2:11pm |

# *NOVEMBER—hath 30 days.*

| | REMARKABLE DAYS, JUDGEMENT OF WEATHER. | | | MOON PHASE LOCATION | ZODIAC SYMBOL | SUN RISE | SUN SET | MOON RISE | MOON SET |
|---|---|---|---|---|---|---|---|---|---|
| 1 | All Saints | | | Last Quarter | ♌ | 8:05am | 6:40pm | --- | 2:48pm |
| 2 | Daniel Boone born in Pa., 1734. | | | | ♌ | 8:06am | 6:39pm | 12:59am | 3:18pm |
| 3 | First State Capitol Bldg occupied, 1794. | | | | ♍ | 8:07am | 6:38pm | 2:04am | 3:43pm |
| 4 | Daylight Savings Time Ends | Second Ky Capitol Bldg. burns, 1824. | | | ♍ | 8:08am | 6:37pm | 3:07am | 4:06pm |
| 5 | J Winston Coleman, author & historian, born near Lexington, 1898. | | | | ♎ | 7:09am | 5:36pm | 3:06am | 3:27pm |
| 6 | John Beckham elected governor, 1900. | | | | ♎ | 7:11am | 5:35pm | 4:05am | 3:48pm |
| 7 | Battle of Belmont, 1861. | | | | ♎ | 7:12am | 5:34pm | 5:04am | 4:11pm |
| 8 | Battle of Ivy Mountain, 1861. | | | | ♏ | 7:13am | 5:33pm | 6:03am | 4:35pm |
| 9 | Martin Van Buren Bates, 'the Kentucky Giant,' born in Letcher County, 1845. He would grow to be 7'11". | | | New Moon | ♏ | 7:14am | 5:32pm | 7:04am | 5:03pm |
| 10 | Your firewood should be stacked by today. | | | | ♏ | 7:15am | 5:31pm | 8:05am | 5:37pm |
| 11 | Veterans Day | Lady Polk' cannon explodes at Belmont: 11 Confederates killed, 1861. | | | ♐ | 7:16am | 5:31pm | 9:05am | 6:16pm |
| 12 | The old raccoon walks late. | | | | ♐ | 7:17am | 5:30pm | 10:03am | 7:04pm |
| 13 | Louis Brandeis born in Louisville, 1856. | | | | ♑ | 7:18am | 5:29pm | 10:55am | 7:58pm |
| 14 | Black Jack Corner created, 1780. | | | | ♑ | 7:19am | 5:28pm | 11:42am | 8:59pm |
| 15 | Commercial flights begin at Louisville's Standiford Field, 1947. | | | | ♒ | 7:20am | 5:27pm | 12:21pm | 10:03pm |
| 16 | Last day for a decent game of horseshoes. | | | | ♒ | 7:21am | 5:27pm | 12:55pm | 11:10pm |
| 17 | Hunting dogs should be trained by today. | | | First Quarter | ♒ | 7:22am | 5:26pm | 1:24pm | ----- |
| 18 | Confederate state government formed, Russellville, 1861. | | | | ♓ | 7:24am | 5:25pm | 1:51pm | 12:17am |
| 19 | George Rogers Clark born, 1752. | | | | ♓ | 7:25am | 5:25pm | 2:17pm | 1:25am |
| 20 | Campbell-Rice religious debates at their peak, Lexington, 1843. | | | | ♈ | 7:26am | 5:24pm | 2:43pm | 2:34am |
| 21 | The turkey gets his way for just one more day! | | | | ♈ | 7:27am | 5:24pm | 3:11pm | 3:47am |
| 22 | Thanksgiving Day | | | | ♉ | 7:28am | 5:23pm | 3:43pm | 5:03am |
| 23 | You should still be thankful for the leftovers. | | | | ♉ | 7:29am | 5:22pm | 4:22pm | 6:22am |
| 24 | Nice night for fishing: Bundle up! | | | Full Moon | ♊ | 7:30am | 5:22pm | 5:11pm | 7:43am |
| 25 | First State Capitol Bldg. burns, 1813. | | | | ♊ | 7:31am | 5:22pm | 6:10pm | 9:00am |
| 26 | Gov Ned Breathitt born, 1924. | | | | ♋ | 7:32am | 5:21pm | 7:19pm | 10:07am |
| 27 | Gen John Hunt Morgan (CSA) escapes from Ohio State Penitentiary, 1863. | | | | ♋ | 7:33am | 5:21pm | 8:32pm | 11:01am |
| 28 | James Buckner Brown, editor of old 'Louisville Herald-Post,' born, 1872. | | | | ♌ | 7:34am | 5:20pm | 9:44pm | 11:44am |
| 29 | Author Harry Caudill dies, Letcher County, 1990. | | | | ♌ | 7:35am | 5:20pm | 10:53pm | 12:18pm |
| 30 | St Andrew | | | | ♍ | 7:36am | 5:20pm | 11:58pm | 12:45pm |

# *DECEMBER—hath 31 days.*

| | REMARKABLE DAYS, JUDGEMENT OF WEATHER. | | MOON PHASE LOCATION | ZODIAC SYMBOL | SUN RISE | SUN SET | MOON RISE | MOON SET |
|---|---|---|---|---|---|---|---|---|
| 1 | George Washington Buckner born into slavery, Green County, 1855: Future doctor and diplomat. | | Last Quarter | ♍ | 7:37am | 5:20pm | - - - - | 1:09pm |
| 2 | Let your presence be the present. | | | ♍ | 7:38am | 5:20pm | 12:59am | 1:31pm |
| 3 | Henry C Burnett of Ky's 1st District expelled from Congress, 1861. | | | ♎ | 7:39am | 5:19pm | 1:59am | 1:53pm |
| 4 | Former Gov. Bert T. Combs drowns in a Powell County flash flood, 1991. | | | ♎ | 7:40am | 5:19pm | 2:57am | 2:15pm |
| 5 | US Army's Camp Breckinridge (between Henderson & Morganfield) closes, 1962. | | | ♏ | 7:41am | 5:19pm | 3:56am | 2:39pm |
| 6 | St Nicholas | | | ♏ | 7:42am | 5:19pm | 4:56am | 3:05pm |
| 7 | Pearl Harbor Re-membrance Day | Martha Layne Collins born, Shelby County, 1936. | | ♏ | 7:42am | 5:19pm | 5:57am | 3:37pm |
| 8 | Frankfort chosen as State Capital, 1792. | | | ♐ | 7:43am | 5:19pm | 6:58am | 4:15pm |
| 9 | James Black ends 7-month term as Ky. Governor, 1919. | | New Moon | ♐ | 7:44am | 5:19pm | 7:57am | 5:00pm |
| 10 | Kentucky admitted into Confederacy without secession, 1861. | | | ♑ | 7:45am | 5:19pm | 8:51am | 5:53pm |
| 11 | Isaac Shelby born, 1750. | | | ♑ | 7:46am | 5:19pm | 9:40am | 6:53pm |
| 12 | William Goebel sworn in as governor, 1899: He'd be assassinated six weeks later. | | | ♑ | 7:46am | 5:20pm | 10:21am | 7:57pm |
| 13 | Confederates rout US troops, Cadiz, 1864. | | | ♒ | 7:47am | 5:20pm | 10:57am | 9:02pm |
| 14 | Lawrence County formed, 1821. | | | ♒ | 7:48am | 5:20pm | 11:27am | 10:08pm |
| 15 | Shuck beans & corn bread weather! | | | ♓ | 7:49am | 5:20pm | 11:54am | 11:15pm |
| 16 | Start looking at those garden catalogs in earnest. | | | ♓ | 7:49am | 5:21pm | 12:19pm | - - - - - - |
| 17 | Campbell County formed, 1794. | | First Quarter | ♈ | 7:50am | 5:21pm | 12:44pm | 12:21am |
| 18 | Kentucky General Assembly considers the idea of public education, 1821. | | | ♈ | 7:51am | 5:21pm | 1:09pm | 1:30am |
| 19 | Buy groceries early, get presents wrapped, when all are stressed, you'll be well-napped. | | | ♉ | 7:51am | 5:22pm | 1:39pm | 2:41am |
| 20 | Barren County formed, 1798. | | | ♉ | 7:52am | 5:22pm | 2:13pm | 3:56am |
| 21 | Cut Christmas tree before the Full Moon. | | | ♊ | 7:52am | 5:23pm | 2:56pm | 5:14am |
| 22 | First Day of Winter | | Solstice | ♊ | 7:53am | 5:23pm | 3:49pm | 6:32am |
| 23 | Young Ewing Allison, author, born, Henderson, 1853. | | | ♋ | 7:53am | 5:24pm | 4:53pm | 7:43am |
| 24 | Kit Carson born, Madison County, 1809. | | Full Moon | ♋ | 7:54am | 5:24pm | 6:05pm | 8:45am |
| 25 | Christmas Day | Gen Hylan Lyon (CSA) orders Taylor County courthouse burned, 1864. | | ♌ | 7:54am | 5:25pm | 7:20pm | 9:34am |
| 26 | Kwanzaa begins | Take your Christmas tree down before it becomes a fire hazard! | | ♌ | 7:54am | 5:26pm | 8:33pm | 10:13am |
| 27 | Fish and visitors stink after three days.' - Benj. Franklin | | | ♌ | 7:55am | 5:26pm | 9:41pm | 10:44am |
| 28 | John Y Brown Jr born in Lexington, 1933. | | | ♍ | 7:55am | 5:27pm | 10:46pm | 11:10am |
| 29 | Bourbon County formed, 1798. | | | ♍ | 7:55am | 5:28pm | 11:48pm | 11:34am |
| 30 | Col John Allen born, 1771 (Allen County was named for him.) | | | ♎ | 7:56am | 5:28pm | - - - - - - - | 11:56am |
| 31 | 2008 is going to be great! | | Last Quarter | ♎ | 7:56am | 5:29pm | 12:48am | 12:18pm |

# PEOPLE
# *Jesse Stuart (1906-1984)*

James M. Gifford, Ph.D.

In 2006 we commemorate the 100th birthday of Jesse Stuart, one of America's best-known and best-loved writers. In 1976 (late in his writing career) the editors of Country Gentleman magazine boldly proclaimed Stuart as "America's Most Famous Chronicler of Rural Life." At that time, nearing the end of a five-decade writing career, Stuart had published nearly 60 books including biographies, an autobiography, essays, and juvenile works as well as poetry and fiction.

Stuart was a famous educator who taught and lectured extensively. His teaching experience ranged from the one-room schoolhouse of his youth in Eastern Kentucky to the American University in Cairo, Egypt. "First, last, always," said Stuart, "I am a teacher... Good teaching is forever, and the teacher is immortal."

Stuart distinguished himself in other ways, too. He was a far-sighted conservationist who spent his adult lifetime purchasing the land his family had sharecropped when he was a boy. In 1980 Stuart assigned his land, less the homeplace, to the state of Kentucky and today it exists as the Jesse Stuart Nature Preserve, managed by the Kentucky State Nature Preserves System. Stuart was also an enthusiastic spokesman for his Kentucky homeland.

Late in life, Stuart assigned his literary estate to the Jesse Stuart Foundation, which has grown into a successful regional press and bookseller headquartered in Ashland. For more information, visit jsfbooks.com.

*James M. Gifford, Ph.D., is Director of the Jesse Stuart Foundation.*

**Jesse Stuart composing on his manual typewriter**
*Source: Jesse Stuart Foundation*

*Did you know...?*

"First, last, always," said Jesse Stuart, "I am a teacher.... Good teaching is forever, and the teacher is immortal."

# Notable Kentuckians

**NOTE** — *Any attempt to list remarkable, distinguished or "notable" individuals carries with it an inherent risk that someone will be omitted. The people named here are a brief cross-section of individuals who have achieved noteworthy accomplishments, some obscure and others with international fame. Other notable Kentuckians may be discussed in other sections of this book. Be assured, many more Kentuckians will be featured in future editions of the Kentucky Almanac and at www.kyalmanac.com.*

**Minnie Adkins**, (1934- ), folk artist, Elliott County

**Sophia Kindrick Alcorn**, (1883-1967), invented methods to teach deaf-blind children, Stanford

**Muhammad Ali**, (1942- ), three-time heavyweight champion of the world, Louisville

**George "Eddie" Arcaro**, (1916-1997), jockey, only jockey to win two Triple Crowns, National Museum of Racing and Hall of Fame (1958), Covington

**John James Audubon**, (1785-1851), artist, "Birds of America," Henderson

**Alben W. Barkley**, (1877-1956), U.S. vice president, Graves County

**Thomas Harris Barlow**, (1789-1865), inventor, Nicholas County

**Ned Beatty**, (1937- ), motion picture, television & stage actor, St. Matthews

**Wendell Berry**, (1943- ), writer & activist, Lexington

John James Audubon

**Bernie Bickerstaff**, (1944- ), youngest college coach in the U.S., Benham

**George Barry Bingham, Sr.**, (1906-1988), president of *The Louisville Courier-Journal* & the *Louisville Times*, Louisville

**George Barry Bingham, Jr.**, (1933-2006), editor and publisher of *The Courier-Journal* from 1971 to 1986, Louisville

**Mary Bingham**, (1904-1995), writer, civic leader & philanthropist, Louisville

**Robert Worth Bingham**, (1871-1937), acquired *The Courier-Journal* and *The Louisville Times* in 1918, ambassador to Great Britain, Louisville

**Sallie Bingham**, (1937- ), philanthropist & writer, Louisville

**Paul Garrett Blazer**, (1890-1966), oil company executive, Lexington

**Thomas Fountain Blue**, (1866-1935), pioneer African-American librarian, Louisville

**Daniel Boone**, (1734-1820), hunter, woodsmen & early explorer, settled Boonesborough in 1775

**Rebecca Boone**, (1738-1813), early settler, Boonesborough

**Anita Y. Boswell**, (1920-2002), first national director for Project Head Start, Shelby County

**James Bowie**, (1796-1836), known for his "Bowie" knife, died at the Battle of the Alamo

**John Bradford**, (1749-1830), first Kentucky printer, Kentucky Gazette 1787, Kentucky Almanac 1788, Lexington

**Louis D. Brandeis**, (1856-1941), U.S. Supreme Court justice, Louisville

**Edward T. "Ned" Breathitt, Jr.**, (1924-2003), governor (1963-1967), signed the Ky. Civil Rights Act into law (1966), Hopkinsville

**James Breckinridge**, (1763-1846), principal author of the public-school system of Kentucky, Lexington.

**John Cabell Breckinridge**, (1821-1875), Ky. politician, U.S. vice-president, U.S. Senator and Confederate secretary of war

**Mary Carson Breckinridge**, (1881-1965), founded the Frontier Nursing Services, Southeastern Ky.

John Cabell Breckinridge

**Belle Brezing (Mary Belle Cox)**, (1860-1940), prototype for Belle Watling in "Gone With the Wind," Lexington

**Foster Brooks**, (1912-2001), comic & actor, Louisville

**Charles N. Buck**, (1879-1930 ), author , books portrayed mountain life, Woodford County

Christopher Kit Carson, (1809-1868), scout & pioneer of the West, Madison County

Harry M. Caudill, (1922-1990), historian & non-fiction writer, Whitesburg

Steve Cauthen, (1960- ), youngest jockey to win the Triple Crown on Affirmed in 1978, Covington

Albert B. "Happy" Chandler, (1898-1991), two-time Governor of Kentucky, Corydon

Willa B. Chappell, (1906-1992), first African-American woman to become licensed as a pilot in the U.S., Glasgow

William H. Childress, (1911-1993), pioneer in Ky. Civil Rights, Louisville

George Rogers Clark, (1752-1818), Revolutionary War general & early Kentucky pioneer, Louisville

Thomas D. Clark, (1903-2005), author & Historian Laureate of Kentucky, Lexington

William Clark, (1770-1838), principal military director of the expedition of the Lewis & Clark western exploration, Louisville.

Anna Mac Clarke, (1919-1944), first female black officer to command a white unit, Anderson County

George Rogers Clark

Cassius Marcellus Clay, (1810-1903), emancipationist & ambassador to Russia, Madison County

Henry Clay, (1777-1852), American statesman & farmer, Lexington

Laura Clay, (1849-1941), early feminist, Madison County

Emma C. Clement, (1874-1952), first African-American woman to be named American Mother-of-the-Year (1946)

Earle Chester Clements, (1896-1985), governor, Morganfield

George Clooney, (1961- ), film & television actor, Augusta

Rosemary Clooney, (1928-2002), actor & premier jazz & pop singer, Maysville

John Colgan, (1840-1916), pharmacist, invented chewing gum, Louisville

Irvin S. Cobb, (1876-1944), humorist & author, Paducah

J. Winston Coleman, Jr., (1898-1983), historian & non-fiction writer, Lexington

Martha Layne Collins, (1936-), first woman governor of Kentucky, Shelby County

Bert T. Combs, (1911-1991), governor of Kentucky, Prestonsburg

Earle Bryan Combs, (1899-1976), professional baseball player, New York Yankees (1924-1935), Owsley County

Houston Conwill, (1947-), painter & sculptor, Louisville

John Sherman Cooper, (1901-1991), U.S. Senator & diplomat, Somerset

Elijah Craig, (1743-1808), early Kentucky preacher, invented distillery of bourbon whiskey, Scott County

Joe Creason, (1918-1974), newspaper writer & columnist, Benton

John Sherman Cooper

John Jordan Crittenden, (1786-1863), political leader, governor., Woodford County

Denzel "Denny" Edwin Crum, (1937- ), college basketball coach, University of Louisville

Diane Crump, (1970- ), first female jockey to ride in a Kentucky Derby (1970)

Harriet Cushman, (1833-1893), Union spy in Confederate camps across Kentucky, Louisville

Billy Ray Cyrus, (1961- ), singer and film & TV actor, Flatwoods

Jefferson Davis, (1808-1889), president of Confederate States of America, Fairview

John "Johnny" Christopher Depp III, (1963- ), actor, Owensboro

George Devol, (1912- ), invented first industrial robot, Louisville

Irene Dunne, (1898-1990), actor, Louisville

Frank Duveneck, (1848-1919), painter & etcher, Covington

Bob Edwards, (1947- ), national radio broadcaster, Louisville

Betty Lou Evans, (1942- ), golfer & coach, inducted in National Golf Coaches Hall of Fame , Lexington

William Stamps Farish III, (1939- ), business magnate & horseman, Woodford County

Charles P. Farnsley, (1907-1990), former state & U.S. congressman, mayor of Louisville (1948-53)

Rev. John G. Fee, (1816-1901), noted abolitionist, founder of Berea College, Berea

John Filson, (1753-1788), Kentucky surveyor & historian, Louisville

Marvin Finn, (1917- ), internationally-known urban folk artist, Louisville

John Fitch, (1743-1798), invented first American steam boat (1786), Nelson County

Mary Elliott Flanery, (1867-1933), first woman to serve in a southern state legislature, Carter County

Larry Flynt, (1942- ), founder of Hustler magazine, Sal-yersville

Wendell Hampton Ford, (1924- ), longest-serving U.S. senator in Kentucky history, Owensboro

John Fox Jr., (1862-1919), novelist, "Little Shepherd of Kingdom Come," Bourbon County

Wendell Ford

**Fontaine Talbot Fox, Jr.**, (1884-1964), nationally syndicated cartoonist, "Toonerville Folks," Louisville

**Ralph Gabbard**, (1945-1996), visionary television newsman & former president of WKYT-TV

**John Ryan Gaines**, (1928- ), horseman, philanthropist, and art collector, Lexington

**Phyllis George**, (1949- ), former Miss America, former First Lady of Kentucky, Lexington

**Jack "Goose" Givens**, (1956- ), first African American All-American in Ky., Lexington

**Sue Grafton**, (1940- ), author of the Kinsey Milhone mystery series, Louisville

**David W. Griffith**, (1880-1948), pioneer movie director & producer, Oldham County

**A.B. Guthrie**, (1901-1991), journalist & novelist, Lexington

**Cliff Hagan**, (1931- ), UK basketball player and athletic director, Hall of Famer, distinguished pro career

**Joe B. Hall**, (1928- ), head UK basketball coach 1972-1985, Cynthiana

**Lionel Hampton**, (1908-2002), jazz musician, composer, Louisville

**Arthur B. Hancock III**, (1943- ), musician & breeder of three Kentucky Derby Winners, Bourbon County

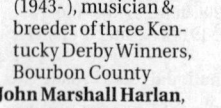

Joe B. Hall

**John Marshall Harlan**, (1833-1911), U.S. Supreme Court Justice, Boyle County

**Benjamin Harrison**, (1745-1808), soldier & pioneer, Cynthiana

**Joel Tanner Hart**, (1810-1877), sculptor, Clark County

**Isaac S. Hathaway**, (1872-1967), internationally known sculptor, first African American to design a U.S. coin, Lexington

**James Morrison Heady**, (1829-1915), known as the "Blind Bard" of Kentucky, Spencer County

**Carl "Kingfish" Helm**, (1926-2001), played guard for the Harlem Globetrotters, Horse Cave

**Richard Henderson**, (1735-1785), American colonizer in Kentucky

**Heather French Henry**, (1975- ), Miss America 2000, lobbyist for veterans, Maysville

**Josiah Henson**, (1789-1883), escaped to Canada & returned to lead others to freedom, believed to be Uncle Tom in Harriet Beecher Stowe's book, "Uncle Tom's Cabin," Owensboro

**John A. "Bud" Hillerich**, (1866-1946), inventor (Louisville Slugger baseball bat), Louisville

**Duncan Hines**, (1880-1959), nationally known food critic, Bowling Green

**Paul "Golden Boy" Hornung**, (1935- ), football player, All-American, Notre Dame, Louisville

**Thomas Morgan Hunt**, (1866-1945), biologist, Nobel Prize winner

**Margaret Ingels**, (1892-1971), first U.S. woman to obtain a mechanical engineering degree, Bourbon County

**Lyman T. Johnson**, (1906-1997), school teacher, led non-violent picketing against racial discrimination, Louisville

**Casey Jones (John Luther Jones)**, (1864-1900), heroic locomotive engineer, Fulton County

**Matthew Harris Jouett**, (1788-1827), portrait artist, Mercer County

**Ashley Judd**, (1968- ), actor & UK graduate, enthusiastic UK basketball fan, Ashland

**Naomi Judd (Diane Ellen Judd)**, (1946- ), singer & actor, Ashland

**Wynonna Judd (Christina Ciminella)**, (1964- ), singer & actor, Ashland

**May Street Kidd**, (1909-1999), businesswoman & Kentucky state representative, Louisville

Naomi Judd

**Arthur Krock**, (1886-1974), Pulitzer Prize winning journalist & author, Glasgow

**Cawood Ledford**, (1926-2001), Hall of Fame sportscaster, "voice" of the UK Wildcats, Harlan County

**Abraham Lincoln**, (1809-1865), 12th U.S. president, Hodgenville

**Mary Todd Lincoln**, (1818-1882), wife of Abraham Lincoln and First Lady,

Cawood Ledford

Mary Todd Lincoln

Lexington

**Brian Littrell**, (1975- ), singer & member of Back Street Boys, Lexington

**Alice Lloyd**, (1876-1962), social reformer, helped establish what is now Alice Lloyd College, Knott County

**Bernadette Locke**, (1958- ), first woman & first African American assistant coach in Division I Men's NCAA basketball, Lexington

**Loretta Lynn**, (1935- ), country songwriter & singer, Butcher Hollow

**John E. Madden**, (1856-1929), horseman, breeder of six Kentucky Derby winners, Fayette County

**Victor Mature**, (1915-1999), actor & producer, Louisville

**Dr. Ephraim McDowell**, (1771-1830), pioneer surgeon, Danville

**Mary T. Meagher**, (1964- ), winner of three gold medals at 1984 Olympic Games, Louisville

**Thomas Merton**, (1915-1968), Trappist monk & writer, Nelson County

**Albert E. Meyzeek**, (1862-1963), African-American educator, civil rights leader, Louisville

Dr. Ephraim McDowell

**Marion Miley**, (1914-1941), internationally-known woman golfer, Lexington

**Lucy Dupey Montz**, (1842-1922), Kentucky's first woman dentist, Warsaw

**David Mogan**, (1952- ), received Lifetime Achievement Award for contributions to Ky. historic preservation (2006), Lexington

**Garrett Morgan**, (1877-1963), African-American, invented gas masks used in WWI, Paris

**Thomas Hunt Morgan**, (1866-1945), Nobel Prize winner 1933 in Physiology or Medicine, Lexington

**Lois Morris**, (1919-1989), founder of National Black Women for Political Action, Louisville

**Thruston Ballard Morton**, (1907-1982), U.S. congressman & Assist. Secretary of State, Louisville

**Tori Murden-McClure**, (1963- ), first woman & first American to row solo across the Atlantic and first woman & first American to ski to the South Pole, Louisville

**Isaac Murphy**, (1861-1896), first jockey to win three Kentucky Derbies, Fayette County

**Carry A. Nation**, (1846-1911), temperance crusader known as "the lady with a hatchet," Garrard County

**Patricia Neal**, (1926- ), Oscar-winning actress, Whitley County

**John Jacob Niles**, (1892-1980), author, composer & balladeer, Louisville

**Warren Oates**, (1928-1982), actor, Louisville

**Rude Osolnik**, (1915-2001), father of contemporary wood turning, Berea.

**Greg Page**, (1958- ), heavyweight boxing champion (1984), record: 58-17-1 with 48 knockouts, Louisville

**Tom Payne**, (1950- ), first African American player to sign with UK, Louisville

**John Ed Pearce**, (1917-2006), Pulitzer Prize winner, writer & columnist for *The Courier-Journal*, Louisville

**Katherine G. Peden**, (1926-2006), first woman appointed Ky. Commissioner of Commerce, Hopkinsville

**Carl Perkins**, (1912-1984), U.S. congressman & teacher, Hindman

**Rick Pitino**, (1952- ), head basketball coach, University of Louisville

**Ersa Hines Poston**, (1921- ), first African-American to hold a presidential cabinet position

**Theodore R.A.M. Poston**, (1906-1974), first African-American reporter for New York Post, Hopkinsville

**Georgia Davis Powers**, (1923- ), first female African-American state

Rick Pitino

Georgia Powers

senator in Ky. (1968)

**William J. Powell, Sr.**, (1899-1942), pilot, lifetime goal was to encourage African-Americans to become pilots, Henderson

**Ed Prichard**, (1915-1984), chairman, Prichard Committee for Academic Excellence, Maysville

**Stanley Reed**, (1884-1980), justice of the U.S. Supreme Court, Maysville

**Kevin Richardson**, (1970- ), singer & member of Back Street Boys, Irvine

**Sanford Thomas Roach**, (1916- ), coach of Dunbar High School, helped pave way for black athletes, Lexington

**Adolph Rupp**, (1901-1977), UK basketball coach, won 875 games in 41 years of coaching, won four NCAA championships, Lexington

**Harvey C. Russell, Jr.**, (1919-1998), first African-American commissioned officer in the Coast Guard WWII, Louisville

Kevin Richardson

**Wiley B. Rutledge**, (1894-1949), U.S. Supreme Court justice, Cloverport

**Col. Harland Sanders**, (1890-1980), restaurateur & founder of Kentucky Fried Chicken, Corbin

**Annie L. Sandusky**, (1900-1976), pioneer in social work, Louisville

**Diane Sawyer**, (1945- ), broadcast journalist, Glasgow

**Gideon Shryock**, (1802-1888), architect, designed the Old State Capitol (Greek Revival style), Lexington

**Moneta Sleet**, Jr., (1926-1996), first African American to win the Pulitzer Prize for photography, Owensboro

Diane Sawyer

**Lucy Harth Smith**, (1844-1955), African-American education pioneer, civil rights advocate, Lexington

**Tubby Smith**, (1951- ), first African American basketball coach at UK, Lexington

**Gene Snyder**, (1928- ), state judge 1957-61, U.S. Representative, Louisville

**Mother Catherine Spalding**, (1793-1858), missionary, founder of Spalding University, Louisville

**Jane M. Spaulding**, ( -1967), first African-American female assistant secretary in the cabinet of a U.S. president

**Tubby Smith**

**James Breckinridge Speed**, (1844-1912), capitalist & philanthropist, Louisville

**George Speri Sperti**, (1900-1991), scientist & inventor (radiation lamp for rheumatism), Covington

**Elvis Jacob Stahr**, Jr., (1916-1998), secy. of U.S. Army & pres. of the National Audubon Society, Hickman

**Frank Leslie Stanley, Sr.**, publisher of the *Louisville Defender*, Louisville

**Adlai Ewing Stevenson**, (1900-1965) vice-president of the United States, Christian County

**Thelma Stovall**, (1919-1994), elected as Kentucky's first female lieutenant governor (1975), Munfordville

**Jesse Stuart**, (1907-1984), teacher & writer, Greenup County

**Nathan B. Stubblefield**, (1860-1928), inventor of the radio (wireless telephony), Murray

**John Orley Allen Tate**, (1899-1979), poet & critic, Winchester

**Jesse Stuart**

**Zachary Taylor**, (1784-1850), 12th president of the U.S. (1849-1850) died in office July 9, 1850, Jefferson Co.

**Byron Temple**, (1935-2002), renowned ceramic artist, Louisville.

**Richard Thomas**, (1951- ), actor, Paintsville

**Hunter S. Thompson**, (1937-2005), "Gonzo" journalist & writer, Louisville

**John T. Thompson**, (1860-1940), invented the Tommygun machine gun, Newport

**Zachary Taylor**

**Thomas Todd**, (1765-1826), Associate justice of the U.S. Supreme Court (1807-1826), Frankfort

**Lily Tomlin**, (1939- ), actress & comedienne, Paducah

**Robert Trimble**, (1776 -1828), Associate Justice of the U.S.Supreme Court, Paris

**Luska J. Twyman**, (1913-1988), first African-American elected to a full term as mayor of a Kentucky city, Glasgow

**Wes Unseld**, (1946- ), played 13 years with the Baltimore Bullets, NBA's seventh all-time leading rebounder, Louisville

**Frederick M. Vinson**, (1890-1953), chief justice of the U.S. Supreme Court (1946-1953), Louisa

**Dr. Thomas Walker**, (1715-1794), physician & surveyor, led an exploratory party to Ky. in 1750

**Frederick M. Vinson**

**Robert Penn Warren**, (1905-1989), poet & writer, Guthrie

**Henry Watterson**, (1840-1921), founded *The Louisville Courier-Journal* in 1868, won Pulitzer Prize in 1918, Louisville

**Davey L. Whitney**, (1930- ), ranked among the top six active coaches, Midway

**Virginia "Jenny" Wiley**, (1760-1831), heroic pioneer mother, buried in Johnson County

**Clarence "Cave" Wilson, Sr.**, (1926-1996), basketball player for Harlem Globetrotters, Horse Cave

**George C. Wolfe**, (1954- ), African-American writer, Broadway producer & director, Frankfort

**Wilson Watkins Wyatt, Sr.**, (1905-1996), former mayor of Louisville, Louisville

**Dwight Yoakam**, (1956- ), country singer, Pikeville

**Col. Charles D. Young**, (1864-1922), highest ranking African-American in WWI, Mays Lick

**Eddie L. Young**, (1923- ), one of the first African-American pilots to fly in Korea and Vietnam, Jenkins.

**Whitney M. Young**, Jr., (1921-1971), executive director of the National Urban League, Shelby County

**William T. Young**, (1918-2004), businessman, horseman, community leader & philanthropist, Lexington

**Whitney M. Young, Jr.**

*Photos:*
*Kentucky Historical Society, Kentucky Department for Libraries & Archives, Sid Webb, Lexington Herald-Leader, and Chandler Foundation*

## PEOPLE

# *They predicted their own deaths*

### Keven McQueen

#### Excerpt from
#### "Kentucky Book of the Dead"

In addition to his many other achievements, Mark Twain accurately predicted his own death. Halley's Comet soared overhead when he was born in 1835, and he always believed his life would end when the comet came back. Twain died in 1910 as the comet reappeared after its allotted seventy-five year absence. A pretty neat trick, one might think, but many people have predicted their own demise with uncanny accuracy. Some have even been Kentuckians.

In March 1880 Mr. Tillman Pierce died at his home on Meeting Creek, Hardin County, after a long illness. His sorrowing family had his body washed, clothed and placed in a casket. Much to their surprise and discomfiture, Pierce suddenly sat up in his casket and announced that he had visited Heaven and Hell while temporarily dead. After describing these places, specifically their climates, he said that he would die again in one day and then would rise again three days afterward; after this final curtain call, he said, he would die and stay dead. Pierce did die at the end of the day, but whether he revived three days later, no one can say. Let's hope he did not, for his spooked family quickly had him buried "fathoms deep." If he did rise again from the dead, a very unpleasant surprise awaited him.

A case reminiscent of Pierce's occurred when Rinda Richie of Hindman, Knott County, died in September 1896. Or at least she put on a good show. After she was dressed in her burial clothes and coffined, Dr. J.T. Walker noticed signs of life and managed to revive her. The fact that she had just missed becoming another victim of premature burial seemed not to trouble her; to the contrary, she told everyone that she had visited Heaven. She further astonished friends and family by telling them that she would die for good in a month. Mrs. Richie spent that month in continu-ous prayer, and true to her word she passed away on October 16.

Andrew Vaughn, a farmer, Mexican War veteran and original California Forty-Niner lived in Harrodsburg, where he was a much-beloved local character. He alarmed many friends by accurately predicting weeks in advance that he would "answer death's bugle call" on August 27, 1895.

In December 1896, the sister of Rockcastle County's Issac Bullen died. He remarked, "One week from today I will be buried." He was right. Bullen obviously was a fellow who liked to be prepared, for he had had his burial clothes and casket made to order twenty-five years before.

Thomas Marshall, originally from Louisville, was at work in a St. Louis poolroom on April 30, 1897, and discussing a Memphis horse race with his friends. Marshall was especially excited by a contestant named Algol, stating: "I'd stake my life on that horse." He even went so far as to place a bet that Algol would finish first. An hour later the news came over the wire that the horse had lost. Marshall fell unconscious at his desk and died later that night. I suppose that means he did not have to pay his wager.

The most distinguished Kentuckian ever to amaze his fellows by revealing his own death date was former Governor Luke P. Blackburn. On September 9, 1887, as he lay on his deathbed, Blackburn overheard a doctor say that he could not live another hour. Blackburn announced: "I will only be with you five days; tell all my relatives and friends." An account in the Atlanta Constitution has the dying man making an even more precise prediction: "I will die on September 14 at 2:30 p.m." Blackburn did die on September 14 at 2:30 p.m. Perhaps Blackburn, himself a physician, had been able to predict his demise with uncanny accuracy by observing his own symptoms.

# PEOPLE

# *International Book Project*

Lynda Jeffries

The International Book Project was founded in 1966 by Mrs. Harriet Van Meter of Lexington. As an example of the ripple effect that can be made by one person, IBP has a unique history of having supplied millions of books worldwide since its beginnings in the basement of Mrs. Van Meter's home. IBP distributes books for institutional use to virtually any location in the world that has access to mail. Many of the requests IBP receives are funded by donors who—by sending an initial mailbag of books—initiate a life-long inter-cultural dialogue. The resulting global friendship that grows between donors and institutions has been the centerpiece of the International Book Project's mission since its inception.

**1966 40 years 2006**
**INTERNATIONAL BOOK PROJECT, INC.**

## How IBP Began

Harriet Drury Van Meter was a life-long activist for literacy in her home state and abroad. In 1966 after a trip to India where she was deeply impressed by the dedication to education in a country where books were expensive and difficult to obtain, she founded the IBP. Her goal was to match American donors of books with schools and libraries in developing countries and to encourage person-to-person international friendships between donors and recipients.

IBP has grown over the years into a federally-registered 501(c)(3) not-for-profit organization that has shipped more than five million books to institutions in 100 countries from Afghanistan to Zambia, including underserved communities within the U.S. Now operating out of a modest warehouse, IBP ships both sea containers of over 20,000 books to large institutions and individually-crafted mailbags, comprised of a few dozen books, to smaller schools, orphanages and libraries. By matching American book donors with recipients abroad, IBP encourages global dialogue and intercultural friendships that are the building blocks for a peaceful tomorrow.

While the IBP is an enduring testament to Mrs. Van Meter's philanthropic legacy, her activism also won recognition during her lifetime. In 1986 in honor of her tireless support of literacy, Mrs. Van Meter was a finalist for the Nobel Peace Prize and in 1989 she was awarded the Kiwanis International World Service Medal.

In 1992 the International Book Project was one of 20 organizations chosen as a Partner for Peace for the services it provides to Peace Corps programming.

**Harriet Drury Van Meter**
*Source: International Book Project*

KENTUCKY GROSS STATE PRODUCT (GSP), BY COMPONENT: 1997-2004 (In Millions of Dollars)

| INDUSTRY | 1997 | 1998 | 1999 | 2000 | 2001 | 2002 | 2003 | 2004 | % CHANGE 1997-2004 |
|---|---|---|---|---|---|---|---|---|---|
| Total Gross State Product | 105,725 | 108,813 | 113,480 | 111,900 | 115,113 | 120,726 | 125,832 | 133,003 | 0.258 |
| Private industries | 91,232 | 94,081 | 98,170 | 96,310 | 98,991 | 103,514 | 107,647 | 113,786 | 0.247 |
| Agriculture forestry fishing and hunting | 2,080 | 1,958 | 1,724 | 2,274 | 1,937 | 1,508 | 1,812 | 2,233 | 0.074 |
| Crop and animal production (Farms) | 1,768 | 1,612 | 1,338 | 1,834 | 1,529 | 1,130 | 1,436 | 1,798 | 0.017 |
| Mining | 2,412 | 2,423 | 2,386 | 2,257 | 2,447 | 2,526 | 2,493 | 2,842 | 0.178 |
| Mining except oil & gas | 2,293 | 2,320 | 2,291 | 2,126 | 2,273 | 2,335 | 2,221 | 2,494 | 0.088 |
| Utilities | 1,858 | 1,864 | 1,855 | 1,794 | 1,928 | 1,896 | 1,999 | 2,131 | 0.147 |
| Construction | 4,291 | 4,605 | 4,898 | 5,088 | 5,318 | 5,268 | 5,455 | 5,740 | 0.338 |
| Manufacturing | 29,378 | 28,974 | 29,548 | 24,163 | 23,473 | 24,810 | 26,027 | 26,275 | -0.106 |
| Durable goods | 17,607 | 17,236 | 18,043 | 14,209 | 13,807 | 14,343 | 15,268 | 15,635 | -0.112 |
| Primary metal manufacturing | 1,454 | 1,499 | 1,411 | 1,303 | 1,255 | 1,926 | 2,200 | 2,113 | 0.453 |
| Fabricated metal product manufacturing | 1,378 | 1,416 | 1,569 | 1,761 | 1,538 | 1,635 | 1,543 | 1,539 | 0.117 |
| Machinery manufacturing | 1,881 | 1,843 | 1,529 | 1,335 | 1,279 | 1,153 | 1,155 | 1,242 | -0.340 |
| Electrical equipment and appliance manufacturing | 1,376 | 1,525 | 1,373 | 1,350 | 1,204 | 1,350 | 1,247 | 1,068 | -0.224 |
| Motor vehicle body trailer & parts manufacturing | 7,835 | 8,279 | 9,381 | 5,513 | 5,345 | 4,992 | 6,126 | 6,258 | -0.201 |
| Other transportation equipment manufacturing | 1,348 | 292 | 315 | 371 | 370 | 230 | 238 | 275 | -0.796 |
| Nondurable goods | 11,772 | 11,738 | 11,505 | 9,954 | 9,666 | 10,466 | 10,759 | 10,640 | -0.096 |
| Food product manufacturing | 5,515 | 5,343 | 5,307 | 3,893 | 3,862 | 4,098 | 4,245 | 4,307 | -0.219 |
| Chemical manufacturing | 1,954 | 2,030 | 2,127 | 1,738 | 1,549 | 1,733 | 2,047 | 1,726 | -0.117 |
| Plastics and rubber products manufacturing | 1,128 | 1,217 | 1,239 | 1,200 | 1,221 | 1,434 | 1,488 | 1,568 | 0.390 |
| Wholesale trade | 5,715 | 6,114 | 6,536 | 6,779 | 7,023 | 7,332 | 7,445 | 8,303 | 0.453 |
| Retail trade | 7,305 | 7,582 | 7,888 | 8,095 | 8,222 | 8,645 | 9,037 | 9,443 | 0.293 |
| Transportation and warehousing excluding Postal Service | 4,219 | 4,782 | 5,187 | 5,394 | 5,424 | 5,651 | 5,985 | 6,317 | 0.497 |
| Truck transportation | 1,224 | 1,369 | 1,451 | 1,435 | 1,436 | 1,506 | 1,549 | 1,643 | 0.342 |
| Other transportation and support activities | 1,318 | 1,619 | 1,802 | 1,960 | 2,068 | 2,058 | 2,170 | 2,355 | 0.787 |
| Information | 2,294 | 2,436 | 2,524 | 2,679 | 2,978 | 3,178 | 3,201 | 3,500 | 0.526 |
| Broadcasting and telecommunications | 1,541 | 1,667 | 1,684 | 1,879 | 2,060 | 2,152 | 2,155 | 2,410 | 0.564 |
| Finance and insurance | 3,978 | 4,084 | 4,228 | 4,688 | 5,541 | 5,871 | 6,065 | 6,535 | 0.643 |
| Federal Reserve banks credit intermediation and related services | 2,159 | 2,251 | 2,380 | 2,414 | 2,825 | 3,143 | 3,255 | 3,409 | 0.579 |
| Insurance carriers and related activities | 1,355 | 1,318 | 1,314 | 1,672 | 2,031 | 2,094 | 2,221 | 2,444 | 0.804 |
| Real estate rental and leasing | 8,408 | 8,742 | 9,460 | 10,022 | 10,697 | 11,486 | 11,547 | 12,044 | 0.432 |
| Professional and technical services | 3,733 | 3,998 | 4,344 | 4,753 | 4,980 | 4,884 | 4,767 | 5,082 | 0.361 |
| Management of companies and enterprises | 1,211 | 1,273 | 1,349 | 1,449 | 1,185 | 1,256 | 1,324 | 1,555 | 0.284 |
| Administrative and waste services | 1,856 | 2,012 | 2,214 | 2,358 | 2,361 | 2,572 | 2,728 | 2,989 | 0.610 |
| Educational services | 416 | 450 | 493 | 550 | 596 | 633 | 680 | 734 | 0.764 |
| Health care and social assistance | 6,807 | 7,111 | 7,656 | 7,869 | 8,642 | 9,347 | 9,992 | 10,621 | 0.560 |
| Arts entertainment and recreation | 516 | 543 | 595 | 634 | 657 | 745 | 805 | 839 | 0.626 |
| Accommodation and food services | 2,590 | 2,793 | 2,842 | 2,923 | 2,998 | 3,206 | 3,331 | 3,530 | 0.363 |
| Government | 14,492 | 14,732 | 15,310 | 15,591 | 16,123 | 17,212 | 18,185 | 19,217 | 0.326 |
| Federal civilian | 2,865 | 2,794 | 2,727 | 2,785 | 2,629 | 3,064 | 3,179 | 3,429 | 0.197 |
| Federal military | 2,010 | 2,033 | 2,142 | 2,314 | 2,428 | 2,582 | 2,962 | 3,155 | 0.570 |
| State and local | 9,617 | 9,905 | 10,441 | 10,492 | 11,066 | 11,566 | 12,044 | 12,633 | 0.314 |

Note: Sub-categories with less than $1 billion were not included in this chart.
Source: U.S. Department of Commerce

From the beginning, Kentucky was all about business. Dr. Thomas Walker, a Virginia physician, led the first organized English expedition into Kentucky in 1750. Dr. Walker didn't come here for his health. He was also a businessman — a land speculator — and he was looking for territory suitable for settlement.

# Business & Economy

Charles Thompson

**Bagdad Roller Mill**
*Photo: Sid Webb*

After months of searching, Walker went home disappointed. He and his party had never gotten beyond the heavily forested hills of eastern Kentucky — good for hunting, Walker noted in his journal, but not for farming.

A more famous businessman arrived by way of North Carolina in 1769. Daniel Boone hunted for deerskins and furs he could sell for a profit back home. He soon learned that business is risky no matter where you are. Kentucky's Native Americans, who had their own centuries-long tradition of doing business with their neighbors, didn't appreciate trespassers. The Shawnee relieved Boone of a small fortune in pelts that he had spent months collecting, and warned him not to come back.

**Mack (L) & Phil Weisenberger in front of Weisenberger Mills**
*Photo: Sid Webb*

Boone and many others ignored that warning. As settlers streamed into Kentucky, entrepreneurs founded businesses to serve them; from banks and general stores to well digging services, taverns, ferries, and even a saltpeter business run by a former slave called Free Frank.

A remarkable number of old Kentucky businesses have survived to the twenty-first century. While there are hardly any from the early pioneer days, there are quite a few from the first half of the nineteenth century, and hundreds that date from 1850 to 1900. About three hundred of these survivors have registered with the Kentucky Historical Society's Centennial Business Program. Most are small businesses which, as historian James C. Klotter has written, "are little known but affect so many people every day. They are the human side of economic history."

How does a business survive for a century, or even two centuries? "Bend over backward and bite your tongue 20 times to satisfy a customer," said Elmore Tonini, third generation president of Tonini Church Supply in Louisville, founded in 1886. Tonini's explanation of his company's longevity is, in so many words, the same one nearly every owner of a century-old business ultimately falls back on. Service, to customers and commu-

nities, is truly the bottom line. It can take many forms, from the local bank that uses its financial power to nurture a community's well being to the pharmacist who's on call to fill a prescription any time, night or day.

"I think the reason we're here today is because we continue to do the same things we were doing a hundred years ago, and that is personal customer service," said Willie D. Patton of Grayson, owner of Horton Bros. and Brown Pharmacy (founded 1889). "We know or soon become acquainted with everyone that comes in our store. I think the people of Grayson have rewarded us for that."

Banks are the biggest category of century-old businesses in Kentucky. Retail establishments and newspapers are close behind. Then come service providers – funeral homes and monument companies are big. Kentucky companies make everything from salsa to shoelaces to hair straighteners.

All these businesses have played a vital role in the commonwealth's history, both as providers of indispensable services and products and as beacons of continuity in an ever changing commercial and cultural landscape. As Thomas D. Clark, the late historian laureate of Kentucky, wrote: "These survivors have established rock-solid

**William Adair January & Wood Co. Maysville, KY**
*Photo: Sid Webb*

assets of integrity, personal service, patron loyalties, and a dedication to the sense of community. Collectively, the centennial businesses have reached far beyond the doorways of their stores and shops to knit a rich Kentucky heritage into a meaningful tradition and history of time and place."

**A list of century-old Kentucky businesses can be found at kyhumanities.org.

## BUSINESS & ECONOMY

# *Pioneer Industries*

Dr. Thomas J. Kiffmeyer

Dr. Gary O'Dell

Kentucky's earliest industries were home-based production of tools and clothing for self-sufficient family farms. Other important early industries included salt mining, iron mining and smelting, hemp and rope production, and niter mining and gunpowder production.

Because it served as a preservative, long hunters and settlers highly valued salt and the production of this mineral represented one the state's first industries. Existing under the state's sandstone formations, salt was deposited in the soils as natural springs leached it from the rock. These deposits, known as "licks" because wild game licked the salt from the ground—became the sites of Kentucky salt works. After pioneer-producers excavated a salt spring, they dug a long trench, the longest was about three miles, which served as a "furnace." Salt makers placed large kettles, some of which held over twenty gallons, over a fire built in the furnace to evaporate the water and leave the salt.

Many salt producers obtained their kettles from yet another of Kentucky's pioneer industries—iron. In 1791 Jacob Myers constructed what probably was Kentucky's first iron furnace near what is now Owingsville, in Bath County. Iron makers constructed stone furnaces forty feet high in which they smelted limestone and ore with charcoal to produce iron. While some furnaces cast finished items including pots and stoves, others simply produced wrought iron for local blacksmiths.

Due to the number of interdependent operations, from woodcutters and miners to highly skilled furnace masters, the larger operations, such as the Aetna Furnace, built in 1816 in Hart County, utilized the labor of hundreds of people, both slave and free. These iron plantations, which included company houses, stores, and schools represented an interesting juxtaposition of antebellum labor systems with the company town system most commonly associated with the modern coal mining industry. The height of Kentucky's

iron industry was in the 1830s and 1840s, when the state ranked third in production behind Pennsylvania and New York. Kentucky's iron industry fell to seventh in the nation in 1870 and all but ceased by 1910.

Evidence indicates that niter mining at Saltpeter

**Carpenter Shop**
**Fort Boonesborough**
*Photo: Sid Webb*

Cave in Carter County became a full-time operation during the War of 1812.

At Great Saltpeter Cave in Rockcastle County and at Mammoth Cave, the works essentially became large saltpeter factories that employed hundreds of laborers, free and slave, and utilized more advanced processing technology. These mines ran twenty-fours hours a day all year at the height of their operations. Moreover, saltpeter mining intensified in the Red River Gorge rockshelters during the war. This increase in niter production gave rise to what was the last, though not least of Kentucky's pioneer industries, gunpowder manufacturing.

Gunpowder, a combination of saltpeter, charcoal and sulfur, production began in Lexington as early as 1793, when Richard Foley advertised gunpowder for sale at his South Elkhorn mill. During the War of 1812 powder mills such as those owned by the Trotter family of Lexington became big business.

# Products manufactured in Kentucky (1810)

| ITEM | MEASURE[2] | US RANK[3] | % US TOTAL[3] |
|---|---|---|---|
| Hemp[1] | 5,755 tons | 1 | 99.9 |
| Hemp bagging | 453,750 yards | 1 | 98.0 |
| Saltpeter[1] | 201,937 lbs | 1 | 47.0 |
| Salt | 324,870 bushels | 2 | 26.2 |
| Maple sugar[1] | 2,471,647 lbs | 2 | 25.6 |
| Blended & unnamed cloths | 4,685,385 yards | 1 | 21.2 |
| Hemp rope | 1,991.5 tons | 2 | 18.4 |
| Distilleries | 2,000 establishments | 3 | 14.0 |
| Gunpowder | 115,716 lbs | 6 | 8.3 |
| Looms for cotton or wool | 23,559 looms | 4 | 7.2 |
| Tanneries | 267 establishments | 5 | 6.2 |
| Cotton manufacturing | 15 establishments | 6 | 5.6 |
| Iron furnaces | 4 furnaces | 9 | 2.6 |
| Paper | 6,200 reams | 8 | 1.5 |
| Spindles | 1,656 spindles | 12 | 1.3 |
| Nails | 196,000 lbs | 11 | 1.2 |
| Carding machines | 75,100 lbs carded | 11 | 1.0 |
| Fulling mills | 53,058 yards fulled | 8 | 1.0 |
| Flaxseed oil | 4,605 gallons | 11 | < 1.0 |
| Bar iron | 52.5 tons | 12 | < 1.0 |

[1] The census noted that these products might not be considered as manufactured and listed them separately from the other products. Notable product groupings NOT shown as manufactured in Kentucky were most metals and metal products, finished wood products (wagons, barrels, furniture, etc.), ceramics and glassware, and chemical products such as paints and dyes.

[2] Measures chosen for this table are those for which data was most complete or best represented production. For these reasons value of production was not used as an indicator for individual products. Value of total US manufacturing production reported as $153,545,397, of which Kentucky's share was $5,153,863 or 3.4 percent.

[3] US ranking and percent of total national production based on data reported for 26 states and territories. Leading manufacturing states, in order according to value of production, were Pennsylvania, New York, Massachusetts, and Virginia.

Source: Coxe, Tench. 1814. A statement of the arts & manufactures of the United States for the year 1810. Philadelphia. Available online at http://www2.census.gov/prod2/decennial/documents/1810v2-01.pdf. The 1810 manufacturers census, the first such, was quite controversial at the time; representatives of several states claimed that production had been greatly underreported. The marshal for Kentucky noted, in particular, that iron production in the state was far greater than reported. This census should therefore be taken as indicative rather than definitive of manufacturing production.

# BUSINESS & ECONOMY
# *Economic Development*

Marvin E. Strong, Jr.

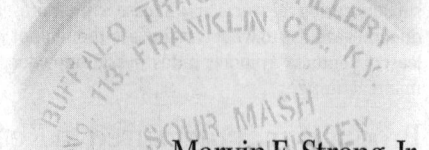

Imagine you're shopping for a new house. You find one that's appealing, you attend a showing, and you and your agent start speaking with the seller and his or her agent. Negotiations begin, it's all running smoothly, and just as you write up your offer, you notice that the agent and the seller have both walked away, to be replaced by two other people you've never met.

You'd get an uneasy feeling, wouldn't you? You

**Toyota plant assembly line, Georgetown**
*Source: Lexington Herald-Leader*

might go ahead with the negotiations, or the sudden change might unnerve you enough to make you walk away from the deal.

This instability existed in the state's economic development efforts prior to 1992, which didn't always result in the best outcome for Kentucky's economy. The art of economic development lies in building relationships. A corporate CEO doesn't wake up one morning and decide, "Hey, I think I'll build my new facility in Kentucky." These things take time, a great deal of study, and a carefully cultivated sense of trust.

Recognizing the value of continuity, the General

Assembly passed House Bill 89 in 1992, creating the Kentucky Economic Development Partnership Board.

The 13-member Board, chaired by the governor, is a true public-private partnership. In addition to the governor, voting members include the secretaries of the state's Finance & Administration Cabinet and Environmental and Public Protection Cabinet, plus eight private-sector members serving staggered terms and representing a variety of business sectors from across Kentucky. The secretaries of the Commerce and Economic Development cabinets serve as non-voting members. This dual structure allows the Board to stay mindful of its duties to the commonwealth while maintaining a business-like approach in its dealings with existing and prospective Kentucky companies.

Under the statute, the Board serves as the governing body of the Cabinet for Economic Development. Not only does it have the authority to hire and fire the Cabinet secretary, it also oversees such functions as strategic planning, finance, business assistance, marketing and promotion, community development, workforce development and innovation – all of which are designed to make it easier for business to prosper here.

And business is indeed prospering in Kentucky. For the period from July 1, 1992, to July 31, 2006, investment announcements in Kentucky's manufacturing and supportive-service sectors totaled more than $34.5 billion. During that period, companies in those sectors made 8,063 announcements of either new locations or expansions of operations in Kentucky, creating 278,800 jobs at full employment.

From 1992-2005, Kentucky's average unemployment rate fell in line with the national average to 5.5 percent, significantly improving from

HH Gregg store
Hamburg Pavillion
Lexington, KY
*Source: Lexington
Herald-Leader*

the state's 8.1 percent average unemployment rate from 1978-1991. Additionally, Kentucky's rank among the 50 states jumped from 41st in 1991 to 33rd in 2004 in average annual wage.

For more than 20 years now, foreign investment

Mining class at the Hager Hill campus
of Big Sandy Community and Technical College
*Source: Lexington Herald-Leader*

has grown increasingly vital to Kentucky's economy. This trend began in a big way in the mid-1980s when Toyota decided to open its manufacturing plant in Georgetown—the company's largest plant outside Japan—and it continues today. In all, foreign companies made 1,014 announcements of new locations or expansions from July 1, 1992, to July 31, 2006. These announcements represented investments of more than $9.4 billion and 46,873 new employees.

While foreign direct investment continues to play a crucial role in the state's economy, Kentucky has also become one of the nation's most aggressive exporters. Over the past decade, Kentucky has ranked sixth in export growth—quite a feat for a state that's not on a coast or an international border. Between 1998 and 2005, exports grew 83.9 percent to nearly $15 billion, providing a growth rate more than twice that of the nation's at 32.9 percent. That figure puts Kentucky seventh in

per capita exports.

To further strengthen the state's high-tech new economy, Kentucky is now implementing a strategic plan to become a world leader in the research, development and marketing of bioscience and life science technologies.

Kentucky's new financial assistance program for technology-driven small businesses puts it in a class of its own. While many states offer programs that match either Phase I or Phase II federal Small Business Innovation Research and Small Business Technology Transfer grants, only Kentucky has the vision to match both phases of funding.

In late 2006 Kentucky high-tech small businesses could begin applying for state grants to match federal Phase I awards under SBIR-STTR grants. In 2007, the state will also offer Kentucky businesses matching funds for Phase II federal SBIR-STTR awards.

The maximum Kentucky matching grant for Phase I testing of the feasibility of an idea or technology is $100,000. Phase II federal awards, which support full-scale research and development, will be matched by Kentucky up to the first $500,000 for each year of the award. The commonwealth offers Phase 0 and Phase 00 award programs as well.

Combined with the continuity and stability provided by the Kentucky Economic Development Partnership Board, such innovations and creativity will assure Kentucky's place in an evermore sophisticated and demanding global economy.

## BUSINESS & ECONOMY

# Kentucky Economic Development Summit

### Dave Adkisson

As competition intensifies, particularly in the global marketplace, Kentucky's business community must closely evaluate the Commonwealth's prospects for success. With Japan, India and China joining the United States as the world's economic powerhouses, the challenge for Kentuckians—and all Americans—is to increase entrepreneurship, innovation and technological ingenuity. That means better educated workers, especially those with high-level math and science skills. If Kentucky is to grow economically, it must improve the education of its citizens and position the state to take advantage of global markets and investment opportunities.

The Kentucky Chamber's Economic Summit, held in July 2006 in Louisville, was designed to evaluate, analyze and understand the current state of business and economics in Kentucky, and explore the strategies needed to shepherd both the local entrepreneur and corporate institution into the emerging global economy.

The summit assembled an exciting array of business leaders, politicians, educators, doctors, economists, researchers and others to present ideas on effective leadership, innovation and practical strategies for success.

Created as an opportunity to assemble a unique mix of professional experience and expertise, the Kentucky Chamber's Economic Summit could not have been timelier. Kentucky carefully balances an economy built on traditional cornerstone industries, such as coal and agriculture, with a yearning to more fully commit to an international marketplace frenzied with new technology, new standards and new applications. The time is now for the business leaders of Kentucky to decide the Commonwealth's future.

But to construct that platform of economic stability and growth, a state must understand its economy. To that end, the summit presented a discussion of several important Kentucky industries—manufacturing, equine, agriculture, research and technology, tourism, and coal—by industry experts—evaluating the future climate of each.

No entity of any kind can expect to achieve its goals without a healthy dose of both awareness and vision—to fearlessly acknowledge shortcomings with a hopeful eye toward the future. The Commonwealth of Kentucky—blessed with natural resources, beautiful landscapes and a diligent workforce—must consistently examine its successes, challenges and possibilities within the shifting paradigms of an emerging global marketplace. The Kentucky Chamber's Economic Summit offered a fantastic opportunity to do just this, giving each Kentuckian a chance to participate in the creation of a new economic outlook, bright and strong as ever.

*Dave Adkisson is president & CEO of the Kentucky Chamber of Commerce, www. kychamber.com.*

**Wayne Martin, Chairman of the Kentucky Chamber and President of Gray Kentucky Television addresses business and education leaders from across the Commonwealth**
*Source: Kentucky Chamber of Commerce*

# BUSINESS & ECONOMY
# *Globalization*

## Gov. Martha Layne Collins

Becoming involved in the global market place can be extremely intimidating because it is an entirely new playing field with new rules that businesses must face. However, as President Bill Clinton wisely put it, "Globalization is not something we can hold off or turn off . . . it is the economic equivalent of a force of nature - - like wind or water." This force of nature has undoubtedly taken Kentucky by storm and has left growth and opportunity in its path. In 2005 Kentucky exported nearly $14.9 billion worth of goods giving our state a 7th place national ranking in exports per capita.

**David Adkisson, President of the Kentucky Chamber of Commerce observes life in China at a local market**
*Source: Kentucky Chamber of Commerce*

equipment, chemicals, computer and electronic equipment, and machinery. Foreign investors are also recognizing Kentucky as a sure bet. Total gross property, plant, and equipment –non-bank was over $26 billion in 2005.

Globalization is inevitable. Like any force of nature, this can seem overwhelming. Flexibility and adaptation are sure methods of survival and will lead to a flourishing Kentucky. Communication barriers are becoming a thing of the past and the environment has never been more right to "go global." Don't think of this as a gamble, but as the best

The process of globalization is not hasty, and necessitates trusting relationships and negotiations in which everyone benefits in some way. The entire Bluegrass region enjoyed the success of last year's exports. For example, $4.1 billion was added to the commonwealth's gross state product and 55,000 jobs were directly created which can only mean an improving quality of life. Often when people hear Kentucky, they think of Bluegrass music, the Derby, and bourbon. Clearly turbojet and turboproller parts aren't the first things that jump to mind. Perhaps they should be, because in 2005 Kentucky was number one of all 50 states in exporting these high demand items. We have a growing list of trade partners that includes Canada, Mexico, France, the UK, China, and Japan, to name a few. Exports from our own backyard experiencing enormous success in foreign markets span a wide range of industries such as transportation

business decision you will ever make.

Doing business beyond Kentucky's borders is one of the greatest challenges any Kentucky company will face, but it is also one of the greatest opportunities. Whether you are a small company just getting started or a well-established large corporation, importing and exporting products and services can prove to be some of the most rewarding and exciting projects you will undertake.

That's where the Kentucky World Trade Center (KWTC) can help. With offices in Lexington, Louisville and Murray, the KWTC is a leading provider of trade services across the state. Kentucky has emerged as a leader among the 50 states in expanding its international trade, and over the past decade, Kentucky ranked sixth in export growth.

*For more information, call 859-258-3139; admin@kwtc.org; or www.kwtc.org.*

## TOTAL U.S. EXPORTS (Origin of Movement) VIA KENTUCKY
## TOP 25 COMMODITIES BASED ON 2005 DOLLAR VALUE
(In Millions of Dollars)

| RANK | HS CODE | COMMODITY | VALUE 2002 | VALUE 2003 | VALUE 2004 | VALUE 2005 | % SHARE 2002 | % SHARE 2003 | % SHARE 2004 | % SHARE 2005 | % CHANGE 2004-2005 |
|---|---|---|---|---|---|---|---|---|---|---|---|
| --- | --- | Total Kentucky Exports and % Share of U.S. Total | 10,607 | 10,734 | 12,992 | 14,899 | 1.5 | 1.5 | 1.6 | 1.6 | 14.7 |
| --- | --- | Total, Top 25 Commodities and % Share of State Total | 5,193 | 4,761 | 6,517 | 7,376 | 49 | 44.4 | 50.2 | 49.5 | 13.2 |
| 1 | 841191 | Turbojet And Turbopropeller Parts | 1,622 | 1,545 | 2,204 | 2,517 | 15.3 | 14.4 | 17 | 16.9 | 14.2 |
| 2 | 870422 | Mtr Veh Trans Gds Com-Ig Int C P E Gvw >5nov20 mtn | 41 | 40 | 231 | 485 | 0.4 | 0.4 | 1.8 | 3.3 | 110 |
| 3 | 870323 | Pass Veh Spk-Ig Int Com Rcpr P Eng > 1500 Nov 3m Cc | 234 | 141 | 406 | 439 | 2.2 | 1.3 | 3.1 | 2.9 | 8.3 |
| 4 | 847330 | Parts & Accessories For Adp Machines & Units | 440 | 288 | 316 | 341 | 4.1 | 2.7 | 2.4 | 2.3 | 8 |
| 5 | 870324 | Pass Veh Spk-Ig Int Com Rcpr P Eng > 3000 Cc | 271 | 133 | 242 | 290 | 2.6 | 1.2 | 1.9 | 1.9 | 19.8 |
| 6 | 870899 | Parts And Accessories Of Motor Vehicles, Nesoi | 320 | 280 | 244 | 267 | 3 | 2.6 | 1.9 | 1.8 | 9.6 |
| 7 | 300210 | Antisera And Other Blood Fractions | 354 | 348 | 288 | 248 | 3.3 | 3.2 | 2.2 | 1.7 | -13.7 |
| 8 | 870829 | Pts & Access Of Bodies Of Motor Vehicles, Nesoi | 65 | 69 | 127 | 226 | 0.6 | 0.6 | 1 | 1.5 | 78.1 |
| 9 | 391000 | Silicones, In Primary Forms | 47 | 134 | 167 | 211 | 0.4 | 1.3 | 1.3 | 1.4 | 26.8 |
| 10 | 870431 | Mtr Veh Trans Gds Spk Ig In C P Eng, Gvw Nov 5 Mtn | 208 | 115 | 225 | 204 | 2 | 1.1 | 1.7 | 1.4 | -9.5 |
| 11 | 847160 | Adp Input Or Output Units, Storage Or Not, Nesoi | 104 | 103 | 137 | 201 | 1 | 1.1 | 1.1 | 1.4 | 47 |
| 12 | 940190 | Parts Of Seats (Ex Medical, Barber, Dental Etc) | 91 | 117 | 200 | 187 | 0.9 | 1.1 | 1.5 | 1.3 | -6.1 |
| 13 | 10190 | Live Horses, Asses, Mules And Hinnies, Nesoi | 24 | 77 | 157 | 182 | 0.2 | 0.7 | 1.2 | 1.2 | 15.8 |
| 14 | 290321 | Vinyl Chloride (Chloroethylene) | 57 | 101 | 124 | 180 | 0.5 | 0.9 | 1 | 1.2 | 45.3 |
| 15 | 870421 | Trucks, Nesol, Diesel Eng, Gvw 5 Metric Tons & Und | 350 | 256 | 375 | 166 | 3.3 | 2.4 | 2.9 | 1.1 | -55.7 |
| 16 | 284420 | Uranium Enriched In U235 Etc. Plutonium Etc. | 208 | 105 | 265 | 164 | 2 | 1 | 2 | 1.1 | -38 |
| 17 | 220830 | Whiskies | 111 | 124 | 149 | 144 | 1 | 1.2 | 1.1 | 1 | -3.3 |
| 18 | 841112 | Turbojets Of A Thrust Exceeding 25 Kn | 107 | 55 | 48 | 128 | 1 | 0.5 | 0.4 | 0.9 | 168.6 |
| 19 | 847990 | Pts Of Mach Mechncl Appl W Indvdul Function Nesoi | 79 | 76 | 153 | 124 | 0.7 | 0.7 | 1.2 | 0.8 | -18.6 |
| 20 | 840790 | Spark-Ign Rcprcing/Rotary Int Combstn Eng, Nesoi | 83 | 91 | 88 | 116 | 0.8 | 0.8 | 0.7 | 0.8 | 32.9 |
| 21 | 847590 | Parts Of Mach For Assmbl Elec Lamp Etc Mfg Glsswre | 0 | 0 | 27 | 114 |  | 0 | 0.2 | 0.8 | 328 |
| 22 | 760612 | Aluminum Alloy Rect Plates Etc, Over .2 Mm Thick | 92 | 104 | 81 | 112 | 0.9 | 1 | 0.6 | 0.8 | 37.8 |
| 23 | 10110 | Purebred Breeding Animal | 164 | 348 | 65 | 110 | 1.5 | 3.2 | 0.5 | 0.7 | 70.3 |
| 24 | 390690 | Acrylic Polymers Nesoi, In Primary Forms | 113 | 97 | 127 | 110 | 1.1 | 0.9 | 1 | 0.7 | -14.1 |
| 25 | 300440 | Alkaloids (No Hormones Or Antibiotics), Dosage Etc | 7 | 16 | 75 | 108 | 0.1 | 0.2 | 0.6 | 0.7 | 44.7 |

## TOTAL U.S. EXPORTS (Origin of Movement) VIA KENTUCKY
## TOP 25 COUNTRIES BASED ON 2005 DOLLAR VALUE
(In Millions of Dollars)

| RANK | COUNTRY | VALUE 2002 | VALUE 2003 | VALUE 2004 | VALUE 2005 | % SHARE 2002 | % SHARE 2003 | % SHARE 2004 | % SHARE 2005 | % CHANGE 2004-2005 |
|---|---|---|---|---|---|---|---|---|---|---|
| --- | Total Kentucky Exports and % Share of U.S. Total | 10,607 | 10,734 | 12,992 | 14,899 | 1.5 | 1.5 | 1.6 | 1.6 | 14.7 |
| --- | Total, Top 25 Countries and % Share of State Total | 9,875 | 10,053 | 12,282 | 14,051 | 93.1 | 93.7 | 94.5 | 94.3 | 14.4 |
| 1 | Canada | 3,652 | 3,424 | 4,633 | 5,087 | 34.4 | 31.9 | 35.7 | 34.1 | 9.8 |
| 2 | Mexico | 469 | 518 | 786 | 1,397 | 4.4 | 4.8 | 6.1 | 9.4 | 77.7 |
| 3 | France | 795 | 740 | 1,084 | 1,288 | 7.5 | 6.9 | 8.3 | 8.6 | 18.8 |
| 4 | United Kingdom | 824 | 850 | 959 | 998 | 7.8 | 7.9 | 7.4 | 6.7 | 4.1 |
| 5 | Japan | 1,003 | 983 | 865 | 783 | 9.5 | 9.2 | 6.7 | 5.3 | -9.5 |

Source: U.S. Census Bureau, Foreign Trade Division

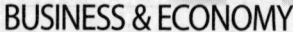

# BUSINESS & ECONOMY
## *Honorary Consuls*

Diplomacy is the primary vehicle by which nations communicate political concerns, negotiate trade deals, settle disputes and protect the interests of their citizens abroad. An embassy or consulate is usually located in the host nation's capital like Washington, D.C., or scattered across the country in a metropolitan area such as Miami, Atlanta or Chicago.

Consulates can be headed by either career diplomats who are citizens of the nation they represent or by honorary consuls. An honorary consul is a private citizen appointed by a foreign government to represent its interests.

In Kentucky, the U.S. Department of State recognizes seven honorary consuls of other countries. The honorary consuls are: Dr. Bernard Strenecky–Barbados, Alfred Welsh–Belgium, Joseph Blackman–Brazil, John Lina–France, Mark Blackwell–Germany, Orn Gudmundsson–Iceland, and Gov.

Martha Layne Collins–Japan. These individuals have been deemed worthy of the position, nominated, and approved by both the foreign country and the U.S. They serve for an indeterminate term at the pleasure of the country they represent and the U.S. Department of State.

Within the diplomatic community, the honorary consul is the first point of contact for a citizen in need of assistance from their embassy or consulate, or with U.S. officials. Honorary consuls work with their consulates to represent the interests of the ordinary citizens of these countries—those in residence and visitors—assist with certain documents that require a personal appearance, promote tourism and trade, provide representation for their country at public events, and generally represent the country locally. The honorary consuls also provide assistance to those who have commercial business interests and need particular information, or assistance, concerning their country. They promote international understanding and goodwill.

Each of the countries represented has a significant presence in the commonwealth and puts a high value on their representation. For example, when an international ambassador visits the commonwealth, it is the honorary consul who makes local arrangements and assures the success of the visit.

Detailed contact information for an honorary consul can be found on the web site of the consulate or embassy of the specific country.

**Governor Martha Layne Collins and Dennis Moore, Public Affairs Officer for the Canadian Consulate General, Detroit at the Kentucky-Canadian Studies Roundtable held at Georgetown College in September 2006**
*Photo: Bobby Clark*

## BUSINESS & ECONOMY
# *Canada – Kentucky's largest trading partner*

Canada is Kentucky's foremost trading partner, purchasing 36 percent of the state's foreign-bound exports in 2004. Total export sales totaled $4.3 billion and Kentucky sold more to its northern neighbor than to its next six largest trading partners combined. Kentucky also imported $3.9 billion worth of goods. Overall, bilateral trade totaled $8.2 billion, an increase of $436 million from 2003. Approximately 69,000 jobs in Kentucky are supported by Canada-U.S. trade.

The transportation sector is the backbone of the Canada-Kentucky trade relationship, generating $3.7 billion in revenue last year. This accounted for 45 percent of the total goods traded between the Bluegrass State and its northern ally. The state supplied Canada with $2.2 billion in transportation goods, making it the state's largest Canada-bound export sector in 2004. Within the sector, Kentucky shipped $823 million in trucks, $662 million in motor vehicle parts (excluding engines), and $582 million in automobiles north of the border. Canadian transportation goods were also in high demand—Canada supplied the state with $1.4 billion worth of goods. Kentucky's purchases included $772 million in motor vehicle parts (excluding engines) and $342 million in motor vehicle engines and parts.

Chemicals generated $900 million in cross-border exchange, making them the second largest trade sector in 2004. Kentucky sent $485 million worth of chemicals to Canada and purchased $415 million worth in return. Bluegrass sales of organic chemicals represented the most profitable chemical commodity, generating $157 million for the state last year. In return, Canada supplied Kentucky with chemicals totaling $415 million, including $123 million in synthetic rubber and plastics.

Kentucky exchanged a total of $1.1 billion in metals products with its northern neighbor last year. The state sold Canada $353 million in these various metal products including $84 million in aluminum and alloys, and $66 million in steel (plate, sheet and strip). Canada reciprocated, supplying Kentucky with $763 million in metals.

Canadians made 275,200 visits to Kentucky last year, enticed by the state's famed Kentucky bluegrass and renowned thoroughbred horses. While visitors to the Bluegrass State pumped $29 million into the Kentucky economy, Kentuckians made 89,500 visits to Canada and spent $36 million over the course of their northern trips.

Alltech is a Lexington-based multinational biotechnology company that incorporated Alltech Canada in 1988. The company provides natural solutions to the feed and food industries, and employs 70 people in Canadian plants.

Montreal-headquartered Alcan is the world's second largest producer of primary aluminum, as well as a global producer of value-added engineered products and composites. The company's operations include key facilities at three Kentucky locations: Sebree, Glasgow and Berea.

*http://www.infoexport.gc.ca/*

| KENTUCKY TRADE | |
| --- | --- |
| Exports to Canada | $4.3 billion |
| Imports from Canada | $3.9 billion |
| Bilateral trade | $8.2 billion |
| Largest export market | Canada |
| KENTUCKY TOURISM | |
| Visits by Canadians | 275,200 |
| $ spent | $29 million |
| Visits to Canada | 89,500 |
| $ spent | $36 million |

## BUSINESS & ECONOMY
# *Sister Cities*                                                   James G. Amato

### CITIZEN DIPLOMACY AT ITS BEST

In 1956 President Dwight Eisenhower hosted a two-day White House summit on citizen diplomacy to foster peace and friendship throughout the world. The post-World War II climate was a fertile environment to launch this effort. With enthusiastic response to the concept, summit participants pledged their support and formed "people-to-people" committees. The "sister city" concept of extending friendship between international cities developed from the Civic Committee.

As envisioned by President Eisenhower, the Sister City program was the ultimate forum for citizen diplomacy. In July 2006, Sister Cities International celebrated its 50th anniversary and stands today as the icon for international citizen diplomacy and cooperation. The Sister Cities program offers communities the opportunity to learn about and participate in international relations; experience other cultures, language, art, music and ideas; understand the economics of world trade and tourism and increase international business partnerships; and participate in cooperative community programs based on diversity. On a one-to-one level, Sister Cities programs encourage and stimulate exchanges and projects in the areas of professional economic development, education, community initiatives, arts and culture, medicine, tourism, and technology.

The Commonwealth of Kentucky has official Sister State relationships with Jiangxi Province, China, and Ecuador. A number of Kentucky cities have long-standing official Sister Cities relationships. For over 40 years, Sister Cities of Louisville has been recognized as an active member of the international citizen diplomacy network. Louisville's Sister Cities are Montpellier, France; Quito, Ecuador; Mainz, Germany; La Plata, Argentina; Tamale, Ghana; Perm, Russia; Jiujiang, China; and Leeds, England (Friendship City Status).

Lexington was one of the first to form a Sister Cities relationship when it twinned with Deauville, France in 1957. Lexington now has three additional Sister Cities: County Kildare, Ireland; Shinhidaka, Japan; and Newmarket, England.

In addition to Louisville and Lexington, the fol-

**A delegation from Lexington visits their sister city, Deauville, France**
*Source: Lexington Sister Cities Commission*

lowing Kentucky cities have official Sister Cities: Bowling Green – Kawanishi, Japan; Danville – pending; Frankfort – San Pedro de Macoris, Dominican Republic; Georgetown – Tahara, Japan; Morehead – Ballymena, Northern Ireland and Yangshuo County, China; Owensboro – Olomouc, Czech Republic; Owensboro Region – Nisshin, Japan (pending); Versailles – pending; and Winchester – Ibarra, Ecuador.

*For more information: Sister Cities International, www. sister-cities.org.*

## BUSINESS & ECONOMY
# *Small Businesses*

Robert G. Clark

Small businesses in the Commonwealth make a significant contribution to Kentucky's economy. More than half of Kentucky's non-farm private output and employment is generated by small firms with 500 or fewer employees. Small business owners, including women, minorities and home-based individuals, continue to be leaders in the state's economy.

The estimated total number of small businesses in Kentucky in 2004 was 317,115. Of the 83,046 employer firms in 2004, 97 percent, or an estimated 80,595, were small firms. The most recent data available show that non-employer businesses numbered 236,520 in 2002.

### KENTUCKY MINORITY-OWNED BUSINESSES

In 1997 there were 12,664 minority-owned firms in Kentucky with $2.46 billion in sales and receipts and 24,572 employees. Minority-owned firms accounted for 4.5 percent of the firms and just over one percent of the sales and receipts in Kentucky's economy. In the U.S. 14.6 percent of the firms were minority-owned, and 3.2 percent of sales and receipts were from minority-owned businesses.

In 2002, Hispanic-owned firms numbered 2,082, an increase of 41 percent from 1997. Black-owned firms numbered 7,595, an increase of 35 percent; and American Indian and Alaska native owned firms numbered 1,324, a decrease of 57 percent.

### KENTUCKY WOMEN-OWNED BUSINESSES

With a total of 77,232 firms, women-owned businesses accounted for 31.4 percent of Kentucky firms in 2002. U.S. women-owned firms accounted for 28.2 percent of total firms. Kentucky businesses owned by women generated $9.5 billion in sales. In 2002, revenues from U.S. women-owned firms comprised 4.2 percent of total business sales and receipts.

Businesses that were equally male-female-owned in 2002 numbered 39,343. Sales receipts from these firms was over $9.5 billion. Women represented 31.4 percent of the self-employed persons in Kentucky.

The estimated number of new employer businesses was 8,807 in 2004.

**Employment.** Small businesses with fewer than 500 employees numbered 69,753 in 2002 and employed 734,027 people or 50.2 percent of the state's non-farm private workforce. Total net employment loss in the state amounted to 16,916 between 2001 and 2002. During the same time period, firms with fewer than 20 employees gained 5,545 jobs.

**Small Business Income.** Small business proprietors' income in 2003 increased by 8.4 percent, from $7.4 billion in 2002 to $8 billion in 2003.

**Finance.** Small firms typically use commercial bank lenders and rely on local bank services. The Small Business Administration Office of Advocacy has identified banks in each state that make the most loans to small businesses. This information is available in its banking studies available at www.sba.gov/advo/research.

For the complete report on Kentucky's small

Nancy Newsom,
Newsom's Aged Country Hams &
Country Store, Princeton
*Photo: Sid Webb*

business profile, go to www.sba.gov/advo/stats/profiles/05ky.pdf.

Resources available to Kentucky small business entrepreneurs:

**Kentucky's Small Business Development Centers** with 15 service centers statewide have experienced and knowledgeable staff for both existing business owners and potential entrepreneurs. This is a free service co-sponsored by the U.S. Small Business

**Mazzonis Cafe, Louisville**
*Photo: Sid Webb*

Administration administered by the University of Kentucky and the Gatton College of Business and Economics, in partnership with regional universities, community and private colleges and the private sector. http://www.ksbdc.org/.

**The Small and Minority Business Branch in Kentucky's Economic Development Cabinet** coordinates Small Business Enterprise, Minority Business Enterprise and Women Business Enterprise activities throughout the state's administrative structure. The branch acts as an advocacy agency for the furtherance and expansion of Kentucky-based small, minority and women-owned businesses through the utilization of resources available through the state or under the purview of the state. www.thinkkentucky.com/SMBD/

**The Kentucky Commission on Small Business Advocacy (KCSBA)** has 19 members appointed by the governor. The mission of CSBA is to act as a business advocate, advising small business owners and helping resolve their concerns and questions about state and federal government regulations. The cost to comply with federal regulations

by Kentucky small businesses is estimated at more than $9.1 billion and this does not include state and local regulations. Kentucky was the eighth state to pass a Regulatory Flexibility Act that gives small businesses a voice in the development of government regulations. www.thinkkentucky.com/advocacy/sba_advocacy.aspx.

**The Small Business Administration (SBA)** provides technical assistance in areas such as entrepreneurial development, SCORE, Small Business Training Network, Womens Business Ownership and International Trade. SBA provides financial assistance through Loan Programs, Investment Division (SBICs), Surety Guarantees and International Trade. SBA also provides contracting assistance through programs like 8a Business Development, HUB-Zone, Government Contracting, Small Disadvantaged Business and Technology (SBIR/STTR). The SBA Kentucky District Office: The Romano Mazzoli Federal Building, 600 Dr. MLK Jr. PL, Louisville, KY 40202, (502) 582-5971 or www.sba.gov/ky.

**One-stop Business Licensing Program**

The Secretary of State offers a One-stop Business Licensing Program. There are over 1,800 business types and over 600 business licenses required from various agencies at the state level in Kentucky. This program allows users to instantly receive a complete listing of all licenses that could be required at the state level. In addition to this streamlined process, users can obtain detailed information about the license or permit, such as the contact person in state government, the fees and requirements for the license, and hyperlinks to forms available on the Internet. http://apps.sos.ky.gov/business/onestop/onestop.aspx

Assistance can also be obtained by contacting the Economic Development Cabinet's Business Information Clearinghouse at (800) 626-2250.

*(Sources: Kentucky Economic Development Cabinet, Small Business Administration and www.sba.gov/advo/research/profiles/05ky.pdf)*

# Home Builders Association Turns 50 Years Old

Bob Weiss

## Providing Kentucky's Housing Needs for Fifty Years

In November of 1957 builders from Louisville, Lexington, Northern Kentucky and Owensboro met and formed the Home Builders Association of Kentucky (HBAK) to provide the housing industry with a strong voice in state government affairs.

The State Association was formed with 300 members from those four local chapters. A part time Executive Director was hired and a small office was opened in Lexington.

Today, fifty years later, the HBA of Kentucky boasts over 7,500 members in 23 local chapters located all across the Commonwealth of Kentucky. The Association currently operates with five staff members in an office building owned by the Association in the State Capital of Frankfort.

During the past fifty years the Association has strived to make Kentucky a desirable place to live, with home ownership opportunities for all citizens.

Throughout the early decades of operation the State Association led the movement to professionalize those working in the housing industry through the adoption of a code of ethics and general construction standards. This led to the adoption of the Statewide Uniform Building Code in 1980.

Certainly, building or remodeling a home is a big decision. In the mid 1990s the Association adopted the voluntary Registered Builder and Remodelor Program, which provides consumers with the comfort of knowing that by using a member of this program that they will deal with a professional in the industry. Prior to becoming a Registered Builder or Remodelor a member must furnish the Association Board with references from the following: banks, previous customers, suppliers, subcontractors. Every Registered Builder and Remodelor must agree to at least five hours of continuing education each year, which keeps them current with the latest information in the housing industry.

Registered Builders and Remodelors have an established reputation with their local subcontractors, financial institutions, suppliers, and with customers. This means the homeowner can take some of the guesswork and worry out of choosing a builder or remodelor. Those in the Registered Builder and Remodelor Program provide their customers with a contract and warranty, proof of proper insurance—and attend continuing education classes to keep up with the latest trends in the industry.

Looking forward to another half a century of

**Kentucky home builders prepare to board an American Airlines plane**
*Source: Home Builders Association of Kentucky*

service to Kentuckians, the Home Builders Association of Kentucky will continue to focus on our main mission on monitoring state legislation and regulations on behalf of the homebuilding industry, and to maintain a full time presence at the State Capitol. Add to this the continued dedication and expanding services to consumers, and we think we'll stay busy for another fifty years.

*Bob Weiss is Executive Director of the Home Builders Association of Kentucky. To find out more about the Association and its members, visit www. hbak.com.*

# BUSINESS & ECONOMY
# *Manufacturing*

In 2004, 4,174 manufacturing establishments in Kentucky employed 263,648 people. However since 1998, the manufacturing sector lost 29,714 jobs or a drop of 10.2 percent. The manufacturing sector contributed $88.6 billion or 39.2 percent of total state industry receipts in 2002, which represents a two percent growth since 1997 with $86.63 billion.

Transportation equipment manufacturing (Ford, General Motors and Toyota) lead the way with $30.3 billion or slightly more than a third of total manufacturing receipts.

The chemical manufacturing sector is the second largest manufacturing group, generating receipts of $7.08 billion in 2002, which was down from the 1997 totals of $7.46 billion. The chemical industry employed 13,231 in 2003, down from 14,331 in 1998.

In 1998 textile mills, textile mill products and apparel manufacturing industry sub-sectors employed 25,641, but in 2003 the number dropped 52 percent or to just 12,291 employees due to moving operations out of Kentucky and overseas. Overall value of shipments by these industry sub-sectors dropped in 1997 from $2.93 billion to $1.77 billion in 2002, a nearly 40 percent drop.

The largest employers in Kentucky are in transportation (42,423), fabricated metal products (26,590) and machinery manufacturing (25,459).

## The Automobile Industry in Kentucky

Auto manufacturers, along with their suppliers and dealers, provide a major driving force in the U.S. economy, and Kentucky has capitalized on this industry. In Kentucky, approximately 2.98 percent of the state's employment is in either the automobile industry or in a job dependent on the auto industry.

The automobile industry has contributed to Kentucky in many ways. For instance, Kentucky's automobile industry represents 5.2 percent of the state's gross state product. Kentucky's automotive industry gross state product for 2002 was over $6.3 billion. Kentucky has the nation's third highest level of auto industry related employment as a percent of total state employment in the United States.

Ford first came to Kentucky in 1913, when Henry Ford began a "factory" at the Summers-Herman dealership in Louisville. In 1925 Henry Ford created what was called "the first modern assembly plant" in Louisville. The plant turned out Model A's and other Ford trucks and cars. During World War II, the plant geared up to produce military equipment.

In 1955, Ford moved its operations to the Louisville Assembly Plant on Fern Valley Road; and in 1969, began operations at the eastern Jefferson County truck plant. The Louisville assembly plant

**Ford truck plant, Louisville**
*Source: Kentucky Department of Tourism*

employs 3,855. In late 1997 Ford announced expansion plans at its Louisville operations, adding 1,000 jobs and 130,000 square feet to the Kentucky truck plant. Total employment at the truck plant is about 6,000. The expanded facility, at 4.6 million square feet, is the second-largest Ford assembly plant in North America.

On June 1, 1981, General Motors moved production of the Corvette from St. Louis to Bowling Green, which remains today the exclusive home of Corvette production. The 1,000 employees in 2003 built over 35,000 vehicles at the one million square foot plant. The new Cadillac XLR has been produced in Bowling Green since the end of 2002.

In 2004, 1,162,681 cars and light trucks were assembled in Kentucky. In addition to the Corvettes and Cadillac XLRs produced in Bowling Green, Kentucky plants produce a number of other models: Ford's Louisville plant produces the Ford Explorer and Mercury Mountaineer SUV models and the Sport Trac. The Ford Kentucky truck plant manufactures Ford Super Duty F Series trucks and Excursion SUV models.

Toyota Motor Manufacturing (TMMK) celebrated its 20th Anniversary in 2006. TMMK has grown to be one of Kentucky's largest employers (about 7,000 team members) and has become Toyota's largest facility in North America (a $5.3 billion investment to date). Economic reports estimate about 35,000 jobs have been generated across the state. Toyota has two vehicle production lines and a powertrain engine and axle facility; more than 7,000 team members build about 500,000 vehicles and nearly 400,000 engines each year. In addition, Toyota's North American headquarters is located in Erlanger, employing 800. Toyota's North American Parts Logistics Division, located in Hebron, employs 400.

Toyota's plant in Georgetown manufactures the Toyota Camry, Avalon and Solara.

TMMK rolled out the first Hybrid Camry built in North America in October 2006. The Georgetown plant plans to build approximately 3,000 to 4,000 Camry Hybrid vehicles per month.

## AUTO MANUFACTURING IMPACT ON THE KENTUCKY ECONOMY

The automobile manufacturing industry's strong presence in Kentucky has grown significantly over the last several years. In 2004, the automobile industry employed over 90,000 in Kentucky, with 19,500 in the motor vehicle manufacturing industry. In Kentucky, employment in the motor vehicle manufacturing industry has grown by more than 35 percent between 1995 and 2000, compared to 14 percent for all industries and 2.5 percent for manufacturing. Kentucky's employment growth in the motor vehicle manufacturing industry between 1995 and 2000 ranks second among the top ten automobile producing states.

The Gross State Product (GSP) for the motor vehicles industry grew at an incredible rate between 1991-2001. The value of shipments for the auto manufacturing industry in Kentucky at over $30 billion.

*Sources: The Alliance of Automobile Manufacturers; Kentucky Cabinet for Economic Development, December 2004; The 1997 and 2002 Economic Census; 2003 and 1998 County Business Patterns.*

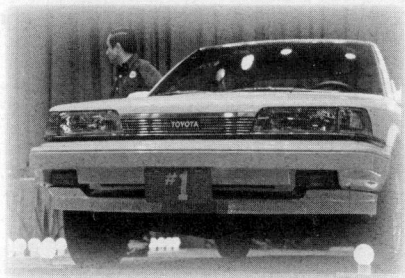

**The first Toyota built in Georgetown**
*Source: Toyota Motor Manufacturing Kentucky*

**2007 Camry on the assembly line**
*Source: Toyota Motor Manufacturing Kentucky*

## Impact of Automobile Manufacturing Industry on Kentucky

|  | Industry | Manufacturing | Auto Manufacturing |
|---|---|---|---|
| Employees (2000) | 1,816,900 | 307,200 | 53,451 |
| Employment Growth (1995 2000) | 11.1% | 2.5% | 37.7% |
| Total Annual Wages | $52,136,852,000 | $11,138,577,000 | $2,624,724,235 |
| GSP (2002 Current Dollars) | $122,282,000,000 | $25,471,000,000 | $6,354,000,000 |
| Real GSP Growth (1991-2001) | 41.38% | 45.95% | 225.14% |
| GSP per Capita (2002) | $29,899 | $6,228 | $1,554 |

# Kentucky Association of Manufacturers Changes Course

Andrew C. Meko

The year 2006 was a year of tremendous change for Kentucky's 95-year-old manufacturing trade association. Formerly known as Associated Industries of Kentucky, the association changed its name to the Kentucky Association of Manufacturers (KAM) in November to better describe its purpose and focus on manufacturing. KAM's mission is to enhance the competitiveness of manufacturers by shaping a legislative and regulatory environment conducive to economic growth, and to increase understanding among policymakers, the media and the general public about the importance of manufacturing to Kentucky's economic strength.

The association's name change helped launch a new statewide campaign designed to educate Kentuckians about the economic power of manufacturing. KAM formed a partnership with the Kentucky Broadcasters Association to air television and radio commercials across the state during 2007 using the tagline, "Manufacturing. Prosperity in the Making." KAM also worked with the Kentucky Press Association to promote the same message in newspapers, business news publications and business magazines across the commonwealth.

An aggressive public relations campaign resulted in hard-hitting commentaries by President and CEO Andrew C. Meko being published on the state's leading editorial pages. The commentaries showcase KAM's unique leadership and expertise on the manufacturing industry and help spur debate on how to best protect and grow Kentucky's

**Joe Bassindale, engineer with Modine Manufacturing Co., Harrodsburg**
*Source: Kentucky Association of Manufacturers*

$29 billion (gross state product), 260,000-employee manufacturing base. In July, Meko delivered a strong message about the future of Kentucky manufacturing at an important economic summit in Louisville. "If we want to keep Kentucky manufacturers here, and attract new companies to Kentucky, we also must ensure they have a properly educated and well-trained pool of labor from which to choose," Meko told the state's business, education and government leaders.

KAM further strengthened its member services and advocacy by providing strategic direction to its administrative and government relations teams. KAM effectively utilizes perhaps the commonwealth's largest, most powerful and experienced lobbying team to bring issues that impact its members to the forefront. Key issues include workforce development, business taxes, economic incentives, global competition, regulations, and the right of workers to freely choose to financially support a union. Administratively, KAM revamped its information technology systems and upgraded its member services as part of an effort to become a nationally renowned association.

KAM continued a longtime tradition by presenting "Manufacturer of the Year" awards on Nov. 3, 2006, in Louisville. Although the 2006 winners were not selected before this publication went to press, the 2005 winners were: Alltech, Blendex, Blue Moon Artworks and Lectrodryer LLC. *For more information, please visit www.aik.org.*

# BUSINESS & ECONOMY

# *Technology*

Dr. Lee Todd

### KENTUCKY'S NEW ECONOMIC FRONTIER: A KNOWLEDGE-BASED ECONOMY

The history of technology in Kentucky is not nearly as storied as that of our agricultural, mining or distilling industries. Technology, however, holds the key to the economic future of the Commonwealth.

This state has traditionally lured good-paying manufacturing jobs through a combination of cheap land, cheap labor and tax incentives. Though traditional Kentucky industries have served this state admirably for decades, economic times are changing in the Commonwealth – and across the globe. The days of recruiting companies to Kentucky by providing cheap land and cheap labor are dwindling. As more and more traditional American businesses choose to expand their operations outside the U.S., Kentucky must find a new way to compete in the global marketplace.

The future of this state's economy must be rooted in the commercialization of knowledge. We must develop a new generation of innovators and entrepreneurs. Of course that mission starts in the classroom, as we prepare Kentucky students for global competition. But after preparing a new generation of critical thinkers, we need to provide them with an economy that will allow them to compete and excel in the modern world.

The recipe for growing and sustaining a successful, modern economy is no secret. Take one look at the hot-beds of innovation across the U.S.

Before there was a Silicon Valley, there was a Stanford University and a University of California-Berkley. Before there was a Research Triangle Park

**UK Coldstream Research Campus**
*Source: University of Kentucky*

in North Carolina, there was a University of North Carolina, a North Carolina State University and a Duke University. Before Massachusetts had a biotechnology corridor, there was a Harvard University and a Massachusetts Institute of Technology.

All these universities have one thing in common – a strong research infrastructure. If Kentucky is serious about competing globally, we must invest resources into expanding and enhancing our research nerve centers. We must realize that our ability to commercialize knowledge is intrinsically tied to the economic health of the Commonwealth.

Even though the development of knowledge is crucial to the future of the Commonwealth, we can not forget our past. We must conduct the type of research that will assist the corporations and companies that already call Kentucky home. We have to add value to our local organizations.

We must conduct research to help make Kentucky's thoroughbred industry even stronger; we must work alongside aluminum manufacturers to ensure that industry can grow and thrive in the Bluegrass; we must help develop clean coal technologies so Kentucky can be an environmental and energy leader; and we must discover new medical technologies so Kentuckians can live healthier, more productive lives.

The Commonwealth of Kentucky needs technology and innovation to be at the forefront of our economic future. We need to invest in education and research. We need to cultivate our new ideas and commercialize our intellectual property. Once we do all these things, we will then provide our next generation of Kentuckians with the type of economy that will allow them to compete in a changing world.

## Kentucky's New Economy Focus

The Dept. of Commercialization and Innovation was created by the Kentucky Innovation Act of 2000; a state-wide strategic plan for development of a technology-centered economy in the Commonwealth was the outcome. Drawing on area-wide strategic plans covering six regions of Kentucky, a state-wide strategic plan focuses on five Priority Research Focus Areas and seven Special Opportunities identified as areas in which Kentucky already has developed a national or international reputation.

Implementation of the plan is being coordinated by the Dept. of Commercialization and Innovation with assistance from the Kentucky Innovation Commission. It includes participation from the Council on Postsecondary Education, Cabinet for Economic Development, the State Chamber of Commerce and other state-wide partners. Kentucky is also focusing on the great potential the Commonwealth has to build a strong biotechnology industry.

Providing young high-tech firms access to capital is critical to growing firms to fuel economic development in the emerging economy. Product development can be expensive and many young firms find it difficult to raise capital. These firms must turn to alternative forms of financing. Since resources are generally not available in Kentucky, the state decided to act aggressively to improve access to capital for fledgling, high-potential technology firms.

The Postsecondary Education Reform Act of 1997 created the Research Challenge Trust Fund to support nationally recognized research programs at the University of Kentucky and the University of Louisville, and to strengthen key programs at the comprehensive universities. These funds, along with the Endowment Match Program (Bucks for Brains), have been used primarily to recruit exceptional faculty to these research universities.

Kentucky has a limited research and development infrastructure as is evidenced in the state's 47th place ranking in per capita R&D spending. The Commonwealth has no significant corporate research and development presence, nor does it have a federal research laboratory. To address these deficiencies the New Economy strategic plan advances the development of a globally competitive research and development infrastructure at Kentucky's research universities. The Commonwealth's resources are deployed to bolster targeted research areas where Kentucky stands to gain national prominence.

The Dept. of Commercialization and Innovation, after consultation with scholars and scientific experts across the Commonwealth, identified five research priority focus areas for Kentucky: (1) Human Health and Development; (2) Biosciences; (3) Information Technology and Communications; (4) Environmental and Energy Technologies; and (5) Materials Science and Advanced Manufacturing

These are the research areas that will afford Kentucky the best opportunity to build centers of research excellence around which competitive technology-based clusters can grow and thrive. These centers and associated business clusters will have the greatest influence on the creation of the New Economy in Kentucky.

*Source: http://www.one-ky.com/*

## McConnell Technology & Training Center

The McConnell Technology & Training Center (MTTC) provides innovative technology enhanced services and solutions for National Defense, business, and workforce customers.

MTTC is a nationally recognized leader for technology services, information and training. The McConnell Technology & Training Center provides technology consulting and training for individuals and businesses, and innovative technology solutions for the U.S. Navy.

MTTC's Fleet Maintenance Reduction Program (FMRP) helps the U.S. Navy resolve nagging and costly shipboard problems by inserting innovative products and technologies. These projects have provided the Navy with significant cost savings, huge manpower savings and important safety improvements. The Navy estimates that the MTTC projects will save approximately $1 Billion over the next fifteen years.

PC Essentials Program: This program helps individuals develop computer literacy and workforce skills. MTTC refurbishes computers donated by companies and individuals, and provides them to people who attend this training class. Over 10,000 families and individuals have completed basic computer training and received personal computers. This program also has trained nearly 2000 Welfare-to-work clients in the Lexington area and holds classes in communities across the commonwealth.

The McConnell Technology & Training Center projects will allow a cost avoidance for the U.S. Navy of approximately $1,000,000,000 over the next 15 years. The MTTC resolves nagging and costly shipboard problems by inserting into the U.S. Fleet commercially available innovative products and technologies, thus providing the Navy with significant cost savings, manpower savings and important safety improvements.

Historically, when refueling U.S. Navy ships at sea, three sailors on each ship used ropes with a flag every 20 yards to show the distance between ships when refueling in order to stay a safe distance from each other. MTTC proposed the use of laser range finders connected to large LED signs on each ship to more precisely measure the distance between ships, provide an immediate digital readout of the distance, and remove sailors from a potentially hazardous task.

MTTC is located in Louisville and may be reached at (888) 778-8786.

**U.S. Navy Replenishment ship**
*Source: McConnell Technology & Training Center*

## BUSINESS & ECONOMY

Bill Caylor
# Mining, Oil & Gas

### THE KENTUCKY COAL INDUSTRY

In 1750 Dr. Thomas Walker was the first recorded person to discover and use coal in Kentucky. Later in 1820, the first commercial mine, known as the "McLean drift bank," opened in Kentucky near the Green River and Paradise in Muhlenberg County. It produced and sold 328 short tons of coal. Prior to the Civil War, Kentucky produced a record 285,760 tons; however, by 1870 production had declined to 150,582 tons. In 1877 a steam-powered shovel was introduced and coal production jumped to more than one million tons in 1879. In 1890 a steam turbine was built and produced 5,000 kilowatts of electricity. By the beginning of World War I, demand for coal increased substantially and Kentucky produced 20.3 million tons.

In 1932 walking dragline excavators were built and four years later coal production jumped to 47.7 million tons. Just as before, World War II increased demand and caused production to soar to 72.4 million tons. By the early 1960s railroads began using unit coal trains, and the first longwall mining operations with powered roof supports was introduced. By 1963 coal production jumped to more than 100 million tons.

In 1972, Kentucky became the leading coal producing state by producing 120.3 million tons. In 1988, for the first time, Wyoming displaced Kentucky as the leading coal producing state but just two years later Kentucky reached a record production level of 179.4 million tons.

### EMPLOYMENT

The Kentucky coal mining industry in 2005

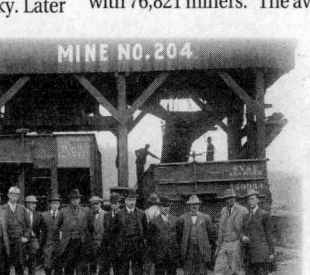

**Big Sandy Operators at
No. 204 Tipple**
*Source: Kentucky Virtual Library*

employed 15,669 miners at an average annual wage of $50,500. Employment peaked in 1949 with 76,821 miners. The average age of a Kentucky miner today is 49 and only 3% of working miners are members of the United Mine Workers of America. Using a conservative multiplier of four, coal generates an additional 61,000 jobs throughout Kentucky at power plants, mine equipment suppliers, law firms, engineering firms, accounting firms, coal sales, trucking, barge, and railroads, to name a very few.

### PRODUCTION

In 2005, 124 million tons was mined. Eighty (80%) percent was mined in Eastern Kentucky, broken down at 57% underground and 43% surface. Twenty (20%) percent was mined in Western Kentucky, broken down by 83% underground and 17% surface. Kentucky's production peaked in

### KENTUCKY COAL PRODUCTION

| YEAR | SURFACE | UNDERGROUND | TOTAL |
|------|---------|-------------|-------|
| 1998 | 58,941,761 | 97,937,265 | 156,879,026 |
| 1999 | 55,150,235 | 89,249,086 | 144,399,321 |
| 2000 | 50,346,219 | 81,499,769 | 131,845,988 |
| 2001 | 53,107,358 | 85,107,965 | 138,215,323 |
| 2002 | 50,595,329 | 80,807,468 | 131,402,797 |
| 2003 | 45,116,482 | 71,849,070 | 116,965,552 |
| 2004 | 45,475,066 | 73,479,407 | 118,954,473 |

*Source: www.omsl.ky.gov/safetyandlicense/annualreports/*

1990 at 179.4 million tons. Kentucky ranks third nationally behind Wyoming (406 million) and West Virginia (151 million).

## ECONOMICS

The current price of coal is around $50 per ton, with most coal sold under long-term contracts to utilities. Kentucky exports 73% of its coal to 23 states and four foreign countries, bringing $3.25 billion into Kentucky. Around 85 cents on each dollar stays here – wages, benefits, operating expenses, royalties, and taxes. Coal pays over $200 million annually in coal severance taxes in addition to the normal business taxes paid by all

**Brenda Schoonover, an equipment operator at Darby Creek Mine grabbed a section of a bolt used to hold up the roof of the mine while operating the roof bolter in Harlan County**
*Photo: Pablo Alcala, Lexington Herald Leader*

Kentucky companies. In 1972, the newly enacted coal severance tax replaced the sales tax on food. With the direct and indirect employment, coal creates economic activity throughout Kentucky totaling $8.97 billion.

## POWER GENERATION

Coal provides 91% of Kentucky's electricity and 52% of our nation's electricity. Kentucky has 113 power plants (58 coal, 15 oil, 10 gas, 30 hydro) producing 15,910 megawatts of electricity. Because of coal, Kentucky has the lowest electricity cost in the nation---4.63 cents/kilowatt-hour.

## SAFETY

Coal miners have one of the safest workplaces in America...with a lower rate of injuries and illnesses per 100 employees than agriculture, construction, or retail trade.

- 1920 – 1929 was deadliest decade with 161 average annual fatalities.
- 1990 – 1999 averaged 12 fatalities per year.
- 2000 – 2005 averaged 7 fatalities.
- 2006 has been a tragic year with 13 fatalities as of Oct. 10, 2006.

## FUTURE OF COAL?

The demand for coal nationally is expected to increase due to the increase in the demand for electricity. Until another viable and economic energy source is found, coal will continue to dominate as the primary source of energy for our nation's electrical needs.

But other markets for Kentucky coal may be on the horizon. The United States currently imports 58% of its oil, up from 36% during the Arab oil embargo in 1973. Coal can help make the U.S. independent from imported oil. Coal-to-liquid fuel is a reality. Germany produced 90% of its fuel needs from coal during World War II. South Africa produces 40% of its fuel needs today.

$1.20 per gallon gasoline? Yes, it can happen. Experts agree, it would take $3 billion to build a coal-to-liquid plant producing 45,000 to 50,000 barrels of liquid fuel a day. The cost to consumers would be $1.20 per gallon, plus taxes. Other new technologies promise the sequestration deep underground of the carbon dioxide emitted when coal is burned at power plants. This new coal-fired plant is called FutureGen. Kentucky hopes to be the site for one of these ultra clean new plants.

## RESERVES

- 250 years of coal reserves in the U.S.
- 100 years of coal reserves in Kentucky
  - 36 billion tons in West Kentucky
  - 52 billion tons in East Kentucky
- U.S. has 27% of world's coal supply

*Sources: Kentucky Geological Survey, www.uky.edu/KGS/, Kentucky Coal Education Web Site, www.coaleducation.org and Kentucky Office of Mine Safety and Licensing, www.omsl.ky.gov/*

*Bill Caylor is President of the Kentucky Coal Association, www.kentuckycoal.com*

# Oil & Gas Industry

Kentucky's oil and gas industry began in the early 19th century with pioneers searching for salt brines for use in tanning, food preservation and livestock agriculture. In 1818 Martin Beatty was searching for brine in what is now the Big South Fork National River and Recreation Area in southeastern Kentucky. This shallow well initially produced up to 100 barrels per day. Between 1818 and the Civil War few oil wells were drilled, but they were often spectacular. The "Old American Well," drilled near Burkesville, produced more than 50,000 barrels from its discovery in 1829 until about 1860. The end of the Civil War began the era of exploration for oil and gas.

The first commercial gas wells in Kentucky were drilled between 1863 and 1865 in Meade County. The gas was used as fuel to evaporate brines and was later delivered by pipeline to Louisville for lighting and domestic heat. Historic production data are sparse. The record for statewide oil production starts in 1883. Western Kentucky natural gas production data are available from 1933 to 1949. Statewide natural gas data are available beginning 1950. These data indicate Kentucky's total historic oil and gas production exceeds 9.85 quadrillion Btu (765 million barrels of oil and 5.4 trillion cubic feet of natural gas).

Two of Kentucky's potential energy resources have largely been ignored because of a lack of information. Preliminary data indicate natural gas is present in coal beds (coal bed methane) in both of the state's coal regions. A small pilot project is currently producing coal bed methane in eastern Kentucky. Natural asphalt, known as tar sand, was mined early in the 20th century for road paving material. The tar sand was successfully produced in the late 1970s and early 1980s when the price of oil was sufficiently high to make this resource economic.

All of Kentucky's counties have been tested to varying depths for oil and gas resources. In 2005, production was reported from 64 counties. In general, oil production dominates in the Western Coal Field and south-central areas of Kentucky; the Eastern Coal Field produces mostly natural gas. Kentucky has an estimated 18,000 producing oil wells and 13,000 producing gas wells. many of these producing wells are in the "stripper" category, having daily production rates of 60 million Btu or less (10 barrels of oil or 60,000 cubic feet of gas). Many wells are reported with initial daily production rates in excess of 580 million Btu (100 barrels of oil or 580,000 cubic feet of gas). Average daily production per well over time is lower, however. Wells completed after 1999 average 11.6 million Btu (2 barrels) per day for oil and 33 million Btu (33,000 cubic feet) per day for gas. In 2005, production totaled 107 trillion Btu (2.45 million barrels of oil and 93 billion cubic feet of natural gas) with a total value of $722 million ($34 million severance tax paid). Annually, Kentucky produces only about 12 percent of the 921 trillion Btu of oil and natural gas consumed in the state.

Petroleum is produced at various depths from limestone, sandstone and shale of Cambrian through Pennsylvanian age. In some areas of the state oil is still produced from depths of less than 100 feet. Wells producing natural gas and condensate from the Cambrian Rome Formation are currently Kentucky's deepest producers, with some zones exceeding 7,500 feet. The overall average total depth of oil and gas wells drilled in the state is less than 1,500 feet. The average depth for wells drilled since 2000 is more than 2,700 feet This increase represents the exploration for deeper producing zones and the continuing efforts to develop the Devonian shale natural gas resource. Both occur primarily in eastern Kentucky.

As the price of oil and gas has increased, interest in coalbed methane, tar sands, and Devonian shale gas production have grown especially in western Kentucky.

*Reprinted with permission from Kentucky Geological Survey, University of Kentucky, www.uky.edu/kgs.*

**Big Sinking Field, Lee County**
*Source: Kentucky Geology:*
*Department of Geology and Forestry (Kentucky Geological Survey), Series 5, Bulletin 4, Frankfort, 266 p.*

# Kentucky—
# Houseboat Capital of the World

In 1951 Wolf Creek Dam was built across the Cumberland River flooding land in Wayne, Russell, Pulaski, Clinton, McCreary, Laurel, and Whitley counties and surrounding riverbanks—giving birth to Lake Cumberland, one of the 10 largest lakes in the U.S. Construction of the project, designed and supervised by the Army Corps of Engineers, began in Aug. 1941. After a three-year delay caused by World War II, the project was completed in Aug. 1952. With its 1,255 miles of shoreline, Lake Cumberland has brought to this region millions of dollars as a result of the tourism industry that has flourished on account of the lake. It is estimated that Pulaski County alone attracts 1.5 million visitors each year.

But part of the economic possibilities of the

**Houseboats come in all shapes and sizes**
*Source: Kentucky Department of Tourism*

newly-impounded Lake Cumberland may have been unforeseen—it spawned a new industry. Sumerset Houseboat Company, started by the Sharpe family of Somerset in 1953, became the first houseboat manufacturer incorporated in America. This one company would become the genesis of regional commerce.

Today it is estimated that the houseboat manufacturing plants in the counties surrounding

Lake Cumberland produce more than half of the nation's houseboats each year. Needless to say, the houseboat industry is a major source of revenue for Kentucky. The price tag for a new houseboat—which can be customized into a veritable floating palace with every imaginable luxury and modern convenience—equates to a home on solid ground. Houseboats can look like a cottage or a villa, and range in size from a 26-foot long houseboat to one resembling a king's mansion, costing as much as $500,000 or more.

And, there's the jobs this industry brings to the area. According to a survey collected by the Ky. Cabinet for Economic Development, Div. of Research & Site Evaluation, nearly a dozen companies—all involved in building houseboats, yachts or luxury cruisers—employ over 800 people in a cluster stretching along the foothills of the Cumberland Plateau from Somerset and Monticello, and Russell Springs to Albany.

Dreaming about owning your own houseboat? Visit the National Houseboat Expo held at the Kentucky Fair & Expo Center in Louisville (one of two such shows in the nation). Each spring over 200 exhibitors display dozens of new houseboats and all the amenities—demonstrating that the elegance and style of a home doesn't have to be compromised just because it has a motor, an aluminum foundation and...floats on water.

*Sources: Somerset Pulaski County Chamber of Commerce, www.spcchamber.com/; National Houseboat Expo, www.nationalhouseboatexpo.com/; Ky. Economic Development Cabinet, Division of Research & Site Evaluation; Al Cross, Institute for Rural Journalism & Community Issues; and US Army Corp. of Engineers, Nashville District, www.orn.usace.army.mil/op/wol/rec/project.htm.*

## NUMBER OF ESTABLISHMENTS BY EMPLOYMENT-SIZE CLASS

| 1997 NAICS CODE | 1997 NAICS DESCRIPTION | ESTABLISHMENTS | | | SALES, RECEIPTS OR SHIPMENTS ($1,000) | | | ANNUAL PAYROLL ($1,000) | | | PAID EMPLOYEES | | |
|---|---|---|---|---|---|---|---|---|---|---|---|---|---|
| | | 2002 | 1997 | % CHG | 2002 | 1997 | % CHG | 2002 | 1997 | % CHG | 2002 | 1997 | % CHG |
| 21 | Mining | 659 | 691 | -4.6 | 4,946,446 | 5,324,568 | -7.1 | 868,157 | 832,468 | 4.3 | 19,886 | 22,400 | -11.2 |
| 22 | Utilities | 342 | 328 | 4.3 | Q | 8,236,037 | N | 529,109 | 505,207 | 4.7 | 9,113 | 11,367 | -19.8 |
| 23 | Construction | 8,807 | 8,878 | -0.8 | 12,631,692 | 9,896,219 | 27.6 | 2,633,289 | 2,000,656 | 31.6 | 83,793 | 76,876 | 9 |
| 31-33 | Manufacturing | 4,282 | 4,218 | 1.5 | 88,320,338 | 86,636,107 | 1.9 | 9,995,730 | 9,198,091 | 8.7 | 261,125 | 288,405 | -9.5 |
| 42 | Wholesale trade | 4,701 | 5,051 | -6.9 | 51,885,133 | 37,242,872 | 39.3 | 2,545,344 | 2,071,234 | 22.9 | 69,558 | 69,309 | 0.4 |
| 44-45 | Retail trade | 16,776 | 17,369 | -3.4 | 40,016,147 | 33,332,675 | 20.1 | 3,818,860 | 3,128,099 | 22.1 | 213,816 | 212,189 | 0.8 |
| 48-49 | Transportation & warehousing | 3,040 | 2,919 | 4.1 | 8,249,830 | 6,288,735 | 31.2 | 2,017,584 | 1,447,860 | 39.3 | 67,163 | 49,545 | 35.6 |
| 51 | Information | 1,549 | 1,261 | 22.8 | N | 5,056,056 | N | 929,663 | 814,710 | 14.1 | 29,668 | 29,098 | 2 |
| 52 | Finance & insurance | 5,841 | 5,373 | 8.7 | N | N | N | 2,584,566 | 1,859,987 | 39 | 68,764 | 60,241 | 14.1 |
| 53 | Real estate & rental & leasing | 3,524 | 3,227 | 9.2 | 2,470,137 | 1,961,641 | 25.9 | 426,014 | 314,279 | 35.6 | 18,019 | 16,284 | 10.7 |
| 54 | Professional, scientific, & technical services | 7,033 | 6,232 | 12.9 | 4,917,995 | 3,853,289 | 27.6 | 1,910,391 | 1,275,347 | 49.8 | 51,650 | 42,481 | 21.6 |
| 55 | Management of companies and enterprises | 640 | 772 | -17.1 | 351,347 | 1,648,582 | -78.7 | 1,710,764 | 1,441,126 | 18.7 | 28,675 | 28,398 | 1 |
| 56 | Administrative, support, waste management, remediation services | 2,790 | 2,848 | -2 | 3,060,399 | 2,147,364 | 42.5 | 1,317,885 | 941,688 | 39.9 | 69,756 | 74,123 | -5.9 |
| 61 | Educational services | 470 | 427 | 10.1 | 258,040 | 134,683 | 91.6 | 77,089 | 36,463 | 111.4 | 4,326 | 2,345 | 84.5 |
| 62 | Health care & social assistance | 9,713 | 8,384 | 15.9 | 16,697,148 | 11,962,976 | 39.6 | 6,732,391 | 5,006,735 | 34.5 | 220,679 | 194,876 | 13.2 |
| 71 | Arts, entertainment, & recreation | 1,223 | 1,170 | 4.5 | 1,005,610 | 772,563 | 30.2 | 273,431 | 189,364 | 44.4 | 16,057 | 15,105 | 6.3 |
| 72 | Accommodation & foodservices | 6,660 | 6,546 | 1.7 | 4,908,331 | 4,056,107 | 21 | 1,397,143 | 1,140,617 | 22.5 | 136,442 | 129,442 | 5.4 |
| 81 | Other services (except public administration) | 6,244 | 6,372 | -2 | 3,115,631 | 2,613,488 | 19.2 | 874,517 | 667,620 | 31 | 39,208 | 36,698 | 6.8 |

N = Not comparable or not available; Q = Receipts not collected at state level for multiestablishment firms

Source: http://www.census.gov/econ/census02/data/comparative/KYCS.HTM

## EMPLOYMENT AND REVENUE BY INDUSTRY SECTOR

| INDUSTRY CODE | INDUSTRY CODE DESCRIPTION | TOTAL ESTABS | 1-4 | 5-9 | 10-19 | 20-49 | 50-99 | 100-249 | 250-499 | 500-999 | 1000 OR MORE |
|---|---|---|---|---|---|---|---|---|---|---|---|
| ------- | Total | 91797 | 46246 | 19169 | 12600 | 8581 | 2819 | 1694 | 453 | 168 | 67 |
| 11----- | Forestry, fishing, hunting, and agriculture support | 308 | 223 | 44 | 24 | 12 | 3 | 2 | 0 | 0 | 0 |
| 21----- | Mining | 632 | 241 | 85 | 99 | 121 | 45 | 26 | 14 | 1 | 0 |
| 22----- | Utilities | 334 | 108 | 76 | 59 | 39 | 30 | 19 | 3 | 0 | 0 |
| 23----- | Construction | 9135 | 5554 | 1682 | 1025 | 602 | 181 | 73 | 15 | 2 | 1 |
| 31----- | Manufacturing | 4174 | 1201 | 671 | 631 | 701 | 370 | 376 | 136 | 68 | 20 |
| 42----- | Wholesale trade | 4595 | 2126 | 947 | 773 | 506 | 145 | 74 | 19 | 4 | 1 |
| 44----- | Retail trade | 16670 | 7175 | 4541 | 2836 | 1382 | 408 | 228 | 87 | 13 | 0 |
| 48----- | Transportation & warehousing | 3076 | 1719 | 488 | 336 | 310 | 116 | 69 | 20 | 12 | 6 |
| 51----- | Information | 1633 | 797 | 321 | 205 | 187 | 66 | 41 | 6 | 8 | 2 |
| 52----- | Finance & insurance | 6181 | 3386 | 1549 | 728 | 361 | 94 | 37 | 15 | 7 | 4 |
| 53----- | Real estate & rental & leasing | 3628 | 2507 | 697 | 293 | 99 | 20 | 10 | 1 | 1 | 0 |
| 54----- | Professional, scientific & technical services | 7882 | 5299 | 1304 | 759 | 363 | 100 | 38 | 14 | 4 | 1 |
| 55----- | Management of companies & enterprises | 619 | 213 | 107 | 110 | 93 | 41 | 35 | 10 | 6 | 4 |
| 56----- | Admin, support, waste mgt. remediation services | 3627 | 1966 | 595 | 412 | 312 | 159 | 143 | 31 | 8 | 1 |
| 61----- | Educational services | 859 | 375 | 163 | 118 | 103 | 43 | 36 | 12 | 8 | 1 |
| 62----- | Health care and social assistance | 10007 | 4146 | 2624 | 1580 | 984 | 274 | 301 | 51 | 21 | 26 |
| 71----- | Arts, entertainment & recreation | 1294 | 682 | 238 | 166 | 127 | 55 | 22 | 4 | 0 | 0 |
| 72----- | Accommodation & food services | 6888 | 1954 | 946 | 1432 | 1858 | 561 | 127 | 9 | 1 | 0 |
| 81----- | Other services (except public administration) | 9844 | 6198 | 2067 | 1006 | 418 | 108 | 37 | 6 | 4 | 0 |
| 99----- | Unclassified establishments | 411 | 376 | 24 | 8 | 3 | 0 | 0 | 0 | 0 | 0 |

*Source:* http://censtats.census.gov/cgi-bin/cbpnaic/cbpsect.pl

## BUSINESS & ECONOMY
# *Utilities*

Paul Wesslund

### POWER IN THE COUNTRY
### THE ELECTRIC CO-OP STORY

Kentucky historian Dr. Thomas Clark, writing about the coming of electricity to rural America in a July 1998 essay in "Kentucky Living" magazine, said, "No other great national enterprise on the globe wrought so quickly so many fundamental modifications in the rural way of life."

Clark added a

Wire swinging in Maysville
Source: *Kentucky Utilities*

personal note about rural electrification coming to his own house: "My father turned on every light on the place. I suggested he turn off most of them; it was costing him money. He retorted, 'Leave them on. I have been in the dark all my life.'"

The results of that excitement over electricity can still be seen in the network of nearly 1,000 local, consumer-owned electric cooperatives that provide power for some 34 million people in 47 states.

In the 1930s, several trends came together for rural America. One was an activist populism that focused on making natural resources available to everyday people. Many of our national parks and economic development projects like the Tennessee Valley Authority came from this movement.

Another force was the effort to end the Great Depression with government programs that targeted different areas of the economy.

But the most powerful force may have been the longing by American farm families as they looked at the glowing cities, and realized they were cut off from the benefits of modern society. Farmers didn't have access to lights, washing machines, radios, irons or indoor plumbing. Power companies didn't believe they could make a profit stringing lines to remote farmsteads.

But several politicians found support for the farmers, and in 1935 President Roosevelt created the Rural Electrification Administration, which offered loans for utilities to serve rural areas.

Power companies still weren't interested, but loan applications poured in from groups of people organizing themselves into cooperatives. REA staff were split over the advisability of lending to these groups. But within months it became obvious that local, member-owned, not-for-profit co-ops would be the primary providers of electricity in the countryside. Local organizers rode from farm to farm, signing up members for $5.

In the 1950s the rural electric co-ops could no longer grow efficiently by buying power from the city utilities. So many of these distribution co-ops that delivered power to their members got together to form power supply co-ops. These generation and transmission co-ops had the resources to build the relatively expensive power plants and lines the distribution co-ops needed.

Today, much of non-urban Kentucky, representing some 1.5 million people, gets electricity from cooperatives. There are 16 distribution co-ops in the eastern part of the state, and they receive their power from East Kentucky Power Cooperative, the generation and transmission co-op based in Winchester. Three co-ops in the west are served by Big Rivers Generation and Transmission Co-op based in Henderson. Five other Kentucky distribution co-ops in the western part of the state receive power from the Tennessee Valley Authority, which produces power for co-ops and municipal utilities in seven states.

Electric co-ops serve about 11 percent of the people in the U.S., and have been keeping pace with other changes under their overall mission of providing a better quality of life. As user-owned, community-based organizations, co-ops are able to fight for other concerns facing people living outside the city. Promoting economic development to keep jobs from moving away, setting up subsidiaries to provide hard-to-find services like cell phones and Internet access in rural areas, and provid-ing more than $100,000 a year in scholarships are examples of how electric co-ops today keep their members connected to the benefits of the modern world.

The Kentucky Association of Electric Cooperatives provides services for the 24 local, consumer-owned electric distribution utilities in the state, as well as the two "generation and transmission" cooperatives. KAEC publishes "Kentucky Living" magazine, which is distributed monthly to more than 500,000 Kentuckians.

## Utilities in Kentucky

The utility industry in Kentucky is big business and in 2002, employed 7,711 people with an annual payroll of $441,701,000. Employment in the utility industry has dropped by almost 32 percent since 1997 when there were 11,367 employees. Annual receipts in 2002 totaled 5.3 billion down from 8.2 billion or an almost 36 percent drop. Below are some of the major utilities operating in Kentucky:

**East Kentucky Power (EKP)** is headquartered in Winchester. The member cooperatives set up EKPC as a not-for-profit generation and transmission utility. Its purpose is to generate energy and ship it to co-ops that distribute it to retail customers. EKPC provides wholesale energy and services to 16 distribution cooperatives through power plants, peaking units, hydro power and more than 2,600 miles of transmission lines. Together, EKPC and member cooperatives are known as Kentucky's Touchstone Energy Cooperatives. The distribution cooperatives supply energy to about 500,000 Kentucky homes, farms, businesses and industries across 89 counties. http://www.ekpc.com/

**Big Rivers Electric Corporation** is based in Henderson Kentucky and serves 22 western Kentucky counties. LG&E entered into a 25-year lease of Big Rivers Electric's generating facilities. Big Rivers is an electric generation and transmission cooperative supplying the wholesale power needs of its

**Linemen at work**
*Source: Kentucky Living Magazine*

three member cooperatives and marketing power to non-member utilities and power markets. These members provide retail electric power and energy to industrial, residential and commercial customers in portions of 22 western Kentucky counties. Big Rivers Electric Corporation serves 98,000 customers. See http://www.bigrivers.coop/ For more information on Kentucky's Rural Electric Cooperatives, visit http://www.kaec.org/.

**Kentucky Power/American Electric Power** provides service to approximately 175,000 customers in all or part of 20 eastern Kentucky counties. Its distribution operations are based in Ashland with service centers in Pikeville and Hazard and area offices in Paintsville and Whitesburg. Kentucky Power maintains 1,233 miles of transmission lines, has 1,060 megawatts of generating capacity and 1.22 billion in assets. See http://www.kentuckypower.com/.

**Louisville Gas & Electric (LG&E)** is a diversified energy services company that is a member of a German family of companies. E.ON is the world's largest investor-owned utility company. LG&E is a regulated electric and natural gas utility, based in Louisville, serving Louisville and 16 surrounding counties. Founded in 1838, investors formed Louisville Gas and Water to provide gas-fired street lighting mandated by Louisville's city fathers to deter crime. The company sold gas from its local coal plant to fuel the gaslights. In 1998, LG&E

Energy acquired KU Energy, which owned neighboring utility, Kentucky Utilities. LG&E serves 384,139 electric customers, 312,146 natural gas customers and their service area covers 700 square miles. LG&E's total regulated generation capacity is 3,514 megawatts. http://www.lgeenergy.com/

**Union Light, Heat and Power (ULH&P)** is owned by Cinergy based in Cleveland, OH. ULH&P serves 129,602 Kentucky customers. ULH&P also serves 87,002 gas customers. Cinergy has 7,055 megawatts of generating capacity serving a total of 1.5 million electric customers and 500,000 gas customers. See http://www.cinergy.com/.

kilowatt-hours of electricity to more than 220,000 households in 28 counties in western and central Kentucky. Distributors of TVA power served more than 47,700 commercial and industrial customers with sales of more than 4.3 billion kilowatt-hours. TVA power revenues in Kentucky totaled more than $733 million. See http://www.tva.gov/.

**Columbia Gas of Kentucky**, based in Lexington, is a subsidiary of Columbia Gas of Kentucky serving over 145,000 energy customers in 31 Kentucky counties in central and eastern Kentucky. See http://www.columbiagasky.com/.

**Atmos Energy** serves 3.1 million natural gas utility customers in 12 states. It ranks as the largest pure gas utility in the U.S. Its nonutility operations serve wholesale customers in 22 states. In 1987, Atmos Energy expanded its operations into Kentucky with the acquisition of Western Kentucky Gas Company. See http://www.atmosenergy.com/

Central Division Meter Reading Crew, 1940
Kentucky Utilities

In fiscal year 2004, **Tennessee Valley Authority (TVA)**, sold more than 7.9 billion kilowatt-hours of electricity to 14 municipal and five cooperatively owned power companies serving customers in Kentucky. Distributors of TVA power provided three billion

Kentucky also has 28 municipal electric utilities. For more information go to the Municipal Electric Power Association of Kentucky at www.mepak.org.

## 2004 ELECTRIC PROFILE

| ITEM | VALUE | U.S. RANK |
|---|---|---|
| National Energy Regulatory Commission Region(s) | | ECAR/SERC |
| Primary Energy Source | | Coal |
| Net Summer Capability (megawatts) | 19,627 | 20 |
|   Electric Utilities | 15,860 | 16 |
|   Nonutility | 3,767 | 24 |
| Net Generation (megawatthours) | 94,529,947 | 18 |
|   Utility | 82,921,402 | 13 |
|   Nonutility | 11,608,545 | 25 |
| Emissions (thousand short tons) | | |
|   Sulfur Dioxide | 469 | 6 |
|   Nitrogen Oxide | 150 | 7 |
|   Carbon Dioxide | 87,270 | 7 |
|   Sulfur Dioxide (lbs/MWh) | 10.9 | 5 |
|   Nitrogen Oxide (lbs/MWh) | 3.5 | 14 |
|   Carbon Dioxide (lbs/MWh) | 2,035 | 7 |
| Total Retail Sales (megawatthours) | 86,521,156 | 15 |
|   Full Service Provider Sales (megawatthours) | 86,521,156 | 15 |
| Direct Use (megawatthours) | 188,482 | 43 |
| Average Retail Price (cents/kWh) | 4.63 | 51 |

*Source: http://www.eia.doe.gov/cneaf/electricity/st_profiles/sept01ky.xls*

## BUSINESS & ECONOMY

# Economic Impact of Tourism

Bob Stewart

An incredible abundance of natural resources, breathtakingly beautiful scenery, and a well-earned reputation for outstanding hospitality offered by its residents are the perfect components for the thriving tourism industry that has evolved in the Commonwealth of Kentucky. These elements, combined with a rich array of significant historic and cultural sites, outstanding state parks,

**Devils Gulch**
*Source: Tour Southern & Eastern Kentucky*

reasonable prices, and the perception of Kentucky as a safe, family-friendly destination have helped to stoke the state's tourism industry to the point where it is undeniably a major economic force.

Visitors come to Kentucky for all sorts of reasons. Visiting family and friends, participating in one of the hundreds of festivals and special events throughout the year, attending the races at one of Kentucky's signature racetracks, or simply checking into a state resort park to enjoy the wonderful natural amenities that are available all across Kentucky are all top reasons visitors give for coming to spend leisure time in the state. Regardless of the reason, visitors love to come to Kentucky and many return over and over again, year after year.

These visitors leave behind a significant amount of money. In 2005, the travel and tourism industry contributed $6.38 billion directly to Kentucky's economy. When factoring in the total impact these travel and tourism activities have once these visitors' dollars are pumped throughout the various sectors of Kentucky's economy, the total economic impact of tourism spending in Kentucky for 2005 totaled $9.44 billion.

This spending also generated $952 million in local, state and federal tax revenues. Additionally, this spending generated and supported 176,200 jobs in Kentucky, with a total payroll of more than $3.3 billion. For every one million dollars spent by tourists, 30 Kentucky jobs are created. These jobs are spread throughout over 3,500 business across the state which directly serve visitors: hotels, motels, resorts, bed & breakfasts, restaurants, campgrounds, marinas, museums, historic sites, race tracks, state parks, and other attractions. These are the obvious tourism-related businesses. However, visitor spending also helps support many other jobs in other sectors as well that may not be so obvious: food & beverage directors at hotels and convention centers, marketing specialists, airport personnel, transportation specialists, and even farmers who grow the produce consumed in state parks and restaurants and sold at farmers markets to visitors all across the state. Also, various goods and services that support the state's bustling meetings and convention industry are also part of the travel and tourism economy. These vendors include special event planners, sound and lighting providers, audio/visual specialists, florists, printers, and caterers to mention only a few.

Competition for the visitor dollar is intense. All 50 states have aggressive marketing campaigns to attract the attention, and spending, of potential visitors. Traditionally, Kentucky has been outspent by half the states, and in some cases dramatically outspent. To help address this, in 2004, a one percent statewide hotel bed tax was passed by the General Assembly that is dedicated specifically to tourism marketing, the first such tax ever approved in Kentucky on a statewide basis. During the 2006-2007 fiscal year, this tax is expected to generate as much as $8 million, which will significantly bolster both the state's advertising budget as well as local and regional tourism organizations' marketing efforts.

Although very important, marketing alone is no longer enough to sustain and grow a vibrant tourism economy. Like other more traditional sectors

**Rolex Three Day Event**
*Photo: Janet Worne, Lexington Herald-Leader*

of Kentucky's economy, such as manufacturing, the tourism industry must be carefully nurtured and continually developed in order to remain fresh and appealing to future and return visitors. In order for this to happen, strategies need to be in place to incent the growth and development of this growing industry.

Recognizing this, the Kentucky General Assembly in 1996 passed the historic Tourism Development Act, the first such legislation in the nation designed specifically to attract tourism business investment to the Commonwealth. Historically, most of Kentucky's economic development incentive programs had been aimed primarily at traditional manufacturing operations. With the estab-

lishment of tourism business incentives, Kentucky became very competitive in the area of attracting development that expands and enhances the state's tourism infrastructure. Essentially what this piece of legislation did was to allow a tourism developer to recover 25 percent of the cost of a project through a rebate of the state sales taxes collected from visitors to the attraction. Initially, in order to qualify for this tax incentive, the project had to cost a minimum of $1 million. In its first seven years, the Tourism Development Act attracted over a half billion dollars in new investment. Projects such as the Newport Aquarium, Newport on the Levee, Hofbrauhaus, and the Kentucky Speedway became reality further bolstering the state's ability to draw visitors.

Additional projects supported by the state and local governments that will benefit future economic impact of the tourism in Kentucky include a new downtown arena in Louisville (estimated completion in 2010) and major additions to the facilities at the Kentucky Horse Park to accommodate major new events scheduled there.

Kentucky's hospitality industry will be in the international spotlight in coming years—particularly when the 37th Ryder Cup international golf tournament is held at Valhalla Golf Club in Louisville in 2008 and the Kentucky Horse Park in Lexington hosts the World Equestrian Games in 2010. Each of these events will bring a significant number of new visitors to the state, generate tremendous media coverage, and dramatically enhance the growing impact of tourism on Kentucky's economy.

*Source of economic impact statistics: Economic Impact Report prepared by the Travel Industry Association (TIA) for the Kentucky Department of Tourism. Source of Tourism Development Act statistics: News Release, Tourism Development Cabinet, September 23, 2003.*

**Breaks Interstate Park**
*Source: Charles Bertram, Lexington Herald-Leader*

# BUSINESS & ECONOMY
# *Equine*

The Kentucky Equine Education Project (KEEP) was formed in May 2004 to raise awareness of Kentucky's horse industry and its economic impact throughout the state. To that end, KEEP brought together horse owners, breeders and trainers of all disciplines and breeds on a scale never seen before to create a unified voice and build a grassroots

ing more horses to remain in Kentucky.

At its core, KEEP endeavors to reach those willing to help foster the horse industry's everyday contributions to the state's agricultural and tourism sectors as well as facilitate public discussions relating to land preservation and the environment. While some 30 percent of Kentucky's modern-day econ-

*Source: Sid Webb*

organization to better inform the public about the equine economy.

Former Kentucky Gov. Brereton Jones (1991-1995) served as the impetus for KEEP's organization and development and was asked to lead the group as its first chairman. Jones and his wife, Libby, own and operate Airdrie Stud farm in Woodford County.

In a little over a year, KEEP has grown its membership ranks to more than 7,000, including members in 114 Kentucky counties representing every breed of horse, not just Thoroughbreds. In addition, KEEP has established a 29-member governing board, added six full-time staff and assigned team leaders in every county in the state. KEEP's maiden lobbying effort during the state legislature's 2005 session yielded legislation that not only established a $15 million breeder incentive fund but also eliminated a tax on out-of-state buyers, encourag-

omy is based on agriculture, including horses, the equine industry has also become a key component of the state's $8 billion tourism trade, the second leading source of revenue and jobs in Kentucky.

KEEP's mission focuses on coalition building among a diverse group of state and local organizations, including chambers of commerce, rotaries, nonprofits, educational foundations, businesses, organized labor and trade associations. KEEP advocates expanding the reach of state-sponsored programs like the Kentucky Thoroughbred and Standardbred development funds — which encourage ownership of Kentucky-bred horses — to include economic incentives and added tax reform to stimulate job growth and spur economic expansion.

Today, roughly 320,000 horses of varied breeds are raised on more than 13,000 farms owned and operated by Kentuckians in every county. Big and small, these farms require feed, fencing, veterinary services, trucks, tractors and manpower to operate, which taken together, create and sustain businesses that contribute more than $4 billion to Kentucky's annual gross domestic product. Incredibly, 100,000 or more jobs are directly or indirectly related to the state's horse industry.

It is estimated that more than half the farm equipment sold in Kentucky, for instance, is used on horse farms. Those farms collectively purchase 400,000 tons of hay and 200,000 tons of feed each year, and the average horse farm builds and maintains roughly 22 miles of fence. Rural and suburban automobile dealerships sell an average of three new trucks for every new car, and no other small business increases the property value of nearby real estate as dramatically as acreage devoted to horses. In short, horse farm operations contribute significantly to the bottom line of businesses across a broad spectrum of industries.

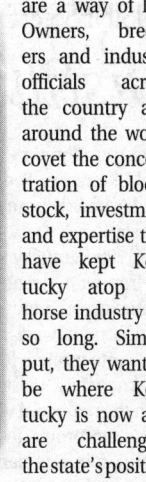

Source: Sid Webb

In Kentucky, horses are not just a business — they are a way of life. Owners, breeders and industry officials across the country and around the world covet the concentration of bloodstock, investment and expertise that have kept Kentucky atop the horse industry for so long. Simply put, they want to be where Kentucky is now and are challenging the state's position like never before.

KEEP's entrance into the public discussion in 2004 on how to best preserve and promote the state's signature industry brought about a renewed sense of purpose for many industry leaders. Indeed, it quantified in real terms, through tax and breeder incentive legislation enacted by the state legislature, the effectiveness of KEEP's broad-based grassroots advocacy and its potential to help shape the industry's future.

*Contributed by the Kentucky Equine Education Project*

## "Well, what about that"

### Keeneland Yearling Sale Establishes World Record
### Lexington, KY (September 21, 2006)

Keeneland set a world record for gross sales at a thoroughbred auction on Thursday, when 10-day totals reached $385,707,000. The milestone, broken when hip 3608 sold for $57,000, surpassed the world record mark of $384,349,900 set at last year's 14-day September sale. Average price for the sale is up 5.4 percent to $148,292 as compared to $140,639 reported last year.

*Source: Keeneland, www.keeneland.com*

# BUSINESS & ECONOMY
## *Distilleries*

Bill Ambrose

Bourbon (bou' r' bon) – 1.) "The Whiskey That Made Kentucky Famous" and 2.) a whiskey distilled primarily from corn and aged in charred oak barrels.

In 1790 Kentucky was still considered the western frontier of the new United States. Even before Kentucky was admitted to the new union in 1792, local farmers were converting their surplus corn crops into a rough form of whiskey. This whiskey was known as "Western Whiskey" to distinguish it from the rye-based whiskies from the east.

Also, according to legend, during this period a Baptist minister named Elijah Craig acquired a number of used oak barrels to store his distilled whiskey. Reverend Craig is said to have burned the insides of these barrels to avoid cleaning the remnants out. The liquor he stored in these barrels turned out to have distinctive characteristics and a rich caramel brown color. Thereafter charred oak barrels were used for shipping bourbon.

In 1833 Oscar Pepper hired Dr. James Christopher Crow as Master Distiller of his family distillery, Glassy Spring Branch of Glenn's Creek in Woodford County. This distillery is still operating today and is known as the Woodford Reserve Distillery. Dr. Crow was a physician trained in Edinburgh, Scotland. Dr. Crow brought a scientific approach to distilling – using the saccharimeter (alcohol measurer) and thermometer to study fermenta-

tion. *Old Crow Bourbon* was named in his honor. He was the first to perfect the sour mash process – where a portion of the "sour" stillage from the prior day was mashed in the next day. This created consistency between batches. Henry Clay, noted Kentucky Senator, would annually ship a barrel of Crow's whiskey to Washington "to lubricate the wheels of government." Other famous customers included Andrew Jackson, John C. Calhoun, Ulysses S. Grant, William Henry Harrison and Daniel Webster.

During the Civil War, the Revenue Act of 1862 authorized the Federal government to impose a

**Four Roses Distillery, Lawrenceburg**
*Photo: Sid Webb*

temporary excise tax on distilled sprits. This tax was signed into law by President Lincoln to offset the cost of the war. The tax was $2.00 per gallon and due at the time the whiskey was distilled. This temporary tax – for some unknown reason – is still being collected to this day. Excise Taxes accounted for twenty-five to fifty percent of the Federal budget between the Civil War and Prohibition.

The distilling industry expanded rapidly after the Civil War, and because of its quality Kentucky Bourbon Whiskey became known as a "gentleman's drink". Fine Kentucky Bourbon was available in most western saloons – a number of lawmen and outlaws in Dodge City were known to partake.

The roots of Prohibition can be traced to the 1890s, with the founding by a group of preachers, teachers and businessmen of the Anti-Saloon League. After the United States entered the First World War the temperance movement made major strides towards a national prohibition. The National Prohibition Act, also known as the Volstead Act after its sponsor Andrew Volstead of Minnesota, was approved in October 1918. President Wilson vetoed this legislation, but Congress quickly overrode his veto. After January 17, 1920 it was against the law to manufacture or sell any beverage with more than one-half of one percent alcohol. The first offense was punishable with a fine of up to $1,000 and a prison term of up to six months. The "Great Experiment" had begun.

After 1919, the remaining bourbon inventory was bottled for medicinal sales. Medical doctors could write a prescription for whiskey, which was then filled at drug stores. Prescriptions were limited to one quart at a time, later one pint every ten days. Doctors were limited to one hundred prescriptions annually, but many turned a blind eye and exceeded these limitations.

Prohibition ended in 1934 but only 34 of 157 distilleries reopened. Over the next 30 years, ownership of these remaining distilleries was consolidated into a half dozen major corporations. In 1968 Congress passed a resolution naming Bourbon Whiskey as America's native spirit.

Kentuckians still celebrate their heritage of fine bourbon whiskey. The Kentucky Bourbon Festival is held annually in Bardstown during September.

**Gethsemani Trappist Fudge**
Photo: Sid Webb

The Kentucky Bourbon Trail was established for tours of Kentucky's operating distilleries. The tour includes Buffalo Trace in Frankfort (*Ancient Age, Buffalo Trace* and *W. L. Weller*); Jim Beam Brands in Clermont (*Booker's, Jim Beam, Knob Creek, Old Crow, Old Grand-Dad, Old Taylor* and *Sunny Brook*); Four Roses Distillery in Lawrenceburg (*Four Roses*); Heaven Hill Distillery in Bardstown (*Elijah Craig, Evan Williams* and *Heaven Hill*) Woodford Reserve in Versailles (*Woodford Reserve*); Maker's Mark Distillery in Loretto (*Maker's Mark*); and Wild Turkey in Lawrenceburg (*Wild Turkey*).

Bourbon whiskey is today one of Kentucky's leading exports with over 400 million dollars in revenue.

## It's a Kentucky Thing!

Bourbon whiskey by federal regulation must contain at least 51 percent but not more than 80 percent corn, and no coloring or flavoring agents can be added. It must be distilled at less than 160 proof and racked into barrels at no more than 125 proof and barrels must be made of new charred oak  To qualify as Kentucky Bourbon the whiskey must be distilled and stored in the commonwealth for at least one year.

*(U.S. Code, Title 27, Part 5, Section 5.22)*

## BUSINESS & ECONOMY

# *Lexington Business Climate*

Tom Martin

Lexington, Kentucky is one of the most interesting medium market cities in the United States—a welcoming place where qualities of life and economy are in balance and the surrounding environs offer some of the nation's most stunning natural beauty.

The Lexington-Fayette County area consistently ranks high in health care, public safety, educational attainment and quality family living. And, the city and surrounding region receive high marks for business location, career relocation, entrepreneurial growth and creativity.

With its signature thoroughbred industry, an array of public and private colleges and universities and a growing high-technology community, the city welcomes diverse cultures, resulting in a cosmopolitan atmosphere.

International events ranging from the Keeneland sales and The Rolex Three-Day Event to the annual Alltech Symposium draw visitors from scores of nations. The much-anticipated 2010 World Equestrian Games will attract even more international guests. More than a few arrive, fall in love with what they discover here, and return to make a new home for themselves and their families.

Agricultural diversification is driving creativity in the regional farming community and leading to the rise of industries associated with biotechnology

**Downtown Lexington**
*Photo: Sid Webb*

**Stan Banks prepares samples for HPLC analysis in the Center for Pharmaceutical Science and Technology at UK.**
*Photo: Charles Bertram, Lexington Herald-Leader*

and aquaculture.

You can live and work in Lexington and be within minutes of some of Kentucky's most beautiful natural areas—Kentucky River Palisades and the Red River Gorge, part of Daniel Boone National Forest. And with more inland waterways than any state except Alaska, Kentucky is a fishing and boating paradise. The rolling countryside of the Bluegrass region provides over 1,000 miles of lightly traveled back roads for bikers and sightseers. Blue Grass Airport offers direct flights to major hubs.

These assets have not been lost on the likes of Forbes magazine, Dun & Bradstreet, Ladies Home Journal or the Places Rated Almanac. These noted industry resources rate Lexington as one of the nation's premier cities for its stunning natural beauty, great schools, innovative health care system and strong economy.

Former governor A.B. "Happy" Chandler once noted that while out of state he rarely crossed paths with a Kentuckian who wasn't on his or her way home. To anyone who has lived, worked and played in Kentucky, that observation comes as no surprise.

*Tom Martin is Editor in Chief for Business Lexington*

## BUSINESS & ECONOMY
# *Louisville*
# *Business Climate*

Joe Reagan

A friendly debate continues on the proper pronunciation of the city's name, but many agree on Louisville's emergence as one of America's most dynamic urban communities.

Since 2003, Louisville has been named: The number one community for relocating families (Worldwide ERC); Twentieth in the U.S. as a desirable location for business expansion or relocation (Expansion Management magazine); Ninth on the list of the Top 20 Hot Headquarters Cities for the 21st century (Business Facilities); and Best city for small business growth (Entrepreneur magazine).

And in March 2006, the National League of Cities named Louisville the number one city for cultural diversity—a reflection of the city's changing face and welcoming attitude.

Originally founded in 1828, Louisville started anew in 2003 when the city and county governments merged. Overnight, Louisville's population ranking soared from the 64th to 16th largest in America. Louisville is home to 695,000 residents living in its 386 square miles and is at the heart of the 25-county, bi-state (Kentucky and Indiana) Greater Louisville region.

Louisville's vibrant downtown features first-rate arts and cultural amenities, lively entertainment and dining venues and a planned multi-purpose arena. A booming downtown housing market offers lofts to high-end condos.

Distinctive neighborhoods meet the needs of all ages and lifestyles—from Victorian mansions to contemporary construction. Outdoor spaces such as the award-winning Waterfront Park and a park system designed by Frederick Law Olmsted contribute to Louisville's beauty.

Two industry sectors energize Louisville's economy – health enterprises and logistics. Hospitals

**Downtown Louisville**
*Source: Greater Louisville, Inc.*

and Fortune 500 headquarters such as Kindred Healthcare Inc. and Humana Inc. represent leadership in health-related industries.

Logistics strength includes companies such as American Commercial Lines' barge-building business on the Ohio River to the UPS international shipping hub, WorldPort, at Louisville International Airport.

With over 20,000 employees, UPS is Louisville's— and the Commonwealth's—largest employer and has made two billion-dollar hub expansions since 1998. UPS also headquarters their Airlines division in Louisville and has helped attract over 90 companies to the area including biotech powerhouses Amgen, Inc. and Genentech, Inc.

Louisville's economic base also includes two Ford Motor Company assembly plants and headquarters for YUM! Brands, Inc., Brown-Forman Corporation, GE Consumer & Industrial, Papa Johns International, Texas Roadhouse, Inc., Churchill Downs, Inc., plus an extensive small business community.

Home of the Kentucky Derby and Louisville Sluggers, Louisville also knows winning requires educational excellence. Business leaders have partnered with Jefferson County Public Schools to develop progressive programs in reading, math and science. The University of Louisville is one of the nation's fastest growing research institutions and Bellarmine University recently announced their vision to become the South's premier independent Catholic university.

Louisville's continued growth and prosperity is a result of successfully integrating legacy and tradition with innovation and progressive thinking.

*Joe Reagan, President and CEO, Greater Louisville Inc.—The Metro Chamber of Commerce.*

## TOP 100 MANUFACTURERS AND/OR SUPPORTIVE SERVICE FACILITIES BY FULL-TIME EMPLOYMENT

| NO | COMPANY | PRODUCTS | EMPL | COUNTY | YR | ADDRESS | CITY | ZIP |
|---|---|---|---|---|---|---|---|---|
| 1 | UPS | Courier services, admin offices, airline offices | 9,942 | Jefferson | 2004 | 1400 N Hurstbourne Pkwy | Louisville | 40223 |
| 2 | Toyota Motor Manufacturing Ky | Automobiles-Camry sedan, Avalon sedan, engines (4 cyl & V6), axles, steering components, blocks/cylinder heads/crankshafts | 7,400 | Scott | 2005 | 1001 Cherry Blossom Way | Georgetown | 40324 |
| 3 | Ford Motor Co | Medium & commercial light truck assembly | 6,000 | Jefferson | 2005 | 3001 Chamberlain Ln | Louisville | 40241 |
| 4 | GE Consumer and Industrial | Major household appliances: dryers, washers, refrigerators & dishwashers | 5,000 | Jefferson | 2005 | AP35-1113 | Louisville | 40225 |
| 5 | Delta Connection Comair | Air terminal, maintenance, training, office facility | 4,900 | Boone | 2006 | 77 Comair Blvd | Erlanger | 41018 |
| 6 | Humana Inc | Back office service calls, claims, enrollment, and IT roles | 3,828 | Jefferson | 2005 | 101 East Main | Louisville | 40202 |
| 7 | Ford Motor Co | Automobile assembly (Ford Explorer, Mercury Mountaineer, Ford Explorer Sport-Trac) | 3,500 | Jefferson | 2005 | 2000 Fern Valley Rd | Louisville | 40213 |
| 8 | Lexmark International Inc | Printers & information processing supplies, headquarters | 3,450 | Fayette | 2005 | 740 W New Circle Rd | Lexington | 40550 |
| 9 | Fidelity Investments | Financial services | 2,900 | Kenton | 2005 | 100 Crosby Pkwy, KP2L | Covington | 41015 |
| 10 | Citicorp Credit Services | Financial services customer service center | 2,500 | Boone | 2005 | 4600 Houston Rd | Florence | 41042 |
| 11 | Humana Inc | Back offices, sales support, and IT roles | 2,042 | Jefferson | 2006 | 500 West Main Street | Louisville | 40202 |
| 12 | Brown-Forman Corp | Distilled spirits, wooden barrels, headquarters | 1,800 | Jefferson | 2005 | 850 Dixie Hwy | Louisville | 40210 |
| 13 | Cagle's Keystone Foods Inc | Fresh & frozen poultry | 1,530 | Clinton | 2005 | RR 4 Box 439 | Albany | 42602 |
| 14 | Tyson Foods Inc | Chicken slaughtering, processing & packaging | 1,350 | Henderson | 2005 | 14660 US Hwy 41 S | Robards | 42452 |
| 15 | Swift & Co | Pork processing | 1,250 | Jefferson | 2005 | 1200 Story Ave | Louisville | 40206 |
| 16 | Pilgrim's Pride | Poultry processing & packing | 1,200 | Graves | 2005 | 2653 State Rt 1241 | Hickory | 42051 |
| 17 | General Motors Corp | Automobiles - Corvette, Cadillac XLR | 1,200 | Warren | 2005 | 600 Corvette Dr | Bowling Green | 42101 |
| 18 | R R Donnelley | Offset printing, computer typesetting, saddle stitch & perfect binding | 1,200 | Barren | 2005 | 120 Donnelley Dr | Glasgow | 42141 |
| 19 | Citicorp Credit Services Inc USA | Customer service call center and collections | 1,200 | Jefferson | 2005 | 12501 Lakefront Place | Louisville | 40299 |
| 20 | Perdue Farms Inc | Chicken slaughtering, processing & packaging | 1,191 | Ohio | 2005 | 489 Cromwell Rd | Cromwell | 42333 |
| 21 | Briggs & Stratton Corp | Lawn mower engines | 1,160 | Calloway | 2005 | 110 Main St | Murray | 42071 |
| 22 | BA Merchant Services | Processor of credit- and debit-card transactions, headquarters | 1,156 | Jefferson | 2005 | 1231 Durrett Ln | Louisville | 40213 |
| 23 | Schwan's Food Manufacturing Inc | Frozen pizzas | 1,150 | Boone | 2005 | 7605 Empire Dr | Florence | 41042 |
| 24 | USEC Paducah Plant | Government & uranium enrichment | 1,150 | McCracken | 2005 | 5600 Hobbs Rd | Paducah | 42001 |
| 25 | AMBRAKE Manufacturing LTD | Automotive disc & drum brakes | 1,134 | Hardin | 2005 | 300 Ring Rd | Elizabethtown | 42701 |
| 26 | NACCO Materials Handling Group | Lift trucks | 1,100 | Madison | 2005 | 2200 Menelaus Rd | Berea | 40403 |
| 27 | Kindred Healthcare Operating Inc | National corporate headquarters, computer service center & help desk; AP reimbursement for hospitals, nursing homes, institutional pharmacies | 1,100 | Jefferson | 2005 | 680 South Fourth St | Louisville | 40202 |
| 28 | Trane Co | Air conditioning, heating & air handling equipment & supplies | 1,100 | Fayette | 2005 | 1515 Mercer Rd | Lexington | 40511 |
| 29 | Nestle Prepared Foods | Specialty microwaveable lunch foods | 1,094 | Montgomery | 2005 | 150 Oak Grove Dr | Mt. Sterling | 40353 |
| 30 | North American Stainless | Stainless steel coils, sheets, and long products (bar, wire, and rod) | 1,091 | Carroll | 2005 | 6870 Highway 42 E | Ghent | 41045 |
| 31 | Cingular Wireless LLC | Wireless service center | 1,055 | Carter | 2005 | 828 East Park Rd | Grayson | 41143 |
| 32 | Dana Corporation | Pick up truck/SUV frames | 1,036 | Hardin | 2005 | 750 N Black Ranch Rd | Elizabethtown | 42701 |
| 33 | Gibbs Die Casting Corp | Aluminum & magnesium die castings, headquarters | 1,000 | Henderson | 2005 | 369 Community Dr | Henderson | 42420 |
| 34 | Wal-Mart Distribution Center 6066 | Distribution | 971 | Christian | 2005 | 690 Crenshaw Blvd | Hopkinsville | 42240 |
| 35 | Bank of America | Data processing (credit/debit card) | 960 | Jefferson | 2005 | 1231 Durrett Ln | Louisville | 40213 |
| 36 | Courier-Journal | Daily newspaper publishing offset printing and mass distribution | 950 | Jefferson | 2005 | 525 W Broadway | Louisville | 40202 |
| 37 | Logan Aluminum Inc | Aluminum rolled sheet stock | 950 | Logan | 2005 | US Highway 431 N | Russellville | 42276 |
| 38 | R R Donnelley | Offset printing, side & saddle stitch binding, patent binding | 921 | Boyle | 2005 | 3201 Lebanon Rd | Danville | 40422 |
| 39 | AK Steel Corp | Steel slabs | 900 | Boyd | 2005 | US Hwy 23 | Ashland | 41101 |
| 40 | SHPS | Corporate Office | 900 | Jefferson | 2005 | 11405 Bluegrass Pkwy | Louisville | 40299 |
| 41 | Publishers Printing Co | Offset & lithographic printing typesetting, saddle stitch & perfect binding | 863 | Bullitt | 2005 | 100 Frank E Simon Ave | Shepherdsville | 40165 |
| 42 | Tokico (USA) Inc | Automobile shock absorbers, struts, brake systems & air compressors | 860 | Madison | 2005 | 301 Mayde Rd | Berea | 40403 |
| 43 | Valvoline Co | Administrative offices and lab | 858 | Fayette | 2005 | 3499 Blazer Pkwy | Lexington | 40509 |
| 44 | L-3 Communications Integrated Sys | Support activities - DOD contract | 850 | Fayette | 2005 | 5749 Briar Hill Rd | Lexington | 40516 |
| 45 | Amazon.com | Fulfillment Center. Receive items available on website into inventory and ship | 850 | Fayette | 2005 | 1850 Mercer Rd | Lexington | 45011 |
| 46 | Publishers Printing Co | Printing publications or magazines | 847 | Bullitt | 2005 | 13487 S Preston Hwy | Lebanon Jnct | 40150 |
| 47 | Catlettsburg Refining LLC | Petroleum refining; gas | 835 | Boyd | 2005 | 11631 US Rt 23 | Catlettsburg | 41129 |
| 48 | Aleris Aluminum | Coils, aluminum tubing and flexible conduits | 830 | Hancock | 2005 | 1372 State Route 1957 | Lewisport | 42351 |
| 49 | Super Service | Freight carrier | 821 | Pulaski | 2005 | 250 Super Service Dr | Somerset | 42501 |
| 50 | Huish Detergents Inc | Detergent | 808 | Warren | 2005 | 385 Southwood Ct | Bowling Green | 42101 |

## TOP 100 MANUFACTURERS AND/OR SUPPORTIVE SERVICE FACILITIES BY FULL-TIME EMPLOYMENT

| NO | COMPANY | PRODUCTS | EMPL | COUNTY | YR | ADDRESS | CITY | ZIP |
|---|---|---|---|---|---|---|---|---|
| 51 | Dart Container Corp | Plastic food containers | 805 | Hart | 2005 | 975 S Dixie St | Horse Cave | 42749 |
| 52 | Toyota Motor Manufacturing NA Inc | Corporate headquarters | 800 | Kenton | 2005 | 25 Atlantic Ave | Erlanger | 41018 |
| 53 | Dana Corporation | Heavy duty truck axles and brakes | 800 | Barren | 2005 | 1320 West Main Street | Glasgow | 42141 |
| 54 | Con Agra Foods | Hams | 800 | Carter | 2005 | 800 Cw Stevens Blvd | Grayson | 41143 |
| 55 | GE Aircraft Engine Div | Aircraft engines, turbines, blades & vanes | 780 | Hopkins | 2005 | 3050 Nebo Rd | Madisonville | 42431 |
| 56 | Century Aluminum of Kentucky LLC | Aluminum castings, sows & smelting | 771 | Hancock | 2005 | 1627 State Rt 271 N | Hawesville | 42348 |
| 57 | Cox Interior Inc | Hardwood moldings, trim, stair parts, interior doors & mantels | 760 | Taylor | 2005 | 1751 Old Columbia Rd | Campbellsville | 42718 |
| 58 | Toyotetsu America Inc | Structural automotive components & stampings | 758 | Pulaski | 2005 | 100 Pin Oak Dr | Somerset | 42503 |
| 59 | Fruit of the Loom | Fabric for underwear & sportswear | 754 | Russell | 2005 | Hwy 127 | Jamestown | 42629 |
| 60 | J P Morgan Chase Bank NA | Check processing and administrative services | 750 | Jefferson | 2005 | Grade Lane Operations | Louisville | 40213 |
| 61 | Eagle Industries LLC | Oak furniture | 750 | Warren | 2005 | 601 Double Springs Rd | Bowling Green | 42101 |
| 62 | J P Morgan Chase Bank NA | Regional loan servicing center | 750 | Warren | 2005 | 201 East Main Street | Lexington | 40507 |
| 63 | Emerson Power Transmission | V-belts, drives, sprockets, gears, ball & roller bearing units, sheaves, bushings, couplings, gear boxes and gear reducers, motorized conveyor pulleys | 750 | Mason | 2004 | 1248 E 2nd St | Maysville | 41056 |
| 64 | Quebecor World | Book publishing & printing; staple saddle stitch & perfect binding | 745 | Woodford | 2005 | 100 US Bypass 60 | Versailles | 40384 |
| 65 | Johnson Controls Inc | Automobile & truck seat frames | 737 | Trigg | 2005 | Hwy 68 E | Cadiz | 42211 |
| 66 | Bowling Green Metalforming LLC | Automotive parts | 730 | Warren | 2005 | 111 Cosma Dr | Bowling Green | 42103 |
| 67 | Hitachi Automotive Products USA | Automobile electric & electronic components | 712 | Mercer | 2005 | 955 Warwick Rd | Harrodsburg | 40330 |
| 68 | Dana Corporation | Truck axles & brake components | 700 | Henderson | 2005 | 1491 Dana Dr | Henderson | 42420 |
| 69 | Mother's Cookie Co | Cookies | 700 | Jefferson | 2005 | 2287 Ralph Ave | Louisville | 40216 |
| 70 | TG Kentucky LLC | Rubber molded & plastic interior automobile parts | 700 | Marion | 2005 | 633 E Main St | Lebanon | 40033 |
| 71 | Kroger Limited Partnership I | Distribution center | 700 | Jefferson | 2005 | 2000 Nelson Miller Pkwy | Louisville | 40223 |
| 72 | Thomson Learning Distribution Ctr | Book distribution center | 700 | Kenton | 2005 | 10650 Toebben Dr | Independence | 41051 |
| 73 | US Bank Home Mortgage | Loan processing and underwriting service center, loan servicing center | 685 | Daviess | 2005 | 4801 Frederica St | Owensboro | 42301 |
| 74 | Tyco Adhesives | Pipeline coatings; industrial, athletic & consumer adhesive tapes & bandages | 676 | Simpson | 2005 | 2320 Bowling Green Rd | Franklin | 42134 |
| 75 | Wal-Mart | Distribution Center | 675 | Laurel | 2005 | 301 Russell Dyche Hwy | London | 40741 |
| 76 | Square D Company | Electrical safety switches & distribution panels, load centers | 666 | Fayette | 2003 | 1601 Mercer Rd | Lexington | 40511 |
| 77 | American Greetings | Distribution and paper product packaging center | 657 | Boyle | 2005 | 2601 Lebanon Rd | Danville | 40422 |
| 78 | Montaplast of North America | Plastic injection molding automotive wheel covers, center caps, and intake manifolds | 651 | Franklin | 2005 | 2011 Hoover Blvd | Frankfort | 40601 |
| 79 | Presbyterian Church [USA] | Headquarters | 650 | Jefferson | 2005 | 100 Witherspoon St | Louisville | 40202 |
| 80 | Dollar General Corp | Storage warehouse | 650 | Allen | 2005 | 427 Beech St | Scottsville | 42164 |
| 81 | Aisin Automotive Casting LLC | Automotive aluminum die cast components | 643 | Laurel | 2005 | 4870 E Hwy 552 | London | 40744 |
| 82 | Alcan Primary Metal Group | Aluminum extrusion billets & ingots | 629 | Henderson | 2005 | 9404 Hwy 2096 | Robards | 42452 |
| 83 | Mid-South Electronics Inc | Injection molded products, printed circuit boards, control panels, ice makers, electromechanical and electronic assemblies | 625 | Jackson | 2005 | 230 Worthington Ct | Annville | 40402 |
| 84 | Pella Corporation | Windows and doors manufacturer | 625 | Calloway | 2005 | 307 Pella Way | Murray | 42071 |
| 85 | McLane Cumberland | Food distribution center | 622 | Jessamine | 2005 | 1040 Baker Ln | Nicholasville | 40356 |
| 86 | ACS Shared Services Inc | Data processing, hosting, and related services | 620 | Laurel | 2005 | 1084 South Laurel Rd | London | 40744 |
| 87 | Papa John's International | Corporate office and make dough | 617 | Jefferson | 2005 | 2002 Papa John Blvd | Louisville | 40299 |
| 88 | AGC Automotive Americas | Automobile glass | 603 | Hardin | 2005 | 1 Auto Glass Dr | Elizabethtown | 42701 |
| 89 | Amazon.com | Fulfillment center. Receive items available on the website into inventory & ship | 600 | Taylor | 2005 | 1050 S Columbia Ave | Campbellsville | 42718 |
| 90 | Topy Corp | Road wheels for passenger cars and light trucks. | 600 | Franklin | 2005 | 980 Chenault Rd | Frankfort | 40601 |
| 91 | Guardian Automotive | Plastic exterior trim | 600 | Rowan | 2005 | 200 Guardian Ave | Morehead | 40351 |
| 92 | Speciality Foods Field Packing Division | Processed meat products | 600 | Daviess | 2005 | 6 Dublin Ln | Owensboro | 42301 |
| 93 | Emerson Electric Co | Hermetic electric motors | 600 | Logan | 2005 | 150 Emerson Bypass Rd | Russellville | 42276 |
| 94 | Dana Corporation | Automobile frames | 600 | Christian | 2005 | 301 Bill Bryan Blvd | Hopkinsville | 42240 |
| 95 | ThyssenKrupp Budd | Automobile parts stamping | 600 | Shelby | 2005 | 1000 Old Brunerstown Rd | Shelbyville | 40065 |
| 96 | DESA LLC | Portable gas heaters & generators | 600 | Warren | 2005 | 2701 Industrial Dr | Bowling Green | 42101 |
| 97 | Electronic Data Systems Corp | In-bound call center | 600 | Clark | 2005 | 1025 Bypass Rd | Winchester | 40391 |
| 98 | American Greetings Corp | Greeting cards | 598 | Nelson | 2005 | 800 American Dr | Bardstown | 40004 |
| 99 | Galls Inc | Corporate office, inbound call center, distribution, shipping | 596 | Fayette | 2005 | 2680 Palumbo Dr | Lexington | 40509 |
| 100 | Grupo Antolin Kentucky Inc | Overhead systems for automobiles | 585 | Christian | 2005 | 208 Commerce Ct | Hopkinsville | 42240 |

Source: Kentucky Economic Development Cabinet - www.thinkkentucky.com/kyedc/pdfs/top200mf.pdf

# BUSINESS & ECONOMY
# *Economic Indicators*

### MAY 2006 INDICATORS
### AS OF JULY 26, 2006

KY Composite Index of Leading Indicators decreased 3.5 percent in May.

- The Leading Index decreased for the second consecutive month.
- The Leading Index rose by 0.4 percent over the same month last year.
- Component indicators were mostly negative, 1:4.
- KY Labor Intensity Index decreased 0.7 percent.
- KY Index of Initial UI Claims decreased by 12.4 percent.
- US Retail Sales increased 1.6 percent.
- Component weights for May are 61.64, 17.31, 12.48, 6.54 and 2.03 respectively.

KY Composite Index of Coincident Indicators increased 0.8 percent in May.

- The Coincident Index is positive for the ninth consecutive month.
- Same-month-last-year growth is positive for the thirty-fourth consecutive month at 2.0 percent.
- Component indicators were mostly positive, 2:1.
- KY Nonagricultural Employment increased 1.5 percent.
- US Industrial Production Index increased 1.8 percent.
- US Personal Income Less Transfers decreased 1.3 percent.
- Component weights for May are 40.47, 25.20 and 20.84 respectively. Component weights do not sum to one because the two US components were discounted to give the Kentucky component more weight.

The Kentucky Leading Index fell by 3.5 percent in May. This is the third decline in four months. The US Leading Index also recorded its second consecutive decline in May. This is cause for concern as many indicators at both the national and state level have been soft for the last four months. The Kentucky Labor Intensity Index, which carries approximately 61 percent of the weight in the Leading Index, has declined for the second consecutive month.

Employment in four of the five manufacturing industries in the Kentucky Labor Intensity Index declined in May. Meanwhile, average weekly hours declined in only two of the five manufacturing industries in May. Four of the five components of the Labor Intensity Index had offsetting employment and average weekly hours changes. As a result, the net movement in four of the five components was near zero. For the most part, the May Labor Intensity Index component changes were small with the exception of the changes in Wood Products industry. Wood Products employment fell by a seasonally adjusted 0.27 percent from April. Wood Products average weekly hours fell by a seasonally adjusted 1.0 percent from April. These two components combined produced enough weight to bring the overall Labor Intensity Index negative. Otherwise the series would have been flat for May. The Labor Intensity Index has hovered around the 105.0 mark since August 2004, with no significant movement in either direction.

The Kentucky Index of Initial Unemployment Insurance (UI) Claims also fell for the second consecutive month. The UI Index is composed of two components, Kentucky First Pays and US Initial Claims. Both were responsible for the strong decline in May. Kentucky First Pays increased by a seasonally adjusted 13.0 percent, while US Initial Claims increased by 5.9 percent. US Initial Claims, being the more stable of the two subcomponents, carries the most weight, approximately 71 percent. Ironically, the Kentucky unemployment rate declined to 5.6 in May. Not only is this a considerable one-month decline, but it is also the first time it has been below 6.0 percent since April 2005.

For a complete description of the Index of Leading Indicators and methodology see University of Kentucky Center for Business and Economic Research Kentucky Annual Economic Report, 2000.

*Source: Office of State Budget Director, www.osbd.ky.gov*

## 2002 SURVEY OF BUSINESS OWNERS

PRELIMINARY ESTIMATES OF BUSINESS OWNERSHIP BY GENDER, HISPANIC OR LATINO ORIGIN AND RACE

| | KY FIRMS (Number) | KY PERCENT | U.S. FIRMS (Number) | U.S. PERCENT | KY SALES & RECEIPTS ($1000) | KY PERCENT | U.S. SALES & RECEIPTS ($1,000) | U.S. PERCENT |
|---|---|---|---|---|---|---|---|---|
| TOTALS | 300,732 | | 22,977,164 | | 284,127,673 | | 22,634,870,406 | |
| Female | 77,232 | 25.68% | 6,492,795 | 28.26% | 9,482,166 | 3.34% | 950,600,079 | 4.20% |
| Male | 174,984 | 58.19% | 13,185,703 | 57.39% | 84,647,270 | 29.79% | 7,096,465,049 | 31.35% |
| Equally male-/female-owned | 39,343 | 13.08% | 2,691,722 | 11.71% | 8,237,792 | 2.90% | 731,051,431 | 3.23% |
| Hispanic | 2,082 | 0.69% | 1,574,159 | 6.85% | 782,891 | 0.28% | 226,468,398 | 1.00% |
| Non-Hispanic | 289,477 | 96.26% | 20,796,061 | 90.51% | 101,584,338 | 35.75% | 8,551,648,161 | 37.78% |
| White | 280,029 | 93.12% | 19,894,823 | 86.59% | 99,681,772 | 35.08% | 8,303,716,399 | 36.69% |
| Black | 7,595 | 2.53% | 1,197,988 | 5.21% | 1,090,724 | 0.38% | 92,681,562 | 1.12% |
| American Indian and Alaska Native | 1,324 | 0.44% | 206,125 | 0.90% | 79,406 | 0.03% | 26,395,707 | 0.12% |
| Asian | 3,243 | 1.08% | 1,105,329 | 4.81% | 1,473,543 | 0.52% | 343,321,501 | 1.52% |
| Native Hawaiian and Other Pacific Islander | S | na | 32,299 | 0.14% | 11,385 | 0.00% | 5,220,795 | 0.02% |
| Publicly-held, foreign-owned, and not-for-profit | 7,333 | 2.44% | 491,715 | 2.14% | 179,737,815 | 63.26% | 13,790,327,139 | 60.93% |

Note: "S" Estimates are suppressed when publication standards are not met. Suppression occurs when one or more of the following criteria are met: the firm count is less than 3; or the Relative Standard Error is 50 percent or more.

Source: U.S. Census Bureau, Company Statistics Division, Economic Census Branch (http://www.census.gov/csd/sbo/state/st21.HTM, http://www.census.gov/csd/sbo/state/st00.HTM)

## INDUSTRY EMPLOYMENT PROJECTIONS 2002 - 2012

| CODE | INDUSTRY | EST YR - PROJ YR | CHANGE | PERCENT CHANGE |
|---|---|---|---|---|
| 110000 | Agriculture, Forestry, Fishing and Hunting | 2002-2012 | 712 | 9.5 |
| 210000 | Mining | 2002-2012 | -5,025 | -25.6 |
| 220000 | Utilities | 2002-2012 | -1,912 | -28.6 |
| 230000 | Construction | 2002-2012 | 12,667 | 15.2 |
| 310000 | Manufacturing | 2002-2012 | 7,913 | 2.9 |
| 420000 | Wholesale Trade | 2002-2012 | 16,976 | 23.7 |
| 440000 | Retail Trade | 2002-2012 | 27,621 | 13 |
| 480000 | Transportation and Warehousing | 2002-2012 | 17,345 | 21.5 |
| 510000 | Information | 2002-2012 | 11,759 | 36.9 |
| 520000 | Finance and Insurance | 2002-2012 | 8,397 | 13.3 |
| 530000 | Real Estate and Rental and Leasing | 2002-2012 | 4,196 | 21.2 |
| 540000 | Professional, Scientific, and Technical Services | 2002-2012 | 14,616 | 25.8 |
| 550000 | Management of Companies and Enterprises | 2002-2012 | 2,017 | 15 |
| 560000 | Administrative and Support and Waste Management and Remediat | 2002-2012 | 15,139 | 17.9 |
| 610000 | Educational Services | 2002-2012 | 38,875 | 24.8 |
| 620000 | Health Care and Social Assistance | 2002-2012 | 46,670 | 23 |
| 710000 | Arts, Entertainment, and Recreation | 2002-2012 | 4,611 | 26 |
| 720000 | Accommodation and Food Services | 2002-2012 | 30,864 | 22.8 |
| 810000 | Other Services (Except Government) | 2002-2012 | 10,137 | 14.8 |
| 900000 | Government | 2002-2012 | 17,048 | 12.3 |
| 910000 | Federal Government | 2002-2012 | -1,997 | -5.3 |
| 920000 | State Government, Excluding Education and Hospitals | 2002-2012 | 4,318 | 10.1 |
| 930000 | Local Government, Excluding Education and Hospitals | 2002-2012 | 14,727 | 25.1 |
| 6010 | Self-Employed Workers, Primary Job | 2002-2012 | 36,472 | 27.9 |
| | Total Employment, All Jobs | 2002-2012 | 316,011 | 16.8 |

Source: http://www.workforcekentucky.ky.gov/

> According to the Ky. Office of Employment and Training, in October 2005, 68.6 percent of high school graduates from the class of 2005 were enrolled in colleges or universities, according to data released today by the U.S. Dept. of Labor's Bureau of Labor Statistics. The college enrollment rate for recent high school graduates was a historical high for the series dating back to 1959.
>
> Source: www.workforcekentucky.ky.gov/

## REAL GROSS STATE PRODUCT (GSP) 2000-2005 (Millions of Current Dollars)

| STATE | GSP 2000 | % | GSP 2001 | % | GSP 2002 | % | GSP 2003 | % | GSI 2004 | % | GSP 2005 | % | % CHANGE 2000-2005 |
|---|---|---|---|---|---|---|---|---|---|---|---|---|---|
| US | 9,749,103 | 1.2% | 10,058,168 | 1.2% | 10,398,402 | 1.2% | 10,896,356 | 1.2% | 11,655,335 | 1.2% | 12,402,967 | 1.2% | 23% |
| Alabama | 114,576 | 1.2% | 118,682 | 1.2% | 123,805 | 1.2% | 130,526 | 1.2% | 141,366 | 1.2% | 149,796 | 1.2% | 26% |
| Alaska | 27,034 | 0.3% | 26,609 | 0.3% | 29,186 | 0.3% | 31,488 | 0.3% | 35,988 | 0.3% | 39,872 | 0.3% | 50% |
| Arizona | 158,533 | 1.6% | 165,358 | 1.6% | 171,942 | 1.7% | 182,414 | 1.7% | 194,246 | 1.7% | 215,759 | 1.7% | 30% |
| Arkansas | 66,801 | 0.7% | 68,927 | 0.7% | 72,203 | 0.7% | 75,564 | 0.7% | 82,712 | 0.7% | 86,802 | 0.7% | 26% |
| California | 1,287,145 | 13.2% | 1,301,050 | 12.9% | 1,340,446 | 12.9% | 1,410,539 | 12.9% | 1,519,202 | 13.0% | 1,621,843 | 13.1% | 25% |
| Colorado | 171,862 | 1.8% | 178,078 | 1.8% | 182,154 | 1.8% | 188,873 | 1.7% | 201,392 | 1.7% | 216,064 | 1.7% | 21% |
| Connecticut | 160,436 | 1.6% | 165,025 | 1.6% | 166,073 | 1.6% | 170,235 | 1.6% | 182,468 | 1.6% | 194,469 | 1.6% | 18% |
| Delaware | 41,472 | 0.4% | 44,206 | 0.4% | 45,324 | 0.4% | 48,109 | 0.4% | 52,298 | 0.4% | 54,354 | 0.4% | 23% |
| District of Columbia | 58,699 | 0.6% | 63,730 | 0.6% | 67,717 | 0.7% | 71,280 | 0.7% | 77,510 | 0.7% | 82,277 | 0.7% | 30% |
| Florida | 471,316 | 4.8% | 497,423 | 4.9% | 522,719 | 5.0% | 556,748 | 5.1% | 609,372 | 5.2% | 674,049 | 5.4% | 36% |
| Georgia | 290,887 | 3.0% | 299,442 | 3.0% | 306,680 | 2.9% | 317,490 | 2.9% | 339,730 | 2.9% | 364,310 | 2.9% | 22% |
| Hawaii | 40,202 | 0.4% | 41,822 | 0.4% | 43,476 | 0.4% | 46,386 | 0.4% | 50,238 | 0.4% | 53,710 | 0.4% | 28% |
| Idaho | 34,989 | 0.4% | 35,631 | 0.4% | 36,651 | 0.4% | 38,468 | 0.4% | 43,509 | 0.4% | 47,178 | 0.4% | 32% |
| Illinois | 464,194 | 4.8% | 476,461 | 4.7% | 487,129 | 4.7% | 509,161 | 4.7% | 533,735 | 4.6% | 560,236 | 4.5% | 18% |
| Indiana | 194,419 | 2.0% | 195,196 | 1.9% | 205,015 | 2.0% | 216,650 | 2.0% | 229,449 | 2.0% | 238,638 | 1.9% | 22% |
| Iowa | 90,186 | 0.9% | 91,920 | 0.9% | 97,356 | 0.9% | 102,358 | 0.9% | 110,210 | 0.9% | 114,291 | 0.9% | 24% |
| Kansas | 82,812 | 0.8% | 86,430 | 0.9% | 89,573 | 0.9% | 93,076 | 0.9% | 98,927 | 0.8% | 105,448 | 0.9% | 22% |
| Kentucky | 111,900 | 1.1% | 115,113 | 1.1% | 120,726 | 1.1% | 125,832 | 1.2% | 133,003 | 1.1% | 140,359 | 1.1% | 22% |
| Louisiana | 131,520 | 1.3% | 133,689 | 1.3% | 134,308 | 1.3% | 146,105 | 1.3% | 160,186 | 1.4% | 166,310 | 1.3% | 24% |
| Maine | 35,542 | 0.4% | 37,129 | 0.4% | 38,625 | 0.4% | 40,197 | 0.4% | 43,258 | 0.4% | 45,070 | 0.4% | 21% |
| Maryland | 180,367 | 1.9% | 192,659 | 1.9% | 204,120 | 2.0% | 214,488 | 2.0% | 230,698 | 2.0% | 244,899 | 2.0% | 27% |
| Massachusetts | 274,949 | 2.8% | 280,509 | 2.8% | 284,386 | 2.7% | 295,938 | 2.7% | 312,700 | 2.7% | 328,535 | 2.6% | 17% |
| Michigan | 337,235 | 3.5% | 334,419 | 3.3% | 349,837 | 3.4% | 362,805 | 3.3% | 366,601 | 3.1% | 377,895 | 3.0% | 13% |
| Minnesota | 185,093 | 1.9% | 190,231 | 1.9% | 198,558 | 1.9% | 209,335 | 1.9% | 224,620 | 1.9% | 233,292 | 1.9% | 23% |
| Mississippi | 64,266 | 0.7% | 65,961 | 0.7% | 68,144 | 0.7% | 72,532 | 0.7% | 77,107 | 0.7% | 80,197 | 0.6% | 22% |
| Missouri | 176,708 | 1.8% | 182,362 | 1.8% | 188,351 | 1.8% | 195,615 | 1.8% | 205,847 | 1.8% | 216,069 | 1.7% | 18% |
| Montana | 21,366 | 0.2% | 22,471 | 0.2% | 23,560 | 0.2% | 25,477 | 0.2% | 27,583 | 0.2% | 29,851 | 0.2% | 33% |
| Nebraska | 55,478 | 0.6% | 57,438 | 0.6% | 59,934 | 0.6% | 64,789 | 0.6% | 67,989 | 0.6% | 70,263 | 0.6% | 22% |
| Nevada | 73,719 | 0.8% | 77,291 | 0.8% | 81,274 | 0.8% | 89,035 | 0.8% | 99,143 | 0.9% | 110,546 | 0.9% | 43% |
| New Hampshire | 43,518 | 0.4% | 44,279 | 0.4% | 46,188 | 0.4% | 48,380 | 0.4% | 52,084 | 0.4% | 55,690 | 0.4% | 26% |
| New Jersey | 344,824 | 3.5% | 362,987 | 3.6% | 372,754 | 3.6% | 388,645 | 3.6% | 410,306 | 3.5% | 430,787 | 3.5% | 19% |
| New Mexico | 50,725 | 0.5% | 51,359 | 0.5% | 52,510 | 0.5% | 57,453 | 0.5% | 63,645 | 0.5% | 69,324 | 0.6% | 35% |
| New York | 777,157 | 8.0% | 808,537 | 8.0% | 821,577 | 7.9% | 847,123 | 7.9% | 906,783 | 7.8% | 963,466 | 7.8% | 19% |
| North Carolina | 273,698 | 2.8% | 285,651 | 2.8% | 296,435 | 2.9% | 307,871 | 2.8% | 323,962 | 2.8% | 344,641 | 2.8% | 21% |
| North Dakota | 17,752 | 0.2% | 18,527 | 0.2% | 19,880 | 0.2% | 21,703 | 0.2% | 22,692 | 0.2% | 24,178 | 0.2% | 31% |
| Ohio | 372,006 | 3.8% | 374,719 | 3.7% | 389,773 | 3.7% | 402,607 | 3.7% | 425,173 | 3.6% | 442,440 | 3.6% | 18% |
| Oklahoma | 89,757 | 0.9% | 94,329 | 0.9% | 97,170 | 0.9% | 103,824 | 1.0% | 111,838 | 1.0% | 120,549 | 1.0% | 28% |
| Oregon | 112,438 | 1.2% | 110,916 | 1.1% | 117,131 | 1.1% | 120,480 | 1.1% | 134,615 | 1.2% | 145,351 | 1.2% | 31% |
| Pennsylvania | 389,619 | 4.0% | 406,713 | 4.0% | 423,110 | 4.1% | 439,241 | 4.0% | 463,752 | 4.0% | 487,169 | 3.9% | 20% |
| Rhode Island | 33,609 | 0.3% | 35,149 | 0.3% | 36,909 | 0.4% | 39,260 | 0.4% | 41,844 | 0.4% | 43,791 | 0.4% | 25% |
| South Carolina | 112,514 | 1.2% | 117,296 | 1.2% | 121,582 | 1.2% | 127,459 | 1.2% | 131,492 | 1.1% | 139,771 | 1.1% | 19% |
| South Dakota | 23,099 | 0.2% | 23,910 | 0.2% | 26,416 | 0.3% | 27,399 | 0.3% | 29,699 | 0.3% | 31,066 | 0.3% | 30% |
| Tennessee | 174,851 | 1.8% | 180,582 | 1.8% | 191,525 | 1.8% | 201,522 | 1.8% | 216,769 | 1.9% | 226,502 | 1.8% | 25% |
| Texas | 727,233 | 7.5% | 762,247 | 7.6% | 783,480 | 7.5% | 828,456 | 7.6% | 903,208 | 7.7% | 982,403 | 7.9% | 29% |
| Utah | 67,568 | 0.7% | 70,109 | 0.7% | 72,665 | 0.7% | 76,180 | 0.7% | 82,546 | 0.7% | 89,836 | 0.7% | 28% |
| Vermont | 17,782 | 0.2% | 18,828 | 0.2% | 19,553 | 0.2% | 20,580 | 0.2% | 21,992 | 0.2% | 23,134 | 0.2% | 23% |
| Virginia | 260,743 | 2.7% | 276,762 | 2.8% | 285,759 | 2.8% | 301,867 | 2.8% | 327,032 | 2.8% | 353,745 | 2.8% | 27% |
| Washington | 221,961 | 2.3% | 225,765 | 2.2% | 231,463 | 2.2% | 240,025 | 2.2% | 253,085 | 2.2% | 268,502 | 2.2% | 19% |
| West Virginia | 41,476 | 0.4% | 43,365 | 0.4% | 45,032 | 0.4% | 46,645 | 0.4% | 49,903 | 0.4% | 53,782 | 0.4% | 24% |
| Wisconsin | 175,737 | 1.8% | 181,936 | 1.8% | 188,600 | 1.8% | 196,316 | 1.8% | 207,739 | 1.8% | 217,537 | 1.8% | 20% |
| Wyoming | 17,331 | 0.2% | 18,941 | 0.2% | 19,619 | 0.2% | 21,806 | 0.2% | 24,092 | 0.2% | 27,422 | 0.2% | 45% |

Source: US Dept of Commerce, Bureau of Economic Analysis, www.bea.gov/bea/regional/gsp

# Family Trends & Society

**Billy Clark**
*Source: Jesse Stuart Foundation*

Billy C. Clark (1928- ), a native of Catlettsburg, is a noted American author and one of Kentucky's most distinguished writers. This is an excerpt from *"A Long Row to Hoe"* (Chapter 9), reprinted with permission of the Jesse Stuart Foundation in Ashland.

"We were no strangers to the hills, least of all Mom. Often when she was in a happy mood she would laugh and tell us how Grandpa Hewlett said he was born so far up the Big Sandy Valley the he'd been able to straddle the river to wash his face. Mom, herself, was born deep in the hills twelve miles up the valley at a toe hold on the hills known as Buchanan, Kentucky. Three miles walk out of the hollow and she could stand on a knoll and stare at the small single-tracked railroad. The train crawled down the valley like a caterpillar worm with its joints loose, smoke puffing from the big malley engine and trailing off over the river. The railroad was the only means of transportation in and out of the valley. The Big Sandy River had been left to pool it; it was so shallow in places that you could wade across it.

When she was twelve, Mom had taken her first ride on the train. This had been a great day. More dreaming had gone into this day than she could tell, and her eyes lighted up even now as she talked of it. Before boarding the train, she needed some sort of luggage to take with her. The fact that she was traveling only twelve miles down river to Catlettsburg didn't matter. Everyone that boarded the train carried luggage. With luggage, there was a feeling of going somewhere. People gathered at the small cowpath station, elected one of their number to flag down the train, and waited hours for it to crawl down the valley. The men wore big handle-bar mustaches, and the women wore their Sunday clothes. They carried 'trading goods' in feed sacks stitched with designs that showed long hours of needlework under oil lamps. Mom's mother had pieced her bag out of a flowered feed sack. There were few bags like this in the valley, and Mom felt proud to hold it. She stood at the station, listening to the people talk.

'How far down you travelin' today, John?'

'All the way. Five miles below Catlettsburg. Clear to Ashland where the train's made up.'

'Lordy! You've a long way to go!'

'Yes sir, a long stretch o' rail. Wouldn't want to make the trip every day.'

Kin gathered to say good-by. The hugged the necks of the people that boarded the train, then crossed over the tracks and ran along the side of the hill to wave until the train was out of sight.

*Jesse Stuart Foundation is deeply committed its dual mission of preserving the literary legacy of Jesse Stuart while fostering appreciation of the Appalachian way of life through its book publishing, bookselling and other activities. Visit www.jsfbooks.com.*

## Steven H. Jones

# FAMILY TRENDS & SOCIETY
# *Gender, Race*
# *& Ethnicity*

This essay focuses on the gender, race and ethnicity of the Kentucky population at the beginning of the 21st century. Gender followed by race represents some of the most salient features of cultural diversity of the state's residents. What follows is an overview of the major social and demographic trends for males, females, Caucasians, African Americans and Hispanics.

### GENDER

The Kentucky population of 4,041,769 is composed of 51.1 percent females and 48.9 percent males. Males and females have roughly the same amount of education at the high school level: 82.9 percent of females have a high school diploma or higher; the comparable percentage for males is 82.6 percent. However, at the college level 22.8 percent of males have a bachelor's degree or higher, while the equivalent figure for females is only 19.9 percent. Kentucky ranks 49th in the U.S. for the number of women aged 25 and older with four or more years of college.

When the average yearly salary of men and women is compared (holding educational level constant for both groups), women in the Commonwealth earn only about 67 percent of the salary of men. As this suggests, women in the state are more poverty stricken than men – 15.6 percent of women live below the poverty line as compared to 11 percent of men. In 1999, 54.4 percent of women in Kentucky participated in the labor force. The most significant national comparison is that Kentucky ranks 40th in the nation for women's labor force participation, and it ranks 47th for women's overall employment and earnings. Many social scien-

tists maintain that these disparities are primarily caused by institutional discrimination. Women in Kentucky, like their counterparts in the nation at large, do not enjoy the same access to economic and political resources that men enjoy.

Women in American society generally, and in Kentucky specifically, play an important role in preserving and enriching family life. Female-centered families represent an especially sensitive barometer of family and female well-being. An examination of the period between 1980 and 2000 indicates that two-parent families in the state decreased

Photo: Sid Webb

from 84 percent of the total number of families to 73 percent. Female-centered families climbed from 16 percent to 26 percent of the state total – a 63 percent increase. In 1999, 43 percent of female-headed families lived in poverty compared to only 18 percent of all families in the state.

### RACE

The major categories based on race are composed of Caucasians and African Americans. In 2003 Caucasians formed 88 percent of the population, and African Americans constituted 8 percent. In order to encourage a general comparison of the Kentucky populace on the basis of gender, race and ethnicity, the socioeconomic categories listed below will generally mirror those presented in the section on gender.

African Americans in Kentucky numbered 305,820 in 2000. In 1990, 61.7 percent of African Americans over the age of 25 had a high school diploma; the comparable figure for Caucasians was 64.7 percent. In 2000, 80.5 percent of African Americans had a high school diploma, and the same figure for Caucasians was 83.3 percent. Differences between blacks and whites in educational attainment are greatest at the college level. In 1990, 25.4 percent of Caucasians over the age of 25 had a bachelor's degree; the comparable figure for African Americans was 14.8 percent. And in 2003, 29.8 percent of whites over age 25 had a bachelor's degree, while only 17.2 percent of blacks had an undergraduate degree.

The median household income for African Americans in 2000 was $22,080 in the Commonwealth, while the median household income for Caucasians was $35,600. The average household size for blacks was 2.44 persons; at the same time the average size of white households was 2.5. When the mean annual income and education level for black females and white females is compared in Kentucky, as income and education increase, the difference in income between the two groups becomes greater. White females earn approximately $2,000 more at the ninth-grade level, and they earn approximately $4,000 more at the doctorate degree level.

Family structure is a key variable in determining African American progress in the nation and the state. A high percentage of female-headed families for a group (especially a gender, racial or ethnic group) usually means elevated levels of poverty. While 22 percent of Caucasian families are headed by females, 63.7 percent of African American families are headed by females in Kentucky. An overwhelming percentage of the mother-centered families live below the poverty line. Thirty-one percent of the black population lives below the poverty level in the state of Kentucky.

African Americans in our state and in the nation face a health care crisis because they suffer from high rates of HIV/AIDS. In 2004 blacks in the U.S. were just under 14 percent of the total population, but they constituted nearly 40 percent of all AIDS cases. By 2005 blacks represented over 50 percent of all AIDS cases in the country. Even though blacks are only about 8 percent of the population in the Commonwealth, they represent 30 percent of all the AIDS cases. There is a ray of hope – the black AIDS rate decreased from 39 percent of the total cases in the state in 1999 to 30 percent in 2004.

*Photo: Sid Webb*

## ETHNICITY

Hispanics numbered approximately 70,910 in 2003, representing 2 percent of the total population in the state. In 1990, 75.6 percent of Hispanics 25 years and older had a high school diploma; in 2000 this number plummeted to 46.5 percent. In 1990, 7.1 percent of Hispanics 25 years and older had a bachelor's degree, but this number had only increased to 7.7 percent by 2000. Thirty-three percent of Hispanics in Kentucky live below the poverty level.

## CONCLUSION

As cultural diversity in Kentucky's population continues to evolve, one trend is striking – high rates of poverty afflict select diverse communities suffering from inadequate socioeconomic resources. There are differences of opinion about causes of this conundrum. Critics of the poor and their way of life and those who blame inefficient institutions agree on one issue: education must play a major role in any solution. Bold new education programs must target women and minorities.

# FAMILY TRENDS & SOCIETY
## Long-Term Care

Bernie Vonderheide

### LONG-TERM CARE IN KENTUCKY

As Kentuckians enter the new millennium people as a whole are living healthier and living longer. As a result, we can expect to live much longer than our ancestors. But increased longevity may also mean the increased probability that one will need long-term care, the assistance required as a result of the natural aging process or a lengthy illness, accident or cognitive impairment.

**In the garden at Ashland Terrace, Lexington**
*Source: Ashland Terrace Retirement Home*

Private long-term care insurance, family savings and other financial resources are among the options for financing long-term care. In Kentucky about 70 percent of individuals in nursing homes are supported by the Medicaid program. Combined federal-state Medicaid payments to nursing homes in the 2005 state fiscal year amounted to more than $640 million. Generally speaking, long-term care is comprised mostly of facilities that care for the elderly, such as nursing homes.

There are some 300 nursing homes in Kentucky – most are for-profit ventures. The remainder are not-for-profit facilities, many owned by religious organizations. In addition to the nursing homes, which provide skilled and intermediate care, there are assisted-living facilities, personal care homes and some family care homes. Each is prescribed by extensive specific state and federal regulations.

There are about 23,000 people in nursing homes in Kentucky. About half of the residents have some type of dementia such as Alzheimer's disease.

Nursing homes are state-regulated—inspectors from the Kentucky Office of the Inspector General visit facilities every nine to 15 months to assess the quality of the care being given, and there are other instances when inspectors are called to check on a problem. Results of these inspections and other information about all nursing homes in Kentucky can be found on-line at www.medicare.gov/NHCompare.

Kentucky's nursing home Ombudsman Program provides valuable oversight of the quality of care and life in nursing homes. Ombudsmen work to resolve resident problems and to advocate for quality care. The Long-Term Care Ombudsman identifies, investigates and helps resolve complaints made by or on behalf of residents of long-term care facilities (including nursing homes, personal care homes and family care homes). The state Long-Term Care Ombudsman may be reached at 1-800-372-2991.

On a statewide level, a relatively new organization, Kentuckians For Nursing Home Reform, works to educate the public on the problems in long-term care and to advocate for better quality care in both the state legislature and the U.S. Congress. You may find this organization at www.KyNursingHomeReform.org.

To report problems in nursing homes, citizens may call the local office of Adult Protective Services or the Office of the State Inspector General at (502) 564-7963. The Kentucky Attorney General has a toll-free number to report elder abuse at 1-877-228-7384.

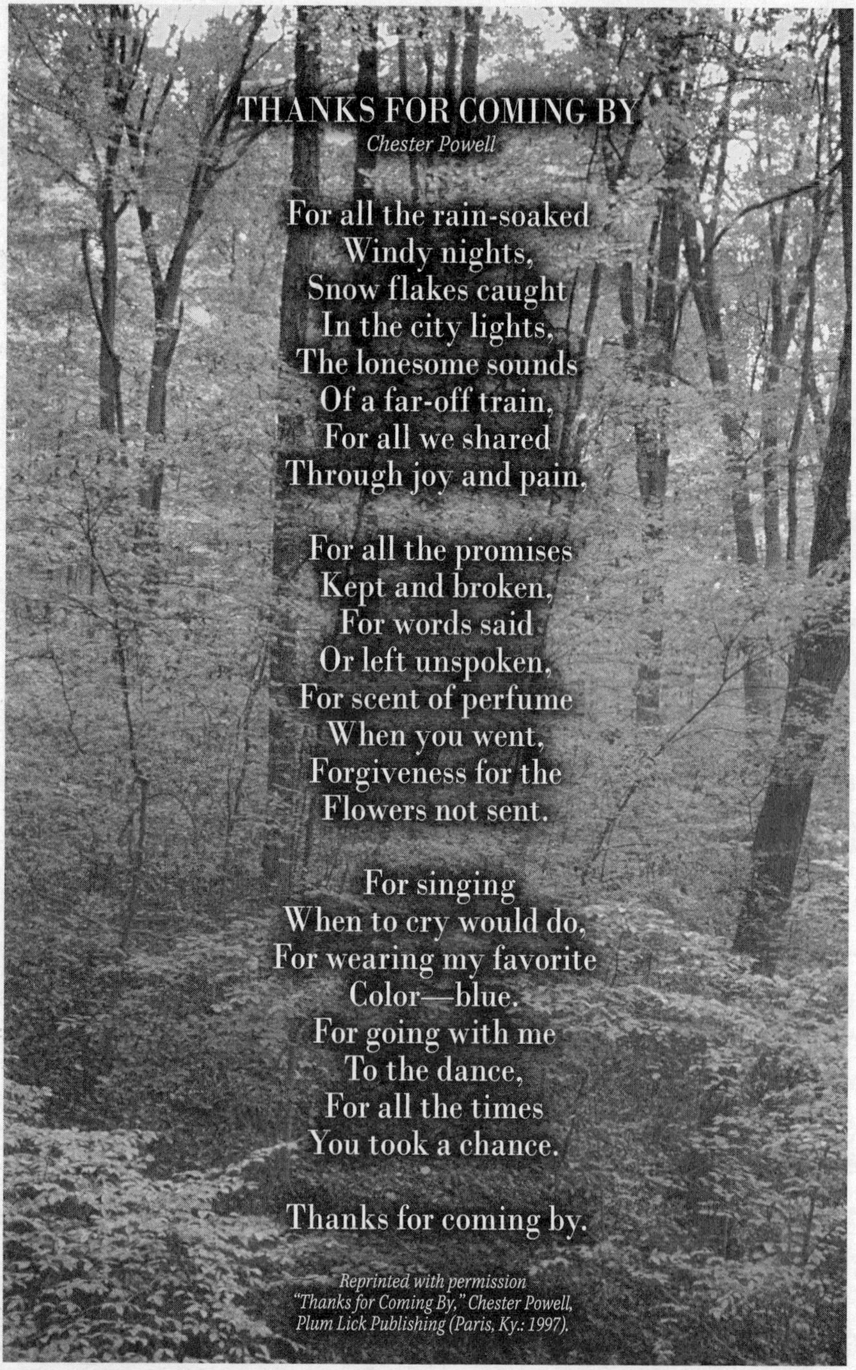

# THANKS FOR COMING BY
*Chester Powell*

For all the rain-soaked
Windy nights,
Snow flakes caught
In the city lights,
The lonesome sounds
Of a far-off train,
For all we shared
Through joy and pain.

For all the promises
Kept and broken,
For words said
Or left unspoken,
For scent of perfume
When you went,
Forgiveness for the
Flowers not sent.

For singing
When to cry would do,
For wearing my favorite
Color—blue.
For going with me
To the dance,
For all the times
You took a chance.

Thanks for coming by.

*Reprinted with permission*
*"Thanks for Coming By," Chester Powell,*
*Plum Lick Publishing (Paris, Ky.: 1997).*

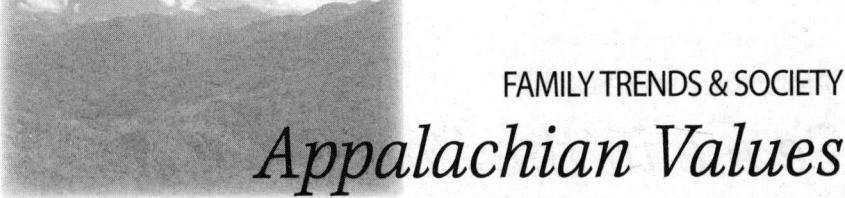

## FAMILY TRENDS & SOCIETY
# *Appalachian Values*

*An excerpt from the book, "Appalachian Values," Loyal Jones, Jesse Stuart Foundation, (Ashland, 1994), reprinted with permission.*

"We mountain people are the product of our history and the beliefs and outlook of our foreparents.

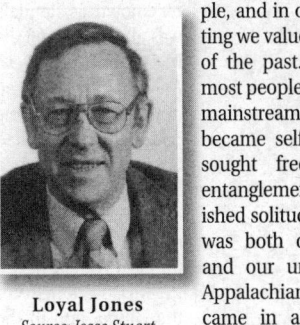

**Loyal Jones**
*Source: Jesse Stuart
Foundation*

We are a traditional people, and in our rural setting we valued the things of the past. More than most people, we avoided mainstream life and thus became self-reliant. We sought freedom from entanglements and cherished solitude. All of this was both our strength and our undoing. Our Appalachian forebears came in almost equal parts from England, Scotland and Germany, although some came from Wales, France, Holland and Africa. And, of course, the Cherokees were here over a thousand years before Europeans settled.

Recent histories have made much of the Scotch-Irish, that is, Scots who settled the counties of northern Ireland after 1610 and whose descendants sailed in large numbers to eastern ports, mostly Philadelphia, in the eighteenth century. Many German, English and Welch people also settled in Pennsylvania, and this conglomeration of peoples overflowed the population reservoirs there and streamed through the Great Valley that separated the Allegheny-Cumberland Plateau on the west from the mighty Blue Ridge on the east, settling the Virginias and the Carolinas and later Tennessee and Kentucky.

They came to a land of great natural beauty—high misty mountains, broad valleys and secluded coves and hollows, clear bouncing waters and frothing waterfalls. Wild game, root and herbs for food and medicine were everywhere. The forests

with their towering trees seemed endless, and underneath were rocks and minerals that would attract outsiders later on. For a people escaping from infringements of church and state, Appalachia was ideal for a new way of life, for a time, away from 'powers and principalities.'

They came for many reasons, but always for new opportunity and freedom—freedom from religious, political, and economic restraints, and freedom to do much as they pleased. The pattern of their settlement shows they were seeking land and solitude.

Although many were literate, evident from their letters, signing of public documents, and their possession of books, for a generation or two they left most formal schooling behind. This was a choice of profound significance for mountain people.

*Source: Kentucky Virtual Library*

Life in the wilderness and the continuing relative isolation of Southern mountaineers made a strong imprint on us. The Appalachian value system that influences attitudes and behavior is different in some ways from that held by our modern countrymen, although it is similar to the value system of an earlier America. Following are some of these values."

…

*Loyal Jones continues to describe these values in his beautiful book, replete with photos by Warren Brunner of haunting scenery and individuals with "character" written on the lines and planes of their faces. The values include religion, independence, self-reliance and pride, neighborliness, humility and modesty, love of place, patriotism, sense of beauty and humor.*

# FAMILY TRENDS & SOCIETY

## *Peace in the Valley*  Benita McCoy Lyons

As a direct descendant of the infamous Hatfield-McCoy feud, I know a thing or two about the McCoys. In fact, my great-great grandfather was the first person killed in the feud, and his son shot the last shot with a Winchester rifle. I have that lever action 1800s gun from the Smithsonian Institute Archives, which was handed down to me through my ancestors.

Now in this 21st century—with the passage of 100 years and through several generations—peace has come to the valley of the Tug Fork, which separates Kentucky from West Virginia. The Hatfields of southern West Virginia and their eastern Kentucky neighbors across the river, the McCoys, live together in harmony, again. For these families started out as friends and neighbors before the terrible War Between the States, and before the animosity that sparked a violent and murderous quarrel.

Mountain people have always been known for their fierce pride, ferocious loyalty and determination—admirable qualities for people living in the wild mountain terrain of eastern America. I composed this story to let the public know that pride—the backbone of a mountain man—can easily destroy if it gets out of hand.

The head of the Hatfield clan, William Anderson

"Devil Anse" Hatfield earned his nickname for Civil War heroics. A legendary marksman and captain in the Confederate Army, Anse held off an entire company of soldiers on a mountaintop called the Devil's Backbone.

**Bad John Wright**
*Source: Kentucky Virtual Library*

Randolf McCoy, better known as Randall, was the leader of the McCoy clan. Like Devil Anse, Randall was an honest, family-loving patriarch. Both had large families, owned land and were thought of as respectable and honest men. During the Civil War, however, the McCoys fought for the Union, and in the Tug Fork Valley—as all over the South—Union forces may have been the declared victor over the Confederates but resentment smoldered even as restoration of the country began.

It was conflict over the Civil War that caused the initial split between the families. After the war, Harmon McCoy, Randall's brother, was found murdered in a cave near a Hatfield cabin. Harmon had been shot and wounded by Anse during the Civil War, and Harmon had made threats against Anse that he didn't live to carry out.

An uneasy peace lasted a few years after this incident, but was shattered in a lawsuit over ownership of a razorback hog. Wounded pride on both sides erupted into the full-blown feud that lasted over 20 years and may have killed as many as 150 people. An eyewitness at the heated trial, Bill Staton, was among many victims found dead in the woods. Bodies were plentiful, but eyewitnesses were not to be found and no trials were held.

Romance between children of feuding families is a tradition that goes back to Romeo and Juliet, and the Hatfield-McCoy feud had its romance as well. Johnsie, the oldest son of Devil Anse, saw Rose Anne McCoy for the first time in August 1880. They fell in love; Rose Anne put aside her loyalties and actually moved into Anse's home to be with Johnsie. It pleased Anse that his enemy's daughter lived in his house, but he refused the lovers permission to marry.

After more than a year in Anse's house, Rose Anne moved to Stringtown, Ky. to live with an aunt Johnsie frequently visited, until Rose Anne's brothers ambushed him. Rose Anne hurried to Anse to warn him that his son had been captured, proving to Anse that Rose Ann loved Johnsie. For the rest of Devil Anse's life, but he regretted not giving his permission for the two to marry.

On election day in 1882, Ellison Hatfield, Anse's brother was stabbed in a fight and died several days later. The three McCoy's present, Tolbert, Phamer, and Randolf, Jr., were captured and executed by the Hatfields. Tolbert was a grown man, Phamer was in his teens, and the worst of all, little Randall was just a child. The Pike County grand jury handed down murder indictments, but the slowness with which they were served brought Kentucky's governor, Simon Buckner, into the feud.

Gov. Buckner hired a lawman to serve the murder indictments, but instead the lawman joined the McCoys on murderous raids into West Virginia against the Hatfields. Devil Anse appealed to his friend, Gov. Willis Wilson, and the feud threatened to escalate into a new war between the states. (The U.S. Supreme Court put an end to the governors' squabbling.s)

In retaliation for the raids, Devil Anse and his clan raided and burned Randall McCoy's home, killing two of his children, and brutally beating his wife. Randal McCoy lost six children to the feud before Devil Anse's immediate family suffered its first casualty. Two of Devil Anse's sons were killed in an early 1890s bar brawl. Their deaths broke Devil Anse's will to continue the bloody feud. He became a devout Christian and ended his fighting days. People say Randall McCoy lost his mind over the deaths of his children and the loss of his home. He died in 1921 still bitter over the feud.

The Hatfields and McCoys came together in the 1970s in front of the cameras of CBS News and officially ended their feud. With passing decades, industries have come to the mountains—modern life goes on in a busy bustle—and there is peace in the Tug Fork Valley.

*Benita McCoy Lyons wants the world to know more about a unique part of Appalachian culture, and that's the Appalachian scratch cooking she loves. By sharing the recipes of her ancestors and their friends, she hopes the impressions of mountain life can be balanced with what is already known about the legendary Hatfield-McCoy feud. Find out more about Benita's company, It's The Real McCoy, Inc., and her new cookbook, "Scratch Cooking 2," at www.kentuckyscratchcooking.com.*

In Beauty, may I walk. All day long, may I walk.

Through the returning seasons, may I walk.

On the trail marked with pollen, may I walk.

With grasshoppers about my feet, may I walk.

With dew about my feet, may I walk.

With Beauty, may I walk.

With Beauty before me, may I walk.

With Beauty behind me, may I walk.

With Beauty above me, may I walk.

With Beauty below me, may I walk.

With Beauty all around me, may I walk.

In old age wandering on a trail of beauty, lively, may I walk,

In old age wandering on a trail of beauty, living again,

may I walk.

It is finished in Beauty.

It is finished in Beauty.

*Beauty Way Prayer from the Navajo Tradition*

DANIEL LAMBERT, *Aged Thirty-six Years.*

"*The* astonishing weight of this man is fifty stone and upwards, being more than seven hundred pounds ; the surprising circumference of his body is three yards, four inches : his leg, on yard and an inch ; and his height, five feet eleven inches ; and though of this amazing size, entirely free from any corporeal defect.

This very remarkable personage received his birth in Leicester : at which place he was apprenticed to an engraver. Until he arrived at the age of twenty years, he was not of more than usual size, but after that period he began to increase in bulk, and has been gradually increasing, until within a few months of the present time.  He was much accustomed to exercise in the early years of this life, and excelled in walking, riding, and shooting ... ."

*Sources: Johnson & Warner's Kentucky Almanac 1810, Lexington, Ky.*

# HEALTH & SCIENCE
# *Frontier Medicine & Nursing*

## Lisa Thompson

As early as 1750 a physician journeyed to the territory that was to become the Commonwealth of Kentucky. Thomas Walker, a doctor and land speculator from Albemarle, Va. led the first organized English expedition through Cumberland Gap into Kentucky.

In 1775 Dr. Frances Jane Coomes arrived in Kentucky and first practiced medicine at Harrod's Fort, she then moved to Bardstown, where she died in 1816. Dr. Coomes performed surgery and made medical compounds in addition to providing medical services. She was the first female doctor to practice in Kentucky.

In 1781 the turbulence of the times is evident in a report that a midwife, "the celebrated Mrs. Harper," was sent for, under armed guard, to McConnell's Station.

It was common for physicians to learn the healing arts through a combination of reading and studying with a mentor. However, with the establishment of Transylvania Medical School in 1799, Kentucky became the second state in the country to provide an opportunity for receiving a formal medical education. Many of the faculty at the time had obtained medical training in Europe.

In 1806 Dr. Walter Brashear performed the first successful amputation at the hip joint in the United States. The patient was a 17-year-old slave from Nelson County.

Dr. Ephraim McDowell performed the nation's first successful ovariotomy on a patient in Danville in 1809, long before the use of anesthesia during surgery.

In the 1840s two of the nation's most prominent medical schools were located in Kentucky: Transylvania Medical School, and Louisville Medical School. More medical training institutions would be established in the following decade, making Kentucky a leader in the training of medical practitioners before the Civil War.

In 1851 Dr. William Loftus Sutton instigated the formation of the State Medical Society. This was the beginning of formal collaboration in the medical community in Kentucky.

The following year, at the urging of the State Medical Society and Dr. Sutton in particular, Kentucky became the first state west of the Alleghenies to collect vital statistics about the population. The recording of birth and death rates would provide valuable information and statistics, aiding in the prevention of disease and a more effective response to epidemics.

Dr. Mary Edwards Walker, the first female surgeon in the U.S. Army and one of two female Medal of Honor recipients, briefly practiced medicine in

**Dr. Mary Edwards Walker, U.S. Army surgeon, wearing her Medal of Honor**
*Source: Library of Congress*

Louisville in 1864-65 upon her release from a Confederate prison.

The State Board of Health was organized in 1878, establishing a governmental regulating agency which dealt chiefly with examining and licensing physicians. Among the board's functions was

**Staff of Frontier Nursing in Hyden, June 26, 1928**
*Source: Kentucky Department of Libraries & Archives*

ated for the education of blacks in 1888. Instrumental in establishing this institution was Dr. J. Henry Fitzbutler, one of the first African-American physicians to practice medicine in Kentucky.

In 1893 in an effort to eliminate medical quackery, the General Assembly passed an anti-empiricism law, requiring certification of physicians practicing in Kentucky. All practicing physicians were required to obtain a license from the State Board of Health by providing proof of medical training. In the absence of formal education, doctors were to provide proof of having begun practicing medicine prior to 1864.

In 1903 a law was passed by the General Assembly which required newly licensed physicians to pass a State Board exam, administered by the Board of Health.

In 1911 legislation was passed making it mandatory to record births and deaths. The Bureau of Vital Statistics was created at this time to administer the process and to compile statistical reports from the information gathered. Guidelines were created, making for a more consistent set of records, which became invaluable in analyzing medical occurrences.

determining which colleges and universities provided acceptable medical training. The board was also required to collect information on vital statistics and dispense information on hygiene and disease in an annual report.

The following year a physician, Dr. Luke Pryor Blackburn, was elected governor. Throughout his years of medical practice (which he resumed in 1883 upon leaving the governor's office), Gov. Blackburn was renowned for his role in the medical community's response to yellow fever.

In 1886 Kentucky's first nursing school was organized at Norton Memorial Infirmary in Louisville. Several more nursing educational institutions were established around this time in Kentucky. Over time training would focus on the medical practices of the nurse as a medical practitioner, rather than as an assistant to a physician.

The Louisville National Medical College was cre-

**Mary Breckinridge,
Frontier Nursing**
*Source: University of
Louisville*

Dr. Lillian South, a Kentucky physician who served as vice president of the American Medical Association in 1913, was instrumental in organizing a reserve corps of female physicians during World War I. She held the position of state bacteriologist on the State Board of Health for 40 years, which involved, among other duties, administering the public school inoculation program.

Further strides in Kentucky's healthcare came when Mary Carson Breckinridge founded the Frontier Nursing Service in 1925. The goal of this organization, based in Hyden, was to provide infant and maternal care in the mountains of southeastern Kentucky, thereby furthering the concept of professional midwifery.

# *Health Statistics*

## POPULATION DISTRIBUTION BY INSURANCE STATUS, STATE DATA 2003 & 2004

|  | 2004 KY TOTAL | 2004 PERCENTAGE | 2003 KY TOTAL | 2003 KY PERCENTAGE | US TOTAL | US PERCENTAGE |
|---|---|---|---|---|---|---|
| Employer | 2,116,980 | 52% | 2,168,220 | 54% | 156,270,570 | 54% |
| Individual | 179,370 | 4% | 179,420 | 4% | 13,593,990 | 5% |
| Medicaid | 568,180 | 14% | 580,430 | 14% | 38,352,430 | 13% |
| Medicare | 557,170 | 14% | 563,640 | 14% | 34,190,710 | 12% |
| Uninsured | 577,650 | 14% | 560,970 | 14% | 44,960,710 | 16% |
| Total | 4,065,700 | 100% | 4,052,680 | 100% | 287,368,410 | 100% |

## DISTRIBUTION OF PERSONAL HEALTH CARE EXPENDITURES BY SERVICE (in millions), FY 2000, FY 2004

|  | 2004 KY TOTAL | 2004 KY % | 2004 US TOTAL | 2004 US % | 2000 KY TOTAL | 2000 KY % | 2000 US TOTAL | 2000 US % |
|---|---|---|---|---|---|---|---|---|
| Hospital Care | 8,308 | 36.7% | 570,756 | 36.6% | 6,208 | 38.7% | 413,131 | 36.4% |
| Physician & Other Professional Services | 6,563 | 29% | 452,603 | 29% | 4,207 | 26.2% | 328,983 | 29% |
| Drugs & Other Medical Nondurables | 3,527 | 15.6% | 188,452 | 12.1% | 2,420 | 15.1% | 151,926 | 13.4% |
| Nursing Home Care | 1,512 | 6.7% | 115,210 | 7.4% | 1,383 | 8.6% | 95,296 | 8.4% |
| Dental Services | 822 | 3.6% | 81,532 | 5.2% | 587 | 3.7% | 60,726 | 5.3% |
| Home Health Care | 524 | 2.3% | 43,181 | 2.8% | 523 | 3.3% | 31,616 | 2.8% |
| Medical Durables | 279 | 1.2% | 22,951 | 1.5% | 184 | 1.1% | 17,750 | 1.6% |
| Other Medical Nondurables | 364 | 1.6% | 32,284 | 2.1% |  |  |  |  |
| Other Personal Health Care | 713 | 3.2% | 53,272 | 3.4% | 514 | 3.2% | 36,687 | 3.2% |
| Total | 22,612 | 100% | 1,560,241 | 100% | 16,027 | 100% | 1,136,115 | 100% |

## DISTRIBUTION OF MEDICAID SPENDING BY SERVICE, FY 2003, FY 2004

|  | 2004 KY TOTAL | 2004 KY % | 2004 US TOTAL | 2004 US % | 2003 KY TOTAL | 2003 KY % | 2003 US TOTAL | 2003 US % |
|---|---|---|---|---|---|---|---|---|
| Acute Care | 2,960,058,744 | 68.7% | 169,893,375,869 | 59% | 2,523,671,975 | 66.1% | 155,517,818,840 | 58.3% |
| Long Term Care | 1,155,457,480 | 26.8% | 100,997,478,517 | 35.1% | 1,126,692,215 | 29.5% | 97,026,007,372 | 36.4$ |
| Disproportionate Share Hospital Payments | 194,861,464 | 4.5% | 17,172,419,431 | 6% | 168,464,730 | 4.4% | 14,273,275,198 | 5.3% |
| Total | 4,310,377,688 | 100% | 288,063,273,817 | 100% | 3,818,828,920 | 100% | 266,817,101,410 | 100% |

| TOTAL SOCIAL SECURITY DISABILITY INSURANCE(SSDI) BENEFICIARIES AGES 18-64 AS A PERCENT OF POPULATION (18-64), 2003 & 2004 | | 2004 KY % | 2004 US % | 2003 KY % | 2003 US % |
|---|---|---|---|---|---|
| | Total Beneficiaries | 6.6% | 3.7% | 6.4% | 3.6% |

## MEDICAID PAYMENTS PER ENROLLEE BY ENROLLMENT GROUP, FY 2001, FY 2003

|  | 2003 KY TOTAL | 2003 US TOTAL | 2001 KY TOTAL | 2001 US TOTAL |
|---|---|---|---|---|
| Children | 1,844 | 1,467 | 1,683 | 1,315 |
| Adults | 2,651 | 1,872 | 2,635 | 1,736 |
| Elderly | 9,526 | 10,799 | 9,487 | 10,619 |
| Blind and Disabled | 7,878 | 12,265 | 7,654 | 10,642 |
| Total | 4,339 | 4,072 | 4,268 | 4,011 |

## FEDERAL MEDICAID EXPENDITURES PER CAPITA, FY2004

|  | KY TOTAL | US TOTAL |
|---|---|---|
| Total Expenditures | $753 | $627 |

## CIGARETTE SMOKING RATE BY GENDER, 2002 & 2005

|  | 2005 KY % | 2005 US % | 2002 KY % | 2002 US % |
|---|---|---|---|---|
| Male | 30.5% | 22.5% | 34.7% | 25.1% |
| Female | 26.9% | 18.3% | 30.3% | 20.0% |

## RETAIL PRESCRIPTIONS FILLED PER CAPITA, 2003 & 2005

|  | 2005 KY TOTAL | 2005 US TOTAL | 2003 KY TOTAL | 2003 US TOTAL |
|---|---|---|---|---|
| No of Prescriptions | 15.3 | 10.8 | 15.5 | 10.7 |

## DISTRIBUTION OF NONELDERLY UNINSURED BY GENDER STATE DATA 2002-2003, U.S. 2003 & STATE DATA 2003-2004, U.S. 2004

|  | 2004 KY TOTAL | 2004 KY % | 2004 US TOTAL | 2004 US % | 2003 KY TOTAL | 2003 KY % | 2003 US TOTAL | 2003 US % |
|---|---|---|---|---|---|---|---|---|
| Female | 271,550 | 47% | 21,129,050 | 46% | 277,690 | 50% | 21,001,460 | 47% |
| Male | 306,100 | 53% | 24,394,520 | 54% | 282,270 | 50% | 23,672,840 | 53% |
| Total | 577,650 | 100% | 45,523,570 | 100% | 559,970 | 100% | 44,674,300 | 100% |

## NUMBER OF BIRTHS BY RACE/ETHNICITY, 2004

|  | KENTUCKY | US |
|---|---|---|
| White | 48,665 | 3,229,814 |
| Black | 4,878 | 612,493 |
| Hispanic | 2,177 | 944,993 |
| Asian/Pacific Islander | 813 | 220,352 |
| American Indian | 95 | 43,931 |

## NUMBER OF TEEN BIRTHS BY RACE/ETHNICITY, 2003

|  | KENTUCKY | US |
|---|---|---|
| White | 5,582 | 174,346 |
| Black | 868 | 97,959 |
| Hispanic | 264 | 128,524 |
| Asian/Pacific Islander | 39 | 7,592 |
| American Indian | 10 | 7,690 |

## NUMBER OF DEATHS PER 100,000 POPULATION BY RACE/ETHNICITY, 2001, 2002

|  | 2002 KY RATE/ 100,000 | 2002 US RATE/ 100,000 | 2001 KY RATE/ 100,000 | 2001 US RATE/ 100,000 |
|---|---|---|---|---|
| White | 994.4 | 828.9 | 981 | 833.7 |
| Black | 1165.5 | 1082.7 | 1,154.5 | 1,099.2 |
| Other | 349.9 | 508 | 330.7 | 521.9 |

## NUMBER OF DEATHS PER 100,000 POPULATION BY GENDER, 2001, 2002

|  | 2002 KY RATE/ 100,000 | 2002 US RATE/ 100,000 | 2001 KY RATE/ 100,000 | 2001 US RATE/ 00,000 |
|---|---|---|---|---|
| Male | 1,228.2 | 1,013.7 | 1,207.9 | 1,023.9 |
| Female | 834.1 | 715.2 | 825.7 | 719.9 |

*Source: Kaiser Family Foundation , http://www.statehealthfacts.org*

## HOSPITALS

| CITY | HOSPITAL | COUNTY | PHONE | NO OF BEDS | OWNER |
|---|---|---|---|---|---|
| Albany | Clinton County Hospital | Clinton | (606) 387-6421 | 42 | Clinton County Hospital, Inc. |
| Ashland | King's Daughters Medical Center | Boyd | (606) 327-4000 | 366 | Ashland Hospital Corporation |
| Ashland | Our Lady of Bellefonte Hospital | Greenup | (606) 833-3333 | 214 | Bon Secours Health System, Inc. |
| Barbourville | Knox County Hospital | Knox | (606) 546-4175 | 42 | Knox County Fiscal Court |
| Bardstown | Flaget Memorial Hospital | Nelson | (502) 350-5000 | 40 | Catholic Health Initiatives |
| Benton | Marshall County Hospital | Marshall | (270) 527-4800 | 25 | Marshall County Fiscal Court |
| Berea | Saint Joseph Berea | Madison | (859) 986-3151 | 48 | Catholic Health Initiatives |
| Bowling Green | Commonwealth Regional Specialty Hospital | Warren | (270) 796-6200 | 28 | Commonwealth Health Corporation |
| Bowling Green | Greenview Regional Hospital | Warren | (270) 793-1000 | 211 | HCA - The Healthcare Company |
| Bowling Green | Rivendell Behavioral Health Services | Warren | (270) 843-1199 | 72 | Universal Health Services |
| Bowling Green | Southern Kentucky Rehabilitation Hospital (SKY) | Warren | (270) 782-6900 | 60 | Vibro Healthcare |
| Bowling Green | The Medical Center/Bowling Green | Warren | (270) 745-1000 | 330 | Commonwealth Health Corporation |
| Burkesville | Cumberland County Hospital | Cumberland | (270) 864-2511 | 25 | Cumberland County Fiscal Court |
| Cadiz | Trigg County Hospital Inc. | Trigg | (270) 522-3215 | 25 | Trigg County Hospital, Inc. |
| Campbellsville | Taylor Regional Hospital | Taylor | (270) 465-3561 | 90 | Taylor County Hospital District |
| Carlisle | Nicholas County Hospital | Nicholas | (859) 289-7181 | 18 | Johnson Mathers Healthcare, Inc. |
| Carrollton | Carroll County Regional Medical Center | Carroll | (502) 732-4321 | 49 | CCMH, Inc. |
| Columbia | Westlake Regional Hospital | Adair | (270) 384-4753 | 25 | Adair County Hospital District |
| Corbin | Baptist Regional Medical Center | Whitley | (606) 528-1212 | 240 | Baptist Healthcare System |
| Corbin | Oak Tree Hospital | Whitley | (606) 523-5150 | 32 | Baptist Healthcare System |
| Covington | NorthKey Community Care | Kenton | (859) 578-3200 | 57 | Northern Ky Mental Health/Mental Retardation Board |
| Cynthiana | Harrison Memorial Hospital | Harrison | (859) 234-2300 | 61 | Harrison Memorial Hospital, Inc. |
| Danville | Ephraim McDowell Regional Medical Center | Boyle | (859) 239-1000 | 177 | Ephraim McDowell Health, Inc. |
| Edgewood | HEALTHSOUTH Rehabilitation Hospital of Northern Kentucky | Kenton | (859) 341-2044 | 40 | HealthSouth Corporation |
| Edgewood | St. Elizabeth Medical Center | Kenton | (859) 301-2000 | 393 | Diocese of Covington |
| Elizabethtown | Hardin Memorial Hospital | Hardin | (270) 737-1212 | 285 | Hardin County, Kentucky |
| Elizabethtown | HEALTHSOUTH Rehabilitation Hospital of Central Kentucky | Hardin | (270) 769-3100 | 40 | HealthSouth Corporation |
| Flemingsburg | Fleming County Hospital | Fleming | (606) 849-5000 | 52 | Fleming County Fiscal Court |
| Florence | Gateway Rehabilitation Hospital | Boone | (859) 426-2400 | 40 | United Rehab |
| Florence | St. Luke Hospital West | Boone | (859) 962-5200 | 153 | St. Luke Hospital, Inc. |
| Fort Thomas | St. Luke Hospital East | Campbell | (859) 572-3100 | 284 | St. Luke Hospital, Inc. |
| Frankfort | Frankfort Regional Medical Center | Franklin | (502) 875-5240 | 173 | HCA - The Healthcare Company |
| Franklin | The Medical Center at Franklin | Simpson | (270) 598-4800 | 25 | Commonwealth Health Corporation |
| Fulton | Parkway Regional Hospital | Fulton | (270) 472-2522 | 70 | Community Health Systems, Inc. |
| Georgetown | Georgetown Community Hospital | Scott | (502) 868-1100 | 75 | LifePoint Hospitals, Inc. |
| Glasgow | T.J. Samson Community Hospital | Barren | (270) 651-4444 | 180 | T.J. Samson Community Hospital, Inc. |
| Greensburg | Jane Todd Crawford Hospital | Green | (270) 932-4211 | 55 | Green County Fiscal Court |
| Greenville | Muhlenberg Community Hospital | Muhlenberg | (270) 338-8000 | 90 | Muhlenberg Community Hospital, Inc. |
| Hardinsburg | Breckinridge Memorial Hospital | Breckinridge | (270) 756-7000 | 27 | Breckinridge County Buildings Commission |
| Harlan | Harlan Appalachian Regional Hospital | Harlan | (606) 573-8100 | 150 | Appalachian Regional Healthcare |
| Harrodsburg | James B. Haggin Memorial Hospital | Mercer | (859) 734-5441 | 50 | Community |
| Hartford | Ohio County Hospital | Ohio | (270) 298-7411 | 68 | Ohio County Fiscal Court |

# HOSPITALS

| CITY | HOSPITAL | COUNTY | PHONE | NO OF BEDS | OWNER |
|---|---|---|---|---|---|
| Hazard | ARH Regional Medical Center | Perry | (606) 439-6600 | 308 | Appalachian Regional Healthcare |
| Henderson | Methodist Hospital | Henderson | (270) 827-7700 | 209 | Community United Methodist Hospital |
| Hopkinsville | ABS Lincs Kentucky, dba Cumberland Hall | Christian | (270) 886-1919 | 52 | Alternative Behavioral Services |
| Hopkinsville | Jennie Stuart Medical Center | Christian | (270) 887-0100 | 194 | Jennie Stuart Medical Center, Inc. |
| Hopkinsville | Western State Hospital | Christian | (270) 889-6025 | 222 | Commonwealth of Kentucky |
| Horse Cave | Caverna Memorial Hospital Inc. | Hart | (270) 786-2191 | 25 | Caverna Memorial Hospital, Inc. |
| Hyden | Mary Breckinridge Healthcare, Inc. | Leslie | (606) 672-2901 | 40 | Frontier Nursing Service, Inc. |
| Irvine | Marcum & Wallace Memorial Hospital | Estill | (606) 723-2115 | 25 | Catholic Healthcare Partners, Cincinnati |
| Jackson | Kentucky River Medical Center | Breathitt | (606) 666-6000 | 55 | Community Health Systems, Inc. |
| Jenkins | Jenkins Community Hospital | Letcher | (606) 832-2171 | 25 | Gregory Johnson |
| LaGrange | Baptist Hospital Northeast | Oldham | (502) 222-5388 | 90 | Baptist Healthcare System |
| Lebanon | Spring View Hospital | Marion | (270) 692-3161 | 65 | Spring View Hospital, LLC |
| Leitchfield | Twin Lakes Regional Medical Center | Grayson | (270) 259-9400 | 75 | Grayson County Hospital Foundation |
| Lexington | Cardinal Hill Rehabilitation Hospital | Fayette | (859) 254-5701 | 108 | The Kentucky Easter Seal Society, Inc. |
| Lexington | Central Baptist Hospital | Fayette | (859) 260-6100 | 371 | Baptist Healthcare System |
| Lexington | Eastern State Hospital | Fayette | (859) 246-7000 | 323 | Commonwealth of Kentucky |
| Lexington | Ridge Behavioral Health System | Fayette | (859) 269-2325 | 110 | Universal Health Services |
| Lexington | Saint Joseph East | Fayette | (859) 967-5000 | 166 | Catholic Health Initiatives |
| Lexington | Samaritan Hospital | Fayette | (859) 226-7000 | 302 | Associated Healthcare Systems Inc. |
| Lexington | Shriners Hospital for Children - Lexington | Fayette | (859) 268-5630 | 50 | Shriners |
| Lexington | St. Joseph Healthcare | Fayette | (859) 313-1000 | 468 | Catholic Health Initiatives |
| Lexington | University of Kentucky Hospital | Fayette | (859) 323-5000 | 473 | Commonwealth of Kentucky |
| Lexington | VA Medical Center - Lexington | Fayette | (859) 233-4511 | 190 | Federal Government |
| London | Marymount Medical Center | Laurel | (606) 878-6520 | 76 | Catholic Health Initiatives |
| Louisa | Three Rivers Medical Center | Lawrence | (606) 638-9451 | 90 | Community Health Systems, Inc. |
| Louisville | Baptist Hospital East | Jefferson | (502) 897-8100 | 407 | Baptist Healthcare System |
| Louisville | Central State Hospital | Jefferson | (502) 253-7060 | 192 | Commonwealth of Kentucky |
| Louisville | Gateway Rehabilitation Hospital at Norton Healthcare Pavilion | Jefferson | (502) 315-8433 | 40 | United Rehab |
| Louisville | Jewish Hospital | Jefferson | (502) 587-4011 | 442 | Jewish Hospital and St. Mary's Healthcare |
| Louisville | Kindred Hospital - Louisville | Jefferson | (502) 587-7001 | 337 | Kindred, Inc. |
| Louisville | Kosair Children's Hospital | Jefferson | (502) 629-6000 | 255 | Norton Hospitals, Inc. |
| Louisville | Norton Audubon Hospital | Jefferson | (502) 636-7111 | 432 | Norton Hospitals, Inc. |
| Louisville | Norton Healthcare at Brownsboro Crossing | Jefferson | (502) 629-8791 | | Norton Hospitals, Inc. |
| Louisville | Norton Hospital | Jefferson | (502) 629-8000 | 719 | Norton Hospitals, Inc. |
| Louisville | Norton Southwest Hospital | Jefferson | (502) 933-8100 | 127 | Norton Hospitals, Inc. |
| Louisville | Norton Suburban Hospital | Jefferson | (502) 893-1000 | 343 | Norton Hospitals, Inc. |
| Louisville | Sts. Mary & Elizabeth Hospital | Jefferson | (502) 361-6000 | 331 | Jewish Hospital & St. Mary's Health Care |
| Louisville | Ten Broeck Hospital - DuPont | Jefferson | (502) 896-0495 | 66 | United Medical Corporation |
| Louisville | Ten Broeck Hospital - KMI | Jefferson | (502) 426-6380 | 82 | United Medical Corporation |
| Louisville | University of Louisville Hospital | Jefferson | (502) 562-3000 | 404 | Commonwealth of Kentucky |
| Louisville | VA Medical Center - Louisville | Jefferson | (502) 287-4000 | 114 | Federal Government |
| Madisonville | Regional Medical Center | Hopkins | (270) 825-5100 | 390 | Trover Foundation |

## HOSPITALS

| CITY | HOSPITAL | COUNTY | PHONE | NO OF BEDS | OWNER |
|---|---|---|---|---|---|
| Manchester | Memorial Hospital Inc. | Clay | (606) 598-5104 | 63 | Adventist Health System |
| Marion | Crittenden Health System | Crittenden | (270) 965-5281 | 50 | Crittenden Health Systems |
| Martin | Our Lady of the Way Hospital | Floyd | (606) 285-6400 | 25 | Catholic Health Initiatives |
| Mayfield | Jackson Purchase Medical Center | Graves | (270) 251-4100 | 107 | LifePoint Hospitals, Inc. |
| Maysville | Meadowview Regional Medical Center | Mason | (606) 759-5311 | 111 | LifePoint Hospitals, Inc. |
| McDowell | McDowell Appalachian Regional Hospital | Floyd | (606) 377-3400 | 25 | Appalachian Regional Healthcare |
| Middlesboro | Middlesboro Appalachian Regional Hospital | Bell | (606) 242-1100 | 96 | Appalachian Regional Healthcare |
| Monticello | Wayne County Hospital, Inc. | Wayne | (606) 348-9343 | 25 | Wayne County Hospital, Inc. |
| Morehead | St. Claire Regional Medical Center | Rowan | (606) 783-6500 | 159 | Sisters of Notre Dame |
| Morganfield | Methodist Hospital Union County | Union | (270) 389-5000 | 41 | Community United Methodist Hospital |
| Mt. Sterling | Gateway Regional Health System | Montgomery | (859) 498-1220 | 64 | Gateway Regional Health System |
| Mt. Vernon | Rockcastle Hospital Inc. | Rockcastle | (606) 256-2195 | 26 | Rockcastle Hospital, Inc. |
| Murray | Murray-Calloway County Hospital | Calloway | (270) 762-1100 | 176 | Murray-Calloway Co. Public Hospital Corp. |
| Owensboro | Owensboro Medical Health System, Inc. | Daviess | (270) 688-2000 | 447 | Owensboro Mercy Health System |
| Owensboro | River Valley Behavioral Health Hospital | Daviess | (270) 689-6500 | 80 | Green River MH/MR Board |
| Owenton | New Horizons Health Systems, Inc. | Owen | (502) 484-2771 | 25 | New Horizon Health System |
| Paducah | Lourdes | McCracken | (270) 444-2444 | 389 | Catholic Healthcare Partners, Cincinnati |
| Paducah | Western Baptist Hospital | McCracken | (270) 575-2100 | 367 | Baptist Healthcare System |
| Paintsville | Paul B. Hall Regional Medical Center | Johnson | (606) 789-3511 | 72 | Health Management Association, Inc. |
| Paris | Bourbon Community Hospital | Bourbon | (859) 987-3600 | 58 | LifePoint Hospitals, Inc. |
| Pikeville | Pikeville Medical Center | Pike | (606) 437-3500 | 261 | Pikeville Medical Center, Inc. |
| Pineville | Pineville Community Hospital | Bell | (606) 337-3051 | 120 | Pineville Community Hospital Assn., Inc. |
| Prestonsburg | Highlands Regional Medical Center | Floyd | (606) 886-8511 | 184 | Consolidated Health Systems, Inc. |
| Princeton | Caldwell County Hospital | Caldwell | (270) 365-0300 | 48 | Caldwell County Fiscal Court |
| Radcliff | Lincoln Trail Behavioral Health System | Hardin | (270) 351-9444 | 77 | Southeastern Hospital Corporation |
| Richmond | Pattie A. Clay Regional Medical Center | Madison | (859) 623-3131 | 105 | Pattie A. Clay Infirmary Association, Inc. |
| Russell Springs | Russell County Hospital | Russell | (270) 866-4141 | 25 | Alliant Management Services, Inc. |
| Russellville | Logan Memorial Hospital | Logan | (270) 726-4011 | 92 | LifePoint Hospitals, Inc. |
| Salem | Livingston Hospital and Healthcare Services | Livingston | (270) 988-2299 | 25 | Livingston Hospital and Healthcare Services Inc. |
| Scottsville | The Medical Center/Scottsville | Allen | (270) 622-2800 | 47 | Commonwealth Health Corporation |
| Shelbyville | Jewish Hospital - Shelbyville | Shelby | (502) 647-4000 | 70 | Jewish Hospital and St. Mary's Healthcare |
| Somerset | Lake Cumberland Regional Hospital | Pulaski | (606) 679-7441 | 222 | LifePoint Hospitals, Inc. |
| South Williamson | Williamson Appalachian Regional Hospital | Pike | (606) 237-1700 | 163 | Appalachian Regional Healthcare |
| Stanford | Fort Logan Hospital | Lincoln | (606) 365-2187 | 43 | Fort Logan Hospital Foundation |
| Tompkinsville | Monroe County Medical Center | Monroe | (270) 487-9231 | 49 | Monroe Medical Foundation, Inc. |
| Versailles | Bluegrass Community Hospital | Woodford | (859) 873-3111 | 25 | LifePoint Hospitals, Inc. |
| West Liberty | Morgan County Appalachian Regional Hospital | Morgan | (606) 743-3186 | 30 | Appalachian Regional Healthcare |
| Whitesburg | Whitesburg Appalachian Regional Hospital | Letcher | (606) 633-3500 | 90 | Appalachian Regional Healthcare |
| Williamstown | St. Elizabeth Medical Center of Grant County | Grant | (859) 824-8240 | 30 | Diocese of Covington |
| Winchester | Clark Regional Medical Center | Clark | (859) 745-3500 | 100 | Clark Regional Medical Center, Inc. |

*Source: Kentucky Hospital Association, www.kyha.com*

# HEALTH & SCIENCE
# *Medical Trends & Advances*

James R. Bean

The pace of change in medical care is fast in 2006, and shows no sign of slowing. Three kinds of advance drive the trend toward more effective medical care in prevention, diagnosis, and treatment.

The first and most important factor in medical advance is new scientific knowledge and technical innovation in treatment. Discoveries in molecular and genetic science, in pharmacology and drug research, and in minimally invasive surgery and procedures have all created the background for new forms of treatment that render current standard therapies and procedures obsolete.

The international Human Genome Project, which aimed to map the entire human genome, completed the 13-year initial work in 2003. The project aimed to identify the 30,000-40,000 human genes, and the sequences of the 3 billion chemical molecular pairs that make up the genes in the human chromosome. Current investigations look to correct genetic defects by using chemical carriers to deliver correct genes to cells in people with genetically faulty or absent genes.

The pace of drug development has led to multiple new forms of therapy for common conditions. For instance, treatment of hypertension now includes multiple different classes of drugs, such as diuretics, beta-adrenergic blockers and angiotensin-converting enzyme (ACE) inhibitors, to name a few.

The second advance driving profound change is new information technology. From a patient's perspective, the Internet provides a wealth of medical information on virtually every medical condition. Information has changed the relationship between doctor and patient, and patients often make treatment choices based in part on information gleaned from the Internet (although accuracy of the data may be questionable).

The third advance creating substantial improvement in health care is educational, administrative and political change. Many conditions are "lifestyle" choices, and are preventable or correctable by changes in daily habits. For instance, obesity has become epidemic in the U.S. and Kentucky population. Two-thirds of adults are now considered overweight, based on the body-mass index (BMI), as compared with one-fourth of adults 40 years ago. Heart attack, stroke, diabetes, gallbladder disease, and colon cancer can be a result of obesity. Dietary change, weight loss, and regular exercise can eliminate future disease, and may increase lifespan by years. Smoking causes emphysema, heart disease, strokes, and lung cancer—second-hand smoke is known to have similar effects. Although Kentucky has the highest adult smoking rate in the nation—about 27.6 percent of adults were regular smokers in 2004 according to the Centers for Disease Control and Prevention—numerous cities and counties have enacted smoking bans in recent years.

A comprehensive description of advances in medical care could fill an entire volume, and this is only a sampling. Surely, the pace of change will render even this update obsolete soon after publication.

*Lexington was the first Kentucky city to impose a 100 percent smoking ban in workplaces, restaurants and bars (effective in 2004). It drew national attention because of tobacco's prominence in Kentucky history. In 2005 Louisville Metro passed an ordinance prohibiting smoking in all buildings open to the public. Numerous city and county governments are following suit in varying degrees. Gov. Ernie Fletcher recently banned smoking in buildings controlled by the executive branch. The regulations are controversial among those who defend "smokers' rights."*

## HEALTH & SCIENCE
# Veterans Affairs

The Department of Veterans Affairs offers a variety of programs and services for the nation's 24.7 million veterans. In Kentucky, the VA spent more than $927 million in 2004 to serve nearly 360,000 veterans who live in the state.

### KENTUCKY VA FACTS, 2004

- 57,173 Veterans and survivors received disability compensation or pension payments from VA
- 6,391+ Veterans, reservists or survivors used GI Bill payments for their education
- 31,119 Owned homes with active VA home loan guarantees
- 720 Were interred in Kentucky's seven national cemeteries

### HEALTH CARE

One of the most visible of all VA benefits is health care. Due to technology and national and VA health care trends, VA has changed from a hospital-based system to a primarily outpatient-focused system over the past eight years. In Kentucky, VA operates major medical centers in Lexington and Louisville.

The Louisville VA Medical Center offers a premier state-of-the-art acute medicine unit that also serves the specialties of hospice and oncology. The facility has 20 beds, including four private and four semi-private rooms. In fiscal year 2005, the Louisville medical center had 6,696 inpatient admissions.

The Lexington medical center has a 16-bed, fully computerized intensive and coronary care suite that is equipped with the most advanced technology available today. In fiscal year 2005, the Lexington medical center had 5,494 inpatient admissions.

### RESEARCH

To provide the highest quality of health care to the nation's veterans, VA sponsors a world-renowned research and development program that addresses some of the most difficult challenges facing medical science today.

The Lexington VA Medical Center is involved in 110 research projects with 46 principal investigators, at a total cost of $4.5 million in research. In Lexington, areas of study include arteriosclerosis, diabetes, small cell lung cancer, HIV, prostate cancer, stroke, Parkinson's disease, epilepsy.

The Louisville VA Medical Center has a medium-sized funded research and development program, including studies in surgical sepsis, heart disease, liver disease, and cancer treatments. There are 100 research projects underway, with 44 principal investigators. VA-funded research totals more than $2 million.

### MEMORIAL AFFAIRS

Most men and women who have been in the military are eligible for burial in a national cemetery, as are their dependent children and usually their spouses. VA has seven national cemeteries in Kentucky

Kentucky opened a veterans cemetery in 2004 at Hopkinsville with VA assistance, which conducted 61 burials, and has submitted pre-applications to build three more cemeteries. VA provided more than 7,000 headstones and markers for the graves of veterans in Kentucky and sent 4,854 Presidential Memorial Certificates to Kentucky survivors of veterans.

*Source: www.va.gov*

### TYPES OF VA FACILITIES IN U.S.

| FACILITY | NO OF LOCATIONS |
|---|---|
| Hospitals | 157 |
| Ambulatory care and community-based outpatient clinics | 869 |
| Vet Centers | 207 |
| Nursing homes | 134 |
| Residential rehabilitation treatment programs | 42 |
| Comprehensive home care programs | 92 |

### BURIALS IN VA NATIONAL CEMETERIES IN KY, 2004

| CEMETARY | LOCATION | NO OF BURIALS |
|---|---|---|
| Camp Nelson National Cemetery | Nicholasville | 376 |
| Cave Hill National Cemetery | Louisville | 2 |
| Danville National Cemetary | Danville | 1 |
| Lebanon National Cemetary | Lebanon | 216 |
| Lexington National Cemetary | Lexington | 0 |
| Mill Springs National Cemetery | Nancy | 70 |
| Zachary Taylor National Cemetery | Louisville | 55 |

## HEALTH & SCIENCE
# Scientists &
# Related Programs

Kentucky has several notable scientists who were born, lived or worked in Kentucky, including William Kelly, inventor of the "air-boiling" process of steel production; David Dale Owen, Kentucky's first state geologist in 1854 and regarded as the premier scientist of the Midwest; Curtis Gates Lloyd, a self-taught botanist of international renown; John Uri Lloyd, chemist and novelist who promoted the use of

**Space Shuttle Discovery
at the International
Space Station**
*Source: NASA*

plant extracts in treating patients and has been called the father of colloidal chemistry.

Robert Shepherd was the first Kentucky scientist elected to the National Academy of Sciences. He was a professor of plant pathology at the University of Kentucky's Tobacco and Health Institute.

George Speri Sperti, a Covington-born scientist and inventor, founded the Basic Science Research Laboratory at the University of Cincinnati, where he concentrated on cancer research. Mary Eugenia Wharton, author, botanist, geologist, educator, and activist was born in Jessamine County and dis-

covered an unnamed species of dewberry in Montgomery County, which was named in her honor, *Rubus Whartoniae*.

One of Kentucky's most famous scientists is Story

**Astronaut Story Musgrave M.D.**
*Source: NASA*

Musgrave (M.D.), a NASA Astronaut. He was born Aug. 19, 1935, in Boston, Mass., but considers Lexington to be his hometown. He graduated from St. Mark's School, Southborough, Mass, in 1953, and entered the U.S. Marine Corps that same year. Dr. Musgrave received his first postsecondary degree at Syracuse University in 1958, graduating with a bachelor of science degree in mathematics and statistics. Since that time, he has received numerous graduate and postgraduate degrees including a doctorate in medicine, physiology and biophysics from the University of Kentucky in 1966. Dr. Musgrave was a U.S. Air Force post-doctoral fellow (1965-1966), working in aerospace medicine and physiology, and a National Heart Institute post-doctoral fellow (1966-1967), teaching and doing research in cardiovascular and exercise physiology. From 1967 to 1989, he continued clinical and scientific training as a part-time surgeon at the Denver General Hospital and as a part-time professor of physiology and biophysics at the University of Kentucky Medical Center.

In 1967 Dr. Musgrave was selected as a scientist-astronaut by NASA. He completed astronaut academic training and then worked on the design and development of the Skylab Program. He was the backup science-pilot for the first Skylab mission, and was a CAPCOM for the second and third Skylab missions. Dr. Musgrave participated in the design and development of all Space Shuttle extravehicular activity equipment including space-suits, life support systems, airlocks, and manned maneuvering units. Dr. Musgrave first flew on STS-6, which launched from the Kennedy Space Center, Florida, on April 4, 1983, and landed at Edwards Air Force Base, Calif., on April 9, 1983. During this maiden voyage of Space Shuttle Challenger, the crew performed the first Shuttle deployment of an IUS/TDRS satellite, and Musgrave and Don Peterson conducted the first Space Shuttle extravehicular activity (EVA) to test the new space suits and construction and repair devices and procedures.

On STS-33, he served aboard the Space Shuttle Discovery, which launched from Kennedy Space Center, Fla., on Nov. 22, 1989. Following 79 orbits, the classified mission concluded on Nov. 27, 1989.

During the first Hubble Space Telescope servicing and repair mission, launched on Dec. 2, 1993, the Endeavour rendezvoused with and captured the HST. During this 11-day flight, the HST was restored to its full capabilities through the work of two pairs of astronauts during a record five spacewalks. Dr. Musgrave performed three of these spacewalks and traveled 4,433,772 miles in 163 orbits of the Earth.

## *Did you Know?*

### *IdeaFestival*
### *Seek New Ways of Thinking — Expand Your Horizons*

*Founded in 2000, the IdeaFestival is a world-class event held in Louisville each year that attracts diverse and leading thinkers from across the nation and around the globe to explore and celebrate innovation and cutting-edge ideas. It is a unique non-linear program designed to stretch people's thinking, utilizing multiple venues to showcase and discuss important ideas in science, the arts, design, business, film, technology, education, etc. The future is created with ideas and innovations, which emerge from and at the intersections of many different fields ("convergence"). Based on the realization that answers are everywhere...the Festival promotes out-of-the-box thinking and cross-fertilization of ideas as a means toward high-speed development of new products, services and creative endeavors. Visit www.kstc.com for more information.*

## RELATED PROGRAMS

Kentucky Science and Technology Corporation (KSTC) is a nonprofit corporation founded in 1987. Its mission is dedicated to advancing entrepreneurial start-up companies and university research ultimately leading to commercial applications and education initiatives.

KSTC manages the Kentucky Enterprise Fund, the Kentucky Science and Engineering Foundation, and Kentucky EPSCoR, each created by the Kentucky Innovation Act of 2000. Since inception of awards in 2001, the Kentucky Enterprise Fund has provided 223 awards totaling $10.6 million, KSEF has provided 231 awards for $10.2 million, and Kentucky EPSCoR has provided 311 awards for $10.6 million. In Jan. 2006, KSTC and the Council on Post-secondary Education announced 105 awards totaling $6 million for business start-ups and faculty research for the first half of the fiscal year. Since 2001, KSTC has distributed an astounding 765 awards totaling $31.4 million.

As directed by the Kentucky Innovation Act of 2000, the Council contracts with KSTC to implement Kentucky's knowledge-based economy programs. All KSTC projects undergo rigorous peer review and fall within the state's five priority research focus areas: biosciences, environmental technologies, human health and development, information technology and communications, and materials science and advanced manufacturing.

Reported benefits to Kentucky's economy have been significant—through June 30, 2005, KSTC investments have resulted in 120 new companies, 1,542 new jobs, three new patents and 56 other invention disclosures and patent applications.

### KENTUCKY ENTERPRISE FUND AWARDS

**University of Louisville, Zhenmin Lei**

Luteinizing Hormone and Alzheimer's Disease

This research will provide crucial insight into the relationship between Alzheimer's disease (AD) and an absence of luteinizing hormone (LH) action in the brain. LH is a hormone found in both men and women whose levels are elevated in older individuals. An understanding of the relationship between LH and AD may lead to novel preventive and therapeutic strategies for the disease.

**Western Kentucky University, Cathleen Webb**

A Novel, Inexpensive Arsenic-Removal System for Rural and Home Drinking Water Supplies

Development of an inexpensive remediation technology for removal or reduction of arsenic from rural water sources.

**University of Kentucky, Eugene Bruce, Fayette County**

Novel Analyses of Human Electroencephalograms for Detection of Brain Injury

Sleep apnea, which may cause deficits in cognitive brain function due to low oxygen levels, is associated with health problems that are common in Kentucky such as obesity, smoking, hypertension, and alcohol use. In order to detect evolving deficits in brain function at an early stage, this project will develop novel methods for analysis of brain electrical activity that are more sensitive to abnormal activity than currently available methods.

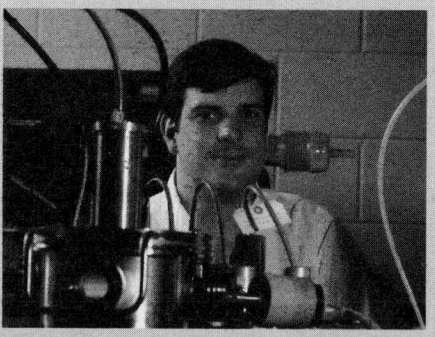

**Professor Bruce Hinds at the University of Kentucky campus with a plasma generator used in the research, which was published in the Journal Science, a prestigious publication for his achievements with nanotubes**
*Photo: Pablo Alcala, Lexington Herald-Leader*

• • •

**The Kentucky Academy of Science** was founded at the University of Kentucky in 1914 to improve scholarly communication among scientists in the commonwealth. See http://kas.wku.edu/kas/.

**Kentucky Science Olympiad** is part of "The Science Olympiad," an international nonprofit organization with a primary purpose to increase student interest in science and to recognize outstanding achievement in science education for teachers and students. Visit www.jctc.kctcs.net/kso/.

**The Kentucky Science Support Network** is designed to provide classroom teachers in Kentucky a direct link to "experts" across the commonwealth. See http://oapd.kde.state.ky.us/kssn/.

# Religion

### Nancy Jo Kemper

entucky religion in 2005 shows all the hallmarks that characterized the religious outlook of the first pioneers. That early environment was characterized by separatism, individualism, local autonomy, biblicism, emotional fervor, and theological diversity. Moreover, the religious culture of Kentucky, over its long history, has played important roles in the nation's religious history and culture.

The majority of pioneers in the first three decades of exploration and settlement, from roughly 1769 to 1800, were either dissenting Baptists or people who were not so much anti-religion as a religious. The long hunters didn't have much time to worry about religion. The Anglican state religion of Virginia had forced many dissenters into North Carolina. Given the wild, sparse and ill-governed nature of the land beyond the mountains, churches had almost no hold on believers. South of Virginia, religion was not organized and churches were weak, due to the

**Statue at the Abbey of Gethsemani, Trappist, KY**
*Photo: Sid Webb*

lack of trained clergy and because of the wide diversity of religious views.

Squire Boone II is said to have preached the first sermon in the state, and the first worship services were held in Harrod's Town in 1776. Two Roman Catholics, a school teacher and a doctor, came to Harrod's Town in 1776 and were the first of their particular professions. Jews also had a hand in early settlements. A Virginia mercantile business of Cohen

and Isaacs secured the services of Daniel Boone to check out possibilities in the new territory for them, and the Gratz family of Philadelphia were among the first settlers of Lexington.

Currently, Baptists remain the largest religious group in the state with 45.4 percent of all religious adherents claiming that they are Baptists. Approximately 18.8 percent of religious adherents claim that they are Roman Catholic. The Jewish community remains strong and vibrant with 11 synagogues or temples around the state, while still amounting to less than 1 percent of all persons who claim some form of religion.

Today, as in the early days, although the state's culture is predominantly Christian and fundamentalist, only 53.4 percent of Kentuckians identify themselves as religious. In the third millennium, moreover, one can see even more religious pluralism in the commonwealth. The state universities have been largely responsible for introducing Asian and middle-eastern immigrants to the population, and these people have brought with them their rich religious heritages as Muslims, Hindus, Jains, Baha'is, and Buddhists. Although small in numbers, these religious traditions add to the cultural and spiritual vitality of the commonwealth.

With the exponential multiplication of population in Kentucky's first three decades, and the establishment in numerous towns in the land beyond the mountains, churches become more numerous. Their diversity, however, and the shortage of clergy, led to the inability of Christians to participate in the Lord's Supper or Holy Communion. With energy trickling down from the Great Revival in New England and new ideas generated by such Enlightenment thinkers as John Locke, coupled with spiritual hunger on the frontier, the ideas generated by these influences began to have consequences.

In Logan County, in 1797, Presbyterian James McGready started a great religious revival. In 1801, a crowd that some estimated at 25,000 gathered at Cane Ridge in Bourbon County, under the leadership of Barton W. Stone, for what would become the Second Great Revival in the history of the fledgling country. Here was born a new movement, known as the Christian Church. "We are not the only Christians," they claimed, "but we are Christians only." They created a more vital, simple, and biblical approach to church life that was to become, at one time in the early 20th century, the largest indigenous American denomination, the Christian Church (Disciples of Christ).

As a result of divisive religious convictions, the descendants of the original followers of Barton W. Stone and another Christian Church founder, Alexander Campbell, are now separated into three branches from that original vine. Today those churches are the Christian Church (Disciples of Christ); the Christian Churches and Churches of Christ (often called Independent Christians); and the (non-instrumental) Churches of Christ. Their numbers together equal that of the United Methodists, which after Baptists and Catholics, formed the third largest denomination in Kentucky in 2005. Two congregations of this Stone-Campbell movement that emerged from the great revival at Cane Ridge are among the largest mega-churches in the United States: Southeast Christian in Louisville and Southland Christian in Lexington.

In 1806 and 1807 learning of the great revival and spiritual vitality in the new state west of the mountains, followers of Mother Anne Lee's United Society of Believers in Christ's Second Appearing, came to Kentucky and established communities near Harrodsburg at Pleasant Hill and at South Union, near Bowling Green. With a strong commitment to communal living, celibacy, the virtues of work and excellence in working, and a rigorous moral code, the Shakers, as they were called, contributed much to Kentucky agricultural life, architecture, tool making, and industry.

Catholics also saw the state of Kentucky as a great fertile place for the creation of religious houses and monasteries. In the area around Bardstown, now known as the "Kentucky Holy Land," a new diocese was created in 1808, and under the leadership of Bishop Benedict Joseph Flaget began to build their cathedral. The Basilica of St Joseph Proto-Cathedral was completed in 1823 with lavish gifts of art and other items from many European royal houses as well as from Pope Leo XII. The official seat of the diocese was moved to Louisville in 1841. Catholics, however, suffered from anti-papal sentiments during riots that occurred in Louisville in 1855. In an election day riot a mob of Know-Nothings entered the Louisville Cathedral, and 25 Irish-Americans were killed.

Nelson and Washington Counties are still home to the great Trappist Monastery of Gethsemani, home to the late writer and theologian Thomas Merton, and to the Sisters of Charity of Nazareth, Ky.

In recent years, two major Supreme Court cases dealing with church and state issues, most notably regarding the Ten Commandments, originated in Kentucky. In 1980, in Graham v. Stone, Superintendent of Public Instruction of Kentucky, the U.S. Supreme Court declared unconstitutional a Kentucky statute that required posting a copy of the Ten Commandments, purchased with private contributions, in each public school classroom in the state. With the issue of the Ten Commandments and their role in American history still simmering in people's memories, county courthouses in McCreary County and in Pulaski County decided to display the Ten Commandments. They were sued successfully by the ACLU. They followed this lawsuit by changing the displays to include other historical documents, and were again sued. Again, a Kentucky case about the Ten Commandments went to the U.S. Supreme Court where it was decided in June 2005, that the displays were unconstitutional because the intention of the counties was substantially to promote religion, and therefore were in violation of the First Amendment.

Today, Kentucky's religious environment might be best described as a kind of moralistic individualism. Christians are the clear majority, and much of the population, even those who do not attend church, would identify themselves as Christian. Christian denominations that believe in local church autonomy and individual responsibility before God predominate the religious landscape of the state. For the majority, the Bible has primary authority in structuring church life and in the formation of the believers' lives. Revivalism continues to be a means of bringing some excitement to small communities, and of reaching out to convert new believers.

# RELIGION
# *Seminaries & Church*
Nancy Jo Kemper                                   # *Related Colleges*

Kentucky has four theological seminaries, accredited by the Association of Theological Schools in the U.S. and Canada.

**Louisville Presbyterian Theological Seminary**
*Established 1853*
  1044 Alta Vista Road
  Louisville, KY 40205
  Ph. (800) 264-1839

**Southern Baptist Theological Seminary**
*Established 1859*
  2825 Lexington Road
  Louisville, KY 40280
  Ph. (800) 626-5525

**Lexington Theological Seminary**
*Established 1865*
  631 S. Limestone
  Lexington, KY 40508
  Ph. (859) 252-0361

**Asbury Theological Seminary**
*Established 1923*
  204 North Lexington Avenue
  Wilmore, KY 40390
  Ph. (800) 2.ASBURY, (859) 858-3581

Kentucky has 17 church-related, accredited colleges, affiliated with the Association of Independent Kentucky Colleges and Universities. They are:

- Asbury College
- Bellarmine University
- Brescia University
- Campbellsville University
- Centre College
- Cumberland College
- Georgetown College
- Kentucky Christian University
- Kentucky Wesleyan College
- Lindsey Wilson College
- Midway College
- Pikeville College
- St. Catharine College
- Spalding University
- Thomas More College
- Transylvania University
- Union College

There are numerous Bible colleges and institutions for preparation for ministry, including: Kentucky Christian University (Grayson); Clear Creek Bible College (Pineville); Kentucky Mountain Bible College (Van Cleve), Louisville Bible College; and Simmons Bible College (Louisville). *For full detail refer to the Education Section.*

Peace demands the most heroic labor and the most difficult sacrifice. It demands greater heroism than war. It demands grater fidelity to the truth and a much more perfect purity of conscience. The Christian fight for peace is not to be confused with defeatism.

*Thomas Merton, Catholic monk & spiritual writer*

## RELIGION

# *Ursuline Sisters of Mount Saint Joseph*

Maple Mount has been home to Ursuline Sisters since 1874, when five German-speaking Ursulines journeyed by flatboat down the Ohio to found Mount Saint Joseph Academy for girls in the rolling hills of Daviess County. Today more than 170 Ursuline Sisters of Mount Saint Joseph minister in Kentucky, Illinois, Tennessee, Louisiana, Missouri, New Mexico, Minnesota, Washington, D.C., and Chile, South America. In their ministry, Ursuline Sisters follow their mission of proclaiming Jesus through education and Christian formation. Sisters serve in schools, parishes, and retreat/spiritual direction, music ministry;

**Memory Meditation Garden, Mount Saint Joseph**
*Source: Ursuline Sisters of Mount Saint Joseph*

outreach to the sick, elderly, and poor; Hispanic ministry; counseling and health care; campus ministry; support for survivors of torture; special ministries to women and children; and the ministry of prayer. Brescia University in Owensboro and Mount Saint Joseph Conference and Retreat Center at Maple Mount are corporate ministries of the Ursuline Sisters of Mount Saint Joseph.

At their 750-acre location 12 miles southwest of Owensboro, the Sisters maintain a Motherhouse residence for active and retired members, and a Conference and Retreat Center. The conference center offers and hosts programs year-round for individuals and groups of all faiths, including directed and private retreats. The Center complex—the former Mount Saint Joseph Academy—

is listed on the National Register of Historic Places. More than 600 acres are dedicated to a working farm, where environment-friendly agricultural methods are used in raising a variety of crops and livestock.

A beautiful renovated chapel features historic stained-glass windows crafted in Germany. The chapel provides a beautiful space for religious celebrations as well as for cultural events. "The Valley," a natural outdoor amphitheatre, offers a location for cul-

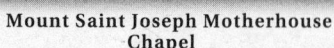

**Mount Saint Joseph Motherhouse Chapel**
*Source: Ursuline Sisters of Mount Saint Joseph*

tural events including a Christian rock concert during the summer. A 25-acre woodland area provides the setting for the annual Mount Saint Joseph Picnic, with Daviess County barbecue and trimmings, and a host of games and prizes. All proceeds from this benefit picnic, held each year on the second Sunday of September, go to the Ursuline Sisters' retirement fund.

*Visitors are welcome to Mount Saint Joseph. For information visit www.ursulinesmsj.org, call Jerry Birge, Director of Communications at 270-229-2007 or e-mail info@maplemount.org.*

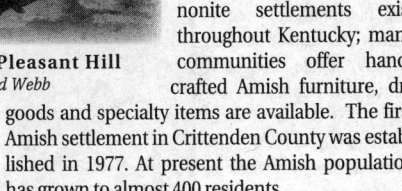

# RELIGION

## Michelle Edwards

# *Amish & Shakers*

The Amish and Mennonites were part of the early Anabaptist movement in Europe, which took place at the time of the Refor- mation. The Anabaptists (late baptizers) believed that only adults who had confessed their faith should be baptized and that they should remain sepa- rate from the larger society. Both Catholics and Protestants put many early Anabaptists to death as heretics, and many others fled to the mountains of Switzerland and southern Ger- many. Here began the tradition of self-sufficient farming and home-based worship services. In 1536, a young Catholic priest from Holland named Menno Simons joined the Anabaptist movement. His writings and leadership united many of the Anabap-

**Shakertown, Pleasant Hill**
*Photo: Sid Webb*

tist groups, who were nicknamed "Mennonites." In 1693, a Swiss bishop named Jacob Amman broke from the Mennonite church. His follow- ers were called the "Amish." Although the two

groups have split several times, the Amish and Mennonite churches still share the same beliefs concerning baptism, non- resistance, and basic Bible doctrines. They differ in mat- ters of dress, technology, lan- guage, form of worship, and interpretation of the Bible. The Amish and Mennonites both settled in Pennsylva- nia as part of William Penn's "holy experiment" of reli- gious tolerance. The first siz- able group of Amish arrived in Lancaster County in the 1720s. In 1824, they declared themselves separate from the home church in Europe.

Today, Amish and Men- nonite settlements exist throughout Kentucky; many communities offer hand- crafted Amish furniture, dry

goods and specialty items are available. The first Amish settlement in Crittenden County was estab- lished in 1977. At present the Amish population has grown to almost 400 residents.

## Shaker Village of Pleasant Hill
### Diana Ratliff

The Shakers, more properly known as the United Society of Believers in Christ's Second Appearing, are one of the most compelling religious and social movements in American life. Originating in the religious ferment of Manchester, England, in the mid-18th century, the "Shaking Quakers" reached fruition after settlement in America in 1774.

"Mother" Ann Lee, the English-born leader of the Shakers, began her public ministry in America in 1780. She lived only until 1784, but her charis- matic preaching had sparked a revolutionary new movement which has had enduring impact on

American religion and culture.

After reading of the great religious revivals being held in Kentucky in the early 1800s, three Shaker missionaries journeyed to Kentucky in 1805 to attend the Cane Ridge meetings in Bourbon County. They quickly converted three Kentuck- ians.

Being a communal society, one of the converts, Elisha Thomas, gave over his 100+ acre farm on the banks of Shawnee Run Creek and began to establish what is known today at Shaker Village of Pleasant Hill in Mercer County.

The Shakers were ardent believers in the millennialist principle of establishing "heaven on earth" through the practice of communitarian social organization, pacifism, celibacy, racial and gender equality, and the public confession of sin. The community at Pleasant Hill reached its peak numbers in the mid 1850s. Pleasant Hill was closed as an operating Shaker village in 1910, and the last Shaker remaining at Pleasant Hill died in 1923.

The restoration began in 1960, opened to the public in 1968 and has served thousands of guests from around the world each year. In "Pleasant Hill and Its Shakers," the late and much beloved Dr. Thomas D. Clark wrote: " 'Shakertown,' or Pleasant Hill, stands not so much as a monument to a narrow religious concept of a celibate society, guided by a willful woman and a prevailing streak of spiritualism, as to the ever-recurring dream in American history that somewhere on this vast continent man could find a hallowed spot to achieve two objectives: first, the redemption of man from his original sin, and, second, the creation of the prefect society in which simplicity, integrity, and quiet love of one's fellowman could prevail free from the machination of a highly materialistic world."

A premier history site, a visitor may talk with costumed interpreters about Shaker life in the 1850s. A National Historic Landmark, it's 34 pristinely restored 19th century buildings are set on 2,900 acres of rolling farmland. Overnight stays, daily programs of Shaker music and dance, skilled artisans demonstrating the 19th century trades of broom making, wood working, coopering, spinning, and weaving are available. Riverboat excursions and horse-drawn wagon rides offer a great way to enjoy the village and surrounding area.

# The Shakers in South Union
*Michelle Edwards*

In 1807 Shakers came to South Union in Logan County and lived there until 1922. The Shakers kept meticulous journals of their activities and from these journals, we catch a glimpse of the history of their daily lives, their belief in work and worship, their inventions and contributions, the birth of the seed industry, textile production and what it was like to live during that period of time. A visit to this wonderful historic site takes one back in time and perhaps gives a better understanding of the challenges facing the Shakers. The Shaker Museum sits upon the historic site of the South Union Shaker Village in the commercial district of South Union. Located in the 40-room 1824 Centre House, the museum houses the nation's largest collection of western Shaker furniture. South Union was one of 24 villages established by the Shakers. During the village's 100-year history, the Shakers acquired and worked 6,000 acres of farmland, constructed over 200 buildings, and maintained industries that developed for them a national reputation.

Built in 1869 the Shaker Tavern was maintained by the Shakers as a thriving business for 40 years, catering to Victorian railroad travelers who stopped at South Union. The Shaker Tavern Bed & Breakfast became a private residence after the Shaker village closed in 1922 and was

**1824 Centre House, South Union**

reopened in 1992. Set in a beautiful country setting and operated by the Shaker Museum, the features include Victorian style furnishings, a full breakfast and admission to the museum.

See: http://www.shakervillageky.org/; http://www.bbonline.com/ky/shaker; http://www.shakermuseum.com/; http://religiousmovements.lib.virginia.edu/nrms/Shakers.html#profile

# Appalachian Pentecostalism

**Patsy Sims**

One of the most popular images of religion in Appalachia is that of serpent handlers. The sensationalism that has popularized this tradition since its inception has condescendingly described its followers, at best, as naive and misguided; at worst, as psychologically disturbed cultists. To themselves, they are ordinary people following their religious beliefs. Historically, serpent handlers as a group are considered to be part of the Pentecostal movement in America, but later they formed independent Pentecostal holiness churches.

There has been much debate over exactly where serpent handling originated, but there is much evidence that it spread out of Tennessee during the early years of the 20th century. The necessary elements were present in Tennessee to encourage the ritual of serpent handling. Vital to its growth was the presence of a fervent fundamentalist religious community with a traditional approach to biblical interpretation — with traditional values that would evoke and reinforce the practice.

Another critical factor in the growth of serpent handling was that it was necessary for the right person to take up a serpent first. This person, at least in East Tennessee, was George Hensley. Hensley may not have been the first person in the 20th century to handle a serpent in obedience to biblical text, but he did lay claim to being the first (Burton, 418). Hensley traveled throughout the South spreading serpent handling throughout the region. He eventually died from a snakebite on July

*Source: Lexington Herald-Leader*

25, 1955 in Florida at the age of 70.

Serpent handlers are fundamentalists, and to the dedicated believers they are just carrying out the words of Jesus in St. Mark 16:17-18: "And these signs shall follow them that believe: in my name they shall cast out devils; they shall speak with new tongues: they shall take up serpents and if they drink any deadly thing, it shall not hurt them; they shall lay hands on the sick and they shall recover."

Most fundamentalist churches take the healing sign, but very few take the Bible literally on serpent handling. Of those that do handle serpents, they are not testing their faith, nor do they feel that they are testing God, as many Christians have accused them of doing. They will not handle snakes unless they are "annointed" or that the power of God was sufficient to protect them. Serpent handlers say that they are "annointed" to pick up serpents and that without this divine intervention, they would be bitten. They feel that they are protected because they take the Bible literally. In serpent handling churches, no one is required to handle the snakes, and in most, no one under the age of 18 is allowed to handle snakes. When they do handle snakes, it is in the summer and fall months when the rattlers, cottonmouths and copperheads which are commonly handled can be caught. Church members capture their own snakes.

*Reprinted with permission of the publisher, University Press of Kentucky, Patsy Sims, "The Snake-Handlers: With Signs Following, Can Somebody Shout Amen,!" The University Press of Kentucky, (Lexington:1996).*

LAW ENFORCEMENT & PUBLIC SAFETY

# *Kentucky Fallen Firefighters Memorial*

## IN HONOR OF SERVICE AND SACRIFICE

On October 11, 1999, a special tribute marked the first memorial service conducted at the Kentucky Fallen Firefighters Memorial, situated at Juniper Park in Frankfort. The memorial was dedicated in honor of the lives of firefighters who made the ultimate sacrifice of duty. The walls of the memorial lists the names of Kentucky firefighters killed in the line of duty and service to their communities. An annual memorial service is held each October in honor of fallen firefighters.

Thirteen names were added to the memorial in 2006—these brave individuals, and the firefighters who preceded them, hold an honored, cherished place in the memories of their comrades and families, and an honored place in the memory of our state.

**Kentucky Fallen Firefighters Memorial**
*Source: Tim Thornberry, Ky. Education Cabinet*

# Law Enforcement & Public Safety

## Dr. Gary Cordner

Kentucky is 46th among the 50 states in the number of state and local police officers per population, with 1.77 police per 1,000 residents. (Louisiana is first with 4.15). In other words, only four states have fewer police officers per population than Kentucky. (They are Minnesota, West Virginia, Vermont and Washington.) That might seem worrisome, except for another statistic – Kentucky has the sixth lowest reported crime rate in the nation. The big picture, then, is that Kentucky has a low crime rate and few police officers, compared to other states.

Every state has a mixture of four types of police officers: (1) federal, such as FBI agents and customs enforcement officers; (2) state, such as state police or highway patrol troopers; (3) local, such as town police officers and sheriff's deputies; and (4) special, such as campus police and game wardens. Kentucky's 7,144 non-federal police officers are distributed as follows:

| | | |
|---|---|---|
| State | 937 | (13.1%) |
| Local | 5,924 | (82.9%) |
| Special | 283 | (4.0%) |

When Kentucky is compared to the other 49 states, it has a typical or average profile in many respects. For example, it is 24th in the number of federal officers, 28th in the number of state and local officers, and 19th in the number of law enforcement agencies (382). It has some other distinctive features.

Kentucky is 4th in the number of sheriff departments (120).

Kentucky is 30th in the number of sheriffs and sheriff's deputies (1,406).

Kentucky is 36th in the average number of sworn officers per agency (18.7). (Hawaii is #1 at 416.3, California #2 at 142.5.)

**Luther Risner
Kentucky State Highway
Patrol**
*Source: Risner Family*

Kentucky is ninth in the portion of its total state and local police officers accounted for by the state police.

These statistics show that Kentucky has many sheriff departments, but they are relatively small. The state also has a large number of town and city police departments, most of which are rather small. The state police in Kentucky represent a larger share of the total law enforcement community than in most other states. In comparative law enforcement terms, Kentucky is a strong state police, weak sheriff state with a heavy preponderance of small town police departments.

### SHERIFF DEPARTMENTS

Kentucky's 120 sheriff departments vary widely in size, from small offices with only a sheriff (Robertson County) or a sheriff and one deputy (Elliott, Lee, Nicholas, and Trimble Counties) to the Jefferson County sheriff's office with 240 deputies. Sheriff departments in Kentucky are authorized to perform police and law enforcement duties, but their primary obligations are to collect certain taxes and fees and serve writs for the courts. These are historically common sheriff functions around the U.S. that hark back to English traditions. Kentucky sheriffs have retained these historical functions to a greater extent than sheriffs in many other states, though, probably due to the Commonwealth's numerous small counties that have not seen fit, or been financially able, to appoint other officials to perform such tasks. As a result, because of these fiscal and civil priorities, many Kentucky sheriff departments do not exercise their police and law enforcement authority to the degree that otherwise might be expected in a predominantly rural state.

Sheriffs, of course, are elected. As such they are

independent of other political and government officials. However, they typically derive part of their funding from the county fiscal court, and consequently have to negotiate with county judge executives and other elected county officials on budgetary matters. Also, they derive much of their funding in the form of a percentage of the taxes and fees that they collect and through fees for serving writs for the court. Realistically, the primacy of these duties follows from their revenue-producing nature.

The most distinctive characteristic of Kentucky sheriffs is something they do not do. They do not run jails. In other states, running the county jail is one of the sheriff's primary responsibilities and jail duties typically account for half or more of sheriff department employees. In Kentucky, however, each county has a separate constitutional office of elected jailer. This unique bifurcation of the sheriff and jailer positions helps explain the small size of many of Kentucky's sheriff offices and the relatively weak role that sheriffs play in Kentucky law enforcement.

**Kentucky Law Enforcement Memorial License Plate**
*Source: Department of Criminal Justice Training*

### TOWN AND CITY POLICE

Kentucky's largest police agency is the Louisville Metro Police Department with 1,192 sworn officers. This agency was formed in 2003 through the merger of the Louisville Police Department and the Jefferson County Police Department, which prior to the merger were the second and third largest police agencies in the state, respectively (after the state police). The second largest local police agency in Kentucky is now the Lexington Division of Police, with 516 authorized sworn officers. Of course, most of Kentucky's municipal police agencies are much smaller. Nationally, 50 percent of police departments have ten or fewer sworn police officers. In Kentucky, 75 percent have ten or fewer officers.

### STATE POLICE

The Kentucky State Police, like state police in other states, were a fairly late addition to the commonwealth's law enforcement system. The Kentucky Highway Patrol was formed in 1936 with 40 officers. It evolved into the Kentucky State Police in 1948.

The Kentucky State Police hired its first black trooper in the 1960s and its first female trooper in the 1970s. The distinctive gray uniform has not changed, but patrol vehicle colors have changed over the years from black to gray to blue and white

to white and finally back to gray. The agency was given its nickname The Thin Gray Line in the 1960s by then Director Ted Bassett.

Today the Kentucky State Police have over 1,000 authorized sworn positions. The agency operates in all 120 counties but particularly in rural areas, providing front-line police patrol and investigations as well as important support services such as central criminal records, the state crime lab, and the Law Information Network of Kentucky (LINK) computer system.

### EDUCATION AND TRAINING

Police education and training programs in Kentucky primarily date from 1966, when Eastern Kentucky University began offering law enforcement classes and the Kentucky Peace Officer's Standards and Training Council was established within state government. The first college course attracted 49 students and initial police training was only one to three weeks in length. From those modest beginnings, EKU's College of Justice and Safety now boasts 44 full-time faculty, 1,500 students, over $60 million per year in federal and state grants and contracts, and the university's Program of Distinction banner. The Kentucky Law Enforcement Council now oversees mandated police recruit training of 16 weeks duration, as well as the 40 hours of in-service training required every year for every peace officer, including chiefs of police. Much of the training is provided by the Department of Criminal Justice Training, a nationally-accredited state agency that operates out of modern, state-of-the-art facilities on the EKU campus.

Kentucky's police training system is the envy of most other states. Part of the credit is owed to a succession of leaders of the Department of Criminal Justice Training, from Robert Stone through Dr. John Bizzack. Importantly as well, the architects of the system in Kentucky had the foresight to establish a surcharge on property and casualty insurance as the funding mechanism for police training. This surcharge has provided steady revenue year after year that self-adjusts for inflation. Without this funding source, the last 40 years of police training in Kentucky would have been much more susceptible to the vagaries of state finances and certainly would not have resulted in the national leadership position now enjoyed.

## LAW ENFORCEMENT OFFICERS KILLED IN THE LINE OF DUTY (1950 - 2005)

| Name | Date | Location |
|------|------|----------|
| Clarence L Meenach | 5/11/50 | Russell |
| Ezra Sutherland | 6/19/50 | Jefferson Co |
| Roy Conway | 7/28/50 | Pike Co |
| Robert R Miller | 2/14/51 | KSP |
| Owen Flack | 6/17/51 | Hopkinsville |
| William M Carrico Sr | 9/15/51 | Carrollton |
| Claude Strong | 1/08/52 | Hickman |
| James B Jasper | 7/03/52 | Pulaski Co |
| Laith Warren | 9/18/52 | Bell Co |
| John P Minogue | 10/04/52 | Louisville |
| Creed J Johnson | 10/31/52 | Lewis Co. |
| Alvin L Keown | 11/08/52 | Jefferson Co |
| Lee T Huffman | 5/04/53 | KSP |
| Robert Hensley | 3/27/54 | Owsley Co |
| Clarence Taylor | 3/27/54 | Owsley Co |
| Henry E StClair | 4/05/54 | Jefferson Co |
| Hubbard Ferguson | 6/18/54 | Gallatin Co |
| William D Porter | 2/25/55 | LaGrange |
| Jack W Ranier Sr | 11/21/55 | Henderson |
| Owen Davenport | 7/13/56 | Corrections |
| Edward R Froedge | 11/04/56 | Owensboro |
| Willie Lewis Sr | 1/01/57 | Leslie Co |
| Luther W Hammond | 2/18/57 | Corrections |
| Novel Mcreynolds | 4/29/57 | Murray |
| Arlin E Curneal | 6/20/57 | Hopkins Co |
| Edward P Nowakowski | 7/10/57 | Louisville |
| Willard C Milstead | 10/15/57 | Princeton |
| Page W Mason | 6/27/58 | Irvine |
| Austin E Vanover Sr | 8/13/58 | Henderson |
| William L Long | 10/04/58 | Louisville |
| Herbert C Bush | 10/11/58 | KSP |
| Stanley Pitakos | 10/16/58 | Newport |
| Elvin Patrick | 1/17/59 | Whitley Co |
| Orville C Trinkle Jr | 3/29/60 | Louisville |
| Delmar Whitworth Sr | 5/24/60 | Jefferson Co |
| Wesley S Fannin | 8/01/61 | Floyd Co. |
| Douglas F Hutton | 12/02/61 | Pulaski Co |
| Sam L Green | 1/01/62 | Rowan Co |
| James C Smith | 7/20/62 | Barbourville |
| Leonard Adams Sr | 12/06/62 | Letcher Co |
| William E Tevis | 5/26/63 | KSP |
| Cosby H Whitted Jr | 8/23/63 | Louisville |
| Elmer Mobley | 5/28/64 | KSP |
| Cecil W Uzzle | 5/28/64 | KSP |
| Warren C Campbell Sr | 8/29/64 | Montgomery Co |
| Harold L Catron Sr | 9/16/64 | Somerset |
| James Sansbury | 2/21/65 | Louisville |
| Delano G Powell | 7/08/65 | KSP |
| Caleb Dehart | 8/22/65 | Leslie Co |
| Glen A Stephens | 9/03/65 | Olive Hill |
| Authur G Dotson | 2/16/66 | Russellville |
| James Strong Jr | 5/28/66 | Corydon |
| Mack E Brady | 11/09/66 | KSP |
| Walter L Meek | 11/26/66 | Johnson Co |
| Danny L Redmon | 1/03/67 | Lexington |
| Cloyd A Charlton | 2/06/67 | Adairville |
| William F Meyer | 9/01/67 | Louisville |
| John L Thomas | 11/21/67 | Lexington |
| Joseph L Price | 11/29/67 | Louisville |
| Donald Ronnebaum | 7/26/68 | Covington |
| Earl J Bertram | 8/18/68 | Jefferson Co |
| James Ryan Sr | 11/04/68 | Danville |
| Oscar Burkhart | 11/07/68 | Harlan Co |
| Donald W Gaskin | 12/30/69 | Louisville |
| James Ratliff | 12/30/69 | Louisville |
| John Schaefer | 5/02/71 | Louisville |
| Wilbur Hayes | 5/02/71 | Louisville |
| Raymond Oyler Jr | 5/08/71 | Louisville |
| Amos A Faulkner Jr | 7/20/71 | Hopkinsville |
| Jack Brock | 12/07/71 | Harlan Co |
| William H Barrett | 12/19/71 | KSP |
| James W Mcneely | 4/08/72 | KSP |
| Lawrence Conley | 4/12/72 | Floyd Co |
| Billy F Wood | 8/08/72 | Williamstown |
| Walter O Thurtell | 9/29/72 | KSP |
| Orie Hicks | 10/08/72 | Harlan Co |
| Tommy Ray | 4/20/73 | Louisville |
| Joe Ward Jr | 4/23/73 | KSP |
| William C Smith | 4/26/73 | KSP |
| Denver Tabor | 7/20/73 | Fish & Wildlife |
| Bristol Taylor | 11/23/73 | Knott Co |
| Jonah D Cox | 2/23/74 | Louisville |
| William C Frederick | 4/24/74 | Paris |
| Armand Vancleave | 4/27/74 | Shively |
| John W Hutchinson | 6/04/75 | KSP |
| Bobby A McCoun Jr | 9/01/75 | KSP |
| William F Pickard | 1/21/76 | KSP |
| Michael T Smith | 3/11/76 | Jefferson Co |
| Wilson McLain | 4/17/76 | Harlan Co |
| William D Cobb | 8/20/76 | Hart Co |
| Mark W Hines | 8/29/76 | Jefferson Co |
| Michael L Williams | 8/29/76 | Salyersville |
| Willis D Martin | 4/26/77 | KSP |
| Gwen Downs | 5/16/77 | Louisville |
| Joe C Lykins | 10/02/77 | Boyle Co |
| Jimmy R Tolson | 6/26/78 | Campton |
| Kenneth R Nally | 11/06/78 | Jefferson Co |
| Lester E Reid | 1/05/79 | Warren Co |
| Clinton E Cunningham | 2/11/79 | KSP |
| Claude E Flinchum | 3/04/79 | Wolfe Co |
| Albert B Sallee Jr | 5/12/79 | Louisville |
| Earl Smith | 5/15/79 | Pike Co |
| Daniel L Hay | 10/16/79 | Maysville |
| Edward R Harris | 11/07/79 | KSP |
| Christopher M Dunn | 4/03/80 | Jefferson Co |
| Hiram A Ritchie | 6/30/80 | Perry Co |
| Horace Hall Jr | 8/14/80 | Bell Co |
| Jerome S Clifton | 10/01/80 | KSP |
| Ronnie E Seelye | 1/27/81 | Louisville |
| Darrell V Phelps | 8/07/81 | KSP |
| Randall Cook | 4/16/82 | Knott Co |
| Alex Eversole | 1/04/83 | Perry Co |
| Charles D Wentworth | 4/12/83 | Shelby Co |
| Jack D Claywell | 6/16/83 | Grayson |
| Ricky A Lafollette | 8/18/83 | Louisville |
| Patricia Ross | 3/01/84 | Corrections |
| Donald R Williams | 6/16/84 | West Point |
| Carnie F Hopkins | 9/09/84 | Livingston Co |
| Anthony E Jansen | 12/30/84 | Newport |
| William R Burns | 7/05/85 | Radcliff |
| Roy H Mardis | 8/23/85 | Lexington |
| Michael R Green | 1/26/86 | Corrections |
| John R Weiss | 2/12/86 | Shively |
| Robert T Walker | 2/16/86 | Irvine |
| Charles F Cash | 5/09/86 | Corrections |
| Jack S Deuser | 7/29/86 | Jefferson Co |
| John R Herron | 12/20/86 | Falmouth |
| Russell J Estep | 1/02/87 | Louisa |
| Robert C Banker | 3/19/87 | Fish & Wildlife |
| James M Richardson | 2/01/88 | Pulaski Co |
| Alton Embry Jr | 5/07/88 | Louisville |
| Thomas A Noonan | 9/10/88 | Highland Heights |
| Joseph M Angelucci | 11/23/88 | Fayette Co |
| Johnny M Edrington | 12/21/88 | KSP |
| Frank W Pysher Jr | 1/10/89 | Jefferson Co |
| Curtis E Lobb | 5/17/89 | Greensburg |
| Shelby W Nease | 7/18/89 | Hazard |
| Terry L Sanders | 9/15/89 | Mayfield |
| Donald L Ferguson | 4/28/90 | Albany |
| Robert P Palmer | 9/25/90 | Elsmere |
| Edward E Flora | 10/26/90 | Warren Co |
| Gary E Kidwell | 1/20/91 | Stanford |
| Kenneth M McCarty | 5/23/91 | Bourbon Co |
| Steve L Bennett | 1/30/92 | Powell Co |
| Arthur C Briscoe | 1/30/92 | Powell Co |
| Cecil E Cyrus | 3/18/92 | Johnson Co |
| Charles K Todd | 8/23/92 | Mayfield |
| Floyd W Cheeks | 10/27/93 | Jefferson Co |
| John L Beck | 1/27/94 | Rowan Co |
| Michael R Carrithers | 8/17/95 | Louisville |
| Eric S Stafford | 6/26/96 | Edmonson Co |
| Gregory Hans | 3/10/97 | Jefferson Co |
| Coleman Binion | 9/05/97 | Carter Co |
| Michael A Partin | 1/04/98 | Covington |
| Brandon H Thacker | 4/16/98 | ABC |
| Regina W Nickles | 10/14/98 | Harrodsburg |
| Joey T Vincent | 6/27/99 | Greenville |
| Jason W Cammack | 4/23/00 | KVE |
| Billy R Walls III | 11/13/01 | Jessamine Co |
| Charles B Morgan Jr | 11/28/01 | Jessamine Co |
| Samuel W Catron | 4/13/02 | Pulaski Co |
| Howard B Callis | 12/10/02 | Corrections |
| Ray B Franklin | 12/02/02 | Charitable Gaming |
| Eddie Mundo Jr | 4/16/03 | LaGrange |
| Douglas W Bryant | 5/19/03 | Fish & Wildlife |
| Robert T Hansel | 10/02/03 | Lynch |
| Steven L Hutchinson | 6/17/04 | Grayson Co |
| Larry D Cottingham | 1/3/05 | Henderson Co |
| Peter A Grignon | 3/23/05 | Louisville |
| Roger D Lynch | 6/2/05 | Livingston Co |

*Source: Kentucky Law Enforcement Memorial Foundation, www.klemf.org*

# LAW ENFORCEMENT & PUBLIC SAFETY
# *Crime*
# *& Traffic Report*

## 2005 KENTUCKY CRIME FACTS

- 115,323 serious crimes were committed in 2005
- A serious crime was committed every 4 minutes, 33 seconds
- Murder was committed every 45 hours, 52 minutes
- Firearms were used in 70% of all murders
- 74% of all murder victims were white; 64% were male
- Rape was committed every 6 hours, 48 minutes
- Robbery was committed every 2 hours, 18 minutes
- 47.4% of violent crimes were solved
- 1,090 police officers were assaulted
- 18.1% of property crimes were solved
- Property crimes outnumbered violent crimes by 9.5 to 1
- 28,785 persons were arrested for DUI
- 46,679 arrests were made for drug violations
- A total of 285,506 arrests were made in 2005

Eight crimes are considered Part I crimes. Part I crimes reported by law enforcement agencies in Kentucky during 2004 and 2005 are shown in the chart below. These overall statistics reflect only offenses reported to or known by the police. The overall crime rate in Kentucky in 2005 increased by 1.5 percent compared to 2004. The categories that show an increase are rape, robbery, aggravated assault, larceny theft and arson. Murder, burglary, and auto theft reflect decreases. The largest per-centage of decrease was in murder, showing 25 fewer reported offenses (-11.6%). The offense of arson shows the largest percentage of increase, 286 more reported offenses (+45.2%). Only fires determined to have been willfully or maliciously set are classified as arson.

Of the 919 arsons in Kentucky, most occurred in the Single Occupancy Residential category with 297 offenses and at an estimated value of property damaged totaling $7,209,098 (average damage $24,273). The most property damage caused by arson was estimated at $50,000,100 in the Industrial/Manufacturing category with only 3 offenses (average damage $16,666,700). 161 arson offenses were in the Motor Vehicles category (Autos, Trucks, Buses, Motorcycles, etc.) with property damage totaling $333,460.

In viewing and comparing this data, it should be noted that these crime statistics are being reported by the number of victims rather than the number of offenses against the same victim. In keeping with the Uniform Crime Reporting guidelines, the Hierarchy Rule is applied in multiple-offense situations. An exception to this rule is Arson, in which each offense (even in the case of multiple charges) is counted for statistical analysis.

Kentucky's "Crime Index" is 2,765.76. The crime index, or rate, is used nationally and is derived from the following formulas:

Population divided by 100,000 = X

Number of offenses divided by X = crime index

**OFFENSES REPORTED, 2004 & 2005**

| | 2005 | 2004 | % CHANGE | % DIST. |
|---|---|---|---|---|
| 1. MURDER | 191 | 216 | -11.60% | 0.20% |
| 2. RAPE | 1,289 | 1,251 | 3.00% | 1.10% |
| 3. ROBBERY | 3,817 | 3,372 | 13.20% | 3.30% |
| 4. AGGRAVATED ASSAULT | 5,685 | 5,232 | 8.70% | 4.90% |
| 5. BURGLARY | 25,673 | 25,784 | -0.40% | 22.30% |
| 6. LARCENY THEFT | 68,123 | 68,478 | -0.90% | 59.90% |
| 7. MOTOR VEHICLE THEFT | 8,635 | 8,669 | -0.40% | 7.50% |
| 8. ARSON | 919 | 633 | 45.20% | 0.80% |
| TOTAL | 115,332 | 113,635 | 1.50% | 100.00% |

*Source: Kentucky State Police, 2005 Crime Report, www.kentuckystatepolice.org.*

Kentucky's crime index for 2005 is based on the current estimated population of 4.17 million.

The crime rate is tabulated on seven major offenses designated Index Crimes by the Federal Bureau of Investigation's Uniform Crime Reporting program. These seven categories include four violent offenses (murder, rape, robbery and aggravated assault) and three nonviolent crimes (burglary, larceny theft and auto theft). Consider the following explanation to help clarify the data classification process:

1) Murder is the unlawful killing of a human being with malice aforethought. Suicides, accidental deaths, negligent manslaughters, assaults to murder, traffic fatalities, and attempted murders are not included. Murder is the most serious of all Part I crimes.

> MURDER was committed every 45 hours, 52 minutes.

2) Rape is defined as the carnal knowledge of a person, forcibly or otherwise, against the person's will. Only forcible rapes are included, together with assaults for the purpose of rape and attempted forcible rapes. Excluded are rapes where the victim is under the age of consent and no force is used.

> RAPE was committed every 6 hours, 48 minutes.

3) Robbery is the felonious taking of the property of another by force, the threat of force, violence, and/or by putting the victim in fear. All attempted robberies are included.

> ROBBERY was committed every 2 hours, 18 minutes.

4) Larceny, or larceny-theft, is the unlawful taking of property or articles of value without the use of force, violence, or fraudulent conversion. Included are such offenses as pocket picking, shoplifting, thefts from autos, and bicycle thefts.

> LARCENY was committed almost every 8 minutes.

5) Assault is the unlawful attack by one person upon another for purpose of inflicting severe or aggravated bodily injury. It is not necessary that injury result from an aggravated assault when a gun, knife, or other weapon is used which could, and probably would, result in serious personal injury.

> ASSAULT was committed every 1 hour, 32 minutes.

6) Burglary is the unlawful entering or remaining in a building with the intent to commit a crime. This includes entries where force of any kind is used to gain entrance, entries where no force was used, and attempts to enter forcibly.

> BURGLARY was committed every 20 minutes, 28 seconds.

7) Auto Theft includes all thefts and attempted thefts of motor vehicles.

> AUTO THEFT was committed every 1 hour, 1 minute.

8) Arson includes any willful or malicious burning or attempt to burn a residence, public building, motor vehicle or aircraft, personal property of another, etc. Only fires determined to have been willfully or maliciously set are classified as arson.

> ARSON was committed every 9 hours, 32 minutes.

## FAMILY OR DOMESTIC VIOLENCE IN KENTUCKY IN 2005

Domestic Violence is a problem that has been of major news focus both nationally and in Kentucky. The number of reported cases and victims assisted in protective shelters is proof that this is a serious public safety issue worthy of priority response. Domestic violence includes any of the following crimes when committed by one family member/partner against another: homicide, kidnapping, sex offenses, stalking, assault, and terroristic threatening.

In Fiscal Year 2005, the Administrative Office of the Courts reported that 26,959 petitions were filed by persons seeking Domestic Violence Protective Orders. There were 26,052 disposition case closings. (AOC does not distinguish between cases dismissed and types of orders issued).

**DOMESTIC VIOLENCE**

| | |
|---|---|
| Total Kentucky Adult Protection Reports Received by DSS in FY'05 (Adult Abuse, Spouse Abuse, Self Neglect, Caretaker Neglect and Exploitation) | 47,796 |
| Total Number of Resulting Allegations | 30,625 |
| Domestic Violence Allegations Investigated (Spouse, Ex-Spouse, Paramour) | 19,693 |
| Adult Abuse Allegations Investigated | 3,693 |
| Caretaker Neglect, Self Neglect and Exploitation Allegations Investigated | 7,239 |
| Percent of Total Adult Protection Allegations due to Domestic Violence | 28.6 percent |
| Percent Change of Domestic Violence Allegations from FY'04 | -13.1 percent |

*Source: Kentucky State Police, 2005 Crime Report, www.kentuckystatepolice.org.*

## HATE BIAS CRIMES IN KENTUCKY IN 2004

A "hate crime" is a criminal offense committed against a person or property which is motivated, in whole or in part, by the offender's bias against a race, religion, disability, ethnicity/national origin, or sexual orientation. These criminal offenses fall into the major crimes (murder, rape, robbery, aggravated assault, burglary, larceny-theft, motor vehicle theft and arson), plus lesser crimes of simple assault, intimidation and vandalism.

The most common offenses involving hate-bias crimes for 2005 were "intimidation," and "destruction/damage vandalism." In 2005 the most commonly reported bias motivation was racial. The second largest percentage was ethnicity/ national origin, followed by sexual orientation for third place, religious for fourth place, and disability for fifth place. By far, individuals (38 or 80.9 percent) were reported to be the main hate crime target.

The most frequently reported location of bias crimes in 2005 was residence/homes. The second most common location was parking lot/garages. The most common race of suspected offender of hate crimes was white.

## DRUG AND DUI ARRESTS IN KENTUCKY IN 2005

There were 46,679 individuals arrested for drug violations in Kentucky in 2005: 6,141 for opium or cocaine; 16,913 for marijuana; 3,036 for synthetic narcotics and 20,589 for other dangerous non-narcotic drugs. DUI (driving under the influence)

**Department for Community Based Services**

**Adult and Child Abuse**

**24-hour Toll Free**

**Reporting Hotline**

**1-800-752-6200**

arrests totaled 28,785; adults counted for 28,253 of the arrests; 23,318 males and 5,451 females; 25,755 were white, 2,446 African Americans, and 396 were in the category of Other.

## ASSAULTS ON LAW ENFORCEMENT OFFICERS IN 2005

In 2005, three Kentucky law enforcement officers paid the supreme sacrifice of their lives in the line of duty for the citizens of this great Commonwealth: **Sergeant Larry Dale Cottingham** of the Henderson County Sheriff's Office, **Officer Peter Grignon** of the Louisville Metro Police Department, and **Deputy Sheriff Roger Dale Lynch** of the Livingston County Sheriff's Department.

A total of 1,090 police officers were assaulted in Kentucky during 2005. Of the officers assaulted, 308 officers received personal injury. This number represents 28.3% of the total number of officers assaulted. 95.4% of the police assaults were cleared.

*Source: Kentucky State Police, 2005 Crime Report, www.kentuckystatepolice.org*

# Traffic Facts

**2004 COLLISION SUMMARY**

| TYPE COLLISION REPORTED | 2003 | 2004 | % CHANGE |
|---|---|---|---|
| Fatal (Public Roads) | 845 | 854 | 1.1 |
| Nonfatal injury (Public Roads) | 31,075 | 29,933 | -3.7 |
| Property Damage Only (Public Roads) | 97,908 | 102,931 | 5.1 |
| Total Number Reported (Public Roads) | 129,828 | 133,718 | 3 |
| Parking Lots/ Private Property | 24,247 | 23,514 | 2.9 |
| Total All Reported | 154,075 | 157,232 | 2 |
| Fatal (Total) | 860* | 866** | 0.7 |
| *Includes 15 fatal collisions on parking lots/private property | | | |
| **Includes 12 fatal collisions on parking lots/private property | | | |

Approximately one of every 4,900 Kentucky residents died as a result of a fatal traffic collision on a public road. About one in 102 Kentucky residents was injured in a traffic collision. [Based on 4,145,922 population estimates.] Approximately one of every 14 drivers licensed in Kentucky was involved in a traffic collision in Kentucky. About one of 2,500 Kentucky drivers was involved in a fatal collision. [Based on 2,888,354 licensed drivers (including learner permits)].

There were 133,718 total collisions in Kentucky. Total collisions increased 3.0 percent from 2003 to 2004.

Collisions with moving motor vehicles (89,932

**DEATH AND INJURY SUMMARY**

|  | 2003 | 2004 | % CHANGE |
|---|---|---|---|
| Persons Killed – Public Roads | 928 | 964 | 3.9 |
| Persons Killed – Parking Lots/Private Property | 17 | 14 | -17.6 |
| Persons Killed (Total) | 945 | 978 | 3.5 |
| Perons Injured – Public Roads | 46,966 | 44,986 | -4.2 |
| Persons Injured – Parking Lots/ Private Property | 1,623 | 1,226 | -24.5 |
| Persons Injured (Total) | 48,589 | 46,212 | -4.9 |

or 65 percent) and collisions with fixed objects (24,661or 24 percent) account for 89 percent of the fatalities and injuries. Sixty-seven (67) percent of all collisions reported involved collisions between two or more moving vehicles (not in a parking lot). Eighteen (18) percent of all collisions involved collisions with fixed objects. Fourteen (14) percent of all collisions did not involve a collision with either a moving vehicle or a fixed object. About 11 percent were other types of collisions.

Fifty (50) pedestrians were killed and 849 were injured in traffic collisions in 2004. Twenty-five (25) percent of the pedestrians killed or injured were 14 years of age or younger, while 7 percent were age 65 or older.

Forty-two (42) percent of all fatal collisions involved a collision with another moving vehicle. Thirty-nine (39) percent of the fatal collisions reported during 2003 involved collisions with fixed objects. Collisions with pedestrians accounted for 6 percent of the fatal collisions. Fourteen (14) percent of the fatal collisions were other type collisions. Most of these (10 percent) were non-collisions (vehicle overturning or other non-collision). Four of the 20 persons killed in hit-and-run collisions were pedestrians and none were pedalcyclists. One hundred three (103) pedestrians and 40 pedalcyclists were injured.

Most collisions (63 percent) occurred in urban areas. However, the majority of fatal collisions (57 percent) took place in rural areas of Kentucky. Although nonfatal injury collisions were divided

**TOTAL DEATH RATES**
(deaths per 100 million miles traveled*)

| YEAR | KILLED | KY | RATE** U.S. |
|---|---|---|---|
| 1989 | 776 | 2.4 | 2.3 |
| 1990 | 851 | 2.5 | 2.2 |
| 1991 | 828 | 2.4 | 2 |
| 1992 | 819 | 2.2 | 1.8 |
| 1993 | 875 | 2.2 | 1.8 |
| 1994 | 791 | 2 | 1.8 |
| 1995 | 856 | 2.1 | 1.8 |
| 1996 | 846 | 2 | 1.8 |
| 1997 | 865 | 1.9 | 1.7 |
| 1998 | 869 | 1.9 | 1.6 |
| 1999 | 819 | 1.7 | 1.5 |
| 2000 | 823 | 1.8 | 1.5 |
| 2001 | 843 | 1.8 | 1.5 |
| 2002 | 915 | 2 | 1.6 |
| 2003 | 945 | 2 | 1.5 |
| 2004 | 964 | 2.1 | 1.5 |

*miles raveled in Kentucky in 2004=47.2 billion
**Includes Public Roads

between urban and rural areas, nearly twice as many property damage collisions were reported in urban areas; 79 percent of all collisions occurred on straight roads and 21 percent on curved roads. Thirty-nine (39) percent of the fatal collisions during 2004 occurred on curved roads.

Seventy-two (72) percent of all collisions reported occurred during daylight hours. Twenty-three (23) percent of all collisions occurred during dark hours, and 5 percent occurred at dawn or dusk. Fifty-six (56) percent of all fatal collisions occurred during daylight hours, 37 percent occurred during dark hours, and 7 percent at dawn or dusk.

Twenty-three (23) percent of all collisions and 32 percent of fatal collisions occurred on weekends (Saturday and Sunday combined). November ranked highest for total number of collisions and February showed the lowest number of total collisions. August reported the highest number of fatal collisions; January showed the lowest.

The total number of persons killed in holiday periods in 2004 was 65 as compared to 44 in 2003. The Labor Day holiday period registered the highest number of fatalities. The lowest number of holiday fatalities occurred over the Christmas holiday.

There were 10,015 collisions in which a truck was involved. This resulted in 137 fatalities and 2,806 injuries. Twenty-three (23) percent of the truck collisions occurred on county or city streets, 20 percent on interstates, and 47 percent on U.S. and state-numbered routes. Twenty (20) percent of the hazardous cargo collisions occurred on interstates and 54 percent on U.S. and state-numbered routes.

Fifty-seven (57) percent of the drivers who were involved in collisions during 2004 (where sex was listed) were male; 43 percent were female. In fatal collisions, 71 percent of the drivers were male and 29 percent were female; there were 640 males versus 324 females killed. Twenty-six (26) percent of all persons killed in traffic collisions were in the 15- to 24-year old age group; there were 154 fatalities in collisions involving a teenage driver (76 of these fatalities were the teenage driver). There were 24 fatalities in alcohol-related collisions involving teenage drivers (10 of these fatalities were the teenage driver).

# LAW ENFORCEMENT & CRIME
# *Federal & State Prisons*

## *Federal Prisons*

### Federal Bureau of Prisons
www.bop.gov
Harley G Lappin, Director
Home Owners Loan Corp Bldg Rm 654
320 1st St NW
Washington DC 20534
(202) 307-3250

### FMC Lexington
Joe W Booker Jr, Warden
3301 Leestown Rd
Lexington KY 40511
(859) 255-6812
An administrative facility for male inmates. It
has a population of approximately 1933.

### FCI Ashland
Linda Sanders, Warden
St Rt 716
PO Box 888
Ashland KY 41105
(606) 928-6414
A low security institution housing 1218 male
inmates.

### FCI Manchester
Jose Barron Jr, Warden
PO Box 3000
Manchester KY 40962
(606) 598-1900
A medium security facility with a male popula-
tion of 1124.

### USP Big Sandy
US Penitentiary
1197 Airport Road
Inez KY 41224
(606) 433-2400
A high security satellite prison camp housing
approximately 1541 male inmates.

### USP McCreary
US Penitentiary
330 Federal Way
Pine Knot, KY 42635
(606) 354-7000
A high security facility that houses 1567 male
offenders.

## *State Prisons*

## ADULT INSTITUTIONS

### Blackburn Correctional Complex - Lexington
Joe Rion, Warden
3111 Spurr Rd
Lexington 40511
(859) 246-2366
Largest adult male minimum security institution (594) providing care, housing, custody, control and governmental services jobs to inmates.

### Eastern KY Correctional Complex - West Liberty
John Motley, Warden
US 460 Index Hill
PO Box 636
West Liberty 41472
(606) 743-2800
A medium security institution with a current
population of 1689.

### Frankfort Career Development Ctr - Frankfort
Kimberly Whitley, Warden
PO Box 538
Frankfort 40601
(502) 564-2120
A 205-capacity minimum security facility. The majority of inmates are assigned to the Governmental Services Program Work Detail.

### Green River Correctional Complex
Patti Webb, Warden
1200 River Rd
PO Box 9300
Central City 42330
(270) 754-5415
A medium/minimum security adult male correctional facility housing 982 inmates.

### KY Correctional Institution for Women - Pewee Valley
Cookie Crews, Warden
Box 337 Ash Ave
Pewee Valley 40056
(502) 241-8454
Houses 726 women. The only adult female institution in the Commonwealth for the purpose of housing felons from all 120 counties.

### KY State Penitentiary – Eddyville
Thomas L. Simpson, Warden
Rt 2 Box 128
Eddyville 42038
(270) 388-2211
The oldest and only maximum-security facility. This facility houses Kentucky's 36 Death-Row inmates. Total population is 856 inmates.

### KY State Reformatory - LaGrange
Larry Chandler, Warden
3001 W Hwy 146
LaGrange 40032
(502) 222-9441
A medium security facility and the state's first largest prison in terms of inmate population with a 1908-bed capacity.

### Little Sandy Correctional Complex - Sandy Hook
Gary Beckstom, Warden
Route 5, Box 1000
Sandy Hook 41171
(606) 738-6133
A medium security institution.

### Luther Luckett Correctional Complex –LaGrange
Tom Dailey, Warden
Dawkins Rd Box 6
LaGrange 40031
(502) 222-0363
A medium/minimum security prison. The population is currently at 1073.

### Northpoint Training Center - Burgin
Steve Haney, Warden
Hwy 33 Box 479
Burgin 40310
(859) 239-7012
A medium-security institution with a current bed capacity of 1,256 inmates.

### Roederer Correctional Complex
James Sweatt, Warden
3001 W Hwy 146
LaGrange 40031
(502) 222-0170
A medium/minimum security facility with 997 inmates.

### Western KY Correctional Complex
Becky Pancake, Warden
374 New Bethel Rd
Fredonia 42411
(270) 388-9781
A medium/minimum security facility.

## PRIVATE PRISONS

### Lee Adjustment Center - Beattyville
Randall Stovall, Warden
Fairground Ridge
PO Box 900
Beattyville 41311
(606) 464-2866
A 400-bed minimum security prison.

### Marion Adjustment Center - St Mary
Arvill Chapman, Warden
95 Raywick Rd
PO Box 10 Hwy 94
St Mary 40063
(270) 692-9622
The first private minimum security prison in the country, it has 826 beds.

### OCCC—Otter Creek Correctional Complex
Joyce Arnold, Warden
Hwy 306 Box 500
Wheelwright 41669
(606) 452-9700

# Receive a Kentucky Almanac with a subscription to the Lexington Herald-Leader!

Subscribe to the Herald-Leader and get the Kentucky Almanac–2nd Edition or give a gift subscription and get the Kentucky Almanac. Whatever you decide, keep the Almanac. If you have a copy, give it as a gift to relatives, friends or business associates!

## For fast service, call now at 1-800-224-0518!

■ ■ ■ ■ ■ ■ ■ ■ ■ ■ ■ ■ ■ ■ ■ ■ ■ ■ ■ ■

Or complete, clip and return this form with your payment information to:

Lexington Herald-Leader, Circulation - R. White
100 Midland Avenue • Lexington, KY   40508-1999

☐ **Daily paid subscription**
(All 7 days, Monday-Sunday)
Save $11.85! • Daily & Sunday $48
*($16/month for 3-months w/Kentucky Almanac)\**
*SD7PKY07*

☐ **Weekend paid subscription**
(4 days, Friday-Monday)
Regular rate • Weekend $36
*($12/month for 3-months w/Kentucky Almanac)\**
*SD4PKY07*

☐ **Please charge my:**
○ debit card or ○ credit card: ○ VISA   ○ MASTER CARD   ○ DISCOVER   ○ AMEX

__ __ __ __ / __ __ __ __ / __ __ __ __ / __ __ __ __   Expires: __ __ __ __ / __ __ __ __

☐ **Please see attached check payment**

NAME _____

ADDRESS _____

CITY _____ STATE _____ ZIP _____

EMAIL _____ PHONE_____
*(required for verification)*

SIGNATURE _____ DATE _____

This offer is valid only for subscribers who have not been an active subscriber in the last 31 days. KY Almanac–2nd Edition is only eligible for paid subscriptions at the time service is started. Available while supplies last. Offer expires March 31, 2007.

*After three months, regular rate of $19.95 for daily service applies. Weekend rate is already the regular rate of $12. Or, continue to save with EZpay by calling 1-800-224-0518.

060713-002-KB

# MEDIA

## Kentucky Journalism Hall of Fame

Established in 1980 by the University of Kentucky Journalism Alumni Association, the Kentucky Journalism Hall of Fame recognizes Kentuckians who made significant contributions to the profession of journalism. The first members of the Hall of Fame were inducted on April 13, 1981. As of 2006, the Kentucky Journalism Hall of Fame has recognized 148 outstanding journalism professionals.

To be considered for this honor, individuals, living or dead, must have made significant contributions to the field of journalism and either be a Kentucky native or spent a substantial part of their career working in journalism-related positions in Kentucky.

### The Pioneers of Kentucky Journalism in chronological order:

**John Bradford** founded the state's first newspaper, the Kentucky Gazette, in Lexington in 1787. Bradford was Kentucky's first public printer and was noted for his pamphlets and book publishing. He was also one of Lexington's leading citizens.

**William Hunter** established one of Kentucky's earliest newspapers, the Mirror, at Washington in Madison County in 1797. The paper was moved in 1798 to Frankfort, where it was renamed the Palladium and continued under Hunter's direction until 1809.

**Samuel Vail** established and operated Louisville's first newspaper, the Farmers Library, which existed from 1801 until 1808.

**Joseph M. Street** was co-founder of the Frankfort newspaper, the Western World, in 1806. He helped expose the Burr conspiracy and Spanish intrigues in Kentucky. Street survived an assassination attempt

brought on by his actions.

**William Worsley** co-founded the Reporter, a prominent central Kentucky newspaper, in 1807. Worsley operated this newspaper until 1819, when he helped establish a paper in Louisville called the Focus.

**Humphrey Marshall** was a staunch Federalist who published the American Republic, later named the Harbinger, in Frankfort between 1810 and 1825. Marshall was a U.S. senator and author of a notable early history of Kentucky.

**Thomas T. Skillman** founded the first religious newspaper west of the Alleghenies, the Evangelical Record and Western Review, in Lexington in 1812. Skillman later edited the Presbyterian Advocate and the Western Luminary.

**Albert Gallatin Hodges** started his career in 1815, when he was 12. Hodges served in various capacities at a number of Kentucky newspapers. In 1833, he established the Frankfort

Commonwealth, which he published for almost four decades.

**Amos Kendall** edited one of the best early Kentucky newspapers, the Argus of Western America, from 1816 to 1829. Kendall was a strong supporter of Andrew Jackson, under whom he was U.S. postmaster general and a member of the "Kitchen Cabinet."

**Francis Preston Blair** was an associate of Amos Kendall and writer for the Argus of Western America. In 1830, Blair went to Washington to become editor of the Jacksonian paper, the Globe, a position he held until 1845.

**Shadrach Penn** founded the Louisville Public Advertising Weekly, which became a semi-weekly and in 1826 became the first daily newspaper in Kentucky. Under Penn's leadership it was a leading paper of Louisville for more than two decades.

**Lewis Collins** was editor of the Maysville Eagle from 1820 to 1828 and again from 1830 to 1847. Collins wrote a history of Kentucky that remains a standard work on the subject.

**Edwin Bryant** was a major figure in the establishment of the Lexington Observer and Kentucky Reporter in 1832. The two papers later became the Lexington Observer and Reporter, of which Bryant was the first editor. He also was associated with the Lexington Intelligencer and the Louisville Dime.

**D.C. Wickliffe** was editor of the Lexington Observer and Reporter from 1838 to 1865. Wickliffe was a friend and supporter of Henry Clay, and after the collapse of the Whigs he became a leader of the Democratic Party. He was Kentucky secretary of state under Gov. Robinson.

**Cassius Marcellus Clay** was an important Kentucky abolitionist. His antislavery newspaper, the True American, was one of the most courageous episodes in the history of Kentucky journalism.

**George D. Prentice** was editor of the Louisville Journal from 1830 to 1868. Prentice, with his outstanding writing and editorial skills, made the Journal the state's most widely read paper and one with national influence. He was a unionist whose efforts helped prevent the secession of Kentucky.

In 1869, Prentice became the first president of the Kentucky Press Association.

**John H. Harney** was editor of the Louisville Democrat, with which he was associated from 1843 until 1868. Harney was a prominent Democratic party leader and an important Louisville journalist of the mid-nineteenth century.

**Walter N. Haldeman** founded the Louisville Courier, which he edited or managed from 1844 until 1868. Haldeman supported the Confederacy and continued to publish the Courier from within Confederate lines during the Civil War. After the war, he helped to establish the Courier-Journal in Louisville, and later became president of that newspaper organization.

**Henry Watterson** was editor of the Courier-Journal from 1868-1919. Established the Courier-Journal both in fact and reputation; made the paper a respected voice throughout the nation but especially in the South. At age 78, won the Pulitzer Prize in 1918 for two editorials supporting American entry into World War I.

*Source: School of Journalism and Telecommunications, University of Kentucky.*

---

## Pioneer Radio & Television Stations

In "Towers over Kentucky, A History of Radio and Television in the Bluegrass State," Francis M. Nash, author and veteran radio station owner, describes the advent of broadcasting and the changes wireless transmissions brought to Kentucky. Published in 1995, the book celebrates the 75th anniversary of the radio broadcasting industry and the 50th anniversary of the Kentucky Broadcasters Association. Although much experimentation with "radiocasts" had been ongoing around the U.S. and within Kentucky since before 1920, the official "first" licensed radio station was WHAS in Louisville. Broadcasting as the "station of the Courier-Journal and Louisville Times," the first show went on the air on July 18, 1922. Both the newspaper and radio station were owned by Robert Worth Bingham.

As anyone who has lived through it, everyday life in America changed dramatically after WWII. "Radios with pictures" was an idea that had been around since experiments in the early 1900s. Kentucky's first television broadcast was a variety show on WAVE-TV in Louisville — it was the evening before Thanksgiving, November 24, 1948. The owner, George Norton, Jr., also owned WAVE radio. It seems that radio station owners had been given early advice by an NBC radio

> "I want to reach to the farthest confines of the state, where a man can string an aerial from his cabin to the nearest pine tree, and setting before the fire, have a pew in church, a seat at the opera, or a desk at the university."
>
> *- Robert Worth Bingham*

official to obtain a TV license as soon as possible. WAVE-TV was the 41st TV station in the U.S.

WHAS-TV went on the air on March 27, 1950 — both WHAS radio and WHAS-TV were owned by Barry Bingham. Estimates indicate that about 25,000 TV sets, which sold for $300-$400 (with five- to seven-inch screens), were being used in the Louisville metropolitan area.

*Source: "Towers over Kentucky, A History of Radio and Television in the Bluegrass State," Francis M. Nash, Host Communications, Inc. (Lexington:1995).*

# History of Newspapers

Jerry Gibson

Kentucky's history of the printed news actually began five years before it became a state. It was conceived as a result of the major political issue of the time — separation from Virginia. It was decided at the second constitutional convention, assembled in Danville, that some publicity was needed for this important topic and that a printing press would be required, primarily to generate public favor. The year was 1785. A special committee was formed to find a printer willing to move to the Kentucky frontier. Looking first to Philadelphia, then Virginia, the committee faced the disappointing reality—no established printer wanted to risk the move. John Bradford, a young Virginian who had settled in Lexington, learned of the plan and approached Gen. James Wilkinson, a member of the special search committee, and offered to establish a newspaper in Kentucky. The committee, meeting again in Danville, accepted Bradford's offer and promised to provide as much public patronage as they could offer. According to a history published by the Kentucky Press Association, the citizens of Danville had expected the paper to be established in their community. However, the trustees of Lexington offered Bradford a location and assistance in setting up the printing shop there.

The first issue of the *Kentucke Gazette* was published in Lexington on Saturday, August 11, 1787 and was distributed to 180 subscribers. Subscribers paid 18 shillings a year for the service. The Gazette was four pages and measured 7 by 8-1/2 inches. No copy of the first edition has survived; however, an original of the second issue, published a week later on August 18, 1787, may be found in the Lexington Public Library. There is evidence that early publications were printed on paper manufactured in Kentucky.

Bradford died at home in Lexington on March 20, 1830, at the age of 80. The *Kentucke Gazette*, operated at times by his sons and others, lasted a total of 60 years ending publication in 1848.

**Historic headline from the Park City Daily News**
*Photo: Sid Webb*

The first competitor to the *Kentucky Gazette* was the *Kentucky Herald*, which began printing in Lexington in 1795. By 1811 several dozen publications had been established. Two papers, *The Mirror* (1806) and *Farmer's Friend* (1809), that started up in Russellville may have been the first publications in the western part of the new state.

Louisville did not have its own paper until 1801 when the *Farmer's Library* was launched. It ceased publication in 1808, after being eclipsed by competition from the new *Louisville Gazette*.

The first daily newspaper appeared in Louisville in 1826 was the *Public Advertiser*, which had begun as a weekly in 1818. It is credited as the first daily newspaper west of the Alleghenies. Publisher Shadrach Penn became one of the most influential men in the state until his paper lost out in very public battles with the new *Louisville Journal*, founded in 1830 by George Prentice. Prentice, who was 21 years old, had come to Kentucky to write a biography of statesman Henry Clay when Clay was running for the office of U.S. president. He engaged in a fiery war of words with Penn and the *Public Advertiser*. Prentice eventually triumphed and became the dominant voice in Louisville and a very strong influence throughout the state.

In western Kentucky the community of Paducah read its first hometown newspaper in 1830. Since then 50 different newspapers have been published there. Many other Kentucky communities can boast of long-established and influential newspapers and strong editors; however, print space herein restricts further elaboration.

One short-lived but historic paper was the *True American*, published by abolitionist Cassius M. Clay of Madison County from offices in Lexington. The paper lasted only three months in 1845, but helped to bring attention to the deprivations of slaves in Kentucky. Published from a shop on North Mill Street, it had 240 subscribers for the first issue and grew to 500 by the second issue.

While George Prentice's *Louisville Journal* continued to gain influence, a former employee, Walter N. Haldeman, began a competing newspaper, *The Morning Courier*, in 1844. While the *Journal* was a strong Union advocate during the Civil War, the *Courier* was run out of Louisville by federal authorities because of its strong support of Confederate causes. Haldeman moved his offices to Nashville and published the paper with a Bowling Green dateline during the war. After the war, the *Courier* was relocated back to Louisville. Meanwhile, Prentice had hired prominent Nashville journalist Henry Watterson to run the *Journal*. Watterson, then 28, approached Haldeman about joining forces. On November 8, 1868, the public was surprised to see the first edition of the *Louisville Courier-Journal*, the merger having been kept quiet. In its history, especially under the influence of the Bingham family, which owned the paper from 1918 to 1987, the newspaper became a predominant publication in Kentucky.

The origins of the *Lexington Herald-Leader*, Lexington's only major newspaper today, can be traced back over 130 years to the *Lexington Daily Press*. Its descendant, the *Morning Herald*, was first published January 1, 1895 and became known as the *Lexington Herald* in 1905. Another large circulating newspaper during this time was the *Kentucky Leader* (formed by a group of Fayette County Republicans in 1888) which eventually became known as the *Lexington Leader* in 1901. In 1937 the owner of the *Leader*, John G. Stoll, bought the *Herald*, and both daily papers were published concurrently (the *Herald* in the morning and the *Leader* in the afternoon) for the next 46 years. The newspapers had a combined Sunday edition, but their editorial policies were quite different. The *Leader* was a Republican, society-based evening edition, and the *Herald* a more political, heavily Democratic morning edition. In 1973 the Herald-Leader Co. was purchased by the Knight Newspapers, Inc., now the Knight-Ridder Corp. The papers were merged in 1983 into a single, morning newspaper that is still published as *The Lexington Herald-Leader*.

# John Ed Pearce (1919-2006)

*"Home is a place you grow up wanting to leave, and grow old wanting to get back to."*

John Ed Pearce, one of Kentucky's premier journalists, died on Sept. 25, 2006, his 87th birthday, in Louisville from complications from cancer. Pearce, a feature writer and columnist during most of his nearly 50 years in journalism, established the Kentucky Oral History Commission along with former Gov. Julian Carroll and Al Smith. Born in Virginia, he came to Kentucky to attend the University of Kentucky. He completed his graduate work at Columbia and Harvard universities. Pearce started his journalism career as a reporter for *Time-Life* and *United Press*, and later edited the *Somerset Journal*. Pearce joined the *Courier-Journal* as associate editor and editorial writer in 1947. Pearce shared in the Pulitzer Prize won in 1967 by the *Courier-Journal* for its fight for stronger strip-mining controls. Pearce, who retired in 1986, was an adviser to four Kentucky governors and a prolific writer. He published "Memoirs: 50 years at the Courier-Journal and other places" in 1997.

# NEWSPAPERS

| CITY | NEWSPAPER | PHONE |
| --- | --- | --- |
| Albany | Clinton County News | (606) 387-5144 |
| Ashland | Independent (The) | (606) 326-2600 |
| Barbourville | Mountain Advocate | (606) 546-9225 |
| Bardstown | Kentucky Standard (The) | (502) 348-9003 |
| Bardwell | Carlisle County News | (270) 628-5490 |
| Beattyville | Beattyville Enterprise (The) | (606) 464-2444 |
| Beattyville | Three Forks Tradition | (606) 464-2888 |
| Bedford | Trimble Banner | (502) 255-3205 |
| Benton | Benton Tribune Courier | (270) 527-3162 |
| Benton | Tribune-Courier | (270) 527-3162 |
| Berea | Berea Citizen (The) | (859) 986-0959 |
| Booneville | Booneville Sentinel (The) | (606) 593-6627 |
| Bowling Green | Bowling Green Daily News | (270) 781-1700 |
| Bowling Green | Clip It Publication | (270) 781-8805 |
| Bowling Green | College Heights Herald | (270) 745-2653 |
| Brandenburg | Meade County Messenger | (270) 422-2155 |
| Breathitt | Breathitt County Voice | (606) 666-8067 |
| Brooksville | Bracken County News | (606) 735-2198 |
| Brownsville | Edmonson News Inc | (270) 597-3115 |
| Burkesville | Cumberland County News | (270) 864-3891 |
| Cadiz | Cadiz Record (The) | (270) 522-6605 |
| Calhoun | McLean County News | (270) 273-3287 |
| Calvert City | Lake News (The) | (270) 395-5858 |
| Campbellsville | Campus Times | (270) 789-5035 |
| Campbellsville | Central Kentucky News Journal | (270) 465-8111 |
| Campbellsville | Central Kentucky News-Journal | (270) 465-8111 |
| Carlisle | Nicholas Countian & Carlisle Mercury (The) | (859) 289-6424 |
| Carlisle | Nicholas News | (859) 289-6425 |
| Carrollton | Carrollton News Democrat | (502) 732-4261 |
| Cave City | Barren County Progress | (270) 786-2679 |
| Cave City | Metcalfe County Light (The) | (270) 786-2679 |
| Cave City | Monroe County Citizen | (270) 786-2679 |
| Central City | Central City Leader News | (270) 754-3000 |
| Central City | Central City Times Argus | (270) 754-2331 |
| Central City | Leader-News | (270) 754-3000 |
| Central City | Times Argus (The) | (270) 754-2331 |
| Cincinnati | Kentucky Post (The) | (859) 292-2600 |
| Clinton | Hickman County Gazette | (270) 653-3381 |
| Columbia | Adair County Community Voice | (270) 384-9454 |
| Columbia | Adair Progress | (270) 384-6471 |
| Columbia | Columbia News | (270) 384-6471 |
| Corbin | Corbin/Whitley News Journal | (606) 528-9767 |
| Corbin | News Journal | (606) 528-9767 |
| Corbin | Times Tribune (The) | (606) 528-2464 |
| Corbin | Tri-County Shopping Guide | (606) 528-2464 |
| Covington | Messenger (The) | (859) 392-1570 |
| Cromona | Letcher County News Press | (606) 855-4541 |
| Cumberland | Tri-City News | (606) 589-2588 |
| Cumberland | Tri-City News (The) | (606) 589-2588 |
| Cunningham | Carlisle Weekly | (270) 642-2841 |
| Cynthiana | Cynthiana Democrat | (859) 234-1035 |
| Danville | Advocate Messenger (The) | (859) 236-2551 |
| Danville | Centre College Cento (The) | (859) 238-5533 |
| Dawson Springs | Dawson Springs Progress | (270) 797-3271 |
| Eddyville | Lyon County Herald Ledger | (270) 388-2269 |
| Edmonton | Herald News | (270) 432-3291 |
| Elizabethtown | Elizabethtown News Enterprise | (270) 769-2312 |
| Elizabethtown | Hardin County Independent | (270) 737-5585 |
| Elizabethtown | News-Enterprise (The) | (270) 769-1200 |
| Elkton | Todd County Standard Inc | (270) 265-2439 |
| Erlanger | Better Living | (859) 727-2970 |
| Evansville | Evansville Courier & Press | (800) 288-3200 |
| Falmouth | Falmouth Outlook (The) | (859) 654-3332 |
| Flemingsburg | Flemingsburg Gazette | (606) 845-9211 |
| Flemingsburg | Messenger (The) | (606) 845-8610 |
| Florence | Campbell County Recorder | (859) 283-0404 |
| Florence | Community Recorder | (859) 283-0404 |
| Florence | Erlanger Recorder | (859) 283-0404 |
| Florence | Florence Recorder | (859) 283-0404 |
| Florence | Kenton Community Recorder | (859) 283-0404 |
| Frankfort | Frankfort State Journal | (502) 227-4556 |
| Frankfort | Kentucky Gazette (The) | (502) 875-8325 |
| Frankfort | Kentucky Monthly | (502) 227-0053 |
| Frankfort | Thoroughbred News (The) | (502) 597-7377 |
| Franklin | Franklin Favorite | (270) 586-4481 |
| Frenchburg | Foothills Courier | (606) 768-6134 |
| Ft Knox | Inside the Turret | (502) 624-1211 |
| Ft Mitchell | Kentucky Enquirer (The) | (859) 578-5500 |
| Fulton | Fulton Leader (The) | (270) 472-1121 |
| Georgetown | Georgetonian (The) | (502) 863-8150 |
| Georgetown | Georgetown News & Graphic | (502) 863-1111 |
| Glasgow | Glasgow Daily Times | (270) 678-5171 |
| Glasgow | Progress (The) | (270) 659-2146 |
| Grayson | Grayson Journal-Enquirer | (606) 474-5101 |

# NEWSPAPERS

| CITY | NEWSPAPER | PHONE |
|---|---|---|
| Grayson | Olive Times | (606) 474-5101 |
| Greensburg | Greensburg Record-Herald | (270) 932-4381 |
| Greenup | Greenup County News Times | (606) 473-9851 |
| Hardinsburg | Breckinridge Herald-News Inc | (270) 756-2109 |
| Harlan | Harlan Daily Enterprise | (606) 573-4510 |
| Harrodsburg | Harrodsburg Herald (The) | (859) 734-2726 |
| Hartford | Ohio County Times News (The) | (270) 298-7100 |
| Hawesville | Hancock Clarion (The) | (270) 927-6945 |
| Hazard | Hazard Herald (The) | (606) 436-5771 |
| Henderson | Gleaner (The) | (270) 827-2000 |
| Hickman | Hickman Courier | (270) 236-2726 |
| Highland Heights | Northerner (The) | (859) 572-5859 |
| Hindman | Troublesome Creek Times (The) | (606) 785-5134 |
| Hodgenville | LaRue County Herald News | (270) 358-3118 |
| Hopkinsville | Fort Campbell Courier | (270) 439-5122 |
| Hopkinsville | Kentucky New Era | (270) 886-4444 |
| Huntington | Huntington Herald Dispatch | (304) 526-4000 |
| Hyden | Leslie County News | (606) 672-2841 |
| Hyden | Thousandsticks News | (606) 672-3399 |
| Inez | Mountain Citizen (The) | (606) 298-7570 |
| Irvine | Citizen Voice & Times | (606) 723-5161 |
| Irvine | Estill County Tribune | (606) 723-5012 |
| Jackson | Intermountain Publishing | (606) 666-2451 |
| Jackson | Jackson Times (The) | (606) 666-2451 |
| Jackson | KY Mountain News | (606) 693-9499 |
| Jamestown | Russell Register (The) | (270) 343-6397 |
| LaCenter | Advance Yeoman | (270) 665-9492 |
| LaCenter | Ballard Weekly | (270) 665-9335 |
| LaGrange | Oldham Era (The) | (502) 222-7183 |
| Lancaster | Central Record (The) | (859) 792-2831 |
| Lancaster | Garrard Central Record | (859) 792-2831 |
| Lawrenceburg | Anderson News (The) | (502) 839-6906 |
| Lebanon | Lebanon Enterprise (The) | (270) 692-6026 |
| Leitchfield | Grayson County News-Gazette | (270) 259-9622 |
| Leitchfield | Leitchfield Record | (270) 259-6061 |
| Leitchfield | Record (The) | (270) 259-6061 |
| Lexington | Business Lexington | (859) 266-6537 |
| Lexington | Cats' Pause | (859) 278-3474 |
| Lexington | Chevy Chaser Magazine | (859) 266-6537 |
| Lexington | Kentucky Kernel | (859) 257-2871 |
| Lexington | La Voz de Kentucky | (859) 621-2106 |
| Lexington | Lexington Herald-Leader (The) | (859) 231-3100 |
| Lexington | Rambler (The) | (859) 233-8315 |
| Lexington | Southsider Magazine | (859) 266-6537 |
| Liberty | Casey County News (The) | (606) 787-7171 |
| London | London Sentinel Echo | (606) 878-7400 |
| London | Sentinel Echo (The) | (606) 878-7400 |
| Louisa | Big Sandy News (The) | (606) 788-9962 |
| Louisville | Aging Well | (502) 895-2805 |
| Louisville | American Baptist Newspaper | (502) 587-8714 |
| Louisville | American Classifieds | (502) 458-5400 |
| Louisville | Bargain Mart | (502) 454-3900 |
| Louisville | Business First Louisville Inc | (502) 583-1731 |
| Louisville | Community | (502) 451-8840 |
| Louisville | Concord (The) | (502) 452-8157 |
| Louisville | Kentucky Journal of Commerce & Industry | (502) 491-4737 |
| Louisville | Kentucky Living | (800) 595-4846 |
| Louisville | Louisville Cardinal (The) | (502) 852-6727 |
| Louisville | Louisville Courier-Journal (The) | (502) 582-4011 |
| Louisville | Louisville Daily Sports | (502) 582-2050 |
| Louisville | Louisville Defender | (502) 772-2591 |
| Louisville | Louisville Eccentric Observer | (502) 895-9770 |
| Louisville | Louisville Magazine | (502) 625-0100 |
| Louisville | Quadrangle | (502) 213-2287 |
| Louisville | Record (The) | (502) 636-0296 |
| Louisville | Seminary Times | (502) 895-3411 |
| Louisville | Southeast Outlook (The) | (502) 253-8650 |
| Louisville | Towers | (502) 897-4310 |
| Louisville | Voice Tribune (The) | (502) 897-8900 |
| Madisonville | Madisonville Messenger (The) | (270) 824-3300 |
| Manchester | Manchester Enterprise | (606) 598-2319 |
| Marion | Crittenden Press (The) | (270) 965-3191 |
| Mayfield | Mayfield Messenger (The) | (270) 247-5223 |
| Maysville | Ledger-Independent (The) | (606) 564-9091 |
| McKee | Jackson County Sun | (606) 287-7197 |
| Middlesboro | Daily News (The) | (606) 248-1010 |
| Monticello | Wayne County Outlook | (606) 348-3338 |
| Morehead | Morehead News | (606) 784-4116 |
| Morehead | Trail Blazer (The) | (606) 783-2697 |
| Morganfield | Union County Advocate (The) | (270) 389-1833 |
| Morgantown | Butler County Banner | (270) 526-4151 |
| Morgantown | Green River Republican | (270) 526-4151 |
| Mt Sterling | Mt Sterling Advocate | (859) 498-2222 |
| Mt Vernon | Banner (The) | (606) 256-9150 |

# NEWSPAPERS

| CITY | NEWSPAPER | PHONE |
|---|---|---|
| Mt Vernon | Mt Vernon Signal | (606) 256-2244 |
| Munfordville | Hart County News-Herald | (270) 524-2481 |
| Murray | Murray Ledger & Times | (270) 753-1916 |
| Murray | Murray State News | (270) 762-4468 |
| Nashville | Nashville Tennessean | (615) 259-8000 |
| New Castle | Henry County Local | (502) 845-2858 |
| Nicholasville | Jessamine Journal (The) | (859) 885-5381 |
| Olive Hill | Olive Hill Times | (606) 286-4201 |
| Owensboro | Messenger-Inquirer | (270) 926-0123 |
| Owensboro | Panogram (The) | (270) 852-3607 |
| Owenton | News Herald (The) | (502) 484-3431 |
| Owenton | Owenton News Herald | (502) 484-3431 |
| Owingsville | Bath County News Outlook | (606) 674-2181 |
| Owingsville | News Outlook | (606) 674-2181 |
| Paducah | Paducah Sun (The) | (270) 575-8600 |
| Paducah | Paducah Sun eXtra | (270) 575-8600 |
| Paducah | West Kentucky News | (270) 442-7389 |
| Paintsville | Paintsville Herald (The) | (606) 789-5315 |
| Paris | Bourbon County Citizen | (859) 987-1870 |
| Paris | Citizen Advertiser (The) | (859) 987-1870 |
| Pikeville | Appalachian News-Express | (606) 437-4054 |
| Pikeville | Bear Facts (The) | (606) 218-5265 |
| Pikeville | Echo (The) | (606) 218-5250 |
| Pikeville | Medical Leader | (606) 218-4952 |
| Pineville | Pineville Sun | (606) 337-2333 |
| Prestonsburg | Floyd County Times | (606) 886-8506 |
| Princeton | Princeton Times Leader | (270) 365-5588 |
| Princeton | Times Leader | (270) 365-5588 |
| Providence | Journal Enterprise (The) | (270) 667-2068 |
| Providence | Providence Journal Enterprise | (270) 667-2068 |
| Radcliff | Radcliff Sentinel | (270) 351-4407 |
| Radcliff | Sentinel (The) | (270) 351-4407 |
| Richmond | Eastern Progress | (859) 622-1881 |
| Richmond | Richmond Register (The) | (859) 623-1669 |
| Russell Springs | Russell County News (The) | (270) 866-3191 |
| Russell Springs | Times Journal (The) | (270) 866-3191 |
| Russellville | News Democrat & Leader | (270) 726-8394 |
| Salyersville | Backroads Buyers Guide (The) | (606) 349-2915 |
| Salyersville | Salyersville Independent | (606) 349-2915 |
| Scottsville | Citizen Times (The) | (270) 237-3441 |
| Scottsville | Citizen Times (The) | (270) 237-3441 |
| Sebree | Sebree Banner (The) | (270) 835-7521 |
| Shelbyville | Landmark Community Newspaper | (502) 633-4334 |
| Shelbyville | Sentinel News | (502) 633-2526 |
| Shelbyville | Sentinel-News | (502) 633-2526 |
| Shepherdsville | Shepherdsville Pioneer News | (502) 543-2288 |
| Smithland | Livingston Ledger | (270) 928-2128 |
| Somerset | Bridge (The) | (606) 679-8501 |
| Somerset | Commonwealth Journal | (606) 678-8191 |
| Springfield | Springfield Sun (The) | (859) 336-3716 |
| Stanford | Interior Journal (The) | (606) 365-2104 |
| Stanton | Clay City Times (The) | (606) 663-5540 |
| Sturgis | Sturgis News (The) | (270) 333-5545 |
| Taylorsville | Spencer Magnet (The) | (502) 477-2239 |
| Tompkinsville | Tompkinsville News | (270) 487-5576 |
| Tompkinsville | T-Ville News Trader (The) | (270) 487-5576 |
| Vanceburg | Lewis County Herald | (606) 796-2331 |
| Versailles | Woodford Sun | (859) 873-4131 |
| Warsaw | Gallatin County News | (859) 567-5061 |
| West Liberty | Elliott County News | (606) 743-3551 |
| West Liberty | Licking Valley Courier | (606) 743-3551 |
| West Liberty | Wolfe County News | (606) 743-3551 |
| Whitesburg | Mountain Eagle (The) | (606) 633-2252 |
| Whitley City | McCreary County Record | (606) 376-5356 |
| Whitley City | McCreary County Voice | (606) 376-5500 |
| Williamsburg | News Journal | (606) 549-0643 |
| Williamson | Williamson Daily News | (304) 235-4242 |
| Williamstown | Grant County News | (859) 824-3343 |
| Winchester | Winchester Sun (The) | (859) 744-3123 |

Source: *The Kentucky Directory Gold Book 2006-2007*

# RADIO & TELEVISION STATIONS

| CITY | COMPANY | PHONE |
|---|---|---|
| Albany | WANY 1390-AM/106.3-FM | (606) 387-5186 |
| Albany | WSBI 1250-AM | (606) 387-8126 |
| Ashland | Daystar WTSF-TV 61 | (606) 329-2700 |
| Ashland | WLGC 1520-AM/105.7-FM | (606) 920-9565 |
| Ashland | WIOKT 1040-AM/WOKU 1080-AM | (606) 928-3778 |
| Barbourville | WYWY 950-AM/WKKQ 96.1-FM | (606) 546-4128 |
| Bardstown | WBRT 1320-AM | (502) 348-3943 |
| Beattyville | WLJC-TV (Channel 65) | (606) 464-3600 |
| Beattyville | WLJC 102.1-FM | (606) 464-3600 |
| Benton | WCBL 1290-AM/99.1-FM | (270) 527-3102 |
| Bowling Green | WBKO/WBWG-TV (Channel 13) | (270) 781-1313 |
| Bowling Green | WKYU-PBS | (270) 745-2400 |
| Bowling Green | WNKY-TV (Channel 40) | (270) 781-2140 |
| Bowling Green | WBGN 1340-AM/WUHU 107.1-FM | (270) 843-0107 |
| Bowling Green | WBVR 96.7-FM/WUHU 107.0-AM/WBGN 1340-AM/WLYE 94.1-FM | (270) 843-3333 |
| Bowling Green | WCVK 90.7-FM/WJVK 91.7-FM | (270) 781-7326 |
| Bowling Green | WGGC 95.1-FM | (270) 651-2142 |
| Bowling Green | WKCT 930-AM/WDNS 93.3-FM | (270) 781-2121 |
| Bowling Green | WKYU 88.9-FM/WDCL 89.7-FM/WKPB 89.5-FM/WKUE 90.9-FM | (270) 745-5489 |
| Bowling Green | WLYE 94.1-FM | |
| Bowling Green | WWHR 91.7-FM | (270) 745-5439 |
| Brandenburg | WMMG 1140-AM/93.5-FM | (270) 422-4440 |
| Burkesville | WKYR 107.9-FM | (270) 433-7191 |
| Cadiz | WHVO 1480-AM | (270) 886-1480 |
| Cadiz | WKDZ 1110-AM/106.5-FM | (270) 522-3232 |
| Calvert City | WCCK 95.7-FM | (270) 395-5133 |
| Campbellsville | WOBP-TV 4 | (270) 789-5210 |
| Campbellsville | WAKY 1540-AM/WGRK 103.1-FM | (270) 789-1464 |
| Campbellsville | WGRK 103.1-FM | (270) 932-7401 |
| Campbellsville | WTCO 1450-AM/WCKQ 104.1-FM | (270) 789-2401 |
| Campbellsville | WVLC 999-FM | (270) 789-0099 |
| Catlettsburg | WTCR 1420-AM/103.3-FM | (606) 739-8427 |
| Central City | WMTA 1380-AM | (270) 754-1380 |
| Central City | WNES 1050-AM/WQXQ 101.9-FM | (270) 754-3000 |
| Columbia | WAIN 1270-AM/93.5-FM | (270) 384-2134 |
| Columbia | WHVE 92.7-FM | (270) 384-7979 |
| Corbin | WCTT 680-AM/107.3-FM | (606) 528-4717 |
| Corbin | WKDP 1330-AM/99.5-FM | (606) 528-6617 |
| Cumberland | WCPM 1280-AM | (606) 589-4623 |
| Cynthiana | WCYN 1400-AM | (859) 234-1400 |
| Danville | WDFB 1170-AM/88.1-FM | (859) 236-9333 |
| Danville | WHBN 1420-AM | (859) 734-4321 |
| Danville | WHIR 1230-AM/WRNZ 105.1-FM | (859) 236-2711 |
| Dry Ridge | WNKR 106.5-FM | (859) 824-9106 |
| East Bernstadt | WJJA 98.5-FM | (606) 843-9999 |
| East Bernstadt | WOBZ-TV (Channel 9) | (606) 843-9999 |
| Eddyville | WWLK 900-AM | (270) 388-9726 |
| Edmonton | WKNK 991-FM | (270) 432-0990 |
| Elizabethtown | WASE 103.5-FM | (270) 766-1035 |
| Elizabethtown | WIEL1400-AM/WTHX 107.3-FM | (270) 763-0800 |
| Elizabethtown | WKMO 106.3-FM | (270) 763-0800 |
| Elizabethtown | WLVK 105.5-FM | (270) 766-1035 |
| Elizabethtown | WQXE 98.3-FM | (270) 737-8000 |
| Elizabethtown | WRZI 101.5-FM | (270) 763-0800 |
| Elizabethtown | WULF 94.3-FM | (270) 765-0943 |
| Elkton | WEKT 1070-AM | (270) 265-5636 |
| Falmouth | WIOK 107.5-FM | (859) 472-1075 |
| Flemingsburg | WYGH 1440-AM | (859) 472-1075 |
| Florence | WFLE 1060-AM/95.1-FM | (606) 849-4433 |
| Florence | ICN6-TV | (859) 392-7685 |
| Frankfort | Kentucky Broadcasters Association | (888) 843-5221 |
| Frankfort | KY Afield | (800) 858-1549 |
| Frankfort | WKYT-TV (Bureau) | (502) 875-5151 |
| Frankfort | Kentucky Public Radio Capitol (Bureau) | (502) 223-6924 |
| Frankfort | WFKY 1490-AM/WKYW 104.9-FM/WKED 103.7-FM/WCND 940-AM | (502) 875-1130 |
| Frankfort | WKYL 102.1-FM | (502) 696-9595 |
| Franklin | WFKN 1220-AM | (270) 586-4481 |
| Frenchburg | WUPX-TV (Channel 67) | (606) 768-9282 |
| Fulton | WFUL-AM 1270 | (270) 472-1270 |
| Fulton | WKZT 1270-AM | (270) 472-1270 |
| Georgetown | WRVG 89.9-FM | |
| Glasgow | WCDS 1440-AM/WHHT 106.7-FM | (270) 651-6050 |
| Glasgow | WCLU 1490-AM/WCLU 102.3-FM | (270) 651-9149 |
| Glasgow | WKLX 100.7-FM | (270) 651-6050 |
| Glasgow | WOVO 105.3-FM | (270) 651-6050 |
| Glasgow | WPTQ 103.7-FM | (270) 651-6050 |
| Grayson | WGOH 1370-AM/WUGO 102.3-FM | (606) 474-5144 |
| Greenville | WKYA 105.5-FM | (270) 338-6655 |

# RADIO & TELEVISION STATIONS

| CITY | COMPANY | PHONE |
|---|---|---|
| Hardin | WAAJ 89.7-FM | (270) 437-4095 |
| Hardin | WHMR-FM 90.1 | (270) 437-4095 |
| Hardin | WVHM 90.5-FM | (270) 437-4095 |
| Hardinsburg | WXBC 104.3-FM | (270) 756-1043 |
| Harlan | WFSR 970-AM/WTUK 105.1-FM | (606) 573-1470 |
| Harlan | WHLN 1410-AM | (606) 573-2540 |
| Harold | WPRG-TV (Channel 5) | (606) 478-1200 |
| Harold | WYMT-TV (Bureau) | (606) 478-5711 |
| Harold | WXLR 104.9-FM/WXKZ 105.3-FM | (606) 478-1200 |
| Hartford | WAIA 1600-AM/WXMZ 106.3-FM | (270) 298-3268 |
| Hartford | WAIA 1600-AM/WXMZ 106.3-FM | (270) 298-3268 |
| Hartford | WSNR 1600-AM/WKHB 106.3-FM | (270) 298-3268 |
| Hartford | WWHK 105.5-FM | (270) 338-2815 |
| Hazard | WYMT-TV (Channel 57) | (606) 436-5757 |
| Hazard | WJMD 104.7-FM | (606) 439-3358 |
| Hazard | WKIC 1390-AM/WSGS 101.1-FM751 | (606) 436-2121 |
| Hazard | WZQQ 97.9-FM | (606) 436-9898 |
| Henderson | WEHT-TV (Channel 25) | (800) 879-8542 |
| Henderson | WSON 860-AM | (270) 826-3923 |
| Highland Heights | WNKU 89.7-FM | (859) 572-6500 |
| Hindman | WKCB 1340-AM/107.1-FM | (606) 785-3129 |
| Hindman | WQXY 1560-AM | (606) 439-0156 |
| Hodgenville | WXAM 430-AM | (270) 358-4707 |
| Hopkinsville | WKAG-TV (Channel 43) | (270) 885-4300 |
| Hopkinsville | WHOP 1230-AM/98.7-FM | (270) 885-5331 |
| Hopkinsville | WNKJ 89.3-FM | (270) 886-9655 |
| Horse Cave | WLOC 1150-AM | (877) 786-4401 |
| Irvine | WIRV 1550-AM | (606) 723-5138 |
| Jackson | WEKG 810-AM/WJSN 106.5-FM | (606) 666-8881 |
| Jamestown | WJRS 104.9-FM | (270) 866-3487 |
| Jenkins | WKVG 1000-AM | (606) 832-4655 |
| Keavy | WVCT 91.5-FM | (606) 528-8604 |
| Kevil | WGCF 89.3-FM/WBEL 88.5-FM | |
| Lebanon | WOGaY-TV | (270) 692-0237 |
| Lebanon | WLBN 1590-AM/WLSK 100.9-FM | (270) 692-3126 |
| Leitchfield | WMTL 870-AM/WKHG 104.9-FM | (270) 259-5692 |
| Lexington | KET-TV (Channels 1-8) | (859) 258-7000 |
| Lexington | WDKY-TV (Channel 56) | (859) 269-5656 |
| Lexington | WKMJ-TV (Channel 15) | (859) 258-7000 |
| Lexington | WKYT-TV (Channel 27) | (859) 299-0411 |
| Lexington | WLEX-TV (Channel 18) | (859) 259-1818 |
| Lexington | WTVQ-TV (Channel 36) | (859) 294-3636 |
| Lexington | WBTF 107.9-FM | (859) 233-1515 |
| Lexington | WBUL 98.1-FM | (859) 422-1000 |
| Lexington | WBVX 92.1-FM | (859) 233-1515 |
| Lexington | WCYN 102.3-FM | (859) 253-5900 |
| Lexington | WKQQ 100.1-FM/WLKT 104.5-FM | (859) 422-1000 |
| Lexington | WLAP 630-AM/WXRA 1580-AM | (859) 422-1000 |
| Lexington | WLRO 101.5-FM/WXZZ 103.3-FM/WLTO 102.5-FM | (859) 253-5900 |
| Lexington | WLXG 1300-AM/WGKS 96.9-FM/WCDA 106.3-FM | (859) 233-1515 |
| Lexington | WLXO 96.1-FM | (859) 233-1515 |
| Lexington | WMJK 105.5-FM | (859) 422-1000 |
| Lexington | WMJR 1380-AM | (859) 278-0894 |
| Lexington | WMKJ 105.5-FM/WMMXL 94.5-FM/WXRA 1580-AM | (859) 422-1000 |
| Lexington | WRFL 88.1-FM | (859) 257-6598 |
| Lexington | WUKY 91.3-FM | (859) 257-3221 |
| Lexington | WVLK 590-AM/WVLK 92.9-FM | (859) 253-5900 |
| Lexington | WWFT 1250-AM | (859) 245-1000 |
| Liberty | WKDO 1560-AM/98.7-FM | (606) 787-7331 |
| London | WFTG 1400-AM/WWEL 103.9-FM | (606) 864-2148 |
| London | WGWL 980-AM | (606) 878-0980 |
| London | WWLT 103.1-FM | (859) 885-7109 |
| London | WYGE 92.3-FM | (606) 877-1326 |
| Louisa | WSAC 92.3-FM | (606) 638-9203 |
| Louisa | WZAQ 92.3-FM | (606) 638-9203 |
| Louisville | WAVE-TV (Channel 3) | (502) 585-2201 |
| Louisville | WBKI-TV (Channel 34) | (502) 809-3400 |
| Louisville | WBNA-TV 21 | (502) 964-2121 |
| Louisville | WDRB-TV (Channel 41) | (502) 584-6441 |
| Louisville | WHAS-TV (Bureau) | (502) 582-7220 |
| Louisville | WHAS-TV (Channel 11) | (502) 582-7840 |
| Louisville | WLKY-TV (Bureau) | (502) 891-4810 |
| Louisville | WLKY-TV (Channel 32) | (502) 893-3671 |
| Louisville | WYCS-TV 24 | (502) 966-0624 |
| Louisville | Kentucky News Network | (888) 566-0001 |
| Louisville | WAMZ 97.5-FM | (502) 479-2222 |
| Louisville | WDJX 99.7-FM/WLRS 105.1-FM/WXMA 102.3-FM | (502) 625-1220 |
| Louisville | WFIA 900-AM/WGTK 970-AM/WFIA 94.7-FM/WRVI 105.9-FM | (502) 339-9470 |

## RADIO & TELEVISION STATIONS

| CITY | COMPANY | PHONE |
| --- | --- | --- |
| Louisville | WFPL 89.3-FM/WFPK 91.9-FM/WUOL 90.5-FM | (502) 814-6500 |
| Louisville | WGTK 970-AM/WRVI 105.9-FM | (502) 339-9470 |
| Louisville | WGZB 96.5-FM/WMJM 101.3-FM | (502) 625-1220 |
| Louisville | WHAS 840-AM/WKJK 1080-AM | (502) 479-2222 |
| Louisville | WJIE 88.5-FM/93.9-FM | (502) 968-1220 |
| Louisville | WLCR 1040-AM | (502) 451-9527 |
| Louisville | WLLV 1240-AM/WLLU 1350-AM | (502) 776-1240 |
| Louisville | WLUE 100.5-FM | (502) 479-2222 |
| Louisville | WPTI 103.9FM/WSFR 107.7-FM | (502) 479-2222 |
| Louisville | WQMF 95.7-FM/WTFX 93.1-FM/WZKF KISS 98.9-FM | (502) 589-4800 |
| Louisville | WRKA 103.1-FM/WVEZ 106.9-FM | (502) 479-2222 |
| Louisville | WTMT 620-AM/WTSZ 105.7-FM | (502) 589-4800 |
| Louisville | WUOL 90.5-FM | (502) 583-6200 |
| Louisville | WXLN 105.1-FM | (502) 814-6513 |
| Louisville | WXXA 790-AM | (502) 777-9956 |
| Madisonville | WFMW 730-AM/WKTG 93.9-FM | (270) 821-4096 |
| Madisonville | WSOF 89.9-FM | (270) 825-3004 |
| Madisonville | WTTL 1310-AM/WYNU 106.9-FM/WWKY 97.9-FM | (270) 821-1310 |
| Manchester | WKLB 1290-AM | (606) 598-2445 |
| Manchester | WTBK 105.7-FM | (606) 598-7588 |
| Marion | WMJL 1500-AM/102.7-FM | (270) 965-2271 |
| Martin | WMDJ 100.1-FM | (606) 874-8005 |
| Mayfield | WDXR 1450-AM/WLJE 94.3-FM | (270) 247-5122 |
| Mayfield | WQQR 94.7-FM | (270) 247-5122 |
| Mayfield | WQQR 94.7-FM/WLLE 102.1-FM | (270) 247-5122 |
| Mayfield | WYMC 1430-AM | (270) 247-1430 |
| Mayking | WTCW 920-AM/WXKQ 103.9-FM | (606) 633-2711 |
| Maysville | WFTM 1240-AM/95.9-FM | (606) 564-3361 |
| McDaniels | W8FI 91.5-FM/W8FI 99.9-FM | (270) 257-2689 |
| Middlesboro | WYMT-TV (Cumberland Valley Bureau) | (606) 248-5702 |
| Middlesboro | WFXY 1490-AM/WXJB 96.5-FM/WANO 1230-AM | (606) 337-2100 |
| Middlesboro | WMIK 560-AM/92.7-FM | (606) 248-5842 |
| Monticello | WFLW 1360-AM/WKYM 101.7-FM | (606) 348-7083 |
| Monticello | WMKZ 93.1-FM | (606) 348-3393 |
| Morehead | WBY-TV Ch7 | (606) 784-7515 |
| Morehead | WIOBM-5 | (606) 784-7515 |
| Morehead | MPRS 90.3-FM | (606) 783-2001 |
| Morehead | WIVY 96.3-FM | (606) 784-9966 |
| Morganfield | WMSK 1550-AM/95.3-FM | (270) 389-1550 |

| CITY | COMPANY | PHONE |
| --- | --- | --- |
| Morgantown | WLBQ 1570-AM | (270) 526-3321 |
| Mt Sterling | WMST 1150-AM | (859) 498-1150 |
| Murray | MSU-TV (Channel 11) | (270) 809-2400 |
| Murray | WKMS 91.3-FM | (800) 599-4737 |
| Murray | WNBS 1340-AM/WRKY 1130-AM/WFGE 103.7-FM | (270) 753-2400 |
| Nicholasville | WVRB 95.3-FM | (859) 885-7109 |
| Nortonville | WKMA-TV 35 | (270) 669-4016 |
| Owensboro | Brescia Broadcast | (270) 685-3131 |
| Owensboro | WKCM 1160-AM/WBIO 94.7-FM | (270) 927-8121 |
| Owensboro | WKWC 90.3-FM | (270) 852-3596 |
| Owensboro | WOMI 1490-AM/WBKR 92.5-FM | (270) 683-1558 |
| Owensboro | WTCJ 105.7-FM/WLME 102.9-FM/WXCM 97.1-FM | (270) 927-8121 |
| Owensboro | WVJS 1420-AM | (270) 927-8121 |
| Owingsville | WKCA-107.7 FM | (606) 674-2266 |
| Paducah | WPSD-TV (Channel 6) | (270) 415-1900 |
| Paducah | WKYX 570-AM/WKYQ 93-FM/WDDJ 96.9-FM/WPAD 1560-AM | (270) 534-9690 |
| Paducah | WLIE 94.3-FM | (270) 247-5122 |
| Paducah | WLLE 102.1-FM | (270) 247-5122 |
| Paducah | WREZ 105.5-FM | (270) 538-5251 |
| Paducah | WZZL 106.7-FM | (270) 538-5251 |
| Paintsville | WKLW 94.7-FM | (606) 789-6664 |
| Paintsville | WKYH 600-AM | (606) 789-3333 |
| Paintsville | WSIP 1490-AM/98.9-FM | (606) 789-5311 |
| Paris | Radio Vida WYGH 1440-AM | (859) 987-1440 |
| Pikeville | WPTJ 90.7-FM | (859) 484-9691 |
| Pikeville | WBPA 1460-AM | (606) 754-5044 |
| Pikeville | WJSO 90.1-FM | (606) 478-2969 |
| Pikeville | WLSI 900-AM/WZLK 107.5-FM | (606) 437-4051 |
| Pikeville | WPKE 1240-AM/WPKE 103.1-FM/WDHR 93.1-FM/WBPA 1460-AM | (606) 437-4051 |
| Pikeville | WPRT 960-AM | (606) 437-4051 |
| Pineville | WRIL 106.3-FM | (606) 337-5200 |
| Pippa Passes | WWJD 91.7-FM | (606) 368-6131 |
| Prestonsburg | WDOC 1310-AM/WQHY 95.5-FM | (606) 886-8409 |
| Princeton | WPKY 1580-AM/WAVJ 104.9-FM | (270) 365-2072 |
| Renfro Valley | WRVK 1460-AM | (606) 256-2146 |
| Richmond | WCBR 1110-AM | (859) 623-1235 |
| Richmond | WEKF 88.5-FM | (800) 621-8890 |
| Richmond | WEKH 90.9-FM | (800) 621-8890 |
| Richmond | WEKU 88.9-FM | (800) 621-8890 |

## RADIO & TELEVISION STATIONS

| CITY | COMPANY | PHONE |
|---|---|---|
| Richmond | WEKY 1340-AM/WCYO 100.7-FM/WKXO 1500-AM/ WLFX 106.7-FM/WIRV 1550-AM | (606) 723-5138 |
| Richmond | WXII (Channel 60) | (859) 622-1885 |
| Russell Springs | WIDS 570-AM | (270) 866-8800 |
| Russell Springs | WJKY 1060-AM | (270) 866-3487 |
| Salyersville | WRLV 1140-AM/WRLV 106.5-FM | (606) 349-6125 |
| Scottsville | WPBM-TV 31 | (270) 618-8831 |
| Scottsville | WLCK 1250-AM/WVLE 99.3-FM | (270) 237-3149 |
| Somerset | WKEQ 97.1-FM/WSEK 93.9-FM/WSFE 910-AM | (606) 678-5151 |
| Somerset | WLLK 102.3-FM | (606) 679-5151 |
| Somerset | WSFC 1240-AM/WSEK 93.9-FM | (606) 678-5151 |
| Somerset | WTHL 90.5-FM | (606) 679-6300 |
| Somerset | WTLO 1480-AM | (606) 678-8151 |
| Stanford | WXKY 96.3-FM | (859) 885-7109 |
| Stanton | WBFC 1470-AM | (606) 663-6631 |
| Stanton | WSKV 104.9-FM | (606) 663-2811 |
| Tompkinsville | WTKY 1370-AM/92.1-FM/WKWY 102.7-FM | (502) 487-6119 |
| Tyner | WWAG 107.9-FM | (606) 287-9924 |
| Upton | WJCR 90.1-FM | (270) 369-8614 |
| Vanceburg | WKKS 1570-AM/104.9-FM | (606) 796-3031 |
| Vancleve | WMTC 730-AM/99.9-FM | (606) 666-5006 |
| Versailles | WCGW 770-AM | (859) 264-9700 |
| Versailles | WCGW 770-AM/WJMM 99.1-FM | (859) 264-9700 |
| West Liberty | WCBI 103.7-FM | (606) 668-9225 |
| West Liberty | WLKS 1450-AM/WLKS 102.9-FM | (606) 743-1029 |
| West Liberty | WMOR 1330-AM/WQXX 106.1-FM | (606) 784-4141 |
| Whitesburg | WEZC 1480-AM | (606) 855-7888 |
| Whitesburg | WIFX 94.3-FM | (606) 633-9430 |
| Whitesburg | WMMT 88.7-FM | (606) 633-0108 |
| Whitley City | WHAY 98.3-FM | (606) 376-2218 |
| Wickliffe | WBCE 1200-AM | (270) 335-5171 |
| Wickliffe | WGKY 95.9-FM | (270) 335-3696 |
| Williamsburg | WEKC 710-AM | (606) 549-3000 |
| Williamsburg | WEZJ 1440-AM/WEZJ 104.3-FM/WEXX 102.7-FM | (606) 549-2285 |

*Source: The Kentucky Directory Gold Book 2006-2007*

### It's a Kentucky Thing

#### Paris Newspaper Celebrates 200 years

In 2006 the longest continuously running newspaper west of the Allegheny Mountains will turn 200 years old. The Citizen-Advertiser may have changed names and owners over time but its dedication to news has been constant.

To celebrate the anniversary, Paris' Hopewell Museum will display machinery, news articles and photos from the newspaper's past and present during an exhibit October through December 2006.

Although the current newspaper is a descendant of Paris' The Kentucky Herald (1795-1807), it officially traces its roots through the name Citizen—beginning with The Western Citizen in 1807, when Kentucky was wilderness and considered "the" West. In 1886 the newspaper merged with The True Kentuckian and was renamed The Kentuckian-Citizen, a name that lasted until 1965 when it was purchased by the Brannon family, the current owners. Hopewell Museum is located at 800 Pleasant Street, Paris. Visit www.hopewellmuseum.org.

# History of the Kentucky Almanac

THE
KENTUCKY
ALMANAC,
FOR THE YEAR OF OUR LORD
1794;

Although John Bradford preserved much of the history of Central Kentucky in the *Kentucky Gazette*, we know little about his educational background, except that he "demonstrated as an adult a proficiency in both writing and mathematics" and was gifted with considerable mechanical ingenuity. Born June 6, 1749, in Prince County, Virginia, he was a descendant of William Bradford, a young man who sailed with his wife Dorothy for America in 1620 aboard the "Mayflower." William Bradford later became governor of the Plymouth Colony.

It 1775 Bradford came to Kentucky to be an assistant to George May, the official surveyor in the future Virginia county, Kentucky County. Like many, he crossed the mountainous

**John Bradford**
*Source: Kentucky Historical Society*

barrier between Virginia and the "west" into mostly unexplored and untamed territory without his wife and children — they stayed behind in the safety of Fauquier County, Va. It would be 10 years (1785 or 1786) before he brought his family to Fayette County.

After a decade of intervening adventures, Bradford established the *Kentucky Gazette*, the first newspaper west of the Allegheny Mountains. The first issue was Aug. 11, 1787. Soon, the press of the *Gazette* was used in printing other pamphlets and books. Starting in 1788 Bradford also published a yearly booklet he called The Kentucky Almanac. Usually containing 30-40 pages, it may have been the first pamphlet printed in the West. Bradford eventually published over 100 books and pamphlets.

The Kentucky Almanac was a combination religious newspaper, short story magazine, scientific journal, farm paper, government bulletin and humor sheet. The price of the almanac was 12-1/2 cents per copy, one dollar per dozen, eight dollars per gross (Jan. 4, 1803) and available for sale in Lexington.

Bradford peppered his almanac with tidbits from Benjamin Franklin, reports from Europe, cures, anecdotes and comic stories. *Note* — Modern-day readers of the old almanac texts must be forewarned: until the late 1780s, American publishers practiced the English method of typesetting the letter "s" as an "f." Benjamin Franklin disapproved of this practice in the late 1780s.

Lawyers, even in 1801, were the brunt of snide comment: *"A LAWYER told his client, his adversary had removed his fuit out of one court into another; to which his client replied, "Let him remove it to the devil if he pleases; I am fure my attorney, for money, will follow it."*

Family advice was frequent: *"There fhould be methinks, as little merit in loving a woman for her beauty, as in loving a man for his profperity; both being equally subject to change."*

The publication of the Kentucky Almanac was, for the most part, continuous from 1794 until 1856. Although it remained in the Bradford family for many decades, the management changed a number of times in later years.

*Sources: "The Voice of the Frontier, John Bradford's Notes on Kentucky," Thomas D. Clark, Ed., University Press of Kentucky (Lexington:1993) and http://www.mayflower-families.com/mayflower/william_bradford.htm.*

## UNIQUELY KENTUCKY
# *Place Names*

Mark Reinhardt

Kentucky has a large number of interesting and odd place names. There are places seemingly named after animals: Monkeys Eyebrow, Possum Trot, Mousie, Bugtussle, Hippo, Wildcat, Turkey, Viper, Lamb, Wolf, Wolverine, Sunfish, Raccoon and Rabbit Hash. We hope that the names Ordinary, Oddville and Blandville are not descriptive of their locations; but that Majestic, Beauty and Lovely are. Everyone will want to visit Goshen, Grace and Halo; Happy and Goody; Fairplay and Goodluck; Gimlet and Bourbon County; Big Beaver Lick, Big Bone Lick and Climax, but you may wish to not go to Quicksand or to Hell for Certain.

Pewee Valley is the highest point within twenty miles. West Liberty is to the east of Liberty. You can go Barefoot in Nicholas County. Is Do Stop an invitation or an order? Typo isn't one. In Floyd County there is a Blue Moon

were named after residents and others, but using only the given name. Floyd County may have the most towns with "first names." There are David and Dana; Melvin, Martin and Minnie; Harold and Hueysville; and Stanville, Allen, Emma and Cliff. Other examples are Ruth, Nancy and Naomi (Pulaski Co.), Daisy and Jeff (Perry County), Martha and Louisa (Lawrence Co.), Inez (Martin), Sidney, Phyllis and Zebulon, after Zebulon Pike, also of Pike's Peak fame (Pike Co.), Stella and Fredville (Magoffin Co.), Gregory, Betsey and Susie (Wayne Co.), Roxanna and Jeremiah (Letcher Co.), Keith

An old iron gate marks the entrance to the King's family cemetery across the street from where the old Hell's Halfacre school once stood near Berry, in Harrison County in June 2006
*Source: David Stephenson, Lexington Herald-Leader*

Sunrise was reflected in the front door at the Peckerwood Grocery Store in Knot Hole September 2006
*Source: David Stephenson, Lexington Herald-Leader*

every month, and there is always a Cyclone in Monroe County.

Many of Kentucky's residents are on a first name basis with their hometowns. Many towns

and Mary Alice (Harlan Co.), Bethany and Mary (Wolfe Co.). There is also Beverly, Helena, Herman, Frances, Maggie, Matthew, Ned, Randolph, Ross, Maud, and Hazel.

It is possible to assemble an impressive sounding itinerary without ever leaving the commonwealth. You can visit Paris and London; Athens or Florence; Berlin or Versailles; Nazareth or Newfoundland; Moscow, Melbourne, or Manila;

Glasgow or Halifax; Heidelberg or Hebron; and Holland or Mexico. For those desiring a more exotic sounding destination; you can go to Globe, Krypton or even to the Moon.

Some Kentucky place names are actually numbers; Number One is in Wayne County, Nineteen is in Ohio County and Seventy Six is in Clinton County.

At one time all of Kentucky was a single county of Virginia. After achieving statehood, it was divided again and again, eventually containing 120 counties; the fourth most in the nation. With this many counties, inconsistencies in county and city names have arisen. For instance, you may expect to find Carlisle in Carlisle County, but it is in Nicholas County, which is where Nicholasville could be, but it is in Jessamine County. You also might expect to find Franklin in Franklin County, but it is in Simpson County; Simpsonville is in Shelby County, while Shelbiana and Shelby Creek are both in Pike County. You might look in Campbell County for Campbellsville, but you need to look in Taylor County, and you will have to look in Spencer County if you want to find Taylorsville. Hardin is in Marshall County, not in Hardin County, but Hardinsburg is in Breckinridge County. It would seem that Madisonville should be in Madison County, but it is in Hopkins County; Hopkinsville is in

**Visitors from all over enjoy 2006 Old-timer's Day in Rabbit Hash**
*Photo: Bobbi Kayser*

Christian County. Neither Russell nor Russellville are in Russell County, but at least Russell Springs is. Neither Morgantown nor Morganfield are in Morgan County; both are in Union County. Both Union and Union Star are in counties other than Union, but at least Uniontown is in Union County. Union is in Boone County, but Boonesville is in Owsley County.

**Carrying a bag of tomatoes given to him by a neighbor, Paul Sexton and his dog Bruiser head home after their usual 40-minute walk in Peasticks in Bath County in August 2006.**
*Source: David Stephenson, Lexington Herald-Leader*

# Kentucky Travel Map

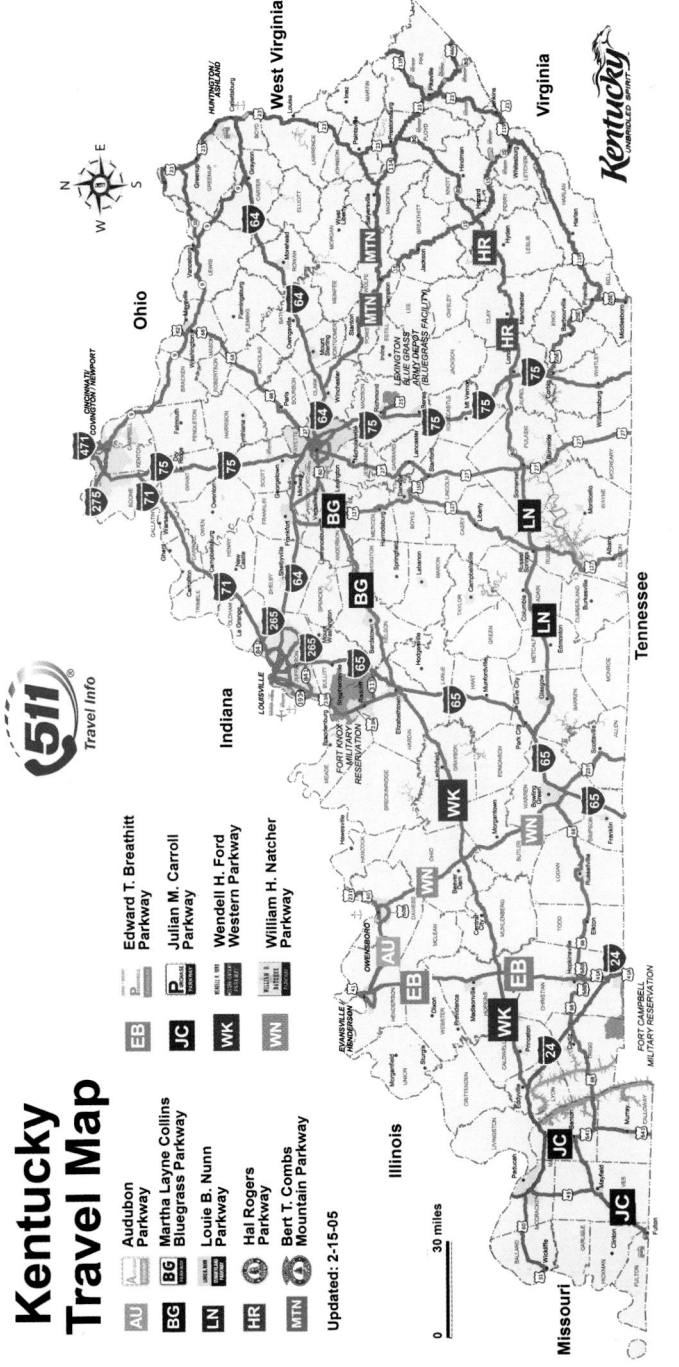

**Updated: 2-15-05**

| | |
| --- | --- |
| AU | Audubon Parkway |
| BG | Martha Layne Collins Bluegrass Parkway |
| LN | Louie B. Nunn Parkway |
| HR | Hal Rogers Parkway |
| MTN | Bert T. Combs Mountain Parkway |

| | |
| --- | --- |
| EB | Edward T. Breathitt Parkway |
| JC | Julian M. Carroll Parkway |
| WK | Wendell H. Ford Western Parkway |
| WN | William H. Natcher Parkway |

0 — 30 miles

511 Travel Info

*Source: Original base map, Kentucky Transportation Cabinet and 511 Travel Information, AASHTO 511.*

# Recreation & Travel

Herb Sparrow

**K**entucky has a long history of attracting tourists. It could be argued that Daniel Boone was the first tourist, as he gazed at the verdant Bluegrass Region from atop Pilot Knob. Although Boone's interest in the state was economic — an untouched area to hunt, trap and settle — he was also enticed by the state's scenic wonders and beauty.

By the early 1800s, just a few years after it became a state, Kentucky was drawing tourists. Curious visitors came to see the saltpeter works at Mammoth Cave shortly after the War of 1812, and by the 1830s "tourists," including notables such as Ralph Waldo Emerson and Swedish soprano Jenny Lind, were traveling rough

*Photo Source: Scott Risner*

roads and staying in a "modernized" log cabin to view the underground wonders of the cave, where black guide Stephen Bishop became a legend during more than 20 years of leading tours by torch light.

Kentucky continued to exert a magnetic allure over the years. In his 1947 bestseller, Inside USA, author John Gunther said Kentucky was the state

**Anglin Falls, Rockcastle County**
*Source: Southern & Eastern Kentucky Tourism Development Association*

**Hiking in Eastern Kentucky**
*Source: Southern & Eastern Kentucky Tourism Development Association*

that the most people wanted to see. Today, tourism is a major industry in the state. Numerous factors help the Bluegrass State draw millions of visitors each year from throughout the United States and many foreign countries.

Kentucky is home to bourbon and bluegrass music; quilts and Louisville Slugger baseball bats; Corvettes and Camrys; Fort Knox's gold and the Run for the Roses; the Niagara Falls of the South and the Grand Canyon of the East; historic mansions and pioneer forts; horse farms and stone fences; black bear and elk; hot browns and barbecue; Shakers and Civil War battlefields; award-winning professional theaters and outdoor dramas; folk art and fine art; horse racing and basketball; small towns and cosmopolitan cities; rolling bluegrass fields and tree-covered mountains.

Kentucky is the state of Abraham Lincoln and Mary Todd Lincoln, Henry Clay and Jefferson Davis, Robert Penn Warren and Alben Barkley, Muham-

mad Ali and Colonel Sanders, Lionel Hampton and Loretta Lynn and sites associated with them. As Americans finally breached the Appalachian Mountains through the Cumberland Gap in the late 18th century and began their relentless push westward, their first stop was Kentucky, bequeathing the state a rich history and heritage. Heritage tourism is one of the top travel trends in the United States, and Kentucky visitors can trace the state's fascinating history at numerous museums and historic sites throughout the state.

Kentucky was a leader in developing state parks. Its system of parks, which includes 17 resort parks with lodges and a range of activities, showcase the state's scenery and history. Many of the parks are located on water, and with Kentucky having more miles of navigable water than any state other than Alaska, water recreation is a major component of the state's tourism scene. Outdoor enthusiasts take to rivers and large manmade lakes throughout Kentucky to fish, swim, water ski, jet boat, sail or just relax aboard houseboats with all the comforts of home. Kentucky's varied scenic wonders also include Cumberland Falls and its unusual moonbow; the 1,000-foot-deep gorge at Breaks Interstate Park; fascinating rock formations of the Big South Fork National River and Recreation Area and the natural arches of the Red River Gorge.

Kentucky's heritage and scenic beauty come together in the Bluegrass Region's horse country, where miles of white and black fence, rock walls, imposing barns and grazing thoroughbreds stamp an indelible image of the state. Other integral parts of Kentucky's appeal are its strong sense of place, its easily accessible location and the warm welcome that visitors receive.

Author Jesse Stuart summed up the universal attraction of his native state:

*"Kentucky is neither southern, northern, eastern, western. It is the core of America.*

*If these United States can be called a body, Kentucky is its heart."*

# RECREATION & TRAVEL
# *Horses*

## *The Kentucky Horse Park*
Bill Cooke

Located on more than 1,300 acres just north of Lexington, the Kentucky Horse Park is the World's only educational equestrian theme park, working horse farm and equestrian event facility. Each year, more than one million visitors utilize its facilities. In addition, the park's National Horse Center now houses 29 private and state equestrian organizations with a workforce of more than 280 employees.

Since the 1930s, Central Kentucky's horse farms have provided an anchor for tourism in the Bluegrass.

**Three Day Event at Kentucky Horse Park**
Source: Kentucky Department of Tourism

During the late 1960s, however, many horse farms closed their doors to the public as a result of vandalism and increased labor costs. In response, Lexington horseman, John R. Gaines and Department of Parks' Commissioner, Jim Host, suggested to Gov. Louie Nunn and members of the Kentucky Legislature, that Kentucky should open a park dedicated to the horse, and the equine industry, in order to boost tourism revenue and to create a public attraction where visitors could experience a Kentucky horse farm and learn about our signature industry. In April 1972 the Commonwealth of Kentucky purchased

Mary Edwards Jenney's Walnut Hall Stud farm for $2.7 million, which was to become the Kentucky Horse Park. Gov. Wendell Ford officially broke ground for the park in 1974.

In 1975 the park was chosen as the site of the 1978 World Three-Day Event Championship, the first equestrian world championship to take place in North America. In the late 70s, the remains of the great Man o' War and African-American jockey, Isaac Bums Murphy, were re-interred at the park. The park opened in September 1978 in conjunction with the World Championship Three-Day-Event.

Today the park features two world-class museums, a visitor center, an outstanding group of retired champions of the track—including the great Cigar and John Henry— and is home to more than 50 breeds of horses (the most housed in any single location in the world). Its 260-site resort campground is one of the finest in the state. The park hosts more than 60 horse shows and events annually, making it the country's premier horse show facility. In the near future these facilities will be enhanced by a new, 6,000-seat indoor arena and a five-star luxury hotel.

In December of 2005, the park was selected by the Fédération Equestre Internationale (FEI) as the site for the 2010 FEI World Equestrian Games. This will be will be the first time the games will be held outside of Europe. In May it was announced that Nicholasville-based Alltech, Inc. would become the games' title sponsor. The Alltech FEI Games will be held September 25 through October 10, 2010, with an expected attendance of between 400,000 and 500,000. It will be the largest sporting event ever hosted by the commonwealth—athletes from around the world will compete in the eight disciplines that make up the games, and for the first time in concurrence with the other seven, para-equestrian games.

# Museums, Carriage Rides, Riding Stables, Camps and Trails & Racetracks

## MUSEUMS

**American Saddlebred Museum** is located in Lexington and is dedicated to Kentucky's oldest native breed of horse, the American Saddlebred (859) 259-2746; The **Carriage Museum** in Maysville showcases transportation before the automobile (606) 759-7305; The Kentucky Horse Park's **International Museum of the Horse** in Lexington is the largest and most comprehensive equestrian museum in the world. It is dedicated to describing the relationship between man and

ing the Mountain Lake Manor & Western Villages (606) 876-5591; **Double J Stables & Horsemans Camp** is located in Mammoth Cave National Park with guided trail rides through Mammoth Cave National Park (270) 286-8167.

**Happy Trails Riding Stables** in Eddyville (270) 871-4370; **Jesse James Riding Stables** in Park City (800) 798-0560; **Keith Stables** in Monticello

Churchill Downs
Source: John Perkins

Studying the Daily Racing Form
Source: Sid Webb

horse (800) 678-8813; **Kentucky Derby Museum** in Louisville with its 10,000 square foot expansion has created a whole new environment full of the sounds, images and artifacts that bring the pageantry and excitement of the Kentucky Derby to life for all visitors. The new exhibits include high-tech computerized hands-on displays and video graphics (502) 637-1111.

## CARRIAGE RIDES

Carriage rides are available at **Annie's Horse-drawn Carriage Rides** in Paducah (270) 210-6095; **Around the Town Carriage** in Bardstown (502) 348-0331; **Buena Vista Carriage** in Louisville (502) 417-7109; **Louisville Horse Trams** (502) 581-0100; and **Lexington Livery Horse Drawn Carriage Tours in Lexington** (859) 259-0000.

## RIDING STABLES, CAMPS & TRAILS

**A Little Bit of Heaven Riding Stables** in Frankfort (502) 223-8925; **Big Red Stables** in Harrodsburg (859) 734-3118; **Deer Run Stables L.L.C.** in Richmond (859) 527-6339; **DH Resorts, Inc.** in Flemingsburg – 1200-acre "Dude Ranch" featur-

(606)561-6458; **Kinlee Stables** in East Bernstadt (606) 843-2645; **Sugar Creek Resort** in Nicholasville (859) 885-9359; **Whispering Woods Riding Stables** in Georgetown (502) 570-9663; and **Wranglers Riding Stables** in Cadiz (270) 752-8266.

## RACETRACKS

**Churchill Downs,** Louisville - (502) 636-4400; **Ellis Park Race Course Inc.,** Henderson - (270) 826-0608; **Keeneland Race Course,** Lexington (859) 254-3412; **Kentucky Downs Race Course,** Franklin, (270) 586-7778; **Players Bluegrass Downs,** Paducah - (270) 444-7117; **Red Mile Harness Track,** Lexington - (859) 255-0752; **Thunder Ridge Racing & Entertainment Complex,** Prestonsburg - (606) 886-7223; **Turfway Park Race Course,** Florence - (859) 371-0200.

*Source: Kentucky Department of Tourism, www.kentuckytourism.com.*

*This information, and more, can be found at the Kentucky Department of Travel's website www.KentuckyTourism.com.*

# RECREATION & TRAVEL
# *Boating*
# *& Marinas*

Lt. Mike Fields

Boating, America's number one family sport, is enjoyed by thousands of new enthusiasts each year. For mid-Americans, Kentucky is the place to come to enjoy cruising, sailing, skiing, fishing and

For canoe and kayak enthusiasts, Kentucky offers waters ranging from tranquil to raging – both found on the Elkhorn Creek in central Kentucky, the Cumberland River near the Cumberland Falls, and on many other waterways that offer the ultimate paddling experience.

Family recreation is endless on the many major impoundments in Kentucky. Since the 1960s, many lakes have been created, such as Barkley, Malone, Barren, Green, Laurel, Cave Run, Fishtrap, Dewey and numerous other state and federal impoundments. During this period, motorboat registration has climbed to over 170,000. In addition to these registered boats,

**Sailboats docked at Land Between the Lakes**
*Source: Kentucky Department of Tourism*

floating in its broad waterway system of lakes, rivers, and streams.

Kentucky offers endless opportunities to boaters of every kind. Whether you enjoy the quietness of floating down a lazy stream in a canoe or kayak, taking a raft through challenging Class 4 rapids, pulling the family behind the boat on a tube or on skis, slowly making your way down the lake on a luxury houseboat filled with friends and relatives, taking a month long trip from one end of the state to the other, or simply trying to catch the "big one," Kentucky has exactly what you are looking for.

there are thousands of non-registered vessels such as canoes, rowboats and sailboats, as well as large houseboats and cruisers that are registered by the Federal Government. And thousands of tourists from neighboring states bring their boats to Kentucky. Although Kentucky's waterways are not yet crowded, it is obvious that boating is growing rapidly.

*Learn more about recreational opportunities on Kentucky's beautiful waterways by contacting the Kentucky Dept. of Fish and Wildlife Resources at 1-800-858-1549 or visit fw.ky.gov.*

## MARINAS

| CITY | REGION | NAME | PHONE |
|------|--------|------|-------|
| Albany | Southern Lakes | Grider Hill Dock & Indian Creek Lodge | (606) 387-5501 |
| Albany | Southern Lakes | Wisdom Dock | (800) 840-8523 |
| Albany | Southern Lakes | Wolf River Resort | (606) 387-5841 |
| Augusta | Northern KY | Augusta River Park Marina | (606) 756-2183 |
| Bellevue | Northern KY | Riverside 4 Marina | (859) 261-8114 |
| Benton | Western Waterlands | Bee Spring Lodge and Marina | (800) 732-0088 |
| Benton | Western Waterlands | Big Bear Resort and Marina | (800) 922-2327 |
| Benton | Western Waterlands | Cedar Knob Resort and Marina | (800) 428-7986 |
| Benton | Western Waterlands | Hester's Spot in the Sun | (800) 455-7481 |
| Benton | Western Waterlands | Hickory Hill 5 Star Resort | (800) 280-4455 |
| Benton | Western Waterlands | King Creek Resort and Marina | (800) 733-6710 |
| Benton | Western Waterlands | Lakeside Campground & Marina Inc. | (270) 354-8157 |
| Benton | Western Waterlands | Malcolm Creek Resort | (800) 733-6713 |
| Benton | Western Waterlands | Shawnee Bay Resort | (270) 354-8360 |
| Benton | Western Waterlands | Sportsman's Anchor Marina | (800) 326-3625 |
| Benton | Western Waterlands | Whispering Oaks Resort | (800) 788-1061 |
| Buckhorn | Boone Country | Buckhorn Lake State Resort Park | (800) 325-0058 |
| Burgin | Bluegrass | Chimney Rock Marina | (859) 748-9065 |
| Burkesville | Southern Lakes | Dale Hollow Lake State Resort Park | (800) 325-2282 |
| Burkesville | Southern Lakes | Hendricks Creek Resort | (800) 321-4000 |
| Burkesville | Southern Lakes | Sulphur Creek Resort | (270) 433-7272 |
| Burnside | Southern Lakes | Burnside Marina | (800) 844-8862 |
| Cadiz | Western Waterlands | Boat Haven Resort & Marina | (888) 557-7638 |
| Cadiz | Western Waterlands | Lake Barkley State Resort Park | (800) 325-1708 |
| Cadiz | Western Waterlands | Prizer Point Marina & Resort | (800) 548-2048 |
| Campbellsville | Southern Lakes | Emerald Isle Resort and Marina | (888) 815-2000 |
| Campbellsville | Southern Lakes | Green River Lake State Park | (270) 465-8255 |
| Campbellsville | Southern Lakes | Green River Marina & Resort | (800) 488-2512 |
| Cawood | Boone Country | Stone Mountain Boat Dock | (606) 573-7352 |
| Clarkson | Derby | Ponderosa Boat Dock | (270) 242-7215 |
| Clarkson | Derby | Wax Marina | (888) 624-9951 |
| Columbia | Southern Lakes | Holmes Bend Marina-Resort | (800) 801-8154 |
| Corbin | Boone Country | Grove Marina | (606) 523-2323 |
| Corinth | Northern KY | Bud's Live Bait Shop | (859) 824-0083 |
| Crittenden | Northern KY | Reynolds Boat Dock | (859) 428-1644 |
| Danville | Bluegrass | Gwinn Island Resort & Marina Inc. | (859) 236-4286 |
| Dawson Springs | Western Waterlands | Pennyrile Forest State Resort Park | (800) 325-1711 |

State Dock is known for the most luxurious rentals on the eastern seaboard, with models to suit every budget. With 1,200 miles of shore, astounding waterfalls and countless secret coves – it's a place where memories are made. Choose from 3, 4 or 7 night vacations.

WHERE MEMORIES ARE MADE.

LAKE CUMBERLAND STATE DOCK

STATEDOCK.COM
1-888-STATEDOCK

## MARINAS

| CITY | REGION | NAME | PHONE |
|------|--------|------|-------|
| Dayton | Northern KY | RiverCity Marina | (859) 292-8688 |
| Dayton | Northern KY | Watertown Yacht Club | (859) 261-8800 |
| Dry Ridge | Northern KY | Ruby's Boat Dock | (859) 824-9967 |
| Dunmor | Bluegrass Blues BBQ | Lake Malone State Park | (270) 657-2111 |
| Eddyville | Western Waterlands | Eddy Creek Marina Resort | (800) 626-2300 |
| Eddyville | Western Waterlands | Holiday Hills Resort | (800) 337-8550 |
| Falls Of Rough | Derby | Rough River Dam State Resort Park | (800) 325-1713 |
| Falmouth | Northern KY | Kincaid Lake State Park | (859) 654-3531 |
| Frankfort | Bluegrass | Frankfort Boat Dock | (502) 227-9481 |
| Frenchburg | Appalachian | Long Bow Marina | (606) 768-2929 |
| Gilbertsville | Western Waterlands | Kentucky Dam Village State Resort Park | (800) 648-2628 |
| Gilbertsville | Western Waterlands | Moors Resort and Marina | (800) 626-5472 |
| Glasgow | Caves Lakes Corvettes | Narrows Marina | (270) 646-5253 |
| Glasgow | Caves Lakes Corvettes | Sawyers Landing Marina | (800) 470-2223 |
| Grand Rivers | Western Waterlands | Green Turtle Bay Houseboat Rentals | (800) 844-8862 |
| Grand Rivers | Western Waterlands | Green Turtle Bay Resort | (800) 498-0428 |
| Grand Rivers | Western Waterlands | Lighthouse Landing | (800) 491-7245 |
| Greenup | Appalachian | Greenbo Lake State Resort Park | (800) 325-008 |
| Hardin | Western Waterlands | Kenlake State Resort Park | (800) 325-0143 |
| Harrodsburg | Bluegrass | Cane Run Fishing Marina | (859) 748-5487 |
| Harrodsburg | Bluegrass | Cummins Ferry Campground & Marina | (859) 865-2003 |
| Harrodsburg | Bluegrass | Pandora Marina | (859) 748-9121 |
| Harrodsburg | Bluegrass | Royalty's Fishing Camp | (859) 748-5459 |
| Harrodsburg | Bluegrass | Walker's Mid-Lake Marina | (859) 748-5520 |
| Jamestown | Southern Lakes | Jamestown Resort and Marina | (800) 830-5131 |
| Jamestown | Southern Lakes | State Dock | (888) 782-8336 |
| Kuttawa | Western Waterlands | Buzzard Rock Resort & Marina | (800) 826-6238 |
| Kuttawa | Western Waterlands | Kuttawa Harbor Marina | (270) 388-9563 |
| Lancaster | Bluegrass | Herrington Marina | (859) 548-2282 |
| Lancaster | Bluegrass | Kamp Kennedy Marina | (859) 548-2101 |
| Lancaster | Bluegrass | Kings Mill Marina | (859) 548-2091 |
| Lancaster | Bluegrass | Sunset Marina | (859) 548-3591 |
| Lawrenceburg | Bluegrass | Beaver Lake Marina LLC | (502) 839-4402 |
| Leitchfield | Derby | Bill's Marina and Service Center | (270) 259-4859 |
| Leitchfield | Derby | Moutardier Marina | (270) 286-4069 |
| Lewisburg | Caves Lakes Corvettes | Shady Cliff Resort & Marina | (270) 657-9580 |
| London | Boone Country | Holly Bay Marina | (606) 864-6542 |
| London | Boone Country | London Dock and Rockcastle Campground | (606) 864-5225 |
| London | Boone Country | Wood Creek Boat Dock | (606) 878-5420 |
| Louisa | Appalacian | Yatesville Lake State Park | (606) 686-2361 |
| Lucas | Caves Lakes Corvettes | Barren River Lake State Resort Park | (800) 699-Boat |
| Maysville | Northern KY | Maysville River Park Marina | (606) 564-2520 |
| Monticello | Southern Lakes | Beaver Creek Resort | (800) 844-8862 |
| Monticello | Southern Lakes | Conley Bottom Resort, Inc. | (606) 348-6351 |
| Morehead | Appalacian | Scott's Creek Marina | (606) 784-9666 |
| Morgantown | Caves Lakes Corvettes | Steamboat Landing Marina | (270) 662-0019 |
| Mount Vernon | Boone Country | Lake Linville Marina and Campgrounds | (606) 256-9696 |
| Murray | Western Waterlands | America's Paradise Resort | (800) 340-2767 |
| Murray | Western Waterlands | Irvin Cobb Resort | (888) 225-2415 |
| Murray | Western Waterlands | Kentucky Beach Resort and Marina | (888) 244-2277 |
| Murray | Western Waterlands | Water's Edge RV Park & Marina | (888) 651-3084 |
| Nancy | Southern Lakes | Lee's Ford Resort Marina | (877) LEES-FORD |
| New Concord | Western Waterlands | Cypress Springs Resort | (270) 436-5496 |
| New Concord | Western Waterlands | Lakeview Cottages & Marina | (877) 895-5876 |
| New Concord | Western Waterlands | Missing Hills Resort | (270) 436-5519 |
| Owensboro | Bluegrass Blues BBQ | Executive Marina of Owensboro | (270) 683-2405 |
| Richmond | Bluegrass | Wilgreen Lake Marina & Bait & Tackle Shop | (859) 623-1881 |
| Russell Springs | Southern Lakes | Alligator #1 | (270) 866-3634 |
| Russell Springs | Southern Lakes | Indian Hills Resort Alligator II Marina & KOA | (877) 363-9911 |
| Sassafras | Boone Country | Carr Creek State Park | (606) 642-4050 |
| Scottsville | Caves Lakes Corvettes | Browns Ford Boat Ramp | (270) 434-2329 |
| Scottsville | Caves Lakes Corvettes | Walnut Creek Marina | (270) 622-5858 |
| Shelbyville | Derby | Guist Creek Marina and Campground | (502) 647-5359 |
| Somerset | Southern Lakes | Buck Creek Boat Dock | (606) 382-5542 |
| Staffordsville | Appalacian | Paintsville Lake State Park | (606) 297-5253 |
| Taylorsville | Derby | Taylorsville Lake Dock | (502) 477-8766 |
| Taylorsville | Derby | Taylorsville Lake State Park | (502) 477-8766 |
| Union | Northern KY | Big Bone Landing Marina & Campground | (859) 384-1713 |
| Union | Northern KY | Farmlands Marina | (606) 384-3140 |
| Warsaw | Northern KY | Dan's Marina and Motel | (888) 326-7386 |
| Warsaw | Northern KY | Pier 99 Marina | (859) 567-8811 |
| Willisburg | Derby | Captain Bobs Boat Dock | (859) 375-0093 |
| Winchester | Bluegrass | Stan's Restaurant and Boat Dock | (859) 527-3146 |

*Source: Kentucky Dept. of Fish & Wildlife*

# RECREATION & TRAVEL
# *Introduction to State Parks*

Jim Carroll

The Kentucky State Park system can be described with superlatives. It has more resort park lodges than any other state. It has three golf courses named among the best in the country by Golf Digest magazine. It preserves some of Kentucky's most valued historic treasures. And Kentucky parks offer easy access to some of the best boating and fishing anywhere.

Kentucky's extensive park system had humble beginnings. In 1924 the Kentucky General Assembly passed a law that established a Kentucky State Parks Commission and allocated the princely sum of $1,100 to help the new board find likely sites for Kentucky state parks. The panel's first director was the state geologist, Dr. Willard R. Jillson.

Within two years, the commission located four properties for park development and moved to acquire them. Three of the sites – encompassing Pine Mountain State Resort Park, Natural Bridge State Resort Park and Old Fort Harrod State Park — remain in the park system today.

The focal point for Kentucky State Parks is 17 resort parks scattered throughout the state. All feature comfortable lodges with modern conveniences, but each has its own atmosphere. In western Kentucky, Kentucky Dam Village and Lake Barkley are large, busy parks. Yet a third park just down the road – Kenlake – has a quiet, inn-like atmosphere. Not far away is another rural gem, Pennyrile Forest State Resort Park.

Some resort parks are known for their natural features – such as Cumberland Falls, Carter Caves, Pine Mountain and Natural Bridge. For others, the big selling point is access to lake activities, including Lake Cumberland, Jenny Wiley, Rough River Dam, Dale Hollow Lake, Buckhorn Lake, Greenbo Lake and Barren River Lake.

Kentucky's unique history is preserved at two resort parks. General Butler in Carrollton maintains the home of a famous military family, while Blue Licks Battlefield marks the site of the last Revolutionary War battle in Kentucky.

Golf is hot in Kentucky state parks. The park system maintains six championship courses dubbed the Signature Series of outstanding courses. Four of the courses are new, having opened in 2003. They are Mineral Mound in western Kentucky, Dale Hollow Lake in south-central Kentucky, and two courses in northeastern Kentucky – Grayson Lake and Yatesville Lake. Pine Mountain's course opened for play in 2001, while the sixth is the popular course at Kentucky Dam Village.

Besides resort parks, the park system maintains 35 other state parks and historic sites. Two of them are urban parks with extensive recreational facilities – E.P. "Tom" Sawyer in Louisville and Ben Hawes State Park in Owensboro. Others interpret Kentucky's history. John James Audubon State Park in Henderson honors the noted 19th century artist and naturalist, while My Old Kentucky Home in Bardstown is the antebellum mansion that tradition holds inspired Stephen Foster to write his famous song.

Reconstructed pioneer forts can be found at Fort Boonesborough and Old Fort Harrod. Columbus-Belmont and Perryville Battlefield mark the sites of important Civil War battles. White Hall near Richmond was the home of emancipationist Cassius M. Clay. The latest addition to the park system, Wickliffe Mounds at Wickliffe in western Kentucky, preserves and interprets a Native American community dating from 1100 A.D.

2004 was an eventful year for the park system, reports Secretary George Ward. Guest rooms were improved with new bedding, hair dryers, and irons and ironing boards. The park system began offering online reservations in the summer of 2004. In August state resort parks began enhancing their dining room menus by buying local produce directly from Kentucky farmers, which makes for excellent fare after a long day of recreation.

Each year, Kentucky parks draw 7 million visitors and contribute $317 million to the economy.

For more information on Kentucky parks, visit http://www.parks.ky.gov

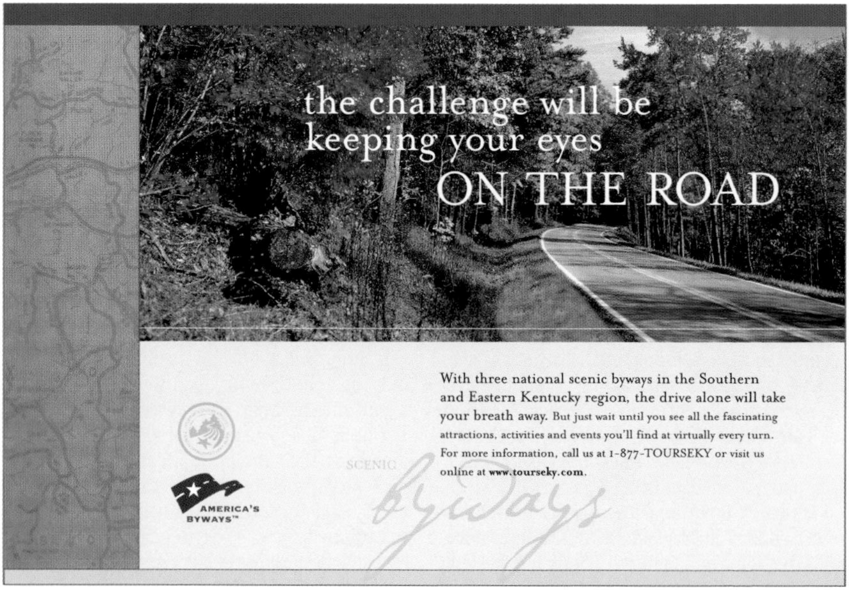

## RECREATION & TRAVEL

# Tourist Attractions, State Parks, Resort Parks & Historic Sites

## Western Lakes Region

**BARDWELL AREA: Carlisle County Chamber of Commerce** (270-628-5459); **Westvaco Wildlife Management Area**—Bottomland hardwood, swamp area and Great Blue Heron Rookery (270-628-5451); **Winford Public Wildlife Area**—237 acres. Waterfowl, rabbit, deer, raccoon, fishing.

**BENTON AREA: Marshall County Tourist Commission** (270-527-3128); (Benton) **Forgotten Past Museum**—gift shop, go carts, bumper cars, mini golf, antique steam engine, museum, and arcade (270-527-9244); **KENTUCKY DAM VILLAGE STATE**

A bridge on US 68 crosses the Cumberland River and Lake Barkley, as it leads into the Land Between The Lakes National Recreation Area
*Photo: Charles Bertram, Lexington Herald-Leader*

**RESORT PARK**—the perfect haven for water sports enthusiasts and also features an 18-hole

Championship Golf Course, full service restaurant, camping, and meeting facilities (270-362-4271); (Calvert City) **Kentucky Lake Motor Speedway**—Race super late models and open wheel modified and limited sportsmen (270-395-3600); (Draffenville) **Kentucky Opry Show**—featuring country, gospel and bluegrass music (888-459-8704); (Gilbertsville) **Henry's Golf Range**—Driving range, mini-golf, batting cages, go-carts (270-362-8170); **Henry's Race Place**—go-kart track (270-362-8170); **Maggie's Jungle Golf and Jungle Run**—Miniature golf, nature trail & petting zoo (270-362-8933); **Mike Wells 4 Rivers Outdoors**—Fishing guide service (270-362-4278); (Hardin) **Hardin Southern Railroad**—two-hour eighteen-mile round trip rail adventure authentically reviving an experience from the past (270-437-4555); **KENLAKE STATE RESORT PARK**—on the western shore of Kentucky Lake, Kenlake offers a choice of quiet relaxation or active recreation. Take to the net at the tennis center, a seasonal facility with temperature-controlled courts, racquet rentals and a pro shop. Nature lovers can explore 200 miles of trails at Land Between the Lakes (270-474-2211) **Mid-South Rail Heritage Foundation**—Collection of historic railroad equipment adjacent to the Hardin Southern Railroad (270-898-8722); **Weakley's Guide Service**—Licensed fishing guides on Kentucky Lake (877-547-3474).

*Sailing on Kentucky Lake*
*Photo: Sid Webb*

**CADIZ AREA: Cadiz/Trigg County Tourist Commission** (270-522-3892); **Canal Loop Trail**—Hiking and biking in the northern part of Land Between the Lakes (270-924-2000); **Elk & Bison Prairie**—Watch elk and bison (800-LBL-7077); **Janice Mason Art Museum**—A mix of local and regional artists (270-522-9056); **Golden Pond Planetarium**—Shows held daily (Mar-Dec) featuring black holes, white dwarves, and life on Mars (270-924-2000); **LAKE BARKLEY STATE RESORT PARK**—The lodge is situated in the wooded shoreline and the grand scale, post-and-beam wood construction features acres of glass offering outstanding views. An outdoor pool overlooking the lake and also has a heated, indoor pool. The Fitness Center offers Nautilus equipment, fitness cycles, a weight room, racquetball court, tanning beds, sauna, whirlpool and fitness trainers. An 18-hole Boots Randolph

**Columbus-Belmont State Park**
*Source: Kentucky Department of Tourism*

golf course, campground, full-service marina, a lighted airstrip and trails for hiking and mountain biking (270-924-1131); **Land Between the Lakes (LBL)**—Located in Western Kentucky and Tennessee, LBL offers 170,000 acres of wildlife, history and outdoor recreation opportunities, wrapped by 300 miles of undeveloped shoreline (800-LBL-7077); **Log House Antiques** (270-522-0610); **Whitetail**

**Creek Outfitters**—Guided whitetail deer hunting (270-924-9639); **Sinking Fork Pay Lake and Fun Park**—swimming, horseshoes, volleyball, picnic area badminton, croquet and fishing (270-235-9677); **The Homeplace**—This living history farm, with 16 original log structures, re-creates the life of a rural farm family before the Civil War. Demonstrations of butter making, tobacco firing, weaving,

**Jefferson Davis
birthplace monument and marker.**
*Photo: Sid Webb*

and plowing (800-LBL-7077); **Woodlands Nature Station**—Hands-on encounter with the natural world the environmental education center nestled in the woods between Honker and Hematite Lakes (800-LBL-7077); **Wrangler's Riding Stables**—Scenic trails at Land Between The Lakes National Recreation Park (270-924-2211)

**CLINTON AREA: Clinton Co. Judge's Office** (270-653-4369); **Hickman County Museum**—1870s home of Captain Henry Watson of the Confederate Army. Local household, farm, business, government, medical & military items (270-653-6587); (Columbus) **COLUMBUS-BELMONT STATE PARK**—site of the November 7, 1861 Battle of Belmont. Confederate General Leonidas Polk while defending Columbus, the "Gibraltar of the West", but was outflanked by Ulysses S. Grant who forced evacuation of the Confederates in 1862. A massive chain and anchor used by the South to block passage of the Union gunboats and the earthen trenches dug to protect 19,000 Confederate troops. The farmhouse was a Civil War hospital is now a museum and the park has a campground (270-677-2327); **JEFFERSON DAVIS STATE HISTORIC SITE**—Jefferson Davis was elected President of the Confederate States of America on February 18, 1861. President Abraham Lincoln and Jefferson Davis were born in Kentucky in log cabins within one year and 100 miles apart. The 351-foot obelisk marks the birthplace of Jefferson Davis. A visitor's center has exhibits and a gift shop. (270-886-1765)

**Eagle feather bonnet**
*Source: Kentucky
Department of Tourism*

**EDDYVILLE/KUTTAWA AREA: Lyon County Joint Tourism Commission** (800-355-3885); **Amaze'n Mazes Fort Venture**—Wild and crazy two-level labyrinth of twists and turns (270-388-7999); **Anderson Woodland Trail**—Beautiful hiking trail with view of Lake Barkley (800-355-3885); **Black Barn Herbs**—Grows pesticide free, hard to find herbs, beautiful perennials and fresh produce (270-365-5023); **Campbell's Orchard**—Peaches and apples and a Gift Shop with preserves, molasses, etc. (270-388-2738); **Eddyville Fun Park**—Go-karts, inflatables, lazer tag, miniature train, snacks & arcade (270-388-9188); **Happy Trails Riding Stables**—Guided horse-back riding through wilderness/nature trails (270-871-4370); **Hook Line & Sinker Guide Service**—Fishing on Kentucky and Barkley Lakes, experienced guides and boats (270-388-0525); **Mineral Mound State Park**—Located on the shores of Lake Barkley and was once owned by author F. Scott Fitzgerald's grandfather. Golf and cruising the lake. The park has a Signature Series 18-hole golf course, a pro shop, a picnic area, a fishing pier and a boat ramp. (270-388-3673); **Rose Hill/Lyon County Museum**—Oldest standing structure in Old Eddyville and is on the National Register (270-388-9986); **Venture River Water Park**—Wave pool, slides and kiddie pool (270-388-7999)

**ELKTON AREA: City of Elkton** (270-265-9877); **Guthrie Railroad Museum**—Renovated caboose from the L&N Railroad (270-483-2683); **Milliken Memorial Community House**—Georgian man-

sion built in 1927 is on the National Register of Historic Places (270-265-9877); **Robert Penn Warren Home**—Home of the nation's first poet laureate and three-time Pulitzer Prize winner is remembered here at his home (270-483-2683)

**GRAND RIVERS/SMITHLAND AREA: Livingston County Tourist Commission** (800-967-0325); **Grand Rivers Tourist Commission** (888-493-0152); **Belle of Grand Rivers**—A 55-foot replica of a turn of the century riverboat that tours Kentucky and Barkley Lake (800-498-0428); **Morris Toy Museum**—Museum displaying toys from the 1800s to the present (270-988-3591); **Grand Rivers Jetty and Walking Trail**—The walkway has benches at the lakefront and a public beach area (270-362-0152); **Kentucky Kayak Kountry**—Paddle sports, recreation, sales and rental of canoes and kayaks. Guided whitewater trips (270-362-0081); **Kentucky Lock and Dam**—Longest dam on the Tennessee River with a major generating plant in the TVA power system (800-467-1388); **Lake Barkley**—Bordering TVA's Land Between the Lakes Recreation Area offers waterfowl hunting, fishing, nature trails, a national battlefield, and a national waterfowl refuge (270-362-8430); **Lake Barkley Lock and Dam**—Lake Barkley connects to Kentucky Lake by a canal (270-362-4236); **Ohio River Public Wildlife Area**—Waterfowl hunting area (502-564-7863); **Patti's 1880s Settlement**—Dining in 1880s atmosphere featuring homemade pies and 2" thick pork chops. Historic log cabin settlement with unique shops, miniature golf and animal park (888-736-2515); **Shawnee Queen River Taxi**—A 48-passenger river taxi on the Ohio River between Golconda, Rosiclare, Elizabethtown, Cave-in-Rock, Illinois and Carrsville, Kentucky (877-677-6123)

**HICKMAN AREA: Hickman Chamber of Commerce** (270-236-2902); **Dorena, Mo - Hickman, Ky Toll Ferry**—Toll Ferry across the Mississippi River (731-285-0390); **R N Henson Broommaker's Museum**—1930s working broom shop now museum with original equipment, photos, and historical mementos (270-236-2360); **Reelfoot Lake Public Wildlife Area**—Trails through flat-bottomed river land with 2,500 acres (901-538-2481); **The Olde House**—The oldest brick house in Hickman probably built as a slave house (731-885-3314); **Warren Thomas Museum**—A century-old church, highlights the history of the area's black community (270-236-2423)

**HOPKINSVILLE/OAK GROVE AREA/FORT CAMPBELL: Hopkinsville/ Christian County CVB** (800-842-9959); **Amazing Acres**—(270-881-2445); **Bravard Vineyards & Winery**—A small, farm/family winery (270-269-2583); **Brushy Fork Creek**—Paul Ferrell is a woodturner and Patricia is a potter with a greenhouse of ferns and orchids (270-424-5988); **Christian Way Farm**—Experience planting, tending or harvesting the crops and feeding the animals (270-269-2434); **Copper Canyon Ranch**—Recreated 1880s mining town, live entertainment, comedy, music, stunts, live reenacted western gunfights, picnic area (270-269-2416); **Dan Cayce Guide Service**—Lake Barkley and Kentucky Lake adjoining the Land Between the Lakes National Park (LBL) offers Crappie and White Bass (Stripe) fishing (270-886-8592); **Don F. Pratt Memorial Museum**—History of the 101st Airborne Division Air Assault the "Screaming Eagles." (270-798-3215); **Fort Campbell Memorial Park**—Commemorates the 248 soldiers

**Wooldridge Monuments Maplewood Cemetery, Mayfield**
*Source: Kentucky Department of Tourism*

who died in a plane crash in Newfoundland (800-842-9959); **Fort Campbell Public Wildlife Area**—85,000 acres with a variety of forest wildlife and farm habitat, sinkholes and beaver lakes which attract wood ducks and shore birds. Trout streams available and 2 lakes with warm water fish species (270-789-2175); (Oak Grove) **War Memorial Walking Trail**—One-mile walking trail lined with markers of all of the United States' wars and conflicts from the French and Indian War to Desert Storm (270-439-5675); **PENNYRILE FOREST STATE RESORT PARK**—Named for the tiny Pennyroyal plant found in the woodlands surrounding this resort and is the perfect back-to-nature hideaway. The resort offers a newly expanded 18-hole golf course; tennis, hiking, canoeing, fishing, swimming and beach. (270-797-3421); **Pennyrile**

**State Forest**— Kentucky's largest state forest with 14,669 acres, native pine, hardwood trees; Pennyroyal Area Museum—See the Night Riders lighting up the sky during the tobacco war...the Cherokee Indians' travails along the Trail of Tears...and clairvoyant Edgar Cayce performing his miracles (270-887-4270); **Trail of Tears Commemorative Park**—Used by the Cherokees on the infamous Trail of Tears and includes the gravesites of Chiefs White Path and Fly Smith (270-886-8033)

**MARION AREA: Marion Tourism Commission** (270-965-5015); **Amish Community**—Over 400 residents, six Amish schools and four church districts. (800-755-0361); **Ben E. Clement Mineral Museum**—Fluorite crystal and other minerals, photographs, letters, records, mining equipment, and other memorabilia (888-965-4263); **Cave-In Rock Ferry**—Free riverboat ferry crosses the Ohio River to Cave-In Rock in Illinois (800-755-0361); **Crittenden County Historical Museum**—Authentic memorabilia from early pioneers (270-965-9257); **Fohs Hall Community Arts Foundation**—National Registry art gallery (270-965-5983); **Mantle Rock Native Education and Cultural Center**—Classes in Native American arts and culture, guides for walking tours of neighboring Mantle Rock, the mid-point on the "Trail of Tears," where hundreds of victims of the Indian Removal Act perished in the winter of 1838–39 (270-965-5882); **Paddy's Bluff Retreat (ATV Park)**—650 acres of forested land along the beautiful Cumberland River. Primitive trails for all terrain vehicles and primitive campsites (270-988-1822); **Paula Collins China Shoppe**—Internationally known china artist displays her work and gives lessons in china painting (270-965-9210)

**MAYFIELD AREA: Mayfield Tourism Commission** (270-247-6101); **Edana Locus House**—Built by multi-millionaire banker Ed Gardner, this circa 1928 home houses the visitor center (270-247-6101); **Icehouse Art Gallery & Western Kentucky Museum**—Hand crafted items and artwork by well known regional artists. Museum displays early industries of Mayfield and Graves County (270-247-6971); **Kaler Bottoms Public Wildlife Area**—Cypress swamps with low-lying wet terrain, swamp, great blue heron rookery, black vulture roost (502-564-4336); **Twilight Cabaret Productions**—Seasonal theatre events and dinner theatre (270-436-2399); **Wooldridge Monuments**—18 figure group of sandstone and Italian marble monuments, "The Strange Procession That Never

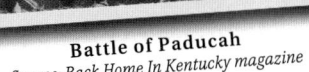

Museum of the American Quilter's Society, Paducah
Source: Kentucky Department of Tourism

Moves." Henry G. Wooldridge, a horse trader who moved to Mayfield around 1840 chose to commemorate his family, pets and himself with life-sized statues grouped around his tomb (270-247-6101)

**MURRAY AREA: Murray Tourism Commission** (800-651-1603); **Clara M. Eagle Gallery**—Canvas to performance, art classics to contemporary (270-762-3052); **Hazel Antique Shopping District**—12 shops and antique malls and 500 antique dealers (270-492-8175); **John Morgan's Guide Service**—Crappie fishing on Kentucky Lake (270-436-2810); **Murray Art Guild**—Provides exhibi-

tions, workshops and demonstrations housed in the Linn House which is on the National Register of Historic Places (270-753-4059); **Playhouse in the Park** (270-759-1752); **Wrather West Kentucky Museum**—Social, cultural and economic development of western Kentucky and the Jackson Purchase.(270-809-4771)

**PADUCAH AREA: Paducah/McCracken County Convention and Visitors Bureau** (800-PADUCAH); **Alben W. Barkley Museum**—Captain William Smedley's 1852 home, listed in the National Register of Historic Places, showcases memorabilia of Alben W. Barkley (270-534-8264); **Annie's Horsedrawn Carriage Rides** (270-210-6095); **Hotel Metropolitan**—An African-American Heritage Museum was a 1908 hotel housed famous African-American entertainers and sports figures during segregation; **Legendary Chief Paduke Statue**—Chief of Sub-tribe of Chickasaw Indians, who lived and hunted in the area until Jackson Purchase, 1818. General William Clark, who founded Paducah, named it in honor of the chief. **Lower Town Arts District**—Studios and galleries of resident artists, including potters, painters, jewelry makers, printmakers and bookbinders (270-444-9191); **Luther F. Carson Four Rivers Center**—Performing arts center hosts Broadway hits, theatre, dance and a musical series with well-known entertainers (270-450-4444);

Battle of Paducah
Source: Back Home In Kentucky magazine

**Maiden Alley Cinema**—Independent films weekly (888-442-7007); **Market House Theatre**—Nationally recognized, award winning community theatre producing plays and musicals (888-648-7529); **Metropolis Lake State Nature Preserve**—Natural lake ringed with bald cypress and swamp tupelo. Five species of rare fish, beaver, wintering place for bald eagles, hiking, birding and nature study; **Museum of the American Quilter's Society**—Quilts and the stories they tell at this national museum (270-442-8856); **Paducah International Raceway**—Racing late model, modified, pre-stock and street stock autos (270-898-7469); **Paducah Railroad Museum**—Contains a model train layout and local and national history exhibits (270-519-7377); **Paducah Wall to Wall Murals**—Renowned artist Robert Dafford's life-sized paintings on the city's floodwall (800-723-8224); **Players Bluegrass Downs**—Live horse racing (270-444-7117); **River Heritage Museum**—Housed in downtown's oldest standing structure, has interactive exhibits that tell the story of the Four Rivers Region (800-PADUCAH); **Steam Locomotive No.1518**—A Mikado steam engine, the last "Iron Horse" used by the Illinois Central Railroad (800-PADUCAH); **West Kentucky Wildlife Management Area**—Deer, squirrels, rabbits, dove, raccoons, ducks. Seven fishing ponds, picnic areas, hiking, primitive camping, horseback riding (270-488-3233); **Whitehaven Mansion/Welcome Center**—This landmark, once destined for destruction, was built in the 1860s (270-554-2077); **William Clark Market House Museum**—Story of a town that has survived tremendous challenges, including the Battle of Paducah and the 1937 flood. Features entire gingerbread woodwork interior of the 1877 **List Drug Store** (270-443-7759); **Yeiser Art Center**—Contemporary art by regional, and national artists. 19th & 20th century American and European art (270-442-2453)

**PRINCETON AREA: Princeton/Caldwell County Chamber of Commerce** (270-365-5393); **Adsmore House Museum and Ratliff Gunshop**—Circa 1857 Greek Revival home restored to late Victorian grandeur and filled with the Smith-Garrett family's personal belongings. **Gunshop restored to early 1840** (270-365-3114); **Big Springs Park on the Trail of Tears**—City park situated on the camping site of the Cherokee Indians in 1838 while they were on the "Trail of Tears" march (270-365-9575); **Caldwell Railroad Museum**—Railroad memorabilia and caboose exhibits (270-365-0582); **Donaldson Creek Hunting Camp**—Offering whitetail deer and turkey hunting (270-365-5118); **Jones-Keeney Public Wildlife Area**—Nature preserve with trails,

scenic overlooks, bow and rifle ranges (502-564-4336); **Princeton Art Guild**—Regional artists featured in a historic building (constructed 1817) that was on the "Trail of Tears." (270-365-3959)

**WICKLIFFE AREA: Ballard County Chamber of Commerce** (270-335-5999); **Barlow House**—11 room house built by local patriarch Clifton Jesse Barlow (270-334-3010); **Ballard County Wildlife**

**Native American burial grounds, Wickliffe**
*Source: Kentucky Department for Libraries & Archives,*
*WPA Collection*

**Management Area**—Sloughs with some hardwoods stands, fishing lakes, and hunting. Eagles can be seen in winter. (270-224-2244); **Fort Jefferson Memorial Cross**—View three states from this 95-foot memorial that stands high upon a bluff at the confluence of the Ohio and Mississippi Rivers (270-335-3438); **Swan Lake Wildlife Management Area**—Near the confluence of the Ohio and Mississippi rivers, this prime wintering area for migratory waterfowl contains numerous sloughs, oxbow lakes and Kentucky's largest natural lake, Swan Lake (270-224-2244); **WICKLIFFE MOUNDS STATE HISTORIC SITE**—An archaeological site of prehistoric Native American village of the Mississippian mound builders. Located on a bluff overlooking the Mississippi river, the village was occupied from about AD 1100 to 1350. The Mississippians built a complex settlement with permanent house and earth mounds situated around a central plaza. The Wickliffe Mounds museum exhibits the excavated features of the mounds, outstanding displays of Mississippian pottery, stone tools, bone and shell implements, the architecture of Mississippian mounds and houses, burial practices of the Mississippians and a bird's eye view of the bluff atop the ceremonial mound. (270-335-3681)

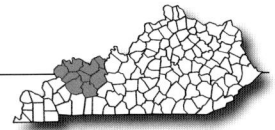

# Bluegrass, Blues & Barbeque

**CENTRAL CITY/GREENVILLE AREA: Central City Tourist Commission** (270-754-9603); **Greater Muhlenberg County Chamber of Commerce** (270-338-5422); **Brewco Motorsports**—Visit the shop of this NASCAR Busch Series two-car team (270-754-2264); Duncan House Museum & Art Gallery – History of coal mining and early settlers, gift shop (270-338-2605); **Everly Brothers Monument**—Tribute to singers Don and Phil Everly; **House of Onyx**—Gemstone dealer, mineral hall and Mexican onyx carvings (800-844-3100); **LAKE MALONE SATE PARK**—788 lake acres is enclosed by dramatic 50-foot sandstone bluffs rising above the water's edge and surrounded by hardwood forests. The park has a campground, marina, beach and hiking trail (270-657-2111); **Rails to Trails**—six-mile multiuse trails which connect Central City and Greenville (270-338-5422); The Palace Theatre – Muhlenberg Community Theater has presented 22 full seasons of comedies, dramas, musicals and children's theatre (270-338-7165)

**DIXON AREA: Webster County Economic Development Corp** (270-639-7015); **Parker Warner Historic Museum**—Historic photography, memorabilia, written and oral history (270-667-5022); **Webster County Civil War Driving Tour**—Several Civil War battle sites and the campsite of General Nathan B. Forrest (270-667-5022)

**HARTFORD/ROSINE AREA: Ohio County Tourism Commission** (270-274-1090); **Bill Monroe's Birthplace**—Guided tours of the restored Boyhood home of Bill Monroe, the "Father of Bluegrass Music." (888-987-6444); **Bluegrass** Motorcycle Museum—Vintage American motorcycles from 1906 to present on display (270-298-7764); **Fordsville Historical Society and Depot Museum**—Depot built in 1916, reminiscent of early L&N train stations, includes relics of Kentucky rural life (270-276-5656); **Ohio County Museum**—features five historic buildings including an 1880 home on the National Historic Register, a small country store, a relocated one-room schoolhouse, and L&N caboose on a track (270-298-3444); **Ohio County Park**—A replica of Old Fort Harrod and nature trails (270-298-4466); **Peabody Public Wildlife Area**—

John James Audubon
*Source: Neville Public Museum*

Yellow-billed Magpie painted by John James Audubon

Reclaimed coal mines with fishing and birding opportunities (502-564-4336); **Rosine Barn Jamboree**—Live jam sessions of Bluegrass, Country and Gospel music (270-274-9744); **Rosine Cemetery**—Early 1860s cemetery includes grave of Bill Monroe (270-274-5552); **Washburn Lake**—Fishing, launching area, boat rentals (502-564-4336)

**HAWESVILLE AREA: Hancock County Tourism** (270-927-8137); **Hancock County Museum**—located in the old Railroad Depot located in the old L&N Railroad Depot and filled with turn-of-the-century memorabilia (270-295-6637); **Hancock County Farm Museum**—See tools and transportation from the past (270-295-3653); **Pate House**—Built in 1822,

**Bill Monroe's birthplace in Rosine.**
*Source: Owensboro-Daviess County Tourist Commission*

the scene of Abraham Lincoln's first trial in which he defended himself against charges of operating a ferry across the Ohio River without a license

**HENDERSON AREA: Henderson County Tourist Commission** (800-648-3128); **Ellis Park Race Course Inc**—Enjoy thoroughbred racing at its best with year-round simulcasting from all major N. America racetracks (800-333-8110); **Henderson Fine Arts Center**—A variety of nationally known artists and top musicians perform throughout the year (270-830-5324); **JOHN JAMES AUDUBON STATE PARK**—Woodland cottages set in the woods where John James Audubon studied and painted birds during his time in Henderson from 1810-1819. A museum and nature center interprets his life through exhibits and a world-renowned collection of his paintings and memorabilia. The wildlife observatory provides the visitor with binoculars and a front row seat to visiting animals. A giant bird's nest is the centerpiece of the Discovery Center with hands-on exhibits and educational programs. (270-826-2247); **Sloughs Wildlife Management Area**—10,000 acres of hunting grounds and wetlands and home to 30,000 Canada geese and 10,000 ducks in winter (270-827-2673)

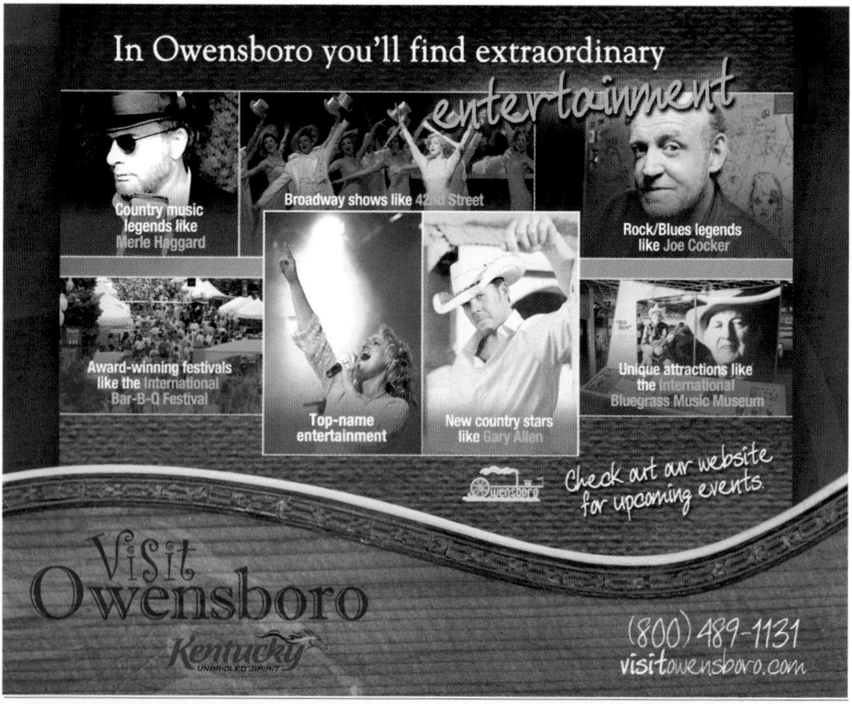

LIVERMORE/CALHOUN AREA: **Livermore Community Library and Art Museum**—Local

color is on display with special showings of quilts and art and crafts. Family historians can visit the genealogy section (270-278-9184)

**MADISONVILLE AREA: Madisonville/Hopkins County Chamber of Commerce** (270-821-3435); **Dawson Springs Museum & Art Center**—Collections, historic photography, memorabilia, written and oral history (270-797-3891); **Glema Mahr Center for the Arts**— Featuring regionally and nationally known performers plus the Anne P. Baker Gallery, a showcase for visual arts exhibits (270-824-8685); **Governor Ruby Laffoon Log Cabin**—Two-

Ice skaters at Winter Wonderland presented by RiverPark Center in Owensboro.
*Source: Owensboro-Daviess County Tourist Commission*

Owensboro's Showcase stage features free Friday night concerts throughout the summer.
*Source: Owensboro-Daviess County Tourist Commission*

room birthplace of Kentucky Governor from 1931-1935, Ruby Laffoon (270-821-3986); **Historical Society of Hopkins Co. Library & Museum**— Browse through volumes of community photos, Civil War and coal mining memorabilia (270-821-3986; **Lake Beshear**—760 acres, fishing and boat ramp; **Madisonville Kart World**—Go-karts, batting cages and large arcade room (270-824-1116); **Sport Shooters**—Indoor shooting range (270-825-1733); **Tradewater Public Wildlife Area**—724 acres, deer, squirrel, raccoon, hiking and birding; **White City Wildlife Management Area**—5,472 acres, rabbit, quail, deer, dove, turkey, waterfowl, fishing, ramp and primitive camping

**MORGANFIELD AREA: Union County Economic Development Foundation** (270-389-9600); **James D. Veatch Camp Breckinridge Museum & Arts Center**—This WWII U.S. Military training center once housed Bob Dole and Jackie Robinson and features the old officer's club with over 40 murals painted on the wall by German POW Daniel Mayer (270-389-4420)

**OWENSBORO AREA: Owensboro/ Daviess County Tourist Commission** (800-489-1131);

**BEN HAWES STATE PARK**—Includes remains of a deep coalmine operation that thrived from the early 1900s through the 1950s. Several buildings remain that can be reached by hiking trails. There is an outdoor classroom for nature classes, 5 miles of trails and 4 miles for mountain biking. 18 hole, 9 hole and par 3 golf available. 270-684-9808; **Executive Inn Rivermont Showroom Lounge**—Riverfront showroom with Las Vegas-style headliner entertainment (800-626-1936); **Fisher Park**—33 acres, includes the Owensboro Softball Complex, a first-class four-field facility hosting over 20 major softball tournaments annually. The park also provides an open picnic shelter and walking trail. ; **Goldie's Best Little Opryhouse in Kentucky**—Live family entertainment every Friday and Saturday night, featuring some of the most talented musicians, singers and comedians (270-926-0254); **Hall of Fame**—"Hometown Hero" Hall of Fame showcases the celebrities that have reached national or international acclaim, from the Owensboro area (800-489-1131); **International Bluegrass Music Museum**—State of the art, interactive museum dedicated to preserving and encouraging the growth of Bluegrass music (888-692-2656); **Lambert Land Maize & Pumpkin Patch LLC**—15 acre interactive corn maize & pumpkin patch (270-764-1448); **Moreland Park**—17 acres, includes a Tennis Center consisting of 12 lighted tennis courts is open to the public, and is host to youth and adult tennis tournaments, as well as high school and college matches; **Owensboro Area Museum of Science and History**— Exhibits on natural, cultural and regional history, Wendell Ford Government Education Center, a SpeedZeum, a permanent motor sports gallery (270-687-2732); **Owensboro Museum of Fine Art**—The permanent collection includes American, European and Asian fine arts and decorative arts dating back to the 14th century (270-685-3181); **Owensboro Symphony Orchestra**—The premier producer of live classical and pops music for the Western Kentucky region, considered among the top twenty Kentucky arts organizations performing over 60 services annually, reaching an estimated audience of over 50,000 per year (270-684-0661); **Panther Creek Park**—7 pavilions, a 6-acre stocked lake, gazebo and butterfly gardens, and 1876 refurbished one-room school house, a fire tower, a swinging bridge (270-685-6142); **Reid's Orchard**—Pick your own fruits

**Sports Illustrated selected Owensboro as Kentucky's #1 Sports Town.**
*Source: Owensboro-Daviess County Tourist Commission*

and vegetables and enjoy the Apple Festival is held the third weekend in October (270-685-2444); **River City Trolley**—Route circles through the historic downtown area (270-687-8570); **River Park Center**—RiverPark Center-Becoming known as Broadway West due to the number of traveling Broadway shows built and premiered in Owensboro, RiverPark Center is Western Kentucky's premiere arts and cultural center offering drama to Broadway, bluegrass to ballet in its 1,500 seat auditorium (270-687-2787); **Shelton Memorial**—Colonel Charles Shelton was the last POW from the Vietnam War (800-489-1131); **Theatre Workshop of Owensboro**—Known as "The Longest Running Show in Town", TWO has offered the finest community theatre in the region for over 40 years (270-683-5003); **Western Kentucky Botanical Gardens**—features six established gardens - Butterfly, Rose, Daylili, Iris, Herb, and Fruit & Berry with hundreds of outstanding plant selections as well as a beautiful location for social gatherings (270-852-8925)

**Interior view of the International Bluegrass Music Museum.**
*Source: Owensboro-Daviess County Tourist Commission*

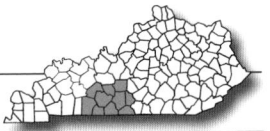

# Caves, Lakes & Corvettes Region

**BOWLING GREEN AREA: Bowling Green Area CVB** (800-326-7465); (Bowling Green) **Barren River Imaginative Museum of Science** (270-843-9779); **Beech Bend Raceway Park & Splash Lagoon**—Campground, amusement park, drag strip, and an oval track (270-781-7634); **Bowling Green Assembly Plant** —Corvette production site (270-745-8019); **Bowling Green Chamber Orchestra, Inc.**—Kentucky's only fully professional chamber orchestra (270-846-2426); **Bowling Green Western Symphony Orchestra** (270-745-7681); **Chaney's**

National Corvette Museum
Source: Kentucky Department of Tourism

**Dairy Barn**—Rolling farmland, Jersey cows, and ice cream (270-843-5567); **Civil War Driving Tour**—Confederate Gen. Simon Bolivar Buckner quickly moved a detachment of troops to occupy Bowling Green on Sept. 18, 1861 (800-326-7465); **College Hill Historic Neighborhood Walking Tour**—Styles, forms and construction methods are mixed freely throughout the district (800-326-7465); **Duncan Hines Scenic Byway**—82-mile route begins at the former home and office of author Duncan Hines, crosses the Green River by ferry (800-326-7465); **Eloise B. Houchens Center**—Greek Revival mansion built in 1904 by Francis Kister, one-time Mayor of Bowling Green

and co-builder of St. Joseph Catholic Church (270-842-6761); **Fountain Square Park**—Built between 1871 and 1872 according to plans of John Cox Underwood (270-782-0222); **Greenwood Park, Inc**—36 holes of mini golf. Go-kart track, bumper boat pool, and batting cage; **Historic L & N Depot & Railpark**—Passenger Depot made of local limestone (270-745-0090); **Jacksons Orchard and Nursery** (270-781-5303); **Kentucky Library and Museum**—History, arts and crafts, Felts House, an 1830s log structure (270-745-2592); **Lost River Cave and Valley**—Kentucky's only underground boat tour (866-274-2283); **National Corvette Museum**—The 68,000 sq. ft. showcase to America's sports car (800-538-3883); **Public Theatre of Kentucky, Phoenix Theatre** (270-781-6233); **Raceworld**—Scale NASCAR cars, a game room with rock climbing wall, and more (270-781-7223); **Riverview at Hobson Grove**—Built by Atwood and Juliet VanMeter Hobson and listed on the National Register, was used for storage of Confederate munitions (270-843-5565); **ShakeRag Historic District Walking Tour**—Bowling Green's first National Register District recognized for its significance to African American history (800-326-7465); **St. Joseph Catholic Church**—On the National Register of Historic Places because of its artistic and historic significance. (270-842-2525); **Upper East Main Street Historic Walking Tour**—Residences built between 1870 and 1930 (800-326-7465); (Woodburn) **Triple H Stables**—Guided trail rides and working farm (270-779-2652)

**EDMONTON AREA: Edmonton/Metcalfe County Chamber of Commerce** (270-432-

3222); **Barn Lot Theater** (270-432-2276); **Historic Metcalfe County Courthouse**—One of the oldest courthouses in Kentucky (888-826-3181)

FRANKLIN AREA: Franklin/Simpson County Tourism Commission (866-531-2040); **African American Heritage Center** (270-586-0099); **Franklin Drive In** (877-586-1905); **Gallery on the Square** (270-586-8055); **Kentucky Downs Race Course**—Live racing in Sept., year 'round simulcast wagering (270-586-7778); **Octagon Hall**—unique octagon shaped house occupied during Civil War by Confederate and Federal troops (270-586-9343); **Old Stone Jail and Simpson County Archives**—Built in 1879 and used until 1986. The buildings house a museum and genealogical archives (270-586-4228)

GLASGOW AREA: **Glasgow/Barren County Tourist & Convention Center** (800-264-3161); (Glasgow) **BARREN RIVER LAKE STATE RESORT PARK**—Lodge and cottages curve around the 10,000-acre lake. Boating, fishing, 18-hole golf course, guided horseback rides, tennis courts, beach, pool and a paved trail

for hiking and biking. (800-325-0057); **Fort Williams**—In October 1863, Confederate forces raided Fort Williams (800-264-3161); **Plaza Theatre**—1934 theatre is a center for cultural events such as music, performing arts and movies (270-361-2101); **Brigadoon State Nature Preserve**—181 acres of rich protected woodlands containing wildflowers and rare species; **South Central Kentucky Cultural Center**—Preservation of the unique history and culture of "the Barrens." (888-256-6941); (Lucas) **Barren River Lake Public Wildlife Area**—20,000 acres for hiking, picnicking, fishing and hunting (270-646-5167)

MAMMOTH CAVE AREA/ CAVE CITY: **Cave City Tourist Commission** (800-346-8908); **Edmonson County Tourist Commission** (800-624-8687); **Big Mike's Mystery House**—Guided tour through mystifying gravity rooms, optical illusions and different oddities (270-773-5144); **Cave Country Go-Carts** (270-773-2299); **Crystal Onyx Cave and Campground**—Beautiful formations such as delicate crystalline draperies, rimstone pools and a prehistoric burial site (270-773-2359); **Dinosaur**

**Mammoth Cave**
*Source: Kentucky Department of Tourism*

**World**—More than 100 life sized dinosaurs in a beautiful natural setting; dig for authentic fossils in the fossil dig (270-773-4345); **Double J Stables & Horseman's Camp**—Guided trail rides through Mammoth Cave National Park and wildlife viewing (800-730-HRSE); **Floyd Collins Museum**—Tells the bizarre and tragic story of Floyd Collins, the explorer who died in Sand Cave (270-773-3366); **Guntown Mountain**—A Wild West town, amusement rides and onyx cave (270-773-3530); **Hillbilly Hound Fun Park**—18 hole miniature golf and go-kart track (270-773-4249); **Ky Action Park/ Jesse James Stables**—Alpine slide, guided scenic trail rides on horseback, go-carts, game room and cave tours in Poutlaw Cave (800-798-0560); **Mammoth Cave Canoe and Kayak**—Canoeing outfitter on the Green River (270-773-3366); **Mammoth Cave Wax Museum**—American history and contributions made by each famous person (270-773-3010); **Mammoth Cave Wildlife Museum**—Kentucky's first and largest wildlife museum including big animals from all over the world (270-773-2255); **Miss Green River Boat Excursion**—A 63-foot twin diesel-powered riverboat for trips on the Green River within Mammoth Cave National Park (270-758-2243); **Onxy Cave**—1/2 hour tour through this unique underground world of columns, stalactites, stalagmites, and other cave formation (270-773-3530); **Outlaw Cave**—Beautiful stalactites, stalagmites, huge column formations from ceiling to floor (800-798-0560); **Bumper Boats**—Includes a miniature golf course (270-773-6027); **Yogi Bear's Jellystone**

Cordell Hull Scenic Byway is called a "Roller Coaster Highway."
*Photo: Sid Webb*

**Park Waterslide** (800-523-1854); (Mammoth Cave) **MAMMOTH CAVE NATIONAL PARK**—Established to preserve the cave system, including Mammoth Cave, the scenic river valleys of the Green and Nolin Rivers. This is the longest recorded cave system in the world with more than 365 miles explored and mapped (800-967-2283); **NOLIN LAKE STATE PARK**—A campground and a 5,795 acre lake (270-286-4240); (Park City) **Diamond Caverns**—Tours for over 143 years features intricate drapery deposits lining the halls in cascades of naturally colorful calcite with thousands of stalactites, stalagmites and flowstone deposits (270-749-2233); **Green River Canoe Outfitters**—Canoeing outpost, full livery service, and self-guided trips (270-749-2041); (Roundhill); **Lazy Acres Trails & Paylake**—Over 1,000 acres available for horseback riding and camping, fully-stocked paylake (270-286-4189)

**MORGANTOWN AREA: Morgantown/Butler County Chamber of Commerce** (270-526-6827); **Green River Museum** (270-526-5342)

**MUNFORDVILLE/HORSE CAVE: Munfordville Tourism Commission** (888-686-3673); **Hart County Tourist Commission** (800-762-2869); (Horse Cave) **American Cave Museum / Hidden River Cave**—Descend 150 feet underneath the streets of historic downtown Horse Cave to the underground river that flows through Hidden River Cave (270-786-1466); **Kentucky Caverns** (800-762-2869); **Kentucky Down Under**—Kangaroos snakes colorful Rainbow Lorikeets in the Aviary (800-

762-2869); **Kentucky Repertory Theatre at Horse Cave**—Kentucky's Professional Festival Theatre (800-342-2177); (Munfordville) **Battle for the Bridge Historic Preserve**—219 acres of the Munfordville Battlefield, site of three Civil War battles (270-524-0101); **Big Buffalo Crossing Canoe & Kayak Rental** (866-233-2690); **Hart County Historical Museum**—Pre-columbian Native Americans and the earliest settlements to the mid-20th Century (270-524-0101)

Kentucky Repertory Theatre in Horse Cave
*Source: Kentucky Department of Tourism*

**RUSSELL-VILLE AREA:**
**Logan County Chamber of Commerce** (270-726-2206); (Adairville) **Red River Meeting House and Cemetery**—Site of the beginning of the Great Revival of 1800 and of the First Camp Meeting in the World (270-539-6528); (Auburn) **Auburn History Museum** (270-542-4677); (Lewisburg) **Century House Winery & Vineyards** (270-755-2807); (Russellville) **Bibb House Museum**—Restored 1829 home of Revolutionary War Maj. Richard Bibb (270-726-4181); **1817 Saddle Factory Museum** (270-726-4181); (South Union) **Shaker Museum at South Union**—The Shakers were a communal religious organization that flourished in America during the 19th century. The Shaker Museum, in a the 40-room 1824 Centre House, is filled with original artifacts (800-811-8379)

**SCOTTSVILLE AREA:** **Scottsville/Adair County Chamber of Commerce** (270-237-4782); **Allen County Historical Museum**—Early 1900s structure includes Civil War memorabilia (270-237-3026); **Mennonite Community** (270-237-4782); **The Tabernacle**—Built in 1897, and the seat of early revivals and gospel singing held in Allen County

**TOMPKINSVILLE AREA:** **Tompkinsville/Monroe County Chamber of Commerce** (270-487-1314); (Gamaliel) **Free-Town Church**—Built in 1846 by freed slaves of Wil-

liam Howard and gave them 400 acres, known as Free-Town (270-487-1314); (Tompkinsville) **Clover Hill Trap Club**—Three field courses for ATA registered birds (270-487-5418); **Cumberland River Ferry**—One of the last remaining free-floating ferries (270-487-1314); **Long C Trails**—2,000 acres of woodland horse back riding/hiking trails with scenic overlooks, waterfalls, wildlife and majestic bluffs, full service campground and cabin rentals; **Mennonite Community** (270-237-4782); **The Tabernacle**—Built in 1897, and the seat of early revivals and gospel singing held in Allen County (270-237-4782)

**TOMKINSVILLE AREA:** **Tompkinsville/Monroe County Chamber of Commerce** (270-487-1314); (Gamaliel) **Free-Town Church**—Built in 1846 by freed slaves of William Howard, who gave them 400 acres, known as Free-Town (270-487-1314); **Clover Hill Trap Club**—Three field courses for ATA registered birds (270-487-5418); **Cumberland River Ferry**—One of the last remaining free-floating ferries (270-487-1314); **Fisherman's Paradise-Kettle Creek Pay Lake** (270-487-1020); **McFarland Creek Outdoors**—4-wheeler nature rides, paint ball games, horseback rides, historic bus tours, nature hikes, carriage rides, petting zoo, water tubing and go cart rides (270-487-5563); **Monroe County Marble Dome**—A wooden structure that covers a 20 x 40-foot marble yard. (270-487-1314); **Old Mulkey Meetinghouse State Historic Site**—The oldest log meetinghouse in Kentucky was built in 1804 during a period of religious revival. Many Revolutionary War soldiers and pioneers, including Daniel Boone's sister, Hannah, are buried here. The structure has twelve corners in the shape of a cross and three doors, symbolic of the Holy Trinity (270-487-8481).

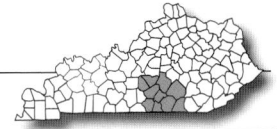

# Southern Lakes & Rivers Region

**BURKESVILLE AREA: Cumberland County Tourist & Convention Commission** (270-433-5133); (Bakerton) **Kentucky Trophy Fishing**—Trophy Striped Bass fishing (270-433-6333); (Burkesville) **DALE HOLLOW LAKE STATE RESORT PARK**—Overlooking a 28,000-acre lake, the lodge has an adjoining conference center and a new 18-hole golf course ranked by Golf Digest as one of the nation's best. There's fishing, boating, scuba diving, swimming and multi-use trails for hiking, horseback riding and mountain biking. The campground has sites for horse owners adjacent to riding trails. (800-325-2282); **Dale Hollow Public Wildlife Area**—Shoreline provides habitat for deer, raccoon, and other small mammals (615-736-5181); **Mud Camp Creek Public Wildlife Area**—Steep, narrow forested ridges to narrow valleys for fishing, primitive camping and hiking (270-465-5039)

**CAMPBELLSVILLE AREA: Taylor County Tourist Commission** (800-738-4719); **Friendship One-Room School House**—A museum that contains historic school memorabilia from 1918-1955 (270-465-5410); **GREEN RIVER LAKE STATE PARK**—Enjoy lakeside fun at the campground on the shores of this 8,200-acre lake with a beach, tie-ups for boats, miniature golf and multi-use trails for hiking, horseback riding and mountain biking (270-465-8255); **Green River Public Wildlife Area**—20,500 acres (270-465-5039); **Hiestand House Museum**—1823 dwelling is one of 12 German stone houses in Kentucky (270-789-4343); **Tebbs Bend-Green River Civil War Battlefield**—Located adjacent to Green

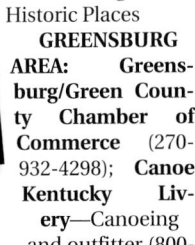

**Big South Fork Scenic Railway**
*Source: Kentucky Department of Tourism*

River Lake (270-465-8726); **The Homeplace on Green River**—1803 working farm museum on 227 acres (270-465-4511); **U.S. Army Corps of Engineers Visitor Center**—Office/Visitor Center (270-465-4463)

**COLUMBIA AREA: Columbia/Adair County Tourism Commission** (270-384-6020); (Columbia) **John B. Begley Chapel**—Neo-Gothic chapel designed by F. Fay Jones, the world's foremost chapel architect (800-264-0138); (Kinfley) **Janice Holt & Henry Giles Home**—The log home of Janice Holt & Henry Giles; listed on the National Register of Historic Places

**GREENSBURG AREA: Greensburg/Green County Chamber of Commerce** (270-932-4298); **Canoe Kentucky Livery**—Canoeing and outfitter (800-Kcanoe-1); **Green River Paddle Trail Park**—Cabins, canoe, and kayak rentals are available (270-932-4298); **Greensburg Walking Tour**—Greensburg 's National Register Historic District and John Hunt Morgan Trail (270-932-4298); **Old Green County Courthouse**—Limestone buildings on the Square, built in 1803, is a museum listed on National Register. Oldest courthouse west of the Alleghenies (270-932-4298); **William Herndon House**—Federal-style birthplace of Herndon, who became Lincoln's lawyer (270-932-4298)

**JAMESTOWN AREA: Russell County Tourist Commission** (888-833-4220); (Jamestown) **Kentucky Off-Track**—Live horse race simulcasts (270-343-3939); **LAKE CUMBERLAND STATE RESORT PARK**—60,000

acres of water and 1,225 miles of shoreline, Lake Cumberland is considered to be one of the finest fishing and boating areas in the Eastern United States. Lure Lodge offers the water-lover panoramic views of the lake and an indoor pool complex. The resort has a 9-hole, par-3 golf course, nature trails and guided horseback rides (270-343-3111); **Shell's Wolf Creek Outfitter** (270-343-2510); **Wolf Creek National Fish Hatchery**—Produces 1,000,000 fish per year (270-343-3797); (Russell Springs) **AJ Guide Service**—Specializing in catching striped bass (270-866-6207); **Bates Guide Service**—Specializes in year round trophy striper fishing (270-866-8703); **Striper Mania Guide Service** (270-866-6717)

**Cumberland River**
*Photo: Sid Webb*

**LIBERTY AREA:** Economic Development Authority of Casey County (606-787-9973); **Clementsville Motorsports**—Mud racing at its finest, truck and tractor pulling (606-787-5541)

**MONTICELLO AREA:** Monticello/Wayne County Chamber of Commerce (606-348-3064); **Keith Stables**—Guided lake rides, tours (606-561-5458); **Mill Springs Mill**—Constructed in 1877, historic grist mill on National Register of Historic Places (606-348-3064); **Victor's Striper Fishing Charter** (800-505-6447)

**SOMERSET AREA:** Somerset/Pulaski County CVB (800-642-6287); (Burnside) **GENERAL BURNSIDE ISLAND STATE PARK**—During the Civil War, Union Gen. Ambrose Burn-

![Water skiing]

**Skiing on Lake Cumberland near Somerset**
*Source: Kentucky Department of Tourism*

side patrolled what was then the Cumberland River surrounding this 400-acre island to keep watch for the Confederates. Campground, boating, fishing and an 18-hole golf course (606-561-4104); **Lake Cumberland Speedway**—3/8 mile dirt round track (606-561-8994); (Nancy) **Haney's Appledale Farm** (606-636-6148); (Somerset) **Beaver Creek Public Wildlife Area**—Fishing, hunting, hiking trails, and wildlife viewing, 17,347 acres (606-376-8083); **D.C. Guide Service**—Fishing boats and latest fishing equipment (800-804-5819); **Lake Cumberland**—Second largest lake in the Cumberland River system (606-679-6337); Mill Springs Battlefield (606-679-1859); **POW/MIA Memorial Garden**—Dedicated to the American servicemen/women listed as Prisoners of War and/or Missing in Action since World War I (606-679-1079); **The Center for Rural Development**—Performing arts and convention facility (606-677-6000)

**STEARNS/WHITLEY CITY AREA:** McCreary County Tourist Commission (888-284-3718); (Stearns) **Big South Fork National River and Recreation Area**—Pristine natural setting panoramic views, hiking, fishing and white water rafting (606-376-5073); **Big South Fork Scenic Railway**—13-mile round trip scenic train ride in enclosed or open air cars through the heart of the Big South Fork National Recreation Area (800-462-5664); **Blue Heron Mining Community**—Coal town tours exhibits & recorded messages. **Oral history recordings in ghost structures, mining artifacts** (606-376-5073); **Koger Barthell Mining Camp**—Reconstructed 1910 mining camp, company store, 12 miner's houses, schoolhouse and 1909-34 antique cars (888-550-5748); **McCreary County Museum**—The 1907 Stearns Coal & Lumber Company office building highlights history from the Indian and Pioneer era through the "Boom" times of the coal and lumber industries (606-376-5730); (Whitley City) **Natural Arch Scenic Area**—Magnificent sandstone arch (50' x 90'), picnicking and hiking (606-679-2010); **Paul Coffey Fishing Guide Service** (606-376-9065); **Yahoo Falls-Big South Fork NRRA**—State's tallest waterfall with hiking trails, overlooks, picnic area (606-376-5073)

**Fly fishing on the Big South Fork National River & Recreation Area**
*Source: Kentucky Department of Tourism*

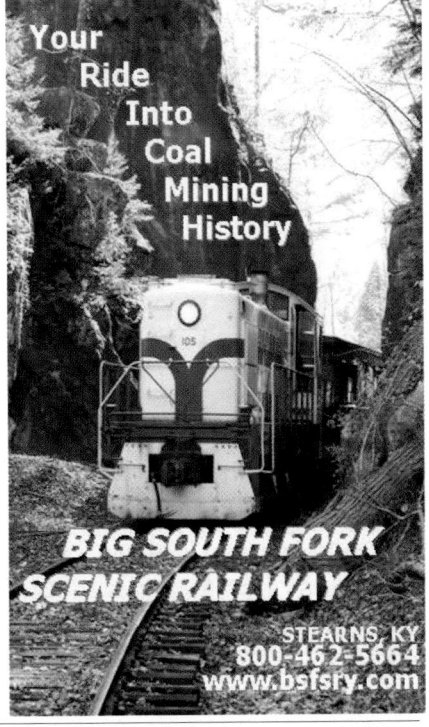

# RECREATION & TRAVEL
# *History of AAA*                    Tom Hicks

AAA has a long-standing history of service in the state of Kentucky. At the turn of the century there were only 600 automobiles in all of Kentucky, with half of them in Louisville. There were no paved roads between cities, no traffic aids, and to make matters worse, most people in the state considered the automobile a useless toy of the rich, that should be severely restricted, if not totally banned. It was because of these conditions that in 1903, 15 owners of automobiles in Louisville came together to found the Louisville Automobile Club, now known as AAA Kentucky.

Their goals were to protect the interests of motorists and automobiles against a hostile public, to encourage the building of and improvements to roads, and to promote the proper use of automobiles. The hard work of being true to these lofty goals quickly began. The dues were set at $5 for active members and $5 for associate members—a significant amount in 1903. By 1906 the club had become a vocal force for the improvement of roads—demanding and getting immediate attention of city planners—and positive changes were the result. Historical highlights of these confrontations and victories include assisting in the creation of Kentucky's first Department of Public Roads in 1912 and writing Kentucky's first automobile laws in 1920.

But, the purpose of the club was not all work. Parades showcased automobiles of various makes and models, and special meeting rooms were established where members could relax and share stories. While the trip would be considered a casual Sunday drive today, a special committee was appointed to plan "runs," such as an expedition to Lexington in which the drivers were required to maintain a strict 12 mph speed on the

Louisville Automobile Club Headquarters in the early 1900s
*Source: AAA*

journey. As a result, the 78-mile drive spanned 15 hours.

AAA Kentucky and its members have come a long way since those early days. The original 27 members have grown to more than 350,000 in the western half of the state. In addition to being the motorists' advocate, various services have been incorporated into member benefits along the way, such as Domestic Travel Service (1906), Emergency Road Service (1922), Bail Bond Service and Personal Accident Insurance (1936), World Wide Travel Agency Service (1950), an Insurance Agency (1973), and a Driver Training Center (1999). The club continues to expand its involvement within the community, being the advocate for and protecting the rights of motorists. This will always be the club's number one priority.

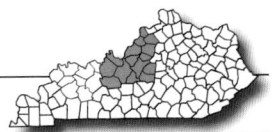

# Kentucky Derby Region

BARDSTOWN AREA: **Bardstown/Nelson County Tourist Commission** (800-638-4877); **Around the Town Carriage**—Narrated tour through historic Bardstown on horse-drawn carriages (502-348-0331); **Bardstown Walking Tour**—Self-guided (800-638-4877); **Basilica of St. Joseph Proto-Cathedral**—First Catholic Diocese west of the Allegheny Mountains (502-348-3126); **Civil War Museum/Old Bardstown Village**—State's largest collection of artifacts featuring the war's Western Theatre (502-349-0291); **Four Roses Distillery Warehouse Operations**—Bottling done by hand, sweet aging Bourbon in white oak barrels (502-543-2264); **Guided Craft Tours**—Kentucky craft artists in their homes and studios (502-349-1777); **Heaven Hill Distilleries Bourbon Heritage Center**—High-tech interactive exhibits and theater (502-337-

1000); **Heaven Hill Distilleries Trolley**—A narrated, introductory tour of historic Bardstown and its attractions (800-638-4877); **My Old Kentucky Dinner Train**—Vintage 1940s dining cars carry passengers through scenic Kentucky countryside for lunch and dinner excursions (502-348-7300); **MY OLD KENTUCKY HOME STATE PARK**—Federal Hill was the inspiration for Stephen Foster's famous ballad, "My Old Kentucky Home." Costumed guides escort you through the stately mansion and formal gardens (502-348-3502); **Old Bardstown Village**—Authentic village of nine log cabins 150-200 years old (502-349-0291); **Old County Jail**—Original 1874 jail and restored Jailer's Inn (800-948-5551); **Oscar Getz Museum of Whiskey History & Bardstown Historical Museum**—Artifacts relating to distilleries, stills, cooperage, antique bottles and advertising art (502-348-2999); **Stephen Foster, The Musical**—Outdoor musical based on the life of America's first great composer. Features many of Foster's most popular songs (800-626-1563); **War Memorial of Mid-America**—Historic buildings feature artififacts from the Revolutionary War through Desert Storm (502-349-0291); **Wildlife/Natural History Museum**—North American animals in natural habitat, fossils and minerals from around the world (502-349-0291); **Women of the Civil War Museum**—Contributions of women during the Civil War (502-349-0291); (Bloomfield) **Springhill Winery**—Kentucky's Wine Heritage and tasting room (502-252-9463); (Nazareth) **Sisters of Charity of Nazareth**—Exhibits illustrate the role of this order in education, healthcare and social services (502-348-1500); (New Haven) **Kentucky Railway Museum**—Ride through the scenic and historic Rolling Fork River Valley on a restored passenger train (800-272-0152); (Trappist) **Abbey of Gethsemani**—The largest and America's oldest order of Cistercian Monks was founded in 1848. The monastery also produces cheese, fruitcake and bourbon fudge; burial site of Thomas Merton. (502-549-4406)

**BEDFORD AREA: Trimble County Tourist**

"Twin Spires, Churchill Downs"
*Source: Kentucky Department of Tourism*

**Commission** (502-255-7196); **Bray Orchards & Roadside Market** (502-255-3607)

**BRANDENBURG AREA: Meade County Tourism** (270-422-3967); **Buttermilk Falls**—Historic hiking trail in a beautiful natural setting (270-422-3626); **John Hunt Morgan Civil War Driving Trail**—Gen. John Hunt Morgan's ride through Meade County (270-422-3626); **Otter Creek Park**—2,600 acres of forest next to the Ohio River (502-574-4583)

**ELIZABETHTOWN/ RADCLIFF AREA-FORT KNOX: Elizabethtown Tourism & Convention Bureau** (800-437-0092); **Radcliff/Ft. Knox Convention & Tourism Commission** (800-834-7540); (Elizabethtown) **Black History Gallery**—Emma Reno Connor collection of the accomplishments and events pertinent to the Black American experience (270-769-5204); **Brown Pusey House**—Built in 1825, example of rural Federal architecture was known as "The Hill House," a boarding house and inn. It once housed Gen. George Custer and his wife in the 1870s (270-765-2515); **Costumed Historic Downtown Walking Tour**—Tour covers 25 historic sites with actors as characters like Sarah Bush Lincoln, Carry Nation, and General George Custer (800-437-0092); **Elizabethtown Historic Driving Tour**—Covering 36 historical sites (800-437-0092); **Har-**

din County History Museum—Story of Hardin County from early Indian inhabitants to modern times (270-763-8339); **Hardin County Schools Performing Arts Center** (270-769-8837); **Lincoln Heritage House**—Double log house crafted in part by Abraham Lincoln's father, Thomas Lincoln (270-765-2175); **Sarah Bush Johnston Lincoln Cabin**—Replica of Sarah Bush Johnston's cabin she lived in when she married Thomas Lincoln (270-765-2175); **Schmidt Museum of Coca-Cola Memorabilia**—World's largest privately owned collection of Coca-Cola memorabilia (270-234-1100); **Swope's Cars of Yesteryear Museum**—50 antique and classic cars (270-765-2181); (Fort Knox) **Patton Museum of Cavalry & Armor**—World-class U.S. Military Museum featuring the history of the Cavalry-Armor Forces including Gen. George S. Patton Jr.'s personal belongings (800-334-7540); (Glendale) **Antiques & Crafts in Historic Glendale**—Carriage rides (270-369-6188); (Radcliff) **Hardin County Playhouse**—Variety of shows (270-351-0577); **Saunders Springs Nature Preserve**—26 acres of hiking, biking and walking trails (800-334-7540); (West Point) **Bridges To The Past**—Walking trail over 3 stone bridges built prior to the Civil War (800-334-7540); **Fort Duffield**—Built in 1861 Kentucky's largest and best preserved Civil War earthen fortification with living history programs (502-922-4574); **Knob Creek Gun Range**—Recreational shooting year 'round, bi-annual Machine Gun Shoot draws 8-10,000 visitors from across the states and abroad (502-922-4457); **Music Ranch USA**—Country jamboree old time Rock, Blues, some Bluegrass and Gospel (502-922-9393); **Tioga Falls National Recreation Trail**—A scenic

**Abraham Lincoln Boyhood Home, National Historic Site, Hodgenville**
*Photo: Sid Webb*

and historic two-mile hike winding over Muldraugh Hill (800-334-7540)

**HODGENVILLE AREA:** **Larue County Chamber of Commerce** (270-358-3411); **Abraham Lincoln Birthplace National Historic Site**—Built at the location of Lincoln's birth, the solid marble, neoclassical monument houses the symbolic cabin of Lincoln's birth (270-358-3137); **Abraham Lincoln Boyhood Home**—Located in Knob Creek and now part of the National Park System as a unit of Abraham Lincoln Birthplace National Historic Site, the Lincoln family residence from 1811 to 1816 (270-358-3137); **Lincoln Jamboree**—Country music showplace (270-358-3545); **Lincoln Museum, Inc.**—Dioramas featuring wax figures trace Lincoln's life from birth to death (270-358-3163)

**IRVINGTON/HARDINSBURG AREA:** **Breckinridge County Tourism** (270-756-0268); (Cloverport) **Cloverport Community Museum**—Historic riverport town in Breckinridge County (270-788-5900); (Hardinsburg) **Breckinridge Co. Historical Society Museum**—Historic Taylor House (270-756-2867); (Irvington) **Broadmoor Gardens and Conservatory**—Kukenhoff Gardens in Holland was the inspiration for this garden, which includes water gardens, a tropical plant conservatory, a rock garden, animal topiaries, an iris garden, a lily garden, an all-white moon garden and a two-mile trail through wildflower meadows (270-547-4200)

**LAGRANGE AREA: Oldham County Tourist & Convention Commission** (800-813-9953); (Crestwood) **Duncan Memorial Chapel**—English Gothic Chapel is built of native stone and located in one of Kentucky's oldest cemeteries (502-241-8392); **Harrods Creek Baptist Church—Organized in 1797; registered on the National Historic Register of Historic Places (502-241-4983); **Yew Dell Gardens**— Rare garden plants and display gardens are one of only 12 American gardens designated as Partnership Gardens by the Garden Conservancy (502-241-4788); (Goshen) **Creasey Mahan Nature Preserve**—Encompasses 100 acres of nature trails, wildlife exhibits, and old springhouse and birds in the avian rehab program (502-228-4362); (La Grange) **Crawford Hot Air Balloons**—Scenic hot air balloon rides; **D.W. Griffith Site**—David Wark Griffith, an Oldham County native, is buried at Mt. Tabor Cemetery in Centerfield. The pioneer filmaker's Civil War epic, "Birth of a Nation," set a new standard for Hollywood in 1915; **Historic District of LaGrange**—Shops are housed in storefronts and homes circa 1840-1930 (502-269-0126); **Little Big Horse Trails** (502-222-1842); **Oldham County History Center** (502-222-0826); **Rob Morris Home**—Stately white frame house is the home of the founder of the Order of the East-

ern Star, Dr. Robert Morris (502-222-0248); (Pewee Valley) **Confederate Cemetery**—Site of the only state burial ground for Southern veterans of the Civil War; **Little Colonel Playhouse** (502-241-9906)

**LEBANON AREA: Lebanon Tourist & Convention Commission** (270-692-0021); (Bradfordsville) **William Clark Quantrill Civil War Driving Tour**—Posing as a Union soldier at times, Quantrill murdered and pillaged along with the James Brothers (270-337-3796); (Lebanon) **Cecil L. Gorley Trail**—3.2 mile naturalist walking trail (270-692-2491); **Goodin View Farm Store and Maze**—Fresh produce, farm raised shrimp, catfish, hybrid striped bass (270-692-0165); **Historic Homes & Landmarks Tour**—Self-guided and driving tours of homes with Civil War history (270-692-0021); **Lebanon Aquatic Center**—34 acre park featuring outdoor tennis and basketball courts, fitness trail, indoor pool, Outdoor 100' slide pool (270-692-6272); **Lebanon Civil War Park**—Major General George H. Thomas (Rock of Chickamauga) led Union forces from Lebanon to Mill Springs in January 1862, first major battle in Kentucky (270-692-6272); **Lebanon National Cemetery**—Built in 1863 to bury Union soldiers killed in Battle at Perryville, also veterans of WWI, WWII, Korean Conflict and Vietnam (270-692-3390); **Scenic Hwy & Byway US 68**—Historic trail used by notables like Andrew Jackson, Jane Todd Crawford and General Lafayette (270-692-0021); (Loretto) **Holy Cross Church**—Site of first Mass in Kentucky and first Catholic Church west of the Allegheny Mountains (270-865-2521) this 5,100 acre lake (270-257-2061); **Calvin Ray's Live Music-Family Entertainment**—Live entertainment with major headliners (270-879-0582); **Maker's Mark Distillery, National Historic Landmark**—Tour bourbon-making process in 19th century distillery, oldest operating (270-865-2099); (Nerinx) **Loretto Motherhouse**—One of the first religious orders of women west of the Allegheny Mountains. 1860 church, 1812 log cabin of founder Fr. Charles Nerinckx (270-865-5811)

**LEITCHFIELD AREA: Blackrock Motor Sports Park**—A statewide natural trained race track with national competitions (270-259-5960); **Grayson County Tourism Commission** (888-624-9951); (Caneyville) **Pine

Knob Theatre—Outdoor live 500-seat theatre (270-879-8190); (Clarkson) **Buck Country Outfitters**—Trophy deer and turkey outfitter offering guided hunts and lodging (270-242-9639); (Falls of Rough) **ROUGH RIVER DAM STATE RESORT PARK**—Surrounded by rolling countryside overlooking a 5,000 acre lake for fishing, jet skis, 18-hole and a 9-hole, par-three golf courses (800-325-1713); **Rough River Lake**—Rocky cliffs add to the beauty of the shoreline of Thomas House; **Grayson Co Historical Society**—Earliest brick house in Grayson County constructed circa 1814 by Jack Thomas (270-230-8989)

**LOUISVILLE AREA:** **Greater Louisville CVB** (888-LOUISVILLE); (Fairdale) **Jefferson County Memorial Forest**—Designated as a National Audubon Society Wildlife Refuge, the forest offers environmental education, adventure programs, hiking, climbing and wildlife watching (502-368-5404); (Harrods Creek) **C Q Princess**—85 foot luxury dinner yacht (502-228-1651); (Louisville) **Actors**

Copper Still,
**Maker's Mark Distillery in Loretto**
*Source: Kentucky Department of Tourism*

**Theatre of Louisville**—Award-winning professional stage company performing comedies, dramas, musicals and the internationally-celebrated Humana Festival of New American Plays (800-4-ATL-TIX); **American Printing House for the Blind**—World's largest company devoted solely to producing products for people who are blind or visually impaired. Founded in 1858, it is the oldest institution of its kind in the United States (800-223-1839); **Art Sparks Interactive Gallery**—Hands-on gallery dedicated to visual arts (502-634-2700); **Art! Art! Barking Dog Dance Company**—Professional modern dance repertory company (502-893-9966); **Belle of Louisville/Spirit of Jefferson**—The Belle of Louisville, built in 1914, is the oldest operating steam-driven paddlewheeler in the country. This beautiful national historic landmark offers sightseeing excursions Cruises originate at the downtown Louisville Wharf (866-832-0011); **Brennan Historic House and Medical Office Museum**—c. 1912 medical office museum, extensive collection of victorian furniture, art, sculpture, china and silver in a restored Italianate brick and limestone residence (502-540-5145); **Broad Run Vineyards**—Operated by three generations of the Kushner-Hyatt family (502-231-0372); **Buena Vista Carriage**—Horse drawn carriage rides through downtown Louisville and Ohio River waterfront (502-417-7109) **Callahan Museum**—Located at the American Printing House for the Blind, history of the education of people who are blind (800-223-1839); **Cathedral of the Assumption**—Recently restored 1852 Cathedral (502-582-2971); **CenterStage Theatre at Jewish Community Center** (502-238-2720); **Churchill Downs**—Officially opened in 1875, became the World's Most Legendary Racetrack and "Home of the Kentucky Derby"

(800-283-3729); **Comedy Caravan**—Award winning comedy theater featuring national touring professional comedians (502-459-0022); **Conrad-Caldwell House Museum**—1895 mansion is among the most ornate in the Old Louisville area (502-636-5023); **Creative Diversity Art Studio**—A venue where artists with disabilities can express, expand and nurture their artistic potential in collaboration with other artists (502-767-4723); **E.P. "TOM" SAWYER STATE PARK**—This 500-acre park is a mecca for indoor and outdoor recreation enthusiasts. Summer aquatics program or one of the team sports scheduled year-round in the park's gymnasium. The park has an outstanding BMX track where the BMX Nationals are held (502-429-7270)

**Embroiderers' Guild of America, Inc.**—The

Reenactors from Historic Locust Grove, the last home of Gen. George Rogers Clark, entertained guests of The Clark Group on the Belle of Louisville on September 26, 2006. The special event was a celebration of the Second Edition of Clark's Kentucky Almanac. Robert Pilkington portrayed explorer William Clark; his sister, Lucy Clark Croghan, mistress of Locust Grove, portrayed by Amanda Dick; Ann Clark Gwathmey & her husband, Owen Gwathmey, played by Janice Sidebottom and James Eiler. The young lady from the neighboring plantation, Springfield, is Sarah Knox Taylor, daughter of Zachary Taylor.
*Photo: Sid Webb*

Margaret Parshall Gallery features exhibits of needlework, library and antique tool display (502-589-6956); **Farmington Historic Home**—Designed from a plan by Thomas Jefferson and completed in 1816 using slave labor, the 14-room house is furnished with antiques from the period. A summer kitchen, springhouse, stone barn, and a recreated early 19th century garden are located on the 18-acre grounds. Abraham Lincoln, a close friend of Speed's son Joshua, spent about three weeks at Farmington in 1841 (502-452-9920); **Filson Historical Society**—Offering an extensive library, museum and a special collections department, the Society is headquartered in the Ferguson Mansion (502-635-5083); **Frazier Historical Arms Museum**—1000 years of history (866-886-7103); **Gheens Science Hall and Rauch Planetarium**—Public astronomy programs, a star show and three different laser light shows (502-852-6664); **Glassworks**—Glass artists and galleries, providing visitors with a rich portrayal of the magic, mystery and beauty of glass (502-584-4510); **Historic Locust Grove**—The ca.1790 Georgian house was the last home of Revolutionary War hero General George Rogers Clark, whose campaign doubled the size of the U.S. The site features nine outbuildings, restored gardens, a museum gallery and museum store (502-897-9845) (See Coupon below); **Hite Art Institute Galleries**—University gallery (502-852-4483); **Iroquois Amphitheater**—Open-air, state-of-the-art proscenium theater on a hillside (502-368-5865); **Kentucky Center for African-American Heritage**—The theme "One More River to Cross" is the state's preeminent black history museum and educational center (502-583-4100); **Kentucky Derby Museum**—Located at Gate 1 of historic Churchill Downs, the museum presents the traditions and excitement of the "greatest two minutes in sports." (502-637-1111); **Kentucky Museum of Art and Craft**—One of the largest selections of handmade Kentucky arts and crafts in the region; museum features 4 exhibition galleries and a permanent collection (800-446-0102); **Little Loom House**—Keeping the art of hand-weaving and its history alive;

housed in three century-old cabins listed on the National Register of Historic Places (502-367-4792); **Louisville Ballet**—The state ballet of Ky., offers classical, neo-classical, and contemporary dance (502-583-3150); **Louisville Bats Professional Baseball**—See advertisement in Sports—Professional baseball. Triple A affiliate of the Cincinnati Reds (502-212-2287); **Louisville Extreme Park**—

**Historic Locust Grove**
*Photo: Sid Webb*

Bikes and Blades extreme park (502-456-8100); **Louisville Free Public Library Galleries**—Free exhibitions and programs on art, culture, books, communications, social and cultural issues (502-574-1600); **Louisville Horse Trams**—Horse and carriage rides in downtown Louisville (502-581-0100); **Louisville Orchestra**—Classical Concert Series, Coffee Concert Series, NightLites Concert Series, Pops Series, Family Concert Series and Summer Concert Series (800-775-7777); **Louisville Science Center & IMAX Theatre**—Engaging hands-on exhibits and an

incredible film in the four-story IMAX Theatre (800-591-2203); **Louisville Slugger Museum & Factory**—Home of the World's Biggest Baseball Bat; bat factory tour (877-775-8443);**Louisville Stoneware**—One of America's oldest producers of hand-made and hand-painted stoneware; retail gift shop, seconds, paint your own pottery and museum (800-626-1800); **Louisville Visual Art Association**—Contemporary visual art center (502-896-2146); **Louisville Zoo**—Over 1,300 animals in natural exhibits with exotic plants throughout the 134-acre zoo, amid rolling hills in the heart of Louisville (502-459-2181); **McAlpine Locks and Dam**—Constructed in 1961-64 by the U.S. Army Corps of Engineers, the dam is 8,627 ft. long and has 9 gates, 22 ft. x 100 ft (502-774-3517); **Muhammad Ali Center**—See advertisement in Sports—An education and cultural center designed to preserve and share the legacy of Muhammad Ali, and further promote respect, hope and understanding across cultural and geographic borders (800-626-5646); **Music Theatre Louisville** (502-589-4060); **Pleiades Theatre Company**—Louisville's premiere Women's Theatre Company (502-637-3064); **Portland Museum**—Showcases Portland and Louisville's river history with an animatronic robot of the first female steamboat captain Mary Miller (502-776-7678); **Riverside, The Farnsley-Moremen Landing**—300-acre historic site is an 1837 Kentucky "I-House" (502-935-6809); **S.A.R. Historical Museum**—National head-

quarters of the Sons of the American Revolution (502-589-1776); **Six Flags Kentucky**

Louisville Slugger Museum & Factory
Photo: Sid Webb

**Kingdom**—Theme and water park located in the heart of Louisville features more than 110 rides and attractions (800-727-3267); **Speed Art Museum**—Holdings include 17th century

Dutch and Flemish paintings, European tapestries and contemporary art (502-634-2700); **Squallis Puppeteers**—Offers arts opportunities (502-544-1299); **Stage One**—Entertaining and professional theatre for the young (800-775-7777); **The Kentucky Center**—Performances in

Covered bridge near Springfield
*Photo: Sid Webb*

the grand Whitney Hall, the intimate Bomhard Theater, the ever-changing Boyd Martin Experimental Theater or the restored W.L. Lyons Brown Theatre (800-775-7777); **The Spirit**—A replica of the fabled river boats of by-gone days (866-832-0011); **Thomas Edison House**—A museum located in an 1850s house where Edison boarded while working as telegrapher in 1866-1867 (502-585-5247); **Whitehall Historic Home**—Built in 1855 and situated on 8.5 acres of grounds and gardens (502-897-2944); **Zachary Taylor National Cemetery**—National Historic Landmark includes the graves of Pres. and Mrs. Zachary Taylor (1784-1850), 12th president of the U.S. (502-893-3852)

**NEW CASTLE AREA: Henry County Chamber of Commerce** (502-845-0806); (New Castle) **Lake Jericho Recreation Area**—137-acre lake with picnic and camping (502-743-5205); **Smith-Berry Vineyard and Winery** (502-845-7091); (Smithfield) **Our Best Restaurant**—Traditional southern items (502-845-7682)

**SHELBYVILLE AREA: Shelbyville/Shelby County Visitors Bureau** (800-680-6388); **American Saddlebred Horse Farm Tours**—

Shelby County has been called "The Saddlebred Capital of the World," with American Saddlebred breeding and training facilities (502-633-6388); **Buffalo Crossing Restaurant and Fun Ranch**—A 1,000-acre working bison farm and attraction with petting zoo, lakes and playgrounds (877-700-0047); **Clear Creek Family Activity Center**—Indoor competition and children's splash pool, walking/running track, gymnasium, game room and outdoor splash pool with water slide (502-633-5059); **Lake Shelby**—Restored authentic log cabin homestead. Near historic site of Squire Boone's Painted Stone Station (502-633-5059); **Wakefield-Scearce Galleries**—Over 30,000 square feet featuring English Antiques, located in Historic Science Hill Girl's School (502-633-4382)

**SHEPHERDSVILLE AREA: Shepherdsville/Bullitt Co. Tourist & Convention Commission** (800-526-2068); (Clermont) **Bernheim Arboretum and Research Forest**—14,000 acres including a 250-acre arboretum with over 2,800 trees and shrubs labeled, a fishing lake, biking and over 50 miles of hiking trails (502-955-8512); **Jim Beam American Outpost**—World-famous Jim Beam Distillery (502-543-9877); (Lebanon Junction) **Junction Jamboree**—Rated the Number One Country Music stage show in Kentucky (502-833-0800); (Shepherdsville) **Bullitt County History Museum**—Located in

**Architectural Antiques, Louisville**
*Photo: Sid Webb*

the century-old front portion of the county courthouse (502-921-0161); **C.R. Wilson Bluegrass Friday Night**—Bluegrass music for the entire family (502-239-8004); **Hawks View Gallery**—Watch as artists create exquisite glass-blown art from start to finish (502-955-1010); **Kart Kountry**—Over 1.5 miles long go-kart track, miniature golf course, batting cages and bumper boats (502-543-9588); **Old Stone Bank**—Built in 1830, this bank is believed to be the first west of the Alleghenies (800-526-2068); **Old Stone Jail**—Built in 1891 and used until 1947 (800-526-2068); Woodsdale One-Room Schoolhouse—Built in 1808, the Schoolhouse represents 145 years of continuous teaching (800-526-2068)

**SPRINGFIELD AREA: Springfield/Washington County Chamber of Commerce** (859-336-3810); (Mt. Zion) **Mt. Zion Covered Bridge**—One of the longest multi-span bridges in Kentucky, built 1871-72; (Springfield) **1851 Historic Maple Hill Manor B&B, Alpaca Farm and Handcrafted Gift Shop**—14 acres includes an orchard of 100+ fruit trees, 200+ raspberry bushes, a nature preserve, alpacas, llamas and pygmy goats (800-886-7546); **LINCOLN HOMESTEAD STATE PARK**—The same spirit of adventure that brought other pioneers to Kentucky led Abraham Lincoln's grandparents to the knolls of Kentucky near the Beech Fork River. The park features the original home of Lincoln's mother, replicas of the 1782 cabin and blacksmith shop where his father was reared and learned his trade, and the home of Mordecai Lincoln, the favorite uncle of the President. Also has a 18-hole golf course (859-336-7461); **Rolling Hills Vineyard and Winery**—(859-262-6154); **St. Catherine Motherhouse**—Home of the first U.S. community of Dominican Sisters (859-336-9303); **St. Rose Proto-Priory**—The first Catholic educational institution west of the Alleghenies (859-336-3121); **Washington County Courthouse**—Completed in 1816, it houses the marriage documents of Abraham Lincoln's parents, Nancy Hanks and Thomas Lincoln. This is the oldest courthouse still in continuous use in Kentucky (859-336-5425); (Willisburg) **Willisburg Lake/Captain Bob's Boat Dock**—Man-made fishing with launching ramp, boat rentals and camping (859-375-0093)

**TAYLORSVILLE AREA: Taylorsville/Spencer County Economic Development Authority** (502-477-3246); **Taylorsville Lake**—Fishing, picnicking and hiking with historic log structures (502-477-8882); **TAYLORSVILLE LAKE STATE PARK**—The campground at this park is a home base from which anglers vie for bass, bluegill and crappie in the 3,050- acre lake. The park has horse campsites and trails for hiking, horseback riding and biking. (502-477-8713)

**Lincoln Homestead**
*Photo: Sid Webb*

# Bluegrass Region

**BEREA/RICHMOND AREA: Berea Tourist Commission** (800-598-5263); **Richmond Tourism Commission** (800-866-3705); (Berea) **Berea Welcome Center**—A must-see stop in the arts and crafts capital of the Commonwealth (800-598-5263); (Richmond) **Acres of Land Winery, Inc** (866-714-WINE); **Battle of Richmond Driving Tour**—Part of the National Trust Civil War Discovery Trail and the Civil War Battle of Richmond (800-866-3705); **Berea Trail**—A driving trail that highlights the cultural heritage and craftsmanship of the artisans in the area (859-622-8439); **Bybee Pottery**—Oldest pottery west of the Alleghenies, handmade crude stoneware (859-369-5350) **Central Kentucky Wildlife Management Area**—1,688 acres with three lakes with regulated hunting and fishing, skeet shooting, field trail and trap shooting (800-858-1549); **Churchill Weavers**—83-year old loom house and gift shop (859-986-3127) **Deer Run Stables L.L.C.**—Horseback riding, trail rides, pony rides, hayrides, bonfires, picnics, and rustic camping. Riding les-

**Churchill Weavers, Berea**
*Source: Tour Southern & Eastern Kentucky*

sons (859-527-6339); **Eastern Kentucky University Hummel Planetarium**—Experience the wonders that await us at the center of the galaxy or simply view the beauty of the sky above us (800-465-9191); **Estill Trail**—Highlights the cultural heritage and craftsmanship of the artisans in the area (859-622-8439); **FORT BOONESBOROUGH STATE PARK**—Daniel Boone reached the Kentucky River on April 1, 1775 and established Kentucky's second settlement. The fort was reconstructed as a working fort complete with cabins, blockhouses and furnishings. Resident artisans, in period clothing, perform craft demonstrations and impart pioneer experiences to modern-day visitors. The Kentucky River Museum in the historic Lockmaster's house on Lock and Dam 10 provides personal glimpses into the lives of families who lived on the river and worked the locks and dams in the 1900s. Camping and swimming pool complex with a water slide. (859-527-3131); **Historic Downtown Richmond**—Over 100 buildings on the National

Register of Historic Places and three National Register Historic Districts (800-866-3705); **Irvinton House Museum** (859-626-1422); **Kentucky Artisan Center**—Showcases and sells Kentucky's outstanding arts, crafts, music, publications and more, and provides travel information about cultural heritage sites (859-985-5448); **Kentucky Artisan Heritage Trails**—The trails include local culture and scenic beauty. Explore quaint towns and rural byways, shop in artisan studios (859-622-8439); **Lake Reba Recreational Complex**—Golf course, fishing, biking, boating, golf and nature trails (859-623-8753); **Richmond Area Arts Center** (859-624-4242); **Richmond Cemetery**—Graves of U.S Rep. Daniel Breck, Cassius M. Clay and tombstones of Civil War Battle of Richmond soldiers (859-623-2529); **Richmond Raceway**—Stock car racing (859-623-9408); **Valley View Ferry**—Kentucky's oldest continuous business, dating back to 1785 (859-258-3611); **WHITE HALL STATE HISTORIC SITE**—Home of Cassius Marcellus Clay – emancipationist, newspaper publisher, Minister to Russia, and friend to Abraham Lincoln. Clay's daughter, Laura Clay, was born at White Hall in 1849 and was politically active for women's suffrage and states' rights. In 1920, Laura Clay became the first woman to be nominated for U.S. President by a major political party. This restored 44-room Italianate mansion was built in 1799 and remodeled in the 1860s. (859-623-9178)

**CARLISLE AREA:** Carlisle/Nicholas County Tourism (859-289-5174); **BLUE LICKS BATTLE-FIELD STATE RESORT PARK**—The salt springs at Blue Licks attracted prehistoric animals, American Indians, pioneers and 19th-century Southerners who came for the therapeutic waters. Blue Licks was also the site of the last Revolutionary War battle in Kentucky, in 1782. Visit the Pioneer Museum to learn more about the fascinating history of Blue Licks. (859-289-5507); **Carnico Lake**—Beautiful man-made lake with beach, fishing and boating

(859-289-7008); **Jailer's Home & Dungeon**—Home built in 1820-24, dungeon cells built 1857 and housed prisoners in the 1850-1890s (859-234-5236); **Nicholas County Depot & Museum**—built 1910 (859-289-4720); **The Mercury Building**—Restored 1820s house began as a saddlery shop and home of the Carlisle Mercury newspaper (859-289-4720)

**CYNTHIANA AREA: Cynthiana/Harrison County Chamber of Commerce** (859-234-5236); **Cynthiana Harrison County Museum**—Historical museum includes items from the Civil War particularly Battles of Cynthiana (859-234-7179); **Quiet Trails State Nature Preserve** (859-234-5382); **Mamas Gone Wild**—Traveling petting zoo with llamas, miniature horses, sheep, rabbits, birds and more (859-234-8664)

**DANVILLE AREA:** Danville/Boyle County CVB (800-755-0076); **Amish/Mennonite Shops**—Farm landscapes, and shops with produce and handmade products (800-755-0076); **Chateau du Vieux Corbeau Winery/Elements Pottery**—Wine tasting and retail purchase. Elements Pottery Studio, hiking trails and the Crow-Barbee House,

**Reenactment of Battle of Blue Licks**
*Photo: Sid Webb*

circa 1780 (859-236-1808); **Central Kentucky Wildlife Refuge**—Six trails for hiking, photography, painting, and nature study enriching to individuals or groups (800-755-0076); **Community Arts Center** (859-236-4054); **CONSTITUTION SQUARE HISTORIC SITE**—Preserves a series of events in Kentucky's history: the constitutional conventions that preceded statehood. For eight years the frontier statesmen who lived in what was then the Kentucky County of Virginia struggled for independence. Finally, on June 1, 1792 Kentucky became the 15th state in the Union and Isaac Shelby, a Revolutionary War hero and convention delegate, was named the first governor. Visit Grayson's Tavern and the first post office west of the Alleghenies; and replicas of the jail, courthouse and meeting house

(859-239-7089); **Isaac Shelby Cemetery State**—Grave of Isaac Shelby, (1750-1826) Kentucky's esteemed first and fifth governor. Shelby is buried at his estate, Traveller's Rest (859-239-7089); **Historic Penn's Store**—A store site since 1845, in the Penn family since 1850. America's oldest country store still in ownership and operation by the same family (800-755-0076); **JFC Museum**—Collections of fossils, rocks, minerals and war memorabilia (800-755-0076); **John W.D. Bowling Model Railroad Museum**—Train layout contains 2,100 linear feet of track and 1.5 miles of wiring. 6,000 handmade trees 1,200 figures, and 160 Structures, it is the largest privately-held permanent layout in Kentucky (859-236-8954); **Kentucky School for the Deaf**—Opened in 1823, Jacobs Hall is the oldest surviving building, constructed in 1855-57 of Italianate design by architect Thomas Lewinski (859-239-7017); **Lightning Valley Motor Sports Park**—Go-Karts (800-755-0076); **McDowell House and Apothecary Shop**—On Christmas Day 1809, the first abdominal surgery was performed by Dr. Ephraim McDowell removing a tumor without anesthetic, from Jane Todd Crawford (859-236-2804); **Norton Center for the Arts**—Designed by a member of the Frank Lloyd Wright Foundation (877-448-7469); **PERRYVILLE BATTLEFIELD STATE HISTORIC SITE**—On October 8, 1862, the rural peace of this tranquil countryside was shattered by cannon explosions and the death moans of young soldiers. Perryville became the site of the most destructive Civil War battle in the state which left more than 6,000 killed, wounded or missing. The park museum tells of the battle that was the South's last serious attempt to gain possession of Kentucky. The battlefield is one of the most unaltered Civil War sites in the nation (859-332-8631); **Pioneer Playhouse Outdoor Dinner Theatre**—Kentucky's original outdoor dinner theater with a New York-based cast (859-236-2747); **The Wilderness Trace Art League Gallery**—Original arts & crafts, created by local artists in a historical building; **West T. Hill Community Theatre**—community theatre, with musicals, dramas, comedies and children workshops

**FRANKFORT AREA: Frankfort/ County Tourism & Convention Commission** (800-960-7200); **A Little Bit Of Heaven Riding Stables**—Trail rides and lessons (502-223-8925); **Bluegrass Theatre Guild**—

**Reenactment of the Battle of Richmond**
*Photo: Sid Webb*

Community theatre (502-223-7529); **Buffalo Trace Distillery**—Distilling began two centuries ago making it the oldest distilling site in the U.S.; set on 110 acres Buffalo Trace Distillery provides for the complete production of whiskeys (800-654-8471); **Canoe Kentucky**—Water adventures and training

on kayaks and canoes (888-226-6359); **Capital City Museum** (502-696-0607); **Country Place Jamboree**—Country music both new and old (502-223-3776); **Daniel Boone's Grave, Frankfort Cemetery**—Gravesite of Daniel and Rebecca Boone, Paul Sawyier, Joel T. Hart, Theodore O'Hara, Vice President Richard M. Johnson, and 17 Kentucky Governors (502-227-2403); **Downtown Frankfort Walking Tour**—Over 70 sites in historic downtown (502-696-0607); **Floral Clock**—Planted with thousands of colorful flowering plants, the face of this clock is 34 feet in diameter and located on the historic Capitol grounds (502-564-3449); **Frank Lloyd Wright's Zeigler House**—Designed for Rev. Jesse R. Zeigler in 1910. National Register (502-875-8687); **Governor's Mansion**—The

**Daniel Boone's Grave**
**Frankfort**
*Photo: Gene Burch*

**Inside Switzer Covered Bridge, Franklin County**
*Photo: Sid Webb*

Archives (502-564-8300); **Kentucky Department of Fish & Wildlife Game Farm**—132-acre recreational/education complex with two fishing lakes, songbird area, small wetland, and Salato Wildlife Education Center (502-564-7863); **Kentucky Military History Museum**—Located in the Old State Arsenal, with historic firearms, edged weapons, artillery, uniforms, flags and personal equipment (502-564-3265); **Kentucky State Capitol**—Completed in 1910 in the Beaux Arts design contains the First Lady Doll Collection (502-564-3449); **Kentucky Vietnam Veteran's Memorial**—The names of the Kentuckians killed in Vietnam are etched in granite beneath the memorial sundial, with the point of the gnomon's shadow actually touching the veteran's name of the anniver-

official governor's residence since 1914, the Beaux Arts mansion, constructed of native limestone, was modeled after the Petit Trianon, Marie Antoinette's summer villa (502-564-8004); **Greenhill Cemetary**—Only monument in the state and one of only 4 in the nation honoring Kentucky's African American Civil War Soldiers (502-564-7005); **Kentucky Department for Libraries & Archives**—Past and present meet in the Cooper Building, which houses the Kentucky Department for Libraries and

sary of his death. Recognized as one of the most original and unusual memorials in the nation; **LIBERTY HALL HISTORIC SITE**—300 Coffee Tree Rd, Georgian house built in 1796 by John Brown, one of Ky.'s first two U.S. Senators (888-516-5101); **Old Governor's Mansion**—The oldest official executive residence in the U.S. still in use. The federal-style mansion was home to 33 Kentucky governors from 1798-1914. Seven U.S. presidents have visited (502-564-8004); **Old State Capitol**—This national

landmark was Kentucky's seat of government from 1831-1910. Greek Revival structure includes a unique, self-supporting staircase held together by preci-

Lexington Art League exhibit at Loudon House
Photo: Sid Webb

sion and pressure (502-564-1792); **Orlando Brown House**—The Greek-Revival Orlando Brown House (1835) is a residence designed by Kentucky's most famous architect, Gideon Shryock. Part of Liberty Hall Historic Site (888-516-5101); **Rebecca Ruth Candy Factory Tours**—"Inventors of Bourbon Candy," began nearly a century ago in 1919 by two women, Rebecca and Ruth (800-444-3766); **Salato Wildlife Education Center**—An educational center with interactive and interpretive exhibits featuring native plants and animals (800-858-1549); **Starway Family Fun Park**—Miniature golf course features waterfalls, streams and bridges and New Rookie karts for younger driver (502-227-1864); **Switzer Covered Bridge**—One of Kentucky's few covered bridges, was built in 1855. Totally restored after floodwaters destroyed bridge; **Thomas D. Clark Center for Kentucky History**—Hands-on activities, interactive exhibits and dynamic collections. Research library contains unique genealogical records for tracing Kentucky ancestors (502-564-1792); **Vest-Lindsey House**—Early 19th century Federal house was home to U.S. Senator George Graham Vest (502-564-6980)

**GEORGETOWN AREA:** Georgetown/Scott County Tourist Commission (888-863-8600); **Amerson Farm Orchard & Winery**—Produce farm, and orchard with garden center and greenhouses

offers delicious seasonal fruits and vegetables, garden plants, and crafts (502-863-3799); **Bi-Water Farm**—seasonal fruits and vegetables and crafts (502-863-3676); **Cardome Centre**—Divided into four basic phases: the earliest years, the Chambers/Robinson years, the Academy years, and the present (502-863-1575); **Cincinnati Bengals Partnership/Georgetown College**—NFL's Cincinnati Bengal's Summer Training Camp at Georgetown College. The only NFL Training Camp in Kentucky (502-868-6300); **Doublestink Hog Farm**—Kids activities on the farm (502-868-9703); **Evans Orchard & Cider Mill, LLC**—Gourmet apples, corn maze, fresh cider and homegrown products (502-863-2255); **Factory Stores of America**—Outlet Mall in Georgetown with over 20 Stores (502-868-0682); **Georgetown & Scott Co Museum**—Located in the former U.S. Post Office (502-863-6201); **Georgetown College**—Founded in 1829 and the oldest Baptist college west of the Alleghenies. The Anne Wright Wilson Fine Arts Building houses one of Central Kentucky's largest galler-

**John Hunt Morgan statue in front of Lexington History Museum**
Photo: Sid Webb

**Bust of Henry Clay**
*Photo: Sid Webb*
*Source: History Museum, Lexington*

ies (800-788-9985); **Toyota Motor Manufacturing KY**—Watch Toyota vehicles from stamping to final inspection (800-866-4485); **Ward Hall**—The largest Greek Revival house in Kentucky and the finest example of Greek Revival Architecture in the south. Prior to 1884, the Kentucky Legislature considered using this great house for the State Capitol (888-863-8600); **Whispering Woods Riding Stables**—12 wonderful horses, 250 acres of woods, creeks and ponds (502-570-9663); **Yuko-En on the Elkhorn**—Official Ky./Japan friendship garden, nearly 6 acres including waterfalls, Koi ponds, arched bridges and Kazan sculpture (502-316-4554)

**HARRODSBURG AREA: Harrodsburg/Mercer County Tourist Commission** (800-355-9192); **Big Red Stables**—Horseback riding on 1,000 acres of lush bluegrass farmlands (859-734-3118); **Canaan Land Farm**—A working sheep farm, this 18th century homestead has a historic wagon road and one of the earliest brick homes in the state (888-734-3984); **Dixie Belle Riverboat at Shaker Village**—The Dixie Belle Riverboat offers public excursions on the Kentucky River along the scenic palisades (800-734-5611); **Downtown Historic District**—Most of the preserved buildings within this National Register of Historic Places District date back to the 1880s and 1890s, walking tours (859-734-2364); **Harrodsburg Historical Society Morgan Row**—Oldest row house in Kentucky (859-734-5985); **OLD FORT HARROD STATE PARK**—In 1774, James Harrod established the first permanent settlement west of the Alleghenies. The fort has been reconstructed near the site of the original. Heavy timbers form stockade walls and enclose the cabins and blockhouses. Craftspeople, dressed in period clothing, perform pioneer tasks such as woodworking, weaving, basketry and blacksmithing and tend the farm animals and gardens. The Lincoln Marriage Temple shelters the original log cabin where Abraham Lincoln's parents were married on June 12, 1806. The Mansion Museum houses Civil War artifacts, an outstanding historical gun display, Native American artifacts and a Lincoln collection. (859-734-3314); **Olde Towne Park**—Includes a unique sculptured 14 x 32 foot cascading fountain, inspired by the dramatic limestone gorge of the Kentucky River known as the "Palisades" (800-355-9192); **Shaker Village of Pleasant Hill**—A premier living history site with 2,900 acres where costumed interpreters chronicle Shaker life and the village has 34 restored buildings. Skilled artisans work at 19th-century trades and historic farming brings the past to life. Riverboat excursions and horse-drawn carriage rides (800-734-5611)

**LANCASTER AREA: Garrard County Chamber of Commerce** (859-792-2282); **Garrard County Jail Museum** (859-792-3065); **Pleasant Retreat Governor William Owsley House**—Ca. 1804, the restored and furnished home of Ky.'s 16th governor, William Owsley (859-792-2500)

**LAWRENCEBURG AREA: Anderson County Chamber of Commerce** (502-839-5564); **Four Roses Distillery LLC**—Tour distillery that was built in the Spanish architectural style (502-839-3436); **Fair Winds At Beaver Lake Inc**—Lake

**Fort Boonesborough**
*Source: Kentucky Department of Tourism*

fishing, camping and a bait and tackle shop (502-839-4402); **Lover's Leap Vineyard and Winery**—Largest vineyard in the state with national award winning wines (502-839-1299); **Wild Turkey-Austin Nichols Distillery**—Home of well-known 101 proof bourbon Wild Turkey (502-839-4544)

**LEXINGTON AREA: Lexington Convention and Visitors Bureau (800-845-3959); Actors' Guild of Lexington**—Contemporary theatre (859-233-7330); **American Saddlebred Museum**—Dedi-

**Keeneland Race Course and Red Mile Harness Track**
*Photos: Sid Webb*

cated to Kentucky's oldest native breed of horse, the American Saddlebred (800-829-4438); **Ashland, The Henry Clay Estate**—This National Historic Landmark houses the Henry Clay Memorial Foundation with a rare collection comprised almost exclusively of original Clay family items (859-266-8581); **Aviation Museum of Kentucky**—Various historical aircraft and interactive displays (859-231-1219); **Blue Grass Tours**—Visit historic Calumet Farm, Keeneland Race Course, Kentucky Horse Park and the famous Man O'War Statue, Thoroughbred Park and historic highlights in downtown Lexington (800-755-6956); **BOONE STATION HISTORIC SITE**—Daniel Boone left Fort Boonesborough and established a pioneer station on this site in 1779. Located north of the Kentucky River, near what is today the town of Athens, the settlement was home to 15 or 20 families in the early 1780s. However, the Boone family suffered many hardships during the three years they lived here, including the deaths of their son Israel and their nephew Thomas at the Battle of Blue Licks. Daniel

**Lexington Public Library**
*Photo: Sid Webb*

Boone's brother, Samuel, is buried at Boone Station (859-527-3131); **Center for Old Music in the New World**—Performance of early music mostly pre-1750 (859-269-2908); **Chrisman Mill Winery & Friends**—Wines, jewelry, gourmet foods, gifts and many Kentucky-made products (859-276-0032); **Explorium of Lexington**—Nine discovery zones with interactive exhibits designed to inspire imagination and curiosity, kids of all ages (859-258-3253); **Flag Fork Herb Farm, Inc**—Restaurant, gourmet food items, crafted items and herbal gardening supplies (859-233-7381); **Gratz Park**—Historic park in downtown Lexington, surrounded by historic homes (Market & Mill); **Headley-Whitney Museum**—Features a diverse collection of objects and hosts international and regional exhibitions (859-255-6653); **Hunt Morgan House & Civil War Museum**—Federal home built in 1814 by John Wesley Hunt, the first millionaire of the new West. John Hunt Morgan, "The Thunderbolt of the Confederacy," and Nobel Prize-winner Thomas Hunt Morgan also resided here; includes local Civil War memorabilia (859-253-0362); **Keeneland Race Course**—Live thoroughbred horse racing (800-456-3412); **Kentucky Horse Park**—Only park of its kind in the world, working horse farm/educational theme park and equine competition facility, more than 1,200 acres, features nearly 50 different breeds of horses (800-678-8813); **Kentucky Theater**—Historic restored theater shows classic, modern and foreign films (859-231-6997); **Latrobe's Pope Villa**—One of three remaining examples of domestic design by B. H. Latrobe, one of the architects of our nation's capitol (859-253-0362); **Lexington Art League**—The Loudoun House is the home for promoting the visual arts (800-914-7990); **Lexington Cemetery**—Historic cemetery (859-255-5522); **Lexington Center/Rupp Arena**—Downtown complex with hotel, retail center, convention halls, and Rupp Arena, home of UK Men's Basketball (859-233-4567); **Lexington Children's Theatre**—Nationally recognized professional theatre (800-928-4545); **Lexington History Museum**—Regional history museum featuring changing exhibits with emphasis on Blue-

grass history, equine, early African-American life (859-254-0530); **Lexington Legends**—Lexington's professional baseball team, a Class A affiliate of the Houston Astros; includes the Kentucky Baseball Hall of Fame Museum (859-252-4487); **Lexington Livery Horse Drawn Carriage Tours** (859-259-0000); **Lexington Opera House**—Built in 1886, offers national touring productions, local music & theatre performances (859-233-4567); **Lexington Philharmonic**—Music Director George Zack (888-494-4226); **Lexington Public Library**—The world's largest ceiling clock, a 74-foot-long Foucault pendulum (859-231-5500); **Loudoun House**—Art Gallery (800-914-7990); **Mary Todd House**—The girlhood home of Mary Todd Lincoln, America's First Lady (859-233-9999); **Raven Run Nature Sanctuary**—A 470+ acre nature sanctuary with 10

miles of trails (859-272-6105); **Red Mile Harness Track**—The oldest (1875) harness track in Kentucky. Site of the Kentucky Futurity, final jewel of trotting triple crown (859-255-0752); **Talon Winery and Vineyards**—Located at historic Fair View Farm in the original 18th century farmhouse (859-971-3214); **The Arboretum**—Features a one-and-a-half acre home demonstration garden (859-257-6955); **The Thoroughbred Center**—Observe trainers with their horses (859-293-1853); **Thoroughbred Park**—2.5 acre park dedicated to the Thoroughbred industry. Seven life-size bronze horses racing to the finish line (859-288-2900); **University of Kentucky Art Museum**—Permanent collection of more than 3,800 European and American paintings, sculptures, prints, drawings, photographs and decorative arts (859-257-5716); **University of Kentucky Basketball Museum**—Relive moments of UK basketball history (800-269-1953); **WAVELAND STATE HISTORIC SITE**—Waveland exemplifies plantation life in Kentucky in the 19th-century; from the acres of grain and hemp waving in the breeze (hence the Waveland name), to the raising and racing of blooded trotting horse. The outbuildings of Waveland, the slave quarters, smokehouses, and icehouses, are important re-minders of the social and economic climate of the time. Today, Waveland prides itself not only as one of Kentucky's best examples of the Greek Revival style, but as a living house museum. (859-272-3611); **Woodsongs Old Time Radio Hour**—Featuring grassroots independent artists from Appalachia and around the world; broadcasts across the U.S. and internationally (859-252-8888)

**NICHOLASVILLE AREA: Nicholasville Tourism Commission** (859-887-7091); **Camp Nelson Civil War Heritage Park**—Union Army Civil War supply depot & training camp. White House, c. 1850, used as the officers' quarters by Union troops during the Civil War, 10,000 African American men gained their freedom at Camp Nelson. **Camp Nelson National Cemetery**—Begun in 1867 with over 2,200 Civil War soldiers buried (859-881-5727); **Chrisman Mill Vineyards & Winery** (859-881-5007); **Harry C. Miller Lock Collection**—America's most comprehensive collection of safe locks (866-LSI-TRAIN); **High Bridge Park**—Eleven-acre park with reconstructed 1879 pavilion and overlook. Site overlooks Kentucky River, Palisades and historic railroad trestle (859-881-9126); **Hickman Creek Nature and Conference Center**—Historic site on Hickman Creek and palisades with log cabins

(859-881-9126); **Jim Beam Nature Preserve** (859-259-9655); **Kentucky River Palisades**—Dramatic cliffs of the palisades is home to at least 25 mammal species and 35 reptile species, two endangered bats, the Gray bat and Indiana bat. It also has the largest concentration of rare plant species (859-881-9126); **Oliver Perry House**—Circa 1850 building constructed by Oliver Perry. Confiscated by Union Army for Civil War 1863-1865 (859-885-5716); **Sugar Creek Re-**

Pisgah Church
*Photo: Sid Webb*

Rebuilding dry stack walls
along Paris Pike
*Photo: Sid Webb*

**sort**—Horseback riding, hiking, tubing, canoeing, rafting, kayaking, birding, picnicking and camping (859-885-9359); **Taylor Made Farm**—Thoroughbred Breeding Farm (859-885-3345); **Valley View Ferry**—Oldest continuously running business, in Kentucky, since 1785 (859-885-4500); **Wilmore Railroad Museum** (859-858-4411); **Wolf Run Wildlife Refuge**—Refuge for wild, domesticated and exotic animals (859-887-2256)

**PARIS AREA: Paris/County Tourism Commission** (888-987-3205); **Birthplace of African-American Inventor-Garrett Morgan**—Garrett Morgan invented the gas mask in 1912 and the tri-color traffic signal in 1923 (888-987-3205); **Bourbon County Courthouse**—Completed in 1905 with marble

hallways and staircase and murals near the large dome (888-987-3205); **Cane Ridge Meeting House & Barton Warren Stowe Museum**—Said to be the largest one-room log structure standing in North America. Scene of August 1801 "Great Revival," largest on the Kentucky frontier (859-987-5350); **Claiborne Horse Farm**—Gravesite of the great Secretariat, 1973 Triple Crown winner and Derby winner Go for Gin (1994) (859-987-2330); **Colville Covered Bridge**—One of 13 covered bridges left in the state, the Colville bridge was built in 1877 (888-987-3205); **Duncan Tavern**—This three-story stone tavern was built in 1788 on the courthouse square in Paris a gathering place for pioneers such as Daniel Boone and Simon Kenton (859-987-1788); **Hopewell Musuem** (859-987-7274); **John Fox, Jr. Genealogical Library**—Duncan Tavern Historical Center (859-987-1788); **Nannine Clay Wallis Home & Arboretum**—Headquarters of the Garden Club of Kentucky, Inc. Seven-acre grounds contains an arboretum (859-987-6158); **Reed Valley Orchard** (859-987-6480)

**STANFORD AREA: Standford/Lincoln County Chamber of Commerce** (606-365-4118); **Cedar Creek Lake**—780-acre sportsman fishing lake (606-365-2533); **Lincoln County Courthouse**—Some of the state's oldest records some on sheep skin (606-365-2533); **Stanford Historic L & N Depot**—Railroad depot museum of Louisville and Nashville (606-365-0207); **WILLIAM WHITLEY HOUSE STATE HISTORIC SITE**—This is the first brick home and circular racetrack in Kentucky, completed in 1794 by William Whitley and his wife

Esther. The estate, known as Sportsman's Hill, is a monument to pioneer ingenuity and re-sourcefulness. The brick house was built in the Flemish bond pattern for great-

**Federal cottage built in 1793 by Capt. Jack Jouett**
*Photo: Sid Webb*

first western frontier (859-745-1358); **Holly Rood Historic Home**—Started 1813 by James Clark (12th governor of Kentucky) was completed in 1814 (859-744-5062); **Leeds Center for the Arts**—Renovated movie theatre built in 1926 (888-772-6985); **Lower Howard's Creek Nature and Heritage Preserve**—Area of settlement outside Fort Boonesborough features a pristine creek with small waterfalls, cliff areas, stone fences and gristmill (800-298-9105)

er strength and has a secret chamber for hiding in the event of an Indian attack. Dubbed the "Guardian of Wilderness Road," the house was a gathering spot for early Kentuckians, including George Rogers Clark and Daniel Boone. 606-355-2881

**VERSAILLES/MIDWAY AREA: Woodford County Tourism Commission** (859-873-5122); **Bluegrass Scenic Railroad and Museum** (800-755-2476); **Boyd Orchards** (859-873-3097); **Buckley Wildlife Sanctuary**—National Audubon Sanctuary with 374 acres with hiking trails, nature center, and bird blind (859-873-5711); **Castle Hill Farm Winery & Vineyard** (859-879-6282); **Equus Run Vineyards**—Small boutique winery in horse country (877-905-2675); **Jack Jouett House**—Federal cottage built in 1793 by Captain Jack Jouett, a prominent leader for Kentucky Statehood, and one of the state's first importers of purebred horses and cattle (859-873-7902); **Nostalgia Station Toy & Train Museum** (859-873-2497); **Pisgah Presbyterian Church**—Established in 1784 as the first Presbyterian church west of the Allegheny Mountains on National Register (859-873-4161); **Thoroughbred Theatre** (859-846-9652); **Woodford Co. Historical Society Library & Museum**—Housed in the former Big Spring Church, built circa 1819 (859-873-6786) **Woodford Reserve**—A National Historic Landmark established on the banks of Glenn's Creek in 1812. The only distiller using the traditional copper pot still method (859-879-1812)

**WINCHESTER AREA: Winchester/County Tourism Commission** (800-298-9105); **Bluegrass Heritage Museum**—History of the Bluegrass, America's

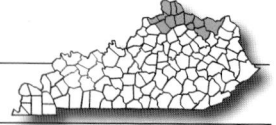

# Northern Kentucky Region

**AUGUSTA AREA:** Augusta Welcome Center (606-756-2183); **Augusta Boatdock and Marina**—Food service and boat launch (606-756-2183); **Augusta Riverwalk** (606-756-2183); **Bracken Berry Farm**—U-pick blackberries and raspberries and pre-picked berries. **Bradford/Payne House**—Site of Underground Railroad activity (606-756-2183); **Historic Augusta**—Beautiful 18th century rivertown (606-756-2183); **Rosemary Cloony House Museum**—Visit where Rosemary lived, largest private collection of "White Christmas' costumes (606-756-2183)

**River front street, Augusta**
Photo: Sid Webb

**CARROLLTON AREA:** Carrollton/Carroll County Tourism & Convention Commission (800-325-4290); **Carroll County Courthouse**—Built in 1884; **GENERAL BUTLER STATE RESORT PARK**—This hilltop resort at the confluence of the Ohio and Kentucky rivers honors a prominent military family. Named for Gen. William Orlando Butler, the family's military fame spanned from Colonial times through the American Revolution, the War of 1812, the Mexican War and the Civil War. The Butler-Turpin House, built in 1859, offers a glimpse of the family history with 18th- and 19th-century heirlooms. Enjoy golfing, hiking, swimming and tennis and the "Two Rivers" Restaurant spotlighting Kentucky cuisine (502-732-4384); **Historic Masterson House**—Historic home c.1790 is the oldest two story brick structure between Cincinnati & Louisville (800-325-4290); **Kentucky Veterans Memorial** (866-462-8853); **Point Park**—Located at the confluence of the Ohio and Kentucky rivers; **The Old Stone Jail**—Built in 1880 (800-325-4290)

**COVINGTON/NEWPORT AREA: Northern Kentucky CVB** (800-STAYNKY); (Alexandria) **Campbell County Log Cabin Museum** (859-635-5913); (Burlington) **Boone County Cliffs State Nature Preserve**—Steep wooded ridges and gentle rolling hills with picturesque creeks and valley. Hiking, birding and nature study (800-628-6800); **Dinsmore Homestead**—A unique historic site of rural life was like in the 19th and early 20th centuries. Nature enthusiasts can enjoy the hiking trails (859-586-6117); (Camp Springs) **StoneBrook Winery**—A small farm family winery (859-635-0111); (Covington) **BB Riverboats**—Riverboat rides on the Ohio (800-261-8586); **Behringer/Crawford Museum**—Native American Prehistory and more (859-491-4003); **Carnegie Visual & Performing Arts Center** (859-491-2030); **Carroll Chimes Bell Tower**—The 100-foot bell tower contains one of the two American-made animated clocks in the world (859-655-4159); **MainStrasse Village**—A restored 19th-century German neighborhood with shoppes and restaurants joined by cobblestone walkways (859-491-0458); **Mother of God Church**—Built in

**Tower Clocks of Mother of God Church, Covington**
Source: Kentucky Department of Tourism

**Big Bone Lick**
*Photo: Sid Webb*

1871 of Italian Renaissance basilica design (859-291-2288); **Railway Museum of Greater Cincinnati**—Interiors of railroad cars, railroad memorabilia and locomotives (859-491-7245); **St. Mary's Cathedral Basilica of the Assumption**—The 100-year-old cathedral is of French-Gothic architecture and resembles Notre Dame in Paris. Second largest stained glass church window in the world (859-431-2060); **Totter's Otterville**—Educational entertainment center for children (859-491-1441); **Workshops of the Restoration Society**—Working graft group producing rugs and furniture (859-491-1292); (Dayton) **Queen City Riverboats**—Public cruises lunch and dinner (859-292-8687); (Florence) **Turfway Park Race Course**—Thoroughbred race track featuring live racing (800-733-0200); (Ft. Mitchell) **Morning Star Pottery Painting Studio** (859-581-3900); **Vent Haven Museum**—World's largest collection of ventriloquist memorabilia (859-341-0461); (Ft. Wright) **James A. Ramage Civil War Museum**—Showcases the defense of Northern Kentucky and Cincinnati during the Civil War (859-344-1145); (Highland Heights) **Museum of Anthropology**—Northern Kentucky University (859-572-5259); (Newport) **East Row Historic District**—Kentucky's second largest historic district (859-292-3666); **Gameworks**—Newport's ultimate destination for a total entertainment experience where you can eat, drink and play (859-581-PLAY);

**Hofbrauhaus Newport**—First authentic Hofbrauhaus outside of Munich Germany with traditional beer hall, and microbrewery (859-491-7200); **Kentucky Symphony Orchestra** (859-431-6216); **Newport Aquarium**—A water wonderland awaits you with thousands of aquatic creatures (800-406-3474); **Newport on the Levee** —An exciting riverfront Town Square with more than 12 restaurants, unique specialty shops, the clubs, theatres, game room (866-538-3359); **Quiet Road Tours, Inc** bike trips (859-431-1300); **Shadowbox Cabaret** (888-887-4236); **The District of Newport**—A quirky, unusual, revitalizing historic main street area (859-292-3666); **World Peace Bell Exhibit Center**—The world's largest free swinging bell, the clapper weighs an amazing 6,878 pounds (800-543-0488); (Rabbit Hash) **Rabbit Hash General Store**—Historic general store (859-586-7744); (Union) **BIG BONE LICK STATE PARK**—Fifteen to twenty-thousand years ago, a great ice sheet covered an area from Canada to the Ohio River. On the edges of this ice sheet, great herds of giant mastodons, wooly mammoths and bison were attracted to the warm salt springs that still bubble from the earth at Big Bone Lick. The salty marsh that attracted the prehistoric visitors also proved to be fatal. Some of the giant creatures became trapped and perished in what the early pioneers called "jelly ground," leaving skeletons and clues about life in prehistoric Kentucky. The extensive fossil collection excavated from this site recognizes Big Bone Lick as the birthplace of American vertebrate paleontology. (859-384-3522); **Boone County Arboretum**—The nations' first arboretum within an active recreation park setting (859-384-4999); **Jane's Saddlebag Big Bone Lick Kentucky**—Reconstructed structures preserve a bygone way of life; and the Spirit of Boone County Flatboat replica of a 1700

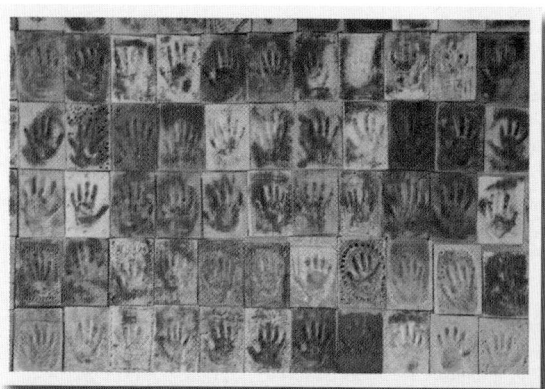

**Hand prints in tile on floodwall, Maysville**
*Photo: Sid Webb*

flatboat (877-724-4266); (Villa Hills) **RiverCity Charter**—Private 40' river yacht on the Ohio River (859-341-8221); (Walton) **Benton Farms U-Pick**—Animals and straw maze (859-485-7000); (Wilder) **Fredericks Landing Rd. Wilder**—Park and boat dock (859-581-8884);

**FALMOUTH AREA: Pendleton County Chamber of Commerce** (859-654-4189); **KINCAID LAKE STATE PARK**—A campground, a 183-acre lake, hiking trails, mini-golf and a new 9-hole golf course – a popular retreat for campers, fishermen, boaters and golfers. Explore the lake in a rental boat from the marina, or soak up the summer sunshine at the lakeside swimming pool. Surrounded by open woodland, the campground offers quiet seclusion with all the modern conveniences campers expect. (859-654-3531); **Kincaid Regional Theatre**—Professional summer theatre (800-647-7469); **Thaxton's Licking River Canoe Rental**—Canoe, kayak, raft and tube the historic Licking River. Riverside cabins and camping (877-643-8762)

**FLEMINGSBURG AREA: Fleming County**

**Chamber of Commerce** (606-845-1223); **Browns Orchard**—Fruit, berries and vegetables at beautiful Park Lake Mountain orchard. The Apple festival is held every weekend mid-September through October (606-845-8936); **DH Resorts, Inc.**—1200-acre "Dude Ranch" featuring the Mountain Lake Manor & Western Villages. Horseback riding, horse riding adventure packages, lodge, cabins, camping, 27-acre lake, pool, restaurant and group programs (800-737-7433); **Franklin Sousley Monument, Elizaville Cemetery**—Sousley was a PFC in the USMCR and helped to raise the flag at Iwo Jima in 1945. Immortalized in the famous photo by AP photographer Joe Rosenthal (606-845-1223); **Flemingsburg Historic District**—Nearly 200 homes and commercial buildings are included on the National Historic Register. (606-845-1223); **Fleming County Public Wildlife Area**—A 2070-acre wildlife area full of a wide range of animals. Fishing and hiking (606-686-3312); **Goddard Covered Bridge**—Only surviving example of Ithiel Town Lattice design in Kentucky. 60 feet long. National Register of Historic Places (606-845-1223); **Grange City Covered Bridge**—86-foot span. National Register of Historic Places (606-845-1223); **Hutton-loyd Tree Farm**—1,125 acres, 860 acres of woodlands, 30 miles of hiking trails (606-876-3423); **Ringo Mills Covered Bridge**—Built in 1867, a single span, Burr truss, without arches. National Register of Historic Places (606-845-1223)

**MAYSVILLE AREA: Maysville-Mason County Tourism Commission** (606-564-9419); (Maysville) **Big Rock ATV & Dirtbike Park**—2,000 acre ATV & dirtbike park (606-564-8283); **Carriage Museum**—Showcases transportation before the automobile: from a basic farmers wagon to an elegant four-seat carriages complete with fringe (606-759-7411); **Downtown Maysville Historic District** (606-564-9419); **Herb Farm at Strodes Run**—A working, 63 acre Organic Herb Farm (606-742-2000); **Hickory Hill Plantation and Nursery**—1861 Kentucky plantation (606-742-2596); **Albert Sidney Johnston House**—Confederate Civil War General Albert Sidney Johnston's home (606-759-7411); **Maysville Flood Wall Murals**—History of the Maysville spanning four centuries; **Mefford's Fort**—Authentic 1787 log cabin (606-759-7411); **Kentucky Gate-**

way Museum Center—An 1881 building allows visitors to experience pioneer life (606-564-5865); **National Underground Railroad Museum**—Slavery artifacts, documents and memorabilia documenting Maysville's role in the abolitionist movement and the role of slavery in America (606-564-3200); **Paradise Breeze Family Entertainment Complex**—Lap pool, arcade, batting cage, slides, paradise pavilion, go-karts, Rainbow Café (606-759-9416); **"R" Farm & More LLC**—A 130-acre farm for children (606-742-2429); **Underground Railroad Driving Tour**—(606-564-9419); (Mays Lick) **Mays Lick Corn Maze** (606-763-6706); **Harriet Beecher Stowe Slavery To Freedom Museum**—The early antebellum home where Harriet Beecher visited and witnessed a slave auction in 1833, which is said to have influenced her writing "Uncle Tom's Cabin" (606-759-4860); **Old Church Museum** (606-759-7411); **Old Washington Historic District**—Established in 1786, home to several authentic log cabins and early 1800s buildings (606-759-7411); **Paxton Inn**—Built around 1810, thought to be a safe house for escaping slaves (606-759-7411); **Simon Kenton Shrine**—Housed in an authentic log cabin built as a pioneer store in the 1780s (606-759-7411); **Johnson Creek Covered Bridge**—Built in 1874, 131-foot Smith truss-designed bridge; **Sunflower Sundries**—An herbal soap factory and organic gardens (606-763-6827)

**OWENTON AREA: Owen County Chamber of Commerce (502-484-9900); Elk Creek Hunt Club** (502-484-4569); **Elmer Davis Lake**—149 acres. Fishing, dock, ramp (502-484-5805); **John A. Kleber Wildlife Management Area**—Steep hillsides, narrow ridge tops and floodplains with a combination of woods, brush, grasslands and wildlife food plots (502-535-6335); **Larkspur Press**—See the art of making books the old-fashioned way (502-

**Tunnel for the Underground Railroad, Covington**
*Photo: Kentucky Department for Libraries & Archives*

484-5390); **Twin Eagle Wildlife Management Area** (502-535-6335)

**VANCEBURG AREA: Lewis County Tourism** (606-792-2722); **Cabin Creek Covered Bridge**—Built in 1867, 114 feet long, burr truss design (606-796-2722); **Sand Hill Christian Church**—Built in 1860, pews facing double entry. Patterned after Alexander Campbell's home church, The Old Meeting House at Bethany WV (606-796-2722); **Union Soldier Monument**—Monument honoring Union soldiers is said to be the only one of its kind south of the Mason-Dixon Line (606-796-2722); **Veterans Memorial Park** (606-796-2722); **WARSAW/SPARTA AREA: Gallatin County Tourism Commission** (859-867-5691); Craig's Creek Lake—Over 1,000-acres of water on the Ohio River; **Hawkins-Kirby House**—House was built circa 1845 by Edmond Waller Hawkins, Judge Advocate of the Northern Kentucky District during the Civil War (859-567-4591); **Kentucky Speedway**—"America's home of championship motorsports" featuring NASCAR, IRL, ARCA, ASA. (888-652-7223); **Markland Dam**—Viewing tower and picnic area (859-597-7661)

**WILLIAMSTOWN/DRY RIDGE AREA: Grant County Visitor's Center** (800-382-7117); **Barkers Blackberry Hill Winery** (859-428-0377); **Corinth Lake**—96-acre lake with fishing, boating, ramp (859-824-0083); **Curtis Gates Wildlife Refuge**—4 miles of dirt roads and trails for hiking, bird watching and a small fishing lake (800-858-1949); **Farmer Bill's**—A working farm with petting zoo and children's playground (859-823-1058); **House of Reptiles LLC**—90 species of reptiles and amphibians (859-824-4577); **Pickin Patch, LLC**—Locally-grown Kentucky produce along with Amish specialty products (859-824-1265); **Williamstown Lake**—A 305-acre water reservoir for fishing, boating, and water skiing.

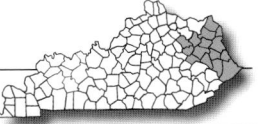

# Eastern Highlands North Region

**ASHLAND AREA:** **Ashland Area Convention & Visitors Bureau** (800-377-6249); (Ashland) **Ashland Area Art Gallery** (606-329-1826); **Ashland Historical Tours** (800-377-6249); **Bar W Rodeo Productions**—Bull riding at its best (606-928-9334); **Clinton Furnace**—Iron furnace built in 1833 by Poage brothers; **Highlands Museum & Discovery Center** (606-329-8888); **Jesse Stuart Foundation**—A non-profit publishing house dedicated to preserving Jesse Stuart's literary works and promoting the culture and literature of Appalachia (606-326-1667); **Paramount Arts Center**—On the National Register of Historic Places, the theatre has a resident ghost "Paramount Joe" and fans still come to see the location of Billy Ray Cyrus' famed "Achey Breaky Heart" video shoot (606-324-3175); (Catlettsburg) **Catlettsburg Floodwall Murals** (606-739-4533); (Princess); **Princess Furnace**—Iron furnace put into operation in 1864 by John Means; (Summit) **Boyd County World War II Memorial** (606-928-9551)

**FRENCHBURG AREA:** **Frenchburg/Menifee County Chamber of Commerce** (606-768-9000); **Broke Leg Falls**—A gorgeous natural waterfall of over 60 feet (606-768-9000); **Clifty Wilderness Area—Red River Gorge**—12,600 acres, features arches, rock shelters, cliffs and back-country camping (606-663-2852)

**GRAYSON AREA: Grayson Tourism & Convention Commission** (606-474-8740); (Grayson) **CARTER CAVES STATE RESORT PARK**—The resort's forested hills has more than 20 twisting caverns. Cascade Cave has a 30-foot underground waterfall or X Cave, where nature has formed luminous stone fans, pipes and spirals. Above ground, enjoy golf, canoeing, hiking, horseback riding and

**Exploring Kentucky**
*Photo: Sid Webb*

mountain biking on 20 miles of single and multi-use trails. In addition to the beautiful fieldstone lodge, the resort offers cottages in a wooded setting (606-286-4411); **Grayson Lake**—Vertical rock cliffs rim the lake's 40

**Oldtown Covered Bridge**
*Source: Tour Southern & Eastern Kentucky*

miles of shoreline (606-474-5815); **GRAYSON LAKE STATE PARK**—Sheer sandstone canyons and gentle slopes contain the 1,512 acres of Grayson Lake. The land was a favorite camping site for Shawnee and Cherokee Indians. The 18-hole golf course, Hidden Cove, was ranked among the best of its type in 2004 by Golf Digest 606-474 -9727; **Grayson Lake Wildlife Management Area** (502-564-4336); (Olive Hill) **Northeastern Kentucky Museum**—Tracing the area's heritage from the Indians to Vietnam (606-286-6012);

**Tygarts State Forest**—Hiking, picnicking and hunting (606-286-4411)

**GREENUP AREA: Ashland Area Convention & Visitors Bureau** (800-377-6249); (Greenup) **Jesse Stuart State Nature Preserve**—733 acres of woods and fields known as W-Hollow (502-573-2886); **Oldtown Covered Bridge**—Built in 1880 on Burr's Patented Design. Two-Span Bridge, 192 Ft Long, on National Register (877-868-7473); (Maloneton) **Bennett's Mill Covered Bridge**—Built 1855, Rare Wheeler Truss Covered Bridge, 155 Feet Long. It has been reported that the bridge was the oldest, longest, single span covered bridge in the world (800-377-6249); **GREENBO LAKE STATE RESORT PARK**—The fieldstone lodge at this resort is named in honor of Jesse Hilton Stuart, (1906-1984) Poet Laureate and native of Greenup County. Enjoy Stuart's writing in the lodge's reading room. Enjoy boating, hiking, horseback riding and mountain biking 606-473-7324; (Wurtland) **Greenup County War Memorial** (606-836-3012); **McConnell House and School**—Georgian architecture house built in 1833 (606-833-9098)

**LOUISA AREA: Lawrence County Tourism Commission** (606-920-9119); **Kentucky's Paveillon**—Five-story tall, 100 feet high paveillon serves as a welcome center of Country Music Highway (606-638-9998); **YATESVILLE LAKE STATE PARK**—Popular with both anglers and recreational boaters, Yatesville Lake State Park is a 2,300 acre mountain reservoir. The Eagle Ridge golf course, built on mountainous terrain, was ranked #3 nationally by "Golf Digest" magazine in their list 2005 best new affordable golf courses. and a campground 606-673-1490

**MOREHEAD AREA: Morehead Tourism Commission** (606-780-4342); **Cave Run Bicycle and Outdoor Center** (606-784-1818); **Cave Run Lake**—8,300 acres surface area is known as the "Muskie Fishing Capitol of the South." (606-784-5624); **Claypool-Young Art Gallery** (606-783-5446); **Cora Wilson Stewart Moonlight School**—One-room school used for adult education in the late 1800s (800-654-1944); **Kentucky Folk Art Center** (606-783-2204); **Minor E. Clark Fish Hatchery**—One of the largest state-owned, warmwater fish hatcheries in the U.S. (606-784-6872); **Shallow Flats Wildlife Observation Area**—Self-guided loop interpretive trail passes near restored wetlands (606-784-5624); **Sheltowee Trace National Recreation Trail**—A 269-mile multiple-use national recreation trail (606-784-6428); **U.S. Forest Service Visitor Center**—The forest stretches over 694,985 acres and 21 counties south to Tennessee (606-784-5624)

**MT. STERLING AREA: Mt. Sterling/Montgomery County Tourism Commission** (866-415-7439); **Gallery For The Arts** (859-498-6264); **Historic Downtown/Main Cross**—Renovated historic block of buildings (859-498-8725); **Ruth Hunt Candy Company**—Started in 1921, produces high quality traditional Kentucky candies (800-927-0302); **The Bramble Ridge Orchard**—U-pick or purchase bagged apples (859-498-9123)

**OWINGSVILLE AREA: Owingsville/Bath County Chamber of Commerce** (606-674-2266); **Bath County Memorial Library**—Works by regional artists and craftsmen (606-674-2531); (Salt Lick) **Tater Knob Fire Tower**—First Fire Tower in the forest is 35 ft. tall (606-784-6428); **White Sulphur ATV Trail** (606-784-6428); **Zilpo Road National Forest Scenic Byway**—11-mile byway tour through the Daniel Boone National Forest (606-784-6428)

**PAINTSVILLE AREA: Paintsville Tourism Commission** (800-542-5790); (Oil Springs) **Oil Springs Cultural Arts and Recreation Center**—Antiques, artifacts collections, pottery, a history study room, arts and crafts library, recycle shop, woodshop, woodshop and music room (606-789-8108); (Paintsville) **Mayo Mansion**—This 43-room mansion was built by John CC Mayo in 1910. Mayo was the first eastern Kentucky coal baron (800-542-5790); **Mayo Memorial United Methodist Church**—Built by John CC Mayo from lime-

stone lifted out of the area's mountains. The Pilcher Organ was donated by Andrew Carnegie (606-789-3296); **US 23 Country Music Highway Museum**—Entertainers featured in the museum are: Billy Ray Cyrus, The Judds, Ricky Skaggs, Hylo Brown, Loretta Lynn, Crystal Gayle, Dwight Yoakam, Patty Loveless, Tom T. Hall, Keith Whitley, Gary Stewart and Rebecca Lynn Howard (800-542-5790); (River) **Jenny Wiley Gravesite**—Cemetery where pioneer heroine Jenny Wiley is

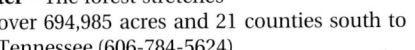

**Loretta Lynn's Birthplace**
*Source: Kentucky Department of Tourism*

buried (800-542-5790); (Staffordsville) **Mountain Homeplace**—Actual working farm as it was in eastern Kentucky in the 1850s (800-542-5790); **PAINTSVILLE LAKE STATE PARK**—Paintsville Lake gleams like a jewel in the crown of mountains of Eastern Kentucky.

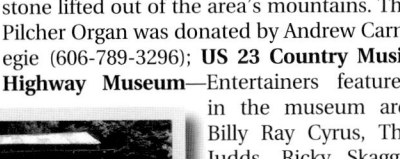

With steep cliffs and wooded coves along the shoreline, this lake provides 1,140 acres of boating, skiing and fishing pleasure. A full-service marina is located near the campground, offering rental houseboats, pontoons and fishing boats. The nearby Mountain Homeplace recreates Appalachian farm life in the mid-1800s (606-297-8486); **Paintsville Lake Wildlife Management** (606-297-6312); (Van Lear) **Butcher Hollow**—Home of country music divas Loretta Lynn and Crystal Gayle, call for availability of guide (606-789-3397); **Coal Miners' Museum**—Displays include Coal Mining Tools, a diorama of the town as it was in the 1930s, Old Town Jail, Van Lear Schools Collection (606-789-8540); **Dewey Dam Recreation Area/Day Use** (606-789-4521) **Van Lear Historical Society** (606-789-8540)

**PIKEVILLE AREA: Pikeville/Pike County Tourism Commission** (800-844-7453); (Elkhorn City) **Artists Collaborative Theatre, Inc** (606-754-5137); **Elkhorn Adventures White Water Rafting**—Russell Fork River (Class IV-Class VI rapids) (800-982-5122); **Elkhorn City Railroad Museum**—Photos, tools, uniforms, and instruments used on the railroad (606-754-8300); (Pikeville) **Big Sandy Heritage Museum**—Preserves the history of the Big Sandy Valley, listed on National Register of Historic Places (606-218-6050); **FISHTRAP LAKE STATE PARK**—1,130-acre lake is narrow and deep. The lake draws its name from the pioneers who noticed the fish traps used by the Native Americans. To this day, the lake has a great reputation for fishing. Also features a privately operated marina and a Corps of Engineers campground (800-844-7453); **Hatfield & McCoy Feud Driving Tour**—Ten actual historic sites where the feud took place (800-844-7453); **Historic Dils Cemetery & Gardens**—Final resting place of the Hatfield

**Owens House, Bath County**
*Source: Tour Southern & Eastern Kentucky*

& McCoy feud chieftain Randolph McCoy and family members, botanical gardens, walking trail and overlook (800-844-7453); **Historic Downtown Pikeville Walking Tour**—53 historic buildings and homes listed on the National Register of Historic Places (800-844-7453); **Pikeville "Cut-Thru Project"**—The project created over 400 acres of usable land by the removal of 18 million cubic yards of earth and is to date the second largest earth moving project in the world (800-844-7453)

**PRESTONSBURG AREA: Prestonsburg Tourism Commission** (800-844-4704); **Dewey Lake**—Wooded hills rise some 700 feet above the lake (606-789-4521); **East Kentucky Science Center**—85-seat Planetarium (877-889-0303); **JENNY WILEY STATE RESORT PARK**—Located deep in the heart of the Appalachians, accented by scenic 1,100-acre Dewey Lake. Activities include shows in the theatre, hiking and golf. (800-325-0142); **Jenny Wiley Theatre** (877-225-5598); **Kentucky Opry**—Country, Bluegrass, Oldies (888-Mac-Arts); **Middle Creek National Battlefield**—The site of the largest and most significant Civil War Battle in Eastern Kentucky (800-844-4704); **Mountain Arts Center**—Country, Bluegrass, Gospel, Pop, Orchestra and Classic (888-622-2787); **Prince Albert Stables**—Features the Rocky Mountain Horse, Full service facility offering training, showing, trailing and breeding (606-874-9219); **Stone Crest Golf Course**—18-hole championship (606) 886-1006; **Archer Park**—Swimming pool, tennis court, ball fields, and picnic shelters (606) 886-6309**; Stone Crest Stables & Show Ring**—Over 200 new stables and numerous horse shows during the year (606) 886-1341; **Samuel May House**—Restored 1817 brick home (606-889-9608); **Thunder Ridge Racing & Entertainment Complex**—live harness racing and year round simulcast wagering (606-886-7223)

**SALYERSVILLE AREA:** Salyersville Tourism Commission (606-349-2409); **Magoffin County Historical Society Log Village** (606-349-1607)

**WEST LIBERTY AREA: West Liberty Tourism Commission** (606-743-3330); **Morgan County Courthouse**—National Register of Historic Places (606-743-3763); **Morgan County Genealogy Center**—Genealogy and Historical Society located in a renovated WRA Jail (606-743-7491); **Old Mill Park**—Historic site of the Well's Grist Mill (606-743-2300); **Paint Creek Log School House** (606-743-2300); **Wrigley Arch And Falls**—features a waterfall and a natural arch (606-743-2300);

Stateline Overlook at the Breaks Interstate Park in Breaks, Virginia, Wednesday, March 7, 2001. The park, which straddles the Ky/Va border, got its name because this is where there is a break in Pine Mountain created by the Russell Fork of The Big Sandy River

*Photo: Charles Bertram, Lexington Herald-Leader*

**BREAKS INTERSTATE PARK**—The Russell Fork River has carved a 250-million year-old masterpiece, a canyon 5 miles long and 1,600 feet deep! Considered the "Grand Canyon of the South," the beauty of Breaks Interstate is showcased along hiking trails and overlooks. The park has a lodge, cottages and campground (800-982-5122)

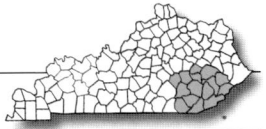

# Eastern Highlands South Region

**BARBOURVILLE AREA: Barbourville Tourism & Recreation Commission** (606-546-6197); (Gray) **Dizney Mountain Arena & Rodeo** (606-546-3210); **DR. THOMAS WALKER STATE HISTORIC SITE**—Dr. Thomas Walker was the first frontiersman in Kentucky, preceding Daniel Boone by 17

**Pioneer Village, Knott Co.**
*Source: Tour Southern & Eastern Kentucky*

years. A physician and surveyor, Walker led the first expedition through Cumberland Gap in 1750. Dr. Walker was an agent for the Loyal Land Company of Virginia and was exploring the western wilderness seeking land for settlement he named the Cumberland river. Dr. Walker built the first cabin in Kentucky, a replica of which stands on the site today (606-546-4400); **Kentucky Communities Craft Village**—Preserves the traditional mountain heritage with a craft workshop (800-880-3152); **Knox Historical Museum** (606-546-4300)

**BEATTYVILLE AREA: Lee County Tourism** (606-464-2888); Three Forks Historical Museum (606-464-2888)

**BOONEVILLE AREA: Owsley County Tourism** (606-593-7296); **Old Drive In**—Shows start at dusk on Friday and Saturday nights in the summer (606-593-5370)

**CAMPTON AREA: Wolfe County Tourism** (606-668-6475); **Old Campton Burial Grounds** (606-668-3040); **Torrent Falls Family Climbing Adventure**—the first climbing adventure park in the U.S. (606-668-6613); **Wolfe County Historical Museum** (606-668-6650); **Swift Creek Arts and Crafts Gallery** (606-725-4860)

**HARLAN AREA: Harlan Tourist & Convention Commission** (606-573-4156); **Cumberland Tour-**

ist & Convention Commission (606-589-5812); (Baxter) **Mountain Outdoors** (606-573-6260); (Benham) **Kentucky Coal Mining Museum**—Exhibits on the miners' home, hospital, commissary, engineering, coal sampling, a mock mine tour and the Loretta Lynn "Coal Miner's Daughter" exhibit (606-848-1530); (Cumberland) **Big Black Mountain**—Kentucky's highest point atop Black Mountain, 4,145 ft (606-848-1530); **Blanton Forest State Nature Preserve**—Kentucky's largest and most diverse old-growth forest. Over 400 different species of plants (502-573-2886); **Godbey Appalachian Cultural & Fine Arts Center**—Appalachian artifacts, oral histories, photographs, art collections, pottery, dulcimer making, and music (606-589-2145); **KINGDOM COME STATE PARK**—With an elevation of 2,700 feet, Kingdom Come is Kentucky's highest state park. Resting near the Kentucky-Virginia border on the crest of Pine Mountain, the park offers scenic vistas second to none. Extraordinary rock formations are featured at this

park, including Log Rock, a natural sandstone bridge, and Raven Rock, a giant monolith that soars 290-feet into the air at a 45-degree angle. Many visitors flock to the park during mild weather to view the park's growing population of black bears. (606-589-2479); (Evarts) **Cloverfork Museum and Highsplint Reunion** (606-837-3220); **Kentucky Mountain Trails of Harlan County** (606-573-4156); (Harlan) **Cranks Creek Public Wildlife Management Area** (606-549-2305); **Harlan County Coal Miners Memorial Monument**—Commemorates memory of Harlan County miners that have lost their lives (800-216-2022); **Kentenia State Forest** (606-573-1460); **Portal 31 Mine Tour** (606-848-1530); **USS Harlan County Archives**—Artifacts of decommissioned US Navy amphibi-

**Buckhorn Log Cathedral**
*Source: Tour Southern & Eastern Kentucky*

ous tank landing ship. (606-573-4156); (Pine Mountain) **Pine Mountain Settlement School**—A National Historic Landmark with weekend nature classes during the spring and fall to students of all ages (606-558-3571); (Smith) **Cumberland Shadow Trail**—Five-mile, backcountry overnight camping trail (606-573-7655); Martins Fork Lake (606-573-7655); **Smith Recreation Area**—Picnic tables, shelters, white sand beach, basketball and more (606-573-7655)

**HAZARD AREA:** Perry County Tourism Commission (888-857-5263); (Buckhorn) **Buckhorn Lake**—Beautiful, mountainous terrain with a historic log structure (606-398-7251); **BUCKHORN LAKE STATE RESORT PARK**—Tucked away in the mountains, Buckhorn is truly the "Great Escape."

The resort is a mecca for nature-lovers and folks who want to get away from it all. Curl up next to the lodge's fireplace or enjoy the mountain air from your private balcony. Surrounded by mist-ringed mountains marching down to the lake's edge, every view from this resort is inspiring. The lodge also features a Conference Center, with all the guest services under one roof. Delicious catered meals are served fresh from the kitchen and guest rooms are only a few steps away. (800-325-0058); **Buckhorn Log Cathedral**—Made of white oak from the surrounding mountains and listed on the National Registry of Historic Places (606-398-7382); (Hazard) **Bobby Davis Museum and Park**—Depicts life in Perry Co. from 1850-1950 (606-439-4325); **Greater Hazard Area Performing Arts** (800-246-7521)

**HINDMAN AREA: Knott County Tourism Commission** (606-785-5881); (Hindman) **Hindman Settlement School/ Marie Stewart Crafts**—Founded in 1902 provides evening folk dances and a crafts shop dedicated to preserving the rich, traditional crafts of the area (606-785-5475); **Kentucky Appalachian Artisan Center**—An art gallery with exhibit changing every 4-8 weeks and a retail sales outlet to market Artisan wares from Eastern Kentucky (606-785-9855); **Kentucky School of Craft** (800-246-7521); **Knott County Historical and Genealogical Society** (606-785-5751); (Sassafras) **CARR CREEK STATE PARK**—Enjoy a variety of activities at this park on Carr Fork Lake. Park your RV or pitch your tent and relax in one of the best campgrounds in southeastern Kentucky.

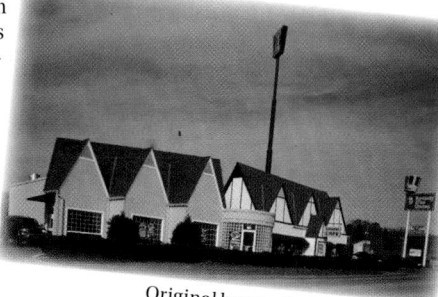

Original home of Kentucky Fried Chicken, Corbin
Source: Tour Southern & Eastern Kentucky

The campground offers all the camper comforts surrounded by mountain scenery. The park also features the longest lakefront sand beach in the Kentucky State Park system. A full-service marina near the park provides lake access as well as fishing and boating supplies. Pleasure boaters and fishermen can explore the 750-acre lake with miles of shoreline and good bass, crappie and walleye fishing (606-642-4050)

**HYDEN AREA: Leslie County Tourism Commission** (606-672-2154); (Wendover) **Frontier Nursing Service**—The oldest American school of nurse-midwifery in existence (1925) Includes the National Historic Landmark home of founder Mary Breckinridge (606-672-2317); (Whitesburg) **Appalshop**—Nationally renowned arts, media, & education center, includes Appalshop Film & Video and Roadside Theater (606-633-0108); **Bad Branch State Nature Preserve** (606-663-0362); **Saint Christopher Chapel**—houses a 15th-century stained glass window (606-672-2317)

**INEZ AREA: Martin County Economic Development** (606-298-2800)

**IRVINE AREA: Estill Development Alliance** (606-732-2450); (Irvine) **Soggy Bottom Farm**—

Mist over the mountains
Source: Tour Southern & Eastern Kentucky

Petting zoo, gift shop, hay rides, pick your own pumpkins, sorghum production (606-723-4568); (Ravena) **Cottage Furnace**—Iron production site during mid to late 1800s; **Fitchburg Furnace**—Built by masons from Ravenna, Italy in 1869, the twin stacks went into operation in 1870 and became the largest charcoal-burning furnace in the world. This is the only double furnace in Kentucky (606-723-2450)

**JACKSON AREA:** Jackson/Breathitt County Chamber of Commerce (606-666-4159); **Breathitt County Museum** (606-666-4159)

**LONDON/CORBIN AREA:** London/Laurel County Tourism Commission (800-348-0095); (Corbin) **Sanders Cafe & Museum**—Colonel Sanders' original restaurant, birthplace of Kentucky Fried Chicken with artifacts and memorabilia from early KFC (606-528-2163); (East Bernstadt) **Kinlee Stables**—Trail rides, buggy, wagon, pony, carousel, and carriage rides, petting zoo, bonfire cookouts, riding lessons and summer camp, family reunions (606-843-2645); (London) **Camp Wildcat Civil War Battlefield**—Recognized as the first Union victory of the Civil War (800-348-0095); **Daniel Boone Motocross Park** (606-877-1364); **Laurel River Lake** (606-864-6412); **LEVI JACKSON WILDERNESS ROAD STATE PARK**—Over 800 acres and includes the Defeated Camp Pioneer Burial Ground, McHargue's Mill and the Mountain Life Museum, which brings visitors into a pioneer settlement. Hike the Wilderness Road and Boone's Trace which carried more than 200,000 settlers from eastern colonies into the western frontier between 1774 and 1796. (606-878-8000); **London Community Orchestra** (606-864-4194); **London Dragway** (606-878-8883); **London Go Karts** (606-864-0761); **McNitt Cemetery** (606-878-8000); **Mountain Life Museum** (606-878-8000); **Rockcastle Adventures Canoe Livery** (606-864-9407);

**MANCHESTER AREA: Manchester/Clay County Chamber of Commerce** (606-598-1754)

**MCKEE AREA: Jackson County Tourism Commission** (606-287-4712); Mill Creek Wildlife Management Area (606-287-7832); Horse Lick Creek Biosphere—This 62-square mile watershed area designated the "Last Great Places" by the Nature Conservancy (606-878-7664)

Natural Bridge
*Source: Tour Southern & Eastern Kentucky*

**MT. VERNON/RENFRO VALLEY AREA:** Mt. Vernon/Rockcastle County Tourist Commission (800-252-6685); **BitterSweet Cabin Museum** (800-252-6685); **Brush Arbor Appalachian Pioneer Log Village** (859-433-3208); **Kentucky Music Hall of Fame and Museum**—Honors Kentucky performers, songwriters, publishers, promoters, managers, broadcasters, comedians and other music professionals who have made significant contributions to the music industry in Kentucky and around the world (877-356-3263); **Renfro Valley Entertainment Center**—Music, singing and comedy where visitors can enjoy some of the best live entertainment in the country (800-765-7464)

**PINEVILLE/MIDDLESBORO AREA: Bell County Tourism Commission** (800-988-1075); (Frakes) **Henderson Settlement** (606-337-3613); (Middlesboro) **Bell County Historical Society Museum** (606-242-0005); **Coal House Museum** (800-988-1075); **CUMBERLAND GAP NATIONAL HISTORICAL PARK**—An 800 ft. deep natural break in the Cumberland Mountains is one of the largest National Historical Parks in the country with 20,305 acres. Overlooks three states (606-248-2817); **Cumberland Gap Tunnel** (606-248-1075); **Hensley Settlement**—The restored isolated Appalachian farmstead flourished during the first half of the 20th century and is on the National Register of Historic Places (606-248-2817); **The Lost Squadron/P-38 Museum**—home of the "Glacier Girl", a World War II P-38 Lightening (606-248-1149); **Wilderness Road Tours** (606-248-2626); (Pineville) **Chained Rock** (800-325-1712); **Kentucky Ridge State Forest** (606-337-3011); **PINE MOUNTAIN STATE RESORT PARK**—Overlooking the Kentucky Ridge State Forest, this mountaintop resort became Kentucky's first state park in 1924 and site of the annual Mountain Laurel Festival. Enjoy beautiful hiking trails, cozy cottages, 18-hole golf course, pro shop and an indoor training center (606-337-3066); **The Bell Theatre** (606-337-3806);

**STANTON/RED RIVER GORGE AREA: Powell County Tourism Commission** (606-663-1161); (Clay City) **Meadowgreen Park Bluegrass Music Hall** (606-663-9008); **Pilot Knob State Nature Preserve**— Considered to be the place where Daniel Boone first stood and looked out over the Bluegrass region of Kentucky (502-573-2886); **Red River Historical Museum** (606-663-2555); **Red River Outdoors**—Climbing lessons and guided trips, canoe rentals, caving and hiking excursions (606-663-ROCK); (Slade) **Kentucky Reptile Zoo**— Over 100 species of reptiles such as mambas, cobras, rattlesnakes, anacondas, lizards, turtles and alligators (606-663-9160); **Natural Bridge Sky Lift Inc.**—Sky lift to the top of Natural Bridge (606-663-

Above: Bert Combs Lake,
Right: Cumberland Falls
State Park
*Source: Tour Southern &
Eastern Kentucky*

2922); **NATURAL BRIDGE STATE RESORT PARK**—It has taken nature millions of years to form the natural sandstone arch from which this park takes its name. Located adjacent to the Daniel Boone National Forest, near the Red River Gorge Geological Area, the bridge spans 78 feet and is 65 feet high. At Natural Bridge, hikers are drawn to this rugged, scenic area of high stone cliffs and stone arches. Hemlock Lodge overlooks a pool complex and Hoedown Island

**Chair lift near Natural Bridge State Resort Park**
*Source: Tour Southern & Eastern Kentucky*

(606-663-2214); (Stanton) **Red River Gorge National Geological Area**—Back-country camping, hiking with more than 80 natural arches, hundreds of miles of hiking trails, a 36-mile looping driving tour, and the Red River (Kentucky's only National Wild and Scenic River) (606-663-2852)

**WHITESBURG AREA: Letcher County Tourism Commission** (606-632-1200); (Blackey) **C.B. Caudill Store & History Center** (606-633-3281); (Seco) **Seco Company Store & Winery**—Restored commissary and camp houses of the South East Coal Company. (606-855-7968); (Whitesburg) **Lilley Cornett Woods**—National natural landmark and state wildlife refuge is one of Kentucky's few remaining tracts of virgin forest. (606-633-5828); **Little Shepherd Trail**—38-mile scenic mountain road meandering along the top of Pine Mountain (606-573-4156); **Pine Mountain Trail** (Under Development)—The trail will showcase the geology, history and spectacular scenery of the central Appalachian Mountains. Ultimately, the trail will be 120 miles long and link Breaks Interstate Park with Cumberland Gap National Park. The trail will traverse the crest of Pine Mountain on the Kentucky-Virginia border, and cross terrain replete with pioneer homesteads, waterfalls, cliffs, rock shelters, caves, upland bogs and scenic overlooks. Currently, 28 miles of the trail are available for hiking and non-motorized vehicles. Trail guides, maps and gear are available at www.pinemountaintrail.com (606-633-2362)

**WILLIAMSBURG/CORBIN AREA: Williamsburg Tourist & Convention Commission** (606-549-0530); (Corbin) **Bill's Riding Stables** (606-528-2066); **Corbin Speedway** (606-526-8899); **Cumberland Falls Rainbow Mist Ride** (800-541-7238); **CUMBERLAND FALLS STATE RESORT PARK**—Water falling 60 feet into a boulder-strewn gorge, a whispering mist that kisses the face and a

The Lost Squadron/P-38 Museum, Middlesboro
*Source: Tour Southern & Eastern Kentucky*

Enjoy a round of golf at the Pine Mountain State Resort Park
*Source: Tour Southern & Eastern Kentucky*

magical moonbow visible on a clear night under a full moon. Known as the "Niagara of the South," the 125-foot wide curtain of water is dramatic day or night. But it is only at night during a full moon that you can see the moonbow (weather permitting), a phenomenon not found anywhere else in the Western Hemisphere! Take a rafting or canoe trip and visit a professional outfitter near the resort or try swimming and horseback riding. Dupont Lodge is built of massive hemlock beams and knotty pine (606-528-4121); **Cumberland Star Riverboat**—Offers sight-seeing, lunch and charter cruises on the Cumberland River and upper Lake Cumberland (800-541-7238); Sheltowee Trace Outfitters (800-541-7238); The Depot on Main-Laugh Tracks Comedy Club (606-523-1117); (Williamsburg) **Cumberland Museum** (800-315-3100); R/C Speedway (606-521-5343); **Hal Rogers Family Entertainment Center**—Home of Kentucky Splash Water Park, miniature golf, go-karts, batting cages, and driving range (866-812-1860)

# Kentucky Travel Time Radio Show

## Super Talk Radio Show WLXO 96.1 FM

Call toll-free 866-831-0311 Tourist Information or www.kytraveltime.com

*Super Talk 96.1 WLXO in Lexington has a new talk radio program, "Kentucky Travel Time." The program is produced by Kentucky's Eastern Highlands North and Eastern Highlands South tourism regions. and airs each Saturday from 12:00 noon to 1:00 pm call in during the show at 859-294-0961. The program hosts deliver a week-to-week travel guide to listeners interested in entertainment, historical sites, heritage and cultural sites, out-of-the-way restaurants, modern lodging facilities, nature-based tourism locations, campgrounds, fall festivals and a host of other under-recognized places to visit, all located in the beautiful mountain area of Kentucky known as the "Kentucky Highlands."*

  Show Sponsors

**Kentucky Depart of Tourism**
www.kentuckytourism.com
**Kentucky Department of Parks**
www.parks.ky.gov
**Kentucky's Country Music Highway Travel Guide**
www.countrymusichighway.com
**Lexington Family Magazine**
www.lexingtonfamily.com
**Tour Southern and Eastern Kentucky**
www.tourseky.com
**The Clark Group—Kentucky Almanac**
www.kyalmanac.com

### Eastern Highlands North
www.kyappalachians.com

**Ashland Area Convention & Visitors Bureau**—www.visitashlandky.com; **Owingsville/Bath County**—606-674-6121; **Elliott County Tourism Council**—606-758-5821; **Frenchburg/Menifee County Chamber of Commerce**—www.frenchburgmenifee.org; **Greenup County Tourism Commission**—www.greenupcountytourism.com; **Lawrence County Tourism Commission**—www.lawrencecokytourism.org; **Martin County Economic Development**—606-298-2800; **Morehead Tourist &.Convention Commission**—www.moreheadtourism.com; **Mt. Sterling/Montgomery County Tourist Commission**—www.mtsterlingtourism.com; **Salyersville Tourism & Convention Commission**—606-349-7678; **Paintsville Tourism & Convention Commission**—www.paintsville.org; **Pikeville/Pike County Tourism Commission**—www.tourpikecounty.com; **Prestonsburg Convention & Visitors Bureau**—www.prestonsburgky.org; **West Liberty Tourism Commission**—www.cityofwestliberty.com;

### East Highlands South
www.danielboonecountry.com

**Barbourville Tourism & Recreation Commission**—www.barbourville.com; **Bell County Tourism Commission**—www.mountaingateway.com; **Corbin Tourist & Convention Commission**—www.corbinkentucky.us; **Cumberland Tourism Commission**—www.kingdomcome.org; **Estill Development Alliance**—www.estillcountyky.net; **Harlan Tourist Commission**—www.harlanonline.net/tourism; **Jackson County Tourism**—www.eastky.net/jacksonco; **Jackson/Breathitt County Chamber of Commerce**—606-666-4159; **Knott County**

**Tourism Commission**—606-785-5881; **Lee County Tourism Committee**—www.beattyville.org; **Leslie County Tourism Commission**—606-672-2154; **Letcher County Tourism & Convention Commission**—606-632-1200; **London/Laurel County Tourist Commission**—www.laurelkytourism.com; **Manchester/Clay County Chamber of Commerce**—www.claycochamber.org; **Mt. Vernon/Rockcastle County Tourism Commission**—www.rockcastlecokytourism.com; **Owsley County Tourism Commission**—606-593-7296; **Perry County Tourism Commission**—606-439-2659; **Powell County Tourism Commission**—www.powellcountytourism.com; **Williamsburg Tourist Commission**—www.williamsburgky.com; **Wolfe County Tourism**—606-668-6475

### Southern Lakes & Rivers
www.mykentuckyvacation.info

**Albany/Clinton Co. Chamber of Commerce**—www.dalehollowlakecumberland.com; **Columbia /Adair County Tourism**—www.columbia-adaircounty.com; **Cumberland County Tourism Commission**—www.cumberlandcounty.com; **Greensburg/Green County Chamber of Commerce**—270-932-4298 or gccityhall@greensburgky.com; **Liberty/Casey County Tourism**—606-787-6463; **McCreary County Tourism Commission**—www.kyvacations.com or 888-284-3718; **Monticello/Wayne County Chamber of Commerce**—www.monticellokychamber.com; **Russell County Tourist Commission**—www.lakecumberlandvacation.com; **Somerset/Pulaski Co. Convention & Visitors Bureau**—www.lakecumberlandtourism.com; **Taylor County Tourist Commission**—www.campbellsvilleky.com

### Northern Kentucky River Region
www.nkytourism.com

**Augusta Welcome Center**—www.augustakentucky.com; **Carrollton/Carroll County Tourism**—www.carrollontourism.com; **Flemingsburg Chamber of Commerce**—www.flemingkychamber.com; **Gallatin County Tourism Commission**—www.gallatincountyky.com; **Grant County Visitor's Center**—www.grantcokytourist.com; **Lewis County Tourism**—606-796-2732; **Maysville /Mason County Tourism Commission**—www.cityofmaysville.com; **Mt. Olivet**—859-289-5507; **Northern Kentucky Convention & Visitors Bureau**—www.staynky.com; **Owen County**—502-484-9900; **Pendleton County**—859-654-4189

## RECREATION & TRAVEL

# *The Belle of Louisville* Kadie Engstrom

When the first steamboat, the *New Orleans*, came down the Ohio River in 1811, it began a chain reaction that led to the development of the country. Before there were railroads and traversable roads, the rivers were the highways, and steamboats were the semitrailers of the 19th century.

Thousands of packet (freight) boats and towboats traveled every navigable waterway in Kentucky, bringing people to settle the towns and cities and work the farms and factories. They carried goods of all kinds – farm products, livestock, tools, grain, tobacco, coal, cotton, wagons, cloth, household supplies – everything needed to advance the commerce of the Commonwealth.

The major rivers – the Kentucky, Big Sandy, Cumberland, Tennessee, Licking, Green, Barren,

*Source: Belle of Louisville*

Ohio – all saw the advent and the progress of the steamboat era. The peak time in history for the hard-working steam-powered vessels was from the 1820s to 1880s, though packets and towboats were still built well into the 20th century.

By the 1960s nearly all the steamboats were gone, lost to fires, snags, ice and explosions, and replaced by diesel-powered towboats. The last of the packet boats is the sternwheel steamer *Belle of Louisville*. Built in 1914 as the *Idlewild* (renamed the *Avalon* in 1948, then the *Belle of Louisville* in 1962), it is the oldest operating steamboat in the country. It is the only steamboat in the United States to ever reach the ripe old age of 90, and the *Belle* will turn 92 on October 18, 2006. The *Belle of Louisville* is a National Historic Landmark and is on the Register of Historic Places. The *Belle*, like many steamboats before it, is an important link to Kentucky's past.

SPORTS

# Louisville Slugger
# Museum & Factory

It takes a special place to craft the Official Bat of Major League Baseball. At Louisville Slugger Museum & Factory, experience history-in-the-making as you stroll through the actual factory where world-famous Louisville Slugger bats are created.

Louisville Slugger began making baseball bats in 1884, when 17-year-old Bud Hillerich crafted the company's first bat for a local superstar hitter. Almost 125 years later, the Hillerich family still owns the business and still prides itself on the customer service that goes into every bat produced for the pros and the general public. The factory tour is a highlight of the visit here, but there's plenty more to enjoy as well.

Admire the World's Biggest Bat – stretching 120 feet into the sky. Crawl through a huge baseball glove, carved from prehistoric limestone. Face down a 90-mph fastball hurled by the major-league pitcher of your choice. Count the homerun notches Babe Ruth carved into his Louisville Slugger bat. Step into the batting cages and take some swings with a replica model of your hero's bat, from Babe Ruth to Derek Jeter. Or, take some cuts with Louisville Slugger's latest line of aluminum and composite TPX and TPS baseball and softball bats. Don't miss the original 13-minute film, "The Heart of the Game," which salutes the art and skill of hitting with some of the greatest players in baseball. Those are just a few of the all-star experiences at Louisville Slugger Museum & Factory. You'll even receive a free souvenir mini-bat at the end of your tour.

You can also create a bat with your own name on it, just like the pros. Your bat can even be personalized with a special message. They make great gifts for all kinds of special occasions, from newborn babies, to groomsmen gifts, to team trophies and more.

Louisville Slugger Museum & Factory is located

*Louisville Slugger Museum & Factory*
*Source: Hillerich & Bradsby*

in downtown Louisville at 800 West Main Street, just a few blocks from the location where the company's first bat was made in 1884.

Call 1-877-7-SLUGGER (1-877-775-8443) or swing by www.sluggermuseum.org for more information.

## RECREATION & TRAVEL

# *Kentucky Tourism Council's "Top Ten" Festivals & Events*

*The Kentucky Tourism Council names its "Top Ten" Festivals & Events four times a year. To be eligible festivals or events must be recommended or produced by a Kentucky Tourism Council member. A panel of impartial judges selects the winners for each season. Criteria for selection include popularity of the event, its impact on the local tourism economy as well as cultural and historical significance.*

### SPRING

**American Quilter's Society 22nd Annual Quilt Show**, Paducah, April 26 - 29. Showcases more than 400 quilts and wallhangings with $100,000 awarded in prizes for outstanding quilts in various categories. (270) 443-8783.

**Kentucky Derby Festival**, Louisville, April 15 – May 6. At 51 years old, it's a whirlwind of fun & entertaining events starting with Thunder Over Louisville and ending with the Kentucky Derby. (502) 584-6383.

**Becky Holder on Courageous Comet during the cross country event at the Rolex Three Day Event on April 29, 2006.**
*Photo: Janet Worne, Lexington Herald-Leader*

**Hillbilly Days**, Pikeville, April 20-22. Shriners and volunteers transform downtown Pikeville into one of the most unique festivals in the world while raising money for the Shriners Hospital. (800) 844-7453.

**International Bar-B-Q Festival** , Owensboro, May 12 -14. Barbecue cooking teams from the area fire up their grills and compete with one another by cooking thousands of pounds of barbecue and burgoo in order to win the coveted trophy. (800) 489-1131.

**MainStrasse Village Maifest,** Covington, May 19-21. Maifest will once again celebrate the German tradition of welcoming the first spring wines by bringing together arts/crafts, food and entertainment. (859) 491-0458.

**Rolex Kentucky Three-Day Event**, Lexington, April 27 –30. The only four-star three-day event in America serving as the primary U.S. Equestrian Qualifying Competition for the World Equestrian Games in Aachen, Germany. (859) 259-4224.

**Chocolate Festival,** Washington, April 8-9. Plan a chocolate getaway to this 18th annual festival where you can indulge yourself with every kind of chocolate you can imagine in a historic atmosphere. (606)-759-7423.

**Kentucky Wine & Vine Fest**, Nicholasville, May 13. Celebrates the heritage of American Viticulture and has been named the official state wine festival of Kentucky. (859) 887-4351.

**Tri-State Railroad Show,** Greenup, March 18-19. A model railroader's smorgasbord of more than 75 vendor tables, model train railroads in all gauges, railroad memorabilia and 1/8th-scale steam and diesel train rides. (606) 834-0007.

**Traditional Bank Mayfest**, Lexington, May 13-14. More than 100 visual artists display their wares for purchase while readings are presented to showcase the written word, along with a Mayfest poster contest. (859) 233-1221.

# SUMMER

**Great American Brass Band Festival**, Danville, June 9-11. An old-time brass band concert in the park with a New Orleans-style parade marching down Main Street followed by music from world-renowned bands. (800) 755-0076

Dan Shields plays his tenor saxophone in the Circle City Sidewalk Stompers Clown Band at the Great American Brass Band Festival in Danville

*Photo: Brad Luttrell, Lexington Herald Leader*

**Kentucky State Fair**, Louisville, August 17-27. This unique festival brings eleven consecutive 16-hour days of excitement to the bluegrass state through concerts, the Kentucky State Fair Thrillway, World Championship Horse Show and delicious food. (502) 367-5000

**Hatfield-McCoy Festival**, Pikeville, June 9-11. After more than 100 years of feuding these two families came together for a reunion and thus was the beginning of the Hatfield-McCoy Festival. (800) 844-7453

**CrabbFest**, Owensboro, July 5-8. Now in its sixth year, Crabbfest is one of the largest Southern gospel festivals in the country with four nights of concerts by 18 major acts. (800) 489-1131

**MainStrasse Village "Original" Goettafest & River Raid**, Covington, June 17-18. Goettafest is a celebration of Goetta, a favorite regional food and the German Heritage of the MainStrasse neighborhood. (859) 491-0458

**Lexington Junior League Horse Show**, Lexington, July 10-15. Held as the first leg of the Saddlebred Triple Crown, it is the world's largest outdoor saddlebred horse show attracting thousands of spectators and nearly 1,000 exhibitors competing for $70,000 in prize money. (859) 233-1221

**W.C. Handy Blues & Barbecue Festival**, Henderson, KY. June 10-17. Celebrates the life, music and cultural heritage of the "Father of Blues" with various forms of music such as Delta & Chicago blues, Dixieland and jazz along with some delicious Henderson-style barbecue. (270) 826-3128

**Mercer County Fair & Horse Show**, Harrodsburg, July 24-29. Held for 177 years, this event is billed as the oldest continuous fair and horse show in the nation and is considered one of the country's top outdoor Saddlebred horse shows. (859) 734-2364

**3rd Annual Francisco's Farm Invitational Fine Art & Craft Show**, Midway, June 10-11. Named for John Francisco, original owner of the property on which Midway stands this event was created to enrich and celebrate the social, cultural and artistic life of the Midway community. (859) 873-5122

**400 Mile Sale Across Kentucky**, Paducah to Maysville, June 1-4. Residents from 60 communities in 24 counties covering 400 miles of scenic Kentucky sell their antiques, collectibles and gently used articles at many yard sales along the US 68/KY 80 corridor. (270) 782-0800

Driver of Hillbilly Choo Choo at Chicken Festival

Source: Kentucky Department of Tourism

## FALL

**Kentucky Bourbon Festival**, Bardstown, September 13-17. Five day international festival hosting 35 events, live music, southern cooking and a huge dose of southern hospitality. (800) 638-4877.

**MainStrasse Village Oktoberfest**, Covington, September 8-10. Nearly 100 artists and craftsmen offer their wares along with food and beverage booths and musical entertainment for the entire family. (859)-491-0458.

**Marion County Country Ham Days** , Lebanon, September 23-24. Family-oriented community festival serving-up country ham with all the trimmings, a PIGasus parade, 5K Pokey Pig Run, classic car show and live entertainment. (270) 692

-0021 .

**World Chicken Festival,** London, September 21-24. Tribute to Colonel Harlan Sanders of Kentucky Fried Chicken with the world's largest skillet, frying-up delicious chicken along with over 200 'eggs-hibitor' booths of arts, crafts and food. (800) 348-0095.

**St. James Court Art Show**, Louisville, October 6-8. This year's show will spill out into six, Old Louisville neighborhoods, display 700 artists, feature food vendor booths and a wide variety of commemorative items. (502) 635-1842.

**Paducah's 12th Ever Barbecue on the River**, Paducah, September 28-30. This three-day charitable event brings circuit cookers and backyard cookers from across the region together to offer some of the most delicious barbecue around. (270) 443-8783.

**Forkland Heritage Festival & Revue,** Gravel Switch, October 13-14. See old friends, reminisce about the past, take a wagon ride, check out the unique exhibits and attend the bean soup Supper Theatre and experience the down home atmosphere of this event. (800) 755-0076.

**The Battle of Perryville**, Perryville, October 7-8. This year's event will host a National Civil War Re-enactment with over 7,000 re-enactors portraying life during our nation's greatest struggle. (800) 755-0076.

**18th Century Market Fair**, Louisville, October 28-29. Historically accurate 18th century Market Days recreating years 1765-1792 where merchants, craftspeople, performers and soldiers gather to socialize, trade goods and entertain. (502) 897-9845.

**Historic Constitution Square Festival**, Danville, Sept. 15-17. Features living history encampments, 75 top-quality juried artists and craftsmen, strolling minstrels and folk music all set among original buildings where Kentucky's forefathers met and debated issues of the day. (800) 755-0076.

## WINTER

**Christmas in the Valley,** Renfro Valley, November 17-December 16. Travel back in time to a nostalgic country Christmas with twinkling lights, clogging elves, St. Nick's workshop and the new,

John Bradford, Kentucky's First Printer, (portrayed by Sam Stephens) with Elizabeth Taylor (portrayed by Elizabeth Taylor Kernen from Stanford) enjoy the 2006 Constitutional Square Festival
*Photo: Sam Stephens*

original production of "Christmas in the Valley" every Friday and Saturday night. (606) 256-2638

**Winter Wonderland**, Owensboro, November 24, 2006-January 1, 2007. Held on the downtown riverfront this festival features the largest outdoor ice rink in the Tri-State area, sleigh rides, snow activities, concessions and visits from Santa. (800) 489-1131

**Santa's Water Wonderland at Newport Aquarium**, Newport, November 24-December 31. Become immersed in the magic of the holiday season by presentations done by a "Scuba Santa" who communicates with guests while interacting with sharks, fish and a loggerhead sea turtle. (859) 815-1432

**Southern Lights: Spectacular Sights on Holiday Nights**, Lexington, November 17-December 31. This is the 13th annual celebration of a nearly 3-mile drive through dazzling lights and animated figures at the Kentucky Horse Park. Indoor activities include a singing Christmas tree, Mini-Train Express and holiday and craft vendors for your shopping pleasure. (859) 259-4224

**Festival of Trees,** Ashland, November 18-26.

Held at the historic Paramount Arts Center this public display features more than 100 professional and community designed trees, elaborate gingerbread houses, wreaths and centerpieces. (606) 329-1007

**Holidays at Woodford Reserve Distillery**, Versailles, November 19-December 30. Enjoy savory culinary delights created by chef-in-residence David Larson, unique holiday shopping in the gift shop and experience genuine "Bluegrass" hospitality on personally guided tours of the distillery nestled amid picturesque horse farms. (859) 879-1934

**Christmas Candlelight Tours at My Old Kentucky Home**, Bardstown, November 24-25 and December 1-2, December 8-9. Guides, dressed in Christmas period attire at Kentucky's most famous home --- Federal Hill mansion, conduct these tours. The house is decorated for the Christmas Holidays, as it would have been in the 1800's. Guests are served refreshments after the tour. (502) 348-3502

**Eagle Watch Weekends, Dale Hollow State Resort Park**, KY Dam Village State Resort Park, Lake Barkley State Resort Park and Kenlake State Resort Park, January 19-21, January 26-28, February 16-17. These weekends offer travelers a chance to view American Bald Eagles from water and land by yachts, pontoon boats and vans. Experts also offer educational opportunities to learn more about eagles and other birds of prey. (502) 564-8110 Ext. 233

**Carter Caves Crawlathon**, Olive Hill, January 26-28. The 26th anniversary of this event provides activities for anyone interested in caves and caving without regard to their level of expertise. A few activities include wild caving, canoeing, pit plunging, sketching workshops, cave photography and proper techniques of caving. (606) 286-4411

**Candlelight Tour**, Frankfort, November 16. Held in the downtown area, sidewalks are lit with luminaries as folks enjoy an evening of strolling, shopping, music carriage rides, food and other events that mark the beginning of the Christmas season. (502) 875-8687

The Kentucky Tourism Council is a 560 member statewide association representing all sectors of the state's tourist industry. The Council's mission is to unite Kentucky's third largest industry through governmental interaction, communication and education. *Source: http://www.tourky.com/.*

# RECREATION & TRAVEL
# *National Parks*
# *& Historic Sites*

## ABRAHAM LINCOLN BIRTHPLACE
## NATIONAL HISTORIC SITE
In the fall of 1808, Thomas and Nancy Lincoln settled on the 348 acre Sinking Spring Farm. Two months later on February 12, 1809, Abraham Lincoln was born in a one-room log cabin near the Sinking Spring. Here the Lincolns lived and farmed before moving to land a few miles away at Knob Creek. The area was established by Congress on July 17, 1916. An early 19th century Kentucky cabin, symbolic of the one in which Lincoln was born, is preserved in a memorial building at the site of his birth.

2995 Lincoln Farm Road, Hodgenville
(270) 358-3137, (270) 358-3138

## BIG SOUTH FORK NATIONAL RIVER &
## RECREATION AREA
The free-flowing Big South Fork of the Cumberland River and its tributaries pass through 90 miles of scenic gorges and valleys containing a wide range of natural and historic features. The area offers a broad range of recreational opportunities including camping, whitewater rafting, kayaking, canoeing, hiking, horseback riding, mountain biking, hunting and fishing. These lands and facilities are operated and maintained by the National Park Service for the benefit and use of the public.

4564 Leatherwood Road
Oneida, TN 37841
(423) 286-7275, (606) 376-5073

## CUMBERLAND GAP
## NATIONAL HISTORIC PARK
The story of the first doorway to the west is commemorated at the national park, located where the borders of Tennessee, Kentucky and Virginia meet. Carved by wind and water, Cumberland Gap forms a major break in the formidable Appalachian Mountain chain. First used by large game animals in their migratory journeys, followed by Native Americans, the Cumberland Gap was the first and

best avenue for the settlement of the interior of this nation. From 1775 to 1810, the Gap's heyday, between 200,000 and 300,000 men, women and children from all walks of life, crossed the Gap into "Kentuckee."

US 25E South, P.O. Box 1848 , Middlesboro
(606) 248-2817

## MAMMOTH CAVE NATIONAL PARK
Mammoth Cave National Park was established to preserve the cave system, including Mammoth Cave, the scenic river valleys of the Green and Nolin rivers, and a section of south central Kentucky. This is the longest recorded cave system in the world with more than 360 miles explored and mapped.

P.O. Box 7, Mammoth Cave
(270) 758-2180

## TRAIL OF TEARS NATIONAL HISTORIC TRAIL
Trail of Tears
Commemorative Park, Hopkinsville

In 1838 the U.S. Army implemented a federal policy to remove American Indian tribes east of the Mississippi River to lands in the western United States. The Cherokee were driven from their homes into stockades scattered throughout the south, and moved to internment camps in southeastern Tennessee. From there, 17 detachments of Cherokees were forcibly moved to Indian Territory (in what is now Oklahoma). Approximately 16,000 men, women, and children made the sorrowful journey accompanied by a high rate of illness and death. The Trail of Tears National Historic Trail was designated in 1987. In 1996 the commemorative park established by the city of Hopkinsville became a certified site on the trail. The city park is the first non-federal property to receive such designation. Visit ww.trailoftears.org/.

# VISIT
# Kentucky National Historic
# Parks & Historic Sites

ABRAHAM LINCOLN
BIRTHPLACE NATIONAL
HISTORIC SITE
http://www.nps.gov/abli/

BIG SOUTH FORK NATIONAL
RIVER & RECREATION AREA
http://www.nps.gov/biso/

CUMBERLAND GAP NATIONAL
HISTORIC PARK
http://www.nps.gov/cuga/

TRAIL OF TEARS
NATIONAL HISTORIC TRAIL
http://www.nps.gov/trte/

MAMMOTH CAVE
NATIONAL PARK
http://www.nps.gov/maca/

# RECREATION & TRAVEL
# *Cave Exploration*                    Dr. Gary O'Dell

Snow-covered mountain peaks. Verdant tropical jungles. The deep ocean abyss. The polar icecaps. The limitless depths of space. These are some of the last frontiers of human endeavor. Most of us can only vicariously experience such exploits through television documentaries and magazine accounts. There is in Kentucky, however, a frontier that remains accessible to the ordinary person. Explorations in the underground wilderness of caves generally require only minimal investment in equipment and the application of plain common sense, along with informal training in safety and methods. Kentucky is home to Mammoth Cave, the world's longest, and thousands of other caverns large and small. Here, sometimes, it is possible to walk in places where no human foot has ever tread.

Caving can be hazardous—caves have slippery slopes, abrupt drop-offs, loose rocks, deep holes, or may be prone to rapid flooding. Among the most serious risks are injuries sustained from falling, drowning and hypothermia. Anyone entering a non-commercial cave should follow these basic safety rules:
• Never go caving alone; preferably go in the company of experienced explorers. Tell someone where you are going, and when you expect to return.
• Carry at least three separate sources of light, along with extra bulbs and batteries.
• Wear head protection: a hardhat or helmet with a chinstrap.
• Dress appropriately; caves in Kentucky have an average interior temperature of about 54 F, but sections may be colder in winter. If entering a wet cave, wear layered clothing to conserve body heat.
• Wear boots with an aggressive tread and ankle protection (never slick-soled shoes).
• Watch the weather closely. Many caves contain active underground streams—an innocuous ankle-deep trickle can become a roaring torrent after a heavy rain. Sticks or leaves stuck to the walls or ceiling can indicate the cave floods completely.
• Don't be a victim in a cave rescue: have proper equipment, experience and training before venturing into a cave.

The flip side is that caves are fragile environments that can be easily damaged by explorers. Heavy visitor traffic through a

Pushing a tight lead in a Rockcastle County cave
*Source: Gary O'Dell*

cave can disrupt the ecosystem; many animal species dwelling in caves are threatened or endangered. Mineral deposits such as stalactites and stalagmites are delicate and can be harmed just by touching, since the oils of human skin can stop growth. These formations are very slow growing and, if broken off, may take centuries to regenerate if at all. Nothing is more disturbing than to enter a cave, once beautifully decorated, and find only broken stubs and piles of trash. The guiding principle of the explorer is to "cave softly." The motto of the National Speleological Society is, "Take nothing but pictures, leave nothing but footprints, kill nothing but time."

Interested in cave exploration? Visit one of Kentucky's many commercial caves to test one's comfort level in an underground environment. Find a local chapter of the National Speleological Society (www.caves.org) for training in the safe and responsible exploration of wild caves in Kentucky.

# RECREATION & TRAVEL

# *State Fair*

Stephanie Darst

On Sept. 22, 1902, the first Kentucky State Fair opened at Churchill Downs in Louisville. The event was designed to boost the state's declining livestock industry, and the legislature provided a $15,000 appropriation, designated solely for premiums to the top livestock, horse and domestic entries.

The State Fair was modeled after Kentucky's many agricultural fairs, the first on Col. Lewis Sanders' Fayette County farm in 1816. These early fairs were stock shows and horse shows, often combined with seed exchanges and lectures to benefit the progressive farmer. Manufacturers of farm implements arranged displays, and competitions were held for "women's work," domestic and culinary classes. Once industrial expositions and world fairs became popular after the Civil War, all of the latest inventions were revealed at the fair.

**Kentucky State Fair**
*Photo: Sid Webb*

That first State Fair drew 75,000 people to see races of steam automobiles, demonstrations of dynamo-powered farm implements and the head-on collision of two locomotives. For the next few years Kentucky communities submitted competitive bids to host the fair. The 1903 Fair occupied the Daviess County Fairgrounds in Owensboro, but very few people attended. The resulting debt, coupled with a lawsuit testing the state's premium appropriation, caused the fair to be cancelled in 1904.

Lexington won the bid in 1905, and large crowds flocked to the fairgrounds later known as the Red Mile, but Louisville's bid was highest in 1906, sending the event back to Churchill Downs. That same year the first official State Fair Board was named, and Louisville was selected as the permanent site

for the Kentucky State Fair.

In September 1908 the Kentucky State Fairgrounds opened in western Louisville. The new facility included a grandstand, half-mile racetrack and livestock pavilion. The Midway featured games of chance, exotic shows, food vendors and the earliest amusement rides, the Ferris wheel and the carousel. The Merchants and Manufacturers Building – the most modern exposition building in America – was dedicated in 1921.

Events at the Kentucky State Fair reflected the trends and happenings of the time, introducing transportation milestones such as airplanes and automobiles and communications advancements from radio to television. The State Fair became the live showcase for new music genres and the largest venue for public education.

The original fairgrounds grew gradually, surviving the Great Depression and benefiting from the New Deal. During World War II, however, the fairgrounds were converted to wartime manufacturing industries, and the 1942 and 1943 State Fairs were cancelled. The State Fair returned to Churchill Downs in 1944 and 1945, but, after the war, plans were drawn up for a brand new year-round, multipurpose facility. The opening of the state-of-the-art Kentucky Fair & Exposition Center was covered live on national television during the 1956 State Fair.

The State Fair has continued to grow and change with the times, showcasing traditional and modern exhibits and entertainment at a site that now ranks as the eighth-largest exposition facility in the United States. In 2004 the 100th Kentucky State Fair was commemorated with a major history exhibition and the publication of a 200-page book.

# RECREATION & TRAVEL

# *Kentucky Bed & Breakfast Inns*

Todd Allen

### CHARM & HOSPITALITY

With abundant choices throughout every region of the state, Kentucky's bed & breakfasts have something to offer every one. Fondly known as B&B's, these inns range from small quaint log cabins in scenic rural settings, to classic mansions and historic farmhouses and inns. For those seeking repose and unique charm, a bed & breakfast offers an opportunity to relax, rejuvenate and enjoy personal attention and distinctive quality accommodations. Many B&Bs offer specialty services including high teas, spa treatments, wedding services, wineries, and meeting spaces— and access to every outdoor recreation imaginable including fishing, hunting, horseback riding, golf, tennis, and hiking. Sometimes even pets are

welcome. These small, charming, privately-owned bed and breakfast inns are an affordable choice for pleasure or business travel. The hosts of these establishments are renowned for their hospitality, breakfasts and as a source of information on local events and things to see and do.

The Bed & Breakfast Association of Kentucky is a statewide professional association of innkeepers, comprised of over 100 members. Membership requires all members to be quality inspected and approved, using the highest of quality standards. Members are dedicated to providing guests with exceptional hospitality, comfort, safety, and satisfaction. Visit www.kentuckybb.com or call 1-888-281-8188 for more information.

# Kentucky Bed & Breakfasts

- Overnight Bed & Breakfast Accommodations
- Bed & Breakfast Gift Certificates Available
- Bed & Breakfast Cookbook for Sale
- Weddings/Special Events
- Meetings/Socials

Bed & Breakfast Association of Kentucky

233 Rose Hill
Versailles, KY 40383-1223

## BED & BREAKFASTS

| LOCATION | BED & BREAKFAST | PHONE |
|---|---|---|
| Albany | Willowtree Bed & Breakfast | 606-387-6450 |
| Auburn | * Federal Grove Bed & Breakfast | 270-542-6106 |
| Augusta | Jane's Riverview B&B | 606-756-2050 |
| Augusta | The Parkview Inn | 606-756-2603 |
| Augusta | White Rose B&B | 800-371-0171 |
| Barbourville | Apple Tree Inn Bed and Breakfast | 606-546-5328 |
| Barbourville | Towne Square Place | 606-545-7256 |
| Bardstown | A Rosemark Haven | 888-420-9703 |
| Bardstown | * Beautiful Dreamer | 800-811-8312 |
| Bardstown | * Colonel's Cottage Inn - Millstone | 800-704-4917 |
| Bardstown | * Colonel's Cottage Inn - Pioneer Park | 800-704-4917 |
| Bardstown | * Homestead Bed and Breakfast and Kentucky Craft Shop | 502-349-1777 |
| Bardstown | * Jailers Inn | 800-948-5551 |
| Bardstown | Old Talbott Tavern | 800-482-8376 |
| Bardstown | * Red Rose Inn | 888-707-0033 |
| Bardstown | Shadowlawn Bed & Breakfast | 502-331-9588 |
| Bardstown | The Veranda | 502-350-3423 |
| Bardstown | Victorian Lights | 502-348-8087 |
| Beattyville | * Paw Paw's Landing | 606-464-3935 |
| Beaver Dam | Corniere Lodging Bed & Breakfast | 877-274-3447 |
| Bedford | * Bedford Inn Bed and Breakfast | 800-459-4536 |
| Bellevue | * Christopher's Bed & Breakfast | 888-585-7085 |
| Bellevue | Cincinnati's Weller Haus Bed and Breakfast | 800-431-4287 |
| Bellevue | * Mary's Rose View Inn Bed & Breakfast | 888-581-8875 |
| Benton | Aire Castle Inn & Stained Glass Art | 866-403-AIRE |
| Berea | * Doctor's Inn Bed and Breakfast | 859-986-3042 |
| Berea | Greathouse Bed and Breakfast | 859-986-7351 |
| Berea | Shady Lane Bed and Breakfast | 859-986-9851 |
| Blaine | Gambil Mansion Bed and Breakfast | 800-485-3362 |
| Bloomfield | * Springhill Winery & Plantation Bed and Breakfast | 502-252-9463 |
| Booneville | Linda's Victorian Rose Bed & Breakfast | 606-593-7662 |
| Bowling Green | 1869 HomeStead Bed & Breakfast | 270-842-0510 |
| Bronston | * Acorn and Fox Inn | 888-561-7755 |
| Brownsville | Raintree Inn | 606-561-5225 |
| Brownsville | Horseshoe Bend Bed and Breakfast | 877-386-8394 |
| Brownsville | * Serenity Hill Bed and Breakfast | 270-597-9647 |
| Burgin | * Lakeview Point | 859-748-8359 |
| Burkesville | Cabin Fever Lodging | 270-358-4415 |
| Burkesville | * Copper Hollow Bed & Breakfast | 270-443-7100 |
| Burkesville | Magnolias Manor | 270-864-1701 |
| Burlington | * Burlington's Willis Graves Bed and Breakfast | 888-226-5096 |
| Cadiz | * Whispering Winds Inn | 270-924-1094 |
| Calvert City | Wildflower Farms Bed & Breakfast | 866-438-8801 |
| Campton | Kathy's Bed and Breakfast | 606-668-6658 |
| Campton | Torrent Falls Bed and Breakfast | 606-668-6441 |
| Carrollton | Highland House B & B | 502-732-5559 |

**BED & BREAKFASTS**

| LOCATION | BED & BREAKFAST | PHONE |
|---|---|---|
| Carrollton | Seppenfeld House | 502-732-9134 |
| Catlettsburg | * The Presidents House | 888-538-4426 |
| Campbellsville | * Swan's Landing Bed & Breakfast | 270-465-9439 |
| Camp Springs | * Camp Springs House | 859-635-4600 |
| Cave City | Rose Manor Bed & Breakfast | 270-773-4402 |
| Cave City | Wayfarer Bed & Breakfast | 270-773-3366 |
| Clinton | Shepherd's Inn | 270-653-4212 |
| Corbin | * Antiques and Accents Bed and Breakfast Inn | 888-926-0646 |
| Corbin | * Flora Lane | 606-526-9765 |
| Covington | * Amos Shinkle Townhouse B & B | 800-972-7012 |
| Covington | The Wallace House Bed & Breakfast | 888-942-8177 |
| Coxs Creek | * Old Kentucky Home Stables & Bed & Breakfast | 502-349-0408 |
| Crestwood | * Foxhollow Manor House Inn | 800-624-7080 |
| Cynthiana | Hawks Nest Bed & Breakfast | 859-235-0440 |
| Cynthiana | Mockingbird Hill House | 859-234-5382 |
| Cynthiana | Seldon Renaker Inn | 859-234-3752 |
| Cynthiana | Side Saddle Inn Bed & Breakfast | 866-761-7336 |
| Danville | Country Lane B & B | 859-236-8671 |
| Danville | Empty Nest Bed and Breakfast | 859-236-3339 |
| Danville | Lincliff Guesthouse | 859-236-0185 |
| Danville | * Morning Glory Manor & Cottage | 859-236-1888 |
| Danville | Old Crow Inn | 859-236-1808 |
| Danville | Pasick's Bed and Breakfast | 800-906-8804 |
| Danville | * The Chambers Bed and Breakfast | 859-236-1693 |
| Danville | The Cottage | 866-453-5466 |
| Danville | The Golden Lion Bed & Breakfast | 800-236-3035 |
| Danville | Walnut and Lace Bed and Breakfast | 859-236-3035 |
| Eddyville | Journey's End Bed & Breakfast | 270-388-5117 |
| Eddyville | * Maple Hill Bed & Breakfast | 270-388-4963 |
| Falls of Rough | * Green Mansion Bed & Breakfast | 270-879-3486 |
| Falls of Rough | Ole Porter Place Bed and Breakfast | 270-879-4095 |
| Falmouth | * Red Brick House | 859-654-4834 |
| Falmouth | Back Inn Time Bed & Breakfast | 859-654-6100 |
| Flemingsburg | Mountain Lake Manor at D.H. Resorts | 800-737-7433 |
| Flemingsburg | * Stockton Station Inn | 606-845-0070 |
| Frankfort | Deercliff Bed & Breakfast | 866-646-7650 |
| Frankfort | * Meek House Bed and Breakfast | 502-227-2566 |
| Frankfort | * The Meetinghouse Bed & Breakfast | 800-768-9308 |
| Franklin | College Street Inn Bed & Breakfast | 800-686-9362 |
| Georgetown | * Blackridge Hall B&B | 877-296-3051 |
| Georgetown | * Bryan House Bed and Breakfast | 502-863-1060 |
| Georgetown | Dundriftin Bunkhouse Bed and Breakfast | 800-360-5774 |
| Georgetown | Gayla Bed & Breakfast | 502-863-5113 |
| Georgetown | Jordan Farm Bed and Breakfast | 502-863-1944 |
| Georgetown | Nine Mile Rest B & B | 859-255-0787 |
| Georgetown | Pineapple Inn Bed and Breakfast | 877-734-6289 |
| Ghent | Ghent House Bed and Breakfast | 502-347-5807 |
| Ghent | The Poet's House | 502-347-0161 |
| Gilbertsville | Magnolia Resort | 270-362-8121 |
| Glasgow | Hall Place Bed & Breakfast | 866-651-3176 |
| Glasgow | * Four Seasons Country Inn | 270-678-1000 |
| Glasgow | Old Victorian Bed & Breakfast | 270-651-1433 |
| Hagerhill | Enchanted Mountain Mansion | 800-467-5547 |
| Hardin | Ross's Landing Bed & Breakfast | 270-354-9596 |
| Harrodsburg | * 1879 Merriman Manor B&B | 888-485-8871 |
| Harrodsburg | * Aspen Hall Manor & Tea Room | 888-809-4457 |
| Harrodsburg | * Baxter House | 888-734-3984 |
| Harrodsburg | * Canaan Land Farm B&B | 877-748-8359 |
| Harrodsburg | Lakeview Point Bed & Breakfast | 859-748-8359 |
| Hartford | Historic Hillside Bed and Breakfast | 270-298-4233 |
| Hartford | Ranney Porch | 270-298-7976 |
| Henderson | * L & N Bed and Breakfast | 270-831-1100 |
| Henderson | * Victorian Quarters Bed & Breakfast | 270-831-2778 |
| Hindman | Knott County Historical and Geneological Society | 606-785-5751 |
| Hodgenville | Old Gait Farm | 877-548-7348 |
| Hyden | Wendover Bed and Breakfast Inn | 606-672-2317 |
| Idlewild | First Farm Inn | 859-586-0199 |
| Irvine | Snug Hollow Farm Bed & Breakfast | 606- |
| Kuttawa | Davis House Bed & Breakfast | 270-388-5585 |
| Lancaster | Hammonds Hall | 859-792-6632 |
| Lawrenceburg | Kavanaugh House B&B and Antique Mall | 800-374-6151 |
| Lebanon | * Myrtledene Bed & Breakfast | 800-391-1721 |
| Leeco | Old School House Bed and Breakfast | 606-464-9991 |
| Lewisport | * The River House Bed and Breakfast | 270-295-4199 |
| Lexington | A True Inn | 866-436-1890 |
| Lexington | George Clarke House B & B | 800-494-9597 |
| Lexington | * Lyndon House Bed & Breakfast | 877-255-1784 |
| Lexington | * Silver Spring Farm | 859-255-1784 |
| Lexington | * Swam's Nest at Cygnet Farm | 859-226-0095 |
| Liberty | Horse & Buggy Country Inn Bed & Breakfast | 800-352-2030 |
| Liberty | Liberty Greystone Manor Bed & Breakfast | 606-787-5444 |
| London | Chesnut House Bed & Breakfast | 606-877-4640 |
| Loretto | The Hill House Bed & Breakfast | 270-865-2300 |
| Louisville | * 1840 Tucker House Bed & Breakfast | 888-297-8007 |
| Louisville | * 1853 Inn at Woodhaven | 888-895-1011 |
| Louisville | * 1882 Aleksander House Bed and Breakfast | 866-637-4985 |
| Louisville | * 1888 Historic Rocking Horse Manor B&B | 888-467-7322 |
| Louisville | 504 B & B | 800-501-1236 |
| Louisville | * Austin's Inn Place | 502-585-8855 |
| Louisville | * Campion House | 502-635-1114 |
| Louisville | * Central Park Bed & Breakfast | 877-922-1505 |
| Louisville | Columbine Bed and Breakfast | 800-635-5010 |

**BED & BREAKFASTS**

| LOCATION | BED & BREAKFAST | PHONE |
|---|---|---|
| Louisville | Culbertson Mansion Bed & Breakfast | 866-522-5078 |
| Louisville | DuPont Mansion Bed & Breakfast | 502-638-0045 |
| Louisville | Fleur de Lis Bed and Breakfast | 502-635-5764 |
| Louisville | Gallery House Bed and Breakfast Art Gallery | 877-597-2744 |
| Louisville | * Inn at the Park | 800-700-7275 |
| Louisville | Laura's Log and Stone Inn Bed & Breakfast | 502-267-0836 |
| Louisville | Pinecrest Cottage and Gardens | 502-454-3800 |
| Louisville | Towne House Bed and Breakfast | 502-636-5673 |
| Lynch | Black Mountain Guest House | 606-848-2766 |
| Madisonville | * Fox Ridge Bed & Breakfast | 270-821-7576 |
| Madisonville | * Hammack-Moore House Bed & Breakfast | 270-821-5812 |
| Madisonville | Ruby Lodge at Spring Lake | 270-825-1666 |
| Marion | * Grace House | 270-965-0010 |
| Marion | Marion Inn | 270-965-5391 |
| Marion | Myers Bed & Breakfast | 270-965-3731 |
| Maysville | * Kleier Haus | 606-759-7663 |
| Maysville | * Moon River Bed and Breakfast | 866-823-1946 |
| McKee | Lakes Creek Bed and Breakfast | 606-287-7953 |
| McKee | Mountain Springs Inn | 606-965-2789 |
| Middlesboro | Cumberland Manor B&B | 606-248-4299 |
| Middlesboro | The Grapevine Inn Bed & Breakfast | 606-248-9249 |
| Midway | Gallery Suites of Midway | 877-477-0778 |
| Midway | * Scottwood Bed and Breakfast | 859-846-5037 |
| Milton | * Green Acres Bed & Breakfast | 877-784-1846 |
| Milton | Richwood Plantation Resort | 866-742-4966 |
| Monticello | Fairchild's Bed & Breakfast | 606-348-5555 |
| Morehead | Brownwood Bed & Breakfast and Cabins | 606-784-8799 |
| Morgantown | * Helm House Bed & Breakfast | 800-441-4786 |
| Mt Vernon | * Singing Hills Inn | 606-256-8283 |
| New Haven | Sherwood Inn | 502-549-3386 |
| Newport | * Cincinnati's Weller Haus Bed & Breakfast | 859-431-6829 |
| Newport | * Gateway Bed & Breakfast | 888-891-7500 |
| Nicholasville | Connemara Bed & Breakfast | 877-571-5777 |
| Nicholasville | * Corner House B&B | 888-727-8336 |
| Nicholasville | Duncan House at Mt. Pleasant B & B | 859-881-8478 |
| Nicholasville | * O'Neal Cabin | 866-988-1006 |
| Oven Fork | Oven Fork Mercantile | 606-633-8909 |
| Owensboro | Helton House Bed and Breakfast | 270-926-7117 |
| Paducah | 1857's Bed and Breakfast | 800-264-5607 |
| Paducah | Fisher Mansion Bed and Breakfast | 866-7-FISHER |
| Paducah | Fox Briar Farm Inn | 888-369-2742 |
| Paducah | Fox Briar Inn at RiverPlace | 877-369-4661 |
| Paducah | Historic Elks Home B&B | 270-442-1231 |
| Paducah | Paducah Harbor Plaza Bed and Breakfast | 800-719-7799 |
| Paducah | * Rosewood Inn Bed and Breakfast | 800-548-3840 |

| LOCATION | BED & BREAKFAST | PHONE |
|---|---|---|
| Paris | * Country Charm Historic Farm Bed & Breakfast | 859-988-1006 |
| Paris | The Treehouse at Stoner Creek Bed & Breakfast | 859-987-6251 |
| Parkers Lake | * Farm House Inn Bed and Breakfast | 606-376-7383 |
| Perry Park | Perry Park Country Club and Bed & Breakfast | 502-484-2159 |
| Prospect | * DuPont Mansion | 502-638-0045 |
| Providence | Magnolia House Bed and Breakfast | 270-667-2642 |
| Renfro Valley | C & J Garden Bed & Breakfast | 606-256-2990 |
| Renfro Valley | Cedar Ridge by Request | 606-256-0037 |
| Renfro Valley | Singing Hills Inn Bed and Breakfast | 877-509-0282 |
| Renfro Valley | Sweet Harvest Inn | 866-606-4534 |
| Richmond | Barnes Mill Bed & Breakfast Guest House | 877-204-3426 |
| Richmond | * Bennett House Bed and Breakfast | 866-354-3567 |
| Richmond | Blue Heron B&B | 859-527-0186 |
| Russellville | Holly Tree Inn | 270-725-8865 |
| Russellville | * Log House Bed and Breakfast | 270-726-8483 |
| Russellville | * Washington House Bed & Breakfast | 866-850-9282 |
| Science Hill | * Four Generations Bed & Breakfast& Tea Room | 606-423-3482 |
| Shelbyville | Sanorosa Farm | 502-647-3324 |
| Shelbyville | Wallace House | 502-633-2006 |
| Simpsonville | Yellow Carriage House B&B Inn | 502-722-2039 |
| Slade | Shadow Mountain Mist Inn | 888-663-2600 |
| Smiths Grove | Cave Spring Caverns and Bed & Breakfast | 270-563-6941 |
| Smiths Grove | * Victorian House Bed & Breakfast and Day Spa | 800-843-5210 |
| Somerset | * Wortman's in the Woods | 866-278-9505 |
| South Union | Shaker Tavern B & B | 800-929-8701 |
| Springfield | * 1851 Historic Maple Hill Manor B&B | 800-886-7546 |
| Stanford | * Howards Inn and Resort | 606-355-2711 |
| Stanford | Stanford Manor | 800-307-0460 |
| Vanceburg | Pine Hill B&B | 606-796-6278 |
| Versailles | * 1823 Historic Rose Hill Inn | 859-873-5957 |
| Versailles | Bluegrass Bed and Breakfast Reservation Service | 859-873-3208 |
| Versailles | Kentucky Mansion | 800-526-9801 |
| Versailles | * Montgomery Inn | 888-219-5181 |
| Versailles | * Rabbit Creek Bed & Breakfast | 877-279-2563 |
| Williamstown | * Storybook Inn | 859-879-9993 |
| Winchester | "Farmer Bill's Country Home" Bed & Breakfast | 859-823-1058 |
| Winchester | * Scott Station Inn Bed & Breakfast | 859-858-0121 |
| Winchester | Guerrant Mountain Mission Bed and Breakfast | 859-745-1284 |
| | * House on Belmont | 859-745-0177 |
| | * Windswept Farm | 859-745-1245 |

* Denotes members of Kentucky Bed & Breakfast Association

Source: Kentucky Department of Tourism

# RECREATION & TRAVEL
# *Hotels & Motels*

**Amerisuites** (800) 833-1516
www.amerisuites.com
Florence, Louisville

**Baymont Inn and Suites** (800) 301-0200
www.baymontinns.com
Corbin

**Best Western** (800) 937-8376
www.bestwestern.com
Cave City, Elizabethtown, Florence,
Louisville, Paris, Russellville, Somerset,
Winchester

**Best Western** (800) 528-1234
www.bestwestern.com
Frankfort, Harrodsburg, Hopkinsville,
Lexington, Louisa, Maysville, Paducah,
Russell

**Comfort Inn** (800) 221-2222
Bowling Green, Cave City

**Comfort Inn** (800) 228-5150
www.comfortinn.com
Bardstown, Brooks, Corbin, Danville,
Erlanger, Franklin, Henderson, La Grange,
Lexington, London, Louisville, Oak Grove,
Paducah, Somerset, Winchester

**Country Hearth Inn** (888) 443-2784
www.countryhearth.com/hotels
Danville, Elizabethtown, Shelbyville

**Country Inn and Suites** (800) 456-4000
www.countryinns.com
Corbin, Georgetown, Lexington, Louisville,
Paducah, Shepherdsville

**Courtyard by Marriott** (800) 321-2211
www.marriott.com
Bowling Green, Covington, Erlanger,
Florence, Lexington, Louisville, Paducah

**Days Inn** (800) 325-2525
www.daysinn.com
Hazard, Kuttawa, Somerset

**Days Inn** (800) 329-7466
www.daysinn.com
Beaver Dam, Berea, Bowling Green,
Carrollton, Cave City, Corbin, Elizabethtown,
Fort Wright, Frankfort, Franklin,
Georgetown, Glasgow, Grayson, La Grange,
Lexington, London, Louisville, Morehead,
Mount Sterling, Murray, Oak Grove,
Owensboro, Paducah, Paintsville, Richmond,
Shelbyville, Shepherdsville, Springfield,
Williamstown

**Days Inn** (800) 325-2525
www.daysinn.com
Hazard, Kuttawa, Somerset

**Drury Inn** (800) 378-7946
www.druryhotels.com
Bowling Green, Louisville, Paducah

**Econo Lodge** (800) 553-2666
www.econolodge.com
Berea, Bowling Green, Georgetown,
Lexington, Radcliff, Richwood

**Embassy Suites Hotel** (800) 362-2779
Covington, Lexington, Louisville

**Extended Stay America** (800) 398-7829
www.extstay.com
Florence, Lexington, Louisville

**Fairfield Inn by Marriott** (800) 228-2800
www.fairfieldinn.com
Ashland, Bowling Green, Brooks, Corbin,
Frankfort, Georgetown, Hopkinsville,
Lexington, Owensboro

**Hampton Inn** (800) HAMPTON
www.hamptoninn.com
Ashland, Bardstown, Bowling Green, Brooks,
Carrollton, Corbin, Covington, Danville, Dry
Ridge, Elizabethtown, Florence, Frankfort,
Franklin, Georgetown, Hazard, Hebron,
Horse Cave, Kuttawa, Lebanon, Lexington,
London, Louisville, Maysville, Owensboro,
Paducah, Richmond, Somerset, Winchester

**Hilton Garden Inn** (800) 445-8667
Lexington, Louisville

**Holiday Inn** (800) 465-4329
www.holiday-inn.com
Berea, Brooks, Carrollton, Corbin,
Covington, Danville, Dry Ridge, Erlanger,
Harlan, Henderson, Hopkinsville, La Grange,
Lexington, London, Louisville, Madisonville,
Middlesboro, Monticello, Morehead, Oak
Grove, Owensboro, Paducah, Pikeville,
Richmond, Richwood, Somerset, Winchester

**Hotel Ivy** (866) IVY-3171
www.ivyhotels.com
Georgetown

**Howard Johnson** (800) 446-4656
Elizabethtown, Florence

**Hyatt Regency** (800) 233-1234
Lexington, Louisville

**Knights Inn** (800) 843-5644
Berea, Corbin, Lexington

**LaQuinta Inn** (800) 531-5900
www.laquinta.com
Lexington, Richmond

**Marriott** (800) 228-9290
www.marriott.com
Lexington

**Microtel Inn** (888) 771-7171
www.microtelinn.com
Bowling Green, Georgetown, Lexington,
Prestonsburg

**Microtel Inns & Suites** (800) 771-7171
www.microtelinn.com
Dry Ridge, Louisville

**Motel 6** (800) 466-8356
www.motel6.com
Bowling Green, Florence, Georgetown,
Lexington, Louisville, Morgantown,
Owensboro, Paducah, Shepherdsville,
Elizabethtown

**National Heritage Inn & Suites**
(877) 256-8600
www.renfrovalleyheritageinn.com
Renfro Valley

**Quality Inn** (800) 228-5151
www.qualityinn.com
Bowling Green, Brooks, Cave City, Corbin,
Louisville, Paducah

**Quality Inn & Suites** (800) 424-6423
www.choicehotels.com
Elizabethtown

**Radisson** (800) 333-3333
www.radisson.com
Covington, Lexington

**Ramada Inn** (800) 272-6232
www.ramada.com
Bardstown, Catlettsburg, Elizabethtown,
Fort Wright, Lexington, London, Louisville,
Maysville, Morehead, Owensboro

**Red Carpet Inn** (800) 251-1962
Paducah

**Red Roof Inn** (800) 733-7663
www.redroof.com
Bowling Green, Florence, Lexington,
Louisville, Richmond

**Residence Inn** (800) 331-3131
www.residenceinn.com
Erlanger, Lexington, Louisville

**Sleep Inn** (800) 753-3746
London, Louisville

**SpringHill Suites by Marriott** (888) 287-9400
www.marriott.com
Lexington, Louisville

**Super 8 Motel** (800) 800-8000
www.super8.com
Berea, Brandenburg, Campbellsville,
Carrollton, Cave City, Central City,
Corbin, Danville, Dry Ridge, Dry Ridge,
Elizabethtown, Florence, Fort Mitchell,
Georgetown, Goody, Grayson, Hazard,
La Grange, London, Louisa, Louisville,
Mayfield, Maysville, Morehead,
Munfordville, Owensboro, Owingsville,
Pikeville, Prestonsburg, Radcliff, Richmond,
Shepherdsville, Somerset, Whitesburg,
Williamsburg

**Travelodge** (800) 578-7878
www.travelodge.com
Florence

# CAMPGROUNDS

| CITY | CAMPGROUND | SITES | PHONE |
|---|---|---|---|
| Albany | Grider Hill Dock & Indian Creek Lodge | 20 | 606-387-5501 |
| Albany | Wolf River Resort | 87 | 606-387-5841 |
| Alexandria | A J Jolly Golf Course & Campground | 25 | 859-635-4423 |
| Bardstown | Holt's Campground | 32 | 502-348-6717 |
| Bardstown | My Old Kentucky Home State Park | 39 | 502-348-3502 |
| Bardstown | White Acres Campground | 100 | 502-348-9677 |
| Beattyville | Lago Linda | 35 | 606-464-2876 |
| Bee Spring | Moutardier Campground CE | 172 | 270-286-4511 |
| Bee Spring | Nolin Lake State Park | 32 | 270-286-4240 |
| Beechburg | Fleming County Wildlife Area | | 800-858-1549 |
| Benton | Bee Spring Lodge and Marina | 15 | 800-732-0088 |
| Benton | Big Bear Resort and Marina | 75 | 800-922-2327 |
| Benton | Birmingham Point RV Park | | 270-354-8482 |
| Benton | King Creek Resort and Marina | | 800-733-6710 |
| Benton | Lakeside Campground & Marina Inc. | 55 | 270-354-8157 |
| Benton | Lakewood Camping Resort | | 270-354-9122 |
| Benton | Malcolm Creek Resort | 42 | 800-733-6713 |
| Benton | Sportsman's Anchor Resort | 53 | 800-326-3625 |
| Benton | Town & Country Resort | 31 | 800-347-1470 |
| Berea | Oh! Ky Campground | 70 | 859-986-1150 |
| Berea | Walnut Meadow Campground | 87 | 859-986-6180 |
| Bowling Green | Beech Bend Park | 500 | 270-781-7634 |
| Bowling Green | Bowling Green KOA | 120 | 800-562-2458 |
| Brandenburg | Otter Creek Park | 250 | 502-574-4583 |
| Bronston | Lake Cumberland RV Park and Golf Driving Range | 60 | 877-461-2404 |
| Buckhorn | Buckhorn Tailwater Campground CE | 30 | 606-398-7220 |
| Burkesville | Dale Hollow Lake State Resort Park | 144 | 800-325-2282 |
| Burkesville | Sulphur Creek Resort | 22 | 270-433-7272 |
| Burlington | River Ridge Park | 75 | 859-586-7282 |
| Burnside | General Burnside Island State Park | 94 | 606-561-4104 |
| Cadiz | Boat Haven Resort & Marina | 12 | 888-557-7638 |
| Cadiz | Devils Elbow Campground C.E. | 20 | 270-924-5878 |
| Cadiz | Goose Hollow Campground & RV Park | 44 | 270-522-2267 |
| Cadiz | Kamptown RV Resort | 93 | 270-522-7976 |
| Cadiz | Lake Barkley State Resort Park | 78 | 800-325-1708 |
| Cadiz | Prizer Point Marina & Resort | 50 | 800-548-2048 |
| Cadiz | Willow Creek Campground & Restaurant | 73 | 270-522-0808 |
| Calvert City | Cypress Lakes Campground | 125 | 270-395-4267 |
| Calvert City | Kentucky Lake KOA | 90 | 800-KOA-8540 |
| Campbellsville | Green River Lake State Park | 157 | 270-465-8255 |
| Campbellsville | Heartland Campground | 101 | 877-822-8552 |
| Campbellsville | Pikes Ridge Campground Green River Lake | 30 | 877-444-6777 |
| Campbellsville | Smith Ridge Campground | 80 | 877-444-6777 |
| Carlisle | Blue Licks Battlefield State Resort Park | 51 | 800-443-7008 |
| Carlisle | Clay Wildlife Area | | 859-289-8564 |
| Carrollton | General Butler State Resort Park | 111 | 866-462-8853 |
| Cave City | Crystal Onyx Cave and Campground | 25 | 270-773-2359 |
| Cave City | Oakes Cabins and Campground | 9 | 270-773-4740 |
| Cave City | Singing Hills RV & Camping Park | 24 | 270-773-3789 |
| Cave City | Yogi Bear's Jellystone Park Camp-Resort | 200+ | 800-523-1854 |
| Central City | Western Kentucky RV Park | 50 | 270-757-0345 |
| Clarkson | Ponderosa Boat Dock | 70 | 270-242-7215 |
| Clarkson | Wax Campground CE | | 270-286-4511 |
| Columbia | Holmes Bend Marina-Resort | 105 | 800-801-8154 |
| Columbus | Columbus Belmont State Park | 38 | 270-677-2327 |
| Corbin | Corbin KOA Campground | 87 | 800-562-8132 |
| Corbin | Cumberland Falls State Resort Park | 50 | 800-325-0063 |
| Corbin | Grove Boat-In Campground | 32 | 606-864-4163 |
| Corbin | Grove Campground | 56 | 606-864-4163 |
| Corbin | Sheltowee Trace Outfitters | | 800-541-7238 |
| Corinth | Three Springs Campground | 18 | 859-806-3030 |
| Crittenden | Cincinnati South Campground (KOA) | 88 | 800-562-9151 |
| Cub Run | Dog Creek Campground CE | 24 | 270-286-4511 |
| Danville | Pioneer Playhouse | 50 | 859-236-2747 |
| Dawson Springs | Pennyrile Forest State Resort Park | 68 | 800-325-1711 |
| Drakesboro | Gregory Lake RV Park | 103 | 270-476-9223 |
| Dry Ridge | Campers Village | 40 | 859-824-5836 |
| Dunmor | Dogwood Lake Camping Resort | 144 | 270-657-8380 |
| Dunmor | Lake Malone State Park | 25 | 270-657-2111 |
| Eddyville | Eddy Creek Marina Resort | 16 | 800-626-2300 |
| Eddyville | Holiday Hills Resort | 100 | 800-337-8550 |
| Eddyville | Hurricane Creek | 51 | 270-522-8821 |
| Eddyville | Indian Point RV Park | 200 | 800-605-8562 |
| Eddyville | Lake Barkley RV Resort | 132 | 800-910-PARK |
| Elizabethtown | Elizabethtown Crossroads Campground | 78 | 800-975-6521 |
| Elkhorn City | Breaks Interstate Park | 60 | 800-982-5122 |
| Falls Of Rough | Cave Creek CE | 86 | 877-444-6777 |
| Falls Of Rough | Peter Cave | | 270-257-8376 |
| Falls Of Rough | Rough River Dam State Resort Park | 66 | 800-325-1713 |
| Falmouth | Kincaid Lake State Park | 84 | 859-654-3531 |
| Frankfort | Elkhorn Campground | 125 | 502-695-9154 |
| Frankfort | Kentucky River Campground | 105 | 866-227-2465 |
| Frankfort | Still Waters Campground & Canoe Trails | 71 | 502-223-8896 |
| Franklin | KOA Franklin | 104 | 800-562-5631 |
| Frenchburg | Lost Hound Campground | 30 | 606-768-6095 |
| Gilbertsville | Kentucky Dam Village State Resort Park | 217 | 800-325-0146 |
| Gilbertsville | Kentucky Lake Resort | 30 | 800-592-5344 |
| Gilbertsville | Moors Resort and Marina | 117 | 800-626-5472 |
| Glasgow | Beaver Creek Campground | 12 | 270-646-2055 |

# CAMPGROUNDS

| CITY | CAMPGROUND | SITES | PHONE |
|---|---|---|---|
| Glendale | Glendale Campground | 91 | 270-369-7755 |
| Golden Pond | Birmingham Ferry Campground | 29 | 800-LBL-7077 |
| Golden Pond | Cravens Bay Campground | 35 | 800-LBL-7077 |
| Golden Pond | Energy Lake Campground | 35 | 800-LBL-7077 |
| Golden Pond | Fenton Campground | 12 | 800-LBL-7077 |
| Golden Pond | Gatlin Point | | 800-LBL-7077 |
| Golden Pond | Hillman Ferry Campground | 247 | 800-LBL-7077 |
| Golden Pond | Jones Creek Lake Access Campground | | 800-LBL-7077 |
| Golden Pond | Land Between the Lakes | 767 | 800-LBL-7077 |
| Golden Pond | Nickell Branch Backcountry Area | 13 | 800-LBL-7077 |
| Golden Pond | Piney Campground | 310 | 800-LBL-7077 |
| Golden Pond | Redd Hollow Backcountry Area | | 800-LBL-7077 |
| Golden Pond | Rushing Creek | 40 | 800-LBL-7077 |
| Golden Pond | Smith Bay Lake Access Campground | 15 | 800-LBL-7077 |
| Golden Pond | Sugar Bay Backcountry Area | | 800-LBL-7077 |
| Golden Pond | Taylor Bay Backcountry Area | | 800-LBL-7077 |
| Golden Pond | Turkey Bay | | 800-LBL-7077 |
| Golden Pond | Twin Lakes Backcountry Area | 14 | 800-LBL-7077 |
| Golden Pond | Wranglers Equestrian Campground | 168 | 800-LBL-7077 |
| Grand Rivers | Canal Campground | 84 | 877-444-6777 |
| Grand Rivers | Exit 31 RV Park | 30 | 800-971-1914 |
| Grand Rivers | Lighthouse Landing | 60 | 800-491-7245 |
| Grayson | Valley Breeze RV Campground | 17 | 606-474-6779 |
| Greenup | Greenbo Lake State Resort Park | 63 | 800-325-0083 |
| Hardin | Aurora Oaks Campground | 50 | 888-886-8704 |
| Hardin | Kenlake State Resort Park | 90 | 800-325-0143 |
| Harlan | Camp Blanton | | 606-573-6811 |
| Harrodsburg | Chimney Rock RV Park | 65 | 859-748-5252 |
| Harrodsburg | Cummins Ferry Campground & Marina | 105 | 859-865-2003 |
| Harrodsburg | Walker's Mid-Lake Marina | 10 | 859-748-5520 |
| Hartford | Ohio County | 75 | 270-298-4466 |
| Hawesville | Vastwood Park of Hancock County | 12 | 270-927-8778 |
| Henderson | John James Audubon State Park | 68 | 270-827-2247 |
| Hillsboro | DH Resorts, Inc. | 10 | 270-737-7433 |
| Horse Cave | Horse Cave KOA Kampground | 65 | 800-562-2809 |
| Hyden | Trace Branch Campground/Rec Area CE | 15 | 606-398-7251 |
| Hyden | Willie Begley Memorial RV Park/ Campground | | 606-672-4875 |
| Jamestown | Kendall Recreation Area | 83 | 877-444-6777 |
| Jamestown | Lake Cumberland State Resort Park | 146 | 800-325-1709 |
| Jamestown | Shell's Wolf Creek Outfitters | 14 | 270-343-2510 |
| Kuttawa | Eureka Recreational Area | 27 | 877-444-6777 |
| Lancaster | Riverview RV | 53 | 606-548-2113 |
| Lawrenceburg | Beaver Lake Marina LLC | 10 | 502-839-4402 |
| Lewisburg | Shady Cliff Resort & Marina | 8 | 270-657-9580 |

| CITY | CAMPGROUND | SITES | PHONE |
|---|---|---|---|
| Lexington | Kentucky Horse Park Campground | 260 | 800-678-8813 |
| Littcarr | Littcarr Campground | 35 | 606-642-3052 |
| Livermore | Livermore RV Park | 31 | 270-499-0779 |
| Livingston | Rockcastle River Outpost | | 606-864-9407 |
| London | Craigs Creek Group Area | | 877-444-6777 |
| London | Holly Bay Campground | 94 | 877-444-6777 |
| London | Levi Jackson State Park | 146 | 606-878-8000 |
| London | London Dock and Rockcastle Campground | 27 | 606-864-5225 |
| London | Westgate R.V. Camping | 14 | 606-878-7330 |
| London | White Oak Boat-In Campground | 50 | 606-864-4163 |
| Louisa | Falls Campground | 60 | 606-686-3398 |
| Louisa | Yatesville Lake State Park | 47 | 606-673-1490 |
| Lucas | Barren River Lake State Resort Park | 99 | 800-325-0057 |
| Lucas | Narrows Campground CE | 90 | 877-444-6777 |
| Lynch | Portal 31 RV Park | 12 | 606-848-1530 |
| Mammoth Cave | Houchins Ferry Campground | 12 | 270-758-2180 |
| Mammoth Cave | Maple Springs Group Campground | 7 | 800-967-2283 |
| Mammoth Cave National Park | Double J Stables & Horsemans Camp | | 800-730-HRSE |
| Mammoth Cave National Park | Mammoth Cave Campground | 109 | 800-967-2283 |
| Marion | Paddy's Bluff Retreat | | 270-836-4297 |
| Marion | S&J RV Park | 10 | 270-965-3338 |
| Mayfield | Kaler Bottoms Public Wildlife Area | | 502-564-4336 |
| Maysville | Hillbilly Haven Campground & Marina | | 606-882-2091 |
| Maysville | Maysville River Park Marina | 33 | 606-564-2520 |
| Mc Daniels | Axtel CE | 158 | 877-444-6777 |
| Mc Daniels | Laurel Branch CE | 77 | 877-444-6777 |
| Mc Daniels | North Fork CE | 106 | 877-444-6777 |
| Mc Kee | S-Tree Campground | 20 | 606-864-4163 |
| Mc Kee | Turkeyfoot Campground | 15 | 606-864-4163 |
| Milton | Helton Camping | 100 | 502-268-3241 |
| Monticello | Conley Bottom Resort, Inc. | 120 | 606-348-6351 |
| Monticello | Cumberland Camping | 40 | 606-348-5253 |
| Morehead | Fall Creek Campground | 10 | 606-348-6042 |
| Morehead | Clay Lick Campground | | 606-784-5624 |
| Morehead | Twin Knobs Campground and Recreation Area | 216 | 877-444-6777 |
| Morganfield | Higginson Henry Wildlife Management Areas | | 270-389-3580 |
| Morganfield | Moffitt Lake Recreation Area | 85 | 270-333-4845 |
| Morgantown | Steamboat Landing Marina | | 270-662-0019 |
| Mortons Gap | Best Western Pennyrile Inn and Campground | 15 | 888-298-2115 |
| Mount Vernon | Nicely Campground | 50 | 606-256-5637 |
| Murray | Bullfrog Campground | 25 | 270-474-1144 |
| Murray | Holly Green RV Park | 36 | 270-753-5652 |

## CAMPGROUNDS

| CITY | CAMPGROUND | SITES | PHONE |
| --- | --- | --- | --- |
| Murray | Water's Edge RV Park & Marina | 55 | 888-651-3084 |
| Murray | Wildcat Creek Recreation Area | 50 | 270-436-5628 |
| Nancy | Pulaski County Park | 45 | 606-636-6450 |
| New Concord | Lakeview Cottages & Marina | 22 | 877-895-5876 |
| Olive Hill | Carter Caves State Resort Park | 89 | 800-325-0059 |
| Olive Hill | Grayson Lake State Park | 71 | 606-474-9727 |
| Owensboro | Diamond Lake Resort | 270 | 270-229-4900 |
| Owensboro | Windy Hollow Campground | 250 | 270-785-4150 |
| Paducah | Duck Creek RV Park | 75 | 800-728-5109 |
| Paducah | Fern Lake Campground | 70 | 270-444-7939 |
| Park City | Diamond Caverns Campground | | 270-749-2891 |
| Parkers Lake | Eagle Falls Resort | 40 | 888-318-2658 |
| Prestonsburg | Jenny Wiley State Resort Park | 117 | 800-325-0142 |
| Putney | Harlan County Campground & RV Park | | 606-573-6424 |
| Ravenna | Aldersgate Camp & Retreat Center | 10 | 606-723-5078 |
| Renfro Valley | Lake Linville Marina and Campgrounds | 36 | 606-256-9696 |
| Renfro Valley | Renfro Valley KOA | 101 | 800-562-2475 |
| Renfro Valley | Renfro Valley RV Park | 79 | 800-765-7464 |
| Richmond | Deer Run Stables L.L.C. | | 859-527-6339 |
| Richmond | Fort Boonesborough State Park | 167 | 859-527-3131 |
| Roundhill | Lazy Acres Trails & Paylake | | 270-286-4189 |
| Russell Springs | Indian Hills Resort & KOA Campgrounds | 110 | 800-KOA-5617 |
| Russell Springs | Indian Hills Resort/Alligator II Marina & KOA | 170 | 800-562-5617 |
| Russell Springs | Pine Crest RV Park and Cabins | 58 | 270-866-5615 |
| Salt Lick | Clear Creek Campground | 21 | 606-784-6428 |
| Salt Lick | Outpost Campground | 52 | 606-683-2311 |
| Salt Lick | White Sulphur Horse Camp | | 606-784-6428 |
| Salt Lick | Zilpo Campgrounds | 172 | 606-768-2722 |
| Sanders | Eagle Valley Campground | 200 | 859-347-9361 |
| Sassafras | Carr Creek State Park | 39 | 606-642-4050 |
| Sawyer | Sawyer Lake Campground | Closed for 2006 | 606-376-5323 |
| Scottsville | Bailey's Point Campground | 215 | 877-444-6777 |
| Scottsville | Barren River Dam & Tailwater Campground | 48 | 877-444-6777 |
| Scottsville | Walnut Creek Marina | 30 | 270-622-5858 |
| Shelbiana | Fishtrap Lake State Park | 28 | 606-437-7496 |
| Shelbyville | Guist Creek Marina and Campground | 26 | 502-647-5359 |
| Shelbyville | Lake Shelby Campground | | 502-633-5069 |
| Shepherdsville | Grand-ma's RV Camping | 38 | 502-543-7023 |

| CITY | CAMPGROUND | SITES | PHONE |
| --- | --- | --- | --- |
| Shepherdsville | Louisville South KOA | 175 | 800-562-1880 |
| Slade | Bee Rock Campground | 10 | 606-663-9199 |
| Slade | Koomer Ridge | 54 | 606-663-2852 |
| Slade | Natural Bridge State Resort Park | 87 | 800-325-1710 |
| Slade | Pumpkin Bottom in the Red River Gorge | | 859-663-9701 |
| Smith | Martins Fork Lake and Recreation Area | | 606-573-1468 |
| Smith | Smith Recreation Area | | 606-573-7655 |
| Smithfield | Lake Jericho Recreation Area | 62 | 502-743-5205 |
| Smithland | Birdsville RV Park | 34 | 270-928-2820 |
| Somerset | Bee Rock Campground | 10 | 606-376-5323 |
| Somerset | Cumberland Point Campground | 30 | 877-444-6777 |
| Somerset | Fishing Creek Recreation Area | 48 | 877-444-6777 |
| Somerset | Little Lick Campground | 6 | 606-679-2010 |
| Somerset | Waitsboro Recreation Area | 25 | 606-561-5513 |
| Sparta | Sparta Campground | 80 | 859-356-9859 |
| Staffordsville | Paintsville Lake State Park | 32 | 606-297-8488 |
| Stearns | Bear Creek Horse Camp | 23 | 423-569-3321 |
| Stearns | Big South Fork - Blue Heron Campground | 45 | 800-365-CAMP |
| Taylorsville | Rolling Hills Camping Resort | 71 | 502-477-1291 |
| Taylorsville | Taylorsville Lake State Park | 55 | 502-477-0086 |
| Tiline | Cumberland River Farm Campground | 13 | 270-928-2180 |
| Union | Big Bone Landing Marina & Campground | 62 | 859-384-1713 |
| Union | Big Bone Lick State Park | 62 | 859-384-3522 |
| Versailles | Lakeside Arena | 60 | 859-873-9155 |
| Versailles | Non-Such Campground | 18 | 859-873-2401 |
| Wallingford | Fox Valley Recreation Area | 100 | 606-849-2143 |
| Wallins Creek | Camp O Cumberland | | 606-664-2909 |
| Walton | Oak Creek Campground | 100 | 877-604-3503 |
| West Liberty | Gamble's Campground and Stable | 28 | 606-522-3400 |
| West Point | Salt River Recreation Area | | 502-922-4065 |
| Whitley City | Alum Ford | 8 | 423-569-9778 |
| Whitley City | Barren Fork Horse Camp | 41 | 606-376-5323 |
| Whitley City | Bell Farm Horse Camp | 5 | 606-376-5323 |
| Whitley City | Great Meadow | 18 | 606-376-5323 |
| Whitley City | Sand Hill Recreation Park | 32 | 606-376-9333 |
| Whitley City | Stampede Run Horse Camp | 24 | 606-376-9666 |
| Williamsburg | Williamsburg RV Park | 30 | 800-426-3267 |
| Willisburg | Captain Bobs Boat Dock | 12 | 859-375-0093 |

*Source: Kentucky Department of Tourism*

## Jerrell Goodpaster

# Hiking

There's no better way to experience the natural beauty of Kentucky than by hiking one of the state's numerous trails. The trails provide access to wildflowers, wildlife and geologic wonders. They can be used for bird watching, backpacking and more. From casual strolls along the Green River, in Mammoth Cave National Park, to exposed ridge top traverses in the Red River Gorge — it can be found in the Bluegrass State. The possibilities are endless.

A visiting hiker might begin a hiking vacation in the east-central part of Kentucky, at Cave Run Lake. The 100 miles of hiking trails near the lake should provide an adequate warm-up for even the most seasoned hiker. Bald eagles, Canada geese, herons and other avian delights can be spotted in this area. The Sheltowee Trace, a 270-mile trail, which follows the Daniel Boone National Forest south to Tennessee, passes through this area and intersects many of the Cave Run trails.

After a few days at Cave Run Lake, the curious hiker can move south a few miles to the Red River Gorge region. This area, combined with the Natural Bridge State Resort Park and

*Source: Sid Webb*

the Clifty Wilderness Area, is home to some of the finest trails in the state. The Auxier Ridge Trail exposes hikers to rugged sandstone cliffs and provides good views of the surrounding topography. The Rock Bridge Trail twists between and beneath giant hemlocks on its way to Creation Falls, which is located just a few feet away from one of the most unique natural arches on the planet. Trails to Natural Bridge, Sky Bridge, Gray's Arch, or one of the other magnificent arches, are sure to please even the most discriminating trail lover.

Visitors who follow the Daniel Boone National

Forest south will find more trails near Yahoo Falls, Cumberland Falls and the Natural Arch Scenic Area. If these fail to satisfy, one can keep traveling south to the Big South Fork National River and Recreation Area. The 50-mile long John Muir Trail will hold anyone's attention for a day or two, but it is only a sample of what the Big South Fork has to offer.

From the Big South Fork, hikers can either move east to more trails and the amazing overlooks of Cumberland Gap National Historical Park and Breaks Interstate Park, or west to the 60 miles of fascinating trails in Mammoth Cave National Park. If the 15 stream crossings on the Wet Prong Loop Trail fail to provide relief from summer heat, a cave tour might do the trick. While visitors are cruising along the extraordinary Cedar Sink Trail, members of the Pine Mountain Trail Conference will be putting the finishing touches on the hundred-mile long Pine Mountain Trail. Hikers who can't wait for its completion can hop further west to the Land Between the Lakes. The 60-mile long North-South Trail is a great place to watch the sun set over Kentucky Lake, or perhaps bring a Kentucky hiking vacation to a close. Of course, a hiker with more time could backtrack and hike the hundreds of miles of trail we skipped over. So many trails, so little time.

Source: Sid Webb

## Well, what about that?

"Many people seem concerned about snakes . . . copperheads and rattlesnakes inhabit the [Red River Gorge]. However . . . they pose only a small statistical risk to hikers. . . . I would confidently suspect that the average person is more likely to be seriously harmed in the Red by hornets, or in a traffic accident."

("Red River Gorge Trail Guide," Jerrell Goodpaster, Lost Branch Publications, Owingsville: 2005)

Lynwood Montell

# RECREATION & TRAVEL
# *Ghosts*
# *& Haunted Places*

"Across the centuries, people have passed along from one generation to the next their cherished heirlooms, such as beliefs, traditions, and historically significant family and community stories. Sitting around fires, or under a shade tree at night, older men and women told stories to entertain, also to explain the unexplainable. Children have always looked to parents, and especially grandparents, for insights into the mysteries of the world about them. Adults told stories about the things they had witnessed or experienced. They often embellished them with their own interpretation of the events described, perhaps even simply to make a good story better.

Kentucky was settled by people with a myriad of social and cultural backgrounds. They were mostly Americans by birth, but of various nationalities and races, being chiefly of English, Scottish, Irish, Scots-Irish, French, German, and African descent. Many of these early ancestors, who moved across the mountains onto the western frontier, preferred the soon-to-be comforts of towns and villages, while others became primarily backwoods people by choice. They fondly accepted the wild freedom of the frontier rural landscape. 'A lonely house in the middle of a great farm was their ideal, and they attained it even before it could be done with safety,' according to geologist Nathan S. Shaler. All of these groups brought with them the folk heritage of their geographical origin. Folk beliefs and narratives of all varieties, told and retold in any given area, reflect the ethnic makeup of the people who live there. Thus it is that the wealth of the stories and beliefs brought to an area by immigrants are translated, and sometimes modified, as they are passed along

**The John Hunt family plot, Lexington Cemetery**
*Source: Sam Stephens*

from generation to generation.

All across the state, Kentuckians have produced a great body of supernatural beliefs, stories, and historical legends. From the pioneer times down to the present, Kentucky has always been rich in ghost legends or personal accounts of ghostly visitations. Traditional stories that tell of ghostly sightings and felt presences of spirits and other supernatural creatures still persists as a vestige of the past, as they help to describe life and times of a bygone era. ...

Back then, it was common practice for a particular member of the family to assume the role as storyteller and tell 'those old scary tales' until the youngsters were often afraid to go to bed at night. In 1976, a resident of Urbana, Illinois, who had grown up in a logging camp in Henderson County, Kentucky, shared the following description of family ghost-telling sessions: 'We lived in this little shack-like house there on the Ohio River when I was a little fellow. It had cracks between the planks in the floor. When my dad would tell them old scary stories of a night, I would sit there, just scared to death. Every now and then, I would look down at the floor, afraid that something would reach up through one of them cracks in the floor and grab me by the leg!

Well, after he had told so many of them old tales, we'd all be scared to death. So me and my brothers would hop up out of our chairs and head for bed. We'd jump into bed, pull the quilts over our heads and stay there that way 'til the next morning. I mean, we was too afraid to get out of bed!'"

*Reprinted with permission from the University Press of Kentucky, "Ghosts Across Kentucky," William Lynwood Montell, pages xii-xiii (Lexington: 2000).*

RECREATION & TRAVEL

# *The Beautiful Ghost*    Keven McQueen

### *Excerpt from*
### *"Kentucky Book of the Dead"*

A tale complete with impressive detail, multiple sightings and at least one reliable witness, was published in the *Cadiz Telephone* in February 1890. The witness was Thomas K. Torian, a livery stable owner described as being "a plain, practical, intelligent gentleman, sober and truthful, and little likely to allow his imagination to mislead him." One Monday evening, Mr. Torian and his carriage driver went to Gracey, Christian County, in order to meet Mrs. Torian, who was returning from a visit to relatives in Russellville. As they made their way back home along on the Cadiz and Hopkinsville road, they passed a small cabin by the roadside. Torian's driver called his attention to a form near the cabin.

The panicked driver immediately took it to be a ghost and said so. Mr. Torian, fearing that his wife would get scared, curtly told the driver that it was only a resident of the cabin. Inwardly, however, he must have had his doubts, for he leaned out the carriage window to get a better look—at the same time deliberately blocking the view from his wife in order that she might not be frightened. Torian saw that a wraithlike woman wearing apparel rather risqué for the era was standing about twenty feet from the road. She turned to face him. Torian later claimed that "he never saw a more beautiful female figure or anyone more graceful in bearing and movement than this strange creature. She wore only one garment, which reached a little below the knees, sleeveless, apparently cut low at the neck, and as colorless as the whitest and purest of marble, as were also her features and all portions of her limbs exposed to view. Her hair, long and luxuriant, was unconfined and reached far below the waist, and, like the rest, was of shimmering whiteness." Torian could compare her only to a beautiful marble statue come to life.

The woman folded her arms across her chest, turned and walked away toward a fence surrounding a nearby cornfield. The carriage clattered on another twenty or thirty yards when Torian decided he had to have another peek at the woman, if woman it was. He looked out the window, expecting her to be far away, but to his amazement she had nearly caught up with the travelers and was standing in the road about thirty feet behind the carriage. This time Torian was satisfied. He closed the curtain and swore he would never mention the incident to anyone.

His driver, however, told some people about it and mentioned that Torian had witnessed it too. The feline was out of the haversack, so to speak, and Torian had a choice: deny that he had seen anything or admit it. He manfully chose to be forthcoming, even allowing the *Cadiz Telephone* to print his name when it ran an account of the sighting. It soon came out that Torian was in good company. Several people in the community had seen the phantom, and unlike most ghosts, which tend to haunt only a single area, this one was something of a wanderer. For example, a well-known farmer who chose to remain anonymous, and who lived several miles from the Cadiz-Hopkinsville road, had a strange encounter with the being the night after Torian saw it. He heard his farm bell ringing, and when he went to investigate he saw the attractive, glowing ghost gliding away from the bell rope. She abruptly vanished before the astounded farmer's eyes. Shortly thereafter two men saw her a short distance from the location of the Torian sighting, and three nights after her appearance before Torian she was sighted, not on a forlorn farm or on the lonely highway, but in the town of Cadiz.

The article made a special point of noting that Thomas Torian considered "all things bearing even a semblance of the supernatural as ridiculous in the extreme." Yet he was at a complete loss to explain what he, his wife, his driver and several other independent witnesses had seen.

# RECREATION & TRAVEL

Jeffrey Abbott

# *Louisville Stoneware*

*For nearly two centuries, Louisville Stoneware has preserved and shaped a rich artistic tradition*

The richness of raw materials. The perfection of a basic form. The poetry of a hand-applied brush stroke. In our machine-driven age, these natural and simple essences seem to have become a lost art.

Since its early beginnings, Louisville Stoneware has been dedicated to the craft of transforming clay into enduring, functional art forms. Working with the basic elements of earth, water, air and fire, skilled artisans create timelessly beautiful dinnerware, bakeware, serving pieces and collectibles that can be enjoyed and cherished for many generations.

Some designs are subtle—others are more striking and exuberant—but what they all have in common is an under-

tion and paint their own unique pieces of art. Visitors choose their canvas, whether it's a plate, mug, bowl, vase, basket or some other handcrafted piece. Louisville Stoneware provides the materials, kilns and expert assistance. No reservations are necessary for parties fewer than five.

## TOURS

Studio One is also where visitors can witness artistry in the making and see how natural stoneware clay is rendered timeless by no fewer than 20 pairs of hands. Tours are available to individuals and groups of 15. Advance registration appreciated.

## LOCATIONS

**STUDIO ONE**, 731 Brent Street, (502) 582-1900, (800) 626-1800, Mon - Sat 9 am – 6 pm, *Paint-Your-Own Art*, Mon – Sat 10 am – 5 pm, *Tours*—Mon – Fri 10:30 am & 1:30 pm; **OXMOOR CENTER**, 7900 Shelbyville Road, Monday – Sat 10 am – 9 pm, Sun Noon – 6 pm; **MALL ST. MATTHEWS**, 5000 Shelbyville Road, (502) 895-9221, Mon - Sat 10 am – 9 pm, Sun Noon – 6 pm.

lying belief that humble, everyday objects have an important place in our lives and homes.

## PAINT-YOUR-OWN ART

At Studio One, Louisville Stoneware's downtown location, visitors can fire up their imagina-

# RECREATION & TRAVEL
# *Planetariums*
# *& Observatories*

The **Arnim D. Hummel Planetarium**, located on the campus of Eastern Kentucky University in Richmond, is open each week for school programs, public programs and special events. Opened in 1988, it contains a Spitz Space Voyager projection system under a 67.5 feet dome. One of the largest and most sophisticated planetariums in the U.S., the Hummel Planetarium has seating for 164 people. Ph. (606) 622-1547, http://www.eku.edu/planetarium/

The **Gheens Science Hall and Rauch Planetarium** in Louisville is designed primarily for astronomy and space science education. The original planetarium, the Rauch Memorial Planetarium, was built in 1962 in honor of Rabbi Joseph Rauch. At the time, it was the first planetarium built in Kentucky. Razed in 1998, it reopened in 2001 as the new Gheens Science Hall and Rauch Planetarium with a 55 foot diameter hemispherical dome. The installation of the Spitz Electric Sky Immersavision technology is only the fourth such installation in the world. Ph. (502) 852-6664, http://www.louisville.edu/planetarium/

The **Weatherford Planetarium** at Berea College in Berea offers students a guided tour through the current sky to discover what's up right now. Using sky mythology, sky imagery and music, students work their way from the North Star to the paths of the planets. Ph: (859) 985-3301, http://physics.berea.edu

The **Hardin Planetarium** at Western Kentucky University in Bowling Green serves university students, the community and the state. Programs at the planetarium are designed to be entertaining and educational. Closed to the public in the summer. Ph. (270) 745-4044 or 3817, www.wku.edu/Dept/Academic/Ogden/Phyast/p4_.htm

The **Golden Pond Planetarium and Observatory**, located in Cadiz at the Land Between the Lakes Visitor's Center, offers a 40-foot dome. Novice astronomers can learn to identify the constellations on a simulated night sky, or visitors can observe the stars through one of four telescopes. Ph. (800) 455-5897 toll-free, http://www.lbl.org/PLGate.html

The **East Kentucky Science Center**, located in Prestonsburg, allows the night sky to capture the imaginations of young and old alike. On a dark

**Gheens Science Hall & Rauch Planetarium located on the University of Louisville campus**
*Source: Kentucky Department of Tourism*

moonless night, the sky is so filled with stars it's hard to tell one from another. Ph. (606) 889-0303, www.wedosience.org

The **Morehead State University Space Science Center,** Morehead, has been established to provide a research and educational facility with state-of-the art laboratories for undergraduate students in space science. The center originated from a joint NASA-Morehead State venture to develop a large aperture radiotelescope, satellite tracking station and associated laboratories and degree programs. Ph. (606) 783-2381, www.moreheadstate.edu

The **StarLab Planetarium**, at the Living Arts & Science Center in Lexington has a 16' x 11' dome with a projector that can display the night sky as it looks from anywhere on the Earth at anytime of the night or year. Open on Thursdays and Fridays in the school year on a first-come, first-served basis. Ph. (859) 252-5222 or 255-2284, www.livingartsandscience.org/science_discovery_field_trips.htm

# Sports

Just as the sun defines the day and the moon puts its signature on the night, it is a sphere that comes to mind when sports in Kentucky is the subject. This particular orb also rises and sets, though rapidly—a dribble, you might say. And few would question its relentless influence on the state's psyche.

Kentucky is, indeed, Planet Basketball. It is the land where glass backboards line the driveways of the well-to-do and rusty hoops are nailed to the sides of barns, where pools of light on late summer nights bathe the

## John A. McGill

baskets in angelic glow as youngsters play another game of pick-up in city parks throughout the state. Say amen.

It's where the Baron of the Bluegrass ruled, where Uncle Ed and the red towel-waving faithful thrived in Bowling Green, where Peck Hickman put the University of Louisville on the map. It's where Joe B. and Denny C. carried on, building their own traditions. It's the place to which Eddie Sutton said he'd crawl, only to eventually limp away under a dark NCAA cloud.

It's where Ricky P. ego tripped all the way from New York to Lexington and later from Boston to Louisville, becoming a Benedict Arnold to many in blue, but the Genius Savior to those in red and black. And it's where a fellow named Tubby established a consistent standard of success while also winning folks over with his admirable character and easygoing ways off the court. It's also where Kentucky Wesleyan, Kentucky State and Georgetown College have made significant contributions to the college basketball landscape, winning national titles in various divisions.

Perhaps most of all, it's where true believers of the bouncing ball reside just this side of Battyville. If the University of Kentucky fails to make it to the Final Four in any given year, for instance, it is wise to keep all sharp objects away from UK followers—who are either mouthing off or in deep mourning over the Shakespearean tragedy of it all. *Et tu, Big Blue?* Still, even though hoops prompt the most hosannas in Kentucky, it is noteworthy to remember that several individuals and teams have had a significant national impact in a number of other sports. A short list would include:

- In horse racing, we find the state's other signature sport, a result not only of having the world's most famous horse race in the Kentucky Derby at Churchill Downs in Louisville, but also by having the world's most lucrative horse sales at Keeneland in Lexington—and an unrivaled collection of magnificent horse farms that, appropriately enough, take the approximate shape of a horseshoe around the city.

- In golf, Lexington's Gay Brewer winning the 1967 Masters, Louisville's Bobby Nichols winning the 1964 PGA Championship, and Louisville's Frank Beard becoming the PGA's leading money winner and named player of the year in 1969.

- In auto racing, Louisville's Danny Sullivan winning the 1985 Indianapolis 500 and the CART Indy Car national championship in 1988; Owensboro's Darrell Waltrip winning the 1989

Daytona 500 and ranked third on the all-time list for career wins in NASCAR with 84; and brother Michael Waltrip winning the Daytona 500 in 2001 and 2003.

- In swimming, Louisville's Mary T. Meagher Plant winning three gold medals in the 1984 Olympics. In 1981 she set a world record in the 100-meter butterfly at 57.93 seconds—a mark that Sports Illustrated has called "the fifth-greatest, single event record of all time in any sport." SI also ranked Mary T. 17th on the list of the 100 greatest female athletes of all time. She was a 14-year-old eighth grader when she set her first world record, beating the previous 200-meter butterfly mark by one-tenth of a second at the 1979 Pan Am Games.

- In football, for all its history of woe, the University of Kentucky having head coaches go into the record books: Paul "Bear" Bryant, whose greater fame came while winning national championships at Alabama, and Blanton Collier, Bryant's successor at UK who later coached the Cleveland Browns to an NFL title.

- Centre College shocking Harvard 6-0 in football in 1921, a game that the New York Times would later call the biggest upset in sports in the first half of the 20th century.

- In National Association of Intercollegiate Athletics football, Georgetown College setting an NAIA record by appearing in four consecutive national championship games from 1999-2002, winning back-to-back titles in 2000 and 2001 to add to a previous championship in 1991.

- And in baseball, Pee Wee Reese, born in Ekron, and later residing in Louisville, becoming a Hall of Fame shortstop with the Brooklyn Dodgers. Meanwhile, back in 1884, Louisville's "Bud" Hillerich turned a wooden bat for Pete "The Old Gladiator" Browning of the Louisville Eclipse baseball team. They called it the Louisville Slugger. It's kind of caught on since.

What follows, then, is a look at Kentuckians who have excelled in a number of sports at every level. While some of the lists cited here can doubtless have more names added to them, we leave that to the day when an almanac devoted exclusively to sports in Kentucky is created—when more categories can be explored and current ones expanded.

In the meantime, we trust the anecdotes and historical data cited here bring you a measure of the diversity of accomplishment to be found in Kentucky's sports history—worthy accompaniment to the ubiquitous bounce of the basketball that remains at the heart of its identity.

SPORTS

# Hunting, Fishing
# & Wildlife
Jon Gassett

The quality, quantity and variety of hunting, fishing and wildlife observation available to Kentucky's residents and visitors are, perhaps, unsurpassed within the continental United States. Hunters enjoy large and healthy populations of deer, wild

and other wildlife. The locations for observation include state parks, wildlife refuges, national forests and nature sanctuaries and preserves.

Since the beginning of our country, fishing and hunting have been significant activities within our culture. Whether for pleasure or necessity, people have always wanted to pursue and take fish and game. Deer, rabbit, squirrel, quail, grouse, elk, bear and hundreds of other species have graced this country, and this wildlife has been taken for granted.

The Bluegrass State was, and is, one of the most abundant and popular places any-

Deer and Elk exhibit, Salato Center
Source: KY Dept. of Fish & Wildlife

turkey, rabbit, squirrel, quail, grouse, dove and waterfowl. With the recent reintroduction of elk to the Commonwealth, hunters have, on a limited basis, the opportunity to pursue one of the largest members of the deer family.

Kentucky's fishing opportunities are also plentiful. The Commonwealth has more miles of navigable waterways than any other state in the continental 48. There are also thousands of smaller streams and ponds for fisherman to enjoy.

The wildlife that may be observed in Kentucky is surprising to many. In addition to the game animals listed above, there are numerous bald eagles, hawks, bobcats, coyotes, beaver, otters, black bears

Students learn about the Salato Center
Source: Source: KY Dept. of Fish & Wildlife

where to enjoy the outdoors. People from all over fish our lakes, hunt our lands and just enjoy our splendid wildlife. But to truly understand what we have and where we are going, we must first look at the past.

Daniel Boone came through the Cumberland

Gap to the prosperous land the Indians called Kentucke. This land was filled with more animals, trees and open land than anyone had ever seen. There were even some species of game that were too plentiful. The new land fell under Virginia law and one of those laws required all male citizens to kill the overabundant squirrels.

By this time, settlers were calling Kentucky home. But still conservation was an unpracticed word, almost unheard. The population of humans were killing off the game and fish at an alarming rate.

The new occupants could not believe the number of species

**White Tail Deer**
*Source: KY Dept. of Fish & Wildlife*

**Wild Turkey**
*Source: KY Dept. of Fish & Wildlife*

game committee, making him the state's first game warden.

In 1792, Kentucky became a state, but not until 1861 was a law established to close seasons on certain game birds and deer. It had taken over 100 years since the first people came through Cumberland Gap to establish some type of law to protect our natural resources.

In 1874, the first fish hatchery was built in Louisville and the Division of Game and Fish was installed with the Department of Agriculture. Two years later a law passed prohibiting destruction of fish by trap, dipnet or seining. After these early decisions by government, things really got moving for the betterment of wildlife.

In February of 1894, one of the biggest steps in the Commonwealth's brief history was made. Kentucky's legislature enacted the first game and fish laws. This provided protection for certain types of fish, wild birds and game, but left the enforcement of the laws to local officials. This was a major feather in the cap of the conservation movement and set the tone for further growth in the 1900s.

The turn of the century saw the beginnings of major change in Kentucky. The Lacey Act of 1900 made it unlawful to transport illegally taken wildlife, and non-resident hunting licenses were first seen around this time. People were really starting to take notice of the problems facing the future of wildlife.

and animals that occupied the new land. In early Europe, only royalty or the upper class could use wildlife in any way. In England, the king owned everything, even the fish, game and birds, until 1215. Here it was all open and free. There was nobody to say what, when or where to hunt and fish. It was an abundance that was new and exciting, but it wouldn't last.

Over the next 20 years, people started to notice that the game wasn't as plentiful as it once was. They had to go as far as 30 miles to find food. People had been able to hunt and take any and as much game as necessary. The huge fish and game populations began thinning out.

What was the reason for all of the destruction of game, fish and birds? One reason is still a problem today: a lack of education. A number of people still have no idea how important conservation and preservation are to nature.

Settlers at Fort Boonesborough decided to do something about the dwindling populations. Daniel Boone was put in charge of the settlement's

Kentucky was not the only state that got involved in the protection of wildlife. Conservation and control of nature was becoming a nationwide topic of discussion. With the election of Theodore Roosevelt in 1901 came an all-new look at conservation in our country. Roosevelt's idea of "conservation through wise use" was used all across the United States. Reproduction of renewable resources before over-harvest was the main idea behind this theory.

The Doctrine of Conservation recognized the importance of a holistic approach to the management of natural resources. The doctrine also made a statement that is true today. Conservation is a responsibility of the public. Conservation isn't something that should be practiced or watched over by sportsmen. It is something for which everyone on the planet should be concerned.

During Roosevelt's "period of conservation," he made sure the Lacey Act was strictly enforced and made numerous other strides to improve wildlife in America. Three other major steps made during his term set a precedent that others tried to follow. The creation of the first federal bird refuge was created at Pelican Island, Florida, the new Division of Forestry was expanded by over 140 million acres of national forest and national parks were greatly improved and expanded.

1904 saw the creation of county "game wardens" in Kentucky, the forefathers of today's Conservation Officers. Their only duty was to enforce fish and wildlife laws and regulations. These men didn't do it for the money; they did it for the love and protection of our natural resources.

One problem with which the early game wardens dealt was landowner rights. There has been an ongoing battle between landowners and sportsmen for many, many years. The main cause of this feud: posted land. In 1878, the Kentucky legislature passed a law making it "unlawful to enter the closed lands of another to hunt, shoot or fish without the consent of the owner after the property has been posted." This was an important law, but it has not kept the illegal hunter off private property. Only the hunter or angler can keep himself or herself off posted land.

Private land covers almost 95 percent of Kentucky. Why is so much of the land posted? Poachers and inconsiderate sportsmen can take most of the

credit. Private landowners don't need the hassle and worry of people leaving gates open or destroying crops. So it is up to the honest sportsmen to improve relations with landowners. Help out the

**Female Canada Goose nesting in Dragonfly marsh at Salato Center**
*Source: KY Dept. of Fish & Wildlife*

farmers with chores, share the game and fish that you remove from the land and just be considerate.

The first 120 years in Kentucky were slow and inconsistent on the conservation front. Most of the moves by government were late coming and could have been much better, but they were making strides. Improvements on the state and national scene were being seen and felt. The "age of conservation expansion" would take place over the next 40 years in Kentucky, but had it not been for a few visionaries in the past two centuries we would have had much less to conserve.

The work and caring of just a few people got the ball rolling in the 1700s; now it is our turn to take over and make sure our state is a better place to live. Using private land is a privilege. Conserving our wildlife resources is a responsibility.

# Hunting
Jon Gassett

Two of the favorite game animals for hunters in Kentucky are whitetail deer and wild turkey. The Kentucky Department of Fish and Wildlife Resources has done an excellent job of managing our abundant natural resources, especially deer and turkey populations.

Whitetail males can attain a height of 3 ½ feet and a weight of 250 pounds. Females usually weigh much less. The size and health of the deer herd has grown remarkably in recent decades. Sixty years ago Kentucky's deer population was less than 1,000. It is estimated that in 2006 the herd num-

bers 900,000. The herd has grown to the point that in some areas the population of deer is too high. The department continues to manage the herd by increasing the length of the hunting seasons as well as the number of deer each hunter may harvest. Despite high deer numbers, Kentucky has become a trophy whitetail destination in recent years. For its land mass, Kentucky has produced more record class white-tailed bucks than any other state or province for the last decade. The Bluegrass State averages 30 plus trophy class whitetails each season. There are seasons for modern firearms, archery and black powder firearms. The deer harvest in 2005 in Kentucky was estimated to be 120,000. A healthy deer herd such as Kentucky's can be reduced by up to 40 percent without negatively affecting its future population. Hunting rarely depletes a herd more than 15 percent.

The wild turkey flock has also shown rapid growth through restoration and restocking efforts of the department. In 1958 the population was approximately 1,500 birds, but has grown to an estimated 230,000, with the 2005 harvest estimated to be 25,000.

It is once again possible to see, hear and hunt elk (also known as wapiti) in the commonwealth, for the first time since the 1850s. Kentucky began its modern-day elk restoration program in December 1997 with the release of seven elk from Kansas. Additional releases totaling 1,500 animals and natural reproduction have increased the herd to over 5,700 in just six years. Kentucky's elk restoration effort was not only the most aggressive and comprehensive ever attempted, but it has now yielded the largest population east of the Mississippi River. The target population is 10,000. Bull elk can reach a height of five feet at the shoulder and a mature weight of 700 pounds, making it one of the largest members of the deer family. The first modern-day elk hunt in Kentucky was in 2001, and was limited to 10 hunters that won a lottery entered by 9,235 hopeful hunters. All 10 hunters successfully harvested an elk. The number of permits issued has increased to 200 in 2006—with more than 26,000 applicants—and will be increased further as the herd increases in number. Eventually close to 1,000 permits are expected to be issued as the herd peaks over the next decade. Viewing the majestic elk on bugling tours in eastern Kentucky has also become quite popular as an offshoot activity of the expanding herd's presence.

The Department of Fish and Wildlife Resources has also led successful restoration projects for grouse and river otter. Squirrel and rabbit seasons are also very popular in Kentucky.

To inquire about hunting licenses or regulations contact the Kentucky Department of Fish and Wildlife Resources via their website at fw.ky.gov, or call the KDFWR Information Center weekdays at (800) 858-1549.

**A close-up view of a bull elk**
*Source: KY Dept. of Fish & Wildlife*

# Fishing
Jon Gassett

Among Kentucky's vast natural resources, water is one of the most prevalent, and our streams, rivers, lakes and reservoirs are literally teeming with an abundance and variety of fish. Fishing—the activity of hunting for fish—is a practice that dates back over the millennia. For many, fishing was a primary means of feeding a family, and now it is a favorite pastime for women, men and children alike. Whether it's the thrill of finding the best "fishin' hole," being out of doors in the beauty of Kentucky's natural wonders, a family tradition, or a means to some solitary moments, fishing continues to be a favorite pastime in the U.S. In 2001, 16 percent of the U.S. population 16 years old and older (34 million anglers) spent an average of 16 days fishing. Many of the most popular fishing destinations for Kentuckians and visitors are major reservoirs found in every region of the commonwealth. Kentucky has 18 major reservoirs over 1,000 surface acres, and is bordered by 600 miles of the Ohio River, it's numerous rivers and their tributaries offer a lifetime's worth of fun, entertainment and the thrill of catching the biggest fish ever. And, of course, that's not counting the countless "fishin' holes" that have been kept family secrets for generations of Kentuckians.

Ted Crowell (back of boat) pitches a jig into cover at Cedar Creek Lake in Lincoln County. The 784-acre lake, which began filling in September 2002, is the state's only designated trophy bass lake. The lake has a 20-inch size and one fish creel limit. Benjy Kinman is shown in the front of the boat in this May 2004 photo.
*Source: KY Dept. of Fish & Wildlife*

## BARREN RIVER LAKE

Let's start with Barren River Lake in mid-western Kentucky—this resource provides high quality fishing for largemouth & spotted (Kentucky) bass, black and white crappie and hybrid striped bass. White bass, bluegill, channel catfish and flathead catfish are also in abundance. Excellent fishing likewise occurs in the tailwaters below Barren River Lake Dam, particularly during the spring and early summer, for crappie, hybrid striped bass and channel catfish. Bluegill, white bass and flathead catfish can also be caught in the tailwaters. You can fish for rainbow trout at Peter Creek, which is less than 10 miles from the state park.

## BUCKHORN LAKE

Buckhorn Lake is one of the best fishing lakes in eastern Kentucky. Anglers can fish for largemouth bass, white crappie, bluegill, channel catfish or muskie. Buckhorn Lake is one of three lakes in Kentucky stocked with muskie by KDFWR. Muskie naturally ranged in the Middle Fork Kentucky River where the lake now stands. Middle Fork Kentucky River below Buckhorn Lake Dam attracts anglers interested in catching white crappie, bluegill, channel catfish, muskie and rainbow trout. KDFWR stocks a total of 5,600 rainbow trout below the dam each year during April through November.

## CEDAR CREEK LAKE

Cedar Creek Lake, Kentucky's newest, serves as the state's only trophy largemouth bass water. Owned and managed by the state fish and wildlife department, bass anglers are limited to keeping one largemouth per day, which has to be at least 20-inches long. It was truly designed with fishermen in mind—no jet skis allowed; fish anywhere from the bank free of other development; plus a tremendous amount of natural cover to enhance fishing success. Cedar Creek Lake covers approximately 800 surface acres.

## CUMBERLAND RIVER AND FALLS

Cumberland Falls and its moonbow are two of Kentucky's greatest natural wonders, and the avid fisherman will find numerous places to fish along this portion of the Cumberland River. Bank fishing is popular just below Cumberland Falls. The Kentucky Wild River section of Cumberland River offers fishing for smallmouth bass, spotted (Kentucky) bass, rock bass, redbreast sunfish, bluegill, walleye and channel catfish. Bark Camp Creek is a 13-mile drive from Cumberland Falls State Resort Park to Forest Road 193 Bridge, where both rainbow and brown trout can be caught. KDFWR stocks a total of 3,600 rainbow trout into this stream during March through June and October—another 500 brown trout are stocked in late winter.

Fishing on Greenbo Lake
Photo: Sid Webb

### DALE HOLLOW LAKE

A fishing trip to Dale Hollow Lake on the Kentucky-Tennessee border will place you at one of the legendary smallmouth and spotted (Kentucky) bass lakes in the Southeast. Good fishing is also the norm for largemouth bass, crappie, bluegill and walleye at Dale Hollow Lake. The Wolf River arm of the lake in Tennessee is open to fishing with a Kentucky fishing license above the reciprocal zone boundary. Fishing is good for trout at the Cumberland River in the Burkesville area. Dale Hollow Lake State Resort Park is the second largest state park in Kentucky.

### DEWEY LAKE

Jenny Wiley State Resort Park borders almost one entire side of Dewey Lake, where anglers can fish for largemouth bass, white crappie, bluegill and channel catfish. The headwaters of Dewey Lake can be float fished on Johns Creek from near the Pike County border at a ford near Thomas off Hwy 194 downstream about five miles to the German Bridge boat ramp. KDFWR stocks a total of 2,200 rainbow trout in this area

A close-up view of a good size trout
Source: KY Dept. of Fish & Wildlife

during April, May, October and November. Johns Creek also offers fishing for largemouth bass, smallmouth bass, spotted (Kentucky) bass, white crappie, bluegill and channel catfish.

### GREENBO LAKE

Greenbo Lake offers some of the best trout fishing in Kentucky, with a total of 15,000 rainbow trout stocked in this lake during January and October each year. The 181-acre lake is the focal point of Greenbo Lake State Resort Park. Anglers can also experience good fishing for largemouth bass, bluegill and channel catfish. Because this lake is so deep and clear, fishing is best during early morning, late afternoon or at night. Greenbo Lake is considered one of the Bluegrass State's top trophy largemouth waters.

### HERRINGTON LAKE

Herrington Lake's winding waters is a destination for many anglers interested in high quality largemouth bass and hybrid striped bass fishing in Central Kentucky. Herrington is a very deep, clear, 2,500-acre reservoir owned by Kentucky Utilities power company. It's tailwater area, accessible by boat only through the Kentucky River, offers good rainbow and brown trout fishing with artificial lures only. In the main lake, bluegill, crappie and white bass are spring favorites in the backs of creeks in timber or along sloping banks.

## KENTUCKY LAKE

There is no better crappie or largemouth bass fishing than at Kentucky Lake in western Kentucky. Kentucky Lake covers 100,000 surface acres in the state, as well as another 50,000 in western Tennessee. It lies on the Tennessee River in the rich Purchase region of Kentucky. The average crappie caught in Kentucky Lake is 10 inches. Two-pound crappie are not uncommon each March and April along shoreline cover, when redbuds and dogwood trees are in full bloom. In addition to excellent largemouth fishing, smallmouth can also be taken on the east side of the lake along the Land Between the Lakes National Recreation Area shoreline. The tailwaters of Kentucky Lake are known for giant blue catfish, channels and flatheads which can be caught from boat or bank.

## KINCAID LAKE

Kincaid Lake in northern Kentucky is home to one of the best populations of largemouth bass in Kentucky. Kincaid Lake is also known for bluegill, crappie and channel catfish. Nearby, the South Fork of the Licking River can be float fished from Cynthiana downstream to Falmouth for smallmouth bass, rock bass, largemouth bass and spotted (Kentucky) bass. This stream is one of the best smallmouth streams in Kentucky. There are several canoe entry and takeout sites along this stretch of South Fork.

## LAKE BARKLEY

Called the "sister" to Kentucky Lake, Lake Barkley's 48,000 acres of water parallel Kentucky Lake, and the two are connected by a canal. Barkley lies completely in Kentucky, and offers outstanding crappie, bass and white bass fishing each spring and fall. Lake Barkley isn't quite as deep as Kentucky Lake, and has many shallow covers and flats where largemouth congregate. Barkley also has superb bluegill and channel catfishing during warmer months along shoreline cover and rip-rapped banks. This large expanse of water, together with Kentucky Lake and Land Between the Lakes (LBL) offers a unique setting for fishing, hiking, camping and hunting all within close proximity.

## LAKE CUMBERLAND

With its 50,000-acre reservoir, Lake Cumberland is the largest lake that lies wholly in Kentucky. Vast, clear and deep waters hold good populations of largemouth bass, smallmouth bass, spot-

ted (Kentucky) bass, crappie, walleye, striped bass, bluegill and channel catfish. The striped bass fishery is one of the best in the U.S. The 75-mile run of Cumberland River from Lake Cumberland Dam downstream to the Tennessee border is known as one of the premier trout fisheries in the Southeast for rainbow and brown trout. The upper 16 miles of river has fishing access for bank and wade anglers just below the dam, near Long

Fishing on Lake Barkley at sunset
Source: Kentucky Historical Society

Bottom, Helm's Landing, Rockhouse and Winfrey's Ferry. Boat anglers can launch at ramps just below the dam, Helms landing and Winfrey's Ferry.

## NOLIN RIVER LAKE

Nolin River Lake provides fishing for walleye in early spring, crappie, largemouth bass and flathead catfish at night during the summer. Situated in the rolling hills of south central Kentucky in Edmonson, Grayson and Hart counties, the dam is located on the Nolin River about 20 miles from Leitchfield. The 5,795-acre Nolin River Lake provides recreational opportunities to over 2 million visitors per year. Bass anglers should concentrate on rocky points and in timbered coves for best success, while crappie fishing is good along shoreline cover in April, and in deeper creek channels in summer.

## THE GREAT OHIO RIVER

The 600-mile stretch of the Ohio River that borders Kentucky provides a tremendous fishing opportunity from one end of the state to the other. This river, which has been such a significant factor in the settlement and growth of Kentucky, is a series of pools, divided by about a half-dozen locks and dams, which allow commercial barge and pleasure boat traffic up and down the waterway. Some of the most productive fishing waters in

Kentucky lie below the dams on the Ohio. Striped bass fishing, cat fishing and sauger fishing in the tailwaters of the Cannelton, McAlpine, Greenup and Newburg dams can be outstanding at various times of the year.

## ROUGH RIVER LAKE

Rough River Lake is situated in Breckinridge, Hardin and Grayson counties. Rough River Lake is a local angler favorite that offers good quality largemouth bass, spotted (Kentucky) bass, white crappie, bluegill, hybrid striped bass and chan-

nel catfish. Rough River below Rough River Lake Dam provides both bank and float fishing opportunities. Over 6,000 rainbow trout are stocked in Rough River from April through September near Hites Falls—another 2,000 rainbow trout are stocked just below Rough River Lake Dam in June.

### SMOKEY VALLEY LAKE

Carter Caves State Resort Park offers a variety of outdoor recreation including fishing at 36-acre Smoky Valley Lake for largemouth bass, bluegill, and channel catfish. Fishing is allowed only during daylight hours on this lake—no internal combustion engine may be operated on the lake. A 12-mile float fishing trip is possible on Tygarts Creek in the spring and after heavy rains in the summer from Olive Hill downstream through a scenic gorge to the Hwy 182 Bridge at the park entrance.

### TAYLORSVILLE LAKE

Taylorsville Lake's 3,000-plus acres provides anglers a great opportunity to catch chunky largemouth bass, nice channel catfish and crappie, and feisty hybrid striped bass. Early

spring anglers go upstream in the Salt River to find hybrids on their annual spawning run, and then return in late summer to tackle these fish in the jumps on the main lake. Lots of natural cover such as stickups and timbered coves provide good cover for largemouth anglers to fish around.

### OTHER LAKES, STREAMS AND PONDS

Excellent fishing is found at a number of other lakes including Yatesville Lake in Lawrence County, McNeely Lake in Jefferson County, Pan Bowl Lake in Breathitt County, Beshear Lake in Caldwell and Christian counties and Guist Creek Lake in Shelby County. Kentucky's farm ponds offer the best early spring fishing in the state because the water warms earlier in these smaller bodies of water. Farm ponds produce numerous trophy-sized fish.

Remember to ask permission before fishing in private ponds, and please practice good stewardship of our waterways and our land.

**David L. Hayes of Leitchfield holds the disputed record smallmouth bass caught in Dale Hollow Lake on July 9, 1955. The fish, whose weight was reported at 11 pounds, 15 ounces, was disqualified as Kentucky's record smallmouth after allegations arose about the fish being stuff with lead weights and outboard motor parts prior to it being weighed. Hayes caught the fish while trolling a white Bomber lure approximately 75 feet off a shale point. The International Game Fish Association, which maintains world records, has reinstated the record for the biggest smallmouth bass ever caught.**
*Photo (B&W): KY Department for Fish & Wildlife*
*Photo (Color): David Hayes*

# Wildlife
*Jon Gassett*

Eagles, bobcats and bears – these are three of the most difficult and most exciting animals to be seen in the wild in Kentucky.

American bald eagles can be observed on a regular basis in the Land Between the Lakes region in Western Kentucky, and occasionally in other portions of the state. These birds, which can have a wingspan of eight feet, have been upgraded from the endangered species list to the threatened species list. They can fly level at 60 miles per hour and dive at 100 miles per hour. Their eyesight is so keen that they can see a rabbit two miles away.

There are approximately 10,000 bobcats (also known as wildcats) in Kentucky. They are difficult to observe due to their nocturnal and solitary habits. Their diet includes mostly small animals such as rabbits, rodents, fish and birds. A large bobcat (they can weigh as much as 30 pounds) can catch a small deer.

In the early 1900s black bears disappeared from Kentucky due to unregulated hunting and a loss of habitat, but they are making a comeback. Bears have been sighted in Eastern Kentucky over the past two decades. Sightings have increased dramatically as roaming bears from surrounding states of Tennessee, Virginia and West Virginia make forays into the state. Bears, which can attain weights in excess of 450 pounds, have been reported in more than two dozen counties in the Cumberland Plateau Region, with the greatest concentrations in Harlan, Bell and Pike counties.

There is a great variety of other wildlife to be seen in Kentucky. The game animals that may be observed include whitetail deer, elk, wild turkey, squirrel and rabbit. Herons, Canada geese and other waterfowl are common throughout the state. Beaver and otters are making a comeback. Peregrine falcons have been reintroduced to the Commonwealth, and coyotes have found their own way in, with an expanding population that may be causing a reduction in fox numbers. Birdwatchers enjoy observing songbirds, hawks and

**Starfire Elk**
*Source: KY Dept. of Fish & Wildlife*

other birds.

One of the best places to see wildlife (although not in the wild) is at the Dr. James C. Salato Wildlife Education Center in Frankfort. There are outdoor live exhibits that include bald eagles, black bear, elk, bobcat, whitetail deer, wild turkey and bison. Indoor exhibits include venomous snakes, frogs and toads, alligator snapping turtle, a bee hive and warm and cold water aquariums. Resident Canada geese and mallard ducks freely roam the grounds. The center has a backyard-style wildlife viewing area, mini wetland, two fishing lakes and a shaded picnic area.

Kentucky has an excellent state park system with abundant wildlife viewing opportunities. The Daniel Boone National Forest, which includes the Red River Gorge and the Big South Fork National Recreation Area are popular wildlife observation destinations. In addition to numerous nature preserves and nature sanctuaries, there are 82 wildlife management areas in Kentucky.

**Bald Eagle**
*Source: KY Dept. of Fish & Wildlife*

The Kentucky Department of Fish and Wildlife Resources offers a Kentucky Wildlife Viewing Guide. This guide contains information including 66 viewing sites, descriptions and special viewing tips. For more information, call (800) 858-1549.

*Article compiled by Mark Reinhardt*

John A. McGill

## SPORTS
# *Boxing*

Given the commanding presence of Muhammad Ali—both for his place in boxing history and for his remarkable charisma that made him a figure of great social significance on the world stage—it is perhaps easy to forget that three other Louisville fighters have also held the world heavyweight title.

**Jimmy Ellis**, Ali's boyhood friend and later his sparring partner, would win the World Boxing Association title in 1968 and keep it until losing to Joe Frazier in 1970. This was the title that the WBA had taken away from Ali after the champion's refusal to be inducted into the U.S. military during the Vietnam War era.

But long before Ali and Ellis, Louisville had a heavyweight champ in **Marvin Hart.** In July of 1905, Hart fought top-ranked Jack Root in Reno, Nevada, for the title that James J. Jeffries had vacated by retiring. Hart had lost to Root, a far more experienced boxer, almost three years earlier, but scored a 12th round knockout. Hart kept the title until losing to Canadian Tommy Burns on Feb. 23, 1906 in Los Angeles. He died in 1931 and is buried in Resthaven Memorial Park in Louisville.

During his rise to prominence, **Greg Page** was considered the second coming of Muhammad Ali for his similar blend of power, quickness and grace. Page would win the WBA heavyweight title in 1984 but lost it five months later. He would have other high points, but he never regained the form and promise he once showed.

During a fight in Erlanger in 2001, Page, then 42, suffered a brain injury that has left him paralyzed on the left side of his body. Last year the American Association for the Improvement of Boxing proposed a "Greg's Law" that would require greater medical oversight to protect fighters.

In addition to the heavyweights, Kentucky has been home to another champion, **Darrin "School Boy" Van Horn** of Lexington. Van Horn, who along with his manager/trainer father, G.L., had moved from Louisiana, attended the University of Ken-

tucky during his meteoric rise in the boxing ranks.

Often entering the ring to the UK fight song, Van Horn became the youngest-ever champion in both

**Muhammad Ali**
*Source: Mark Cornelison, Lexington Herald-Leader*

the junior middleweight (he was 20 years, 4 months and 28 days old) and the super middleweight (22 years, 8 months, 11 days) divisions.

With famed trainer Lou Duva in his corner, Van Horn defeated Robert Hines in a 12-round unanimous decision for the IBF junior middleweight title in Atlantic City in 1989. He would lose his first title defense to Gianfranco Rosi. Van Horn wasn't finished, however. Moving up to the super middleweight division, he shocked IBF champion Lindell Holmes with an 11th round knockout in May of 1991. Van Horn would run into a buzzsaw in Iran Barkley in his second title defense in January of 1992, losing in a second round technical knockout.

# Muhammad Ali Center

**MUHAMMAD ALI** is believed by many to be the most recognizable person on the planet. He is one of a select few individuals ever to have transcended his athleticism into a symbol of larger societal issues. Once the "King of the World," today, Ali is a United Nations Messenger of Peace who belongs to the world, and forever will be Kentucky's own.

Born in Louisville on January 17, 1942, Cassius Marcellus Clay, Jr. grew up in a small home in one of Louisville's black neighborhoods located in the city's West End. Cassius learned as a child, confidence from his father and respect for others and spiritual nurturing from his mother.

At age 12, Clay found boxing and dedicated himself to the sport. Ali's accomplishments in the ring were legendary—winning the Gold Medal for the United States at the 1960 Olympic Games in Rome and then going on to win an unprecedented three heavyweight championship titles. But there was always more to Muhammad Ali than what took place in a boxing ring.

Ali's societal and religious convictions paralleled the challenges of the Civil Rights era and antiwar movement of the 1960s. Although some opposed his outspoken views, many were inspired by his confidence and courage.

Upon retiring from boxing in 1981, Muhammad expanded his global humanitarian efforts—attending goodwill missions, providing millions of meals to the world's hungry, and helping secure the release of 15 United States hostages in Iraq. In addition to his international work, Muhammad is equally devoted to helping charities at home, visiting countless soup kitchens, hospitals, and many other important charities.

When Ali lit the Olympic cauldron at the 1996 Games in Atlanta, his life's purpose was rekindled, while also sending 3 billion viewers an inspiring message of courage and character. In November 2005, Ali symbolically passed the torch to the Muhammad Ali Center—a longtime dream of Muhammad and Lonnie Ali—in their hometown of Louisville. Its mission is *to preserve and share the legacy and ideals of Muhammad Ali, to promote respect, hope and understanding, and to inspire adults and children everywhere to be as great as they can be.*

The 93,000 sq. ft. center serves as both a destination site and an international educational and cultural center that carries on Muhammad's legacy and continues his life's work. Visitors are motivated by 2 ½ levels of media and interactive exhibits that tell Ali's life story and offer the encouragement to achieve one's own "personal greatness." Ali's biographical storyline is told through six core values of Muhammad's life: *respect, confidence, conviction, dedication, spirituality, and giving*, which also serve as the foundation for the Ali Center's public outreach, global initiatives, membership and educational programming.

**Inside the Muhammad Ali Center**
*Source: Muhammad Ali Center*

In addition to the exhibits, the Ali Center features two changing exhibit galleries—the Howard L. Bingham Gallery and LeRoy Neiman Gallery, classrooms, an auditorium, meeting and event space, a library and archives, distance learning facilities, retail store, and café.

For more information about the Muhammad Ali Center, visit www.alicenter.org, or call (502) 584-9254.

# Muhammad Ali's Boxing Record

Total bouts: ................................................. 61
Knockouts: ................................................. 37
Won by Decision: ...................................... 19
Loss by Decision: ........................................4
Knocked Out:...............................................1

## ALI'S YEAR-BY-YEAR FIGHT RESULTS
*(\*\*\* = Heavyweight Title bouts)*

| Date | Opponent | Site | Result |
|------|----------|------|--------|
| **1960** | | | |
| 29-Oct | Tunney Hunsaker | Louisville | W6 |
| 27-Dec | Herb Siler | Miami Beach | KO4 |
| **1961** | | | |
| 17-Jan | Anthony Sperti | Miami Beach | KO3 |
| 7-Feb | Jim Robinson | Miami Beach | KO1 |
| 21-Feb | Donnie Fleeman | Miami Beach | KO7 |
| 19-Apr | Lamar Clark | Louisville | KO2 |
| 26-Jun | Duke Sabedong | Las Vegas | W10 |
| 22-Jul | Alonzo Johnson | Louisville | W10 |
| 7-Oct | Alex Miteff | Louisville | KO6 |
| 29-Nov | Willie Besmanoff | Louisville | KO7 |
| **1962** | | | |
| 10-Feb | Sonny Banks | New York City | KO4 |
| 28-Feb | Don Warner | Miami Beach | KO4 |
| 23-Apr | George Logan | Los Angeles | KO6 |
| 19-May | Billy Daniels | New York City | KO7 |
| 20-Jul | Alejandro Lavorante | Los Angeles | KO5 |
| 15-Nov | Archie Moore | Los Angeles | KO4 |
| **1963** | | | |
| 24-Jan | Charlie Powell | Pittsburgh | KO3 |
| 13-Mar | Doug Jones | New York | W10 |
| 18-Jun | Henry Cooper | London, England | KO5 |
| **1964** | | | |
| 25-Feb | Sonny Liston | Miami Beach | TKO7\*\*\* |
| **1965** | | | |
| 25-May | Sonny Liston | Lewiston, Maine | KO1\*\*\* |
| 22-Nov | Floyd Patterson | Las Vegas | KO12\*\*\* |
| **1966** | | | |
| 29-Mar | George Chuvalo | Toronto, Canada | W15\*\*\* |
| 21-May | Henry Cooper | London, England | KO6\*\*\* |
| 6-Aug | Brian London | London, England | KO3\*\*\* |
| 10-Sep | Karl Mildenberger | Frankfurt, Germany | KO12\*\*\* |
| 14-Nov | Cleveland Williams | Houston | KO3\*\*\* |
| **1967** | | | |
| 6-Feb | Ernie Terrell | Houston | W15\*\*\* |
| 22-Mar | Zora Folley | New York City | KO7\*\*\* |

| Date | Opponent | Site | Result |
|------|----------|------|--------|
| **1970** | | | |
| 26-Oct | Jerry Quarry | Atlanta | KO3 |
| 7-Dec | Oscar Bonavena | New York City | KO15 |
| **1971** | | | |
| 8-Mar | Joe Frazier | New York City | L15\*\*\* |
| 26-Jul | Jimmy Ellis | Houston | KO12 |
| 17-Nov | Buster Mathis | Houston | W12 |
| 26-Dec | Jurgen Blin | Zurich, Switzerland | KO7 |
| **1972** | | | |
| 1-Apr | Mac Foster | Tokyo, Japan | W15 |
| 1-May | George Chuvalo | Vancouver, Canada | W12 |
| 27-Jun | Jerry Quarry | Las Vegas | KO7 |
| 19-Jul | Alvin Lewis | Dublin, Ireland | KO11 |
| 20-Sep | Floyd Patterson | New York City | KO8 |
| 21-Nov | Bob Foster | Stateline, Nevada | KO8 |
| **1973** | | | |
| 14-Feb | Joe Bugner | Las Vegas | W12 31- |
| Mar | Ken Norton | San Diego | L12 |
| 10-Sep | Ken Norton | Los Angeles | W12 20- |
| Oct | Rudy Lubbers | Jakarta, Indonesia | W12 |
| **1974** | | | |
| 28-Jan | Joe Frazier | New York City | W12 |
| 30-Oct | George Foreman | Kinshasa, Zaire | KO8\*\*\* |
| **1975** | | | |
| 24-Mar | Chuck Wepner | Cleveland | KO15\*\*\* |
| 16-May | Ron Lyle | Las Vegas | KO11\*\*\* |
| 30-Jun | Joe Bugner | Kuala Lampur, Malaysia | W15\*\*\* |
| 1-Oct | Joe Frazier | Quezon City, Phillipines | KO14\*\*\* |
| **1976** | | | |
| 20-Feb | Jean-Pierre Coopman | Hato Rey, Puerto Rico | KO5\*\*\* |
| 30-Apr | Jimmy Young | Landover, Md. | W15\*\*\* |
| 24-May | Richard Dunn | Munich, Germany | KO5\*\*\* |
| 28-Sep | Ken Norton | New York City | W15\*\*\* |
| **1977** | | | |
| 16-May | Alfredo Evangelista | Landover, Md. | W15\*\*\* |
| 29-Sep | Earnie Shavers | New York City | W15\*\*\* |
| **1978** | | | |
| 15-Feb | Leon Spinks | Las Vegas | L15\*\*\* |
| 15-Sep | Leon Spinks | New Orleans | W15\*\*\* |
| **1980** | | | |
| 2-Oct | Larry Holmes | Las Vegas | KO'd11\*\*\* |
| **1981** | | | |
| 11-Dec | Trevor Berbick | Nassau, Bahamas | L10 |

# 2010 Alltech® FEI World Equestrian Games™

Jack Kelly

On Dec. 6, 2005, Kentucky history was made when the Fédération Equestre Internationale (FEI) — the governing body for worldwide equestrian sport — announced Lexington as the site of the 2010 World Equestrian Games. Preparation for the Games actually began months earlier when the Kentucky Horse Park committed itself to hosting this prestigious event by submitting its multi-million dollar bid to the FEI. Following months and years of planning and preparation, in 2010, Kentucky will become the first non-European city to host the elite championships that have been dubbed the "equestrian Olympics."

Greatly assisted by a record-setting $10 million financial commitment from Nicholasville-based Alltech, the Alltech® FEI World Equestrian Games™ 2010 will take place between Sept. 25 and Oct. 10, 2010. Not only will this be the first time that the U.S. hosts the FEI World Equestrian Games, it will also be the debut for the FEI's eighth recognized discipline – para-equestrian. The other seven Games disciplines include the three Olympic equestrian disciplines of dressage, eventing and show jumping as well as non-Olympic disciplines of driving, endurance, reining and vaulting.

Among a number of "firsts" for these Games is the title sponsorship by Alltech, a global leader in animal health and nutrition, whose commitment set a record for equestrian sport. In yet another first, the 2010 Games will be pre-

**International Three Day Eventer Cathy Wieschhoff presents Alltech's colors at the entrance to the Kentucky Horse Park**
*Source: 2010 Alltech FEI World Equestrian Games*

senting all eight disciplines on one site, utilizing the more than 1,200 acres that comprise the renowned Kentucky Horse Park.

Held every four years, the World Equestrian Games will be the largest equestrian sporting event ever to be held in the United States. The Games held their inaugural event in 1990 in Stockholm, Sweden; were then contested in 1994 in The Hague, Netherlands; in Rome, Italy in 1998; and in Jerez, Spain in 2002. The most recent 2006 World Equestrian Games were held in Aachen, Germany.

Kentucky is a state with a rich equine heritage. It is the home of not only world-famous thoroughbreds but also some of the most passionate horse owners, horse-industry workers and horse fans in the country. In addition, many who don't call Kentucky home will make the long trek to the 2010 Games to see an equestrian event with no rival in the United

A crowd of over 40,000 overflows Aachen's Main Stadium in Germany — Aug. 20 - Sept. 3, 2006
*Source: Alltech FEI World Equestrian Games*

over the course of two weeks. Some of the other expected numbers for the 2010 Games include approximately 800 athletes and 900 horses, representing more than 60 countries, which are expected to compete at the 2010 Games.

The goal of the Alltech® FEI World Equestrian Games™ 2010 is nothing short of creating a truly memorable world-class event for the competitors, spectators, horse owners and sponsors of the world. The anticipated economic impact in Kentucky — estimated at $150 million — includes the development of a new $34 million indoor, climate-controlled arena, a new luxury hotel on the grounds of the Kentucky Horse Park, airport improvements, road widening and the creation of an integrated hospitality program for spectators and corporate VIPs.

The Kentucky Horse Park is more than just the future host of these upcoming world equestrian championships. It also encompasses the National Horse Center — home to more than 30 top equine organizations including the U.S. governing body for equestrian sport, the United States Equestrian Federation®. Also within a short radius from the park are two of the country's finest equine hospitals. These attributes plus the incomparable physical beauty of the 1,200-acre site of rolling bluegrass hills, white plank fences and equestrian facilities, truly make the Kentucky Horse Park the ideal spot for a World Equestrian Games that will go down in history.

Reiner Aaron Ralston slides to a stop on quarter horse stallion, Smart Paul Olena
*Source: Alltech FEI World Equestrian Games*

States. While it is anticipated that 400,000 to 500,000 spectator tickets will be sold over the two weeks of competition, with an average of two tickets per person, it is possible that those numbers could be exceeded if the prior Games are any indication. At the Aachen Games, 570,000 spectators viewed the competition

# SPORTS
# *Horse Racing*

Ed Bowen

### THE INDUSTRY
*As Kentucky cash crops go,*
*nothing tops the horse.*

The horse is the leading cash crop in Kentucky. Its sales of more than $1 billion exceeds the individual totals from the poultry, tobacco and cattle industries. The economic impact on Kentucky has been placed at more than $4 billion annually. The thoroughbred is the leading breed in the horse industry in terms of economic impact.

The industry is concerned with three major areas: breeding, racing and sales. Here is a closer look at each element.

### BREEDING
Kentucky produces more than 25 percent of all thoroughbreds born in North America. The foal crop of 2004 was 9,731 out of a national total of 33,864. There are more than 350 thoroughbred stallions standing in the state and they are bred to more than 20,000 mares. Although fewer

*Photo: Sid Webb*

than 10 percent of thoroughbred stallions in the nation stand in Kentucky, they account for 35 percent of all breedings—a result of the concentration in the state of the best and therefore most utilized stallions.

Another indicator of Kentucky's prominence in breeding is found in the concentration of mares that are stabled permanently in the state or are brought into the state to be bred. (Artificial insemination is not allowed in the registration of thoroughbreds, so mares mated with Kentucky stallions have to be physically present.) One of many statistics underscoring Kentucky's leadership among breeding states is the fact that 98 of the 131 Kentucky Derby winners (75 percent) and eight of the 11 Triple Crown winners were foaled (born) in the state.

Kentucky's 450 thoroughbred farms maintain green space covering approximately 1,350,000 acres devoted to breeding and raising horses. The state's horse industry provides 100,000 jobs, directly and indirectly. A vast network of supporting industries includes feed, tack, veterinary services and supplies, fencing, barn building, painting, landscaping, tree trimming, horse van hauling, advertising, purchasing and selling agencies, printing, signage, sale companies, and information distributors.. At the race track, trainers, grooms, exercise riders, mutuel clerks and various other occupations swell the number of those employed employed.

In addition, the equine industry has an $8.8 billion impact on state tourism, accounting for an additional 14,600 jobs. The Kentucky Horse Park in Lexington is devoted solely to the horse. It covers 200 acres and attracts nearly a million visitors annually.

### RACING
Kentucky thoroughbred tracks conducted 259 racing programs in 2005, staging 2,552 races, with purses totaling $78,999,981. The majority of purse distribution comes from the "takeout" from the total amounts bet on the races, including on-site wagering and simulcast wagering from other sites around the country. Takeout is set by the state. Specific percentages are earmarked for the purse account, the operation of the track and the state. In addition, $9 million is offered in purse supplements from the Kentucky Thoroughbred Development Fund. The KTDF was established by state statute in 1978 and receives three-quarters of 1 percent of money wagered at Kentucky tracks and 2 percent of simulcast wagering from elsewhere. The fund provides premiums to owners of Kentucky-breds that win races in the state. Through efforts of the Kentucky Equine Education Program, about $12 million from the 6 percent sales tax on stallion services is earmarked for additional premiums to breeders .

## SALES

Two major thoroughbred auction companies are headquartered in Kentucky: Keeneland and Fasig-Tipton Co. Both are located in Lexington.

For many years, Kentucky breeders tended to send their yearlings to market in New York, but during World War II, restrictions on train travel prompted the formation of Breeders' Sales Company, a cooperative that began conducting sales on the grounds of Keeneland's race course. Later, Breeders' Sales was folded into the Keeneland Association and Keeneland's yearling sales became the most fashionable thoroughbred auction in the world.

The success of Keeneland sale graduates around the world bring leading buyers from Europe, Japan, and Dubai as well as from across North America. Sixteen Kentucky Derby winners and five Epsom Derby winners have been sold at Keeneland. The record price for a thoroughbred sold at auction is $13,100,000—paid for Seattle Dancer as a Keene-land yearling in 1985. By contrast, Kentucky Derby and Preakness winner Canonero II brought only $1,200 as a yearling in 1969.

Keeneland currently conducts four separate sales annually—for yearlings, weanlings, 2-year-olds and breeding stock. In 2005, these sales required a total of 33 days and saw 7,827 horses sell for a total of $744,411,300, an average of $95,108.

Fasig-Tipton Co., centered in New York, has conducted auctions throughout North America. It had a presence in Kentucky prior to the emergence of Breeders' Sales, and Fasig-Tipton returned to the state to establish a permanent division in the 1970s. Triple Crown winner Seattle Slew, Kentucky Derby and Belmont winner Bold Forbes and filly Derby winner Genuine Risk quickly established Fasig-Tipton's Lexington sale ring as another prime source of thoroughbreds. In 2004, Fasig-Tipton conducted five separate auctions in Kentucky, during which 1,523 horses were sold for a total of $89,560,800, an average of $58,806.

# Regulation & Organizations of the Industry

## KENTUCKY HORSE RACING AUTHORITY

Gov. Ernie Fletcher abolished the Kentucky State Racing Commission in 2004 and replaced it with the Kentucky Horse Racing Authority. The new authority has the regulatory roles traditionally in the hands of the old commissions, along with a responsibility to promote the industry. Members of the old commission and the new authority are appointed by the governor. The authority is responsible for the integrity of racing and licenses those involved in the day-to-day jobs of the race track. The testing of horses for illegal medication is an example of its responsibilities. Other states and provinces in North America have similar racing commissions. Thus there is no central government authority controlling the industry nationwide.

## THE JOCKEY CLUB

Organized in New York in 1894, The Jockey Club originally had a regulatory position in several states, and its rules of racing were widely recognized. Over the years, however, state racing commissions were assigned the responsibility of racing oversight in their individual purviews.

The Jockey Club remains an important organiza-tion, however, in another way. In the late 19th Century, the club acquired the rights to the fledgling

*Photo: Sid Webb*

American Stud Book, a breed registry. Ever since, the club has fulfilled the role of registering North American thoroughbreds and ensuring the integrity of the Stud Book. All states and provinces in North America recognize The Jockey Club as the sole source of registration in order for a thoroughbred to be permitted to participate in a pari-mutuel race.

The Jockey Club maintains offices in New York

City and Lexington. The Jockey Club family of companies now includes The Jockey Club Information Systems, which provides some 27,000 catalogue pages for thoroughbred auctions throughout North America; Equineline, which provides racing and breeding information to more than 15,000 customers from 60 countries; Equibase, the official database of the racing industry, which is a partnership with the Thoroughbred Racing Association and collects, produces and stores statistics on all races at North American tracks; InCompass, which provides computerized accounting/management systems to race tracks; and The Jockey Club Technology Services, which provides technical support for all the other companies.

## NATIONAL THOROUGHBRED ASSOCIATION/ BREEDERS' CUP LIMITED, LEXINGTON

The first running of the Breeders' Cup, the "Super Bowl" of thoroughbred racing, was held in 1984. The series first involved seven races and now has eight—each with a purse of $1 million or more. The Breeders' Cup, held near the end of the year, has a large bearing on which horses are named champions of their various age/gender divisions. The Breeders' Cup, whose offices are in Lexington, is joined organizationally with the National Thoroughbred Racing Association, which undertakes many of the industry's promotional roles, including television and lobbying efforts in Washington, D. C.

## GRAYSON-JOCKEY CLUB RESEARCH FOUNDATION, LEXINGTON

An affiliate of The Jockey Club, the foundation has financial headquarters in New York and staff offices in Kentucky. The foundation's membership is open to all who care for horses, and its sole role is to raise funds to support veterinary research—specifically to promote the health and soundness of the horse.

In 2006, the foundation budgeted more than $950,000 to university researchers throughout North America and in England for 20 specific projects addressing diseases and injuries, including state of the art techniques such as DNA vaccination, gene therapy and adult stem cell treatment. Since 1983, the Grayson-Jockey Club has provided more than $13 million to conduct more than 210 projects at 32 institutions. Among the key institutions receiving funds is the Maxwell Gluck Equine Research Center at the University of Kentucky, which was founded by a joint funding effort involving the estate of breeder/owner Gluck, the Commonwealth of Kentucky and the thoroughbred industry.

## THOROUGHBRED OWNERS AND BREEDERS ASSOCIATION, LEXINGTON

TOBA was formed in 1961 and is a national trade organization of leading thoroughbred horse breeders and owners. It has approximately 3,000 members and seven employees. TOBA's mission is to "improve the economics, integrity and pleasure of the sport on behalf of thoroughbred owners and breeders." Projects managed by TOBA include the American Graded Stakes Committee, The Greatest Game LLC, Sales Integrity Program, and Claiming Crown. TOBA is also represented on the board of directors of the National Thoroughbred Racing Association as a founding member and on the American Horse Council. TOBA is the owner of The Blood-Horse magazine.

## AMERICAN ASSOCIATION OF EQUINE PRACTITIONERS, LEXINGTON

Founded by a small group of equine specialists in 1954 during a meeting in Louisville, the American Association of Equine Practitioners has grown into an international organization of more than 8,500 members. Offices are located in Lexington. Kentucky resident membership totaled 284 in 2005. Despite the rural nature of the state, this number ranks Kentucky within the top five states in AAEP membership, illustrating the concentration of expertise in the commonwealth. The AAEP holds an annual meeting in different American cities, presenting papers on state of the art aspects of veterinary care for horses, as well as sponsoring continuing education seminars for members.

## KENTUCKY THOROUGHBRED ASSOCIATION AND KENTUCKY THOROUGHBRED OWNERS AND BREEDERS, LEXINGTON

A conjoined organization of some 1,000 members, the KTA-KTOB supports and promotes the industry through various programs and lobbying efforts in the state capital of Frankfort. The KTA also is responsible of administering the Kentucky Thoroughbred Development Fund. One of the KTA's most important functions is its role, in conjunction with the Kentucky Horsemen's Benevolent and Protective Association, in representing horsemen (owners) in negotiating purse contracts with two of the state's tracks, Keeneland and Churchill Downs.

## THE KENTUCKY HORSEMEN'S BENEVOLENT AND PROTECTIVE ASSOCIATION, LOUISVILLE

With 6,000 members, the KHBPA focuses on representing horsemen (owners) in negotiating purse contracts with the state's race tracks. (In the cases of Keeneland and Churchill Downs, the KHBPA shares this function with the KTA.) The KHBPA, like sister organizations in other states and the national umbrella HBPA organization, provides various benevolent services to members of the thoroughbred racing community.

SPORTS

# Horse Racing
# Thoroughbreds

Ed Bowen

### HISTORY

The thoroughbred horse was developed in England and the first horse regarded as a thoroughbred to come to the Colonies was Bulle Rock, imported to Virginia in 1730. In Kentucky, racing originally was conducted through the streets. As early as 1791, three-day meetings were held over what was known as the Lexington Course, and during that decade race meetings were also held in Georgetown, Danville, Versailles, Bardstown and Shelbyville.

Henry Clay was among the original members of the first Kentucky Jockey Club, which was established in 1979 in a meeting at John Postlethwait's Tavern in Lexington. This organization conducted race meetings in Maysville, Winchester, Paris, Versailles, Flemingsburg, Harrodsburg and Richmond, in addition to Lexington.

(In those days, the phrase Jockey Club described an organization of men involved in the sport rather than a group of jockeys, as the word is used today. England's Jockey Club had been established several decades earlier, and the phrase was adopted by many organizations, including both ruling bodies and companies owning racetracks.)

Kentucky racing was originally a sport of short dashes, more like quarter horse racing than the thoroughbred racing of today. The rising popular-

*Photo: Sid Webb*

ity of four-mile heat races gave rise to the need for improved and more established stock. The first thoroughbred stallion known to have been brought to Kentucky was Benjamin Wharton's Blaze, which was advertised at stud in Georgetown in 1797.

During the 19th century, racing was conducted in several locations, including Louisville's handsome Woodlawn Course. In 1832, the Kentucky Association track in Lexington was renovated and became the second track "stripped" of grass, as the Union

**Man O'War (Kentucky Horse Park)**
*Photo: Sid Webb*

limestone that is the undergirding of the rolling hills and flowing creeks in Central Kentucky.

Bluegrass, which gives its name to the area (officially *poa pratensis*) was not native to the region, but was used as lush pasture grass as the area was cleared.

Another element that made Kentucky inviting was the fact that the area was less ravaged during the Civil War than was the horse country of Tennessee, which had been another burgeoning center of successful racehorse breeding.

The concentration of breeding in Central Kentucky in the aftermath of the Civil War gave rise to an increased degree of professionalism among horsemen in the area, which further strengthened the Bluegrass region's status. The state became a supplier not only for local horsemen but for non-resident owners—as it is to this day.

A. J. Alexander (see "Noted Kentucky Breeders") raised his horses in Kentucky at Woodburn Stud and was among the first to be a commercial breeder, producing horses specifically for the market rather than racing them himself.

Course in New York had been a decade earlier. The Kentucky Association had been formed in 1828.

Racing on dirt ovals became common and was instrumental in determining the shape of racing in this country. While English racing continued to be conducted in short three- or four-day meetings, the use of dirt surfaces rather than more delicate grass made possible the extended race meetings that still prevail in the United States.

Long race meetings also meant that stables were provided at various racetracks, whereas in England horses were trained in private yards and had to be transported to the racecourse for each start.

The breeding of thoroughbreds was established in the Upper Atlantic and Tidewater regions and spread south and west. The Bluegrass became the leading area for thoroughbred breeding, one key reason being the mineral-providing Ordovician

Many Kentucky horses were sent as yearlings to where the buyers were. For example, the great Domino was bred in Kentucky by Maj. Barak Thomas and sent to be sold at the Tattersall's annual auction in New York City, where he was purchased by Wall Street tycoon James R. Keene for $3,000 in 1892.

At the same time, out-of-state sportsmen also supported the development of Kentucky breeding by purchasing farms in the Commonwealth. Keene established Castleton Stud (see "Historic Farms"), and such other major New York industrialists as August Belmont I, August Belmont II, members of the Whitney family and Walter Salmon—along with Pennsylvanians Samuel D. Riddle and Joseph E. Widener—bought or leased farms in Kentucky.

Chicago tycoons William Monroe Wright and John D. Hertz also purchased farms—Calumet and Stoner Creek, respectively. More recently, the list includes Texan Nelson Bunker Hunt, South African minerals tycoon Graham Beck, Gulfstream Jet founder Allen Paulson, Khaled Abdullah of Saudi

Airdrie Stud, the old property is owned by former Kentucky Gov. Brereton C. Jones and Mrs. Jones, a descendant of the Alexanders.

**Runnymede Farm:** Established near Paris by Col. Ezekiel Clay Runnymede following the Civil War, the farm was owned by Col. Clay and his brother-in-law, Col. Catesby Woodford. They bred several major Kentucky racehorses and breeding

**Early morning exercise**
*Photo: Sid Webb*

Arabia, and the Maktoums, the ruling family of Dubai. All of them have purchased Kentucky farms and hired professional managers to run them.

Other major businessmen prefer to breed in Kentucky by sending their mares to be boarded on the professional, commercial farms. They have included William Woodward Sr., Marshall Field, Charles Engelhard, Mrs. Henry Carnegie Phipps and her son and grandson, Ogden and Ogden Mills Phipps.

All of these patterns continue into the present, although the number of Kentucky-raised horses sent to be sold outside the state is far fewer than those that are auctioned at the sales held in Lexington by both Keeneland and Fasig-Tipton.

**SOME HISTORIC KENTUCKY FARMS**

**Woodburn Stud** (see A. J. Alexander)**:** Now called

animals. The best included Ben Brush, winner of the 1896 Kentucky Derby and many other races. Ben Brush later became the sire of leading stallions Broomstick and Sweep.

Another Runnymede-bred was Hanover, a champion of the 1880s which returned to Kentucky and was the nation's leading sire four times. Clay and Woodford were not the official breeders of record of Miss Woodford, but they raised her, the first Thoroughbred to earn $100,000. The farm has remained in the family and today is run by Catesby Woodford Clay, a grandson of Ezekiel Clay. Recent horses bred by Runnymede include the 2005 Illinois Derby winner, Greeley's Galaxy.

**Hamburg Place** (see John E. Madden)

**Castleton Stud:** Established by James R. Keene

in 1893. Keene, a Wall Street tycoon, became a dominant breeder and owner although he was said to visit the farm only rarely. He entrusted its care to his brother-in-law, Maj. Foxhall Daingerfield. Keene bred 13 champion horses in addition to buying and racing the great horse Domino. Commando, a champion son of Domino, sired Colin, which was an unbeaten in15 races. Sysonby, another Keene champion, was so revered that after his death in 1906, it was estimated that a crowd of 4,000 attended his funeral. He was later exhumed and his skeleton placed in the American Museum of Natural History in New York City.

**Idle Hour Stock Farm/Darby Dan Farm:** Established by Col. E. R. Bradley (see above), Idle Hour was home to major stallions such as Black Toney, Blue Larkspur, and North Star III during the 1920s and 1930s. Col. Bradley also imported the foundation French-bred mare La Troienne. Col. Bradley won the Kentucky Derby four times. He died in

ners Chateaugay (1963) and Proud Clarion (1967), Preakness/Belmont Stakes winner Little Current (1974) and English Derby winner Roberto (1972). Darby Dan is now operated by a daughter and grandson of Galbreath, Mrs. Jody Phillips and her son, John Phillips.

**Calumet Farm:** The Lexington property purchased in 1924 by William Monroe Wright of Chicago was renamed Calumet Farm for the baking powder company that Wright owned. He turned it into a successful standardbred farm. After his death in 1931, his son, Warren Wright Sr., converted the operation to thoroughbreds.

Throughout the rest of Warren Wright's life (which ended in 1950) and continuing with his widow (later Mrs. Gene Markey), Calumet dominated American racing as no other farm has ever done. From 1941-1958, Calumet bred and raced a record seven Kentucky Derby winners: Whirlaway (1941), Pensive (1944), Citation (1948), Ponder

Photo: Esther Webb

1946 and the core of the farm later was acquired by John W. Galbreath and renamed Darby Dan Farm. Galbreath, a real estate developer and builder from Columbus, Ohio, imported European champions Ribot and Sea-Bird II to stand at stud there, as well as acquiring the champion Swaps and other top-level stallions. Under Galbreath's direction, Darby Dan bred and raised Kentucky Derby win-

(1949), Hill Gail (1952), Iron Liege (1957) and Tim Tam (1958). A large measure of that success could be attributed to Calumet's famed trainers, Ben and Jimmy Jones.

Whirlaway and Citation were also Triple Crown winners. Calumet was the nation's leading breeder 14 times and the leading owner 12 times between 1941 and 1961. Wright and Mrs. Wright/Markey bred 17 champions, including Horse of the Year designees Whirlaway, Twilight Tear, Armed, Citation and Coaltown. In 1968, Mrs. Wright's Forward Pass became Calumet's eighth homebred Derby winner, but the farm's fortunes declined after that.

It was not until the late 1970s—when Alydar, Our Mims, Davona Dale and other outstanding runners emerged—that Calumet regained a measure of its former prestige. After Mrs. Markey's death in 1982, the farm was managed by a relative, J. T. Lundy, until it was sold due to insolvency in 1992. During that time, Calumet added another Derby winner, Strike the Gold (1991), as breeder, bringing the total to nine, and also bred and raced another Horse of the Year, Criminal Type (1990). The farm was sold at auction for $17 million to Henryk de Kwiatkowski. It has been run by his widow and children ever since his death in 2003.

**Faraway Farm:** Located outside Lexington, Faraway enjoyed it greatest fame as the home of Man o' War as a stallion. Man o' War stood most of his stud career (1920-47) at the farm and was an enormous attraction to tourists from around the world. Will Harbut, his groom, became famous for his eloquent spiel about what he called the "mostest hoss that ever was."

Faraway was owned for many years by Man o' War's owner, the eastern sportsman Samuel R. Riddle, along with Mr. and Mrs. Walter M. Jeffords Sr. (Mrs. Jeffords was Mrs. Riddle's niece.) Today, the barn where Man o' War stood has been renovated and that portion of the old Faraway is now part of Greg Goodman's Mt. Brilliant Farm.

**Claiborne Farm:** (See Arthur Hancock Sr. et al)

**Spendthrift Farm:** (See Leslie Combs II)

**The Whitney Studs:** Harry Payne Whitney followed his father, W. C. Whitney, into racing. He leased a farm in New Jersey as he was establishing a leading stable in the East. Whitney then purchased property in Lexington. He bred champions Equipoise, Top Flight and others among a record (for the time) 191 stakes winners. After his death in 1930, his son, C. V. Whitney, took over the stable and farm. He had a similar and lengthy career as a leading breeder and owner.

Whitney's Fisherman was the first American

*Photo: Sid Webb*

horse to win the Washington, D. C., International, a pioneering international race run in Maryland. Adjacent to the Harry Payne Whitney and C. V. Whitney property was Greentree Stud, established by Harry Payne Whitney's sister-in-law, Mrs. Helen Hay Whitney.

Mrs. Whitney won the Kentucky Derby with Twenty Grand in 1931 and Shut Out in 1942. After her death in 1944, Greentree passed to her children, New York *Herald-Tribune* publisher John Hay (Jock) Whitney and Mrs. Charles S. Payson. The farm's success continued under their management. Greentree bred the champion Capot and purchased and raced the 1953 Horse of the Year, Tom Fool, who later became an important sire.

C. V. Whitney's widow, Marylou Whitney, resumed the breeding and racing operation after his death and won the 2004 Belmont Stakes with homebred Birdtown. Part of the old Whitney complex is now known as Payson Stud and is operated by Mrs. Virginia Kraft Payson, who had married Charles S. Payson after his first wife's death. Most of the Whitney property was sold in various parcels to Gainesway Farm, first owned by founder John R. Gaines and later purchased by Graham Beck.

**The Maktoum Studs:** Beginning in the early 1980s, the ruling family of Dubai became a major presence in sales, racing and breeding, both in this country and abroad. Sheikhs Maktoum al Maktoum, Mohammed al Maktoum and Hamdan al Maktoum established elaborate, highly professional and successful farms in Kentucky: Gainsborough, Shadwell and Darley at Jonabell.

The *Blood-Horse* magazine estimated in 2005 that the family had invested about $7 billion in horses, farms, a racetrack in Dubai, veterinary centers and racing-related items. The family has been so active in the yearling market that in 1989 and 1990, the Maktoums accounted for more than 40 percent of gross sales at the Keeneland summer sale.

Sheikh Mohammed alone has purchased more than $650 million worth of horses at public auction. The best go into the various breeding operations owned by the family in Kentucky and e l s e w h e r e .

Photo: Sid Webb

Among the champions bred in Kentucky by the Maktoums and exported to race abroad were Epsom Derby winners Erhaab, Nashwan and Lammtarra.

**Juddmonte Farm:** Just as the Maktoums did, Prince Khaled Abdullah of Saudi Arabia established a superb Kentucky farm as one of his bases for an international breeding operation. In addition to its many major victories in Europe, Juddmonte also has raced a strong division in this country. Its more than 100 grade/group 1 winners, including Empire Maker, the Belmont Stakes winner of 2003.

**Lane's End Farm:** (See William S. Farish)

**Overbrook Farm:** (See W. T. Young)

## *Well, what about that...?*

### The Great Man O'War (1917-1947)

He had a distinctive blazing white star on his forehead and a deep, rich red coat, and a huge personality. Arguably the most famous horse in the world, Man O'War passed away one month after his lifetime companion, Will Harbut. Man O'War was embalmed and lay in state in a specially-made casket, lined with his racing colors. He is the yardstick that greatness is still measured against in horse racing.

# Famous Kentucky-bred Horses
Ed Bowen

*Kentucky-breds have a rich*
*and famous history*
*Here are thumbnail portraits of famous horses bred*
*(born) in Kentucky. Names in parentheses indicate the*
*sire (father), dam (mother), and maternal grandsire.*

**ALYDAR**, foaled 1975 (Raise a Native-Sweet Tooth, by On-and-On) Bred and raced by Calumet Farm. Raced 1977-79. Won 14 of 26 races, earned $957,195.

**ALYSHEBA**, foaled 1984 (Alydar-Bel Sheba, by Lt. Stevens) Bred by Preston Madden, raced by Dorothy and Pam Scharbauer. Raced 1986-88. Won 11 of 26 races, earned $6,679,242.

**A.P. INDY**, foaled 1989 (Seattle Slew-Weekend Surprise, by Secretariat) Bred by William S. Farish & Partners, raced by Tomonori Tsurumaki. Raced 1991-92. Won 8 of 11 races, earned $2,979,815.

**AZERI**, foaled 1998 (Jade Hunter-Zodiac Miss, by Ahonoora) Bred by Allen Paulson, raced by Paulson's Living Trust. Raced 2001-2004. Won 17 of 24 races, earned $4,079,820, a record for females. Azeri was the champion older female for three consecutive years (2002-04) and was also overall Horse of the Year in 2002.

**BARBARO**, foaled 2003 (Dynaformer---La Ville Rouge, by Carson City). Bred and raced by Mr. and Mrs. Roy Jackson. Raced 2005-06. Won 6 of 7 races, earned $2,302,200. Dominant, unbeaten winner of the Kentucky Derby in 2006, Barbaro was severely injured in the Preakness two weeks later but remained a national hero as modern veterinary practice undertook a prolonged effort to save his life.

**BOLD RULER**, foaled 1954 (Nasrullah-Miss Disco, by Discovery) Bred and raced by Mrs. Henry Carnegie Phipps (Wheatley Stable). Raced 1956-58. Won 23 of 33 races, earned $764,204. Eight time leading sire.

**BROOMSTICK**, foaled 1901 (Ben Brush-Elf, by Galliard) Bred by Col. Milton Young, raced by Capt. Samuel S. Brown. Raced 1903-1905. Won 14 of 39 races, earned $74,730. Leading sire.

**BUCKPASSER**, foaled 1963 (Tom Fool-Busanda, by War Admiral) Bred and raced by Ogden Phipps. Raced 1965-67. Won 25 of 31 races, earned $1,462,014.

**BULL LEA**, foaled 1935 (Bull Dog-Rose Leaves, by Ballot) Bred by Coldstream Stud, raced by Calumet Farm. Raced 1937-39. Won 10 of 27 races, earned $94,825. Leading sire.

**CITATION**, foaled 1945 (Bull Lea-Hydroplane II, by Hyperion) Bred and raced by Calumet Farm. Raced 1947-1951. Won 32 of 45 races, earned $1,085,760. Triple Crown winner.

**COLIN**, foaled 1905 (Commando-Pastorella, by Springfield) Bred and raced by James R. Keene. Raced 1907-08. Won 15 of 15 races, earned 178,110.

**COUNT FLEET**, foaled 1940 (Reigh Count-Quickly, by Haste) Bred and raced by Mrs. John D. Hertz. Raced 1943-44. Won 16 of 21 races, earned $250,300.

**DAMASCUS**, foaled 1964 (Sword Dancer-Kerala, by My Babu) Bred and raced by Mrs. Edith W. Bancroft. Raced 1966-68. Won 21 of 32 races, earned

**Calumet Farm**
*Photo: Sid Webb*

$1,176,781.

**DANZIG**, foaled 1977 (Northern Dancer-Pas de Nom, by Admiral's Voyage). Bred by Derry Meeting Farm and William S. Farish, raced by Henry de Kwiatkowski. Raced in 1980. Won 3 of 3 races, earned $32,400. Leading sire.

**DISCOVERY**, foaled 1931 (Display-Ariadne, by Light Brigade). Bred by Walter Salmon's Mereworth Farm, raced by Alfred G. Vanderbilt. Raced 1933-36. Won 27 of 63 races, earned $195,287.

**DOMINO**, foaled 1891 (Himyar-Mannie Gray, by Enquirer) Bred by Maj. Barak Thomas, raced by James R. Keene and Foxhall Keene. Raced 1893-95. Won 19 of 25 races, earned $193,500.

**EASY GOER**, foaled 1986 (Alydar-Relaxing, by Buckpasser) Bred and raced by Ogden Phipps. Raced 1988-90. Won 14 of 20 races, earned $4,873,770.

**EQUIPOISE**, foaled 1928 (Pennant-Swinging, by Broomstick) Bred by Harry Payne Whitney, raced by C. V. Whitney. Raced 1930-35. Won 29 of 51 races, earned $338,610.

**EXTERMINATOR,** foaled 1915 (McGee-Fair Empress, by Jim Gore) Bred by F. D. (Dixie) Knight, raced primarily by Willis Sharpe Kilmer. Raced 1917-1924, won 50 of 100 races, earned $252,996.

FAIR PLAY, foaled 1905 (Hastings-Fairy Gold, by Bend Or) Bred and raced by August Belmont II. Raced 1907-1909. Won 10 of 32 races, earned $86,950. Sire of Man o' War.

**FOREGO**, foaled 1970 (Forli-Lady Golconda, by Hasty Road) Bred and raced by Lazy F. Ranch. Raced 1973-78. Won 34 of 57 races, earned $1,938,957.

**GALLANT FOX,** foaled 1927 (Sir Gallahad III-Marguerite, by Celt) Bred and raced by William Woodward Sr.'s Belair Stud. Raced 1929-30. Won 11 of 17 races, earned $328,165. Triple Crown winner.

**HAIL TO REASON,** foaled 1958 (Turn-to-Nothirdchance, by Blue Swords) Bred by Bieber-Jacobs Stable, raced by Patrice Jacobs. Raced in 1960. Won 9 of 18 races, earned $328,434.

**HANOVER,** foaled 1884 (Hindoo-Bourbon Belle, by Bonnie Scotland) Bred by Catesby Woodford and Ezekiel F. Clay, raced by Mike and Phil Dwyer. Raced 1886-87. Won 32 of 50 races, earned $118,887.

**HINDOO,** foaled 1878 (Virgil-Florence, by Lexington) Bred by Daniel Swigert, raced by Mike and Phil Dwyer. Raced 1880-82. Won 30 of 35 races, earned $71,875.

**John Henry**
*Source: Ky. Department of Tourism*

**JOHN HENRY,** foaled 1975 (Ole Bob Bowers-Once Double, by Double Jay) Bred by Robert Lehman, raced by Sam Rubin. Raced 1977-84. Won 39 of 83 races, earned $6,597,947.

**KELSO,** foaled 1957 (Your Host-Maid of Flight, by Count Fleet) Bred and raced by Mrs. Richard C. du Pont Jr. Raced 1959-66. Won 39 of 63 races, earned $1,977,896. Five-time Horse of the Year.

**LEXINGTON,** foaled 1850 (Boston-Alice Carneal, by Sarpedon) Bred by Dr. Elisha Warfield, raced by Richard Ten Broeck. Raced 1852-55. Won 6 of 7 races, earned $56,600. Sixteen-time leading sire.

**MAN O' WAR,** foaled 1917 (Fair Play-Mahubah, by Rock Sand) Bred by August Belmont II, raced by Samuel D. Riddle. Raced 1919-20. Won 20 of 21 races, earned $249,465.

**MISS WOODFORD,** foaled 1882 (Billet-Fancy Jane, by Neil Robinson) Bred by George Bowen, raced primarily by Mike and Phil Dwyer. Raced 1882-86. Won 37 of 48 races, earned $118,270. Miss Woodford was the first American race horse of either gender to earn as much as $100,000.

**MR. PROSPECTOR,** foaled 1970 (Raise a Native-Gold Digger, by Nashua) Bred by Spenthrift Farm, raced by A. I. Savin. Raced 1973-74. Won 7 of 14 races, earned $121,171. Leading sire.

**NASHUA,** foaled 1952 (Nasrullah-Segula, by Johnstown) Bred by William Woodward Sr. Raced by William Woodward Jr. and Leslie Combs II. Raced 1952-56. Won 22 of 30 races, earned $1,288,565.

**NATIVE DANCER,** foaled 1952 (Polynesian-Geisha, by Discovery) Bred and raced by Alfred G. Vanderbilt. Raced 1952-53. Won 21 of 22 races, earned $785,240. First Thoroughbred TV hero.

**OMAHA,** foaled 1932 (Gallant Fox-Flambino, by Wrack) Bred and raced by William Woodward Sr.'s Belair Stud. Raced 1934-36. Won nine of 22 races, earned $154,755. Triple Crown winner.

**PERSONAL ENSIGN,** foaled 1984 (Private Terms-Grecian Banner, by Hoist the Flag). Bred and raced by Ogden Phipps. Raced 1986-88. Won 13 of 13 races, earned $1,679,880.

**ROUND TABLE,** foaled 1954 (Princequillo-Knight's Daughter, by Sir Cosmo) Bred by Claiborne Farm, raced by Travis M. Kerr. Raced 1956-59. Won 43 of 66 races, earned $1,749,869.

**RUFFIAN,** 1972 (Reviewer-Shenanigans, Native Dancer) Bred and raced by Mr. and Mrs. Stuart Janney Jr. Raced 1974-75. Won 10 of 11 races, earned $313,429.

**SEABISCUIT,** foaled 1933 (Hard Tack-Swing On, by Whisk Broom) Bred by Mrs. Henry Carnegie Phipps, raced primarily by Charles S. Howard. Raced 1935-40. Won 33 of 89 races, earned $437,730.

**SEATTLE SLEW,** foaled 1974 (Boldnesian-My Charmer, by Poker) Bred by Ben Castleman, raced by Jim and Sally Hill and Karen and Mickey Taylor. Raced 1976-78. Won 14 of 17 races, earned $1,208,726. Triple Crown winner.

**SIR BARTON,** foaled 1916 (Star Shoot-Lady Sterling, by Hanover) Bred by John E. Madden and Vivian Gooch, raced by Comdr. J. K. L. Ross. Raced 1918-20. Won 13 of 31 races, earned $116,857. First Triple Crown winner.

**SPECTACULAR BID,** foaled 1976 (Bold Bid-

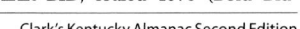

der-Spectacular, by Promised Land) Bred by Mrs. William Jason and Mrs. William Gilmore, raced by Harry Meyerhoff and family. Raced 1978-80. Won 26 of 30 races, earned $2,781,608.

**SUNDAY SILENCE**, foaled 1986 (Halo-Wishing Well, by Understanding) Bred by Oak Cliff Thoroughbreds, raced by Arthur Hancock III and partners. Raced 1988-90. Won 9 of 14 races, earned $4,968,554.

**SYSONBY**, foaled 1902 (Melton-Optime, by Orme) Bred and raced by James R. Keene. Raced 1904-05. Won 14 of 15 races, earned $184,438.

**TOM FOOL,** foaled 1949 (Menow-Gaga, by Bull Dog). Bred by Duval Headley, raced by Greentree

Stable. Raced 1951-53. Won 21 of 30 races, earned $570,165.

**TWILIGHT TEAR,** foaled 1941 (Bull Lea-Lady Lark, by Blue Larkspur) Bred and raced by Calumet Farm. Raced 1943-45. Won 18 of 24 races, earned $202,165.

**WAR ADMIRAL**, foaled 1934 (Man o' War-Brushup, by Sweep) Bred and raced by Samuel D. Riddle. Raced 1936-39. Won 21 of 26 races, earned $273,240. Triple Crown winner.

**WHIRLAWAY,** foaled 1938 (Blenheim II-Dustwhirl, by Sweep) Bred and raced by Calumet Farm. Raced 1940-43. Won 32 of 60 races, earned $561,161. Triple Crown winner.

# Renowned Breeders
Ed Bowen

**R. A. ALEXANDER** (1819-1867)—With an inheritance from an uncle in Scotland, Alexander established Woodburn Stud in Woodford County (now known as Airdrie Stud and still an operating thoroughbred farm). Alexander helped shape the thoroughbred industry along modern lines with professional management and annual auctions of his yearlings.

**COL. E. R. BRADLEY** (1859-1946)—Legend places Col. Bradley as a steel worker in his native Pittsburgh, then a cowboy, prospector and miner. But when he testified in Congress he described himself as a gambler. Bradley developed gambling halls in various cities, most fashionably in Palm Beach, Fla. He also took a great interest in thoroughbred breeding and racing and won four runnings of the Kentucky Derby with Behave Yourself (1921), Bubbling Over (1926), Burgoo King (1932) and Broker's Tip (1933).

**HENRY CLAY** (1777-1852)—Known in world affairs for the Treaty of Ghent and for his four attempts to be elected president, Henry Clay was also an avid agriculturalist. Among animals raised at his home, Ashland, in Lexington, were thoroughbreds. Some of his stock became ancestors to important horses still found in the thoroughbred gene pool. A total of 11 Kentucky Derby winners trace to Clay's mares Magnolia and Margaret Wood.

**LESLIE COMBS II** (1901-1990) — Combs took the concept of syndication of stallions to a new level and launched an era in which ownership of virtually all highly commercial stallions was divided into 32 to 40 shares. The most noteworthy of these transactions included his syndication of Nashua, the 1955 Horse of the Year, for $1,252,100, making him the

first horse sold for as much as $1 million.

**WILLIAM S. FARISH** (1939- )—William S. Farish was born in Texas, where his family had launched Humble Oil, but he moved to Kentucky and established Lane's End Farm in Versailles as one of the world's leading thoroughbred operations. In partnerships, he has bred and sold winners of each of the Triple Crown races: Kentucky Derby winner Charismatic, Preakness winner Summer Squall and Belmont Stakes winners A.P. Indy and Lemon Drop Kid.

**JOHN R. GAINES** (1928-2005)—John R. Gaines established two versions of Gainesway Farm in Lexington and created a highly successful commercial breeding and selling operation. He was instrumental in establishing the Breeders' Cup, the Kentucky State Horse Park and the National Thoroughbred Racing Association.

**JAMES BEN ALI HAGGIN** (1821-1914)—A grandson of a Turkish Army officer, Haggin was born in Kentucky but roamed the West and South America, mining gold, copper and silver. He raised horses on the 44,000-acre tract he acquired in California and then came back to Kentucky, where he acquired Elmendorf Farm and increased it to some 9,000 acres. Part of the property still carries the name Elmendorf, while other parcels became separate — and important — breeding farms, including Spendthrift, Gainesway, Greentree, Normandy, Payson Stud and C. V. Whitney Farms.

**ARTHUR B. HANCOCK SR.** (1875-1957)—Hancock expanded his family's Virginia breeding operation into Kentucky with the establishment of Claiborne Farm near Paris on land inherited by his wife. Claiborne became one of the world's renowned farms both in breeding its own horses and in standing stallions and boarding mares and raising foals for many prestigious clients. During Hancock's lifetime, Claiborne's important sire acquisitions included Celt, Wrack, Sir Gallahad III, Double Jay, Princequillo and Blenheim II. Sir Gallahad was purchased in France in partnership with key Claiborne clients William Woodward Sr., Marshall Field and R. A. Fairbairn.

**ARTHUR B. HANCOCK JR.** (1910-1972)—Claiborne Farm's status in the thoroughbred world was maintained and perhaps enhanced by Arthur B. (Bull) Hancock Jr., who ran it from 1947 when his father became ill until his own death in 1972. Bull Hancock continued the pattern of acquisition of top stallions, including five-time leading sire Nasrullah and English Triple Crown winner Nijinsky II.

**SETH W. HANCOCK** (1949-)—He was only 23 when his father passed away, and he soon found himself running Claiborne far earlier than he had anticipated. Hancock proved himself early on by syndicating Secretariat for more than $6 million, a record at the time. The great horse came to stand at Claiborne after winning the Triple Crown in 1973. Hancock has continued the tradition of his father and grandfather, both as a breeder and in acquiring stallions and raising horses for clients. During his tenure, Claiborne was the leading breeder in 1984 when homebred Swale won the Kentucky Derby and Belmont Stakes.

**HAL PRICE HEADLEY** (1888-1962)—An exemplar of the versatile agriculturist and businessman, Kentucky native Headley was the breeder and owner of champion filly and producer Alcibiades and importer of English-bred stallion Pharamond II. The latter sired Headley's champion, Menow. Headley was the prime inspiration and initial leader in creation of Keeneland Race Course, which returned racing to Lexington in 1936 after the old Kentucky Association track had closed.

**WARNER L. JONES JR.** (1916-1994)—Warner Jones Jr. was involved in virtually every aspect of racing and breeding. He was on the board of Churchill Downs for more than 50 years and was chairman for a dozen years. At the same time, he ran a commercial operation at his Hermitage Farm in Louisville, where he bred 1953 Kentucky Derby winner Dark Star and more than 130 other stakes winners. Jones also stood leading sire Raja Baba and he twice consigned world-record priced yearlings to the Keeneland summer sale in vastly different eras.

**JOHN E. MADDEN** (1856-1929)—Born in Pennsylvania, Madden moved to Lexington and established Hamburg Place, part of which is still a farm owned by grandson Preston Madden. The other part has become a major shopping development carrying the same name. Madden converted from a successful career with standardbreds and became a leading thoroughbred breeder, owner and seller. He also was a trainer and adviser to some of the most successful owners in the East. Madden was the nation's leading breeder in races won annually from 1917-1927 and the leader in earnings from 1917-1923. He bred five Kentucky Derby winners — Old Rosebud (1914), Sir Barton (1919), Paul Jones (1920), Zev (1923) and Flying Ebony (1925). Sir Barton became the first Triple Crown winner. Years later, grandson Preston Madden added to that legacy by breeding the 1987 Derby winner, Alysheba.

**H. P. McGRATH** (1814-1881)—Born near Lexington but lured to the life of gambling clubs in New Orleans and the East, McGrath returned to his roots to establish McGrathiana as a thoroughbred farm. He bred and raced Aristides, which in 1875 won the first Kentucky Derby.

**DANIEL SWIGERT** (1833-1912)—Once the manager of Woodburn, Daniel Swigert acquired his own farms—first Stockwood and then Preakness Stud, which he renamed Elmendorf. Among the many champions he bred was Kentucky Derby winner Hindoo, later the sire of Domino. Swigert bred two other Derby winners, Apollo and Ben Ali. He also owned Derby winner Baden-Baden. The unbeaten 2-year-old Tremont and the champion mare Firenze were also among the horses he bred.

**MAJ. BARAK THOMAS** (1826-1906)—Maj. Thomas had various jobs before launching into thoroughbred breeding. He was one of the first to approach it as a full-time occupation, and this emphasis on professionalism had a role in establishing Kentucky as the center of the industry. He established Dixiana Farm and Hira Villa Stud in Lexington and was the breeder of both Himyar and his bellwether son, Domino.

**W. T. YOUNG** (1918-2004)—W. T. Young was a prominent businessman, philanthropist and leader in Kentucky. Among his major gifts was $5 million to help build the University of Kentucky library that is named for him. Young did not venture into the thoroughbred industry until the 1970s, but he developed Overbrook Farm and quickly made a mark. He bred and raced Storm Cat and returned the horse to stand at stud at Overbrook. Storm Cat became the leading sire of 1999 and 2000 and has been the leading sire of 2-year-olds seven times. Young won the Kentucky Derby in 1996 with his homebred, Grindstone. Tabasco Cat, which he bred and raced in partnership, won the Preakness and Belmont Stakes in 1994.

# Thoroughbred Race Tracks
*Ed Bowen*

### CHURCHILL DOWNS
### Louisville

Home of the Kentucky Derby, Churchill Downs was established as the Louisville Jockey Club in 1875. Churchill Downs is the oldest track in the United States to have had racing annually, without interruption. While the Derby is the track's centerpiece, several other important stakes races are held—including the **Kentucky Oaks**, companion piece to the Derby which was also inaugurated in 1875. Now run on the day before the Derby, the Oaks is a 1 1/8 mile race for 3-year-old fillies.

**Churchill Downs**
*Source: Department of Commerce,
Creative Services*

The **Kentucky Jockey Club Stakes** is a 1 1/16-mile race for 2-year-olds that serves as a test of each horse's prospects of becoming a Derby entrant the following spring. The **Clark Handicap** is for 3-year-olds and older. The **Stephen Foster Handicap** is for 3-year-olds and up. **The Breeders' Cup** has been hosted by Churchill Downs in 1988, 1991, 1994, 1998 and 2000. In 2005, Churchill Downs

unveiled a massive expansion and renovation that cost $121million. Adjacent to the grandstand and clubhouse is the Kentucky Derby Museum.

### KEENELAND
### Lexington

The Kentucky Association track in Lexington closed in 1933, ending its run as the oldest racetrack in America (dating from 1828). Hal Price Headley and other horsemen worked with business leaders to found a new racing association and Keeneland was born in 1936. Beginning in the World War II era, thoroughbred auctions were held on the grounds. Keeneland subsequently rose to the top of the world's horse sales. The **Blue Grass Stakes** was first run in 1911 and immediately was regarded

**Mary Lou Whitney and her guest, Ivana Trump, are on the 4th floor balcony at Churchill Downs at the 132nd running of the Kentucky Derby, Louisville, Saturday May 6, 2006.**
*Photo: David Perry, Lexington Herald-Leader*

as a Kentucky Derby prep. The race was revived at Keeneland in 1937 and now has a $750,000 purse.

The **Phoenix Breeders' Cup,** first contested in 1831, is the oldest race in America still being run, but not continuously. The **Ashland Stakes** for 3-year-old fillies has a purse of $500,000. **The Spinster**, open to fillies and mares 3 years old and up, is run at 1 1/8 miles with a purse of $500,000. The **Queen Elizabeth II Challenge Cup** began in 1984 and its first running was viewed by the woman it was named after, Queen Elizabeth II of England. **The Royal Chase for the Sport of Kings** is a steeplechase that has played host to Her Majesty Princess Anne. A number of Keeneland's races are sponsored by companies and horse farms, including the Blue Grass Stakes, supported by Toyota.

*Photos: Sid Webb*

### TURFWAY PARK
### Florence

Turfway was known as Latonia when it opened in 1959. The spring meeting's signature has long been the **Lane's End Stakes**. **The Kentucky Cup Day of Champions** presents five stakes races and is an annual feature of late summer/early autumn.

### ELLIS PARK
### Henderson

The track opened in 1922 as Dade Park and was operated by James C. Ellis for most of its first 30 years. The track's **Gardenia Stakes** is a graded race for fillies and mares and carries a purse of $200,000.

### KENTUCKY DOWNS
### Franklin

Kentucky Downs has year-round simulcast wagering. There is a short live race meeting each September. Key race is the $200,000 **Kentucky Cup Turf Handicap**, run in conjunction with Kentucky Cup Day at Turfway Park.

**Barbaro winning the 2006 Kentucky Derby**
*Photo: Ron Garrison, Lexington Herald-Leader*

# Keeneland Unveils New Racetrack

Nick Nicholson

Seventy years after its inaugural season of racing, Keeneland debuted a new racetrack and numerous improvements for its 2006 fall meet. The Polytrack surface on the main track is the centerpiece of the renovations, which took place during the summer of 2006.

The top layer of the new track—comprised of silica sand, fibers and recycled materials—provides a soft cushion for horse and rider. It is covered in a wax coating that allows water to flow through the top surface to the sub layers below and helps avoid a freezing or inconsistent racetrack—even in inclement weather. The sub layers and vertical drain pipes below provide a safer, more consistent racing surface compared to a conventional dirt track.

Statistics show that Polytrack is superior to conventional dirt tracks because it provides a safer racing surface for horses and jockeys—and a soft surface is kinder to horses' joints and legs.

A Polytrack surface remains consistent regardless of weather. Keeneland is the third North American racing facility to announce that it will install Polytrack as its main racing surface. Turfway Park, in Florence, Ky., installed the surface in August 2005, and Woodbine, in Toronto, Ontario, installed Polytrack in 2006.

The renovation marks a significant step forward for Keeneland in its goal to be one of the world's safest and most beautiful racetracks, while adhering to its original mission of being a model racetrack.

Keeneland is well known for its traditions and doing what is best for the horse is at the heart of those traditions. We aspire to have the safest, most modern racetrack in the world. While removal of our old surface may seem revolutionary to some, it actually is very true to our mission.

Also in the fall of 2006, Keeneland became the first racetrack in the U.S. to offer Trakus video race technology to its patrons. Trakus provides the ability—via sensor chips carried in saddlecloths and antennas positioned around the racetrack—to track each horse in a race electronically and digitally in real time.

For more information about Keeneland, visit www.keeneland.com/.

**Polytrack Layers**

Loose Polytrack (about 3 inches)

Compact Polytrack (about 7 inches)

Porous Macadam (asphalt)

Clean Stone

Dense Grade Aggregate

Dirt

Perforated Drainage Pipes

Keeneland is the third North American racing facility to install Polytrack as its main racing surface. Turfway Park, in Florence, Ky., installed the surface in August 2005. Keeneland became the first racetrack in the U.S. to offer Trakus video race technology to its patrons.
*Source: Keeneland*

# The Kentucky Derby
*Ed Bowen*

### They run for roses, and a page in racing history

Widely regarded as the most famous horse race in the country and one of the great races of the world, the Kentucky Derby is the goal of virtually all horsemen. In fact, the mating patterns of thousands of thoroughbreds are made with the Derby in mind. Of the 132 Derby winners, 99 were bred (born) in Kentucky.

The Derby is run at Churchill Downs in Louisville on the first Saturday in May. At 1 1/4 miles, it almost always represents the longest test its entrants have yet faced. The Derby is exclusively for 3-year-olds and is the first race in the Triple Crown series, followed by the Preakness Stakes in Maryland and the Belmont Stakes in New York.

The Derby has been an annual event ever since its inaugural race in 1875. Col. M. Lewis Clark formed the Louisville Jockey Club and envisioned the Derby to be a counterpart of the famous Epsom Derby in England. The track had become known as Churchill Downs after the family from which the property was acquired.

The race rose to regional fame, but the track's health and the race's importance waned over the years. By 1902 a local tailor, Col. Matt Winn, was induced to take over management in an attempt to save the track and the race.

**Infield at the Kentucky Derby**
*Source: Lexington Herald-Leader*

Col. Winn promoted the Derby by catering to the New York media and by convincing railroad lines to take blocks of tickets and schedule extra cars to Louisville. By 1915, when Harry Payne Whitney, a major Eastern owner, won the race with the filly Regret, he proclaimed the race the greatest in America. With that seal of approval from a nationally renowned horseman, the Derby was secure.

By 1946, Churchill Downs boasted a crowd of 100,000 annually. That figure was not actually reached according to Kentucky Racing Commission records until 1969, but it has been far surpassed since. The record crowd is 163,628, which attended the 100th running of the event in 1974. The 2005 running, won by 50-1 longshot Giacomo, attracted the second-largest crowd, 156,435. In 2005, parimutuel betting on the Derby at Churchill Downs and at simulcasting locations totaled $103,325,518.

## KENTUCKY DERBY FACTS

- **Fastest time:** Secretariat, 1:59 2/5 in 1973
- **Longest odds of a winner:** 91.45-1, Donerail, 1913
- **Shortest odds of a winner:** 2-5, Calumet Farm entry (Citation & Coaltown), 1948; and Count Fleet, 1943
- **Percentage of winning favorites:** 38% (50 of 131)
- **Most wins, breeder:** Calumet Farm, 9
- **Most wins, owner:** Calumet Farm, 8
- **Most wins, trainer:** Ben A. Jones, 6
- **Jockey, most wins:** Eddie Arcaro and Bill Hartack, 5 each
- **Stallion, most winners sired:** Falsetto, Virgil, Sir Gallahad III, and Bull Lea, 3 each
- **Largest field:** 23, in 1974 (the field is now limited to 20)
- **Smallest field:** 3, in 1892 and 1905
- **Filly winners:** Regret, 1915; Genunie Risk, 1980; Winning Colors, 1988
- **Largest winning margin:** 8 lengths (Old Rosebud, 1914; Johnstown, 1939; Whirlaway, 1941; Assault, 1946)
- **Largest winner's purse:** Giacomo, $1,639,600 in 2005
- **Triple Crown winners:** 11 (Sir Barton, 1919; Gallant Fox, 1930; Omaha, 1935; War Admiral, 1937; Whirlaway, 1941; Count Fleet, 1943; Assault, 1946; Citation, 1948; Secretariat, 1973; Seattle Slew, 1977; Affirmed, 1978)

*Source: Churchill Downs*

# Kentucky Derby Winners

| YR | WINNER | OWNER | TRAINER | JOCKEY | SECOND | THIRD | TIME | MONEY |
|---|---|---|---|---|---|---|---|---|
| 2006 | Barbaro, b. c. | Mr. & Mrs. Roy Jackson | Michael Matz | Edgar Prado | Bluegrass Cat | Steppenwolfer | 02:01.4 | $1,453,200 |
| 2005 | Giacomo, gr/ro. c. | Mr. & Mrs. Jerome S. Moss | John Shirreffs | M. Smith | Closing Argument | Afleet Alex | 02:02.8 | $1,639,600 |
| 2004 | Smarty Jones, ch. c. | Someday Farm | John Servis | S. Elliott | Lion Heart | Imperialism | 02:04.1 | †5,854,800 |
| 2003 | Funny Cide, ch. g. | Sackatoga Stable | Barclay Tagg | J. Santos | Empire Maker | Peace Rules | 02:01.2 | 800,200 |
| 2002 | War Emblem, dkb/br. c. | The Thoroughbred Corp. | Bob Baffert | V. Espinoza | Proud Citizen | Perfect Drift | 02:01.1 | †1,875,000 |
| 2001 | Monarchos, gr/ro. c. | John C. Oxley | John T. Ward Jr. | J. Chavez | Invisible Ink | Congaree | 02:00.0 | 812,000 |
| 2000 | Fusaichi Pegasus, b. c. | Fusao Sekiguchi | Neil Drysdale | K. Desormeaux | Aptitude | Impeachment | 02:01.1 | 1,038,400 |
| 1999 | Charismatic, ch. c. | Robert & Beverly Lewis | D. Wayne Lukas | C. Antley | Menifee | Cat Thief | 02:03.3 | 886,200 |
| 1998 | Real Quiet, b. c. | Mike Pegram | Bob Baffert | K. Desormeaux | Victory Gallop | Indian Charlie | 02:02.4 | 738,800 |
| 1997 | Silver Charm, gr/ro. c. | Robert & Beverly Lewis | Bob Baffert | G. Stevens | Captain Bodgit | Free House | 02:02.4 | 700,000 |
| 1996 | Grindstone, dkb/br. c. | Overbrook Farm | D. Wayne Lukas | J. Bailey | Cavonnier | Prince of Thieves | 02:01.1 | 869,800 |
| 1995 | Thunder Gulch, ch. c. | Michael Tabor | D. Wayne Lukas | G. Stevens | Tejano Run | Timber Country | 02:01.3 | 707,400 |
| 1994 | Go for Gin, b. c. | W. Condren-J. Cornacchia | Nicholas P. Zito | C. McCarron | Strodes Creek | Blumin Affair | 02:03.7 | 628,800 |
| 1993 | Sea Hero, b. c. | Rokeby Stable | MacKenzie Miller | J. Bailey | Prairie Bayou | Wild Gale | 02:02.4 | 735,900 |
| 1992 | Lil E. Tee, b. c. | W. Cal Partee | Lynn S. Whiting | P. Day | Casual Lies | Dance Floor | 02:03.0 | 724,800 |
| 1991 | Strike the Gold, ch. c. | Brophy-Condren-Cornacchia | Nicholas P. Zito | C. Antley | Best Pal | Mane Minister | 02:03.1 | 655,800 |
| 1990 | Unbridled, b. c. | Frances A. Genter Stable | Carl A. Nafzger | C. Perret | Summer Squall | Pleasant Tap | 2:02 | 581,000 |
| 1989 | Sunday Silence, dkb/br. c. | Gaillard-Hancock-Whittingham | Charles Whittingham | P. Valenzuela | Easy Goer | Awe Inspiring | 2:05 | 574,200 |
| 1988 | Winning Colors, ro. f. | Mr. & Mrs. Eugene Klein | D. Wayne Lukas | G. Stevens | Forty Niner | Risen Star | 2:021/5 | 611,200 |
| 1987 | Alysheba, b. c. | Dorothy & Pamela Scharbauer | Jack Van Berg | C. McCarron | Bet Twice | Avies Copy | 2:032/5 | 618,600 |
| 1986 | Ferdinand, ch. c. | Mrs. Howard B. Keck | Charles Whittingham | W. Shoemaker | Bold Arrangement | Broad Brush | 2:024/5 | 609,400 |
| 1985 | Spend a Buck, b. c. | Hunter Farm | Cam Gambolati | A. Cordero Jr. | Stephan's Odyssey | Chief's Crown | 2:001/5 | 406,800 |
| 1984 | Swale, dkb/br. c. | Claiborne Farm | W.C. Stephens | L. Pincay Jr. | Coax Me Chad | At the Threshold | 2:022/5 | 537,400 |
| 1983 | Sunny's Halo, ch. c. | David J. Foster Racing Stable | David C. Cross Jr. | E. Delahoussaye | Desert Wine | Caveat | 2:021/5 | 426,000 |
| 1982 | Gato Del Sol, gr. c. | Hancock III & Peters | Edwin Gregson | E. Delahoussaye | Laser Light | Reinvested | 2:022/5 | 428,850 |
| 1981 | Pleasant Colony, dkb/br. c. | Buckland Farm | John P. Campo | J. Velasquez | Woodchopper | Partez | 2:02 | 317,200 |
| 1980 | Genuine Risk, ch. f. | Mrs. B.R. Firestone | LeRoy Jolley | J. Vasquez | Rumbo | Jaklin Klugman | 2:02 | 250,550 |
| 1979 | Spectacular Bid, gr. c. | Hawksworth Farm | Grover G. Delp | R. Franklin | General Assembly | Golden Act | 2:022/5 | 228,650 |
| **1978** | **Affirmed, ch. c.** | Harbor View Farm | Lazaro Barrera | S. Cauthen | Alydar | Believe It | 2:011/5 | 186,900 |
| **1977** | **Seattle Slew, dkb/br. c.** | Karen L. Taylor | W.H. Turner Jr. | J. Cruguet | Run Dusty Run | Sanhedrin | 2:021/5 | 214,700 |
| 1976 | Bold Forbes, dkb/br. c. | E. Rodriguez Tizol | Lazaro Barrera | A. Cordero Jr. | Honest Pleasure | Elocutionist | 2:013/5 | 165,200 |
| 1975 | Foolish Pleasure, b. c. | John L. Greer | LeRoy Jolley | J. Vasquez | Avatar | Diabolo | 2:02 | 209,600 |
| 1974 | Cannonade, b. c. | John M. Olin | W.C. Stephens | A. Cordero Jr. | Hudson County | Agitate | 2:04 | 274,000 |
| **1973** | **Secretariat, ch. c.** | Meadow Stable | Lucien Laurin | R. Turcotte | Sham | Our Native | 1:592/5 | 155,050 |
| 1972 | Riva Ridge, b. c. | Meadow Stable | Lucien Laurin | R. Turcotte | No Le Hace | Hold Your Peace | 2:014/5 | 140,300 |
| 1971 | Canonero II, b. c. | Edgar Caibett | Juan Arias | G. Avila | Jim French | Bold Reason | 2:031/5 | 145,500 |
| 1970 | Dust Commander, ch. c. | Robert Lehmann | Don Combs | M. Manganello | My Dad George | High Echelon | 2:032/5 | 127,800 |
| 1969 | Majestic Prince, ch. c. | Frank McMahon | John Longden | W. Hartack | Arts and Letters | Dike | 2:014/5 | 113,200 |
| 1968 | #Forward Pass, b. c. | Calumet Farm | Henry Forrest | I. Valenzuela | Francie's Hat | T. V. Commercial | 2:021/5 | 122,600 |
| 1967 | Proud Clarion, b. c. | Darby Dan Farm | Loyd Gentry | R. Ussery | Barbs Delight | Damascus | 2:003/5 | 119,700 |
| 1966 | Kauai King, dkb/br. c. | Michael J. Ford | Henry Forrest | D. Brumfield | Advocator | Blue Skyer | 2:02 | 120,500 |
| 1965 | Lucky Debonair, b. c. | Mrs. Ada L. Rice | Frank Catrone | W. Shoemaker | Dapper Dan | Tom Rolfe | 2:011/5 | 112,000 |
| 1964 | Northern Dancer, b. c. | Windfields Farm | Horatio Luro | W. Hartack | Hill Rise | The Scoundrel | 2:00 | 114,300 |
| 1963 | Chateaugay, ch. c. | Darby Dan Farm | James Conway | B. Baeza | Never Bend | Candy Spots | 2:014/5 | 108,900 |
| 1962 | Decidedly, gr. c. | El Peco Ranch | Horatio Luro | W. Hartack | Roman Line | Ridan | 2:002/5 | 119,650 |
| 1961 | Carry Back, br. c. | Mrs. J.A. Price | J.A. Price | J. Sellers | Crozier | Bass Clef | 2:04 | 120,500 |
| 1960 | Venetian Way, ch. c. | Sunny Blue Farm | Vic Sovinski | W. Hartack | Bally Ache | Victoria Park | 2:022/5 | 114,850 |
| 1959 | Tomy Lee, b. c. | Fred Turner Jr. | Frank Childs | W. Shoemaker | Sword Dancer | First Landing | 2:021/5 | 119,650 |
| 1958 | Tim Tam, dk. b. c. | Calumet Farm | H.A. Jones | I. Valenzuela | Lincoln Road | Noureddin | 2:05 | 116,400 |
| 1957 | Iron Liege, b. c. | Calumet Farm | H.A. Jones | W. Hartack | Gallant Man | Round Table | 2:021/5 | 107,950 |
| 1956 | Needles, b. c. | D & H Stable | H.L. Fontaine | D. Erb | Fabius | Come On Red | 2:032/5 | 123,450 |
| 1955 | Swaps, ch. c. | R.C. Ellsworth | M.A. Tenney | W. Shoemaker | Nashua | Summer Tan | 2:014/5 | 108,400 |
| 1954 | Determine, gr. c. | A.J. Crevolin | Willie Molter | R. York | Hasty Road | Hasseyampa | 2:03 | 102,050 |
| 1953 | Dark Star, br. c. | Cain Hoy Stable | Edward Hayward | H. Moreno | Native Dancer | Invigorator | 2:02 | 90,050 |
| 1952 | Hill Gail, dk. b. c. | Calumet Farm | B.A. Jones | E. Arcaro | Sub Fleet | Blue Man | 2:013/5 | 96,300 |
| 1951 | Count Turf, b. c. | J.J. Amiel | Sol Rutchick | C. McCreary | Royal Mustang | Ruhe | 2:023/5 | 98,050 |
| 1950 | Middleground, ch. c. | King Ranch | Max Hirsch | W. Boland | Hill Prince | Mr. Trouble | 2:013/5 | 92,650 |
| 1949 | Ponder, dk. b. c. | Calumet Farm | B.A. Jones | S. Brooks | Capot | Palestinian | 2:041/5 | 91,600 |
| **1948** | **Citation, b. c.** | Calumet Farm | B.A. Jones | E. Arcaro | Coaltown | My Request | 2:052/5 | 83,400 |

| YR | WINNER | OWNER | TRAINER | JOCKEY | SECOND | THIRD | TIME | MONEY |
|---|---|---|---|---|---|---|---|---|
| 1947 | Jet Pilot, ch. c. | Maine Chance Farm | Tom Smith | E. Guerin | Phalanx | Faultless | 2:06 4/5 | 92,160 |
| **1946** | **Assault, ch. c.** | King Ranch | Max Hirsch | W. Mehrtens | Spy Song | Hampden | 2:06 3/5 | 96,400 |
| 1945 | Hoop, Jr., b. c. | F.W. Hooper | Ivan H. Parke | E. Arcaro | Pot o' Luck | Darby Dieppe | 2:07 | 64,850 |
| 1944 | Pensive, ch. c. | Calumet Farm | B.A. Jones | C. McCreary | Broadcloth | Stir Up | 2:04 1/5 | 64,675 |
| **1943** | **Count Fleet, br. c.** | Mrs. John Hertz | G.D. Cameron | J. Longden | Blue Swords | Slide Rule | 2:04 | 60,725 |
| 1942 | Shut Out, ch. c. | Greentree Stable | John M. Gaver | W.D. Wright | Alsab | Valdina Orphan | 2:04 2/5 | 64,225 |
| **1941** | **Whirlaway, ch. c.** | Calumet Farm | B.A. Jones | E. Arcaro | Staretor | Market Wise | 2:01 2/5 | 61,275 |
| 1940 | Gallahadion, b. c. | Milky Way Farm | Roy Waldron | C. Bierman | Bimelech | Dit | 2:05 | 60,150 |
| 1939 | Johnstown, b. c. | Belair Stud | James Fitzsimmons | J. Stout | Challedon | Heather Broom | 2:03 2/5 | 46,350 |
| 1938 | Lawrin, br. c. | Woolford Farm | B.A. Jones | E. Arcaro | Dauber | Can't Wait | 2:04 4/5 | 47,050 |
| **1937** | **War Admiral, br. c** | Glen Riddle Farms | George Conway | C. Kurtsinger | Pompoon | Reaping Reward | 2:03 1/5 | 52,050 |
| 1936 | Bold Venture, ch. c. | M.L. Schwartz | Max Hirsch | I. Hanford | Brevity | Indian Broom | 2:03 3/5 | 37,725 |
| **1935** | **Omaha, ch. c.** | Belair Stud Stable | James Fitzsimmons | W. Saunders | Roman Soldier | Whiskolo | 2:05 | 39,525 |
| 1934 | Cavalcade, br. c. | Brookmeade Stable | R.A. Smith | M. Garner | Discovery | Agrarian | 2:04 | 28,175 |
| 1933 | Brokers Tip, br. c. | E.R. Bradley | H.J. Thompson | D. Meade | Head Play | Charley O. | 2:06 4/5 | 48,925 |
| 1932 | Burgoo King, ch. c. | E.R. Bradley | H.J. Thompson | E. James | Economic | Stepenfetchit | 2:05 1/5 | 52,350 |
| 1931 | Twenty Grand, b. c. | Greentree Stable | James Rowe Jr. | C. Kurtsinger | Sweep All | Mate | 2:01 4/5 | 48,725 |
| **1930** | **Gallant Fox, b. c.** | Belair Stud Stable | James Fitzsimmons | E. Sande | Gallant Knight | Ned O. | 2:07 3/5 | 50,725 |
| 1929 | Clyde Van Dusen, ch. g. | H.P. Gardner | Clyde Van Dusen | L. McAtee | Naishapur | Panchio | 2:10 4/5 | 53,950 |
| 1928 | Reigh Count, ch. c. | Mrs. John Hertz | B.S. Mitchell | C. Lang | Misstep | Toro | 2:10 2/5 | 55,375 |
| 1927 | Whiskery, b. c. | H.P. Whitney | Fred Hopkins | L. McAtee | Osmand | Jock | 2:06 | 51,000 |
| 1926 | Bubbling Over, ch. c. | E.R. Bradley | H.J. Thompson | A. Johnson | Bagenbaggage | Rock Man | 2:03 4/5 | 50,075 |
| 1925 | Flying Ebony, blk. c. | G.A. Cochran | W.B. Duke | E. Sande | Captain Hal | Son of John | 2:07 3/5 | 52,950 |
| 1924 | Black Gold, blk. c. | Mrs. R. M. Hoots | Hanley Webb | J. D. Mooney | Chilhowee | Beau Butler | 2:05 1/5 | 52,775 |
| 1923 | Zev, br. c. | Rancocas Stable | D.J. Leary | E. Sande | Martingale | Vigil | 2:05 2/5 | 53,000 |
| 1922 | Morvich, br. c. | Benjamin Block | Fred Burlew | A. Johnson | Bet Mosie | John Finn | 2:04 3/5 | 46,775 |
| 1921 | Behave Yourself, b. c. | E.R. Bradley | H.J. Thompson | C. Thompson | Black Servant | Prudery | 2:04 1/5 | 38,450 |
| 1920 | Paul Jones, br. g. | Ral Parr | Wm. Garth | T. Rice | Upset | On Watch | 2:09 | 30,375 |
| **1919** | **Sir Barton, ch. c.** | J.K.L. Ross | H.G. Bedwell | J. Loftus | Billy Kelly | Under Fire | 2:09 4/5 | 20,825 |
| 1918 | Exterminator, ch. g. | Willis Sharpe Kilmer | Henry McDaniel | W. Knapp | Escoba | Viva America | 2:10 4/5 | 14,700 |
| 1917 | Omar Khayyam, blk. c. | Billings & Johnson | C.T. Paterson | C. Borel | Ticket | Midway | 2:04 3/5 | 16,600 |
| 1916 | George Smith, blk. c. | John Sanford | Hollie Hughes | J. Loftus | Star Hawk | Franklin | 2:04 | 9,750 |
| 1915 | Regret, ch. f. | H.P. Whitney | James Rowe Sr. | J. Notter | Pebbles | Sharpshooter | 2:05 2/5 | 11,450 |
| 1914 | Old Rosebud, b. g. | H.C. Applegate | F.D. Weir | J. McCabe | Hodge | Bronzewing | 2:03 2/5 | 9,125 |
| 1913 | Donerail, b. c. | T.P. Hayes | T.P. Hayes | R. Goose | Ten Point | Gowell | 2:04 4/5 | 5,475 |
| 1912 | Worth, br. c. | H.C. Hallenbeck | Frank M. Taylor | C. H. Shilling | Duval | Flamma | 2:09 2/5 | 4,850 |
| 1911 | Meridian, b. c. | R.F. Carman | A. Ewing | G. Archibald | Governor Gray | Colston | 2:05 | 4,850 |
| 1910 | Donau, b. c. | William Gerst | George Ham | F. Herbert | Joe Morris | Fighting Bob | 2:06 2/5 | 4,850 |
| 1909 | Wintergreen, b. c. | J.B. Respess | C. Mack | W. Powers | Miami | Dr. Barkley | 2:08 1/5 | 4,850 |
| 1908 | Stone Street, b. c. | C.E. Hamilton | J.W. Hall | A. Pickens | Sir Cleges | Dunvegan | 2:15 1/5 | 4,850 |
| 1907 | Pink Star, b. c. | J. Hal Woodford | W.H. Fizer | A. Minder | Zal | Ovelando | 2:12 3/5 | 4,850 |
| 1906 | Sir Huon, b. c. | George J. Long | Peter Coyne | R. Troxler | Lady Navarre | James Reddick | 2:08 4/5 | 4,850 |
| 1905 | Agile, b. c. | S.S. Brown | Robert Tucker | J. Martin | Ram's Horn | Layson | 2:10 3/4 | 4,850 |
| 1904 | Elwood, b. c. | Mrs. C. E. Durnell | C.E. Durnell | F. Pryor | Ed Tierney | Brancas | 2:08 1/2 | 4,850 |
| 1903 | Judge Himes, b. c. | C.R. Ellison | J.P. Mayberry | H. Booker | Early | Bourbon | 2:09 | 4,850 |
| 1902 | Alan-a-Dale, ch. c. | T.C. McDowell | T.C. McDowell | J. Winkfield | Inventor | The Rival | 2:08 3/4 | 4,850 |
| 1901 | His Eminence, b. c. | F.B. VanMeter | F.B. VanMeter | J. Winkfield | Sannazarro | Driscoll | 2:07 3/4 | 4,850 |
| 1900 | Lieut. Gibson, b. c. | Charles H. Smith | Charles H. Hughes | J. Boland | Florizar | Thrive | 2:06 1/4 | 4,850 |
| 1899 | Manuel, b. c. | A.H. & D.H. Morris | Robert J. Walden | J. Taral | Corsini | Mazo | 2:12 | 4,850 |
| 1898 | Plaudit, br. c. | J.E. Madden | J.E. Madden | W. Simms | Lieber Karl | Isabey | 2:09 | 4,850 |
| 1897 | Typhoon II, ch. c. | J.C. Cahn | J.C. Cahn | F. Garner | Ornament | Dr. Catlett | 2:12 1/2 | 4,850 |
| 1896 | Ben Brush, b. c. | M.F. Dwyer | Hardy Campbell | W. Simms | Ben Eder | Semper Ego | 2:07 3/4 | 4,850 |
| 1895 | Halma, blk. c. | Byron McClelland | Byron McClelland | J. Perkins | Basso | Laureate | 2:37 1/2 | 2,970 |
| 1894 | Chant, b. c. | Leigh & Rose | Eugene Leigh | F. Goodale | Pearl Song | Sigurd | 2:41 | 4,020 |
| 1893 | Lookout, ch. c. | Cushing & Orth | Will McDaniel | E. Kunze | Plutus | Boundless | 2:39 1/4 | 3,840 |
| 1892 | Azra, b. c. | Bashford Manor | John H. Morris | A. Clayton | Huron | Phil Dwyer | 2:41 1/2 | 4,230 |
| 1891 | Kingman, b. c. | Jacobin Stable | Dud Allen | I. Murphy | Balgowan | High Tariff | 2:52 1/4 | 4,550 |
| 1890 | Riley, b. c. | Edward Corrigan | Edward Corrigan | I. Murphy | Bill Letcher | Robespierre | 2:45 | 5,460 |
| 1889 | Spokane, ch. c. | Noah Armstrong | John Rodegap | T. Kiley | Proctor Knott | Once Again | 2:34 1/2 | 4,880 |
| 1888 | Macbeth II, b. g. | Chicago Stable | John Campbell | G. Covington | Gallifet | White | 2:38 1/4 | 4,740 |
| 1887 | Montrose, b. c. | Labold Brothers | John McGinty | I. Lewis | Jim Gore | Jacobin | 2:39 1/4 | 4,200 |
| 1886 | Ben Ali, br. c. | J.B.A. Haggin | Jim Murphy | P. Duffy | Blue Wing | Free Knight | 2:36 1/2 | 4,890 |
| 1885 | Joe Cotton, ch. c. | J.T. Williams | Alex Perry | E. Henderson | Bersan | Ten Booker | 2:37 1/4 | 4,630 |
| 1884 | Buchanan, ch. c. | W. Cottrill | William Bird | I. Murphy | Loftin | Audrain | 2:40 1/4 | 3,990 |
| 1883 | Leonatus, b. c. | Chinn & Morgan | Raleigh Colston | W. Donahue | Drake Carter | Lord Raglan | 2:43 | 3,760 |
| 1882 | Apollo, ch. g. | Morris & Patton | Green B. Morris | B. Hurd | Runnymede | Bengal | 2:40 1/2 | 4,560 |
| 1881 | Hindoo, b. c. | Dwyer Brothers | James Rowe Sr. | J. McLaughlin | Lelex | Alhambra | 2:40 | 4,410 |
| 1880 | Fonso, ch. c. | J.S. Shawhan | Tice Hutsell | G. Lewis | Kimball | Bancroft | 2:37 1/2 | 3,800 |
| 1879 | Lord Murphy, b. c. | Geo. W. Darden & Co. | George Rice | C. Shauer | Falsetto | Strathmore | 2:37 | 3,550 |
| 1878 | Day Star, ch. c. | T.J. Nichols | Lee Paul | J. Carter | Himyar | Leveler | 2:37 1/4 | 4,050 |
| 1877 | Baden Baden, ch. c. | Daniel Swigert | Ed Brown | W. Walker | Leonard | King William | 2:38 | 3,300 |
| 1876 | Vagrant, b. g. | William Astor | James Williams | R. Swim | Creedmoor | Harry Hill | 2:38 1/4 | 2,950 |
| 1875 | Aristides, ch. c. | H.P. McGrath | Ansel Williamson | O. Lewis | Volcano | Verdigris | 2:37 3/4 | 2,850 |

**(Triple Crown winners in bold.)**

## SPORTS

# *The chance of a lifetime...* Billy Reed

*Four springs ago, two men, not now identified, laid plans which are about to come to fruition. One was planning the mating which led to the winner of the Kentucky Derby. The other was lighting a fire under the mash at the Brown-Forman Distillery. Strength to them both.*

*—Joe Palmer, Spring, 1952*

As legend has it, thoroughbred racing and bourbon whiskey both came to prosper in Kentucky as nowhere else because of the rich limestone soil and the minerals in the water, particularly in the central part of the commonwealth. The soil and the water produced a strain of grass that, it was said, looked blue if held to a flame. And thus did Kentucky become the Bluegrass State, known internationally for its horse farms, race tracks and distilleries.

The proximity of the horses and the bourbon led to the invention of a drink known as the mint julep, which was served at the most prestigious breeding farms to buyers who had come to inspect the young horses that were for sale. And thus did Kentucky develop its own brand of Southern hospitality.

A decade after the Civil War, when the Old South was deep in the throes of reconstruction, a couple of Louisville businessmen opened a racetrack in the city's South End. It was named Churchill Downs, after the family who owned the property, and it had a couple of spires — twin spires, as they came to be known — atop the grandstand to give it a touch of class.

In the spring of 1875, the track sponsored a stakes race known as the Kentucky Derby, modeled after the Epsom Derby in England, in order to give the state's breeders a showcase for their best young horses. The first Derby was won by a little red colt named Aristides, who saved the day for owner H.P. McGrath when his stablemate, the favored Chesapeake, faltered and "spit out the bit," as horsemen put it.

Among the crowd that day was a youngster named Matt Winn, who watched the Derby from his father's wagon parked in the track infield. He grew up loving Churchill Downs and the Derby to the point that, when the track was on the brink of bankruptcy in the early 1900s, Winn put together a group of investors to save it.

From that time until his death in 1948, Winn lived and breathed the Kentucky Derby. Far ahead of his time in the areas of marketing and promotion, Winn personally built the Derby into the world's best-known and most-coveted race. At some point, he adopted the honorary title of "Colonel," which enhanced his image as a Southern gentlemen.

While Winn was building the Derby and Churchill Downs, racing also prospered in other parts of the state. In Northern Kentucky, Latonia (now Turfway) provided the legal gambling action for guys and dolls who patronized the area's nightclubs, casinos and gin joints. And in Central Kentucky, the breeders, weary of the trouble and expense of sending their sales yearlings to Saratoga in upstate New York, founded a combination race track and sales company in 1936. Named Keeneland, in honor of founder Jack Keene, the picturesque plant outside Lexington represented "racing as it was meant to be," and sales yearlings that were literally the cream of the international crop.

Every year, more than 35,000 thoroughbreds are born throughout the world. Only one can win the Kentucky Derby in the spring of his 3-year-old year, which is why the singer Dan Fogelberg called it "the chance of a lifetime in a lifetime of chance" in his song, "Run for the Roses."

Virtually next door to Keeneland on the Versailles Pike, just across from the Blue Grass Field airport, lies Calumet Farm, which still is the home of more Kentucky Derby winners (eight) than any other owner. Of the 11 horses that have won racing's Triple Crown (Derby, Preakness and Belmont Stakes), two carried Calumet's devil's red-and-blue silks — Whirlaway in 1941 and Citation in 1948.

Through the years, as tobacco, coal and bourbon have fallen out of favor with many, horse racing has become Kentucky's signature industry. It's what separates Kentucky from, say, Ohio or West Virginia. And a virtual cottage industry has grown around the Derby.

Although the race itself generally lasts only a couple of minutes (Secretariat's 1973 time of 1:59 2/5 for the mile and a quarter still is the Derby record), the festival celebrating it begins two weeks earlier and includes a hot-air balloon race, a steamboat race, a parade, a fireworks display that draws 400,000 to the banks of the Ohio River and some of the most celebrated parties this side of Hollywood.

On Derby Day, it's *de rigeur* for women to wear outlandish hats. For the men, it's ties and sports jackets in colors and patterns that seldom are seen away from the golf course. And it's expected that everyone will knock back a mint julep or two, make many trips to the betting windows and shed a tear when Stephen Foster's melancholy "My Old Kentucky Home" is played as the Derby horses come on the track.

The owner, trainer and jockey who are lucky enough to win the Derby — and, make no mistake, luck is every bit as important as pedigree and talent — win more than a gold trophy. They win a little slice of immortality. Have you ever won the Kentucky Derby? Inevitably, that's the first question a horseman gets asked when he or she meets a stranger.

In 2005, longshot Giacomo won the Derby and paid $102.60 for a $2 win bet, second highest in Derby history. The superfecta, which requires picking the top four horses in order, was worth more than $1 million.

Out in Arizona, a bettor had a winning superfecta ticket, but couldn't find it. He looked everywhere, going through bags and bags of trash. No luck. Finally he shared his plight with the pari-mutuel clerk who had sold him the ticket. She looked around her work area and found the ticket. The new millionaire gave her a generous tip. He might even have bought her a mint julep or two.

Strength to them both.

"On Derby Day, it's de rigeur for women to wear outlandish hats."

*Source: Kentucky Derby Museum*

# SPORTS

# *Horse Events*
# *Saddlebreds*

Tolley Graves

Kentucky is home to America's only native breed of horse, the American Saddlebred. A very special breed of horse – beautiful, intelligent, fun to ride or drive and adaptable to any use – this is a horse for every horse person.

The American Saddlebred is easily recognized in a backyard or in a show ring. His proud head and tail carriage, combined with size and substance, clearly distinguish this elegant horse from any other light horse breed.

The conformation of the breed is striking and enables him to perform well at many endeavors. With his long legs and sloping pasterns, the ideal Saddlebred has high stepping action along with a ground-covering stride. A long, arching neck and large expressive eye complete the picture of beauty and refinement.

**Kentucky Horse Park**
*Photo: Sid Webb*

By the initial publication of the Kentucky Almanac in 1788, the foundation had begun for the horse known as the Kentucky Saddler through most of the 1800s. The name American Saddle Horse became official in 1891 with the formation of the registry. Common usage prompted another change in the latter half of the 20th century, and this popular and versatile breed is now known as the American Saddlebred.

The Saddlebred was developed by 18th century colonists who sought a good-looking, sensible, adaptable and comfortable animal to ride and drive. The American Saddlebred is a composite of several breeds, including the Narragansett Pacer, the Thoroughbred, the Morgan, the Hackney and the Canadian Pacer.

Early breeders took care to maintain the easy gaits of the first Saddlers, and added quality, size and strength. A utility horse of beauty, high intelligence and good disposition these horses were the mainstay of the Confederate cavalry during the Civil War and the choice mount of many generals on both sides of the war. Some noted "Saddlers" serving in the war were Robert E. Lee's Traveller, Ulysses S. Grant's Cincinnati, Sherman's Lexington, Stonewall Jackson's Little Sorrel, John Hunt Morgan's Black Bess and General Meade's Baldy. After the war, General Grant allowed the Southerners to take their horses home, thus ensuring their breeding programs would continue.

Kentucky has always been the center of the Saddlebred industry. The first known horse show was held just north of Lexington in 1816. With the invention of the steam engine, many people switched their horses from work to recreational activities and horse shows grew in popularity. As the Saddlebreds' favorite thing to do is show off, many spectators were attracted to their proud carriage, lively expression and high leg action. From their ancestors Saddlebreds inherited the ability to perform at the slow gait and rack, distinct four-beat gaits where only one hoof hits the ground at a time.

The characteristics that have contributed to the Saddlebred's reputation as the "peacock of the show ring" also make him an excellent sport horse. Smoothness of gaits, speed coupled with intelligence, powerful muscling plus an innate desire to please, enable him to do whatever is asked of him. Saddlebreds compete successfully in a variety of disciplines including jumping, barrel racing, driving, dressage, endurance riding, etc. A Saddlebred is capable of almost any task he is asked to perform and will do it with extraordinary style.

Saddlebreds have even attained celebrity status. Buffalo Bill Cody's mount, Columbus, was a star in his 1890s Wild West Show. Mr. Ed and Fury became television stars in long-running hit shows. William Shatner, an owner and exhibitor of American Saddlebreds, had some of his horses appear in scenes from Star Trek Generations. Other Saddlebreds have been cast as Black Beauty and Toronado, Zorro's dashing mount.

The first Kentucky State Fair was held in 1902, with the Saddle Horse Show a prime attraction. Louisville is still the location every August for the World's Grand Championship Horse Show. If you visit Kentucky in the summer, chances are there will be a Saddlebred horse show near you. County fairs featuring Saddlebreds are held every weekend throughout the state. Louisville's prestigious Rock Creek Show is held in June, followed by the largest outdoor Saddle Horse show in the world at Lexington's Red Mile in July.

Visitors to the area seeking more Saddlebred information should stop at the beautiful Kentucky Horse Park in Lexington. The American Saddlebred Museum is located on the Horse Park grounds and also houses the offices of the American Saddlebred Registry and Association. The museum features permanent, special and interactive exhibits. An award winning feature movie on the breed plays in the theater along with various videos stationed throughout the museum. If you are looking for Saddlebreds in your home location you may find them on the computer-based locator program that prints out a list of farms. A child-friendly area of the museum features a touch screen question and answer game and two large Saddlebred rocking horses, a favorite ride for visitors of all ages.

Many of the legendary Saddlebred show horses lived in Kentucky, and many are buried here in the Bluegrass, including six-time Five-Gaited World's Champions Wing Commander and My-My. Five-Gaited World's Grand Champions Imperator, Sky Watch and Wild-Eyed And Wicked are buried at the Horse Park's Hall of Champions. The remains of Rex Peavine, Five-Gaited Grand Champion at the Kentucky State Fair in 1903, are also located at the American Saddlebred Museum.

A thrilling show horse, a true and loyal companion, the American Saddlebred is the horse for everyone. More than 100 years of careful development through selective breeding have produced a horse that is as uniform in its style and conformation today as the saddle horses of Civil War times. A bit more polished and refined, but still the same hard-working, intelligent and graceful breed that deserves the title "The Horse America Made."

*Tolley Graves, is Executive Director of the American Saddlebred Museum.*

## BREEDS OF HORSES IN KENTUCKY

Yes, we love Thoroughbreds, Standardbreds, Quarter Horses...and many other horse breeds that Kentuckians adore for their beauty, gait, temperament, style and personality. These breeds include: American Gaited Pony, American Miniature, American Paint, American Saddle Horse, American Shetland Pony, American Walking Pony, American Warmblood, Appaloosa, Arabian, Barb, Belgian, BelgianWarmblood, Buckskin, Donkey, Clydesdale, Dutch Warmblood, Friesian, Hackney Horse, Half Arabian, Highland Pony, Irish Hunter, Lipizzaner, Lusitano, Missouri Fox Trotter, Morgan Horse, Mountain Pleasure Horse, Mule, Mustang, National Show Horse, National Spotted Saddle Horse, New Forest Pony, Paint, Palamino, Peruvian Paso, QuArab Horse, Racking Horse, Rocky Mountain Horse, Tarpan, Tennessee Walking Horse, Shetland Pony, Spanish Barb, Welsh pony and ... Zebra.

*Source: Kentucky Horse Park and http://cowboyfrank.com*

# SPORTS
# *Horse Racing Standardbreds*

Origins of the Standardbred trace back to Messenger, an English Thoroughbred foaled in 1780, and later exported to the U.S. Messenger was the great-grandsire of Hambletonian 10, to whom every Standardbred can trace its heritage. The name "Standardbred" originated because the early trotters (pacers would not come into favor until much later) were required to reach a certain standard for the mile distance in order to be registered. The mile is still the standard distance covered in nearly every harness race.

The first Standardbred races were contested along roads, with men challenging their friends to see who had the swifter horse. Often the streets of cities were cleared for racing—that's why so many cities have a Race Street.

In many respects, the Standardbred resembles its ancestor the Thoroughbred. It does not stand as tall, averaging 15.2 hands, although it has a longer body. The head is refined, set on a medium-sized neck. The quarters are muscular yet sleek. The clean hind legs are set well back. This breed appears in varying colors, although bay, brown and black are predominant; weight varies between 800 and 1000 pounds.

Standardbred racing is contested on two gaits, the trot and the pace. Trotters move with a diagonal gait; the left front and right rear legs move in unison, as to the right front and left rear. It requires much skill by the trainer to get a trotter to move perfectly at high speeds, even though the trotting gait is a natural one in the animal world.

Pacers, on the other hand, move the legs on one side of their body in tandem: left front and rear, and right front and rear. This action shows why pacers are often called "sidewheelers." Pacers, which account for about 80 percent of the performers in harness racing, are aided in maintaining their gait by plastic loops called hobbles, which keep their legs moving in synchronization.

## The Red Mile

The date was Tuesday, Sept. 28, 1875, and it was the inaugural opening day of the Great Fall Trots at The Red Mile, sponsored by the newly reorganized Kentucky Trotting Horse Breeders Association. The Red Mile, located just one mile from downtown Lexington and well-known for its fast, red clay and one-mile track, is the second oldest harness track in the world.

The Red Mile offers showcase horse racing each year plus full-card simulcasting 365 days a year from top harness outlets such as Meadowlands, Mohawk and Woodbine (including simulcasts of quarter horse racing from Los Alamitos, Sunland Park and other tracks).

In 2004, the Red Mile hosted its inaugural Quarter Horse meet, which marked the first time that breed had raced in the Bluegrass in more than a decade. The Red Mile hosts numerous other events, such as horse sales, wedding receptions, holiday parties, concerts, circuses, reunions, corporate meetings and many more events.

The Round Barn, a picturesque building listed on the National Register of Historic Places, offers a charm all its own. It is available for a host of events and can accommodate up to 200 guests; for non-seated events it will easily hold more.

Leading drivers at the Red Mile are: Wins: Josh Sutton (Spring) – 31; David Miller (Grand Circuit) – 37; UDR: Mike Zeller (Spring) - .387; John Patterson, Jr. (Grand Circuit) - .0379; Purses: John Meittinis (Spring) - $84,680; and David Miller (Grand Circuit) - $1,280,060. Leading trainers are: Clint Binkley (Spring) – 16 and Brett Pelling and Charles Sylverster (Grand Circuit) – 11.

*Reprinted with permission from The Red Mile (www. theredmile.com) and the U.S. Trotting Association (www.ustrotting.com).*

SPORTS
# *Baseball*

## John A. McGill

*Four Kentuckians
have made it to Cooperstown,
but many others have made their mark.*

It wasn't that easy for Jackie Robinson to break the color barrier in baseball in 1947, and it was a pair of Kentuckians who played significant roles in helping him make history.

Gov. Albert B. "Happy" Chandler, born near Corydon, was the commissioner of major league baseball at the time and worked behind the scenes to pave the way for Robinson to be signed to a major league contract. And Pee Wee Reese, the Brooklyn Dodgers shortstop and team captain, was the player who refused to sign a petition by his teammates threatening a boycott if Robinson joined the team.

Robinson joined the Dodgers, and on his first road trip, which was to Cincinnati, fans began to heckle him. Reese, however, walked over to Robinson and put his arm across Robinson's shoulder. It silenced the crowd.

Reese, who some regard as being from Louisville but actually was born in Ekron, was as good at playing baseball as he was at doing the right thing. He was an All-Star selection 10 times during a career that stretched from 1940 to 1958. The Dodgers won the National League pennant seven times in that period.

Both Chandler and Reese are in baseball's Hall of Fame. Two other Kentuckians have joined them in Cooperstown: U.S. Sen. Jim Bunning of Southgate and Earle Combs of Pebworth.

Bunning is the only pitcher to throw no-hitters in both the American and National Leagues—and one of them was a perfect game, coming while pitching for Philadelphia in a 6-0 win over the New York Mets in Shea Stadium on June 21, 1964. Bunning had a career record of 224-184 with a 3.27 ERA. He was a minor league manager for several years before entering politics.

Combs was the leadoff hitter for the 1927 New York Yankees, the team that was dubbed "Murderers' Row." Joining Combs were talents such as

Babe Ruth and Lou Gehrig. The 1927 Yankees are still regarded as one of the greatest teams in history. Combs batted .356 that year with 231 hits, a club record that held until 1986 when Don Mattingly topped it. Combs had a career batting average of .325, and although he attempted a come-

Ronnie Martinez was the starting pitcher for the Legends, Lexington Legends vs Greensboro Grasshoppers baseball game, Applebee's Park, Lexington
*Source: Lexington Herald-Leader*

back after fracturing his skull crashing into an outfield wall (they weren't padded back then), he retired after a comeback attempt in 1935. Combs, who had a 29-game hitting streak in 1931, was replaced by none other than Joe DiMaggio.

Others from the Bluegrass State have had significant major league careers.

Don Gullett of South Shore was a 19-year-old rookie when he was hastily called in to pitch for Cincinnati after the Reds' ace, Jim Maloney, hurt himself running the bases. In his first major league appearance in April of 1970, Gullett pitched five scoreless innings and picked up the decision. It wasn't long after that that manager Sparky Anderson was saying that Gullett would become a sure Hall of Fame pick one day.

Gullett had a 16-6 record with an impressive 2.64 ERA and led the National League in winning percentage at .727. He had a 61-26 record with the Reds over a four-year period that included the Reds' world championship years of 1975 and 1976, where he started Game One in both World Series. He became a free agent in 1977 and went to the Yankees, going 14-4 in a year when New York won the World Series. Chronic shoulder problems led to severe rotator cuff damage and cut short his career. Gullett would become the longtime pitching coach for the Reds.

Gus Bell of Louisville started with the Pittsburgh Pirates in 1950 but made his mark after being traded to Cincinnati, where he hit a career-high 30 home runs in 1953. Bell was with the Reds for nine years and had more than 100 RBI four times. Gus, the father of Buddy Bell, was a four-time All-Star.

Lou Johnson of Lexington played a key role for the Los Angeles Dodgers when they won the World Series in 1965, hitting the decisive home run in Game 7. Earlier in the season, he scored the lone run in Sandy Koufax's perfect game—earning the nickname "Sweet Lou."

Woodie Fryman, the tobacco farmer from Ewing, was slow to make it to professional baseball, not signing until he was 25. But his career went into hyperspeed after that. With only 12 minor league appearances, the lefthander was called up for the 1966 season by the Pittsburgh Pirates and threw three straight shutouts. It was the start of an 18-year career that saw him throw four one-hitters and twice be named an All-Star.

Doug Flynn of Lexington was a reserve infielder on The Big Red Machine, the nickname given to the Cincinnati Reds of the 1970s, who won back-to-back World Series championships in 1975 and 1976 and are regarded along with the 1927 New York Yankees as one of the greatest teams in baseball history. Even though he was known far more for his glove work than his batting, Flynn tied the modern major league record with three triples in a single game against Montreal on Aug. 5, 1980.

Joe Cowley of Lexington set an American League pitching record by striking out the first seven Texas Rangers batters to open a game on May 28, 1986, and in September of that year threw a no-hitter against the California Angels despite issuing seven walks. Cowley did this with the Chicago White Sox, but his major league debut came with the Yankees. After eight years in the minors, he was named a starter by New York in July of 1984. He won eight straight decisions and finished 9-2.

There are many more, including: Clint Johnson, an Ashland native who was a star in the old Negro leagues and was elected to the Kentucky Athletic Hall of Fame. Others who were standouts in the old Negro leagues included Louisville's John Beckwith, who played seven positions and hit 54 home runs for the Homestead Grays in 1928, and Greenup's Clinton (Hawk) Thomas, who hit .407 for the Philadelphia team in 1924.

Steve Hamilton, the Morehead native who pitched 11 years in the major leagues, mostly for the Yankees, is one of only three men who played on both a World Series and an NBA championship team. Paul Derringer was a 20-game winner for the Reds in the late 1930s and early 1940s. John Shelby Sr. of Lexington played for the Dodgers, including when L.A. won the World Series over Oakland in 1998.

Few may recall that Cotton Nash, one of the most popular and productive players in UK basketball history, also briefly played in the majors (with the White Sox and Twins from 1967-70). Steve Finley of Paducah first made it to the majors in 1989, played for the 2001 World Series champion Arizona Diamondbacks and is now with the San Francisco Giants. He came into 2005 with 293 career home runs. Austin Kearns of Lexington, Terry Shumpert of Paducah, Brad Wilkerson of Owensboro, pitcher Paul Byrd of Louisville and pitcher Brandon Webb Wright of Ashland are among other Kentuckians currently playing.

Unfortunately, two Kentucky natives also were involved in one of the most tragic incidents in baseball history.

In 1920, Cleveland Indians shortstop Ray Chapman, a native of Beaver Dam, was hit in the temple by a pitch and died in the hospital 12 hours later, the only modern era major league player to be fatally injured in a game. Chapman was a talented player, stealing 52 bases in 1917—a record that wasn't broken until 1980. The Yankees pitcher who threw the fateful pitch was Carl Mays of Liberty.

### Alan Stein

# SPORTS
# *Minor League Baseball*

Minor League Baseball is an organization that has endured more than a century of social, political and cultural changes. Through the pioneering spirit of its membership and leaders, minor league baseball has evolved and remains a vital component of the American landscape. Today, minor league baseball touches the lives of people and cultures throughout the world.

In 2005, a record-setting 40 million fans attended regular season games, breaking the attendance record that had stood since 1949. Total regular season attendance has increased in 20 of the last 24 seasons and has surpassed 33 million in each of the last twelve seasons. This enormous fan base, drawing more fans than the NBA, the NFL and the NHL combined, is centered on minor league baseball's attractiveness to all spectrums of our communities – the young and the young-at-heart, families of all sizes and varieties and diverse economic sectors — all coming together for America's favorite game.

In Lexington, the Lexington Legends are drawing people from all over the Bluegrass region and surrounding states to Applebee's Park. It's the entire family that is coming, and businesses, too, because Lexington Legends baseball is fun. It has something for the young and the young at heart.

Kids can play in the Kid Zone and ride the carousel; families can sit down to eat in the Maker's Mark club restaurant and watch the field on our in-house television feed, or visitors can spread out a picnic blanket along the outfield line catching foul balls; and businesses can entertain their clients in a corporate suite surrounded by the

glamour and ambience of base-ball. All can watch the antics of mascots and fans alike as they enjoy their days and their evenings watching America's game.

The Lexington Legends are about entertainment and our commitment to customer ser-vice is unparalleled. From beginning to end of the fan's experience, we make sure everything is done to make your visit to Applebee's Park fun and entertaining. We invest - along with our sponsors and advertis-ers - in your experience because we have learned that you will return.

Our philosophy is simple. We focus on you, the fans—we know what you want and what you like. We strive to bring clean, safe entertainment to Kentucky where fans get great

**The first pitch of the Lexington Legends vs the Hagerstown Suns at the Lexington Legends home opener on April 9, 2001 in Lexington**
*Photo: David Stephenson, Lexington Herald-Leader*

value for their discretionary dollar, and, more importantly, their discretionary leisure time. Come join the fun.

# History of River City Baseball

Baseball has some of its deepest roots embed-ded in Louisville as the River City was an original member of the National League. Hall of Famers such as Honus Wagner and Carlton Fisk played here as well as Kentucky native Pee Wee Reese.

The relationship between Louisville and the national pastime dates back over 130 years to 1874 when professional baseball was first played in Louisville and has been in town for all but 19 years.

The Louisville Redbirds became the first Minor League team in history to have one million fans in one season, accomplishing the feat in 1983. By being the first franchise to break the one mil-lion mark in attendance, Louisville set the stage for the renaissance of Minor League baseball's popularity which continues to escalate today.

Much has transpired in regards to professional baseball in Louisville since the early days of the 1980s. Cardinal Stadium was vacated for the state-of-the-art Louisville Slugger Field which opened in 2000. After a 16-year working agree-ment with the St. Louis Cardinals, the franchise became the top farm club of the Milwaukee Brewers in 1998 followed by the Cincinnati Reds in 2000.

The team name was changed from the Red-

birds to the RiverBats and then to the Bats since the franchise's inception in 1982. Though the team has experienced a number of changes, one thing that remains constant is this area's affinity for professional baseball.

*Contributed by Megan Dimond, Assistant Direc-tor of Media & PR, Louisville Bats.*

## Did You Know?

The Florence Freedom baseball team was founded in 2002. Shortly after moving to Florence the original owners filed for bank-ruptcy. In January 2005 Northern Kentucky businessman Clint Brown bought the team.

Since 2005, the team has flourished. The '05 Freedom hit 124 home runs, shattering the league record. In '06 almost 100,000 fans came to Champion Window Field to cheer on the Freedom.

The spirit of the team is evident in its slogan, "America's Game...Northern Ken-tucky's Team!" This team's brand of base-ball is an affordable way to entertain your family all summer long. For more informa-tion visit: www.florencefreedom.com.

# Little League Baseball

## VALLEY SPORTS AMERICAN

### 2002 Little League World Series Champion

When Louisville's Valley Sports American all-star team reached the championship game of the Little League World Series in 2002, it became the first Kentucky team to accomplish the feat in the then 56-year history of the event.

But Valley Sports was just warming up. They went on to beat Japan 1-0 for the championship to become the first United States team to win it all since 1998—and only the 10th U.S. champion over a 35-year span.

Valley's triumph produced only the third 1-0 score in the history of Little League World Series championship games as the team closed out with a 24-game winning streak.

Members of the team: Aaron Alvey, Justin Elkins, Ethan Henry, Alex Hornback, Wes Jenkins, Casey Jordan, Shane Logsdon, Blaine Madden, Zach Osborne, Jake Remines, Josh Robinson, Wes Walden.

Coaches: Troy Osbourne, Keith Elkins, Dan Roach.

# KHSAA Boys Baseball

## MOST STATE CHAMPIONSHIPS

| School | Titles |
|---|---|
| Louisville Manual | 6 |
| Owensboro | 6 |
| Louisville St. Xavier | 5 |
| Newport Catholic | 4 |
| Ashland Blazer | 3 |
| Harrison Co. | 3 |
| Lexington Lafayette | 3 |
| Lexington Tates Creek | 3 |
| Lou. Pleasure Ridge Park | 3 |

## PAST STATE CHAMPIONS

| Year | Champion |
|---|---|
| 1940 | Newport |
| 1941 | Newport |
| 1942 | Louisville St. Xavier |
| 1943 | Louisville Male |
| 1944 | (no tournament held) |
| 1945 | Louisville St. Xavier |
| 1946 | Newport Catholic |
| 1947 | Louisville Manual |
| 1948 | Prestonsburg |
| 1949 | Louisville St. Xavier |
| 1950 | Newport Catholic |
| 1951 | Louisville St. Xavier |
| 1952 | Louisville Manual |
| 1953 | St. Joseph |
| 1954 | Newport Catholic |
| 1955 | Louisville Manual |
| 1956 | Newport Catholic |
| 1957 | Louisville Manual |
| 1958 | Maysville |
| 1959 | Louisville Manual |
| 1960 | Paducah Tilghman |
| 1961 | Caverna |
| 1962 | Louisville Manual |
| 1963 | Covington Holmes |
| 1964 | Owensboro |
| 1965 | Bowling Green |
| 1966 | Ashland |
| 1967 | Ashland |
| 1968 | Ashland |
| 1969 | Owensboro |
| 1970 | Elizabethtown |
| 1971 | Daviess Co. |
| 1972 | Caverna |
| 1973 | Lexington Henry Clay |
| 1974 | Somerset |
| 1975 | Elizabethtown |
| 1976 | Owensboro |
| 1977 | Owensboro |
| 1978 | Lexington Tates Creek |
| 1979 | Shelby Co. |
| 1980 | Lexington Tates Creek |
| 1981 | Louisville St. Xavier |
| 1982 | Madison Central |
| 1983 | Owensboro |
| 1984 | East Carter |
| 1985 | Owensboro Catholic |
| 1986 | Lexington Tates Creek |
| 1987 | Owensboro |
| 1988 | Lexington Lafayette |
| 1989 | Lexington Lafayette |
| 1990 | Paintsville |
| 1991 | Franklin-Simpson |
| 1992 | Lexington Lafayette |
| 1993 | Harrison Co. |
| 1994 | Lou. Pleasure Ridge Park |
| 1995 | Lou. Pleasure Ridge Park |
| 1996 | Lou. Pleasure Ridge Park |
| 1997 | Harrison Co. |
| 1998 | Harrison Co. |
| 1999 | Lexington Catholic |
| 2000 | Henderson Co. |
| 2001 | Boyd Co. |
| 2002 | Covington Catholic |
| 2003 | Lexington Paul Dunbar |
| 2004 | Christian Co. |
| 2005 | Lexington Christian |
| 2006 | Lexington Catholic |

## MOST HITS (CAREER)

| No. | Player | School | Years | Hits |
|---|---|---|---|---|
| 1. | J.B. Schmidt | Harrison Co. | 1994-00 | 275 |
| 2. | B.J. Foley | Corbin | 1995-02 | 236 |
| 3. | Scott Fryman | Harrison Co. | 1990-94 | 228 |
| 4. | Brent Hampton | Harrison Co. | 1990-95 | 227 |
| 5. | Will Renaker | Harrison Co. | 1994-98 | 226 |
| 6. | Noochie Varner | Harrison Co. | 1995-99 | 223 |
| 7. | Brad Wilkerson | Apollo | 1991-95 | 221 |
| 8. | Derrick Alfonso | Warren Central | 1999-04 | 220 |
| 9. | Jeff Derrickson | Bryan Station | 1997-01 | 204 |
| 10. | Ryan Cox | Taylor Co. | 1997-00 | 202 |

## MOST HOME RUNS (CAREER)

| No. | Player | School | Years | Home Runs |
|---|---|---|---|---|
| 1. | Paul Morse | Danville | 1989-92 | 62 |
| 2. | Shon Walker | Harrison Co. | 1989-92 | 52 |
| 3. | Corey Hart | Greenwood | 1998-00 | 48 |
| 3. | Kendall Withers | Harrison Co. | 1995-99 | 48 |
| 5. | Dion Newby | Harrison Co. | 1990-93 | 46 |
| 6. | Glen McDonald | Middlesboro | 1993-96 | 45 |
| 7. | Will Renaker | Harrison Co. | 1994-98 | 43 |
| 7. | Brad Allison | Harrison Co. | 1988-92 | 43 |
| 7. | Chris Snopek | Harrison Co. | 1986-89 | 43 |
| 10. | Noochie Varner | Harrison Co. | 1995-99 | 37 |

## MOST RUNS BATTED IN (CAREER)

| No. | Player | School | Years | RBI |
|---|---|---|---|---|
| 1. | Will Renaker | Harrison Co. | 1994-98 | 253 |
| 2. | Paul Morse | Danville | 1989-92 | 230 |
| 3. | B.J. Foley | Corbin | 1995-02 | 220 |
| 4. | Noochie Varner | Harrison Co. | 1995-99 | 207 |
| 5. | J.B. Schmidt | Harrison Co. | 1994-00 | 202 |
| 6. | Brad Wilkerson | Apollo | 1991-95 | 198 |
| 7. | Kendall Withers | Harrison Co. | 1995-99 | 195 |
| 7. | Scott Fryman | Harrison Co. | 1990-94 | 195 |
| 9. | Brandon Gupton | Taylor Co. | 1998-01 | 191 |
| 10. | Brian Coffman | Bullitt Central | 1997-00 | 186 |

## HIGHEST BATTING AVERAGE (CAREER)

| No. | Player | School | Years | Avg. |
|---|---|---|---|---|
| 1. | David Owens | Rockcastle Co. | 1975-78 | .584 |
| 2. | Noah Welte | St. Patrick | 1997-00 | .568 |
| 3. | Soren Wolf | Monticello | 1998-01 | .526 |
| 4. | Brandon Coffey | Walton-Verona | 1997-00 | .502 |
| 5. | Aaron McClure | Hickman Co. | 1997-01 | .486 |
| 6. | Will Renaker | Harrison Co. | 1994-98 | .464 |
| 7. | David Goodwin | Powell Co. | 1977-80 | .458 |
| 8. | Matt Durham | Scott Co. | 1997-99 | .444 |
| 9. | Michael Evans | Hickman Co. | 1997-00 | .443 |
| 9. | Brad Wilkerson | Apollo | 1991-95 | .443 |

## MOST PITCHING WINS (CAREER)

| No. | Player | School | Years | Wins |
|---|---|---|---|---|
| 1. | Mark Galvin | Elizabethtown | 1996-00 | 42 |
| 2. | Mike Blakeman | Green Co. | 1965-68 | 41 |
| 3. | Daniel Carrender | Pulaski Co. | 1995-99 | 37 |
| 3. | Eric Asbury | Harrison Co. | 1992-96 | 37 |
| 3. | Brad Wilkerson | Apollo | 1991-95 | 37 |
| 6. | Jon Kirby | Estill Co. | 1999-02 | 33 |
| 7. | Shane Smith | Nicholas Co. | 1999-01 | 32 |
| 8. | Jeremy Sowers | Ballard | 1998-01 | 31 |
| 8. | Andy Baldwin | Taylor Co. | 1997-00 | 31 |
| 8. | John Smith | Middlesboro | 1988-92 | 31 |

## LOWEST EARNED RUN AVERAGE (CAREER)

| No. | Player | School | Years | ERA |
|---|---|---|---|---|
| 1. | David Slovak | Eastern | 2002-04 | .085 |
| 2. | Jimmy Osting | Trinity | 1993-95 | 1.09 |
| 3. | Mark Galvin | Elizabethtown | 1996-00 | 1.36 |
| 4. | Brad Wilkerson | Apollo | 1991-95 | 1.58 |
| 5. | Clint Brodsky | Boone Co. | 2001-03 | 1.59 |

## MOST SHUTOUTS (CAREER)

| No. | Player | School | Years | Total |
|---|---|---|---|---|
| 1. | Mike Blakeman | Green Co. | 1965-68 | 18 |
| 2. | Jeremy Sowers | Ballard | 1998-01 | 17 |
| 3. | Mark Galvin | Elizabethtown | 1996-00 | 13 |
| 4. | Jon Kirby | Estill Co. | 1999-02 | 12 |
| 4. | Jimmy Osting | Trinity | 1993-95 | 12 |

## ALL-TIME WINNINGEST COACHES

| No. | Coach | Schools | Wins |
|---|---|---|---|
| 1. | Larry Gumm* | Green Co. | 974 |
| 2. | Don Richardson | Madison Central | 952 |
| 3. | Charlie Adkins* | Paintsville | 785 |
| 4. | Mac Whitaker* | Harrison Co. | 730 |
| 5. | Charlie Taylor | Somerset | 702 |
| 6. | G.J. Smith* | South Laurel | 696 |
| 7. | Bill Tom Wayne* | Henderson Co. | 665 |
| 8. | Greg Shelton | Franklin-Simpson | 643 |
| 9. | Ron Myers | Elizabethtown | 613 |
| 10. | Jack Hicks | Owensboro | 606 |

* Active

## KENTUCKY MR. BASEBALL WINNERS

| Year | Player | School |
|---|---|---|
| 1989 | Tab Brown | St. Xavier |
| 1990 | Darren Burton | Pulaski Co. |
| 1991 | Trever Miller | Trinity |
| 1992 | Shon Walker | Harrison Co. |
| 1993 | Dion Newby | Harrison Co. |
| 1994 | Scott Downs | Pleasure Ridge Park |
| 1995 | Brad Wilkerson | Apollo |
| 1996 | Aaron McGlone | Greenup Co. |
| 1997 | Scott Hodges | Henry Clay |
| 1998 | Austin Kearns | Lafayette |
| 1999 | Joseph Blanton | Franklin-Simpson |
| 2000 | Spencer Graeter | Ballard |
| 2001 | Jeremy Sowers | Ballard |
| 2002 | Brad Corley | Pleasure Ridge Park |
| 2003 | Josh Ellis | Paul Dunbar |
| 2004 | Collin Cowgill | Henry Clay |
| 2005 | Chaz Roe | Lafayette |
| 2006 | TBA | |

*(Source: KHSAA Sports Information)*

**Practicing before a game in the Lou Johnson T-ball and Small Fry League that is named after the first Major League baseball player from Lexington**
*Source: Lexington Herald-Leader*

# John A. McGill

# *Basketball*

Kentucky teams have generated enough stories of national championships and All America players—even a pro title—to fill any almanac on their own—but none more intriguing than Kentucky State's.

At the start of the 1970s decade, the Thorobreds won three consecutive National Association of Intercollegiate Athletics, or NAIA, championships with talent that many observers felt might well be capable of defeating the University of Kentucky.

There's certainly cause to dispute that claim—at least in the 1969-70 season, when Adolph Rupp's Wildcats, led by Dan Issel, were ranked No. 1 in the nation much of the year before losing in a regional final to Jacksonville and 7-foot Artis Gilmore.

That same season, Kentucky State was fashioning the first of its three straight NAIA titles—and rapidly gaining a national reputation that went far beyond the norm for a small college team.

That's because the Frankfort-based school had a pair of remarkable players: Travis "The Machine" Grant and Elmore Smith, both of whom would later become first round NBA draft picks.

Grant, a 6-foot-7 forward, was also sometimes called "Machine Gun," an apt description of his ability to shoot over an opponent at will. Grant had an incredible career field goal accuracy of 63.8 percent.

**Jamal Mashburn played for the UK basketball team from 1991 to 1993**
*Source: Lexington Herald-Leader*

Smith, a 7-foot center, averaged nine blocked shots a game and his rebounding average of 24.2 rebounds per game in 1970-71 remains an NAIA record.

They were coached by Lucias Mitchell, who later would become coach at Norfolk State but before leaving gave Kentucky State its most illustrious era in basketball, by far.

Smith and Grant played together when Kentucky State won national titles in 1970 and 1971, but Smith declared hardship to enter the NBA draft and missed his senior season. Not that it mattered. Grant led the Thorobreds to yet another championship in 1972. It is worth noting that to win these titles, Kentucky State had to survive the NAIA's 64-team tournament, and then play in Kansas City.

Smith was the first pick of the Buffalo Braves in the 1971 NBA draft (and third pick overall). A year later, Grant was chosen by the Los Angeles Lakers as their first pick (and 13th overall).

Kentucky's rich basketball tradition is reflected in many ways—not the least of which being UK's seven NCAA titles, Louisville's two NCAA titles, Kentucky Wesleyan's eight NCAA Division II titles, and Georgetown's one NAIA crown. Add to that the American Basketball Association crown that the Kentucky Colonels won in 1975.

But for sheer audacity, it is hard to top Kentucky State's brief but golden era of basketball excellence.

# KHSAA Boys Basketball

## ALL-TIME WINNINGEST SCHOOLS

| Rank | School | Wins |
|------|--------|------|
| 1. | Ashland Blazer | 1,737 |
| 2. | Paducah Tilghman | 1,656 |
| 3. | Central City | 1,578 |
| 4. | Monticello | 1,234 |
| 5. | Paris | 1,195 |
| 6. | Lexington Lafayette | 1,187 |
| 7. | Wayne Co. | 1,149 |
| 8. | Newport Central Catholic | 1,149 |
| 9. | Paintsville | 1,201 |

## BOYS' SWEET 16 STATE CHAMPIONS

| Year | Champion | Score | Runner-Up |
|------|----------|-------|-----------|
| 1918 | Lexington | 16-15 | Somerset |
| 1919 | Lexington | 21-17 | Somerset |
| 1920 | Lexington | 56-13 | Ashland |
| 1921 | Louisville Manual | 32-17 | Union Academy |
| 1922 | Lexington | 55-27 | Frankfort |
| 1923 | Louisville Manual | 41-17 | Clark County |
| 1924 | Lexington | 15-10 | Ft. Thomas |
| 1925 | Louisville Manual | 40-11 | Winchester |
| 1926 | Louisville St. Xavier | 26-13 | Danville |
| 1927 | M.M.I. | 34-25 | London |
| 1928 | Ashland | 13-11 | Carr Creek |
| 1929 | Heath | 21-16 | Corinth |
| 1930 | Corinth | 22-20 | Kavanaugh |
| 1931 | Louisville Manual | 34-23 | Tolu |
| 1932 | Hazard | 15-13 | Louisville Male |
| 1933 | Ashland | 33-25 | Horse Cave |
| 1934 | Ashland | 26-13 | Danville |
| 1935 | Louisville St. Xavier | 32-18 | Newport |
| 1936 | Corbin | 24-18 | Nebo |
| 1937 | Midway | 30-22 | Inez |
| 1938 | Sharpe | 36-27 | Maysville |
| 1939 | Brooksville | 42-39 | Hindman |
| 1940 | Hazel Green | 35-29 | Ashland |
| 1941 | Inez | 35-27 | Louisville St. Xavier |
| 1942 | Lexington Lafayette | 44-32 | Harlan |
| 1943 | Hindman | 29-26 | Louisville St. Xavier |
| 1944 | Harlan | 40-28 | Dayton |
| 1945 | Louisville Male | 54-42 | Central City |
| 1946 | Breckinridge Training | 68-36 | Dawson Springs |
| 1947 | Maysville | 54-40 | Brewers |
| 1948 | Brewers | 65-48 | Maysville |
| 1949 | Owensboro | 65-47 | Lexington Lafayette |
| 1950 | Lexington Lafayette | 55-51 | Clark County |
| 1951 | Clark County | 69-44 | Cuba |
| 1952 | Cuba | 58-52 | Louisville Manual |
| 1953 | Lexington Lafayette | 84-53 | Paducah Tilghman |
| 1954 | Inez | 63-55 | Newport |
| 1955 | Hazard | 74-66 | Adair County |
| 1956 | Carr Creek | 72-68 | Henderson |
| 1957 | Lexington Lafayette | 55-52 | Louisville Eastern |
| 1958 | Louisville St. Xavier | 60-49 | Daviess County |
| 1959 | North Marshall | 64-63 | Louisville Manual |
| 1960 | Louisville Flaget | 65-56 | Monticello |
| 1961 | Ashland | 69-50 | Lexington Dunbar |
| 1962 | Louisville St. Xavier | 62-58 | Ashland |
| 1963 | Louisville Seneca | 72-66 | Lexington Dunbar |
| 1964 | Louisville Seneca | 66-56 | Breckinridge County |
| 1965 | Breckinridge Co. | 95-73 | Covington Holy Cross |
| 1966 | Shelby County | 62-57 | Male |
| 1967 | Earlington | 54-53 | Covington Catholic |
| 1968 | Glasgow | 77-68 | Louisville Seneca |
| 1969 | Louisville Central | 101-72 | Ohio County |
| 1970 | Louisville Male | 70-69 | Madison |
| 1971 | Louisville Male | 83-66 | Anderson County |
| 1972 | Owensboro | 71-63 | Elizabethtown |
| 1973 | Louisville Shawnee | 81-68 | Louisville Male |
| 1974 | Louisville Central | 59-54 | Louisville Male |
| 1975 | Louisville Male | 74-59 | Lexington Henry Clay |
| 1976 | Edmonson County | 74-52 | Christian County |
| 1977 | Louisville Ballard | 68-59 | Louisville Valley |
| 1978 | Shelby County | 68-66 | Covington Holmes |
| 1979 | Lexington Lafayette | 62-52 | Christian County |
| 1980 | Owensboro | 57-56 | Louisville Doss |
| 1981 | Simon Kenton | 70-63 | Mason County |
| 1982 | Laurel County | 53-51 | North Hardin |
| 1983 | Lexington Henry Clay | 35-33 | Carlisle County |
| 1984 | Logan County | 83-70 | Bourbon County |
| 1985 | Hopkinsville | 65-64 | Clay County |
| 1986 | Pulaski County | 47-45 | Pleasure Ridge Park |
| 1987 | Clay County | 76-73 | Louisville Ballard |
| 1988 | Louisville Ballard | 88-79 | Clay County |
| 1989 | Pleasure Ridge Park | 75-73 | Wayne County |
| 1990 | Louisville Fairdale | 77-73 | Covington Holmes |
| 1991 | Louisville Fairdale | 67-63 | Lexington Tates Creek |
| 1992 | University Heights | 59-57 | Lexington Catholic |
| 1993 | Marion County | 85-77 | Lexington Paul Dunbar |
| 1994 | Louisville Fairdale | 59-56 | Lexington Paul Dunbar |
| 1995 | Breckinridge Co. | 70-63 | Pleasure Ridge Park |
| 1996 | Paintsville | 71-53 | Ashland Blazer |
| 1997 | Louisville Eastern | 71-59 | Ft. Thomas Highlands |
| 1998 | Scott County | 89-78 | Paintsville |
| 1999 | Louisville Ballard | 71-47 | Scott County |
| 2000 | Elizabethtown | 79-69 | Lexington Catholic |
| 2001 | Lexington Lafayette | 54-49 | Louisville Male |
| 2002 | Lexington Catholic | 83-53 | Paducah Tilghman |
| 2003 | Mason County | 86-65 | Louisville Ballard |
| 2004 | Warren Central | 66-56 | Mason County |
| 2005 | South Laurel | 72-59 | Warren Central |
| 2006 | Jeffersontown | 61-48 | Apollo |

## ALL-TIME LEADING SCORERS (CAREER)

| Rank | Player | School | Points |
|------|--------|--------|--------|
| 1. | Kelly Coleman | Wayland | 4,337 |
| 2. | Charlie Osborne | Flat Gap | 3,647 |
| 3. | Harry Todd | Earlington | 3,567 |
| 4. | Chris Harrison | Tollesboro | 3,542 |
| 5. | Charles Thomas | Harlan | 3,365 |
| 6. | Clem Haskins | Taylor Co. | 3,325 |
| 7. | Ty Rogers | Lyon Co. | 3,300 |
| 8. | Fred Hale | Williamstown | 3,233 |
| 9. | Ervin Stepp | Phelps | 3,228 |
| 10. | Manual Forrest | Lou. Moore | 3,226 |

## MOST POINTS SCORED (GAME)

| No. | Player | School | Year | Points |
|-----|--------|--------|------|--------|
| 1. | Wayne Oakley | Hanson | 1954 | 114 |
| 2. | Danny Cornett | Breck.Training | 1964 | 87 |
| 3. | Wayne Golden | Lou. Shawnee | 1970 | 84 |
| 3. | Jack Winders | Morton's Gap | 1954 | 84 |
| 5. | Bob Slusher | Lone Jack | 1957 | 83 |
| 5. | Bill Burnett | Paris | 1916 | 83 |
| 7. | Roger Bolton | Lynn Camp | 1968 | 78 |
| 8. | Ervin Stepp | Phelps | 1980 | 75 |

| 8. | Kelly Coleman | Wayland | 1956 | 75 |
| 10. | Chris Harrison | Tollesboro | 1991 | 73 |

## ALL-TIME LEADING REBOUNDERS (CAREER)

| No. | Player | School | Rebounds |
|---|---|---|---|
| 1. | Harry Todd | Earlington | 2,188 |
| 2. | Tim Stephens | McCreary Co. | 2,157 |
| 3. | J.R. VanHoose | Paintsville | 2,069 |
| 4. | Brian Saylor | Red Bird | 1,558 |
| 5. | Keith Blackburn | Eminence | 1,506 |
| 6. | Charles Thomas | Harlan | 1,441 |
| 7. | Edward Congleton | Lee Co. | 1,388 |
| 8. | Dennis Johnson | Harrodsburg | 1,347 |
| 9. | Chase Gibson | Pikeville | 1,344 |
| 10. | Parke Congleton | Lee. Co. | 1,323 |

## ALL-TIME WINNINGEST COACHES

| No. | Coach | Schools | Wins |
|---|---|---|---|
| 1. | William Kean | Central | 856 |
| 2. | Russ Williamson | Inez | 793 |
| 3. | Bobby Keith | Clay Co. | 767 |
| 4. | Pearl Combs | Vicco/Hindman | 760 |
| 5. | Don Parsons | Madisonville | 714 |
| 6. | John Bill Trivette | Pikeville | 709 |
| 7. | Ron Bevars* | North Hardin | 679 |
| 8. | Marvin Meredith | Russell | 677 |
| 9. | Al Prewitt | Henry Co./Henry Clay | 654 |
| 10. | David Fraley* | Powell Co./Pulaski Co. | 640 |

* active

## KENTUCKY MR. BASKETBALL WINNERS

| Year | Player | School |
|---|---|---|
| 1956 | Kelly Coleman | Wayland |
| 1957 | Billy Ray Lickert | Lexington Lafayette |
| 1958 | Ralph Richardson | Russell Co. |
|  | Harry Todd | Earlington |
| 1959 | Pat Doyle | North Marshall |
| 1960 | Jeff Mullins | Lexington Lafayette |
| 1961 | Randy Embry | Owensboro |
| 1962 | Mike Silliman | Louisville St. Xavier |
| 1963 | Mike Redd | Louisville Seneca |
| 1964 | Wes Unseld | Louisville Seneca |
| 1965 | Butch Beard | Breckinridge Co. |
| 1966 | Mike Casey | Shelby Co. |
| 1967 | Jim McDaniels | Allen Co. |
| 1968 | Terry Davis | Shelby Co. |
| 1969 | Ron King | Louisville Central |
| 1970 | Robert Brooks | Richmond Madison |
| 1971 | Jimmy Dan Conner | Anderson Co. |
| 1972 | Jerry Thurston | Owensboro |
| 1973 | Wesley Cox | Louisville Male |
| 1974 | Jack Givens | Lexington Bryan Station |
| 1975 | Dom Fucci | Lexington Tates Creek |
| 1976 | Darrell Griffith | Louisville Male |
| 1977 | Jeff Lamp | Louisville Ballard |
| 1978 | Doug Schloemer | Covington Holmes |
| 1979 | Dirk Minniefield | Lexington Lafayette |
| 1980 | Ervin Stepp | Phelps |
| 1981 | Phil Cox | Cawood |
| 1982 | Todd May | Virgie |
| 1983 | Winston Bennett | Louisville Male |
| 1984 | Steve Miller | Lexington Henry Clay |
| 1985 | Tony Kimbro | Louisville Seneca |
| 1986 | Rex Chapman | Owensboro Apollo |
| 1987 | John Pelphrey | Paintsville |
| 1988 | Richie Farmer | Clay Co. |
| 1989 | Allan Houston | Louisville Ballard |
| 1990 | Dwayne Morton | Louisville Central |
| 1991 | Jermaine Brown | Louisville Fairdale |
| 1992 | Tick Rogers | Hart Co. |
| 1993 | Jason Osborne | Louisville Male |
| 1994 | Elton Scott | Marion Co. |
| 1995 | Charles Thomas | Harlan |
| 1996 | Daymeon Fishback | Greenwood |
| 1997 | Brandon Davenport | Owensboro |
| 1998 | J.R. VanHoose | Paintsville |
| 1999 | Rick Jones | Scott Co. |
| 2000 | Scott Hundley | Scott Co. |
| 2001 | Josh Carrier | Bowling Green |
| 2002 | Brandon Stockton | Glasgow |
| 2003 | Ross Neltner | Fort Thomas Highlands |
| 2004 | Chris Lofton | Mason Co. |
| 2005 | Dominic Tilford | Jeffersontown |
| 2006 | Walt Allen | South Laurel Co. |

# KHSAA Girls Basketball

## ALL-TIME WINNINGEST SCHOOLS

| No. | School | Wins |
|---|---|---|
| 1. | George Rogers Clark | 575 |
| 2. | Paris | 504 |
| 3. | Henderson Co. | 500 |

## GIRLS' SWEET 16 STATE CHAMPIONS

| Year | Champion | Score | Runner-Up |
|---|---|---|---|
| 1920 | Paris | 32-10 | Nicholasville |
| 1921 | Ashland | 22-11 | Clark Co. |
| 1922 | Ashland | 39-7 | Sardis |
| 1923 | West Louisville | 8-5 | Cresent Springs |
| 1924 | Ashland | 13-11 | Georgetown |
| 1925 | Georgetown | 40-0 | Hardyville Memorial |
| 1926 | Maysville | 23-16 | Henderson |
| 1927 | West Louisville | 19-18 | Georgetown |
| 1928 | Ashland | 27-11 | Oddville |
| 1929 | Ashland | 23-10 | Oddville |
| 1930 | Hazard | 23-18 | Woodburn |
| 1931 | Woodburn | 24-19 | Ashland |
| 1932 | Woodburn | 25-20 | Paintsville |
| 1975 | Louisville Butler | 60-43 | Barren Co. |
| 1976 | Lou. Sacred Heart | 68-55 | Butler |
| 1977 | Laurel Co. | 48-46 | Paris |
| 1978 | Laurel Co. | 63-48 | Breathitt Co. |
| 1979 | Laurel Co. | 43-36 | Lafayette |
| 1980 | Louisville Butler | 65-49 | Franklin Co. |
| 1981 | Pulaski Co. | 50-42 | Marshall Co. |
| 1982 | Marshall Co. | 48-44 | Mercy |
| 1983 | Warren Central | 57-49 | Whitesburg |
| 1984 | Marshall Co. | 55-53 | Belfry |
| 1985 | Whitley Co. | 38-37 | Atherton |
| 1986 | Oldham Co. | 49-48 | Franklin-Simpson |
| 1987 | Laurel Co. | 50-48 | Doss |
| 1988 | Louisville Southern | 57-34 | Oldham Co. |
| 1989 | Clay Co. | 48-44 | Clark Co. |
| 1990 | Henry Clay | 62-50 | Southern |
| 1991 | Laurel Co. | 33-31 | Clark Co. |
| 1992 | Louisville Mercy | 44-38 | Clay Co. |
| 1993 | Nicholas Co. | 48-46 | Warren East |
| 1994 | M.C. Napier | 88-56 | Highlands |
| 1995 | Scott Co. | 68-45 | Pulaski Co. |
| 1996 | Union Co. | 44-37 | Central Hardin |
| 1997 | Hazard | 54-38 | Elizabethtown |
| 1998 | Elizabethtown | 45-37 | Montgomery Co. |
| 1999 | Lexington Catholic | 57-42 | Assumption |
| 2000 | West Carter | 58-50 | Shelby Co. |
| 2001 | Lexington Catholic | 36-34 | Manual |
| 2002 | Lou. Sacred Heart | 57-46 | Jackson Co. |
| 2003 | Lou. Sacred Heart | 42-40 | Lexington Catholic |
| 2004 | Lou. Sacred Heart | 43-34 | Lexington Catholic |
| 2005 | Lexington Catholic | 59-54 | Clinton Co. |
| 2006 | Lexington Catholic | 69-52 | Rose Hill Christian |

## ALL-TIME LEADING SCORERS (CAREER)

| No. | Player | School | Points |
|---|---|---|---|
| 1. | Jaime Walz | Ft. Thomas Highlands | 4,948 |
| 2. | Geri Grigsby | McDowell | 4,385 |
| 3. | Kim Mays | Knox Central | 3,952 |
| 4. | Carolyn Alexander | Hazard | 3,726 |
| 5. | Lisa Harrison | Louisville Southern | 3,469 |
| 6. | Mandy Harmon | Sheldon Clark | 3,280 |
| 7. | Marialice Jenkins | Fordsville | 3,266 |
| 8. | Erica Hallman | Covington Holmes | 3,187 |
| 9. | Sherry Mitchell | Muhlenberg Central | 3,155 |
| 10. | SeSe Helm | Warren Central | 3,144 |

## MOST POINTS SCORED (GAME)

| No. | Player | School | Year | Points |
|---|---|---|---|---|
| 1. | Geri Grigsby | McDowell | 1975 | 81 |
| 2. | Beverly Smallwood | Dorton | 1987 | 71 |
| 3. | Heather Benton | Leslie Co. | 2004 | 66 |
| 3. | Melissa Brandon | Oneida Baptist | 1996 | 66 |
| 5. | Jody Sizemore | Leslie Co. | 1999 | 63 |
| 5. | Sondra Miller | M.C. Napier | 1983 | 63 |
| 7. | Heather Benton | Leslie Co. | 2004 | 60 |
| 7. | Jaime Walz | Ft. Thomas Highlands | 1995 | 60 |
| 9. | Jody Sizemore | Leslie Co. | 1998 | 58 |

## ALL-TIME LEADING REBOUNDERS (CAREER)

| No. | Player | School | Rebounds |
|---|---|---|---|
| 1. | Sarah Elliott | Jackson Co. | 1,843 |
| 2. | Jaime Walz | Ft. Thomas Highlands | 1,762 |
| 3. | Megan Gray | Harrison Co. | 1,754 |
| 4. | Lisa Harrison | Louisville Southern | 1,716 |
| 5. | Kyra Elzy | Oldham Co. | 1,703 |
| 6. | Jessica Schmidt | Walton-Verona | 1,674 |
| 7. | Jade Perry | Muhlenberg North | 1,647 |
| 8. | Angela Brown | Clinton Co. | 1,569 |
| 9. | Amanda Collins | Pike Co. Central | 1,491 |
| 10. | Jenni Benningfield | Louisville Assumption | 1,480 |

## ALL-TIME WINNINGEST COACHES

| No. | Coach | Schools | Wins |
|---|---|---|---|
| 1. | Howard Beth* | Marshall Co. | 703 |
| 2. | Randy Napier* | M.C. Napier/Perry Co. Central | 623 |
| 3. | John High* | Whitesburg/Breathitt Co. /Montgomery Co. | 559 |

| 4. | Wendell Wilson* | Leslie Co. | 564 |
|---|---|---|---|
| 5. | John "Hop" Brown | West Carter | 514 |
| 6. | Bill Goller | Holy Cross | 512 |
| 7. | Doug & Sue Kincer | Fleming-Neon | 484 |
| 8. | Roy Bowling | Laurel Co./Lou. Mercy | 483 |
| 9. | Bill Brown | Lou. Southern/Lou. Ballard | 475 |
| 9. | Willis McClure | Owensboro Apollo | 475 |

*\* active*

## KENTUCKY MISS BASKETBALL WINNERS

| Year | Player | School |
|---|---|---|
| 1976 | Donna Murphy | Newport |
| 1977 | Geri Grigsby | McDowell |
| 1978 | Irene Moore | Breathitt Co. |
| 1979 | Beth Wilkerson | Paris |
| 1980 | Lisa Collins | Laurel Co. |
| 1981 | Lillie Mason | Olmstead |
| 1982 | Connie Goins | Frankfort Western Hills |
| 1983 | Clemette Haskins | Warren Central |
| 1984 | Carol Parker | Marshall Co. |
| 1985 | Brigette Combs | Whitesburg |
| 1986 | Kris Miller | Owensboro Catholic |
| 1987 | Mary Taylor | Marshall Co. |
| 1988 | Kim Pehlke | Louisville Doss |
| 1989 | Lisa Harrison | Louisville Southern |
| 1990 | Kim Mays | Knox Central |
| 1991 | Ida Bowen | Sheldon Clark |
| 1992 | Becky McKinley | Bullitt East |
| 1993 | Brandi Ashby | Webster Co. |
| 1994 | Laurie Townsend | Owensboro Apollo |
| 1995 | Ukari Figgs | Scott Co. |
| 1996 | Jaime Walz | Fort Thomas Highlands |
| 1997 | Rachel Byars | Union Co. |
| 1998 | Beth Vice | Montgomery Co. |
| 1999 | Jody Sizemore | Leslie Co. |
| 2000 | Jenni Benningfield | Louisville Assumption |
| 2001 | Katie Schweggman | Louisville Bishop Brossart |
| 2002 | Erica Hallman | Covington Holmes |
| 2003 | Megen Gearhart | West Carter |
| 2004 | Crystal Kelly | Louisville Sacred Heart |
| 2005 | Carly Omerod | Louisville Sacred Heart |
| 2006 | Arnika Brown | Christian Co. |

*(Source: KHSAA Sports Information)*

**Girls & Boys High School Basketball**
*Source: Kentucky High School Athletic Association*

Louis Stout

# SPORTS
# *Coach*
# *William L. Kean*
## *Giant of Kentucky High School Sports History*

Of all Kentucky prep coaches, black or white, Louisville Central's William L. Kean may have been the greatest. And not at just one sport, either. Kean carved out an amazing legacy as a basketball and football coach. For four decades, Kean's mighty Yellow Jackets pounded opponents into submission, capturing numerous state and national championships along the way.

Kean came to Louisville Central after graduating from Howard University, where he was a star quar-

**(Left) Coach William Kean and his team**
*Source: Louis Stout*

terback. Although he was small (5'7", 140 pounds), Kean, known as "Pee Wee," had a warrior's heart and a fierce winner's mentality, which he brought with him when he took over at Louisville Central.

Kean ruled Louisville Central sports from 1923 until his death in 1958. His football teams had a winning percentage of 81.9 (225-45-12), while his basketball teams did even better, fashioning an overall won-loss record of 856-83 for an incredible 91.1 winning percentage. Kean's 856 wins puts him at the top on the all-time list for Kentucky coaches.

Under Kean's guidance, the Yellow Jackets captured three national basketball championships and seven state titles. His 1956 club, arguably his greatest, finished with a flawless 38-0 record.

Kean's teams played modern-day basketball, utilizing the controlled fastbreak, in-your-face man-to-man defense and a relentless 1-2-1-1 full-court trapping press.

But as extraordinary as Kean's record was in hoops, it may take second place to his accomplishments on the gridiron. His football Yellow Jackets won 20 straight Thanksgiving Day contests against such schools as Chicago DuSable, Indianapolis Crispus Attucks, East St. Louis High and Gary (Ind.) Roosevelt.

The 1943 season could serve as the model for Kean's Louisville Central teams. That group finished with a perfect 10-0 mark that included a victory over Lincoln Grant, and two wins each over Lexington Dunbar, Indianapolis Crispus Attucks, Knoxville Austin High and St. Louis Vashon High.

However, Kean's greatest victory took place away from the playing field. He was among the first to push for games against all-white schools. In 1952, Louisville St. Xavier agreed to schedule Kean's Yellow Jackets. This was an amazing and ground-breaking accomplishment, considering that the Brown v. Board of Education decision mandating school integration was still two years away.

Few individuals have had a more powerful or longer-lasting impact on Kentucky prep sports than William L. Kean. In every way, he was truly one of the giants of Kentucky high school sports history.

*Adapted by Tom Wallace from "Shadows of the Past" by Louis Stout (Lexington, Host Communications— 2006).*

*Louis Stout retired as Executive Director of the Kentucky High School Athletic Association in 2002.*

# Colleges & Universities

## CAMPBELLSVILLE COLLEGE
### MEN'S BASKETBALL

### ALL-TIME LEADING SCORERS

| No. | Player | Pts. |
|-----|--------|------|
| 1. | Van Berry | 2,615 |
| 2. | Benji Kelly | 2,121 |
| 3. | Todd Armes | 1,880 |
| 4. | James Boulware | 1,723 |
| 5. | Cecil Ellis | 1,676 |
| 6. | Ramont Smith | 1,517 |
| 7. | Marcio Kardosh | 1,488 |
| 8. | Steve Bugg | 1,422 |
| 9. | Jeff Gumm | 1,369 |
| 10. | Ray Wilson | 1,346 |

*(Source: Campbellsville College Sports Information)*

## CENTRE COLLEGE
### MEN'S BASKETBALL

### CENTRE COLLEGE BY THE NUMBERS
- Overall Record: 579-634
- 5 20-win seasons
- 3 NCAA Division III Final Four appearances
- 11 Southern Collegiate Athletic Conference titles
- 8 NCAA Tournament appearances
- 30 players named All-SCAC
- 7 SCAC Player of the Year selections

### CENTRE COLLEGE ALL-AMERICANS
Danny Johnson (1989)
David Hicks (1991)
Reggie Magnusson (2006)
Kevin Lavin (1987)

### ALL-TIME LEADING SCORERS

| No. | Player | Pts. |
|-----|--------|------|
| 1. | David Hicks | 1,921 |
| 2. | Kevin Lavin | 1,814 |
| 3. | Bill Kazee | 1,660 |
| 4. | Danny Johnson | 1,553 |
| 5. | Mike Marks | 1,487 |
| 6. | Mike Pharris | 1,440 |
| 7. | Mark Holbrook | 1,414 |
| 8. | Bryan Bates | 1,400 |
| 9. | Buddy Baker | 1,336 |
| 10. | David DeMarcus | 1,290 |

### ALL-TIME LEADING REBOUNDER
Coy Zerhusen     857

### ALL-TIME ASSIST LEADER
Coby DeVary     451

## CENTRE COLLEGE
### WOMEN'S BASKETBALL

### CENTRE COLLEGE BY THE NUMBERS
- 2 NCAA Division III Final Four appearances
- 6 NCAA Tournament appearances

- 6 SCAC Championships since 1990
- 32 players named All-SCAC
- Wendie Austin named SCAC Player of the Year in 1993 and 1994
- Shannon Collins Hodge is Centre's all-time leading scorer — male or female — with 2,000 career points

### CENTRE COLLEGE ALL-AMERICANS
Shannon Collins Hodge (1989)
Susan Yates (1990)

### MEMBERS OF 1,000 POINT CLUB
Shannon Collins Hodge
Wendie Austin
Debi Bennett
Sarah Green
Angela Ice
Beth Johnson
Becky Jorgenson
Kimey Kyker
Cheryl Lewis
Jennifer Patterson
Susan Yates

*(Source: Centre College Sports Information)*

## CUMBERLAND COLLEGE
### MEN'S BASKETBALL

### CUMBERLAND COLLEGE BY THE NUMBERS
- Overall record: 915-467
- 5 30-win seasons
- 20 20-win seasons

### ALL-TIME LEADING SCORERS

| No. | Player | Years | Games | Pts. | Avg. |
|-----|--------|-------|-------|------|------|
| 1. | Roger Richardson | 1980-84 | 138 | 2,068 | 15.0 |
| 2. | Wilford Jackson | 1960-64 | 107 | 1,945 | 18.1 |
| 3. | Bob Long | 1967-70 | 65 | 1,830 | 28.1 |
| 4. | Ivan Johnson | 1998-03 | 134 | 1,815 | 13.5 |
| 5. | Maurice Byrd | 1970-74 | 106 | 1,809 | 17.1 |
| 6. | Garrett Gregory | 1983-87 | 135 | 1,782 | 13.2 |
| 7. | Brian Key | 1992-96 | 129 | 1,690 | 13.1 |
| 8. | Brad Gover | 1994-97 | 99 | 1,573 | 15.9 |
| 9. | Larry Gorman | 1977-79 | 73 | 1,501 | 20.6 |
| 10. | Larry Hurt | 1971-74 | 83 | 1,475 | 17.7 |

### ALL-TIME CAREER SCORING AVERAGES

| No. | Player | Years | Games | Pts. | Avg. |
|-----|--------|-------|-------|------|------|
| 1. | Bob Long | 1967-70 | 65 | 1,830 | 28.1 |
| 2. | Larry Gorman | 1977-79 | 73 | 1,501 | 20.6 |
| 3. | Wilford Jackson | 1960-64 | 107 | 1,945 | 18.1 |
| 4. | Larry Hurt | 1971-74 | 83 | 1,475 | 17.7 |
| 5. | Maurice Byrd | 1970-74 | 106 | 1,809 | 17.1 |

### ALL-TIME LEADING REBOUNDERS

| No. | Player | Years | Rebounds | Avg. |
|-----|--------|-------|----------|------|
| 1. | Maurice Byrd | 1970-74 | 1,281 | 11.9 |
| 2. | Wiley Brown | 1960-64 | 1,054 | 10.0 |
| 3. | Melvin Harris | 1971-75 | 1,033 | 9.2 |
| 4. | Garrett Gregory | 1983-87 | 962 | 7.1 |
| 5. | Steve Banks | 1975-78 | 920 | 10.8 |
| 6. | Raymond Cox | 1966-70 | 911 | 9.3 |
| 7. | Jerry Brown | 1964-67 | 864 | 10.2 |
| 8. | Jim Rollins | 1964-67 | 859 | 11.5 |

| 9. | Bob Long | 1967-70 | 832 | 12.8 |
| 10. | Joe Dallas | 1977-80 | 808 | 10.9 |

| 9. | Allison Smith | 1985-87 | 634 | 11.3 |
| 10. | Kim Feistritzer | 1990-94 | 627 | 5.0 |

## ALL-TIME ASSISTS LEADERS

| No. | Player | Years | Assists | Avg. |
|---|---|---|---|---|
| 1. | Tony Pietrowski | 1994-99 | 654 | 3.9 |
| 2. | John McCoy | 1982-86 | 625 | 4.6 |
| 3. | Larry Gorman | 1977-79 | 624 | 8.6 |
| 4. | Junie Hemphill | 1984-88 | 585 | 4.4 |
| 5. | Ivan Johnson | 1998-03 | 451 | 3.4 |
| 6. | Brian Key | 1990-94 | 378 | 3.3 |
| 7. | Garry Patton | 1975-78 | 358 | 5.0 |
| 8. | Scott Thomas | 1982-86 | 327 | 2.7 |
| 9. | Ed Bowen | 1980-82 | 273 | 7.4 |
| 9. | Doug Oak | 1990-94 | 273 | 2.2 |

## ALL-TIME ASSISTS LEADERS

| No. | Player | Years | Assists |
|---|---|---|---|
| 1. | Missie Irvin | 1989-94 | 634 |
| 2. | Jessie Holt | 1998-02 | 474 |
| 3. | Konnie Irvin-Snyder | 1985-89 | 414 |
| 4. | Hope Peace-Akins | 1986-91 | 408 |
| 5. | Betsy Rains | 1982-86 | 366 |
| 6. | Mandy Calihan | 1994-98 | 354 |
| 7. | Candi Fannin | 1990-93 | 345 |
| 8. | Monica Hang | 2002-04 | 335 |
| 8. | Lisa Pflueger | 1980-84 | 335 |
| 10. | Soni Smith | 1980-84 | 327 |

## ALL-TIME STEALS LEADERS

| No. | Player | Years | Steals |
|---|---|---|---|
| 1. | Ivan Johnson | 1998-03 | 229 |
| 2. | Tony Pietrowski | 1994-99 | 214 |
| 3. | Brian Key | 1990-94 | 176 |
| 4. | Don Skipper | 1988-90 | 128 |
| 4. | Steve Glenn | 1989-91 | 128 |
| 6. | Jerry Williams | 1999-01 | 106 |
| 7. | Doug Garth | 1993-97 | 99 |
| 8. | Mark Vernon | 1998-02 | 94 |
| 9. | Demorrius Thomas | 2001- | 91 |
| 10. | Eric Bailey | 1996-98 | 74 |

*(Source: Cumberland College Sports Information)*

## ALL-TIME FREE THROW PERCENTAGE (CAREER)

| No. | Player | Years | FTA | FTM | PCT. |
|---|---|---|---|---|---|
| 1. | Betsy Rains | 1982-86 | 292 | 241 | .825 |
| 2. | Jessie Holt | 1998-02 | 279 | 226 | .810 |
| 3. | Christy Webster | 1994-98 | 304 | 245 | .806 |
| 4. | Lindsay Holder | 1999-02 | 139 | 111 | .799 |
| 5. | Konnie Irvin-Snyder | 1985-89 | 116 | 92 | .793 |
| 6. | Haven Aldridge | 1994-98 | 351 | 278 | .792 |
| 7. | Charline Gibson | 1990-94 | 242 | 186 | .769 |
| 8. | Barbara Spratling | 1986-88 | 218 | 167 | .766 |
| 9. | Missie Irvin | 1990-94 | 321 | 245 | .763 |
| 10. | Annette Wormsley | 1987-90 | 273 | 207 | .758 |

*(Source: Cumberland College Sports Information)*

## CUMBERLAND COLLEGE
### WOMEN'S BASKETBALL

## CUMBERLAND COLLEGE BY THE NUMBERS
- Overall record: 473-389
- 10 20-win seasons

## ALL-TIME LEADING SCORERS

| No. | Player | Years | Games | Pts. | Avg. |
|---|---|---|---|---|---|
| 1. | Soni Smith | 1980-84 | 101 | 2,015 | 19.9 |
| 2. | Hope Peace-Akins | 1986-91 | 124 | 1,622 | 13.0 |
| 3. | Jamie Walker | 1999-03 | 126 | 1,492 | 11.8 |
| 4. | Haven Aldridge | 1994-98 | 120 | 1,490 | 12.4 |
| 5. | Jessie Holt | 1998-02 | 123 | 1,404 | 11.4 |
| 6. | Lisa Barton Nantz | 1982-86 | 108 | 1,394 | 12.9 |
| 7. | Candi Fannin | 1990-94 | 117 | 1,358 | 11.6 |
| 8. | Missie Irvin | 1989-94 | 123 | 1,356 | 11.0 |
| 9. | Charline Gibson | 1990-94 | 125 | 1,353 | 10.7 |
| 10. | Betsy Rains | 1982-86 | 110 | 1,315 | 11.9 |

## ALL-TIME CAREER SCORING AVERAGES

| No. | Player | Years | Games | Pts. | Avg. |
|---|---|---|---|---|---|
| 1. | Soni Smith | 1980-84 | 101 | 2,015 | 19.9 |
| 2. | Nicole LaVan | 1999-01 | 54 | 902 | 19.3 |
| 3. | Barbara Spratling | 1986-88 | 54 | 989 | 18.3 |
| 4. | Anita Ledbetter | 1976-80 | 45 | 702 | 15.6 |
| 5. | Hope Peace-Akins | 1986-91 | 124 | 1,622 | 13.0 |

## ALL-TIME LEADING REBOUNDERS

| No. | Player | Years | Rebounds | Avg. |
|---|---|---|---|---|
| 1. | Rhonda Hodges | 1979-83 | 861 | 7.4 |
| 2. | Mioshi Moore | 1988-92 | 779 | 6.7 |
| 3. | Geri Antrobus | 1991-95 | 767 | 6.7 |
| 4. | Susan Zellner | 1976-80 | 755 | 8.2 |
| 5. | Lisa Barton Nantz | 1982-86 | 741 | 6.9 |
| 6. | Carrie Dawson | 1979-83 | 682 | 6.4 |
| 7. | Allison Wilburn | 1981-84 | 643 | 7.9 |
| 8. | Jana Newman | 1985-87 | 640 | 6.2 |

## EASTERN KENTUCKY UNIVERSITY
### MEN'S BASKETBALL

## EKU BY THE NUMBERS
- Overall record: 1,043-986
- 4 20-win seasons
- 6 NCAA Tournament appearances

## ALL-TIME LEADING SCORERS

| No. | Player | Years | Pts. | Avg. |
|---|---|---|---|---|
| 1. | Antonio Parris | 1983-87 | 1,723 | 16.9 |
| 2. | John Allen | 1990-94 | 1,635 | 14.1 |
| 3. | Arlando Johnson | 1991-95 | 1,617 | 14.1 |
| 4. | Carl Brown | 1972-76 | 1,592 | 16.2 |
| 5. | Eddie Bodkin | 1963-66 | 1,587 | 21.1 |
| 6. | James Tillman | 1978-80 | 1,514 | 27.0 |
| 7. | Charles Mitchell | 1970-73 | 1,507 | 20.6 |
| 8. | Jack Adams | 1953-56 | 1,460 | 20.6 |
| 9. | DeMarkus Doss | 1992-96 | 1,442 | 13.2 |
| 10. | Kenny Elliott | 1975-79 | 1,353 | 13.3 |

## ALL-TIME CAREER SCORING AVERAGES

| No. | Player | Years | Pts. | Avg. |
|---|---|---|---|---|
| 1. | James Tillman | 1978-80 | 1,514 | 27.0 |
| 2. | Eddie Bodkin | 1963-66 | 1,587 | 21.1 |
| 3. | Charles Mitchell | 1970-73 | 1,507 | 20.6 |
| 4. | Jack Adams | 1953-56 | 1,460 | 20.6 |
| 5. | George Bryant | 1969-72 | 1,345 | 19.5 |

## ALL-TIME LEADING REBOUNDERS

| No. | Player | Years | Rebounds | Avg. |
|---|---|---|---|---|
| 1. | Mike Smith | 1988-92 | 977 | 8.6 |
| 2. | Jim Baechtold | 1948-52 | 933 | 10.6 |
| 3. | Garfield Smith | 1965-68 | 884 | 13.2 |
| 4. | Jack Adams | 1953-56 | 870 | 12.3 |
| 5. | Mike Oliver | 1974-78 | 859 | 8.9 |
| 6. | Eddie Bodkin | 1963-66 | 812 | 11.0 |

| 7. | Carl Greenfield | 1968-71 | 802 | 11.8 |
|----|-----------------|---------|-----|------|
| 8. | Dave Bootcheck | 1976-80 | 728 | 7.4 |
| 9. | Elmer Tolson | 1949-53 | 716 | 8.2 |
| 10. | Willie Woods | 1967-70 | 693 | 10.8 |

## ALL-TIME WINNINGEST COACHES

| Coach | Years | Record | Pct. |
|-------|-------|--------|------|
| Paul McBrayer | 16 | 219-144 | .603 |
| Max Good | 8 | 96-129 | .427 |
| Guy Strong | 6 | 78-65 | .545 |
| James E. Baechtold | 5 | 70-57 | .551 |
| Ed Byhre | 5 | 69-63 | .523 |
| Charles T. Hughes | 6 | 68-40 | .630 |

*(Source: Eastern Kentucky University Sports Information)*

# EASTERN KENTUCKY UNIVERSITY
## *WOMEN'S BASKETBALL*

### EKU BY THE NUMBERS
- Overall record: 489-425
- 4 Ohio Valley Conference championships
- 1 NCAA Tournament appearance
- 6 20-win seasons
- 1 WNIT appearance

### ALL-TIME LEADING SCORERS

| No. | Player | Years | Pts. |
|-----|--------|-------|------|
| 1. | Lisa Goodin | 1980-84 | 1,920 |
| 2. | Jaree Goodin | 1989-93 | 1,679 |
| 3. | Peggy Gay | 1975-79 | 1,674 |
| 4. | Katie Kelly | 2000-04 | 1,626 |
| 5. | Kim Mays | 1992-95 | 1,587 |
| 6. | Charlotte Sizemore | 1997-02 | 1,561 |
| 7. | Kelly Cowan | 1987-91 | 1,515 |
| 8. | Angie Cox | 1988-92 | 1,425 |
| 9. | Tina Wermuth | 1979-83 | 1,403 |
| 10. | Laphelia Doss | 1994-98 | 1,378 |

### ALL-TIME LEADING REBOUNDERS

| No. | Player | Years | Rebounds |
|-----|--------|-------|----------|
| 1. | Laphelia Doss | 1994-98 | 1,027 |
| 2. | Sandra Mukes | 1978-82 | 975 |
| 3. | Jaree Goodin | 1989-93 | 914 |
| 4. | Tina Wermuth | 1979-83 | 866 |
| 5. | Carla Coffey | 1984-88 | 751 |
| 6. | Maisha Thomas-Blanton | 1991-95 | 711 |
| 7. | Teresa McNair | 1999-03 | 631 |
| 8. | Shannon Brady | 1981-85 | 625 |
| 9. | Charlotte Sizemore | 1997-02 | 611 |
| 10. | Tina Cottle | 1983-85 | 577 |

### ALL-TIME ASSISTS LEADERS

| No. | Player | Years | Assists |
|-----|--------|-------|---------|
| 1. | Angie Cox | 1988-92 | 488 |
| 2. | Katie Kelly | 2000-04 | 395 |
| 3. | Cheryl Jones | 1989-92 | 394 |
| 4. | Mikki Bond | 1998-02 | 389 |
| 5. | Lisa Goodin | 1980-84 | 374 |
| 6. | Samantha Young | 1991-96 | 350 |
| 7. | Charlotte Sizemore | 1997-02 | 344 |
| 8. | Zoey Artist | 1998-02 | 307 |
| 9. | Kim Mays | 1992-95 | 297 |
| 10. | Maisha Thomas-Blanton | 1991-95 | 270 |

### ALL-TIME STEALS LEADERS

| No. | Player | Years | Steals |
|-----|--------|-------|--------|
| 1. | Teresa McNair | 1999-03 | 406 |

| 2. | Angie Cox | 1988-92 | 327 |
|----|-----------|---------|-----|
| 3. | Maisha Thomas-Blanton | 1991-95 | 236 |
| 4. | Charlotte Sizemore | 1997-02 | 228 |
| 5. | Mikki Bond | 1998-02 | 227 |

## ALL-TIME WINNINGEST COACHES

| Coach | Years | Record | Pct. |
|-------|-------|--------|------|
| Larry Joe Inman | 17 | 286-192 | .598 |
| Dianne Murphy | 7 | 96-101 | .487 |
| Shirley Duncan | 4 | 41-59 | .410 |

*(Source: Eastern Kentucky University Sports Information)*

# GEORGETOWN COLLEGE
## *BASKETBALL*

### GEORGETOWN BY THE NUMBERS:
- Overall record: 1610-824
- One NAIA national title (1998)
- 3 first team All Americans
- 3 Coach of the Year awards

### FIRST TEAM ALL AMERICANS
Kenny Davis
Dick Vories
Will Carlton

### WINNINGEST COACHES
Jim Reid (529)
Bob Davis (415)
Happy Osborne (309)

### ITEMS OF NOTE
- Georgetown holds the NAIA record for most consecutive trips to the national championship with 14 (1992-2005).
- Georgetown defeated Southern Nazarene (Okla.) 83-69 in the 1998 title game.
- Bob Davis was NAIA Coach of the Year in 1959, Jim Reid in 1994 and Happy Osborne in 1998.

*(Source: Georgetown College Sports Information)*

# KENTUCKY STATE UNIVERSITY
## *MEN'S BASKETBALL*

### K-STATE BY THE NUMBERS
- Overall record: 902-721
- 1 NCAA Tournament appearance (1962)
- 3 NAIA national championships (1970, 1971, 1972)
- 10 NAIA district championships
- 1 SIAC Tournament championship (2001)
- 4 First Team All Americans (selected 8 times)
- 5 Coach of the Year awards

### K-STATE FIRST TEAM ALL AMERICANS
Travis Grant, forward (1970, 1971, 1972)
Elmore Smith, center (1971)
Gerald Cunningham, forward (1975, 1976, 1977)
Billy Ray Bates, forward (1978)

### ITEMS OF NOTE
- Coach Lucias Mitchell led the Thorobreds to NAIA championships in 1970, 1971 and 1972. His powerful 1970-71 team posted the school's best record, 31-2.
- Elmore Smith's 22.6 career rebounding average ranks among college basketball's all-time best. He pulled down 36 rebounds in a win over Lincoln.

- Legendary three-time All-American Travis "The Machine" Grant once scored 75 points in a single game, making good on 35 field goals. The total points likely would have been considerably higher had the three-point field goal rule been established.) He finished his career with 4,045 points and a 33.4 scoring average.
- The Thorobreds scored 159 points in a game on two occasions.
- Harvey Carmichael handed out 21 assists in a win over Carson-Newman.

## ALL-TIME LEADING SCORERS

| No. | Player | Years | Games | Pts. | Avg. |
|-----|--------|-------|-------|------|------|
| 1. | Travis Grant | 1968-72 | 121 | 4,045 | 33.4 |
| 2. | Gerald Cunningham | 1973-77 | 121 | 2,635 | 21.8 |
| 3. | Elmore Smith | 1968-71 | 85 | 1,813 | 21.3 |
| 4. | Billy Ray Bates | 1974-78 | 107 | 1,723 | 16.1 |
| 5. | Lewis Linder | 1972-76 | 116 | 1,574 | 13.6 |
| 6. | Mike Busby | 1977-81 | 111 | 1,483 | 13.0 |
| 7. | Harvey Carmichael | 1971-75 | 123 | 1,318 | 10.7 |
| 8. | Fred Bowles | 1981-85 | 95 | 1,309 | 13.8 |
| 9. | Tyrone Jordan | 1978-82 | 106 | 1,246 | 11.8 |
| 10. | Alfred Smith | 1978-82 | 88 | 1,238 | 14.1 |

## ALL-TIME CAREER SCORING AVERAGES

| No. | Player | Years | Games | Pts. | Avg. |
|-----|--------|-------|-------|------|------|
| 1. | Travis Grant | 1968-72 | 121 | 4,045 | 33.4 |
| 2. | Gerald Cunningham | 1973-77 | 121 | 2,635 | 21.8 |
| 3. | Elmore Smith | 1968-71 | 85 | 1,813 | 21.3 |
| 4. | Billy Ray Bates | 1974-78 | 107 | 1,723 | 16.1 |
| 5. | Alfred Smith | 1978-82 | 88 | 1,238 | 14.1 |

## ALL-TIME LEADING REBOUNDERS

| No. | Player | Years | Rebounds | Avg. |
|-----|--------|-------|----------|------|
| 1. | Elmore Smith | 1968-91 | 1,917 | 22.6 |
| 2. | Travis Grant | 1968-72 | 1,121 | 9.4 |
| 3. | Gerald Cunningham | 1973-77 | 1,023 | 10.3 |
| 3. | William Graham | 1967-71 | 1,023 | 9.3 |
| 5. | Roy Smith | 1974-77 | 910 | 11.7 |
| 6. | Andre Hampton | 1971-75 | 847 | 11.7 |
| 7. | Billy Ray Bates | 1974-78 | 784 | 7.3 |
| 8. | Charles Tyron | 1977-80 | 758 | 6.5 |
| 9. | Arthur Box | 1971-75 | 679 | 6.7 |
| 10. | Sam Sibert | 1971-72 | 664 | 20.1 |

## ALL-TIME ASSISTS LEADERS

| No. | Player | Years | Assists |
|-----|--------|-------|---------|
| 1. | Harvey Carmichael | 1971-75 | 972 |
| 2. | Jerry Stafford | 1969-73 | 909 |
| 3. | Lewis Linder | 1972-76 | 687 |
| 4. | Johnny Mitchell | 1975-78 | 456 |
| 5. | Jerome Brister | 1976-81 | 449 |
| 6. | Leonard Williams | 1978-80 | 381 |
| 7. | Michael Douglas | 1993-97 | 358 |
| 8. | Toby Joseph | 1989-93 | 302 |
| 9. | Travis Grant | 1968-72 | 267 |
| 10. | Bruce Coles | 1978-80 | 255 |

## ALL-TIME WINNINGEST COACHES

| Coach | Years | Record | Pct. |
|-------|-------|--------|------|
| Lucias Mitchell | 8 | 192-47 | .803 |
| Joseph G. Fletcher | 10 | 149-85 | .637 |
| James B. Brown | 7 | 93-70 | .571 |

*(Source: KSU Sports Information)*

# KENTUCKY WESLEYAN COLLEGE
## *MEN'S BASKETBALL*

## KWC BY THE NUMBERS

- Overall record: 1,416-701
- 8 NCAA Division II national championships (1966, 1968, 1969, 1973, 1987, 1990, 1999, 2001)
- 18 Final Four appearances
- 20 Elite Eight appearances
- 91 NCAA Tournament wins
- 14 Great Lakes Valley Conference titles
- 5 GLVC Tournament championships
- 6 30-win seasons
- 27 Top 10 national poll finishes
- 3 National Player of the Year award winners
- 17 First Team All Americans
- 6 National Coach of the Year award winners

## FIRST TEAM ALL AMERICANS

Mason Cope (1957)
Sam Smith (1967)
Dallas Thornton (1968)
George Tinsley (1969)
Jyronna Ralston (1974)
Rod Drake (1984)
Dwight Higgs (1984)
J.B. Brown (1988)
Corey Crowder (1990)
Willis Cheaney (1995)
Antonio Garcia (1998)
Dana Williams (1999)
Leroy John (2000)
Lorico Duncan (2001)
Tyrus Boswell (2002)
Ronald Evans (2002)
Marlon Parmer (2003)

## OTHER KWC ALL AMERICANS

Fairce Woods (1946, 1949)
Joe Roop (1955)
Bill Bibb (1957)
Kelly Coleman (1959)
Gary Auten (1961)
Dick O'Neill (1969)
John Duncan (1970, 1971)
Jim Smith (1970)
Willie Johnson (1976)
Ray Harper (1985)
Dave Bennett (1985, 1986)
Sam L. Smith (1987)
Alex Kreps (1992)
Carlos Skinner (1993)

## ITEMS OF NOTE

- Kentucky Wesleyan College is the all-time Division II winner with 1,416 victories.
- Fairce Woods was the first Panther to earn All-America recognition and the first to score 1,000 career points.
- KWC has won eight NCAA Division II national titles under five different coaches (Guy Strong, Bob Daniels, Bob Jones, Wayne Chapman and Ray Harper).
- Wayne Chapman won 82 percent of his games and two NCAA championships during his five-year tenure as head coach.
- KWC's eight national titles ranks second only to UCLA's 11 among all Division I, II, III programs.
- The Panthers notched their first victory by beating Eastern Kentucky 44-22 in 1908.
- The legendary "King" Kelly Coleman averaged 27.7 points per game during his three seasons at KWC, scoring 40 or more points on four occasions. Coleman averaged 30.3 ppg

in 1960, third best in the nation.
- Corey Crowder 1991, Antonio Garcia (1999) and Marlon Parmer (2003) won National Division II Player of the Year awards.
- Thirty-six former Panthers have played at the professional level.

## ALL-TIME LEADING SCORERS

| No. | Player | Years | Games | Pts. | Avg. |
|---|---|---|---|---|---|
| 1. | Corey Crowder | 1988-91 | 118 | 2,282 | 19.3 |
| 2. | Dwight Higgs | 1981-84 | 120 | 2,228 | 18.6 |
| 3. | Kelly Coleman | 1958-60 | 75 | 2,077 | 27.7 |
| 4. | George Tinsley | 1966-69 | 119 | 2,014 | 16.9 |
| 5. | Dallas Thornton | 1965-68 | 112 | 1,929 | 17.5 |
| 6. | Gary Auten | 1959-62 | 102 | 1,774 | 17.4 |
| 7. | Rod Drake | 1981-84 | 120 | 1,664 | 13.9 |
| 8. | Mike Williams | 1971-73 | 87 | 1,568 | 18.0 |
| 9. | Fairce Woods | 1946-49 | 89 | 1,424 | 16.0 |
| 10. | Gino Bartolone | 1998-01 | 133 | 1,361 | 10.1 |

## ALL-TIME CAREER SCORING AVERAGES

| No. | Player | Years | Games | Pts. | Avg. |
|---|---|---|---|---|---|
| 1. | Kelly Coleman | 1958-60 | 75 | 2,077 | 27.7 |
| 2. | Corey Crowder | 1988-91 | 118 | 2,282 | 19.3 |
| 3. | Sam Smith | 1966-67 | 58 | 1,102 | 19.0 |
| 4. | Dwight Higgs | 1981-84 | 120 | 2,228 | 18.6 |
| 5. | Jyronna Ralston | 1973-74 | 57 | 1,031 | 18.1 |
| 6. | Mike Williams | 1971-73 | 87 | 1,568 | 18.0 |
| 7. | Dave Bennett | 1985-86 | 61 | 1,083 | 17.8 |
| 8. | Sam L. Smith | 1986-87 | 63 | 1,115 | 17.7 |
| 9. | Dallas Thornton | 1965-68 | 112 | 1,929 | 17.5 |
| 9. | Lorico Duncan | 2000-01 | 68 | 1,193 | 17.5 |

## ALL-TIME LEADING REBOUNDERS

| No. | Player | Years | Rebounds | Avg. |
|---|---|---|---|---|
| 1. | George Tinsley | 1966-69 | 1,115 | 9.4 |
| 2. | James Greene | 1970-73 | 1,088 | 10.2 |
| 3. | Antonio Garcia | 1998-99 | 997 | 14.2 |
| 4. | John Duncan | 1968-71 | 974 | 10.1 |
| 5. | Larry Morris | 1969-72 | 945 | 9.3 |
| 6. | Kelly Coleman | 1958-60 | 904 | 12.1 |
| 7. | Dallas Thornton | 1965-68 | 903 | 8.1 |
| 8. | Corey Crowder | 1988-91 | 806 | 6.8 |
| 9. | J.B. Brown | 1985-88 | 797 | 6.6 |
| 10. | Willie Johnson | 1974-76 | 723 | 9.4 |

## ALL-TIME ASSISTS LEADERS

| No. | Player | Years | Assists | Avg. |
|---|---|---|---|---|
| 1. | Willis Cheaney | 1992-95 | 635 | 5.6 |
| 2. | Rod Drake | 1981-84 | 458 | 3.8 |
| 3. | Patrick Critchelow | 1996-99 | 454 | 3.6 |
| 4. | Ray Harper | 1983-85 | 442 | 7.1 |
| 5. | Andra Whitlow | 1984-87 | 438 | 3.7 |
| 6. | Junebug Rakes | 1988-91 | 415 | 3.6 |
| 7. | Kim Clay | 1986-89 | 411 | 3.8 |
| 8. | Steve Divine | 1990-93 | 405 | 3.4 |
| 9. | Kris Kemp | 1994-97 | 361 | 3.1 |
| 10. | Dwight Higgs | 1981-84 | 328 | 2.7 |

## ALL-TIME WINNINGEST COACHES

| Coach | Years | Record | Pct. |
|---|---|---|---|
| Ray Harper | 9 | 242-45 | .843 |
| Robert Wilson | 15 | 204-141 | .591 |
| Wayne Boultinghouse | 6 | 129-45 | .741 |
| Wayne Chapman | 5 | 128-29 | .815 |
| Bob Jones | 8 | 119-90 | .569 |
| Mike Pollio | 5 | 117-35 | .770 |
| Bob Daniels | 5 | 110-36 | .753 |

(Source: Kentucky Wesleyan College Sports Information)

# KENTUCKY WESLEYAN COLLEGE
*WOMEN'S BASKETBALL*

## KWC BY THE NUMBERS
- Overall record: 279-455
- 3 All Americans
- 10 All Great Lakes Valley Conference players (selected 11 times)

## KWC ALL AMERICANS
Stacy Calhoun (1989)
Octavia Dean (1992)
Jill Burness (1995 Academic)

## ITEMS OF NOTE
- Ex-UK Wildcat Randy Embry led the Lady Panthers to a 17-1 record during his second (and final) season as head coach.
- In 1984, Margie Speaks led the nation in free throw shooting, making good on 89.2 percent of her attempts.
- The 1991-92 team is the school's only 20-game winner, finishing with a 21-7 record.
- The 1983-84 team led the nation in free throw accuracy by hitting 75.9 percent of its free throws.

## ALL-TIME LEADING SCORERS

| No. | Player | Years | Games | Pts. | Avg. |
|---|---|---|---|---|---|
| 1. | Angie Johnson | 1996-99 | 109 | 1,782 | 16.3 |
| 2. | Stacy Calhoun | 1987-90 | 110 | 1,672 | 15.2 |
| 3. | Brenda Britt | 1981-84 | 99 | 1,532 | 15.5 |
| 4. | Carrie Bridgeman | 1996-99 | 110 | 1,373 | 12.5 |
| 5. | Kerrie Moore | 1992-96 | 111 | 1,320 | 11.9 |
| 6. | Alice Shade | 1988-91 | 111 | 1,312 | 11.8 |
| 7. | Janice Johnson | 1979-82 | 84 | 1,232 | 14.7 |
| 8. | Leslie Warren | 2000-03 | 105 | 1,156 | 11.0 |
| 9. | Margie Speaks | 1982-85 | 97 | 1,064 | 11.0 |
| 10. | Amy Gruen | 1988-91 | 83 | 1,029 | 12.4 |

## ALL-TIME LEADING REBOUNDERS

| No. | Player | Years | Rebounds | Avg. |
|---|---|---|---|---|
| 1. | Jenny Boyd | 1991-94 | 807 | 7.5 |
| 2. | Alice Shade | 1988-91 | 708 | 6.4 |
| 3. | Kerrie Moore | 1992-96 | 689 | 6.2 |
| 4. | Brenda Britt | 1981-84 | 688 | 6.9 |
| 5. | Carrie Bridgeman | 1996-99 | 649 | 5.9 |
| 6. | Janice Johnson | 1979-82 | 642 | 7.7 |
| 7. | Angie Johnson | 1996-99 | 627 | 5.8 |
| 8. | Willia Hayes | 1985-88 | 578 | 5.8 |
| 9. | Amy Gruen | 1988-91 | 572 | 6.8 |
| 10. | Jill Burness | 1994-95 | 518 | 9.8 |

## ALL-TIME ASSISTS LEADERS

| No. | Player | Years | Assists | Avg. |
|---|---|---|---|---|
| 1. | Kelly Brewer | 1996-99 | 478 | 4.3 |
| 2. | Stacy Calhoun | 1987-90 | 465 | 5.2 |
| 3. | Tracey Wilson | 1988-91 | 403 | 4.0 |
| 4. | Brandy Reynolds | 2001-04 | 376 | 3.5 |
| 5. | Tina Ashby | 1979-82 | 368 | 4.4 |
| 6. | Brenda Britt | 1981-84 | 360 | 3.6 |
| 7. | Amanda Peters | 2001-03 | 334 | 4.2 |
| 8. | Kim Baughn | 1993-95 | 314 | 4.3 |
| 9. | Angie Johnson | 1996-99 | 306 | 2.8 |
| 10. | Margie Speaks | 1982-85 | 272 | 2.8 |

## ALL-TIME STEALS LEADERS

| No. | Player | Years | Steals |
|---|---|---|---|
| 1. | Stacy Calhoun | 1987-90 | 303 |
| 2. | Kelly Brewer | 1996-99 | 210 |

| 3. | Tracey Wilson | 1988-91 | 190 |
| 4. | Angie Johnson | 1996-99 | 185 |
| 5. | Brandy Reynolds | 2001-04 | 178 |
| 6. | Jenny Boyd | 1990-94 | 152 |
| 7. | Willia Hayes | 1983-87 | 144 |
| 8. | Amanda Peters | 2001-03 | 129 |
| 9. | Tracy Watson | 1986-90 | 120 |
| 10. | Carrie Bridgeman | 1996-99 | 114 |

## ALL-TIME WINNINGEST COACHES

| Coach | Years | Record | Pct. |
|---|---|---|---|
| Scott Lewis | 3 | 48-33 | .593 |
| Brent Matthew | 4 | 47-47 | .500 |
| Michele Rupe | 4 | 38-72 | .345 |
| Gene Minton | 3 | 31-52 | .400 |
| Mike Simpson | 3 | 31-53 | .369 |
| Tandy Bradford | 3 | 21-59 | .263 |
| Randy Embry | 2 | 20-14 | .588 |

*(Source: Kentucky Wesleyan College Sports Information)*

# LINDSEY WILSON COLLEGE
*MEN'S BASKETBALL*

## LINDSEY WILSON COLLEGE BY THE NUMBERS
- Overall record: 369-260
- 8 National Championship appearances
- 1 Mid-South Conference championship
- 2 MSC Tournament championships
- 4 KIAC championships
- 1 KIAC Tournament championship
- 13 players named NAIA All-Americans
- 19 players named Mid-South All-Conference
- 18 players named KIAC All-Conference

## ALL TIME LEADING SCORERS

| No. | Player | Years | Pts. |
|---|---|---|---|
| 1. | Cetric Anderson | 2001-05 | 1,932 |
| 2. | Scott Cook | 2002-06 | 1,630 |
| 3. | Joe McGeorge | 1990-94 | 1,444 |
| 4. | Chris Dickerson | 1987-90 | 1,266 |
| 5. | Jared Barnes | 2001-05 | 1,135 |
| 6. | Matt Bennett | 1993-97 | 1,132 |
| 7. | Mark Butcher | 1993-97 | 1,103 |
| 8. | Michael Resch | 1996-01 | 1,086 |
| 9. | Brent Conley | 1998-00 | 1,063 |
| 10. | Stephen Russell | 2003-06 | 977 |

## ALL TIME LEADING REBOUNDERS

| No. | Player | Years | Pts. |
|---|---|---|---|
| 1. | Jared Barnes | 2001-05 | 554 |
| 2. | Stephen Russell | 2003-06 | 532 |
| 3. | Michael Resch | 1996-01 | 498 |
| 4. | Cetric Anderson | 2001-05 | 487 |
| 5. | Nelson Cundiff | 1987-91 | 443 |

## ALL TIME ASSIST LEADERS

| No. | Player | Years | Pts. |
|---|---|---|---|
| 1. | Scott Cook | 2002-06 | 672 |
| 2. | Cetric Anderson | 2001-05 | 418 |
| 3. | Jared Barnes | 2001-05 | 308 |
| 4. | Nelson Cundiff | 1987-91 | 296 |
| 5. | Brandon Davenport | 1999-01 | 288 |

*(Source: Lindsey Wilson College Sports Information)*

# LINDSEY WILSON COLLEGE
*WOMEN'S BASKETBALL*

## LINDSEY WILSON BY THE NUMBERS
- Overall record: 341-235
- 4 National Championship appearances
- 5 KIAC championships
- 2 players named NAIA All-Americans
- 16 players named Mid-South All-Conference

## ALL-TIME LEADING SCORERS

| No. | Player | Years | Pts. |
|---|---|---|---|
| 1. | Donna Burden | 1988-93 | 2,213 |
| 2. | Ronyeld Shirley | 1997-01 | 1,293 |
| 3. | Lyndsay Howard | 2000-04 | 1,210 |
| 4. | Amy Lankford | 1995-99 | 1,205 |
| 5. | Heather Baker | 1998-00 | 1,155 |
| 6. | Shelia Isenberg | 1986-90 | 1,103 |
| 7. | Jennifer Crawley | 1994-99 | 954 |
| 8. | Kristi Murphy | 1996-98 | 944 |
| 9. | Allisia Stewart | 2002-04 | 938 |
| 10. | Tonya Feese | 1989-93 | 903 |

## ALL-TIME LEADING REBOUNDERS

| No. | Player | Years | Pts. |
|---|---|---|---|
| 1. | Ronyeld Shirley | 1997-01 | 896 |
| 2. | Shelia Isenberg | 1986-90 | 844 |
| 3. | Donna Burden | 1988-93 | 721 |
| 4. | Amy Lankford | 1995-99 | 664 |
| 5. | Sonya Fudge | 1986-90 | 488 |

## ALL-TIME ASSIST LEADERS

| No. | Player | Years | Pts. |
|---|---|---|---|
| 1. | Tonya Feese | 1989-93 | 630 |
| 2. | Leah Hamrick | 1993-97 | 587 |
| 3. | Tiffany Reid | 2003-05 | 336 |
| 4. | Rebecca Husband | 2002-05 | 331 |
| 5. | Jenny Jones | 1997-01 | 307 |

*(Source: Lindsey Wilson College Sports Information)*

# MIDWAY COLLEGE
*WOMEN'S BASKETBALL*

## MIDWAY BY THE NUMBERS
- Overall record: 145-300
- The basketball program is the oldest athletic program at Midway College.
- 1 NAIA All American
- 2 NAIA All American Scholar-Athletes
- 2 National Small College All Americans
- 4 All Region XII athletes
- 14 KIAC All Conference selections

## ALL-TIME LEADING SCORERS

| No. | Player | Years | Pts. |
|---|---|---|---|
| 1. | Natalie Dial | 2002-06 | 1,683 |
| 2. | Michella Hopkins | 1994-98 | 1,633 |
| 3. | Amy Klein | 1999-03 | 1,094 |
| 4. | Jill Potts | 1993-97 | 1,029 |
| 5. | Karen Frasure | 1992-96 | 1,023 |
| 6. | Jessica Eden | 1997-02 | 1,016 |

## ALL-TIME LEADING REBOUNDERS

| No. | Player | Years | Rebounds |
|---|---|---|---|
| 1. | Jill Potts | 1993-97 | 836 |
| 2. | Natiaie Dial | 2002-06 | 808 |

| No. | | Years | |
|---|---|---|---|
| 3. | Michella Hopkins | 1994-98 | 692 |
| 4. | Susan Sullins | 1994-98 | 606 |

## ALL-TIME ASSISTS LEADERS

| No. | Player | Years | Assists |
|---|---|---|---|
| 1. | Amy Klein | 1999-03 | 511 |
| 2. | Jenny Wiley | 1993-96 | 343 |
| 3. | Courtney Kerr | 1993-95 | 316 |
| 4. | Tia Garrett | 2002- | 277 |
| 5. | Whitney Allison | 1996-99 | 263 |

## ALL-TIME STEALS LEADERS

| No. | Player | Years | Steals |
|---|---|---|---|
| 1. | Jenny Wiley | 1993-96 | 220 |
| 2. | Amy Klein | 1999-03 | 201 |
| 3. | Jill Potts | 1993-97 | 194 |
| 4. | LaChae Churn | 2001-04 | 158 |
| 5. | Tia Garrett | 2002- | 138 |
| 6. | Jessica Eden | 1997-02 | 137 |
| 7. | Michella Hopkins | 1994-98 | 133 |

*(Source: Midway College Sports Information)*

# MOREHEAD STATE UNIVERSITY
## *MEN'S BASKETBALL*

## MOREHEAD STATE BY THE NUMBERS

- Overall record: 944-907
- 5 NCAA Tournament appearances (1956, 1957, 1961, 1983, 1984)
- 7 All Americans (selected eight times)
- 9 Ohio Valley Conference titles (1956, 1957, 1961, 1963, 1969, 1972, 1974, 1984, 2003)
- 2 OVC Tournament championships (1983, 1984)
- 4 OVC Player of the Year selections
- 4 coaches voted OVC Coach of the Year (selected 5 times)
- 51 All OVC players (selected 84 times)
- 2 KIAC championships (1941, 1944)

## MOREHEAD STATE ALL AMERICANS

Earl Duncan, forward (1943)
Warren Cooper, center (1945)
Sonny Allen, guard (1950)
Dan Swartz, center (1955, 1956)
Steve Hamilton, forward (1957)
Harold Sergent, guard (1963)
Leonard Coulter, forward (1972)

## ITEMS OF NOTE

- The Eagles claimed their first win when they defeated Cumberland 37-25 in 1929.
- Ellis Johnson, Morehead State's all-time winningest coach, was an All American as a guard on Adolph Rupp's first University of Kentucky team. Johnson is still regarded as one of the greatest all-around athletes in UK history.
- Ex-Eagle player and athletics director Steve Hamilton played in a World Series with the New York Yankees and an NBA championship series with the Los Angeles Lakers. Hamilton once had 38 rebounds in a game against Florida State.
- Current Eagles coach Kyle Macy was an All-American at UK. Macy later spent several seasons in the NBA.
- In the 2001-02 season, Morehead State led all NCAA Division I schools in free throw percentage (78.4).
- The 2003-04 Morehead State team led all Division I schools in field goal accuracy, hitting 51 percent.
- All-American guard Harold Sergent was a standout member

of the powerful 1961 state champion Ashland Tomcats, a team many still rank as the best ever in Kentucky high school basketball history.

## ALL-TIME LEADING SCORERS

| No. | Player | Years | Games | Pts. | Avg. |
|---|---|---|---|---|---|
| 1. | Ricky Minard | 2000-04 | 114 | 2,381 | 20.9 |
| 2. | Herbie Stamper | 1975-79 | 99 | 2,072 | 20.9 |
| 3. | Dan Swartz | 1953-56 | 69 | 1,925 | 27.5 |
| 4. | Sonny Allen | 1946-50 | 92 | 1,923 | 20.8 |
| 5. | Steve Hamilton | 1954-58 | 102 | 1,829 | 17.8 |
| 6. | Brett Roberts | 1988-92 | 107 | 1,788 | 16.7 |
| 7. | Leonard Coulter | 1971-74 | 77 | 1,781 | 23.1 |
| 8. | Granny Williams | 1959-62 | 76 | 1,637 | 21.5 |
| 9. | Harold Sergent | 1962-65 | 63 | 1,469 | 23.2 |
| 10. | Ted Hundley | 1973-77 | 100 | 1,450 | 14.5 |

## ALL-TIME CAREER SCORING AVERAGES

| No. | Player | Years | Games | Pts. | Avg. |
|---|---|---|---|---|---|
| 1. | Dan Swartz | 1953-56 | 69 | 1,925 | 27.5 |
| 2. | Harold Sergent | 1962-65 | 63 | 1,469 | 23.2 |
| 3. | Leonard Coulter | 1971-74 | 77 | 1,781 | 23.1 |
| 4. | Granny Williams | 1959-62 | 76 | 1,637 | 21.5 |
| 5. | Ricky Minard | 2000-04 | 114 | 2,381 | 20.9 |
| 6. | Herbie Stamper | 1975-79 | 99 | 2,072 | 20.9 |
| 7. | Sonny Allen | 1946-50 | 92 | 1,923 | 20.8 |
| 8. | Earl Duncan | 1939-43 | 74 | 1,430 | 19.3 |
| 9. | Warren Cooper | 1942-45 | 54 | 1,011 | 18.5 |
| 10. | Steve Hamilton | 1954-58 | 102 | 1,829 | 17.8 |

## ALL-TIME LEADING REBOUNDERS

| No. | Player | Years | Rebounds | Avg. |
|---|---|---|---|---|
| 1. | Steve Hamilton | 1954-58 | 1,675 | 16.4 |
| 2. | Norm Pokley | 1960-63 | 1,046 | n/a |
| 3. | Leonard Coulter | 1971-74 | 961 | 12.5 |
| 4. | Lamar Green | 1966-69 | 914 | n/a |
| 5. | Ted Hundley | 1973-77 | 901 | 9.0 |
| 6. | Brett Roberts | 1988-92 | 897 | 8.4 |
| 7. | Bob McCann | 1984-87 | 862 | 10.5 |
| 8. | Doug Bentz | 1989-93 | 808 | 7.2 |
| 9. | Willie Jackson | 1966-69 | 793 | 11.3 |
| 10. | Thornton Hill | 1956-59 | 781 | n/a |

## ALL-TIME ASSISTS LEADERS

| No. | Player | Years | Assists |
|---|---|---|---|
| 1. | Marquis Sykes | 1999-03 | 606 |
| 2. | Ricky Minard | 2000-04 | 417 |
| 3. | Howard Wallen | 1971-74 | 411 |
| 4. | Ted Docks | 1995-99 | 356 |
| 5. | Jeff Fultz | 1980-84 | 336 |
| 6. | Guy Minnifield | 1981-84 | 284 |
| 7. | Pat Tubbs | 1989-92 | 254 |
| 8. | Jeff Griffin | 1985-87 | 249 |
| 9. | Marty Cline | 1992-95 | 237 |
| 10. | Rocky Adkins | 1978-82 | 231 |

## ALL-TIME WINNINGEST COACHES

| Coach | Years | Record | Pct. |
|---|---|---|---|
| Ellis Johnson | 15 | 196-158 | .553 |
| Bobby Laughlin | 12 | 166-120 | .580 |
| Wayne Martin | 9 | 130-120 | .520 |
| Kyle Macy | 9 | 106-144 | .424 |

*(Source: Morehead State University Sports Information)*

# MOREHEAD STATE UNIVERSITY
## *WOMEN'S BASKETBALL*

## MOREHEAD STATE BY THE NUMBERS
- Overall record: 176-253
- The 1978-79 Lady Eagles posted the program's best record at 28-4.
- Lady Eagle teams have topped the 100-point mark on 15 occasions.
- 11 First Team All-Ohio Valley Conference players (selected 16 times)
- 3 Lady Eagles named OVC Player of the Year
- 3 Lady Eagle coaches voted OVC Coach of the Year

## FIRST TEAM ALL OVC PLAYERS
Donna Murphy (1978, 1979, 1980)
Donna Stephens (1979, 1980, 1981)
Michelle Stowers (1979)
Priscilla Blackford (1982, 1983)
Connie Appelman (1985)
Kelly Stamper (1987)
Julie Magrane (1992)
Bev Smith (1993)
Amy Kieckbusch (1997)
Tasha Gales (2002)
Travece Turner (2003)

## ALL-TIME LEADING SCORERS

| No. | Player | Years | Games | Pts. | Avg. |
|---|---|---|---|---|---|
| 1. | Donna Murphy | 1976-80 | 105 | 2,059 | 19.6 |
| 2. | Donna Stephens | 1978-82 | 93 | 1,710 | 18.4 |
| 3. | Julie Magrane | 1988-92 | 107 | 1,697 | 15.9 |
| 4. | Tasha Gales | 1999-03 | 105 | 1,602 | 15.3 |
| 5. | Robin Harmon | 1978-82 | 121 | 1,599 | 13.2 |
| 6. | Bev Smith | 1988-03 | 111 | 1,592 | 14.3 |
| 7. | Kandi Brown | 2000-04 | 114 | 1,583 | 13.9 |
| 8. | Priscilla Blackford | 1980-84 | 94 | 1,481 | 15.8 |
| 9. | Michelle Stowers | 1976-80 | 109 | 1,459 | 13.4 |
| 10. | Megan Hupfer | 1992-96 | 106 | 1,444 | 13.6 |

## ALL-TIME LEADING REBOUNDERS

| No. | Player | Years | Rebounds | Avg. |
|---|---|---|---|---|
| 1. | Donna Murphy | 1976-80 | 1,442 | 13.7 |
| 2. | Priscilla Blackford | 1980-84 | 1,075 | 11.4 |
| 3. | Donna Stephens | 1978-82 | 1,044 | 11.2 |
| 4. | Julie Magrane | 1988-92 | 1,034 | 9.7 |
| 5. | Bev Smith | 1988-93 | 879 | 7.9 |
| 6. | Michelle Stowers | 1976-80 | 846 | 7.8 |
| 7. | Tasha Gales | 1999-03 | 822 | 7.8 |
| 8. | DeVonda Williams | 2000-04 | 800 | 7.0 |
| 9. | Megan Hupfer | 1992-96 | 792 | 7.5 |
| 10. | Kelly Stamper | 1985-89 | 722 | 6.6 |

## ALL-TIME ASSISTS LEADERS

| No. | Player | Years | Assists |
|---|---|---|---|
| 1. | Irene Moore | 1978-82 | 499 |
| 2. | Susann Brown | 1975-79 | 455 |
| 3. | Kelly Stamper | 1985-89 | 454 |
| 4. | Rita Berry | 1980-84 | 449 |
| 5. | Robin Harmon | 1978-82 | 429 |
| 6. | Hilary Swisher | 1993-98 | 425 |
| 7. | Stacey Spake | 1990-94 | 379 |
| 8. | Kandi Brown | 2000-04 | 363 |
| 9. | B.J. Bradford | 1987-91 | 353 |
| 10. | Tiphanie Bates | 1983-87 | 332 |

## ALL-TIME STEALS LEADERS

| No. | Player | Years | Steals |
|---|---|---|---|
| 1. | B.J. Bradford | 1987-91 | 198 |
| 2. | Kelly Stamper | 1985-89 | 191 |
| 3. | Hilary Swisher | 1993-98 | 181 |
| 3. | Stacey Spake | 1990-94 | 181 |
| 5. | Kandi Brown | 2000-04 | 177 |
| 6. | Sherita Joplin | 1991-95 | 170 |
| 7. | DeVonda Williams | 2000-04 | 153 |
| 8. | Tiphanie Bates | 1983-87 | 148 |
| 9. | Shawne Marcum | 1993-97 | 136 |
| 10. | Julie Magrane | 1988-92 | 131 |

## ALL-TIME WINNINGEST COACHES

| Coach | Years | Record | Pct. |
|---|---|---|---|
| Mickey Wells | 9 | 156-01 | .632 |
| Loretta Marlow | 9 | 110-116 | .487 |
| Laura Litter | 9 | 76-144 | .345 |

*(Source: Morehead State University Sports Information)*

# MURRAY STATE UNIVERSITY
## *MEN'S BASKETBALL*

## MSU BY THE NUMBERS
- Overall record: 1,340-771
- 13 NCAA Tournament appearances
- 20 Ohio Valley Conference titles (1951, 1964, 1968, 1969, 1980, 1982, 1983, 1988, 1989, 1990, 1991, 1992, 1994, 1995, 1996, 1997, 1998, 1999, 2000, 2006)
- 11 Racers named OVC Player of the Year
- 53 All OVC players (selected 97 times)
- 5 OVC Athletes of the Year (selected seven times)
- 7 OVC Coach of the Year awards (selected 11 times)

## OVC PLAYERS OF THE YEAR
- Jim Jennings, center (1964) – led the team in scoring all three seasons. Finished career with 1,370 points and 1,147 rebounds and averaged 19.3 points per game.
- Claude Virden, forward (1969) – Averaged 23.5 ppg as a junior in 1969 and had 1,490 career points. Averaged 11 rebounds per game. Hit 86 percent of his free throws in 1967-68 season.
- Les Taylor, guard (1972, 1973) – MSU's first two-time OVC Player of the Year. Scored 1,477 points and averaged 21.1 ppg. Averaged 25.6 ppg in 1971-72 season.
- Gary Hooker, forward/center (1980) – Averaged 18.6 points and 12.3 rebounds while shooting 55 percent from the field in 1979-80 season.
- Glen Green, guard/forward (1983) – Ended his career with 1,557 points after twice leading the club in scoring. Had career marks of 49 percent shooting from the field and 77 percent free throw shooting. Also had 423 assists and 141 steals.
- Jeff Martin, forward (1988, 1989) – MSU's all-time leading scorer with 2,484 points. Career scoring average of 21.2 ppg. Averaged 26.0 in 1987-88. Made good on 52 percent of his field goal attempts. His 806 points during 1987-1988 campaign is an MSU record.
- Popeye Jones, forward (1990, 1991) – MSU was the only Division I school to offer him a scholarship. Became a superstar after shedding 40 pounds. Scored 2,057 points. MSU's all-time leading rebounder with 1,374. Led the nation in rebounds in 1990-91.
- Marcus Brown, guard (1995, 1996) – MSU's third all-time leading scorer with 2,236 points. His 26.4 scoring average in 1995-96 is the school's best for a single season. Hit 85 percent of his free throws. Connected on 173 three-pointers during his career.
- De'Teri Mayes, forward (1998) – His 21.26 career scoring average is MSU's best. Only played 63 games but still managed to score 1,340 points. Holds the school record

for three-point goals with 103. Hit 41 percent of his three-point attempts. Shot 80 percent from the free throw line.
- Aubrey Reese, guard (2000) – Ended his career with 1,291 points. Connected on 105 three-pointers, including 54 during the 1999-2000 season. Had 383 assists and 134 steals.
- Cuthbert Victor, forward (2004) – Twice led the club in scoring and had 1,485 career points and 935 rebounds. Averaged 10.2 rebounds as a senior. Shot a blistering 63 percent from the field in his final season, and 59 percent for his career. Had 167 steals and a MSU all-time best 160 blocked shots.

## OTHER MSU PLAYERS WITH RETIRED JERSEYS
- Garrett Beshear, forward/center, three-time All-OVC selection; scored 1,716 points while twice leading the club in field goal percentage.
- Howie Crittenden, guard, a prep school legend at Cuba High School and still the holder of six MSU records; scored 2,019 points and averaged 19.4 ppg; made a school-best 731 free throws, including 19 in a single game on three different occasions.
- Johnny Reagan, forward, twice led the team in scoring.
- Bennie Purcell, guard, two-time All-OVC pick who finished his career with 1,054 points; averaged 18.3 as a senior in 1951-52; shot 77 percent from the charity stripe that season.
- Joe Fulks, forward, twice led the team in scoring; went on to become an NBA legend; credited with introducing the jump shot into the game; once called the "Babe Ruth of basketball."
- Paul King, forward, All-OVC pick in 1990; scored 1,108 points; made 173 treys while shooting 40 percent from beyond the three-point line; finished with 99 blocked shots.

## ITEMS OF NOTE
- MSU won nine OVC titles in the 1990s, tops among all Division I programs. In all, MSU has won 19 OVC championships, the most by any conference school.
- Prior to taking over at MSU, Mick Cronin served as an assistant to Cincinnati's Bob Huggins and Louisville's Rick Pitino.
- Three generations of the Goheen family excelled at college hoops. Robert and Bennie played for MSU, while Bennie's son, Barry, was a standout at Vanderbilt.
- Ex-Racer Bennie Purcell's son, Mel, is a former pro tennis champion. Mel is now MSU's men's tennis coach.

## ALL-TIME LEADING SCORERS

| No. | Player | Years | Games | Pts. | Avg. |
|---|---|---|---|---|---|
| 1. | Jeff Martin | 1985-89 | 117 | 2,484 | 21.2 |
| 2. | Isaac Spencer | 1997-01 | 127 | 2,248 | 17.7 |
| 3. | Marcus Brown | 1993-96 | 118 | 2,236 | 18.9 |
| 4. | Popeye Jones | 1988-92 | 123 | 2,057 | 16.7 |
| 5. | Howie Crittenden | 1952-56 | 104 | 2,019 | 19.4 |
| 6. | Lamont Sleets | 1079-84 | 111 | 1,902 | 17.1 |
| 7. | Vincent Rainey | 1994-97 | 113 | 1,888 | 16.7 |
| 8. | Frank Allen | 1989-93 | 116 | 1,811 | 15.6 |
| 9. | Garrett Beshear | 1951-53 | 112 | 1,716 | 15.3 |
| 10. | Glen Green | 1979-83 | 115 | 1,557 | 13.5 |

## ALL-TIME LEADING REBOUNDERS

| No. | Player | Years | Rebounds |
|---|---|---|---|
| 1. | Popeye Jones | 1988-92 | 1,374 |
| 2. | Dick Cunningham | 1965-68 | 1,292 |
| 3. | Jim Jennings | 1961-64 | 1,147 |
| 4. | Stewart Johnson | 1963-66 | 981 |
| 5. | Isaac Spencer | 1997-01 | 976 |
| 6. | Cuthbert Victor | 2000-04 | 935 |

| 7. | Marcelous Starks | 1971-74 | 875 |
|---|---|---|---|
| 8. | Ron Johnson | 1968-71 | 837 |
| 9. | Quitman Sullins | 1954-58 | 791 |
| 10. | Claude Virden | 1967-70 | 778 |

## ALL-TIME ASSISTS LEADERS

| No. | Player | Years | Assists |
|---|---|---|---|
| 1. | Don Mann | 1985-89 | 531 |
| 2. | Lamont Sleets | 1979-84 | 459 |
| 3. | Glen Green | 1979-83 | 423 |
| 4. | Chad Townsend | 1996-98 | 383 |
| 4. | Aubrey Reese | 1997-00 | 383 |
| 6. | Frank Allen | 1989-93 | 364 |
| 7. | Kevin Paschel | 2000-04 | 363 |
| 8. | Isaac Spencer | 1997-01 | 357 |
| 9. | Grover Woolard | 1973-77 | 341 |
| 10. | Brian Stewart | 1980-84 | 322 |

*(Source: Murray State University Sports Information)*

# NORTHERN KENTUCKY UNIVERSITY
*MEN'S BASKETBALL*

## NKU BY THE NUMBERS
- Men's overall record: 582-409
- 130-win seasons
- NCAA Division II national runner-up in 1997

## NKU NATIONAL PLAYERS OF THE YEAR
Michelle Cottrell, basketball (2001, 2002)
Krystal Lewallen, softball (2004)

## ALL AMERICANS
Michelle Cottrell, basketball (2000, 2001, 2002)
Derek Fields, basketball (1989)
Paul Cluxton, basketball (1997)
LaRon Moore, basketball (1997)
Craig Sanders, basketball (2002)
Brenden Stowers, basketball (2003)
Kristin Koralewski, volleyball (n/a)
Krystal Lewallen, softball (2004)
Ricki Rothbauer, softball (n/a)
Stephanie Leimbach, softball (n/a)
Curtis Phelps, golf (n/a)
Kim Keyer-Scott, golf (n/a)

## NKU ATHLETIC HALL OF FAME MEMBERS
Richard Derkson, basketball (1971-75)
Peggy Vincent, basketball (1975-79)
Peggy Ludwig, volleyball (1975-78)
Gary Wall, baseball (1974-78)
Johnny Lott, cross country (1975-79)
Dan Doellman, basketball (1975-79)
Jeff Stowers, basketball (1972-76)
Russ Kerdolff, baseball (1975-79)
Julie Thomas Perry, volleyball (1976-79)
Marilyn Moore, basketball/volleyball coach (n/a)
Derek Fields, basketball (1985-89)
Melissa Wood-Fleming, basketball (1983-87)
Kevin Cieply, soccer (1981-84)
Gary Flowerdew, baseball (1985-88)
Brenda Ryan, basketball/softball (1978-82)
Roger Klein, tennis coach (1975-88)
Paul Steenken, tennis (1983-86)
Brady Jackson, basketball (1979-83)
Julee Hill, volleyball/basketball (1975-78)
Barbara Harkins, basketball (1978-82)
Dave Krebs, soccer (1981-82)
Bill Aker, baseball coach (1972-2000)

Dr. Jim Bilbo, team physician (1986-present)
Diane Redmond, basketball (1975-79)
J.T. Roberts, soccer (1993-96)
Amy Flaugher, basketball/softball (1978-82)
Tim Grogan, baseball (1975-79)
Nancy Berger, volleyball (1979-82)
Paul Cluxton, basketball (1993-97)
John Toebben, men's soccer coach (1990-2002)
2000 NCAA Division II women's basketball national
   champions
Amy Flaugher, basketball/softball (1978-82)
Tim Grogan, baseball (1975-79)
Nancy Berger, volleyball (1979-82)
Paul Cluxton, basketball (1993-97)
John Toebben, men's soccer coach (1990-2002)
2000 NCAA Division II women's basketball national
   champions

## ITEMS OF NOTE

- Paul Cluxton set an NCAA all-time record in 1996-97 by connecting on 94 percent of his free throws. His career mark was 93.4 percent.
- Michelle Cottrell was a three-time NCAA Division II All-American and was twice named National Player of the Year. She was also named Most Outstanding Player of the 2000 Division II Elite Eight.
- The NKU women's team won the 2000 NCAA Division II national title by beating North Dakota State 71-62 in overtime. Nancy Winstel was the head coach.
- Peggy Vincent is the women's all-time leading scorer with 1,883 points and the all-time leading rebounder with 1,166.
- Bill Aker retired with 806 wins in 29 seasons as Norse baseball coach.

## ALL-TIME LEADING SCORERS

| No. | Player | Years | Pts. |
|---|---|---|---|
| 1. | Craig Sanders | 1998-02 | 2,007 |
| 2. | Brady Jackson | 1979-83 | 1,980 |
| 3. | Richard Derkson | 1971-75 | 1,927 |
| 4. | Dan Doellman | 1975-79 | 1,920 |
| 5. | LaRon Moore | 1993-97 | 1,866 |
| 6. | Derek Fields | 1985-89 | 1,664 |
| 7. | Mike Kelsey | 2001-05 | 1,595 |
| 8. | Shawn Scott | 1984-88 | 1,533 |
| 9. | Craig Conley | 1997-01 | 1,502 |
| 10. | Paul Cluxton | 1993-97 | 1,495 |

## ALL-TIME LEADING REBOUNDERS

| No. | Player | Years | Pts. |
|---|---|---|---|
| 1. | LaRon Moore | 1993-97 | 859 |
| 2. | Steve Jesse | 1980-84 | 812 |
| 3. | Dan Doellman | 1975-79 | 784 |
| 4. | Todd Svoboda | 1989-92 | 770 |
| 5. | Tony Faehr | 1975-78 | 686 |

## ALL-TIME ASSIST LEADERS

| No. | Player | Years | Pts. |
|---|---|---|---|
| 1. | Craig Conley | 1997-01 | 530 |
| 2. | Shannon Minor | 1993-97 | 529 |
| 3. | Kevin Listerman | 1995-00 | 501 |
| 4. | Craig Wilhoit | 1989-93 | 420 |
| 5. | Derek Fields | 1985-89 | 406 |

*(Source: Northern Kentucky University Sports Information)*

# NORTHERN KENTUCKY UNIVERSITY
*WOMEN'S BASKETBALL*

## NORTHERN KENTUCKY BY THE NUMBERS
- Overall record: 672-261
- NCAA Division II national champions in 2000
- Best season record: 32-2 in 2000
- Longest win streak: 34 games

## ALL-TIME LEADING SCORERS

| No. | Player | Years | Pts. |
|---|---|---|---|
| 1. | Michelle Cottrell | 1998-02 | 2,241 |
| 2. | Peggy Vincent | 1975-79 | 1,883 |
| 3. | Barb Harkins | 1978-82 | 1,585 |
| 4. | Michele Tuchfarber | 1997-01 | 1,509 |
| 5. | Lori McClellan | 1989-93 | 1,501 |
| 6. | Linda Honigford | 1986-90 | 1,482 |
| 7. | Pam King | 1982-86 | 1,442 |
| 8. | Amy Mobley | 1999-03 | 1,398 |
| 9. | Melissa Wood | 1983-87 | 1,393 |
| 10. | Christie Freppon | 1987-91 | 1,339 |

## ALL-TIME LEADING REBOUNDERS

| No. | Player | Years | Pts. |
|---|---|---|---|
| 1. | Peggy Vincent | 1975-79 | 1,166 |
| 2. | Michelle Cottrell | 1998-02 | 1,103 |
| 3. | Barb Harkins | 1978-82 | 876 |
| 4. | Pam King | 1982-86 | 857 |
| 5. | Christie Freppon | 1987-91 | 850 |

## ALL-TIME ASSIST LEADERS

| No. | Player | Years | Pts. |
|---|---|---|---|
| 1. | Katie Kelsey | 1995-99 | 514 |
| 2. | Amy Flaugher | 1978-82 | 466 |
| 3. | Diane Redmond | 1975-79 | 462 |
| 4. | Brenda Ryan | 1978-82 | 416 |
| 5. | Annie Levens | 1988-92 | 398 |

# PIKEVILLE COLLEGE
*MEN'S BASKETBALL*

## PIKEVILLE COLLEGE BY THE NUMBERS
- Overall record: 679-662
- 10 20-win seasons

## ALL-TIME LEADING SCORERS

| No. | Player | Pts. |
|---|---|---|
| 1. | Bart Williams | 2,736 |
| 2. | Todd May | 2,225 |
| 3. | Brian Johnson | 2,188 |
| 4. | Donnis Butcher | 2,080 |
| 5. | Jody Thompson | 2,061 |
| 6. | John Lee Butcher | 2,010 |
| 7. | Hoskins Carroll | 1,812 |
| 8. | David Rowe | 1,617 |
| 9. | Reggie Gravely | 1,572 |
| 10. | Mike May | 1,395 |

## ALL-TIME LEADING REBOUNDER
Vern Woods        1,208

## ALL-TIME ASSIST LEADER
John Kitchen                    756

## ALL-TIME WINNINGEST COACHES
| Coach | Years | Record | Pct. |
|---|---|---|---|
| Paul Butcher | 11 | 153-133 | .535 |
| Randy McCoy | 5 | 134-71 | .654 |
| Wayne Martin | 4 | 90-33 | .732 |

# PIKEVILLE COLLEGE
## WOMEN'S BASKETBALL

## PIKEVILLE COLLEGE BY THE NUMBERS
- Overall record: 388-386
- 3 20-win seasons

## ALL-TIME LEADING SCORERS
| No. | Player | Years | Pts. |
|---|---|---|---|
| 1. | Renee Brewer | 2,333 | |
| 2. | Teresa Ray | 2,234 | |
| 3. | Amanda Collins | 2,215 | |
| 4. | Allyson Preece | 1,791 | |
| 5. | Teccoa Gallion | 1,717 | |
| 6. | Rosemary Gilliam | 1,711 | |
| 7. | Crystal Slone | 1,572 | |
| 8. | Melody Sturgill | 1,556 | |
| 9. | Karissa Carter | 1,553 | |
| 10. | Autumn Damron | 1,464 | |

## ALL-TIME LEADING REBOUNDER
Rosemary Gilliam              1,312

## ALL-TIME ASSIST LEADER
Tammy Tussey                 750

## ALL-TIME WINNINGEST COACHES
| Coach | Years | Record | Pct. |
|---|---|---|---|
| Roy Cutright | 14 | 217-206 | .513 |
| Bill Watson | 8 | 145-119 | .549 |
| Randy Roberts | 3 | 35-52 | .402 |

*(Source: Pikeville College Sports Information)*

# ST. CATHARINE COLLEGE
## MEN'S BASKETBALL

## ALL-TIME LEADING SCORERS
| No. | Player | Pts. |
|---|---|---|
| 1. | Butch Joyner | 1,100 |
| 2. | Arnold Gore | 544 |
| 3. | Kenny Hayes | 424 |

# ST. CATHARINE COLLEGE
## WOMEN'S BASKETBALL

## ALL-TIME LEADING SCORERS
| No. | Player | Pts. |
|---|---|---|
| 1. | Ashley Butler | 1,250 |
| 1. | Heather Taylor | 1,250 |

*(Source: St. Catharine College Sports Information)*

# THOMAS MORE COLLEGE
## MEN'S BASKETBALL

## THOMAS MORE BY THE NUMBERS
- Overall record: 598-815
- 12 Intercollegiate athletic teams
- Winning percentage of .533 (96-74) in Connor Convocation Center

## ALL-TIME LEADING SCORERS
| No. | Player | Years | Pts. |
|---|---|---|---|
| 1. | Rick Hughes | 1992-92 | 2,605 |
| 2. | Brian O'Conner | 1977-81 | 2,078 |
| 3. | Larry Staverman | 1954-58 | 1,673 |
| 4. | Brian Clapp | 1985-89 | 1,492 |
| 5. | Steve Butcher | 1985-89 | 1,466 |
| 6. | Dan Tieman | 1958-62 | 1,454 |
| 7. | John Wendefer | 1968-72 | 1,404 |
| 8. | Dan Schmidt | 1955-59 | 1,315 |
| 9. | Dave Faust | 1977-81 | 1,285 |
| 10. | Frank Emmerich | 1960-63 | 1,252 |

## ALL-TIME LEADING REBOUNDERS
| No. | Player | Years | Rebounds |
|---|---|---|---|
| 1. | Brian O'Conner | 1977-81 | 1,180 |
| 2. | Larry Staverman | 1954-58 | 1,114 |
| 3. | Todd Bender | 1974-78 | 1,010 |
| 4. | Gary Alhrich | 1958-61 | 906 |
| 5. | Rick Hughes | 1992-96 | 897 |
| 6. | John Wendefer | 1968-72 | 895 |
| 7. | Steve Butcher | 1985-89 | 803 |
| 8. | Dan Lenihan | 1980-84 | 727 |
| 9. | Brian Clapp | 1985-89 | 712 |
| 10. | Don Schmidt | 1955-59 | 678 |

## ALL-TIME ASSISTS LEADERS
| No. | Player | Years | Assists |
|---|---|---|---|
| 1. | Jim Nestheide | 1978-82 | 454 |
| 2. | Jim Weyer | 1954-58 | 435 |
| 3. | David Green | 1995-99 | 399 |
| 4. | Ron Dawn | 1974-78 | 375 |
| 5. | Billy Arthur | 1989-92 | 362 |
| 6. | Dave Faust | 1977-81 | 344 |
| 7. | Les Stewart | 1959-62 | 331 |
| 8. | Bob Beck | 1969-73 | 322 |
| 9. | Dan Tieman | 1958-62 | 319 |
| 10. | Mark Klein | 1999-03 | 311 |

## ALL-TIME STEALS LEADERS
| No. | Player | Years | Steals |
|---|---|---|---|
| 1. | Billy Arthur | 1989-92 | 223 |
| 2. | David Green | 1995-99 | 191 |
| 3. | Mark Klein | 1999-03 | 186 |
| 4. | Rick Hughes | 1992-96 | 146 |
| 5. | Tim Cutter | 1989-93 | 124 |
| 6. | Lath Kirk | 1984-89 | 111 |
| 7. | Markel Snyder | 1993-97 | 110 |
| 8. | Andrae Woodard | 2002- | 109 |
| 8. | Adam Gergen | 1995-99 | 109 |
| 10. | Andy Helmers | 1993-97 | 106 |

## ALL-TIME WINNINGEST COACHES
| Coach | Years | Record | Pct. |
|---|---|---|---|
| Charlie Wolf | 5 | 81-67 | .547 |
| Larry Cox | 8 | 96-95 | .503 |
| Jim Weyer | 18 | 208-259 | .445 |
| Gerald Orosz | 4 | 22-37 | .373 |
| Jim Connor | 12 | 133-235 | .361 |
| Terry Connor | 7 | 58-122 | .322 |

# THOMAS MORE COLLEGE
## WOMEN'S BASKETBALL

### ALL-TIME LEADING SCORERS

| No. | Player | Years | Pts. |
|---|---|---|---|
| 1. | Amy Burk | 1995-99 | 1,706 |
| 2. | Kim Prewitt | 1992-95 | 1,501 |
| 3. | Sherry Clinkenbeard | 1994-98 | 1,229 |
| 4. | Holly Roberts | 1998-03 | 1,219 |
| 5. | Shawnta Neely | 1990-94 | 1,188 |
| 6. | Jamie Boehl | 1986-89 | 1,181 |
| 6. | Bridget New | 1998-02 | 1,181 |
| 8. | Joanna Bess | 2000-04 | 1,136 |
| 9. | Kim Byron | 1988-92 | 1,134 |
| 10. | Brenda Simon | 1983-87 | 1,051 |

### ALL-TIME LEADING REBOUNDERS

| No. | Player | Years | Rebounds |
|---|---|---|---|
| 1. | Kim Byron | 1988-92 | 917 |
| 2. | Brenda Simon | 1983-87 | 784 |
| 3. | Bridget New | 1998-02 | 757 |
| 4. | Amy Burk | 1995-99 | 703 |
| 5. | Sherry Clinkenbeard | 1994-98 | 610 |
| 6. | Rita Haneburg | 1974-77 | 567 |
| 7. | Sue Lally | 1981-85 | 511 |
| 8. | Laura Richter | 1986-89 | 469 |
| 9. | Christy Hoffediz | 1995-99 | 454 |
| 10. | Joanna Bess | 2000-04 | 420 |

### ALL-TIME ASSISTS LEADERS

| No. | Player | Years | Assists |
|---|---|---|---|
| 1. | Shannon Galbraith | 1994-98 | 430 |
| 2. | Jamie Boehl | 1986-89 | 354 |
| 3. | Joanna Bess | 2000-04 | 276 |
| 4. | Shawna Kelly | 1998-02 | 273 |
| 5. | Dawn Franzen | 1993-95 | 199 |
| 6. | Nancy West | 1989-91 | 176 |
| 7. | Jodi Schroeder | 2000-04 | 169 |
| 8. | Chris Long | 1988-92 | 167 |
| 9. | Kim Prewitt | 1992-95 | 156 |
| 10. | Michelle Parnell | 1988-91 | 151 |

### ALL-TIME THREE-POINT GOALS (CAREER)

| No. | Player | Years | FGM |
|---|---|---|---|
| 1. | Kim Prewitt | 1992-95 | 242 |
| 2. | Amy Burk | 1995-99 | 144 |
| 3. | Allison Byars | 2001-04 | 133 |
| 4. | Holly Roberts | 1998-03 | 128 |
| 5. | Allison Ramsey | 1994-96 | 105 |
| 6. | Joanna Bess | 2000-04 | 96 |
| 7. | Ashley Will | 1999-03 | 95 |
| 8. | Sherry Clinkenbeard | 1994-98 | 87 |
| 9. | Jodi Schroeder | 2000-04 | 86 |
| 10. | Bethany Vice | 1998-02 | 80 |

*(Source: Thomas More University Sports Information)*

# TRANSYLVANIA UNIVERSITY
## MEN'S BASKETBALL

### TRANSY BY THE NUMBERS
- Overall record: 1,088-906
- 2 first team All Americans
- 1 NAIA National Player of the Year
- 8 Academic All Americans

### FIRST TEAM ALL AMERICANS
Vince Bingham (1998)
Collier Mills (2001)

### ITEMS OF NOTE
- Transy finished its first season in 1903 with a 3-1 record. Among its victims were Georgetown and State College of Kentucky, later to become the University of Kentucky.
- Former governor and baseball commissioner Albert B. "Happy" Chandler captained the 1920-21 Transy team that had a 4-4 record.
- Former Transy head coaches include C.M. Newton and Lee Rose.
- Don Lane spent 26 years as Transy's head coach, retiring after the 2001 season with an all-time record of 509-241.
- Collier Mills was a first-team All-American and National Player of the Year in 2001. Collier's father, Terry, and older brother, Cameron, both played for the University of Kentucky.

### ALL-TIME LEADING SCORERS

| No. | Player | Years | Pts. |
|---|---|---|---|
| 1. | Vince Bingham | 1994-98 | 2,109 |
| 2. | Daniel Swintosky | 1990-95 | 2,000 |
| 3. | Jeff Blandon | 1985-88 | 1,906 |
| 4. | Dale Cosby | 1971-74 | 1,881 |
| 5. | Everett Bass | 1969-72 | 1,875 |
| 6. | Jennis Stidham | 1958-61 | 1,867 |
| 7. | Collier Mills | 1997-01 | 1,774 |
| 8. | Andre Flynn | 1982-85 | 1,670 |
| 9. | Jim Hurley | 1966-68 | 1,628 |
| 10. | Jack Lucas | 1960-63 | 1,611 |

### MISCELLANEOUS STATISTICAL LEADERS (CAREER)

| Category | Player | Years | Total |
|---|---|---|---|
| Rebounds | Everett Bass | 1969-72 | 1,308 |
| Assists | James Clay | 1961-65 | 560 |
| Blocked Shots | John Tyler | 1984-88 | 247 |
| Field Goal Percent | Orbrey Gritton | 1985-89 | 59.6 |
| Three-point Percent | Rod Runyon | 1987-91 | 49.1 |
| Free Throw Percent | Larry Kopczyk | 1977-80 | 85.7 |

### ALL-TIME WINNINGEST COACHES

| Coach | Years | Record | Pct. |
|---|---|---|---|
| Don Lane | 26 | 509-241 | .679 |
| C.M. Newton | 14 | 176-167 | .513 |
| Lee Rose | 8 | 160-57 | .737 |

*(Source: Transylvania University Sports Information)*

# TRANSYLVANIA UNIVERSITY
## WOMEN'S BASKETBALL

### TRANSY BY THE NUMBERS
- Overall record: 495-336
- 6 20-win seasons
- 1 first team All American

### FIRST TEAM ALL AMERICAN
Marcia Webb (1999)

### ITEMS OF NOTE
- From 1902 to 1930, Transy's women's team had a 68-27 record, far superior to their male counterparts.
- The 1922-23 state champion women's team finished with an 8-0 record, allowing opponents only nine field goals the entire season.

- Pat Deacon coached for 17 seasons, guiding the school to its first 20-win season (21-6) in 1986-87.
- Current coach Mark Turner took the Pioneers to the NAIA national tournament for the first time in 1996-97.

## ALL-TIME LEADING SCORERS

| No. | Player | Years | Pts. |
|---|---|---|---|
| 1. | Joretta Carney | 1988-92 | 1,670 |
| 2. | Elaine Russell | 1994-98 | 1,664 |
| 3. | Kathy Hill | 1978-82 | 1,621 |
| 4. | Tari Young | 1999-03 | 1,586 |
| 5. | Ashley Sanders | 1995-99 | 1,574 |
| 6. | Marcia Webb | 1996-99 | 1,570 |
| 7. | Mary Jean Rogers | 1980-84 | 1,320 |
| 8. | Martha Bruner | 1989-93 | 1,270 |
| 9. | Karen Server | 1989-93 | 1,212 |
| 10. | Beth Lucas | 1982-86 | 1,164 |

## MISCELLANEOUS STATISTICAL LEADERS (CAREER)

| Category | Player | Years | Total |
|---|---|---|---|
| Rebounds | Elaine Russell | 1994-98 | 1,085 |
| Assists | Lisa Doyle | 1986-90 | 577 |
| Blocked Shots | Marcia Webb | 1996-99 | 139 |
| Field Goal Percent | Joretta Carney | 1988-92 | 54.8 |
| Three-point Percent | Melissa Butcher | 1991-94 | 43.2 |
| Free Throw Percent | Amber Smith | 1990-93 | 78.5 |

## ALL-TIME WINNINGEST COACHES

| Coach | Years | Record | Pct. |
|---|---|---|---|
| Mark Turner | 18 | 312-175 | .640 |
| Pat Deacon | 16 | 175-146 | .545 |

*(Source: Transylvania University Sports Information)*

# UNION COLLEGE
*MEN'S BASKETBALL*

## UNION COLLEGE BY THE NUMBERS
- Overall Record: 883-871
- 10 20-win seasons

## UNION ALL-AMERICANS
Ernest Trosper (1955)
Bill Trent (1966)
Paul Andrews (1968)
Ken Meibers (1968)
James Anderson (1985)
Nalice Hart (1994)
Chris McKissic (1997)
Durrell Robinson (2001)

## ALL-TIME LEADING SCORERS

| No. | Player | Years | Pts. |
|---|---|---|---|
| 1. | Paul Andrews | 1966-70 | 2,552 |
| 2. | Mike Sammons | 1974-78 | 2,284 |
| 3. | Ken Meibers | 1966-70 | 2,171 |
| 4. | Durkee Davidson | 1976-80 | 2,118 |
| 5. | Ernie Trosper | 1951-55 | 2,040 |
| 6. | Chris McKissic | 1994-98 | 1,923 |
| 7. | Bill Swafford | 1969-73 | 1,752 |
| 8. | Matt Arthur | 1996-00 | 1,569 |
| 9. | Jon Castleberry | 1989-93 | 1,513 |
| 10. | Terry Smallwood | 1968-72 | 1,493 |

## ALL-TIME LEADING REBOUNDERS

| No. | Player | Years | Rebounds |
|---|---|---|---|
| 1. | Ken Meibers | 1966-70 | 1,591 |
| 2. | Paul Andrews | 1966-70 | 1,577 |
| 3. | Bill Trent | 1963-66 | 1,210 |
| 4. | Joe Bramlage | 2002-06 | 1,002 |
| 5. | Steve Jones | 1973-77 | 912 |

## ALL-TIME WINNINGEST COACHES

| Coach | Years | Record | Pct. |
|---|---|---|---|
| Pete Moore | 20 | 253-325 | .438 |
| Brian Evans | 7 | 116-105 | .525 |
| Charlie Fenske | 5 | 94-65 | .591 |

*(Source: Union College Sports Information)*

# UNION COLLEGE
*WOMEN'S BASKETBALL*

## UNION COLLEGE BY THE NUMBERS
- Overall record: 342-442
- 3 20-win seasons

## UNION ALL-AMERICANS
Malissa Hutchins (1988)
Amber Spencer (1993)
Chasity Nunn (2004)

## ALL-TIME LEADING SCORERS

| No. | Player | Years | Pts. |
|---|---|---|---|
| 1. | Amber Spencer | 1989-93 | 2,273 |
| 2. | Michelle Lewallen | 1998-02 | 1,385 |
| 3. | Regina Hubbard | 1981-85 | 1,374 |
| 4. | Amanda Vance | 1999-03 | 1,287 |
| 5. | Leslie Wagner | 1994-98 | 1,228 |
| 6. | Malissa Hutchins | 1984-88 | 1,156 |
| 7. | Chasity Nunn | 2002-04 | 1,089 |
| 8. | Cathy Abbott | 1986-90 | 1,042 |
| 9. | Andrea Whitehead | 2002-present | 967 |
| 10. | Mindy Wynn | 1998-02 | 959 |

## ALL-TIME LEADING REBOUNDERS

| No. | Player | Years | Rebounds |
|---|---|---|---|
| 1. | Amber Spencer | 1989-93 | 1,178 |
| 2. | Michelle Lewallen | 1998-02 | 972 |
| 3. | Shanica Jackson | 1997-99 | 628 |
| 4. | Leslie Wagner | 1994-98 | 605 |
| 5. | Amanda Vance | 1999-03 | 456 |

## ALL-TIME WINNINGEST COACHES

| Coach | Years | Record | Pct. |
|---|---|---|---|
| Debbie D'Anna | 10 | 111-161 | .408 |
| Tim Curry | 6 | 81-80 | .506 |
| Tamra Cash | 5 | 53-70 | .431 |

*(Source: Union College Sports Information)*

# UNIVERSITY OF KENTUCKY
*MEN'S BASKETBALL*

## UK BY THE NUMBERS
- Overall record: 1,926-596-1
- 7 NCAA championships (1948, 1949, 1951, 1958, 1978, 1996, 1998)
- 2 National Invitation Tournament titles (1946, 1976)
- 43 Southeastern Conference titles (1933, 1935, 1937, 1939,

1940, 1942, 1944, 1945, 1946, 1947, 1948, 1949, 1950, 1951, 1952, 1954, 1955, 1957, 1958, 1962, 1964, 1966, 1968, 1969, 1970, 1971, 1972, 1973, 1975, 1977, 1978, 1980, 1982, 1983, 1984, 1986, 1995, 1996, 1998, 2000, 2001, 2003, 2005)
- 25 SEC Tournament championships (1933, 1937, 1939, 1940, 1942, 1944, 1945, 1946, 1947, 1948, 1950, 1952, 1984, 1986, 1992, 1993, 1994, 1995, 1997, 1998, 1999, 2001, 2003, 2004)
- 15 first team All Americans (selected 21 times)
- 87 All SEC players (selected 145 times)
- 8 Olympic Gold Medal winners
- 4 coaches named National Coach of the Year

## FIRST TEAM ALL AMERICANS

- Aggie Sale, forward/center (1932, 1933) – National Player of the Year in 1933; scored the first two points for Adolph Rupp at UK; the Cats' first big-time scorer; Rupp always listed Sale among the best players he ever coached.
- Leroy Edwards, center (1935) – nicknamed "Cowboy," he only played one season at UK, earning National Player of the Year honors; extremely strong, physical player; his 16.3 scoring average was UK's best until Alex Groza showed up a decade later.
- Bob Brannum, center (1944) – only 17 when he earned All-America honors; another tough, bruising player; left UK after his freshman season, joined the military, then returned to UK, only to find himself on the bench; transferred to Michigan State.
- Ralph Beard, guard (1947, 1948, 1949) – fiery competitor and a brilliant player; still regarded as the yardstick by which all UK guards are measured; UK was 130-10 during the four years Beard and Wah Wah Jones played; graced the first cover of Sports Illustrated magazine.
- Alex Groza, center (1947, 1948, 1949) – quick agile center and the first UK player to average 20 points per game; two-time Final Four MVP; left UK as the all-time leading scorer with 1,744 points.
- Bill Spivey, center (1951) – UK's first seven-footer; only played two seasons, but scored 1,213 points and led the 1951 club to the NCAA title; ruled ineligible for his senior season and later banned from the NBA even though he was never found guilty of being involved in the point-shaving scandal of the late 1940s.
- Cliff Hagan, forward/center (1952, 1954) – two-time All-American and one of the few athletes to win championships at the high school, college and pro levels; very graceful, and the owner of a lethal hook shot; teamed with Frank Ramsey to give UK one of the greatest 1-2 combos in college basketball history.
- Johnny Cox, forward (1959) – lean and tough, he helped guide the "Fiddlin' Five" to the 1958 NCAA title; ended his career with 1,461 points and 1,004 rebounds, making him one of only four Wildcats to crack the 1,000 mark in those categories.
- Cotton Nash, forward/center (1964) – one of the most charismatic Wildcats of all-time; also, one of the greatest; three-time All-American, he left as UK's all-time leading scorer with 1,770 points; only Wildcat to average 20 points per game three times; reached the 1,000-point club faster than any other Wildcat, surpassing the mark in his 45th game.
- Dan Issel, center (1970) – UK's all-time leading scorer with 2,138 points; the only Wildcat to average more than 30 points per game for a season; averaged 33.9 points and 13.2 rebounds as a senior; hit for a school record 53 points against Ole Miss; went on to have a brilliant pro career.
- Kyle Macy, guard (1980) – arguably the most popular Wildcat of all-time; a smooth backcourt player with a deadly jumper and nerves of steel; averaged 12.5 points for the powerful 1978 NCAA title club; hit 89 percent of his free throws, a UK all-time best.

- Kenny Walker, forward/center (1986) – two-time All-American and second only to Issel in scoring with 2,080 points; known as "Sky," he was the leading scorer for Joe B. Hall's last UK team and Eddie Sutton's first; twice chosen SEC Player of the Year.
- Jamal Mashburn, forward (1993) – the single most important Wildcat in the post-probation era; could pass, score, rebound and defend; scored 1,843 points despite playing in only 98 games; turned pro after three seasons at UK.
- Tony Delk, guard (1996) – UK's fifth all-time leading scorer with 1,890 points and the school's all-time leader with 283 three-point buckets; had seven treys in UK's championship win over Syracuse in 1996; Final Four and SEC tourney MVP in 1996; once scored 70 points in a high school game.
- Ron Mercer, forward/guard (1997) – easily ranks among the most gifted and multi-dimensional Wildcats of all-time; accounted for 1,013 points despite playing just two seasons; scored 20 points against Syracuse in the 1996 NCAA title game; SEC tourney MVP in 1997.

## OTHER UK PLAYERS WITH RETIRED JERSEYS

- Basil Hayden (1920-22) – UK's first All-American (1921); later coached UK for one season.
- Burgess Carey (1925-26) – earned All-America recognition for his great defensive prowess; captain of the 1925-26 club.
- Carey Spicer (1929-31) – holds the distinction of being Rupp's first All-American player; also earned All-America recognition in 1929 under John Mauer; instrumental in helping bring success to Rupp's up-tempo, fast-breaking style.
- Adolph Rupp (1930-1972) – won 876 games, four NCAA titles, one NIT crown and 27 SEC championships during his 42 years at the helm; four-time National Coach of the Year; seven-time SEC Coach of the Year; inducted into Naismith Hall of Fame in 1969.
- Frenchy DeMoisey (1932-34) – Rupp's third All-American, a prolific scorer and one of the first players to shoot a hook shot; once scored 39 points in 39 minutes during a two-game span; one sportswriter called him a "whirling dervish."
- Mickey Rouse (1938-40) – three-year backcourt starter and the first U.K. player to have his jersey retired; earned All-SEC honors for his play during the 1939-40 season.
- Kenny Rollins (1943, 1947-48) – smooth, unselfish guard and captain of the great "Fabulous Five" club that won the 1948 NCAA title and, later, an Olympic gold medal in London games; once held high-scoring Bob Cousy to three points.
- Wah Wah Jones (1946-49) – Maybe the greatest all-around athlete to ever play at UK; an All-American in basketball and All-SEC in football; also excelled at baseball; a four-time All-SEC and All-SEC tourney selection; a genuine Kentucky legend.
- Cliff Barker (1947-49) – oldest member of the "Fabulous Five," he was a magician with the basketball; it was once said that he could do everything with a basketball except make it talk; spent time in a German POW camp during World War II.
- Frank Ramsey (1951, 1953-54) – probably the most-successful on-court Wildcat of all-time; won an NCAA title at UK and enough NBA championship rings with Boston to open a jewelry store; a slashing, driving player; Rupp once said, "if we win by 30, Frank gets three points; if we win by three, he gets 30."
- Lou Tsioropoulos (1951, 1953-54) – the super strong "Golden Greek" teamed with Hagan and Ramsey to lead UK to its only perfect season (25-0); superb rebound and defender, he once held LSU's Bob Pettit to 17 points, 13 below his average.

- Billy Evans (1952, 1954-55) – a much underrated player and a key contributing member of the unbeaten 1953-54 squad; a member of the 1956 U.S. team that captured the Olympic gold medal; also excelled at tennis.
- Gayle Rose (1952, 1954-55) – two-year backcourt starter, he averaged 6.7 points for the unbeaten 1953-54 team; came back as a senior to help lead UK to a 23-3 record and another SEC title.
- Cawood Ledford (1953-92) – the legendary "Voice of the Wildcats" for 39 years and one of the most-beloved figures in UK history; named Kentucky Sportscaster of the Year 22 times; elected to the Kentucky Athletic Hall of Fame and the Kentucky Journalism Hall of Fame.
- Jerry Bird (1954-56) – two-year starter, he averaged 16.2 points as a senior in one of Kentucky's greatest sports families; brothers Calvin, Rodger and Billy played football at UK, while son Steve was a standout receiver at Eastern Kentucky University.
- Phil Grawmeyer (1954-56) – an outstanding performer whose career was hampered by injuries; a valuable member of that powerful 1953-54 team; grabbed 703 rebounds in just 71 games.
- Bob Burrow (1955-56) – Rupp's first JUCO player; scored 1,023 points and pulled down 823 rebounds in his two seasons at UK; scored 50 points against LSU; his 34 rebounds against Temple remains UK's single-game best.
- Vernon Hatton (1956-58) – will forever be remembered for hitting a last-second 47-footer in the first overtime to keep UK alive in its three-overtime win over Temple; later hit the game-winning bucket against Temple in the NCAA semifinal game; scored 30 against Seattle in the championship game; SEC Sophomore of the Year in 1956.
- Bill Keightley (1962-present) – the man known as "Mr. Wildcat" has been UK's equipment manager for more than 40 years; the last remaining connection to the Rupp Era.
- Louie Dampier (1965-67) – another extremely popular Wildcat, and arguably the finest long-range shooter in school history; averaged 21.1 points for "Rupp's Runts" during the memorable 1965-66 season; shot 50.8 percent from the field and 84.4 percent from the free throw line; went on to become the all-time leading scorer in ABA history.
- Pat Riley (1965-67) – averaged 22 points and 8.9 rebounds for the "Runts"; scored 1,464 points as a Wildcat; played several years in the NBA, then went on to coach the Lakers to four NBA titles in the 1980s; named NBA Coach of the Decade.
- Joe B. Hall (1973-85) – had the daunting task of following Rupp, the only coach most UK fans had ever known; had a record of 297-100 in 13 seasons; led the Cats to one NCAA title and the 1976 NIT crown; played at UK in the late 1940s.
- Kevin Grevey (1973-75) – two-time All-American, his 21.4 career scoring average trails only Issel and Nash; a lefty with a deadly outside jumper; scored 34 points in the 1975 NCAA title game loss to UCLA; played several years in the NBA.
- Jack Givens (1975-78) – another deadeye southpaw, "Goose" blistered Duke with a towering 41-point performance in the 1978 NCAA championship game; UK's third all-time leading scorer with 2,038 points; Final Four MVP in 1978.
- Rick Robey (1975-78) – scored 20 points and grabbed 11 rebounds in the 1978 title game win over Duke; shot 63.5 percent from the field as a senior; led the club in rebounding three times; shot 81 percent from the free throw line during the 1974-75 season.
- Richie Farmer (1989-92) – one of the "Unforgettables" who helped bring UK basketball back after NCAA probation; hit six crucial free throws to seal UK's stunning 100-95 upset of LSU; a true prep legend after leading Clay County High to five straight Sweet 16 appearances, including the 1987 championship.
- Deron Feldhaus (1989-92) – a rugged second-generation Wildcat who blended a hard-nosed inside game with a soft outside shooting touch; averaged 14.4 points on Rick Pitino's first UK team; had 13 rebounds against LSU and Shaquille O'Neal; his father, Allen, played at UK in the early 1960s.
- John Pelphrey (1989-92) – a remarkably intelligent and shrewd player who used his high basketball IQ to beat more naturally gifted players; scored 16 points in the classic loss against Duke in an NCAA regional final; hit 160 three-pointers during his career; also had 327 assists and 173 steals.
- Sean Woods (1990-92) – a fierce competitor best remembered for sinking a daring bank shot over Duke's Christian Laettner that gave UK a one-point lead with 2 seconds to play in the regional final; led the SEC in assists as a sophomore; had 21 points and nine assists in the classic against Duke; finished his career with 482 assists.
- Rick Pitino (1990-97) – brought UK out of the darkness imposed by NCAA sanctions; posted a 219-50 record at UK; led the powerful 1995-96 club to the NCAA title; came back the nest year, and despite an injury to Derek Anderson, led UK to the title game, losing in overtime to Arizona; left UK to coach the Boston Celtics.

# ITEMS OF NOTE

- UK (then State College) recorded its first win when it defeated Lexington YMCA 11-10 on Feb. 18, 1903.
- Athletic teams were officially christened "Wildcats" in 1909.
- UK claimed its first championship in 1921 by defeating Tulane, Mercer, Mississippi A&M and Georgia in the Southern Intercollegiate Athletic Association title game. That year, Basil Hayden became UK's first All-American.
- Alumni Gym opened on Dec. 13, 1924. Critics called it a "white elephant."
- Adolph Rupp is named UK coach on March 23, 1930.
- Ralph Beard's free throw gives UK a 46-45 victory over Rhode Island in the NIT championship game.
- Members of the 1947-48 NCAA title team are nicknamed the "Fabulous Five." They are Ralph Beard, Wah Wah Jones, Alex Groza, Kenny Rollins and Cliff Barker. That group would later help the U.S. win the gold medal in the 1948 Olympic Games held in London.
- In 1949, UK captures its second consecutive NCAA title by defeating Oklahoma A&M 46-36 in Seattle.
- Memorial Coliseum opens on Dec. 1, 1950. Critics call it a "white elephant."
- UK wins the 1951 NCAA title by stopping Kansas State 68-58 in the final game.
- UK is suspended by the NCAA for the 1952-53 season.
- Cawood Ledford broadcasts his first UK game on Dec. 5, 1953.
- UK wins the 1958 NCAA championship by beating Seattle 84-72 in Louisville.
- UK beats Tennessee 69-66 on Jan. 18, 1969 to become the first school to win 1,000 games.
- On June 9, 1969, Tom Payne becomes the first black player to sign with UK.
- Adolph Rupp coaches his last game at UK on March 18, 1972, a 73-54 loss to Florida State in the NCAA tournament.
- Joe B. Hall coaches his first game at UK, a 75-66 win at Michigan State.
- UK falls to UCLA 92-85 in the 1975 NCAA championship game.
- UK beats NC-Charlotte 71-67 to win the 1976 NIT title.
- On Dec. 10, 1977, as top-ranked UK is defeating Kansas on "Adolph Rupp Night" in Lawrence, Kansas, Rupp dies in Lexington.
- Jack "Goose" Givens erupts for 41 points to lead UK to a 94-88 victory over Duke in the 1978 NCAA championship game.

- Joe B. Hall announces his retirement on March 22, 1985.
- On Nov. 22, 1985, Eddie Sutton coaches his first game at UK, a 77-58 win over Northwestern (La.) State.
- On March 10, 1989, in the wake of an NCAA investigation, Eddie Sutton resigns as UK coach. Two months later, the NCAA places UK's basketball program on probation.
- Rick Pitino is named UK coach on June 2, 1989.
- On Nov. 28, 1989, Rick Pitino wins his first game at UK, a 76-73 victory over Ohio University.
- Rick Pitino makes history by naming Bernadette Locke an assistant on his coaching staff.
- On March 28, 1992, in what many call the greatest NCAA Tournament game ever played, UK loses to Duke on a last-second shot by Christian Laettner. It is also Cawood Ledford's last game as "Voice of the Wildcats."
- UK clips Syracuse 76-67 to win the 1996 NCAA championship.
- UK returns to the NCAA championship game in 1997, losing to Arizona 84-79 in the final game. Two months later, Rick Pitino resigns as UK coach.
- On May 12, 1997, C.M. Newton introduces Orlando "Tubby" Smith as UK's new coach.
- Tubby Smith wins his first game at UK, defeating ex-Cat Kyle Macy's Morehead State squad 88-49.
- UK's "Comeback Cats" rally from a 10-point halftime deficit to defeat Utah 78-69 in the 1998 NCAA championship game.
- After a long illness, Cawood Ledford dies at his home in Harlan on Sept. 5, 2001.

## ALL-TIME LEADING SCORERS

| No. | Player | Years | Games | Pts. | Avg. |
|---|---|---|---|---|---|
| 1. | Dan Issel | 1968-70 | 83 | 2,138 | 25.8 |
| 2. | Kenny Walker | 1983-86 | 132 | 2,080 | 15.8 |
| 3. | Jack Givens | 1975-78 | 123 | 2,038 | 16.6 |
| 4. | Keith Bogans | 2000-03 | 135 | 1,923 | 14.2 |
| 5. | Tony Delk | 1993-96 | 133 | 1,890 | 14.2 |
| 6. | Jamal Mashburn | 1991-93 | 98 | 1,843 | 18.8 |
| 7. | Kevin Grevey | 1973-75 | 84 | 1,801 | 21.4 |
| 8. | Tayshaun Prince | 1999-02 | 135 | 1,775 | 13.1 |
| 9. | Cotton Nash | 1962-64 | 78 | 1,770 | 22.6 |
| 10. | Alex Groza | 1945-49 | 120 | 1,744 | 14.4 |

## ALL-TIME CAREER SCORING AVERAGES

| No. | Player | Years | Games | Pts. | Avg. |
|---|---|---|---|---|---|
| 1. | Dan Issel | 1968-70 | 83 | 2,138 | 25.8 |
| 2. | Cotton Nash | 1962-64 | 78 | 1,770 | 22.7 |
| 3. | Kevin Grevey | 1973-75 | 84 | 1,801 | 21.4 |
| 4. | Bob Burrow | 1955-56 | 51 | 1,023 | 20.1 |
| 5. | Louie Dampier | 1965-67 | 80 | 1,575 | 19.7 |
| 6. | Bill Spivey | 1950-51 | 63 | 1,213 | 19.3 |

| 7. | Cliff Hagan | 1951-54 | 77 | 1,475 | 19.2 |
|---|---|---|---|---|---|
| 8. | Jamal Mashburn | 1990-93 | 98 | 1,843 | 18.8 |
| 9. | Mike Casey | 1968-71 | 82 | 1,535 | 18.7 |
| 10. | Pat Riley | 1965-67 | 80 | 1,464 | 18.3 |

## ALL-TIME LEADING REBOUNDERS

| No. | Player | Years | Rebounds | Avg. |
|---|---|---|---|---|
| 1. | Dan Issel | 1968-70 | 1,078 | 12.9 |
| 2. | Frank Ramsey | 1951-54 | 1,038 | 11.4 |
| 3. | Cliff Hagan | 1951-54 | 1,035 | 13.4 |
| 4. | Johnny Cox | 1957-59 | 1,004 | 12.0 |
| 5. | Cotton Nash | 1962-64 | 962 | 12.3 |
| 6. | Kenny Walker | 1983-86 | 942 | 7.1 |
| 7. | Chuck Hayes | 2002-05 | 910 | 6.8 |
| 8. | Sam Bowie | 1980-84 | 843 | 8.8 |
| 9. | Rick Robey | 1975-78 | 838 | 8.0 |
| 10. | Bob Burrow | 1955-56 | 823 | 16.1 |

## ALL-TIME ASSISTS LEADERS

| No. | Player | Years | Assists | Avg. |
|---|---|---|---|---|
| 1. | Dirk Minniefield | 1980-83 | 646 | 5.3 |
| 2. | Anthony Epps | 1994-97 | 544 | 3.9 |
| 3. | Roger Harden | 1983-86 | 498 | 4.1 |
| 4. | Wayne Turner | 1996-99 | 494 | 3.3 |
| 5. | Sean Woods | 1990-92 | 482 | 5.3 |
| 6. | Kyle Macy | 1978-80 | 470 | 4.8 |
| 7. | Cliff Hawkins | 2001-04 | 468 | 3.7 |
| 8. | Ed Davender | 1985-88 | 436 | 3.4 |
| 9. | Travis Ford | 1992-94 | 428 | 4.3 |
| 10. | Saul Smith | 1998-01 | 363 | 2.5 |

## ALL-TIME WINNINGEST COACHES

| Coach | Years | Record | Pct. |
|---|---|---|---|
| Adolph Rupp | 42 | 876-190 | .822 |
| Joe B. Hall | 13 | 297-100 | .748 |
| Rick Pitino | 8 | 219-50 | .814 |
| Tubby Smith | 9 | 241-71 | .772 |

# UNIVERSITY OF KENTUCKY
## WOMEN'S BASKETBALL

### UK BY THE NUMBERS
- Overall record: 557-419
- 1 NWIT championship (1990)
- 1 Southeastern Conference championship (1982)
- 4 Top 20 finishes (1980, 1981, 1982, 1983)

UK coach Mickie DeMoss watched from the sidelines during the UK vs. Chattanooga, first round Women's NCAA basketball March 18, 2006
*Source: Janet Worne, Lexington Herald Leader*

- 5 All America players (selected 7 times)

## UK ALL AMERICANS

- Pam Browning, center (1977) – scored 1,598 points; twice hit for a career high 35 points.
- Maria Donhoff, forward (1978) – ended with 1,187 points; scored 20 points in her first varsity game.
- Valerie Still, center (1981, 1982, 1983) – UK's all-time leading scorer (2,763 points), men or women; also the school's top rebounder with 1,525; scored more than 30 in a game on 23 occasions.
- Kristi Cushenberry, guard (1990) – ninth all-time leading scorer with 1,358 points; hit a school-best 39.7 percent of her three-point attempts.
- Vanessa Foster-Sutton, center (1990) – twice led the team in rebounding; shot 59 percent from the field in 1990.

## ITEMS OF NOTE

- UK women played their first game on Feb. 21, 1903.
- The 1924 UK women went 10-0, winning the championship of the South.
- After a 50-year hiatus, women began playing again at UK in the 1970s, reaching varsity status in 1974. Sue Feamster was the first coach.
- Debbie Yow took over as coach in 1976.
- In 1979, UK upset second-ranked Tennessee 66-64 in front of 4,500 fans in Memorial Coliseum.
- Terry Hall was named head coach in 1980.
- UK broke the national attendance record for a women's collegiate game when 10,622 fans saw the Cats beat Old Dominion 80-66 in Memorial Coliseum on Feb. 5, 1983.
- Sharon Fanning became the new head coach in 1987.
- The 1990 club finished with a 23-8 record, winning three tournament titles, including the NWIT.
- In 1995, Bernadette Locke-Mattox became the fifth UK women's coach.
- In 2003, Valerie Still became the first Lady Cat to have her jersey retired. Still is married to ex-Wildcat Rob Lock. Her brother, Art, was an All-American for the football Wildcats; Long-time Tennessee assistant coach Mickie DeMoss named head coach at UK.
- Former Cat guard Stacey Reed is married to former UK guard Jeff Sheppard.

## ALL-TIME LEADING SCORERS

| No. | Player | Years | Games | Pts. | Avg. |
|-----|--------|-------|-------|------|------|
| 1. | Valerie Still | 1979-83 | 119 | 2,763 | 23.2 |
| 2. | Leslie Nichols | 1982-86 | 111 | 1,797 | 18.2 |
| 3. | Pam Browning | 1974-78 | 107 | 1,598 | 14.9 |
| 4. | Sara Potts | 2002-05 | 117 | 1,563 | 13.4 |
| 5. | Liz Lukschu | 1977-81 | 119 | 1,488 | 12.5 |
| 6. | SeSe Helm | 2000-04 | 108 | 1,487 | 13.8 |
| 7. | Stacey Reed | 1991-95 | 114 | 1,482 | 13.0 |
| 8. | Tiffany Wait | 1995-00 | 122 | 1,445 | 11.8 |
| 9. | Jodie Whitaker | 1985-89 | 111 | 1,433 | 12.9 |
| 10. | Kristi Cushenberry | 1988-92 | 118 | 1,358 | 11.5 |

## ALL-TIME CAREER SCORING AVERAGES

| No. | Player | Years | Games | Pts. | Avg. |
|-----|--------|-------|-------|------|------|
| 1. | Valerie Still | 1979-83 | 119 | 2,763 | 23.2 |
| 2. | Leslie Nichols | 1982-86 | 111 | 1,797 | 18.2 |
| 3. | Pam Browning | 1974-78 | 107 | 1,598 | 14.9 |
| 4. | Belitta Croley | 1984-88 | 94 | 1,339 | 14.2 |
| 5. | SeSe Helm | 2000-04 | 108 | 1,487 | 13.8 |

## ALL-TIME LEADING REBOUNDERS

| No. | Player | Years | Rebounds | Avg. |
|-----|--------|-------|----------|------|
| 1. | Valerie Still | 1979-83 | 1,525 | 12.8 |
| 2. | Leslie Nichols | 1982-86 | 877 | 7.9 |
| 3. | Debra Oden | 1976-80 | 785 | 7.2 |
| 4. | Kim Denkins | 1994-98 | 762 | 7.1 |
| 5. | Liz Lukschu | 1977-81 | 722 | 6.1 |
| 6. | LaTonya McDole | 1998-02 | 711 | 6.1 |
| 7. | Jocelyn Mills | 1989-93 | 703 | 6.8 |
| 8. | Maria Donhoff | 1977-81 | 692 | 5.7 |
| 9. | SeSe Helm | 2000-04 | 672 | 6.2 |
| 10. | Karen Mosely | 1982-86 | 633 | 5.8 |

## ALL-TIME ASSISTS LEADERS

| No. | Player | Years | Assists | Avg. |
|-----|--------|-------|---------|------|
| 1. | Patty Jo Hedges | 1980-83 | 731 | 6.1 |
| 2. | Sandy Harding | 1983-87 | 706 | 6.4 |
| 3. | Jodie Whitaker | 1985-89 | 464 | 4.2 |
| 4. | Lea Wise | 1979-83 | 464 | 3.7 |
| 5. | Stacey Reed | 1991-95 | 442 | 3.9 |
| 6. | Rita Adams | 1999-03 | 400 | 3.6 |
| 7. | Tracye Davis | 1987-91 | 367 | 3.2 |
| 8. | Tiffany Wait | 1995-00 | 339 | 2.8 |
| 9. | Lisa Collins | 1980-84 | 325 | 2.8 |
| 10. | Leslie Nichols | 1982-86 | 323 | 2.9 |

## ALL-TIME WINNINGEST COACHES (BY PERCENTAGE)

| Coach | Years | Record | Pct. |
|-------|-------|--------|------|
| Terry Hall | 7 | 138-66 | .676 |
| Debbie Yow | 4 | 79-40 | .664 |
| Sue Feamster | 5 | 64-39 | .621 |
| Sharon Fanning | 8 | 134-97 | .580 |
| Bernadette Mattox | 8 | 91-135 | .402 |

*(Source: University of Kentucky University Sports Information)*

# UNIVERSITY OF LOUISVILLE
*MEN'S BASKETBALL*

## U OF L BY THE NUMBERS

- Overall record: 1,505-806
- 2 NCAA championships (1980, 1986)
- 1 NIT championship (1956)
- 32 NCAA appearances (1951, 1959, 1961, 1964, 1967, 1968, 1972, 1974, 1975, 1977, 1978, 1979, 1980, 1981, 1982, 1983, 1984, 1986, 1988, 1989, 1990, 1992, 1993, 1994, 1995, 1996, 1997, 1999, 2000, 2003, 2004, 2005)
- 1 NAIB title (1948)
- 1 Conference USA championship (2005)
- 5 first team All Americans
- 1 Final Four Most Valuable Player

## FIRST TEAM ALL AMERICANS

- Charlie Tyra, center (1957) – scored 1,728 points and grabbed 1,617 rebounds; led the 1956 Cardinals to the NIT championship.
- Wes Unseld, center (1967, 1968) – earned All-America recognition all three years at U of L; twice had 30 rebounds in a game; only player to be named NBA MVP and Rookie of the Year in the same season.
- Darrell Griffith, guard (1980) – arguably the greatest U of L player of all-time; an incredible athlete with out-of-this-world leaping ability; carried the Cards to the 1980 NCAA title.
- Pervis Ellison, center (1989) – made his mark as a freshman by helping the Cards capture the 1986 NCAA crown; finished his career with 2,143 points.
- Clifford Rozier, center (1994) – averaged 17 points per game and 11 rebounds as a Cardinal.

## OTHER U OF L ALL AMERICANS
Don Goldstein, forward (1959)

John Turner, forward (1961)
Butch Beard, guard (1969)
Jim Price, guard (1972)
Junior Bridgeman, guard (1975)
Allen Murphy, guard (1975)
Phil Bond, guard (1976)
Wesley Cox, forward (1977)
Rick Wilson, guard (1978)
Lancaster Gordon, guard (1984)
DeJuan Wheat, guard (1997)
Reece Gaines, guard (2003)

## ALL-TIME LEADING SCORERS

| No. | Player | Years | Games | Pts. | Avg. |
|-----|--------|-------|-------|------|------|
| 1. | Darrell Griffith | 1976-80 | 126 | 2,333 | 18.5 |
| 2. | DeJuan Wheat | 1993-97 | 136 | 2,183 | 16.1 |
| 3. | Pervis Ellison | 1985-89 | 136 | 2,143 | 15.8 |
| 4. | Reece Gaines | 1999-03 | 125 | 1,945 | 15.6 |
| 5. | Milt Wagner | 1981-86 | 144 | 1,836 | 12.8 |
| 6. | Derek Smith | 1978-82 | 131 | 1,826 | 13.9 |
| 7. | LaBradford Smith | 1987-91 | 133 | 1,806 | 13.6 |
| 8. | Charlie Tyra | 1953-57 | 95 | 1,728 | 18.2 |
| 9. | Herbert Crook | 1984-88 | 142 | 1,723 | 12.1 |
| 10. | Wes Unseld | 1965-68 | 82 | 1,686 | 20.6 |

## ALL-TIME CAREER SCORING AVERAGES

| No. | Player | Years | Games | Pts. | Avg. |
|-----|--------|-------|-------|------|------|
| 1. | Wes Unseld | 1965-68 | 82 | 1,686 | 20.6 |
| 2. | Butch Beard | 1966-69 | 83 | 1,580 | 19.0 |
| 3. | Darrell Griffith | 1976-80 | 126 | 2,333 | 18.5 |
| 4. | Charlie Tyra | 1953-57 | 95 | 1,728 | 18.2 |
| 4. | John Reuther | 1962-67 | 74 | 1,346 | 18.2 |
| 6. | Jim Price | 1969-72 | 87 | 1,490 | 17.1 |
| 7. | Clifford Rozier | 1992-94 | 65 | 1,104 | 17.0 |
| 8. | John Turner | 1958-61 | 86 | 1,451 | 16.9 |
| 9. | Allen Murphy | 1972-75 | 89 | 1,453 | 16.4 |
| 10. | Mike Grosso | 1968-70 | 59 | 958 | 16.2 |

## ALL-TIME LEADING REBOUNDERS

| No. | Player | Years | Rebounds | Avg. |
|-----|--------|-------|----------|------|
| 1. | Charlie Tyra | 1953-57 | 1,617 | 17.0 |
| 2. | Wes Unseld | 1965-68 | 1,551 | 18.9 |
| 3. | Pervis Ellison | 1985-89 | 1,149 | 8.4 |
| 4. | Fred Sawyer | 1958-61 | 1,040 | 12.0 |
| 5. | Rodney McCray | 1979-84 | 1,029 | 7.6 |
| 6. | Billy Thompson | 1982-86 | 930 | 6.5 |
| 7. | John Turner | 1958-61 | 919 | 10.6 |
| 8. | Derek Smith | 1978-82 | 884 | 6.7 |
| 9. | Herbert Crook | 1984-88 | 877 | 6.2 |
| 10. | Don Goldstein | 1956-59 | 868 | 10.7 |

## ALL-TIME ASSISTS LEADERS

| No. | Player | Years | Assists | Avg. |
|-----|--------|-------|---------|------|
| 1. | LaBradford Smith | 1987-91 | 713 | 5.4 |
| 2. | Phil Bond | 1972-77 | 528 | n/a |
| 3. | DeJuan Wheat | 1993-97 | 498 | 3.7 |
| 4. | Keith Williams | 1986-90 | 482 | n/a |
| 5. | Reece Gaines | 1999-03 | 475 | 3.8 |
| 6. | Billy Thompson | 1982-86 | 459 | 3.2 |
| 7. | Milt Wagner | 1981-86 | 432 | 3.0 |
| 8. | Rick Wilson | 1974-78 | 394 | n/a |
| 9. | Everick Sullivan | 1988-92 | 393 | n/a |
| 10. | Darrell Griffith | 1976-80 | 383 | 3.0 |

## ALL-TIME DUNKS LEADERS

| No. | Player | Years | Dunks |
|-----|--------|-------|-------|
| 1. | Pervis Ellison | 1985-89 | 162 |
| 2. | Alvin Sims | 1993-96 | 123 |
| 3. | Darrell Griffith | 1976-80 | 117 |

| 3. | Cornelius Holden | 1988-92 | 117 |
|----|------------------|---------|-----|
| 5. | Rodney McCray | 1979-83 | 103 |

## ALL-TIME WINNINGEST COACHES

| Coach | Years | Record | Pct. |
|-------|-------|--------|------|
| Denny Crum | 30 | 675-295 | .696 |
| Peck Hickman | 23 | 443-183 | .708 |
| Rick Pitino | 5 | 118-48 | .710 |
| John Dromo | 4 | 68-23 | .747 |

*(Source: University of Louisville Sports Information)*

# WESTERN KENTUCKY UNIVERSITY
*MEN'S BASKETBALL*

## WKU BY THE NUMBERS

- Overall record: 1,530-754
- 19 Ohio Valley Conference titles (1949, 1950, 1952, 1954, 1955, 1956, 1957, 1960, 1961, 1962, 1966, 1967, 1970, 1971, 1972, 1976, 1980, 1981, 1982)
- 9 OVC Tournament championships (1949, 1952, 1953, 1954, 1966, 1967, 1976, 1978, 1981)
- 6 Sun Belt Conference titles (1987, 1994, 1995, 2001, 2002, 2003)
- 5 Sun Belt Tournament championships (1993, 1995, 2001, 2002, 2003)
- 19 NCAA Tournament appearances (1940, 1960, 1962, 1966, 1967, 1970, 1971, 1976, 1978, 1980, 1981, 1986, 1987, 1993, 1994, 1995, 2001, 2002, 2003)
- 13 National Invitation Tournament appearances (1942, 1943, 1948, 1949, 1950, 1952, 1953, 1954, 1965, 1982, 1992, 2005, 2006)
- 27 All Americans (selected 35 times)

## WKU ALL AMERICANS

William "Red" McCrocklin, center (1938)
Carlisle Towery, center (1940, 1941)
Oran McKinney, center (1943)
Dee Gibson, guard (1948)
Don Ray, forward (1948)
Odie Spears, forward (1948)
Bob Lavoy, center (1949, 1950)
John Oldham, guard (1949)
Buddy Cate, forward (1950)
Rip Gish, forward/center (1951)
Tom Marshall, forward (1953, 1954)
Art Spoelstra, center (1953)
Ralph Crosthwaite, center (1958)
Bobby Rascoe, guard (1962)
Darel Carrier, guard (1964)
Clem Haskins, forward (1965, 1966, 1967)
Jim McDaniels, center (1969, 1970, 1971)
Johnny Britt, guard (1976)
Craig McCormick, center (1982)
Kannard Johnson, forward (1984)
Tellis Frank, forward (1987)
Brett NcNeal, guard (1989)
Darnell Mee, guard (1993)
Chris Robinson, forward/guard (1996)
Chris Marcus, center (2001, 2002)
Nigel Dixon, center (2004)
Mike Wells, guard (2004)

## ITEMS OF NOTE

- Legendary coach Ed Diddle won his first game at WKU in 1922 when his Hilltoppers posted a 103-7 victory. Diddle also served as WKU football coach for seven seasons (1922-28), compiling a 38-24-2 won-loss record.

- The first Hilltoppers to have their jerseys retired were Ed Diddle, Clem Haskins, Tom Marshall, Jim McDaniels, John Oldham and Carlisle Towery.
- Dr. Kelly Thompson, Ed Diddle, L.T. Smith, Ted Hornback, Nick Denes, Dr. Dero Downing and John Oldham were elected to the Ohio Valley Conference Hall of Fame.
- Clem Haskins, Tom Marshall and Jim McDaniels were named to the Ohio Valley Conference Half-Century team.
- Clem Haskins, Wayne Chapman, Jim McDaniels and Johnny Britt were all chosen OVC Player of the Year.
- Were it not for a highly controversial officiating call that resulted in a loss to Michigan, the Hilltoppers would have met UK's Rupp's Runts in the Mideast Regional final of the 1966 NCAA Tournament. Western led Michigan by one point when the ball was tied up between Cazzie Russell and WKU's Greg Jones with one second to play. This was before the change of possession arrow rule, so a jump ball was called. Jones was whistled for a foul as he jumped for the tip and Russell hit both ends of a one-and-one with no time left on the clock to give Michigan a 79-78 win.
- Wayne Chapman transferred to WKU after playing on the University of Kentucky freshman team with Pat Riley and Louie Dampier.
- Led by Jim McDaniels' 35 points and 11 rebounds, the Hilltoppers ripped UK 107-83 when the two clubs finally clashed in the 1971 NCAA tourney.
- Wes Strader served as radio play-by-play man for Hilltopper basketball and football for 36 years (1964-2000).

## ALL-TIME LEADING SCORERS

| No. | Player | Years | Games | Pts. | Avg. |
|-----|--------|-------|-------|------|------|
| 1. | Jim McDaniels | 1968-71 | 81 | 2,238 | 27.6 |
| 2. | Ralph Crosthwaite | 1955-59 | 103 | 2,076 | 20.1 |
| 3. | Tom Marshall | 1950-54 | 100 | 1,909 | 19.1 |
| 4. | Brett McNeal | 1985-89 | 120 | 1,856 | 15.5 |
| 5. | Johnny Britt | 1972-76 | 103 | 1,765 | 17.1 |
| 6. | Kannard Johnson | 1983-87 | 126 | 1,738 | 13.8 |
| 7. | Clem Haskins | 1964-67 | 76 | 1,680 | 22.1 |
| 8. | Bobby Rascoe | 1959-62 | 80 | 1,670 | 20.9 |
| 9. | Chris Robinson | 1992-96 | 120 | 1,656 | 13.0 |
| 10. | Art Spoelstra | 1951-54 | 92 | 1,510 | 16.4 |

## ALL-TIME CAREER SCORING AVERAGES

| No. | Player | Years | Games | Pts. | Avg. |
|-----|--------|-------|-------|------|------|
| 1. | Jim McDaniels | 1968-71 | 81 | 2,238 | 27.6 |
| 2. | Clem Haskins | 1964-67 | 76 | 1,680 | 22.1 |
| 3. | Bobby Rascoe | 1959-62 | 80 | 1,670 | 20.9 |
| 4. | Ralph Crosthwaite | 1955-59 | 103 | 2,076 | 20.1 |
| 5. | Darel Carrier | 1961-64 | 69 | 1,318 | 19.1 |
| 5. | Tom Marshall | 1950-54 | 100 | 1,909 | 19.1 |
| 7. | Johnny Britt | 1972-76 | 103 | 1,765 | 17.1 |
| 8. | Charlie Osborne | 1958-61 | 80 | 1,359 | 17.0 |
| 9. | Art Spoelstra | 1951-54 | 92 | 1,510 | 16.4 |
| 10. | Wayne Chapman | 1965-68 | 79 | 1,292 | 16.3 |

## ALL-TIME LEADING REBOUNDERS

| No. | Player | Years | Rebounds | Avg. |
|-----|--------|-------|----------|------|
| 1. | Ralph Crosthwaite | 1954-58 | 1,309 | 12.7 |
| 2. | Tom Marshall | 1950-54 | 1,225 | 12.3 |
| 3. | Jim McDaniels | 1968-71 | 1,118 | 13.8 |
| 4. | Art Spoelstra | 1951-54 | 1,043 | 11.3 |
| 5. | Bob Daniels | 1953-57 | 964 | 9.9 |
| 6. | Greg Smith | 1965-68 | 932 | 11.8 |
| 7. | Harry Todd | 1959-62 | 924 | 11.6 |
| 8. | Dwight Smith | 1964-67 | 856 | 11.0 |
| 9. | Kannard Johnson | 1983-87 | 840 | 6.7 |
| 10. | Clem Haskins | 1964-67 | 809 | 10.6 |

## ALL-TIME STEALS LEADERS

| No. | Player | Years | Steals |
|-----|--------|-------|--------|
| 1. | Darnell Mee | 1990-93 | 259 |
| 2. | Chris Robinson | 1992-96 | 203 |
| 3. | Brett McNeal | 1985-89 | 148 |
| 4. | Darius Hall | 1991-95 | 146 |
| 5. | Darrin Horn | 1991-95 | 139 |
| 6. | Mark Bell | 1991-93 | 135 |
| 7. | Bobby Jones | 1980-84 | 134 |
| 8. | Derek Robinson | 1998-02 | 124 |
| 9. | Joe Harney | 1995-99 | 121 |
| 10. | Patrick Sparks | 2001-03 | 119 |

## ALL-TIME WINNINGEST COACHES

| Coach | Years | Record | Pct. |
|-------|-------|--------|------|
| Ed Diddle | 42 | 759-302 | .715 |
| John Oldham | 7 | 146-41 | .781 |
| Jim Richards | 7 | 102-84 | .548 |
| Clem Haskins | 6 | 101-73 | .580 |
| Dennis Felton | 5 | 100-54 | .649 |

*(Source: Western Kentucky University Sports Information)*

# WESTERN KENTUCKY UNIVERSITY
## *WOMEN'S BASKETBALL*

### WKU BY THE NUMBERS
- Overall record: 720-351
- 1 National Runner-Up (1992)
- 3 NCAA Final Fours (1985, 1986, 1992)
- 3 NCAA Sweet 16s (1991, 1993, 1995)
- 15 NCAA Tournament appearances (1985, 1986, 1987, 1988, 1989, 1990, 1991, 1992, 1993, 1994, 1995, 1997, 1998, 2000, 2003)
- 7 Sun Belt titles (1989, 1990, 1992, 1993, 1997, 2003, 2004)
- 8 Sun Belt Tournament championships
- 5 NWIT appearances
- 1 KWIC championship (1929)
- 3 First Team All Americans

### WKU FIRST TEAM ALL AMERICANS
Lillie Mason, forward (1986)
Clemette Haskins, guard (1987)
Tandreia Green, forward (1989)

### ITEMS OF NOTE
- The Lady Toppers appeared in 11 consecutive NCAA Tournaments (1985-1995).
- The Lady Toppers have appeared in 41 different invitational tournaments, winning 15 while posting a 63-27 record overall.
- In 2000, Lillie Mason became the first Lady Topper to have her jersey retired.
- The Lady Toppers won their first game in 1914, beating Logan College 12-8. Win number 600 came on Dec. 4, 2000 with a 99-80 win over Tennessee Tech.
- Hall of Fame men's coach Ed Diddle served as WKU women's coach for two seasons, finishing with an 11-6 record.
- Paul Sanderford posted a career record of 365-120, leading his teams to post-season play in 14 of his 15 years at the helm.

### ALL-TIME LEADING SCORERS

| No. | Player | Years | Games | Pts. | Avg. |
|-----|--------|-------|-------|------|------|
| 1. | Lillie Mason | 1982-86 | 125 | 2,262 | 18.1 |
| 2. | ShaRae Mansfield | 1998-01 | 127 | 1,804 | 14.2 |
| 3. | Kami Thomas | 1983-86 | 128 | 1,796 | 14.0 |
| 4. | Tandreia Green | 1987-90 | 125 | 1,781 | 14.2 |
| 5. | Clemette Haskins | 1984-87 | 128 | 1,762 | 13.8 |
| 6. | Natalie Powers | 1998-02 | 117 | 1,641 | 14.0 |

| 7. | Kim Pehlke | 1989-92 | 127 | 1,487 | 11.7 |
| 8. | Beth (Lane) Blanton | 1976-79 | 116 | 1,446 | 12.5 |
| 9. | Brenda Chapman | 1975-78 | 94 | 1,436 | 15.3 |
| 10. | Shae Lunsford | 1996-99 | 118 | 1,386 | 11.7 |

| 7. | Traci Patton | 1985-88 | 744 | n/a |
| 8. | Dianne Depp | 1981-84 | 735 | 7.2 |
| 9. | Brigette Combs | 1986-89 | 717 | n/a |
| 10. | Gina Brown | 1982-85 | 712 | 5.8 |

## ALL-TIME CAREER SCORING AVERAGES

| No. | Player | Years | Games | Pts. | Avg. |
|---|---|---|---|---|---|
| 1. | Lillie Mason | 1982-86 | 125 | 2,262 | 18.1 |
| 2. | Pam Hart | 1976-79 | 83 | 1,325 | 16.6 |
| 3. | Leslie Logsdon | 2001- | 92 | 1,373 | 14.9 |
| 4. | ShaRae Mansfield | 1998-01 | 127 | 1,804 | 14.2 |
| 4. | Tandreia Green | 1987-90 | 125 | 1,781 | 14.2 |
| 6. | Natalie Powers | 1998-02 | 117 | 1,641 | 14.0 |
| 6. | Kami Thomas | 1983-86 | 128 | 1,796 | 14.0 |
| 8. | Clemette Haskins | 1984-87 | 128 | 1,762 | 13.8 |
| 9. | Laurie Heltsley | 1979-82 | 88 | 1,153 | 13.1 |
| 10. | Beth (Lane) Blanton | 1976-79 | 116 | 1,446 | 12.5 |

## ALL-TIME ASSISTS LEADERS

| No. | Player | Years | Assists |
|---|---|---|---|
| 1. | Clemette Haskins | 1984-87 | 731 |
| 2. | Renee Westmoreland | 1990-93 | 477 |
| 3. | Dawn Warner | 1993-96 | 440 |
| 4. | Kelly Smith | 1988-91 | 398 |
| 5. | Camryn Whitaker | 2000- | 388 |
| 6. | Kim Pehlke | 1989-92 | 374 |
| 7. | Debbie O'Connell | 1986-89 | 348 |
| 8. | Jaime Walz | 1997-00 | 336 |
| 9. | Kami Thomas | 1983-86 | 335 |
| 10. | Kristina Covington | 1998-03 | 299 |

## ALL-TIME LEADING REBOUNDERS

| No. | Player | Years | Rebounds | Avg. |
|---|---|---|---|---|
| 1. | Lillie Mason | 1982-86 | 1,012 | 8.1 |
| 2. | ShaRae Mansfield | 1998-01 | 1,000 | 7.9 |
| 3. | Shea Lunsford | 1996-99 | 883 | 7.5 |
| 4. | Tandreia Green | 1987-90 | 875 | 7.0 |
| 5. | Donna Doellman | 1976-79 | 823 | 8.4 |
| 6. | Alicia Polson | 1978-81 | 747 | 6.6 |

## ALL-TIME WINNINGEST COACHES

| Coach | Years | Record | Pct. |
|---|---|---|---|
| Paul Sanderford | 15 | 365-120 | .753 |
| Steve Small | 4 | 88-40 | .688 |
| Mary Taylor Cowles | 3 | 62-33 | .652 |
| Eileen Canty | 4 | 50-62 | .446 |
| Julia Yeater | 2 | 44-18 | .710 |

*(Source: Western Kentucky University Sports Information)*

## *Natalie Dial*
## 2006 KIAC FEMALE ATHLETE
## OF THE YEAR

**Midway, KY** – Midway College student athlete Natalie Dial has been named the 2006 Kentucky Intercollegiate Athletic Conference (KIAC) Female Athlete of the Year. Dial, a 2006 Midway College graduate, broke several basketball records, including All-Time Leader in Points Scored (1,683), Career Field Goals Made (632), and Career Field Goal Percentage (51.1%). She is the second All-Time Leader in Rebounds (808) and Career Games Played (129). Dial has been chosen as First Team All-KIAC all four years and has ranked in the Top 7 in the KIAC in scoring all four years.

Dial maintained a 3.404 GPA throughout her career and earned a degree in Business Administration with a minor in Computer Information Systems.

# SPORTS
# *Football*

John A. McGill

For a state known for basketball, Kentucky has nevertheless produced a considerable amount of football buzz over the years. In fact, state schools have produced seven national championships.

Georgetown College has won three NAIA national titles, Eastern Kentucky University has won two NCAA Division I-AA titles (and was in the title game four straight years from 1979 to 1982), Western Kentucky won the NCAA Division I-AA title in 2002 and the University of Kentucky was recognized as the 1950 NCAA Division I-A champion in a recent rating system done by Jeff Sagarin.

Kentucky's football history doesn't stop there. For instance:

**Centre College's win over Harvard** in 1921 not only would later be deemed the biggest sports upset in the first 50 years of the 20th century by the *New York Times*, it also prompted one of the excited faithful in Danville to paint the side of a cow "C6 H0"—which wasn't some rudimentary chemistry equation but, rather, the game's final score.

Known as "The Praying Colonels" because they knelt on the field before each game in prayer, there was perhaps more than the usual need for prayer prior to the Harvard game. That's because many of the players reportedly placed large bets on themselves the night before in Boston pool halls. (It was, needless to say, a decidedly different world back then.)

Numerous other noteworthy individuals and events have spiced the state's football history, among them:

**Paul "Bear" Bryant,** the last coach to compile an overall winning record as the University of Kentucky football coach, going 60-23-5 and making four bowl appearances. Bryant left U.K. to coach at Texas A&M, then took over at Alabama, where he won a slew of national titles. Bryant's record in 38 years at Maryland, Kentucky, Texas A&M and Alabama was 323-85-17.

Louisville native **Paul Hornung,** aptly nicknamed "The Golden Boy," won the Heisman Trophy at Notre Dame in 1956 and became a star running back for Vince Lombardi's Green Bay Packers. His 176 points in 1960 still remains an NFL record for single-season scoring.

**Howard Schnellenberger,** another Louisville native, was an All America tight end at U.K. before launching a stellar coaching career. Schnellenberger revived programs at Miami, where he won a national title in his fourth year, and at Louisville, where he laid the groundwork for the school's current success. His U of L teams beat such teams as Texas, Michigan State, North Carolina, West Virginia and Virginia. But his biggest win at Louisville came in the 1990 Fiesta Bowl when the Cardinals beat Alabama 31-7. In 2001, he fielded the first-ever team

**Morehead**
*Source: Herald-Leader*

at Florida Atlantic University, which already has wins over Division I teams, the most notable an upset of Hawaii its only home loss in 2004.

**Johnny Unitas** starred at the University of Louisville before becoming one of the NFL's greatest quarterbacks in a 17-year career with the Baltimore Colts. Inducted into the pro football Hall of Fame in 1979, Unitas led the Colts to one Super Bowl title and three NFL championships. In the 1958 NFL title game, Unitas engineered a pair of 80-yard drives in a 23-17 win over the New York Giants that is still considered by many to be the greatest pro game ever played.

Quarterbacks in this state have been particularly impressive. U.K. quarterbacks **Babe Parilli** and **George Blanda** have been inducted into the College Football Hall of Fame and Pro Football Hall of Fame, respectively. U.K. quarterback **Tim Couch** was the No. 1 draft pick of the Cleveland Browns and Louisville has boasted such quarterbacks as **Johnny Unitas, Chris Redman, Jeff Brohm** and **Stefan LeFors.**

Quarterback **Phil Simms,** who grew up in Louisville and played college ball at Morehead State, was named the MVP of Super Bowl XXI after he completed 22 of 25 passes to lead the New York Giants to a 39-20 win over the Denver Broncos, giving the Giants their first-ever Super Bowl title. Simms, who played 15 years, is now a key analyst for network NFL telecasts.

**Kentucky's Sugar Bowl win over top-ranked Oklahoma** broke the Sooners' 31-game winning streak. That U.K. team was recently recognized as the 1950 national champion by Jeff Sagarin, whose college football rating index has been a staple of *USA Today* since 1985. Sagarin applied his rating system to the seasons that determined champions prior to bowl games and as a result named UK the 1950 champions—a designation that is now listed in the NCAA record book.

In addition to having UK tackle **Bob Gain** become the first SEC player to win the Outland Trophy as the nation's best lineman in 1950, Bear Bryant also had standouts such as All American quarterback **Babe Parilli**, **George Blanda** and **Jerry Claiborne**, who would become UK coach in 1982.

Eastern Kentucky coach **Roy Kidd** was inducted into the College Football Hall of Fame in 2003 after compiling a 315-123-8 record, including two national titles, in 39 years at the school. Kidd was a two-time Division I-AA national Coach of the Year.

Though not a native, **Buddy Ryan** lived on a 200-plus acre farm in Lawrenceburg when he was the architect of the Chicago Bears' "46" defense that helped produce a Super Bowl champion and later as head coach with the Philadelphia Eagles and Arizona Cardinals. **Twin sons Rex and Rob Ryan** got their coaching starts here, Rex at Morehead State and Eastern Kentucky and Rob at Western Kentucky. Both are now defensive coordinators in the NFL, Rex with the Baltimore Ravens and Rob with the Oakland Raiders.

# KHSAA Football

## ALL-TIME WINNINGEST SCHOOLS

| Rank | School | Wins |
|---|---|---|
| 1. | Louisville Male | 760 |
| 2. | Ft. Thomas Highlands | 745 |
| 3. | Mayfield | 720 |
| 4. | Paducah Tilghman | 680 |
| 5. | Danville | 666 |
| 6. | Owensboro | 631 |
| 7. | Hopkinsville | 588 |
| 8. | Louisville Manual | 586 |
| 9. | Middlesboro | 584 |
| 10. | Ashland Blazer | 576 |

## MOST ALL-TIME CHAMPIONSHIPS

| | | |
|---|---|---|
| 1. | Ft. Thomas Highlands | 16 |
| 1. | Louisville Trinity | 16 |
| 3. | Louisville St. Xavier | 11 |
| 4. | Danville | 10 |
| 5. | Beechwood | 9 |
| 6. | Mayfield | 7 |
| 7. | Louisville Male | 6 |
| 8. | Boyle Co. | 5 |
| 8. | Covington Catholic | 5 |
| 10. | Bardstown | 4 |
| 10. | Lynch | 4 |

## ALL-TIME LEADING SCORERS (CAREER)

| No. | Player | School | Points |
|---|---|---|---|
| 1. | Herbie Phelps | Old Kentucky Home | 722 |
| 2. | Kelvin Turner | Danville | 702 |
| 3. | Monquantae Gibson | Louisville Moore | 696 |
| 4. | Derek Homer | Fort Knox | 680 |
| 5. | Shaun Alexander | Boone Co. | 662 |
| 6. | Josh Gross | Russell | 632 |
| 7. | Mike Minix | Paintsville | 618 |
| 8. | Jeremy Britt | Danville | 602 |
| 9. | Jon Chapman | Pikeville | 594 |
| 10. | Michael West | Lawrence Co. | 584 |

## ALL-TIME LEADING RUSHERS (CAREER)

| No. | Player | School | Years | Yards |
|---|---|---|---|---|
| 1. | Derek Homer | Fort Knox | 1993-96 | 8,224 |
| 2. | Jeremy Britt | Danville | 1995-98 | 7,839 |
| 3. | Michael West | Lawrence Co. | 1998-01 | 7,725 |
| 4. | Kelvin Turner | Danville | 2001-04 | 7,170 |
| 5. | Scott Russell | Evarts | 1988-91 | 7,090 |
| 6. | Quinton Henson | Lynn Camp | 1996-99 | 7,148 |
| 7. | Monquantae Gibson | Lou. Moore | 1998-01 | 6,741 |
| 8. | Mark Higgs | Owensboro | 1980-83 | 6,721 |
| 9. | Brent Coleman | Pikeville | 1993-96 | 6,696 |
| 10. | Shaun Alexander | Boone Co. | 1991-94 | 6,662 |

## ALL-TIME LEADING PASSERS (CAREER)

| No. | Player | School | Years | Yards |
|---|---|---|---|---|
| 1. | Tim Couch | Leslie Co. | 1991-95 | 12,167 |
| 2. | Brian Brohm | Lou. Trinity | 2001-03 | 10,579 |
| 3. | Kyle Moore | Breathitt Co. | 1995-98 | 10,026 |
| 4. | Brandon Smith | Boyle Co. | 2001-04 | 8,796 |
| 5. | Andy Ahrens | Lou. Ballard | 1998-01 | 8,686 |
| 6. | Ryan Jones | Madison Cent. | 1996-99 | 8,662 |
| 7. | John W. Monin | Bardstown | 1998-01 | 8,268 |
| 8. | Neil Warren | South Laurel | 1996-99 | 8,138 |
| 9. | Zach Barnard | O'boro Catholic | 2002-04 | 8,124 |
| 10. | Dustin Gruza | Mason Co. | 2000-03 | 8,040 |

## MOST TOUCHDOWN PASSES (CAREER)

| No. | Player | School | Years | TDs |
|---|---|---|---|---|
| 1. | Tim Couch | Leslie Co. | 1991-95 | 133 |
| 2. | Brian Brohm | Lou. Trinity | 2001-03 | 119 |
| 3. | Brandon Smith | Boyle Co. | 2001-04 | 116 |
| 4. | Jeff Duggins | Boyle Co. | 1998-01 | 112 |
| 4. | Jacob Doss | Lex. Catholic | 1999-02 | 112 |
| 6. | Kyle Moore | Breathitt Co. | 1995-98 | 111 |
| 7. | Neil Warren | South Laurel | 1996-99 | 104 |
| 8. | Chris Redman | Lou. Male | 1991-94 | 102 |
| 9. | John Wesley Monin | Bardstown | 1998-01 | 99 |
| 10. | Allen Sperry | Breathitt Co. | 1999-00 | 92 |
| 10. | Gino Guidugli | Ft. Thomas High. | 1998-00 | 92 |

## ALL-TIME LEADING RECEIVERS (CAREER)

| No. | Player | School | Years | Rec. | Yards |
|---|---|---|---|---|---|
| 1. | Montrell Jones | Lou. Male | 1997-00 | 266 | 4,345 |
| 2. | Gerad Parker | Lawrence. Co. | 1996-99 | 238 | 4,736 |

| No. | | Coach/Name | Schools | Years | | |
|---|---|---|---|---|---|---|
| 3. | Jason Reynolds | Bullitt East | 1991-94 | 227 | 2,852 |
| 4. | Maurice Marchman | Lou. Ballard | 1999-01 | 178 | 2,867 |
| 5. | Chris Lofton | Mason Co. | 2001-03 | 175 | 3,511 |
| 6. | Ben Smith | Taylor Co. | 1997-99 | 163 | 2,283 |
| 6. | Michael Bush | Lou. Male | 1999-02 | 163 | 3,031 |
| 8. | Clay Wolford | Lex. Catholic | 1997-00 | 155 | 2,586 |
| 9. | Neal Brown | Boyle Co. | 1994-97 | 154 | 2,327 |
| 10. | Dan Baker | Leslie Co. | 1991-94 | 149 | 2,410 |

## ALL-TIME WINNINGEST COACHES

| No. | Coach | Schools | Wins |
|---|---|---|---|
| 1. | Bob Schneider | Newport Central Catholic | 302 |
| 2. | Joe Jaggers | North Hardin | 292 |
| 3. | Mojo Hollowell | Henderson Co. | 285 |
| 4. | Dudley Hilton* | Bell Co. | 283 |
| 5. | Phillip Haywood | Belfry | 281 |
| 6. | Walter Brugh | Paintsville | 280 |
| 7. | Bob Redman* | Lou. Male | 277 |
| 8. | Garnis Martin | Bardstown | 271 |
| 9. | Sam Harp | Danville | 264 |
| 10. | Mike Glaser | St. Xavier | 261 |

## KENTUCKY MR. FOOTBALL AWARD WINNERS

| Year | Player | School |
|---|---|---|
| 1986 | Frank Jacobs | Newport Central Catholic |
| 1987 | Kurt Baber | Paducah Tilghman |
| 1988 | Jeff Brohm | Louisville Trinity |
| 1989 | Pookie Jones | Calloway Co. |
| 1990 | Damon Hood | Warren Central |
| 1991 | Scott Russell | Evarts |
| 1992 | Billy Jack Haskins | Paducah Tilghman |
| 1993 | Jeremy Simpson | Lincoln Co. |
| 1994 | Shaun Alexander | Boone Co. |
| 1995 | Tim Couch | Leslie Co. |
| 1996 | Derek Homer | Fort Knox |
| 1997 | Dennis Johnson | Harrodsburg |
| 1998 | Jared Lorenzen | Highlands |
| 1999 | Travis Atwell | Hancock Co. |
| 2000 | Montrell Jones | Louisville Male |
| 2001 | Jeff Duggins | Boyle Co. |
| 2002 | Michael Bush | Louisville Male |
| 2003 | Brian Brohm | Louisville Trinity |
| 2004 | Curtis Pulley | Hopkinsville |
| 2005 | Micah Johnson | Fort Campbell |

*(Source: KHSAA Sports Information)*

# Colleges & Universities

## EASTERN KENTUCKY UNIVERSITY
*FOOTBALL*

### EKU BY THE NUMBERS:
- Overall record: 516-323-38
- 2 national championships (1979, 1982)
- 17 Division I-AA playoff appearances
- 1 bowl championship (1967)
- 18 Ohio Valley Conference titles
- 3 undefeated teams (1940, 1954, 1982)
- 56 All Americans
- 216 All OVC players
- 2 College Football Hall of Fame inductees
- 1 OVC Hall of Fame inductee

### ITEMS OF NOTE:
- EKU won its first game in 1927, beating St. Mary's 32-6.
- Roy Kidd ended his career with a 315-123-8 record. He was a two-time National Coach of the Year award winner and a 10-time OVC Coach of the Year selection. He was inducted into the College Football Hall of Fame and the OVC Hall of Fame in 2003.
- Ex-Colonel defensive back George Floyd was inducted into the Divisional Class for the College Football Hall of Fame in 1999. Floyd was a first-team All-America pick and OVC Defensive Player of the Year in 1980.
- EKU ranks first in OVC history with a conference record of 263-104-7.
- Wally Chambers, a first-team All-America pick in 1972, was voted NFL Defensive Rookie of the Year in 1973 as a tackle with the Chicago Bears.
- Current coach Danny Hope, a 1981 EKU graduate, has participated in nine bowl games while serving as an assistant at Louisville, Wyoming and Purdue.
- Assistant coach and Corbin native Steve Bird, a first-team All-American receiver at EKU, comes from one of the most-celebrated athletic families in Kentucky sports history. His father, Jerry, played basketball at UK under Adolph Rupp while his uncles Calvin, Rodger and Billy all played football at UK.
- The Colonels have a 171-36-1 all-time record at Kidd Stadium.

### INDIVIDUAL CAREER RECORDS

| Category | Player | Years | Total |
|---|---|---|---|
| Scoring | Elroy Harris | 1985-88 | 355 |
| Rushing Yards | Markus Thomas | 1989-92 | 5,552 |
| Rushing Average | Markus Thomas | 1989-92 | 6.6 |
| Passing Yards | Jim Guice | 1965-68 | 5,041 |
| Touchdown Passes | Jim Guice | 1965-68 | 46 |
| Receptions | Bobby Washington | 1994-97 | 154 |
| Receiving Yards | Rondel Menendez | 1995-98 | 2,990 |
| TD Receptions | Rondel Menendez | 1995-98 | 27 |
| Total Offense | Markus Thomas | 1989-92 | 5,552 |
| Field Goals | Dale Dawson | 1983-86 | 49 |
| PATS | David Flores | 1977-80 | 126 |
| Interceptions | George Floyd | 1978-81 | 22 |

### ALL-TIME WINNINGEST COACH

| Coach | Years | Record | Pct. |
|---|---|---|---|
| Roy Kidd | 39 | 315-123-8 | .716 |

*(Source: Eastern Kentucky University Sports Information)*

## GEORGETOWN COLLEGE
*FOOTBALL*

### GEORGETOWN BY THE NUMBERS
- Overall Record: 462-415-20
- Three NAIA national titles (1991, 2000, 2001)
- 2 First Team All Americans
- 2 Coach of the Year awards

### FIRST TEAM ALL AMERICANS
- Eddie Eviston
- John Michael Sullivan

### ITEMS OF NOTE
- Bill Cronin was named NAIA Coach of the Year in 2000 and 2001.
- Bill Cronin's overall coaching record at Georgetown is 88-14 (1999-present).

# KENTUCKY STATE UNIVERSITY
*FOOTBALL*

## K-STATE BY THE NUMBERS
- Overall record: 339-396-26
- 7 bowl appearances (1928, 1935, 1943, 1948, 1971, 1975, 1997)
- 2 perfect seasons (1934, 1937)
- 30 All Americans (selected 43 times)

## ITEMS OF NOTE
- William Coleman and George "Big Bertha" Edwards both earned All-America recognition in each of the four years they played for the Thorobreds.
- Henry A. Kean posted a 73-17-6 record (.760 percent) during his 12 years as head coach. Kean also coached the basketball and baseball teams.
- The Thorobreds own a 4-3 record in bowl games.

## K-STATE ALL AMERICANS
William Coleman, tackle (1932, 1933, 1934, 1935)
Alphonso Bumphas, guard (1934, 1935)
George "Big Bertha" Edwards, halfback (1934, 1935, 1936, 1937)
William "Bus" Davidson, tackle (1934, 1935)
Robert Hardin, end (1934)
Joe Kendell, quarterback (1934, 1935, 1936)
Eugene Toomer, tackle (1937, 1938)
William Scaife, tackle (1938)
Melvin Bailey, center (1938)
Asbury Rogers, guard (1938)
Redford Rogers, quarterback (1939)
Hoy Thurman, halfback (1941)
Herbert Trawick, guard (1940, 1941, 1942)
Warren George, center (1941)
Warren Cyrus, end (1942)
James Williamson, tackle (1946)
Pierre "Red" Jackson, center (1948)
Richard "Chick" Corbin, halfback (1948)
Alvin Hanley, halfback (1948)
Harry Daniels, tackle (1948)
D'Artagnan Martin (1970)
Wiley Epps (1972)
Frank Oliver (1974)
Marcus Dover (1997)
Michael Mason (1997)
Cletidus Hunt (1998)
Travis Hardin, offensive line (1998)
Seneca Gray, offensive line (1999)
Alvon Brown, running back (1999)
Lakunta Farmer, linebacker (1999)

## ALL-TIME WINNINGEST COACHES
| Coach | Years | Record | Pct. |
| --- | --- | --- | --- |
| Henry A. Kean | 12 | 73-17-6 | .760 |
| LeRoy Smith | 13 | 65-62-3 | .512 |
| George Small | 6 | 33-40 | .452 |
| George Edwards | 6 | 27-27-1 | .500 |

*(Source: Kentucky State University Sports Information)*

# MOREHEAD STATE UNIVERSITY
*FOOTBALL*

## MOREHEAD STATE BY THE NUMBERS
- Overall record: 293-391-22
- 10 All Americans (selected 11 times)
- 2 Ohio Valley Conference Player of the Year selections

- 3 OVC Coach of the Year awards
- 5 Academic All Americans
- 62 All OVC players (selected 74 times)
- 2 All Pioneer Football League Coach of the Year awards

## MOREHEAD STATE ALL AMERICANS
John "Buck" Horton, center (1938)
Stanley Radjunas, guard (1939)
Paul Adams, center (1940)
Vincent "Moose" Zachem, center (1942)
Joe Lustic, running back (1946)
Dave Haverdick, defensive tackle (1969)
John Christopher, punter (1981, 1982)
Billy Poe, offensive guard (1986)
Darrell Beavers, defensive back (1990)
David Dinkins, quarterback (2000)

## ITEMS OF NOTE
- The 1941 Eagles routed Rio Grande, 104-0.
- Ellis Johnson, the school's winningest basketball coach, also coached football for 16 seasons, posting an overall record of 54-44-10.
- Quarterback Phil Simms, the 1977 OVC Player of the Year and eventual Super Bowl MVP with the New York Giants, threw for 5,545 yards during his four years at Morehead State.
- David Dinkins scored a school-record 32 points in a 2000 win over Kentucky Wesleyan.

## MOREHEAD STATE FOOTBALL RECORDS (CAREER)

| | |
| --- | --- |
| Most Points | David Dinkins (384) |
| Most Yards Passing | Chris Swartz (9,028) |
| Most Touchdown | Passes: Chris Swartz (55) |
| Most Yards Rushing | David Dinkins (3,765) |
| Most Rushing Touchdowns | David Dinkins (63) |
| Most Pass Receptions | Jerome Williams (166) |
| Most Total Offense | David Dinkins (9,337) |
| Most Field Goals | Lenn Duff (18) |
| Longest Field Goal | Charlie Stepp (54 yards) |
| Best Punting Average | John Christopher (42.4) |
| Longest Punt | Don Rardin (78 yards) |
| Most Tackles | Tommy Warren (270) |
| Most Interceptions | Vic Williams (16) |

## ALL-TIME WINNINGEST COACHES
| Coach | Years | Record | Pct. |
| --- | --- | --- | --- |
| Matt Ballard | 11 | 64-53 | .547 |
| Ellis Johnson | 16 | 54-44-10 | .551 |
| Guy Penny | 8 | 39-39-2 | .500 |
| George D. Downing | 8 | 28-32-3 | .467 |
| Jake Hallum | 4 | 22-17-1 | .546 |

*(Source: Morehead State University Sports Information)*

# MURRAY STATE UNIVERSITY
*FOOTBALL*

## MSU BY THE NUMBERS
- Overall Record: 423-340-37
- 8 Ohio Valley Conference titles (1948, 1950, 1951, 1979, 1986, 1995, 1996, 2002)
- 10 All America players
- 12 OVC Player of the Year selections
- 1 National Coach of the Year
- 4 OVC Coach of the Year selections
- 211 All OVC players

## MSU ALL AMERICANS

- Al Giordano, guard/LB (1955) – tough, hard-nosed player who excelled on both offense and defense. Also played professional baseball.
- Gary Foltz, end (1962) – outstanding pass catcher. Led the team in receptions in 1960 and 1962.
- Don Clayton, TB (1973) – holds the MSU rushing record with 2,804 yards. Ran for 1,403 yards in 1973 and 1,257 yards in 1974.
- Eddie McFarland, DB (1977) – ranks eighth on the all-time tackles list with 332. Had his best year in 1977 with 94 tackles.
- Terry Love, DB, (1979) – excellent defender and team leader. Opposing quarterbacks rarely threw in his direction.
- Charlie Wiles, G (1986) – outstanding player who helped guide the Racers to a 6-1 league record and OVC title.
- Derrick Cullors, RB (1995) – holds MSU single-season records for rushing (1,765 yards), touchdowns (20) and scoring (120). Ran for 253 yards in 1995 game against Western Illinois.
- William Hampton, DB (1995, 1996) – Holds the school record for career interceptions with 19. Returned five for touchdowns. Had 115 interception return yards against Akron in 1984.
- Reggie Swinton, WR (1996) – Second all-time receiver with 2,346 career yards. Finished with 139 catches. Had career totals of 26 TDs and 156 points.
- Shane Andrus, PK (2001) – Kicked 26 field goals and holds the MSU record for longest field goal, a 52-yarder against Eastern Illinois in 2002.

## MSU OVC PLAYERS OF THE YEAR

John Wheeler, Lineman (1964)
Larry Tillman, QB (1968)
Rick Fisher, RB (1971)
George Greenfield, RB (1972)
Danny Lee Johnson, RB (1978)
Terry Love, DB (1979)
Gino Gibbs, QB (1981)
Michael Proctor, QB (1989)
Derrick Cullors, RB (1995)
William Hampton, DB (1995)
Mike Cherry, QB (1996)
Justin Fuente, QB (1999)

## WINNINGEST COACHES BY PERCENTAGE

| Coach | Years | Record | Pct. |
|---|---|---|---|
| Carlisle Cutchin | 6 | 37-11-4 | .771 |
| Mike Gottfried | 3 | 22-11-1 | .667 |
| Houston Nutt | 4 | 31-16-0 | .660 |
| Frank Beamer | 6 | 42-23-2 | .646 |
| Roy Stewart | 12 | 60-33-11 | .645 |

## ITEMS OF NOTE

- Each spring, Racer players wrap up their off-season conditioning with the Iron Horse Challenge, a three-day competition that tests strength, speed, desire and teamwork. The Iron Horse Challenge was the brainchild of MSU strength and conditioning coach Mike Vinson.
- Three MSU coaches have been voted OVC Coach of the Year: Bill Furgerson (1968), Mike Gottfried (1979) and Houston Nutt (1995, 1996).
- Houston Nutt won the Eddie Robinson Award as National Coach of the Year in 1995.
- A thoroughbred runs a 400-meter lap around the Stewart Stadium track every time the Racers score.
- Brien Bivens holds the MSU record for longest punt, 90 yards in a 2002 game against Southeast Missouri.
- In 1928, MSU defeated Will-Mayfield by the score of 119-6.
- MSU won its first game in 1924, beating Lambuth 7-0. Win number 400 came in 1999 when the Racers beat Kentucky Wesleyan 53-0.

## ALL-TIME LEADING SCORERS

| No. | Player | Years | Pts. |
|---|---|---|---|
| 1. | Paul Hickert | 1984-87 | 263 |
| 2. | Greg Miller | 1997-00 | 212 |
| 3. | Chris Dill | 1991-95 | 206 |
| 4. | Rob Hart | 1996-97 | 183 |
| 5. | Willie Cannon | 1983-87 | 174 |
| 6. | Reggie Swinton | 1994-97 | 156 |
| 6. | Terrence Tillman | 1998-00 | 156 |
| 8. | Jeff Lancaster | 1980-83 | 153 |
| 9. | Greg Duncan | 1988-90 | 145 |
| 10. | Stan Watts | 1968-71 | 141 |

## ALL-TIME LEADING RUSHERS

| No. | Player | Years | Yards |
|---|---|---|---|
| 1. | Don Clayton | 1972-74 | 2,804 |
| 2. | Danny Lee Johnson | 1977-81 | 2,522 |
| 3. | Willie Cannon | 1983-87 | 2,370 |
| 4. | Rick Fisher | 1969-71 | 2,297 |
| 5. | Rodney Payne | 1985-87 | 2,189 |
| 6. | Waynee McGowan | 1991-94 | 2,099 |
| 7. | Anthony Downs | 1996-97 | 2,037 |
| 8. | Ron Lane | 2002-04 | 2,011 |
| 9. | Nick Nance | 1978-81 | 1,928 |
| 10. | Billy Blanchard | 2001-02 | 1,796 |

## ALL-TIME LEADING PASSERS

| No. | Player | Years | Yards |
|---|---|---|---|
| 1. | Michael Proctor | 1986-89 | 8,632 |
| 2. | Stewart Childress | 2000-03 | 7,581 |
| 3. | Justin Fuente | 1998-99 | 6,392 |
| 4. | Larry Tillman | 1965-68 | 5,037 |
| 5. | Kevin Sisk | 1983-85 | 4,917 |
| 6. | Mike Cherry | 1995-96 | 4,490 |
| 7. | Tony Fioravanti | 1960-63 | 3,449 |
| 8. | Matt Haug | 1967-70 | 3,407 |
| 9. | Tom Pandolfi | 1972-74 | 2,970 |
| 10. | Mike Dickens | 1976-78 | 2,677 |

## ALL-TIME LEADING RECEIVERS

| No. | Player | Years | Rec. |
|---|---|---|---|
| 1. | Terrence Tillman | 1998-00 | 146 |
| 2. | Reggie Swinton | 1994-97 | 139 |
| 3. | Deandre Green | 2002-03 | 126 |
| 4. | Lee McCormick | 1982-85 | 122 |
| 5. | Shaun Boykins | 1998-00 | 111 |
| 6. | James Huff | 1987-90 | 107 |
| 7. | Jack Wolf | 1967-70 | 101 |
| 8. | Joe Perez | 1998-99 | 100 |
| 9. | Billy Hess | 1967-70 | 96 |
| 10. | Glen Arterburn | 1986-89 | 95 |

*(Source: Murray State University Sports Information)*

# THOMAS MORE COLLEGE
*FOOTBALL*

## THOMAS MORE BY THE NUMBERS

- Overall record: 103-44
- Second fastest Division III school to reach 100 wins
- 3 undefeated regular season records (1991, 1995, 2001)
- 2 NCAA Division III championship playoff appearances (1992, 2001)

## ALL-TIME LEADING SCORERS

| No. | Player | Years | PTS |
|---|---|---|---|
| 1. | Will Castleberry | 1997-00 | 296 |
| 2. | Derrick Jett | 1991-94 | 222 |

| 3. | Ryan Reynolds | 1991-94 | 210 |
| 4. | Carlton Carter | 1992-95 | 198 |
| 5. | Jeff Runion | 2000-03 | 189 |
| 6. | Erik Ward | 1993-95 | 160 |
| 7. | Justin Frisk | 2001-02 | 156 |
| 8. | Curtis Williams | 1998-01 | 152 |
| 8. | Dan Calhoun | 1992-96 | 152 |
| 10, | Tyran Thompson | 2002- | 102 |

## ALL-TIME LEADING RUSHERS

| No. | Player | Years | Att. | Yards | TDs |
|---|---|---|---|---|---|
| 1. | Will Castleberry | 1997-00 | 944 | 4,546 | 45 |
| 2. | Ryan Reynolds | 1991-94 | 669 | 3,666 | 31 |
| 3. | Derrick Jett | 1991-93 | 563 | 2,686 | 37 |
| 4. | Dan Calhoun | 1992-96 | 493 | 2,386 | 24 |
| 5. | Carlton Carter | 1992-95 | 448 | 2,289 | 31 |
| 6. | Curtis Williams | 1998-01 | 419 | 2,218 | 22 |
| 7. | Tyran Thompson | 2002- | 433 | 1,938 | 22 |
| 8. | Justin Frisk | 2001-02 | 330 | 1,888 | 23 |

## ALL-TIME LEADING PASSERS

| No. | Player | Years | Com. | Att. | Int. | Yards | TD |
|---|---|---|---|---|---|---|---|
| 1. | Dustin Hicks | 1995-98 | 442 | 868 | 36 | 5,745 | 35 |
| 2. | Jesse Lowery | 1999-01 | 304 | 647 | n/a | 4,357 | 38 |
| 3. | Larry Hutson | 1992-95 | 346 | 620 | 22 | 4,042 | 40 |
| 4. | John Paul Case | 1990-93 | 326 | 620 | 24 | 3,757 | 32 |
| 5. | Nate Berkley | 2003- | 170 | 345 | 26 | 2,780 | 26 |

## ALL-TIME LEADING RECEIVERS

| No. | Player | Years | Rec. | Yards | Avg. |
|---|---|---|---|---|---|
| 1. | Todd Newman | 1991-94 | 108 | 1,741 | 16.1 |
| 2. | Andy Shields | 1995-98 | 98 | 1,262 | 12.9 |
| 3. | Chris Kent | 1994-97 | 86 | 1,201 | 14.0 |
| 4. | Will Castleberry | 1997-00 | 69 | 716 | 10.4 |
| 5. | Chris Wagner | 1990-93 | 66 | n/a | n/a |
| 6. | Craig Rieck | 1996-99 | 65 | 1,501 | 23.1 |
| 7. | Jeff Krohmer | 1997-99 | 60 | 973 | 16.2 |
| 8. | Greg Stofko | 1990-93 | 59 | 722 | 12.2 |
| 9. | Lee Turner | 1995-96 | 57 | 860 | 15.1 |
| 10. | Ryan Reynolds | 1991-94 | 52 | n/a | n/a |

## ALL-TIME WINNINGEST COACHES

| Coach | Years | Record | Pct. |
|---|---|---|---|
| Vic Clark | 9 | 61-29 | .678 |
| Dean Paul | 5 | 40-12 | .769 |
| Mike Hallett | 1 | 4-6 | .400 |

*(Source: Thomas More University Sports Information)*

# UNIVERSITY OF KENTUCKY
*FOOTBALL*

## UK BY THE NUMBERS

- Overall Record: 537-536-44
- One national title (1950)
- Eight Bowl Appearances
- Two Southeastern Conference titles (1950, 1976)
- 15 first-round NFL draft choices
- 22 first team All Americans (selected 26 times)
- 9 Academic All Americans
- 65 first team All SEC players (selected 87 times)

## FIRST TEAM ALL AMERICANS

- Derek Abney, kick returner (2002) – set six NCAA records, 11 SEC records and 14 school records, including NCAA marks for most kick return touchdowns in a season (6, four on punts and two on kickoffs) and in a career (8, 6 on punts and 2 on kickoffs).
- Sam Ball, tackle (1965) – three-year letterman at offensive tackle and first-round NFL draft choice by Baltimore Colts
- Rodger Bird, halfback (1965) – also a two-time All-SEC player who had 646 yards rushing and 12 touchdowns in 1965 and had a career-high 157 yards rushing against Virginia Tech in 1963
- Warren Bryant, tackle (1976) – Also won the Jacobs Award in 1976 as the outstanding SEC blocker; named to the Lakeland (Fla.) Ledger 25-year All-SEC team (1961-85)
- Ray Correll, guard (1953) – Named defensive most valuable player in UK's 20-7 win over TCU in the 1952 Cotton Bowl and named to the All-Time Cotton Bowl team.
- Tim Couch, quarterback (1998) – Led the nation in pass completions while second in completion percentage, passing yardage and touchdown passes; fourth in Heisman Trophy voting; Gave up senior year of eligibility and was No. 1 NFL draft pick (by Cleveland) in 1999.
- Bob Gain, tackle (1949, 1950) – Four-year letterman who, in addition to winning the 1950 Outland Trophy, was a three-time All-SEC selection.
- Irv Goode, center and linebacker (1961) – While primarily recognized for his ability at center, Goode had 23 tackles against national champion Ole Miss in 1960. Thirteen-year NFL veteran and two-time Pro Bowl selection.
- Clyde Johnson, tackle (1942) – UK's first All American; played two years in the NFL with the Los Angeles Rams.
- Lou Michaels, tackle (1956, 1957) – Named the SEC's Outstanding Lineman in 1956 by Birmingham TD Club and the SEC's Outstanding Player by the Nashville Banner in 1957; also averaged 39.8 yards as a punter; inducted into the College Football Hall of Fame in 1992
- Steve Meilinger, end (1952, 1953) – Named to Quarter Century All-SEC team by Birmingham QB Club (1950-74); had 75 career catches for 1,210 yards (16.1 average) while also rushing for 714 yards and intercepting six passes.
- Doug Moseley, center (1951) – Also played linebacker on Bear Bryant teams that went 28-8 and won an SEC title; Co-captain of the 1951 team that went 8-4 and beat TCU 20-7 in the Cotton Bowl
- Rick Norton, quarterback (1965) – Held UK season record for passing with 1,823 yards and 11 TDs in 1965; threw for 373 yards against Houston in 1965; first round draft pick of the Miami Dolphins in 1966
- Rick Nuzum, center (1974) – Was named UK's MVP in 1974 and played three seasons in the NFL
- Glenn Pakulak, punter (2002) – Holds UK modern era records for best average yards per punt in a season (45.58 in 2002) and in a career (44.43, 2000-2002)
- Babe Parilli, quarterback (1950, 1951) – Finished fourth and third in Heisman Trophy voting as a junior and senior; held school record for career TD passes with 50; completed 331 of 592 passes for 4,351 yards in three years as UK went 28-8, won an SEC title, and played in the Orange, Sugar and Cotton Bowls.
- Mike Pfeifer, offensive tackle (1989) – Strong offensive lineman who was also a first-team All SEC selection
- Howard Schnellenberger, end (1955) – Won four varsity letters at both offensive and defensive end; co-captain of 1955 team; 44 career receptions for 618 yards (14.0 average) and 11 touchdowns; Caught a 22-yard TD pass from Bob Hardy for a 14-13 win over Tennessee in 1954; later coached Baltimore Colts, then returned to college ball to revive University of Miami football and win the national championship in 1983; laid the groundwork for University of Louisville's rise in football, including a win over Alabama in the Fiesta Bowl.
- Elmore Stephens, tight end (1974) – A Time magazine selection, but was not picked to All-SEC first or second teams
- Art Still, end (1977) – Set school single-season record for tackles behind the line with 22 in 1977; Named SEC Outstanding Senior Player in 1977 by the Birmingham TD Club and to the 25-year All-SEC Team (1961-75) by the

Lakeland (Fla.) Ledger; played 12 years in the NFL with Kansas City and Buffalo.

- Herschel Turner, tackle (1963) – Played both offensive and defensive tackle and also was a first-team All-SEC pick. Played two years with St. Louis in the NFL.
- James Whalen, tight end (1999) – Originally a walk-on player, set UK single-season record for receptions with 90 (for 1,019 yards) in1999 and is fifth in career receptions with 120 (for 1,324 yards)

## OTHER UK PLAYERS WITH RETIRED JERSEYS

- George Adams, running back, first team All-SEC 1984
- Ermal Allen, quarterback (1939-41), also played basketball; 22 years with the Dallas Cowboys as an assistant coach and director of research and development
- Calvin Bird, do-everything player (running back, defensive back, receiver and returner) named SEC Sophomore of the Year in 1958
- George Blanda, quarterback and punter/kicker, four-year letterman (1945-48) and first player in pro football to score 2,000 career points (2,002 total). Member of Pro Football Hall of Fame
- Paul (Bear) Bryant (honorary), coach, led UK to its first national and SEC championships in 1950 and went 60-23-5 in eight years; In addition to consecutive appearances in the Orange, Sugar and Cotton Bowls from 1950-52, led UK to its first-ever bowl game, the Great Lakes Bowl in 1947; coached eight first-team All Americans
- Jerry Claiborne, end and defensive back, holds the UK single-season record for interceptions with nine for 130 yards in 1949; named Coach of the Year in three different conferences (Southern in 1963, ACC in 1973-75-76 and SEC in 1983); 179-122-8 in 28 yars as a coach at Virginia Tech, Maryland and UK, where he went 41-46-3 despite an 0-10-1 start; elected to the College Football Hall of Fame in 1999
- Blanton Collier (honorary), coach, went 41-36-3 in eight seasons, including a 7-3 record in his first year (1954) as successor to Bear Bryant, winning SEC Coach of the Year award by the Nashville Banner; hailed for his 5-2-1 record against arch-rival Tennessee; played at Paris High School, where he also began his head coaching career in 1927; left job as Cleveland Browns assistant to take UK position, returned to Browns as head coach and went 76-34-2 from 1963-1970 with an NFL title in 1964 and four division titles
- Sonny Collins, halfback, first team All-SEC for three seasons (1973-75) and the Nashville Banner's SEC Player of the Year in1974
- Bob Davis, halfback, 2083 yards rushing from 1935-37
- Dermontti Dawson, offensive line, All-SEC in 1987, seven-time Pro Bowl selection while playing with Pittsburgh Steelers
- Joe Federspiel, linebacker, first-team All-SEC and team MVP in 1971, named to SEC All-Decade Team for the 1970s by the Atlanta Journal-Constitution
- Mark Higgs, running back, third in UK history with 2,892 rushing yards who averaged school records of 6.6 yards per carry (one season) and 5.43 yards (career)
- Tom Hutchinson, split end, all-time leading receiver until 1977 with 94 catches for 1,483 yards, first team All-SEC 1960-61-62
- Wallace "Wah Wah" Jones, end, first team All-SEC in 1948 who is the only UK athlete to have his jersey retired in both football and basketball. Four-year lettermen in both sports, plus baseball
- Ralph Kercheval, all-around athlete in 1931-33 who is still regarded as perhaps the finest punter in SEC history. Still holds several SEC records including single-game punting average (52.0 average with minimum of 10 punts). Second longest punt in UK history (78 yards) and career average of 44.8 yards per punt

- Rick Kestner, first-team All-SEC offensive end in 1964-65. Caught nine passes for 185 yards and three touchdowns in UK's 27-21 upset of top-ranked Ole Miss in 1964.
- Jim Kovach, linebacker, all-time leading UK tackler, first team All-SEC 1978
- Dicky Lyons, do-everything player, first-team All-SEC 1967-68; first player in SEC history to have 1,000 yards in rushing, punt returns and kickoff returns; career punt return average of 15.4 yards per return still a UK record
- Charlie McClendon, defensive end, cornerback and tight end; helped lead Bear Bryant's 1949 team to the Orange Bowl and 1950 team to the Sugar Bowl. As head coach at LSU for 18 years, had a 137-59-7 record and went to 13 bowl games.
- Derrick Ramsey, quarterback, first-team All-SEC and third team All-American in 1977; and named Outstanding SEC Quarterback by the Birmingham Touchdown Club. Led UK to 9-3 and 10-1 records his last two seasons.
- Jay Rhodemyre, center and linebacker, first-team All-SEC in 1947; named to UK's All-Time Team by both the Lexington Herald-Leader and Louisville Courier-Journal
- Dave Roller, defensive lineman, first-team All-SEC in 1969-70. Ten-year NFL career.
- Larry Seiple, runner, receiver, returner and punter; holds UK records for everage reception in a season (23.5 yards in 1965) and career (19.8); famous for his fake punt and run on fourth-and-41 yards to go that went 70 yards for a touchdown against Ole Miss and keyed a 16-7 win.
- Washington "Wash" Serini, center, earned four varsity letters while playing for three different coaches (A.D. Kirwan, Bernie Shively, Paul Bryant); first-team All-SEC in 1944
- Bernie A. Shively (honorary), head coach for one season (1945) and athletics director for 30 years (1938-67); credited with the construction of 11,000-seat Memorial Coliseum in 1950 when many regarded it as a "white elephant" that would rarely if ever see capacity attendance.
- Harry Ulinski, center and linebacker; four-year letterman undr Paul Bear Bryant and captain of the 1949 team that went 9-3; first-team All-SEC in 1949.
- Jeff Van Note, defensive end, team's MVP as a senior in 1968; played 18 years with the Atlanta Falcons as a center and a six-time Pro Bowl selection

## ITEMS OF NOTE:

- The first college football game in the South was at UK's Stoll Field when Centre played Kentucky University (now Transylvania) in 1880.
- In 1881, UK became the first Southeastern Conference team to introduce football. The school was then known by a variety of names: A&M College, Kentucky State College and/or State University of Kentucky.
- "The Immortals" were the only undefeated, untied and unscored upon team in UK history. They went 7-0-0 in 1898.
- Shipwreck Kelly rushed for a then school record 280 yards in 57-0 win over Maryville in 1930. He also was first team All Name.
- UK tackle Bob Gain won the 1950 Outland Trophy as the nation's best lineman, becoming the first SEC player to be so honored.
- Kentucky's Nat Northington was the first African American player to sign with an SEC team and the first to play in a league game, versus Ole Miss in 1967.
- In 1983, UK became the first school in NCAA history to go to a bowl game after being winless the previous season as Jerry Claiborne's team earned a spot in the Hall of Fame Bowl in Birmingham.
- In 1989, UK became the first SEC school to win the College Football Association Academic Achievement Award with a graduation rate of 90 percent (18 of 20 of their 1983

freshman signees earning diplomas).
- Bear Bryant's UK record: 60-23-5 in eight seasons (1946-1953).
- Successor Blanton Collier's UK record: 41-36-3 in eight seasons and a 5-2-1 record against arch-rival Tennessee. (Collier would go on to coach the Cleveland Browns to an NFL title.)

## ALL-TIME LEADING SCORERS

| No. | Player | Years | TD | FG | PAT | PTS |
|---|---|---|---|---|---|---|
| 1. | Joey Worley | 1984-87 | 0 | 57 | 75 | 246 |
| 2. | Seth Hanson | 1997-01 | 0 | 35 | 127 | 232 |
| 3. | Taylor Begley | 2002-05 | 0 | 36 | 118 | 226 |
| 4. | Craig Yeast | 1995-98 | 32 | 0 | 0 | 192 |
| 5. | Doug Pelfrey | 1990-92 | 0 | 34 | 65 | 167 |
| 6. | George Adams | 1981-84 | 27 | 0 | 2 | 166 |
| 7. | Moe Williams | 1993-95 | 27 | 0 | 1 | 164 |
| 8. | Dicky Lyons | 1966-68 | 26 | 1 | 4 | 163 |
| 9. | Rodger Bird | 1963-65 | 27 | 0 | 0 | 162 |
| 10. | Sonny Collins | 1972-75 | 26 | 0 | 2 | 160 |

## ALL-TIME LEADING RUSHERS

| No. | Player | Years | Att. | Yards | Avg. | TD |
|---|---|---|---|---|---|---|
| 1. | Sonny Collins | 1972-75 | 777 | 3835 | 4.9 | 26 |
| 2. | Moe Williams | 1993-95 | 618 | 3333 | 5.4 | 26 |
| 3. | Mark Higgs | 1984-87 | 532 | 2892 | 5.4 | 25 |
| 4. | George Adams | 1981-84 | 638 | 2648 | 4.2 | 25 |
| 5. | Artose Spinner | 1999-2002 | 438 | 2105 | 4.8 | 17 |
| 6. | Marc Logan | 1983-86 | 389 | 1769 | 4.5 | 11 |
| 7. | Derrick Ramsey | 1975-77 | 446 | 1764 | 3.9 | 25 |
| 8. | Anthony White | 1996-99 | 364 | 1758 | 4.8 | 11 |
| 9. | Rodger Bird | 1963-65 | 397 | 1699 | 4.2 | 21 |
| 10. | Derek Homer | 1997-2000 | 353 | 1689 | 4.8 | 11 |

## ALL-TIME LEADING PASSERS

| No. | Player | Years | Com. | Att. | Int. | Pct. | Yards | TD |
|---|---|---|---|---|---|---|---|---|
| 1. | Jared Lorenzen | 2000-03 | 862 | 1514 | 41 | .569 | 10,354 | 78 |
| 2. | Tim Couch | 1996-98 | 795 | 1184 | 35 | .671 | 8435 | 74 |
| 3. | Bill Ransdell | 1983-86 | 469 | 816 | 29 | .575 | 5564 | 22 |
| 4. | Rick Norton | 1963-65 | 298 | 598 | 44 | .498 | 4514 | 26 |
| 5. | Babe Parilli | 1949-51 | 331 | 592 | 37 | .559 | 4351 | 50 |
| 6. | Randy Jenkins | 1979-83 | 363 | 699 | 53 | .519 | 4148 | 24 |
| 7. | Pookie Jones | 1991-93 | 263 | 504 | 19 | .522 | 3459 | 16 |
| 8. | Dusty Bonner | 1997,99 | 313 | 479 | 13 | .653 | 3380 | 26 |
| 9. | Jerry Woolum | 1960-62 | 216 | 407 | 24 | .531 | 2759 | 11 |
| 10. | Bernie Scruggs | 1969-71 | 239 | 493 | 31 | .485 | 2704 | 13 |

## ALL-TIME LEADING RECEIVERS

| No. | Player | Years | Rec. | Yards | Avg. | TD |
|---|---|---|---|---|---|---|
| 1. | Craig Yeast | 1995-98 | 208 | 2899 | 13.9 | 28 |
| 2. | Derek Abney | 2000-03 | 197 | 2339 | 11.9 | 18 |
| 3. | Anthony White | 1996-99 | 194 | 1520 | 7.8 | 8 |
| 4. | Derek Homer | 1997-2000 | 129 | 1052 | 8.2 | 2 |
| 5. | James Whalen | 1997-99 | 120 | 1324 | 11.0 | 13 |
| 6. | Quentin McCord | 1996-2000 | 112 | 1743 | 15.6 | 15 |
| 7. | Kevin Coleman | 1995-98 | 107 | 1428 | 13.3 | 13 |
| 8. | Tom Hutchinson | 1960-62 | 94 | 1483 | 15.7 | 9 |
| 9. | Felix Wilson | 1977-79 | 90 | 1508 | 16.8 | 10 |
| 10. | Derek Smith | 1999-2001 | 89 | 1224 | 13.8 | 9 |

*(Source: University of Kentucky Sports Information)*

# UNIVERSITY OF LOUISVILLE
*FOOTBALL*

## U OF L BY THE NUMBERS
- Overall record: 414-404-17
- 11 first team All Americans
- 8 USA Conference Player of the Year award winners (selected 12 times)
- 12 bowl appearances (1958, 1970, 1977, 1991, 1993, 1998, 1999, 2000, 2001, 2002, 2003, 2004, 2006).

## FIRST TEAM ALL AMERICANS
Tom Lucia (1949)
Lenny Lyles (1957)
Ken Kortas (1963)
Tom Jackson (1972)
Otis Wilson (1979)
Roman Oben (1994)
Jamie Asher (1995)
Sam Madison (1996)
Ibn Green (1999)
Anthony Floyd (2000)
Elvis Dumervil (2005)

## ITEMS OF NOTE
- Ex-Cardinal Johnny Unitas went on to become one of the greatest NFL quarterbacks of all-time with the Baltimore Colts. Unitas is a member of the NFL Hall of Fame.
- Lenny Lyles, a 1957 All-American, also had a long and successful career in the NFL.
- The 1991 Cardinals scored what is arguably the greatest win in school history by topping Alabama 34-7 in the 1991 Fiesta Bowl. Quarterback Browning Nagle threw for three touchdowns in the lopsided upset win.
- Former U of L coach Howard Schnellenberger is generally credited with being the driving force that led to the annual Louisville-Kentucky game.

## ALL-TIME LEADING SCORERS

| No. | Player | Years | TD | FG | PAT | PTS |
|---|---|---|---|---|---|---|
| 1. | Lenny Lyles | 1954-57 | 49 | 0 | 6 | 300 |
| 2. | Nate Smith | 2000-03 | 0 | 44 | 143 | 275 |
| 3. | Michael Bush | 2003- | 38 | 0 | 0 | 228 |
| 4. | Art Carmody | 2004- | 0 | 140 | 26 | 218 |
| 5. | David Akers | 1993-96 | 0 | 35 | 111 | 216 |
| 6. | Ibn Green | 1996-99 | 33 | 0 | 0 | 198 |
| 7. | Arnold Jackson | 1997-00 | 32 | 0 | 2 | 196 |
| 8. | Ron Bell | 1987-90 | 0 | 36 | 82 | 190 |
| 9. | Eric Shelton | 2003-04 | 30 | 0 | 0 | 180 |
| 10. | Jon Hilbert | 1996-99 | 0 | 22 | 114 | 180 |
| 10. | Howard Stevens | 1971-72 | 30 | 0 | 0 | 180 |

## ALL-TIME LEADING RUSHERS

| No. | Player | Years | Att. | Yards | Avg. |
|---|---|---|---|---|---|
| 1. | Walter Peacock | 1972-75 | 811 | 3,204 | 4.0 |
| 2. | Nathan Poole | 1975-78 | 517 | 2,903 | 5.6 |
| 3. | Lenny Lyles | 1954-57 | 394 | 2,786 | 7.1 |
| 4. | Howard Stevens | 1971-72 | 509 | 2,723 | 5.3 |
| 5. | Frank Moreau | 1995-99 | 499 | 2,599 | 5.2 |
| 6. | Tom Lucia | 1947-50 | n/a | 2,542 | n/a |
| 7. | Michael Bush | 2003- | 418 | 2,386 | 5.7 |
| 8. | Deon Booker | 1985-88 | n/a | 2,363 | n/a |
| 9. | Ralph Dawkins | 1990-93 | 525 | 2,159 | 4.1 |
| 10. | Anthony Shelman | 1991-94 | 459 | 2,114 | 4.6 |

## ALL-TIME LEADING PASSERS

| No. | Player | Years | Com. | Att. | Pct. | Yards | TD |
|---|---|---|---|---|---|---|---|
| 1. | Chris Redman | 1996-99 | 1,031 | 1,679 | .614 | 12,541 | 84 |
| 2. | Dave Ragone | 1999-02 | 685 | 1,180 | .581 | 8,596 | 74 |
| 3. | Jay Gruden | 1985-88 | 572 | 1,049 | .545 | 7,024 | 44 |
| 4. | Stefan LeFors | 2001-04 | 416 | 630 | .660 | 5,853 | 38 |
| 5. | Ed Rubbert | 1983-86 | 430 | 873 | .493 | 5,496 | 28 |
| 6. | Jeff Brohm | 1989-93 | 402 | 715 | .562 | 5,451 | 38 |
| 7. | Marty Lowe | 1991-95 | 416 | 767 | .542 | 4,861 | 27 |
| 8. | Browning Nagle | 1989-90 | 333 | 597 | .558 | 4,653 | 32 |

| 9. | John Madeya | 1970-72 | 364 | 746 | .488 | 4,504 | 34 |
| 10. | Dean May | 1980-83 | 328 | 602 | .545 | 4,359 | 29 |

## ALL-TIME LEADING RECEIVERS

| No. | Player | Years | Rec. | Yards | Avg. | TD |
|-----|--------|-------|------|-------|------|-----|
| 1. | Arnold Jackson | 1997-00 | 299 | 3,670 | 12.3 | 31 |
| 2. | Ibn Green | 1996-99 | 217 | 2,830 | 13.0 | 33 |
| 3. | J.R. Russell | 2001-04 | 187 | 2,619 | 14.0 | 19 |
| 4. | Miguel Montano | 1994-97 | 175 | 2,305 | 13.2 | 5 |
| 5. | Jamie Asher | 1991-94 | 153 | 1,741 | 11.4 | 5 |
| 6. | Ralph Dawkins | 1990-93 | 151 | 1,667 | 11.0 | 12 |
| 7. | Deion Branch | 2000-01 | 143 | 2,204 | 15.4 | 18 |
| 8. | Lavell Boyd | 1997-99 | 135 | 1,775 | 13.1 | 10 |
| 9. | Zek Parker | 1998-01 | 128 | 1,804 | 14.1 | 13 |
| 9. | Jim Zamberlan | 1965-67 | 128 | n/a | n/a | 11 |

## ALL-TIME WINNINGEST COACHES

| Coach | Years | Record | Pct. |
|-------|-------|--------|------|
| Frank Camp | 23 | 118-95-2 | .556 |
| Howard Schnellenberger | 10 | 54-56-2 | .491 |
| John L. Smith | 5 | 41-21-0 | .661 |
| Bobby Petrino | 3 | 29-8-0 | .784 |
| Lee Corso | 4 | 28-11-3 | .690 |
| Tom King | 6 | 27-21-0 | .563 |

*(Source: University of Louisville Sports Information)*

# WESTERN KENTUCKY
## *FOOTBALL*

## WKU BY THE NUMBERS

- Overall record: 496-317-30
- 1 NCAA Division I-AA national championship (2002)
- 8 NCAA I-AA playoff appearances
- 8 Ohio Valley Conference championships (1952, 1963, 1970, 1971, 1973, 1978, 1980, 2000)
- 2 bowl appearances (1952, 1963)
- 16 first team All Americans
- 3 OVC Coach of the Year award winners (selected five times)
- 97 All OVC players (selected 128 times)

## WKU FIRST TEAM ALL AMERICANS

Jimmy Feix, quarterback (1952)
Jim Hardin, guard (1957)
John Mutchler, End (1963)
Dale Lindsey, linebacker (1964)
Lawrence Brame, defensive end (1970)
Jim Barber, linebacker/academic (1971)
Virgil Livers, defensive back (1974)
John Bushong, defensive tackle (1974)
Dave Carter, center (1976)
Chip Carpenter, guard (1977)
Pete Walters, guard (1980)
Tim Ford, defensive end (1980)
Donnie Evans, defensive end (1980)
Patrick Goodman, center (1999)
Melvin Wisham, linebacker (2000)
Bobby Sippio, defensive back (2000)

## ITEMS OF NOTE

- Western defeated McNeese State, 34-14, to win the NCAA Division I-AA national championship in 2002.
- Ex-Hilltopper standout Romeo Crennel is currently the head coach of the Cleveland Browns. Crennel served as assistant coach for 24 years with the New England Patriots, including the position of defensive coordinator since 2001.
- Jimmy Feix, Virgil Livers and Willie Taggart were the first WKU players to have their uniform jerseys retired. Feix would later become one of the school's most successful coaches.
- Wes Strader was the Hilltoppers' radio play-by-play announcer for 36 years (1964-2000).
- Legendary WKU basketball coach Ed Diddle was the head football coach for seven seasons (1922-28), compiling a 38-24-2 won-loss mark.
- WKU has participated in two bowl games, winning both. In the 1952 Refrigerator Bowl, the Hilltoppers beat Arkansas State 34-19. Quarterback Jimmy Feix was named the game's MVP. In the 1963 Tangerine Bowl, the powerful Hilltoppers, led by MVP quarterback Sharon Miller, blanked the Coast Guard Academy 27-0.
- John Mutchler, Dickie Moore, Lawrence Brame, Lonnie Shuster, Virgil Livers, Rick Green, Biff Madon and John Hall all earned OVC Player of the Year recognition.

## ALL-TIME LEADING SCORERS

| No. | Player | Years | Pts. |
|-----|--------|-------|------|
| 1. | Willie Taggart | 1995-98 | 286 |
| 2. | Peter Martinez | 2000-02 | 279 |
| 3. | Jeff Poisel | 1996-99 | 265 |
| 4. | Clarence Jackson | 1970-73 | 252 |
| 5. | Dan Maher | 1985-88 | 250 |
| 6. | Dickie Moore | 1965-68 | 206 |
| 7. | Joe Arnold | 1985-88 | 192 |
| 8. | Antwan Floyd | 1993-96 | 166 |
| 9. | Jim Vorhees | 1966-69 | 164 |
| 10. | Max Stevens | 1950-53 | 162 |

## ALL-TIME LEADING RUSHERS

| No. | Player | Years | Att. | Yards |
|-----|--------|-------|------|-------|
| 1. | Willie Taggart | 1995-1998 | 721 | 3,997 |
| 2. | Antwan Floyd | 1993-96 | 697 | 3,775 |
| 3. | Joe Arnold | 1985-88 | 642 | 3,570 |
| 4. | Dickie Moore | 1965-68 | 607 | 3,560 |
| 5. | Clarence Jackson | 1970-73 | 563 | 2,707 |

## ALL-TIME LEADING PASSERS

| No. | Player | Years | Com. | Att. | Yards |
|-----|--------|-------|------|------|-------|
| 1. | Jeff Cesarone | 1984-87 | 735 | 1379 | 8,566 |
| 2. | Johnny Vance | 1966-69 | 289 | 592 | 4,046 |
| 3. | John Hall | 1977-80 | 286 | 571 | 3,876 |
| 4. | Justin Haddix | 2003-present | 239 | 438 | 3,851 |
| 5. | Jimmy Feix | 1949-52 | 272 | 554 | 3,780 |

## ALL-TIME LEADING RECEIVERS

| No. | Player | Years | Rec. | Yards |
|-----|--------|-------|------|-------|
| 1. | Jay Davis | 1968-71 | 131 | 2,236 |
| 2. | Alan Mullins | 1982-85 | 124 | 1,866 |
| 3. | Keith Paskett | 1983-86 | 123 | 2,117 |
| 4. | Robert Coates | 1986-89 | 119 | 1,445 |
| 5. | Cedric Jones | 1984-88 | 117 | 1,632 |

## ALL-TIME WINNINGEST COACHES

| Coach | Years | Record | Pct. |
|-------|-------|--------|------|
| Jimmy Feix | 16 | 106-56-6 | .649 |
| Jack Harbaugh | 14 | 91-68-0 | .572 |
| Nick Denes | 11 | 57-39-7 | .587 |
| Jack Clayton | 9 | 50-33-2 | .602 |

*(Source: Western Kentucky University Sports Information)*

# John A. McGill

# SPORTS
# *Motorsports*

In 1982 when he was a rookie at the Indianapolis Motor Speedway, Louisville's Danny Sullivan was on a practice lap when the fiberglass cowling surrounding his cockpit flew off and sent the car into a spin. He crashed hard into the third turn wall. Later, while being looked over in the track's infield hospital, Sullivan, who was unhurt, said from behind the examining curtain: "You know what? You really DO know you're going 200 miles an hour when it's backwards."

Three years later, Sullivan would become a part of Indy 500 lore when he again went backwards. This time it was while attempting to pass Mario Andretti for the race lead and launching into a full 360-degree spin. But he emerged unscathed and pointed in the right direction. Later, Sullivan tried an identical pass on Andretti, again for the lead and this time succeeded. For a guy with Hollywood looks, it was a Hollywood script. They called Sullivan's 1985 Indy 500 victory the "Spin and Win" race. He would also win the CART Indy Car national title in 1988. Sullivan is the only prominent driver from Kentucky in the ultra-fast world of open wheel, open cockpit racing (he also drove in Formula One), but a number of other drivers—most notably Owensboro brothers Darrell and Michael Waltrip—have been major forces in NASCAR stock car racing.

Owensboro's Darrell Waltrip won three national titles and the 1989 Daytona 500 when the series was known as the Winston Cup. His 84 career wins are the most by any driver in the modern

**Kentucky Speedway part-owner Jerry Carroll on the track with the speedway's pace car (a Mustang). Kentucky Speedway is in Sparta**
*Photo: David Perry, Lexington Herald-Leader*

NASCAR era, which began in 1971. And younger brother Michael is a two-time Daytona 500 winner. They are the most famous of drivers from Owensboro, but hardly the only ones. In fact, this city of only 54,076 has produced an astounding number of world-class drivers in several forms of racing.

Owensboro had six drivers in the 2003 Daytona 500, a number that no other city could come close to matching. Six still compete in various NASCAR series, most of them in the Nextel Cup, the sanctioning body's highest level. Bill Sterrett, Sr. won three world championships in hydroplane racing, and his son Bill Jr. was also a prominent racer. Brother Terry Sterrett also competed in the Miss Owensboro hydroplane, while Jim McCormick was one of the sports most dominant drivers in the 1960s and 1970s.

Owensboro's Cooper Hayden, meanwhile, won a top fuel national drag racing championship in 1968. Owensboro also has produced three world class motorcycle racers: brothers Nicky, Tommy and Roger Lee Hayden. Jeremy Mayfield and the Green brothers (Jeff, David and Mark) also have made names for themselves in NASCAR. But the man who preceded them all was Owensboro native G.C. Spencer, who dominated small tracks throughout the Midwest in the 1940s and 1950s with his "Flying Saucer" car. Spencer eventually made it to NASCAR, finishing fourth in the 1965 point standings.

# SPORTS

## *Golf*

John A. McGill

The 1960s were the golden era for Kentucky professional golfers. Louisville's Bobby Nichols won the PGA championship in 1964, Lexington's Gay Brewer won the Masters in 1967 and Louisville's Frank Beard was the PGA's leading money winner and winner of the PGA Player of the Year award in 1969.

No decade has seen as many Kentucky golfers record as many important victories since, but oth-

**Kenny Perry, (left) shakes hands with Mark Brooks after Brooks won the PGA Championship on the first hole of a sudden-death playoff on Aug. 11, 1996.**
*Photo: Michelle Patterson, Lexington Herald-Leader*

ers have made significant accomplishments.

Topping the list is **Kenny Perry** of Franklin, who

remains a prominent PGA tour regular and has earned more than $18 million with nine career wins—six of which have come since he turned 40. Perry, who played high school golf in Paducah and college golf at Western Kentucky University, was a member of the U.S. Ryder Cup team in 2004.

Perhaps his most compelling tournament was one he lost—the 1996 PGA Championship at Louisville's Valhalla Golf Club. Then a relative unknown, Perry led the event despite a bogey on the 72nd hole. It proved costly, however, when Mark Brooks birdied the final hole to force a playoff. Perry lost on the first extra hole.

**Larry Gilbert** of Lexington was, as Sports Illustrated called him, "a hero to the nation's club pros." Gilbert won three National Club Pro Championships and played in several U.S. Opens and PGA Championships, but opted to stay close to his family rather than join the PGA tour.

In 1993 he and his wife Brenda took the last $4,000 out of their bank account to have a go at the Senior PGA tour. Gilbert won $516,000 as a rookie and in July of 1997 won his first major, the Senior Players Championship. By then his career earnings had crossed $3.2 million. Six months later, Gilbert, 55, died of lung cancer.

Lexington's **Myra VanHoose Blackwelder**, became the first woman to earn a full sports scholarship at the University of Kentucky, went on to become LPGA Rookie of the Year in 1980. She won more than $90,000 in 1988 and finished on the top 10 money list three times.

**Jodie Mudd** of Louisville won four PGA events and finished fifth on the PGA money list in 1990. He had a seventh-place finish in the 1989 Masters and tied for fourth in the 1990 British Open.

Others who have made their mark on the national stage include Paducah's **Russ Cochran**, Middlesboro's **George Cadle**, Lexington's **Jim O'Hern**, Louisville's **Ted Schulz**, Madisonville's **Brad Fabel**, Pikeville's **Robert Damron** and Union's **Steve Flesch**, who ranks 47th in all-time PGA career earnings.

## WOMEN'S STATE AMATEUR
### *Golf Champions*

| Year | Champion | Tournament Site |
|------|----------|-----------------|
| 1923 | Mrs. Charles McCraw | Audubon CC |
| 1924 | Mrs. Charles McCraw | Lexington CC |
| 1925 | Emma Peffer | Twin Oaks CC |
| 1926 | Mrs. Charles McCraw | Louisville CC |
| 1927 | Mrs. Walter Hopkins | Paris CC |
| 1928 | Emma Peffer | Middleboro CC |
| 1929 | Mrs. Harvey Meyers | Lexington CC |
| 1930 | Mrs. Elvina LeBus | Fort Mitchell CC |
| 1931 | Marion Miley | Big Spring CC |
| 1932 | Marion Miley | Ashland CC |
| 1933 | Mrs. Willard Johnson | Owensboro CC |
| 1934 | Marion Miley | Winchester CC |
| 1935 | Marion Miley | Audubon CC |
| 1936 | Mrs. Willard Johnson | Owensboro CC |
| 1937 | Marion Miley | Ashland CC |
| 1938 | Marion Miley | Louisville CC |
| 1939 | B. Little | Bellefonte CC |
| 1940 | B. Little | Lexington CC |
| 1941 | Mrs. Willard Johnson | Ft. Mitchell CC |
| 1946 | Miss Verna Lee Stone | Winchester CC |
| 1947 | Mrs. Willard Johnson | Big Spring CC |
| 1948 | Verna Lee Stone | Idle House CC |
| 1949 | Betty Rowland | Bellefonte CC |
| 1950 | Mrs. S. D. W. Seaver | Audubon CC |
| 1951 | Betty Rowland | Owensboro CC |
| 1952 | Betty Rowland | Summit Hills CC |
| 1953 | Betty Rowland | Lexington CC |
| 1954 | Charlene Cross | Boiling Springs CC |
| 1955 | Charlene Cross | Owensboro CC |
| 1956 | Katty Wylie | Paintsville CC |
| 1957 | Mrs. Charlene C. Baumgarten | Louisville CC |
| 1958 | Mrs. Gaines Wilson, Jr. | Hopkinsville CC |
| 1959 | Mrs. Gaines Wilson, Jr. | Idle Hour CC |
| 1960 | Mrs. Gaines Wilson, Jr. | Paxton Park CC |
| 1961 | Mrs. Gaines Wilson, Jr. | Bellefonte CC |
| 1962 | Margaret Jones | Big Springs CC |
| 1963 | Mrs. Gaines Wilson, Jr. | Village Green CC |
| 1964 | Brenda High | Owensboro CC |
| 1965 | Mary Lou Daniel | Summit Hills CC |
| 1966 | Kaye Beard | Paintsville CC |
| 1967 | Anne M. Combs | Tates Creek CC |
| 1968 | Margaret Jones | Mayfield CC |
| 1969 | Kaye Beard | Wildwood CC |
| 1970 | Margaret Jones | Big Elm CC |
| 1971 | Margaret Jones | Owensboro CC |
| 1972 | Brenda High | Hopkinsville CC |
| 1973 | Mrs. Ronald C. Hacker | Bellefonte CC |
| 1974 | Anne M. Combs | Winchester CC |
| 1975 | Myra Van Hoose | Indian Hills CC |
| 1976 | Myra Van Hoose | London CC |
| 1977 | Anne M. Combs | Lone Oak CC |
| 1978 | Anne M. Combs | Paintsville CC |
| 1979 | Anne Rush | Spring Lake CC |
| 1980 | Mrs. Kaye Beard Potter | Wildwood CC |
| 1981 | Julie Zembrodt | Calvert City CC |
| 1982 | Julie Zembrodt | Lincoln Homestead CC |
| 1983 | Anne M. Combs | Bellefonte CC |
| 1984 | Mrs. Jessica Cornelius | Eagle's Nest CC |
| 1985 | Mrs. Gaines Wilson, Jr. | Owensboro CC |
| 1986 | Sandy Byron | Arlington CC |
| 1987 | Debbie Blank | Glenwood Hall CC |
| 1988 | Joan Rizer | Paintsville CC |
| 1989 | Joan Rizer | Big Elm CC |
| 1990 | Joan Rizer | Madisonville CC |
| 1991 | Joan Rizer | Lincoln Homestead CC |
| 1992 | Laurie Goodlett | Fox Run CC |
| 1993 | Laurie Goodlett | Calvert City CC |
| 1994 | Joan Rizer | Gibson Bay CC |
| 1995 | Christine Ridenour | Summit CC |
| 1996 | Cynthia Powell | Crooked Creek CC |
| 1997 | Jenny Throgmorten | Henderson CC |
| 1998 | Heather Kraus | Kearney Hill Golf Links |
| 1999 | Whitney Wade | Eagle Trace CC |
| 2000 | Whitney Wade | Perry Park CC |
| 2001 | Whitney Wade | Mayfield G & CC |
| 2002 | Mandy Goins | Woodson Bend Golf Resort |
| 2003 | Katie Fraley | Stone Crest Golf Course |
| 2004 | Lauren Scholl | Lafayette Golf Club |
| 2005 | Taryn Durham | Shelbyville CC |
| 2006 | Krista Burton | Owensboro Summit CC |

*(Source: Women's Kentucky State Golf Association, www.wksga.org)*

## Did you know?

Tori Murden-McClure is a daring woman who has conquered many challenges—in December 1999, she became the first woman and first American to row solo across the Atlantic Ocean. In 81 days she rowed 3,333 miles from the Canary Islands to Guadeloupe in the Caribbean. Tori was also the first woman to ski to the South Pole and the first woman to climb Lewis Nunatuk in the Antarctic. A Louisville native, Tori Murden-McClure holds a divinity degree from Harvard and a law degree from the University of Louisville.

*Sources: KET, http://www.ket.org/pressroom/2006/k and Greater Louisville Sports Commission, http://www.louisvillesports.org/hometownathletes.htm.*

**Tori Murden-McClure**
*Source: Tori Murden-McClure*

# SPORTS

## *Olympics*

Mark Maloney

Deciding on the most significant contributions to the Olympic Games made by athletes with Kentucky connections is a debate of—appropriately enough—Olympic proportions.

Kentucky's first Olympic medalists, in the 1904 St. Louis Games, were a pair of track and field athletes from Louisville, Ralph Waldo Rose and Nate Cartmell.

Rose, the first man ever to break the 50-foot barrier in the shot put, won the gold in his specialty and also won a silver (discus) and bronze (hammer throw). Cartmell earned silvers in the 100- and 200-meter dashes.

Cartmell returned to add an individual bronze and two relay golds while Rose earned his second gold in the shot put in London in 1908. Rose would also win gold and silver medals at the 1912 Stockholm Games.

What Rose is best remembered for, though, is for carrying the United States flag during opening ceremonies of the 1908 Games. Of 18 nations participating, only the U.S. – Rose – failed to dip the flag as it passed England's King Edward VII.

The American flag has dipped only once at an Olympics since, at the 1932 Winter Games in Lake Placid, N.Y., Billy Fiske, a bobsledder, dipped to then-New York Gov. Franklin D. Roosevelt. Since 1942, it has been national law that the U.S. flag should not be dipped "to any person or thing."

Any "Kentucky Olympic" debate would also have to include the Fabulous Five and A Great Eight.

The University of Kentucky basketball team's Fab Five, which had won the NCAA title, combined with the Phillips Oilers to win the 1948 gold in Lon-

**UK's Aronda Primault during her uneven bars routine**
*Source: Lexington Herald-Leader*

don. Cliff Barker, Alex Groza and native sons Ralph Beard Jr. (Hardinsburg), Wallace "Wah Wah" Jones (Harlan) and Kenny Rollins (Wickliffe) represented U.K., along with coach, Adolph Rupp, who served as an assistant.

The U.S. Naval Academy fielded A Great Eight, the name given to the 1952 eight-oared shell with coxswain rowing team that won by the largest margin ever at Helsinki. Wayne Frye of Trinity rowed in the seven seat for a squad that also won a record three national championships and 29 races in a row.

Dr. Dot Richardson, a University of Louisville medical school graduate, hit a two-run home run in the first-ever gold-medal softball game (Atlanta, 1996), leading the U.S. to a 3-1 win over China. She also helped the team rebound from three straight defeats – to Japan, China and Australia – in the 2000 Sydney Games to successfully defend the gold. In the medal round, the Americans beat the same three teams they had lost to earlier.

But was Richardson more significant than Louisville's Mary T. Meagher? "Madame Butterfly" swam to three golds in three days at the 1984 Los Angeles Games.

Still, a case can be made that the greatest contribution by a Kentuckian to the Olympics was The Greatest himself—Muhammad Ali.

He first excelled as Cassius Clay, winning the light heavyweight gold medal at the 1960 Rome Games just one year out of Louisville Central High School. He would become the three-time heavyweight champion of the world. The story goes that Clay, dismayed after being hassled and refused service at an all-white Louisville restaurant following his accomplishment, threw his gold medal into the Ohio River.

The International Olympic Committee presented Ali with a replacement medal at the 1996 Atlanta Games—but that was only prelude to one of the Games' most touching moments.

The final person to light the fire at opening ceremonies is always a well-kept secret. In Atlanta, it turned out to be Ali. Even though a physical shell of his former self, even though his body was shaking from Parkinson's syndrome, Ali appeared and took the Olympic flame from swimmer Janet Evans, ascending the steps with the torch to light the cauldron as thousands cheered and millions more watched worldwide.

It was, without question, one of most touching and inspiring moments the Games have ever produced.

Kentucky has a rich history in the Olympic Games. Along with the medalists and moments listed here, many other non-medal winners have represented their state and country with grace and true sportsmanship.

The most significant contribution? The choice is yours.

## OLYMPIC MEDAL WINNERS

**SUMMER GAMES**

**Athletics: Track and Field (*demonstration sport)**

1904 – Nate Cartmell, Louisville (100-meter dash SILVER, 200 SILVER); Ralph Rose, Louisville (shot put GOLD, discus SILVER and hammer throw BRONZE)

1908 – Nate Cartmell, Louisville (4x400 relay GOLD, 200-meter dash BRONZE, sprint medley relay GOLD*); Ralph Rose, Louisville (shot put GOLD)

1912 – Ralph Rose, Louisville shot put, both hands GOLD and shot put SILVER)

1924 – Eugene Oberst, Owensboro (javelin BRONZE)

1932 – Percy Beard, Hardinsburg (110-meter high hurdles SILVER)

1972 – Ralph Mann, University of Kentucky faculty (400-meter hurdles SILVER)

1992 – LaVonna Martin, former Lexington resident (100-meter hurdles SILVER)

1996 – Tim Harden, University of Kentucky (4-x-100 relay SILVER)

2000 – Passion Richardson, University of Kentucky (4-x-100 relay BRONZE)

2004 – Dwight Phillips, University of Kentucky (long jump GOLD)

**Baseball**

1988 – Ty Griffin, Fort Campbell (GOLD*)

1996 – Chad Green, University of Kentucky (BRONZE)

2000 – Jon Rauch, Westport, Morehead State; and Brad Wilkerson, Owensboro (GOLD)

**Basketball**

1948 – Cliff Barker; Ralph Beard Jr., Hardinsburg; Alex Groza; Wallace Jones, Harlan; Kenny Rollins, Wickliffe; all University of Kentucky (GOLD, with Adolph Rupp, assistant coach)

1956 – Bill Evans, University of Kentucky (GOLD)

1960 – Adrian Smith, Farmington, University of Kentucky (GOLD)

1964 – Jeff Mullins, Lexington (GOLD)

1968 – Mike Silliman, Louisville (GOLD)

1972 – Kenny Davis, Georgetown College (SILVER). (USA team refused

medals because of disputed finish loss to the Soviet Union in the gold-medal game)

1984 – C.M. Newton (manager, gold-medal team)

1996 – Ceal Barry (women's team leader, gold-medal team); Clem Haskins (men's assistant coach, gold-medal team)

2000 – Alan Houston, Louisville (GOLD); Tubby Smith, University of Kentucky, and Gene Keady, Western Kentucky, (assistant coaches, gold-medal team)

**Boxing**

1952 – Norvel Lee, Covington (light heavyweight GOLD)

1960 – Muhammad Ali (then known as Cassius Clay), Louisville (light heavyweight GOLD)

**Diving**

1972 – Micki King, University of Kentucky administrator (women's 3-meter springboard GOLD)

**Gymnastics**

2004 – Jason Gatson, Winchester (team SILVER)

**Judo**

1984 – Ed Liddie, Cumberland College (extra-lightweight BRONZE)

**Rowing**

1952 – Wayne Frye, Trinity (Eight-oared shell with coxswain GOLD)

1964 – Thomas Amlong, Fort Knox (Eight-oared shell with coxswain GOLD)

**Sailing**

1932 – Temple Ashbrook (6-meter class individual SILVER)

**Shooting**

1920 – Willis "Ching" Lee, Natlee (Military rifle 300+600 team GOLD, 300-meter prone team GOLD, 300-meter standing team SILVER, 600-meter prone team GOLD; Miniature rifle 50-meter team GOLD, team free rifle GOLD, Running deer, single shot BRONZE)

1984 – Patty Spurgin, Murray State (air rifle GOLD)

2000 – Nancy Napolski Johnson, University of Kentucky (air rifle GOLD)

**Softball**

1996 – Dot Richardson, University of Louisville Medical School (GOLD)

2000 – Dot Richardson, University of Louisville Medical School (GOLD)

**Swimming**

1972 – Gary Conelly, University of Kentucky coach (4-x-100 freestyle relay GOLD, 4-x-200 freestyle relay GOLD)

1976-2004 – Mark Schubert, University of Kentucky graduate (coach of multiple medal winners)

1984 – Mary T. Meagher, Louisville (100-meter butterfly GOLD, 200-meter butterfly GOLD, 4-x-100 medley relay GOLD)

1988 – Mary T. Meagher, Louisville (200-meter butterfly BRONZE, 4-x-100 medley relay SILVER)

1992 – Megan Kleine, Lexington (4-x-100 medley relay GOLD; coached by John Brucato, Lexington)

2000 – Nate Dusing, Covington (4 x 200 freestyle relay SILVER)

2004 – Nate Dusing, Covington (4-x-100 freestyle relay BRONZE); Rachel Komisarz, University of Kentucky (women's 4-x-200 freestyle relay GOLD); Annabel Kosten, University of Kentucky (Netherlands' women's 4-x-100 freestyle relay, BRONZE)

**Volleyball**

1984 – Rich Duwelius, Benton (GOLD)

**WINTER GAMES**

1980 – Warren Strelow, Kentucky Thorougblades (GOLD-medal hockey team goalie coach)

1994 – Ville Peltonen, Kentucky Thoroughblades (hockey BRONZE, Finland)

1998 – Jan Caloun, Kentucky Thoroughblades (hockey GOLD, Czech Republic); Ville Peltonen, Kentucky Thoroughblades, (hockey BRONZE, Finland)

2002 – Brian Shimer, Morehead State (four-man bobsled driver) BRONZE; Doug Sharp, University of Louisville track staff (four-man bobsled side-pusher), BRONZE; Warren Strelow, Kentucky Thoroughblades (silver-medal hockey team goalie coach); Walter Bush, Kentucky Thoroughblades owner, recipient of the Olympic Order

2006 – 2006 – Mikael Samuelsson, Kentucky Thoroughblades (hockey GOLD, Sweden); Ville Peltonen, Kentucky Thoroughblades (hockey SILVER, Finland); Filip Kuba, Kentucky Thoroughblades (hockey BRONZE, Czech Republic)

# SPORTS

# *Tennis*                                    Tom Wallace

Mel Purcell knows what it's like to topple giants. During his 10-year career on the pro tennis circuit, Purcell consistently knocked off higher-ranked players, including future Hall of Fame greats Boris Becker and Ivan Lendl.

Purcell was ranked among the top 30 in the world for five of his 10 seasons on the tour, reaching a personal best ranking of No. 17 from 1981-83. The highlight of that period came in 1983, when Purcell reached the quarterfinals at Wimbledon.

It didn't take Purcell long to make his presence felt once he left the University of Tennessee for life in the professional ranks. In his first year, the shaggy-haired Murray native was named the tour's Rookie of the Year.

**Mel Purcell**
*Source: Murray State University*

ley Conference championships along the way.

Purcell captured the 1977 Kentucky High School singles title as a senior at Murray High School. Following graduation, he spent a year at the University of Memphis, where he won Metro Conference singles and doubles titles. The following year, he transferred to the University of Tennessee, earning All-America honors in 1980 after capturing Southeastern Conference singles and doubles championships.

In 1980, Purcell teamed with fellow Volunteer Rodney Harmon to win the NCAA doubles crown.

For the past 14 years, Purcell has served as coach at Murray State, the first five years spent as an assistant to his father, the past nine

During his career, Purcell won three singles titles and four doubles titles. His championship-winning partners included Stan Smith and Tim Wilkinson. Before retiring in 1987, Purcell earned just under $800,000 in prize money.

Those on the pro circuit shouldn't have been surprised by Purcell's immediate success; he'd been winning tennis matches from the time he first picked up a racket. Purcell had an excellent teacher, too. His father, Bennie, was a superb player who spent 28 seasons as tennis coach at Murray State University, leading his teams to 11 Ohio Val-

as head coach. He has twice guided the Racers to OVC championships and NCAA tourney bids. For his efforts, Purcell was named OVC Coach of the Year in 2001 and 2002.

In addition to overseeing a highly successful tennis camp, Purcell still finds time to occasionally participate on the Jimmy Connors Champions Tour, where he bumps heads against old rivals like Connors, Bjorn Borg, John McEnroe and Roscoe Tanner. Purcell has also served as the color commentator for TV broadcasts of the Champions Tour.

# UNIVERSITY OF KENTUCKY
*MEN'S TENNIS*

## UK BY THE NUMBERS
- Overall record: 974-564
- 1 SEC Championship (1992)
- 7 Top 10 Finishes
- 3 NCAA Elite Eight Finishes
- 3 ITA National Team Indoor Final Four Finishes
- 2 NCAA Singles Runners-Up
- 17 NCAA Tournament Bids
- 20 Top 25 Finishes
- 14 Players named All-American

## UK ALL AMERICANS
| | |
|---|---|
| Greg Van Emburgh | Andy Potter |
| Rich Benson | Micahel Hopkinson |
| Mario Rincon | Mahyar Goodarz |
| Adam Malik | Cedric Kauffmann |
| John Yancey | Carlos Drada |
| Ian Skidmore | Jesse Witten |
| Scott Hulse | Tigran Martirosyan |

## ITEMS OF NOTE
- UK Coach Dennis Emery was inducted into the Kentucky Tennis Hall of Fame in 2000.

## ALL-TIME WINNINGEST COACHES
| Coach | Years | Seasons | Record | Pct. |
|---|---|---|---|---|
| Dennis Emery | 1983- | 23 | 427-262 | .620 |
| H.H. Downing | 1922-46 | 29 | 172-110-6 | .597 |
| Richard E. Vimont | 1964-71 | 8 | 115-45-2 | .710 |
| Graddy Johnson | 1972-80 | 9 | 167-82 | .671 |
| Ballard Moore | 1960-63 | 4 | 46-23 | .667 |

# UNIVERSITY OF KENTUCKY
*WOMEN'S TENNIS*

## UK BY THE NUMBERS
- 1 SEC Championship (2005)
- 7 Top 10 Finishes
- 4 SEC Singles Champions
- 1 SEC Doubles Championship
- 8 Players named All-American
- 14 All-SEC Singles Selections
- 8 All-SEC Doubles Selections

## UK ALL AMERICANS
| | |
|---|---|
| Sonia Hahn | Sarah Witten |
| Tamaka Takagi | Amy Trefethen |
| Susan Klingenberg | Aibika Kalsarieva |
| Carolina Mayorga | Sarah Foster |

## ITEMS OF NOTE
- Sonia Hahn (1987), Chris Karges (1986, 87) and Caroline Knudten (1987) all won SEC Singles titles. The Karges-Knudten team captured the SEC doubles title in 1986.
- Sarah Witten was the first UK player to earn All-America recognition three consecutive years.
- Aibika Kalsarieva is the only UK player to earn All-America honors in her first season.
- Ex-Wildcats Susan Klingenberg, Sonia Hahn and Tamaka Takagi are all members of the UK Tennis Hall of Fame

# UNIVERSITY OF LOUISVILLE
*MEN'S TENNIS*

## UL BY THE NUMBERS
- 4 NCAA bids since 1998
- 1 Regional final appearance
- 1 player named All-American
- 1 Coach of the Year (2000)
- No. 24 ranking in 2005
- 8 players named Academic All-Americans
- 10 players nationally ranked
- 6 ex-Cardinals went on to play at the professional level

## ITEMS OF NOTE
- Rex Ecarma named USA Coach of the Year in 2000.
- Michael Mather earned All-America recognition in 1998 after going through the season with a perfect 22-0 dual match record.

## MOST SINGLES WINS (CAREER)
| No. | Player | Years | Wins |
|---|---|---|---|
| 1. | Andy Schrecker | 1988-92 | 119 |
| 2. | Brendan Burke | 1984-87 | 105 |
| 3. | Rex Ecarma | 1983-87 | 100 |
| 4. | Paulo Carvalho | 1999-03 | 92 |
| 5. | Cody Conley | 1999-03 | 90 |
| 5. | Todd Arterburn | 1984-87 | 90 |

## MOST DOUBLES WINS (CAREER)
| No. | Player | Years | Wins |
|---|---|---|---|
| 1. | Brendan Burke | 1984-87 | 95 |
| 2. | Rex Ecarma | 1983-87 | 92 |
| 3. | Todd Arterburn | 1984-87 | 88 |
| 4. | Brent McCombe | 1999-02 | 86 |
| 4. | Cody Conley | 1999-03 | 86 |

## ALL-TIME WINNINGEST COACHES
| Coach | Years | Seasons | Record | Pct. |
|---|---|---|---|---|
| Rex Ecarma | 1990- | 15 | 222-168 | .569 |
| Kevin Walsh | 1980-90 | 10 | 132-108 | .550 |

# UNIVERSITY OF LOUISVILLE
*WOMEN'S TENNIS*

## UL BY THE NUMBERS
- 3 consecutive 20-win seasons
- 3 players earned All-Conference in 2005

## ITEMS OF NOTE
- Cardinals had biggest turnaround in the nation, going from a 6-19 record in 2002 to 22-7 in 2003.
- Cardinal coach Greg Davis has never had a team post fewer than 20 wins in a season.

## MOST SINGLES WINS (CAREER)
| No. | Player | Years | Wins |
|---|---|---|---|
| 1. | Kelly Ford | 1997-00 | 102 |
| 2. | Meg Peavy | 1979-81 | 100 |
| 2. | Julie Guess | 1989-92 | 100 |
| 2. | Manisha Patel | 1996-99 | 100 |
| 5. | Angie Schneider | 1995-98 | 99 |

## MOST DOUBLES WINS (CAREER)

| No. | Player | Years | Wins |
|-----|--------|-------|------|
| 1. | Manisha Patel | 1996-99 | 113 |
| 2. | Meg Peavy | 1979-81 | 100 |
| 3. | Kelly Ford | 1997-00 | 79 |
| 4. | Kelly Taylor | 2002-05 | 74 |
| 5. | Kim Hull | 1985-89 | 72 |

# EASTERN KENTUCKY UNIVERSITY
## MEN'S TENNIS

### EKU BY THE NUMBERS
- 1 Ohio Valley Conference championship (1951)
- 1 OVC Player of the Year
- 1 Coach of the Year
- 11 players named to All-OVC team

### ITEMS OF NOTE
- Joe Shaheen named OVC Player of the Year in 1975
- Jack Adams was voted OVC Coach of the Year in 1966
- Rob Oertel coaches both the EKU men's and women's teams. His four-year record as men's coach is 47-52.

### EKU ALL-OVC SELECTIONS

| | |
|---|---|
| Sam Nutty (1963) | Joe Shaheen (1975) |
| Lewie Heil (1963) | David Ghanayem (1983) |
| Lindy Riggins (1966) | Jamie Sellars (1998) |
| Mike Jeffries (1967) | John Kellert (2003) |
| Tom Davis (1967, 68) | |

# EASTERN KENTUCKY UNIVERSITY
## WOMEN'S TENNIS

### EKU BY THE NUMBERS
- 2 players named OVC Player of the Year (3 times)
- 1 Coach of the Year
- 13 players named All-OVC

### ITEMS OF NOTE
- Deanna Addis (1980) and Nikki Wagstaff (1988, 89) were selected OVC Player of the Year.
- Sandy Martin was selected OVC Coach of the Year in 1992.
- Rob Oertel's four-year record as women's coach is 48-51.

### EKU ALL-OVC SELECTIONS

| | |
|---|---|
| Mandy Jackson (1979) | Pam Wise (1988) |
| Deanna Addis (1980) | Yael Soresman (1990) |
| Susan Wilson (1983) | Samantha Roll (1990) |
| Claudia Porras (1984) | Amy Scott (1992) |
| Kristi Spangenberg (1984) | Lindsay Herrera (2003, 05) |
| Tina Peruzzi (1987, 90) | Meredith Giles (2005) |
| Nikki Wagstaff (1988, 89) | |

# MURRAY STATE UNIVERSITY
## MEN'S TENNIS

### MSU BY THE NUMBERS
- All-time record: 787-429
- 19 Ohio Valley Conference championships
- 4 players named OVC Player of the Year (7 times)
- 4 coaches named OVC Coach of the Year (12 times)
- 2 30-win seasons (1983, 1985)
- 14 20-win seasons

### ITEMS OF NOTE
- Nick Barone (1965), Bobby Montgomery (1984), Tony Wretlund (1985, 88) and Nikola Aracic (1999, 01, 02) were all named OVC Player of the Year.
- Bennie Purcell was voted OVC Coach of the Year 8 times.
- Mel Purcell was named OVC Coach of the Year twice, while Jim Harris and Chad Stewart each earned the honor once.
- For 10 years, from 1980-1989, Murray captured the OVC title, posting a remarkable 253-106 record during that period.
- Won a school-best 33 matches during the 1984-85 season.
- Coach Mel Purcell was ATP Rookie of the Year after turning professional. During his pro career, he posted wins over Boris Becker and Ivan Lendl. He also won four doubles titles, playing with such noted partners as Stan Smith and Tim Wilkinson.

# MURRAY STATE UNIVERSITY
## WOMEN'S TENNIS

### MSU BY THE NUMBERS
- Overall record: 579-294
- 5 Ohio Valley Conference championships
- 2 coaches voted OVC Coach of the Year (6 times)
- 3 players named OVC Player of the Year (4 times)
- 1 30-win season (1980-81)
- 4 20-win seasons
- 2 undefeated seasons (1967-68, 1972-73)

### ITEMS OF NOTE
- April Horning (1983), Sally Henle (1987) and Melissa Spencer (2003, 04) were all named OVC Player of the Year.
- Connie Keasling has been named OVC Coach of the Year five times. Ken Purcell won the honor once (1984).
- Won a school-best 30 matches in 1980-81.

### MOST SINGLES WINS (CAREER)

| No. | Player | Years | Wins |
|-----|--------|-------|------|
| 1. | Sheri Chong | 1985-89 | 104 |
| 2. | Sally Henle | 1985-89 | 94 |
| 3. | Jorunn Eid | 1980-84 | 91 |
| 4. | Bobbi Koehn | 1986-90 | 90 |
| 5. | Jaclyn Leeper | 2001-05 | 88 |

### MOST DOUBLES WINS (CAREER)

| No. | Player | Years | Wins |
|-----|--------|-------|------|
| 1. | April Horning | 1980-84 | 100 |
| 2. | Martha Zimmer | 1994-98 | 93 |
| 3. | Brooke Berryman | 1995-99 | 92 |
| 3. | Jorunn Eid | 1980-84 | 92 |
| 5. | Melissa Spencer | 2000-04 | 87 |

### ALL-TIME WINNINGEST COACHES

| Coach | Years | Record | Pct. |
|-------|-------|--------|------|
| Connie Keasling | 16 | 251-155 | .618 |
| Nita Head | 16 | 208-71 | .746 |
| Sherryl Rouse | 4 | 58-26 | .690 |
| Ken Purcell | 2 | 35-26 | .574 |

# Sponsors & Advertisers Index

*(Sponsors are indicated in bold)*

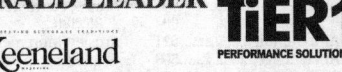

# General Index

*Note: Due to space constraints many of the remarkable individuals named in the various charts in the Sports section are not listed in this index. Also, for Sponsors and Advertisers, see index on page 749.*

# We invite you to join us in the continuation of a historical publication — the Kentucky Almanac and Book of Facts, Second Edition.

Granted, our adventure in publishing the first Kentucky Almanac since 1856 doesn't reach the challenges Dr. Thomas Walker or Christopher Gist faced as they entered the Kentucky wilderness. But, publishing an almanac is an enormous job, even the second time around. Last year's Premier Edition became a holiday best seller in less than sixty days.

We feel quite satisfied with our accomplishments to make the Second Edition even better. We are very proud of our new almanac and hope you find it informative, enlightening and enjoyable to read.

We wish to extend our deepest thanks to our many sponsors, advertisers and contributors. We trust that all of these supporters will be pleased and proud to have played such an important part in the Second Edition of this truly historic publication.

Despite all our efforts, we know it isn't perfect. Certainly, we want it to be flawless, but we acknowledge that inadvertent mistakes have been made, important events and people unintentionally omitted. Send us corrections, additions, opinions, helpful hints and obscure, but significant facts, covering any topic pertinent to our understanding of Kentucky — where we've been and where we're going.

Call us with your comments at 1-800-944-3995; email us at info@ theclarkgroupinfo.com. We will use your suggestions and guidance as we prepare for the next edition and other publications.

Sincerely,
**The Staff of The Clark Group**
Lexington, Kentucky
Publishers of Clark's Kentucky Almanac and Book of Facts, Second Edition

The **Clark** Group